PSYCHOLOGY TODAY
AN INTRODUCTION
Fifth Edition

Psychology Today An Introduction

FIFTH EDITION

ACADEMIC ADVISORS

Richard R. Bootzin
Northwestern University

Elizabeth F. Loftus
University of Washington

Robert B. Zajonc
University of Michigan

WRITER

Elizabeth Hall

WITH PART INTRODUCTIONS BY ISAAC ASIMOV

SPECIALIST CONTRIBUTORS

Randolph Blake
Northwestern University

Joseph LoPiccolo
State University of New York at Stony Brook

Charles J. Holahan
University of Texas at Austin

Sandra W. Scarr
Yale University

RANDOM HOUSE   NEW YORK

Fifth Edition
9876543

Library of Congress Cataloging in Publication Data

    Rev. ed. of: Psychology today / Jay Braun, Darwyn E.
Linder. 4th ed. c1979.
    Bibliography: p.
    Includes indexes.
    1. Psychology. I. Bootzin, Richard R., 1940–
II. Loftus, Elizabeth F., 1944–   . III. Zajonc,
Robert B. (Robert Boleslaw), 1923–   . IV. Braun,
Jay, 1938–   . Psychology today. [DNLM:
1. Psychology. BF 121 P9727]
BF121.P85 1983   150   82–20450
ISBN 0-394-32581-8

Manufactured in the United States of America

Cover design: Arthur Ritter, Inc.
Cover sculpture: Lawrence Van Pelt, Arthur Ritter, Inc.
Cover photograph: Ralph Tornberg Studio, John Coghlan
Text design: Leon Bolognese
Photo research: R. Lynn Goldberg

A Note from the Publisher

In the late 1960s the publishers of *Psychology Today* magazine decided to go into the college textbook business. It was time, they thought, to apply to textbooks the concepts that had made the magazine a success. CRM textbooks would be written in a lively conversational style, designed in an open and inviting magazine format, and sprinkled generously with exciting full color illustrations. The idea seemed just right for the new "media generation" of college students.

CRM's first venture into the field was *Psychology Today*. The text was produced by an illustrious crew of 38 academics who provided chapter drafts written in academic language. These were then rewritten by professional writers in language more appealing to students.

The first edition took the market by storm, selling more copies in its first year than any other psychology text *ever!* The advantages of the CRM style were speed, currency, and catchy prose. The disadvantages were unevenness in style and reading level, a lack of integration from chapter to chapter, an overemphasis on pop topics, and a tendency to slight basic psychological research.

When Random House bought CRM Books in 1974, the third edition of *Psychology Today* was nearly completed. The fourth edition, published in 1979, was the first edition that was truly a Random House book. We kept the exciting graphics program that had made the book popular with students, but we improved the academic content. For the first time, *Psychology Today* appealed as much to faculty as it did to students. The book provided the instructor with solid coverage in all areas of psychology.

We knew, though, that we could improve the book still further. In this fifth edition, we feel we have at last achieved our goal for *Psychology Today*. A team of three distinguished academic advisors supervised the entire revision, making certain that the coverage of each area of psychology was current and complete.

Our team was headed by **Richard R. Bootzin,** professor and Chairman of the Department of Psychology at Northwestern University. Dr. Bootzin is a specialist in personality and abnormal psychology, and a prominent researcher in the areas of sleep and sleep disorders, principles of behavior change, and mental health evaluation. He is the coauthor of *Abnormal Psychology: Current Perspectives,* 3d edition, published in 1980 by Random House.

Elizabeth F. Loftus, professor of psychology at the University of Washington, Seattle, was the second member of our team. Dr. Loftus is a specialist on learning and memory, and she has been nationally recognized for her research on eyewitness testimony. Her book on the subject, *Eyewitness Testimony,* was published by Harvard University Press in 1979, and it won an APA National Media Award in 1980.

The third distinguished member of our team was **Robert B. Zajonc,** professor of psychology at the University of Michigan and Director of its Research Center for Group Dynamics. Dr. Zajonc, a specialist in social psychology, is known for his research on the effects of mere exposure, social facilitation, family structure and intellectual development, and emotion and cognition. In 1978 he won the APA Distinguished Scientific Contribution Award.

The breadth of coverage in introductory psychology is so great that we asked four specialist contributors to assist us. The chapters on sensation and perception were supervised by **Randolph Blake,** professor of psychology at Northwestern University. Dr. Blake is a specialist in visual psychophysics and perception.

The chapters on early development and personality development were supervised by **Sandra W. Scarr,** professor of psychology at Yale University. Dr. Scarr is a specialist in developmental psychology and in behavior genetics. She is editor of the journal *Developmental Psychology.*

The chapter on sexuality was supervised by **Joseph LoPiccolo,** professor of psychiatry at the State University of New York at Stony Brook. Dr. LoPiccolo is a specialist in sexual function and dysfunction.

The chapter on environmental psychology was supervised by **Charles J. Holahan,** associate professor of psychology at the University of Texas at Austin. Dr. Holahan has done research in a wide variety of urban, residential, and organizational settings.

Even with this eminent team of psychologists in charge, we faced one more concern from previous editions: the writing style and reading level were uneven in places and the book lacked integration from chapter to chapter. So we turned to Elizabeth Hall, who has been an intermediary between psychologists and the public for a number of years. Ms. Hall is the coauthor of *Child Psychology Today,* published by Random House in 1982, and of *Developmental Psychology Today,* whose fourth edition was published by Random House in 1983. She was Editor-in-Chief of *Human Nature* magazine and was on the staff of

Psychology Today magazine from its first year of existence. As managing editor of *Psychology Today,* Ms. Hall interviewed many eminent psychologists, including Jean Piaget, Jerome Bruner, B. F. Skinner, and Bruno Bettelheim. Her skills and experience have made this the best-written edition yet.

The work of our team is now complete. The fifth edition of *Psychology Today* is one of the most exciting educational tools on the market. We hope that students will continue to enjoy it and to learn from it for many more editions.

A Note from the Academic Advisors

When we planned the fifth edition of *Psychology Today,* we had several goals in mind. We knew we needed to strengthen the book's exposition of basic concepts and expand the coverage of physiology. At the same time we wanted to bring to the book our excitement about the work being done on the frontiers of psychological research today. We also wanted to give students a feel for how psychology developed by retaining the classic studies that changed the direction of the field. Our modifications took the following form:

Table of Contents. The text still consists of twenty-eight chapters divided into eight parts, but their sequence has been rearranged. Because most psychology instructors prefer to cover physiology and awareness early in the course, this material has been moved closer to the beginning. The former Part Four, Biological and Perceptual Processes, is now Part Two (Chapter 3, The Brain and Behavior; Chapter 4, Sensation and the Senses; Chapter 5, Perception; and Chapter 6, Varieties of Consciousness).

We have added a totally new chapter, Environmental Psychology (Chapter 28), covering one of the newest research areas in the field. The chapter explores the spatial dimension of our relationships with others and the behavioral effects of the settings in which we live and work.

To keep the book the same length, we have condensed the four social psychology chapters into three: Chapters 25, 26, and 27. The new Chapter 25 is still concerned with attitudes and attitude change, but more attention has been paid to the ways attitudes are formed. This chapter now emphasizes the circumstances under

which attitudes influence behavior and when behavior influences attitudes. The new Chapter 26 considers the relationship between attitudes and social perception. Thus, person perception and interpersonal attraction are seen in a new context that helps to tie the entire unit together. The new Chapter 27 on social influence begins with the simplest form of influence—the mere presence of another person—and ends with the complex influence that affects cooperation and competition.

Chapter Revisions. All chapters have been thoroughly updated and the text carefully examined and rewritten to improve clarity. The book is now more integrated—both within each chapter and as a whole, making relationships within the field of psychology apparent. The following revisions deserve special attention:

· The treatment of neuroscience has been strengthened by the inclusion of the latest research on split brains, on the relationships between pain and endorphins, and between neurotransmitters and psychopathology (Chapters 3, 5, 23, and 24).
· Reorganization of the chapter on learning to emphasize the relationship between learning and cognition (Chapter 8).
· New research on the psychological effects of marijuana and other drugs (Chapter 6).
· New material on the reliability of eyewitness testimony, and on how a person's mood can affect memory (Chapter 9).
· New findings on the competency of the newborn—the development of their ability to per-

ceive depth and color, their capacity to locate sounds in space, and their imitation of adult facial expressions (Chapter 11).

- Recent advances in pragmatics that allows discussion of the intimate connection between language and social interaction (Chapter 13).
- A reorganized discussion of motivation to include the motivational consequences of various cognitive states, such as cognitive dissonance, and the question of why people persist at some tasks and not at others (Chapter 16).
- An expansion of the discussion of emotion to give equal attention to all its components (physiological, cognitive, and behavioral) as well as a discussion of the opponent-process theory of emotion (Chapter 15).
- New sections that evaluate theories of personality, psychopathology, and therapy (Chapters 18, 19, and 24).
- New material on the relationship between psychological factors and physical illness (Chapter 21).
- An emphasis on social cognition that links the social psychology chapters to the rest of the book (Chapters 25, 26, and 27).

Special Features. In response to the suggestions of users and reviewers, we have made several changes in the special features. The Isaac Asimov introductions to each chapter have been dropped in favor of an introduction by Asimov to each part. The boxed feature in each chapter is shorter, running about a half-page in length instead of two pages. Each box highlights a topic on the cutting-edge of psychology that pertains to the chapter, and twenty-three of the boxes are entirely new. The new boxes consider such topics as:

- Can brain tissue renew itself? (Chapter 3)
- Endorphins: the body's own painkiller (Chapter 4)
- The psycholinguistics of violence (Chapter 13)
- The effects of day care (Chapter 14)
- Does pornography cause sex crimes? (Chapter 17)
- Freud, his father, and the Oedipal theory (Chapter 18)

Pedagogical Aids. Each chapter is followed by a summary, written in paragraph form instead of in the outline style of the fourth edition. A list of key terms has been added for each chapter. An annotated list of recommended readings is also included for each chapter. There is now a complete glossary with full definitions at the back of the book. There are also name and subject indexes.

Illustrations. New photographs, charts, and tables have been selected on the basis of their educational value, and the entire illustration program retains the special flair of previous editions.

All these innovations and improvements make this the best edition yet of *Psychology Today*. Students can embark on their introduction to psychology with full confidence that they will find the experience enjoyable and rewarding. It is our hope that instructors will find this new edition a valuable review of past research integrated with the newest research and ideas in the field of psychology.

Acknowledgments. We were fortunate to have worked with a number of talented people on this revision. First, we must acknowledge the many outstanding psychologists who contributed to earlier editions. Next, we are indebted to the reviewers, listed facing the title page, who reviewed the chapters of the new edition and whose comments and suggestions were invaluable.

Our special thanks go to the Random House editorial staff: Barry Fetterolf, Mary Falcon, and Suzanne Thibodeau, who guided the entire project; Cele Gardner, Judith Kromm, and Betty Gatewood, who shaped the chapter drafts; Elaine Rosenberg, who supervised the copy-editing process and the illustration program; and Alisa Carse, who coordinated the communication with the reviewers.

The production team at Random House has our gratitude for turning the manuscript into a handsome book: Stacey Alexander, production supervisor; Leon Bolognese, designer; and R. Lynn Goldberg, photo editor.

We would also like to thank Judith Solomon, research assistant. Finally, we must acknowledge our personal gratitude to Mitzi and Geoffrey.

RRB
EFL
RBZ

Contents

X Contents

Special Features

PART ONE

About Psychology

There is no question in my mind that psychology is, of all the branches of science, the most attractive, tantalizing, and useful. To show you what I mean, let me explain each adjective.

1) *Attractive*. No person who lives in the world can help but pick up aspects of science whether she or he knows it. You can't play billiards without learning a lot about the practical aspects of mechanics. You can't be a gardener without becoming an amateur biologist, or learn to be a cook without developing a feel for some aspects of chemistry. What science does is supply a *method* for learning that makes it possible to gather numerous details that you miss in ordinary living. Nevertheless, practical experience does give you certain skills and understandings that books and theory don't always supply.

And where can you possibly have already learned more through experience than in connection with psychology. You spend your whole life living with people, learning how to deal with them and react to them, growing interested in, and perhaps exasperated by, their peculiarities. Even if, by some chance, you led the life of a recluse, you would nevertheless have yourself to deal with, and *you* are people, too, and sufficiently complicated all by yourself.

Consequently, in learning psychology, you are dealing with something you already know a great deal about and are bound to be very interested in—and what can be more attractive than that?

2) *Tantalizing*. Anything too easy isn't very interesting. Children love to play tick-tacktoe, but it is a game that can be quickly and completely analyzed and once that has been done, there is no further point in playing it.

No branch of science is actually *too* easy, but surely psychology, if the most familiar of sciences, is also the least "easy." It deals, basically, with the human brain, which is built up of 10,000,000,000 neurons, each connected to a very large number of others so that the number of neuronic pathways is too high a number to make easy sense when it is written down. The three pounds of human brain is much more complex than any three pounds of anything else in the universe that we know of. One brain is much more complicated than one star, which is why we know so much about stars and so little about the brain. What's more, we are trying to comprehend the brain with what?— With the brain!

What a challenge! And what can be more tantalizing than that?

3) *Important*. It isn't hard to see that this science, at once so attractive and so tantalizing, is also tremendously important. If humanity has advanced through its history, it has been through the activity of the human brain, which has brought us material security and every aspect of culture. And if humanity has been placed in danger, it has been through the activity of the human brain, for it is human motivations, carefully thought out and justified by the brain— greed, envy, rage, lust—that produce the wars, violence, alienation, cruelties that other motivations—sympathy, love, desire to give and build and create—fight so endlessly.

What can possibly be more important than to understand both the destructive and constructive aspects of human thought, emotion, and personality, in order that we might fight the one and encourage the other?

ISAAC ASIMOV

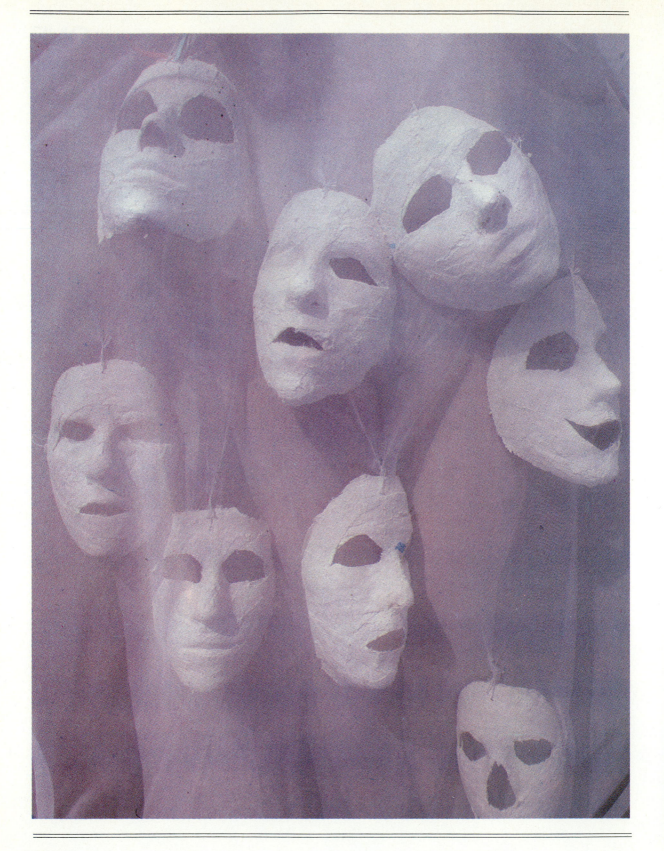

CHAPTER 1

Understanding Psychology: An Introduction

Although this course marks your formal introduction to psychology, you have been studying behavior all your life. If you could not predict how people are likely to react in certain situations, if you did not have theories about why people behave as they do, if you did not—on occasion—manipulate other people, you could not function as a human being. But the common-sense understanding of human nature sometimes leads people astray. Look for a moment at the following list of statements. True or false?

1. For the first week of life, a baby sees nothing but a gray blur, regardless of what she or he "looks at."
2. Children learn to talk more quickly if adults habitually repeat the words they try to say, using proper pronunciation.
3. The best way to get a chronically noisy schoolchild to settle down and pay attention is to punish her or him.
4. Slow learners remember more of what they learn than fast learners.
5. Highly intelligent people—"geniuses"—tend to be physically frail and socially isolated.
6. On the average, you cannot predict from a person's grades at school and college whether she or he will do well in a career.
7. A third or more of the people suffering from severe mental disorders are potentially dangerous.
8. The more severe the disorder, the more intensive the therapy required to cure it; for example, schizophrenics usually respond best to psychoanalysis.
9. The only way to get people to like you is to be nice to them all the time.
10. A hypnotic trance is very similar to light sleep.

How many of these statements seem true? All? Most? Research by psychologists has shown them all to be false. As you will discover again and again, much common sense about human behavior turns out to be nonsense. For that reason, this book is likely to challenge many of your assumptions and perhaps change your view of yourself.

Since its birth about a century ago, psychology has become a wide-ranging discipline that embraces an almost endless array of basic research problems and a broad range of practical matters. Although most psychologists would agree that **psychology** is the study of behavior, the meaning of behavior varies among psychologists. To encompass all psychologists, our definition of **behavior** will include thoughts, feelings, and dreams—anything a person does or experiences.

As this expanded definition indicates, the subject matter of psychology is extraordinarily diverse. Psychologists study behavior in the hope of discovering why we fall in love, how soon a baby can recognize its mother, why some people are creative, why other people become schizophrenic, whether your personality is partially determined before you are born, what happens in hypnosis, how drugs affect human functioning, and whether chimpanzees and dolphins can acquire language. Psychologists investigate everything from how flatworms learn to how a symphony is created, from the seemingly undifferentiated howls of a hungry infant to the complex reactions of an adult to the death of a spouse.

Psychology is not, of course, the only scientific study of human behavior; it overlaps with both the biological and the other behavioral sciences. For example, neurophysiologists and biochemists have made strides toward discovering physiological influences on mental disorders. Anthropologists, through their investigation of the customs, manners, morals, and social structures of other societies, have shown psychologists that their focus on technological societies has given them a narrow view of human nature. Some psychologists have begun to collaborate with researchers in these other fields, further broadening the scope of the discipline. No corner of our lives escapes the interest of psychologists, for every aspect of human behavior—from the moment of conception to the moment of death—raises issues that are important if we are finally to understand why human beings do what they do.

The Growth of Psychology

Psychology broke away from philosophy and physiology and emerged as a separate discipline just over 100 years ago. In the past century, this young and fertile discipline has undergone a series of expansions in both subject matter and research methods. The tremendous growth of psychology (see Figure 1.1) is perhaps best portrayed by examining a few of the major ideas about its fundamental nature as they have been elaborated over the years.

Psychology as the Study of Conscious Experience

Psychology had its formal beginnings in Leipzig, Germany, where Wilhelm Wundt founded the

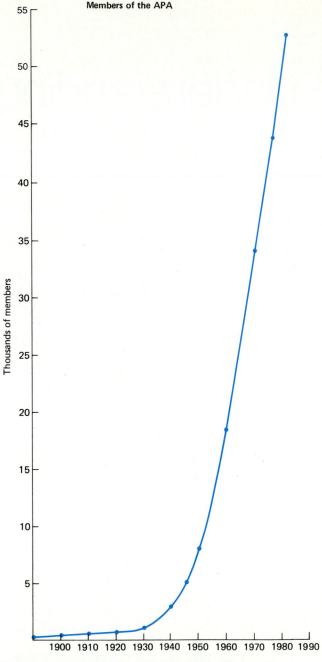

Figure 1.1 The growth of membership in the American Psychological Association over the past fifty years. (Updated from Daniel, 1975.)

first psychological laboratory in 1879. Wundt is considered the first psychologist, as opposed to the philosopher or physiologist who was also interested in psychology (Boring, 1957). He stringently limited the subject to the study of conscious experience. Wundt believed that all our conscious experiences are merely intricate combinations of elemental sensations—that is, intellectual towers made of sensory building blocks. In much the same way that a chemist uses certain processes to discover the basic elements composing all the complex substances in the world. Wundt attempted to use introspection to find the basic sensations. He trained people carefully in the technique of introspection, teaching them to observe and report the "content" or "elements" of awareness in a particular situation. Wundt also tried to discover the principles—the "mental chemistry"—by which those sensations combine to become conscious experience. In essence, Wundt's approach to establishing a discipline of psychology was confined to analyzing detailed descriptions of how people perceive things in the world, and psychology was formally defined as the study of conscious experience. Would-be psychologists flocked to Wundt's laboratory from Europe and North America, and the first generation of American psychologists was trained by him (Bringmann, 1979).

Psychology as the Study of Unconscious Processes

For Sigmund Freud, a physician who practiced in Vienna until 1938, conscious experiences were only the tip of the iceberg. Beneath the surface, he believed, lay primitive biological urges that seek expression but are in conflict with the requirements of society and morality. According to Freud, these unconscious motivations and conflicts are powerful influences on our conscious thoughts and actions; they thus are responsible for much human behavior, including many of the physical symptoms that troubled Freud's patients (R. Watson, 1963).

Since unconscious processes could not be directly studied through introspection, Freud employed an indirect method for their study. In this technique, known as **free association**, a patient said everything that came to mind, making no attempt to produce logical, meaningful statements out of what seemed like absurd or irrelevant thoughts. Freud sat and listened, and then interpreted the associations. Free associations, Freud believed, reveal the operation of unconscious processes. He also believed that dreams express primitive unconscious urges. To learn more about these urges he developed dream analysis, an extension of free association in which the patient free-associated to his or her dreams (Freud, 1949).

While working out his ideas, Freud took meticulous notes on his patients and treatment sessions. He used these records, or case studies, to develop and illustrate a comprehensive theory of personality—that is, of the total, functioning person (Hall and Lindzey, 1978). Freud's theory of personality is discussed in Chapter 18.

In many areas of psychology, Freud's view of unconscious motivation remains a powerful and controversial influence. Modern psychologists may support, alter, or attempt to refute it—but most have a strong opinion about it. (Freud's theories are discussed in Chapters 14, 18, and 23.) The technique of free association is still used by psychoanalysts, and the method of intensive case study is still a tool for investigating behavior.

Psychology as the Study of Individual Differences

A lasting impact on psychology came from a nineteenth-century Englishman's concern with the way in which biology causes one person's abilities, character, and behavior to differ from those of other people. In searching for the determinants of these individual differences, Sir Francis Galton (1869) traced the ancestry of various eminent people. He found that greatness runs in families. (Such a finding was appropriate, for Galton himself was considered a genius and his family included at least one towering intellectual figure—a cousin named Charles Darwin.) Galton concluded that genius or eminence is a hereditary trait—a premature conclusion. He did not consider the possibility that the tendency of genius to appear in eminent families might well be a result of the exceptional environments and socioeconomic advantages that also tend to run in such families.

The data Galton used were based on his study of biographies. Not content to limit his inquiry to indirect accounts, Galton went on to invent procedures for testing human abilities and characteristics. These tests were the primitive forebears of the modern personality and intelligence tests that most people take at some time in their lives. Galton also devised statistical techniques that are still used today (see Chapter 2).

What makes each person unique? The nineteenth-century English physiologist Francis Galton studied the biological determinants of individual differences and concluded that genius is hereditary. He spent immense time collecting, collating, and analyzing thumbprints in order to identify inherited characteristics.

Although Galton began his work before psychology emerged as an independent discipline, his theories and techniques quickly became central aspects of the new science. His book, *Inquiries into Human Faculty and Its Development* (1883), is regarded as having defined the beginnings of individual psychology. Galton's writings raised the issue of whether behavior is determined by heredity or environment—a subject that has remained a focus of heated controversy (see Chapters 7, 11, and 20). Galton's influence can also be seen in the widespread use of psychological tests, in the continuing controversy over their use, and in the statistical methods employed to evaluate their findings (see Chapter 20).

Psychology as the Study of Observable Behavior

A Russian physiologist, Ivan Pavlov, charted a different course for psychological investigation. Pavlov, who received the Nobel Prize in 1904 for his early work on digestive secretions, conducted a series of studies with dogs that were to have a major influence on the development of psychology. In one experiment, Pavlov (1927) set a metronome ticking each time he gave a dog some meat powder. At first the dog salivated the moment it saw the meat powder; after the procedure was repeated several times, the dog would salivate each time it heard the metronome, even if no food appeared.

The concept of the conditioned reflex that grew out of these studies gave psychologists a new tool with which to explore the development of behavior. By applying this concept, in which a response (salivation) is brought about by a stimulus (the metronome) different from the one that first produced it (food), psychologists could begin to account for behavior as the product of prior experience (see Chapter 8). This enabled them to explain certain behavior and certain differences among individuals as the result of learning.

Pavlov was part of a school of Russian neurophysiologists who rejected the introspective approach to psychology in favor of a strictly objective, experimental approach that was to become the hallmark of behaviorism (Kazdin, 1978). Pavlov and his colleagues simply pursued this method of study; it was left for others to turn it into a program for a new psychology.

It is John B. Watson (1878–1958), an American psychologist, who is credited with founding **behaviorism**, the approach to psychology that limits its study to observable responses to specific stimuli—responses that can be measured. He contended that all behavior, even behavior that appeared to be instinctive, is the result of conditioning and that it occurs in response to an appropriate stimulus. Watson (1913) maintained that introspection, the subjective analysis of thoughts and emotions used by Wundt, was as inappropriate in psychology as it was in chemistry. Theology, not psychology, was the proper place for introspection, he argued. The province of psychology was behavior, and its goal was the prediction and control of that behavior.

Watson did not succeed in restricting psychology to the study of observable behavior. In fact, he expanded the field considerably by extending the range of problems and phenomena with which psychologists could deal. In this sense his emphasis on the mechanisms of learning and on the significance of the environment in developing and maintaining behavior were major contributions. By using conditioned reflexes and other techniques for the study of learning processes, Watson also contributed to the development of such areas of psychological investigation as learning (see Chapter 8), memory (see Chapter 9), and problem solving (see Chapter 10).

Although it was Watson who defined and solidified the behaviorist position, it was B.F. Skinner, the contemporary American psychologist, who refined and popularized it. Skinner both narrowed the specific predictive claims of behaviorism and broadened its social implications.

Skinner sought to show that the consequences of behavior provide the basic mechanism for predicting and shaping future behavior. He even wrote a utopian novel, *Walden Two* (1948), to indicate how learning principles might be applied to an entire society.

Skinner exerted great influence on both the general public and the science of psychology. His face became familiar to nationwide television audiences, and his book *Beyond Freedom and Dignity* (1971) was a best seller. Walden Two communities have been formed in various parts of the country, and many people toilet train their children, lose weight, quit smoking, and learn new skills by using methods inspired by Skinner.

Skinner has been widely criticized, for many are convinced that "manipulative" conditioning could limit personal freedom; however, others have applauded him as a social visionary. The theories and methods developed by Skinner have permeated psychology. Behaviorist-inspired techniques vie with traditional psychotherapy for primacy in the treatment of various psychological disorders. The techniques of reinforcement, or controlling the consequences that follow behavior, have become increasingly popular in education, and Skinner's teaching machine was the forerunner of modern programmed education. Moreover, a vast number of today's psychologists use Skinner's research methods to obtain precise findings in their laboratory experiments (Herrnstein, 1977).

As we have seen, psychology has expanded from an infant discipline characterized by a focus on conscious experience to a vast modern science that embraces the study of all behavior. This brief survey is far from comprehensive, touching as it does on only a few of the most important contributions to the scope, substances, and methods of psychological investigation. A look at the practice of psychology today will give some further idea of the field's expansion.

Psychology Today

Although only 100 years have passed since psychology emerged as an independent discipline, its roots can be traced back to ancient Greece and to speculations about the nature of sensation, perception, reason, emotion, dreams, and memory (Klein, 1970). Developments in many countries over many years have contributed to the modern science of psychology, which now flourishes around the world: in Germany, where Wundt established his laboratory; in England, where Galton worked; in Russia, where Pavlov discovered the conditioned reflex; in Japan, where the discipline is still relatively new; and in numerous other countries. Significant strides in psychology have been taken on every continent. However, it is in the United States that psychology has the most support for research, the greatest degree of public acceptance, and the greatest diversity. Of the estimated 260,000 psychologists in the world, about 100,000 live in the United States and Canada. A look at the major fields of specialization in which American psychologists engage will give some idea of the discipline's present diversity.

Fields of Specialization

The national professional organization for psychologists, the American Psychological Association (APA), was founded in 1892 to advance the science of psychology by encouraging research, increasing professional competence, and disseminating psychological knowledge (APA,

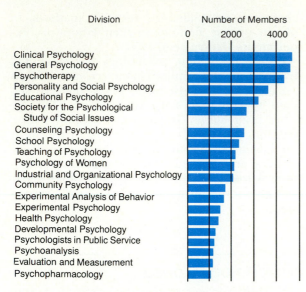

Division	Number of Members
	0 2000 4000

Clinical Psychology
General Psychology
Psychotherapy
Personality and Social Psychology
Educational Psychology
Society for the Psychological
  Study of Social Issues
Counseling Psychology
School Psychology
Teaching of Psychology
Psychology of Women
Industrial and Organizational Psychology
Community Psychology
Experimental Analysis of Behavior
Experimental Psychology
Health Psychology
Developmental Psychology
Psychologists in Public Service
Psychoanalysis
Evaluation and Measurement
Psychopharmacology

Figure 1.2 Membership in the twenty largest divisions of the American Psychological Association's thirty-nine divisions in 1981. Note that a psychologist may be a member of more than one division. Psychotherapists and clinical psychologists, for example, are likely also to be members of the Personality and Social Division.

1981). In 1981, the APA had more than 52,000 members, most of whom belonged to one or more of thirty-nine specialized divisions. Twenty of these divisions have more than 1,000 members, and their relative sizes are shown in Figure 1.2. Some members belong to several divisions, but the list gives an idea of the variety of psychological specialties and the range of psychologists' interests. The following brief descriptions of problems and research taken from some of the major specialties further indicate the diversity of concerns among psychologists, whose interests run from the firing of a single brain cell to the formulation of public policies.

Experimental and Physiological Psychology Have you ever been trying to read an article assigned by your economics instructor and been distracted when your roommate tuned in a radio talk show? Caught in this common but annoying situation, most of us find it impossible to follow the article we have been reading. We either request that the offending program be turned off, leave the room to read elsewhere, or put aside the assigned article. Nobody, we say, can do two things at the same time. Yet experimental psy-

chologists have trained students to read and understand stories while at the same time they copied dictated sentences—which they also understood—showing that it *is* possible to do two things at once (Hirst, Neisser, and Spelke, 1978). The skill was difficult to master, and the students required a number of training periods before they could follow both trains of thought. Such divided attention has been displayed outside the laboratory, however, for air traffic controllers and simultaneous translators at the United Nations could not handle their jobs unless they had some mastery of divided attention.

Divided attention is only one concern of **experimental psychology**, which investigates basic behavioral processes that are shared by various species. Although experimental psychologists generally use laboratory experiments to pursue their study, it is not the use of the controlled experiment alone that distinguishes psychologists who pursue this specialty; rather, it is the basic nature of the process studied, which may be

Experimental psychologists have shown that the ability to divide our attention among several different stimuli—as in this television control room—is a skill that can be learned.

Figure 1.3 Do animals think?

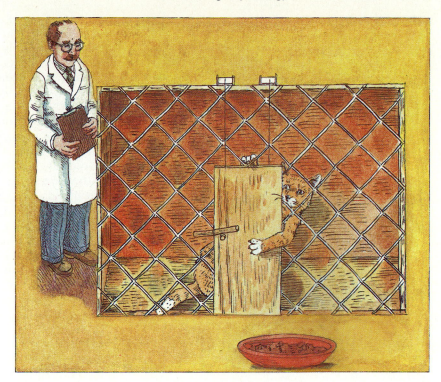

sensation, perception, learning, memory, problem solving, communication, emotion, or motivation.

Experimental psychologists have sought answers to such questions as: What is the basis for the love between mother and baby? Can we learn while we sleep? Can animals think (see Figure 1.3)? What is the role of the brain in memory? How do visual experiences during infancy affect later vision? Not all experimental psychologists study human beings. Some work with rats; others use mice, kittens, monkeys, or even octopuses to study such questions. For example, the discussion in Chapter 14 shows how a baby's love for her or his mother has been explored by raising rhesus monkeys in different ways (Harlow and Harlow, 1966). Research with rats has helped explain the strong connections we make between food and illness. For example, most of us have at some time eaten an unusual food, say lobster thermidor, and then become nauseated. But some people find they can never again eat the dish that they believe made them ill. The sight or even the thought of a lobster shell filled with chunks of lobster meat in a rich, sherry-flavored sauce makes their stomachs churn. John Garcia's (Garcia and Koelling, 1966) experiments with rats have shown that these rodents learn similar associations—indeed that making the connection helps the species to survive. From such studies, we have discovered that learning is a more complicated phenomenon than Pavlov's experiments with dogs had led psychologists to believe. Garcia's studies, which are discussed in Chapter 8, provide another example of the way animal research leads to human research that can give us insight into the behavior of our own species.

Some experimental psychologists focus on the underlying physical bases of behavior. Researchers who attempt to untangle the connections between the nervous and endocrine systems and behavior practice **physiological psychology** or **neuropsychology**. The physiology of dreaming, the effect of specific areas of the brain on obesity, or the role of specific nerve cells in the perception of shapes and colors are among the topics physiological psychologists or neuropsychologists study.

Most experimental and physiological psychologists work in academic settings, because there freedom of inquiry allows basic research, which aims to advance knowledge, to flourish. However, because of the special training in mathematics and computer sciences received nowadays by most experimental psychologists, the rapidly growing computer industry has been

One bad experience with escargots, and we may never want to eat them again. Experiments with animals have suggested that this aversion to foods that have made us ill has probably had survival value for our species.

hiring many holders of advanced degrees in psychology. Another group of experimental psychologists who sometimes work in industry practice **psychopharmacology**, the relationship between drugs and behavior. Many are employed by pharmaceutical companies to assess the psychological effects of drugs that are under development. Using various standardized behavioral testing procedures, a psychopharmacologist might examine the effects of a particular drug on an organism's learning ability, perception, reaction time, emotions, or sleep and waking cycles.

Developmental Psychology   As children pass from infancy to childhood, their understanding of the world expands enormously. One task a child must master is that of understanding that other people do not see precisely what the child sees. This growth in the realization that the world is

made up of many people, each with her or his own viewpoints, thoughts, and feelings, has been studied extensively by developmental psychologists. One aspect of this development was demonstrated when a developmental psychologist sat at a table with a child and together they looked at white cards. Either the child, the experimenter, or both wore colored glasses; the psychologist's glasses had yellow lenses, the child's had green lenses. About half the three-year-olds always predicted that the experimenter saw the card as they did—green or white— but six-year-olds always predicted exactly how the card would appear to the psychologist (Liben, 1978).

The work of developmental psychology is not confined to the study of children. All aspects of behavioral development over the entire life span are the concern of **developmental psychology**. Every psychological concept—learning, memory, motivation, perception, personality, thinking, and so on—can be examined from the standpoint of its change and development through life. Some developmental psychologists specialize in studying the capabilities of the newborn infant. Others concern themselves with the development of these capabilities in the child, and still others focus on changes through adulthood. There has been increasing interest in the developmental tasks connected with aging, and the past decade has seen the rapid growth of a life-span developmental psychology, which focuses on age-related behavioral change from birth to death (Goulet and Baltes, 1970).

As we shall see in Chapters 11, 12, 13, and 14, the questions posed by developmental psychologists cover a range of topics as broad as psychology itself. How soon can babies perceive depth? Why are the sleep patterns of infants so different from those of adults? How do children develop a concept of self? Is the acquisition of language simply a matter of biological maturation, is it the result of learning, or does it grow out of social interaction? And why do all normal children accomplish such a difficult task with seeming ease? Are psychological differences between boys and girls genetic or social? Is the development of conscience dependent upon the way parents discipline a child? How does sexual maturation affect the self-esteem of adolescents? Why do people differ in intelligence quotient (IQ) scores? Is a person's degree of masculinity or femininity stable, or does it change in various phases of life? How does aging affect memory and problem solving? And how do people come to terms with death?

Developmental psychologists work in a wide variety of settings: as consultants to children's television programs; in federal programs such as Head Start; in private practice; in institutions, where they may do psychotherapy with emotionally disturbed children; in industry, where they may try to determine how an employee's attitude to work changes with age; and in schools, where they may work with children who have learning problems. Most of them, however, work in university settings conducting research on developmental processes.

Personality Psychology   Some people are highly competitive, hostile when thwarted, and behave as if they were always racing the clock. This pattern of behavior, called Type A, is associated with the development of heart disease, even when such traditional predictors as family history, smoking, high blood pressure, and high cholesterol levels are controlled. Type A people seem to have a strong need to maintain control in stressful situations (Glass, 1977). Although Type A people are often quite productive and frequently outperform Type B people, who tend to be relaxed and who do not feel the continual pressure of time, in some situations the Type A

personality pattern can lead to trouble. In one experiment (Brunson and Matthews, 1981), people with Type A and Type B personalities were asked to solve various problems and to think out loud as they worked at the solutions. After the subjects had solved several of the problems, the experimenters gave both groups a series of insoluble problems. By the time the fourth insoluble problem had been presented, the subjects with Type A personalities were frustrated and annoyed, saying that the task was too hard and they lacked the ability to handle it. They seemed to give up, sticking with the same incorrect answer despite the fact they had been told it was wrong. Type B subjects, on the other hand, were unhappy and bored when given the series of insoluble problems, but they continued trying to find a solution and seemed optimistic about their eventual success.

This study of the relation between personality and behavior is an example of research in **personality psychology**, a field in which individual differences in behavior are studied. Such differences reflect the fact that not all people react the same way in the same situation, and personality psychologists attempt to explain why this is so. They also try to discover why people tend to behave in a fairly consistent manner in various situations. It is this combination of differences among individuals and consistency within in-

Traditionally, the drama of human life has been interpreted by writers, artists, and musicians. Today, however, psychologists also contribute insights into our understanding of what is human.

dividuals that creates personality, so that each of us is known for having a specific set of characteristics, our own ways of behaving, of getting along in the world, and of interacting with others.

As Chapter 14 indicates, personality psychologists are interested in how personality develops, whether it changes over time, and if so, how. They want to know whether individual traits and temperament are inherited or the product of the environment. Personality psychologists explore individual differences in aggression, compassion, obedience to authority, sociability, independence, and adherence to ethical codes. From such investigations have come various theories of personality, which are discussed in Chapters 18 and 19, and explanations for different ways of adjusting to life's stresses, which are discussed in Chapter 21.

Most personality psychologists work in academic settings. However, some who specialize in the assessment of personality work in psychiatric hospitals, where they diagnose patients, or in industry, where they assist in personnel selection.

Social Psychology Studies conducted in several countries have demonstrated that a steady diet of media violence seems to increase the aggressive behavior of juvenile delinquents (Parke et al., 1977). Delinquent boys who watched aggressive or violent movies such as *Bonnie and Clyde* and *The Dirty Dozen* engaged in more acts of physical aggression after seeing these movies than did delinquent boys who watched such neutral movies as *Lili* or *Daddy's Fiancée*. In another study (Hoyt, 1970), when male college students saw a film in which violence was justified, they were more likely to give other people strong (simulated) electric shocks than when the violence they saw was never justified. Further, violence that was justified as vengeance, as is done in many films, led to stronger shocks than violence that was justified as self-defense. These attempts to assess the connection between violence in the mass media and aggressive behavior are typical of one concern of **social psychology**, the study of the behavior of people in groups, paying special attention to the influence of other people on individuals.

Each of us is enmeshed in a network of social relationships with people we encounter at work, at school, in the neighborhood, and within our family. Social psychologists study the ways in which these relationships develop. They want to know who likes whom—and why. They are interested in the attitudes that people have toward social issues and in the way those attitudes are formed and changed by society. They also want to know how those attitudes affect our thought processes. For example, in one study (Judd and Kulik, 1980) college students read statements on women's rights, capital punishment, and majority rule in South Africa and indicated whether they agreed or disagreed with them. The next day the students were asked to write out as many of the statements (such as "The Equal Rights Amendment should be supported by all who believe that discrimination is wrong" and "Majority rule would only complicate the lives of most South Africans") as they could. Students judged statements more rapidly and remembered them better when they either were highly consistent with their own attitudes or clashed violently with them, indicating that our social attitudes affect how rapidly we think and how well we remember certain types of information.

Social psychology has become an extremely wide-ranging field of psychology. Among the topics studied are friendship formation, romantic attraction, perception of other people, social influence, behavior in groups, bargaining and conflict (see Chapters 25 through 27), with psychologists always searching for the way these aspects of life are affected by the situation—and especially by what others do or say. Social psychologists are particularly interested in the relevance of their research to society, and in 1936 founded the Society for the Psychological Study of Social Issues, which focuses on human problems in the group, the community, the nation, and the world.

Social psychologists generally work in academic settings, but not always in the psychology department. Some social psychologists who are interested in group processes and decision making can be found in schools of business, and others work in industry. The rising interest in applying social psychology to concrete problems has attracted social psychologists into political and legal settings and the health fields.

Educational and School Psychology Since in many colleges and universities student evaluation of instructors plays a part in determining faculty salaries and promotions, it is important to discover the basis for students' judgments. In one study (Naftulin et al., 1973), adults enrolled in a course were asked to judge the teaching ability of a guest instructor, who was actually an actor. The actor delivered his lecture in a fascinating manner, but its content was garbled, self-contradictory, illogical, and full of non sequiturs and nonsense words. Yet these adult students, who were psychologists, psychiatrists, social workers, and educators, rated the bogus instructor as a highly capable teacher. The teacher's lack of knowledge and absence of scholarly ability had no effect on the ratings, supporting the proposition advanced by other psychologists (Kulik and McKeachie, 1975) that students judge teachers, not on their mastery of the subject, but simply on how well they talk.

Student evaluation of teachers is only one concern of **educational psychology**, which investigates all the psychological aspects of the learning process. At just one professional conference, educational psychologists presented research on creative thinking in fifth-graders, gender differences in mathematical ability, television's effect on study habits, anxiety in education, teachers' effects on students' behavior, the identification of gifted children, attention in learning-disabled children, and a host of other topics. Most educational psychologists work in colleges or universities, where they conduct research and train teachers and psychologists. A few work on curriculum development, materials and procedures for schools, and in government agencies, business, and the military.

Educational psychology differs considerably from **school psychology**. Most school psychologists work in elementary and secondary schools, where they assess children with learning or emotional problems and work out ways for parents and teachers to help them. School psychologists also administer personality, intelligence, and achievement tests in the schools.

Industrial and Organizational Psychology In most areas of life, physical attractiveness is an asset, but when it comes to getting a job, it can be a hindrance—if you're a woman. When people rated job applications for vacancies in an insurance firm, attractive women who applied for managerial jobs were discriminated against in ratings of their qualifications, decisions to hire them, and starting salaries. In addition, the more attractive the woman, the more stereotypically feminine she seemed to the raters. On applications showing similar backgrounds, qualifications, and interests, unattractive women and attractive men did much better than attractive women, receiving higher ratings and generally being recommended for the position. When the application was for a clerical job, attractiveness paid off for both men and women, with attractive applicants of either sex consistently rated higher than unattractive applicants (Heilman and Saruwatari, 1979).

The workings of personnel departments and the factors that influence job selection are

Break time in a factory. Industrial psychologists have given increasing attention to work conditions, job-related stress, and employee morale.

among the topics considered in **industrial psychology** and **organizational psychology**, in which the relationship between people and their jobs is studied. Work occupies a large part of our waking hours, and psychologists have given increasing attention to the conditions and effects of employment. They investigate employee morale, job-related stress, the qualities that make a good boss, how to enrich jobs, and ways to make working hours more flexible. In **human-factors psychology** the psychologists consider the purpose of a particular machine or environment and the capabilities of the probable user, then devise the most convenient, comfortable, and efficient design that matches the two.

Less than half of all organizational and industrial psychologists are found in colleges or universities; the majority work in business or industry, in government agencies, or as consultants to business or government. Some of these psychologists practice **personnel psychology**; they screen job applicants, evaluate job performance, and recommend employees for promotion. Other industrial and organizational psychologists specialize in **consumer psychology**, studying the preferences, buying habits, and responses to advertising of consumers. Such psychologists might, for example, study ways to persuade people to conserve energy, advise on the design of a new container for salad dressing, or conduct surveys to determine the market for a new product.

Clinical Psychology Patients who have spent many years in a mental hospital often are either excessively withdrawn or behave so bizarrely that life on the unit is unpleasant and unmanageable —for both patients and staff. In one study (Paul and Lentz, 1977) that will be discussed in Chapter 24, psychologists used techniques developed by behaviorists to make radical changes in the way such a unit was run. Patients were no longer treated as "sick people" but as residents of a dormitory or boarding house. They were expected to function appropriately and to pay for both necessities (meals) and luxuries with tokens they earned by their behavior. They made their beds, kept themselves groomed, bathed, behaved properly at mealtime, and participated in ward activity. Such behavior won praise and attention from the hospital staff and earned the patients the vital tokens. Life on the unit changed dramatically, and the benefits extended

far beyond routine. The program worked so well that after seven months most of the patients (who had spent an average of seventeen years in mental hospitals) had improved enough to be released to a shelter facility within the neighboring community.

The study, diagnosis, and treatment of abnormal behavior is the province of **clinical psychology**. Clinical psychologists have developed diverse ways of treating various disorders. In studying the basis of any disorder, they look for possible biological, biochemical, educational, and environmental causes. About half of all clinical psychologists work in hospitals and clinics or have private practices.

Some clinical psychologists who practice **community psychology** have the primary aim of preventing mental disorders. Their ultimate goal is to change the aspects of the environment that lead to disorder; they can be found in outpatient clinics, advising community workers on how to handle psychological problems, staffing emergency services, and supervising halfway houses and hot lines.

Other clinical psychologists have specialized in **health psychology**, with the aim of preventing and treating disease that involves psychological factors. The role of emotional stress in heart disease and ulcers is widely known, but only within the past few years has the effect of psychological factors in other diseases—from colds to cancer— been suspected. For example, some health psychologists look for factors that lead people to smoke, overeat, ignore symptoms of disease, or ignore their physicians' prescriptions, and they devise ways of helping people to overcome these behaviors. Other health psychologists might work at identifying the psychological components of chronic pain, at helping people change life styles that make them candidates for heart disease, or at helping people develop effective ways of coping with serious diseases or disorders.

Emerging Specialties As the field of psychology develops and our knowledge of human behavior broadens, psychology is applied to new areas of human life. Among these new fields of specialization is **environmental psychology**, the study of the relationship between people and their physical settings (see Chapter 28). As human beings live in the world, they modify their environment, but they are also modified by that

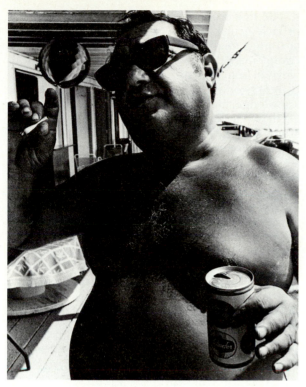

Identifying the psychological factors that may lead some people to overeat or drink too much is one concern of health psychologists.

environment. Environmental psychologists investigate such influence, studying such problems as the effects on city dwellers of crowding, noise, or the perception of danger. Some environmental psychologists explore the effects of building design upon social interaction or the quality of life. In one such study (Holahan, 1982), environmental psychologists investigated the feelings of university students about their living conditions. They found that students who lived in high-rise dormitories were much more dissatisfied with their living quarters than were students who lived in low-rise dormitories, and that students who lived on the higher floors in the high-rise buildings were the most dissatisfied of all. Apparently, other students found the higher floors of these dormitories relatively inaccessible, so they tended to stay away, making it more difficult for students who lived on these floors to meet people and to make friends.

A second emerging field is that of **forensic psychology**, whose practitioners apply psychological principles to the problems of law enforcement and the courts. Many forensic psychologists are found in psychology or specialized law programs in academic settings, where they research problems concerning eyewitness testimony, jury selection, the process of jury decision, and the testimony of expert witnesses (Loftus, 1979; Pennington and Hastie, 1981). Some forensic psychologists work in community mental health centers, where they consult with the police, the courts, and prison officials. Others work in police departments, where their duties run from screening recruits and training officers in how to handle family quarrels, crowds, suicide threats, and hostage crises to helping officers who have emotional problems and assisting in the investigation of crimes. The assistance of forensic psychologists in criminal investigations may involve using clues to construct personality profiles of probable criminals or hypnotizing defendants, victims, or eyewitnesses to enhance their memory, as discussed in Chapter 6. (Although hypnosis is generally accepted as an investigative technique, the results are not always reliable and most courts refuse to accept information gained in this way as evidence.) Some forensic psychologists work in prisons, where they provide counseling and psychotherapy to inmates.

A third field of specialization that has recently developed is **program evaluation** and policy research, in which psychologists evaluate the effectiveness and cost of government programs meant to alleviate social problems. Such evaluation can help to prevent waste and make sure that programs are actually moving a community toward specific goals. Psychologists' training in experimental methods enables them to measure and compare the factors that affect a particular program and the results they lead to. Although economists, political scientists, and sociologists are also involved in the evaluation of programs and policies, many psychologists—including those who practice **quantitative psychology**, which specializes in measurements and statistics —are engaged in evaluating programs for the Congressional Budget Office and the General Accounting Office of the federal government; others evaluate programs in the field of education. The increasing need to make every dollar count is bringing program evaluations into the fields of health care, employment, transportation, energy conservation, and criminal rehabilitation.

Psychology: Basic and Applied Science

This look at major fields of specialization makes it plain that psychology is both a basic and an applied science. In **basic science**, knowledge is acquired for its own sake to advance our understanding of the nature of things; the potential usefulness of the knowledge gained is not a consideration. In **applied science**, findings from basic science are used to accomplish practical goals. Most biologists and physicists, for example, practice basic science; most physicians and engineers practice applied science. Psychologists may practice either—or both. Some psychologists who do basic research study a particular topic because they are aware that any knowledge gained will be relevant to practical problems. A developmental psychologist who studies the ability of infants to perceive patterns is doing basic research. Her purpose has nothing to do with the design of crib toys, but if her findings are applied by a psychologist in his job as a consultant to a toy manufacturer, the science becomes applied. Similarly, a social psychologist who studies the friendships among a group of office workers—who likes whom, how much, and why—is doing basic science. If he discovers that one member of the group has no friends at all and another has so many friends she hardly has time to work, the psychologist might try to understand and explain the situation, but he would not try to alter it. He would leave that to a clinical or industrial psychologist who practices applied psychology.

The distinction is not always clear to beginning psychology students. In the first weeks of a course, students sometimes ask about the relation of psychology to everyday life, and their tone of voice is often challenging. Psychology, they imply, is not telling them what they want to know; it is not doing what it ought to be doing. One student may object because psychology is too slow, too painstaking, too plodding. Intricate studies, many of them conducted with animals by rigorously objective researchers, seem boring and provide no insight into the nature of humanity. Another student may object because psychology is too abstract, too remote, a concoction of grandiose theories, animal studies (again), and experiments that turn on such inconsequential matters as the smallest change in the brightness of a light that a person can perceive. This student may wonder what use or value any of this information can have.

The first student, who finds the scientific approach incompatible with his own way of looking at things, might still find psychology a valuable complement to the literary and philosophical views of human nature. The second student, who is interested in the application of psychological knowledge, may find herself developing an interest in psychology as a basic science. For example, students who find mnemonic (memory-jogging) devices useful may begin to wonder why they work, and thus discover an interest in the way memories are organized in the brain. People who reward their children with privileges or money for doing chores that are checked off on a chart as they are completed may become curious about the principles of learning on which such systems are based. People who think they need psychotherapy may want to know not only what type would be best for them but why any therapy is effective; they may also want to know what psychologists have discovered about the causes of mental disorders.

Psychology as a Vocation

Some students find they have more than a casual interest in psychology and wonder about a possible vocation in the field. As we have seen, psychology is practiced by men and women in a number of professions, and various professions have different educational requirements.

Whether they are engaged in basic research to uncover fundamental laws of behavior, in applied research to solve specific problems, or in providing counseling and therapy to people suffering from psychological problems, the majority of psychologists have earned a PhD in the discipline of psychology. To earn a PhD, a psychologist must complete a four-to-six-year graduate program in a department of psychology at a university. Typically, this program includes broad exposure to the theories and findings of psychology, a special focus on a subdiscipline (e.g., developmental or social psychology), and extensive training in research methods. Each PhD candidate must complete an original research project of fairly wide scope, under the direction of experienced researchers on the graduate faculty, and must then submit the findings as a doctoral dissertation.

Students who want to become clinical or counseling psychologists must either meet the requirements for the PhD or else enroll in a professional school of psychology (which may or may not be associated with a university), where they must meet the requirements for a PsyD (doctor of psychology), a degree that places more emphasis on application and less on research. No matter which course they follow, clinical psychologists must complete specialized training in diagnosis and psychotherapy as well as a year of training at an institution that has an internship program accredited by the American Psychological Association.

Yet many students who are interested in psychology either do not want or cannot afford graduate training. In the last decade or so, psychology has become one of the most popular majors in the college curriculum, chosen by thousands of students who have no intention of completing a graduate degree. According to the National Center for Education Statistics, 41,000 BAs in psychology were awarded during the academic year 1979–1980, but only 2,773 PhDs. To a considerable extent, psychology has become a general major, like English or history—fascinating, informative, worthwhile, and a useful basis for many careers and interests.

Looking Ahead

Reading this book and taking an introductory psychology course will not make you a psychological researcher or qualify you to conduct psychotherapy. But you will learn a good deal about the ways in which biological, environmental, and psychological factors shape human behavior.

This introduction to the study of behavior will acquaint you in Chapter 2 with the methods psychologists use in research. Part Two explores the role of the brain in behavior, delving into sensation, perception, and the varieties of consciousness. Part Three considers the basic aspects of behavior, with special emphasis on learning, memory, and problem solving. Part Four traces human development in all its complexity: physical, cognitive, and language development, and the foundations of personality and social behavior. Part Five investigates motivation, emotion, and sexuality. Part Six describes theories of personality and the assessment of personality and intelligence. Adjustment, behavior disorders, and approaches to treatment are the subjects of Part Seven. Finally, in Part Eight, we look at social behavior and the role of the environment, discovering what psychology can tell us about, and do for, society.

This book may sharpen your taste for further exploration in psychology. If you choose to go on in the field, it should provide a solid foundation for future studies. If your interest remains casual, this text should at least enrich and augment your understanding of some of the forces that influence your life.

SUMMARY

1. Although the field of **psychology** has changed and broadened over the past century, it is still best defined as the study of behavior, provided that **behavior** is understood to include thoughts, feelings, and dreams—anything a person does or experiences. Psychologists study every aspect of human behavior from conception to death.

2. Psychology broke away from philosophy and physiology in 1879 when Wundt founded the first psychological laboratory in Leipzig, Germany. Wundt defined psychology as the study of conscious experience. To Freud, unconscious processes were also an important area of study, and he used the free associations of his patients to get to underlying unconscious experiences. The study of individual differences was added to psychology by Galton. He invented the forebears of modern personality and intelligence tests and devised statistical techniques that are still used today. With the research of Pavlov, a Russian physiologist, psychology became the study of observable behavior and the role of learning came to dominate the discipline. **Behaviorism**, the study of observable and measurable responses to specific stimuli, was founded by Watson, an American psychologist. Skinner refined and popularized behaviorism, narrowing its predictive claims and broadening its social implications.

3. The major fields of specialization indicate the broad range of psychologists' interests. **Experimental psychologists** investigate basic behavioral processes shared by various species, using controlled experiments to investigate the nature of sensation, perception, learning, memory, problem solving, communication, emotion, or motivation. Experimental psychologists who attempt to untangle the connections between the nervous and endocrine systems and behavior are called **physiological psychologists** or **neuropsychologists**. Experimental psychologists who study the relationship between drugs and behavior are known as **psychopharmacologists**. **Developmental psychologists** study all aspects of behavioral development over the entire life span. **Personality psychologists** study the relation between individual attitudes and behavior. **Social psychologists** study the behavior of people in groups, paying special attention to the influence of other people. **Educational psychologists** investigate all the psychological aspects of the learning process, while **school psychologists** work with children who have learning or emotional problems and administer personality, intelligence, and achievement tests. **Industrial psychologists** and **organizational psychologists** study the relationship between people and their jobs. Some of these psychologists, called **human-factors psychologists**, design machines or environments that match the capabilities of their users; others, called **personnel psychologists**, screen job applicants, evaluate job performance, and recommend employees for promotion. Other industrial and organizational psychologists specialize in **consumer psychology**, studying the preferences, buying habits, and responses to advertising of consumers. **Clinical psychologists** are engaged in the study, diagnosis and treatment of abnormal behavior. Some clinical psychologists, known as **community psychologists**, aim at preventing mental disorders; they are found in the community, at outpatient clinics, emergencies services, halfway houses, and hot lines. Other clinical psychologists, known as **health psychologists**, focus on preventing and treating diseases that involve psychological factors. **Environmental psychologists** study the relationship between people and their physical settings. **Forensic psychologists** apply psychological principles to the problems of law enforcement and the courts. **Program evaluators** and **quantitative psychologists** assess the effectiveness and cost of government programs meant to alleviate social problems.

4. In **basic science**, knowledge is acquired for its own sake to advance our understanding of the nature of things; its usefulness is never a consideration. In **applied science**, findings from basic science are used to accomplish practical goals. Psychology is both a basic and an applied science.

5. The majority of psychologists have a PhD in psychology, which requires the completion of a four-to-six-year graduate program in psychology at a university, including a dissertation based on an original research project. Clinical or counseling psychologists, however, have the option of completing a PhD or earning a PsyD (doctor of psychology) from a professional school of psychology—which may or may not be associated with a university.

KEY TERMS

applied science	environmental psychology	personality psychology
basic science	experimental psychology	personnel psychology
behavior	free association	physiological psychology
behaviorism	forensic psychology	program evaluation
clinical psychology	health psychology	psychology
community psychology	human-factors psychology	psychopharmacology
consumer psychology	industrial psychology	quantitative psychology
developmental psychology	neuropsychology	school psychology
educational psychology	organizational psychology	social psychology

RECOMMENDED READINGS

AMERICAN PSYCHOLOGICAL ASSOCIATION. *Careers in Psychology*. Washington, D.C.: American Psychological Association, 1980. Prepared by the major national organization of psychologists. This booklet describes the subdisciplines and various career opportunities within psychology.

BORING, E. G. *A History of Experimental Psychology*. 2nd ed. New York: Appleton-Century-Crofts, 1950. The classic comprehensive presentation of the history of psychology from antiquity to the twentieth century.

COHEN, I. S. (ed.). *Perspectives on Psychology: Introductory Readings*. New York: Praeger, 1975. A well-chosen collection of readings by major contributors to psychology, providing a broad sample of issues and perspectives in the field.

HEARST, E. (ed.). *The First Century of Experimental Psychology*. Hillsdale, N.J.: Lawrence Erlbaum, 1979. A collection of contributed chapters that trace the history of specific topic areas. Contains photographs of most of the important figures of experimental psychology.

MARX, M. H., and W. A. HILLIX. *Systems and Theories in Psychology*. 2nd ed. New York: McGraw-Hill, 1973. A historically oriented discussion of major psychological systems and theories, comprehensive but primarily experimental in emphasis.

SCHULTZ, D. *A History of Modern Psychology*. 3rd ed. New York: Academic Press, 1981. Focuses on the past century of development psychology and includes brief biographies of major historical figures.

WATSON, R. I. *The Great Psychologists*. 4th ed. Philadelphia: Lippincott, 1978. Describes the contributions of great psychologists from the Greek philosophers through modern times.

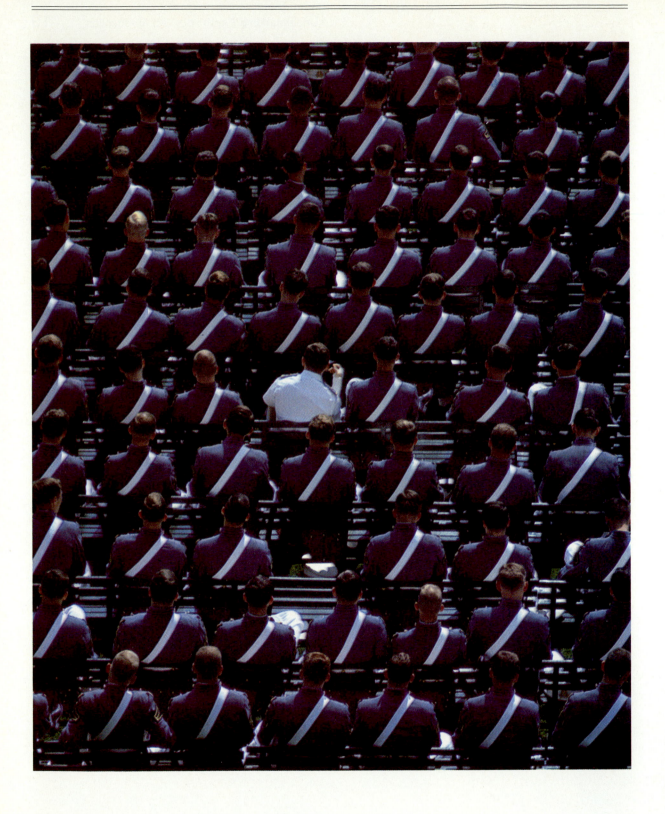

CHAPTER 2

Doing Psychology: Methodology

If we are to understand why human beings behave as they do, we must have some way to investigate human thought and behavior. Suppose you became interested in the effects of marijuana on the reaction time of college students. How would you set about discovering whether the drug has any effects? It would seem logical to have some students smoke marijuana and then test their reaction time, using various standard tests. But designing an experiment that would give you the answer you seek is in reality complicated. Many seemingly unimportant details could, if not taken into consideration, have such a strong influence on the students' behavior that your experiment would be meaningless. There are details involving your subjects: perhaps marijuana affects men and women differently; perhaps students with any illness should be excluded, since a person's physiological condition might alter the effects of the drug; or perhaps users and nonusers react differently to marijuana. The marijuana itself poses other problems, because unless each student smokes a drug of the same purity and potency, your results will be worthless. If you test only students who have smoked marijuana, you still cannot be sure of your findings. There would be no way to be certain that any alteration in their reaction time was not the result of the atmosphere surrounding the experiment or their own expectations that they were going to experience a high. So half your students must not actually get any drug, although none of them can know whether they are smoking marijuana or some inactive substance. Finally, what about your own expectations? Your knowledge as to which students have marijuana could affect how closely you observe a smoker or the concern you show toward any reactions. Only if you have controlled all these aspects of your experiment can you hope to discover anything about the effects of marijuana on reaction time (Badia and Runyon, 1982).

All these aspects of **methodology**, or methods used in the investigation, would concern any psychologist who set out to study the question. The methods used by psychologists in their investigations are similar to the methods used in other scientific fields. They provide scientists with a way of testing their **theories**, or sets of logically related statements that, in the case of psychologists, explain human behavior. Theories help a scientist to organize a multitude of observations, relating them in a coherent manner. The relationship between theory and research works both ways: theories guide research by suggesting **hypotheses** (propositions or beliefs to be tested), and research affects theory by providing information that modifies or revises a theory (Badia and Runyon, 1982).

The experimental method used to investigate the effects of marijuana on reaction

21

time is not the only means of testing a theory. Psychologists also ask people to respond to carefully worded questions, observe people in their natural environments, or intensively study individuals.

There is no one best method for studying all aspects of thought and behavior; each has certain advantages as well as limitations. The method a psychologist uses to answer a particular question often arises from the question itself. In general, research attempts to describe both mental and physical behavior, to explain the reasons for that behavior, and to predict the circumstances under which it might occur again. To accomplish these goals, researchers may choose separate strategies, each providing the answer to a specific question. For example, a study of attitudes toward sexual practices may require a survey, which is a method designed to discover the frequency with which people hold a particular attitude toward sexual behavior. To understand the origin of these attitudes, researchers might then do a series of experiments, which would help explain the various attitudes and predict the sort of behavior that might follow from them.

No matter what method psychologists use in their research, they follow the same general procedure. First, they generate a hypothesis; then they decide what kind of data would give a meaningful answer to the question they are investigating; then they gather the data by means of one or more methods; and finally, they analyze the data, usually by means of statistical techniques.

Gathering the Data

Each method of studying behavior has a place in psychological investigation, and certain aspects of information collecting go beyond a single method. These wider aspects include the factors involved in, and the nature of, the population studied.

When gathering their data, psychologists focus on certain **variables** (factors or events) that are capable of change. The answers to questions about behavior come from the changing relationship between these variables. Any factor whose change is expected to affect the event that is being studied is called an **independent variable**. The event that is being studied and that is expected to change when the independent variable is altered is called a **dependent variable**. A

researcher's hypothesis can always be rephrased into an "if/then" statement: "If the smoking of marijuana affects people's reaction time, then people under the drug's influence will react differently on tests of reaction time than people who have no marijuana in their systems." The variable that follows the word "if" is the independent variable; the variable that follows the word "then" is the dependent variable.

Since researchers cannot collect all possible data concerning a question, they gather a **sample**, or a selected segment, of the possible data. A sample must be large enough to reflect the universe of information it is meant to represent. For example, an opinion poll meant to reflect the opinions of all Democrats in the United States could not rely on a sample of only six people. Given that millions of people identify themselves as Democrats, such a small sample is almost certain to produce biased results. If, by chance, four of the six people in the sample come from Mississippi and Alabama, the findings of this poll would also be biased toward the views of Southern Democrats (which are often different from those of other Democrats). The principal requirement of a sample is that it represent the population under consideration, and this requirement demands either a random or a representative sample.

In a **random sample**, every member of the population has an equal chance of being included in the sample. If you wanted to survey people in a small town to discover how racial prejudice affects the way people vote, you could choose a random sample from voter registration lists. In other words, the method we use to sample people has no biases that favor some people over others. A bias of this sort could occur if, for example, we chose only people who lived in the poor sections of the town.

In some cases, a random sample is not adequate because it will miss members of a certain group such as voters who belong to a political party whose numbers are small in proportion to the town's population. To avoid missing such groups, surveys often use a **representative sample**, a sample in which people known to possess certain characteristics are included in proportion to their numbers in the population being studied. If we knew that 4 percent of the town's voters belonged to the Libertarian Party, we would want to make sure that 4 percent of our sample was drawn *at random* from their membership. In public opinion polling, a sample is constructed

If these anti-abortion marchers were surveyed for their views on the defeated Equal Rights Amendment, a large majority would probably be found to have been against it. Such a sample would be unrepresentative of the American population as a whole.

so that both sexes, each ethnic minority, educational level, and geographic region is represented in the same proportion as it exists in the general population.

Under most circumstances, random sampling and representative sampling lead to an adequate representation of whatever characteristic of the population is of interest. Haphazard sampling, which involves examining the most convenient or first members of the population encountered, usually does not adequately represent the characteristics of the group being studied.

The problem of a representative sample goes beyond the choice of subjects. Psychologists must also make certain that the specific items to which people in a study respond are an adequate sample of the possible items. For example, if we wanted to find out whether people prefer color to black-and-white photographs, we would have to show them a large collection of photographs. If we used only two or three photographs of each type, our collection would be unrepresentative, and our findings might reflect simply a preference for the subject matter of the particular photographs (dogs, landscapes, portraits) or the skill of the particular photographer instead of a preference for color or black-and-white.

Once they have selected their sample, psychologists generally collect data using one of five methods: the experiment, correlational research, the survey, the case study, or naturalistic observation.

The Experiment

Many psychologists regard the experiment as the "method of choice," because it allows them to infer cause-effect relationships with more confidence than do other methods. In an **experiment** researchers actively control the presence, absence, or intensity of factors that may affect whatever behavior is under study. The effect of all other factors is held constant. The main advantage of the experiment over other data-gathering methods is that the experimenters' control enables them to rule out all influences on the subjects' behavior except the factors being considered and to make inferences based on objective findings. The experiment's main disadvantage is that ruling out extraneous influences sometimes makes the situation so unnatural that behavior shown during the experiment may not resemble its counterpart in daily life.

The best way to illustrate the essential characteristics of an experiment is to follow a relatively simple one through its design, execution, and analysis. Aware that studies had consistently found that physical attractiveness affects friendships, popularity, and dating, a pair of psychologists (Kenrick and Gutierres, 1980) wondered whether the extremely beautiful women portrayed in the mass media affected men's judgments concerning the attractiveness of women they met in their daily lives. The psychologists formulated the hypothesis that a woman would appear less attractive to a man if his first sight of her came just after he had seen a beautiful model.

The subjects were male undergraduates who had volunteered to take part in an experiment described as a study of first impressions. The subjects were to look at a yearbook photograph and then fill out a "personality rating," judging the person in the photograph on such qualities as "likeable-unlikeable;" "selfish-unselfish," "warm-cold," "beautiful-ugly." (The woman in the photograph was moderately attractive, and the rating of interest to the experimenters was "beautiful-ugly.") While the researcher described the experiment, students in the **experimental group** saw a "sample" photograph—a black-and-white slide of Farrah Fawcett-Majors —which was the independent variable.

A second group of students heard the same instructions and rated the same picture, but saw no photograph of Farrah Fawcett-Majors. These students formed a **control group**, which is an important part of an experiment, because it has the same characteristics as the experimental group but is not exposed to the independent variable.

The experimenters' hypothesis was supported. Subjects who had first seen the photograph of Fawcett-Majors judged the moderately attractive woman in the "yearbook photograph" significantly less beautiful than subjects who saw only the yearbook photograph. Although such reactions may be short-lived, the researchers pointed out, first impressions of potential romantic partners could be adversely affected if they take place in the context of recent exposure to media beauty.

Not all experiments take place in a laboratory. Some are conducted on street corners, in subways, hospitals, schools, airports, and offices. In these **field studies**, researchers can introduce the independent variable, but they have no control over other variables and often cannot assign subjects to the experimental group.

An interesting field experiment was conducted by two psychologists who wanted to find out if people who initially complied with a small request would be more likely to comply with a large request (Freedman and Fraser, 1966). In the study a group of housewives was asked some questions about what products they used around the house (a small request). Several days later, the same experimenter called the housewives and asked if they would allow some men to come into their house and classify all their household products (a large request). These housewives were found to be far more likely to comply with the large request than another group who had not been asked for the smaller favor.

This study is a good example of a field study since it was conducted in the homes where these women lived. Thus the experimenters did not have to worry about whether the setting of the experiment was artificial, and indeed this is one of the major advantages of the field study in general. Experimenters using this method usually cannot be criticized for collecting data in an artificial environment. As in this example, it is often possible for the experimenter to introduce an independent variable; however, the researcher cannot always control many of the other variables that might influence the major observation.

Correlational Research

Sometimes it is impossible to conduct an experiment that will test a hypothesis. For example, suppose we wanted to know about the relationship between parental discipline and juvenile delinquency, and wondered whether permissive or strict discipline was more likely to lead to juvenile delinquency. To do an experiment that would answer this question, we would make parental discipline the independent variable and manipulate it by requiring some parents of newborns to be strict with their children and others to be lenient. Then, when the children reached adolescence, we could count instances of delinquent behavior in each group and compare them. Obviously, few parents would agree to participate in such a study and intervening in children's lives in this manner would be unethical. If we want to know about the relationship between the two variables of discipline and delinquency, we must use some other method. One way to explore such a relationship is through correlational research.

A correlational study of the relationship between discipline and juvenile delinquency could be set up by selecting a random sample of adolescents and interviewing their parents. The interview would assess the strictness of discipline in the home by asking such questions as "How often did you spank your child when she (he) was small?" Then we could look at court records to determine instances of delinquency in our sample and compare the two variables, looking for correlations.

A **correlation** is an indication of the degree of relatedness between two variables. In some instances the relationship between the two variables turns out to be close and positive, meaning that a high rank on one measure is usually accompanied by a high rank on the other. Such a strong **positive correlation** exists between socioeconomic level and years of schooling: people at upper socioeconomic levels tend to have extensive education; people at lower socioeconomic levels tend to have less education. In other instances, a close relationship between the two variables is negative, meaning that a high rank on one measure is usually accompanied by a low rank on the other. This strong **negative correlation** appears between musical ability and tone deafness (an inability to distinguish the pitch of musical notes). The more tone-deaf a person is, the less likely it is that she or he will be able to play an instrument or compose music that people will want to listen to. Often there is little or no relationship—either positive or negative—between two variables. For example, there is no relationship between eye color and education or between hair color and tone deafness. In a later section of the chapter, we will explore correlation as a statistical tool.

In a **correlational study**, psychologists select a group (such as juvenile delinquents or left-handed people) and assess the relationship between already existing variables. Since the variable has been manipulated by life and not in a laboratory, it is impossible to control other factors that might affect the outcome. Thus, the disadvantage of a correlational study is the lack of control over the variables. Despite this lack of control, a correlational study has two major advantages: its correspondence to daily life and its availability when practical or ethical questions rule out an experiment.

A problem with correlations is that people often misinterpret them. Instead of seeing a correlation as indicating merely that two things tend to occur together, they see it as indicating cause and effect. However, the two variables may be correlated because of a third variable that has not been measured, or even considered, but that affects both the variables being compared. For example, suppose there were a positive correlation between the number of tattoos on a motorcycle owner's body and the likelihood that she or he has been involved in a motorcycle accident.

Since tattoos cannot cause accidents (or vice versa), some third factor, perhaps a preference for taking risks, is affecting the rate of tattoos and accidents among motorcycle owners.

Sometimes a correlation suggests a cause-effect relationship that can be supported by an experiment. A number of years ago correlational studies kept finding a strong positive correlation between cigarette smoking and lung cancer. It was possible, however, that some third factor (such as a genetic predisposition) was responsible for both smoking and lung cancer. Not until researchers had used cigarette smoke to produce lung cancer in laboratory animals were scientists convinced that the correlation did reflect causation and that a third, unidentified, factor was not responsible (Snodgrass, 1977).

Correlations, then, say nothing about cause and effect between two factors. However, they do allow us to make predictions about events. If we know that a young girl comes from an upper-middle-class home, we can predict that she will probably go to college; if we know that a man is tone-deaf, we can predict that he is not likely to compose an interesting piece of music; if we know that a motorcycle owner is tattooed, we can predict that he has a good chance of smashing up his bike. Yet in all of these cases, our prediction could be wrong. Few events are perfectly correlated so that one factor always (or never) accompanies the other.

The Survey

A good deal of correlational research comes out of **surveys**, in which information about people's characteristics, attitudes, opinions, or behavior is obtained by asking them all the same questions. The largest survey in the United States is conducted each decade by the Bureau of the Census to establish the size, distribution, and characteristics of the population. Attempts are made to contact every household in the country and to count every person. The results from this survey tell us a great deal about people. For example, the 1980 census indicates that for the first time, the population of rural areas and small towns is growing faster than that of metropolitan centers, that the population is aging as members of the baby-boom generation get older, more people live longer, and people have fewer children; and that 6 million of the 226 million residents of the United States live in groups as opposed to sin-

A study might show that a tattooed motorcyclist is statistically more likely to be involved in a crash than is a nontattooed cyclist. Although tattoos and accident-proneness would be correlated, the relationship would not be one of cause and effect.

gle-family households (Hauser, 1981). Such information helps the government plan programs and estimate budget needs, and enables businesses to predict markets for goods.

Questioning every household produces accurate information, but such completeness is beyond the budget, staff, and time of psychologists. For this reason, most surveys select a sample of individuals and query them about a matter of interest. In 1972, the National Crime Survey was begun by the Law Enforcement Assistance Administration (LEAA) to keep track of crime and its impact on society. Every six months, poll takers visit thousands of homes and interview residents about their experience with crime during the preceding six months (*Surveying Crime*, 1976). For example, people who were part of the 1980 sample were asked, "Did anyone beat you up, attack you, or hit you with something, such as a

rock or bottle?" and "Did anyone try to rob you by using force or threatening to harm you?" If the answer to such questions is "yes," the person is asked about the circumstances, the effects the crime had on her or him, and whether it was reported to the police.

Although the aim of the National Crime Survey is laudable, some researchers are concerned that it may lead to inflated reporting of crime. As we shall see in Chapter 9, human memory is not always reliable, and one problem that is likely to distort the National Crime Survey is people's tendency to distort time in their recollections. For example, crimes that occurred seven, or eight, or nine months previously may be recalled as happening within the past six months. Since this is a common memory fault, it could lead to an overreporting of many crimes (Loftus and Marburger, 1982).

In surveys like the National Crime Survey, researchers select existing variables (such as gender, age, education, and occupation) and compare their relationship with another variable of interest (such as being robbed). By using computers, these relationships can be quickly derived from an enormous amount of data.

Surveys are often used by themselves, but they are sometimes used in connection with experiments that take place outside the laboratory. For example, researchers might arrange to have the same course taught in two different ways (manipulating the teaching environment), then survey the students to find out which approach to the subject is preferred.

Surveys can be oral (interviews) or written (questionnaires). Interviews have the advantage of letting the investigators see the subjects; they also allow them to modify the questions if it seems advisable. Questionnaires take less time to administer and so are particularly useful in gathering information from a large number of people.

In conducting a survey of either sort, investigators must try to ensure that the sample is truly representative of the group being studied. In 1936, a poll by *Literary Digest* magazine predicted a massive victory for Republican candidate Alf Landon over Democratic incumbent Franklin D. Roosevelt, but Roosevelt won by a landslide (Badia and Runyon, 1982). The problem was that the magazine had polled people whose names appeared on lists of telephone subscribers and automobile owners. In those Depression days, people who had telephones and cars tended to be wealthy, and, then as now, wealthy people were more likely to be Republicans. Thus the population sampled did not represent the voting population, and the results of the survey were misleading.

Numerous sex surveys have been done during the past thirty years. One problem with such surveys is the difficulty of finding a representative sample. People who responded to a survey conducted by *Psychology Today* magazine in 1969, for example, were readers of the magazine and they were younger, more highly educated, more liberal, wealthier, and less religious than the American population as a whole (Athanasiou, Shaver, and Tavris, 1970). In addition, since they volunteered to fill out the questionnaire, they may have differed in important ways from *Psychology Today* readers who chose not to participate.

Social psychologists often use surveys to gather data on people's attitudes and beliefs. In doing this, they sometimes encounter people who give misleading answers, either deliberately or accidentally. Some people answer "yes" whenever they can, just to be agreeable; others seem to have a built-in tendency to say "no." If a survey concerns a touchy area, such as sex, money, or race relations, people are especially likely to claim that they believe whatever they think they *ought* to believe. The psychologist conducting a survey can often control for this problem by including several differently worded questions on the same topic. Thus a person might say in answer to one question that she or he has no objection to a certain sexual practice and then, in answer to another, that she or he has never engaged in the practice and certainly never intends to. In such a case, the psychologist would suspect that the subject's attitude toward the practice was somewhat less positive than the first answer seems to have suggested.

The Case Study

Some questions about human behavior cannot be answered by experiments, correlational studies, or surveys. Suppose we wanted to discover whether experience with language in the first few years of life is necessary if a person is ever to acquire a language. It would be unethical to deprive a group of infants of any contact with language for fifteen years to test our hypothesis. Nor could we do a correlational study, since virtually every child has continual experience with

language from birth. The scarcity of children without early language experience also eliminates the survey as our research tool.

If, however, we should discover a child who for some reason has lived shut away from human contact, a golden opportunity would present itself. We could gather information on the question by means of a **case study**, an intensive investigation of one or a few individuals, usually with reference to a single psychological phenomenon—in this instance, the effect of language deprivation.

From time to time such children are found. In 1799, for example, Jean-Marc Gaspard Itard, a French doctor, discovered a boy of about twelve wandering naked through the forest. Victor, a "wild child" who lived on nuts and potatoes, trotted on all fours like an animal and could not speak. After working with the boy for five years, Itard managed to teach him to understand some language and to read simple words and phrases, but the boy never learned to speak (Lane, 1976). Nearly two centuries later, a thirteen-year-old girl was discovered who had spent her life isolated in a room. Genie, a malnourished child who could not stand erect, had been beaten whenever she made a sound. Since her father permitted no one to speak in her presence, she had grown up without any contact with language. When she was found, Genie knew no language, but after years of intensive work with psychologist Susan Curtiss (1977), Genie learned to understand what others said and to put words together so as to make herself understood. As we shall see in Chapter 13, Genie never developed a normal command of language. Cases like those of Victor and Genie are extremely rare, but they can give us information that can be obtained in no other way.

Case studies provide a wealth of information about any phenomenon of interest as it is displayed by the person or persons being studied. They allow for considerable depth of analysis and may imply the existence of certain behavioral laws; they do not, however, demonstrate that any law is actually operating.

Sometimes case studies take the form of an experiment, in which certain variables that affect a person are manipulated and repeated observations are made. In this situation, the person's original behavior serves as the control condition. However, results from an experimental case study may not be generalized to other people.

Two important principles govern the use of

case studies. The first is the observation of regularity, a lawfulness or patterning of behavior that indicates that the behavior is organized around some principle. The second is the need for subsequent case studies that repeat the pattern of behavior observed and again show the operation of behavioral laws developed in earlier case studies.

Case studies are especially useful when the question being explored makes it impossible or unethical to use an experiment in which subjects are randomly assigned to different treatments. For example, the recovery of function from brain damage has been researched primarily through case studies. Individuals who have suffered severe head injuries in accidents have been observed over long periods to determine the impact of the injury on psychological functioning and to observe the way in which some psychological functions are gradually recovered. In such cases, it would be unethical to inflict brain injuries deliberately in order to study their effects or to withhold medical treatment in order to observe the effects of accidental injuries.

Although the case-study method does not allow us to establish psychological laws or principles, it provides valuable insights into the regularity and patterning of behavior. In the hands of a brilliant psychologist, the case-study method can be a powerful tool, as when Sigmund Freud based his theory of personality development (described in Chapter 18) on case studies of patients who came to him for treatment. Jean Piaget's theory of intellectual development, described in Chapter 12, began with intensive observations of the behavior of his own three children, whom he studied almost from the moment of their birth.

Naturalistic Observation

Armed with the experiment, the correlational study, the survey, and the case study, psychologists still find themselves unable to explore some questions. Suppose, for example, we wanted to find out whether men and women smile at each other more in a supermarket or at a car wash. No laboratory experiment could provide an answer, and the survey, the correlational study, and the case study can tell us nothing about such differences in behavior. To answer this question, we would have to visit a number of supermarkets and car washes and watch men and women, noting each time one of them smiled at another.

This method of **naturalistic observation**, in which psychologists carefully observe and record behavior in natural settings, is commonly used by ethologists as a first step in studying the behavior of an animal species. A social psychologist might use naturalistic observation to study leadership roles within a commune or a therapy group. A developmental psychologist might use it to study the way four-year-olds interact at a preschool. An experimental psychologist might use it to study a species' behavior before designing an experiment meant to find out what kind of problems members of that species can solve and how they go about it.

In most naturalistic observation, the investigator is passive, unobserved, and does not intrude into the situation being studied. Among the sorts of behavior that might be observed are exterior physical signs that indicate current or past behavior, such as beards, tattoos, or skirt lengths; expressive movement, such as the direction of a person's gaze or smiles in the supermarket; physical location, such as where people sit or stand in relation to one another; conversation; and time duration, such as the length of time children play with particular toys (Webb et al., 1966).

Naturalistic observation has an enormous advantage: the situation is directly applicable to daily life and people are more likely to behave normally in such settings than in a laboratory. There are, however, disadvantages to this method of studying behavior. The experimenter has no control over any of the variables. Suppose we discover that men and women consistently smile more at one another in the car wash than in the supermarket. Because we cannot manipulate any of the variables, we are at a loss for an explanation. Car washes may be happier places than supermarkets; supermarkets may remind shoppers of tight budgets; or perhaps people smile more when they are outdoors and the car wash's outdoor location, not the nature of the business, is responsible for the smiles. This lack of control flaws another naturalistic study aimed at detecting differences in the way people habitually think. The psychologist (Moore, 1922) who believed that what people talked about toward the end of the day indicated what they were most interested in, walked a twenty-two block stretch of Broadway in New York City every evening for several weeks. He recorded all the bits of conversation he overheard and noted whether the speaker was male or female and whether the people with the speaker were of the same or the opposite sex. In analyzing his data, he found that when men talked to each other, 8 percent of their conversation was about women, but when women talked together, 44 percent of their conversation was about men. The psychologist had no control over the subjects in his study, and we have no way of knowing whether people strolling along Broadway at 7:30 P.M. are typical of the population at large—or even of Manhattan residents. Nor do we know about the content of conversation that was too soft to be overheard. It is possible that men dropped their voices when talking to other men about women.

A problem with many observational studies is the effect of the observer on the behavior of subjects. The psychologist who walked Broadway probably blended into the crowd and had no effect on the conversation of passers-by. But in other situations the effect of the researcher's presence may be profound. For example, a study of nursery-school children (Bruner, 1980) showed that the presence of an adult doubled the length of time children kept at an activity despite the fact that the adult never spoke to the child or interacted with the child in any way. For this reason, a cardinal rule of naturalistic observation is that the investigator should stay out of the way —for example, by observing animals from inside a camouflaged enclosure or children from behind a one-way window. When such concealment is impossible, the observer tries to blend into the background and refrains from recording any behavior until her or his presence has been taken for granted.

Psychologists sometimes use **participant observation**, in which members of a research team actually join an existing group to record events and impressions that are accessible only to group members. For example, three social psychologists (Festinger, Riecken, and Schachter, 1956) joined a secretive "doomsday" group that had predicted that the world would end in great floods and earthquakes on a certain date and at a certain time. As members of the group, the psychologists were present when the fateful moment came and went, and they could observe the way in which the failure of the prophecy influenced the behavior of group members. Instead of disbanding, the group ended its secrecy and became active in publicizing its views and attracting new members.

In observational research, it is important to develop ways of recording data that avoid the problems of subjective interpretation. Investiga-tors must develop explicit rules for categorizing and recording what the observer sees, so that two observers can come up with comparable results. How do we know the doomsday group became less secretive after its prophecy failed? Because the researchers kept a careful record of their observations. By examining such data, other psychologists can determine whether the conclusions are reasonable. The record of observations can be kept as a set of notes, as tape recordings, or as ratings on forms used for such studies. The important principle is that the data can be examined directly by researchers other than the original observer. Thus the observer's possible biases and idiosyncratic interpretations can be detected.

Analyzing the Data: Statistical Tools

No matter what method of collection is used, once the data are gathered, they must be quantified for psychologists to decide what they mean. Psychologists rely on statistics to help them summarize and interpret their findings. Statistics can be descriptive or inferential.

Descriptive Statistics

Descriptive statistics simply summarize data collected for a sample population. For example, your grade-point average (GPA) is a descriptive statistic that summarizes the results of your academic efforts, and the results of the latest Gallup poll summarize public attitudes toward the president's policies. Using descriptive statistics, investigators can say something meaningful about their findings with a few words and figures.

Describing Distributions of Scores Suppose a member of Congress wants to know about the concerns of people in her district. She wonders whether her constituents worry about many problems or if most are concerned about only a few issues. She hires a team of psychologists who make up a questionnaire containing forty-seven questions that can be answered "yes" or "no"— for example, "I am extremely concerned about

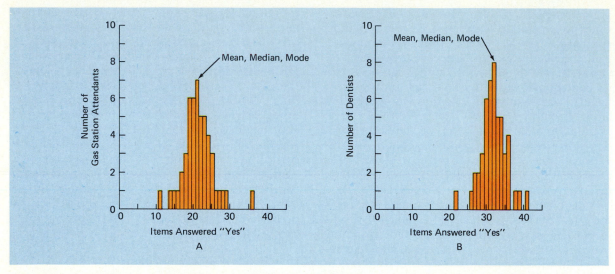

Figure 2.1 Two frequency distributions. In each figure, the vertical scale shows the frequency with which a score on the horizontal scale was observed. (A) The distribution of the scores from an imaginary group of gas-station attendants on an imaginary questionnaire. (B) The distribution of the scores of an imaginary group of dentists on the same test. Note that these distributions are similar in range but different in their averages. Also note that mean, median, and mode—the three measures of central tendency—are the same in both of these normal, symmetrical distributions.

the easy availability of handguns''; ''I believe that inflation is our most serious economic problem.'' The psychologists then give the questionnaire to a group of fifty people from a deteriorating section of the district and to another group of fifty people who live in a middle-class section of the district. Afterward, they tally the results for each group separately, so that they will be able to see how socioeconomic level affects concern. Now they are ready to describe their findings in terms of range, frequency distribution, and central tendency.

The psychologists find that some of the people worry about many issues and others worry about only a few. But among the first group no one worries about fewer than 11 issues, and no one worries about more than 36. The **range** of scores in this group is therefore 26 (that is, $36 - 11 + 1 = 26$). Among the second group, worries vary from 22 to 41, giving a range of 20.

By plotting the scores of each group on a graph, as shown in Figure 2.1, the psychologists have displayed their findings in a form that is easy to grasp. This method of describing the scores is known as a **frequency distribution**, which is an arrangement of data that shows the number of instances of each value of a variable.

On a graph of frequency distribution, the frequency (in this case frequency of people who

worried about various numbers of problems) is plotted along the vertical axis, and the values (in this case, the number of problems that concern people) are plotted along the horizontal axis. (When plotting frequency distributions from an experiment, the independent variable [which is manipulated by the researcher] is plotted along the horizontal axis, and the dependent variable [which reflects changes induced by the independent variable] is plotted along the vertical axis.)

The psychologists' next task is to choose a method for comparing the responses of the two socioeconomic groups that will provide a descriptive statistic—a single number that characterizes each distribution. One way to do this is to compare the central tendencies of the two distributions. A **central tendency** is a statistic that locates the center of the distribution, and the way the central tendency is measured depends partly on how the scores are distributed.

There are three measures of central tendency: the mean, the median, and the mode. The **mean**, which is the arithmetic average, is found by adding all the scores and then dividing the sum by the number of people who took the test. As shown in Figure 2.1, the mean score for the inner-city constituents was about 21; for the middle-class constituents, it was about 32. The second measure of the central tendency is the

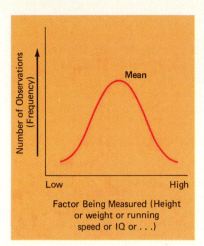

Figure 2.2 The "bell" shape of an ideal normal distribution of frequencies. The mean is at the middle of a normal distribution.

median, which is the score that falls in the exact middle of a distribution, when all scores are arranged from highest to lowest. For example, when the heights, in inches, of five players on a hypothetical basketball team are ranked (86, 84, 78, 77, 70), the median height is 78. The third measure of central tendency, the **mode**, is the score that most frequently appears in a distribution.

The examples in Figures 2.1A and B both show a symmetrical distribution, in which mean, median, and mode are the same. This equivalence of the measures of central tendency characterizes a **normal distribution**, and when such a distribution is plotted on a graph, the resulting curve has a characteristic bell shape. Such a shape, as shown in Figure 2.2, generally appears when a very large sample of scores is plotted.

However, few distributions ever exactly match the bell shape of the normal curve. Consider the graph in Figure 2.3, which represents the distribution of salaries at a plastics company. The mean income of its fifty employees is $36,000 a year, but look at the distribution. The president of the company earns $140,000 a year; he pays three executives $80,000 and four executives $60,000. There are six managers at $40,000 and six salespeople who earn $30,000. The majority of the employees, the thirty people who run the machines, all earn $25,332 or less. Although the mean of all fifty salaries is $36,000, this measure of central tendency is not a fair representation of the actual distribution of salaries.

In the case of the plastics company, the median is a better measure of central tendency, because it tells us the point at which the same number of salaries fall above and below it. The median income is $25,332. However, the mode, or the most frequent salary, is only $12,666 a year; more people make this salary than make any other.

Thus the way in which scores are distributed is extremely important. Even in the case of a symmetrical distribution, the range of scores often differ, as they do in Figures 2.1A and B. For this reason, psychologists need an additional descriptive statistic that tells them how the scores vary around the mean.

Variability and Standard Deviation The measures that show how closely clustered or how widely spread any distribution of scores is are called **measures of variability**. Range, discussed earlier, is one measure of variability, but it is a poor measure because a single score can have a dramatic effect on it. For example, salaries in a small company might range from $10,000 a year to $50,000 a year—a range of $40,000. If the president's salary is raised to $200,000 a year, the range suddenly becomes $190,000, yet only one salary has been increased. Therefore psychologists generally use a measure of variability that is not so dependent on a single score.

Figure 2.3 The distribution of incomes in an imaginary plastics company. Note that the shape of this distribution is completely different from the shapes in Figure 2.2. Note also that the mean, median, and mode are not identical in this distribution. Frequency distributions of this kind—and of many other kinds—occur in psychology, but normal distributions are the most common.

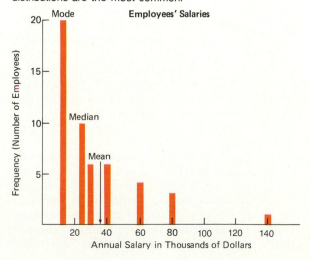

How to Find the Standard Deviation

Ascertaining the standard deviation is not difficult, although it is tedious to compute without the aid of a calculator. To calculate the standard deviation:

(1) Determine the mean of the scores.
(2) From each score, subtract the mean and square the difference. (Scores are squared to eliminate the negative signs that result when dealing with scores that fall below the mean.)
(3) Add the squares together.
(4) Divide the sum by the number of scores.
(5) Take the square root of the value you have obtained. This figure is the standard deviation.

The **standard deviation**, the measure generally preferred, tells us how much figures in a given set of data vary from the mean. This measure is related to the mean but it gives equal importance to all scores. The standard deviation can be computed by means of a simple formula (see accompanying box). Knowing the standard deviation, we can relate a score to the mean by comparing it with the standard deviation. Suppose that a large group of students takes a quiz with 100 questions, in which the mean score is 60 and the standard deviation is 10. Since the typical score will fall within 10 units of the mean, a student with a score of 90 (3 standard deviations above the mean) obviously is doing outstanding work, and a student with a score of 30 (3 standard deviations below the mean) is unlikely to pass the course. But students with scores varying from 50 to 70 are within the expected range for the typical student in this course.

If you were to measure almost any trait in a large group of people—height, weight, intelligence quotient (IQ), friendliness—you would find a normal distribution of scores. The largest number of people would fall near the mean, and fewer and fewer people would fall at each level on either side of the mean. Any normal distribution can be described by the mean and the standard deviation. And when these descriptive statistics are given, normal distributions are easy to compare. The mean locates each distribution on the measured dimension and allows you to see any differences in central tendency. The standard deviation allows you to compare the variability of scores within a given distribution with the variability of scores within other distributions.

Correlation Coefficients   Correlational research, which was discussed earlier in the chapter, has its own descriptive statistic. Psychologists who wish to assess the strength of a correlation (the degree and direction of relation between two variables) use the **correlation coefficient**. The correlation coefficient is a number ranging from −1, which indicates a perfect negative correlation between the two variables, through 0, which indicates no correlation, to +1, which indicates a perfect positive correlation. Thus the closer a correlation coefficient is to +1 or −1, the stronger the relationship—positive or negative—between the two variables. Thus, a correlation coefficient of −.65 between two variables is just as strong as a correlation coefficient of +.65. The sign (+ or −) of the correlation is disregarded when considering the strength of the relationship between variables. For example, if at some university, there is a correlation of −.42 between the students' GPAs and the number of traffic tickets they have received and a correlation of +.26 between their GPAs and their speed on the 100-yard dash, the figures demonstrate a stronger relationship between traffic violations and GPA than between athletic ability and GPA. In this fictitious example, traffic violations do a better job of predicting student grades than does running ability. A minus sign in front of a correlation coefficient simply indicates that as one variable gets bigger, the other tends to get smaller—like the relationship between the length and the thickness of a rubber band as it is stretched, which probably has a correlation near −1.

Correlations come in all sizes, but few ever attain a perfect +1 or a −1. For example, the correlation between the height of a parent and the height of the parent's child of the same sex is about +.50; the correlation between IQ scores and school grades is about +.45; the correlation between physical punishment by a mother and physical aggression by her child is about +.20. The existence of correlations can be discovered by using a scatter plot to organize the data, as

Figure 2.4 Data that are being examined for the existence of correlations are often plotted in the manner shown here. These "scatter plots" reveal visually the degree to which two variables are related. In both of these plots the set of lighter points shows a zero correlation. The darker-colored set of points in A represents a moderate positive correlation. The darker points in B represent a strong negative correlation.

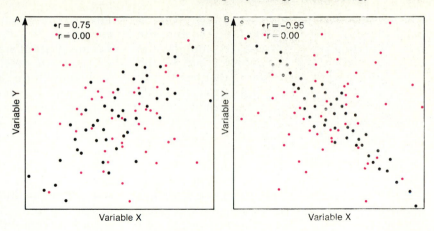

shown in Figure 2.4. Knowing the correlation between two variables is not always enough to allow us to use them in predicting events; for this purpose, we need inferential statistics.

Inferential Statistics

Once data from a study have been summarized in descriptive statistics, **inferential statistics** allow researchers to judge how likely it is that their findings did not occur simply by chance. Thus, inferential statistics provide ground rules for determining whether the hypothesis that guided the research was supported and whether researchers can infer (draw a reasonable conclusion) that their findings apply to the group from which the sample was drawn.

To draw such inferences from their findings, researchers must first disprove the **null hypothesis**, which states that all the differences found between the experimental and the control group were due to chance. They must rely on probability and statistical significance to invalidate the null hypothesis so that they can accept the hypothesis that guided the experiment (Anderson, 1971).

Probability   **Probability** is a basic tool of inferential statistics. It is a complex area of mathematics that was developed so that researchers and statisticians can estimate reasonably accurately the chances that a particular event will occur.

Suppose you toss a coin a hundred times. If it lands heads up fifty-three times, is the coin biased? What if it lands heads up seventy-nine times? A statistician would tell you that the prob-

ability of a tossed coin landing heads up on any one throw is .50: there is a 50 percent chance that the outcome will be heads and a 50 percent chance that it will be tails.

Assume, for example, that you have tossed a coin ten times and that it has landed heads up each time. You are about to toss it again. Reflect for a moment on the next toss. There are three possible predictions: (1) another head will turn up; (2) a tail will turn up; or (3) the odds are still .50, so it's impossible to tell. If you predicted that the next toss would produce a tail, you committed a common error known as the gambler's fallacy. It is a fallacy because there is no reason to expect that the probability of a tail turning up on this toss is any higher than .50.

Since the probability of getting a head on any

Figure 2.5 A frequency distribution of the outcomes of two hundred tosses of ten pennies at a time. Each tally represents the occurrence of a particular number of heads and tails among the ten pennies on one toss. (Note that if this distribution is looked at sideways, it has a "normal" shape. The most common outcome in this demonstration was five heads and five tails, but an eight-to-two ratio also occurred a number of times. Suppose you had tossed the coins just once and obtained nine tails and one head. Would you have been justified in judging the coins to be biased?

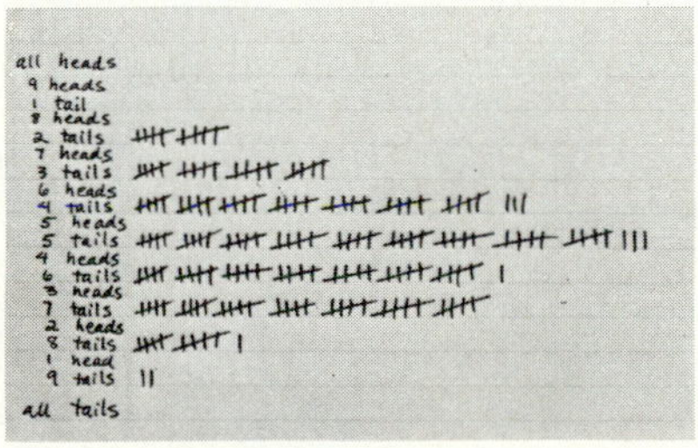

given toss is .50, the odds are always 50–50: a head will turn up half of the time. To find the odds of getting two heads in a row, multiply the odds for getting one event (one head) by the odds for getting the second (another head): 1/2 × 1/2 is 1/4. For four heads in a row, the odds would be 1/16 that such an event would occur by chance alone (1/2 × 1/2 × 1/2 × 1/2). The probability that a coin will come up heads ten times in a row is 1/2 raised to the tenth power (1/1,024), so that the odds against such a sequence occurring by chance with a fair coin are 1,024 to 1. If you now suspect that your earlier coin-tossing results were not a matter of chance and that the coin was biased (see Figure 2.5), you can appreciate the value of inferential statistics. Psychologists use probability to determine the significance of their results.

Statistical Significance   Suppose that a group of 50 children has been given vitamin C each day for a month. In the next month, 8 of these children get colds. A control group of 50 children takes a **placebo** pill (a substance that has no physiological effect) to ensure that any difference in the number of children who catch colds in each group is not due to the fact that the children in one group took pills and the other group did not. The control group gets 11 colds. The problem is to decide whether the difference between 8 and 11 is large enough to indicate that the vitamin C reduced the number of colds or whether the results might merely be due to chance. Psychologists and other scientists have adopted an arbitrary convention for making such decisions. Using statistical procedures, we can estimate the amount of difference that we would expect between the two groups by chance. Then we can compare the expected difference to the difference that was actually found. If the actual difference (3 colds, in this example) is quite a bit greater than chance predicts, we can say that the difference is a real difference.

How do we decide whether our difference is a real difference or one that occurred by chance? Using standard statistical procedures, we can calculate the probability that the result was due to chance. In some cases, it might be 1 chance in 10 or 1 chance in 100 or 1 chance in 1,000. It is common practice among researchers to use the values 1 chance in 20 (0.05) or 1 chance in 100 (0.01). If we calculate the probability that our result was due to chance to be as small as 0.05,

then we can conclude that we have a real difference.

Thus, tests of **statistical significance** allow researchers to determine exactly how small the probability is that their results have come about by chance. If computations of probability indicate that the outcome could occur by chance only once in twenty times, the probability of that outcome is 0.05. Stated in another way, less than 5 times out of 100 would an investigator expect the difference between the two groups to be due to chance. In such a case, an investigator would summarize the findings by saying that the results had attained the "0.05 level of statistical significance," inferring that the null hypothesis can be rejected. Some investigators choose more stringent levels of significance, say 0.01 (or 99 to 1 odds). No matter what level of statistical significance is selected, the probability that the results occurred solely by chance is computed, and only if that probability is low does the researcher assert that the results support the experimental hypothesis.

Selected Methodological Problems

In describing the methods and statistical techniques that psychologists commonly use, we have, for the sake of clarity, greatly simplified the process of conducting a research study. However, although inferential statistics allow researchers to reject the possibility that their findings are the result of chance, they cannot detect the presence of constant error—some additional factor that was always present in the experimental condition but was not recognized. To detect constant error, researchers must inspect the design of the experiment. Problems and pitfalls confront every researcher, and unless they are coped with successfully, they can invalidate the interpretation of a psychological study.

Experimenter Bias

In psychology, as in other fields, people tend to find what they expect to find, and experimenters' expectations can radically affect their findings. These biases arise when researchers inadvertently influence the subjects' responses or perceive the subjects' actions in terms of their own hypothesis. For example, if investigators are conducting a study in which they interview subjects face to face, they can affect a subject's responses by unwittingly communicating positive or negative feelings, as by smiling when the subject's responses corroborate the theory and frowning when they contradict it.

Psychologists have studied **experimenter bias,** as this phenomenon is called, and discovered that it also appears when students are asked to do research. In one study (Rosenthal and Fode, 1963), students were supposed to train rats to run mazes. When they received their rats, half the students were told that their animals had been bred to be "maze bright" and the other half were told that their rats were "maze dull." There was really no difference between the rats given to the two groups of students. Yet rats belonging to students who had expected their animals to be bright learned the maze rapidly, and rats belonging to students who had expected dull animals took a long time to learn the maze.

The same sort of experimenter bias affected a group of elementary-school teachers studied by Robert Rosenthal (1966), who told them that some of their pupils had made high scores on special tests and were sure to show unusual intellectual development during the school year. Actually, these pupils were picked at random and hence were no different from the rest of the children. Later in the year, the teachers rated the "bloomers" as more interested, more curious, and happier than other students. And when all the children were given IQ tests at the end of the year, the "bloomers" showed a significantly greater gain in IQ than did the "nonbloomers," as Figure 2.6 shows. This effect was strong in the early grades—among first-graders, the "bloomers" gained an average of 15 IQ points more than did the control "nonbloomers"—but similar differences in IQ gains did not appear in the fifth and sixth grades. Although young children seem to be especially susceptible to encouragement from their teachers, the effect may well have been the result of the teachers' expectations. Since there was little information in school records to contradict Rosenthal's statements about the younger children, teachers were particularly receptive to outside suggestions about their students' ability.

Researchers use several methods to overcome experimenter bias. Because they know that differences in physiological and psychological

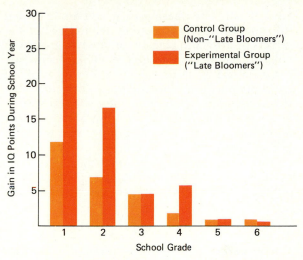

Figure 2.6 Teachers in each of the six grades of an elementary school were led to believe that certain of their pupils had been discovered to be "late bloomers" on the basis of a special test and would show great academic gains during the year. In fact, the pupils were selected at random. Intelligence tests were given both at the beginning and at the end of the school year. This histogram shows the relative IQ gains during the year of the control group (pupils not expected to be "late bloomers" by their teachers) and the experimental group (pupils who were expected to be "late bloomers"). Both groups gained in the lower grades, but the experimental group gained more. However, in the upper grades there was little effect, perhaps because the teachers already had strong expectations about the pupils based on their performances in earlier grades. (After Rosenthal, 1966.)

make-up lead human beings to perceive the world differently, investigators often use two or more observers in studies that involve observing or rating behavior (Ray and Ravizza, 1981). When observations made by two or more people are highly correlated, the findings are less likely to be contaminated by any person's subjective perceptions.

Another way for a researcher to avoid experimenter bias is to use the **double-blind technique**, in which neither the experimenter nor the subjects know which subjects belong to the experimental group and which belong to the control group. In an experiment testing the effects of a tranquilizing drug, for example, the experimental group would be given the tranquilizer and the control group would receive a placebo, perhaps in the form of a sugar pill. Only some outside party, such as the pharmacist who supplied the pills, would know which group received which kind of pill. The pharmacist would not give that information to the experimenter until after the effects of drug and placebo on the two groups of subjects had been recorded. A similar technique can be used in natural studies. For example, if psychologists were looking for a possible correlation between IQ and psychological adjustment and were using interviews as one way to assess adjustment, it would be important that they not know their subjects' IQ scores until after completing the interviews and recording their conclusions concerning the subjects' psychological adjustment.

Demand Characteristics

The investigator is not the only one who can bias the results of a study; equally disrupting effects can come from the subjects, because they are human beings who interpret each situation in which they find themselves. For this reason, an independent variable does not always evoke a subject's natural reaction. In any experiment, subjects may respond in three ways: (1) they may react to themselves (by responding naturally); (2) they may react to the experimenter (by responding in ways they think will please her or him); or (3) they may react to the experimental situation (by trying to figure out the situation and responding in accordance with their thoughts about the experiment; Ray and Ravizza, 1981).

When a subject's response is strongly determined by the research setting, psychologists say that **demand characteristics** are operating—the subject is responding in ways that seem to be demanded by the situation. For example, some years ago all babies were assumed to go through a period of intense "stranger anxiety" that began toward the end of the first year, when they became extremely upset at the approach of any stranger. Later studies found that it was the strange setting of the laboratory and not the strangeness of the person that was primarily responsible for the anxiety and tears. Tested in their homes, the babies seemed unafraid and interested when a stranger appeared (Tracy, Lamb, and Ainsworth, 1976). Because the earlier extreme reactions were the result of demand characteristics, the phenomenon is now called "stranger wariness," indicating that although most babies regard strangers with caution— which they reveal by an increased heart rate (Campos, 1976)—infants become fearful only

when the situation seems strange and perhaps threatening.

Demand characteristics also appeared in studies of hypnosis (Orne, 1969; Orne and Evans, 1966). In these studies, there was a group of hypnotized subjects and a second, "quasi-control" group whose members had been asked to act "as if" they were hypnotized. In the middle of the experiment, a tape recorder suddenly stopped and a desk lamp went out; the hypnotist, saying a fuse had blown, left the room. The purpose of the bogus blown fuse was to discover what happened to people in a hypnotic trance when the hypnotist left them. In this instance, the quasi-control group continued to act as if they were hypnotized, but the hypnotized subjects gradually came out of the trance and seemed confused. When members of the quasi-control group were interviewed, it became apparent that they had figured out that the power failure was a hoax, assumed they were being observed, and continued to pretend they were in a trance. In a second study that controlled for demand characteristics by moving the experiment to a room where there was no one-way observation window and by stopping *all* electrical equipment in the room (including the room lights and a polygraph), the quasi-control group's behavior changed. When the hypnotist left the room, most of them dropped the pretended trance and behaved normally. Apparently, in the earlier study these subjects were reacting to a situation they had figured out.

Sometimes merely the fact of being part of an experiment can dramatically affect subjects' behavior. More than fifty years ago, a group of workers at a plant in Hawthorne, Illinois, were studied to see how various factors in the working environment (such as lighting and working hours) affected production. No matter what the researchers did, production increased. Even when the independent variable should have reduced the workers' output—as when they had to labor in bad light—production went up. Many psychologists believe that the special attention these workers received during the studies was in itself enough to make them work harder, although others have pointed out the existence of uncontrolled variables that could have been responsible for the effect (Rice, 1982). Since that time, however, investigators have been conscious of the **Hawthorne effect**, as the influence of attention that accompanies an experiment is called, and they often take steps to control for it.

Problems of Measurement

A third problem that faces psychologists concerns the selection of behavioral measures that will answer the question they are studying. When the goal is to measure IQ, the IQ test is the obvious choice. There are other standard ways of measuring psychological phenomena. For example, the maze-running ability of a rat can be assessed either by timing the animal's run through the maze on successive trials or by seeing how many trials are needed before the rat can run the maze without error. But in many cases, deciding how to measure the variable under study can be a major methodological problem.

Among the difficulties that face psychologists is the possibility that there is no meaningful difference between the experimental condition and the control condition. Although investigators think they are manipulating the independent variable, it actually remains the same for both groups. Before methods of recording brain waves were developed, for example, psychologists studying sleep had to assume that those subjects with closed eyes were asleep. But closed eyes can accompany states other than sleep, so that investigators could not be positive that the independent variable had indeed been manipulated.

The selection of behavioral measures becomes particularly acute when researchers are studying infants who cannot talk. Suppose, for example, you wanted to know whether a baby could tell the difference between a mother saying "yes" and "no." How would you find out? Because psychologists are interested in how soon babies can discriminate between sounds, they have devised ingenious ways of discovering such things. In one popular technique, babies are given a nipple to suck; connected to the nipple is a device that records the rate of sucking. Although babies get nothing through the nipple, they will suck at a constant rate as long as nothing new attracts their attention. A sudden change in stimulation, however, is invariably followed by a burst of rapid sucking. So you would record a woman's voice saying "yes . . . yes . . . yes" over and over again, then play the recording until the baby's sucking at the nipple had slowed to the steady rate. At that time you would switch the recording from her voice saying "yes" to "no"; if the baby suddenly begins sucking rapidly, you would know the infant had detected a difference between the two words. Using this technique, re-searchers have found that babies only a month old can tell the difference between sounds as similar as "ba" and "pa" (Eimas and Tartter, 1979).

Replication

During their training, psychologists are taught to anticipate and avoid methodological errors, for example, by adopting the double-blind technique when there is a danger that experimenter bias may affect their findings. Despite such precautions, however, errors sometimes occur. For this reason, a scientific study should be subject to **replication**, that is, duplication with the same results. Replication is obviously important if psychology—or any science—is to accumulate reliable data. If particular findings appear only once or twice, they may be due to chance or to defects in experimental design.

When psychologists speak of replication, they are usually referring to whether the findings of one researcher or team of researchers have been duplicated by another. For example, if Smith, Jones, and Schwartz perform an experiment that finds that jogging five miles a day relieves depression, and four similar studies done by different researchers on different subjects reach the same results, the original findings are said to be replicated. This kind of replication is known as **intersubject replication**, or replication with different subjects. Although a single experimenter may test his or her findings on a number of different groups of subjects, the strongest type of intersubject replication is that achieved when different researchers find the same results with different groups of subjects.

Intrasubject replication, on the other hand, is replication with the *same* subjects. This kind of replication is often sought by scientists as part of a single experiment, as a means of testing the reliability of their own findings. For example, in our hypothetical jogging experiment, the investigator might identify fifteen depressed subjects, who would then be put on a program of daily jogging, eventually working up to five miles of jogging a day. After a given period (four months, perhaps), the subjects would be examined to see whether they were more or less depressed than they had been at the start of the experiment. After recording these findings (say, that most of the subjects were significantly less depressed), the experimenter would ask the subjects to *stop* jogging for a period of time significant enough for their bodies to lose their new level of fitness (four more months, perhaps). Once again, the subjects would be examined: Were they again depressed? Finally, the subjects would be asked to repeat their jogging program for a period. If the depression-reducing effect appeared again, the experimenters could have some confidence in their findings. If the experimental intervention had made a permanent change in the subjects, intrasubject replication would be impossible. If subjects in our hypothetical experiment did not become depressed again after they stopped jogging, we would not be able to achieve intrasubject replication in our experiment. This would not mean that our findings were worthless, however. If intersubject replication could be achieved, we still would have a reliable and interesting bit of data worthy of examination in further experiments.

Ideally, replication studies clarify, correct, and extend the findings of the first study, so that some point about behavior can be regarded as having been conclusively demonstrated. On occasion, however, attempts at replication raise more questions than they answer.

Some years ago, for example, investigators (Bakan, 1971) reported that eye movements revealed that most people tended to rely on one side of the brain when processing information. In people who consistently shifted their glance to the left when answering a question, the brain's right cerebral hemisphere predominated. In people who consistently shifted their gaze to the right, the left cerebral hemisphere predominated. Thus, the direction of gaze became a measure of individual difference. Other researchers (Schwartz, Davidson, and Maer, 1975) failed to replicate these findings. Instead, they said, people looked to the right when answering questions that required verbal analysis, arithmetic, or logic. They looked to the left when drawing on musical skills, answering questions that involved spatial relations, or questions that evoked emotion. According to these researchers, direction of gaze was a measure of the kind of processing going on in the brain. Then a third group of researchers (Gur, Gur, and Harris, 1975) reported that researchers had been seeing too much in their data: the direction of gaze was related to anxiety levels provoked by the presence of an experimenter. When the experimenter sat directly in front of the subjects (as in the first experiment), they became anxious and tended to rely on the side of the brain that was most compatible with their own cognitive style.

When the experimenter was out of the room and eye movements were videotaped (as in the second experiment), the direction of gaze was linked with the content of the question. But even these findings did not settle the debate. About half the studies involving eye movement failed to find *any* of the predicted differences. Thus, there has been no consistent replication, and whatever link exists between brain activity and eye movement appears to be weak and indirect (Springer and Deutsch, 1981).

When it comes to meeting the replication requirement, psychologists are not perfect. Not all studies—even some very important ones—have been replicated. Sometimes findings escape critical analysis and attempts at replication for years. When they do so, it may be because the findings corroborate the prevailing scientific attitude. Replicating a study whose findings seem obviously correct promises much drudgery and little reward. In addition, the inability to replicate a study does not necessarily mean that the hypothesis behind the study had been disproved. Replication studies are as open to experimenter bias and other methodological problems as are original studies.

Ethical Principles in Psychological Research

At several points in this chapter, we have said that a research project could not be conducted because it would be "unethical." For example, shutting infants away from human contact for their first few years to determine whether early experience with language is necessary for its eventual acquisition would clearly be unethical. Such a procedure could cause irreparable harm; therefore, this sort of research should never be conducted with human subjects, regardless of the potential significance of the outcome. Although the great bulk of psychological research involves no risk—either physical or psychological—to participants and poses no ethical questions, some cases are not so clear-cut.

Suppose, for example, that you are approached by a private investigator and asked to participate in a burglary. And suppose, further, that following a meeting at which the proposed burglary was discussed, you agreed to help out with the understanding that you would be guaranteed immunity from prosecution. Afterward you are told that you have just participated in an experiment aimed at discovering what sort of situations lead people to break the law and how they perceive their actions. Would you be angry? Embarrassed? Ashamed? Relieved? Happy to have contributed to the advancement of knowledge? Or would your self-esteem plummet because you realized that you were capable of breaking the law? Is it possible that after agreeing to participate in this bogus burglary you might find it easier to contemplate breaking the law in the future?

Just such an experiment has been conducted as part of an attempt to understand the perceptions of people involved in the wiretapping and burglary case at the Watergate complex in Washington, D.C., which ultimately led to the resignation of President Richard M. Nixon (West, Gunn, and Chernicky, 1975). Some people who were approached by the investigator were told that the burglary was to be done for a government agency; some were told that they would receive a large sum of money; some were told that they would receive immunity from prosecution; and the rest, who formed a control group, were given no inducement of any kind. It has been charged that this study violated the psychologists' code of ethics because taking part in it could have negative effects on the participants and because its similarity to the Watergate break-in would result in wide publicity once the findings were published (Cook, 1975).

Because psychologists have an ethical obligation to protect the dignity and welfare of the people who participate in research, the American Psychological Association (1981) has drawn up a set of ethical principles to guide the conduct of research that involves human subjects. This code sets up several conditions aimed at protecting human subjects, including privacy, voluntary participation, informed consent, and freedom from harm. All complaints against psychologists are investigated by the APA's Committee on Scientific and Professional Ethics, and when charges are substantiated, the psychologist is suspended or expelled from the APA (Hare-Mustin and Hall, 1981).

Participants in an experiment have the right to privacy. Their thoughts and feelings may not be revealed without their consent. Thus, to use findings from studies such as the one that involved an invitation to crime, researchers must keep all personal data private and report their findings in such a way that the identity of participants cannot be determined—whether by ordinary citizens, by the press, by government, or by other scientists.

Participation in an experiment must also be voluntary; a person must be free to decide whether or not to take part. Further, if a subject wants to drop out of the experiment at any point, she or he must be free to do so.

Before a person can decide whether to participate, she or he must have some sort of information about the experiment. Psychologists are supposed to tell potential subjects what they will have to do during an experiment and whether any harm might possibly come from taking part in the study. Thus voluntary participation should be based on informed consent.

Finally, no lasting harm should come from participating in the experiment. Indeed many psychologists believe that no effects of any kind should linger after the experiment is over and contact between researcher and subject has been terminated.

In addition to being obliged to protect the people who participate in their research, psychologists are also obligated to try to find the answers to important scientific, psychological questions. At times these obligations conflict. To conduct important studies, psychologists may have to use procedures that involve some risk of physical or psychological harm to some of the participants. For this reason, research involving human subjects is generally reviewed by a panel of other psychologists who determine whether the subjects will be adequately protected. They also decide whether the proposed experiment will allow subjects to participate voluntarily through informed consent. Such review is required by the U.S. government for all research funded by federal grants, and most universities require such review of all research.

Yet sometimes a study could not be undertaken if the participants knew its details and purpose. If psychologists want to find out, for example, whether a bystander will report a theft, telling potential subjects about the experiment would destroy its value. Most people would behave the way they think they should behave. In a study (Latané and Elman, 1970) that used deception, researchers staged the blatant theft of a case of beer while the cashier was in the rear of a beverage store. Among people who watched the theft by themselves, 35 percent failed to report it to the cashier. And when two or more people watched the theft, in only 56 percent of the cases did even one of them report it. The discovery of which conditions lead people to report crimes or come to the aid of strangers in distress can have important implications for society.

Another sort of objection has been raised to informed consent by some psychologists (Loftus and Fries, 1979) who point out that human beings are very suggestible and that giving them detailed information, such as possible side effects of a drug in a double-blind test of its effectiveness, can lead subjects to experience these effects. The psychologists describe a study conducted with informed consent, in which some of the people who were given the placebo reported the strongest possible side effects—nausea, vomiting, dizziness, mental depression—despite the fact that they had received no drug. One subject who got the placebo said the side effects were so severe that they led to an automobile accident. In such cases, full information can cause harm instead of preventing it.

Although some psychologists maintain that deception is always unethical, most believe that under some circumstances deception is necessary. The APA code of ethics recognizes that concealment or deception is sometimes necessary, but stipulates that in such cases researchers tell subjects about the deception—and the reason for it—after the experiment has been completed.

What about the Watergate study we discussed earlier? When the researchers were challenged, they described four procedures they had used to protect the subjects. First, after the study was over, all subjects were told about the nature of the experiment, that they had been deceived, and that the investigators regretted having had to use deception. Second, the meeting at which the robbery was discussed in detail was a second meeting, which took place only after the subjects had been approached and asked to come to a different location to discuss "a project you might be interested in." Third, the researchers tried to set up a study that did not involve deception, but could find no way to study the question without using deceit. Finally, both the state attorney's office and a lawyer who was also a psychologist had advised the researchers, and the latter had helped plan the study so as to protect the rights of all participants (Ray and Ravizza, 1981).

Human subjects are not the only focus of concern in experiments. In some instances research that cannot be done with human participants is performed on animals: rats, cats, pigeons, monkeys, and many other species. For example, a psychologist may study the importance of visual experience by raising one group of rats in complete darkness and another group under normal

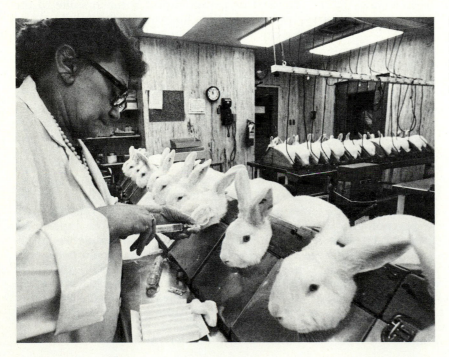

Some research cannot ethically be performed on human subjects. Often animals are used instead. But protests against the Draize test, which uses rabbits to determine the safety of cosmetics, are growing.

The Practical Benefits of Basic Research

It is often difficult to see what use can come from the absorption of psychologists in the behavior of rats, pigeons, or chimpanzees, but what is learned in such experiments sometimes directly benefits human beings. The achievements of Sarah, a chimpanzee who learned to connect oddly shaped bits of colored plastic with things in her world, has made life better for many people. In a lengthy research program, David Premack (1971; Premack and Premack, 1972) taught Sarah to communicate, using a different piece of plastic for each word, such as a blue triangle for "apple." Sarah's vocabulary included most parts of speech; she knew such words as "under," "red," "three," and "take." Sarah answered questions by placing symbols on a board, and she also learned to follow the instructions contained in symbols arranged by her trainers. Although, as we shall see in Chapter 13, Sarah may not have learned a true language, she could certainly exchange information with human beings.

Those same bits of colored plastic that Sarah used to "talk" with her trainers have been used in similar ways to broaden the communicative skills of handicapped people. In one program (Glass, Gazzaniga, and Premack, 1973), the Premack system enabled patients whose language ability had been damaged by a stroke to communicate again. These patients had at one time been able to talk fluently, but prior acquisition of language is not required for human applications of the program. The Premack system has also been successful with the mentally retarded. For example, sixty retarded children who had failed in a conventional language therapy program learned to "talk" fluently with a modified version of Sarah's symbols (Carrier and Peak, 1975). In another program (Deich and Hodges, 1977), people so severely retarded they could not talk at all also learned to communicate with the symbols, "saying" such things as "Teacher put candy in box." One patient, Charlie, who had a mental age of only three years, eight months, learned to "talk" so well with the plastic bits that he could be trained in sign language and placed in a class for the trainable mentally retarded. Thus, it is possible that any program in basic research will ultimately have practical use.

lighting conditions. Although researchers may use procedures with animals that would be unethical to use with people, stringent standards govern the treatment of animal subjects. State and federal regulations specify procedures and standards for animal care—housing, feeding, and cleaning. Ethical standards prohibit the researcher from inflicting unnecessary pain. As with human beings, the importance of the research is weighed against the potential harm to the animals involved.

When researchers are suspected of violating these standards, they can be held responsible. In one case, a prominent researcher who had been experimenting on monkeys to find ways of helping stroke victims regain the use of their limbs was charged with cruelty to animals (Holden,

Animals experience pain and fright, too, and experimenters must observe ethical standards in their treatment of animal subjects.

1981). The monkeys had had the nerves in one arm severed, or deafferented, and their good arm had been bound to their bodies to force them to use the deafferented arm. Because monkeys have no feeling in a deafferented limb, it is often injured and the monkeys treat it as a foreign object, perhaps even chewing off their own fingers. An animal-welfare activist who had volunteered to work at the laboratory became concerned at the monkeys' physical condition and at what he regarded as appalling conditions within the laboratory and called authorities. In this case, it was not the research on the animals that was questioned, which has important human applications, but the lack of veterinary care for the monkeys and the living conditions in the laboratory. According to the researcher, he had been on vacation during the period involved, and the workers whose responsibility it was to clean, feed, and care for the animals had not been doing their jobs. When the case came to court, the researcher was exonerated of charges that the laboratory conditions were unacceptable or that he had inflicted unnecessary pain or suffering on the animals. He was, however, found guilty on six counts of cruelty to animals for failure to provide adequate medical care for six of the monkeys, and he was fined $3,015.

Scientific investigation, then, cannot be conducted in an ethical vacuum. Psychological research, which not only affects human beings and animals but depends on them for subjects, must necessarily be subject to rigorous ethical constraints.

Now that our methodological survey is complete, we are ready to explore the field of psychology. Although some of the material in this chapter may have seemed esoteric, it lies at the heart of any progress in understanding human behavior. Even a cursory knowledge of the various methods used by psychologists enables us to understand the research presented in this book and to analyze more critically some of the glowing reports that often appear in the mass media.

SUMMARY

1. The procedure psychologists use to conduct studies involves formulating a **hypothesis**, or propositions being tested, deciding what kind of data could answer the question under investigation, gathering the data, and then analyzing it—usually by means of statistical techniques. The particular method of gathering data depends on the nature of the question the psychologist wants to answer. Researchers collect a **sample**, or selected segment, of the data pertaining to their hypothesis. The sample is either a **random sample**, in which every member of the population has an equal chance of being included, or a **representative sample**, in which people known to possess certain characteristics are included in proportion to their numbers in the population being studied.

2. In an **experiment**, the psychologist actively controls the presence, the absence, or the intensity of those factors thought to affect the behavior being studied and holds all other factors constant. Subjects in the **experimental group** undergo the experimental treatment; subjects in the **control group** have the same characteristics as the experimental group except that they do not undergo the experimental treatment. A **variable** is any factor in the experiment that is capable of change. The variable that is manipulated by the experimenter is the **independent variable;** the variable that changes when the independent variable changes is the **dependent variable.** Not all experiments take place in a laboratory. In a **field study,** researchers introduce the independent variable into a natural setting.

3. **Correlational studies** indicate the degree of relatedness between two variables. In a **positive correlation**, a high rank on one variable is usually accompanied by a high rank on the other. In a **negative correlation**, a high rank on one variable is usually accompanied by a low rank on the other. Although a correlation does not indicate cause and effect, it allows predictions about the likelihood of two things occurring together. A **survey** attempts to estimate the opinions, characteristics, or behavior of a population, generally based on a representative sample. A **case study** is an intensive investigation of one or a few individuals, usually with reference to a single psychological phenomenon. In **naturalistic observation**, behavior is observed and re-

corded under natural conditions. In **partici-pant observation**, researchers join an existing group to record events and impressions that are accessible only to group members.

4. Researchers generally analyze data by means of descriptive or inferential statistics. **Descriptive statistics** reduce a mass of data to a manageable and understandable form. For example, individual scores can be compared by describing the way they are distributed. The **range** of a set of scores is the difference between the highest and lowest scores. Another way of describing a group of scores is to use the **central tendency**, which may be the **mean**, or the arithmetical average; the **median**, or the score that falls in the exact middle of the distribution; or the **mode**, which is the most frequently obtained score. When the mean, the median, and the mode are equivalent, the distribution is symmetrical, or a **normal distribution**. Measures of variability indicate how closely clustered the distribution of scores is. The most commonly used measure of variability is the **standard deviation**, a number that indicates the extent to which figures in a given set of data vary from the mean. **Correlation coefficients** assess the strength of a relationship between two variables. A correlation coefficient is a number ranging from -1 (a perfect negative correlation) through 0 (no correlation) to $+1$ (a perfect positive correlation).

5. **Inferential statistics** are used to determine whether the original hypothesis was clearly supported by the data or whether the **null hypothesis** (which states that the results were due primarily to chance) was upheld. Probability is an area of mathematics that deals with the likelihood of certain events. Tests of **statistical significance** allow researchers to decide whether chance might have been responsible for experimental findings.

6. **Experimenter bias** refers to the fact that the expectations of investigators can influence their findings. One way for a researcher to avoid experimenter bias is to use two or more independent observers; another way is to use the **double-blind technique** in which neither the experimenter nor the subjects know which subjects belong to the experimental group and which belong to the control group. When the subject's response is determined more by the research setting than by the independent variable, **demand characteristics** are affecting the research results. In the **Hawthorne effect**, the attention that accompanies the experiment influences the experimental results. Deciding how to measure the factor under study can be a major methodological problem. Before findings of a study are accepted by the profession, they should be **replicated** in a study by at least one other psychologist at a different laboratory. The second investigator may either modify or attempt to reproduce the conditions of the original study.

7. Certain psychological studies may involve risk of physical or psychological harm to some of the participants. The American Psychological Association has developed a set of principles to guide the conduct of researchers; this code calls for the subjects' privacy, voluntary participation, informed consent, and freedom from harm. When research cannot ethically be done with human subjects, it can sometimes be performed on animals. State and federal regulations specify standards for the use of animals in research and procedures for their care.

KEY TERMS

case study	dependent variable	frequency distribution
central tendency	descriptive statistics	Hawthorne effect
control group	double-blind technique	hypotheses
correlation	experiment	independent variable
correlation coefficient	experimental group	inferential statistics
correlational study	experimenter bias	intersubject replication
demand characteristics	field studies	intrasubject replication

mean	null hypothesis	representative sample
measures of variability	participant observation	sample
median	placebo	standard deviation
methodology	positive correlation	statistical significance
mode	probability	surveys
naturalistic observation	random sample	theories
negative correlation	range	variables
normal distribution	replication	

RECOMMENDED READINGS

CRAIG, J. R., and L. P. METZE. *Methods of Psychological Research.* Philadelphia: Saunders, 1979. This book discusses how to conduct psychological research, the ethics of such research, and how to write a research report, among other topics.

MARKEN, R. *Methods in Experimental Psychology.* Monterey: Brooks/Cole, 1981. Another fine discussion of methods of conducting and writing up research.

RAY, W. J., and R. RAVIZZA. *Methods Toward a Science of Behavior and Experience.* Belmont, Calif.: Wadsworth, 1981. An introductory text on methods in psychology. Nicely written, with good examples.

RAYNOLDS, P. D. *Ethics of Social Science Research.* Englewood Cliffs, N.J.: Prentice-Hall, 1982. This paperback book helps students and researchers develop their own strategies for analyzing ethical problems in social science research.

SIEGEL, M. H., and H. P. ZEIGLER (eds.). *Psychological Research: The Inside Story.* New York: Harper & Row, 1976. This book, now in paperback, contains chapters by psychologists in which they describe how they got into doing the particular research that they do. They talk about their mistakes and their triumphs.

PART TWO

Biological and Perceptual Processes

In 1798, William Wordsworth, writing of a dull and unimaginative clod, said:

A primrose by a river's brim
A yellow primrose was to him,
And it was nothing more.

How I despised the person in question, when, as a youngster, I first read that passage. How he must have been deaf to poetry, blind to beauty, lost to imagination. How pleased I was that *I* was not like that; that I could see the primrose with the eyes of wonder.

And yet—Science must limit itself to the material aspects of that primrose and nothing more. It must avoid poetry, dismiss beauty, and carefully discipline imagination. There can be nothing in the primrose that cannot be weighed, measured, and, in one way or another, sensed not only by myself but by others.

I must find in the primrose only that which others, following my description of my investigation, will find as well. Results must be sensible and reproducible.

Why?—If I find something about the primrose I cannot describe, or, having described it, cannot persuade others to find as well, the result is of no use to anyone but myself. If I per-

suade some to find it but not others, that is of only limited use.

The universe of science deals with those phenomena on which all reasonable human beings can agree. (Who are "reasonable"?—Well, that's one of the problems that occupies the science of psychology.)

Does that mean that the scientist is unbearably limited to a life of dull materialism and numbers?

Don't you believe it! The methodology of science may be of no use outside the limits of the scientific universe, but within those limits it uncovers wonders and beauty that the undisciplined imagination, unaware of the uses of science, can never grasp.

The microscope applied to the primrose petal produces vistas of order and dainty interrelationships the unaided eye cannot see. Chemistry reveals the molecular structure of pigments that no one could dream of otherwise. Turning to the plant that bears the blossom, there is the complex interrelationship of the components of the photosynthetic mechanism that makes it possible for the plant to turn the energy of sunlight into material struc-

tures, and the whole is more beautiful than anything Wordsworth ever sensed in a primrose, however impassioned it may have made him feel.

And yet surely there is something beyond that. When one listens to a Beethoven symphony, is there any way of analyzing the sound waves that will produce something that will duplicate the sensation of the unanalyzed sound? Can any acoustical study, any explanation of the tonal interrelationships supply what we feel when we listen in ignorance? If we hold the hand of someone we love, what analysis of tactile stimulation will explain our sensation? How careful a chemical breakdown will suffice to make us understand the effect of the smell of a roasting chicken when we are hungry, or of freshly cut grass when we are dreamily relaxed on a summer afternoon?

But then, questions like that also fall within the scientific universe, for one branch of science does take up the question of perception—all conceivable varieties of it. That is psychology, to which nothing human (however nonscientific) can be alien.

ISAAC ASIMOV

45

CHAPTER 3

The Brain and Behavior

The experiences of J. W., a bright twenty-six-year-old man, are helping scientists to unravel the workings of the human brain. In a typical experiment, a black-and-white drawing of a hunter's cap was flashed on a screen before him. J. W. could not name the drawing, but he was aware that he had seen "something." A game of twenty questions began. "Is it an object or a living thing?" a researcher asked. "An object," was the reply. In response to further questions, J. W. said that it wasn't a vehicle, a tool, or any kind of household utensil. Asked if the picture was an article of clothing, J. W. said that it was. Then he could also say that the article of clothing in the picture was usually worn by men, that it was worn during the autumn, and that it was usually red. At last, by this process of elimination, he identified the object as a hunter's cap.

J. W.'s difficulty in naming an object that he could clearly see lay in the fact that a few weeks earlier he had undergone surgery in an attempt to halt the massive epileptic seizures that afflicted him. The surgeons had partially severed the connection between his **cerebral hemispheres**, which make up 85 percent of the human brain, disrupting communication between them. Using an ingenious device, researchers flashed a picture that was sent only to the right side of his brain. Since, like most people, J. W. processed language in his left cerebral hemi-

sphere and the left side of his brain had not seen the picture, he was unable to put what he had seen into words.

Gradually, J. W. developed a way to transfer information from one cerebral hemisphere to the other, but he was never able to transfer the visual image of the object he had seen. Instead, he transferred complicated information about the context in which the pictured object might be found. For example, the picture of a knight flashed to his right cerebral hemisphere led him to say, "I have a picture in mind but can't say it. . . . Two fighters in a ring . . . Ancient . . . wearing uniforms and helmets . . . on horses . . . trying to knock each other off . . . Knights?"

Because his seizures continued, J. W. had a second operation that completed the split between his cerebral hemispheres. The transfer of information ceased. Then when his right cerebral hemisphere saw a picture, he would say, "I didn't see anything" (Sidtis et al., 1981).

As we shall discover, the existence of split-brain patients like J. W. has provided a rich source of information about the functioning of the human brain. Yet despite enormous strides in our knowledge of the brain, much of this complex organ is but dimly understood. Indeed, David Hubel (1979, p. 52), who shared the Nobel Prize for his discoveries about the brain's function in vision, has said, "How long it will be before one is able to say that the brain—or the mind—is in broad outline understood . . . is anyone's guess.''

We do know that there is an intimate relationship between the brain and behavior. Damage to the brain can be followed by disturbances of speech, sight, or hearing, a preoccupation with sex, gross overeating, the inability to store new memories, the disruption of muscle control, coma, or the inability to fall asleep. Stimulating the brain can make a person feel sexy, angry, or happy. It can also cause specific muscles to move, produce complex hallucinations, and evoke detailed patterns of behavior that are commonly found in a species.

A large and active group of specialists, called **neuropsychologists**, study these relationships in human beings, examining the structure of the nervous system and how it relates to the other organs and parts of the body. Their primary goal is to discover how information—whether it comes from the environment or from within the body—is changed into a form that the brain can use, and how this new form of information is then changed into feelings, thoughts, and actions. Neuropsychologists also seek to understand just how the human brain is related to the action of muscles and glands. Although such study focuses on the brain, that organ is always seen in the context of the entire nervous system, for it is through the rest of the system that brain function is translated into behavior.

The Nervous System

Every living organism is equipped with specialized structures that integrate information from many sources and translate it into appropriate responses. In single-celled animals, such as amoebae and paramecia, different parts of the single cell are related to different behavioral functions. In more complex animals, special cells have distinct roles in behavior. Stimulation from the environment is handled by **receptor cells** that lie within the sense organs. Muscle contraction and glandular secretion are the job of **motor cells**, which specialize in movement. Signals from one part of the body to another are transmitted by **neurons**, cells that connect receptor cells with motor cells so that their activities can be carried out smoothly. Neurons are of special

interest because they interconnect and combine to form the nervous system.

Divisions of the Nervous System

The **nervous system** constitutes a network of communication channels that spreads to every part of the body. For convenience of discussion, the nervous system is usually subdivided into various parts, but in actual operation the parts act together and the distinctions become somewhat blurred.

The **central nervous system (CNS)**, consisting of the brain and the spinal cord, contains most of the neurons. The central nervous system controls all human behavior, from the blink of an eye at a puff of air to the solution of a complex problem in symbolic logic. The **peripheral nervous system (PNS)**, consisting of **nerves** (bundles of neuron fibers) and **ganglia** (collections of neu-

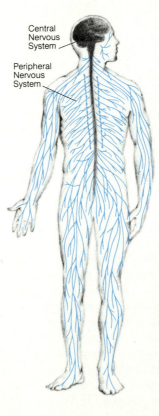

Central Nervous System

Peripheral Nervous System

Figure 3.1 The central nervous system (CNS) and the peripheral nervous system (PNS) in the human body. Both of these systems are made up of billions of nerve cells, or neurons, each of which is capable of transmitting a train of chemical-electrical signals in one direction. In the CNS, these neurons form an immensely complex network that organizes, stores, and redirects vast quantities of information. In the PNS, neurons in every pathway carry information either from receptors (such as the sense organs) toward the CNS or away from the CNS to effectors (in the muscles, for example). There is a close match between information going to the CNS and information coming from it. Every muscle, for example, not only receives from the CNS directions to contract or relax but also sends back information about its present state of contraction or relaxation.

ron cell bodies found principally along the spinal column), leads from the central nervous system to all parts of the body. The peripheral nervous system carries messages, connecting sensory receptors with the central nervous system and the central nervous system with muscles and glands. The central and peripheral nervous systems are shown in Figure 3.1.

The peripheral nervous system itself has two divisions: the somatic and the autonomic. The **somatic nervous system**, which consists of both sensory and motor neurons, is related to the external world. It controls the skeletal muscles, which move the bones. We usually think of somatic activity as being under voluntary control: for example, pointing a finger or walking are movements we can control at will. The **autonomic nervous system** regulates the internal environment. It controls the visceral muscles (blood vessels, heart, and intestines) and the glands. Autonomic activity is considered involuntary, for it generally occurs with little awareness or control, as when muscles lining the digestive tract contract or the heart beats. Despite the "involuntary" nature of these activities, some people have learned to influence some of them—heart rate, blood pressure, or skin temperature—under some conditions (Stoyva, 1976).

The autonomic nervous system is further divided into the sympathetic and parasympathetic divisions. Both divisions send nerves into almost every visceral muscle and gland in the body. The **sympathetic nervous system** dominates in emergencies or stressful situations, responding in ways that promote energy expenditure—increasing blood-sugar levels, heart rate, and

blood pressure and halting digestion. The **parasympathetic nervous system** dominates in relaxed situations, responding in ways that conserve energy. For example, after a large meal, the parasympathetic nervous system decreases the heart rate and slows the flow of blood to the skeletal muscles as it enhances digestion. However, the division of labor is not rigid. When a person is anxious, the sympathetic nervous system responds by increasing blood pressure and heart rate, but the parasympathetic nervous system also responds, sometimes causing indigestion, diarrhea, and urination in extremely stressful situations. The two systems work together in many actions. For example, sexual arousal is the business of the parasympathetic division, but sexual orgasm is a response of the sympathetic division. The relationships of the parts of the nervous system are diagrammed in Figure 3.2.

Neurons

There are many billions of neurons in the human body. These cells are extremely small, varied in shape, and closely packed together. As basic units of the nervous system, they transmit messages in the form of electrochemical impulses. Neurons conduct messages in several ways: some carry information from the sense organs to the brain and spinal cord; some from the brain and spinal cord to the muscles and glands; and some carry messages from one neuron to another. Such relationships between neurons are translated into thoughts, feelings, perceptions, and memories.

Figure 3.2 Diagram of the relationship between the parts of the nervous system.

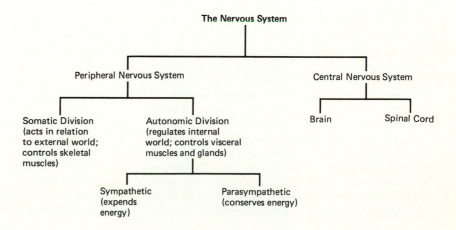

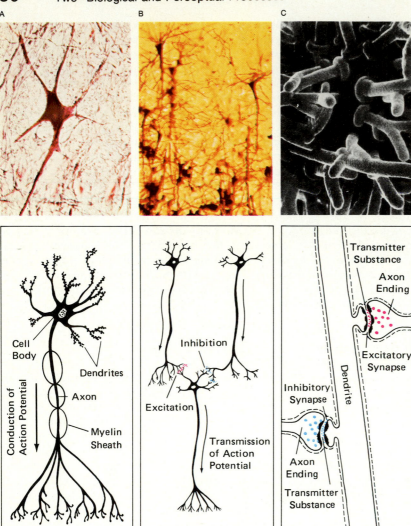

A

B

C

Figure 3.3 The fundamental structures in the nervous system. (A) A photomicrograph and a diagram of the parts of a single neuron. The dendrites are the receiving end of the neuron; the axon is the sending end. An action potential is transmitted along the axon of a neuron only when its dendrites have been sufficiently excited. (B) A photomicrograph and a simplified diagram of neurons in the cerebral cortex. Note that one neuron may have either an excitatory or an inhibitory effect on another and that the action potentials are transmitted in only one direction along the firing neuron. (C) An electron micrograph and a diagram of the structures at the synapse. Note the correspondence between the axon endings and the small protrusions on the dendrites in the diagrams in C and B. When an action potential reaches the end of the axon of a neuron, small amounts of transmitter substances are released from storage areas across the synapse to the dendrites of another neuron. The substances from some neurons are excitatory in their effect; the substances from others are inhibitory. If the receiving neuron gets sufficient excitation (and not too much inhibition), it in turn fires.

In the nervous system, neurons are vastly outnumbered by smaller cells called **glia** ("glue"). Their role is largely undefined, but they seem to provide nutrients and structural support to the neurons, as well as a barrier to certain substances from the bloodstream (Stevens, 1979). Although glial cells are important, the neurons appear to play the major role in behavior.

Neurons have three characteristic features: a cell body, dendrites, and an axon. The **cell body** contains the nucleus; because it is the cell's metabolic center, the nucleus provides energy for neural action. The numerous **dendrites** are short fibers that branch out from the cell body to make connections with other neurons. The **axon** is a long fiber that leads away from the cell body and connects with the dendrites of other neu-

rons. Specialized areas of the dendrites—and sometimes parts of the axon and cell body—receive messages from other neurons. These messages usually travel in the same direction: from the dendrites through the cell body and down the length of the axon (see Figure 3.3).

Transmission of Neural Signals

Messages are conducted through the nervous system by means of an electrochemical process. Chemicals in the body normally exist as ions—electrically charged molecules or atoms. The passage of these ions in and out of a neuron is regulated by the cell membrane. When in a resting state, the membrane causes the interior of the cell to be negatively charged, while the exterior, immediately outside the membrane, is positively charged. The cell is said to be **polarized**—negative inside and positive outside. If a stimulus affects the cell with great enough intensity, the membrane temporarily becomes open to a sudden inrush of certain ions, changing the cell's polarity at the point of stimulation; the cell interior momentarily becomes positive and the exterior negative. The resulting electrical charge races down the length of the axon, its speed depending on the properties of the axons. Many axons are wrapped in a fatty, whitish substance, known as a **myelin sheath**, which serves as insulation and thereby increases the speed of the message. Myelinated axons form the **white matter** of the nervous system; nonmyelinated axons, dendrites, and cell bodies form the **gray matter**.

Any stimulus usually produces a burst of electrical charges, which send nerve impulses traveling down the axon much as a spark travels down a fuse. Once a charge has passed, the cell enters a brief **refractory period**, during which it cannot fire, or transmit an impulse. However, the neuron's polarity is soon restored, so it can conduct rapid bursts of consecutive impulses. When impulses reach the end of the axon, they activate muscles, glands, or other neurons.

Different messages are conveyed by the axons' rates and patterns of firing. Among neurons that convey information about the intensity of a stimulus, the more intense a stimulus, the higher the firing rate (Stevens, 1979; see Figure 3.4). Some neurons fire so rapidly that they can transmit about 1,000 impulses per second. Which neural

pathway a message takes also determines the nature of the message; thus, stimulation of the visual nerves by any means (e.g., by pressure) produces a visual sensation, and stimulation of the nerves of hearing and taste produces auditory and taste sensations.

The Synapse   When an impulse has sped along an axon and reached the buttonlike tips of its tiny branches, the message faces a gap, called a **synapse**, that separates the end of one neuron and

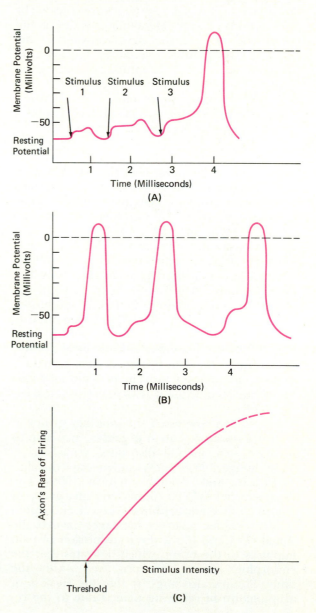

Figure 3.4   Records of an axon's response to excitatory stimuli. (A) The arrows indicate the points in time at which three different stimuli were presented to the neuron. The first two stimuli were below the intensity level required to produce a response—in this case, an action potential. The minimum level of intensity necessary for a stimulus to produce a response is called the threshold level. The third stimulus was above the threshold, and therefore an action potential was produced. (B) A series of action potentials are produced by several above-threshold stimuli. When an action potential reaches the end of an axon, it causes a release of the neurotransmitter substance, which in turn produces an effect (either excitatory or inhibitory) on the adjacent neurons, muscles, or glands. (C) Graph illustrating that as the intensity of a stimulus increases, so does the axon's rate of firing. (Stevens, 1966.)

the beginning of the next. The message crosses the gap by means of **neurotransmitters**, chemicals that are produced in the cell body and stored in sacs at the tip of the axon. The arrival of an impulse at the axon tip releases a neurotransmitter into the synapse. A typical neuron has from 1,000 to 10,000 synapses and may receive information from about 1,000 other neurons (Stevens, 1979).

The released chemicals fill the synapse between the axon and the connecting neuron, transmitting a message to the neuron by changing its voltage. The message is usually received by a dendrite, but some messages are received by the cell body or axon. Depending on the chemical composition of the neurotransmitter, the message may be either **excitatory**, causing a receiving neuron to fire, or **inhibitory**, decreasing or preventing the neuron's firing. When a neuron is firing at a rapid rate, more neurotransmitter is released by the arrival of each impulse, increasing the strength of the message.

Implications of Chemical Transmission   Since information relies on neurotransmitters for its passage along the nervous system, chemicals may be the basis for much of our behavior. Human moods, mental disorders, sleep, memory, and perceptions of pain and pleasure may be largely a matter of which neurotransmitters are being released within the brain at a particular time. For example, norepinephrine is believed to play a role in arousal, pleasure, dreaming, and mood, while serotonin may affect body temperature, sensory perception, and the onset of sleep (Iverson, 1979). A third prevalent neurotransmitter, **dopamine**, is thought to regulate emotional response and complex movements, and may also have some connection with memory (Brozoski et al., 1979).

It has been suggested that another group of neurotransmitters, called **peptides,** may help to regulate pain, mental disorders, sexual drive, thirst, hunger, drowsiness, and perhaps the ability to learn and remember (Gurin, 1979). The relief of pain has been connected with a group of peptides called **endorphins.** When an endorphin activates certain neurons, messages travel to the spinal cord and block the transmission of pain impulses to the brain, which indicates that the endorphins are opiates produced within the body. Studies also suggest that the success of acupuncture in relieving pain is due to the release of endorphins in response to the stimulation caused by the many needles involved (Carlson, 1980).

Different pathways in the brain apparently use different neurotransmitters. Since each neurotransmitter can activate only neural receptors that are designed to fit its molecular structure, the neurotransmitter acts much like a key placed into a lock. The receptors for endorphins also accept opiates such as morphine or heroin because their chemical structures are similar to those of endorphins. In fact, the existence of two endorphins was discovered because of this similarity (Snyder, 1980). The role of endorphins in relieving pain and producing pleasure is discussed further in Chapter 4.

Neurotransmitters have been associated with a number of psychological and physical disorders. As we shall see in Chapter 23, excessive dopamine activity has been linked with schizophrenia. The gradual destruction of the pathways that carry dopamine leads to the development of Parkinson's disease, a progressively chronic condition that involves involuntary shaking of the extremities, neck, and jaw (Kety, 1979). It is also believed that some forms of depression are the result of a deficiency of particular neurotransmitters. Bipolar disorder, in which people swing from hyperactivity accompanied by euphoria and disorganized behavior to deep depression, may also be linked with neurotransmitters. Some people who suffer from this disorder are greatly improved by doses of lithium, which may affect the movement of neurotransmitters and the sensitivity of neural receptors to them (Tosteson, 1981).

The discovery of the connection between neurotransmitters and behavior offers the hope of relieving pain, curing illness, and inducing peak performance, sharpened memory, and heightened pleasure through synthetic drugs that mimic the neurotransmitters' actions. The task of developing such drugs, however, may be more difficult than some think. The first artificial pain-killing substances related to endorphins proved to have the same serious drawback as morphine and heroin: they were addictive. However, some synthetic transmitters may not be addictive. In fact, one synthetic drug, which is based on a peptide that leads rats to mate and restores sexual potency to human males, is now being tested for use as either a fertility drug or a contraceptive, depending on the dosage (Gurin, 1979).

Reflex Arcs and the Spinal Cord

Not all connections between neurons in the central nervous system are complicated; the simplest is the **reflex arc**, a connection between sensory and motor signals that has been described as the basic functional unit of the nervous system.

The simplest reflex arc takes place within a single segment of the spinal cord. For example, the knee-jerk reflex, which occurs when the tendon below the kneecap is tapped, involves only two kinds of neurons: **sensory neurons**, which carry messages from the sense organs to the spinal cord, and **motor neurons**, which carry signals from the cord to muscles or glands (part A of Figure 3.5). Sensory neurons convey information about stimulation of the tendon to the spinal cord. This information must cross only one synapse within the gray matter of the spinal cord, and it causes motor neurons to stimulate the thigh muscles that jerk the knee. Most reflexes, however, are more complicated than the two-neuron knee jerk; for example, in the pain-withdrawal reflex (part B of Figure 3.5), three types of neurons are involved: sensory, motor, and **interneurons** (neurons that connect only with the other two types of neurons). When a leg that is exposed to pain is withdrawn, these neurons pass information to the opposite leg, so that body weight is shifted off the exposed leg.

Such simple reflex arcs occur without direct recourse to the brain. Thus, the spinal cord constitutes a simplified model of a neurological system. It receives sensory information, processes it, and then delivers neural impulses to the muscles that initiate and coordinate motor activity.

The spinal cord is also the main communication "cable" between the brain and the peripheral nervous system. A cross section shows that it consists of a central butterfly-shaped area of gray matter; this is a site of intensive synaptic activity. The surrounding area of white matter consists of axons carrying information to and from the brain and to other parts of the spinal cord.

This communication means that the brain has some involvement even in reflexive behavior that takes place without direct brain control. For instance, the painful stimulation that triggers a withdrawal reflex must travel to the brain in order to be experienced as painful. Yet the reflex response often occurs before the pain is felt. Most people can recall touching a hot object,

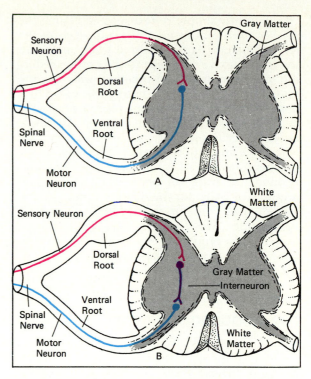

Figure 3.5 (A) A diagram of a two-neuron reflex arc, such as the one present in the knee-jerk response. This is the simplest form of reflex arc. (B) A diagram of a three-neuron reflex arc. The pain reflex, which causes a quick withdrawal from the painful stimulus, is an example of this type of reflex arc. It involves one set each of motor and sensory neurons (as in the two-neuron reflex arc), but in addition, an interneuron is present in the gray matter of the spinal cord. The extra neuron means that the information now crosses two synapses. (Gardner, 1975.)

withdrawing their hand, and becoming aware of the pain only after the withdrawal. Awareness and voluntary control over reflex activity is possible, however, because neurons travel the length of the spinal cord to the brain and back again. Ask someone to tap the tendon below your kneecap; your leg will jerk reflexively. Now have the person tap the same place while you concentrate on blocking the response. The pathways that link the brain to the spinal cord should enable you to inhibit the involuntary kick. If these pathways were severed, you could not control the jerking of your leg, and you would not know that your leg had kicked unless you saw it.

Reflex arcs are present throughout the nervous system, and what appear to be simple reflex networks are often part of complicated behavior.

An apparently simple reflex, such as dilating the pupil of the eye, can involve many levels of the nervous system. At the simplest level, pupil dilation is a reflexive response to the sudden reduction of light: neurons act together, widening the pupil so that more light enters the eye. On a more complex level, this same response is part of an emotional reaction that involves the whole body. For example, our pupils widen when we experience anger or fear, even if the light source remains constant. At yet another level, pupil dilation may interact with our learned reading and interpretive skills, for the dilation reflex also occurs when we come upon an interesting sight. A book entitled *Naked Bodies* is likely to call forth a more intense pupillary response than a book labeled *The History of Psychology*.

The Endocrine System

Neurons transmit impulses rapidly, sending messages through the nervous system in a thousandth of a second and using up a good deal of energy in the process. But not all behavior requires the sort of immediate response demanded when you inadvertently placed your hand on a hot stove. When behavior does not depend on speed, the body relies on the slower **endocrine system,** which communicates by means of **hormones,** chemical substances that are produced by the **endocrine glands** and secreted directly into the bloodstream. Some hormones are similar in structure to some neurotransmitters, but hormones act in the bloodstream instead of within the synapse. Several seconds are required for the stimulation, release, and transport of a hormone. Once released from the endocrine glands, hormones influence a wide variety of behavior by selective action that is confined to certain target organs. Physical growth, emotional response, motivation, the availability of energy, and sexual function are among the processes directly affected by hormones.

However, the endocrine system does not work in isolation. In the case of sexual behavior, neurons carry information from sense organs about a sexual situation, the brain decides whether the stimulation is attractive, and the spinal cord is involved in the reflexive movements of sexual intercourse and in erection and ejaculation. But male and female hormones affect neurons in both the spinal cord and the brain, perhaps increasing the skin's sensitivity to sexual stimulation (Carlson, 1980).

The interaction of endocrine and nervous systems is especially apparent in the function of the pituitary gland. The **pituitary gland,** which lies at the base of the brain, has often been called the "master gland" of the endocrine system, because it secretes many hormones that control the output of other endocrine glands. Yet, through its control of the pituitary, the brain is ultimately responsible for the activities of the endocrine system. Some of the hormones that are poured into the bloodstream by the pituitary gland are produced in the brain and only stored in the pituitary gland. Further, the release of pituitary hormone is controlled by the brain, which monitors the amount of hormones in the blood and sends messages to correct deviations from the proper level.

This control works through the mechanism of feedback; a look at the interaction of the pituitary and thyroid glands illustrates how feedback operates (see Figure 3.6). The **thyroid gland** regulates body metabolism. Among its products is the hormone **thyroxin,** which promotes key chemical reactions that affect the entire body. Too little thyroxin leads to lethargy and depression, and too much results in hyperactivity and anxiety. The amount of thyroxin released by the thyroid gland is controlled by the pituitary's secretion of a thyroid-stimulating hormone into the bloodstream. When this hormone reaches its target, the thyroid gland, that gland secretes additional thyroxin. In turn, the level of thyroxin in the blood affects the amount of thyroid-stimulating hormone that the pituitary produces when signaled by the brain. High blood levels of thyroxin reduce the output of thyroid-stimulating hormone, while low blood levels of thyroxin lead to increased production of the hormone. In this way, under the executive control of the brain, the pituitary and thyroid glands interact to regulate and balance general body metabolism.

This process of maintaining a balanced internal environment through feedback is an example of **homeostasis,** or self-regulation. The basic principle of homeostasis is that deviations from a certain level of a substance automatically activate processes that will eliminate that deviation, restoring the original level. A thermostat is a familiar homeostatic mechanism; deviations in room temperature signal the thermostat to turn a furnace on or off. As a result of similar homeo-

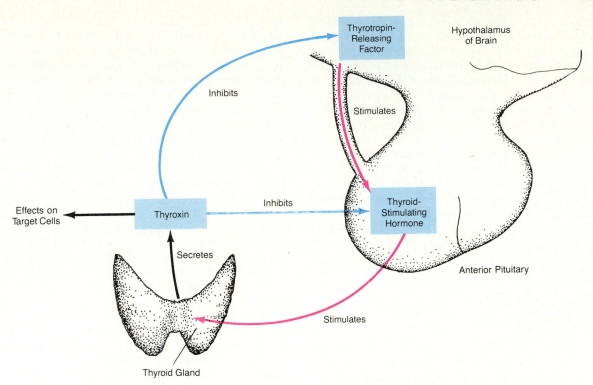

Figure 3.6 The feedback mechanisms regulating the amount of thyroxin that the thyroid gland secretes. A portion of the brain called the hypothalamus produces a hormone known as thyrotropin-releasing factor (TRF). TRF travels to the anterior portion of the pituitary gland, where it triggers the release of thyroid-stimulating hormone (TSH). TSH, in turn, stimulates the thyroid gland to release thyroxin, which spreads throughout the body. Upon reaching the brain, however, high levels of thyroxin inhibit the secretion of both TRF and TSH, thus causing the release of thyroxin to be temporarily "turned off." Finally, when thyroxin levels drop to a low enough point, the whole cycle starts all over again.

static processes, the level of thyroxin in the blood is kept in **equilibrium**—a state of balance due to the equal action of opposing forces.

The importance of maintaining equilibrium can be seen by considering the **adrenal glands,** a pair of glands located just above the kidneys. These glands secrete hormones that affect emotions and the body's reaction to stress. When a person faces sudden danger, experiences intense pain, or is frightened, the sympathetic nervous system signals the adrenal glands to produce two hormones that speed up the heart, increase the blood supply to the skeletal muscles, raise the blood pressure, accelerate breathing, and elevate glucose levels in the blood. In conjunction with the sympathetic nervous system, the adrenal glands thus prepare the person under stress to flee or to fight. Sometimes, however, this life-preserving reaction can be lethal. When the individual is faced with life-threatening danger but is helpless either to combat it or to get away, the adrenal glands keep pumping hormones into the bloodstream. This continuous flow of hormones can kill cells in the heart, disrupting its rhythm and leading to heart failure. The individual is literally frightened to death ("Scared to Death," *Science Digest,* 1980). Such deaths are rare, but this overwhelming loss of equilibrium apparently explains cases of voodoo death, in which people who believe that someone has put a spell on them suddenly fall ill and die (Cannon, 1942).

The **gonads,** or sex glands, secrete hormones that—in conjunction with hormones produced by the pituitary gland—regulate reproduction. In females, the ovaries secrete hormones that affect secondary sex characteristics (such as the development of the breasts), the menstrual cycle, and the production of milk after the birth of a baby. In males, the testes secrete hormones that affect secondary sex characteristics (such as deepening of the voice and growth of facial hair) and the production of sperm. As we shall see in

Chapter 17, these hormones play an essential role in sexual development. Sex hormones have radical effects on sexual behavior in other animals as well as in humans. In human adults, however, the connection between hormones and sexual behavior is less direct; human sexual behavior is primarily under the control of psychological factors. This psychological control shows most clearly when medical problems require the removal of the gonads. Most women whose ovaries have been removed continue to experience their former levels of sexual desire and to maintain successful sexual relations. And although some men whose testes have been removed find that their sexual capacity and responsiveness gradually declines, others continue to function normally (Thompson, 1975).

The Brain

The brain is an organ of tremendous complexity that exerts some sort of control over every aspect of human action, whether it be breathing, sleeping, eating, playing tennis, or writing a poem. The adult human brain weighs about three pounds and is composed of numerous substructures with specific, interrelated functions. It regulates behavior in three major ways. First, it maintains and controls vital internal bodily functions, such as temperature and digestion. Second, it receives sensory information about the external world and issues motor commands in response to this information. Third, it uses past experience to select or create new ways of responding to the environment.

The brain is best understood by regarding it as composed of three overlapping layers—the central core, the limbic system, and the cerebral cortex—with each layer representing a consecutive stage in the evolution of the brain. As we shall see, different parts of the brain appear to be involved in different types of behavior, a concept known as **localization of function.**

The Cerebral Hemispheres

The **cerebral hemispheres,** the most prominent feature of the human brain, are what most people think of as "the brain." The cerebral hemispheres are heavily involved in information processing: learning, speech, reasoning, and memory. The two distinct halves, the right and left hemispheres, are roughly mirror images of each other but have different functions. Much of the **limbic system** lies within them, and the **cerebral cortex** is the covering that surrounds them ("*cortex*" means "bark" or "outer coverings").

Although the cerebral hemispheres account for 85 percent of the brain's weight, no one knows just how much of this tissue is required for normal functioning. In fact, studies of hydrocephalics by John Lorber, a British neurologist, have ignited a controversy in neurological circles. Hydrocephalics are people who were born with a defect in the nervous system that causes fluid to be trapped in the brain so that the fluid gradually fills a larger and larger area, compressing normal brain tissue against the skull and often expanding the **cranium,** the portion of the skull that houses the brain. Lorber has turned up nearly sixty hydrocephalics whose craniums are 95 percent fluid, including one young man who earned an honors degree in mathematics at Sheffield University and who showed no social abnormalities of any kind. This man's skull was only slightly larger than normal and he had virtually no cerebral hemispheres. Although many in the group studied are severely disabled, half of them have IQs greater than 100, indicating an intelligence functioning at or above average levels (Lewin, 1980).

No one is sure exactly how to interpret Lorber's findings, but researchers have suggested three explanations: (1) the existence in most people of large areas of unused brain capacity; (2) hitherto unsuspected functions carried out in the primitive areas of the brain; or (3) a pattern of destruction of brain tissue that spares essential cells. Whatever the explanation, the cases uncovered by Lorber indicate that the human brain can work under conditions generally considered impossible.

The Cerebral Cortex   The cerebral cortex, composed of gray matter that covers the cerebral hemispheres, is the most recently evolved portion of the nervous system. To accommodate its billions of neurons, this thin (about 1/12 inch thick) covering is highly convoluted, or wrinkled.

Several prominent landmarks on the cortical surface are used as guides in locating regions of the brain. Each hemisphere has two deep fissures that divide it into four sections, or lobes. As Fig-

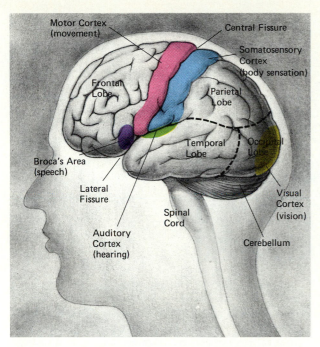

Figure 3.7 An external view of the left hemisphere of the cerebral cortex. The diagram shows the two major fissures and the four cerebral lobes. Colored regions identify parts of the cortex involved in speech, hearing, vision, sensory, and motor functions.

ure 3.7 shows, the **central fissure** separates the frontal lobe from the parietal lobe, and the **lateral fissure** marks the top boundary of the temporal lobe. Less obvious markers separate the occipital lobe from the temporal and parietal lobes.

The **occipital lobe,** located at the back of the brain, is the major area for the reception and analysis of visual information. Sensory receptors in the eye send information to the occipital lobe through the optic nerve and thalamus, an area buried in the hemispheres at the top of the brain stem. Injury to this part of the human cortex can produce blind spots in the visual field.

Within the **temporal lobe** are the auditory reception areas as well as additional areas for the processing of visual information. A good deal of our knowledge about the function of the temporal lobe has come from studies of epileptic patients undergoing surgery. When Canadian neurologist Wilder Penfield (Penfield and Perot, 1963) applied electrical stimulation to various points of the temporal lobe of patients under local anesthesia, the patients responded by describing complex auditory or visual hallucina-

tions or vivid memories of past events, depending on the area stimulated. Although some patients felt they were reliving, not remembering, the experiences, a close inspection of the reports indicates that the memories were not exact reproductions of the original experiences, but resembled dreams (Loftus and Loftus, 1980). For example, a woman who relived the experience of childbirth indicated that she was *watching* herself go through the process of giving birth, and another woman heard a mother calling her little boy in a lumberyard—a location she had never visited.

The **frontal lobes** are located at the front of each cerebral hemisphere. Because the human frontal lobes are considerably larger than those of any other animal, Franz Joseph Gall, a nineteenth-century Viennese anatomist, considered the frontal lobes to be the seat of human intellect. This idea is no longer accepted, for some people seem to handle intellectual tasks normally after massive amounts of frontal lobe tissue have been removed or destroyed. In fact, the young mathematician studied by Lorber had virtually no frontal lobes. The involvement of the frontal lobes in behavior seems to be quite general, and whatever behavioral defects result from damage to them appear to involve the ability to order stimuli, sort out information, and maintain attention to a task despite distraction, rather than the kind of intellectual abilities involved in academic tasks (Milner, 1964).

The area of the frontal lobes next to the central fissure, known as the **motor cortex,** is responsible for the regulation of voluntary movements. Another part of the left frontal lobe is involved in the use of language, and damage to this area affects speech.

The area of the **parietal lobes** just behind the central fissure, known as the **somatosensory cortex,** is the primary area for the reception and interpretation of sensation from the skin and for the sense of bodily position. Damage to this portion of the cortex generally impairs the sense of touch. Damage that extends beyond the primary sensory area in the right parietal lobe interferes with spatial organization and may distort perception of personal body image.

The function of the motor and somatosensory cortex has been defined with more precision than that of any other cortical area (see Figure 3.8). The amount of cortex devoted to a particular body part's motor activities and sensory impressions depends on the degree of precise

The section of the frontal lobe that regulates voluntary movements, such as dancing, is called the motor cortex.

motor control or sensitivity of that body part—not on its size or muscle mass. Thus the fingers, which can make precise movements, have much larger representation in the motor cortex than does the hip. The lips, which can also make fine movements and are extremely sensitive to touch, have a large area of the sensory cortex devoted to them. These two representations correspond to the behavioral capacities that best set human beings apart from other animals—tool use and speech.

Despite the precision with which they have been able to define the brain's sensory and motor areas, neuropsychologists have had little success in localizing the areas where abstract mental processes are carried out. It is assumed that areas without sensory or motor function, called the **association cortex,** are involved in abstract thought. The association areas, which have no direct connections outside the cortex, make up about three-fourths of the cortical area. They apparently act on information that has al-

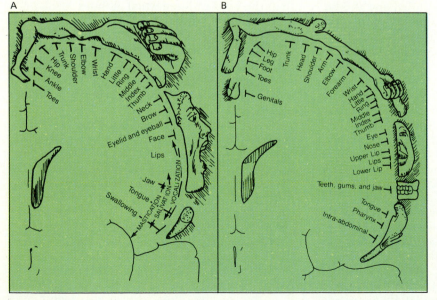

Figure 3.8 Both A and B represent the right hemisphere of the brain, which controls the voluntary muscles on the left side of the body. (A) A diagram representing the location and amount of cortical space devoted to the motor capacities of various body parts. Areas of the body capable of the most complex and precise movements take up the largest quantities of space in the motor cortex. For example, the eyelid and eyeball (capable of many precise movements) have a larger representation than the face. (B) A diagram representing the location and amount of cortical space devoted to the sensory capacities of various body parts. In the sensory realm, those organs capable of the highest sensitivity have the largest representations in the somatosensory cortex. (Penfield and Rasmussen, 1950.)

ready gone through several stages of processing and take part in the processes we call learning, memory, emotion, intelligence, and conscious behavior.

The Two Sides of the Brain As the connection between language impairment and left-hemisphere damage indicates, the two cerebral hemispheres differ in composition and have specialized functions. Both hemispheres contain the same amount of neural tissue, but the ratio of gray matter to white matter is significantly higher in the left hemisphere (Gur et al., 1980). In general, the left half of the brain receives sensations from and controls the voluntary muscles on the right side of the body; and the right half of the brain does the same for the left side of the body. Thus a stroke that damages functioning in the right cerebral hemisphere may cause paralysis on the left side of the body.

In most people, the left cerebral hemisphere is somewhat larger than the right. It is also true that in most people the left hemisphere is the site of language ability. Damage to this hemisphere often results in severe speech disturbances. The right cerebral hemisphere is the site of spatial skills, visual imagery, and musical abilities (see Figure 3.9). Damage to this hemisphere has subtle effects on behavior, perhaps because whatever abilities are handled by the right cerebral hemisphere are distributed over larger areas of tissue than is the case of abilities handled by the left cerebral hemisphere (Springer and Deutsch, 1981). People with right-hemisphere damage may find it difficult to draw, to find their way from one place to another, or to build a model from a plan (Kimura, 1975). They may also respond in inappropriate ways because they cannot recognize the emotions expressed by others; for example, they often confuse jokes with anger (Geschwind, 1979).

The cerebral hemispheres also process material differently, the left hemisphere using a logical, sequential manner and the right hemisphere, a simultaneous, intuitive manner (Springer and Deutsch, 1981). Hemispheric specialization does not mean that each cerebral hemisphere can process only certain kinds of information, but that each hemisphere is more efficient at certain tasks. Some research indicates that the left hemisphere's proficiency in language derives from its superior processing speed. When speech is slowed perceptibly, the right hemisphere can process it (Schwartz and Tallal, 1980). However,

lateralization—the establishment of functions in one hemisphere or the other—exists in all of us, and one hemisphere or the other tends to dominate, depending on the type of activity performed.

The two halves of the brain also seem to store different types of information, but this division in hemispheric functioning usually escapes detection because the two halves of the brain work together as a coordinated unit. The cerebral hemispheres are connected by a large cable of neural fibers called the **corpus callosum,** which carries messages back and forth between the left and right side of the brain (Sperry, 1964, 1975). When this connection is severed surgically to relieve epileptic seizures, as was done in the case

Figure 3.9 This drawing, though greatly simplified, suggests the sensory input and the types of information processing handled by the cortical hemispheres of the brain. (Adapted from Eccles, 1973.)

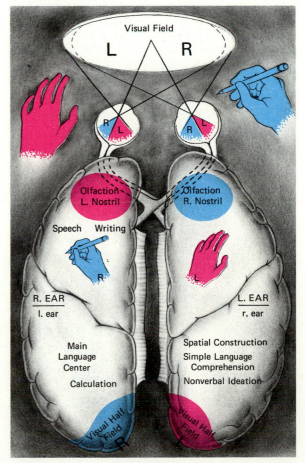

of J. W., the two halves of the brain function independently, almost as if two different consciousnesses inhabited one brain (Sperry, 1969; Gazzaniga, 1967). A forty-year program of research with these split-brain patients has demonstrated the specialized functions of each hemisphere and led to a Nobel Prize for Roger Sperry, who has directed the program (Gazzaniga, 1981).

Severing the corpus callosum seems to produce two separate minds in a single body, each operating without awareness of the other (Gazzaniga, 1977). After surgery, only the mind in the left cerebral hemisphere can speak or write, be-cause it contains the major language-processing area. But because each mind controls the opposite side of the body, the mind in the right cerebral hemisphere can communicate by gesturing with the left hand. In addition, only the left hand can draw objects in their entirety—a skill that requires the perception of spatial relationships. The mind in the right cerebral hemisphere does retain some language ability; it understands words but takes longer than the mind in the left cerebral hemisphere to process them (Zaidel, 1978).

Thus, if an object is briefly flashed to the left half of the brain, the split-brain patient can say

Figure 3.10 Experimental apparatus used for testing split-brain patients. When a written word is presented on a screen in one half of the visual field, this information is transmitted exclusively to the opposite hemisphere. In a person with an intact corpus callosum, this information is first received by the hemisphere opposite to the visual half-field in which the word was presented, and then this information is transmitted to the other hemisphere across the corpus callosum. In split-brain patients the hemispheres are disconnected, and therefore their independent functions can be studied. If the word "spoon" were presented in the right half of the visual field (transmitted to the left hemisphere), and patients were asked to verbally identify the word they saw, they would readily say "spoon." If, however, the same word was presented in the left half of the visual field (transmitted to the right hemisphere), patients would be unable to name the word. This is because speech mechanisms are found only in the left hemisphere in most people. Although the right hemisphere cannot name the item, it "knows" what the item is. The left hand, which sends its touch information primarily to the right hemisphere, is able to pick the correct item from several objects hidden behind a screen, as illustrated here. (After Gazzaniga, 1972.)

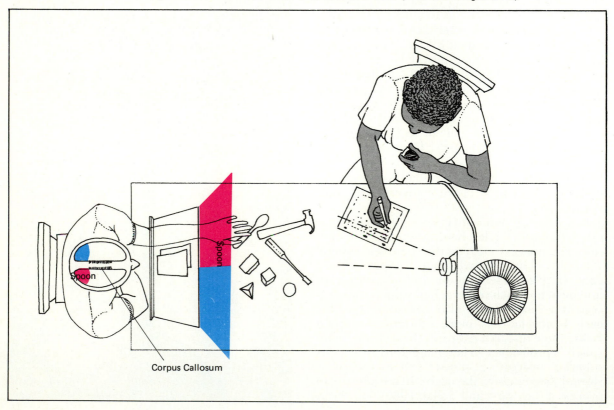

Corpus Callosum

what has been seen. However, if the same object is flashed to the left side of the visual field, and therefore to the right side of the brain, the person cannot say what has been seen but can identify by touch alone a similar object from a group of objects screened from view (see Figure 3.10). In these cases, the mind in one-half of the brain literally does not know what the mind in the other half has seen. In one experiment a picture of a nude woman was flashed to the right cerebral hemisphere of a split-brain patient. The patient laughed but said that she saw nothing. Though the vocal left brain had not seen the nude, the right brain had not only seen it but had also reacted to it. When the woman was asked why she had laughed, she seemed confused and could not explain (Gazzaniga, 1967).

J. W., whose case was discussed at the beginning of the chapter, differs from most of these split-brain patients because his corpus callosum was severed in stages. Until the final operation, his right and left cerebral hemispheres were able to pass some information across the intact portion of the corpus callosum. However, many split-brain patients learn to use cues to pass information between the cerebral hemispheres. For example, if the patient's task is to identify an object by touch, stroking the surface of, say, a comb, with the left hand can create sounds that alert the left cerebral hemisphere to the nature of the object (Gazzaniga, 1967).

The exploration of cerebral hemispheric function has been complicated by the existence of left-handed people and two sexes. Nearly all right-handed people and about 60 percent of the left-handed process language in the left hemisphere; the rest use either the right hemisphere or both sides of the brain—as many ambidextrous people do. The exact relationship between brain organization and handedness is unclear, but right-handers tend to perform better on language-related tasks, while left-handers tend to be better at the perception of tones and to have superior artistic ability (Herron, 1979).

Gender introduces other difficulties into the study of hemispheric function. Females tend to do better than males in language-based skills and males tend to do better in tasks of a spatial nature (Springer and Deutsch, 1981). Males are also more proficient at mathematics—but not at arithmetic. Although cultural expectations, as well as the different ways in which boys and girls are reared, undoubtedly affect their development of these skills, the varying effects of brain

damage point to a difference in brain organization in the two sexes. Among men, the removal of a portion of the left temporal lobe (to prevent epileptic seizures) often leads to disturbances in language, and removal of part of the right temporal lobe causes disturbances in spatial skills. But this effect does not appear among women (Lansdell, 1962). Other researchers (McGlone, 1978) have found that language disturbance after damage to the left cerebral hemisphere is three times more frequent in men than in women. Such findings point to greater lateralization in males than in females and suggests that females may use both hemispheres to some degree in both types of skills. For practical purposes, the difference between the sexes is not important because the average difference between the groups is small, and some women are better at spatial abilities than most men, while some men are better at language skills than most women (Springer and Deutsch, 1981). For the purpose of understanding the brain, however, such sex-related differences are both puzzling and important.

The Limbic System   Within the cerebral hemispheres and above the central core lies the **limbic system** ("limbic" means "bordering"). Its highly interrelated structures (the **hippocampus**, the **amygdala**, and the **septal area**) ring the top of the central core, connecting with it and with the cerebral cortex (see Figure 3.11).

The limbic system, the second of the three brain layers to develop, was added to the central core about 100 million years ago (Fishbein, 1976). Although the structure's original purpose was olfactory—the analysis of odors to identify food, potential mates, and predators—the limbic system now has a much wider role. It seems to play a major part in such behavior as eating, fighting, drinking, self-defense, and mating (MacLean, 1958). Damage to the system can alter such behavior radically, depending on the area involved. After limbic system damage, fierce wild animals have become docile, and tame domestic cats have turned savage. In addition, marked changes in sexual behavior and eating patterns also follow limbic system damage (Klüver and Bucy, 1939). All this behavior has some motivational or emotional component, and in each case the animal must decide whether to approach or avoid some object (food, water) or creature (mate, predator). Although the limbic system

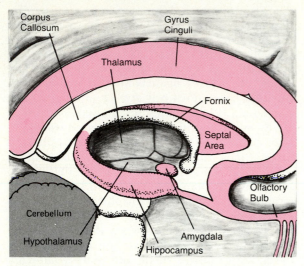

Figure 3.11 A schematic diagram of the limbic system. Structures within this system play a significant role in a variety of emotional behaviors. Damage to various regions of the limbic system may cause wild animals to become tame, or tame animals to become vicious. Other limbic lesions may radically alter sexual and feeding behavior. The olfactory bulb (responsible for the sense of smell) is closely associated with other limbic structures, suggesting the importance of this sense to several limbic system functions

seems heavily involved in such approach-avoidance decisions, it is not the only part of the brain involved in emotion; the cortex also enters into emotional response and the recognition of emotions in others (Geschwind, 1979).

The limbic system's role in emotion is spotlighted by the discovery of specific sites that seem intimately connected with pure pleasure. The discovery of these pleasure centers came about when James Olds and Peter Milner (1954) discovered that rats would ignore all other stimuli to get mild electrical stimulation delivered through electrodes implanted in certain parts of the limbic system. The animals found the brain stimulation so compelling that even after fasting for twenty-four hours they would leave food untasted while they stopped to receive their electric charge. Given a chance to control the stimulation themselves, they pressed the controlling lever every few seconds. Not all pleasure centers are in the limbic system; when electrodes were placed in some areas of the hypothalamus, for example, rats pressed the lever again and again to get the pleasurable stimulation. Brain stimulation is not always so pleasant: in some parts of the hypothalamus and

limbic system it is neutral; in other parts it seems to be painful.

Pleasure centers are not limited to rats; human beings who have received similar stimulation in attempts to alleviate serious medical conditions, such as epilepsy, have reported feeling "drunk," "happy," "great," and as if they were building up to a sexual orgasm (Heath, 1963). The most pleasurable sensations are located in the septal area of the limbic system.

The Central Core

In both appearance and function, the central core of the human brain resembles the brains of all animals that have backbones (see Figure 3.12). The **central core** was the first layer of the brain to evolve, and it contains structures that carry out functions necessary for survival: sleeping, waking, breathing, and feeding. The structures that make up the central core are shown in Figure 3.13.

The Brain Stem   Within the skull, the spinal cord swells to form the **brain stem**, which contains several important structures. The **medulla** controls salivation, chewing, and facial movements and plays an essential role in such autonomic activities as breathing and circulation. Above the medulla is the **pons** (or "bridge"), which connects the two halves of the cerebellum. The pons transmits motor information from the higher brain areas and the spinal cord to the cerebellum and integrates movements between the right and left sides of the body. A small structure called the **midbrain** lies near the top of the brain stem. Through this structure passes all neural information sent between the brain and the spinal cord. The midbrain also contains centers for visual and auditory reflexes, including the "startle" reflex to sudden, intense stimuli and "orienting" reflexes that allow us to locate and follow moving objects with our eyes or ears. In species that rely on auditory and visual reflexes for survival, these areas of the midbrain are relatively large. For example, bats, which locate their prey by sound, have prominent auditory areas in the midbrain, whereas birds that must sight, track, and capture their prey in flight have prominent and bulging visual areas.

The **reticular formation** is a latticework of neural fibers and cell bodies that extends from

Figure 3.12 A comparison of the brains of several animals possessing backbones. The human cerebrum is much larger than that found in other animals. As the cerebrum increases in size, it begins to form folds, called convolutions. These folds enable the surface area of the cerebrum to increase without producing a great increase in the brain's volume. (Truex and Carpenter, 1969.)

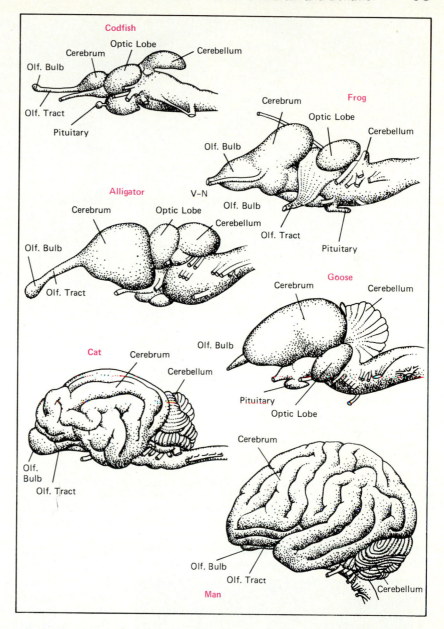

the spinal cord through the brain stem and into the thalamus. It appears to regulate consciousness and attention, arousing the higher brain when information related to survival must be processed. The reticular formation also seems to screen extraneous sensory input, especially during sleep. Damage to the reticular formation disrupts the natural sleep-waking cycle and can result in an almost permanent, comalike state of sleep (Magoun, 1963).

The Cerebellum The **cerebellum** (or "little brain"), which looks like a miniature version of the cerebral hemispheres, lies above the pons. The cerebellum's chief functions are to coordinate voluntary movement and to regulate posture and physical equilibrium. It does this by monitoring both incoming and outgoing information. Before transmitting motor commands from the higher brain to the muscles, the cerebellum processes the information. It then com-

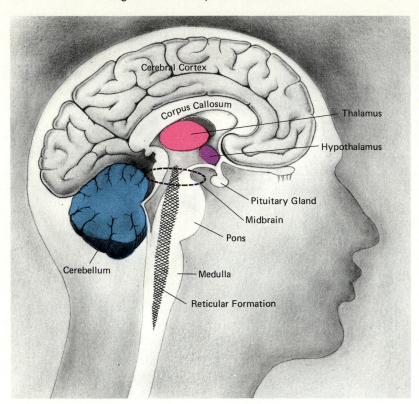

Figure 3.13 The structures composing the central core of the brain. (This illustration shows the left hemisphere of the brain as it would appear if it were sliced exactly in half from front to back.) The structures represented in this figure are the first to receive incoming information, and they regulate the most fundamental processes of the body. The reticular formation, which controls the most general responses of the brain to sensory input, is located in the area that connects the brain to the spinal cord and to the rest of the nervous system. The thalamus has a central location in the brain and the hypothalamus is very close to the pituitary gland, which controls the activity of the other endocrine glands. A few brain structures that evolved more recently than the central core are also shown here. Note particularly the corpus callosum, the large band of nerve fibers that connects the two hemispheres of the cerebral cortex.

The human brain is distinguished by its large cerebral hemispheres. But its central core is similar to those of other vertebrates. The central core consists of the brain stem—which contains the medulla, pons, midbrain, and reticular formation—the cerebellum, the thalamus, and the hypothalamus. These various structures control the functions that are essential to survival: sleeping, waking, breathing, and feeding.

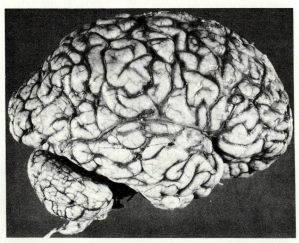

pares these messages with the continuous flow of information it receives concerning muscle tension and position, reconciles any difference in the messages, and sends the messages out in a way that ensures smooth and balanced motor responses (Eccles, Ito, and Szentagotnaik, 1967). Damage to the cerebellum may be followed by **ataxia**, a condition in which a person is afflicted with severe tremors, drunken movements, and a lack of balance. Such a person lacks the control involved in simple movements; for example, an ataxic person might accidentally hit a friend in the stomach while reaching out to shake hands.

The Thalamus   At the top of the brain stem and within the cerebral hemispheres lies the **thalamus**, a pair of egg-shaped structures. These connected structures surround a fluid-filled chamber within the brain that was once believed to be responsible for all brain processes. Although emphasis on the cavity was mistaken, the surrounding thalamus does have an important role in human behavior. It provides a crucial link between the cerebral hemispheres and the sense organs. One of its duties is to act as a relay station, sorting information from the sensory receptors and routing it to appropriate areas of the higher brain. The thalamus also processes information from various parts of the cerebral hemispheres, interrelating it before sending it on to the cerebellum and the medulla. By connecting areas of the brain in this way, the thalamus performs a major integrative role.

The Hypothalamus   Just below the thalamus lies a small structure (about the size of the tip of your index finger) called the **hypothalamus.** It monitors changes in the body's internal environment and sends out signals that maintain the person's internal state at some balanced optimal level. The hypothalamus influences behavior on which life depends: feeding, internal temperature regulation, emotional and physiological responses to stress, and sexual function. Different areas of the hypothalamus are primarily involved in such homeostatic functions as the regulation of body temperature. When a warm-blooded animal is exposed to cold, signals from the hypothalamus cause blood vessels in the skin to contract, reducing heat loss from body surfaces. Other hypothalamic signals instruct the pituitary gland to produce the hormone that triggers thyroxin production, increasing body metabolism and generating heat to compensate for external cold. High levels of thyroxin induce shivering, which leads to the production of even more heat. When the animal is exposed to external heat, the hypothalamus mobilizes the body's cooling resources, causing the body to dilate blood vessels in the skin, to sweat, and to slow its metabolism, thereby cooling itself. In this way, parts of the hypothalamus act as a kind of thermostat to maintain the body at its optimal temperature.

Other hypothalamic areas maintain other homeostatic functions such as the regulation of hunger. At one time it was believed that the hypothalamus contained feeding and satiety centers. That is, after destruction of one area a rat would refuse to eat and would die of starvation unless force-fed (Anand and Brobeck, 1951), whereas destruction of another area led the animal to gorge itself, eating until it became exceedingly obese (Hetherington and Ranson, 1942). It appears, however, that neurotransmitters are deeply involved in these reactions, with the critical factor being not damage to a feeding or satiety center, but the destruction of pathways that carry particular neurotransmitters (Carlson, 1980). Obesity develops when destruction of a pathway alters an animal's metabolism so that fat cells continuously convert nutrients to fat (Friedman and Stricker, 1976).

Since most obese people have an intact hypothalamus, psychologists have looked for other explanations for obesity. Some researchers (Rowland and Antelman, 1976) have found that when a rat's tail is gently pinched twice a day, the animal's food consumption more than doubles. Again neurotransmitters are involved—the stress of the pinch releases dopamine in the brain. These researchers suggest that stress (including the stress of being fat in a society that thinks only thinness is beautiful) can cause people to overeat.

Disorders of the Brain

Sometimes, because of accident or disease, a normally functioning brain goes awry, resulting in abnormal motor, emotional, or cognitive be-

After destruction of a small part of the lower middle area of the hypothalamus (known as the ventromedial nucleus), the rat shown here has overeaten to such an extent that it weighs 1,080 grams. (The dial has gone beyond the 1,000-gram capacity of the scale and registers an additional 80 grams.) In contrast, a normal rat would weigh about 320 grams. A rat with this type of lesion will not work for extra food, although it will eat huge amounts if the food is tasty and readily available.

havior. One common cause of brain damage is a **stroke**, which is usually caused by a rupturing of blood vessels on the surface of the brain. The rupture stops the supply of nutrients, and pressure from released blood destroys brain structures. Brain cells in the affected area stop functioning, and a variety of disorders can appear.

Patients may become paralyzed on one side of the body or may develop some type of **aphasia** —an inability to speak although the vocal apparatus is intact, or an inability to understand spoken language although hearing is intact and the patient can write and speak. Severe head injuries or tumors can affect behavior in a similar fashion.

Widespread damage to the left cerebral hemisphere may produce global aphasia, in which all language function is disrupted. But damage to the language area of the left frontal lobe produces Broca's aphasia, named for Paul Broca, who first discovered that speech difficulties usually follow damage to the left side of the brain. In Broca's aphasia, the patient speaks haltingly, often omitting prepositions, conjunctions, or articles, and has difficulty in getting the intended words out. The patient is aware of the errors and has no trouble understanding the speech of others. Damage to the left temporal lobe results in Wernicke's aphasia, in which the patient speaks fluently but may utter meaningless sentences. These patients are generally unaware that their speech is garbled and have trouble understanding the speech of others.

Damage to the temporal lobe can also result in **amnesia**, or loss of memory. In one case, a soldier who was struck in the left temporal lobe by a bullet became deaf as well as amnesic. The soldier lost some memories and some information he had learned before the injury, but found his inability to remember current events extremely annoying. To get around his disorder, he began to keep a notebook in which he jotted down events as they happened—but he kept misplacing the notebook (Whitty and Zangwill, 1977).

Injury to the left temporal lobe can also lead to an auditory **agnosia**, or the inability to recognize sounds such as running water, ringing telephones, or musical tones. Injury to the parietal

Can Brain Tissue Renew Itself?

Until a few years ago, it was assumed that most brain injuries in adults resulted in permanent damage. Since neurons, unlike other body cells, do not reproduce, it was taken for granted that axons and dendrites could not regenerate. When adults did recover, their recovery was attributed to one of three causes: (1) the existence of undamaged tissue that possessed the same abilities as the tissue that had been destroyed; (2) the assumption of function by other brain tissue—a view based on the belief that all brain tissue was interchangeable; or (3) a recovery of function by cells that had been shocked by the injury so that they simply stopped working for a time (Pines, 1976). Research with rats, hamsters, and monkeys has found, however, that in these mammals, at least, axons and dendrites can regenerate and that the "sprouting" of fibers from cell bodies appears to be triggered by glial cells that migrate to the affected area. The arrival of these cells is followed by activity in the neurons, which results in the establishment of new neural circuits (Lynch et al., 1975). Some areas of the brain appear to repair themselves more readily than others, but in some regions losses are permanent—even in young animals (Goldman, 1976). Studies of the aftermath of brain damage in human beings indicate that adults recover about as well as do children, and that recovery after an injury such as a bullet wound or a blow to the head is better than recovery after disease or stroke (St.James-Roberts, 1979).

Sometimes the body cannot repair nerve damage. The neurons may indeed begin to regenerate, sprouting new connecting fibers, but the growth is haphazard and the fibers never find their appropriate targets. If this happens, the damaged connections are not reestablished and the disability is permanent. When nerves in the spinal cord are severed, for example, the person is usually paralyzed below the level of the injury (Marx, 1979).

and occipital lobes of the right cerebral hemisphere can also cause agnosia, in this case a visual agnosia, or the inability to recognize objects or faces.

Some kinds of epilepsy, in which large numbers of neurons fire together in rhythm, can be traced to injury or infection that leaves a scar on the brain surface. Apparently, the scar periodically becomes the focus of a gradually spreading electrical activity that affects the normal neurons around it. Other forms of epilepsy may be due to a deficiency or abnormality in a neurotransmitter that inhibits neural firing (Kety, 1979).

Bacterial infections, such as meningitis, tuberculosis, and syphilis, can cause brain damage, although much of the havoc wrought by such diseases has been almost eliminated by antibiotics. Viral infections, such as measles, mumps, influenza, and herpes, can also damage the brain. Sometimes herpes or a strain of influenza quietly inhabits the nervous system for years before its effects appear. Poliomyelitis, a viral infection that has been nearly wiped out by the development of a vaccine, is a disease of the motor neurons that a few decades ago often resulted in permanent paralysis and sometimes in death.

Chronic alcoholism can lead to an irreversible impairment of judgment and loss of memory. (Vitamin deficiencies associated with alcoholism probably contribute to these effects.) Recently, cross-sectional X-ray photographs of brain tissue revealed structural changes in the brains of alcoholics in their twenties and thirties. The left cerebral hemispheres of these young alcoholics (both men and women) had diminished in density compared with the left cerebral hemisphere of a matched control group. Among the control group, the left cerebral hemisphere was composed of denser neural tissue than the right; among the alcoholics, the right cerebral hemisphere tended to be denser than the left (Golden et al., 1981). These findings suggest that in chronic alcoholics the left cerebral hemisphere's advantage over the right is reduced.

Studying Brain-Behavior Relationships

Much that we have learned about the brain's function has come from the study of brain injury. By carefully observing damage in other animals and humans and by using techniques developed to study the brain from the outside of the skull, scientists have mapped many of the brain's intricate structures and pathways. The hope is that such detailed study will lead to eventual understanding of the brain's role in human behavior.

Clinical Observations

Most early clinical observations concerned the effects of damage to the cortex. Medical practitioners observed that patients who had suffered strokes or other types of localized brain damage tended to show particular disruptions in behavior. By relating the type of disruption to the specific area of brain damage, scientists hoped to discover the relationships between the brain and behavior. When patients with brain damage died, the examination of their brains made the precise location of damage possible, and consistencies between the site of the damage and behavioral disruptions were noted.

Such observations have established some general relationships between the brain and behavior: for example, the concept that each side of the body is controlled by the opposite side of the brain and the realization that the left side of the brain generally dominates speech processes.

Neuropsychologists observing disruptions in behavior no longer have to wait for their patients' deaths to connect these observations with the region of brain damage. A precise location can be made while the patient is alive. Brain scans, which are produced when computers combine X-rays taken from many angles, can show cross sections of the brain's structure at any level. Without these scans, research advances like the discovery of structural changes in the brains of young alcoholics would be impossible.

Stimulation

Many of the basic relationships noted by early physicians have been confirmed by modern neurosurgical techniques. In one such method, mild electrical stimulation is applied to different areas of the brain; the electricity acts like the electrochemical impulse, stimulating neurons to fire. By using this method, Wilder Penfield (Penfield and Rasmussen, 1950), whose work was discussed earlier, applied weak electrical current to points on the cerebral cortex in an attempt to discover the focal point of his patients' epilepsy. When he stimulated the frontal lobe next to the central fissure, muscles on the opposite side of a patient's body moved. Patients stimulated in one area of the left cerebral hemisphere made sounds, but, stimulated in another area, they could not utter a word. Patients stimulated in the sensory cortex claimed they had been touched; the location on their bodies of the supposed touch corresponded to a specific location in the brain.

The brain can also be stimulated by chemicals, and scientists have used this technique in other animals. After implanting a small tube in an animal's brain so that the end touches the area under study, a researcher sends a small amount of chemical through the tube to the area. Such experiments have shown, for example, that different chemicals applied to the hypothalamus can affect an animal's feeding and drinking (Grossman, 1960). Other research has found that applying female hormones to parts of the hypothalamus causes a female rat without ovaries to become sexually receptive (Davis, McEwen, and Pfaff, 1979), and implanting male hormones in the hypothalamus of a castrated male rat will restore its sexual behavior (Johnson and Davidson, 1972).

Research involving stimulation has made possible the mapping of the motor and somatosensory cortex (see Figure 3.8). Findings from such research are also useful in the treatment of certain medical problems. For example, an electrical current delivered through electrodes implanted in particular areas of the brain brings temporary relief from pain and is sometimes used to relieve the intolerable suffering of patients with such illnesses as terminal cancer. Brain stimulation has also been used to control violently aggressive behavior in mental patients for whom all other methods of restraint have failed. A single session of stimulation appears to calm such patients for a day or more, and transistorized belt units have been developed that allow patients to calm themselves by pushing an "anti-hostility" button whenever aggressive feelings begin to build up (Moyer, 1971).

Brain-Lesion Techniques

Another method of discovering brain-behavior relationships is the creation of a **lesion** in an animal's brain—the selective destruction or removal of small amounts of tissue. After the surgery, researchers compare the animal's behavior with its activity before surgery, carefully noting any changes or disruptions. Since the brains of animals such as cats and monkeys are organized much like the brains of humans, the results of this research often provide information that applies to human functioning.

Observations of animal behavior following selective brain lesions generally support the information provided by clinical observations and brain stimulation. Indeed, brain lesions and stimulation techniques can be used together to understand certain brain-behavior relationships. As noted earlier, destruction of certain pathways in the hypothalamus is associated either with extreme overeating or with undereating to the point of starvation. Stimulating the same areas in a normal animal has opposite effects. Mild electrical stimulation in the region whose destruction leads to self-starvation makes an animal eat, even when it has just finished a meal; the animal behaves as if it is hungry although it needs no food (Miller, 1957). Stimulation in the region whose destruction leads to gross obesity makes an animal stop eating, even if it is starving. The neurotransmitters that pass through this area of the hypothalamus apparently affect the animal's ability to recognize when it is full.

Similar combinations of stimulation and lesion procedures have been used to analyze other brain-behavior relationships. In general, it seems that if electrical stimulation of a specific area is followed by an increase in some behavior, lesions in that same area will decrease the behavior. Similarly, if stimulation blocks a behavior, lesions may cause it to occur more frequently and vigorously.

Evoked Potentials

The electrical activity of the nervous system can be studied by placing electrodes on the scalp at various places and recording the voltage emitted by the brain. Any change in the brain's electrical activity in response to stimulation presented by the researcher, such as a sight or a sound, is called an **evoked potential**, and the technique has supplied useful information about brain-behavior relationships.

A change in electrical activity in a specific area of the brain after stimulation of a sense organ indicates a relationship between that part of the brain and the sense organ. For example, sounds cause marked evoked potentials at the top of the temporal lobe over the auditory cortex; light produces evoked potentials around the tip of the occipital cortex; and skin pressure produces evoked potentials in the parietal lobe next to the central fissure. Each of these cortical areas has a detailed and specific relationship with the particular sense that it processes. For instance, the musical scale is represented in a more or less orderly fashion along the auditory cortex, from low to high, with low notes producing evoked potentials at one end of the auditory cortex, high notes at the other end, and middle notes in between (Woolsey, 1961). Similar detailed arrangements have been found for other areas of the sensory cortex.

Most evoked potentials are recorded from outside the skull, but surgery to locate the focus of epileptic activity allows researchers to use the process on the surface of the brain itself. When the left hemisphere was exposed in such surgery, evoked potentials were recorded from ten different sites while patients silently identified objects shown on slides, then at a visual signal answered aloud a prearranged question about them ("Do the names of the two objects rhyme?"). The patients also matched lines on slides, a spatial task. Silent naming and replies to the question were accompanied by brain activity in two sites, activity that was absent when the patient was visually matching lines; these findings indicate a clear link between language behavior and brain activity in specific sites (Fried, Ojemann, and Fetz, 1981).

Single-Unit Recording

Evoked potentials record the activity of a group of neurons. Using a process called **single-unit recording**, psychologists can record the electrical activity of a single neuron. In this procedure, a microelectrode is placed very close to an individual neuron in the nervous system.

Our understanding of the brain's organization and function has been advanced through the application of this technique. For example, when researchers used it to record the activity of neurons in the visual cortex of cats and monkeys, they found that individual neurons are responsive to highly specific visual stimuli. A horizontal line moving across the retina from left to right might cause one neuron to fire, while another might fire only in response to a vertical or a diagonal line (Hubel and Wiesel, 1962). This sort of finding has been duplicated for other areas of the brain in many different animal species, with some neurons responsive only to temperature, to situations that require learning, or to numbers—firing only after a certain number of rhythmic auditory or visual stimuli have been sensed (Thompson et al., 1970). Individual neurons respond in a highly specific fashion, and this selectivity is apparently the basis for the behavioral and perceptual capacities of animals and human beings.

The Debate Over "Mind Control"

As researchers discover more about the brain, various methods of applying that knowledge have been devised. Some of these techniques have become the center of enormous controversy.

As noted earlier, mild electrical stimulation of the brain can calm violently aggressive mental patients or make people feel "happy" or near sexual orgasm. The use of stimulation to inhibit violence has been criticized because it has been seen as a form of mind control (Valenstein, 1973). In contrast, inducing pleasurable sensations by stimulating the limbic system has been criticized as ethically and socially undesirable. Those who hold this view argue that the person who places the pleasure-giving electrodes in another person's brain is in the powerful, manipulative position of a drug pusher (Rose, 1973).

The most heated controversy has arisen over **psychosurgery**, the destruction or removal of brain tissue for the purpose of altering behavior: thoughts, emotional reactions, personality, or patterns of social response (Valenstein, 1973). Psychosurgery can be done with a scalpel; often, however, electrodes are used as they are in brain stimulation, but in this case the electricity is used to destroy, not to stimulate. As with brain stimulation, the goal in some cases is to alleviate pain. But brain lesions have also been used to curb outbursts of uncontrollable violence, and the practice invariably meets opposition. For example, a thirty-six-year-old man who had murdered, then raped, a nurse and who had been in a mental hospital for eighteen years agreed to undergo psychosurgery. His parents also consented to the operation, but the procedure was challenged in court on the grounds that since the patient had agreed to psychosurgery in the hope of being released, he could not have freely given the informed consent required before surgery can be performed. Others have suggested that informed consent to psychosurgery is never possible, since "the damaged organ is the organ of consent" (Holden, 1973).

Some researchers (Mark, 1974) have urged the judicious use of psychosurgery, but others have called for a halt to it until an impartial evaluation of its risks and benefits can be carried out (Chorover, 1979). Again, the specter of brain control has been raised, and opponents of psychosurgery have warned that such irreversible physiological intervention is potentially a more serious problem than the violence it is intended to eliminate (cited in Moyer, 1971).

The Complex Behavioral Functions of the Brain

Despite all we have learned about the brain, we are still in the dark about much of that organ's functioning. And we know least about the sort of behavior that holds the greatest interest for psychologists: learning, memory, perception, and intellectual activity. Our lack of knowledge can be attributed in great part to the fact that these processes do not seem to be localized in the way that movements and the senses are.

In fact, many parts of the brain are involved in most behavior; conversely, any one area of the brain may be involved in many different kinds of behavior. For example, in addition to being involved with complex behavior, the cortex also plays a part in spinal reflexes, sleep and wakefulness, sexual behavior, and eating (Braun, 1975). Similarly, the hypothalamus is involved with a great deal more than regulating the pituitary gland and controlling patterns of feeding and drinking. Research has shown that rats with hypothalamic damage also suffer learning deficits (Teitelbaum, 1971). Thus, the brain functions as a single unit, and to understand the relationship between brain and behavior, we must look at the functioning brain of a living organism as well as at the activity of individual neurons.

SUMMARY

1. In multicelled animals there are three main types of specialized cells: **receptor cells**, which receive sensory information from the environment; **motor cells**, which control muscle movements and glandular secretions; and **neurons**, which transmit information throughout the body.

2. The **nervous system**, which acts as a communication network among all body cells, is divided into the **central nervous system**, which consists of the brain and the spinal cord and is the major control center for behavior, and the **peripheral nervous system**, which relays information from sensory receptors to the central nervous system and sends out messages to muscles or glands. The divisions of the peripheral nervous system are the **somatic nervous system**, which is related to external behavior and is generally under voluntary control, and the **autonomic nervous system**, which controls the visceral muscles and glands and is generally involuntary. The autonomic system is subdivided into the **sympathetic nervous system**, which expends energy in coping with stressful situations, and the **parasympathetic nervous system**, which conserves energy, functioning during normal or relaxed situations.

3. The basic structural units of the nervous system are neurons and **glia**, which provide structural support and nutrients to the neurons and bar certain substances from the bloodstream. Among the specialized neurons are **sensory neurons** that transmit information from the sense organs to the brain and spinal cord; **motor neurons** that transmit information from the brain and spinal cord to the muscles and glands; and **interneurons** that connect neurons to one another and integrate sensory and motor activity. Neurons consist of a **cell body**, which contains the nucleus; **dendrites**, which are relatively short fibers that extend from the cell body; and an **axon**, which is a long fiber that leads away from the cell body.

4. In a resting state, the cell is **polarized**: its interior is negatively charged while its exterior is positively charged. A stimulus allows positive ions to penetrate the cell membrane, reversing the polarization and resulting in an electrochemical charge, or firing. The intensity of a stimulus is conveyed by the rate of firing and by the numbers of neurons activated. Messages are transmitted from one neuron to another by **neurotransmitters** (chemicals stored in sacs at the axon tip), which are released into the **synapse** (a small space separating one neuron from another) by the arrival of an action potential. Messages are either **excitatory** (causing the receiving neuron to fire) or **inhibitory** (keeping the receiving neuron from firing).

5. Much behavior depends on which neurotransmitter is released, so that a good deal of human behavior is chemically based. Each transmitter can activate only neural receptors that are designed to fit its molecular structure. **Endorphins**, one variety of neurotransmitter, are similar in structure to opiates and are implicated in pain and pleasure. Because of the similarity in structure, receptors designed to fit endorphins will accept opiates.

6. The spinal cord connects the brain and the peripheral nervous system, and within the spinal cord are **reflex arcs**, the simplest chain of connecting neurons.

7. The nervous system transmits rapid messages that require a good deal of energy, but the **endocrine system** transmits slower, energy-conserving messages, by means of chemical substances called **hormones**. Hormones are produced by the **endocrine glands**, which secrete these chemicals directly into the bloodstream, through which they reach their particular target organs. The level of a hormone in the blood is kept in a state of balance, or **equilibrium**, through a self-regulation process called **homeostasis**. Hormones affect sexual arousal, emotional response, motivation, physical growth, and metabolism.

8. The brain consists of three overlapping layers: the central core, the limbic system, and the cerebral hemispheres. The **cerebral hemispheres** are involved in learning, speech, reasoning, and memory. The **cerebral cortex** is the **gray matter** that covers the cerebral hemispheres. The **occipital lobe**, which is located at the back of the brain, is primarily involved in the reception and analysis of visual information. Areas for auditory reception and for processing visual information are found in the **temporal lobe**. The **frontal lobe** is quite generally involved in behavior, and that part of it that lies next to the central fissure is concerned with the regulation of voluntary movements and is called the **motor cortex**. In the **parietal lobe** is the **somatosensory cortex**, which receives touch and positional information from different areas of the body. About 75 percent of the cortex has no specific function; these areas are called the **association cortex**. The cerebral hemispheres are composed of two halves (the right and left hemispheres); the left half of the brain generally controls the right half of the body, and vice versa. The left hemisphere is involved with language and logical thought; it processes information in a logical, sequential manner. The right hemisphere is involved in spatial skills, musical ability, and visual imagery; it processes information in a simultaneous, intuitive manner. The two hemispheres communicate through a thick band of neural fibers called the **corpus callosum**. The brains of males and females may be organized differently, with females using both hemispheres to some degree in all types of skills. The **limbic system** is involved in motivational and emotional processes. It plays a role in feeding, fighting, fleeing, and mating. Damage to the limbic system produces marked changes in aggressive, feeding, and sexual behavior.

9. The **central core** of the brain, consisting of the brain stem, the cerebellum, the thalamus, and the hypothalamus, carries out the basic functions of survival. The **brain stem** is composed of the **medulla**, which is involved in breathing, circulation, chewing, salivation, and facial movements; the **pons**, which connects the two halves of the cerebellum and acts as a relay station; the **midbrain**, which is a center for visual and auditory reflexes; and the **reticular formation**, which arouses the higher brain areas to incoming information and maintains the sleep-waking

cycle. The **cerebellum**, which is divided into two hemispheres, coordinates voluntary muscle activity and maintains physical balance. The **thalamus** sorts messages from sensory receptors, sends them to the appropriate regions of the higher brain, and integrates information coming from the cerebral hemispheres. The **hypothalamus** monitors changes in the internal environment and sends out signals that maintain equilibrium. It signals the autonomic nervous system to respond to environmental changes and influences the pituitary gland, thereby affecting the production of hormones throughout the endocrine system. The hypothalamus has a major effect on feeding, internal temperature regulation, responses to stress, and sexual function.

10. Accident or illness can disrupt brain functioning, resulting in abnormal motor, emotional, or cognitive behavior. One common cause of brain damage is a **stroke**, in which blood vessels on the surface of the brain suddenly rupture. As a result, the afflicted person may be paralyzed or develop **aphasia**— an inability to speak or to understand spoken language. Epilepsy, bacterial infections, viral infections, and alcoholism can all affect brain functioning.

11. Several techniques are used in the study of the relationship between brain functioning and behavior. Clinical observations relate disruptions in behavior after brain damage to specific sites of damaged tissue. Mild electrical stimulation, which causes neurons to fire, elicits specific behavior, as does chemical stimulation. Research on brain stimulation has produced maps of the sensory and motor cortex and provided treatment of certain medical problems, such as intractable pain. Selectively destroying or removing small amounts of brain tissue, thereby creating **lesions** in the brains of animals, has also helped to clarify the connections between brain function and behavior. Recording **evoked potentials**, or changes in the brain's electrical activity in response to stimulation, has also been helpful in determining brain-behavior connections. The **single-unit recording** technique, in which electrodes are inserted close to individual neurons within the brain, has shown that individual neurons respond to highly specific stimuli.

12. The application of knowledge about the brain to alter behavior has generated a debate over "mind control." The use of brain stimulation to calm violent patients and the use of stimulation to create pleasurable states are both highly controversial techniques; but most debate centers on **psychosurgery**, the destruction or removal of brain tissue to change behavior.

KEY TERMS

adrenal glands	cerebral hemispheres	hippocampus
agnosia	corpus callosum	homeostasis
amnesia	cranium	hormones
amygdala	dendrites	hypothalamus
aphasia	dopamine	inhibitory
association cortex	endocrine glands	interneurons
ataxia	endocrine system	lateral fissure
autonomic nervous system	endorphins	lateralization
axon	equilibrium	lesion
brain stem	evoked potential	limbic system
cell body	excitatory	localization of function
central core	frontal lobes	medulla
central fissure	ganglia	midbrain
central nervous system (CNS)	glia	motor cortex
cerebellum	gonads	motor cells
cerebral cortex	gray matter	motor neurons

myelin sheath
nerves
nervous system
neurons
neuropsychologists
neurotransmitters
occipital lobe
parasympathetic nervous
  system
parietal lobe
peptides

peripheral nervous system
  (PNS)
pituitary gland
polarized
pons
psychosurgery
receptor cells
reflex arc
refractory period
reticular formation
sensory neurons
septal area

single-unit recording
somatic nervous system
somatosensory cortex
stroke
sympathetic nervous system
synapse
temporal lobe
thalamus
thyroid gland
thyroxin
white matter

RECOMMENDED READINGS

BLAKEMORE, C. *Mechanics of the Mind.* New York: Cambridge University Press, 1977. An introduction to how the mind works and its relationship to the brain.

CARLSON, N. R. *Physiology of Behavior.* 2nd ed. Boston: Allyn & Bacon, 1980. A good introductory text on physiological psychology. Explains complex concepts in a clear way.

ROSE, S. *The Conscious Brain.* New York: Knopf, 1975. A British scientist gives a personal account of brain research. Fun to read.

SCHNEIDER, A. M., and B. TARSHIS. *An Introduction to Physiological Psychology.* 2nd ed. New York: Random House, 1979. A good introduction to physiological psychology. Provides helpful explanations with a minimum amount of difficult language.

SPRINGER, S. P., and G. DEUTSCH. *Left Brain, Right Brain.* San Francisco: W. H. Freeman, 1981. A discussion of all the recent research on the two hemispheres of the brain, with a well-written discussion of neuroanatomy in the Appendix.

The Brain. San Francisco: Freeman, 1979. Contains eleven articles, all by eminent brain researchers, that appeared in the September 1979 issue of *Scientific American.* Many good illustrations.

VALENSTEIN, E. S. *Brain Control: A Critical Examination of Brain Stimulation and Psychosurgery.* New York: Wiley, 1973. Fine discussion of brain stimulation and psychosurgery. Contains both scientific evidence and many interesting case histories.

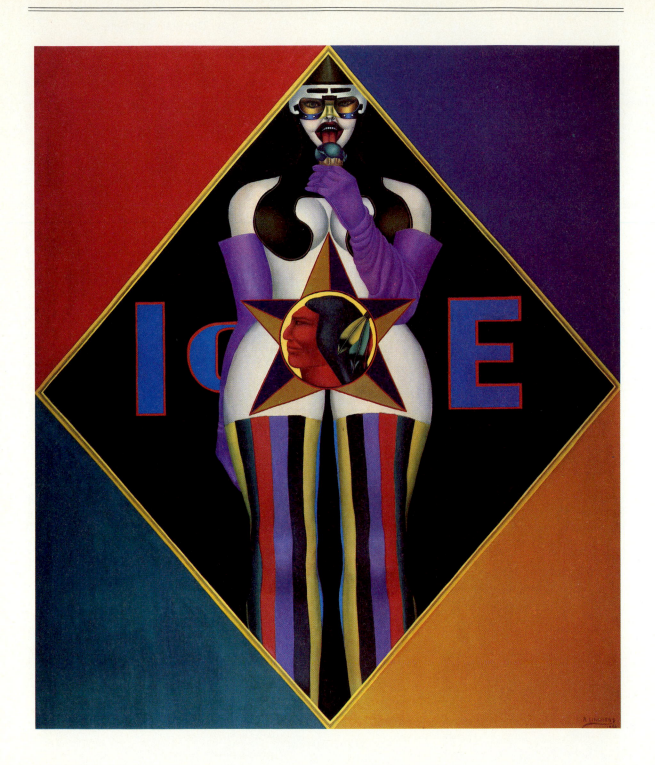

CHAPTER 4

Sensation and the Senses

Our ability to deal with the environment—to locate food and to distinguish friend from foe—depends on the acquisition of information about events around us. Our only source for this information is provided by our senses, those specialized receptor and nervous system structures that put us in touch with the external world. The senses are our life lines to reality.

Because our sensory experience is so rich, it is natural to assume that all environmental events are available to us. This is a mistake. Each of our senses is a custom-designed device that responds to only a limited range of sensory information, and the sensory systems of different species vary remarkably in their selectivity. For example, many nocturnal species are color-blind but have a highly developed sense of hearing. Certain moths are deaf to all frequencies of sound except those emitted by the hunting bats that prey on them. Many birds have an acute sense of vision but a poor sense of smell. Human beings have a relatively keen sense of smell but cannot, for example, detect the aroma exuded by earthworms that betrays their presence to worm-eating snakes. Thus we can see that sensory systems are like filters that accentuate or suppress information about the world, depending on the kinds of information that the organism needs to survive.

The study of sensory processes is one of the oldest research areas in psychology, dating back over a century. Historically, the study of sensory processes has consisted of two major branches: sensory physiology and psychophysics. **Sensory physiology** investigates the means by which environmental information is captured and transformed by the receptors and then processed in the nervous system. **Psychophysics** is devoted to establishing the relationship between physical stimulation and the resulting sensory experience. The two branches are closely related, and advances in one branch often lead to research in the other. Using results obtained through both approaches, this chapter examines sensation and its neural basis.

Stimuli and Sensations: Psychophysics

The external world consists of various forms of energy that can impinge on sensory receptors. Any form of energy that can evoke a response is a **stimulus,** which can be described in either physical or psychological terms. In the physical domain, a stimulus is measured by such instruments as photometers, thermometers, or weight scales, and the resulting measures are expressed as luminance, degrees, or kilograms. In the psychological domain, a stimulus is described in terms of its subjective attributes, through the use of such words as brightness, warmth, and heaviness.

Human beings respond psychologically to stimuli along two principal dimensions: quality and quantity. The *quality* of a stimulus refers to the kind of sensation it produces. For instance, color—or hue—is a quality related to visual stimulation, whereas pitch on the musical scale is a quality related to auditory stimulation. Such differences in sensory quality appear to correspond to neural activity within different sensory regions of the brain. For this reason, we can neither hear sunsets nor see melodies.

Quantity is related to the amount of stimulation. The brightness of a color represents a quantity of light, and loudness represents a quantity of sound. These characteristics—hue, brightness, pitch, loudness—are examples of psychological dimensions of sensation; that is, they are the subjective properties of sensory experience as perceived by the stimulated person.

In studying the relationship between stimuli and sensations, psychologists tend to focus on three basic problems: (1) the minimum amount of stimulation required to evoke a discernible sensation; (2) the amount by which a stimulus must change along some dimension for that change to be detected; (3) and the factors that influence these sensory judgments.

The Limits of Sensation

There are limits to the fidelity of our senses. A tone may be too weak to be heard, or the difference in color between a pair of lights may be too small to detect. In discussing such limitations, psychologists use the concept of threshold. There are two types of threshold: the **absolute threshold,** which refers to the weakest stimulus that produces a detectable sensation, and the **difference threshold**, or **just noticeable difference (jnd)**, which refers to the smallest change in a stimulus that produces a change in sensation.

A psychologist might establish an absolute threshold for light by having a person watch for a light in a dark room. Using a machine that projects low-intensity light beams, the psychologist projects a very dim beam on the wall, gradually increasing the light's intensity until the person says, "I see it." Alternatively, the psychologist can start by projecting a visible beam and then gradually decrease its intensity until the

person says, "I can't see it." These procedures are generally repeated a number of times with the same person, and the lowest intensity at which the person reports seeing the light half the time is considered the absolute threshold.

The difference threshold is established by a procedure similar to that used with the absolute threshold. The psychologist might gradually increase the difference between two visible light beams until the person says, "Yes, one light is brighter than the other." This technique makes it possible to identify the smallest increase in light intensity that is noticeable to the human eye.

When conditions are ideal, absolute thresholds are quite low, so that only minute amounts of stimulation are required to produce sensations. For example, the human sense of smell can detect one drop of perfume in a three-room apartment. The sense of taste can detect a teaspoon of sugar dissolved in two gallons of water. And on a clear, dark night, the human eye can detect the light of a candle burning thirty miles away (Galanter, 1962).

Yet ideal conditions rarely prevail. In terms of absolute threshold, a person ideally would never detect the light when its intensity fell below the absolute threshold and would always detect it when it exceeded this value. This ideal performance can be expressed graphically as a **psychometric function**, a plot depicting the change in an individual's performance that takes place as some aspect of a stimulation varies. If a fixed, stable threshold existed, this plot would take the form of an abrupt step like the one shown in Figure 4.1. However, this ideal outcome is never realized in an experiment, and instead psychometric functions more nearly resemble the smooth curve also shown in Figure 4.1. In actual experience, each person's response varies within a range of stimulation. Sometimes a person says, "Yes, I see it," at a particular intensity of light that on other occasions brings the response, "No, I don't." So in the strict sense, there is no absolute threshold. Because of this variation in detection, psychologists have arbitrarily designated the absolute threshold as the intensity that is detected on half the trials.

The ability to detect stimuli varies for several reasons. First, because of fluctuations in the internal state of our sensory apparatus and our readiness (e.g., our levels of attention or fatigue), the same physical stimulus can evoke neural responses of different magnitude. Second, sensory systems appear to contain internal

Noise—whether external or internal—is only one factor that can affect our ability to perceive stimuli. Others include level of attention, fatigue, and motivation.

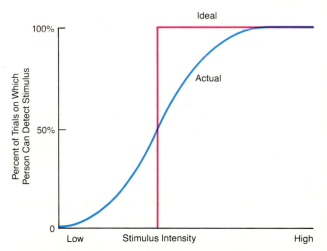

Figure 4.1 Under ideal conditions there would exist a specific point at which the intensity of a stimulus was great enough for a person to detect it. Below that point, the stimulus would never be detected, while above that point it would always be perceived. This ideal threshold of sensation is depicted by the red line on the graph. Such ideal conditions rarely prevail, however. A person's ability to detect a stimulus is influenced by a variety of things, including fatigue or alertness, motivation, and the level of spontaneous neural activity within the sensory system. As a result, low intensity stimuli are sometimes perceived and sometimes not, as the blue curve on the graph reveals. So psychologists arbitrarily define the absolute threshold as the weakest stimulus that a person can detect 50 percent of the time.

"noise"—spontaneous neural activity independent of external stimulation. Because of this internal noise, a stimulus, or signal, occurs against a background level of activity that introduces the same sort of variability caused by external noise. Third, a person's level of motivation may strongly influence performance on tests of signal detection.

Such judgments are seen by some scientists (e.g., Green and Swets, 1966) as a process that can be separated into two components: the sensation and the person's report of it. Realizing that internal and external factors affect threshold, these researchers have advocated **signal detection theory**, which proposes that there is no single absolute threshold for a stimulus. This theory assumes that noise can interfere with signal detection and that decisions about weak signals depend on nonsensory factors. These researchers have also developed testing procedures that either are immune to factors that influence decisions or explicitly manipulate these factors so that their influence can be studied.

Theories of sensory limits and signal detection have important applications in decision making, because much of the machinery of modern society requires people to detect minimal stimuli, no matter what external or internal noise may be present. For example, a radar operator must be able to detect an airplane on a radar screen even when the operator is tired or when the blip from the plane is faint and difficult to distinguish from blips caused by a flock of birds or bad weather. The radar operator's decision can be crucial when guiding airliners or when detecting enemy planes during wartime, yet such judgments are affected by many factors over which the operator has no control.

Sensory Scaling

Measuring the physical magnitude of a stimulus, as temperature is measured in degrees or sounds are measured in decibels, is a straightforward procedure, because we have calibrated instruments that provide scaled values of magnitude. However, measuring the subjective magnitude of the sensation that a stimulus produces is *not* straightforward, because a sensation is a private event and inaccessible to measuring instruments. This inaccessibility would be no problem if sensation varied directly with the magnitude of stimulation, but it does not. For example, doubling the light produced by a bulb (a physical event) does not double a person's sensation of brightness.

This disparity between changes in the magnitude of a stimulus and changes in the sensation the stimulus produces was first systematically studied by Ernst Weber in the nineteenth century. He found that although people notice small changes in a weak stimulus, they notice only large differences in a strong stimulus. For instance, if one pound is added to a bag containing a loaf of bread, the sensation of weight is greatly increased. But if one pound is added to a seventy-pound backpack, the increase in weight is imperceptible.

Weber (1834) formalized this relation as **Weber's law**, which states that the amount of stimulus needed to produce a just noticeable difference in sensation is a constant fraction of the intensity of the stimulus. For example, the JND for 100-pound backpack is about 2 pounds for most people. Thus, for a 50-pound backpack the JND would be about 1 pound, and for a 10-pound backpack, about 1/5 of a pound. For the sensation of weight, then, the proportion necessary for a JND is about 1/50. Some sensory systems are less sensitive than this: that is, they can detect changes only after larger fractional changes in stimulation. For example, the fractional increase that produces a JND in the intensity of a tone is 1/10, in skin pressure 1/7, and in the saltiness of a liquid 1/5.

Although Weber's law was an important advance, Weber did not offer it as a scale of sensation. Instead the generalization was made by his contemporary, Gustav Fechner (1860). Fechner proposed that successive JNDs be considered as equal intervals on a psychological scale of sensation, just as successive frequencies make up the musical scale. He devised several techniques for measuring difference thresholds, which could be used indirectly to derive the values for this scale. Much of what we know about sensation was discovered through the use of these techniques. Fechner also derived a general psychophysical law, known as **Fechner's law**, which takes the form of an equation:

$$S = k \log I$$

in which S is the magnitude of the sensation, I is the intensity, and k is a constant that is produced by Weber's law. According to this formula, the magnitude of a sensation increases less rapidly than does the intensity of the stimulus.

After Fechner, most psychologists assumed it was necessary to use some indirect technique to measure sensation, since people were unable to behave like yardsticks or thermometers. Then, a few decades ago, S. S. Stevens (1957) argued that people can indeed directly rate the intensity of various stimuli. To achieve this rating, Stevens devised a method of magnitude estimation in which people assigned numbers to each sensation. For example, a light that seemed twice as bright as a standard light was given a number twice as large as the standard. Stevens found that people could reliably assess their own subjective experiences, and from these judgments he produced a direct scale of subjective magnitude. Using such scaling techniques, Stevens found that the relationship between subjective experience and physical intensity was not as Fechner had proposed it, but that a sensation was instead proportional to the intensity of a stimulus raised to a certain power. According to **Stevens' power law**, different sensory domains have different exponents, which means that the increase of sensation with intensity is different for each sense (see Figure 4.2). For example, the physical intensity of light must be increased eightfold before it looks twice as bright. The physical intensity of a sound must be more than three times as intense before we hear it as twice as loud.

Debate continues over the validity of direct sensory scaling and the correct form of the true "psychophysical law." Recent advances in sensory physiology have led some psychologists to look to the nervous system itself to provide a final answer to this question.

Sensory Adaptation

All of us have walked from a sunny sidewalk into a dimly lit theater and discovered that we were unable to see which seats were occupied, or even the rows of seats themselves. This temporary blindness is an example of **adaptation**, which refers to an adjustment in sensitivity after prolonged and constant stimulation. All sensory systems display adaptation. Some senses, like smell and touch, adapt quickly, but others, like the sense of pain, adapt very slowly.

The resulting decrease in sensitivity should not be regretted. The process of adaptation allows us to operate efficiently over an enormous range of stimulus intensities. For example, visual adaptation makes it possible to see in broad daylight as well as at night, although the illumination under these two conditions may differ by a millionfold. A steady level of stimulation, whether pressure, light, sound, or odor, provides no new information. By de-emphasizing old information, adaptation increases our alertness to new stimulation. For instance, a sleeping person adapts to the sound of a playing radio and awakens when the radio is turned *off*.

In addition to decreasing sensitivity, adaptation can distort sensation. A blatant form of this distortion can be experienced in the following experiment. Place one hand in icy water and the

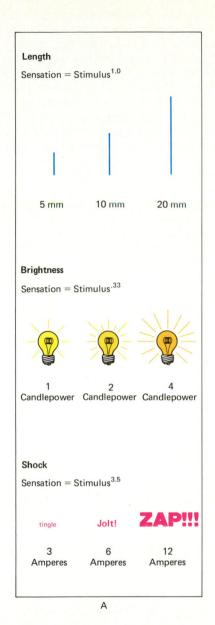

Length

Sensation = Stimulus$^{1.0}$

5 mm   10 mm   20 mm

Brightness

Sensation = Stimulus$^{.33}$

1 Candlepower   2 Candlepower   4 Candlepower

Shock

Sensation = Stimulus$^{3.5}$

tingle   Jolt!   ZAP!!!

3 Amperes   6 Amperes   12 Amperes

A

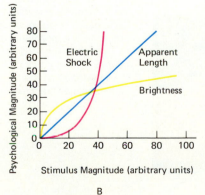

Psychological Magnitude (arbitrary units)

Electric Shock   Apparent Length   Brightness

Stimulus Magnitude (arbitrary units)

B

Figure 4.2 (A) S. S. Stevens has shown that the psychological magnitude (size) of a sensation varies according to some power of the physical magnitude of the stimulus. The size of the power, or exponent, to which the stimulus intensity must be raised, is different for different stimulus dimensions. (top) The equation for the psychological magnitude of line length has an exponent of 1.0; this means that when a line is doubled in length, it does in fact look twice as long. (middle) Brightness has an exponent of 0.33; when you double the amount of light coming from a bulb, your sensation of brightness increases only about one-fourth. (bottom) Electric shock has an exponent of 3.5; this means that doubling the intensity of the electricity produces a feeling of shock 11.3 times greater, on the average. (B) The three relationships plotted as graphs, to show the growth of psychological magnitude as physical magnitude grows. (After Stevens, 1962.)

other in water as hot as you can stand it. After you have adapted to the temperatures, plunge both hands into a bucket of tepid water. The initial sensation will be a bizarre contradiction between the messages sent by the two hands. The water will feel both hot and cold, although you know that it is neither.

Perceived sensations are not determined solely by the present stimulus, but are also affected by immediately preceding stimuli. For instance, the same weight may feel heavy or light, depending on weights that have been lifted just before the weight in question is handled. The adaptation level to a particular amount of stimulation seems to influence sensory judgment by providing a frame of reference for evaluating new sensations (Helson, 1964).

The Senses: Sensory Physiology

The five senses commonly referred to are those detected by the five obvious sense organs: eyes, ears, nose, tongue, and skin. Actually, human beings have more than five senses. Within the skin are receptors for at least four kinds of sensation (touch, warmth, cold, and pain). An organ in the inner ear, called the **vestibular apparatus**, provides a sense of balance and equilibrium. Receptors in the muscles, joints, and tendons provide a sense of body position and movement. Finally, other receptors located in the brain itself monitor vital information about blood chemistry and temperature, acting as sensors of internal physiological states. Although this discussion is restricted to the classic five senses and to the

sense of balance and movement, *all* sense organs operate according to similar principles.

Each sense organ contains special receptors that are sensitive to particular types of stimuli. However, the basic job of all sensory receptors is the same: to convert environmental stimuli into neural impulses, the language of the nervous system. This process of transformation is known as **transduction**. The neural information then travels over specialized nerve pathways to specialized sensory areas in the brain. Here it undergoes refined analysis and ultimately produces conscious experience and sometimes motor behavior.

Vision

Vision is the richest human sense and provides us with a wealth of information. The eyes receive light reflected from objects in the world, and from this light we perceive shape, color, depth, texture, and movement.

Light, the basic stimulus for vision, makes up only a small portion of the electromagnetic spectrum. As Figure 4.3 shows, this spectrum also contains radio and infrared waves, ultraviolet rays, X-rays, and gamma rays, which are outside the range of human visual sensitivity and must be measured with special instruments. The electromagnetic spectrum is scaled in units called **wavelengths**, and that portion visible to the human eye ranges from just below 400 μm (millimicrons) to about 780 μm. Even within this range, the human eye is not uniformly sensitive to all wavelengths; it is most sensitive in the middle of the visible region, so that less energy is required to detect a dim light when it is composed of

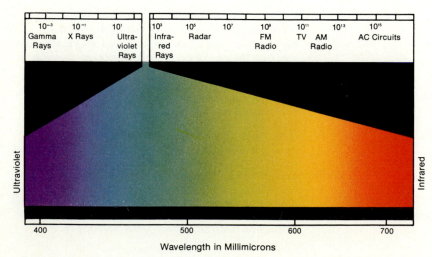

Figure 4.3 The spectrum of electromagnetic energy. The small portion of this spectrum to which the human eye is sensitive is shown expanded. The scale on the large spectrum is a logarithmic scale of wavelength: each step on the scale corresponds to a tenfold increase in the wavelength of the electromagnetic radiation.

A

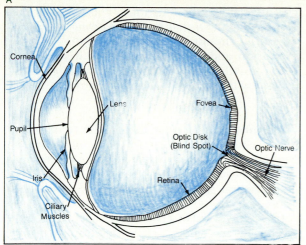

Human Eye

Figure 4.4 The structure of the human eye and retina. (A) Incoming light passes through the cornea, pupil, and lens and eventually hits the retina. (B) From the outer surface of the retina the light must filter through several layers of cells before reaching the rods and cones. The rods and cones register the presence of light and pass on an electrical potential to the adjacent bipolar cells. From here the impulses travel to the ganglion cells, the axons of which form the fibers of the optic nerve leading to the brain. Note that in or near the fovea a single cone may connect to its own exclusive bipolar cell, thus enhancing visual acuity. (After Coren, Porac, and Ward, 1979.)

B

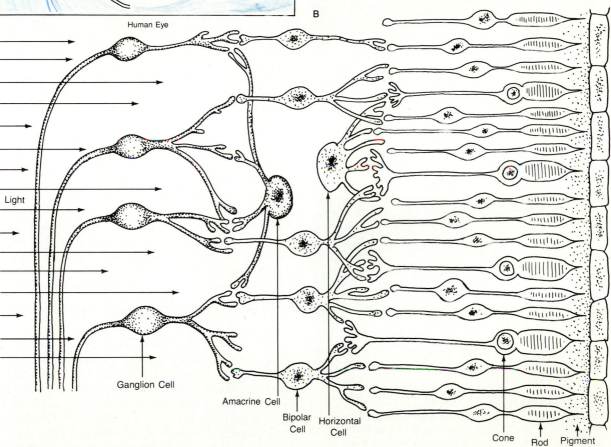

wavelengths from the middle of the visible spectrum than when the wavelengths come from either extreme.

The Structure of the Eye Basically, the human eye consists of the cornea, the iris, the lens, and the retina (see Figure 4.4). Light enters the eye through the **cornea**, the transparent covering in front of the eye. The cornea, which is sharply curved, serves as a preliminary lens, helping to focus the light. Behind the cornea is the **pupil**, the opening in the center of the eye that appears black. The amount of light that enters the eye through the pupil is regulated by the **iris**, a ring of muscle whose pigmentation gives the eye its color. Light passes through the pupil to a transparent structure called the **lens**. The ciliary mus-

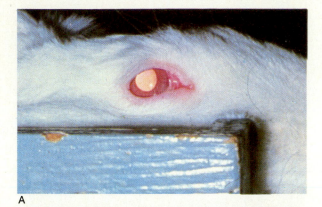

A

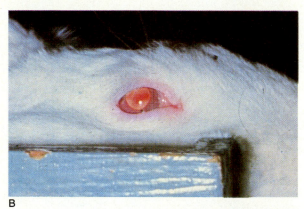

B

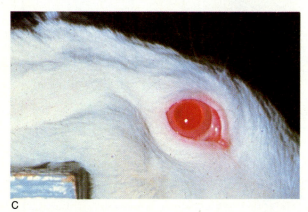

C

Photograph A shows a rabbit's eye after it has been in bright light for some time. The pigment rhodopsin has been "bleached" away by the light (the same would be true of your eye after a few minutes on a sunlit beach, though it would not be as noticeable to an observer). Photograph B shows the same eye after two minutes in a completely dark room (the photo was taken with a brief flash). Notice that some of the pigment has returned. Photograph C was taken after ten minutes in the dark; the recovery of the eye from bleaching is nearly complete, and the eye is said to be dark-adapted.

cles attached to the lens modify its curvature to focus the light so that it makes a clear image on the **retina**, the surface at the back of the eye. The expansion and contraction of the iris and the ciliary muscles are reflexive, reacting to changes in light without our conscious control.

The Retina and Receptor Cells   The retina is an intricate network of receptor cells and neurons, where light energy is converted into neural impulses that can be transmitted to the brain. The major neural structures of the retina and their interconnections, which are diagramed in Figure 4.4B, are involved in a chain of visual processing.

The first stage in this chain that leads to vision occurs within the visual receptors. Located at the very back of the retina, these specialized cells convert light energy into an electrical potential, behaving much like a photoelectric cell that senses the absolute amount of light in a tiny, dotlike region. The retina actually contains two receptor systems. One system, composed of **rods**, is responsible for vision in dim light; it signals information about brightness but not color. The other system, composed of **cones**, operates in increased light and is responsible for detailed vision and for color perception.

Rods and cones differ in several ways. In terms of sheer numbers, rods far outstrip cones, by 120 million to 6 million. In addition, the two types of receptors are unevenly distributed throughout the retina. Cones are highly concentrated in the central region of the retina and are the only receptors in the very center of the **fovea**, the retinal area that lies almost directly opposite the pupil. Rods predominate in peripheral regions of the retina.

All rods contain **rhodopsin**, a light-sensitive molecule, or **photopigment**, that is much more sensitive than photopigments in the cones. As a result, rods can operate in dim light that renders cones useless. There are three varieties of photopigments in the cones, each sensitive to different wavelengths. As we shall see, this property enables the cones to play their role in color vision. In this respect, the eye resembles a camera loaded with two entirely different types of film, a highly sensitive black-and-white film and a less sensitive, high-resolution color film.

After photochemically registering the presence of light, rods and cones pass their electrical potential through the **bipolar cells** to the **ganglion cells**. In the fovea a single cone recep-

Figure 4.5 Although you are never normally aware of it, the blind spot is literally blind. To demonstrate this fact to yourself, hold this figure at arm's length, cover your left eye, and focus on the center of the X. Slowly move the figure toward you, staring continuously at the X. At some point, you will no longer be able to see the red spot. This is the point at which the red spot's image has fallen on the blind spot in your right eye. The red spot will reappear if you move the figure even closer. Blind spots are not ordinarily noticed because they are off center, so that one eye fills in much of what the other is missing. In addition, the continual movement of the eyes shifts the area of the blind spot, enabling the brain to fill in the rest of the missing information.

tor may connect with only one ganglion cell, whereas in more peripheral parts of the retina, many receptors (rods or cones) may converge on a single ganglion cell. This narrow communication between cones and ganglion cells in the fovea is one reason for the superior visual acuity of this retinal area——the fovea is used when looking closely at details. By the same token, the convergence of many peripheral receptors (predominantly rods) on a single ganglion cell allows information from a relatively large area to be combined, producing an enhanced sensitivity to dim light. This extensive connection makes it easier to see a dim star by looking out of the corner of the eye. Between the receptors and the ganglion cells, two other types of neurons, the **horizontal cells** and the **amacrine cells**, form lateral networks at two different levels, enabling neighboring retinal areas to influence each other (see Figure 4.4B).

The axons of the 1 million ganglion cells in each eye form the **optic nerve**, which leaves the eye through an area of the retina known as the **optic disc**, or blind spot, as shown in Figure 4.4A. The blind spot is aptly named, because it contains no receptor cells and creates an actual blind spot in the visual field of each eye. Using Figure 4.5, you can experience your own blind spot. After leaving the eyeball, the optic nerves meet at a junction called the **optic chiasm**, where they are rerouted. Fibers from the left half of each eye go to the left cerebral hemisphere, and fibers from the right side of each eye go to the right cerebral hemisphere. From here the majority of axons lead to the **lateral geniculate nucleus**, a grouping of cell bodies in the thalamus; the remainder of the axons lead to the superior **colliculus** and other midbrain structures concerned with the control of eye movements and other visual reflexes. Axons of geniculate cells in turn travel to the **visual cortex**, where the processing associated with the emergence of conscious visual perception occurs.

At each of these stages of processing (retinal cells, lateral geniculate nucleus, visual cortex), individual neurons respond to light stimulation falling within a restricted region of the retina. This region is known as the cell's **receptive field**. Together, the millions of receptive fields (one for each cell) form a mosaic that registers information over the entire field of vision. Much of the experimentation that established the function of these receptive fields was done by David Hubel and Torsten Wiesel (1979), who received the Nobel Prize for their research.

Each receptive field is divided into two regions: an ON and an OFF. Turning on a light increases the cell's firing rate in the ON region but decreases it in the OFF. Some cells have their ON region in the center while others have it in the surrounding area.

As stimulation progresses from retina to cortex, the shapes of the receptive fields become increasingly more specialized. As shown in Figure 4.6, retinal receptive fields tend to be roughly circular, with their ON/OFF regions arranged concentrically. As a result of this arrangement, retinal cells respond best to roughly circular spots or to edges of light and not at all well to diffuse light (Frisby, 1980). Cells in the lateral geniculate nucleus respond in much the same way. In the visual cortex, receptive fields are elongated, with their ON and OFF regions located side by side. Consequently, cortical cells respond to lines or bars of light, with various cells responding to lines of specific orientations. The visual cortex is also where input from both eyes is combined to produce stereoscopic vision, adding depth to our world. The properties of the

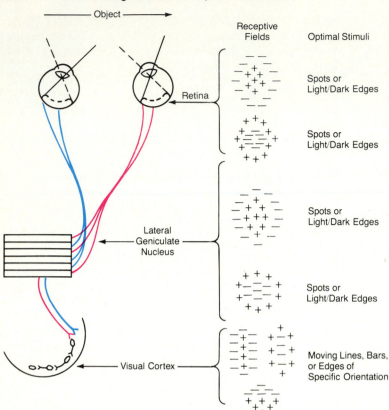

Object

Receptive
Fields

Retina

Lateral
Geniculate
Nucleus

Visual Cortex

Optimal Stimuli

Spots or
Light/Dark Edges

Spots or
Light/Dark Edges

Spots or
Light/Dark Edges

Spots or
Light/Dark Edges

Moving Lines, Bars,
or Edges of
Specific Orientation

Figure 4.6   A schematic diagram that shows the first three major stages in visual processing—the retina, the lateral geniculate nucleus, and the visual cortex. To the right are shown the characteristic spatial layouts of receptive fields in these stages. The minus signs indicate the OFF regions, while plus signs denote the ON regions. Cells at successively higher stages tend to respond to more specialized features. This particular diagram refers to the visual pathways in the cat, but the same general scheme applies to higher primates, including humans. (After Barlow, Narasimhan, and Rosenfeld, 1972.)

receptive fields at each stage of visual processing may provide the neural basis for the ability to recognize distinctive features, a process that is discussed in Chapter 7.

Color Vision   Color perception is a complex process that depends on psychological as well as physiological processes. Although each color or hue perceived in the visual spectrum corresponds to a certain range or combination of wavelengths (see Figure 4.3), the experience of color also depends on the intensity of light, the way it is reflected from a surface, and the color of surrounding objects. The color of any object is neither in the object itself nor in the light rays reflected from it; instead, color is a perceptual experience that results when the properties of light stimulate various types of receptors, initiating a chain of visual processing that eventually excites particular cells in the visual cortex.

How does the visual system translate different light wavelengths into the experience of color? Two major explanations, the trichromatic theory and the opponent-process theory, have been developed to explain color vision, and each explains certain aspects of it. Most investigators now accept some form of dual process theory

that incorporates elements of both these leading theories.

The **trichromatic theory** was first advanced in the nineteenth century by Thomas Young and later elaborated by the physiologist Hermann von Helmholtz. It proposes that color vision is based on three types of cones thought to be mingled in a mosaic pattern throughout the central retina. Each type is most sensitive to different wavelengths, with some cones responding best to red light, others to green light, and still others to blue light. The proportion of each kind of cone activated determines the color that is perceived. When red-sensitive cones are stimulated, we see red. When red-sensitive and green-sensitive cones are equally stimulated, we see yellow, because the wavelengths defining yellow are between red and green on the spectrum. According to the theory, any color of the visible spectrum can be produced from some combination of the three kinds of cones (MacNichol, 1964).

Support for the trichromatic theory comes from color-matching experiments in which a person mixes together several different wavelengths to produce a color that matches a comparison light of a single wavelength. Most people must use three different wavelengths to achieve a match and find it impossible to get a match with only two. Presumably, the requirement of three wavelengths is related to the three types of receptors.

A small proportion of people can make satisfactory matches using only two wavelengths. These people, called **dichromats**, have difficulty discriminating wavelengths in certain regions of the spectrum: they confuse colors that most people can distinguish. Dichromats are believed to have only two types of cones, instead of the normal three. An even rarer and more severe deficiency is complete color blindness. People who are color-blind are called **monochromats**; they see the world only in shades of gray, as if they were watching a black-and-white film. Presumably, their retinas contain only one kind of cone.

Opponent-process theory, which also dates back to the nineteenth century, proposes the existence of three antagonistically organized systems, with two of the systems composed of pairs of opposite colors. Color opposites are demonstrated on the color wheel in Figure 4.7. When complementary colors (colors on opposite sides of the wheel) are combined, they are seen as colorless—either gray or white, a phenomenon known as **color cancellation**. The antagonistic systems involved in the opponent-process theory are based on the complementary pairs of colors, red-green and yellow-blue, as well as a third colorless (light-dark) system (see Figure 4.8). According to this theory, cells that respond to one color are inhibited by its opposite.

Several aspects of color vision favor this theory. It explains the nature of colored **afterimages**, or sensory impressions that persist after removal of the stimulus. To experience an afterimage, rest your eyes for a few minutes and then stare intently at the lower right-hand star of the flag in Figure 4.9 for forty-five seconds. Transfer your gaze to a white area, such as a blank sheet of paper. You should see the flag in its correct colors, which are the complements of those shown in the figure. By a similar process, you are likely to see blue shortly after a brief flash of intense yellow light, or red after a brief flash of green light.

Opponent-process theory also best explains the tendency of the color in one part of a visual scene to cause a shift in the perceived color of a neighboring area, an effect called **simultaneous color contrast**. For example, when a patch of

Figure 4.7   The color wheel. Any two colors that are opposite each other are complementaries; that is, combining them produces gray.

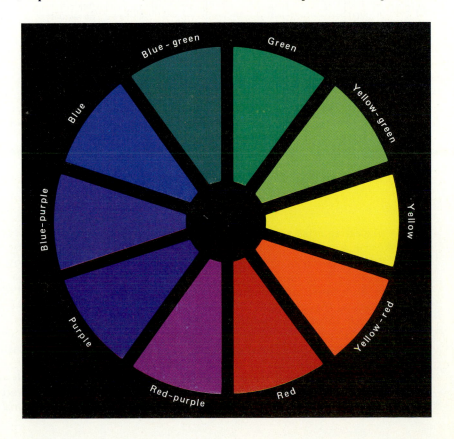

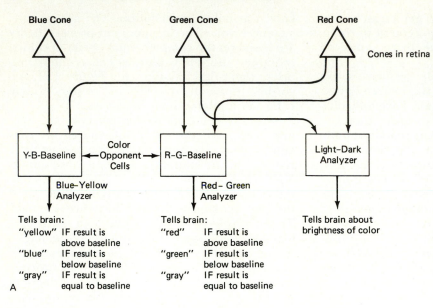

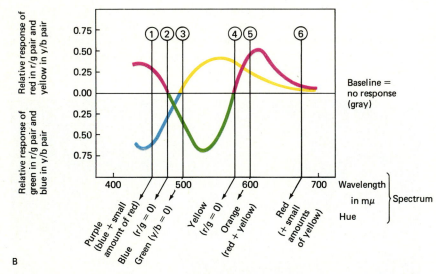

Figure 4.8 The interaction of the trichromatic and opponent-process aspects of color vision. Part A of the figure shows one way in which three types of cones might give information to color-opponent cells. The "red" cell is actually sensitive to both red and yellow. Each of the analyzer cells produces a moderate output called the "baseline" output when it is not stimulated, or if its two kinds of input are equal. If the blue-yellow analyzer produces an output much below baseline (due to a predominance of input from the blue cones), while the red-green analyzer produces an output somewhat above baseline (due to receiving greater input from the red cone than from the green cone), the result will be a mixture of red and blue that the brain will perceive as purple.

This example can be visualized more easily in part B, where it is shown as line 1. This shows the output of the blue-yellow and the red-green color opponent analyzer cells, both of which are taken into account by the brain in perceiving the color of any given patch of light. The other numbered lines show how we see other colors, according to the opponent-processes theory of color vision. For example, line 4 shows that when the red-green analyzer is at baseline (which means gray to the brain) and the blue-yellow analyzer responds at above baseline, we see yellow. (After Hochberg, 1978.)

gray is placed against a green background, the gray takes on a reddish hue (the complementary color). But if a patch of green is placed upon a complementary (red) background, the green will appear to be a more intense shade of green.

Experimental evidence has led to the general acceptance of the notion that color vision involves both trichromatic and opponent-processing systems. Research (MacNichol, 1964) in support of the trichromatic theory has demonstrated the existence of three different cone photopigments, each most sensitive to wavelengths in different regions of the visible spectrum. Other research indicates that after this initial stage, color processing is carried out in accordance with opponent-process theory. Many cells in the retina and in the lateral geniculate nucleus are excited when the eye is stimulated with one color but inhibited by its complement (DeValois, 1965). This sort of opponent response becomes even more specialized among cells within the visual cortex of the brain (Zeki, 1980).

The crucial role of the brain in color vision is further demonstrated by patients with injuries to particular portions of the cortex. One patient

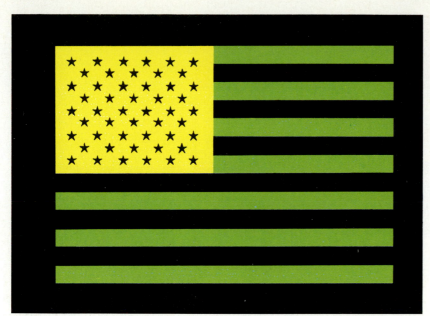

Figure 4.9 The text explains how this drawing can be used to demonstrate the phenomenon of afterimage—a sensory impression that persists after removal of the stimulus that originally caused it. The afterimage will show the flag in its "proper" red, white, and blue colors, thus demonstrating that color opposites are somehow paired in the brain.

with brain lesions in this area found color drained from his world, complaining that it was like watching a black-and-white movie. However, he perceived some colors as "very pale pink," "very pale blue," or "light orangey." Given a set of brightly colored felt-tipped markers and asked to color appropriately a picture of vegetables, the man used brown to color carrots, mushrooms, and a tomato; blue to color the tomato's stem; and blue and green to color the carrot tops and lettuce. The fact that this destruction of his color vision had no effect on any other aspect of his sight, including visual acuity, visually guided eye movements, and depth perception indicates that the final analysis of color is located in a distinct portion of the cortex (Pearlman, Birch, and Meadows, 1979).

Hearing

Just as visual receptors in the eyes respond to light, transducing it into neural signals, so auditory receptors in the ears respond to sound waves to produce neural signals. Sound waves are caused by pressure changes in the atmosphere, which generate vibrations among the air molecules. In the case of a radio, the amplifier makes the speaker vibrate. This vibrating speaker alternately pushes against the air in front of it, compressing it, and pulls away from the air, making it less dense, or expanding it. The waves of compressed and expanded air particles travel through the air and strike the eardrum. Then the eardrum is rapidly pushed and pulled by the compressions and expansions and, as a result, vibrates in the same patterns as the loudspeaker did originally, though with much less intensity.

Waves of compression and expansion, which are illustrated in Figure 4.10, move through the air in much the same way as waves of water move through the ocean: the vibration of each molecule of air or water sets the next molecule in motion around an average resting place, but the individual molecules do not advance with the wave. The molecules of water in an ocean wave ten yards from shore are not the same molecules that break against the beach—ocean waves are simply pulses of energy that travel through the medium of water. In the same way, sound waves are pulses of compression and expansion traveling through a medium of air or water. In a vacuum, where there is no medium to transmit the waves, there can be no sounds.

All waves have two obvious physical attributes: frequency and intensity. Frequency refers to the number of waves passing a given point in a given period, so that the **frequency** of a sound wave is the number of compression-expansion cycles that occur within one second, expressed in a unit known as a Hertz (Hz). The **pitch** of a sound depends on the frequency: the higher the fre-

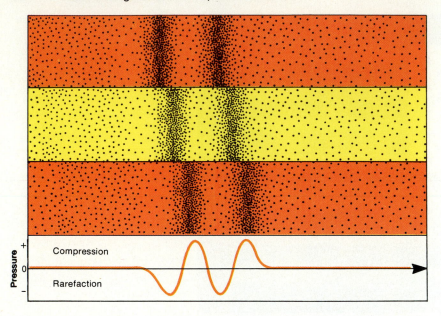

Figure 4.10 Sound is created when an object vibrates. This motion is transmitted to surrounding air molecules and emanates out in a wave. In the top part of this figure, we see the same air molecules at three different points in time as two cycles of a sound wave pass by. Below we see a graph of this wave in which air pressure is plotted as it varies over time. As the sound wave passes any given point, air pressure first rises above its resting point (compression), then falls below it (rarefaction), then returns to the resting point again. This cycle of compression and rarefaction is repeated in adjacent molecules of air, as long as sufficient energy to move the molecules remains. The number of cycles per second defines the frequency of the wave and gives the sound its pitch. The more cycles per second, the higher the pitch. The intensity of the sound depends on the force that the original vibration created. The greater the force, the greater the number of molecules affected, and the louder the sound we hear.

quency, the higher the pitch. Young adults can hear sounds as low as 20 Hz (that is, 20 cycles per second) and as high as 20,000 Hz. As people age, this audible range is reduced, especially at the high-frequency end. Among commonly heard frequencies, the human voice ranges from 120 to 600 Hz, middle C on a piano is 256 Hz, and the highest note on a piano is 4,100 Hz. People do not hear the sound of a dog whistle because it produces frequencies greater than 20,000 Hz, but dogs hear the sound because their auditory systems are sensitive to frequencies in this range.

The other physical attribute of sound waves is **intensity**, which can be thought of as the amplitude of the air-pressure wave. Amplitude is usually expressed in a unit of measurement called the **decibel (dB)**, which is calculated according to a logarithmic formula. Each increase of 20 dB in

a sound increases the amplitude tenfold. The physical attribute of amplitude is related to the subjective experience of loudness. Among common sounds, a whisper is generally about 30 dB, normal conversation about 60 dB, and the roar of a subway train, 90 dB. Sounds above 120 dB are likely to be painful to the human ear, and a sonic boom is 128 dB. At zero dB, near the threshold of hearing, human beings should be able to hear the sound of a single air molecule striking the eardrum. However, only in completely quiet surroundings is this detection possible, because such tiny deflections are normally masked by background sounds.

The Structure of the Ear   The ear has three major divisions: (1) the outer ear (the external

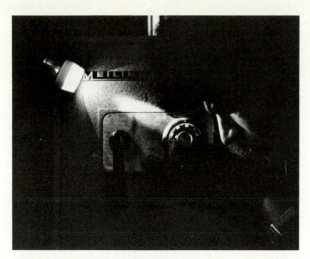

Only in a very quiet environment, such as an empty building at midnight, would one be able to hear a sound like the click of a combination lock. Normally, such a sound would be masked by common background noises.

projecting portion, called the pinna, and the auditory canal); (2) the middle ear (separated from the outer ear by the eardrum and containing three small bones collectively called ossicles); and (3) the inner ear, or cochlea (see Figure 4.11A). (The three semicircular canals, located in the inner ear, are not part of the auditory system; they provide cues to body position and movement.)

When a sound wave enters the ear, it passes down the auditory canal and strikes the **tympanic membrane (eardrum)**, causing it to vibrate. On the other side of the eardrum are the **ossicles**, a series of delicate little bones known as the **hammer**, the **anvil**, and the **stirrup** (so named for their shapes). These three bones of the middle ear are linked and suspended in such a way that when the eardrum moves the hammer, it in turn moves the anvil, which moves the stirrup. This lever action amplifies the sound wave by 20 to 30 dB. Further amplification occurs when the pressure exerted at the eardrum is concentrated onto the much smaller area of the stirrup. This enables the stirrup to apply increased pressure to the **oval window**, a flexible membrane on the side of the spiral-shaped, fluid-filled inner chamber called the **cochlea** (see Figure 4.11B). If the cochlea were entirely rigid, the stirrup would be unable to move the fluid within. But there is a second membranous spot

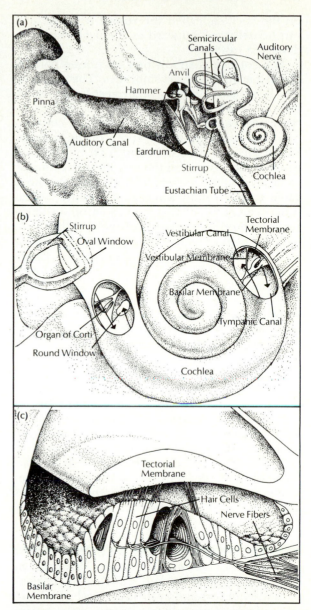

Figure 4.11 The hearing process. (A) Cross-section showing the outer, middle, and inner ear. Sound waves pass through the auditory canal and are transformed into mechanical vibration by the eardrum. The three small bones amplify this motion and transmit it to the oval window of the cochlea, which is depicted in (B). The motion of the oval window sends pressure waves through the fluid in the cochlea in the directions shown by the arrows. (C) Closeup cross-section of the organ of Corti, within the cochlea. Waves in the cochlear fluid cause the basilar membrane to vibrate, which in turn disturbs the hair cells, the receptor cells of hearing.

on the cochlea, called the **round window**, that can be deflected outward as the oval window is deflected inward.

The cochlea is subdivided into three parallel canals partitioned by membranes. The oval window lies at the beginning of the **vestibular canal**, and the round window lies at the end of the **tympanic canal**. These two canals are continuous only at the tip of the spiral of the cochlea. Vibrations introduced in the fluid by the oval window must travel all the way up the vestibular canal around the corner and back down the other canal to the round window. Therefore, vibrations are continuously traveling in opposite directions on opposite sides of the cochlea.

Embedded in the central, or cochleal, canal is the actual organ of hearing—the **organ of Corti**, which consists of a string of receptors positioned between two membranes separating the canals (see Figure 4.11C). The receptors, called **hair cells**, lie in the **basilar membrane**, but the tips of the cell extensions, or hairs, project through the fluid and touch the **tectorial membrane**. As the fluids of the canals vibrate in opposite directions, these two membranes likewise move in opposite directions, so that the hairs between them are bent in a kind of rubbing or shearing motion. As a result of this bending, the hair cells produce neural signals that travel to the brain along the adjacent **auditory nerve**.

As we shall see, individual neurons are attached to different portions of the basilar membrane, each responding to different frequencies and carrying this information to the **auditory cortex** in the temporal lobe of the brain. Within the auditory cortex itself, a significant proportion of the neurons respond not to frequency or intensity, but to more complex features of sounds such as clicks and whistles. Some neurons will not respond to steady tones but will fire when frequencies change, some only to increased frequencies (a rise in pitch) and others only to decreased frequencies (a falling pitch; Evans, 1974).

Neural Coding by the Ear   The brain has no trouble distinguishing between high and low tones, but we do not fully understand how it does so. Two distinct mechanisms appear to be involved, one described by the place theory, the other by the volley theory. According to the **place theory** of pitch, the particular location (place) on the basilar membrane where sound

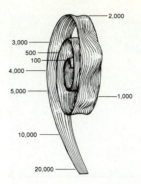

Figure 4.12   The place theory. This diagram shows waves traveling down the basilar membrane and indicates the points at which the waves are largest for a number of different frequencies. Because greater displacement produces more stimulation of the organ of Corti, the brain could use the location of the most rapidly firing cells in the organ of Corti as a code for the frequency of the sound.

waves produce the greatest displacement (hence the most intense stimulation of the organ of Corti) signals a sound's frequency to the brain. A version of this theory was first advanced by von Helmholtz and later supported by Georg von Békésy (1956), who discovered that waves of a given frequency do not produce a uniform vibration of the basilar membrane. Rather, he found, high-frequency waves have the greatest effect on the region near the oval window, and low-frequency waves have the greatest effect near the top of the cochlea.

The place theory has been supported by two kinds of data. First, among elderly patients who could no longer hear certain high-frequency tones, groups of receptors along specific portions of the basilar membrane were found to be damaged, as shown in Figure 4.12 (Crowe, Guild, and Polvogt, 1934). Second, mild electrical stimulation of small groups of neurons leading from different places along the basilar membrane results in the experience of different pitches, depending on the place along the basilar membrane that is stimulated.

The place theory explains the detection of high- and medium-frequency sounds, but it cannot explain how we can tell the difference between very similar low tones, since there is a great deal of overlap in the areas of maximum displacement at low frequencies. To get around this problem of overlap, the **volley theory** of pitch (Wever, 1949) emphasizes the timing of individual nerve impulses within the auditory nerve. Like a company of riflemen firing a volley on command, an ensemble of neurons fire in coordination, producing a frequency of firing that mirrors the frequency of the tone stimulus. Presumably, the group action enables the ensemble to overcome the limitations on the firing rate of each individual neuron, which can fire no more than about 1,000 impulses per second. To fire in time with the stimulus requires a fine degree of synchrony among neurons, particularly at frequencies above 5,000 Hz.

Contemporary researchers subscribe to a combination of the place theory and the volley theory. At low frequencies, timing is thought to be important, whereas at higher frequencies the place mechanism comes into play.

The capacity to hear any frequency depends on the integrity of the hair cells of the basilar membrane. If a sound of excessive intensity strikes the ear, the vibrations of the fluids may tear the hairs apart, leading to irreversible loss of hearing in that frequency range. Although muscles can damp, or moderate, the movement of the stirrup in response to high-intensity sound,

they cannot prevent damage from continual excessive noise. Consequently, an extensive amount of hearing loss has been caused by modern technology—from factories to jet planes to loud music.

The Skin Senses

Skin sensations take four basic forms: touch, warmth, cold, and pain. Receptors for these sensations lie at various depths within the skin, as Figure 4.13 shows, and connect with neurons that transmit information from the receptors to the brain. The relationship between the type of receptors and the experience of various sensations is not clearly understood. Stimulation of receptors around the roots of hair cells appears to be followed by the sensation of touch on the skin, while other receptors seem to respond to pressure within muscles and internal organs. At one time it was believed the only the sensation of pain could be transmitted by receptors in free

Modern music—often loud and driving—has been blamed for a substantial amount of hearing loss.

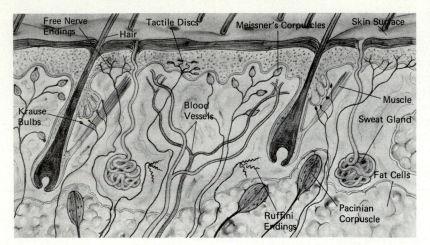

Figure 4.13 A cross-sectional diagram of human skin. A number of different kinds of receptors have been identified near the surface of the skin, but there is considerable uncertainty about their functions. Meissner's corpuscles are believed to be pressure sensitive. Pacinian corpuscles may be additional receptors for "deep" pressure.

Free nerve endings may be important in the sensation of pain. It is speculated that Krause bulbs are responsive to cold and Ruffini endings responsive to warmth.

nerve endings in the skin (in contrast to encapsulated nerve endings). But the cornea of the eye, which almost exclusively contains free nerve endings, is responsive to pressure and temperature as well as pain. Thus confusion still exists about the role of these free nerve-ending receptors (Geldard, 1972).

Warmth and Cold   No sensation of temperature —warmth or cold—is felt when the skin is touched with stimulators that are at skin temperature, usually 32 degrees Celsius; the temperature at which there is no sensation is referred to as **physiological zero.** Warmth is felt at temperatures greater than physiological zero, and cold is felt at temperatures lower than physiological zero.

Nor are warmth and cold felt at every point on the skin. If one square centimeter of skin is stimulated, cold will be felt at about six spots within that area and warmth sensed at only one or two spots. The separate identity of warm and cold spots is generally accepted, partly because stimulating a cold spot with a hot stimulus sometimes yields a cold sensation. The name for this phenomenon is **paradoxical cold.**

The sensation of "hot" appears to be produced by the simultaneous activation of both warmth and cold receptors in a particular area of the skin, so that information from the two kinds of receptors is mixed. This synthesis of sensation is another example of the economical design of sensory systems. The phenomenon can be demonstrated using an apparatus like the one depicted in Figure 4.14. Cold water flows through one of the tubes, and warm water

through the other. If either of these tubes is touched, the appropriate sensation is perceived —either warmth or cold. However, if a hand lies across the coils so that warm and cold stimuli are side by side on certain areas of the skin, a stinging hot sensation will be felt, like that caused by touching a hot oven rack barehanded. This apparatus "fools" the sensory system into sending a message of hot in the absence of the normally appropriate stimulus.

Figure 4.14 With ice water flowing through one of the tubes of this coil, and warm water at about 105° F. flowing through the other tube, the person placing a hand on the coil will feel a burning hot sensation.

Touch Pressure-sensitive receptors in the skin are more responsive to changes in pressure than to steady states. Once the skin has been displaced to accommodate the source of the pressure, adaptation occurs and the sensation of pressure usually disappears—rapidly, if the force exerted is small. If this were not true, we would be constantly aware of the gentle pressure of clothes, eyeglasses, and so on.

Sensitivity to touch varies enormously over different portions of the body. Our fingers and lips, for example, are exquisitely sensitive, but portions of the back are relatively insensitive. This variation is partly related to the fact that a disproportionately large area of the sensory cortex is devoted to the fingers and mouth, as we saw in Chapter 3 (see Figure 3.8).

Pain Pain is not limited to the skin. However, we know little about pain from the interior of the body except that it seems to be deep, difficult to pinpoint, and often more unpleasant than the bright, localized pain from the skin. Many kinds of stimuli—scratch, puncture, pressure, heat, cold, twist—can produce pain. Their common property is real or potential injury to bodily tissue.

The experience of pain is greatly influenced by emotional factors, and in the excitement of combat—whether on the battlefield or the soccer field—perception of pain may temporarily vanish. **Pain thresholds**, or the points at which pains are first perceived, vary considerably from person to person or from time to time. People who are anxious have lower pain thresholds than those who are not; women tend to have lower pain thresholds than men; and clerical workers tend to have lower thresholds than laborers and miners (Merskey, 1973). It was once thought that most chronic pain had no organic basis and was probably due to stress or conflict, but this idea has been greatly discounted (Liebeskind and Paul, 1977).

No direct way exists to measure the intensity of pain sensations, and most studies of pain rely on subjective accounts. In the laboratory, people report that skin pain disappears with prolonged stimulation, but under ordinary circumstances, there is little adaptation to pain. Since pain signals that something is amiss, it is fortunate that we do not adapt to it. The value of pain as a danger signal is clearly indicated by the situation of people who are born without the ability to feel

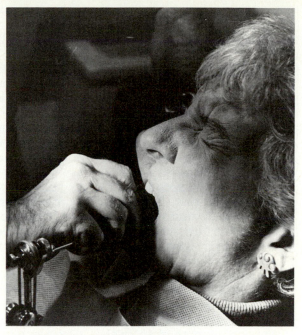

Pain thresholds vary from person to person and from time to time. Women, for example, generally have lower pain thresholds than do men. If this woman is anxious when she visits the dentist, her pain threshold may be especially low at this moment.

pain. Such people may experience severe burns, broken bones, or even a ruptured appendix, but feel no pain signals that would alert them either to protect themselves against further injury or to seek medical attention.

For years it was assumed that specialized nerve fibers carried pain signals to specific regions of the brain, as is the case with the other senses. Then during the late 1950s, research demonstrated clearly that the sensation of pain is not associated with one particular specialized nerve. This discovery led to the notion that information about pain is carried in the pattern of neural discharges. In 1965, the idea was explicitly set forth by Ronald Melzack and P. D. Wall in their **gate-control theory** of pain, which asserts that the sensation of pain depends on the balance of activity between large- and small-diameter nerve fibers within the spinal cord. Activity predominantly within small fibers opens the spinal gate, allowing pain signals to pass and leading to the experience of pain, whereas activity in the large fibers tends to close the gate and thus prevent pain. There has been a good deal of debate over

The Quest for a Nonaddictive Painkiller

In laboratories around the world, researchers are seeking to develop nonaddictive painkillers that are as effective as morphine. The search was spurred nearly ten years ago by the discovery of endorphins, a group of neurotransmitters discussed in Chapter 3, which help the body turn off its response to pain. Endorphins, whose name means "the morphine within," block the transmission of pain impulses to the brain. Although first discussions of endorphins referred to them as "mimicking opiates" (Marx, 1976), it appears that opiates actually mimic endorphins and that the chemical structure of an opiate molecule fits the brain's receptors for endorphins as a key fits a lock.

Endorphin receptors are not scattered randomly throughout the brain, but are found in regions associated with moods and with the perception of pain (Marx, 1976). Most of these receptors are located at synapses between neurons, where messages of pain could most effectively be blocked.

There are two major types of endorphins: beta-endorphin, a large peptide molecule that is several times more effective than morphine, and enkephalins, two smaller peptide molecules that produce powerful pain relief lasting for only a few minutes. Both types have been the focus of the search for a nonaddictive painkiller.

When endorphins were first discovered, it was thought that duplicating their chemical structure would surely produce the long-sought "natural opiate." Since endorphins were nonaddictive, their chemical analogues should also be free from the threat of addiction. Such hopes were destroyed in tests with laboratory animals. The effects of these new opiates were all too similar to those of morphine. Laboratory animals first developed tolerance, requiring larger injections to achieve the same effects, and then developed dependence, showing a reversal of the drug's effects as the new opiate wore off. Tolerance and dependence are the hallmarks of addiction; thus, the new opiates were just as addictive as morphine. In fact, when an endorphin antagonist (which blocks the effects of endorphins) was injected into animals, they went through the same symptoms seen in addicts who are withdrawing from heroin (Marx, 1976). To make matters worse, the new opiates also had such side effects as severe abdominal cramps (Gurin, 1979).

Why are the endorphin analogues addictive when neither beta-endorphin nor enkephalins create addiction? A barrier between the brain and the bloodstream protects the nervous system from unwanted substances by filtering out many chemicals that course through the body. Creating an endorphin analogue that can penetrate the blood-brain barrier may require modifying the molecular structure so much that the drug's properties are altered (Gurin, 1979). After all, the addictive opiates have structures similar to those of endorphins. Further, the fleeting effect of enkephalins, probably the result of the peptides' rapid breakdown within the brain, may be the reason the body does not become addicted to enkephalins —the truly natural opiate. Altering the structure of the drug to prolong its effect may also switch an opiate from being nonaddictive to being addictive.

Scientists are still searching for the nonaddictive "natural" opiate, but they no longer see their quest as either certain or simple. Most peptides play multiple roles within the brain, so that attempting to design an analogue with a single effect, controlling only one kind of behavior (such as pain), may be beyond our grasp (Gurin, 1979).

---

the gate-control theory, and the evidence concerning it is mixed (Nathan, 1976). Despite a general inconsistency in the findings, some people with chronic pain have been successfully treated by electrical stimulation of the large fibers, a method that accords with the theory.

The Chemical Senses

The chemical senses of taste and smell are so closely associated that we often confuse their messages. This confusion develops because receptors for these two senses are located close together in the mouth, throat, and nasal cavity, causing smell and taste to interact, particularly in the appreciation of food. Without a sense of smell, the subtleties of food flavor cannot be appreciated. For instance, if you taste an apple and a raw potato while blocking your nose, you will have difficulty distinguishing between them. In the same way, food flavors are often flat and uninteresting to a person with a bad head cold.

Smell   Many people consider **olfaction**, or the sense of smell, to be one of the "lower" senses. This view may stem from the fact that olfaction does not provide as much information for the "higher" mental functions (such as reasoning and memory) as do vision and hearing. Among human beings, a principal function of smell is apparently to warn us of potentially dangerous stimuli—to alert us to odors of toxic substances that we might otherwise eat or inhale. Thus unpleasant odors may receive the most attention from us. However, odors are also involved with human pleasure. Because food flavors depend so heavily on odor, an enormous spice and condiment industry has developed, and our enjoyment of pleasant odors has created the perfume industry. The sense organ for olfaction is the **olfactory epithelium**, located at the top of the nasal passages and connected to the base of the brain. Millions of hair cells projecting from the olfactory epithelium are sensitive to molecules of volatile substances, and they transduce this kind of information into neural impulses. Unlike other sensory receptors, these hair cells are constantly being replaced, and there is a complete turnover of cells approximately every four to five weeks.

Most odors to which human beings respond are organic compounds, but the exact physical basis of odor sensation remains a mystery. According to the "stereochemical" theory, the quality of an odor is related to the physical size and shape of the molecules that make up the odorous substance. Research (Amoore and Venstrum, 1967) has shown that in many cases people do judge odors from substances with similar molecular structures to be similar. However, not all substances show this similarity between chemical structure and subjective odor. We still cannot say why people can smell some substances and not others or why certain groups of odors smell alike.

A number of attempts have been made to classify odors strictly on the basis of subjective judgments. The most popular classification scheme is Hans Henning's smell prism, shown in Figure 4.15 (Henning, 1916). Six supposedly pure qualities form the corners of the prism, and the intermediate qualities lie along the surface. The reason for the development of such a scheme is that it may provide a clue to the chemical properties that distinguish one class of odors from another.

Some animal species communicate by means of odors. They release **pheromones**, chemicals that trigger a behavioral reaction in other animals of the same species. Since pheromones travel on air currents, they can communicate over great distances, but they move slowly and leave a lingering message because they take a long time to fade away. A major purpose of pheromone production is to attract the opposite sex, and sex-attractant pheromones have been found in many species, including crabs, spiders, moths, fish, amphibians, reptiles, and monkeys (Wilson, 1975). Smell apparently plays an important role in the sexual behavior of monkeys. Vaginal secretions of the female monkey contain volatile fatty acids whose odor stimulates sexual

Figure 4.15 Henning's smell prism. Supposedly, every possible smell sensation can be located somewhere on the surface of this solid. This theoretical description of smell implies that certain smells are impossible. For example, a putrid, flowery, burned, spicy smell should be possible, but not a putrid, flowery, resinous smell. Where on this surface would you place the smell of a fresh, ripe peach?

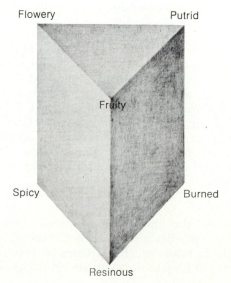

Some animals produce pheromones, scented chemicals that linger in the air to attract the opposite sex. Human beings do not seem to depend on such substances, but we manufacture a wide variety of perfumes that perform a similar function.

behavior in male monkeys. The same fatty acids have been found in the vaginal secretions of healthy young women with regular menstrual cycles. Fatty acid production peaks in the middle of the menstrual cycle—the time of highest probable fertility—then declines until menstruation. This cyclical rise in the production of fatty acids ceases in women who take birth control pills. Such women show a steady, low production of the acids, at about the level found in other women during menstruation (Michael, Bonsall, and Warner, 1974). The effect of these fatty acids on human behavior is unknown, but, as the investigators point out, the same substances serve as a powerful sex-attractant pheromone in other primates.

Taste As the discussion of smell indicated, when people describe how food "tastes," they include its odor, which circulates from the back of the mouth up to the olfactory receptors. Taste is, however, a more restricted sense than olfaction. The source of an odor can be detected and identified from a distance, but the source of a taste must be in contact with the mouth. Most people can identify and discriminate hundreds of odors, but when odor and other sensory qualities, such as texture, are eliminated, they perceive only four basic taste categories: sweet, sour, salty, and bitter. Mixtures of these four basic qualities are apparently responsible for all other taste sensations (Bartoshuk, 1971).

Different areas of the tongue are especially sensitive to each of the four basic taste qualities, as shown in Figure 4.16. These taste qualities seem to be somewhat independent: they can be selectively suppressed and are differently affected by certain drugs. For example, if you eat sugar after chewing the leaves of a certain plant *(Gymnema sylvestre)*, the sugar no longer tastes sweet and it feels like sand (Bartoshuk et al., 1969). The drug cocaine temporarily eliminates taste sensations in a certain order: first bitter

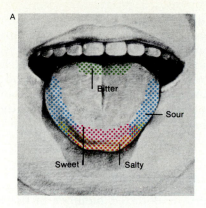

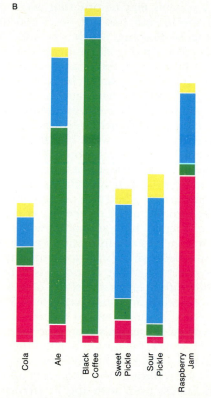

disappears, then sweet, then salty, and finally sour (Moncrieff, 1966).

The specific sensation of taste results from stimulation of the **taste buds** in the mouth and tongue. The surface of the human tongue contains about 10,000 of these structures, grouped in projections known as **papillae**. Taste buds contain receptor cells for taste stimuli, and these cells are connected to nerve fibers that carry taste information to the brain. In several species of animals, the individual nerve fibers leading from these cells respond to more than one kind of taste (Pfaffman, 1955), suggesting that taste detection is a more complicated process than would result if each nerve fiber simply reported about only one of the four basic taste stimuli. Perhaps the neural code for different tastes is based on particular patterns of activity in the thousands of taste nerve fibers leading from the tongue.

Balance, Posture, and Movement

We are continually aware of our balance, posture, movement, and orientation in space. This awareness is produced by the cooperation of the vestibular and kinesthetic senses.

The Vestibular Sense   The **vestibular sense** contributes to balance. The vestibular sense organ lies in the inner ear, buried in the bone above and to the rear of the cochlea. Its major structures are the three fluid-filled **semicircular canals,** which lie at right angles to one another, as shown in Figure 4.17. A movement of the head causes the fluid in the canals to move against and bend the endings of receptor hair cells. The hair cells connect with the vestibular nerve, which joins the auditory nerve on its way to the brain.

Vestibular responses are stimulated by rotational or linear acceleration, falling, and tilting the body or head. Such stimuli interact with eye-movement systems. For example, rapid rotation on the longitudinal axis of the body, such as that produced by spinning on skates, can result in vestibular nystagmus, a rapid back-and-forth motion of the eyes. Vestibular nystagmus can also occur when a person stops spinning, though in this instance it results from continued movement of fluid in the semicircular canals after spinning has stopped. Another type of nystagmus can be induced by running hot water into

Figure 4.16 (A) A map of the human tongue showing the areas of maximum sensitivity to the four fundamental kinds of taste sensation. (B) The tastes of a number of foods analyzed into the four components of taste shown in A. The length of the colored bars indicates the amount of each component judged to be present in the taste of the food by a number of subjects in a psychophysical experiment. (Data from Beebe-Center, 1949.)

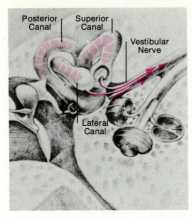

Figure 4.17 The vestibular system. Compare this figure with Figure 4.11 to see where it is located in the ear. The organs of balance are three fluid-filled semicircular canals arranged at right angles to one another. The inertia of the fluid inside at least one of the canals causes it to move relative to the walls of the canals whenever the motion of the head speeds up, slows down, or changes direction. The motion of the fluid drags tiny stones over hair cells in the walls of the canals, and the hair cells transmit impulses to the brain.

the external ear canal. The heat of the water transfers to the semicircular canals and the fluid within them moves, resulting in caloric nystagmus. Warm water running into an ear during a shower often produces this effect.

The Kinesthetic Sense   **Kinesthesis** is the sense of body movement and position. It cooperates with the vestibular and visual senses to maintain balance and equilibrium. The receptor cells for the kinesthetic sense are in the nerve endings in and near the muscles, tendons, and the more than one hundred body joints. The nerve endings in the joints are especially important in sensing bodily movements; which receptors re- spond depends on the direction and angle of movement. Together, the various kinesthetic receptors provide the feedback necessary for regulation of active body movement. Efficient and coordinated locomotion is thus produced by the kinesthetic and vestibular senses, but vision also contributes to the process, indicating once again that the senses generally act as a team.

The Homing Sense?

A hitherto undetected member of the team of sensory systems may be one that exists in many animal species but has not been considered a human sense: **homing**, which is an internal sense of navigation. Among the animals that can find their way home after being taken away and then released are lobsters, snails, bees, fish, amphibi- ans, turtles, rodents, bats, and birds. Recently, the sense appears to have been demonstrated by human beings. In Manchester, England, groups of university students were blindfolded, driven in a roundabout way to a point thirty-two miles from the university, then—before the blindfolds were removed—asked to indicate the direction of the university. The students tended to make accurate indications of direction, as did a later group of English high-school students. Neither group was able to orient themselves by the heat of the sun, because on both occasions the sky was heavily overcast. What is more, weighting the blindfold with a magnet instead of a brass bar caused a decline in this navigational sense, in- dicating that among humans there possibly is a sensitivity to the earth's magnetic field (Baker, 1980). However, the notion of a homing sense in human beings is still highly controversial. At- tempts to replicate the experiments in the United States, even with the assistance of the original English researcher, so far have failed (Gould and Able, 1981).

SUMMARY

1. Our senses are our only source of informa- tion about the environment, yet each sensory system responds to only a limited range of stimuli. The study of human sensory systems is divided into **sensory physiology**, which investigates the means by which information is captured and transformed by receptors and then processed in the nervous system, and **psychophysics**, which establishes the re- lationship between physical stimulation and sensory experience.

2. A **stimulus** is any form of energy to which our senses respond, such as light waves or

sound waves. Stimuli can be measured physically (as with a light meter or a thermometer) or psychologically (in terms of subjective sensations). Psychological reports of a stimulus describe its **quality** (or the kind of sensation produced) and **quantity** (or the amount of sensation produced).

3. The minimum stimulus required for a person to experience a specific sensation is referred to as the **absolute threshold**. The smallest physical change in a stimulus that produces a change in sensation is known as the **difference threshold**, or **just noticeable difference (jnd)**. The state of a person's sensory apparatus, readiness, motivation, and the degree of external and internal noise continually vary, affecting human response to stimuli. Therefore, according to **signal detection theory**, there is no single absolute threshold for a stimulus, and noise often interferes with its detection.

4. The magnitude of a stimulus and the magnitude of its corresponding sensation can be described as a ratio between the two quantities, and three major descriptions of the relationship have been advanced. *Weber's law* states that the amount of a stimulus required to produce a just noticeable difference is always a constant proportion of the intensity of the stimulus. *Fechner's law* states that the intensity of a sensation increases proportionately with the magnitude of the stimulus. *Stevens' power law* emphasizes that the exact properties of the relationship differ for each of the senses.

5. Following prolonged stimulation, an adjustment in sensory capacity, known as **adaptation**, occurs. Adaptation decreases sensitivity and may distort sensation; however, adaptation allows the senses to work over a larger range and keeps us alert to changes in the environment.

6. All our sense organs operate on similar principles. In each sense organ are receptors sensitive to specific types of stimuli, and each type of receptor converts environmental stimuli into neural impulses—a process called **transduction**.

7. The basic stimuli involved in vision are light waves, which are scaled in units called **wavelengths**. The major structures of the eye are the **cornea**, the **iris**, the **lens**, and the **retina**. Light enters the eye through the **pupil**, an opening in the center of the eye through which light passes to the lens. Ciliary muscles attached to the lens change its curvature, focusing the light and producing a clear image on the retina. The retina contains four types of neural cells: **bipolar cells, horizontal cells, amacrine cells**, and **ganglion cells**. In the retina, light is transduced into neural impulses by two types of receptors: **rods** and **cones**. These receptors stimulate bipolar cells, which pass their information to ganglion cells; the axons of ganglion cells form the **optic nerve**, which leaves the eye through the **blind spot** and relays visual information to the brain. At the **optic chiasm**, the optic nerves meet and are rerouted, with a majority of the axons going to the **lateral geniculate nucleus**. At each stage of processing, each neuron responds only to light that falls within its **receptive field**. Cones are involved in color perception and are especially concentrated in the area of the retina called the **fovea**, where they are also responsible for detailed vision. Rods provide vision of light and dark; less light is required to stimulate them than the cones. Color vision seems to involve two mechanisms. One process, according to the **trichromatic theory**, uses three types of cones: one type highly sensitive to red light; another, to green light; and the third, to blue light. Different wavelengths of light stimulate different cones, and the color seen depends on how many cones of each type are stimulated. Various kinds of color blindness can be explained by this theory. A person with normal color vision is believed to have all three cone photopigments; a person in whom one of the cone systems is missing or deficient is called a **dichromat**; and a totally color-blind person, who can see only shades of gray, is called a **monochromat**. The other color vision process, according to the **opponent-process theory**, involves ganglion cells, cells in the lateral geniculate nucleus, and cells in the visual cortex that are stimulated by one color and inhibited by its opposite, or complementary, color. The phenomena of **afterimages** and **simultaneous color contrast** can be explained by this theory.

8. In the auditory system, auditory receptors in the ears transduce sound waves into neural signals. Waves of air particles strike the eardrum, causing it to vibrate. The **frequency** of a sound wave is determined by the number of wave cycles that occur within one second, measured in Hertz (Hz), and the sound's **pitch** depends on that frequency. The **intensity** of a sound wave, measured in **decibels (dB)**, corresponds to the amplitude of the wave and is reflected in the sound's loudness. The outer ear is composed of the pinna and the auditory canal. The **tympanic membrane** (eardrum) separates the outer ear from the middle ear, which contains three small bones, or **ossicles**, known as the **hammer**, the **anvil**, and the **stirrup**. The stirrup is attached to a membrane called the **oval window**, which separates the middle ear from the inner ear. The inner chamber of the ear, called the **cochlea**, is filled with fluid and is divided into the **vestibular canal**, the **tympanic canal**, and the central or cochleal canal, which contains the organ of hearing—known as the **organ of Corti**. In the organ of Corti are the sound receptors, or **hair cells**, which lie in the **basilar membrane** but which reach through the fluid to touch the **tectorial membrane**. When canal fluids vibrate in response to an auditory stimulus, the membranes move in opposite directions, bending the hair cells and producing neural signals that travel to the brain through the auditory nerve. Sounds of very high intensity may damage the hair cells, resulting in an irreversible hearing loss. The detection of pitch is described by two theories. The **place theory** of pitch states that the site of maximum displacement on the basilar membrane indicates to the brain the specific frequency of sound, and the **volley theory** states that the entire basilar membrane vibrates at the resonant frequency, causing the auditory nerve to fire in synchrony, thus signaling pitch.

9. There are four basic types of skin sensations: pressure, warmth, cold, and pain; receptors for these sensations lie at various depths within the skin. These receptors are connected to neurons that relay the sensory information to the brain. If the skin is touched by a stimulator that is at skin temperature, no sensation of temperature will be felt; this temperature is called **physiological zero. Paradoxical cold**, in which stimulation of a cold spot with a hot stimulus results in a cold sensation, indicates the existence of separate temperature-sensitive spots on the skin. Receptors of pressure vary in sensitivity, and the most sensitive body areas are the fingertips, the lips, and the tip of the tongue. **Pain thresholds** vary among people and over situations. Pain acts as a danger signal, alerting us to real or potential bodily injury. The **gate-control theory** of pain suggests that the sensation of pain depends on the balance of activity between large- and small-diameter nerve fibers within the spinal cord, with small-fiber activity opening the gate so that pain signals can travel to the brain and large-fiber activity closing the gate and preventing pain.

10. The chemical senses of taste and smell are closely associated. The major function of **olfaction** (the sense of smell) is to warn us about potentially toxic substances, although we also attend to pleasant odors. The hair cells projecting from the **olfactory epithelium** transduce olfactory information into neural impulses. There are only four basic categories of taste (sweet, sour, salty, and bitter), and they can be detected only through direct mouth contact. The surface of the human tongue contains about 10,000 **taste buds**, which contain receptor cells for taste stimuli.

11. The **vestibular sense** has to do with balance. The vestibular sense organ is made up of three fluid-filled **semicircular canals** above the cochlea. Head movements cause the fluid within the canals to move, bending the receptor hair cells. These hair cells connect with the vestibular nerve, which joins the auditory nerve on the way to the brain. **Kinesthesis**, the sense of body movement and position, works with the vestibular and visual senses to maintain balance and equilibrium. Receptor cells for this sense are found in nerve endings in and near joints, muscles, and tendons. *Homing*, a navigational sense, exists in some animals but has not been proved to exist in humans.

KEY TERMS

absolute threshold
adaptation
afterimage
amacrine cells
anvil
auditory cortex
auditory nerve
basilar membrane
bipolar cells
cochlea
colliculus
color cancellation
cones
cornea
decibel (dB)
dichromats
difference threshold
Fechner's law
fovea
frequency
ganglion cells
gate-control theory
hair cells
hammer
homing
horizontal cells

intensity
iris
just noticeable difference
   (jnd)
kinesthesis
lateral geniculate nucleus
lens
monochromats
olfaction
olfactory epithelium
opponent-process theory
optic chiasm
optic disc
optic nerve
organ of Corti
ossicles
oval window
pain thresholds
papillae
paradoxical cold
pheromones
photopigment
physiological zero
pitch
place theory
psychometric function
psychophysics

pupil
receptive field
retina
rhodopsin
rods
round window
semicircular canals
sensory physiology
signal detection theory
simultaneous color contrast
Stevens' power law
stimulus
stirrup
taste buds
tectorial membrane
transduction
trichromatic theory
tympanic canal
tympanic membrane
vestibular canal
vestibular apparatus
vestibular sense
visual cortex
volley theory
wavelength
Weber's law

RECOMMENDED READINGS

BORING, E. G. *Sensation and Perception in the History of Experimental Psychology.* New York: Appleton-Century-Crofts, 1942. Essential for an historical appreciation of sensation and psychophysics. This classic book is especially noteworthy for its treatment of the attributes of sensation and the historical antecedents of modern color theory.

FRISBY, J. P. *Seeing: Illusion, Brain, and Mind.* Oxford: Oxford University Press, 1980. Discusses the psychophysical, physiological, and computer-simulation approaches to the study of vision. The book is richly illustrated with pictures demonstrating various phenomena of vision.

GESCHEIDER, G. *Psychophysics: Methods and Theory.* Hillsdale, N.J.: Erlbaum, 1976. An introduction to the problem of measuring sensation, with many examples provided from all the senses. The descriptions of direct and indirect scaling and of signal detection theory are thorough and understandable.

GOLDSTEIN, E. B. *Sensation and Perception.* Belmont, Calif.: Wadsworth, 1980. An up-to-date general text on sensation and perception. While emphasizing vision, the book includes coverage of the other senses and contains an interesting chapter on the perception of music.

CHAPTER 5

Perception

The process of perceiving is always an act of construction, in which the brain uses sensory data to build a meaningful hypothesis about the existence of an object or event. If necessary, the construction process will fill in any gaps in the available sensory information. Many times when we are processing information we fail realize that our perceptual mechanisms can fool us into seeing things that do not exist. In fact, if you noticed the missing word in the last sentence, you are very unusual, because the context of the entire passage influences your perception of the sentence as a whole.

Normally, we process sensory information from the environment without being aware that we are doing so. We read the words on a page without noticing how we interpret the patterns of lines and letters in order to read. We can listen to a train in the distance and tell whether it is coming from the north or south, but we are not aware of precisely how we determine the train's location and direction of travel. Such information processing takes place quickly, without conscious effort. Only when our attention is called to something like the sentence with the missing word do we realize that our brain has supplied nonexistent information and that it requires an interpretive process to transform sensation into perception.

From Sensation to Perception

Perception can be defined as an organism's awareness of objects and events in the environment, brought about by stimulation of the organism's sense organs. Although it is impossible to completely separate perception from sensation, the perceptual process has traditionally been considered to be more complex, because perception presents an organism with a meaningful interpretation of its basic sensations. The sensations of "redness" and "roundness," for example, contribute to our visual perception of an apple. In the dark, a certain odor, crunchy sound, sweet taste, and smooth, waxy feel yield the same perception—an apple—but the perception is based on sensations different from the ones we experience when we see the object. What we call an "apple" is all these sensations and more, of course, but we need only a few of them to accurately and automatically interpret what we are sensing as an apple.

Two features of perception sharply distinguish it from sensation. First, in some cases different sensory input can produce the same perception. For example, in bright sunlight the sail of a ship looks white; should the sun go behind a cloud, the sail will continue to be perceived as white, although the

Figure 5.1 This drawing is a classic demonstration of figure-ground ambiguity. What you perceive as figure and as ground depends on a number of factors, including your expectation.

amount of light reflected from the sail to the eye is sharply diminished. Second, in other cases the same sensory input can yield different perceptions, as when the drawing in Figure 5.1 is alternately interpreted as a vase or face-to-face human profiles.

What happens in the brain obviously is crucial to our ability to understand what is "out there," for the brain organizes and gives meaning to the limited information gathered by our senses. As we saw in the opening paragraph, when sensory information is incomplete, brain processes often create a complete perception by "filling in" missing details. In some instances, the brain provides us with **subjective contours**, which are lines or shapes that appear to be part of a figure but are actually not physically present. In the drawings in Figure 5.2, the various shapes are perceived as having distinct outlines. If you examine them closely, however, you will discover that some of the lines that define the shapes are simply not there. The lines are perceptually present but physically absent. Subjective contours appear naturally when we encounter certain types of stimuli. Our perception of these contours is the result of the brain's automatic attempt to enhance and complete the details of an image (Kanizsa, 1976).

The same process seems to operate in the perception of Figure 5.3. Most people interpret the

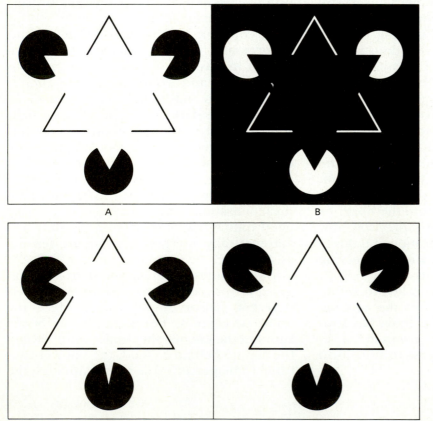

Figure 5.2 Subjective contours. The brain seeks to tie the components of an incomplete picture together by creating the perception of contours that complete the picture. (A) The subjective contours form a white triangle in the middle of this visual image. (B) In this case, the outline of a center triangle is perceived once again, but this time the triangle appears black as the result of the background color. C and D illustrate the fact that subjective contours may be curved as well as straight. (After Kanizsa, 1976.)

Figure 5.3 Although this version of da Vinci's *Mona Lisa* is highly distorted, our brain is capable of enhancing the perceptual details of this picture in such a way that we are able to recognize its resemblance to the original painting. Such block portraits are made with a flying-spot scanner, a device similar to a television camera. (After Harmon, 1973.)

coarsely grained distribution of light and dark squares as the familiar *Mona Lisa*. Although the sensory impression is merely a degraded shadow of the elegant and detailed da Vinci painting, brain processes fill in the missing details to make the image resemble the original painting (Harmon, 1973). Notice how the picture seems to become more detailed if you move farther away from it and squint your eyes.

Brain processes can do more than provide missing information; they can also compensate for misleading distortions in information. A striking example of this ability is provided in the work of G. M. Stratton (1896), who wore spectacles that turned the retinal image upside down. When Stratton first put on the glasses, he had trouble coordinating vision and movement, because he saw everything inverted, with right and left reversed as well as top and bottom. After about a week, however, he adjusted and could walk, read, eat, write, and carry out other activities successfully. Although he adapted so well that he sometimes forgot he was living in an inverted world, Stratton reported the experience as being like bending over and looking through his legs. When he finally removed the spectacles, the world looked abnormal, although he did not perceive it as being upside down. In such experiments, adaptation does not occur unless the person moves about and interacts with the distorted environment, a further indication that perception is not a passive but an active process (Rock, 1966).

This same "compensation" phenomenon was studied using prism goggles that distorted vision by making straight lines appear curved (Kohler, 1962). With the goggles in place, people at first described their environment as fluid and unstable. Within a relatively short time, however, they began to compensate for the distortions produced by the goggles and reported little difficulty in coordinating their movements within their newly stabilized perceptions. When the goggles were removed, people found it difficult to adjust to the world after wearing the prisms for several weeks or months. They behaved as if they were now wearing goggles that distorted in the opposite direction from those originally used. If the goggles had curved all lines to the left, for example, people now saw all lines as curved to the right. These compensatory distortions lingered for days before they disappeared and the world again seemed normal.

Brain activity can also create perceptions even in the absence of appropriate sensory stimulation. We sometimes have visual experiences without using our eyes, as in dreams, auditory experiences without using our ears, and so on. As we shall see in Chapter 6, subjects who took part in experiments that eliminated most external stimulation saw colors, patterns, objects, or scenes despite the fact that their goggles cut off all visual stimulation (Bexton, Heron, and Scott, 1954).

Perhaps the most convincing evidence of the brain's role in perception comes from the results of research using electrical brain stimulation, as described in Chapter 3. Although such stimulation is applied directly to the brain, and therefore completely by-passes the sense organs, subjects often report a clear perception of nonexistent sights, sounds, and feelings.

Helen Keller could not see, hear, or speak, but she overcame these handicaps to become a distinguished author and educator. Her achievements show that brain processes can compensate for missing perceptual stimuli.

It seems clear that perception is not simply the detection of stimuli by sensory receptors. Instead, the perceptual process depends on the way the brain organizes those stimuli to create meaning.

Perceptual Organization

The world we perceive through this process of perceptual organization is extremely complex. We see objects of various sizes, shapes, and colors; we see them as separate units distinguished from other visual units; we see them arranged in three-dimensional space, as moving or stationary. We perceive a three-dimensional world, yet the images received by the retina are two-dimensional and upside down. We perceive a stable environment, although the retina receives constantly changing stimuli. Several explanations have been advanced to account for human perception, including the Gestalt approach, which emphasizes entire organized patterns, and the feature-analysis approach, which emphasizes the decomposition of a pattern into its parts.

Gestalt Principles

In the Gestalt view of perception, human beings constantly group the information received by their sensory receptors, organizing the pieces into meaningful patterns, or **gestalts**, after the German word for "form" or "shape." Because of the organization of the black patches in Figure 5.4, for example, we can perceive the form of a dog; a slight rearrangement of the patches would obscure this perception. The dog's form is a gestalt, a perceptual whole. Although we can see each element in the pattern, we perceive more than the separate elements; we recognize the whole form of the dog. Therefore, the gestalt is said to be greater than the sum of its parts.

Gestalt psychology began early in this century when Max Wertheimer, Kurt Koffka, and Wolfgang Köhler attempted to account for perception in terms of the organizational processes of the brain. In their research, the early gestalt psychologists presented people with various patterns—often consisting of dots or musical tones—and simply asked the people what they saw or heard. From their data they formulated a number of principles that they believed described the brain's natural organizing principles. These innate tendencies of the brain explained how it structured sensory stimuli to produce the perception of gestalts. Two of the major gestalt concepts are grouping and figure and ground.

Grouping **Grouping** is the organizing of sensory data, and several of its principles are shown in Figure 5.5. In part A, because dots of equal size are shaped equally across a field, no stable distinguishing pattern is perceived. In part B, the dots are seen as forming a series of four parallel lines, because some dots have been moved closer

Figure 5.4 A stable differentiation of the elements of this picture into figure and ground is difficult at first, and would probably be impossible if you had no previous knowledge of or experience with Dalmatian dogs. The knowledge that there is a Dalmatian dog in this picture, however, makes it possible to differentiate one set of spots as figure and the other spots as undifferentiated ground.

together; this demonstrates the principle of **proximity**, the grouping of stimuli that are close together. In part C, when a few dots are added, these four lines are seen as two curved lines. In this case, the principle of **continuity** overrules the influence of proximity: dots that form a single, continuous grouping are seen as a gestalt. Another organizing principle is **similarity**; in part D, a cross is perceived in the original pattern of dots because of the similarity of the dots making up the cross.

The principles of grouping apply to all the senses. For instance, both proximity and continuity influence the gestalt of a musical composition. The notes of a melody are automatically grouped according to their proximity in time. However, when a composition, such as a Bach fugue, includes two melody lines played simultaneously, continuity overrides proximity. That is, if two notes are played close together in time, but are not part of the same melody, they are not perceived as a gestalt.

Figure 5.5 A demonstration of some of the gestalt principles of organization. The pattern of equally spaced identical dots in A is not easily organized. It is seen either as an undifferentiated field or as a set of unstable overlapping patterns. In B a stable perception of parallel lines emerges because of the *proximity* of some dots to others. When some of these lines are made *continuous* with one another in C, dots that are physically quite distant from one another are seen as belonging to a single curved line. In D a very stable organization emerges suddenly because some of the dots have been made *similar* to one another and different from the rest.

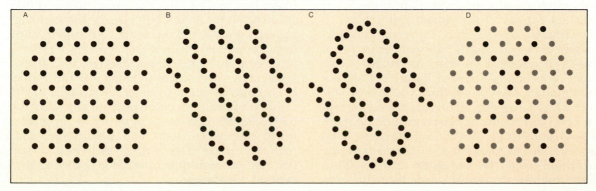

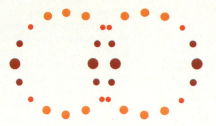

Figure 5.6 An illustration of the perceptual tendency toward simplicity. Despite conflicting cues, this figure is seen as two intersecting circles. The circle is among the simplest of perceived forms and provides by far the simplest means of interpreting this pattern.

As several researchers (e.g., Hochberg, 1978; Attneave, 1954) have pointed out, all the principles of grouping can be integrated under a single concept: **simplicity**. Simple patterns are perceived more easily than are complex patterns. This is so whether the simplicity results from proximity, continuity, similarity, or some other principle of perceptual organization. For example, despite conflicting cues and possible interpretations, Figure 5.6 is seen as two interlocking circles, by far the simplest way to perceive it.

Figure and Ground Another basic perceptual tendency is the division of what we see into figure and ground. When we look at a scene, we automatically separate it into regions that represent objects, or **figure**, and regions that represent spaces between objects, or **ground**. This ability to distinguish objects from space does not seem to depend on past experience. When people who have been blind from birth have an eye operation that enables them to see, they soon become able to separate figure from ground, although they have had no experience with visual details (von Senden, 1960).

Although visual experience is not absolutely necessary for perceiving figure and ground, it does seem to have an effect on perception, particularly when most of the normal sensory cues have been removed. At first, for example, the various dots and blotches of Figure 5.4 are not differentiated. After some effort, you may be able to see a Dalmatian dog. In this case, your perception of a single figure against a ground depends on your knowledge of what a Dalmatian looks like; without any knowledge of Dalmatians, the perception would be extremely difficult. Most young children are unable to see these blotches

as a single figure (Thurstone, 1944), indicating that experience allows figure and ground to be distinguished more easily. The same perceptual qualities that blend the Dalmatian into the background are the basis of camouflage, an attempt to reduce the patterning that distinguishes figure from ground for the purpose of hiding the presence of an object—whether a military unit or a duck hunter.

Figure-ground perceptions are not merely visual. For example, many fragrances fill the air in a cosmetics department, but if you catch the odor of your favorite perfume, it suddenly becomes the figure, leaving the other fragrances as the ground. Or suppose you are in a crowded restaurant, following the voice of your dinner companion. That voice is the figure and the rest of the restaurant noise is the ground. But suppose someone at the next table says something outrageous that catches your attention. Suddenly that person's voice becomes the figure and your companion's voice part of the ground.

Most psychologists who study perception have accepted the explanations of perception advanced by gestalt and the principles of perceptual patterning, but they have gone beyond this analysis to focus on still other processes that influence the way we organize sensory information.

Perceptual Constancy

Our organization of sensory information is greatly aided by the process of perceptual constancy, which affects several aspects of vision. When we move toward a tree, for example, the image that it casts on the retina gets larger, its color grows more distinct, and the details of the branches and trunk become sharper. Yet we know that the tree is not becoming larger, more colorful, or more detailed. In the same way, the image cast by a car that is moving away becomes smaller, but we do not perceive the car as changing size. Nor, when we see a coin rolling away from us on its edge, do we perceive any lessening of its round shape, despite the fact that at that moment it casts an oval image on the retina. Even large moment-to-moment changes in the sensory information received from objects in the environment tend to be ignored in favor of a world that is constant and predictable. This tendency to perceive objects as having certain constant (or stable) properties is known as **perceptual constancy**.

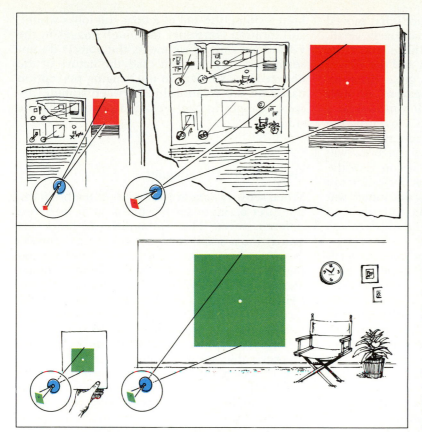

Figure 5.7 Following the instructions given in the text, stare at the dot, then at a sheet of white paper, then at a blank wall. The farther away the wall is, the larger the afterimage will appear to be. The drawings at the left explain why this happens. (top) Normally, the more distant an object is from the eye, the smaller the image projected onto the back of the eye. The brain compensates for this effect by scaling up the apparent size of distant objects. The result is size constancy: objects do not appear to change size just because they move closer or farther. But when the image in the eye is held constant, as it is with an afterimage (bottom), the brain's compensation for changes in distance creates large changes in apparent size.

One type of perceptual constancy is **size constancy**. The farther away an object is, the smaller the size of the image it projects on the retina; however, we automatically take into account any information we have about the object's distance and translate the projected size into the object's real size.

To see how size constancy works, hold one hand at arm's length and the other hand half that far from your eyes, and note the relative size of your hands. They look very much the same size, even though the near hand projects a larger image onto the eye. If you now move the near hand so that it hides part of the far hand from view, you will perceive a disparity between the sizes of the two images. The partial overlapping highlights this size disparity, which normally goes unnoticed.

The relationship between size and distance can be demonstrated more precisely with afterimages—images that persist after the original stimulus is removed. Stare for forty seconds in adequate lighting at the dot in the red square in Figure 5.7. Then hold a piece of white paper a foot from your eyes and look at the center of it. If you have trouble seeing an afterimage of the square, focus on one spot on the paper. Now move the paper to about two feet in front of your eyes and look at it: the square probably looks twice as large. If you look at a more distant surface, such as a white wall, the afterimage will appear to be even larger. Obviously, the size of the afterimage does not really change, because it is based on your original fixation on the red square. What does change is the perceived size of the image: as your eyes focus at greater distances, your brain interprets the afterimage as representing a larger object. The afterimage seems to be twice as large at two feet as at one foot because your brain tells you that an object that is twice as far away as another object, yet still projects the same size image onto the eye, has to be twice as large as the second object.

Size constancy is also responsible for the moon illusion, which most people notice and comment on. As the moon rises above the horizon, it appears enormous, but once it has moved into the skies, it appears comparatively small. The horizon is responsible for this effect, as its interposition between the moon and the viewer alerts the brain to the moon's great distance. When the moon is high in the heavens, no such cues to distance are provided. If you look at a rising moon through a tube, thus separating the moon from any cues on the horizon, the illusion of great size will be destroyed and the moon will appear much smaller. Similarly, if you view the moon at its zenith through an artificial horizon drawn on a large transparency, the moon will suddenly seem much larger. As with the red square, perceived size depends upon perceived distance.

This relationship between an object's projected size and its distance is the same for both the eye and a camera. There is an inverse relationship between the distance of an object and its projected image—the greater the distance, the smaller the projected image. When an object's distance from the eye or camera is doubled, for example, its projected size is halved. Thus, if you photograph a tree, first from 100 feet and then from 200 feet, the tree will be twice as large on the first photograph as on the second. Brain processes can contribute to size constancy only if distance can be inferred: by taking into account the relationship between size and distance, accurate inferences are made about real size.

When cues for size and distance are in conflict, a person automatically opts for one or the other —usually in favor of the more likely conclusion. In World War II, the Allies used a strategy based on this phenomenon to confuse the Germans during the invasion of Normandy. At dawn the Allies dropped two-foot dummies of paratroopers in areas miles inland from the planned landing site. The impact of the dummies on the ground set off a series of small explosions that sounded like rifle fire. Because of the poor light and general confusion, the Germans believed the dummies were real paratroopers, attacking from a distance. The Germans set out to fight the invading army; not until they moved close to the dummies did they realize that they had been misled by the small size of the figures. Their mistake gave the Allies extra time to put real troops ashore on the coast.

Size constancy is only one important perceptual constancy. There is also shape constancy (the coin rolling away from us retains its round shape); color constancy (when the sun goes be-hind a cloud, the sail of a boat still looks white); and location constancy (although images in the visual field shift as we move, the objects do not seem to move). In each case, the nature of the **constancy** is similar: an unchanging perception based on the relationship between stimuli, despite changes in the sensation provided by the stimuli.

Resolution of Ambiguity

When sensory data are ambiguous, the brain can interpret a single set of stimuli in at least two different ways. This ambiguity can block the search for a stabilized perception that conveys meaning. Sometimes figure and ground are ambiguous, as in Figure 5.1. In this drawing, figure and ground alternate so that the perception switches back and forth between a vase and two faces in profile. Another type of perceptual ambiguity involves a figure that can be seen in two different perspectives, such as the well-known Necker cube, shown in Figure 5.8. The figure provides no information as to which side of the cube is the front and which is the back. In these two examples, there is no correct perception. Presented with such a dilemma, the brain apparently entertains alternate hypotheses and, since both possibilities are equally plausible, a person never decides between them.

Normally, we resolve perceptual ambiguity by choosing the most likely possibility that accounts for the available sensory information. We generally use **context**—the setting in which the stimuli appear—to go beyond the available sensory information and to determine what it ought to mean. For example, the two lines at the top of Figure 5.9 are not entirely clear. When they are placed into the sentence "Fido is drunk," their features are clarified: they become the word "is." However, when they are placed into the number 14,157,393, their features are clarified in a different way: they become the numbers 1 and 5.

Context is also important in our perception of speech. If a person hears a random series of words, such as "Lives mountain man on that a," embedded in a great deal of noise, few of the words will be recognized. However, if the words are placed in the meaningful order, "That man lives on a mountain," most of the words will be recognized despite the noise. The context provided by a meaningful arrangement of the words is a clear aid to recognition (Miller, 1962). We all

Figure 5.8 The Necker cube is a classic case of perceptual ambiguity. The tinted surface sometimes appears as the front of the cube and sometimes as the back. (After Gregory, 1968.)

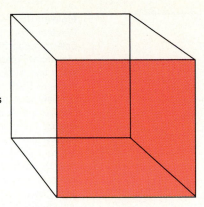

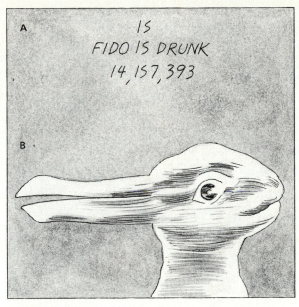

Figure 5.9 (A) The stimulus above the handwriting can be interpreted as either 15 or IS, depending on its context. (B) This figure is also ambiguous, and depending on the context in which it is found, it may be perceived as either a rabbit or a duck. (B after Lanners, 1977.)

use context to make sense of what we hear in a noisy situation, such as a loud party.

We also draw upon past experience and stored knowledge to provide a context for resolving ambiguity and organizing nonsense (Lindsay and Norman, 1972). Consider, for instance, your ability to accurately identify the source of inspiration for the following nonsensical rhyme as you read it aloud.

Mister Merry,
Cute and scarry,
Cow fuzz gore guard ingrown?
Wet sliver balls,
Uncock eel smells,
Ungritty made fall sinner moan.

When you ignore the meaning and bizarre imagery of the words, rhythm and sound provide a context for the jingle, which then becomes a greatly distorted version of a familiar nursery rhyme.

Feature Analysis

Context aids perception by providing meaning for a pattern of stimuli; feature analysis aids perception by breaking up the pattern. **Feature analysis** is the process by which sensory information is identified according to its distinctive characteristics or features. For example, you would not be able to read this sentence if you could not recognize the letters that compose it.

To understand how feature analysis works, researchers have developed computer models of the process. In 1959, Oliver Selfridge programed a computer to recognize the letters of the alphabet. Selfridge's system, which is portrayed in Figure 5.10, is based on the fact that a small set of distinctive features can be used to identify all the capital letters of the alphabet. Each letter is defined by a unique set of characteristics. For example, both L and T have one vertical and one horizontal angle, but L has one right angle and T has two right angles. To distinguish Ls from Ts, a computer must be programed to analyze three different features: horizontal lines, vertical lines, and right angles. To analyze the entire alphabet, the computer must analyze a series of such features and then find the best match in the information it has stored about the features of each letter. For instance, the unique combination of one horizontal line, two vertical lines, and four right angles will be identified as an H.

Computer models provide a convenient means for describing how feature analysis may operate in our own perceptual processes. For example, the demons in Selfridge's system could be construed as analogous to the receptive fields of cells in the visual cortex, which respond to line segments and their orientation (see Chapter 4). Such computer models are not analogous merely

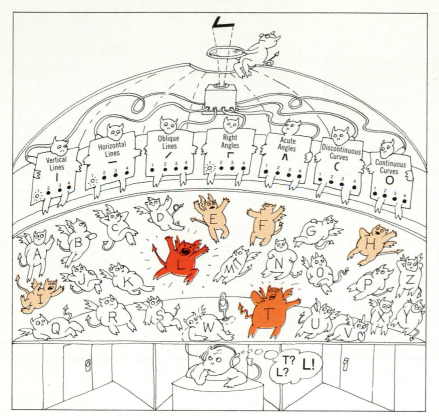

Figure 5.10 Selfridge's Pandemonium. In this model of pattern recognition, image demons register an image of the outside world and display it to the feature demons. Each feature demon is specialized to perceive a certain feature; the demon examines the image for the presence of that feature and reports its findings to the cognitive demons. Each of the cognitive demons represents a particular pattern that might be expected to come in from the outside world. A cognitive demon starts yelling if the features that have been identified match the features that are found in its particular pattern. The better the match, the louder it yells. The decision demon listens to the resulting uproar and chooses the pattern corresponding to the noisiest cognitive demon. Presumably it is its pattern that has appeared in the outside world.

to our identification of letters; the extraction of features also takes place when we recognize paintings by famous artists, songs performed by different musicians, constellations of stars in the sky, and the odors of different flowers.

Although computer models are useful in identifying the elements of feature extraction, they do not tell the whole story of this perceptual process. Selfridge's program enabled the computer to identify only the capital letters of a standard-print alphabet. Yet people can recognize letter patterns despite wide variations in the ways that the letters are printed (Lindsay and Norman, 1972). Whether an F is big or small, plain or fancy, slanted or straight, upside down or right side up, people can abstract the features necessary to identify its pattern. Irregularities in the shape of a letter can tax a computer, but with little effort, human beings accommodate such irregularities in their recognition processes.

Depth Perception

Recognition is one aspect of perception; the other aspect is location. In a three-dimensional world, we need to be able to perceive three-dimensional space, and our bodies have been constructed to make such distinctions possible. For example, because we have one ear on each side of our heads, sounds that come from the left side produce sound waves that arrive at the left ear earlier than at the right ear (and vice versa), as Figure 5.11 shows. Consequently, we can localize sound, determining approximately which direction any sound comes from.

Our most important sense for judging the position of objects in space is vision. **Depth perception**, or the ability to tell how far away an object is, is constructed from several kinds of information. One source is provided by anatomy: the eyes, like the ears, are set apart, so that the retinal image received by each eye is slightly different. This difference is called **binocular disparity.** You can discover binocular disparity by holding a finger in front of you and looking at it with one eye at a time; the image registered by the right eye will be slightly left of center, and that registered by the left eye will be slightly right of center. Now, line up your finger with an object that is some distance away, and look at

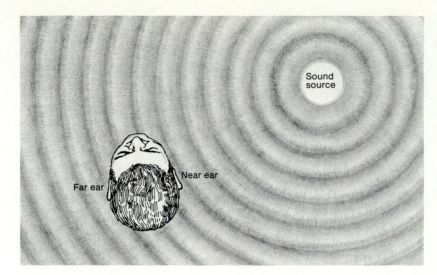

Figure 5.11 Human beings are able to perceive the direction of sound sources by making comparisons between the times at which a particular sound reaches each of the two ears. Because the ears are not very far apart, the difference between the sound's arrival time at the two ears is quite small; human beings are able to detect a difference of about thirty-millionths of a second. It is this amazing sensitivity to small time differences that makes your perception of stereophonically reproduced sound so different from your perception of monaurally reproduced sound. (After Lindsay and Norman, 1972.)

both your finger and that object with one eye at a time. As you switch from eye to eye, your finger will seem to jump back and forth in relation to the more distant object, because the binocular disparity of far objects is less than that of near objects. We use this difference in disparity to judge the distance of an object. As we look at objects with both eyes, the combined information gives a perception of depth, called **stereopsis.** The stereoscope, a device that helps an observer fuse the images of two photographs

taken from slightly different angles, takes advantage of this perceptual phenomenon and allows a two-dimensional, photographed scene to be perceived as if it had three dimensions, as illustrated in Figure 5.12.

Just as some people are color-blind, others are blind to binocular disparity, a condition called **stereoblindness.** This disorder, which affects about 5 percent of the population, probably results from a scarcity of cells in the visual cortex that receive sensory input from both eyes. In

Figure 5.12 The interaction of the two eyes in the perception of depth is analogous to the interaction of the two ears in the perception of direction. The brain combines two slightly different two-dimensional images of the same stimulus into one perception that is three-dimensional. The two photographs shown here were taken from slightly different positions in order to reproduce the slightly different images received by your two eyes. If you look down the sides of a tall piece of cardboard placed on the line dividing the two photographs, as the woman in the sketch is doing, you can deliver one of these images to your left eye only and the other to your right eye only. If you are able to fuse these images, that is, to visually superimpose them exactly, the scene will jump out in depth. A popular toy, the "Viewmaster," operates on the same principle.

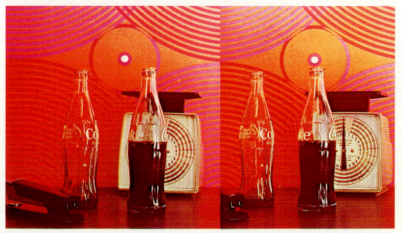

An example of texture gradient as a cue to depth perception.

Artists were aware of monocular cues to depth perception long before these cues became the subject of psychological study. Since paintings are static as well as two-dimensional, the impression of depth must rely on cues that do not involve motion. One such aid to monocular depth perception is **interposition**, in which one object partially blocks the view of another object, creating the illusion that the second object is farther away. A second cue to depth is **linear perspective**, which is produced by the apparent convergence of parallel lines, like those in the photograph of railroad tracks in Figure 5.14D (see p. 117). A third depth cue is **relative size**, the rela-

Duccio's *Maetrà, Retro, Entrata a Gerusalemme,* a Gothic painting, displays a rudimentary attempt to indicate depth.

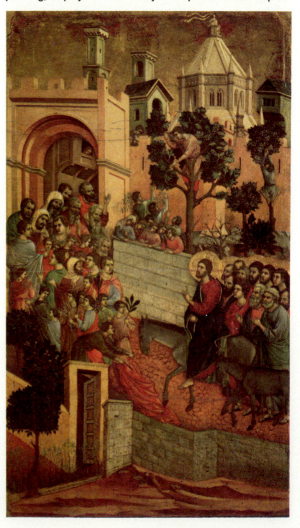

many instances, this reduction in such cells can be traced to early childhood disorders that prevented the normal, coordinated use of the eyes (Lema and Blake, 1977). Although unable to use the cue of binocular disparity, stereoblind people can discern depth by relying on **monocular cues**—information that does not require the cooperation of both eyes. Monocular cues are not as precise as binocular disparity, but they are adequate for depth perception, as you can judge by simply closing one eye and looking around you.

One monocular cue to depth is **motion parallax**, the differences in the relative movements of retinal images that occur when we move or change position. You can demonstrate motion parallax by looking toward two objects, one near you and the other some distance away. Close one eye so that binocular disparity is eliminated, and move your head back and forth. The near object will seem to move more than the far object. We use this difference in movement to perceive depth. Because of this difference, when we drive along a highway, trees and telegraph poles beside the road seem to whizz by while distant mountains appear motionless. As we shall see in Chapter 11, research using a device called the visual cliff indicates that motion parallax enables animals and human beings alike to perceive depth shortly after birth, suggesting that the capacity is inborn.

tionship between the size of the retinal image produced by an object and the apparent distance of that object from an observer: the larger the retinal image, the closer the object appears to be. Finally, **texture gradient**, the graduated differences that occur as distance increases, also provides a cue to depth. In a scene in which texture is obvious, such as the one shown in the accompanying photograph, the nearer stones appear larger and coarser and the more distant ones, smaller and finer.

Over the centuries, artists' appreciation of monocular cues to distance grew, and the improvement in the ability to convey depth can be seen in the accompanying paintings. In the Gothic painting, the use of perspective and relative size to indicate depth is rudimentary compared with the highly developed use of monocular cues in the Renaissance painting.

Perception of Movement

Another aspect of location that is characteristic of the perceptual world is movement, produced both by ourselves and by the objects around us. We know when we are in motion, and so we relate the movements of our own bodies to the resulting changes in what we see. When we look from one side of a room to another, what we see changes constantly, but we perceive the changes as resulting from the movement of our own eyes, and not from movement of the room.

We can also tell that we are moving even though we are not producing the movement ourselves, as when we ride in a car that someone else is driving. In this case, what we see in the world outside the car is **global motion parallax**, a constant flux in what is seen, which produces our perception that we are moving through space (J. Gibson, 1966).

Motion is sometimes perceived although no real motion is taking place. In **apparent motion**, a rapid succession of motionless stimuli that mimic the changes that occur in true movement leads to the perception of motion. One example of apparent movement, the **phi phenomenon**, was described by Gestalt psychologist Wertheimer (1923), who pointed out that when lights are switched on sequentially, as in some neon signs, we see movement although nothing is actually moving. The phi phenomenon is the basis of motion pictures. We perceive that people in films are moving, although the stimuli producing the perceived motion are a series of still photographs that flash by at a rate of at least sixteen frames per second. In both these examples of apparent movement, the rapid succession of visual stimuli reproduces the changes in sensory information that occur in real movement, producing an illusion of movement.

You can experience another kind of apparent movement when riding in a train. When the train stops, the scenery outside will, for a time, appear to move slowly backward. This aftereffect of motion, called the waterfall illusion, was so named because one of its discoverers (Adams, 1834) found that his prolonged gaze at a waterfall was followed by the illusion that the riverbank was drifting gradually upward. In the waterfall illusion, the apparent movement is always in the

The Renaissance painting *Delivery of the Keys,* by Perugino, employs a relatively sophisticated use of monocular cues to show depth.

opposite direction from the previous real movement, and it is probably caused by sensory adaptation, in which the responsiveness of direction-selective cells in the visual cortex is temporarily reduced (Blakemore, 1973). Just as color-opponent cells respond to stimulation by one color and not by another (see Chapter 4), so direction-selective cells respond to movement in one direction and not in another. If the normal detection of movement is produced by a comparison of the outputs from direction-selective cells, the reduced responsiveness of cells sensitive to movement in one direction would allow greater activity among cells sensitive to the opposite motion, thereby producing the waterfall illusion. The eerie feeling that accompanies this aftereffect probably arises because the visual neurons that detect position have not adapted, so that despite the riverbank's apparent movement, it keeps its position relative to its surroundings. As a result, the brain is getting contradictory information from two classes of neurons (Blakemore, 1973).

Illusions

Neural adaptation of detector cells in the visual cortex may be responsible for other illusions besides the motion aftereffect. An **illusion** is a perception that does not correspond to a real object or event, and it is produced by physical or psychological distortion. A number of other temporary illusions can be explained as aftereffects that result when a particular class of visual neurons adapts to stimulation. For example, the tilt aftereffect involves neurons that respond to line segments and their orientations; it may be experienced with the stimuli in Figure 5.13. Look steadily at the tilted lines on the left in the figure for one minute, focusing on the bar between them. Now focus on the dot between the vertical lines on the right. Since the cells responsive to a leftward tilt have adapted, the lines should appear to tilt to the right.

Such illusions demonstrate important perceptual processes that go unnoticed under ordinary conditions. By studying these illusions in the lab-

Figure 5.13 This figure demonstrates the tilt afterimage, as explained in the text. View it with the book propped up about nine feet away from you. (After Blakemore, 1973.)

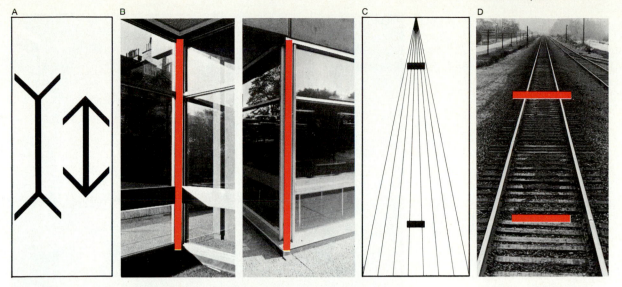

Figure 5.14 Two famous illusions and possible explanations for how they work. The vertical lines of the figures in the Müller-Lyer illusion (A) are identical in length, but they do not appear to be. An explanation for this illusion, suggested in B, is that the arrow markings on the lines in A cause them to be perceived as three-dimensional objects that have corners. The corners seem to induce a size-constancy effect: The vertical line that appears to be distant is perceived as larger. The horizontal lines in the Ponzo illusion (C) are also identical in length. As the photograph in D suggests, this figure, too, could easily be perceived as three-dimensional, and again size constancy would cause the apparently more distant "object" to be scaled up in apparent size relative to the "nearer object." (After Gregory, 1970.)

oratory, researchers hope to discover more about visual neurons and just how human beings process visual information.

Some optical illusions, such as desert and arctic mirages, are not due to sensory adaptation but are produced by physical distortion. They are examples of the physical principle of light refraction and have been used to explain cultural beliefs about the nature of the world. For instance, the arctic mirage was probably responsible for the medieval Norse explorers' belief that the earth was saucer-shaped, with an up-curved rim. In this illusion the distant horizon of the sea appears rimlike and higher than the observer; the illusion is produced when relatively warm air lies against a cold surface, such as the Arctic Ocean. The resulting temperature inversion gives the air a refractive capacity much like that of a prism or a glass of water. Distant land masses that should be obscured by the curvature of the earth become visible because the air refracts their images upward (Sawatzky and Lehn, 1976). It seems likely that the Norse belief in a saucer-shaped earth may have delayed European acceptance of the theory of a spherical earth.

Psychologists are interested in illusions that cannot be explained by physical phenomena, such as the temporary illusions due to adaptation

and the subjective contours discussed at the beginning of this chapter. Psychological illusions reflect the psychological contribution to perception by demonstrating a disparity between physical stimulation sensation and perception.

It has been suggested that some psychological illusions result from a misapplication of size constancy during perception (Gregory, 1970). For example, the lines in Figure 5.14A appear to be of different lengths, but if you measure them with a ruler you will see that they are identical. This figure, called the Müller-Lyer illusion, has features similar to those that indicate distance to the eye. The arrows act like outlines of corners, as illustrated in Figure 5.14B. As a result, the "shorter" line is interpreted as being closer to the observer than the "longer" line, which is interpreted as being recessed into the page. Because both lines project the same size image onto the retina, the line that is interpreted as being closer is perceived as smaller, in accordance with size constancy. A related effect can be seen in the Ponzo illusion (Figure 5.14C), in which the converging lines are like parallel lines that extend away from the observer. In Figure 5.14D, the same illusion is demonstrated using railroad tracks. The horizontal bar that is farther down the track is perceived as larger; once again, size

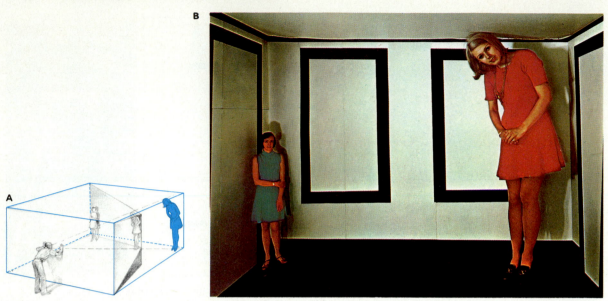

Figure 5.15   The Ames room. In A the actual construction of the room is compared with the way the room is perceived. The photograph in B shows the room as it is seen through the peephole. The illusion is produced by people's inexperience with any rooms except rectangular ones with flat floors. The brain infers that both women standing against the back wall are at the same distance from the eye and interprets the difference between the size of their images as a real difference in size.

constancy dictates that when two objects project the same-size image on the retina, but one object is perceived as more distant than the other, the far object must be larger.

Striking visual illusions have been created by building models that trick the visual system into misapplying size and shape constancy. The best example is the Ames room, shown in Figure 5.15B: the two women inside the room look dramatically different in size because we perceive the room as rectangular (Ames, 1951). In fact, Figure 5.15A shows that the room is not rectangular; the back wall is farther away on the left side than on the right. Perspective and size cues have been cleverly changed to fool us into seeing the room as rectangular. Since we see it as a rectangular room, we perceive the women to be standing the same distance from us. Once again, size constancy dictates that if two people are the same distance away, but one projects a larger-size image onto the eye, then that person must be larger. The Ames room illusion works only if we view the room without adequate perception of depth. Although Figure 5.15B portrays the room as having only three walls, laboratory models of it have four. The observer looks at the room through a peephole; this serves to remove important depth cues such as binocular parallax

(because the observer can use only one eye at a time) and motion parallax (because the observer cannot move around to see the room from different positions).

If observers are allowed to explore the surfaces of the Ames room with a stick inserted through a hole in the wall, they are less susceptible to the illusion. Gradually, they see the room for what it really is: a set of trapezoids joined to form acute and obtuse angles—that is, a distorted room. Mere intellectual knowledge of how the room is shaped does not prevent the illusion; only active exploration of the room is effective.

In these illusions based on the inappropriate application of size constancy, incorrect perceptual inferences are made about distance and size because features of the illusions mimic the patterns of corners, parallel lines, and rectangular rooms that are seen in the world about us. As these illusions show, perception does not simply reflect the world, but interprets it. The interpretive role of perception is necessary, because sensory input is often sketchy and misleading. By compensating for inadequate sensory information, perception puts us in contact with the environment, telling us what is out there in the world and where it is in relation to us, helping us to survive in a hostile environment.

The Influence of Experience on Perception

A recurrent theme in our discussion of perception has been the role of experience and expectation in shaping our interpretation of sensory events. Obviously, our ability to derive meaning from the black squiggles printed on this page is based on our past experience with letters and words. Similarly, our expectations influence our perccptions as we read. Because of your expecta-

tions, you may not have noticed the misspelled word in the last sentence, and as the opening of the chapter demonstrated, the omission of an entire word can also escape notice.

Expectations and previous experience constantly interact with one another to influence our perception of sensory events such as pain (as we saw in Chapter 4). As for the effect of expectations on visual perception, look at Figure 5.16B; then glance at Figure 5.16A. Do you see a young woman? Now look at Figure 5.16C and then at Figure 5.16A. Do you now see an older woman? The experience of viewing one drawing influences how you perceive the ambiguous figure.

A

B

C

Figure 5.16 (A) This drawing (like that in Figure 5.1) is perceptually ambiguous. The effect of personal experience and set on what is perceived here is particularly strong. Many people have difficulty in seeing a young woman in this drawing. Others have equal difficulty in seeing an old woman. (B) This is a version of drawing A that has a strong tendency to be interpreted as a representation of a young woman. Does viewing B affect your perception of A? (C) This version of drawing A is likely to be interpreted as a representation of an old woman. Does viewing C affect your perception of A? One tends to use whatever is familiar in interpreting an ambiguous stimulus pattern. (After Boring, 1930.)

Seeing Without Seeing

On the television screen a group of attractive young people cavort in the California surf, accompanied by the sounds of a singing commercial. Throughout the commercial the words "Drink Ziggy Cola" flash on the screen, but each exposure is so brief that the eye does not detect it. If sales increase in areas where the flashing command was superimposed on the commercial as compared with sales in areas where the commercial ran without the command, advertisers would decide that they had made effective use of **subliminal perception,** or the registration of sensory information that influences behavior without producing any conscious experience of the stimulus. The information can be a sight, a sound, or an odor.

Just how persuasive subliminal messages are is a matter of debate. Although some critics have warned that subliminal persuasion can be used by politicians and corporations to control the public's behavior, others have dismissed the phenomenon as ineffective and trivial.

Psychologists have been trying to establish whether subliminal perception exists and, if it does, whether it can change our attitudes and behavior. One problem that plagues research in this area is to determine whether such messages are actually subliminal, since subtle biases can affect people's replies to such questions as "Did you see 'Drink Ziggy Cola' flashed on the screen?" Observers may be reluctant to report seeing a stimulus if they believe that their perceptions might differ from those of others or if seeing a particular stimulus might make them seem odd. When flashed stimuli used in early subliminal research were sexual words or drawings, this effect created a real problem (Elms, 1972).

Several studies (e.g., Zajonc, 1968) have shown that people develop positive attitudes toward things with which they are familiar. For example, a nonsense syllable, a word, a painting, or a piece of music that has become familiar through repeated exposure is also judged as increasingly attractive. This finding has been used in attempts to establish the existence and effectiveness of subliminal perception. In one study (Kunst-Wilson and Zajonc, 1980), researchers first established a level of exposure that was too brief to be identified by flashing objects on a screen and systematically reducing the length of exposure until they had found a level that was below the absolute threshold (see Chapter 4). Then, with a new group of subjects, they flashed a series of irregular black octagons on the screen at this subliminal level, with half of the observers being exposed to one set of ten octa-

Perception is also substantially influenced by our motivation and needs. When in a particular motivational state, we tend to notice stimuli that in the past have been associated with the satisfaction of that state. For example, a hungry traveler is likely to notice stimuli, such as restaurant signs, that would be ignored just after a meal. In fact, an increased tendency to perceive food-related stimuli when we are hungry can operate even in the absence of such stimuli. In one experiment, people who had fasted for varying amounts of time tried to identify pictures that a researcher said would be dimly projected onto a screen. Although the researcher manipulated the projector, no pictures were ever flashed onto the screen. Yet the subjects said they saw pictures, and the longer they had fasted, the greater the proportion of food-related pictures they perceived (McClelland and Atkinson, 1948).

Our expectations, past experiences, and psychological states combine, setting us to perceive the world in certain ways. This readiness to perceive stimuli in a specific way, ignoring some types of stimulation and becoming sensitive to others, is called our **perceptual set**. Although the perceptual sets of the reader and the hungry traveler last only until the book is laid aside or a meal is eaten, our experiences early in life and those common to our culture lead to enduring ways of perceiving the world.

Early Life Experiences

We know that certain early experiences can markedly affect our perceptual responsiveness to the world. There is evidence that some perceptual processes develop only when an individual

gons and the other half to a different set. Afterward, when the observers were shown pairs of octagons (one from each set) and asked which of the pair was more attractive, most observers selected octagons they had seen subliminally even though they could not recognize the ones they had previously seen. Thus, it appears that subliminal perception does exist and that it can turn the unknown into the familiar at a level below conscious awareness. In similar research, investigators (Marcel, in press; Fowler et al., 1981) have found evidence that people can process words without being aware that they have seen them. Words were flashed so briefly that they were unrecognizable, yet subjects' replies to questions concerning the invisible words indicated that although they could not say what words they had "seen," they had some awareness of the words' meaning.

Subliminal perception may also be related to **blindsight,** the ability of the blind to sense the existence and location of stimuli. People in whom the visual cortex has been destroyed and who therefore cannot see, when asked to turn their eyes toward the source of a flashing light, generally move their eyes in the correct direction. Asked to reach toward the light, they tend to stretch their hands in the direction of the flashes. Yet they say they have no sensation of the flashes and feel that they are guessing (Poeppel, Held, and Frost, 1973).

Blindsight may be explained by the existence of a second visual system located in the midbrain, which operates without our awareness and which ordinarily supplies the cortical visual system with information regarding the location of stimuli. As noted in Chapter 3, the midbrain controls visual reflexes. When the visual cortex is damaged or destroyed, the processing of visual stimuli in the second system continues, providing at the subconscious level the sort of information that allows the blind to reach toward a target. There is evidence that if the cortex is damaged early in development, subcortical visual capacities may increase. Researchers (Perenin and Jeannerod, 1979) have described two patients in whom such damage occurred when they were only seven years old. The pair not only could point toward a target, but could perceive patterns and shapes as well, distinguishing between horizontal and vertical lines and between triangles and circles.

Subliminal perception and blindsight indicate that we may often make decisions on the basis of information that is out of conscious awareness and that cannot be put into words—a possibility that raises questions about the nature of consciousness (see Chapter 6).

is raised with exposure to a normal visual environment. As mentioned in the discussion of depth perception, human beings do not develop normal binocular depth perception unless there is a coordinated use of both eyes early in life. Experience also plays an important role in the depth perception of animals, for kittens reared without light show no apparent capacity for depth perception and readily venture into situations that normally reared kittens avoid for fear of falling (E. Gibson and Walk, 1976). Such experiences can be reversed, for when light-deprived kittens are subsequently permitted to explore freely a lighted and patterned environment, they quickly learn to discriminate depth cues. In contrast, light-deprived kittens that are subsequently moved around in a patterned environment by a mechanical device (see Figure 5.17) rather than by their own movements do not develop depth perception (Held and Hein, 1963). Thus it seems that for an organism to develop depth perception, it must *actively* explore its environment.

As we shall see in the discussion of perceptual development in Chapter 11, human infants develop depth perception by the time they are five months old, yet they do not seem to relate this perceptual ability to the danger of falling until after they have experience in crawling. Although babies enter the world with a functioning visual system, early experience plays an important role in the development of visual processing. Early visual deprivation in kittens is known to reduce the number of cells that respond to stimulation, and abnormal visual experience in the first year of life can have serious effects on various aspects of human vision (Held, 1979). For example, visual acuity suffers in babies with strabismus, a

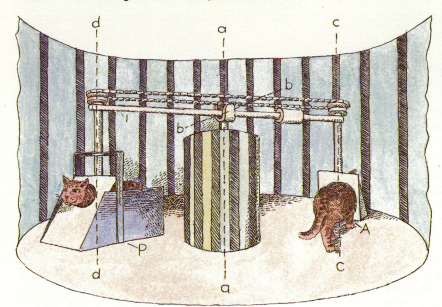

Figure 5.17 Apparatus used in the experiment by Held and Hein. Although the "passive" kitten on the left receives about the same amount of visual stimulation as the "active" one on the right, it does not develop depth perception, while the active kitten does. Feedback from self-induced movement seems to be an important element in learning how to see things in depth. (After Held and Hein, 1963.)

condition in which the eye muscles do not work in coordination so that the two eyes focus on different points. When one eye turns too far toward the nose, babies rely on the other eye to look at interesting objects, and by the time they are six months old, the clarity of vision in the turned eye has decreased. Early astigmatism, in which the curvature of the cornea is not uniform, causing images in one direction to blur, can lead to reduced acuity for lines in a particular orientation by the time a child is three years old.

Cultural Influences

The effects of experience on perception are not limited to early abnormal experiences; the normal perceptual experiences of a culture may lead its members to develop perceptual biases, a phenomenon called **cultural relativism**. For example, members of technologically advanced cultures easily translate the two-dimensional, sharply bordered, gray-shaded stimulus of a photograph into a representation of the world. But not all cultures provide the experiences that make this translation so simple. For example, when an African Bushwoman was shown a photograph of her son, she had great difficulty making sense of the shadings of gray she saw (Segall, Campbell, and Herskovits, 1966). Without any experience in perceiving photographs, she could not recognize her own son until the details of the picture were explained to her.

Some psychologists have hypothesized that cultural factors have great impact on the ways that people from different societies view the world. For example, most children in Western societies are exposed to pictures and picture books, and these experiences teach them to translate two-dimensional drawings into a three-dimensional world. Some psychologists have suggested that this special cultural experience makes us susceptible to the Müller-Lyer illusion, which is based on our tendency to see acute and obtuse angles on a printed page as right angles in the real world. People who have not had this special experience, such as members of the Zulu tribe in Africa, are much less susceptible to the illusion. In addition, Western children live in houses constructed with straight lines, corners, and right angles, while Zulus grow up in an environment characterized by roundedness and a lack of "carpentered" structure. Thus, Westerners learn to use the angles in the Müller-Lyer illusion to infer distance, while Zulus make no such automatic inference (Segall, Campbell, and Herskovits, 1966).

Culture also seems to affect susceptibility to the Ponzo illusion, the tendency to infer depth from two converging lines. In one study (Leibowitz and Pick, 1972), investigators showed this illusion to two groups of Ugandans: university students and rural villagers. Both groups lived in an environment filled with such converging-line depth cues as roads, buildings, and plowed fields. However, when the Ugandans looked at

Figure 5.18 The stimuli used in the study of examining cultural differences in susceptibility to the Ponzo illusion. All the horizontal lines presented in this figure are of equal length. (After Leibowitz and Pick, 1972.)

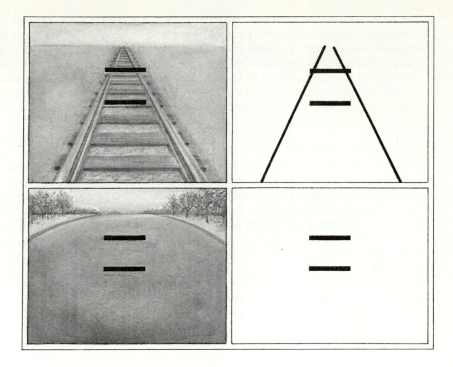

the stimuli pictured in Figure 5.18, the students among them were as likely as students in Pennsylvania to see the illusion, but few of the Ugandan villagers could perceive it. Experiences connected with schooling appear to explain the difference between the students and the villagers. University students, in both Uganda and Pennsylvania, have extensive exposure to books, photographs, newspapers, and the like, from which they learn to perceive three-dimensional space in a two-dimensional representation. In contrast, the Ugandan villagers were more sensitive to the flatness of a two-dimensional representation. The investigators concluded that because the villagers were unable to disregard the flatness of the photograph, they were less likely to see the cues necessary for perceiving the illusion of depth. Such responses demonstrate the pervasive influence of experience and expectations on the ways in which human beings perceive and react to the world around them.

SUMMARY

1. **Perception** is an organism's awareness of objects and events in the environment brought about by stimulation of its sense organs. When sensory information is incomplete, the brain fills in missing details, as when it provides **subjective contours**.

2. The brain's organization of stimulation into perception has been explained in various ways. According to Gestalt psychologists, bits of information are organized into meaningful patterns, called **gestalts**. When presented with an array of stimuli, the brain uses **grouping** to achieve perceptual **simplicity**. The principles of grouping include **proximity, continuity,** and **similarity**. Brain processes also organize sensations by dividing stimuli into **figure**, regions that represent objects, and **ground**, the spaces between figures.

3. Although retinal images of objects change according to one's distance or angle from them,

the brain tends to interpret objects as unchanging, according to the principle of **perceptual constancy**. In **size constancy**, the visual system takes into account the fact that the farther away an object is, the smaller the retinal image. Similar processes are used to achieve constancy in shape, color, and location.

4. When the brain is presented with ambiguous sensory data, it uses the **context** of the stimuli to determine the best perceptual organization. In **feature analysis**, sensory information is identified according to its distinctive characteristics. **Depth perception** is the ability to tell how far away an object is. In **binocular disparity**, the brain uses the slight differences in information received by each eye to perceive depth; people who suffer from **stereoblindness** cannot detect binocular disparity and must rely on **monocular cues** that require information from a single eye. Such cues include **motion parallax**, differences in the relative movements of retinal images as we change position; **interposition**, in which one object partially blocks the view of another; **linear perspective**, the apparent convergence of parallel lines in the distance; **relative size**, the relationship between the size of the image projected on the retina and the distance of the object from the observer; and **texture gradient**, the apparent differences in the texture of objects as distance increases.

5. Movement in the perceptual world can be produced by ourselves or by the objects around us. Through **global motion parallax**, the constant flux of objects leads to the perception of movement that is not produced by the observer, as when riding in a car. **Apparent movement**, or the illusion of motion, can be created by a rapid succession of motionless stimuli. For example, motion pictures use the **phi phenomenon**, in which apparent motion is created by rapidly flashing still pictures.

6. **Illusions**, perceptions that do not correspond to real objects or events, are produced by physical or psychological distortions. Physical illusions are misperceptions in response to actual changes in light refraction, as in desert mirages. Some psychological illusions, such as the waterfall illusion, are the result of sensory adaptation and occur when cells sensitive to a particular kind of stimuli adapt and their responsiveness is reduced. Other psychological illusions, such as the Müller-Lyon, Ponzo, and Ames room illusions, result from a misapplication of the principles of size or shape constancy.

7. Perception is also affected by our expectations, previous experiences, and psychological states, which create **perceptual set**—a readiness to attend to and perceive certain stimuli in a specific way and to ignore other stimuli. Certain perceptual processes, such as size, shape, and depth perception, seem to develop only if the organism's early life experience includes active exploration of the environment. Cultural learning can lead to the development of perceptual biases, producing **cultural relativism**. For example, the perception of such phenomena as optical illusions and photographs can be influenced by cultural experiences.

KEY TERMS

apparent motion	ground	proximity
binocular disparity	grouping	relative size
blindsight	illusion	similarity
context	interposition	simplicity
continuity	linear perspective	size constancy
cultural relativism	monocular cues	stereoblindness
depth perception	motion parallax	stereopsis
feature analysis	perception	subjective contours
figure	perceptual constancy	subliminal perception
gestalt	perceptual set	texture gradient
global motion parallax	phi phenomenon	

RECOMMENDED READINGS

GREGORY, R. L. *The Intelligent Eye.* New York: McGraw-Hill, 1970 (paper). Gregory stresses the importance of perceptual inference, arguing that perception is a set of simple hypotheses about reality that depend upon sensory experience. The book is particularly strong in the area of visual illusions.

HOCHBERG, J. E. *Perception* (2nd ed). Englewood Cliffs, N.J.: Prentice-Hall, 1978 (paper). A nicely illustrated update of a popular text. The author discusses research findings within the context of theory and places various problems within a historical framework.

LINDSAY, P., and D. NORMAN. *Human Information Processing.* New York: Academic Press, 1972. The first half presents a clear, readable account of information-processing analyses of perception.

ROCK, I. *Introduction to Perception.* New York: Macmillan, 1975. This book takes a more cognitive approach to perception. The author adopts a constructivist position wherein perception is treated as a representational process. He argues that it is premature to analyze this process at the neuronal level.

CHAPTER 6

Varieties of Consciousness

One day in 1962, Canadian neurologist Wilder Penfield flew to Moscow to examine a new patient, Nobel-Prize-winning physicist Lev Landau. Landau had been unconscious for six weeks, following an auto accident that left him with severe head injuries. Landau's limbs were paralyzed, his eyes were open but unfocused, and it seemed clear to Penfield that his patient neither saw nor understood anything. When Penfield recommended a minor diagnostic operation, Landau's estranged wife came to Moscow and with Penfield visited her husband for the first time since the accident. As she told her unconscious husband about the proposed operation, Landau's eyes suddenly focused on his wife and he appeared to see, hear, and understand her. Her voice had roused him, and although he could not speak and had no motor control except over the muscles that moved his eyes, Landau had regained consciousness. A hemorrhage in the midbrain blocked all impulses below the eye-movement center although it allowed messages to pass between the brain stem and the cortex. In this case, consciousness and understanding were present, although motor control and the ability to lay down new memories were lost (Penfield, 1979). Landau began a long, slow recovery, but remembered nothing of the meeting with Penfield nor any events that took place within several months after his accident.

Consciousness, then, is different from processes in the lower parts of the brain, from memory, and from the ability to control the body, but no precise and satisfactory definition has been produced. Loosely defined, **consciousness** is an awareness of the thoughts, images, sensations, and emotions that flow through the mind at any given moment (Marsh, 1977). This definition closely resembles seventeenth-century philosopher John Locke's idea of consciousness as the perception of what passes in a person's mind. As such, consciousness is subjective—a private world, accessible mainly through introspection.

Primarily for this reason, some psychologists have refused to consider the nature of consciousness on the grounds that the subject is meaningless. Early behaviorists believed that mind, consciousness, and awareness could not be analyzed scientifically and therefore had no place in the study of psychology. Today, however, many psychologists, including some behaviorists, have rejected this position. They have begun to study the physiological activities that accompany changes in awareness, such as those produced by hypnosis, drugs, meditation, and dreaming, and have discovered much about the workings of consciousness.

The Nature of Consciousness

Most psychologists would agree that consciousness is limited, that it is related to brain activity, and that it has various modes. Beyond that, ideas about consciousness vary widely. Psychologist William James (1902) proposed that our normal waking consciousness is only one type of consciousness and that other potential forms of consciousness are separated from it by the "filmiest of screens." Since much research into consciousness has explored these other forms, the material presented in this chapter may seem like a hodge-podge of unrelated topics. But as we shall see, consciousness appears to vary along a continuum, and these various topics represent different points along that continuum.

The Limits of Consciousness

Human consciousness is limited in that most of the activity in the world around us and within our bodies takes place without our awareness. This lack of awareness comes in part from the relatively narrow range of our perceptual capacities. The world would seem quite different to us if we could see X-rays, hear the high-frequency sounds that guide porpoises and bats, smell the faint odors that provide information to dogs and insects, or sense the functioning of our internal organs. Because each of our sensory channels is limited, our consciousness is constricted.

A second reason for this lack of awareness is the narrow extent to which our minds can process diverse information simultaneously. So many sensations, feelings, thoughts, and memories are accessible at any given moment that attending to all of them would overwhelm us and perhaps leave us unable to act at all. But much of the information that is available to consciousness is automatically screened out, allowing us to attend to some things by becoming unaware of others. For example, the wide receiver is so intent on the quarterback's signals that he does not hear the screaming spectators in the football stadium.

Consciousness, then, is limited in two ways: by the inaccessibility to the human mind of certain stimuli and by constraints on the focus of human attention.

The Relation of Consciousness to Brain Activity

For centuries it has been believed that consciousness and brain activity are tightly linked, and research supports the notion. As we saw in Chapter 3, stimulating parts of the cerebral cortex can produce conscious experiences, such as sights or sounds or the sudden interpretation of a present event as familiar or strange (Penfield, 1969).

The evidence clearly shows that subjective

Modern research confirms the long-held belief that altered states of consciousness are related to variation in the activity of the brain. Researchers studying sleep, for instance, routinely monitor a subject's brain waves using electrodes applied to the scalp, as shown here. They have discovered that very distinctive brain wave patterns are associated with the stages of sleep.

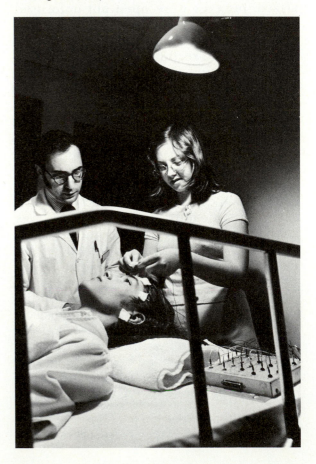

awareness and brain activity are closely related, but the nature of this relationship is not clear. Many neuroscientists (e.g., Rose, 1973) have argued that the distinction between consciousness (or mind) and the brain is purely semantic. Consciousness, they say, is simply the sum total of brain activity—nothing more.

Psychobiologist Roger Sperry (1977) disagrees with this definition and proposes an interactional view: mind has a role in directing brain activity, but brain activity is necessary for mind to emerge. Despite such insights, the puzzle of the connection between consciousness and brain activity has not been solved. Indeed, Sperry (1976) feels that it is "one of the most truly mystifying unknowns remaining in the whole of science."

The Modes of Consciousness

Psychologists agree that there are several modes of consciousness, and their methods of studying these modes have been partly responsible for the jumble of topics that are considered under consciousness. Some researchers have approached consciousness from the anatomy of the brain, basing their work on patients whose cerebral hemispheres have been surgically severed, while others have looked at a particular state of consciousness, such as dreaming, or the effect of manipulations, such as sensory deprivation, on consciousness.

The Split Brain   Research with epileptic patients has led some psychologists to suggest that within each of us exist two separate modes of consciousness: one logical and analytic, the other intuitive and artistic (Ornstein, 1977). The two separate consciousnesses that seem to emerge after surgery like that described in Chapter 3 tend to go to sleep and wake up at about the same time and to have generally similar personalities, but they seem to lack any direct access to each other's awareness.

However, since much of the two-consciousness theory is based on findings from research with epileptic patients, we should be cautious in our interpretation. The findings may reflect early brain damage from the affliction as well as shifts in function by the brain to compensate for the damage (Springer and Deutsch, 1981). We still

do not know how the lateral specialization of the brain is related to the various states of consciousness a normal human being can experience.

The Continuum of Consciousness   Under differing conditions, our conscious awareness can vary greatly, so that it is possible to enter many diverse states of consciousness, each with its own distinctive quality of subjective experience (Tart, 1975). Some states occur naturally, and these have been described as existing on a continuum that stretches from normal waking consciousness to dreaming (Martindale, 1981). Between these two poles lie five other states: realistic fantasy, autistic fantasy, reverie, and hypnagogic states. **Realistic fantasy,** which takes a narrative form and is often problem oriented, is most like normal consciousness; **autistic fantasy** lacks any orientation toward reality. **Reverie** has neither coherence nor control by the fantasizer, but consists of unrelated images, scenes, or memories. The **hypnagogic state** lies between waking and sleep, and its automatic images may consist of vivid sights or intense sounds. Dreams are also automatic and less coherent than we usually assume, for it appears that their structure is generally imposed by the waking mind in its attempt to recall them.

Some states of consciousness are deliberately induced by hypnosis, drugs, biofeedback, meditation, or sensory deprivation. Each of these methods of altering consciousness either increases or decreases the level of cortical arousal, which is controlled by the brain's limbic system, a structure linked with emotion and motivation (Martindale, 1981). Like normal states of awareness, these altered states can be placed on a continuum, but this time it takes the form of a curve (see Figure 6.1). On this curve, which was proposed in a provocative article entitled, "A Cartography of Ecstatic and Meditative States" (Fischer, 1971), as arousal decreases consciousness shifts from relaxation into tranquility and then into states associated with meditation. Increases in arousal shift consciousness in the other direction, from the level of daily routine through creativity and into states associated with irrational behavior and ecstasy. Most research on consciousness has centered on describing and explaining the nature of these various states, particularly those that involve dramatic alterations in normal waking awareness.

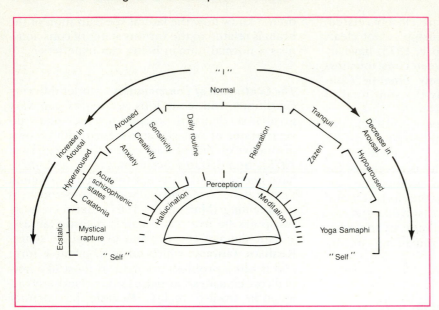

Figure 6.1 Most altered states of consciousness can be classified according to how much they increase or decrease the arousal of the brain's cortex. Thus, altered states can be arranged on a continuum from those associated with very high arousal to those associated with very low. (After Fischer, 1971.)

Sleep and Dreams

Few people consider sleep as a stage of consciousness, but despite our feeling that dreamless sleep is a mental vacuum, the mind during sleep remains relatively active. It is especially active during dreams, and everyone dreams—including people who claim they never do—although most of us find it difficult to recall these sleeping fantasies (Dement, 1974).

The Stages of Sleep

Much of what we know about sleep has come from records of the brain's electrical activity (**electroencephalograms, or EEGs**), eye movements, and muscle activity during sleep (Dement, 1979). In a typical sleep experiment, electrodes are attached to a volunteer subject's scalp and face and connected to a device that monitors brain waves, eye movements, and changes in muscle tension while the subject sleeps overnight in the laboratory.

Such studies have revealed the presence of four stages of sleep, through which the sleeper progresses—from wakefulness to deepest sleep and back again to light sleep—in regular cycles that occur about every ninety minutes (see Figure 6.2). The most reliable way to identify sleep is by the character of the EEG, for each stage in the process of falling asleep is dominated by certain brain-wave frequencies, measured in cycles per second. Beta waves are the fastest, and they predominate in the EEG of a person who is fully awake and alert with eyes open. A person who is awake, but relaxed with eyes closed, typically displays a predominance of slower alpha waves. As a person begins to fall asleep (stage 1, Figure 6.3), the pattern of waves changes, and a few very slow theta waves and occasional burst of high-frequency beta waves are mixed in with the alpha waves. As sleep becomes progressively deeper (stage 2), extremely slow delta waves begin to predominate (stage 3).

When a person is in deep sleep (stage 4), muscles relax and heart rate and respiration are slow and regular. Because it is so difficult to rouse someone in deep sleep, the nature of consciousness during stage 4 is unknown. By the time a person is awake, it is impossible to tell whether whatever is recalled from sleep took place during stage 4 or during the wakening period. Yet the brain is active because sleep disorders such as sleepwalking, sleep talking, and night terrors occur during this stage. (For a discussion of night terrors, see the box on page 132.)

REM Sleep

Sleepers gradually return from deep sleep to the stage 1 pattern, then again begin the descent to

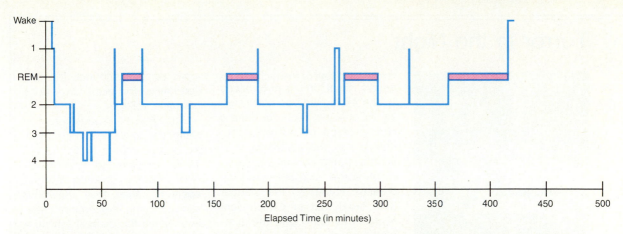

Figure 6.2 The kinds of sleep and their durations, as measured from midnight on, during a normal night's sleep of a twenty-five-year-old male. The horizontal axis indicates minutes elapsed. The vertical axis indicates types of sleep. Shaded bars represent periods of rapid eye movement (REM) sleep. (After Bootzin, 1981.)

stage 4. When they reach stage 1, however, they do not wake up but remain asleep. At this time, their eyes move rapidly back and forth beneath closed eyelids, causing the sleep to be known as **REM (rapid eye movement) sleep.** REM sleep occupies about 22 percent of sleeptime, or from one and a half to two hours each night, so that the average person goes through four or five episodes each night, beginning with the first return to stage 1 sleep. Despite the division of sleep into four stages, the distinction between REM and other stages of sleep (collectively called **non-REM,** or **NREM sleep**) is the clearest and most important (Dement, 1979).

REM Sleep and Dreaming The movement of sleepers' eyes led researchers to suspect that REM sleep might be related to dreaming. When they woke sleeping subjects, their suspicions were confirmed: those wakened during REM periods reported dreams with vivid visual imagery at least 80 percent of the time (Webb, 1973). In contrast, sleepers wakened during a NREM period rarely reported the coherent episodes we normally define as dreams; instead, mental activity appeared to consist of drifting, unstructured thought and images.

After studies had established the connection between rapid eye movements and dreams, sleep researcher William Dement (1974) proposed that these movements reflected the movement of the dreamers' eyes while watching a dream unfold. Dement developed this "scanning hypothesis" on the basis of anecdotal reports from

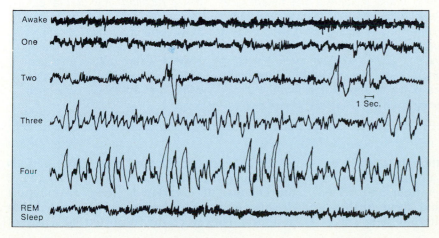

Figure 6.3 Records of the electrical activity of the brain (EEG) in a person in various stages of sleep and in the relaxed waking state known as "alpha." Note that in the deeper stages of sleep the high-frequency, small-amplitude waves give way to lower-frequency, large-amplitude waves. This change is thought to reflect the fact that the neurons in the brain are all firing at about the same level and in about the same pattern. Note also that the EEG pattern in REM sleep is very similar to stage 1.

Terror in the Night

A five-year-old child who has been sleeping peacefully suddenly sits up in bed, screams, and stares wildly at some imaginary object. Her mother rushes to the bedside and finds her daughter agitated but still asleep, although her breathing is labored and her pulse is beating wildly. None of the mother's consoling words or caresses have any effect on the obviously terrified child, who seems dazed, talks incoherently, and continues to stare wide-eyed. After a few minutes the girl's pulse and breathing return to normal and, without ever completely awakening, she returns to a tranquil sleep. In the morning she has no memory of the attack. The child's experience is known as a night terror, and it bears little resemblance to the familiar nightmare. Night terrors generally occur within the first two hours of sleep; nightmares occur during the second half of the night. Night terrors occur during deep sleep (stage 4); nightmares occur during REM sleep. Night terrors are characterized by sudden sharp changes in the autonomic nervous systems—pulse and respiration surge, skin resistance increases markedly, the sleeper may break out in perspiration. Nightmares show only the autonomic changes associated with REM sleep. A person in the grip of a night terror may get up and walk about; a person having a nightmare cannot move because of the muscle paralysis that accompanies REM sleep. Finally, night terrors are accompanied by amnesia, but a person who has a nightmare can relate its frightening content at length ("the vampire was chasing me and then I ran down a corridor and opened a door and it leaped out at me").

Night terrors are most common among children between the ages of three and eight years old, although adults sometimes experience them. For this reason, sleep researcher Ernest Hartmann (1981) has suggested that they are linked with the development of the nervous system and may indicate a mild neurological disorder due to faulty maturation in the brain stem. During stage 4 sleep, the brain responds to some unknown internal stimulus with a minor electrical discharge that sets off the terror. The discharge is similar to a minor epileptic seizure, although the person having the night terror does not have epilepsy.

Since these episodes generally disappear by adolescence, other sleep researchers (Mitler et al., 1975) recommend that when night terrors in children have no apparent cause, they should be allowed to run their course. However, since the sleeper having a night terror can move about, parents should make sure that such children sleep in a room where they can come to no harm while sleepwalking.

Stress apparently increases the frequency of night terrors. When the terrors begin after a child's parents are divorced or the child has been in a serious accident, reassurance or psychotherapy may help lessen them (Hartmann, 1981). Occasionally —especially if the sufferer is an adult—night terrors can be treated with Valium, which suppress slow-wave sleep. In one case (Mitler et al., 1975), a man kept his family awake by screaming in the night and holding garbled conversations with some unknown person. Although he disrupted the household, the man never recalled any of the episodes. After recordings in the sleep laboratory had confirmed that the attacks came during stage 4 sleep, researchers prescribed Valium. The night terrors ended and the family slept once more.

subjects in his laboratory. Attempts to verify the scanning hypothesis often involve studies of blind sleepers (Schwartz, Weinstein, and Arkin, 1978). People who are blind from birth go through the same cyclical pattern of sleep stages as do sighted people, and they have periods resembling REM sleep except for the lack of eye movements. If awakened, they also report dreams, except the dreams are not visual, but auditory. However, the reported absence of rapid eye movements among blind dreamers may be the result of eye damage that alters the electrical activity monitored in the sleep laboratory. Some researchers have reported rapid eye movements in blind sleepers that were not being detected by monitoring equipment. It is difficult to test the scanning hypothesis among sighted dreamers because most REM sleep is characterized by a complicated mixture of eye movements, with few clear, testable patterns. REM sleep is clearly more important than the simple scanning hypothesis implies, but its function is not yet clear.

The Paradoxes of REM Sleep   Although the person in REM sleep is obviously not awake, the EEG pattern shows more arousal than would be expected from a sleeper. In addition, there is an irregular and highly varied heartbeat, breathing rate, and blood pressure, along with signs of sexual arousal. These physiological signs resemble those of a person who is not only awake but highly excited as well. To add to the paradox, such medical disasters as heart attacks and acute worsening of duodenal ulcers and emphysema sometimes occur during this stage of sleep (Snyder, 1965; Armstrong et al., 1965; Trask and Cree, 1962).

By other measures, however, the person is more deeply asleep than in other stages. During REM sleep, people are difficult to awaken and do not respond to touch or sound as quickly as during stages 2 and 3. Despite the aroused physical activity of REM sleep, major body muscles lose their tone and become limp. Because of these contradictory physical signs, REM sleep is sometimes called "paradoxical sleep": people seem to be awake, yet deeply asleep.

The loss of muscle tone during REM sleep temporarily paralyzes the muscles. Yet in the deepest sleep of stage 4, muscles retain their tone. During NREM sleep the body does not move because it has no order from the brain to do so; during REM sleep the body does not move because it cannot (Dement, 1979). The marked drop in muscle-tension levels is a sure indicator of REM sleep, and it appears that stimulation of a specific part of the brain causes this loss of motor control. When this part of a cat's brain is removed, the animal no longer lies still during episodes of REM sleep. Instead, it gets up, leaps, shows rage or fear, or plays with its paws as if a mouse were between them (Jouvet, 1975). The cat's behavior suggests that the paralysis that accompanies REM sleep keeps us from acting out our dreams.

Do We Need REM Sleep?   On the supposition that REM sleep might play a vital role in human functioning, Dement (1974) deliberately deprived people of the opportunity to dream. Each time sleepers entered a REM period, Dement woke them. Over a series of nights, it became increasingly difficult to arouse a sleeper as a REM stage began, and the longer sleepers were denied REM sleep, the more often it appeared. When, on the fifth night, sleepers were allowed to stay in REM sleep, there was a "REM rebound" effect: time spent in REM sleep doubled over the person's normal level.

Since our bodies automatically compensate for a loss of REM sleep, it apparently fills some psychological or physiological need, but its precise function remains unclear. Any restorative function of sleep can be demonstrated only by inference from sleep deprivation. Most deprivation studies have shown personality and behavioral changes, such as aggressiveness, childish behavior, and increased appetite (Webb, 1973), but deprivation of any sleep stage may make a person tired or irritable. We also compensate for lack of stage 4 sleep (Agnew, Webb, and Williams, 1967), and it has been suggested that our need for a particular sleep stage depends on the nature of our fatigue—on whether it results from heavy physical activity or from intense intellectual or emotional activity. A study of long-distance runners revealed that stages 3 and 4 sleep increased dramatically for two nights after they had run in a 92-kilometer marathon (Shapiro et al., 1981). Thus, physical tiredness may increase the need for deep sleep, whereas intellectual activity or emotional stress may increase the need for REM sleep, perhaps in part because REM sleep may restore the ability to focus attention (Hartmann, 1979).

Some evidence suggests that the brain adapts to waking experiences during REM sleep. In one study, medical students wore goggles with distorting lenses for several days. At night the students slept in the laboratory. While they were adapting to the lenses, the students spent more time than usual in REM sleep; but once they had adjusted to the lenses, REM sleep returned to normal (Luce, 1971).

Indirect evidence that REM sleep helps maintain the responsiveness of the brain comes from the fact that time spent in REM sleep steadily decreases as people age. Newborns spend about half their sleep time in REM sleep, infants under two years 30 to 40 percent, and adolescents and adults about 20 to 25 percent. As people reach their seventies, there is a further slight decrease in REM sleep (Williams, Karacan, and Hursch, 1974). Some researchers suggest that REM sleep stimulates the brain, enhancing the growth and maintenance of neural tissue (Anders and Roffwarg, 1973). This self-generated neural activity may prepare sensory and motor areas to handle the load of stimulation received from the environment during waking hours. The need for this sort of rehearsal should be greatest in newborns and decrease with age, and this is precisely the REM pattern (Roffwarg, Muzio, and Dement, 1966).

The Content of Dreams

The average person has about 150,000 dreams during the first seventy years of life (Snyder, 1970), but those dreams do not represent hours of exciting drama. Although the dreams we remember and tell others about tend to be relatively coherent, interesting, and sexy stories, those collected in sleep laboratories tend to be pedestrian or even dull (Webb, 1979). Either we recall dreams selectively, remembering the more exciting ones and forgetting the rest, or else, since the home dreamer remembers only the last dream before awakening, dreams from random awakenings during earlier REM periods are less interesting than the final dream.

One reason dreams may seem so mysterious is that they are not bound by time and space, by the constraints of attention, or by critical evaluation (Webb, 1979). Past and future coexist, as do locations. The dreamer's attention is not focused, and minute details may seem more important than the purpose or demands of the dream. Finally, the dreamer is not critical, accepting events no matter how impossible, frightening, or disgusting they may be.

Although such stimuli as sounds, temperature changes, or touches near a sleeping person do not induce dreams, if the sleeper is already in a REM period they may be incorporated into the dream's content. When water was sprayed on the faces of some volunteer sleepers, they reported more dreams involving water than did sleepers

Dreams are mysterious: the dreamer's world is not bound by time or space or by the conventions of waking life.

who were undisturbed (Dement and Wolpert, 1958).

A dream's content can sometimes reveal the dreamer's mind. Sigmund Freud (1900) proposed that dreams express the hidden needs and desires of the unconscious mind and believed that dreams had two levels of content—one obvious and the other hidden. The obvious, or **manifest content,** is a weaving of daily events, sensations during sleep (such as bladder tension), and memories. However, this manifest content veils the dreamer's unconscious wishes in symbolic images that are acceptable to the dreamer, and these unconscious wishes—primarily from unresolved early emotional conflicts —make up the dream's **latent content.**

During the past few decades, psychoanalysts have shifted away from Freud's theory of dreams; few still slavishly follow his method of dream interpretation. According to Calvin Hall (1979), dreams are not meant to conceal but to reveal, and their symbolism is not an attempt to veil early conflicts. However, in their reflection of the unconscious, dreams use visual metaphors. Since people are accustomed to expressing their ideas in words, not images, the visual metaphor seems mysterious, whereas verbal metaphors are a common part of daily conversations. Among other investigators (for example, Ullman, 1962; Foulkes, 1964), a preoccupation with latent content has given way to an analysis of direct meaning. For example, when a student dreams that she has written an exam in disappearing ink, she is not trying to resolve an emotional conflict that dates back to infancy, but is simply worried about tomorrow's chemistry test.

Recalling and Controlling Dreams Some people always seem to have a new dream to report, whereas others say that they rarely, or never, dream. Certain differences have been found between the two groups: those who often recall dreams tend to daydream frequently, to be good at creating visual imagery, and to have better visual memory than do people who rarely recall dreams. There appears to be no difference in auditory memory between the two groups (Cohen, 1979).

Since nearly all sleepers who are awakened during REM sleep report dreams, researchers have looked for additional explanations. It may be that habitual dream recallers tend to wake up from REM sleep, whereas those who rarely recall dreams generally awaken from NREM sleep (Webb and Kersey, 1967). Mood has been found to affect dream recall, with negative moods before sleep being followed by an increase in dream recall (Cohen, 1979). Perhaps the unpleasant mood before sleep leads to poor sleep, which results in the sleeper awakening from REM instead of NREM sleep. Another reason for poor recall of dreams may be interference. If dreamers awaken slowly, or if their attention is distracted upon awakening, they are less likely to recall a dream than those who experience little interference during awakening. People who were asked to telephone the weather bureau as soon as they woke up and to write down the temperature before they recalled their dreams remembered about half as many dreams as did people who were asked to recall their dreams immediately on wakening (Cohen, 1979).

There is some indication that people can increase their recall of dreams. Dream recall may be a skill made up of an interest in dreams, paying attention to them, practice in recalling them, and a habit of relating dream experiences to others (Cohen, 1979). Learning to control dreams is more difficult. From time to time there appear reports of tribal societies that make a regular practice of cultivating dream consciousness, mastering their dreams and using them to work out social problems (e.g., Stewart, 1972), but as yet none has been substantiated.

Hypnosis

According to the popular conception of hypnosis, the state of a hypnotized person resembles that of a sleepwalker, who has lost touch with waking awareness and control but who behaves as if she or he were awake. Yet there are enormous differences between the sleepwalker and the hypnotized person. For one thing, their EEGs are different. The sleepwalker's brain waves are the slow waves of stage 3 or stage 4 sleep; the hypnotized person's brain waves are like those of a waking person. Second, unlike the hypnotized person, the sleepwalker pays no attention to other people and does not follow instructions. Third, the sleepwalker does not remember sleepwalking, whereas the hypnotic subject remembers the details of the hypnotic state unless there have been instructions to forget them (Barber, 1975). Finally, after a person goes to sleep, oxygen consumption gradually decreases, but during hypnosis there is no change in the consumption of oxygen (Wallace and Benson, 1972).

Hypnosis is obviously not sleep, but after years of research psychologists still cannot say exactly what it is. Since hypnosis can be defined only by the behavior of hypnotized people, many psychologists doubt whether it should be considered a separate state of consciousness. Although hypnosis has been successfully applied in medicine and therapy, where it is used to anesthetize patients during surgery and to treat psychosomatic allergies, migraine headaches, and insomnia, there is little agreement as to how hypnotism works. In addition, the recent uncritical acceptance of hypnosis by some law enforcement officials has led to certain abuses of the process, which will be discussed later in this section.

Hypnotic Susceptibility

Most people are familiar with the process by which a person becomes hypnotized. The hypnotist induces a trance by slowly persuading the subject to relax, lose interest in external distractions, and focus on the hypnotist's suggestions. It is not necessary to swing a pocket watch or other object back and forth, but a hypnotist sometimes does so to focus the subject's attention and to increase the hypnotist's perceived authority and expertise. Once the subject is relaxed the hypnotist typically gives a few simple suggestions—such as that the subject's arm will rise. Only after the subject has complied with these easy suggestions will the hypnotist proceed to more difficult ones, such as that the subject will feel no pain, or will not bleed when stuck with a pin.

According to one estimate, about nine in ten people can be hypnotized to some degree if they want to be and if they trust the hypnotist (Williams, 1974). Hypnotists stress that the relationship between a hypnotist and a subject is one of cooperation, not domination. The ability to spot people who can be easily hypnotized is the key to success for a stage hypnotist. This can be done by telling the audience that they will discover how easy it is to relax through the power of suggestion alone. After telling them repeatedly to relax and close their eyes, the hypnotist suggests that they will find it difficult to open their eyes. The hypnotist then goes through the audience and chooses people whose eyes are still closed to be subjects onstage.

Psychologists measure the trait of hypnotic susceptibility more systematically, through tests such as the Stanford Hypnotic Susceptibility Scale. In this test, after inducing hypnosis in the subject, the hypnotist offers a series of suggestions, such as "Your left arm will become rigid." Subjects who respond with an inability to bend the arm more than two inches and who similarly follow a dozen such suggestions, which include seeing an imaginary fly buzzing around the room, are considered highly susceptible to hyp-

nosis. Among more than five hundred college students who took this test, about 10 percent scored as highly susceptible (E. Hilgard, 1965), although no more than 5 percent were potential hypnotic virtuosos—those people who experience everything the hypnotist suggests, no matter how bizarre (E. Hilgard, 1977). A number of similar scales have been developed to assess hypnotic susceptibility, and the results on many of them appear to be correlated.

People who score high on such scales tend to become absorbed in reading novels, listening to music, or appreciating the beauty of nature. They also tend to experience trancelike states in which they feel separated from the usual way of experiencing the world (Bowers, 1976). The ability to become deeply absorbed in experiences may develop in early childhood, for studies (J. Hilgard, 1970; 1974) indicate that highly susceptible people often have a childhood history of daydreaming and imaginary companions. Apparently, developing fantasy skills in childhood makes people open to hypnotic suggestion as adults.

The Hypnotic State

Since no single objective measure correlates with hypnotic trance and a hypnotized person shows no specific physiological changes, the status of hypnosis has not been settled. Some researchers, among them Ernest Hilgard (1975), take the position that we simply lack the appropriate measures. It has been only three decades since researchers discovered that rapid eye movements signaled a dreaming state. Until then, although personal experience testified to its uniqueness, there was no scientific evidence that classified dreaming as a discrete state of consciousness. Similarly, says Hilgard, hypnosis is a state that we can all recognize but cannot yet measure.

In the absence of psychophysiological measures of the hypnotic state, Ernest Hilgard (1977) lists the changes in behavior that hypnotists have long recognized as signs that a subject has been hypnotized. These include: increased suggestibility; enhanced imagery and imagination, including visual memories from early childhood; compliance with the hypnotist's instructions; avoidance of initiative; and the uncritical acceptance of distortions of reality. The hypnotized person firmly believes she or he is in

Table 6.1   Subjective Reports Based on an Inquiry Following Attempted Hypnosis

Inquiry	Affirmative Replies to Inquiry as Related to Hypnotic Susceptibility (Percent)*			
	High (N = 48)	Medium (N = 49)	Low (N = 45)	Slightly susceptible (N = 17)
Were you able to tell when you were hypnotized?	65	60	47	31
Any similarity to sleep?	80	77	68	50
Disinclination to act:				
to speak?	89	79	68	31
to move?	87	77	64	50
to think?	55	48	32	12
Feeling of compulsion?	48	52	20	6
Changes in size or appearance of parts of your body?	46	40	26	0
Other feelings of changes:				
of floating?	43	42	25	12
of blacking out?	28	19	7	6
of dizziness?	19	31	14	0
of spinning?	7	17	0	6
of one or more of the prior four feelings?	60	60	39	25

*Based on an inquiry following the taking of one of the two forms of the Stanford Profile Scales of Hypnotic Susceptibility, after having scored at least 4 on SHSS-A; the insusceptible are not included.

Source: From E. R. Hilgard, *Divided Consciousness: Multiple Controls in Human Thought and Action.* New York: Wiley-Interscience, 1977, Table 10, p. 164.

an altered state, and reports following attempted hypnosis show major differences in the experience of those who are highly susceptible and those who show only slight susceptibility (see Table 6.1).

However, some researchers contend that these changes do not indicate a special state of consciousness because all of them can be induced outside hypnosis. In support of this view, Theodore Barber (1965) argues that unhypnotized subjects can do all the feats attributed to hypnotized subjects, if the unhypnotized subjects are given brief instruction, urged to try hard, and assured that the tasks are easy. Under such conditions, unhypnotized subjects can become a human plank, lying rigid with no other support than one chair beneath their shoulders and another beneath their feet, or even stick needles through their hands. If Barber is correct, the existence of hypnosis as a separate state of consciousness is called into question.

Despite numerous attempts, no one has satisfactorily established the reality of hypnosis. In one study, Frank Pattie (1935) tried to induce temporary blindness in only one eye through hypnosis, setting up elaborate precautions to eliminate any fraud. After inducing hypnosis, Pattie stimulated the person's eyes in a way that

made it impossible for the subject to tell, without cheating, which eye had been stimulated. Pattie also tried to eliminate possible ways to cheat, such as blinking one eye or moving the eyes from side to side. If the supposedly blind eye was indeed blind, Pattie would have convincing evidence that hypnosis can actually block the registration of sensory impulses from the eyes.

After testing several people, Pattie did find one subject who, under hypnosis, seemed to become blind in one eye. However, an extremely subtle test showed that the woman was not blind at all. Pattie asked her to look at the top line of Figure 6.4 with a red filter over her seeing eye and a green filter over her "blind" eye. If the woman were truly blind in the green-filtered eye, she would have seen only what appeared through the red filter, as in the bottom line of Figure 6.4. But she saw the entire display. Although she failed this test, she insisted that she was indeed blind in one eye and she apparently believed that she had not cheated.

Two explanations have been advanced to account for the woman's denial. The first explanation, called neodissociation theory, claims that she was in a hypnotic state and, despite the normal physiological response of her blind eye, she was unaware of what that eye was seeing. The

Figure 6.4 The technique used by Pattie to expose a suspected cheater in an experiment on hypnotically induced blindness. The subject was required to look at a line (top) of mixed colored letters and numbers with a red filter over her "good" eye and a green filter over her "bad" eye. The effects of the red filter are shown in the bottom line. If the subject had really been blind, she would have seen only a line of distinct letters and numbers. (After Pattie, 1935.)

second explanation, called role enactment theory, contends that the woman had done a skillful job of acting out the role of a hypnotized person as she understood it.

Two Explanations: Neodissociation Theory and Role Enactment Theory

The **neodissociation theory** of hypnosis, which was proposed by Ernest Hilgard (1973; 1977), is based on the notion that consciousness depends on multiple systems (such as cognition and emotion) that are coordinated through hierarchies of control. During hypnosis, those controls shift, and the system that governs behavior during normal consciousness is no longer a part of awareness. Although information continues to be registered and processed, it is no longer represented in consciousness (E. Hilgard, 1978). Thus, the woman's insistence that she was blind in one eye—despite evidence to the contrary—was the result of a split in consciousness between her visual system and her awareness during the hypnotic state.

The **role enactment theory** holds that hypnosis is not a special state of consciousness, but is simply a special case of role playing. In this view, the person acts *as if* hypnotized, just as an actor plays a role. By establishing expectations for the subject and giving explicit instructions, the hypnotist prepares the subject for the role. During hypnosis, role expectations become more explicit as the hypnotist defines the subject's understanding of the role through increasingly explicit instructions. If the subject continues to meet the hypnotist's changing role demands, the transition to the role of hypnotized person is complete. The experiences reported by the subject are those she or he believes are appropriate for

someone under hypnosis (Sarbin and Coe, 1972). Thus, the woman's insistence that she was blind in one eye was typical of someone acting "as if" she were hypnotized. The question of whether a hypnotized subject is in a unique state of consciousness or simply role playing is also raised by the "regressive" handwriting shown in Figure 6.5.

It is impossible to reconcile these two interpretations of hypnosis, although by comparing scores on two different hypnotic susceptibility scales, Ernest Hilgard (1977) has distinguished the presence of two different groups of "susceptible" people. He suggests that one group is truly hypnotizable while the other group is highly suggestible. Whether neodissociation or role enactment provides a better explanation for hypnosis, the phenomenon is remarkable, for by trance or by suggestion people can be "set" to tolerate severe pain. But no matter how hypnosis is eventually explained, its effects make it worthy of investigation.

Figure 6.5 Signatures obtained from hypnotized subjects with eyes closed under "normal" and "regression" conditions. In the "regression" condition each subject was asked to return to the second grade. Were the subjects temporarily re-entering their past, or were they instead acting out an imagined second-grade self? A definitive answer to this question has not yet been found. (Hilgard, 1965.)

Uses and Abuses of Hypnosis

Hypnosis has been used in therapy, in medicine, and in the courtroom, and as long as its limitations are understood, it can be used profitably in all three places. The use of hypnosis in therapy or medicine primarily affects the person who is hypnotized, so any misuse has fewer consequences. But when hypnosis is used in a courtroom, it can affect the lives of other people. This broad influence makes knowledge of its limitations imperative.

In legal cases, hypnosis is used primarily to enhance memory—the memory of the defendant, whose recall might prove innocence; the memory of the victim, whose recall might identify a culprit; or the memory of the eyewitness, whose recall might establish guilt or innocence. In most cases, courts have refused to admit as evidence information gained by hypnosis, but its use by both defense and prosecution continues to grow.

Yet after reviewing both criminal and civil cases, Martin Orne (1979) urged caution in the legal use of hypnosis. He points out that people can pretend to be hypnotized and that the pretense is sometimes so skillful that it fools experts. Further, there is no guarantee that information recalled in a hypnotic trance is true. A hypnotized person is uncritical and compliant and, at the hypnotist's suggestion, obligingly fills in requested details. The problem is that many of these details are not recalled but imagined. As we shall see in Chapter 9, due to the nature of human memory, the imaginary details become thoroughly incorporated into the subject's memory, and she or he becomes convinced that they are real. For this reason, when hypnosis is used to aid in the identification of a criminal, authorities should be certain that neither the subject, the authorities themselves, nor the hypnotist has any preconceptions about the criminal's identity. If they do—and if those preconceptions are wrong—innocent people can be identified as criminals.

Orne sets forth four proposals that he believes would make the use of hypnosis in legal cases far more reliable than it is today. First, only a specially trained psychologist or psychiatrist who has received no verbal information about the case should be used as a hypnotist. Second, the entire encounter between hypnotist and subject should be videotaped so that any suggestions inadvertently implanted by the hypnotist can be detected. Third, no observer should be present during the session, because the reactions of observers to the hypnotized person's statements can shape that person's "recollections." Finally, videotapes of all interrogations should be available to check for information that might have been implanted during earlier questioning. If hypnosis is used cautiously following these suggestions, Orne believes, it can produce helpful information and any harm that might come from misinformation will be avoided.

The Self-Regulation of Consciousness

Like hypnosis, self-regulating techniques such as meditation and biofeedback have a wide range of clinical uses, from the control of pain and psychosomatic disorders to psychotherapy. Furthermore, each technique has forced us to revise our ideas about the degree of control people can exert over their own minds and bodies.

The realization that people might regulate their own consciousness led researchers to begin serious study of the practice. In an early study, investigators monitored the brain waves of a yogi (an expert practitioner of the spiritual school of yoga) as he meditated. Once the EEG tracings showed a steady flow of alpha waves coming from the yogi's brain, the experiment began. A psychologist struck a tuning fork and held it next to the yogi's ear. The unbroken stream of alpha waves indicated that the yogi's brain had not recorded the sound. Nor was there any neural response to the sound of a hand clap or the burning sensation of a hot test tube on his bare skin. The yogi's awareness seemed separated from his senses; external stimulation produced no evoked potentials (see Chapter 3; Anand, Chhina, and Singh, 1961).

Since that study was performed, other approaches to the self-regulation of consciousness have been explored in the laboratory. Techniques of self-regulation vary in the way they alter consciousness and change bodily function. In addition, because they are under the individual's control, they are different from the altered states already discussed. For example, neither changes in consciousness during sleep nor action in the hypnotic state (once the subject has voluntarily surrendered control) seems under the individual's power, but the changes involved in meditation and biofeedback are willed by the subject.

Meditation

The oldest method of self-regulation is **meditation**, a retraining of attention that induces an altered state of consciousness (Goleman, 1977). Some form of meditation is used in every major religion, including Judaism and Christianity. There are, however, two major paths to the meditative retraining of attention and each leads to a different state of consciousness, as indicated in Figure 6.1. The path of concentration described in the early experiment characterizes yoga, transcendental meditation, and sufism. In it, the mind focuses on a specific object—whether actual or mental. The path of mindfulness, in which the mind observes itself, characterizes the meditation techniques of Gurdjieff and Krishnamurti. Buddhism uses both forms of attention (Goleman, 1977).

Learning to Meditate   In concentrative meditation, the person sits quietly with eyes closed, focusing attention on one thing. When practicing transcendental meditation (TM), which the Maharishi Mahesh Yogi developed from classical Indian techniques, the object of attention is a **mantra,** a sound that the meditator chants over and over. The object of attention can take any form: short prayers (such as the early Christian *Kyrie eleison,* or "Lord have mercy"), a picture, a candle flame, a spot in the lower abdomen, a bodily sensation, or a mandala, a design constructed so that the gaze always returns to the center, as seen in Figure 6.6. During this concentrative meditation, when awareness is focused on an unchanging source of stimulation, such as a mantra or a mandala, the effect is to turn off the meditator's consciousness of the external world (Ornstein, 1977).

In mindful meditation, attention is on the body, on internal sensations, on mental states, or on the workings of the mind. In one form of **zazen,** a set of techniques used by Zen Buddhists, the meditator simply notices the normal flow of breathing, without trying to control it in any way. During mindful meditation, the object is to open up awareness by realizing the random nature of stimuli that make up reality (Goleman, 1977).

Figure 6.6   To meditate, it is necessary to empty the mind of distracting thoughts by focusing on a simple pattern or thought that will not lead to distractions. In some forms of meditation the meditator concentrates on a visual pattern such as the mandala shown here, which continually returns the gaze to its center.

Physiological Changes During Meditation   As a person meditates, body functioning changes to resemble the state of deep relaxation with its slowed metabolism. Among individuals practicing TM, oxygen consumption fell markedly, breathing and heart rates slowed, skin resistance to electrical conduction rose abruptly, and blood pressure dropped. After comparing these measures with those typical of sleep and hypnosis, the researchers (Wallace and Benson, 1972) concluded that meditation produces a state unlike either sleep or hypnosis.

The physiological changes of meditation resemble those of relaxation (Woolfolk, 1975), but the meditative state is not exactly like relaxation. A major difference lies in brain-wave patterns. Brain-wave activity shows few changes in a relaxed person, but the brain waves of a meditator may change radically. The nature of the changes depends in part on the kind of meditation being done. Alpha waves, at eight to twelve cycles per second, are normally found in large amounts only in people whose eyes are closed. However, in laboratory experiments, supplying the eyes with uniform visual input (such as that which results when halved ping pong balls are placed on the eyes) leads to a complete absence of any sense of vision. This condition is associated with bursts of alpha rhythm. In meditation, the mantra or mandala provides unchanging input and the effect on the brain is somewhat similar (Ornstein, 1977). Studies of meditators practicing TM show increased slow alpha waves (eight to nine cycles per second) along with the occasional appearance of even slower theta waves (Wallace and Benson, 1972). When Zen monks practicing zazen were tested, their EEG tracings showed alpha waves as soon as they began meditating, although their eyes were wide open (Kasamatsu and Hirai, 1966). As meditation continued, the tracings gradually shifted to theta waves—a wave not customarily seen in a person with open eyes. There is, then, solid evidence that in altering the way we respond to the world, meditation also affects physiological functioning.

Biofeedback

Scientists have been attracted to the study of meditation because meditators seem to have control over bodily processes, such as blood pressure and heart rate, that had been considered involuntary. Now, however, electronic technology has made it possible to control normally involuntary processes without meditation. By means of **biofeedback,** in which electronic devices present a continuous flow of information regarding some physiological function, many people can learn to attain voluntary control over that function (Yates, 1980). The monitored information can be in the form of lights, clicks, changes in sound volume, or displays on an oscilloscope screen (a cathode ray tube much like a television screen). Using this information, people can attempt to alter some function and discover immediately whether they have succeeded. By trial and error, some gradually learn to influence the function.

As we shall see in Chapter 21, by helping people to regulate bodily processes, biofeedback has been successfully used to treat stress-related ailments. For example, a patient who suffers from an irregular heartbeat is connected to a machine that monitors heart rate. When the heart is beating in an appropriate rhythm, an amber light glows; should it beat too slowly, a green light flashes; too quickly and a red light flashes. By attending to slight body cues associated with changes in heart rate, the patient slowly learns to keep the amber light on, thereby developing some ability to keep the heart beating within the healthy range. Biofeedback is also used routinely to treat Raynaud's syndrome, a condition in which the blood vessels of the hand become so constricted that it turns cold, and any stress makes it blue and painful. Whether the feedback is from hand temperature, blood flow, or the diameter of blood vessels, a patient may learn to regulate hand temperature and, with practice, to control the size of the blood vessels (Brown, 1980). The same general procedure—using biofeedback to learn to control a specific physiological response, then controlling it without biofeedback—has been tried successfully with numerous disorders, such as high blood pressure and chronic muscle-tension headaches. Such accomplishments indicate that active learning is going on as people gain control over these involuntary processes; yet the learners cannot say *how* they exert control, although some may say that they have put themselves into "another state of mind" (Brown, 1980).

Control through biofeedback is not easy, and some of the first claims that gained attention have been questioned—especially those in the area of alpha-wave production (Miller, 1974). It had been asserted that biofeedback training increased the production of alpha waves and led to a state of calm, blissful euphoria (e.g., Brown, 1974), but later research indicated no reliable connection between alpha-wave activity and such a subjective state (Plotkin and Cohen, 1976). In fact, other studies showed that people generate no more alpha waves through biofeedback than they do by closing their eyes and relaxing (Lynch, Paskewitz, and Orne, 1974).

The notion that alpha-wave production is primarily an indication of relaxation was supported by a study (Lindholm and Lowry, 1978) in which a computer gave members of one group false feedback about their alpha-wave rhythms. This group produced as much alpha-wave activity as did members of another group that received accurate biofeedback. Thus, the increased alpha-wave production among subjects in early studies may have been no more than the result of gradual relaxation as subjects began to feel comfortable in the experimental situation.

Although biofeedback has failed to alter consciousness when used with alpha waves, it appears to have successfully altered consciousness when providing information on theta-wave production (Budzynski, 1979). When people use biofeedback to reduce the tension of forehead muscles, some become relaxed enough to learn to produce theta waves and thus to enter the hypnagogic state that lies between reverie and sleep —a state in which EEG tracings bear some resemblance to those of the Zen Buddhists in zazen.

Although biofeedback has had little educational application, it might one day be used routinely in study. For example, while reading most people have had the experience of suddenly realizing that the words on the page before them are not registering. If a student were hooked to a biofeedback arrangement with a computer so that information was presented only when the physiological indicators of attention were present, attentional lapses in the student would be immediately followed by the disappearance of information from the display, serving notice that the student needed to refocus attention (Ornstein, 1977).

Sensory Deprivation

Meditation and biofeedback involve a kind of attention that shuts out the rest of the world and that can alter consciousness. The requirements of some occupations, such as flying intercontinental airplanes or long-distance truck driving, can have a similar effect. For example, most truckers who have driven interstate highways in the western United States have had hallucinations, some of them leading to accidents when the trucker slammed on the brakes to avoid a stalled car that existed only in his mind (Hebb, 1969). Such reports, along with the experiences of shipwrecked sailors and prisoners in solitary confinement, have led researchers to investigate the effects on human consciousness of **sensory deprivation,** in which stimulation (visual, auditory, and tactual) is sharply reduced.

Adverse Effects   The first sensory deprivation experiments indicated that the experience was completely negative (Bexton, Heron, and Scott, 1954). Male college students lay on beds in partly soundproofed cubicles, cut off from the sensory stimulation of daily life. Translucent goggles eliminated the sense of vision, the hum of fans and an air conditioner masked any meaningful sounds, and gloves and cotton cuffs eliminated tactile sensations (see Figure 6.7). After an initial period of boredom, the students became restless, irritable, and unable to concentrate. Many of them hallucinated, some seeing colors or patterns and others seeing objects or scenes (a procession of squirrels with sacks over their

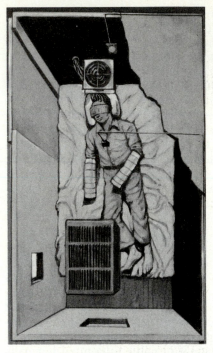

Figure 6.7   In a classic series of experiments on sensory deprivation conducted at McGill University in the 1950s, subjects were isolated in sound-resistant cubicles. Gloves and cotton cuffs prevented input to their hands and fingers; a plastic visor diffused the light coming into their eyes; a foam pillow and the continuous hum of the air conditioner and fan made input to the ears low and monotonous. Except for eating and using the bathroom, the subjects did nothing but lie on the bed. Few chose to remain longer than three days. (After Heron, 1957.)

shoulders marching across the snow). Some students lost the sense of their bodies, and one of them said, "My mind seemed to be a ball of cotton-wool floating above my body." Many students found the situation so unpleasant that they refused to continue it, and when they emerged from the cubicles, most showed a temporary disturbance of vision, handwriting, and performance on tests of intellectual functioning.

While these subjects were in the cubicles, they became susceptible to persuasion. As compared with a control group, sensorily deprived students who heard taped messages advocating a receptive attitude toward extrasensory perception (ESP) were more likely to change their attitudes toward ESP in a favorable direction. Such findings led writers to call the experience "brainwashing" and to compare it with the procedures reportedly used for "reeducation" in China. However, subsequent studies indicated that during sensory deprivation subjects are open to change only on topics that are trivial or on which the subject has formed no opinion and that highly intelligent subjects become hostile to the persuasive message (Suedfeld, 1969). Although sensory deprivation seems related to the experience of solitary confinement or to the isolation experienced by the shipwrecked sailor, it has little in common with brainwashing, in which the techniques of stimulus overload, lack of privacy, lack of sleep, and constant indoctrination are used for political reeducation (Suedfeld, 1977).

Sensory deprivation apparently leads to a hypnagogic state, whose hallucinations can be compared with the intense images most of us experience as we drift off to sleep, and it is induced by a prolonged reduction in sensory information. Sensory and cognitive changes that accompany sleep, meditation, or biofeedback are expected, and so are not regarded as threatening. But when, for example, a sensorily deprived person unexpectedly hallucinates—whether in a solitary cell, alone at sea, behind the wheel of a truck, or in a deprivation chamber—she or he may regard this normal reaction to the condition as a symptom of mental derangement and therefore find the experience frightening and unpleasant (Suedfeld, 1979).

Beneficial Effects As further studies were conducted, it became clear that the experience of sensory deprivation was not always negative and that in certain circumstances it was even beneficial. The stress of sensory-deprivation experiments indeed appears to be in part the result of the subject's expectations. Whether the experiment is carried out under conditions similar to those used in the first experiment or whether the subject is "tanked"—immersed in a tank of highly saline, buoyant water in a dark, soundproofed room—some people find the experience highly unpleasant, but most find it neutral and some find it highly pleasant and ask to repeat it (Suedfeld, 1977). In early studies, subjects were led to expect that the situation might be unpleasant or even harmful, because they were given medical release forms to sign and "panic buttons" to push if the situation became too stressful. When people go through such preliminaries and are then simply placed in a normally lighted room by themselves for a few hours, they find the experience much more stressful than people who undergo the same isolation without preliminary

warnings (Orne and Scheibe, 1964). Those who adapt well to sensory deprivation seem to be the ones who relax and enjoy the sensations instead of becoming anxious. Because sensory deprivation increases most people's acceptance of persuasion, it has been used with all kinds of psychotherapy, in the treatment of phobias, and to help people stop smoking (Suedfeld, 1977). For example, after a few days of sensory deprivation, some psychiatric patients relate better to their psychiatrists, and their self-image, contact with reality, and social interaction improve.

Drug-Altered Consciousness

Changes in consciousness also follow the ingestion of **drugs,** which may be defined as any inorganic substance that can interact with a biological system (Iversen and Iversen, 1975). Accordingly, almost all of us use drugs, since this definition encompasses such substances as aspirin, antibiotics, and vitamins. In relation to consciousness, however, only **psychoactive drugs,** or drugs that interact with the central nervous system to alter mood, perception, and behavior, are of interest. As we saw in Chapter 3, chemicals have profound effects on behavior, and each drug that changes the chemistry of the brain induces a distinctive state of consciousness (Goleman and Davidson, 1979). Among the psychoactive drugs are such commonplace substances as the caffeine in coffee and most soft drinks as well as such powerful substances as marijuana, alcohol, amphetamines, and LSD that sharply alter consciousness.

Psychoactive drugs are beneficial when used to treat physical or psychological disorders and detrimental when they create addiction. But our interest lies in those psychoactive drugs that are intentionally taken to change mood or thought or to alter consciousness.

The Effects of Certain Drugs on Consciousness

Since 90 percent of the drugs used in the 1970s were not even known during the 1960s, it is highly probable that new varieties of consciousness-altering drugs will continue to appear (Combs, Hales, and Williams, 1980). At present, caffeine and nicotine, which stimulate the central nervous system; alcohol, which depresses the central nervous system; and marijuana are the drugs most commonly used to alter consciousness in the United States.

Marijuana   Marijuana has a long history of use in Eastern societies and is an accepted psychoactive drug in some cultures that forbid the use of alcohol. Only within the past two decades has it become widely used in the United States, although it has been common among various subcultures. For example, jazz musicians have customarily been extensive users. Since the 1960s, marijuana has become so popular that, according to government figures, about one out of every seven Americans over the age of fifteen uses it in any given week.

The consciousness-altering agent in marijuana is tetrahydrocannabinol (THC), a complex molecule that occurs naturally in three varieties of wild hemp, or cannabis. The plant can be dried to produce marijuana or the resin exuded by the flowers of the female plants can be used to make hashish, a gummy powder that is up to ten times as concentrated as marijuana. Although marijuana and hashish are generally smoked, both can be mixed with food.

The effects of THC vary from person to person and appear to be heavily influenced by the setting in which the drug is taken. However, regular users generally agree as to marijuana's effects (Tart, 1970). The drug appears to heighten most sensory experiences: music sounds fuller, colors are brighter, smells are richer, food tastes better, and sexual sensations are more intense. A person taking the drug becomes euphoric and may find new meaning in the world or a profundity in mundane events. The sense of time is greatly distorted. A short sequence of events may seem to last for hours. An ordinary object may seem so beautiful and compelling that the user sits and stares at it for a very long time. A short phrase of music may seem to last so long that it becomes isolated from the rest of the composition and the hearer perceives it as never before.

There is also a negative side to marijuana: it can heighten unpleasant experiences. The drug may intensify an already frightened or depressed mood until the user experiences acute anxiety accompanied by paranoid thoughts and may believe that she or he is ill, dying, or going insane.

This effect is most likely to appear in an inexperienced user who takes an extremely heavy dose and is unprepared for its effects (Grinspoon, 1977). Cases have been reported in which already unstable people who used marijuana developed psychological disturbances.

Although anecdotal accounts of marijuana's effects are plentiful, there was no well-controlled research on the drug until the late 1960s. One of these early experiments studied college students, some of them experienced users and others who had never used the drug. All the experienced users but only one of the inexperienced participants got "high" (reported the typical euphoria). None of the experienced users but all the inexperienced subjects showed impaired intellectual and motor skills (Weil, Zinberg, and Nelsen, 1968). However, other studies have found that reaction time, attention, time estimation, motor coordination, and driving skills are generally impaired by marijuana but that experienced users appear to be able to "come down" when necessary to carry out a task (Grinspoon, 1977). One consistent finding is that marijuana appears to interfere with some aspects of memory. The storage of information for later recall seems to be disrupted whether marijuana is eaten in brownies or smoked, and when users smoke it they may find that they cannot recall information that they have been given only a few seconds previously (Loftus, 1980). This effect has been measured by asking intoxicated subjects to recall information that has just been learned (Darley et al., 1973; Casswell and Marks, 1978). Practice in focusing attention may, however, enable a "stoned" user to remember nearly as well as when sober, because when people smoke marijuana every day for a month in laboratory studies, their memory at first declines and then improves (Dornbush, 1974).

Although some studies claim to find brain damage, fetal malformation, or intellectual impairment from chronic marijuana use, careful examination has found no convincing evidence that habitual use causes such permanent damage (Grinspoon, 1977). The first study (Schaeffer, Andrysiak, and Ungerleider, 1981) of long-term use among Americans found no cognitive effects after more than seven years of extremely heavy use. Intellectual functioning among these ten adults was above average and virtually identical with that shown in tests they had taken fifteen to twenty years previously.

However, a report commissioned by the Institute of Medicine (1982) indicates that chronic marijuana use may affect the lungs. Since marijuana smoke contains about 50 percent more carcinogenic hydrocarbon than does tobacco smoke and since laboratory exposure of human lung cells to marijuana smoke produces changes that are characteristic of early cancer, health authorities are concerned that heavy, prolonged marijuana use could lead to lung cancer. There also appears to be a mild, temporary effect on the body's immune system so that users might be more susceptible to infection. The amotivational syndrome (apathy, loss of ambition, difficulty in concentrating) does exist among marijuana smokers, but there is some indication that it may be primarily an accentuation of existing behavior (Maugh, 1982).

Stimulants   Drugs that stimulate the central nervous system increase heart rate, blood pressure, and muscle tension. The heart contracts more strongly, blood vessels constrict, the bronchial tubes and the pupils of the eyes dilate, and the adrenal glands go into action (Combs, Hales, and Williams, 1980). The major **stimulants** used to alter consciousness are nicotine, caffeine, cocaine, and amphetamines.

The arousal of the central nervous system by cigarette smoking, the commonest method of nicotine ingestion, is accompanied by a reduction in the amount of alpha-wave production and an increase in the speed of the remaining alpha waves—just the opposite of meditation. EEGs of smokers also show increased high-frequency beta-wave activity. These EEG changes are reversed when users stop smoking, and nicotine withdrawal is often followed by depression, irritation, anxiety, tension, restlessness, drowsiness, and an inability to concentrate. Nicotine-related EEG changes are reflected in behavior: chronic smokers often have trouble sleeping. Studies in the sleep laboratory show that it takes smokers longer than nonsmokers to fall asleep. When smokers abruptly give up nicotine, they immediately begin to sleep better, despite the discomfort that follows the withdrawal of the drug (Soldatos et al., 1980).

Caffeine, another central nervous system stimulant, is found in tea, soft drinks, chocolate, and cocoa, but the commonest source is coffee. Unlike many drugs, which are associated with recreation, caffeine is associated with work. Since it increases alertness and reaction time, most users

feel that it improves their daily performance. Excessive doses of caffeine can lead to restlessness, irritability, and sleep disturbance, and abrupt withdrawal from the drug is often followed by headaches and depression.

Cocaine, a product of the leaves of certain coca plants, is a potent stimulant that is usually taken in the form of a white powder. When it is inhaled, or "snorted," into the nostrils, cocaine is absorbed into the bloodstream through the mucous membranes. It may also be injected intravenously. Cocaine was once an ingredient of Coca-Cola, which was originally sold as an invigorating tonic. Today, although cocaine is both illegal and expensive, it has become popular as a recreational drug among the upper-middle class.

Most of the information we have on the effects of cocaine comes from interviews of users (Grinspoon and Bakalar, 1976). One of the few laboratory studies (Resnick, Kestenbaum, and Schwartz, 1977) of the drug indicated that a moderate dose produces a euphoria that can last more than half an hour. Users claim that it improves attention, reaction time, and speed in simple mental tasks, and sharpens memory; they find it helpful for work that requires alertness and a free flow of associations. It also appears to suppress boredom and fatigue. Because of their euphoria, people who have taken cocaine often overestimate both their own capacities and the quality of their work. Because cocaine is a stimulant, it produces a burst of energy, but when the drug wears off, physical exhaustion, anxiety, and depression may follow (Resnick, Kestenbaum, and Schwartz, 1977).

Long-term use or large doses of cocaine can have harsher effects. Repeated use can irreversibly damage the mucous membranes of the nasal septum, which separates the nostrils. Chronic use can also result in a general poisoning of the system, characterized by mental deterioration, weight loss, agitation, and paranoia. Taken in large doses, cocaine can produce hallucinations, especially the conviction that bugs are crawling beneath the skin. This hallucination may be the result of hyperactivity of nerves in the skin that is induced by the drug. When cocaine is injected in extremely large doses, it can cause headaches, hyperventilation, nausea, convulsions, coma, or even death.

Amphetamines, generally called "speed," are synthetic drugs. In moderate doses they produce euphoria and energy, increase alertness, and improve reaction time and physical coordination. Anxiety and irritability often accompany the use of amphetamines, but the real danger is amphetamine psychosis, which produces a condition nearly indistinguishable from schizophrenia. For the user to reach a "high," doses of amphetamines must be continually increased, and users may switch from pills to intravenous injections, each containing the amphetamines normally found in about twenty pills. The addict, or "speed freak," injects the drug every three to four hours over a period of nearly a week, then "crashes" and sleeps for several days. Awakening is accompanied by acute hunger and a depression that responds only to more amphetamines. While such massive doses of amphetamines are being taken, amphetamine psychosis may appear. This condition is characterized by paranoia and the compulsive repetition of trivial behavior—for example, one adolescent spent hours counting cornflakes (Snyder, 1979).

Amphetamine psychosis can probably be traced to the drug's chemical structure. Because amphetamines resemble certain neurotransmitters, they causes these transmitters to build up around nerve endings, leading them to fire again and again and exaggerating behavior that is governed by that part of the nervous system where the transmitters function (Snyder, 1979). The resemblance between such amphetamine-produced behavior and the behavior of schizophrenics may provide clues that will enable researchers to untangle the genetic, chemical, and environmental causes of schizophrenia and perhaps lead to a way of preventing or curing this serious mental disorder.

Depressants **Depressants** retard the action of the central nervous system, so that neurons fire more slowly. In small doses they produce intoxication and euphoria, but they also decrease alertness, reaction time, and motor coordination. Large doses produce slurred speech, unsteadiness, and unconsciousness. The major depressants are alcohol, barbiturates (often known as "reds," "yellow jackets," or "blues"), and tranquilizers, such as Librium or Valium. When taken together, depressants are **synergistic**— that is, the effect of two depressants is greater than the sum of the two drugs' effects. For example, if alcohol is drunk with a barbiturate, the effect is four times (not twice) as great as that of either of the drugs taken alone (Combs, Hales, and Williams, 1980).

The initial effects of alcohol, the most commonly used depressant, depend upon the mood of the drinker and the setting and may be euphoric or depressing. A couple of drinks often produce a sense of relaxation and well-being, lightheadedness, and a release of inhibitions. Since the depressive influence of alcohol affects inhibitory centers of the brain, people using alcohol often say or do things they ordinarily would not. Alcohol also affects memory, impairing the ability to process and store new information, although it has a minimal effect on the ability to recall old information while intoxicated (Loftus, 1980). This effect on information storage is stronger when a person is becoming intoxicated than when she or he is beginning to recover from the peak period of intoxication.

The long-term effects of alcohol on memory and information processing depend upon how much alcohol is generally drunk at a time, not upon the total amount consumed over the years. People whose drinking patterns show heavy inebriation on widely separated occasions are more likely to show intellectual impairment than people who spread the same amount of alcohol over longer periods of time. Apparently the brain can handle a drink each day better than it can handle seven drinks on one day followed by six days' abstinence (Parker and Noble, 1977).

Memory blackouts, occasions when the drinker sobers up and cannot remember what happened the night before, are most common among chronic alcoholics but are sometimes experienced by social drinkers. Blackouts seem most likely to occur when the drinker gulps a lot of alcohol quickly, is extremely tired, or takes another depressant while drinking (Loftus, 1980).

Hallucinogens **Hallucinogens**—which get their name from their ability to produce hallucinations—have been used to alter consciousness from the beginnings of recorded history (Schultes, 1976). Because some people believe these drugs demonstrate the potential for an expansion of human consciousness, they are also called "psychedelic," or "mind-manifesting."

Hallucinogens are found in many common plants, including belladonna, henbane, mandrake, datura (Jimson weed), morning glory, peyote cactus, some mushrooms, and cannabis.

Although one or two drinks may produce a state of pleasant relaxation and light-headedness, consuming a large amount of alcohol—particularly at one sitting—can result in memory impairment.

Synthetic hallucinogens include lysergic acid diethylamide (LSD) and phencyclidine (PCP). Although the precise effect of these chemicals on the brain is unknown, some appear to mimic the activity of neurotransmitters and thus alter the activity of brain cells.

Mescaline, which comes from the peyote cactus, is used by the Native American Church of North America in its religious rituals. The drug produces vivid hallucinations and its effects were carefully described by the British writer Aldous Huxley (1979), who believed that mescaline opened "the doors of perception." Huxley found that his visual perceptions were intensified while under the drug's influence—a small bouquet of flowers became a miracle "shining with their own inner light" and full of the significance of all existence. As visual impressions were heightened for Huxley, place, time, and distance lost all interest and meaning. Afterward Huxley speculated that a major effect of mescaline might be to open up the central nervous system to experience, allowing all the sensations that are generally filtered out by the nervous system to reach awareness—a situation that would overwhelm us during waking consciousness.

One of the synthetic hallucinogens, PCP, or "angel dust," may be taken by mouth, smoked along with marijuana, snorted, or injected. In low doses it produces hallucinations, but in large doses it can produce stupor, coma, or death.

The other major synthetic hallucinogen, LSD, is one of the most powerful drugs known. Extensive studies have indicated that it is 4,000 times stronger than mescaline. After taking an average dose (100 to 300 micrograms), the user embarks on a "trip" that lasts from six to fourteen hours.

An LSD trip is unpredictable because the situation in which the drug is taken, and the user's initial mood, beliefs, and expectations of the drug's effect have a powerful influence on the experience, which can be euphoric or terrifying. Since the drug affects mood, the user may go through a series of intense moods that shift rapidly. Perceptual hallucinations are common and generally start with simple geometric forms, which change to complex images and then to dreamlike scenes (Siegel, 1977). Distortions in perception may be so pronounced as to make familiar objects unrecognizable. A wall, for example, may seem to pulsate, breathe, or even melt. Sensory impressions become crossed, so that the user may claim to "see" sounds and "hear" sights. The self may seem to split into one being who observes and another who feels. Time may speed up or stretch out interminably. As with marijuana and mescaline use, a single stimulus may catch the attention and absorb the user for hours.

LSD can have unpleasant side effects; the most common are panic reactions, and they can be terrifying. Panic usually develops among users who try to ignore or shake off the sensations produced by the drug and discover that it is impossible to do so. When the panic is severe, medical attention may be required.

Researchers have found LSD helpful in their study of the brain's biochemical functioning. The chemical structure of the LSD molecule is related to serotonin, a neurotransmitter that may play an important role in the regulation of sleep and emotion. LSD appears to block the effects of **serotonin** on brain tissue, perhaps by mimicking the neurotransmitter at the neural receptors. This blocking effect may account for some of LSD's effects on behavior, but exactly how the drug works is not known (Iverson, 1979).

Extrasensory Perception

Extrasensory perception (ESP) refers to the reception of knowledge about the environment that does not arrive through a known sensory channel, and the study of ESP is called **parapsychology** ("beyond psychology")—the psychology of events that go beyond what is considered possible. Some parapsychologists are convinced that extrasensory abilities exist and propose that their occurrence is linked with altered states of consciousness (Shapin and Coly, 1978).

Studies in which instances of ESP seem to have appeared indicate that the same experimental procedures that induce such altered states as meditation, hypnosis, and dreaming are associated with the presence of ESP (Tart, 1978). It has been proposed that the appearance of ESP during sleep or hypnosis, for example, is not the result of being in another state of consciousness but the result of the change in awareness, and that ESP abilities are most likely to be present during large and rapid shifts in consciousness (Parker, 1975). For that reason, a great deal of interest in states during which the processing of sensory information is altered has been developed among parapsychologists.

Three forms of ESP are generally considered: telepathy, precognition, and clairvoyance. **Telepathy**, or mind reading, refers to the transference of thought from one person to another. **Precognition** refers to the ability to see the future. And **clairvoyance** involves the knowledge of events not detectable by normal senses. A clairvoyant person could, for example, sense the suit and number of a card sealed in an envelope. Telepathy and clairvoyance are hard to separate and for that reason are generally studied together. For example, the person who correctly identified the card sealed in the envelope might have been using clairvoyance or might have relied on telepathy, reading the mind of the person who placed the card in the envelope. Finally, a paranormal phenomenon that is related to ESP is **psychokinesis (PK),** the ability to move objects without touching them.

The basic problem is whether ESP and PK even exist. To the extreme skeptic, they do not exist and any reported incidents can be explained by natural laws, coincidence, or trickery. To the believer, there is no doubt of the existence of ESP and PK and the explanation may contradict known scientific laws. A moderate view is that **paranormal phenomena** (phenomena outside the range of normal events) may exist although no one has yet proved that they do, and that reports should be investigated carefully because a satisfactory demonstration of ESP, followed by its explanation, could greatly increase our knowledge of human beings and of the universe.

Explanations of ESP

Many events that are reported as instances of ESP can be explained without resorting to parapsychology. For example, married couples often swear that on occasion they read each other's thoughts. Yet people who live together for years have a store of common memories, and when both think of the same topic simultaneously, the coincidence is likely to be due to some barely noticed sight or sound or smell that triggers the same memory in both minds. A car that is driven in a television drama might, for example, resemble the car owned by friends, so that when the wife says, "We ought to ask Susan and Michael over this weekend," the husband says with good reason, "I was just thinking about them."

A similar explanation was at the basis of what one psychiatrist had believed was his own extrasensory ability (Hall, 1977). It seemed that whenever the psychiatrist worried about a former patient, the patient would call within a day or so, report being upset, and ask to see him. When the psychiatrist kept careful records of his worries, he discovered that he was neither telepathic nor clairvoyant. His concerns about his former patients and their own upsets almost invariably took place on the anniversary of some event that the course of therapy had made clear was a source of great disturbance. The common memory of the earlier event was often triggered in the psychiatrist's mind by some stimulus that caused him to think of the patient. For example, his concern over one patient was initiated by a falling acorn on the anniversary of a disturbing autumn event in the life of a patient who had explicitly connected autumn, falling acorns, and his own depression while in therapy.

When attempting to account for supposedly paranormal events, we should search for the simplest possible explanation. As long as these explanations contradict the basic principles of science, most scientists will continue to regard them with skepticism. For example, Donald Hebb (1974) writes that while telepathy is not inconceivable, believers violate basic scientific laws when they say that distance makes no difference in the transmission of thoughts. In the same way, precognition violates what scientists know about time: so far, there is no scientific explanation for how someone can jump ahead to see the future and then jump back to tell about it. Psychokinesis violates what scientists know about space, since there are no known ways that an individual can move an object by sheer force of thought.

But before we can attempt to explain why supposedly paranormal events occur, we must be able to validate their occurrence. Most apparently paranormal events have few witnesses and afterward it is virtually impossible to verify them. Other problems have plagued attempts to study ESP and PK in the laboratory.

The Problem of Scientific Validation

Scientific investigations into the existence of ESP and PK have been conducted in the United States since the early 1900s. Joseph B. Rhine, the best-known researcher in the area, tried to use scientific methodology to prove the existence of ESP. For example, he tested for telepathy by having a "sender" focus on each card in a special deck, one at a time. A "receiver," locked in a distant room, stated which card the sender had turned up and was thinking about. Studies of this sort produced mixed results: some researchers found individuals who could correctly identify more cards than would be expected by chance, while other researchers could find no one who was able to do this. Ultimately, Rhine (1974) expressed his own doubts that telepathy could be verified through acceptable scientific procedures, although he never doubted the existence of the phenomenon.

The major reason that most scientists do not accept the results of experiments that support ESP or PK is the instability of the findings. A basic principle of scientific research is that one scientist should be able to replicate another scientist's results. Not only do different experiments yield contradictory findings, but the same individual seems to show ESP or PK on one day but not on the next. Proponents of ESP or PK argue that such research cannot be consistently replicated because paranormal abilities demand a friendly environment for their emergence.

However, statisticians have pointed out that despite decades of criticism, most experiments conducted in sympathetic surroundings are poorly designed, badly run, and inappropriately analyzed (Diaconis, 1978).

Although ESP may indeed be a fragile phenomenon, the inability to replicate results and the difficulty of verifying paranormal results are crucial problems. Until researchers develop a type of study that is friendly enough for the phenomenon to emerge yet so carefully controlled that the results can be analyzed with confidence, skepticism about the existence of ESP and PK will remain (Diaconis, 1978).

How do all the altered states of consciousness described in this chapter fit together? Researchers cannot agree. As noted earlier, one explanation connects the shift from one state into another with the degree of arousal, but another highly speculative suggestion is that they are all connected in some way with lateral specialization of the brain. Researchers who study dreaming suggest that waking imagery and dreaming may be processed primarily by the right cerebral hemisphere (Cohen, 1979); researchers in hypnosis suggest that highly hypnotizable people tend to rely on right-hemisphere processing of information (Bowers, 1979); and other researchers propose that meditation allows the intuitive thought of the right cerebral hemisphere to emerge (Ornstein, 1977). Researchers in biofeedback agree, suggesting that the process of theta-wave conditioning switches off the left cerebral hemisphere's critical judgment and allows right-hemisphere abilities to emerge (Budzynski, 1979), and researchers in parapsychology propose that ESP and PK are right-hemisphere skills (Ehrenwald, 1976). Whatever the connection between brain physiology and altered states of consciousness, most of the altered states do tend to have in common alpha- or theta-wave production, relaxation, and an absence of the logical information processing of daily life. At present, however, these suggestions remain at the level of conjecture, for the evidence is incomplete, inconclusive, and sometimes contradictory.

SUMMARY

1. **Consciousness** is an awareness of the thoughts, images, sensations, and emotions that flow through the mind. Consciousness is limited by the narrow range of human perceptual capacities and by the narrow extent of the mind's processing capacity. The precise nature of the connection between consciousness and brain activity has not been established,

with some neuroscientists arguing that consciousness is the total of brain activity and others proposing that the mind directs the brain's activity but that brain activity is necessary for the mind to emerge. It has also been proposed that two separate modes of consciousness coexist within each person, related to functional differences between the right and left halves of the brain. The consciousness of the left cerebral hemisphere is logical and analytic; that of the right, artistic and intuitive. The natural states of consciousness appear to lie on a continuum that consists of normal waking consciousness, **realistic fantasy, autistic fantasy**, **reverie,** the **hypnagogic state**, and sleep. Deliberately altered states of consciousness can lead to irrationality and ecstasy when the alteration arouses the nervous system, or to tranquility and meditation when the alteration lowers arousal.

2. Mental activity goes on during all or most of sleep. **Electroencephalograms (EEGs)** of the brain's electrical activity during sleep indicate four stages of sleep, each dominated by certain brain-wave frequencies, measured in cycles per second. Beta waves are the fastest, followed by alpha waves, theta waves, and delta waves. During a night's sleep, a person progresses through these four stages in a regular cyclical pattern that recurs about every ninety minutes. **REM sleep**, characterized by rapid eye movements, occurs when the brain waves indicate a return to the waking pattern (stage 1) without waking. In **non-REM (NREM) sleep**, the mind's activity consists of drifting, unstructured thoughts and images, but REM sleep is characterized by vivid dreams. The function of REM sleep is unclear, but some evidence suggests that during REM sleep the brain adapts to daily experiences.

3. Some of the content of a dream comes from stimuli near the sleeping person, but the rest is supplied by the dreamer's mind. Freud believed that the **manifest content** of a dream derives from daily events, sensations during sleep, and memories, and that the **latent content** consists of disguised unconscious wishes, primarily from early emotional conflict. Most psychoanalysts have either modified or abandoned Freud's theory of dreams. People who frequently remember dreams may waken directly from REM sleep, while those who rarely recall them may waken from NREM sleep. Some failure to recall dreams may be due to interference by slow awakening or distracted attention.

4. The difficulty of defining hypnosis except by describing the behavior of hypnotized people has caused many psychologists to doubt that hypnosis represents an altered state of consciousness. People who are highly susceptible to hypnosis tend to become deeply absorbed in reading or music and as children to develop skills in fantasy. No specific set of physiological changes has been found to correlate with the hypnotic state, but two major theories have been advanced. **Neodissociation theory** suggests that consciousness depends upon multiple systems that are coordinated in hierarchies of control; during hypnosis the controls shift and the system that normally governs behavior is no longer aware of processed stimuli. **Role enactment theory** sees hypnosis as a special case of role playing, in which the subject is guided by the hypnotist and his or her own beliefs concerning the hypnotic experience. Hypnosis is used in medicine, therapy, and the legal system, but when used in civil and criminal cases, precautions must be taken to avoid the subject's incorporation of fantasy into memory.

5. Consciousness can be self-regulated by such techniques as meditation, biofeedback, and sensory deprivation. These techniques vary in the altered states and bodily changes they can produce. **Meditation** alters consciousness by retraining attention. **Biofeedback** provides a continual flow of information about a person's physiological functioning, thereby allowing the person to learn to control the monitored function. **Sensory deprivation** alters consciousness by sharply reducing all stimulation.

6. **Psychoactive drugs** interact with the central nervous system to alter a person's mood, perception, and behavior. Marijuana enhances most sensory stimuli and can heighten both pleasant and unpleasant sensations; its effects vary with the person and the setting. **Stimulants**, including nicotine, caffeine, cocaine, and amphetamines, stimulate the central nervous system and speed up other physiological

systems. Cocaine provides energy, alertness, and feelings of confidence, but large doses or long-term use can lead to physical and psychological impairment. Amphetamines produce euphoria, energy, and alertness, but prolonged, heavy dosage can lead to amphetamine psychosis, a condition that closely resembles schizophrenia. **Depressants**, including alcohol, barbiturates, and tranquilizers, retard the action of the central nervous system. In small doses they produce euphoria as they decrease alertness, reaction time, and motor coordination; in large doses they produce unsteadiness and unconsciousness. **Hallucinogens,** such as mescaline, PCP, and LSD, produce hallucinations. Their exact chemical effects on the brain are unknown, but they may mimic the activity of certain neurotransmitters.

7. **Extrasensory perception (ESP)** refers to the reception of knowledge about the environment that does not arrive through a known sensory channel. The major forms of ESP are **telepathy,** the transference of thought from one person to another; **precognition,** the ability to see the future; and **clairvoyance,** the knowledge of events not detectable by normal senses. Related to ESP is **psychokinesis (PK),** the ability to move objects without touching them. Many events reported as instances of ESP or PK can be explained without resorting to the paranormal. Scientific investigation has failed to verify the existence of ESP and PK, primarily because of the instability of the findings, and most scientists remain skeptical of its existence.

8. It has been speculated that altered states of consciousness are connected with the functioning of the right cerebral hemisphere, but evidence for this physiological connection is incomplete, inconclusive, and sometimes contradictory.

KEY TERMS

autistic fantasy
biofeedback
clairvoyance
consciousness
depressants
drugs
electroencephalogram (EEG)
extrasensory perception (ESP)
hallucinogens
hypnagogic state

latent content of dreams
manifest content of dreams
mantra
meditation
neodissociation theory
non-REM or NREM sleep
paranormal phenomena
parapsychology
precognition
psychoactive drugs
psychokinesis (PK)

realistic fantasy
REM sleep
reverie
role enactment theory
sensory deprivation
serotonin
stimulants
synergistic
telepathy
zazen

RECOMMENDED READINGS

DEMENT, WILLIAM C. *Some Must Watch While Some Must Sleep.* San Francisco: Freeman, 1974. One of the pioneers in modern dream research presents a brief, readable, up-to-date account of what is known about sleep and dreaming. Gives special attention to the relationship between sleep and psychological disorders, including insomnia and mental illness.

HILGARD, ERNEST. *Divided Consciousness: Multiple Controls on Human Thought and Action.* New York: Wiley, 1977. A presentation of neodissociation theory, developed by Hilgard.

ORNSTEIN, R. E. *The Psychology of Consciousness.* 2nd ed. New York: Harcourt Brace Jovanovich, 1977. Introduces a wide variety of research on human consciousness. It is well written and covers a broad range of topics.

PETERSEN, ROBERT E. (ed.). *Marijuana Research Findings: 1976.* Research Monograph 14. National Institute on Drug Abuse, 1977. A broad, thorough, and objective summary of research findings on all aspects of marijuana: chemistry, behavioral effects, physiological effects. Can be obtained from the National Institute on Drug

Abuse, 11400 Rockville Pike, Rockville, Md. 20852.

RAY, OAKLEY, *Drugs, Society, and Human Behavior.* St. Louis: Mosby, 1978. A lucid, lively, and thorough presentation of drug research and the impact of "recreational" drugs on society. Includes a section on psychotherapeutic drugs.

SARBIN, THEODORE, and WILLIAM COE. *Hypnosis.* New York: Holt, Rinehart and Winston, 1972. An analysis of hypnosis from the standpoint of role theory.

TEYLER, TIMOTHY J. *Altered States of Awareness.* San Francisco: Freeman, 1972. A collection of important articles from *Scientific American* dealing with the split brain, sleep and dreaming, drugs, meditation, and sensory deprivation.

PART THREE

Learning and Cognition

A little over a year ago, I was asked to write an article about my word processor and I was forced to confess that I did not own one. I was rather embarrassed for I knew that many writers had by then switched to word processors. The magazine that asked for the article did not flinch, however. Within a couple of weeks they arranged to have a word processor, together with a printer, delivered to my home.

If I had been embarrassed before, I was now appalled.

After all, I had been using an electric typewriter for a quarter-century and I was used to it. Besides, the word processor looked formidable.

The company that manufactured it sent people to instruct me in its use and they very kindly showed me how to manipulate the material that appeared on the television screen; how to add, how to delete, how to change, how to give the machine various instructions, how to work the printer, and so on.

It all seemed very complicated.

They also handed me several instruction manuals that terrified me by their mere size and weight.

For a month thereafter I tried to learn to use the word processor, but had very little luck. I read the instruction manuals assiduously and listened to the cassettes that accompanied them, but I seemed to be getting nothing at all out of it.

I grew increasingly embarrassed. I am a grown man and, supposedly, a highly intelligent one, and yet I seemed to be an idiot at the new machine. My natural reaction was to blame the word processor and to want to call up the company and tell them to take the miserable object out of my home.

I had about made up my mind to do that, too, when one morning I sat down for my daily bout of frustration with the instrument and found, to my utter astonishment, that I could work it. All the things I had been taught, I could do. If I momentarily forgot the precise manner of signaling instructions to the machine, I could look up the needed steps in the instruction manual, which suddenly made sense.

Ever since then I have been using the word processor routinely for all final copies, and for some first drafts as well. These introductions are being written entirely on the word processor.

Naturally, I was curious. What had happened overnight that switched me from nothing to something?

It seemed mysterious, but the more I thought of it, the more it seemed to me it had happened before. When I had first put on roller skates as a small boy, for instance, I had promptly fallen down. For days I mostly fell down, but I stuck to it because I was too ashamed to quit, and then one day, I put on the skates, started off and found myself skating. I *didn't* fall down. (Well, only once in a long while.)

So it seems clear that learning is not necessarily an obvious process that you can watch at every stage. A lot of it goes on under the surface, where it simply isn't visible, and you may be making progress even when you think you aren't. And when, finally, the underbrush is cleared away—there you are!

The important thing is to stick to it.

ISAAC ASIMOV

CHAPTER 7

Perspectives on Behavior

Like all sciences, psychology seeks to discover basic uniformities and regularities. It deals with behavior not as it occurs in life but as an abstraction. In this sense, "behavior" is the sort of abstraction in psychology that "motion" is in physics. Despite all we know about the laws of motion, we cannot predict the trajectory of a particular boulder tumbling down the side of a particular mountain on a particular day. There are too many uncontrolled and unknown factors involved in the boulder's flight that we can neither evaluate nor measure. The laws of motion do not consider the sudden gust of wind that changes the boulder's course or the effect of the boulder's striking small rocks or bushes growing in its path. At present there is simply no way to evaluate every factor that might influence the boulder's trajectory.

The fundamental principles that govern behavior also disregard the many causes of variation among organisms and ignore circumstances that may affect their actions. In the *basic* study of motion, we think of objects as having only mass and velocity, and we ignore where they came from and whether these objects are made of lead or polyester. In the study of behavior, we hope that our examination of the effects of experiences on an organism's behavior will lead to a principle that applies equally to the neighbor's child, to children everywhere, and perhaps to members of similar species. We hope that

the principle has always applied in the past and that it will continue to apply in the future.

Today not very many laws of behavior can be established so firmly. We cannot expect that all principles will apply to all populations or to all situations. But some principles are basic. To discover the basic principles of any science, it is necessary to study phenomena in their most elementary forms. Thus, in the study of motion, researchers examine not boulders tumbling down a mountain, but billiard balls moving on a smooth plane. Similarly, in the study of human behavior, the difficulty—and ethical problems—involved in controlling extraneous factors leads researchers to examine behavior as it occurs in a simple form—among lower species. When we study animals, many factors that influence human behavior can be held constant. For example, the effects of language and culture are immediately excluded. Because we can raise animals in laboratories, we are able to control an animal's past experiences. Because we can breed many species in colonies, we are able to control an animal's genetic background. Finally, we can conduct studies with animals that simply could not be carried out on human beings. For instance, we could not rear a human child in total isolation or expose a person to severe stress.

From studies of animals, a basic psychological principle has emerged: behavior

155

is the result of innate (i.e., instinctive) and environmental factors working together. A newly hatched duckling will readily take to water, but a newly hatched chick will avoid it. The duck's attraction to water and chick's aversion to it are both innate predispositions and need not be learned from experience. Yet virtually all behavior is also affected by environment and experience. A hungry frog that gobbles up a bee the first time that one flies within reach quickly learns that bees should be excluded from its diet. A major purpose of this chapter is to show how hereditary and environmental factors interact to bring about some behavior that traditionally has been considered "instinctive" and other behavior that has been regarded as "learned."

The discussion that follows reviews some of the insights we have gained by studying animal behavior. It points out issues that have been clarified by such studies and the problems that arise when information about animal behavior is applied to human beings.

ronment. For example, the shape of an animal's teeth is generally related to its diet, so that meat-eating animals have teeth that are adapted to tearing flesh. In developing an evolutionary position, ethologists could rely on the evidence of fossil records when analyzing changes in form. But since there was no fossil record of function, much more imaginative approaches than excavation and classification were applied to the evolution of behavior.

Ethologists asked an important question about behavior: What is its **adaptive significance** for the animal? That is, how does an animal's behavior help it to survive and reproduce? In searching for answers, ethologists observed the way animals in their natural habitat behave in social, predatory, migratory, maternal, and other situations. Each kind of behavior was then analyzed to determine its role in the animal's and species' adaptation. Although ethologists recognized that animals do learn, their primary focus was on innate determinants of behavior.

Animal Studies: The Historical Background

Our knowledge of animal behavior is based on contributions from two disciplines: ethology and comparative psychology. These fields of study now overlap substantially, but originally they were quite different.

Ethology and Comparative Psychology

Ethology was developed by European zoologists who sought to explain animal behavior in evolutionary and physiological terms. For their principal source, they turned to Charles Darwin, who in such works as *On the Origin of Species* (1859) and *The Expression of the Emotions in Man and Animals* (1872) furnished evidence that behavioral traits evolve according to many of the same principles that govern anatomical and physiological evolution. Ethologists came to believe that certain patterns of behavior are innate, and they regarded those patterns as a product of evolution. They held that the evolution of form (body structure and physiology) and function (behavior) are interdependent and that the form and functions of any species are inherited adaptations to its envi-

Would a researcher such as the man shown here be more likely to be a comparative psychologist or an ethologist?

The focus of comparative psychology, however, was on the role of learning in behavior. Psychologists compared the behavior of different species, hoping to find certain underlying similarities that would suggest general "laws of behavior." But, unlike ethologists who studied animal behavior in natural habitats, comparative psychologists relied on laboratory experiments, in which the life histories, the early experiences, and sometimes the genetic histories of the animals were carefully controlled and examined.

This initial separation of interest was reflected both in the principal methodologies—field research versus laboratory research—and in the species they most frequently studied. Ethologists concentrated on birds, fish, and insects; comparative psychologists concentrated on rats, monkeys and human beings. Given these differences, it is not surprising that ethologists emphasized the role of instinct in animal behavior and comparative psychologists the role of learning and experience. Although at one time these different emphases were the focus of a major debate among psychologists, the interests of ethologists and comparative psychologists have tended to merge and the contributions of both views have been incorporated into general psychology (Mason and Lott, 1976).

The Nature Versus Nurture Issue

Although today it is obvious that an animal's behavior is the product of its heredity *and* environment, psychologists have not always thought so. In the early part of the twentieth century there were vigorous debates over whether certain behavior could be considered "instinctive" *or* "learned." When the issue was human behavior, the debate became heated. At one extreme were psychologists such as William McDougall (1908), who considered human behavior to be essentially instinctive. At the other extreme were psychologists such as John B. Watson (1930), who considered virtually all human behavior to be learned.

The controversy between psychologists holding one or the other of these opinions became known as the **nature versus nurture** issue. Those who held McDougall's view that there is no fundamental difference between animals and human beings argued that human behavior reflects basic natural instincts, just as the behavior of other animals can be said to reflect their instinct. Those who held Watson's view that human beings are fundamentally different from lower animals argued that human behavior is principally a product of the way the individual has been nurtured: experience with the environment is the major determinant of human behavior.

Central to the nature-nurture controversy was the problem of defining "instinct." Psychologists thought of instinctive behavior as different from reflexes on the one hand and from learned behavior on the other. Instinctive behavior was a concept used to describe patterns of unlearned, organized behavior involving the entire animal. It applied to activities, such as feeding, mating, and aggression, that serve the individual and the species. Reflexes were viewed as components of instincts, having the same relationship to instinctive behavior that the individual notes of a melody have to a musical composition. Thus, to be considered instinctive, a behavior pattern (1) had to develop even if there was no opportunity to practice it; (2) had to occur in its complete form at the earliest opportunity; (3) had to be universal among all members of the species; and (4) required specific neurophysiological processes and structures for its onset, maintenance, and inhibition.

In his classic essay "The Descent of Instinct" (1955), Frank Beach pointed out the futility of attempting to characterize animal behavior as either instinctive or learned. Using the example of nest building in the pregnant female rat, Beach pointed out that this complex behavior seems to fit the criteria for "instinctive" behavior. Pregnant female rats build nests in a standard manner the first time they become pregnant. They do so even if they have been raised in isolation, which would eliminate the opportunity to learn about nest building by watching other rats do it. However, if rats are raised from birth in cages that contain no objects they can carry, and thus have no experience in carrying things around, when they become pregnant they will not built nests, even if nesting materials are available (Lehrman, 1953). Apparently, the early experience of manipulating materials is necessary for the proper development of nesting behavior in later life.

The extreme positions of McDougall and Watson illustrate the search for basic principles of behavior. Both psychologists put forward hypotheses concerning what each thought was the fundamental process underlying behavior. Both excluded all other processes as unimportant. McDougall and Watson were both wrong—but they were also both right. They were wrong in disregarding all other processes, and they were right in underscoring the significance of the process on which each focused. But such extremism is not peculiar to psychology; in any scientific field suppositions are often tested in an extreme form, because their proponents are trying to see how much they can explain with a simple, elegant principle.

Species-Specific Behavior

Because of the problem of defining instinct, the notion has been replaced by the concept of "species-specific behavior," a concept formulated by ethologists. Instead of asking whether behavior is innate, modern psychologists try to account for both innate and environmental factors that are responsible for it. **Species-specific behavior** is considered behavior that is typical of a particular species whose members share a common genetic background and a common environment that provides similar influences and experiences. Thus, the concept of species-specific behavior integrates the two major influences on behavior.

Contemporary research in species-specific behavior often combines the field approach of ethology with the laboratory approach of comparative psychology. The analysis of singing in birds provides a good example of the way these approaches are coupled.

From field studies, we know the basic development of the song of the wild chaffinch, a member of the sparrow family. In the first nine months after it hatches, the bird progresses from producing only simple food-begging calls to singing the notes and the "syllables" that will make up its final song. But these notes and trills are not sung in any distinct order. During the tenth month a characteristic song pattern begins to form, and by the time the chaffinch is twelve months old its singing crystallizes into the specific song that the bird will sing for the rest of its life. Other field studies have found that the song is most vigorously sung during nesting season, suggesting that the song's principal function is related to identifying other members of the species and to selecting mates.

Building on these field studies, laboratory studies have demonstrated the limits of this species-specific behavior and the effects of experience on its development. W. H. Thorpe (1961) removed young chaffinches from other birds as soon as they hatched, keeping each of them isolated for a year. When the birds grew up, they did not develop the song of a mature chaffinch. However, if the young birds heard tape recordings of normal chaffinch songs during their first four months of isolation, they later developed virtually normal songs. Apparently, the early experience of hearing the chaffinch song is essential for its normal development, and the first few months of the chaffinch's life is a **sensitive period**—a relatively restricted interval during

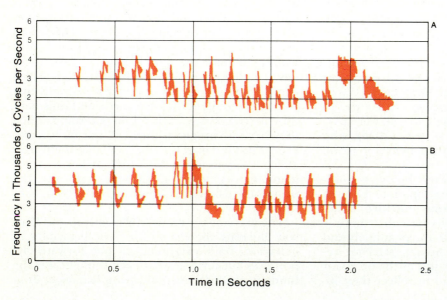

Figure 7.1 Sound spectographs of two chaffinches. (A) The song of a normal adult. (B) The song of a chaffinch reared in isolation and exposed during a sensitive period to a tape recording of a normal song spliced in such a way that the ending came in the middle. This bird's song reflects both learned and innate influences. It sings with the "splice" heard on the tape, but it also sings with the overall broadening and deepening trend of the normal song. It would not sing in this way if it were merely mimicking the tape. (After Thorpe, 1961.)

which an animal is especially susceptible to particular influences that may have lasting effects on behavior. In the case of the chaffinch, the young birds seem to "learn" the song in the early months even though they will not be able to reproduce it until months later. In further research, Thorpe found that if birds are exposed to an electronically rearranged form of the normal song, their adult song will reproduce that rearranged version, as shown in Figure 7.1. There are, however, limits on the flexibility of the song's form: chaffinches will not learn the songs of species that are very different from their own. These laboratory studies reveal the flexibility of the song within certain hereditary limits and the importance of experience in its development.

Some birds develop local dialects, so that a species' song varies distinctively from location to location. In this case, learning sharply limits a species-specific behavior: birds that sing in one dialect do not respond to birds singing in an alien dialect. For example, among the white-crowned mountain sparrows of Colorado, females respond to the male song by tilting back their heads, squatting, fluttering their wings, lifting their tail, and vocalizing. This response apparently signals the female's sexual receptivity. When juvenile and adult females heard their local song played in the laboratory, both the young and the mature birds responded with the characteristic display. But neither responded when they heard the alien dialect. Exposure to the local song during the sensitive period sensitizes the birds to their own dialect (Baker, Spitler-Nabors, and Bradley, 1981).

Factors that Influence Behavior

As the chaffinch and mountain sparrow examples illustrate, no single influence can account for a particular behavior pattern. Genes, maturation, environment, and experience interact in almost every case. By examining the roles of inheritance, environment, and learning, research into animal behavior provides insight into the particular behavior patterns of a species.

Innate Factors that Influence Behavior

The more complex a behavior, the more likely it is generally that the behavior has been acquired through experience. No one would suspect that reading and doing calculus are innate, but we would expect nursing to be an innate behavior. But innate influences are not limited to simple behavior patterns; as we shall see, some very complex achievements have been credited to innate factors. In each case, these complex patterns involve special sensory and perceptual capacities that make an organism particularly sensitive to certain aspects of the environment. This complex behavior also involves motor pat-

This bee has not accidentally alighted on this flower. Because of their sensitivity to differences in ultra-violet light, bees can discriminate between flowers that simply look white to human beings.

terns that enable the organism to act appropriately on the information it receives through its sense organs.

Sensory Capacities Animals experience the world quite differently from the way we do, and examining their sensory capacities can provide valuable insight as to how and why a certain behavior occurs. As Karl von Frisch (1950, 1967) showed in a series of experiments, honeybees find their way unerringly from distant locations back to the hive because they can perceive polarized light. This inherited perceptual ability enables them to identify the position of the sun even on overcast days and then use its position as a navigational guide as they go to and from the hive to forage for nectar, often over long distances. In addition, the bees' visual sensitivity to differences in ultraviolet light explains how they can discriminate, at a distance, between flowers that simply look white to us.

Other species rely on quite different senses. The bat locates objects in space by responding to the echoes of high-frequency sounds that it continuously emits while flying, a capability that explains how bats avoid crashing into obstacles and how they can intercept flying insects in the dark.

In the case of salmon, an unusual sense of smell enables them, after spending several years traveling thousands of miles in the ocean, to find and spawn in the stream in which they were born. Studies of the migration patterns of salmon have discovered that the fish have a sense of smell that can discriminate among subtle chemical differences in water (Hasler and Larson, 1955). Moreover, salmon can remember these differences, including the odor of the stream in which they were born. When they reach sexual maturity after several years in the ocean, salmon swim up the coast until they encounter the familiar odor of their own stream and then "follow their noses" home. When the salmon's nose is plugged up, it becomes incapable of finding its way up the proper stream or tributary. Thus homing salmon have two unusual abilities: the sensory capability to smell subtle differences in water and the ability to recognize the odor of the stream of their birth.

The fish inherit the special sensory and brain mechanisms that provide a foundation for this behavior, but there is no way to determine why such an intricate specialized mechanism evolved in the first place. We can only speculate as to why

salmon do not swim up any stream to spawn, because, as noted earlier, there are no fossil records of early behavior patterns. However, we do know that some streams dry up seasonally; others have the wrong temperature for the proper nurturing of salmon eggs; and in others the salmon are in great danger from predators. The salmon's return to the stream of its birth would appear to ensure that breeding will occur in a place where the cycle has been successful at least once before. But it is quite possible that this—and other—behavior patterns evolved by accident.

Fixed Action Patterns In addition to special sensory capacities, motor patterns also play a role in inherited behavior. Careful observation of any animal shows that much of its species-specific behavior consists of relatively stereotyped and often-repeated patterns of movements, known as **fixed action patterns.** These may range from simple behavior such as pecking to the more complex patterns of courtship. We do not know how such patterns develop because they usually appear in full form the first time they are performed. We do know, however, that these patterns are somehow "wired" into the animal's nervous system.

An animal can be made to perform fixed action patterns by stimulating its brain electrically, as research with chickens has demonstrated. When electrodes are placed at various sites in the chicken's brain stem, as shown in Figure 7.2, stimulation in some places produces one behavior pattern and stimulation in other places yields different patterns. Stimulating some areas produces simple actions—the chicken stands up or sits down or turns its head to the side. Other areas elicit more complex patterns—grooming, attack, fleeing, eating, or courtship (von Holst and von St. Paul, 1962).

By stimulating two different areas of the brain at the same time, investigators (von Holst and von St. Paul, 1962) evoked two fixed action patterns simultaneously. Stimulation of one area in the brain stem causes a chicken to stretch out its neck and flatten its feathers; stimulation of another area makes it fluff up its feathers. When both areas were stimulated simultaneously, the animal stretched out its neck and flattened its feathers; after the stimulation stopped, it fluffed its feathers. That is, the chicken showed first one fixed action pattern and then the other. In other

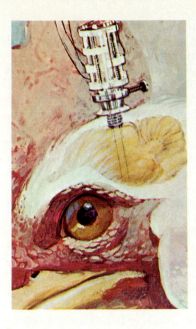

Figure 7.2 A pair of electrodes has been implanted in the brain of this chicken and is held in place by an apparatus through which electrical stimulation may be delivered.

instances, both action patterns occurred at once, as when simultaneous stimulation of the area that produces looking to the left and the area that produces sitting led the hen to sit and look to the left at the same time.

These examples of the effect of brain stimulation on fixed action patterns suggest that the behavior produced was the result of characteristic patterns of brain organization. Brain stimulation has been used to evoke species-specific behavior in other animals. Laboratory-raised cats that have never seen a rat or killed another animal will kill a rat when the appropriate part of the brain is electrically stimulated (Flynn et al., 1970). The cats display a form of attack that is almost identical to the form seen in the wild when experienced cats attack and kill prey (Berntson, Hughes, and Beattie, 1976). These observations strongly indicate that inherited brain mechanisms underlie species-specific behavior.

Selective Breeding Experiments The most compelling illustrations of heredity's role in behavior have come from the results of selectively breeding animals to accentuate particular behavioral traits. Various breeds of dogs show behavioral specialties that have been deliberately fostered during centuries of selective breeding. German shepherds have been bred to display ferocious protectiveness; retrievers have been bred to ex-

hibit a willingness and ability to retrieve such objects as game birds and rabbits.

In the laboratory, experiments with fruit flies have also shown that certain behavioral tendencies are heritable. For example, if fruit flies are put into a long glass tube that has a light at one end and is dark at the other, some of the flies will move to the light end of the tube while others will stay in the dark. Movement toward light in this situation is called **phototaxis.** Experiments have shown that phototaxis will become more prevalent in a fly population when flies that display the behavioral trait are bred together (Hirsch and Boudreau, 1958). Apparently, the difference in behavior between moving and not moving toward a light has a genetic foundation.

Similar breeding experiments have shown that some kinds of learning ability are heritable. Individual members of a species generally differ in their ability to learn. Noting this, R. C. Tryon (1940a, b) conducted a series of experiments to test whether such differences could be augmented through selective breeding. Using food as a reward, he trained a large group of rats to find their way through a complicated maze. Each rat ran the maze every day for nineteen consecutive days. The rats showed wide variations in initial learning ability, as measured by the total number of errors (wrong turns) made during the trials (see Figure 7.3). Tryon then developed two strains of rats by breeding the fastest learners together and the slowest learners together. When the offspring of the first generation matured, he trained them in the maze and again selectively bred them, bright to bright and dull to dull, repeating the process through twenty-five generations over a period of fifteen years. By the eighth generation, as shown in Figure 7.3, the two strains of rats were quite distinct in their ability to learn the maze: the brightest slow learners were about equivalent in maze performance to the dullest fast learners.

Learning ability in rats was thus shown to be heritable—at least the ability to learn mazes. Later studies (Searle, 1949) showed that the "bright" rats who learned the maze quickly were not necessarily the best learners in other situations. For example, when escape from water was the measure of learning, the "maze-dull" rats were superior. However, the experiments did clearly demonstrate that inheritance contributes to the capacity to learn in a specific situation.

Just what changes in the rats' genetic structure took place during these experiments, what genes

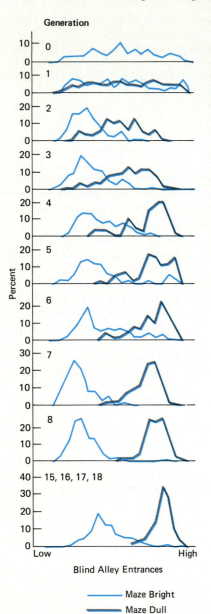

Figure 7.3
Progress of selection in rats for low and high errors in a seventeen-unit maze. By the eighth generation of selection the maze-bright and maze-dull lines were well separated, and further selection resulted in no improvement. (After Tryon, 1940c.)

were involved, and how genetic changes were transformed into psychological processes that led to differences in learning speed is unknown. The principal change might have been in perceptual acuity, the speed of response, the ability to retain spatial information, immunity to distraction, or some other factor—or combination of factors. Until we have specific knowledge of genetic changes, the question of precisely what is inherited in transmission between generations will remain open.

Although genetic effects are often difficult to establish for individuals, they are clear and important for populations, especially in the case of psychologically significant factors. The differences between individual effects and population effects are difficult to appreciate, but an effect that has minor consequences for an individual can have major consequences for a population. Suppose we were able to change intelligence by five points, so that instead of 100 the average IQ was 105. Five points in IQ is not much of a change for an individual—two IQ measures taken on the same day can easily show such a difference. And a difference so small would be unlikely to lead to differences in school performance or other manifestations of intellectual functioning. But if we examine the normal distribution of scores discussed in Chapter 2, we can easily calculate what would happen to a population if the average IQ were suddenly to change from 100 to 105. The standard deviation of IQ is 15 points, which tells us that a community of 1,000 individuals with a mean IQ of 100 would have about 22 individuals with an IQ of 130 (two standard deviations above the mean) and about 22 individuals with an IQ of 70 (two standard deviations below the mean). Individuals with an IQ of 130 or more are likely to benefit the community in a number of ways, but individuals with an IQ of 70 must be cared for and are a burden. If the mean IQ of this same community changed from 100 to 105, the number of very able people (IQ 130 or above) would suddenly increase from 22 to 50. At the same time, the number of members who require special assistance would shrink from 22 to 11. A pool of 50 very able people is likely to develop many more new inventions, creative products, or ingenious solutions to social and technical problems than a pool of only 22. And when the number of people whose mental maturity is so low they must be cared for drops from 22 to 11, the costs and burden to the community are greatly reduced. Thus, what may be a negligible difference at the level of the individual becomes an enormous difference at the level of the population—talent doubles and the proportion of mentally deficient is halved.

Environmental Stimuli

Behavioral scientists have long understood that specific stimuli in the environment often seem to serve as signals for fixed action patterns as well

Motionless, this tick is waiting for a meal. Only the distinctive odor of a mammal's skin glands leads the tick to fall off its leaf and onto its host.

as for more complex kinds of behavior. In fact, such stimuli determine whether or not the behavior will occur at all.

Sign Stimuli   The role of a specific stimulus is especially apparent in the behavior of the hungry female tick, which climbs into the branches of a bush and waits for weeks, if necessary, for a mammal to pass directly beneath her (von Uexküll, 1921). As she waits, the tick seems unresponsive to the barrage of sights, sounds, and odors about her. Only one stimulus will elicit a response: the distinctive odor of a mammal's skin glands (caused by butyric acid). Its detection signals an approaching meal and stimulates the tick to drop onto her host. The odor is considered a **sign stimulus,** because it released the fixed action pattern of feeding in the tick.

Sometimes it is the size of the stimulus that releases the response. Niko Tinbergen (1961) reported that herring gulls, offered an egg several times larger than one of their own eggs, prefer the larger egg—even when it is so large that the bird cannot assume a normal brooding position, as shown in the accompanying photograph.

Color is the key element in many sign stimuli. The red underside of several species serves as a sign stimulus to its predators or enemies. Red breast feathers on another bird, for example, are a sign stimulus that encourages attack by a male robin protecting its territory. Tinbergen (1952) found that the male stickleback fish will attack a crude model of another stickleback if the model has a red belly—regardless of the model's shape. Thus, the stickleback ignores models that seem fishlike to human beings, but quickly attacks models that seem unfishlike but have a red underside (see Figure 7.4).

Innate Releasers or Novel Experience?   Because the male stickleback acquires its brilliant red belly during mating, Tinbergen (1952) proposed that stickleback attacks against red targets are a manifestation of "reproductive aggression": the attacks serve to distribute the stickleback population more efficiently over their habitat, reducing crowding and overexploitation of resources. Subsequent research has found, however, that stickleback aggression is restricted neither to

A herring gull attempting to brood an egg many times the size of the egg it lays. For this species and for a number of other birds, size is a key element of the sign stimulus that elicits brooding behavior.

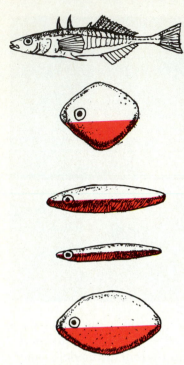

Figure 7.4 Tinbergen found that a male stickleback will attack any of the bottom four of these models before it will attack the top one, which closely resembles a stickleback in everything but the red belly. The red belly acquired by male sticklebacks during the mating season is a sign for attack that outweighs all other stimuli.

fishlike objects nor to the color red. The red belly of the stickleback and its brilliant emerald eyes appear only *after* the fish has constructed its nest. Yet a great deal of aggression among male sticklebacks takes place when nesting territories are being chosen and while the fish's belly is still gray. In a series of experiments (Muckensturm, 1969), male sticklebacks saw fishlike plastic targets with bellies of various colors—yellow, red, violet, and gray. The red-bellied models were attacked less often than the violet- or yellow-bellied models, despite the fact that there is no yellow at all in the stickleback's environment. It appears that what was originally considered reproductive aggression is aggression directed toward novelty. Most animals react to novelty in two ways: if the new stimulus is overpowering, the animal flees, seeking shelter; if the stimulus moves slowly, is not noisy, and looks manageable, the animal attacks. Other studies revealed that the stickleback's aggression toward red targets decreases markedly with experience, showing again how genetic, environmental, and experimental factors combine to control complex patterns of behavior.

The study of stickleback aggression was part of research on what were called **innate releasers,** or specific stimuli in the environment of a given species that release a chain of behavior with sub-

stantial adaptive value. It was believed that the tendency to respond to these releasers had evolved through natural selection and that it eventually became an innate neural mechanism. The red belly of the stickleback at first appeared to be such an innate releaser, but no neural process related to the aggressive response to red stimuli was ever discovered. And since the attacks declined with familiarization, the innate character of the response is questionable.

An innate releaser dependent on the shape of the stimulus was proposed by Konrad Lorenz (1939) and Tinbergen (1951). It appeared that chicks and ducklings reacted with fear to overhead shapes resembling birds of prey. Researchers suspended a cardboard shape, such as the one in Figure 7.5, on a wire a few feet above the young fowl and moved the shape back and forth. When the shape was moved in a direction that made it resemble a goose (long neck), the chicks and ducklings were quite calm. But when the shape was moved in the opposite direction, so that it resembled a bird of prey (short neck), the young birds reacted with fear. Since the experiment was performed on very young animals, their reaction to bird shape appeared to develop without any prior experience. Thus, the ethologists believed they had found a complex behavior pattern with clear adaptive value that was released by a specific stimulus configuration.

Subsequent research has shown, however, that the major factor in the birds' panic was neither the shape nor the direction of movement but, once again, its novelty. Birds bred in a laboratory under controlled conditions and deprived of any experience with the shape reacted with fear to both movements (Hirsch, Lindley, and Tolman, 1955). As the birds became accustomed to the movements, they stopped showing fear of the shape's movements in either direction. Other research indicates that with experience, young birds lose their fear even of a live hawk (Martin and Melvin, 1964).

These results contradict the view that the short-necked shape was an innate releaser and they also damage the hypothesis that the behavior pattern evolved through natural selection. If this were the case, the birds would not adapt to the shape. On the contrary, birds would have to retain their fear of a hawk even after they had repeatedly escaped from its claws. In every case, however, the birds reacted with fear when confronted with a novel stimulus (Melzack, Penick, and Beckett, 1959).

Social Interaction and Sex Change: A Fish Story

One of the clearest interactions between overt adaptive behavior and biological processes appears in fish that live among the coral reefs off the Philippine Islands. If the proportion of males drops among this species *(Anthias squamipinnis),* enough females will become male— changing their exterior sex, their color, their gonads, and their behavior—to restore the sexual composition of the group. When such fish are examined, they contain testes but evidence of the former ovaries is also present.

In an effort to discover what causes the sex change, a researcher (Shapiro, 1980) studied twenty-six groups of fish, in which the typical group contained about ten males and sixty females. The social groups of this fish vary in size, but there are always more females than males. One male was removed from each control group and three to nine males from each experimental group.

Because the color of males and females in this species is so different, the sex reversal can be followed simply by observing the alteration in color. In the typical control group, one of the females began changing her sex on about the third day after the single male was removed. In the experimental groups, the females began to change their sex on about the fifth day after the males were removed. A total of fifty-eight males were removed from the experimental groups, and fifty-seven females changed their sex. But when several males were removed from a group, not all the females changed their sex at once. Instead, first one female would begin the reversal, then approximately two days later another female would start to change.

The researcher speculates that several social mechanisms are involved in this one-to-one sex change. First, the large groups of fish may be composed of smaller groups, each containing one male and several females, and the smaller groups form a social hierarchy within the large group. Since interaction within each small group is determined by its ranking, the spacing of the female's reversal would be determined by the relative rank of her own group. The ranking of females within the small groups may also play a part. This female hierarchy could either suppress or enhance the process of sex reversal. When the first female begins to change her sex, she may interact with a lower ranked female in such a way as to suppress the onset of the lower-ranked fish's change by approximately two days. Alternatively, the second female to change sex may depend upon some kind of interaction with the first female to trigger her own change—an interaction that may require several days. Whatever combination of social interaction is involved, it produces a powerful biological effect and maintains the sexual composition of the group.

Goose →

← Hawk

Figure 7.5 A typical shape used in studies of innate fear releasers in young precocial birds, such as goslings, chicks, turkeys, quail, and ducklings.

Sequential Stimuli By determining which stimuli appear to be most closely associated with the onset of behavior, we can begin to gain some insight into such complex behavioral patterns as the northward flight of some birds in spring. These seasonal migrations are examples of patterns of behavior that depend on **sequential stimuli**, or a chain of environmental stimuli that is required to trigger the behavior. The spring migration of some species of snowbirds and crows apparently depends upon the gradual lengthening of the day as spring approaches. This was demonstrated by capturing a number of these birds and placing them in a room with artificial illumination. When the birds received gradually increasing amounts of light, mimicking the lengthening of daylight as spring draws near, they tended to fly north when released, even in the dead of winter. If they received gradually decreasing amounts of light, as occurs with the approach of winter, the birds tended to fly south when released (Rowan, 1931). Apparently, increases and decreases in the amount of light are sequential stimuli that determine migratory flight in these birds.

The chain of stimuli leading to a behavior like reproduction can be quite a long one, as studies of ring doves have shown (Lehrman, 1964). Each step in the process—courting, mating, nest building, and caring for the young—occurs only in response to distinctive stimuli. These stimuli provoke hormonal changes in the birds, and the hormonal changes in turn produce behavioral changes that serve as some of the stimuli for the next link in the chain.

Learning

One fruitful way to study species-specific behavior is to observe its development in animals (especially those that are young). In this way, we have discovered that (1) the ability of an animal to acquire certain behavior patterns is itself species-specific to some degree; and (2) much species-specific behavior must be learned.

Species-Specific Learning Animals vary considerably in their learning capacities and in the flexibility they bring to bear on a new situation. Some species learn one behavior pattern readily, yet are extremely inflexible when the situation demands a new pattern. As Tinbergen (1951) observed, the hunting wasp digs a nest, flies once or twice around the site, then heads off and ranges widely in search of food. The wasp easily finds its way back to the nest. The wasp obviously learns landmarks rapidly. If those landmarks are moved a little, however, as shown in Figure 7.6, the wasp becomes hopelessly disoriented and cannot find the nest, even if it is in plain view.

It is not always clear just what animals learn when they become acquainted with a given environment. Do they acquire territorial "maps," based simply on what they see (or smell), or do they relate their own movements to the world as they learn to move about? Some insight into this question was gained by a study in which kittens

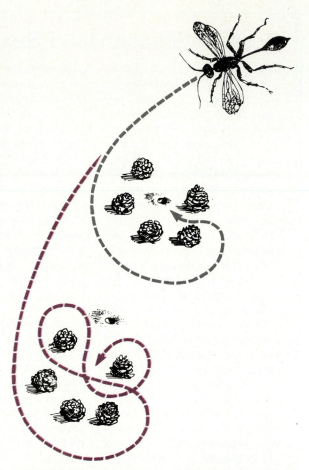

Figure 7.6   The hunting wasp's ability to find its way back to its nest is an example of a behavior that depends on both learning and inherited capacities. The gray dotted line shows that the wasp can locate the nest unerringly once it has learned the nest's position. Apparently, the wasp uses the four surrounding clumps of vegetation as navigational landmarks, for when these clumps are moved slightly to one side the wasp behaves as if the nest were still in the middle (purple dotted line). The learning the wasp displays here is therefore quite rigid. The animal is totally lost even though the nest is only a short distance away.

were reared in darkness from birth, then allowed to explore a lighted environment (Held and Hein, 1963). Half the animals explored the space on their own, whereas the rest were wheeled about in a cart. Kittens that were free to walk about and explore appeared to become familiar with the new space more rapidly and more extensively than those who were passive explorers, although both groups were exposed to the same area for the same length of time.

An animal's ability to learn relationships is related to its particular sensory or motor capabilities. Rats, for example, readily learn to solve complex problems involving odor discrimination; by comparison they do poorly when they try to solve the same problem by sight.

Some kinds of learning based on the senses can be powerful and yet limited. For example, the ability to learn through taste is very powerful in rats. Rats who eat a small amount of distinctively flavored toxic food thereafter avoid that food, even though several hours elapse between food intake and their illness. A series of experiments by John Garcia and his colleagues (1966; 1972; 1974) have shown that rats also make this association when the illness is caused not by the food but by a drug or X-rays administered several hours after the ingestion of the flavored food. This learning can take place even if the animal is unable to connect its internal state to any specific environmental source. In one study (Garcia and Rusiniak, 1980), the investigators anesthetized rats after they ate and administered the toxic substance while the animals were unconscious. On later occasions the rats still avoided the food. However, the resulting food aversion is limited to novel foods; if rats become ill after eating a familiar food, they will continue to eat that food.

Other studies (Braun and McIntosh, 1973) have shown that rats that experience motion sickness when rotated on a turntable after drinking distinctively flavored water "blamed" the sickness on the flavored water rather than on the dizzying rotation. Learning the relationship between taste and illness is much more powerful in rats than learning relationships between other kinds of sensory events. For example, although rats associate a light or tone with a shock to the feet, the connection between the events must be close. If there is a delay of even a few minutes between the tone and the shock, rats will not learn to associate them.

Sea and air sickness in human beings may be related to the same phenomenon that results in taste aversion among rats. Certain toxic plants, when eaten, produce semihallucinatory states accompanied by unstable visions: the horizon seems to move and rock. If the plant is eaten, it will kill the organism within hours unless the food is vomited or the stomach is pumped. It has been proposed that, in protecting themselves

against these effects, human beings evolved a tendency to vomit whenever the horizon seemed to rock (Treisman, 1980). But the horizon also rocks when we are on a ship or in an airplane, something that early evolution could not have anticipated. Thus, a response that protected early human beings against poison plants that have vanished from today's diet has become an annoying vestigial effect.

Imprinting   As the discussion of species-specific behavior indicated, early exposure is sometimes necessary for a behavior pattern to develop in its mature form. Chaffinches will produce an abnormal song if they are prevented from hearing other members of their species during a sensitive period in the first few months of life. Research with other animals indicates that sensitive periods occur in the lives of a number of species, when they are especially susceptible to certain kinds of learning. The classic example of a sensitive period is the phenomenon of **imprinting**, the process by which some species of birds and mammals form early social attachments. Konrad Lorenz (1965) first found that a newly hatched duckling or gosling will form an attachment, or "imprint," to the first moving object it encounters and will then follow the object. In the wild that first object is usually the bird's mother. In the laboratory the newly hatched bird can be exposed to other objects and become imprinted inappropriately, learning to follow a human being (see the accompanying photograph), a box on wheels, or a bird of a different species.

Imprinting. A few hours after they were hatched (during a sensitive period), these goslings saw Konrad Lorenz instead of their mother. Thereafter they followed him around as if he were the real mother.

It is not difficult to see the importance of these attachments for young birds. Early attachments to adult members of the infant's species seem to be the first stage of participation in social systems for many birds. In other words, imprinting appears to be a primary mechanism for the development of necessary social bonds. These bonds can be highly resistant to change. Lorenz describes an extreme case, in which a goose that he raised not only followed him but when it reached sexual maturity, attempted to mate with him.

In the case of imprinting, the length of the sensitive period is fairly restricted. A slightly older duckling or gosling (sometimes only a few hours older) does not form these attachments as easily. However, sensitive periods should not be interpreted solely in terms of age or time elapsed since birth, but in terms of what experiences have occurred during the given period. It is possible, for example, to imprint a chick prenatally by playing a series of tones near the eggs during the third week of incubation (Grier, Counter, and Shearer, 1967). After hatching, such chicks heard either the familiar tone or a new one. They moved in the direction of the familiar tone and seemed to avoid the novel sound. Sensitive periods can also be prolonged if experiences that might produce attachment are restricted. In another study (McDonald, 1968), the investigator anesthetized chicks after they hatched and kept them in a stupor for several days. After the anesthesia wore off, he was able to imprint them with utter success, although they were considerably past the normal sensitive period.

Imprinting occurs mainly through repeated exposure, so that it changes an unfamiliar object that may have evoked fear into a familiar one that does not. By following the familiar imprinted object (e.g., the mother hen), the growing organism is prevented from becoming familiar with other objects, thus the attachment (and the protection that it provides) becomes increasingly stabilized. Only if the original object of attachment is removed from the young animal's environment will the animal become attached to another object (Salzen and Meyer, 1968).

Imprinting clearly demonstrates our earlier conclusions about the relationship between learning and species-specific behavior. First, birds that show imprinting exhibit a species-specific ability to learn. Second, imprinting demonstrates that learning can play a role in the development of species-specific behavior. In many species (e.g., sheep, dogs, cats, birds, perhaps even human beings) the learning that occurs during sensitive periods seems to be essential for the development of normal social behavior (Scott, 1962).

Life Experiences   Species-specific behavior that appears as natural to an animal as breathing may depend heavily upon the environment's provision of experiences that allow the behavior to develop. A dramatic example of an "instinctive" behavior that depends upon experience is the cat's inclination to kill rats. The cat's predatory behavior is species-specific because it is common among wild cats and because it can be produced by brain stimulation, as we saw earlier. But rat killing by cats does not appear to be inevitable.

In a classic series of studies, Zing Yang Kuo (1930) found the relationships between these two "natural enemies" to be flexible. Cats reacted to rats in a variety of ways, from congeniality to fear to killing, depending upon what their experience had taught them about rats when they were kittens. The majority of kittens raised with a rat-killing mother eventually killed the rodents. Kittens raised in isolation from rats and who had no chance to watch a rat-killing mother did not automatically kill rats when given the opportunity. But after observing other cats kill rats, they became rat killers themselves. However, kittens that were raised with rats would not kill them even after they watched other cats kill rats. As a final demonstration of the role of learning in the cat's predatory behavior, Kuo showed a rat to a cat and then punished the cat; when the cat was later confronted with a rat, the cat ran away.

The dependence of the cat's predatory behavior on learning and experience is quite clear from this study. As Kuo (1930, p. 234) concluded, "Our study has shown that kittens can be made to kill a rat, to love it, to hate it, to fear it, or to play with it: it depends on the life history of the kitten." Studies of "instinctive" behavior in other species also show the influence of experience on a basic species-specific behavior, indicating that behavior simply cannot be separated into learned and unlearned components (Hailman, 1969). For example, experience can heavily influence the affiliative preferences of animals. In one study (Dennenberg, Hudgens, and Zarrow, 1964), mice were raised under several different conditions. One group was raised in the normal manner by a mouse mother with a litter of other mice; a second group was raised by a foster rat mother in a litter of rats; and a third group was kept in isolation after weaning, with neither rats nor mice for company. Sometime after the mice were weaned they were given a choice of another mouse or a rat as a companion. Mice that had been raised by a rat mother in a litter of rats clearly preferred the rat but other mice—whether raised by a mouse or in isolation—preferred mice as companions.

Interpreting Behavior

Although the purpose in studying animals is to shed some light on human behavior, we are often tempted to observe and describe an animal's actions from our own point of view. We tend to look for purpose in the behavior of animals, to attribute human values and motives to them, and to make unjustified generalizations from one species of animal to another. By following a few guidelines and considering some questions, we can avoid these temptations.

What Is the Adaptive Significance of a Trait?

One of the assumptions guiding the study of animal behavior is that any trait consistently displayed by a species of animal in its normal habitat must have some sort of adaptive significance for the animal. In evolutionary theory, the adaptive significance of a trait refers to the way in which it helps the species to survive in its ecological niche—its special part of the environment. For example, the behavior involved in nest building can be viewed as increasing the probability that offspring—and hence the species—will survive. By keeping offspring alive to mature to a breeding age, the species is perpetuated. Sometimes the adaptive significance of a trait is obvious, as in most instances of feeding, but in other cases it is obscure.

Sometimes extensive field research and sometimes only laboratory experiments can determine the adaptive significance of a behavior trait. For example, some moths and butterflies have evolved striking and highly colorful circular patterns on their wings, as the photograph of the Io moth on this page shows. When the resting moth is touched or startled, it suddenly throws open its wings but does not take off. What is the possible adaptive significance of this behavior? Are the wing pattern and the behavior related? One possibility is that the pattern is related to protective coloration (camouflage), except that the sudden wing flicking is bound to attract the attention of a predator. Another possibility is that the pattern aids in mate selection, as do the brilliant feathers of the peacock, except that the moth's colorful pattern combined with its attention-getting behavior seem to make the insect vulnerable to predators.

An Io moth. The circular pattern on its wings has an unexpected adaptive significance for the moth—and for its predators.

Finally, since the circular patterns resemble eyes, their sudden display to a potential predator, such as a bird, may frighten the predator off. A clever laboratory experiment (Blest, 1957a, b) showed that this last suggestion appears to be correct: sudden exposure of the wing pattern tends to inhibit predation. Birds seemed reluctant to eat a mealworm that had eyelike spots projected onto it, but they showed no such hesitation toward a worm that had some other kind of projected patterns (crosses or parallel lines). The adaptive significance of this wing display in some moths shows how simple behavior in one species can be related to or dependent on the behavior of another species. Presumably, avoiding large and widely spaced eyelike patterns has its own adaptive significance for birds.

How Purposive Is Behavior?

It is often tempting to talk about the adaptive significance of some behavioral characteristic as though the behavior indicated some "purpose" on the part of the animal. We may say, for example, that the frog's purpose in striking at flies is to get food. We would be less inclined, however, to interpret the ensnarement of a fly by the Venus flytrap plant as being anything other than the reflexive closing of the plant's leaves when triggered by the stimulus of a fly crawling over them. The relationship of the behavior in each case to survival (i.e., food getting) is obvious. But can we say that either the frog or the flytrap perceives the consequence of ensnaring a fly? Or is fly catching simply an automatic reaction that contributes to the survival of these two organisms?

The more similar an animal is to human beings, the more inclined we are to attribute intention to the animal and to interpret the behavior as having some purpose, as human behavior usually does. To ascribe purpose to behavior, in the sense that the behavior is caused by the animal's perception of the act's consequences, unnecessarily complicates explanations of animal behavior. As the following example suggests, such explanations are often unjustified.

At the beginning of this chapter, we saw that normally raised female rats build a nest the first time they become pregnant. It would be tempting to describe the nest building of pregnant rats as having the purpose of providing warmth and seclusion for their as yet unborn offspring. New-born rats are unable to maintain their body temperature adequately, and the nest site and insulating nesting material help to keep them warm. Nests also help to keep the young rats contained in one place where their mother can protect them from predators.

However, closer observation of this behavior reveals that any rat will construct a nest if it gets cold. One of the side effects of pregnancy in the rat is a lowering of body temperature, which is promoted by changes in the animal's blood chemistry. It would appear that nest building by the pregnant rat is a simple response to getting cold and that it has no direct connection with intentional preparations for the arrival of offspring. If the temperature of the nesting areas in a laboratory is kept extremely warm, many pregnant rats do not build nests. Nest building in the pregnant rat does provide a warm brooding area for the litter and thus is certainly adaptive. But we cannot assume that it was foreseen by the mother. The stimulus of lowered body temperature alone was enough to trigger a rat's nest building.

The example of nest building in the pregnant rat illustrates the general scientific **principle of parsimony**, which states that given two equally reasonable explanations of any situation, always choose the simpler. Years ago, in reaction to the tendency of naturalists to attribute human characteristics to the animals they observed, the naturalist Lloyd Morgan proposed that comparative psychologists adopt this conservative principle (which has since been labeled "Morgan's canon"). As Morgan (1894) stated the principle, "In no case may we interpret an action as the outcome of the exercise of a higher psychical faculty, if it can be interpreted as the outcome of the exercise of one which stands lower in the psychological scales." He believed that to make our interpretations of animal behavior overly complex often interfered with our understanding of the behavior.

The example of the nest-building rat also tells us something about the pitfalls in ascribing **teleological** explanations (i.e., those that invoke purpose) to human behavior. Researchers find it difficult to resist interpreting the behavior of human subjects in terms of some purpose, but there is no way to verify their interpretations. Although we can always ask people why they behaved in a certain way, the answers we get may mislead us. It is entirely possible that people are either not aware of their true purposes or that

Territoriality among human beings: while animals establish territories to meet their needs for food and shelter, human beings do so to meet their needs for privacy and status as well.

they are distorting them. Such unawareness or distortion affects mundane acts as well as important decisions. For example, when people are asked to chose the pair of hose they preferred from four identical pairs, most people choose the pair on the far right. Despite the fact that location dominates their choice, people will offer seemingly plausible reasons for it and deny that the position of the object has any influence on their evaluation (Nisbett and Wilson, 1977). No matter how logical people's explanations of their actions sound, there is no way to verify whether the stated purpose accurately reflects their motives. There is simply nothing—besides a meaningful sequence of behavior—with which we can compare personal reports of purposes and intentions.

Generalizing to Human Behavior

In the nineteenth century it was a common practice to ascribe human values and motivation to animal behavior (anthropomorphism).

In recent years it has been popular to do the opposite—to account for human behavior, in a simplistic way, as similar to the behavior of animals. Julian Edney (1974) labeled this approach the "beastopomorphic" interpretation and used as an example explanations of human territoriality.

According to the beastopomorphic view, said Edney, human beings share with other animals the inherited and irrevocable drive to claim, defend, and compete for territory. But there are significant differences between territoriality in animals and in human beings. In animals the use of space tends to follow stereotypical, fixed patterns, but among human beings its use is highly varied (e.g., nomadic or sedentary, hunting-and-gathering or farming). This wide range in the ways human beings use space suggests that human territoriality is largely based on cultural traditions, as we shall see in Chapter 28. For lower animals, territoriality serves primarily physiological needs, such as providing food and shelter; for human beings it serves a far greater range of needs, such as privacy, status, and ideology. In this case, animal analogies fall far short of accounting for human behavior.

Similarly, many writers, from Freud to Lorenz, have suggested that aggression is an inescapable part of our basic animal inheritance. This view too has been sharply criticized (Pilbeam, 1972), not only because it promotes what its critics believe is an unnecessarily pessimistic view of human nature but also because it runs counter to much of the evidence. We know that human aggression can be modified to take many forms, some of which are less destructive than others. We also know that just as cats appear to learn to control their species-specific predatory behavior, human beings can learn to suppress, control, and rechannel their aggression.

Behavior represents ways of adapting to the environment and as we have seen, much behavior has proved over many generations to have adaptive significance for animals in their natural habitats. A search for similar adaptive significance in human behavior has been urged by sociobiologists, who study the hereditary basis of behavior in animals and human beings, trying to determine whether various social behavior is inherited from remote ancestors. According to Harvard zoologist Edward O. Wilson, **sociobiology** is "the systematic study of the biological basis of all social behavior" (1975, p. 4).

Sociobiologists hope to develop general laws concerning the evolution and biology of social behavior and to identify a hereditary origin for many of its forms, such as aggression and altruism. The basis of sociobiology is the extensive comparison of the behavior of social species, and the explanation is made in terms of genetic advantage (Wilson, 1978).

Since any society must have some sort of cooperative organization to survive, sociobiologists have been particularly interested in altruism (Wilson, 1975). Altruistic behavior often entails harm to the helper, and since death precludes further reproduction, it seems unlikely that altruism could have any genetic advantage. Yet death and injury from acts of altruism are common in animal species. The soldier ant, which is sterile, dies to protect its queen, which then lives to produce more of the soldier ant's kind. The bee gives its life in stinging an intruder and thereby protects the entire hive. Such behavior seems contrary to evolutionary principles.

An attempt to explain this paradox has been advanced by sociobiologists (Dawkins, 1976; Wilson, 1975). William Hamilton (1963) proposed that organisms are not motivated by a desire for survival, but by a tendency to protect their own genes. The protection of one's own genes, of course, includes the protection of one's own life, since individual survival offers the possibility of transmission of genes through reproduction. These concepts of kin selection and of **inclusive fitness**, in which the individual sacrifices its own fitness (or chance to have offspring) to increase selectively the fitness of its relatives, explain why animals sacrifice themselves to protect others. Sacrifices meant to protect genes occur in a hierarchical order—the greatest sacrifice is made for those who share the most genes with the individual: children or parents. Siblings, because they share only one quarter of the genes, will be on the receiving end of altruism less often and the sacrificial acts will be less intense, and cousins—who share one-eighth of the genes—will receive even less.

Although the application of this concept to human altruism has not been established, studies (Freedman, 1979) of adolescents have indicated at least a verbal agreement with the concept. Asked about risking their own lives in a series of fictional situations, adolescents said they would help brothers before cousins, sisters before girl friends, family before strangers. What is more, they were ready to steal to save a relative's life, but not to save a stranger.

Some critics of sociobiology, notably Richard Lewontin, Steven Gould, and other members of the Harvard-based Sociobiology Study Group, point out that explaining behavior on a genetic level can lead to the notion that since our social organizations have been determined by our genes, they are virtually impossible to change (Sociobiology Study Group, 1978). Thus sociobiology can be used to defend warfare and the domination of women as evolutionary adaptations.

Other critics of sociobiology point out that there is no hard evidence that specific genes exist for altruism, aggression, or other social behavior —only theories and guesswork (Washburn, 1978). They also point out that animals at times behave with extreme selfishness. Among the lions of the Serengeti Plain in East Africa, lionesses have been observed driving their own cubs away from food if the catch was small; many of these cubs have died of starvation. Of 1,400 herring gull chicks studied during one period, 23 percent were killed by attacks from adults of their own species as they strayed from the nest (Marler, 1976).

Genes may indeed be an important component of human social behavior, but they cannot determine it without the assistance of appropriate experiences. If the children of two great athletes are never permitted to exercise, their genes will never make them athletes. The flexibility of human social behavior, the extreme differences manifested in various cultures and in different contexts is uniquely human (Pilbeam, 1972).

The question of the extent to which heredity constrains variation in human social behavior is far from settled. Given the cautions against direct analogies between human and animal behavior, how is our understanding of ourselves enriched by the vast amount of information we have gathered about other animals? For one thing, some analytic tools borrowed from animal studies have been valuable in clarifying human behavior. For example, the concept of species-specific behavior has been used to study the development of human language (Marler, 1970; Lenneberg, 1967). A child needs the vocal apparatus and the brain organization to control speech. In this respect, language ability is inherited. But language is also environmentally determined, in the sense that its expression is shaped by experience with a particular language. Like the other behavior we have discussed, language is neither strictly innate nor strictly learned; it is a product of both factors. Without the innate capacity or the experience, a child could not develop a formal language.

Another value of animal research is that in many cases (even though we are cautious about the use of direct analogies) the results do appear to be applicable to human beings. This conclusion will be evident throughout the rest of this book. But the application of animal research to human social behavior cannot be made in specific cases, such as altruism, nest building, begging for food, or voting for political parties. Instead, its legitimate application is in general laws that apply to abstract forms of behavior found in all species, such as attraction, avoidance, learning, and threat, laws that help to organize the vast store of information that is collected in various branches of psychology.

SUMMARY

1. In seeking to discover basic laws of behavior, psychologists deal with "behavior" as an abstraction, ignoring particular organisms or particular circumstances. A basic concept that has emerged from animal research is that behavior is the result of the interaction of innate and environmental factors.

2. **Ethology's** major concern with behavior was with its **adaptive significance**—its importance in helping the animal to survive and reproduce successfully, and ethologists relied heavily on field research for their data. Comparative psychologists were concerned primarily with the influences of experience on behavior, and they relied mainly on controlled laboratory experiments. Contemporary research into animal behavior often combines the field approach of ethology with the laboratory approach of comparative psychology.

3. The debate over whether certain behavior could be considered as "instinctive" (inborn) or "learned" (environmentally determined) became known as the **nature-versus-nurture** issue. But as nest building in the pregnant rat demonstrates, it is futile to try to characterize animal behavior as either instinctive or learned—both factors must be considered in the explanation of any behavior. The concept of **species-specific behavior** has replaced the classical notion of instinct. Species-specific behavior is behavior that is typical of a particular species, the members of which share a common inheritance and a common environment.

4. The behavior pattern of a species is influenced by genetic, developmental, environmental, and life-experience factors. Innate, or genetic, factors influence physical traits, sensory systems, and the organization of the brain, determining an animal's behavioral capacities. For example, an examination of an animal's sensory capacities can often provide insight into some behavior. **Fixed action patterns** are relatively stereotyped and frequently repeated patterns of movement that appear in full form the first time they are performed and are somehow "wired" into an animal's nervous system.

5. Specific stimuli in the environment often seem to serve as signals for fixed action patterns as well as for complex behavior. A **sign stimulus**, which may be an odor, color, or shape, releases a fixed action pattern in an animal, but sign stimuli are not as specific as once was thought. An animal's tendency to respond to innate releasers, or specific stimuli that release a chain of behavior with survival value, was thought to be an innate neural mechanism, but this view is now questioned. Some complex behavioral patterns are associated with **sequential stimuli,** and the

chain of stimuli leading to a particular pattern can be a long one.

6. Developmental studies of species-specific behavior in young animals have shown that the ability of an animal to learn is in some degree species-specific and that learning is essential for the development of much species-specific behavior. Animals vary in their species-specific learning capacities and in the flexibility of their behavior in new situations. **Sensitive periods** are certain times in the lives of animals when they are especially susceptible to particular kinds of learning, and the experiences during that period—not the period itself—are responsible for influencing some forms of early learning. **Imprinting,** the process by which some species of birds and mammals form early social attachments, appears to be a primary mechanism for the development of social bonds. Sensitivity to imprinting is highest shortly after birth.

7. Any trait consistently displayed by a species in its natural habitat usually has some adaptive significance for the animal, but laboratory experiments may be necessary to determine the adaptive significance. Ascribing purpose to an animal's behavior, in the sense of saying that the animal acts with some awareness of the behavior's consequence, makes explanations of behavior unnecessarily complex. The **principle of parsimony** suggests that, given two possible explanations of an animal's behavior, we should always select the one that results from a lower rather than a higher mental faculty.

8. It has become popular to account for human behavior as similar to the behavior of animals, but such explanations are often too simple. A search for adaptive significance in human behavior has been promoted by **sociobiologists,** who study the evolutionary basis of behavior in animals and human beings by comparing social species. However, sociobiologists, who explain social behavior in terms of genetic advantage, have found no hard evidence to support their theories in human beings. Despite the various controversies, concepts borrowed from the study of lower animals, such as the concept of species-specific behavior, have contributed to the analysis and understanding of human behavior.

KEY TERMS

adaptive significance
ethology
fixed action patterns
imprinting
innate releasers

inclusive fitness
nature versus nurture
phototaxis
principle of parsimony
sensitive period

sequential stimuli
sign stimulus
sociobiology
species-specific behavior
teleology

RECOMMENDED READINGS

ALCOCK, JOHN. *Animal Behavior: An Evolutionary Approach.* Sunderland, Mass.: Sinauer, 1975. A broad, biologically oriented discussion of animal behavior processes; thorough and well-written.

DARWIN, CHARLES. *The Descent of Man* (1871). Philadelphia: West, 1902. The evolutionary case for the idea that humans and some other mammals are descended from common ancestors.

DAWKINS, R. *The Selfish Gene.* New York: Oxford University Press, 1976. This is an engaging and informative review of the new concepts of sociobiology.

DE THIER, VINCENT G. *To Know a Fly.* San Francisco: Holden Day, 1962. A delightful, readable account of the behavior of flies.

DEWSBURY, DONALD A. *Comparative Animal Behavior.* New York: McGraw-Hill, 1978. A comprehensive, up-to-date textbook on animal behavior from the perspective of a comparative psychologist.

EISENBERG, J. F., and W. S. DILLON (eds.). *Man and Beast: Comparative Social Behavior.* Washington, D.C.: Smithsonian Institution Press. This edited volume includes well-written and comprehensive summaries of recent work in this area by such pioneers of sociobiology as William D. Hamilton and Edward O. Wilson, and observers of primate behavior Hans Kummer and John H. Crook, Robin Fox, and Irven DeVore. It also contains discussions about the nature-nurture controversy that include papers by the philosopher Susanne K. Langer and by the late anthropologist Margaret Mead.

LORENZ, KONRAD. *King Solomon's Ring.* New York: Crowell, 1952. A light, easy-to-read book of essays about Lorenz's many interesting experiences with animals.

TINBERGEN, NIKO. *Animal Behavior.* New York: Time-Life Books, 1965. A beautifully illustrated book on animal behavior for the general public, with an excellent running narrative by one of the world's leading ethologists.

CHAPTER 8

Learning

At the Naval Oceans System Center in Honolulu, Hawaii, pigeons, taught to spot human survivors of helicopter crashes at sea, are being trained as members of rescue missions. In cages strapped to the underside of a searching helicopter, the birds will peck at a switch whenever they spot life vests, life rafts, or signal flares in the water, alerting the helicopter pilot to the presence of possible survivors below. These pigeons are not gifted, nor do they know the significance of their pecking; instead, they are ordinary birds being trained according to basic principles of learning. The birds are rewarded with grain each time they peck a switch after they have seen the colors orange, yellow, or red—the colors of vests, rafts, and flares. When the pigeons are on flight duty and spot one of these colors amid the gray, green, or blue waters below, their pecks will make a light in the cockpit flash, telling the pilot where to look for possible survivors and which bird to reward with grain. The birds already have passed practice flights in which they pecked at the sight of a sixteen-inch practice buoy from 500 feet in the air while they were traveling at 100 miles per hour. The buoy was a quarter of a mile away when the pigeons spotted it, long before a human being would have picked it out (Diamond, 1979). In fact, on tests of their spotting ability, pigeons are accurate about 90 percent of the time as compared with an accuracy of about 40 percent for human flight crews.

Unless psychologists understood some of the basic principles of learning, they would be unable to turn pigeons into members of rescue operations. Learning is basic to psychology: no matter what area of psychology we consider, learning plays a central role in its study. Among other activities an industrial psychologist searches for the best way to train employees to be safety conscious. An educational psychologist looks for more efficient ways to teach children with learning disabilities. An environmental psychologist wonders whether urban background noise affects the way people learn. A developmental psychologist explores the possibility that children learn in different ways at different ages. A social psychologist wants to know how people learn prejudicial attitudes toward other ethnic groups. A school psychologist looks at the effect of reward and punishment on classroom behavior. A physiological psychologist studies the effects of drugs on the learning process. And a clinical psychologist searches for ways to teach a client who is afraid of dogs to approach them without panic.

Learning and Performance

Learning is fundamental to all aspects of life, but just what is it? A good general definition of **learning** is: a relatively enduring change in behavior caused by experience or practice. Learning must be inferred from changes in an organism's performance, because we cannot observe the learning process directly (Ellis, 1978).

Inferring learning from changes in performance is not as simple as it may seem, because not all changes in performance are the result of learning. Maturation can lead to permanent changes in performance, but the changes do not depend upon practice and are not attributable to learning. Similarly, drugs, fatigue, or motivation can lead to changes in performance, but the changes are temporary and have no connection with practice so they cannot be attributed to learning.

Improvements in performance are not always the result of more thorough learning. For example, a professional tennis player's victory over an opponent who had previously defeated him could be due to a variety of reasons. During the last match he may have been bothered by blisters or concerned about an argument with his wife, or winning this match may have been especially important to him. Even if he had learned a more efficient serve during recent practice, we cannot be certain that his improved performance resulted only from this new knowledge.

Nor can we be sure that when performance deteriorates it is because something that was learned has been forgotten. For example, a hungry rat can be taught to run a maze for a reward of food. If the rat runs the maze faster on trial 20 than on trial 1, the experimenter can tentatively conclude that the animal's increased efficiency is a sign that learning has taken place. But by trial 40, the rat may have eaten its fill and its performance may begin to decline. Although the animal's performance is impaired, the impairment may be due to lowered motivation or to fatigue, and what it has learned by having run the maze will probably be retained. When the rat is hungry again, it will demonstrate the response it learned as diligently as it had before. Thus, although learning remains constant, performance can vary. The point to remember is that learning, as inferred from performance, is a *relatively enduring* change that accompanies experience. Although this general definition covers virtually all learning, learning can also be divided into several different types: classical conditioning, which is involved in our emotional responses; operant conditioning, which explains a good deal of our voluntary behavior; and social learning, which accounts for the way we learn by observing others.

Classical Conditioning

A young woman who has just graduated from law school and been hired by an influential law firm develops cancer. She is put on chemotherapy, a treatment whose side effects include nausea. When she reports to the hospital for her third weekly treatment, she becomes nauseated and begins vomiting as soon as she crosses the threshold. Several days later, she is shopping in the local supermarket and sees the nurse who administers the drug to her; a wave of nausea sweeps over the young lawyer and she begins to retch uncontrollably. She has been classically conditioned to associate the hospital and those connected with her treatment with her drug-induced nausea, so that both the hospital and the nurse evoke the same response from her that was originally produced by the drug. The association seems obvious, but to understand the learning principles that explain it, we must explore how classically conditioned responses are established, how they can be generalized beyond the original setting, and how they can be eliminated.

The Conditioned Response

Classical conditioning (sometimes called Pavlovian conditioning) involves reflex behavior. A simple reflex is an involuntary response that is elicited (brought on) by a specific stimulus. For example, the salivary reflex in a dog is elicited by a stimulus—food in the dog's mouth—that elicits a response—salivation. Other stimuli, such as ringing bells or flashing lights, do not normally cause salivation. So far as salivation is concerned, they are neutral. However, in classical conditioning, a neutral stimulus, when it is repeatedly presented with another stimulus that normally evokes a reflexive response, comes to elicit that response when presented by itself, as shown in Figure 8.1. For example, the Russian physiologist Ivan Pavlov (1849–1936) found that if a neutral stimulus, such as the sound of a bell, regularly occurs just before a dog is given food, the bell itself gradually comes to elicit the dog's salivation response. Thus, the salivation reflex

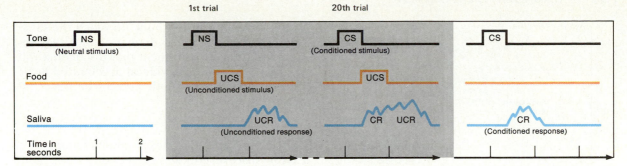

1st trial   20th trial

Tone	NS (Neutral stimulus)	NS	CS (Conditioned stimulus)	CS
Food		UCS (Unconditioned stimulus)	UCS	
Saliva		UCR (Unconditioned response)	CR UCR	CR (Conditioned response)
Time in seconds	1 2			

Figure 8.1 The relationship of events in classical conditioning (from left to right). *Before*—A stimulus such as a tone that elicits no salivary response can be described as a neutral stimulus (NS) with respect to salivation. This stimulus, the tone, is paired with an unconditioned stimulus (US) food, which elicits the unconditioned response (UCR) of salivation. *During conditioning*—Repeated pairing of the tone and the food begins to elicit salivation in response to the tone as well as to the food. Because the previously neutral tone is no longer neutral, but capable of calling forth salivation, the tone itself becomes a conditioned stimulus (CS) and the salivation it elicits now becomes a conditioned response (CR). *After*—Finally, a test with the tone alone is sufficient to elicit salivation.

has become associated with a new stimulus that does not normally evoke that response; the reflex can be said to have been classically conditioned. Through the process of conditioning, an insignificant stimulus has become highly significant to the dog.

The food in the mouth is an **unconditioned stimulus (UCS).** It elicits the **unconditioned response (UCR)** of salivation. The term "unconditioned" is used because the response does not depend on the organism's previous experience with the stimulus—it does not have to be learned. The new stimulus that elicits salivation after repeated association with the UCS is called the **conditioned stimulus (CS).** The animal's salivation in response to the conditioned stimulus is called the **conditioned response (CR).** It

has been conditioned by the animal's experience, in which the food (the UCS) was repeatedly paired with the bell (the CS). Many sights, sounds, or touches can act as conditioned stimuli for salivation: a flash of light, the ticking of a metronome, a tap on the skin.

Pavlov's Experiments Pavlov (1927), who discovered classical conditioning, put dogs in harnesses like the one in Figure 8.2. Before confining the animals, a tube had been inserted into each dog's cheek so that saliva would flow from the salivary gland into a glass container. The mechanical device on the far left of the drawing kept track of the number of drops secreted. In front of the dog was a tray in which the animal's food was placed.

Figure 8.2 The apparatus used in early studies of classical conditioning. Saliva dropping from a tube inserted into the dog's cheek strikes a lightly balanced arm, and the resulting motion is transmitted hydraulically to a pen that traces a record on a slowly revolving drum. Pavlov's discovery of conditioned salivation was an accidental by-product of his researches into the activity of the digestive system.

179

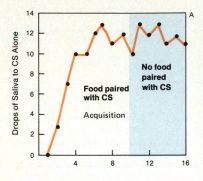

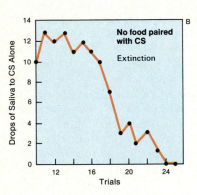

Figure 8.3 (A) Acquisition of a conditioned response. On early test trials—with light alone—there is little salivation. Later in the series the light alone (CS) elicits considerable salivation. A conditioned response (CR) has been acquired. (B) Extinction of a conditioned response. When the light-food pairings are eliminated, the amount of salivation (CR) to the light alone (CS) drops steadily until the relationship between the CS and the CR is destroyed.

In a typical classical conditioning study, the experimenter presented a stimulus—perhaps a tone—and several seconds later food was dropped into the dog's tray. As the dog began to eat the food (the UCS), its presence in the mouth caused salivation; this was the unconditioned response. The tone and the food were repeatedly associated. Then, every few trials the tone was presented alone, without food, and as Figure 8.3A shows, before too long, the tone by itself elicited salivation. This salivation to the tone was the conditioned response.

In a similar manner, Pavlov conditioned other reflexes. For example, an electric shock to a dog's forepaw elicited a withdrawal response—the dog pulled its paw away from the stimulus. If the unconditioned stimulus of shock was regularly preceded by a neutral stimulus, such as the ticking of a metronome, the dog soon learned to pull its paw away in response to the sound alone. However, conditioning will not take place unless the conditioned stimulus consistently precedes or accompanies the unconditioned stimulus.

Pavlov gave the name **stimulus substitution** to this tendency to react to the previously neutral stimulus as though it were the unconditioned stimulus. His dogs responded to a light or bell as if it were food and to the ticking of a metronome

as if it were an electric shock. In much the same way, a man waiting in a dentist's office may respond to the announcement that the dentist will see him next (the CS) with an accelerated heart rate, as if a decayed tooth were to be filled immediately (the UCS).

The Garcia Effect   For nearly a half century after Pavlov discovered classical conditioning, psychologists believed that a reflex response could be conditioned with equal ease to any neutral stimulus. Further, they believed that unless the unconditioned stimulus accompanied the conditioned stimulus or followed close on its heels, conditioning would not occur. But psychologist John Garcia and his associates (Garcia and Koelling, 1966; Garcia, Ervin, and Koelling, 1966) demonstrated that both beliefs were false. Animals quickly connected some types of neutral stimuli with unconditioned responses and almost never connected other types of stimuli with unconditioned responses. What is more, if the neutral stimulus was one that animals seemed prepared to connect with a response, the delay between the stimulus and the response could be lengthy—in some cases up to twelve hours (Andrews and Braveman, 1975).

In one of his experiments, Garcia fed a group of rats sweetened water; afterward, the rats were either shocked on the foot or nauseated by radiation or a toxic injection. On subsequent occasions, rats who had been nauseated refused to touch sweetened water, but rats who had received an electric shock drank it without hesitation. A second group of rats were fed plain water, but each time this group drank, lights flashed and loud noises erupted. Afterward, these rats, too, were either shocked on the foot or nauseated. On subsequent occasions, rats who had been shocked avoided the "noisy, bright" water, but rats who had become nauseated drank it immediately.

According to Garcia, rats' evolutionary history has prepared them to connect tastes with illness and pain with sights and sounds, because such connections have been essential to their survival. In the rats' world, pain is likely to be accompanied by contact with dangerous objects that are seen and heard. The connection between illness and taste is generally delayed. Rats are scavengers who sample each new food they come upon. Since strange substances are sometimes poisonous, rats must be able to avoid poisons if they are to survive. Yet it often takes several hours for the effects of poison to be felt. But if the rats' nervous system is programed to connect the taste of any food eaten before a gastric illness with that illness, rats who consume poison and survive will avoid that particular poison in the future, thereby increasing their chances of survival.

When human beings become ill, they seem prepared to connect taste with illness just as rats do. For example, young cancer patients were given Mapletoff, a distinctively flavored ice cream, just before receiving chemotherapy—a treatment that generally is followed by nausea. Several months later, three-fourths of them rejected that flavor, but among cancer patients in a control group who had not received chemotherapy after their ice cream, half preferred the Mapletoff to another flavor (Bernstein, 1978). This experiment with cancer patients supports the experience of many people, who find that when they become ill after eating a distinctive food (such as Béarnaise sauce, lobster, or mince pie), the taste or even the thought of the offending food nauseates them (Seligman and Hager, 1972).

Generalization and Discrimination

Once an organism has been conditioned to respond in a specific way, as when Pavlov's dogs salivated when they heard a tone or Garcia's rats reacted with distaste to sweetened water, **generalization** may occur; that is, a response learned in one situation may be elicited by other, similar situations. Generalization is as common among human beings as it is among rats or dogs. For example, if you have an extremely warm relationship with your Aunt Ellen, you may find that your liking for Aunt Ellen generalizes to women with the same name you later meet, so that you begin your acquaintance with any Ellen expecting to like her.

The more similar a stimulus is to a conditioned stimulus, the more likely it is that the response to it will be generalized. If one of Pavlov's dogs were conditioned to salivate at the sound of a tone at 1,000 cycles per second (cps), the dog would also respond to a tone at 950 cps; if the tone's pitch drops to 600 cps, the animal would probably salivate but not nearly so much; and it might not respond at all to a tone at 250 cps. This increased tendency to respond as the resemblance between a new stimulus and a condi-

tioned stimulus becomes closer is called a **generalization gradient,** and if the responses of several conditioned dogs to tones of varying pitches were averaged and plotted on a graph, the generalization gradient would show a typical curve.

Although responses often generalize to similar stimuli, organisms can be trained to differentiate among similar stimuli, responding to one and not responding to others. This process is called **discrimination,** and it results when the unconditioned stimulus regularly follows one stimulus and never follows other, similar stimuli. Suppose that one of Pavlov's dogs learned to salivate to a 1,000-cps tone and promptly generalized its response to tones of varying pitches. If Pavlov sounded tones at other frequencies without putting food into the dog's tray but continued to place food in the tray just after the dog heard the 1,000-cps tone, the dog would soon discriminate among the tones, salivating only to the 1,000-cps tone. In fact, after this sort of training, one of Pavlov's dogs learned to salivate at the sight of a circle, but not at the sight of an ellipse; another learned to salivate when four tones were heard in a specific order, but not when the same tones were sounded in any other order (Pavlov, 1927).

Generalization is important in daily life because it allows us to behave adaptively in various situations. Without generalization, none of us would survive for long, because we would have to learn separately the significance of each stimulus in the world. Without generalization, a pedestrian stepping off a curb without looking would react only to blaring automobile horns and might be run over by the first car that sounded a musical horn. Generalization allows us to be flexible, transferring information learned in one situation to another, somewhat different condition. It is our ability to discriminate, however, that keeps us from blindly generalizing what we learn. We notice the relevant features of new stimuli and can respond appropriately. For example, we distinguish among the quite similar stimuli *d*, *p*, *b*, and *g*. And without hesitation, we put a carton of milk into the refrigerator instead of into the oven, despite the fact that both appliances have square compartments with enameled doors.

Extinction of a Classically Conditioned Response

Although a classically conditioned response often becomes firmly established, it may not en-

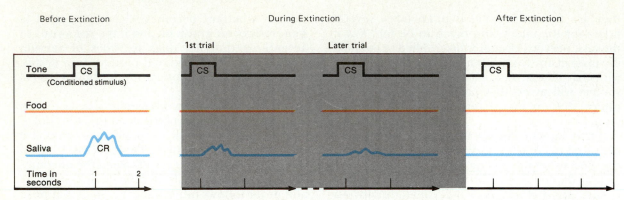

Figure 8.4 The relationship of events in the extinction of a classically conditioned response. The CS is presented repeatedly without the UCS. As a result, the CR gradually diminishes until it is no stronger than it was before conditioning.

dure forever. The response lasts only as long as the conditioned stimulus and the unconditioned stimulus occasionally occur together. But if the two stimuli are never again paired, the conditioned response will gradually fade away. For example, if the young lawyer's chemotherapy is successful and later she repeatedly visits the hospital to see a friend who is in traction following an automobile accident, the nausea that strikes her as she enters the building will slowly disappear. As Pavlov discovered, a dog that has been conditioned to salivate in response to a tone coupled with food will produce less and less saliva if the tone is repeatedly presented by itself. As shown in Figure 8.3B the drops of saliva produced gradually diminish until the dog ceases to drool. This slow decline and eventual disappearance of a conditioned response is called **extinction** (see Figure 8.4).

Classical Conditioning and Human Behavior

The findings from Pavlov's research had a powerful effect on American psychology. Nowhere was their impact stronger than on behaviorism and on John B. Watson, its founder (see Chapter 1). Watson proposed that all learning could be explained as the product of classical conditioning. He pointed out, for example, that fear can be classically conditioned, and he demonstrated his point by conditioning an eleven-month-old boy to fear white rats (Watson and Rayner, 1920). When Albert first saw a white rat, he showed no signs of fear and even tried to play with the animal. Then Watson and his colleague,

Rosalie Rayner, began their classical conditioning procedure: at regular intervals they placed the rat near the infant and whenever Albert touched it, they used a hammer to strike a steel bar held just behind the infant's ear. The loud clang made Albert start violently, bury his head in the mattress, and whimper. After the rat and the noise had been paired on several occasions, Albert began to show conditioned fear whenever he saw the rat, even if the noise was not sounded. In fact, Albert's conditioned fear generalized to other furry objects and animals—a rabbit, a dog, a Santa Claus mask, and even a fur coat. There was a generalization gradient to Albert's fear,

We learn fear of animals through the process of classical conditioning. The same process can be used to enable us to overcome such fears, and it has been adapted as a treatment for animal phobias.

and some of the objects frightened him more than others. More than a month after the infant first showed generalized fear, he was tested again. This time he showed fear of a rat, a rabbit, a dog, a fur coat and the mask. However, despite his visible fear of the rabbit and the coat, Albert reached out for both and attempted to make contact with them (Harris, 1979).

Watson also studied ways in which conditioned fears, like Albert's, can be reduced or eliminated. The most successful technique described by Watson (1924) was what he called "unconditioning," in which feared objects were paired with pleasant things. In one study, Mary Cover Jones (1924) unconditioned three-year-old Peter, who feared rabbits and a number of other things. A caged rabbit was gradually brought nearer and nearer to the table where the child ate a snack of milk and crackers. After several days, Peter was able to hold the rabbit without showing fear, stroking the animal with one hand while he ate with the other. At the same time, the child lost his fear of cotton, fur coats, and feathers, and his fear of rats was greatly reduced. This technique is similar to those now used successfully for treating phobias in children and adults.

Although few behaviorists today agree with Watson's notion that all learning can be explained through classical conditioning, virtually no one questions its importance in many types of learning.

Operant Conditioning

Some behaviorists believed that learning that was not explained by classical conditioning could be explained by **operant conditioning,** or **instrumental conditioning,** in which learning is explained by the way the consequences of behavior affect an organism's behavior in the future. Research that anticipated later studies of operant conditioning was done by Edward Thorndike (1874–1949), a hard worker, a prolific writer, and a great innovator, who was interested in animal intelligence. His first subjects at Harvard University were chickens, and until his landlady's protests became "imperative," Thorndike kept his chickens in his room, doing his experiments at home (Thorndike, 1936).

In his most famous experiments, Thorndike (1898) put cats into puzzle boxes. Food was placed outside the box, but to reach it the cat had to escape from the box—a feat that required the animal to unlatch the door. The latch could be tripped by a simple maneuver, such as stepping on a treadle. According to Thorndike, the cats at first used simple trial and error, biting at the bars or trying to squeeze between them, and finally released themselves by accident. As the cats were put back into the same puzzle box time and again, they gradually became so skillful that they immediately released the latch. Thorndike concluded that the connection between the cats' successful response and their escape was strengthened by repetition, and he explained this strengthening of the association between stimulus and response by formulating the **law of effect.** According to this law, responses (such as stepping on the treadle) that are followed by a satisfying consequence tend to be repeated, but responses that are followed by annoying consequences tend to disappear.

During the 1930s, B. F. Skinner began studying the learning process in animals, and the results of his studies led him to believe that human, as well as animal, learning could be explained by the principles of operant conditioning. Skinner (1981) tries to manage his life by applying these principles to his own behavior, and he has extended them to society in his utopian novel, *Walden Two* (1948b), and his analysis of culture, *Beyond Freedom and Dignity* (1971). Skinner explains most daily events with operant principles. For example, he points out that the efficiency of hearing aids is increased because people respond to the sight of a hearing aid by raising their voices, and that although the white canes of the blind may enable them to sense obstacles, their effectiveness is increased because people respond to the sight of these canes by getting out of the way (Skinner, 1981).

A basic difference between classical and operant conditioning is that operant conditioning applies to voluntary behavior, while classical conditioning applies to reflexes. Reflexes are sometimes called **respondent behavior,** to contrast them with **operant behavior**, which is voluntary. For example, when an animal salivates in response to food in its mouth, the salivation is a reflex (a "respondent"). Operant behavior, on the other hand, is spontaneous behavior that "operates" on or has an effect on the environment and is not associated with an obvious stimulus. For example, no stimulus is necessary to

Study Tips for Efficient Learning

By applying tactics that are derived from learning theory, you can learn to study more efficiently. Some effective learning techniques focus on the nature of the material to be learned, some on learning strategies, and others on the state of the learner.

Make the Material Meaningful
Research shows that meaningfulness is an important variable affecting learning. The more meaningful the material—that is, the more it relates to what you already know—the more readily it

sinks in. Test yourself with the following lists of syllables. Study each list in turn for one minute, then see how many of the five items you remember.

1	2	3
boy	mas	zoj
tan	pul	vaf
car	tal	zyt
dip	fer	jyz
hut	dod	giw

(Based on Glaze, 1928)

You probably found list 1 the easiest to learn, because it contains familiar, meaningful words. For a similar reason—because the items resemble English words—the nonsense syllables in list 2 should have given you less trouble than the syllables in list 3, which bear no resemblance to any words in English.

One way to apply the principle of meaningfulness to study is to tackle new material in stages, making sure that you have mastered one stage—have made that material meaningful—before you move on to the next. Another technique is to think of the mate-

rial in a way that makes it relevant to your own experience.

Add Some Novelty
A second variable that affects the efficiency of learning is novelty. Novelty can either increase or decrease the efficiency of learning. Suppose that you are presented with the following information: The animal with the longest gestation period is the elephant, which carries its young for twenty-two months. The novelty of this fact, as presented in the context of a psychology textbook, will probably enable you to remember it quite easily. However, if the same statement were presented in a textbook on elephant physiology, it would be just one novel statement about elephants among a mass of other data and it would be difficult to recall. Thus, too much novelty may hinder learning, but a small amount engages the learner's attention and thereby increases learning efficiency. You can structure some novelty into your study periods, perhaps by studying with friends or at the library instead of studying alone or at home.

induce a rat to explore its cage or to persuade a human infant to babble.

Operant behavior is influenced by environmental factors—by the rewards and punishments that follow it. In other words, operant behavior is affected by its consequences, and behavior that results in pleasant consequences is likely to be repeated, while behavior that results in unpleasant consequences is likely to disappear. Thus, Thorndike's law of effect has become Skinner's law of reinforcement.

Reinforcement and Punishment

The consequences of behavior are classified according to the kind of effect they have on subse-

quent behavior. Consequences that lead to an increase in the frequency of behavior are called **reinforcement,** or **reward.** Consequences that lead to the suppression or decrease in the frequency of behavior are called **punishment.** A consequence that is a reward for one person may be punishment for another. For example, some people look forward to spending vacations camping in the wilderness, but others regard the absence of plumbing, good beds, and air conditioning as punishment.

Any consequence that increases the frequency of behavior is reinforcement. In **positive reinforcement,** the presentation of a stimulus (such as food or praise) following a response strengthens the response. In **negative reinforcement,**

Organize the Material

A different sort of variable in learning is the principle of organization. You will generally find it easier to learn new information by rule than by rote—by studying the forest rather than the isolated trees. Try memorizing the following words by rote:

bad dab bag gab
ban nab bat tab

You probably found yourself tediously repeating the words. Now see if you can discover some patterns that relates all these words. If you notice that each word begins with the final letter of the word that precedes it, that *a* is always the middle letter, and that reversal and alphabetical order are also involved, then you have organized the list in such a way that it is easy to learn. In addition, you will probably remember the list longer than you would if you had simply learned it by rote.

Rehearse

Rehearsal is a strategy that seems to help everyone learn. The more you practice something, the better you will remember it.

Rehearsal is especially effective when it is active. Instead of passively reading and rereading the material you want to learn, try writing summaries from time to time or asking yourself questions about what you have read. Such techniques force you to organize information, and this organization should make learning easier.

Overlearn

When you rehearse a skill or fact more than is necessary for immediate performance, you overlearn it. Overlearning is what makes it possible to ride a bicycle or type or recite the Pledge of Allegiance even if you have not done so for years. If you overlearn for one exam and cram all night for another, you may get similar grades, but the overlearned facts will probably remain with you long after the exam while the crammed facts will probably be forgotten almost immediately after the test.

Space Your Study Time

Although cramming remains a popular study technique, research has shown that such "massed practice" is generally less efficient than "distributed practice," or study that is spread out over time. If you do have to cram, take a short break every hour. Increased efficiency will more than compensate for the time lost.

Relax—But Not Too Much

Your own feelings and motives can also affect your study effectiveness and your performance in the classroom. In general, extremely high and extremely low levels of anxiety affect performance adversely, while a moderate level seems beneficial. That is, neither the student who is in terror of flunking nor the student who could not care less is likely to do as well on an exam as a moderately anxious student (Sarason, Mandler, and Craighill, 1952).

Motivation seems to have a similar effect on performance. If you are poorly motivated, you will probably perform poorly, and if you are overly motivated, your high emotional arousal may interfere with your performance.

---

the response is strengthed by the *removal* of a stimulus (usually something unpleasant, such as electric shock) following the response. Removing something that is unpleasant can be as satisfying as presenting something that is pleasant, so either kind of consequence can reinforce—or strengthen—a response.

Punishment, on the other hand, involves any unpleasant event (such as shock or denial of privileges) that follows a response and weakens it. If each time a rat presses a lever, it receives a punisher in the form of electric shock, the rat will soon stop pressing the lever. Negative reinforcement and punishment are often confused because they both involve unpleasant stimuli, but they have opposite effects: negative reinforcers strengthen a response (electric shock ceases when the rat presses a lever), while punishers eliminate a response (electric shock starts when the rat presses a lever).

Psychologists disagree about the efficiency or value of punishment in learning. Skinner (1938) believes that punishment does not really eliminate a response that has formerly been rewarded (such as pressing a lever to get food or bullying another child to get a toy). Instead, he argues, the response is simply suppressed; as soon as the punishment stops (an electric shock to the rat's paw or a spanking for the young bully), the organism will resume the response. A much more effective way of eliminating an undesired response is to stop reinforcing it so that the response is extinguished (the rat never gets food when it presses the lever) or to reinforce incompatible responses (the bully gets a reward for sharing toys). However, it often takes a long time to eliminate undesirable responses with positive reinforcement, and although punishment may only suppress the behavior, it does work when it immediately follows the response. In fact, the suppression may last for a very long time.

Yet there are disadvantages to the use of punishment. Punishment can generalize, so that not only the undesirable behavior disappears but desirable behavior as well. A child who is regularly and severely punished for aggression may stop fighting but may also become passive, giving up assertiveness along with aggression. In addition, the punished animal or person tends to avoid the individual who did the punishing and the situation in which it occurred. Although punishment clearly tells a person what not to do, it gives no hint as to what the individual should do, so that it simply eliminates inappropriate behavior instead of establishing behavior that is appropriate. Finally, although punishing a learned response may be done without harm to the individual, punishing an innate response, such as eating or drinking, may lead to neurosis. Dogs that received electric shocks while they were eating tended to become either aggressive or sluggish, and some developed tremors and on later occasions retched when food was put before

them; another group of dogs that received shocks while food was being put into their dishes showed no ill effects (Lichtenstein, 1950).

Not all learning is the result of an actual relationship between an act and its consequences. Sometimes behavior is strengthened because it happens to be followed by a reinforcer. The relationship between the behavior and the reinforcer is coincidental, but the person assumes that the behavior causes the reinforcement, and so the response increases. This kind of behavior change is called **superstitious behavior.** Examples of such behavior abound on any televised baseball game. Batters can be seen tugging at their caps, rubbing their noses, or tapping the plate or their left foot with the bat three times before they move into the box—rituals that are supposed to guarantee them hits. Since most batters hit safely about a quarter of the time, each hit they get reinforces the superstitious behavior.

Similar superstitions appeared in pigeons when Skinner (1948a) fed them at regular intervals, no matter what the birds happened to be doing. Although there was no connection between behavior and reinforcement, the pigeons soon developed ritualistic, stereotyped behavior patterns, such as bowing, turning in circles, and hopping from one foot to the other. The pigeons acted as if they believed that whatever they happened to be doing at the moment of food deliv-

Figure 8.5 The conditioning of superstitious behavior. Note the sense of continuity Skinner draws between the behavior of the pigeon and that of human beings.

"The bird behaves as if there were a causal relation between its behavior and the presentation of food. A few accidental connections between a ritual and favorable consequence suffice to set up and maintain the behavior in spite of many unreinforced instances. The bowler who has released the ball down the alley but continues to behave as if he were controlling it by twisting and turning his arm and shoulder is (a) case in point. These behaviors have no real effect upon one's luck or upon the ball . . . just as food would appear as often if the pigeon did nothing--or, strictly speaking, did something else."
(B. F. Skinner, 1948)

ery was responsible for the appearance of the food. In this case, although reinforcement did not depend upon a pigeon's behavior (as the baseball player's single did not depend upon his tapping the plate), it nevertheless had an effect on that behavior (see Figure 8.5). Skinner (1971) concluded that the results of these experiments strongly support the law of effect.

Establishing and Maintaining Operantly Conditioned Responses

By studying the effects of reinforcement and punishment in animals, psychologists have learned a good deal about the workings of operant conditioning. In such situations, it is possible to maintain complete control over the presentation of reinforcement.

Shaping   By exercising control over reinforcement, psychologists have used shaping to train animals to perform unusual behavior. The process of shaping is at the basis of a well-defined operant response: bar pressing by rats. Bar pressing is easy for a rat to perform, and easy to record automatically. Although an untrained rat already knows all the components of behavior necessary for bar pressing, the animal rarely executes the sequence spontaneously. To press the bar, the rat must approach it, rise up on its hind legs, put its front paws on the bar, and push it down toward the floor. Instead of waiting for the rat to stumble onto the correct response, the experimenter uses a procedure called **shaping,** a form of operant conditioning based on the reinforcement of ever-closer approximations of a desired behavior. The shaping process, developed by Skinner, is effective only if the animal has some reason, such as hunger or thirst, to work for reinforcement.

Shaping begins by reinforcing the rat's first response in the right direction—in the case of bar pressing, approaching the bar. After this behavior has been reinforced several times, the rat approaches the bar regularly. Then to get further reinforcement, the rat must also rise slightly off the floor. At first, the rat may be rewarded for lifting one paw; gradually reinforcement comes only if the rat lifts both paws high enough to reach the bar. Finally, reinforcement is withheld

A

Rat exploring box, accidentally approaches bar.

Hears click as food is dropped into cup.

Gets food and afterward tends to approach the bar again. Each time it does, it receives food.

B

Rat no longer reinforced simply for approaching the bar.

Experimenter now waits for animal to rise up on its hind legs; then click sounds as food drops into cup.

Rat eats food and afterward tends to rise up near the bar again. Each time it does it receives food.

C

Rat no longer reinforced simply for rising up near the bar.

Now must actually press bar for food to be dropped into cup.

Rat then eats food and afterward tends to press bar again. Each time it does it receives food so bar-pressing becomes very frequent.

Figure 8.6 Shaping the bar-press response. The idea behind shaping is to reinforce ever-closer approximations of a desired behavior, until eventually that behavior is performed. In this illustration the bar-press response is shaped in only three steps: the rat is first rewarded for approaching the bar, then for rising up near it, and finally for pressing it. In reality, of course, the researcher may have to progressively reward a longer series of discrete behaviors, each one only a very small step beyond what the rat was doing before.

Shaping is often used to teach circus animals their tricks. What steps might be involved in teaching these elephants to dance on their hind legs?

until the rat presses the bar. This process is illustrated in Figure 8.6.

The same technique can be used to train animals to do intricate tricks. Pigeons have been taught to play Ping-Pong and to tap out simple tunes on a toy piano; dolphins have been taught to "hula" while balancing on their tails; and bears have been taught to ride unicycles. Human behavior can also be shaped with similar procedures. For example, two psychologists (Azrin and Foxx, 1974) have devised a way to toilet train young children by reinforcing each step in the sequence of walking toward the potty chair, lowering their pants, sitting down, and urinating. Shaping has also been used effectively by behavior therapists, who have applied the techniques to adults with various behavior disorders (Lanyon and Lanyon, 1978).

Schedules of Reinforcement   While new behavior is being established, experimenters generally reinforce an animal each time the behavior occurs. But once it is established, behavior can be maintained by regulating the relationship between behavior and reinforcement. This is done by altering the basis on which the animal is rewarded; that is, by changing the **schedule of reinforcement.**

An animal that is reinforced for every response—for example, a rat given a food pellet each time it presses the bar—is on a **continuous reinforce-**ment schedule. A schedule in which an animal is reinforced after only some of its responses is called a **partial reinforcement schedule.** In general, animals work harder (pressing the bar more often for each bit of food) when they are on partial reinforcement schedules than when reinforcement follows every response. This fact is fortunate, for if continuous reinforcement were required to maintain a response, operant conditioning would have little application outside the laboratory, since few responses in the world are reinforced every time they are made.

In one type of partial reinforcement schedule, an animal is rewarded each time it makes a specified number of responses, say, fifteen presses of the bar. This is called a **fixed ratio schedule** and is analogous to the automobile factory worker who gets paid each time a certain number of cars rolls off the assembly line. Placed on a fixed ratio schedule, a rat works fairly quickly, pressing the bar at a more rapid rate than if it were rewarded after each bar press. And for good reason: the faster the rat works, the more it eats.

Sometimes, however, a rat is placed on a **fixed interval schedule,** in which reinforcement comes for the first response after a specified period, say a minute. Thus, no matter how hard the rat works, rewards come no oftener than once each minute. Shortly after a rat is placed on a fixed interval schedule, it adjusts its response rate to the schedule, working just hard enough to maintain reinforcement. After a food pellet arrives in the cup, the rat tends to stop working until near the end of the fixed interval; then it slowly increases its bar pressing, only to stop again after the next food pellet arrives. This schedule is roughly analogous to a person receiving a weekly wage because there is no relationship between effort and reward; the employee who does a minimum amount of work is paid as regularly as the one who works at a rapid pace.

As the analogies indicate, regular schedules of reinforcement are also used to regulate the behavior of people. For example, most people are paid on a fixed interval schedule—weekly or monthly. But agricultural laborers and those who do sewing at home get paid on a piecework basis—by the number of boxes of produce they pack or the number of garments they make.

Not all partial schedules of reinforcement are based on such regular relationships between behavior and reinforcement. Irregular or unpredictable partial reinforcement schedules are even more efficient than fixed schedules in increasing desired behavior.

In a **variable ratio schedule,** reinforcement may come after an *average* of ten responses. However, the reinforcement does not arrive after the tenth response, but at an unpredictable time; it may come after every response for a while and then only after twenty or thirty responses. In a **variable interval schedule,** reinforcement may come on the *average* of once each minute. Again, because of its unpredictable occurrence, reinforcement may come after ten seconds or after ten minutes. Because of the unpredictability of these schedules, the animal whose behavior is being reinforced is always alert to the possibility of a reward, hence it tends to respond at a high rate.

The persistent behavior of an animal on a variable schedule is analogous to the actions of a gambler at a slot machine. Because both the amount of reinforcement and its schedule are highly varied, slot machines have a compelling effect on the behavior of the person pulling the handle. Since the machine pays out unpredictable amounts at unpredictable times, the player continues to hope that the next pull will bring the jackpot.

The power of irregular schedules to maintain behavior often leads to the maintenance of undesirable responses. For example, new parents often find their baby's cries difficult to deal with,

Variable reward schedules tend to result in very high rates of response because there is always a chance that the next response will yield the desired payoff. This is what makes slot machines so compelling. If slot machines were operated on fixed reward schedules, it would be unlikely that anyone would play them.

so they rush to comfort the wailing infant. But it is easy to reinforce crying with parental attention. The infant soon learns that crying is the way to get taken out of the crib—especially if the parents rarely pick up the baby when she or he is not crying. When parents try to break the cycle by ignoring the wails, the infant may cry harder. Even if the parents are sometimes successful, particularly prolonged periods of crying may lead them to pick up their baby. The infant is then on a highly efficient, irregular partial reinforcement schedule, which can be ended only by a steadfast refusal to award attention-getting crying.

Conditioned Reinforcers

After an animal—or a person—learns some behavior to get a **primary reinforcer** (i.e., a stimulus such as food, water, sleep, or sex that fulfills some basic need), the organism may perform that same behavior under the control of a different reinforcer. In such a situation, the power of the primary reinforcer has generalized to a **secondary reinforcer,** or a **conditioned reinforcer.** A conditioned reinforcer is a stimulus that signals that the primary reinforcer will soon appear. For example, the click as pellets are released into a food cup signals that the primary reinforcer, food, is on the way. If the click consistently precedes the arrival of the food, it may acquire the power to elicit the learned behavior, just as the trainer's whistle evokes tail slaps and leaps from a dolphin because the sound signals that fish is on the way.

The regularity with which a primary reinforcer follows learned behavior in the laboratory is rarely encountered in daily life. In most cases, a conditioned reinforcer covers the interval between a response and its reinforcement. For example, money is a highly effective conditioned reinforcer, and people are willing to work for it because they know it can be exchanged for primary reinforcers, such as food or shelter. But money retains this power only as long as it has value. If it becomes worthless, people will no longer work for it, beg for it, or steal it. In Europe, during the depression of the 1930s, people refused money and would work only for the primary reinforcers of goods and services.

The power of conditioned reinforcers is suggested by the fact that chimpanzees are willing to work for tokens that can be used to buy fruit from a vending machine called a Chimp-O-Mat (Wolfe, 1936; see Figure 8.7). The chimpanzees' labor demonstrates that conditioned reinforcers —in this case, the tokens—can span lengthy delays between the completion of a task and the arrival of a primary reinforcer, such as food. Without the tokens, even a short interval between the task's completion and the arrival of food made the chimpanzees reluctant to keep working.

Conditioned reinforcers can also be used to establish new behavior, because a conditioned reinforcer can generalize to new learning situations. For instance, the tokens that maintain a chimpanzee's bar pulling are also effective in establishing some new response, such as bell ringing. Used in this way, conditioned reinforcers can establish and maintain long sequences of learned behavior. A chimpanzee working for tokens carries out at least three separate responses in sequence, and the first two of them are maintained by conditioned reinforcers. The chimpan-

Figure 8.7 A powerful conditioned reinforcer in daily human life is money. Wolfe showed in an important series of experiments that chimpanzees, too, could learn to use "money." Chimps could be conditioned to pull down a heavily weighted handle in order to obtain tokens (poker chips), which could then be inserted into a machine that vended peanuts or bananas. The value of the tokens to the chimps was evident from the fact that they would work for them and save them—and would sometimes try to steal them from each other. (After Wolfe, 1936.)

zee first pulls a handle to get a token from the token-dispensing machine, then drops the token into a slot on the Chimp-O-Mat to get a grape, and finally eats the grape.

Just as the chimpanzees' tokens generalize to new situations, so money and similar reinforcers generalize to a wide variety of human behavior. A conditioned reinforcer that has been particularly effective in recent years is the manufacturer's coupon. People spend hours clipping these coupons from their newspapers, sorting them, filing them, and trading them before they finally exchange them in partial payment for food (a primary reinforcer) at the supermarket.

Generalization and Discrimination

Generalization and discrimination occur in operant conditioning, just as they do in classical conditioning. A pigeon trained to peck a red key to get food will also peck an orange key. This sort of stimulus generalization is common in everyday life. A young child who has just learned to call the family dog "doggie" may start calling cats and rabbits by the same name. Similarly, an adult who customarily drives a car with a standard shift will often try to depress the nonexistent clutch pedal when driving a car with an automatic transmission. Generalization sometimes has unfortunate consequences. For example, when a member of a minority group commits a socially unacceptable act, observers tend to generalize that action to the rest of the minority group, creating or maintaining prejudice.

As with classical conditioning, discrimination between quite similar stimuli is not difficult to learn. Precise stimulus control can be established through a procedure called **discrimination training,** in which the organism is reinforced for responding to one stimulus but not reinforced for responding to a slightly different stimulus. In the case of the pigeon, a key is illuminated by a red or a yellow light, which are the **discriminative stimuli.** When the red light is on, the pigeon's pecks are reinforced; when the yellow light is on, they are not. Eventually, the pigeon learns to respond to the red light (the **positive discriminative stimulus**) but not to the yellow light (the **negative discriminative stimulus**). The pigeon's pecking has come under the control of the lights, because the color of the lighted key gives the pigeon information about the availability of reinforcement. Through the same process of discrimination training, the child who calls all animals "doggie" comes to call some of them "kitty" and others "bunny."

Aversive Conditioning

Most of the techniques for behavior control described so far have relied on positive reinforcers —food, money, or similar rewards that increase the frequency of the behavior that precedes them. Another method of controlling behavior involves the use of unpleasant, or aversive, stimuli. **Aversive conditioning** relies on negative reinforcement and punishment, and the problems involved with this sort of conditioning were discussed earlier.

The distinction between the two techniques becomes clear when we consider a small boy who throws a temper tantrum because his parents do not want him to play in the mud. When the parents try to prevent his messy play, the boy punishes them by yelling and screaming. However, if the parents give in and permit him to play in the mud, they have responded to negative reinforcement: as soon as they act, the annoying tantrum stops.

Negative reinforcement can take various forms, and sometimes occurs naturally. When you step out into the bright noonday sun, you immediately reach for your sunglasses, which in the past have ended the unpleasant glare. Negative reinforcement can also be used deliberately. In one case, psychologists used loud noise to increase conversation among mental patients (Heckel, Wiggins, and Salzberg, 1962). Each time the group of patients lapsed into silence for longer than one minute, a speaker hidden in an air-conditioning vent began to make an uncomfortably loud noise. As soon as one of the patients began to talk, the noise stopped. Very quickly, there was a sharp rise in the amount of conversation among the patients.

Mild electric shock has been used as negative reinforcement, but only after other methods of treatment have failed. For example, a retarded child who had developed a habit of severely beating his head was given mild shock, coupled with a loud buzzer, to make him stop. The shock could be ended by touching a toy, for when the child was holding a toy he did not strike himself. When the shock was first used, an experimenter guided the boy's hands to a toy, and the shock stopped. After several trials, the shock was eliminated and only the secondary reinforcer of the buzzer was used. The buzzer sounded when the boy released a toy and stopped when he picked it up again. As a result of this treatment, the boy stopped his self-injurious behavior (Kazdin, 1975).

Punishment is meant to decrease or suppress behavior. There are many kinds of punishment —spanking children, jailing lawbreakers, flunking students—and punishment can be a useful means of controlling behavior. Certainly "accidental" punishment can effectively suppress the repetition of a particular behavior: a child has to touch a hot stove only once.

Sometimes punishment takes the form of removing a positive event, as when a boy who misbehaves is exiled to his room for a half-hour, or when a motorist who is caught driving seventy-five miles an hour is fined for speeding. In the first case, companionship was denied the child; in the second, money was removed from the motorist. Punishment by denial was used in an attempt to get young boys to stop sucking their thumbs. Each boy watched a series of animated cartoons and whenever he began to suck his thumb, the film was stopped. Thumb sucking fell off dramatically; however, when the cartoons were shown without interruption, the boys sucked their thumbs nearly as often as before (Baer, 1962).

Punishment is probably most effective when used in conjunction with positive reinforcement, so that as the unwanted behavior is punished, desirable behavior is reinforced. For example, a six-year-old girl whose bizarre climbing activities had caused her several serious injuries was given a mild shock on the leg each time she started to climb the furniture. At the same time, the experimenter (Risley, 1968) reinforced her with food whenever she sat down quietly or made eye contact with him. In this case, the combination of punishment and positive reinforcement effectively ended the dangerous climbing.

Practical Applications of Operant Conditioning

The concepts of operant conditioning are applied every day in ordinary situations. Computer-assisted instruction and behavior modification are two areas of widespread practical application.

Computer-Assisted Instruction Animals learn fastest when their reinforcement comes immediately after a response, because immediacy allows the animal to use information about the availability of reinforcement to alter its behavior. That is, animals learn more efficiently when they get immediate feedback. **Feedback** is reinforcement in the form of information about past performance that is used to alter future behavior, and the feedback principle is the basis of computer-assisted instruction.

In **computer-assisted instruction (CAT)**, each student sits at a computer terminal, answers questions or carries out tasks under the computer's instructions, gets immediate feedback, and moves ahead at her or his own pace. The computer adjusts the course to the student's abilities, branching off into remedial or supplementary steps if necessary to improve the student's comprehension. The computer can also be programed to jump back to the start of a sequence that is causing difficulty or to jump forward to a new sequence for the fast learner. Finally, the computer can maintain a record of each student's progress and use this information to structure subsequent work.

More than 50,000 computers are being used in schools today, and students in elementary school learn reading, mathematics, biology, and music theory with the help of computers (Williams et al., 1981). Computers have been used in a wide variety of college courses, with promising results. For example, when university students learned introductory Russian from a computer, they did significantly better on final exams than students taught in a regular Russian course, fewer computer students dropped out, and more computer students went on to enroll in an ad-

Computer-assisted instruction allows students to progress at their own pace and adjusts lessons to their varying levels of ability.

vanced Russian class (Suppes and Morningstar, 1969).

Computer-assisted instruction does have its drawbacks. Working alone with a machine for lengthy periods may be distasteful to some students who miss the intellectual stimulation, social interaction, and competition of the classroom. However, many computers are being used in conjunction with regular classroom work, and the newest generation of microcomputers provides versatile instructional programs that lessen boredom and provide enrichment for gifted students (Williams et al., 1981).

Behavior Modification   **Behavior modification,** the application of operant techniques to human behavior, has been used in homes, schools, hospitals, prisons, and the community at large. Although most behavior modification programs rely on positive reinforcement and extinction as their primary tools, some use negative reinforcement and punishment; the studies described in the discussion of aversive conditioning were examples of behavior modification.

An extremely successful program of behavior modification that primarily used positive methods was carried out in a California junior-high school with seven students who had been declared incorrigible by police, school officials, and the probation department (Gray, Graubard, and Rosenberg, 1974; Graubard and Rosenberg, 1974). These twelve- to fifteen-year-olds had long histories of trouble at school, and teachers tended to be hostile and suspicious toward them. The students were given formal instruction in behavior modification techniques for one period each day, during which they were taught how to shape their teachers' behavior using positive reinforcement for favorable comments and actions, and either mild punishment (such as the statement, "It's hard for me to do good work when you're cross with me") or extinction (simply ignoring an action) to discourage unfavorable behavior. Within five weeks, the school atmosphere had changed. The formerly "incorrigible" students were now liked and respected by their teachers and the students found school a pleasant place. During a test period, students stopped reinforcing their teachers for two weeks, and the teachers' positive comments dropped while their negative comments increased sharply. Then the students went back to behavior modification on an informal basis and school

again became tolerable. The teachers thought the students had changed; the students were sure the teachers had changed. Both were right.

An entirely different approach to behavior modification was used in the mountains near Logan, Utah, where positive reinforcement proved to be an inexpensive way to eliminate litter (Osborne, Powers, and Anderson, 1974). An unsupervised area, approximately a half-mile long and a quarter-mile wide, was first cleared of 1,676 pounds of litter by Boy Scouts. Then the researchers set up two litter stations along the road, placing in them large oil drums for litter disposal. After ascertaining how much litter people would pick up on their own, the researchers began the program. Plastic bags were provided and signs were attached to the drums, stating that for every bag of litter collected, an individual could fill out a card good for either a 25-cent payment or a chance in a $20 weekly lottery. With these inducements, ten times as much litter was deposited in the drums as when people were left to their own devices. Since most of the people chose the chance in the lottery, the cost was nominal—certainly less than the cost of preparing billboards and television and radio advertisements that urge people not to litter.

Comparison of Classical and Operant Conditioning

Both classical and operant conditioning involve the establishment of a relationship between stimuli and responses; however, there are distinct differences in the procedures that establish the relationship (see Table 8.1).

First, in classical conditioning, the reinforcer, or UCS, precedes the response—for example, food is placed in the mouth before salivation occurs. The opposite relationship characterizes operant conditioning; here, the reinforcer follows the appropriate response—food follows a bar press. Second, in classical conditioning, a specific stimulus is responsible for the response, but in operant conditioning, because there are many stimuli, it is impossible to say just which stimulus is responsible. Third, in classical conditioning, the response is elicited by the specific stimulus (food in the mouth causes salivation); but in operant conditioning, the response is

Table 8.1 Comparison of Classical and Operant Conditioning

Type of comparison	Classical Conditioning	Operant Conditioning
1. Response-reward sequence	1. UCS precedes response	1. Response precedes reward
2. Role of stimuli	2. Specific stimulus produces the response	2. No specific stimulus produces a response
3. Character of response	3. Response is elicited	3. Response is emitted
4. Observed changes	4. Change in effectiveness of formerly neutral stimulus on magnitude of response	4. Change in speed, force, or frequency of response
5. Involvement of nervous system	5. Usually involves autonomic nervous system	5. Usually involves somatic nervous system
6. What is learned	6. Emotions such as fears, attitudes, feelings	6. Instrumental (goal seeking) behavior

Source: Adapted from H. C. Ellis. *Fundamentals of Human Learning, Memory and Cognition.* 2nd ed. Dubuque, Iowa: Wm. C. Brown, 1978., p. 19.

emitted (the bar does not cause the rat to press it). Fourth, in classical conditioning, a formerly neutral stimulus (the tone) becomes increasingly effective at substituting for the UCS in eliciting the response (salivation), while in operant conditioning, a response is emitted more often, more quickly, or more forcefully than before. Fifth, in classical conditioning, the response generally involves the autonomic nervous system, while in operant conditioning, the response involves the somatic nervous system. This separation of nervous system responses is not always distinct, since in some cases both parts of the nervous system are involved in either kind of conditioning. Finally, in classical conditioning, organisms learn emotions, attitudes, and expectations, while in operant conditioning, organisms learn responses that are directed toward a goal (Ellis, 1978).

Despite these differences, both types of conditioning appear to involve the same learning process. The outcome, in which reinforcement establishes particular responses, is the same in both. Both generalize to other situations, both are subject to discrimination training, and in both, the removal of the reinforcer leads to the eventual extinction of the response.

Social Learning Theory

An approach to learning that combines traditional learning theory with a concern for human thought processes has been developed by social learning theorists. In **social learning theory,** as put forth by Albert Bandura (1977), learning is not simply a matter of reacting to stimuli; instead people apply cognitive processes to the stimuli they encounter, selecting, organizing, and transforming them. As a result, stimuli are seen as information, and it is people's interpretations of stimuli and not the stimuli themselves that control behavior.

The way that cognitive processes can affect the power of reinforcement was shown in a study in which people were rewarded for manual responses on a variable interval schedule, receiving reinforcement about once each minute (Kaufman, Baron, and Kopp, 1966). Some of the people were told that they would be rewarded after approximately 150 responses (on a variable ratio schedule); some were told they would be rewarded once each minute (on a fixed interval schedule); and some were told, correctly, that they would be rewarded approximately once each minute (on a variable interval schedule). Everybody got the same rewards at the same rate, but the performance of each group was quite different. Those who thought they were on a fixed interval schedule averaged 6 responses; those who thought they were on a variable ratio schedule averaged 259 responses; and those who thought they were on the actual variable interval schedule averaged 65 responses. In other words, their expectation of reinforcement and not the reinforcement itself was the strongest determinant of their performance.

Such anticipation of reinforcement influences what people notice, and what they notice is important because, say social learning theorists, much of what we learn is the result of **observational learning.** Instead of learning everything by trial and error, with our successes reinforced and our failures punished, we pay attention to what other people do and say and notice the consequences of their behavior. Most important behavior is learned in this way. Indeed, learning to drive a car or to perform brain surgery by operant conditioning, in which reinforcements and punishments gradually shaped us into drivers or surgeons, would be costly to both individuals and society.

In observational learning, other people serve as models and from them we learn complete patterns of behavior, instead of acquiring a pattern bit by bit in response to reinforcement. From watching a model, we can learn a new pattern of behavior, learn to stop behaving in a certain way, behave in previously forbidden ways, or behave in an old way that had been forgotten but was recalled by the model's performance (Bandura and Walters, 1963). We may store information about a modeled behavior in memory—how to perform a new dance step, how a friend gets dates, the consequences of writing a best seller —and use this information to structure our behavior in the future. Many people imitate parents, teachers, or friends, but some imitate the behavior of people they will never meet—movie stars, fictional characters, athletes, or other media personalities. More is learned through observation than overt behavior; people also can acquire a full range of attitudes, emotions, and social styles in this way.

Observational learning has been applied in a wide variety of settings. For example, instructors are urged not to force poor readers to read but

Much of our behavior is the result of observational learning. Once a behavior is modeled for us a few times (a new dance step, for example), we find it easy to join in.

to encourage them by having other children of the same age read aloud (Di Vesta, 1974). The successful readers serve as models, demonstrating the possibility of learning to read and the reinforcements the good reader receives both in praise from others and in the satisfaction that accompanies success.

Learning theories that do not consider the active role played by human thought in the acquisition and regulation of behavior seem to ignore a crucial aspect of human experience. Cognitive models of learning have influenced most areas of psychology, including personality and social development, psychopathology, and psychotherapy. The cognitive approach provides the major foundation for Chapter 9 on memory.

SUMMARY

1. **Learning** can be described as a relatively enduring change in behavior caused by experience or practice. Learning must be inferred because the process cannot be observed directly. Changes in performance are not always the result of learning, but may be caused by maturation, drugs, fatigue, or motivation. Learning can be divided into three different types: classical conditioning, operant conditioning, and social learning.

2. In **classical conditioning,** a neutral stimulus (a tone), when it is repeatedly presented with an **unconditioned stimulus** (e.g., food) that normally evokes a reflex, or **unconditioned response** (e.g., salivation), comes to elicit that response when presented by itself. Once the neutral stimulus elicits the original response, the previously neutral stimulus has become a **conditioned stimulus** and the original response has become a **conditioned response.**

This tendency to react to a previously neutral stimulus as though it were the unconditioned stimulus was called **stimulus substitution** by Pavlov, who discovered classical conditioning. Some limits to conditioning were discovered by Garcia. He found that animals quickly connect some kinds of neutral stimuli with unconditioned responses and almost never connect other kinds of stimuli with unconditioned responses. Garcia also found that if the neutral stimulus is one that animals seem prepared to connect with a response, the delay between stimulus and response can be lengthy.

3. Once an organism has been conditioned to respond in a specific way, the response may **generalize,** that is, a response learned in one situation may be elicited by other, similar situations. The more similar a situation is to a conditioned stimulus, the more likely it is that the response will generalize. The process by which animals are trained to differentiate among stimuli, responding to one and not responding to others, is called **discrimination.** Unless the conditioned stimulus and the unconditioned stimulus are occasionally presented in conjunction with each other, a classically conditioned response will eventually disappear, a process known as **extinction.** Pavlov's work had a profound influence on behavioral psychology. Watson, for example, maintained that the principles of classical conditioning could account for all learning—whether animal or human.

4. Behavioral psychologists who believed that classical conditioning could not explain all learning followed a line of research pioneered by Thorndike. Thorndike's **law of effect** states that responses that are followed by satisfying consequences tend to be repeated, but responses that are followed by annoying consequences tend to disappear. As a result, **operant conditioning,** in which learning is explained by the way the consequences of behavior affect an organism's future behavior, was developed by Skinner. **Operant behavior** is spontaneous behavior that has an effect on the environment and is not associated with an obvious stimulus; it is influenced by the consequences that follow it.

5. The consequences of behavior are classified according to the kinds of effect they have on subsequent behavior. Consequences that lead to an increase in the frequency of behavior are called **reinforcement.** Consequences that lead to the suppression or decrease in the frequency of behavior are called **punishment.** In **positive reinforcement,** the reinforcer is anything following a response that strengthens the response. In **negative reinforcement,** the reinforcer is anything that strengthens the response that led to the reinforcer's removal. Punishment is anything unpleasant following a response that weakens the response.

6. Once established, operantly conditioned responses can be maintained by various **schedules of reinforcement,** or the basis on which the organism is rewarded. Providing reinforcement each time a response occurs is called **continuous reinforcement,** a technique used to establish new behavior. Once the behavior is established, the best way to maintain it is through one of the **partial reinforcement** schedules. On a **fixed ratio schedule,** the organism is reinforced after it has made a specified number of responses. On a **fixed interval schedule,** the organism is reinforced after a fixed interval of time, regardless of the number of responses made. On a **variable ratio** schedule, reinforcement comes after an average number of responses. On a **variable interval schedule,** reinforcement comes after an average amount of time has elapsed.

7. A **conditioned reinforcer** is a stimulus that signals that the **primary reinforcer** (the original reinforcer) is on the way. If the conditioned reinforcer consistently precedes the primary reinforcer, the conditioned reinforcer will acquire the power to elicit the learned behavior by itself. Because conditioned reinforcers generalize to new learning situations, they can be used to establish new behavior. When an organism produces an operantly conditioned response to another stimulus, **generalization** has occurred. **Discrimination training,** in which reinforcement and extinction are used together, will train an organism to confine a response to a particular stimulus. A **positive discriminative stimulus** informs the organism that reinforcement is available; a **negative discriminative stimulus** informs the organism that responses will not be reinforced.

8. **Aversive conditioning** can also be used to control behavior through the techniques of negative reinforcement and punishment. **Computer-assisted instruction** uses **feedback,** reinforcement in the form of information about past behavior, to teach students. **Behavior modification,** the application of operant techniques to human behavior, relies primarily upon positive reinforcement and extinction to change behavior, but some programs also use aversive conditioning.

9. In **social learning theory,** as formulated by Bandura, learning is not simply a matter of reacting to stimuli, but to people's interpretations of stimuli after they have been processed. Instead of learning by trial and error, much of our learning comes from watching others, or from **observational learning,** in which we pay attention to what other people do and say, and notice the consequences of their behavior. In observational learning, people serve as models and we learn complete patterns of behavior from them. Attitudes and emotions, as well as actual behavior, can be learned in this way.

KEY TERMS

aversive conditioning
behavior modification
classical conditioning
computer-assisted instruction
  (CAI)
conditioned reinforcer
conditioned response (CR)
conditioned stimulus (CS)
continuous reinforcement
  schedule
discrimination
discrimination training
discriminative stimuli
extinction
feedback
fixed interval schedule
fixed ratio schedule

generalization
generalization gradient
instrumental conditioning
law of effect
learning
negative discriminative
  stimulus
negative reinforcement
observational learning
operant behavior
operant conditioning
partial reinforcement
  schedule
positive discriminative
  stimulus
positive reinforcement
primary reinforcer

punishment
reinforcement
respondent behavior
reward
schedule of reinforcement
secondary reinforcer
shaping
social learning theory
stimulus substitution
superstitious behavior
unconditioned response
  (UCR)
unconditioned stimulus
  (UCS)
variable interval schedule
variable ratio schedule

RECOMMENDED READINGS

HOUSTON, J. P. *Fundamentals of Learning and Memory.* 2nd ed. New York; Academic Press, 1981. This book emphasizes experimental investigation of learning and memory. It presents the basic data on both animal and human learning, along with the theories that researchers have devised to explain those data.

PAVLOV, I. P. *Conditional Reflexes.* New York: Oxford University Press, 1927. All about Pavlovian conditioning.

SCHWARTZ, B. *Psychology of Learning and Behavior.* New York: Norton, 1978. This text is about research on learning, with strong emphasis on recent developments in learning research.

SKINNER, B. F. *The Behavior of Organisms.* New York: Appleton-Century-Crofts, 1938. All about operant conditioning—straight from the horse's mouth.

WARSON, D. L., and R. G. THARP. *Self-directed Behavior: Self-modification for Personal Adjustment.* 2nd ed. Monterey: Brooks/Cole, 1977. This book tells you how to use learning principles to modify your own behavior. It is an interesting how-to-do-it book.

CHAPTER 9

Memory

Imagine being handed a list of fifty unrelated words, then after about three minutes' study, recalling them perfectly, forward or backward. A Russian newspaper reporter who was studied extensively by Alexander Luria (1968) found this feat no more difficult than you would find recalling what you ate for breakfast this morning. What is more, the Russian, whom Luria called S, could repeat the list without any previous warning after a lapse of fifteen or sixteen years.

In such a situation, reported Luria, S would sit with his eyes closed and say:

> Yes, yes . . . This was a series you gave me once when we were in your apartment . . . You were sitting at the table and I in the rocking chair . . . You were wearing a gray suit and you looked at me like this . . . Now, then, I can see you saying . . .

With that, the list would come tumbling out, each word in order and never confused with the words of another list. Foreign languages posed no problem; S once memorized long passages of *The Divine Comedy* in Italian, which he did not speak, and fifteen years later recalled them with ease.

These amazing feats of memory depended upon mental imagery. When memorizing a list of words, S often imagined a walk down a familiar street, and mentally placed an image corresponding to each word in a distinctive place along the street. To recall the list, he simply repeated his mental stroll and called off each item as he passed it. He also turned strings of letters or numbers into stories, using standard images for each letter and number. For example, his image for the number 2 was a high-spirited woman.

Faced with final exams, you might long for a memory like S's, but his incredible memory became a curse as well as a blessing. S could not forget. Images he had created to help him remember haunted him, intruding into his awareness and making it difficult to concentrate on his daily business. He became confused, finding it impossible to follow simple conversations because someone's words would trigger a host of associated images. Unable to hold regular employment, S was forced to work at the only job his amazing memory suited him for—that of a performer who displayed his curious ability in one town after another.

Although S's skill at recalling meaningless lists is remote from everyday experiences with memory, the study of such an unusual ability can increase our understanding of memory. In S's case, the techniques he used make it clear that the way information is organized can greatly increase the chances of recalling it.

What Is Memory?

All of us would agree that S had a "good memory"; people who cannot remember

Good memories are important in some professions: actors and actresses, for example, may need to recall their lines from several plays without error.

appointments or who continually mislay their glasses or car keys often say they have a "bad memory." To understand what we mean by the notion of a good or bad memory, it is useful to view **memory** as a function: the capacity to register, retain, and retrieve information.

Memory can be demonstrated by recognizing information when it is reencountered at a later time or by recalling stored information. Picking out your own stolen jewelry from a police department display of recovered earrings, cufflinks, and watches is an example of recognition; recommending a restaurant because of the wonderful lobster you have eaten there is an example of recall.

When recognition and recall are flawless, the demonstration of memory is easy, but all of us register more information than we can recall.

Final exams provide a common experience of the failure to recall stored information. Although a question has been expected and the material carefully studied, the mind goes blank and, no matter how great the effort, the information remains elusive. Students give various reasons for poor performance on examinations, and a list of fourteen common excuses has been collected (Wingfield and Byrne, 1981; see Figure 9.1). Poor performance is at the basis of the reasons in the first group; the student had stored the information but failed to recall it. Lack of knowledge or capacity is responsible for failures in the second group; the student either did not or could not store the information. Reasons in the third group are unclassified; they could represent poor performance, lack of knowledge, or incapacity.

As the students' excuses show, it is often difficult to discover whether the inability to remember is due to a failure in recall or to a failure to store the information in the first place. For this reason, discovering why the process of recognition or recall sometimes goes awry is one interest of researchers. The study of human memory is an attempt to understand the entire memory system, from the first registration of information to its recall for use at a later date. In examining the workings of memory, psychologists distinguish three basic memory functions or processes: acquisition, retention, and retrieval.

Acquisition involves transforming raw information into the form in which it will be stored. This process is also called **encoding**, but not all aspects of information we wish to remember are encoded. When two people see the same situation, each may attend to different aspects of it and their later discussions will show that although their memories overlap, they are also different. In addition to attention, an understanding of the material to be remembered and the strategies used to encode it also affect the acquisition process. For example, S's use of imagery was an encoding strategy.

Once information is encoded, it must be retained, and **retention**, or maintaining information in storage, is the second memory process. When retention fails, information is forgotten, and studies have shown that most forgetting can be traced to interference from more recent information.

Retrieval, the third memory process, refers to the ability to get encoded information out of storage and back into awareness. The process of

Figure 9.1

GROUP	RESPONSES
I. Performance/Behavior	**1.** My pencil kept breaking (I broke my glasses) so I wrote too slowly.
	2. I was tired (sick) when taking the examination.
	3. I knew the answers, but I just couldn't think of them.
	4. I was too nervous during the exam, and had a mental block.
	5. The questions misled me as to what was wanted for an answer.
	6. I was preoccupied with personal problems and just couldn't think.
II. Knowledge/Capacity	**1.** I was tired (sick) when trying to study for the exam.
	2. I just didn't study enough.
	3. I learned the individual facts, but couldn't see how they related to each other.
	4. I couldn't understand the material.
III. Uncategorizable	**1.** I didn't know the exam was today.
	2. I just wasn't up for it.
	3. A flying saucer landed in my bedroom and . . .
	4. I never do well on objective exams.

Figure 9.1 Fourteen reasons why I failed the last examination. (Wingfield and Byrnes, 1981.)

All the onlookers here are observing the same event, but their memories of it are likely to be quite different, depending on where their attention was focused.

retrieval involves an organized search of retained material, and the search employs a variety of strategies.

Not all memories are alike, and only some of what we encode is retained for any length of time. Research on the acquisition, retention, and retrieval of information has led many psychologists to assume that there are three different types of memory stores: sensory memory, short-term memory, and long-term memory (Atkinson and Shiffrin, 1968).

Sensory memory, the first type of storage, refers to the momentary persistence of sensory information after stimulation has ceased, such as the image on a frame of movie film. The memory can be a sight, a sound, a touch, a smell, or a taste, and unless it is processed, thereby transferring it to another part of the system, the memory will fade in about a second. Sensory memory can hold a great deal of information at one time, but because the information is unprocessed, it has no meaning.

Information that has been transferred to **short-term memory**, the second type of memory storage, is retained for about fifteen seconds. The information in short-term memory has meaning; the sensory information (the black shapes of the letters in this sentence) has been transformed into words that carry a message. Short-term memory can hold only a limited amount of information.

Long-term memory, the third type of memory storage, has a limitless capacity and information is stored there indefinitely. Information that is transferred to long-term memory is related meaningfully to other information already in storage. Long-term memory makes society possible; it enables us to recognize friends, cook a meal, hold a job, and enjoy a book or a film.

Some researchers (e.g., Cermak and Craik, 1979) prefer to talk about memory in another way, pointing out that instead of transferring information from one type of storage to another, human beings process the information at increasingly deeper levels. With **levels of processing**, whether material is retained depends on the depth to which it is processed and the extent to which it is elaborated (i.e., related to other material that has already received deep processing). Although neither the structural nor the levels-of-processing explanation can account for all aspects of human memory, each has been useful to researchers.

Types of Memory

Once an item of information enters the memory system, it must be stored or it will fade quickly and disappear. Since it is impossible to observe the way information is stored in the system, psychologists make inferences about storage by examining the performance of subjects on memory retrieval tasks. Each type of memory—sensory, short-term, and long-term—handles information in a different way and retains it for a different length of time (see Figure 9.2).

Sensory Memory

No one is certain just how much information can be held in sensory memory. It is generally supposed that this first type of memory contains all the information registered by the various sense organs at any given instant, but that the information decays almost immediately.

Understanding Sensory Memory Information that stimulates the eye is held in **iconic memory,** and since vision is a major source of information

Figure 9.2 A diagram of the human memory system showing the relationship among sensory memory, short-term memory, and long-term memory. (Wortman and Loftus, 1981.)

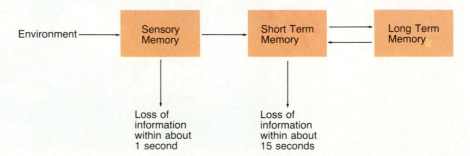

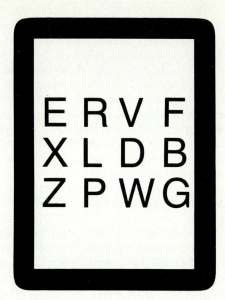

Figure 9.3 When exposed to this array of unrelated letters for a brief period, people typically recall no more than four or five of them. But if subjects are signaled immediately after the exposure to recall just one of the lines, they can always recall all four letters correctly. This evidence suggests that people "read" the information from some sort of complete sensory image of the stimulus, which fades in the time it takes to say the names of the letters in the image.

about the world, this visual sensory memory has received a good deal of attention from researchers. Each fixation of the eye presents the brain with another image, and if information did not fade quickly from iconic memory, human vision would be confused and the visual field would resemble a snapshot made with multiple exposures. But researchers were not sure how long visual images persisted until George Sperling (1960) conducted a series of classic experiments. He first discovered that when four letters or numbers were flashed before them for 50 milliseconds (.05 second), most people could correctly report all four of them. But no matter how many more letters he presented during that brief period, people generally could report no more than five. Yet people consistently said that they saw more than five letters; the problem was that by the time they had reported the first four or five, they had forgotten the rest.

To find out whether all the information in a display was held in iconic memory, Sperling showed people a pattern like the one in Figure 9.3. This time, just as the array went off, he sounded a high, medium, or low tone. When his subjects heard the high tone, they were to report

the top line; when they heard the medium tone, they were to report the middle line; when they heard the low tone, they were to report the bottom line. Under these conditions, people displayed almost perfect recall; they reported accurately whichever line Sperling designated. Apparently the entire display was in iconic memory.

By gradually lengthening the time between the flash and the tone, Sperling was able to test the duration of iconic memory. He found that people's performance got progressively worse and then leveled off when the flash and tone were separated by a second. With this delay, they could report only one—or sometimes two—of the letters in any line. Again, since they could report from any line, four or five letters must have been available to them, but by the time one line had been reported, the rest were gone. Thus, iconic memory apparently begins to fade immediately, and within about a second, any information that has not been coded and transferred to short-term memory has vanished.

Iconic memory is just one type of sensory memory. Each of the other senses has its own type of memory, but of them, only auditory sensory memory has been studied to any degree. Auditory sensory memory, or **echoic memory**, is more enduring than iconic memory; the memories of sounds begin fading almost immediately, but in most cases they are not completely gone until about four seconds have passed (Darwin, Turvey, and Crowder, 1972). Without echoic memory, language would be impossible, because by the time a speaker had finished a sentence—or even a word—the hearer would have forgotten the first part of the communication.

Selective Attention Since information fades so rapidly from sensory memory, it must be transferred to short-term memory if it is to be useful. However, no one can use all the myriad sights, sounds, and other sensations that continually stimulate the central nervous system. As Sperling's study of iconic memory showed, human beings control the selection of material from sensory memory, processing whatever they choose. This control process is called **selective attention**.

A good example of selective attention that almost everyone has experienced is the cocktail party phenomenon. At a crowded cocktail party, our ears receive a confusing babble of auditory information. Although the racket of other voices, the clink of glasses, and the sounds of music form a complex jumble of sounds, we have no problem in following our partner's words—the message we have selected for processing. It may seem that we accomplish this feat by shutting out all other sounds, but research indicates that the unattended sounds do get an elementary form of attention. Selective attention permits some processing of additional information that has not been selected for attention.

The cocktail party phenomenon has been studied extensively by psychologists. One way to explore selective attention is with the technique of **dichotic listening**, in which a person wearing a set of earphones hears two different messages played simultaneously, one in each ear. The subject is told to "shadow" the message coming into one ear; that is, to repeat it aloud as it is received.

In shadowing, the listener's voice, like a shadow, follows immediately behind the recorded message. Early experiments (Cherry, 1953) found that people could report the shadowed message about as well when there was a competing message fed into the opposite ear as when they heard the message in isolation. Like a guest at a cocktail party, however, they had consciously attended to only one message. When asked to recognize or recall material from the nonshadowed message, they could remember nothing of its content, nor could they say whether the voice had relayed a meaningful message or a stream of nonsense syllables.

Yet some information had been processed; listeners could report whether the voice coming into the other ear had been that of a man or a woman—and whether the sex of the speaker had changed at some point in the message. They also

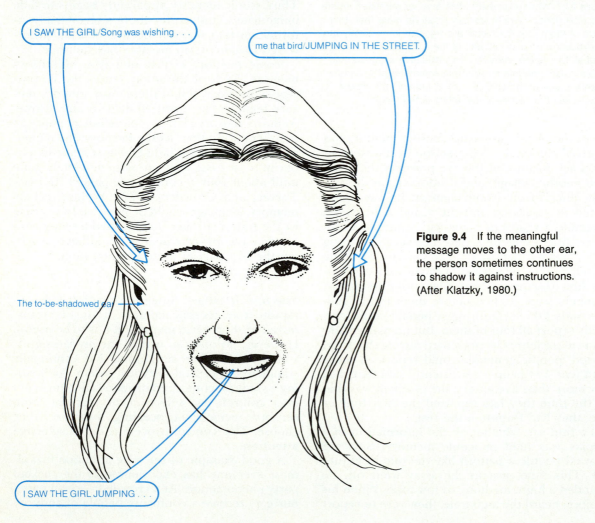

I SAW THE GIRL/Song was wishing . . .

me that bird/JUMPING IN THE STREET.

The to-be-shadowed ear

I SAW THE GIRL JUMPING . . .

Figure 9.4 If the meaningful message moves to the other ear, the person sometimes continues to shadow it against instructions. (After Klatzky, 1980.)

heard their own name when it was inserted into the nonshadowed message. In fact, if the insertion of the listener's name was followed by an instruction to switch shadowing from one ear to another, about a third of the listeners heard it and at once complied (Moray, 1959).

Meaning appears to have a powerful effect on selective attention. When a person is following a message in one ear and ignoring a message in the other, should the messages suddenly cross so that the message that had been coming into the shadowed ear moves to the unshadowed ear, the person's attention will jump to the previously unshadowed ear (see Figure 9.4). Under such a condition, attention will jump despite the researcher's instructions to repeat only the message coming into the designated ear (Treisman, 1960). What is more, most people are completely unaware that they have made the switch.

The influence of meaningfulness has appeared in other types of shadowing experiments. If a meaningful sequence jumps back and forth between the two ears, listeners will follow and report it. For example, in one study, researchers (Gray and Wedderburn, 1960) asked listeners to recall the items they heard in any order they wished. When each ear heard a sequence of digits, listeners tended to recall all the numbers presented to one ear before recalling the numbers presented to the other. But when they heard a sequence such as "dogs six fleas" in one ear and "eight scratch two" in the other, they tended to report "dogs scratch fleas" and "eight six two" (see Figure 9.5).

Other evidence also indicates that stimuli we have chosen to ignore do get into sensory memory. If a listener is stopped in the middle of a shadowing experiment and asked about the non-

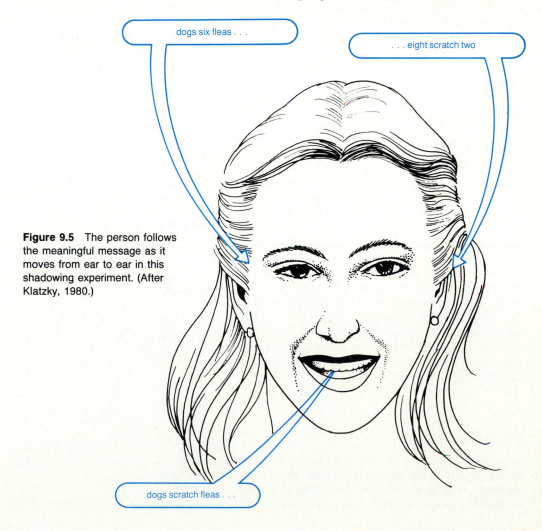

Figure 9.5 The person follows the meaningful message as it moves from ear to ear in this shadowing experiment. (After Klatzky, 1980.)

shadowed message, she or he will be able to recall the last few words of the message despite the fact that other questions about its content draw a blank (Loftus and Loftus, 1976). As we saw earlier, nonattended information fades rapidly and cannot be remembered.

Not everything we do requires selective attention. For example, many of the processes involved in routine driving, such as steering, flipping on a turn indicator, or downshifting a sports car, become automatic. Apparently, most processes that receive extensive practice, such as typing, playing a piano, or riding a bicycle, become automatic and no longer require attention.

Visual aspects of **automaticity**, as these automatic actions are called, have been investigated in relation to sensory memory. In one study (Schneider and Shiffrin, 1977), people watched a series of brief visual displays consisting of letters alone or letters and a number. As the displays were flashed on a screen, subjects reported the presence of a target letter or number. Sometimes the target was a single letter to be found among groups of other letters; at other times the target was a number to be picked from among groups of letters. The crucial aspect of the study was the relationship between the target and the surrounding letters; whether both were members of the same or different categories played a vital part in the results. For example, people needed to see the displays for only 80 milliseconds to pick a number from a group of letters, but had to see each display for 400 milliseconds to pick a specific letter from the group. In addition, when picking a number from a group of letters, it made little difference whether the display contained one, two, or three letters. When asked to pick a letter from among other letters, however, people became progressively less accurate as more letters appeared in the display. Apparently the process of discriminating numbers from letters is automatic and the entire display can be processed at once. But when a particular letter must be picked out of a group of letters, each letter in the display must be inspected.

Short-Term Memory

Since information in sensory memory is unprocessed, it must be transferred into short-term memory if it is to become meaningful. In the shadowing experiments, the information reported by the listeners had been recognized as having meaning, and in the process of recognition, the information moved from sensory to short-term memory. Material in short-term memory is available, but its use is limited by two basic characteristics of short-term memory: it can hold information for only a brief period, and it has a limited capacity.

The brief retention span of short-term memory is a frequent source of annoyance. For example, short-term memory is efficient at holding a telephone number that has just been looked up long enough to dial it, but if the line is busy, the number slips away and must be looked up again when an attempt to redial it is made.

Such everyday experiences have been verified by research that has established just how long it takes information to decay from short-term memory. In a typical experiment (e.g., Peterson and Peterson, 1959), a person read a combination of three consonants (BXY) for a period of two seconds, then—either immediately or after a delay—attempted to recall them. During the delay, the person counted backward by threes to interfere with any attempt to repeat the words and thus to maintain them in memory. When there was no delay, retention was always perfect, but as the delay lengthened, recall kept dropping for about fifteen seconds, then leveled off (see

Figure 9.6 The results of Peterson and Peterson's experiment to measure the length of time that short-term memory lasts without the aid of rehearsal. Subjects were shown a three-consonant combination (CPQ, for example) that they were to remember; immediately after they saw it, they began to count backward by threes from some number supplied by the experimenter. The longer the experimenter let them count before asking them to recall the combination, the less likely the subjects were to recall it correctly.

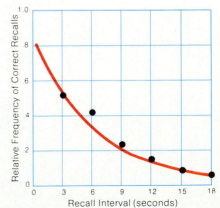

Figure 9.6). By this time, a person could remember the consonants on only about 10 percent of the attempts. Presumably, information retained for more than fifteen seconds had been transferred to long-term memory, because there was no further drop in accuracy after that time.

Information can be kept in short-term memory indefinitely by rehearsing it, or repeating it over and over. There are two kinds of rehearsal, maintenance rehearsal and elaborative rehearsal, each with its own function (Craik and Lockhart, 1972). **Maintenance rehearsal** maintains information in short-term memory. The information is stored in a transient acoustical code, so that no matter how long the rehearsal goes on, the information is forgotten about fifteen seconds after the repetition stops. For example, a person might rehearse items on a shopping list (bread, garlic, asparagus, chicken) for quite some time, but once the items have been purchased, the list will fade from memory. However, maintenance rehearsal can transfer material to long-term memory, as indicated by repeated findings that people who use maintenance rehearsal in laboratory studies can later accurately select words they have rehearsed from a much longer list (Anderson, 1980). **Elaborative rehearsal** transfers information into long-term memory so that it may later be retrieved. In elaborative rehearsal, information is associated with other information, images are created, or the information is organized in some way. The Russian with the astounding memory used elaborative rehearsal to memorize lists of words.

The amount of material that can be maintained through rehearsal is limited by the capacity of short-term memory. Most people can maintain about seven items in short-term memory, although the number varies from person to person (Miller, 1956). That limit of seven items can take many forms, however, so that it is best described as seven "chunks," a chunk being a grouping with some sort of individual representation in long-term memory. The chunks can be seven letters, seven numbers, seven words, seven phrases, or seven sentences. Information can be chunked by recoding it. For example, it is possible to recode the string of digits, 149162536496481100121, into a single chunk of information. All that is required to remember this string of twenty-one digits is to think of it as the square, in succession, of the numbers 1 through 11 ($1^2 = 1$; $2^2 = 4$; $3^2 = 9$; $4^2 = 16$; and so on).

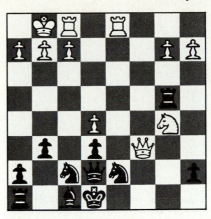

Figure 9.7A Study this arrangement of chess pieces for five seconds. Then turn to the empty chess board on page 208 and try to reproduce the arrangement. The amount you are able to recall correctly represents approximately seven of the chunks you have developed for processing information about chess games.

Memory chunks need not be verbal; in fact some of the most useful chunks are visual, as were those of the Russian memory expert. After a five-second exposure, an excellent chess player can reproduce the entire board shown in Figure 9.7A. (Figure 9.7B, page 208, gives you this opportunity.) Yet these masters' memory range is no greater than the average college student's. The masters' superiority lies in their ability to recognize familiar visual configurations or chunks; therefore, chess masters cannot reproduce chessboards if the pieces are arranged in a random pattern that is unlikely to occur in a game between good players.

In a recent experiment, an average college student (S. F.) increased his memory span from seven to seventy-nine digits (Ericsson, Chase, and Faloon, 1980). It took the student 230 hours of practice over a year and a half, but in that period he managed to rival the feats of professional memory experts (see Figure 9.8). The student, who was a long-distance runner, recoded the numbers he was given into running times for various races. For example, he recoded the number 3,492 as "3 minutes and 49 point 2 seconds, near world-record mile time." As the study went on, the student also added age codes (see 893 as "89 point 3, very old man") and date codes (coding 1,944 as "near the end of World War II"). In addition to recoding the numbers, the student increased recall by organizing the groups he had constructed from the digits into a hierarchy and recalling them in terms of the hierarchy.

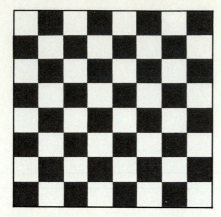

Figure 9.7B   Turn to Figure 9.7A on page 207, if you have not already looked at it, and study it for five seconds. Then try to reproduce the arrangement shown there on this empty chess board. Your success in doing so will depend heavily on your experience with the game of chess.

Since the student used elaborative rehearsal, we would expect him to retain some of the digits in long-term memory, and that is just what he did. When he was tested to see if he could recognize digit sequences he had memorized earlier, he recognized three- and four-digit combinations that had been presented to him several days previously. The student's memory did not violate the seven-chunk capacity of short-term memory. His method of recoding required him to handle only four chunks at any one time, and

his rehearsal group never exceeded six chunks. The student's memory span was still climbing when the study was terminated, which indicates that the limits of human memory have not yet been reached.

Long-Term Memory

Long-term memory can be considered the repository of permanent knowledge. The amount of material in this final storage is almost beyond comprehension. In fact, some theorists (e.g., Penfield, 1959) suggest that every fact that enters long-term memory remains there in some form throughout life, although this idea has recently been challenged (Loftus and Loftus, 1980).

As yet no one understands precisely how information is transferred from short-term to long-term memory. It is generally believed that the transfer depends upon the elaborative rehearsal cycle: the longer the information remains in the cycle and the better it is organized, the more likely the transfer. We cannot observe transfer processes directly, but there is increasing evidence to support the existence of short-term and long-term memory.

Rationale for a Dichotomous Memory   Although the idea of dividing memory into short-term and long-term storage has been around since the end of the nineteenth century, when William James (1890) proposed that human beings had both a primary (short-term) and a secondary (long-term) memory, the division found little favor in the first half of this century. Since that time, experimental evidence and the experiences of some epileptics have combined to convince many psychologists that there is more than one kind of memory process.

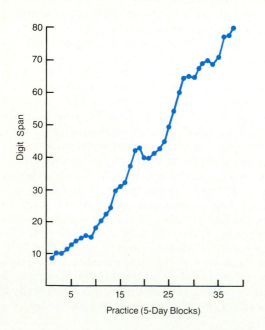

Figure 9.8   Average digit span for S. F. as a function of practice. Digit span is defined as the length of the sequence that is correct 50 percent of the time; under the procedure followed, it is equivalent to average sequence length. Each day represents about 1 hour's practice and ranges from 55 trials per day in the beginning to 3 trials per day for the longest sequences. The 38 blocks of practice shown here represent about 190 hours of practice; interspersed among these practice sessions are approximately 40 hours of experimental sessions (not shown). (After Ericsson, Chase, and Faloon, 1980.)

Experimental evidence for the existence of two memory processes has come in the form of experiments in **free recall**. In a typical free-recall experiment, a person hears a list of, say, twenty words, read one at a time. As soon as the last word is read, the person recalls as many of the words as possible (Murdock, 1962). The results can be plotted as a **serial-position curve**, which shows the probability of recalling a word in relation to its position on the list. In Figure 9.9A, such results have been averaged over several subjects and many trials. As the serial-position curve shows, memory is best for the last few words on the list, next best for words at the beginning of the list, and weakest for words in the middle.

We can suppose that memory is best for the last words, because these items are still in short-term memory at the time of recall, and that memory is good for the first words because they received the most rehearsal as the subject heard the list. However, if there is only a single, unitary memory process, those last words are remembered best simply because they have been studied more recently. The proposal that memory is dichotomous can be tested by manipulating the conditions of the experiment. When people are asked to count backward by threes as soon as the final word is read, memory for the last words in the list drops sharply, becoming as weak as memory for words in the middle of the list (Postman and Phillips, 1965). Results from such an experiment are shown in Figure 9.9B. If memory were unitary, recall of words at the end of the list might have dropped slightly under these conditions but should have remained better than recall

for words in the middle of the list, because the final words were studied last. However, the serial-position curve for this experiment is what we would expect if there are two kinds of memory processes. Apparently as the capacity of short-term memory was filled with numbers, words that had already been transferred to long-term memory were unaffected, but the unrehearsed final words decayed.

Laboratory evidence for a dichotomous memory has been supported by studies of epileptics who have undergone brain surgery to prevent seizures. These patients obtained relief from epileptic seizures, but they sometimes suffered a serious side effect: they could no longer learn from and retain new experiences.

According to Brenda Milner (1966), who analyzed a number of such cases, damage to the part of the brain called the hippocampus is responsible for this disruption of memory. She described a twenty-seven-year-old man who had undergone radical brain surgery to prevent severe seizures. When Milner interviewed him two years after the operation, he still reported his age as twenty-seven. He retained little memory of the operation and kept repeating, "It is as though I am just waking up from a dream; it seems as though it just happened." The man had little, if any, memory of events since the operation, but there was no impairment in his intellectual functioning. Indeed, he did slightly better on an IQ test than he had done before the surgery. His memory for events before the operation was intact, but because he could not memorize new information simple acts of daily life presented great obstacles to him. For instance, when his

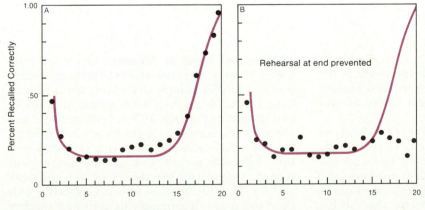

Figure 9.9 The results of a series of experiments by Murdock (A) and by Postman and Phillips (B) that elegantly demonstrate the separate contributions of short-term memory (STM) and long-term memory (LTM) to the serial-position curve. The black dots show the percentage of correct recalls as a function of the position of the word in the list. The colored line in A represents the idealized form of the data there and is repeated in B for purposes of comparison. In B, the contribution of STM has been completely eliminated by the prevention of rehearsal, but LTM's contribution is unchanged.

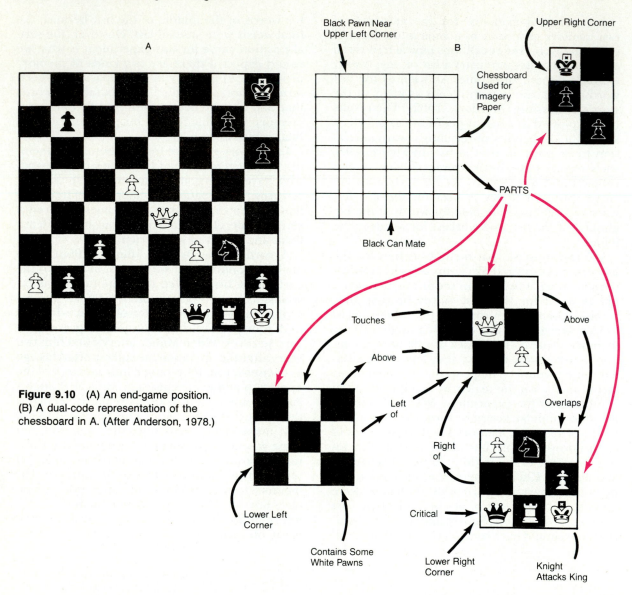

Figure 9.10 (A) An end-game position. (B) A dual-code representation of the chessboard in A. (After Anderson, 1978.)

family moved to a new house, he was unable to learn the new address and kept returning to his old home. He reread magazines without finding their content familiar. He forgot where household items were kept.

Cases like this support the idea of two kinds of memory storage. Short-term memory is unimpaired; a patient can retain items, but with any momentary distraction and shift of attention, the memories are lost. Since long-term memory is also intact, we must conclude that the mechanism that moves information from short-term to long-term memory is damaged.

Episodic and Semantic Memory Once the existence of two memory stores has been established, a further complexity arises. We appear to have two kinds of long-term memory: episodic and semantic (Tulving, 1972). Both episodic and semantic memory store information indefinitely, but the information in each is a very different sort. **Episodic memory** is an autobiographical record, a record of the things we see and hear and do. The information in it is connected with time and place. Remembering a former teacher who had a terrible temper, the menu from a special dinner, an appointment scheduled for tomorrow, or receiving a ticket for speeding last month are examples of episodic memory. **Semantic memory** is organized knowledge about words and symbols and their meanings, their relationships and referents, and the rules for manipulating them. It is not connected with time and place. Remembering that the plural of "mouse" is "mice," that a mile equals 1.6 kilometers, that apples are red, and that a whale is a mammal are examples of semantic memory.

Information in episodic memory is much more likely to be changed or forgotten than is information in semantic memory. The reason for this disparity can be traced to the basic difference in the contents of these memory stores. Retrieving information from semantic memory leaves its contents unchanged, but retrieving information from either kind of memory is an episode in a person's life and must itself be entered in episodic memory. Free-recall experiments are studies of episodic memory, because what is encoded is not the meaning of the words on the list but their fleeting presence in a particular episode (a psychology experiment). As we shall see in the section on memory retrieval, semantic memory can have important effects on episodic memory, indicating that the two kinds of long-term memory are not isolated from each other.

Representation of Information in Memory   When information is placed into memory, what form does the representation take? This question gets at one of the most complex areas in the field of memory research, and if it could be answered accurately, we would have a much clearer picture of the memory system and of human thought processes. Two major theories have been advanced to account for the mental representation of information: the dual-code theory and the propositional-code theory.

Dual-code theorists propose that information is represented by visual images and by words (Paivio, 1971). The images are not regarded as accurate snapshots of an entire scene; rather, they are overlapping fragments connected with associations and perhaps accompanied by clarifying phrases (Anderson, 1978). In this view, the images are incomplete and often inaccurate, and may be regarded as perceptual chunks of information (see Figure 9.10). When information is stored in words, its form resembles the original auditory perception of the information or the articulatory generation of the words (the motor acts of speaking; Anderson, 1980).

Propositional-code theorists propose that information is represented in an abstract manner that uses neither sounds nor sights nor motor acts, and that the abstractions take the form of rule-governed propositions. In this view, information is reduced to its basic meaning, and unimportant details are not represented. Several types of propositional representations have been advanced, and one of the most popular is the **semantic network model**, in which memory is seen as a network of interconnected nodes (Anderson and Bower, 1973; Norman, Rummelhart, and the LNR Research Group, 1975). Each node is an idea, a concept, or an event, and the nodes are connected in terms of their relationships.

Some research favors the dual-code theory, but other studies support the propositional-code theory. For example, the dual-code theory has been supported by experiments in which people scanned imagined sentences or line diagrams, signaling information about the sentence or diagram as they scanned it (Brooks, 1968). When people scan sentences, they can give such information as whether each word is a noun much more rapidly by tapping with their hands (right hand for "yes," left hand for "no") than by simply saying "yes" or "no" for each word in the sentence. But when they mentally scan block diagrams (see Figure 9.11), they can give information (such as whether each corner is at the extreme top or bottom of the figure) much more rapidly with words than by pointing. It appears, therefore, that speaking interferes with the mental processes involved in the representation of words and that pointing interferes with mental processes involved in the representation of figures, indicating that words and visual events are represented in different ways. These results are not easily explained by the propositional-code theory.

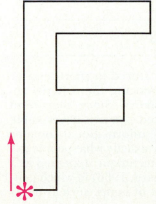

Figure 9.11 A simple block diagram used by Brooks (1968) to study the scanning of mental images. The asterisk and arrow showed the subject the starting point and the direction for scanning the image. (After Brooks, 1968. Copyright © 1968 by the Canadian Psychological Association. Reprinted by permission.)

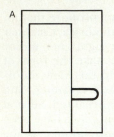

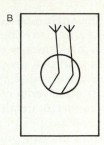

Figure 9.12 "Droodles." (A) A midget playing a trombone in a telephone booth. (B) An early bird who caught a very strong worm. (After Bower, Karlin, and Dueck, 1975.)

However, other research that supports propositional-code theory indicates problems with the dual-code theory. It appears that we store the meaning of pictures we see, and not copies of the pictures. In one experiment (Bower, Karlin, and Dueck, 1975), investigators showed people "droodles," like those in Figure 9.12, then asked that the picture be redrawn from memory. When a meaningful label had been attached to the drawing, 70 percent of the subjects could reproduce it, but when the picture had been shown without any label, only 51 percent of the subjects could reproduce it. In addition, once a representation is retrieved, it has moved from long-term to short-term memory, so the fact that people have visual images does not demonstrate that the information that produced the images is stored in visual form (Norman, 1976).

The question of representation remains unsettled, and it may be that representation takes more than one form in memory. No matter what the form of representations, however, they must be organized and stored in such an interrelated manner that there are many ways to reach them (Norman, 1976).

Memory Retrieval

Whether information is stored in short-term or long-term memory, producing the material requires a search of memory. Since short-term memory has such a limited capacity, it is possible to search through all the information it contains —and that appears to be exactly what people do. This exhaustive search technique appeared in a series of studies (Sternberg, 1966) in which people looked at a small set of items, such as digits or letters. After the items were in short-term memory, an additional item was shown and subjects decided as quickly as possible whether this new item had been part of the set they had just seen. The number of items in the set varied from one to six, and people had no trouble in matching the new item to the items in their short-term memory. However, the more items in the set (and thus the more information in short-term memory), the longer it took people to decide whether the new item had been part of the set, indicating that they searched the entire store of short-term memory in the identification process.

The mass of information in long-term memory is so enormous that an exhaustive search is impossible. In fact, the more we know about a subject, the longer it takes us to retrieve specific items of information about it, a feature of memory called a **fan effect** (Anderson, 1980). However, information in long-term memory is stored in an orderly fashion, so if the search can be directed to a particular area, it is much easier to locate the item being sought. Search of long-term memory is directed and speeded by the use of retrieval cues.

Retrieval Cues

A **retrieval cue** is a piece of information that helps us to retrieve information from long-term memory. It can be a word, a sight, an odor, a texture that reminds us of the information we are seeking—or that summons unbidden an event from the past. For example, the odor of evergreens may suddenly evoke the memory of Christmases past. Retrieval cues are taken seriously by the legal system and often used in court to remind a witness of some event. In one court decision, the range of possible retrieval cues was described as "the creaking of a hinge, the whistling of a tune, the smell of seaweed, the sight of an old photograph, the taste of nutmeg, the touch of a piece of canvas" (*Fanelli* v. *U.S. Gypsum Co.,* 1944). Many aspects of memory—including recognition and recall, state-dependent memory, and the elusiveness of information that remains stubbornly on the tip of the tongue—can be understood by applying the concept of retrieval cues.

Recognition and Recall Retrieval takes two basic forms: recognition and recall. **Recognition** requires us to realize whether something that is before us has been seen or heard in the past. The process seems to occur automatically and is usually accurate. A familiar act of recognition occurs in answering multiple-choice questions. Three possible answers are in view; the task is to recognize the correct item. **Recall** requires us to retrieve specific pieces of information in the information's absence. The process often demands an active search of long-term memory. To answer the question, "What is your mother's family name?" the item must be recalled from memory.

Recognition is easier than recall because the most effective possible retrieval cue is present— the original information. There is no need to search long-term memory for it. Recognition for visual memories is often extraordinarily good. In one experiment (Haber and Standing, 1969), people looked at 2,560 photographs of various scenes, studying each for ten seconds. When shown a group of photographs on a subsequent day, the subjects were able to recognize between 85 and 95 percent of the pictures they had seen before.

In contrast, recall is often difficult because retrieval cues may be sparse or absent. The most common recall failure is the inability to retrieve any information at all, as when people grope for a word they want or fail to remember a name they thought they knew. False recall is rare. When it does occur, it can usually be explained in terms of strong familiar associations. For example, most grandchildren are used to having a grandparent call them by a parent's name.

Relearning   Sometimes information can be neither recalled nor recognized with certainty, as when a student seems to have forgotten everything learned in last year's German class. Yet if that student were to begin studying German again, she would be able to relearn the language in less time than the original learning required. Although the information is no longer accessible, it apparently leaves a trace in long-term memory that facilitates new storage and retrieval, when cued by relearning.

Thus, like recognition and recall, relearning appears to be a way to assess memory. These subtle traces of memory can be discovered by means of the **relearning score**, or **savings score**, a measurement devised a century ago by Hermann Ebbinghaus (1885). Using himself as a subject, Ebbinghaus recorded the number of repetitions he needed to learn a list of unrelated items accurately. Then he waited until he seemed to have forgotten the items and relearned the list, again recording the number of repetitions required to master it. The difference in the number of trials between the original and the relearning session he called the savings score. As Figure 9.13 indicates, the shorter the time between the first and second sessions, the fewer the trials needed for relearning and the higher the savings score.

State-Dependent Memory   Many people have experienced an inability to recall on the following morning events that accompanied heavy drinking the night before. Such losses of memory may be due in part to the absence of retrieval cues, for several experiments (e.g., Weingartner et al., 1976; Bartlett and Santrock, 1979) have shown that a person's internal state—whether sober or drunk, happy or sad—can serve as a retrieval cue. In **state-dependent memory**, information

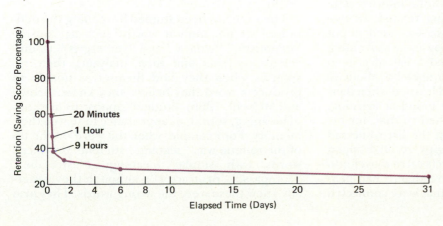

Figure 9.13 Relearning. The saving score (time saved in relearning a set of nonsense syllables) as a function of time since the first learning. (After Ebbinghaus, 1885.)

learned while in one physiological state is difficult to retrieve when a person is in a different state, but when the original condition is restored, the information can again be retrieved.

In a typical test of state-dependent memory, some people learn material while they are in a normal state and others learn the same material while under the influence of alcohol or other drugs. On a later occasion, some people are tested under the condition in which they learned the information, while others are tested in the opposite condition. If the information is remembered better when the state of encoding matches the state of retrieval than when the states do not match, the memories are state dependent (Klatzky, 1980). One study (Goodwin, Crane, and Guze, 1969) showed that memory loss was greater for subjects going from an intoxicated to a sober state than for those going from sobriety to intoxication, indicating that there may also be some interference with encoding while under the influence of alcohol.

In a study using marijuana (Eich et al., 1975), the role of a person's internal state as a retrieval cue was made especially plain. People learned a list of words divided into categories (flowers, animals, and so forth), then recalled them in either the same or the opposite state (normal versus after smoking marijuana). As expected, with the internal state as a retrieval cue, the state-dependent effect turned up: subjects recalled more words when they were in the state in which they learned them, whether drugged or undrugged. But when category names were given as retrieval cues, the state-dependent effect disappeared; all groups did equally well, no matter what state they were tested in. In this case, the category names substituted for the internal state as retrieval cues.

Similar effects appear when the internal state is emotional rather than drug related. In one study (Bower, 1981), hypnosis was used to put college students into a happy or a sad mood, then the students memorized a list of sixteen words. Later, students could remember about 80 percent of the words they had learned when their mood at recall matched the mood at learning, but when moods were switched so that, for example, students who learned the list while sad tried to remember it while happy, recall dropped to about 45 percent. The effects carried over into daily life. When the same investigator had people keep a diary of incidents that were connected with emotion, he found that people tended to remember events from the diaries that matched their moods at recall.

Restoring an internal state restores the situation to its original **context**, or setting, for the context acts as a retrieval cue, directing attention to the appropriate area of memory. Physical context can also have a powerful effect on memory. If, for example, you spent the summer traveling in Europe and spotted a familiar face in a London pub, you might well have some trouble attaching a name to the face. But if the familiar person said, "We shared a bathroom in our freshman year," thereby placing the face in the context of a college dormitory, you would find it easier to retrieve the missing name. The context of a learning environment has a similar effect, as a study of underwater divers showed (Godden and Baddeley, 1975). In this experiment, members of an underwater diving club learned a list of words; half the members learned the list on dry land, the other half learned the list thirty feet below the surface. When the standard recall test was given, divers who learned underwater recalled more words underwater and divers who learned ashore recalled more words ashore.

"Tip-of-the-Tongue" Phenomenon   Sometimes we produce our own retrieval cues internally, although they're not always successful, as the **"tip-of-the-tongue" phenomenon** indicates. When we have a word or a number on the tip of the tongue, we are certain that we know the word but simply can not pull it out of storage. The condition has been described as "a state of mild torment, something like the brink of a sneeze" and when the word is finally retrieved, there is a feeling of considerable relief (Brown and McNeill, 1966).

The state has been studied by reading the definitions of uncommon words, such as "apse," "nepotism," "cloaca," and "ambergris," to university students and then analyzing their responses when they find themselves unable to produce a word they believe they know (Brown and McNeill, 1966). Students appear to use cues of meaning, sound, or appearance to search their memory. For example, when the word on the tip of the tongue was "sextant," students produced words with similar meanings ("astrolabe," "compass," "protractor"), although they generally knew these were the wrong words. They also

Flashbulb Memories

Most people can remember exactly where they were and what they were doing when they heard about the assassination of President John F. Kennedy, and their memory of the event seems almost as clear as if it had happened an hour before. Such a brief, highly illuminated moment of the past is called **flashbulb memory**, because it seems like a photograph taken with a flashbulb. Yet the memories are not complete. A man who recalls the moment when he heard about the assassination with clarity ("I was sitting in my sixth-grade music class . . . the class started yelling . . . my homeroom teacher was crying") may not recall the way his informant was dressed or may find that other details of the scene are missing.

When psychologists (Brown and Kulik, 1977) studied flashbulb memories, they found that virtually all of the people they asked, black or white, had flashbulb memories of the presidential assassination. In the case of Martin Luther King Jr.'s assassination, however, three-fourths of the blacks but only about a third of the whites had such memories. Nearly all of these people also had flashbulb memories of at least one extraordinary personal event, such as hearing of a close friend's accidental death.

An analysis (Brown and Kulik, 1977) of Kennedy assassination memories showed that most contained six kinds of information: (1) the place in which the person heard the news, (2) the event that was interrupted, (3) the informant who bore the message, (4) the emotions of the informant, (5) the person's own emotions, and (6) some immediate personal aftermath. Idiosyncratic details—the weather, an object held in the hand, the taste of a fish soup, the feel of an unusual surface underfoot—were also common.

Flashbulb memories at one time may have had adaptive significance for our species. These memories appear to develop when emotional arousal is accompanied by great surprise and the perception of major consequences. To survive, our ancestors had to be able to respond to events that placed them in danger. The flashbulb memory process allowed them to store for future guidance any highly significant event they encountered, such as the first appearance of a new dangerous carnivore in their territory or a serious injury to a dominant group member (Brown and Kulik, 1977). Many aspects of the event were stored, because our ancestors had no way of knowing which aspects would later prove to be important.

No one knows just how the process works. It has been speculated that the shock of a highly significant event releases some substance, perhaps a neurotransmitter, into the central nervous system. At almost the same moment, synapses across the brain's cortex receive the substance, which causes them to "fix" their ongoing activity, storing the highly vivid memory for later use (Benderly, 1981).

As we noted above, flashbulb memories are typically incomplete: we may remember some details clearly, but we forget others. It is also possible that what we think we remember clearly is not an accurate picture of what actually took place. Critics point out that there have been few attempts to verify the accuracy of people's flashbulb memories, and that it is possible to find instances when a clear flashbulb memory was wrong (Loftus, 1980). Since most people have had the experience of telling and retelling their experiences of unusually disturbing events, it is likely that certain details are added or subtracted in the retelling, and the memory is thus distorted. Indeed, the retelling may account for why the memories seem so clear after the passage of time.

produced words with similar sounds ("secant," "sextet," "sexton,"). Sometimes the similar-sounding words were not English words at all ("sekrant," "saktint"), but had the right number of syllables. Students also frequently could produce the first and last letters of the word.

The way internal cues are generated in a "tip-of-the-tongue" search was demonstrated by the case of a fifty-four-year-old man whose left cerebral hemisphere had been damaged as the result of a war injury (Wingfield, 1979). The man had great trouble remembering words he knew very well, and as he searched his memory for a word, the verbal record of his search showed that he used his own internal cues to direct it. For example, shown a picture of an anchor, over the next several minutes he said:

> It's one of those things that belongs to a boat (context cue) . . . Now what do they call it? . . . Not hanger, no (sound cue) . . . Oh crumbs, that's simple . . . It's one of those . . . Do they throw it on the boat? (context cue) . . . A something . . . Not hanger (sound cue) . . . Oh, it's coming out in a minute . . . Something like hammer (sound cue) . . . Hanger, er . . . ank, ank—(sound cue) . . . Anchor (Wingfield, 1979).

Presumably, the students searching for words to match definitions went through a similar, silent process.

It has been suggested that tip-of-the-tongue searches are not always as informed as the earlier study of university students indicated (Koriat and Lieblich, 1974). In this view, the students made mental bets regarding the formal features (sound, number of syllables) of the word, based on what they knew about similar words. They combined those bets with information gleaned from the conditions of the experiment (English word, uncommon) and the definition (in the case of "sextant," navigational instrument) as cues to guide the search.

Remembering as Reconstructing

The struggles involved in tip-of-the-tongue searches show that memories do not always surface intact; sometimes only fragments of a word can be retrieved. Because retrieval is often more than a passive playback of stored information, fragmentary information plays an unnoticed role in many recollections. Retrieval frequently involves an active reconstruction of the past in which we piece out bits of stored information about an event with guesses and inferences based on our general knowledge. In most cases, we do this without any awareness that our reconstruction is different from the recalled event.

The way inferences based on preconceptions shape memory has been known for a half century. In a classic experiment (Carmichael, Hogan, and Walter, 1932), people were shown a group of figures and later asked to reproduce them. The form the later drawings took was largely determined by the way the figures were described at the original showing. The descriptions set up preconceptions, so that when a pair of circles connected by a straight line were called "eyeglasses," viewers inferred that the figure must have had a typical eyeglass shape. When the same figure was called "dumbbell," reproductions were based on inferences drawn from a typical dumbbell shape, as in Figure 9.14.

Preconceptions led to false inferences in the

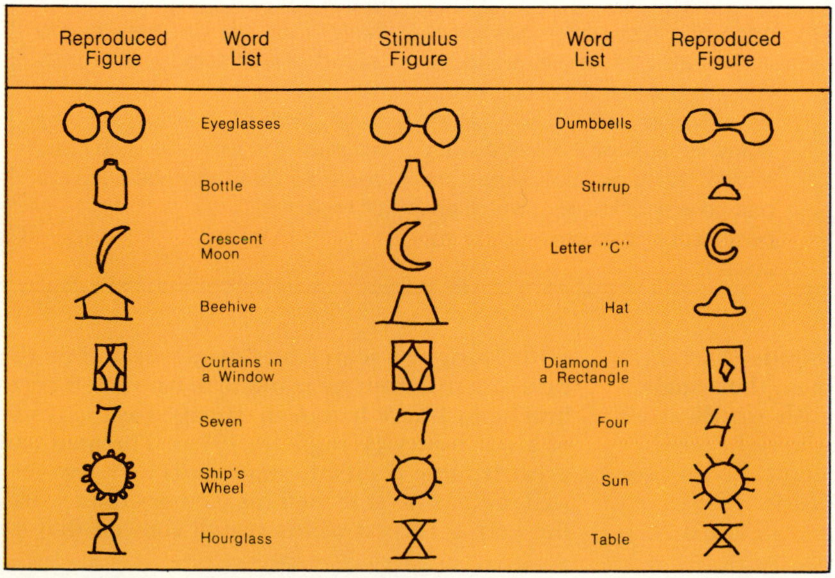

Reproduced Figure	Word List	Stimulus Figure	Word List	Reproduced Figure
	Eyeglasses		Dumbbells	
	Bottle		Stirrup	
	Crescent Moon		Letter "C"	
	Beehive		Hat	
	Curtains in a Window		Diamond in a Rectangle	
	Seven		Four	
	Ship's Wheel		Sun	
	Hourglass		Table	

Figure 9.14 Carmichael, Hogan, and Walter designed an experiment to study the influence of set on perception. Subjects were shown the line patterns in the middle column of this figure, and these stimuli were described as drawings of various objects. Later, when the subjects were asked to reproduce from memory the patterns they had seen, they made the drawings shown in the right and left columns. You can see how the naming of the patterns influenced their drawings. (After Carmichael, Hogan, and Walter, 1932.)

The critical slides used by Loftus, Miller, and Burns (1978) to test the accuracy of recollection. Half the subjects saw the photo with the stop sign and half the photo with the yield sign.

reproduction of the figures, but information received *after* an event can also be woven into our memories, transforming what we thought we experienced. This feature of memory can have serious consequences when we consider the number of court cases that are decided on the basis of eyewitness testimony. In one study (Loftus et al., 1978), people saw thirty color slides that depicted an accident in which a red automobile stopped at an intersection before it turned right and hit a pedestrian. Half the people saw a slide in which there was a stop sign on the corner; the rest saw a yield sign in the same place. Afterward the people answered a series of questions about the accident, and one of the questions assumed the existence of a sign. Half the people who saw the stop sign heard a question that presupposed a yield sign, and half the people who saw a yield sign heard a question that presupposed a stop sign. The rest heard a question consistent with the slide they actually had seen. When these people later were shown both slides of the stopped car, 41 percent of those who had been asked an inconsistent question chose the slide with the wrong sign as the one they had seen. Among those who had been asked a consistent question, only 25 percent chose the wrong slide.

In other experiments (Loftus and Palmer, 1974), people saw a filmed traffic accident and were then asked questions about it. One of the questions involved the speed of the two cars at the time of the collision, but half the people heard the verb "smashed" used in the question and the other half heard the verb "hit." A week later these people were again questioned about the film. When asked whether they had seen any broken glass in the movie, 32 percent of those who had earlier heard "smashed" agreed that they had seen imaginary broken glass; only 14 percent of those who had heard "hit" claimed to have seen the imaginary glass. There is a limit to such manipulations of memory. For example, when people see a large red wallet figure prominently in a filmed theft, they will not incorporate into their recollections a statement that the wallet was brown (Loftus, 1979).

Our reconstructions can also be affected by motivation, as can most human activities. High motivation can lead to the memory error called **confabulation**, in which a person who is unable to retrieve an item from memory reconstructs an appropriate recollection. Confabulation explains the apparent ability of people in deep states of hypnosis to give detailed reports of events that occurred during childhood, an effect that impressed psychologists in the days when memory was regarded as a faithful copy of past experience. In such an instance, a hypnotist asks a subject to describe his sixth birthday. Typically, the man, if in a deep trance, gives a lengthy and quite impressive account of a birthday party complete with cake, candles, presents, and guests. He seems absolutely convinced that the report is accurate, but objective evidence usually contradicts him. It can almost always be shown that the subject has confabulated, combining several birthday parties and inventing missing details. Even so, under further questioning, the subject is not able to distinguish the true parts of the story from the imaginary additions.

Aiding Retrieval

It is possible for anyone to improve her or his memory, as the experience of the long-distance runner made clear. **Mnemonic**, or memory-assisting, systems have been known for thousands of years and were practiced in ancient Greece. Mnemonic systems organize information so that it can be remembered, using imagery, association, and meaning to accomplish their purpose, and they all make use of information already stored in semantic memory. However, the boost to ordinary memory they provide will not take the work out of learning. At first these devices may take more time than traditional rote memorization, but people who learn to use mnemonic systems gain two advantages. First, routine things are memorized more efficiently, freeing their minds for tasks that involve understanding and reason. Second, facts required for tasks involving reasoning and understanding are remembered better (Higbee, 1977).

Although these systems are quite efficient, none will produce a photographic memory so that the recollection is an exact and enduring copy of a scene, a list of words, or the pages of a book. Such a memory is unknown, although a very small percentage of the human population possesses a unique ability that is somewhat similar, an ability known as **eidetic imagery**. Most of us maintain more or less vague visual images, but people with eidetic imagery can visualize a scene with almost photographic clarity. Research with children indicates that only about 5 percent have this ability, and the figure drops sharply after adolescence (Haber, 1969). Although the eidetic child can describe in detail many of the elements of a complex picture, this ability does not seem to aid long-term memory processes. The scene fades quickly and once it is gone, it cannot be recaptured. In addition, if an eidetic child is asked to describe a picture while in the act of viewing it, the eidetic image is not formed. It seems that verbal processes interfere with the formation of the image, and that the eidetic child is no better than other children at storing verbal information.

Method of Loci One mnemonic system used by the Russian memory expert described at the beginning of this chapter is called the **method of loci**, and it involves the use of a series of loci, or places, that are firmly implanted in memory. Items to be remembered are placed along a familiar route.

Anyone can use this method. Suppose, for example, that you must learn the names of the presidents of the United States in chronological order. Simply visualize a familiar place—say, the house in which you grew up—and imagine each president in a particular location: George Washington greeting you at the front door, John Adams and Thomas Jefferson talking in the entrance hall, James Madison playing backgammon with John Quincy Adams on the stairway, and so on until you find Ronald Reagan chopping wood in the back yard. Thus, by taking a mental journey through the house along the same route, you will be able to visualize and recall the presidents. The same loci could be used to recall information about each of Shakespeare's plays or the chemical reactions involved in photosynthesis.

Another mnemonic system based on loci is called the peg-word system, which uses twenty simple words as loci. Once memorized, these words act as pegs upon which any arbitrary series of information can be hung. Each of the twenty words stands for one of the numbers from one to twenty. For example:

One is a bun.
Two is a shoe.
Three is a tree.
Four is a door.
Five is a hive.
Six is sticks.
Seven is heaven.
Eight is a gate.
Nine is a line.
Ten is a hen.

Each item to be remembered is visualized as interacting with one of these words. Suppose the memory task involves a shopping list, consisting of tomato soup, potatoes, spaghetti, and pickles. Imagine tomato soup being poured over a large bun, a potato resting in a shoe, strands of spaghetti hanging over a tree limb, and pickles sticking like knives into a door. Once at the market, it's fairly easy to run through the familiar peg words and recall the image that has been hung on each. The list of presidents could be learned the same way with, for example, George Washington gnawing on a bun, John Adams complaining of a hole in his shoe, and so forth.

Imagery The method of loci is based on imagery and uses the principle that it is easier to remember something if the object can be pictured in some way. Imagery is most helpful when the items to be remembered are concrete rather than abstract. For example, compare the word combinations "gorilla-piccolo" and "omniscience-euphony." The first pair of words, both concrete nouns, immediately suggests specific images, but the second pair, both abstract nouns, either suggests no images at all or suggests images that are not uniquely tied to the words to be remembered. Abstract nouns can be remembered through images, but there is always the risk that "choir," chosen as the image for "euphony," will bring "harmony" instead of "euphony" to mind on later recall.

Memory for visual images improves further if the images are woven into some sort of scene. Studies (e.g., Bower, 1973) have shown that when a pair of words, such as "pig-ice," must be remembered, people who imagine the words interacting in some way, such as a pig skating on ice, will remember the words better than someone who creates unconnected images for both words. The images need not be bizarre—ordinary scenes work just as well. But it is helpful to imagine a scene with a strong emotional impact. In one study (Sadalla and Loftness, 1972), people were shown lists of noun pairs and told to form images about the words that would later help them to recall the second noun in the pair when they were given the first. Some of the people were instructed to form neutral images, vivid but without emotional content; others to form positive images, full of pleasant feelings; the rest to form negative images, which were "horrifying" and "uncomfortable to think about." On later memory tests it was clear that associating any strong emotion with an image was more effective than none; both positive and negative images helped people recall misssing words far better than did neutral images.

Why imagery is such a powerful tool of memory is not completely understood. It may be because imagery is processed in the nonlinguistic systems of the brain. In this view, words plus images are more likely to be remembered than words alone for the same reason that it is better

Figure 9.15 A visualization that might aid a person to remember the word pair *locomotive—towel*.

to have two reminder notes—one at home and one in a pocket—than to have only one. The two kinds of "notes"—verbal and visual—make it twice as likely that the message will be remembered.

Research with people who are totally blind from birth indicates that imagery can be used to improve memory even among those who have never had visual experiences. In one experiment (Jonides, Kahn, and Rozin, 1975), both sighted and congenitally blind adults showed improved memory when they were given word pairs such as "locomotive-dishtowel" and told to imagine a relationship between the words of each pair—for example, the locomotive wrapped in the dishtowel (see Figure 9.15). The fact that imagery instructions improved the memory of blind subjects as well as sighted ones indicates that imagery effects do not rely on vision. The reason for imagery's effectiveness with the blind is unclear; attempts to relate its success to other sensory channels, such as hearing or touch, have been unsuccessful.

The Key Word System The key word system has been successfully used to learn foreign languages, and it relies on linking English words (key words) with foreign words that have similar sounds. The imagery used is much like that suggested to the blind. For example, if the word to be learned is *pato* (pronounced "pot-o"), the Spanish word for duck, an effective image is a duck with a *pot* (key word) on its head. To learn the French word for skin, *peau* (pronounced "poe"), imagine Edgar Allan Poe with a beautiful complexion. Students who use this method have learned almost twice as many words in the same study time as students who use rote memorization. In addition, since some key words are better than others, the system works best if an instruction booklet suggests the key word but students create their own images (Bower, 1978).

Rhymes and Acronyms   Unlike the mnemonic systems we have been discussing, rhymes and acronyms are specific. They can be used only once, so that although they are effective, they require a good deal of effort to create. Most, therefore, are handed down and apply to common information that many people must learn. There are many mnemonic rhymes: *"I* before *E* except after *C"; "Thirty days hath September, April, June, and November . . .";* and so on. The rhyme system is based on the fact that people have no difficulty remembering the individual items (the letters or the months); the problem is remembering something about them (letter order, number of days). Acronyms are created by taking the first letter of each word in a series that must be remembered and making a word for them. For example, ROY G. BIV represents the order of the colors in the spectrum: red, orange, yellow, green, blue, indigo, violet.

Forgetting

Everyone forgets: the plot of a movie seen six months ago; the menu at dinner last Tuesday night; the date of a friend's birthday; the promise to send an acquaintance a magazine article. What happens to information that was once known but now cannot be remembered? Either it has been lost from memory, or the information is still in storage but for some reason cannot be retrieved. In either case, two explanations have been suggested as the cause of forgetting: decay and interference.

Retrieval Failure

The tip-of-the-tongue phenomenon is one example of retrieval failure, and in this case there is a realization that a piece of information cannot be retrieved from storage. But sometimes there is no sense of searching for well-known information; it is as if the material had been wiped out of storage or had never been known. Yet even this form of forgetting may be the result of retrieval failure. If retrieval failure explains forgetting, then the forgotten material is simply inaccessible and the right retrieval cue would bring the information out of storage (Loftus and Loftus, 1976).

A condition called **retrograde amnesia**, in which people are unable to remember events preceding some kind of brain damage, suggests that retrieval failure does explain some forgetting. Memory loss in retrograde amnesia may apply only to events immediately preceding the injury, or the loss may extend back over days or years.

In most cases of retrograde amnesia, the memories are not lost but have become inaccessible. They may begin to return in a few minutes or over a period of years, depending on the severity of the injury. As people recover, memories gradually come back, and the span of time covered by amnesia lessens. Memories of the distant past are usually the first to reappear. Sometimes memories of events that occurred seconds before the injury are never recovered, probably because these memories were never transferred from short-term to long-term memory.

Although most cases of retrograde amnesia are the result of head injuries, it may also be produced by other types of damage to the brain. For instance, the patient undergoing electroconvulsive shock therapy usually experiences memory loss, as may the victim of carbon monoxide poisoning. The extent of the memory loss appears to be related to the severity of the damage to the brain. Some patients with head injuries have anterograde amnesia as well as retrograde amnesia. A person with **anterograde amnesia**, like the epileptic patient described in the section on dichotomous memory, can no longer lay down new memories because the process that moves information from short-term memory to long-term memory is damaged.

Decay

Although there is no way to show that memories have ever been permanently lost, the oldest theory of forgetting assumes that they wear away, or decay, with the passage of time. Decay theory presumes that when a new fact is learned or a

Memories fade with time, but we may remember certain childhood experiences quite clearly even in advanced age.

new experience occurs, a **memory trace**, which is a physiological change, is formed in the brain. As time passes, the trace decays and may disappear altogether. When this happens, the information is forgotten. The only way to increase the strength of the memory trace is to make use of, or practice, the information. Decay theory appears to account for the transience of the fragile sensory and short-term memory stores, but the application of decay theory to long-term memory is open to question.

The proposal that memories fade with time fits our subjective experiences. For instance, the memory of last week's football game is usually stronger and more detailed than the memory of a game from last season. However, many long-term memory phenomena cannot be explained by decay theory. Motor skills tend to be remembered over long periods without practice; for example, an adult who has not been on ice skates for years can generally demonstrate the skill for a child. A senile person who cannot remember what happened yesterday may readily recall childhood experiences. Also, research has demonstrated that people forget substantially less if they sleep for several hours after learning something than if they stay awake (see Figure 9.16). These facts are difficult to explain if we assume that memories simply decay with the passage of time.

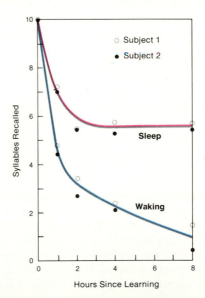

Figure 9.16 Two subjects were given lists of nonsense syllables to learn (BIK, QAJ, NIC, for example) and were tested after various periods of time. When the subjects were allowed to sleep during the time interval between learning and recall, they remembered much more than they did if they had stayed awake. (After Jenkins and Dallenbach, 1924.)

Interference

Another explanation of forgetting attributes it to **interference**, assuming that other material blocks out the memory. According to this explanation, any apparent decay of the memory of last year's football game is caused by interference from all the other events, including football games, since that time. Had no other games been seen in the past year, the memory might have faded less. Although interference probably does not explain all forgetting, it does account for the experimental results presented in Figure 9.16. People who learned nonsense syllables, then went to sleep and so were not subject to interference, recalled the syllables better than people who continued their waking activities. After eight hours, the subjects who remained awake remembered only about 10 percent of the material; those who slept recalled about 60 percent (Jenkins and Dallenbach, 1924).

Research has shown that interference near the beginning of the storage process can prevent new material from passing into long-term memory (McGeoch, 1942). In a typical experiment, people memorize the adjectives in list A of Table 9.1, then they learn the adjectives in list B. When asked to recall list A, people who memorized list B will not remember as many of the adjectives as people in a control group who memorized only list A. The information in list B interferes with the information in list A; since the interference comes from the learning of a subsequent list, psychologists call this **retroactive interference**, indicating that the interference has moved backward ("retro-") from list B to list A.

Interference can work both ways. When people who learned both lists are tested on list B, they will not remember as many adjectives from that list as will people who did not memorize list A. When interference moves forward ("pro-"), it is called **proactive interference**. In other words, proactive interference comes from learning that

takes place *before* the information in question is learned; retroactive interference comes from learning that takes place during the retention period, *after* the information in question is learned.

It may be that interference does not cause the loss of information, but only makes it inaccessible. In one study (Postman and Stark, 1969), information that could not be recalled could be recognized. That is, people who had forgotten many items in list A because of retroactive interference were able to pick out some of the forgotten words from a long list of adjectives.

The greater the similarity between the materials to be memorized, the greater the interference during subsequent recall. This information can be applied to study habits in order to minimize the effects of interference. For example, it may be wise not to study highly similar subjects—such as math and physics, or psychology and sociology—close together in time. By separating the study of similar kinds of material, both proactive and retroactive interference between the subjects are reduced. Sleep provides the best protection from interference, for during sleep no new information that can interfere with the studied material is absorbed. This fact indicates that studying before bedtime or napping after a study period would reduce interference.

Motivated Forgetting

The failure to retrieve an item from memory is sometimes the result of human motivations. Motives can interfere with recall, producing distortions of memory and other negative effects. This kind of forgetting is a matter of suppression or **repression**, a conscious or unconscious decision to "forget" unpleasant or disturbing memories. Although the material has not disappeared from storage, the retrieval mechanism by-passes routes that lead to the repressed memory. However, indications that the forgotten material is still available often appear in behavior—a person may pause or fumble for words when discussing events related to the critical memory, or may show other signs of anxiety, such as sweating or blushing.

Motivations also can cause us to remember ourselves in a more favorable manner than we deserve, so that our memories become self-serving (Loftus, 1980). In one study by French pschologist Jean-Paul Codel, each person in

Table 9.1 Lists of Adjectives Used in Testing Long-Term Memory

List A	List B	List C
happy	gay	58
big	large	22
hard	solid	18
funny	humorous	19
thin	slender	33
calming	soothing	71
neat	tidy	45

groups of four estimated the length of a rod; afterward the rod was measured and the correct length announced. Later, when asked how their own estimates compared with those of the rest of their group, most people recalled that their estimates had been one of the most accurate—no matter how poorly they had actually done.

As time goes on, our recollections become even more favorable to ourselves. In 1974, 1,300 Iowa men who had been interviewed a decade before were recontacted and asked the same questions (Powers, Goudy, and Keith, 1978). On some of the questions (such as "Had you made a will in 1964?") the answers corresponded with the answers on the earlier survey. But when asked in 1974, "What was your income in 1964?"

60 percent of the men gave inaccurate answers and the inaccuracies generally erred in the direction of higher incomes. In answering most of the questions, men tended to paint a more flattering picture of their past than appeared in their 1964 replies. Although sometimes people may lie to create a good impression, it is probable that most inaccurate recollections reflect a person's actual memories. In the discussion of reconstructive memory, it became clear that small incidents can change memories in important ways. It is probable that our self-serving memories are not attempts to deceive others, but reconstructions that bolster our self-esteem, so that we can continue to think of ourselves in a positive manner (Loftus, 1980).

SUMMARY

1. **Memory** is the human capacity to register, retain, and retrieve information. Memory can be demonstrated by recognizing information when it is reencountered at a later date or by recalling stored information. There are three basic memory processes: acquisition, retention, and retrieval. **Acquisition**, also called **encoding**, is the transformation of raw information into the form in which it will be stored. **Retention** refers to the maintenance of information in storage, and **retrieval** refers to the ability to get encoded material back into awareness. There are also three different types of memory store: sensory memory, short-term memory, and long-term memory. Instead of viewing information as being transferred from one type of storage to another, some psychologists see information as being processed at increasingly deeper levels, from a shallow sensory level to deep levels of meaning.

2. **Sensory memory** contains all the information registered by the sense organs at any given moment, but the information decays in about a second. Information that enters sensory memory through the eye is held in **iconic memory**. **Selective attention**, a control process that selects information for processing from sensory memory, has been studied primarily in terms of **echoic memory**, or information that enters sensory memory through the ear. One way to study selective attention is with the **dichotic listening** technique, in which a person wearing a set of earphones hears two different messages played simultaneously, one in each ear. People can easily follow ("shadow") the message coming into one ear, but they know nothing of the content of the message in the other ear. They can, however, hear their own name when it is inserted into the unshadowed message. Processes such as driving, typing, and playing a piano become automatic with constant practice and no longer require selective attention; this condition is called **automaticity**.

3. **Short-term memory** has limited capacity (about seven items) and a short retention span (about fifteen seconds). Information can be kept in short-term memory by rehearsing it. In **maintenance rehearsal**, the information fades after the rehearsal stops; in **elaborative rehearsal**, the information is organized and transferred into long-term memory. The amount of material that can be maintained in short-term memory can be increased by "chunking" it; that is, by reorganizing it so that individual items of information are recoded as larger groups (such as organizing words into phrases).

4. **Long-term memory** is the repository of permanent knowledge, and its capacity is almost limitless. Information is stored in either **episodic memory**, an autobiographical record of

events, or **semantic memory**, organized knowledge about words and symbols and the rules for manipulating them. **Dual-code** theorists believe that information in long-term memory is represented by visual images and by words; **propositional-code** theorists believe that information is represented by abstract propositions. Both theories have received some experimental support, but both have problems.

5. Information is retrieved from storage by means of **retrieval cues**, pieces of information that direct the search. Recognition is easier than recall, because in **recognition** the retrieval cue is the information itself; there is no need to search storage. In **recall**, there must be an active search of long-term memory. In **state-dependent memory**, information that is learned during one internal state (intoxication, anger) is difficult to retrieve when a person is in a different state (sobriety, happiness). When the original state is restored, the information is again available. In such instances, the physical state serves as a retrieval cue. Retrieval often involves an active reconstruction of the past, in which bits of information are pieced out with guesses and inferences drawn from general knowledge. The process takes place without our awareness, and information encountered after an event takes place can be woven into memories of the event.

6. **Mnemonic**, or memory-assisting, systems organize information so that it can be remembered, using imagery, association, and meaning. Many mnemonic systems rely on imagery, and they may be so effective because they add an additional (visual) way of processing information that is stored by verbal methods.

7. When information is forgotten, it may still be in storage but be temporarily unavailable. If so, the right retrieval cue will make it available again. The **decay** theory of forgetting presumes that the **memory trace** (a physiological change in the brain) gradually decays and disappears, an explanation that accounts for forgetting from sensory memory and short-term memory. The **interference** theory of forgetting assumes that additional material, encountered either before or after the forgotten information was learned, makes information unavailable.

KEY TERMS

acquisition
anterograde amnesia
automaticity
confabulation
context
dichotic listening
dual-code theory
echoic memory
eidetic imagery
elaborative rehearsal
encoding
episodic memory
fan effect
flashbulb memory
free recall

iconic memory
interference
levels of processing
long-term memory
maintenance rehearsal
memory
memory trace
method of loci
mnemonic
proactive interference
propositional-code theory
recall
recognition
relearning score
repression
retention

retrieval
retrieval cue
retroactive interference
retrograde amnesia
savings score
selective attention
semantic memory
semantic network model
sensory memory
serial-position curve
short-term memory
state-dependent memory
"tip-of-the-tongue"
    phenomenon

RECOMMENDED READINGS

BADDELEY, A. D. *The Psychology of Memory*. New York: Basic Books, 1976. An excellent, comprehensive textbook on memory.

DAVIES, G., H. ELLIS, and J. SHEPHERD. *Perceiving and Remembering Faces*. New York: Academic Press, 1981. A book that is all about the processes by which we recognize—or fail to recognize—another face. This book brings together new information in the form of a set of review articles, each written by a leading researcher in the field.

HIGBEE, K. L. *Your Memory: How It Works and How to Improve It*. Englewood Cliffs, N.J.: Prentice-Hall, 1977. This book discusses research on memory and how to remember better. The author's strategy is to learn some useful techniques and add a pinch of hard work, and you can have a better memory.

KLATZKY, R. *Human Memory: Structure and Processes.* San Francisco: Freeman, 1975. An introduction to memory from a cognitive perspective.

LOFTUS, E. F. *Memory*. Reading, Mass.: Addison-Wesley, 1980. Written for laypeople, this book contains many examples of how the memory system works and discusses the malleability of memory.

LURIA, A. R. *The Mind of a Mnemonist.* New York: Basic Books, 1968. This wonderful little book describes a famous Russian memory expert named S. Luria studied this man for over thirty years.

CHAPTER 10

Cognition

For centuries, scurvy has killed more seamen than accidents, warfare, or all other diseases put together. On Vasco da Gama's famous voyage around the Cape of Good Hope in 1497, 100 of his crew of 160 men died of the disease. Two and a half centuries later, James Lind, a physician on the British ship *Salisbury,* had an infirmary full of scurvy patients and devised an experiment to discover the best treatment for this dangerous disease (Mosteller, 1981). He set up six groups of patients, placing two scurvy-ridden sailors in each group. The first group got six spoonfuls of vinegar each day; the second got a half pint of sea water; the third got a quart of cider; the fourth, seventy-five drops of vitriol elixir; the fifth, two oranges and a lemon; and the sixth, nutmeg. The sailors who were given a daily ration of citrus fruit were cured in a few days —at least they were well enough to get out of bed and help nurse the other patients.

In 1747, vitamins were unknown, so Lind could not know that scurvy was the result of a vitamin C deficiency and that citrus fruits were a concentrated source of the vitamin. How did Lind decide to include oranges and lemons among his unlikely assortment of treatments? He had heard of an earlier English expedition on which sailors in one of the ships received three teaspoons of lemon juice each day and escaped the disease. When he faced the infirmary full of scurvy patients, Lind had a difficult problem to solve, so he combined all the bits of information he had gathered about the disease with other things he knew, including his memory of the earlier use of lemon juice as a preventive and his knowledge that lemons and oranges were similar fruits. To solve his problem, he applied various pieces of information to different experimental groups. This process of organizing information to solve a problem is an example of cognition in action.

Problem solving is one type of **cognition**, which is the process of knowing; cognition also encompasses thinking, decision making, reasoning, judging, imagining—all the higher mental processes human beings engage in. These very diverse mental activities may seem to be a jumble of topics without any common elements, but a common ground underlies them all: they all depend upon learning and memory. This chapter on cognition, then, examines the operation of learning and memory in complex situations.

The modern study of cognition has developed within the last three decades. During the nineteenth century, psychologists studied cognition by using **introspection**, a method in which trained observers reported their own mental activities under controlled conditions. It amounted to a self-observation of the mind. Introspection fell out of favor when it became clear that reports from various laboratories often contradicted one another and that observers generally found whatever the theory guiding their own research predicted would be found.

With introspection discredited, psychologists stopped studying cognition. During the

1920s, behaviorism became the dominant field in psychology, and although behaviorists were willing to admit that mental events existed, they refused to study them on the grounds that cognition could not be studied objectively. John Watson (1930) even declined to use the term "thinking" in connection with psychology.

The modern study of cognition emerged after World War II, when the information-processing approach to handling knowledge was first developed. It became possible to think of human beings in terms of gathering, processing, storing, and using information. Then as computer science grew and researchers began to work with the concept of artificial intelligence, cognitive psychologists started to apply concepts used with computers to the analysis of human thought. However, the return to the study of cognition did not mean a return to the subjective methods of the nineteenth-century psychologists. Cognitive psychologists apply objective methods, just as behavioral psychologists do, but their basic interests are different. Any interest modern behaviorists take in thought processes is for the purpose of explaining behavior. Cognitive psychologists, on the other hand, are interested in behavior to the extent that it helps explain thought processes.

The broad array of processes included in cognition makes it impossible to cover the entire topic in a single chapter. We will, therefore, limit the discussion to three major areas of cognitive functioning: problem solving, decision making, and creativity.

Problem Solving

All problems have certain elements in common: an individual is prevented by a barrier, either physical or psychological, from reaching some goal, and an effort must be made to circumvent or surmount the barrier. But problems vary greatly in their complexity and in the effort required to solve them. Because each type of problem demands a particular combination of knowledge and thought, some strategies are better than others for surmounting the barriers that prevent the solution of various types of problems.

The Importance of Past Experience

Problem solving requires the use of past knowledge—both knowledge that is specific to a problem (such as Lind's knowledge that lemon juice seemed to prevent scurvy) and general knowledge (Lind's knowledge that oranges and lemons are closely related fruits). When an individual is faced with a problem, the problem serves as a retrieval cue that brings information related to the problem out of storage. Once the individual has the information, imagination takes over; the individual must decide whether the retrieved information will lead to the problem's solution (Anderson, 1980).

If the problem is identical with an earlier problem and the objects used to achieve the goal in the earlier problem are at hand, the identical past experience is cued and the old solution is simply repeated. For example, when a lamp stops working, the same solution that solved the problem before—replacing the light bulb—generally solves it again. But suppose replacing the bulb has no effect on the darkened lamp. Now the situation presents only a partial match between experience and the problem. More information is retrieved and the person tries to recognize the situation as similar to something that has happened in the past. Recalling past power failures, the individual might check the circuit box to make sure the current is on or the wall plug to see if the lamp is plugged in. If neither of these solutions works, the match between the problem and past solutions becomes less likely, and if a match cannot be made, no effective action can be carried out. At this point, a person with no knowledge of electricity might decide that further action was futile and take the lamp to an electrician. A person with a larger store of electrical knowledge would stop and think about the problem, recalling additional information about electricity, such as the fact that wires sometimes fray and break and that contact points wear out, then examine the cord or the socket to see if it is worth trying to replace either the cord or the contact points.

All these solutions are examples of **reproductive thinking**, the direct application of previous knowledge to a new problem. In other cases, **creative thinking** is required: because previously learned rules are unavailable, new rules based on other stores of information must be generated. We will examine this process later in the chapter.

Problem-Solving Strategies

Whether a problem requires reproductive or creative thinking, the problem-solving process uses various strategies. In some cases, systematic hypothesis testing will lead directly to a solution; it can rely on either algorithms or heuristics to simplify the task.

Hypothesis Testing   Retrieving past information and using it to imagine possible solutions is at the basis of **hypothesis testing**, in which various ways a goal can be reached are formulated and then tested. It is a strategy commonly used by scientists to solve problems, but it is just as applicable to problems in daily life. Suppose a mechanic is trying to discover why a car will not start. Any one of several conditions could be responsible, and it is the mechanic's job to discover which is the culprit. To do so, the mechanic uses the strategy of hypothesis testing, formulating possible reasons for the car's failure and testing them, one at a time. He might first decide that the battery is dead and test this hypothesis by turning on the headlights. If the lights work, he may decide that gasoline is not getting to the engine and test this hypothesis by disconnecting the fuel line where it enters the carburetor. If gas flows out of the line when the engine is cranked, his second hypothesis is wrong, and he may hypothesize that the spark plugs are not firing, and so on, developing and testing hypotheses until one of the tests reveals that a hypothesis is correct (see Figure 10.1).

Hypothesis testing involves several steps: (1) generate a hypothesis; (2) devise a test of the hypothesis; (3) evaluate the outcome; (4) if the hypothesis is incorrect, go back to step 1 and generate a new hypothesis. New hypotheses are developed and tested until a solution is reached. In applying hypothesis testing to a problem, we can use either an algorithmic or a heuristic approach.

Algorithms   An **algorithm** is a simple set of rules arranged in a logical order that will solve all instances of a particular set of problems. For example, the rules for subtraction work for all

Figure 10.1   Table of hypotheses generated about why a car won't start. (After Einhorn and Hogarth, 1981.)

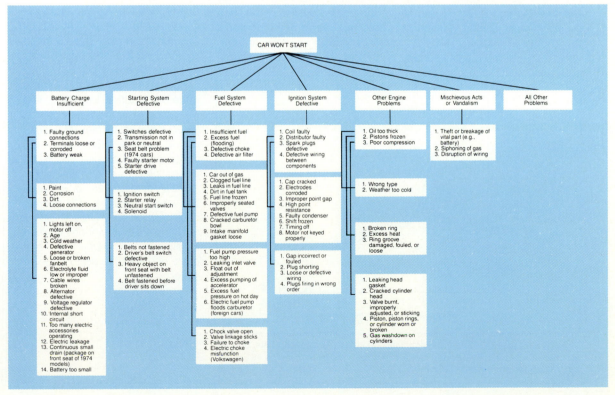

Learning to Learn

You have probably noticed that someone who is extremely good at playing one videogame generally learns a new one rapidly. If Ray consistently wins at Asteroids and David has never before played a videogame, it is not hard to predict that Ray will beat David when they both play Pac-Man for the first time. Ray will win because when people are exposed repeatedly to the same types of problems, they develop problem-solving strategies. The acquisition of such strategies is called "learning to learn," and it forms the basis for hypothesis testing, heuristics, and algorithms.

Harry Harlow (1949) discovered the process while studying the ability of monkeys to solve problems. In one of his studies, monkeys had to find a raisin that had been placed under one of two lids. At first a red lid and a green lid were placed in front of the monkey, with the raisin always beneath the green lid. Har-

low kept changing the position of the lid until the monkey learned that color was the cue that indicated the presence of the raisin. Then Harlow switched the cue from color to shape, using triangular and round lids of the same color. After a number of tries, the monkey learned that the shape of a lid revealed the raisin's hiding place. After solving hundreds of such problems, the monkey learned that the appearance of the lids, not their position, was always the key to the solution. It also learned that the solution to each new problem was independent of previous solutions and that cues that had been rewarded in the past were irrelevant to a new problem. Eventually, the monkey learned the principle that ran through all the problems and paid attention only to the characteristics of the lid. It could now solve such problems with no more than a single error.

In learning to learn, the mon-

keys formed a **learning set**, which they could use appropriately in many situations. Learning sets enable monkeys—or people —to transfer what they learn in performing one task to some other problem (Harlow and Harlow, 1949). Such **transfer of training** is important in problem solving and in all learning. Learning sets have been studied by having people learn lists of words. Such lists consist of pairs of words ("red/soft";"dog/ moon"), and the task is to memorize the list so that when the subject is shown a word from a pair, the second word is recalled. When a group of people learned sixteen such lists on sixteen successive days, they soon developed a learning set. They transferred their learning strategy to new lists. Although it took them nearly forty attempts to learn the list given them on the first day, by the sixteenth day they learned the new list in fewer than twenty attempts (Ward, 1937).

Such a transfer of knowledge is generally positive. Someone who has learned to play the clarinet usually learns to play the saxophone quickly and easily, because clarinet playing and saxophone playing are similar skills. But sometimes transfer is negative and interferes with solving new problems. A clarinet player may find that the motions learned in playing the clarinet make it more difficult to learn to play the guitar.

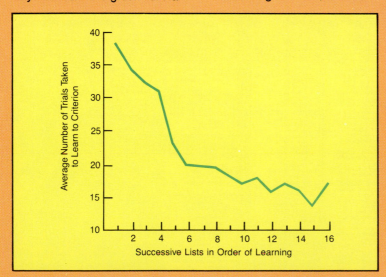

The learning to learn effect. Subjects learned sixteen successive lists, one per day. Notice that the last list was learned in about half as many trials as the first list. (Adapted from Ward, 1937.)

subtraction problems, regardless of the particular numbers that compose the problems. If these rules are followed, they guarantee success (see Figure 10.2). If we used an algorithm to solve an anagram, such as KECA, we should systematically work through all the possible combinations of the letters until a combination turned up that made a word. The advantage of an algorithm is that its rules are clear and precise. The algorithm for solving the anagram might begin: Move the final letter one place to the left (KEAC). Does it make a word? If not, move the letter one more place to the left (KAEC). Does it make a word? If not, move the letter one more place to the left (AKEC). And so on.

Using algorithms, unskilled people learned to find the source of trouble in disabled radios after only a week's instruction. In fact, they did better in a trouble-shooting test than did people who had been trained in a conventional manner (Davies, 1970). Algorithms appear to be especially useful when applied to such things as contracts

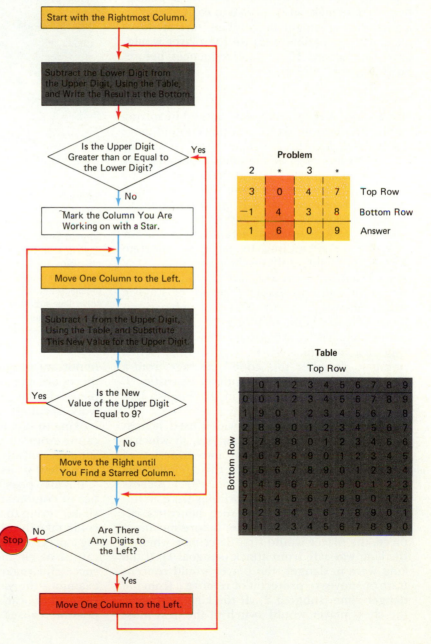

Figure 10.2 An algorithm for subtraction of whole numbers. An infinite number of subtraction problems can be correctly solved by following this precise set of rules. To use the algorithm to solve the sample problem, begin at step 1 and continue down the chart, as directed. Try making up your own subtraction problem and using the algorithm to get the answer. (Adapted from Lewis and Papadimitriou, 1978.)

and income tax regulations. In one study (Lewis et al. 1967), people who used algorithms solved problems concerning tax regulations much faster and more accurately than people who simply followed the official government instructions.

Since algorithms test all possible solutions, they are not always practical, because some problems have more solutions than can reasonably be tested. For instance, before each move a chess player who used algorithms would have to test every possible response that the opposing player could make in response to each move the algorithm user might make. This sort of chess playing is impossible because the player would have to evaluate 10^{120} play sequences before moving a chess piece.

Heuristics   A relatively quick method of solving problems and one that chess players find more useful than algorithms is heuristics, a strategy that relies on a person's familiarity with the task or with some parts of it. A **heuristic** may be thought of as a rule of thumb that provides a general direction for solving problems. Although a heuristic approach does not guarantee success, it often leads to a rapid solution. For example, in attempting to solve the anagram KECA, we could apply the heuristic that CVCV (c=consonant, v=vowel) and CVVC combinations are more probable features of English words than CCVV or VVCC combinations. Thus, we could begin by trying the CVCV combinations. Heuristics are also used in solving cryptograms, like the one in Figure 10.3. When trying to decipher this coded message from a Sherlock Holmes tale, start with the heuristic, "E is the most common letter in the English language."

An extremely general, but widely used, heuristic is the use of **subgoal analysis**, in which a difficult problem is divided into a series of smaller problems, or subgoals, that are relatively easy to solve (Newell and Simon, 1972). A chess player who realized that algorithms were an impractical guide would find such heuristics extremely helpful. For example, before moving a piece, the player would first determine whether the king was safe from attack (subgoal 1). If the king were in danger, the player would concentrate on moves to protect it or remove it from the danger zone (subgoal 2). If the king were safe, the chess player would switch to the next most

Figure 10.3   Match your skill against that consummate expert in deductive problem solving, Sherlock Holmes. The case of Hilton and Elsie Cubitt began when client Hilton handed Sherlock the first hieroglyphic fragment. Several days later Sherlock received three more samples; shortly afterward the last example came. Sherlock rushed into action after seeing the last fragments. Why? What message did these last figures contain? How would you solve this puzzle of the "dancing men"? What heuristics, or rules of thumb, might be helpful? Check your solution with the one explained in the caption for Figure 10.10.

important subgoal, which is to ensure that other pieces are not in danger (subgoal 3). If the other pieces do not need defending, the player would work through a series of offensive subgoals, looking to see, for example, if it were possible to capture one of the opponent's major pieces. In subgoal analysis, each of the subgoals constitutes a problem in its own right.

It is also possible to use algorithms and heuristics in combination. For example, the auto mechanic trying to determine why a car will not start could take the algorithmic approach and, following a precisely stated set of rules, test all possible causes of engine failure. He will ultimately be successful regardless of the order in which he examines the various systems, searching for the cause of the car's refusal to start. However, some possible causes are more likely than others, so the mechanic will probably solve the problem faster if he uses heuristics to determine the order in which he tests the systems. For example, if defective spark plugs are very common, the mechanic might test the ignition system, checking to see if the plug is shorting, if the gap is incorrect, and so forth. However, if it is a cold morning and the driver had been trying to start the car for some time, the mechanic might begin by applying a test to the battery. Applying heuristics in this way increases efficiency in problem solving.

Categorizing the World

To solve problems, human beings depend upon an elaborate set of concepts they have developed to categorize the world. Without a knowledge of such concepts as "car," a mechanic would not be able to apply to a Pontiac knowledge gained from working on a Plymouth. By studying how human beings develop categories, we can deepen our understanding of the problem-solving process.

Early research into categorization used artificial concepts. A typical experiment involved simple figures that varied in size (small, large); color (red, blue); and shape (circle, square). Subjects were told that each figure belonged in either category A or category B and that their task was to figure out the appropriate category for each figure. In most cases, a simple rule would solve the problem. For example, red figures belong to category A, blue figures belong to category B. But subjects were not told the rule. They were simply shown the figures (e.g., a large blue circle) one at a time and asked to indicate the category to which each figure belonged. After each guess, the subjects were given *feedback* (told whether they were right or wrong). Using the feedback, they eventually solved the problem.

Psychologists found that subjects did not simply memorize the correct category for each stimulus, remembering that the small red circle and the large red square belonged in category A and the small blue circle in category B. Instead they developed and tested hypotheses about the rule in the experimenter's mind. When feedback indicated that a hypothesis was wrong, the subjects tried a new one until eventually they arrived at the correct rule for categorizing the figures.

Membership in a category appears to depend upon family resemblance; that is, an object is considered a good example of a category if it is similar to many members of that category and not similar to members of another category, so that a horse is considered a good example of a mammal, but a bat is not (Rosch, 1977). Although people agree on typical members of a category, the vagueness of category boundaries leads to disagreement and uncertainty about objects that are not typical. In one study (McCloskey and Glucksberg, 1978) in which thirty people judged whether items belonged in particular categories, all said that "cancer" was a disease, but sixteen said that "stroke" was a disease while fourteen said it was not. A month later, the same people were asked to judge the same items, and eleven of the thirty had changed their minds as to whether stroke was a disease.

Learning which objects belong to a category and which should be excluded may be accomplished by forming a **prototype**, a hypothetical best—or most typical—example of the category. The prototype of a category is developed by averaging its specific members. For example, a person's prototype for the bird category would be a sort of average of all the individual birds the person had seen, and it might look something like a robin. According to this view, people decide whether an object is a member of a category by determining how similar it is to the category prototype (Anderson, 1980).

After wondering if people do form a hypothetical prototype for each category, psychologists tried to find out. In a series of studies (Posner and Keele, 1968; 1970), people looked at examples of four different patterns made up of scattered dots. Each pattern had a prototype, which was nine dots scattered in a random pattern (see Figure 10.4), but subjects never saw the prototypes. Instead they looked at four distortions of each prototype, each distortion varying from the prototype in a different way. The subjects studied these sixteen distorted patterns until they could correctly sort them into the four patterns. Later the subjects were given another sorting task, which included the sixteen distorted patterns, additional distortions they had never seen before, and the four prototypes. They sorted 80 percent of the familiar patterns correctly, 68 percent of the prototypes, and 50 percent of the unfamiliar distortions. Apparently, people are fairly proficient at extracting from a number of instances the central characteristics of a category, for if they remembered only the specific instances they had studied, their sorting of prototypes and unfamiliar distortions would

Prototype

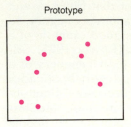

Distortion 1

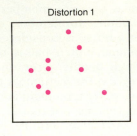

Distortion 2

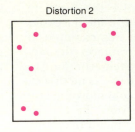

Figure 10.4 Examples of the stimuli used in experiments by Posner and Keele (1970), which demonstrated subjects' ability to extract a central category from a series of instances. Subjects studied distortions of a prototype, such as the two examples on the right. (After Posner and Keele, 1970.)

have been much lower. But since they remembered the studied patterns better than the prototypes, they must have remembered specific instances they had seen as well.

Other cognitive psychologists (e.g., Anderson et al., 1979) propose that instead of forming an idea of a best example, people notice what sets of features tend to accompany category membership and develop the category around these features. For example, they notice that beak, feathers, wings, two legs, and the power of flight are features that occur together in birds. But a bird's color or the fact that it has two eyes is not relevant to the category and so not included in the category's features. Confusion arises when a bird lacks some of the distinguishing features, as when a bird neither flies nor has typical feathers (penguin) or when members of another category have some of the features that distinguish birds (the bat has wings and flies). In this approach to category formation, there is no prototype, but an incomplete set of features that often occur together.

Computer Simulation

A knowledge of the way people form categories is important in **computer simulation**, which involves the construction of computer programs that act as much like people as possible. The purpose of computer simulation is to explain cognitive processes and to make predictions that can be tested experimentally with human beings. The computer program is, in fact, the theory, and it is an especially clear form of theory: each logical step is completely specified, and precise predictions about human thought can be made by running the program under various conditions. These predictions about human cognition are tested by observing human beings as they perform under the conditions specified in the program.

The belief that heuristics influence all goal-directed thinking provided the basic premise for the development of a computer program called the General Problem Solver (GPS), which has solved many diverse problems in logic, algebra, and chess (Newell and Simon, 1972). The program is written so that the computer uses common heuristics (such as subgoal analysis) either singly or in combination, in a way that simulates the behavior of a human being solving the same problem. The GPS cannot solve all problems, but it can handle any problem that can be put in a general format specifying the current situation, the desired goal, and permissible methods of reaching the goal. According to Herbert Simon and Allen Newell (1970), who developed the GPS, comparisons of the operations carried out by computers while solving a problem with those used by college students solving the same problem show that both computers and college students tend to notice the same things about a problem, establish the same subgoals, operate on the problem in the same way—and run down the same blind alleys. However, the solutions reached by the GPS do not use memory in the same way that human solutions do, and its methods have no reference to the subject matter of the problem being solved.

The GPS solves problems by abstracting them from the world of experience; programs developed by Roger Schank and Robert Abelson (1977) give the computer knowledge about concepts that can be applied to problems, along with a set of rules covering the possible relationships of these concepts. For example, the computer is provided with knowledge concerning common situations (such as automobile accidents, taking the subway, dining in a restaurant) and with the knowledge required to infer probable human intentions and goals.

Computers programed by these methods have come closer to duplicating human thought processes than any previous computers, but an enormous gulf between the computer and human cognition remains. Computers are rigid and uncreative, have small memories, are devoid of emotion, are incapable of development and change, and have always been unable to handle human experience. Some computer specialists (e.g., Weizenbaum, 1978) are certain the gulf between computers and human intelligence can never be bridged, but by enabling computers to interpret the world in terms of human experience—however haltingly—the new programs have begun to reduce the size of the gap.

Impediments to Problem Solving

Factors that have nothing specific to do with a problem can interfere with a person's ability to solve it. One such factor is related to that essential aspect of problem solving, past experience; the other is related to the problem solver's emotional or motivational state.

Fixation   Automatically applying an inappropriate strategy to a problem and then rigidly clinging to the obviously ineffective approach is known as **fixation**. It can inhibit or prevent successful solutions.

Attempts by thousands of people under many

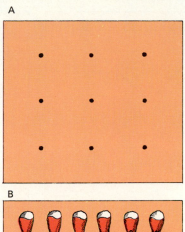

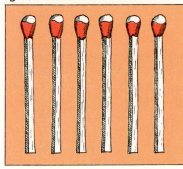

Figure 10.6   Two mind-teasers designed by Martin Scheerer (1963). (A) Nine dots are arranged in a square. The problem is to connect them by drawing four continuous straight lines without lifting pencil from paper. (B) Six matches must be assembled to form four congruent equilateral triangles each side of which is equal to the length of the matches. (If you don't have matches, any six objects equal in length will do.) Check your answers with those given in Figure 10.7.

Figure 10.5   Luchins' classic demonstration of set in problem solving. In each of the problems in this series you must work out how you could measure out the quantities of liquid indicated on the right by using jars with the capacities shown on the left. Try the series yourself before reading on. After solving the first five problems, nearly two-thirds of Luchins' subjects were unable to solve the sixth. The sixth problem actually requires a simpler strategy than the first five, and it would be easily solved were it not for the set established by the first five.

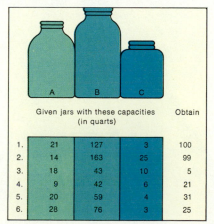

	Given jars with these capacities (in quarts)			Obtain
	A	B	C	
1.	21	127	3	100
2.	14	163	25	99
3.	18	43	10	5
4.	9	42	6	21
5.	20	59	4	31
6.	28	76	3	25

different conditions to solve a series of six arithmetic problems show how strong the fixation of newly acquired habits or sets can be. The first six problems in Figure 10.5 can be solved in the same way: Fill the largest jar (jar B), then from it fill the middle-sized jar (jar A) once and the smallest jar (jar C) twice. This method can be stated in a simple formula: $B - A - 2C$. The sixth problem requires a different solution.

In a series of studies (Luchins, 1946), most people who were given the sixth problem first solved it readily. However, people who solved the other five problems before attempting to solve the sixth problem found it extremely difficult. Two-thirds of these people persisted in using the $B - A - 2C$ formula although it was inappropriate for the problem. Their fixation was so strong that many gave up, while others staunchly maintained that the formula worked, insisting that $76 - 28 - 3 - 3 = 25$.

A
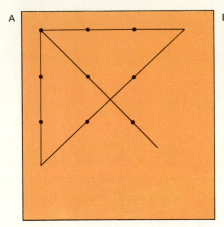

B
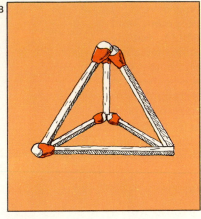

Figure 10.7 Solutions to the mind-teasers in Figure 10.6. The principal impediment in both of these problems is perceptual fixation. (A) The dot problem is solved by extending the lines beyond the dots; most people assume that they must stay within the perceived square structure. (B) The match problem is solved by building a three-dimensional pyramid; most people assume that the matches must lie flat, as they were first perceived.

What appears to be a simple case of fixation may sometimes be quite different. A traditional example of perceptual fixation is the square composed of nine dots shown in Figure 10.6. The task is to connect all the dots by drawing four straight lines without lifting the pencil from the paper. Most people perceive the nine dots as a square and assume that the pencil lines must be drawn within the boundaries of the square. Actually, the only way to solve the problem is to draw lines that extend beyond the perceptual boundaries of the square (see Figure 10.7). Thus, people who fixate on the dots as representing a square supposedly find that this limited frame of reference leads to a faulty assumption about the rules and blocks the ability to solve the problem (Scheerer, 1963). However, it has been pointed out that the dot problem is more complex than has been supposed, and that when people are told the solution requires going outside the square, 80 percent of them still cannot solve it. What is more, after they have been shown the solution, many people cannot reproduce it. Although this traditional demonstration may involve perceptual fixation, other factors seem to be heavily involved (Weisberg, 1980).

Another type of fixation involves **functional fixedness**, the inability to use a familiar object in an unfamiliar way. For example, a person is shown into a room where a candle, tacks, and a box of matches lie on a table. The person's job is to mount the candle on the wall so that it burns properly, using any of the objects on the table (see Figure 10.8). Tacking a candle directly to the wall will not solve the problem. The matches are in their original box, which emphasizes the box as a container and so encourages the problem solver to fix upon this familiar function. As

long as the box is seen only as a container, the problem solver will be unable to view it as a candleholder (Duncker, 1945).

Functional fixedness was again demonstrated when researchers suspended two cords from the ceiling and asked people to tie the cords together (Birch and Rabinowitz, 1951). However, the cords were so far apart that a person could not reach one while holding onto the other. The problem could be solved by tying a weight to the end of one of the cords, then swinging it like a pendulum until it could be caught while the person held the other cord. In the room with the

Figure 10.8 A problem used by K. Duncker to demonstrate functional fixedness: He gave subjects the materials shown and asked them to mount a candle on a wall so that it could be used to give light. Try to solve the problem yourself. (The use of the term "functional fixedness" gives you a clue to the solution of the problem that Duncker's subjects did not have.) The solution is given in Figure 10.10.

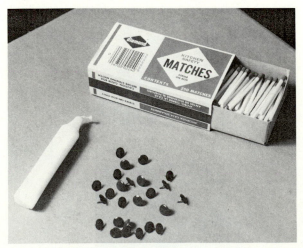

strings were two objects that could be used as weights: a switch and a relay. Before confronting the strings, one group of people solved a problem that involved wiring the switch into an electrical circuit, fixing its function as an electrical switch; a second group solved a problem using the relay in a circuit, thus fixing the function of the relay. A control group was given no prior experience with the two objects. After the pretest period, each person faced the two-string problem. All the subjects who had solved their pretest problem by using the relay selected the switch to create a pendulum, but most of the subjects who had previously used the switch selected the relay. People in the control group were equally likely to use the switch or the relay. Prior experience with either of the weighted objects caused people to see those objects in a way that interfered with their ability to assign a new function to them.

Both types of fixation demonstrate the same phenomenon: the production of a **mental set**, or a tendency to keep repeating solutions that worked in other situations. Inappropriate mental sets lead to counterproductive behavior when previously acquired knowledge is transferred to new situations where it does not apply.

Motivational Level   The effects of past experience on problem solving may be long-lived and stable. In contrast, the emotional and motivational states of the problem solver are relatively short-lived influences. Research has indicated that there is an optimal motivational level for efficient problem solving and that the optimal level appears to vary with the type of problem. At low levels of motivational arousal, performance is poor. As motivation increases (due to stress or other emotional arousal), performance improves, but only up to a point. After a certain point, called the **optimal arousal level**, further increases in motivation cause performance to deteriorate. The relationship, diagramed in Figure 10.9, is called the **Yerkes-Dodson law**, after the two psychologists who noted it in 1908.

Students who have done poorly on tests, either because they were unmotivated or because they were so hypermotivated that their emotional state interfered with their performance, are familiar with the practical effects of the Yerkes-Dodson law. Investigators have pointed out that soldiers in combat regularly demonstrate that portion of the law regarding hyperarousal, with as many as three-fourths of the soldiers who han-

dle their rifles effectively in practice not even firing their weapons during combat (Keegan, 1976). For example, more than 200 of the muzzle-loading rifles found on the field after the Battle of Gettysburg during the American Civil War had been loaded at least five times without being fired (Baddeley, 1972).

In a study that simulated the dangers of battle, army recruits taking part in a tactical exercise were informed that their lives were actually in danger. After being told that their unit was mistakenly being shelled by live ammunition, recruits had to repair a broken radio to notify headquarters of the mistake. Predictably, the performance of the recruits suffered (Berkun et al., 1962). Because of changed ethical standards regarding research, such studies are no longer done, but later studies of parachutists, rock climbers, and deep-sea divers have shown that the relationship between stress and performance may be different in novices and in veterans. Apparently, with regular exposure to a particular kind of danger, people learn to inhibit performance-disrupting anxiety (Baddeley, 1972). Even among veterans, however, extreme stress eventually leads to a breakdown in performance.

Figure 10.9   The relationship between motivational arousal and the effectiveness of performance may be represented as an inverted "U." For a given task there is an optimal amount of arousal; a greater or a lesser degree of activation will result in less efficient behavior. This result is known as the Yerkes-Dodson law. The peak of the curve varies with the nature of the task: Optimal arousal for a complex, intricate task such as repairing an electron microscope may be far below the optimal arousal for a simple physical task like washing dishes. (After Yerkes and Dodson, 1908.)

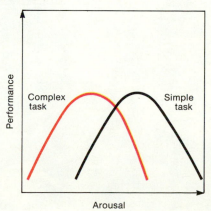

Decision Making

Making the right decision is fundamental to the problem-solving process. Some decisions have only minor consequences: it makes little difference whether a person buys a blue suit or a brown one, takes a bus or a subway, orders roast beef or broiled fish. But other decisions can have serious consequences: choices concerning marriage, careers, and investments can change lives; congressional choices on tax laws can affect the economy; and military decisions can alter the face of the whole planet. When making decisions, people often ignore important information. For example, residents of a flood plain tend to ignore the hazards of their location. Few of them buy flood insurance and most rebuild homes destroyed by floods on exactly the same

sites (Slovic, Kunreuther, and White, 1974). Such seemingly irrational decisions can be explained by research during the last decade into the decision-making process. Interest in this area has grown so rapidly that by the mid-seventies more than a thousand books and articles on decision making in business, government, ecology, law, and psychology had been published (Barron, 1974; Kleiter, Gachowetz, and Huber, 1976). Evidence indicates that human decisions are based on heuristics, that errors in judgment arise when the heuristics are misapplied, and that the way choices are framed can tip a decision in one direction or another.

Heuristics in Judgment

Decisions rely on heuristics, just as does the search for solutions to problems; as with problem solving, past experience often plays a greater role than pertinent information when a choice must be made. Heuristics allow us to decide quickly on the value of a certain action or the probability of certain consequences, without deliberating over a heuristic's appropriateness to a particular situation. The two major heuristics are representativeness and availability, and without them, it would take an inordinate amount of time to make the many decisions each of us faces every day.

Representativeness   When using the heuristic of **representativeness**, people base their predictions on resemblances between the predicted event and a typical example, or on the degree to which a predicted outcome is typical of its generating process. Suppose the problem is to predict political attitudes. The first prediction is for a man described as a vice president of a small-town bank who is clean-shaven; customarily wears dark, three-piece suits, white shirts, and a gold watch chain; belongs to the local Chamber of Commerce; and regularly attends the Baptist church. On the basis of the resemblance between

Many of our everyday decisions have minor consequences: it matters little what pair of shoes we select. If we choose the wrong spouse or career, however, the consequences can be extremely serious. In recent years, psychologists have become increasingly interested in how we come to make such decisions.

the banker and the prototypical conservative, it would be fairly safe to predict this man's political attitudes as conservative.

Now suppose the prediction has to do with the sex of all babies born in Chicago during the course of a year. On the basis of the knowledge that the generating process produces an almost equal distribution of sex, a prediction that Chicago births will be roughly half boys and half girls would be a wise use of the representativeness heuristic. This heuristic is also a dependable guide when it is applied to decide that an all-male jury or an all-white jury is probably the result of a biased selection procedure, since an unbiased jury would more closely reflect the sexual and racial composition of the community (Nisbett and Ross, 1980).

Availability When using the heuristic of **availability**, people base predictions on a comparison of the current situation with similar situations in the past, and their judgment depends upon the range of past examples they recall. When similar situations have been experienced frequently, it is probable that future events will resemble them, and the relevant situations will be easy to recall. Indeed, we regard easily recalled information as typical. For example, suppose a friend has been late on many occasions; when she fails to arrive at the restaurant on the stroke of one, your judgment, based on easily recalled examples, will be "I should have known I would have to wait for her." And you are probably right; your friend may habitually underestimate traffic and its effect on travel time.

In cases where past exposure and attention have resulted in the storage of unbiased information, availability is a useful tool. For example, if you are asked whether there are more apartment houses or single-family dwellings in your neighborhood, your own experiences and your recollections of them would probably produce an accurate answer drawn from an unbiased sample.

Biases in Judgment

Heuristics are not always reliable. The use of a particular heuristic leads people to ignore other sources of information, and when the ignored information has greater relevance than information called for by the heuristic, judgment will be biased and decisions will be erroneous.

Biases in Representativeness When relying on representativeness, a close resemblance to a stereotypical example often leads people to discard other information in their possession. Consider the following example:

> Two psychologists have a friend who is a professor. He likes to write poetry, is rather shy, and is small in stature. Which of the following is his field? (1) Chinese studies or (2) psychology?

Did you choose Chinese studies or psychology? If you used the heuristic of representativeness, you chose Chinese studies, since the description more closely resembles the occupational stereotype for Sinologists than for psychologists. But a moment's reflection on the relative proportions of Sinologists and psychologists and on the likelihood of psychologists making friends among members of their own profession should lead you to select psychologist (Nisbett and Ross, 1980).

In a study (Kahneman and Tversky, 1973) involving a somewhat similar judgment, 100 brief personality descriptions were prepared, and two groups of people were told that the paragraphs described lawyers and engineers, then were asked to sort the descriptions by profession. But each group also got a different bit of information: the first group heard that 70 percent of the paragraphs described lawyers and 30 percent described engineers; the second group heard that 30 percent of the paragraphs described lawyers and 70 percent described engineers. This important piece of information should have led the first group to ascribe more of the descriptions to lawyers and the second to ascribe more descriptions to engineers. Yet both groups discarded the information and sorted the descriptions similarly, assigning the paragraphs purely on the basis of a match between personality and occupational stereotype.

Representativeness can also lead people to ignore the size of the sample involved in their predictions; yet as noted in Chapter 2, information gathered from a small sample is often unreliable. This tendency appeared in a study (Kahneman and Tversky, 1972) based on the following example:

> A certain town is served by two hospitals. In the larger hospital about forty-five babies are born each day, and in the smaller hospital

about fifteen babies are born each day. As you know, about 50 percent of all babies are boys. However, the exact percentage varies from day to day. Sometimes it may be higher than 50 percent, sometimes lower.

For a period of one year, each hospital recorded the days on which more than 60 percent of the babies born were boys. Which hospital do you think recorded more such days?

(1) the larger hospital
(2) the smaller hospital
(3) about the same (i.e., within 5 percent of each other).

More than half the people who judged these probabilities chose the last alternative, assuming that it more nearly reflects the generating process that produces sex distribution in the population. Yet daily births in the small hospital are so few that the probability of producing more than 60 percent boys on any one day is much greater for it than for the larger hospital.

In the same way, people fall prey to the gambler's fallacy, which was mentioned in Chapter 2. Gamblers know that the probability of the number 13 coming up on a roulette wheel is 1 in 38. Therefore, many assume that if 13 has not come up after numerous spins of the wheel, then the "law of averages"—the generating process—makes it likely that 13 will come up soon. This assumption ignores the mathematical fact that each spin of the wheel is completely independent of the last spin. The wheel has no memory, and the probability of any number coming up will not be affected by the numbers that have come up in the last hundred, or even thousand, spins—unless the wheel is rigged.

Biases of Availability   The availability heuristic will lead to biased judgments when easily retrieved examples are themselves biased. A study in which people were given lists of newsworthy individuals, then asked whether the list contained more men or women, demonstrates how familiar information can lead to erroneous judgments (Tversky and Kahneman, 1973). When the list included famous men but less well-known women (John F. Kennedy, Millicent Fenwick), people judged that the list contained more men's than women's names. But when the women on the list were more famous than the men (Elizabeth Taylor, Placido Domingo), the judgment

was reversed; people said there were more women on the list. Because famous names are more easily recalled (are more available), the relative fame of the people on the list distorted people's recollections. This distortion produced a biased judgment.

The same researchers (Tversky and Kahneman, 1973) asked people whether the letter "k" was more likely to appear in the first or third position in words. People almost always said that "k" more often appears as the first letter, when the opposite is true. But since there is little reason to store words according to their third letter, it is difficult to retrieve words by that method: "kiss," "knife," "knuckle," "knowledge," and "king," are easier to retrieve from storage than "awkward," "poker," "elk," "bake," "like," and "sake."

Availability also affects people's judgment as to the cause of social interactions. In one study (Jones and Nisbett, 1972), observers of interactions tended to attribute such behavior as giving money to a panhandler as due to the generosity of the donor, whereas the donor saw the action as due to the situation (perhaps the panhandler looked especially needy). Other studies (Taylor and Fiske, 1978) have shown that when an observer's attention is manipulated (e.g., by placing a single black or a single female in a group or by changing a seating arrangement), the observer's judgment as to the causes of any interaction will also shift, since those aspects of interaction that receive attention are easiest to recall.

Another influence on availability is the vividness of information. Concrete, arresting anecdotal information often seems to have more influence on human decisions than more reliable statistical information (Nisbett and Ross, 1980). For example, in 1974 after Mrs. Gerald Ford and Mrs. Nelson Rockefeller both had mastectomies, cancer-detection clinics were overrun with women seeking examinations for breast cancer. The vivid accounts of the two famous cases made the possibility of breast cancer highly available to women. Yet the pallid—but sobering—statistic that one woman in twenty will develop cancer of the breast had had little impact despite publicity campaigns to bring it to the attention of American women.

The impact of vivid information was further demonstrated in a study involving the assessment of a defendant's guilt on a drunk-driving charge (Thompson, Reyes, and Bower, 1979). Sometimes the prosecutor's information regarding the defendant's condition was vivid (he staggered against a table, knocking over a bowl of "guacamole dip" and "splattering guacamole all over the white shag carpet"); the rest of the time, the prosecutor's information was pallid (the defendant merely staggered against a table, knocking a bowl to the floor). Sometimes the defense's information regarding the defendant's alertness was vivid (he leaped out of the way of a "bright orange Volkswagen"); the rest of the time it was pallid (he leaped out of the way of a "car"). When vivid information was presented by the prosecution, assessments of the case shifted toward guilty, and when vivid information was presented by the defense, assessments shifted toward innocent—but only under certain conditions. When the defendant was portrayed as having a bad character, or when assessments of guilt were taken immediately after the subjects read the information, vividness had no effect. By the next day, however, the effect of the vivid information on cases involving the defendant with good character became clear, supporting the premise that highly memorable information can bias subsequent judgment.

Several reasons have been advanced to account for the impact of vivid information (Nisbett and Ross, 1980). First, human attention is limited, and time spent processing vivid information means that less time is spent processing pallid information that may be equally or more important than the vivid information that catches attention. Second, vivid information remains in thought longer than pallid information does, thereby recalling images from similar incidents (the time a friend got drunk and pulled a tablecloth off a laden table). Third, the longer information remains in thought, the more it is rehearsed, making subsequent recall easier. Finally, vivid information may keep returning to thought, making people attribute more importance to it (the image of green guacamole splattering across white carpet is hard to put aside).

Biases in Anchoring The starting point from which decisions are made can also bias judgment, an effect called **anchoring**. Anchoring has this effect because it focuses attention on the starting point (or anchor) to the neglect of other relevant information (Dodd and White, 1980). For example, if a stock-market analyst is asked to predict the Dow-Jones high for the current year after being told last year's *high,* the analyst will come up with a higher figure than if given the Dow-Jones *average* for the previous year.

An arithmetical study that demonstrated the effect of anchoring found that when people were asked to predict the product of $1 \times 2 \times 3 \times 4 \times 5 \times 6 \times 7 \times 8$ within five seconds, they came up with a lower estimate than if asked to predict the product of $8 \times 7 \times 6 \times 5 \times 4 \times 3 \times 2 \times 1$ (Tversky and Kahneman, 1973a). Although the products are identical, starting with the larger figures consistently led to the expectation of a larger product for the incompleted calculation.

Biases of Hindsight Human judgment is also biased when based on **hindsight**, which involves looking back on events after they have occurred. When they hear about an event, people often tend to regard its occurrence as inevitable and to maintain that their knowledge of the event had no effect on their belief that it would occur (Fischhoff, 1977; Slovic and Fischhoff, 1977). The bias of hindsight is apparent in almost every sports fan who berates a baseball manager for not changing pitchers when it was "obvious" that the next pitch would be hit out of the park, or a football coach for calling a play up the middle when "anyone could see" that the defensive line was ready for it. In fact, that notorious example of hindsight, the Monday morning quarterback, is a familiar American figure.

Hindsight may be yet another example of the availability heuristic in action, since once people hear about an outcome, that outcome becomes easy to recall when considering possibilities (Nisbett and Ross, 1980). In a study of hindsight (Slovic and Fischhoff, 1977), people were given descriptions of a psychology experiment and asked to estimate the probability of two possible, but opposing, findings. Half were told the actual results of the study and the other half were not. People who knew the outcome and were thus operating with the benefit of hindsight gave the actual outcome a much higher probability of success than did people who had to rely on foresight —a factor to keep in mind the next time someone responds to the results of a psychology experiment with "Anyone with a little common sense already knows that."

Framing Decisions

Most problems can be posed in more than one way, and the way a problem is phrased—its **frame**—can affect the decision that is made. Consider the following problem:

Imagine that the U.S. is preparing for the outbreak of an unusual Asian disease, which is expected to kill 600 people. Two alternative programs to combat the disease have been proposed. Assume that the exact scientific estimate of the consequences of the program are as follows:

If Program A is adopted, 200 people will be saved.

If Program B is adopted, there is 1/3 probability that 600 people will be saved, and 2/3 probability that no people will be saved.

Which of the two programs would you favor? (Tversky and Kahneman, 1981).

When the problem is phrased this way, in terms of saving lives, most people choose program A, which promises certain salvation for 200. However, if the frame of the problem is changed to reflect the probability of losing lives, the decisions are reversed. For example:

If Program A is adopted 400 people will die.

If Program B is adopted there is a 1/3 probability that nobody will die, and 2/3 probability that 600 people will die.

Which of the two programs would you favor? (Tversky and Kahneman, 1981).

Given this frame, people become willing to take the risk they shunned in the first instance, and most choose to risk all 600 lives.

Amos Tversky and Daniel Kahneman (1981) sum up the results of research into the framing of decisions by stating that when choices involve possible gains, people tend to be risk averse, but that when the choices involve possible losses, they become risk takers. This is the case whether the potential gain or loss involves lives, money, or time, and reflects the fact that most people find the displeasure connected with loss greater than the pleasure that comes from gain. When losses are seen as certain, their unpleasantness is much stronger than when they are seen as probable. As a result, when problems are seen in terms of certain losses, judgments can suddenly change.

Other research has shown that when people are presented with an epidemic that is caused by one of two possible viruses, they will choose a hypothetical vaccine that is sure to be effective in half the cases—no matter which virus is the carrier—over another vaccine that will not affect the epidemic at all if virus A is the carrier but will certainly wipe it out if the carrier is virus B (Slovic, Fischhoff, and Lichtenstein, unpub.). Apparently, people prefer the certain elimination of some risk to the possible elimination of all risk. That may be the reason that insurance salesmen point out that fire insurance can eliminate all financial risk from fire instead of stressing that it reduces the overall probability of property loss (since floods and earthquakes are not covered).

According to Tversky and Kahneman, people regard an outcome in reference to a neutral anchor, and by manipulating the anchoring point, the evaluation of the same outcome can be changed from a gain to a loss, as in the example of the epidemic. Thus, anchoring becomes an important factor in framing problems. For example, people are pleased when the utility company offers them a slight "discount" for prompt payment, and the practice is viewed as offering a gain from the "neutral" figure printed on the statement. If, however, the bill came with the "discounted" amount already subtracted, the discounted amount would become neutral, and people would regard the tardy payment of the full amount as a surcharge, hence a loss. Since losses are less pleasant than gains, people much prefer the discount to the surcharge, despite the fact that the identical amount of money changes hands in both situations.

In most cases, people are not aware that decisions can be framed in alternative ways, and that changing the frame can change their preferences. For that reason, suggest Tversky and Kahneman, it is better to think about the possible outcome of a decision in terms of "What will I feel then?" instead of in terms of "What do I want now?"

Creativity

Creativity involves innovative solutions and discoveries, and covers the entire range of possibilities from an original solution for a practical problem to the creation of a poem or the development of a scientific theory. In the creative process, two previously unconnected elements are combined in a new and useful way, and the greater the distance between the elements, the higher the level of creativity shown by the combination (Mednick, 1962). Each new combination results when its creator perceives an analogy between two or more elements, in effect recategorizing members of two separate classes as members of the same larger class (Martindale, 1981).

The Creative Process

In Wolfgang Kohler's (1925) classic study, chimpanzees demonstrated the creative process in problem solving when they saw an analogy between sticks and methods of obtaining food, reclassifying the sticks as tools. Kohler placed food outside the bars of a chimpanzee's cage but inside the cage left several sticks that could be locked together. Tantalized by the food, the chimpanzee at first tried what might look like reproductive thinking: it stretched its arms through the bars in attempts to reach the food outside the cage, but all methods that had worked in the past failed.

When this attempt failed, the chimpanzee often paused for a time, as if studying the problem. Suddenly, the chimpanzee seemed to experience **insight**: it perceived a relationship between the goal of food and the use of sticks as tools. When this happened, the chimpanzee quickly assembled the interlocking sticks and used them to rake the food within reach. Once the chimpanzee had reorganized its perceptions in this way, it had little difficulty in solving similar problems, but its subsequent solutions involved reproductive thinking. Only the original insight required creative thinking.

However, creative thinking does not appear out of nowhere. In another study (Birch, 1945), chimpanzees who had never played with sticks, and thus had no experience to draw on, could not perceive sticks as tools and so did not solve the problem. But chimpanzees who had had lengthy experience playing with sticks when no food was present, and thus had developed a partial match between stored information and the problem, solved the problem in less than a half minute. These latter chimpanzees had used the sticks in so many ways that their solutions probably did not require insight.

When it comes to the highest forms of human creativity, experience also plays an important part. Although a poet customarily uses creative thought, the poet who has no scientific background will not experience a sudden insight that

results in a scientific discovery. Creative solutions, like reproductive solutions, are firmly based on past experience (Weisberg, 1980).

When asked about the source of their ideas, artists and scientists are usually at a loss to explain them, often reporting that brilliant advances came in a dream or just simply "appeared" (Ghiselin, 1952). Indeed, the reports of writers and scientists are often strikingly similar. For example, the English novelist William Thackeray (1899) said, "I have been surprised at the observations made by some of my characters. It seems as if an occult power was moving the pen. The personage does or says something, and I ask, how the dickens did he come to think of that?" The French mathematician Henri Poincaré (1913) found it just as difficult to account for his discoveries:

One evening contrary to my custom, I drank black coffee and could not sleep. Ideas rose in crowds; I felt them collide until pairs interlocked, so to speak, making a stable combination. By the next morning I had established the existence of a class of Fuchsian functions, those which come from the hypergeometric series; I had only to write out the results, which took but a few hours.

In the same way, the German chemist Friedrich August Kekule suddenly solved the problem of the arrangement of carbon atoms within the benzene molecule when he fell into a half-sleep and saw atoms twining in a snakelike chain until the snake grabbed its tail in its mouth, forming a ring —the exact arrangements of the six carbon atoms (Ghiselin, 1952).

To step in at the moment of seemingly effortless creativity is, however, to enter the creative process near its end. Creativity appears to progress through four successive stages: (1) preparation, when the individual works at a problem but can find no solution; (2) incubation, when the problem is set aside and not consciously worked on; (3) illumination, when the solution arrives in a sudden burst of insight; and (4) verification, when the solution is tested or elaborated (Wallas, 1926).

The Creative Person

Some people are highly creative, others are not; and psychologists have studied many people in the hope of discovering just what differences in cognitive processes lead to creativity. A review of the research on creativity indicates that creative people daydream more often than uncreative people, remember their night dreams better, are more susceptible to hypnosis, more willing to take risks, and more freely admit negative or pathological things about themselves (Martindale, 1981).

Creative people also show different patterns of attention from those found in uncreative people, and it has been theorized that the secret of creativity is individual differences in attention (Mendelsohn, 1976). In a shadowing study (Dykes and McGhie, 1976) like those discussed in Chapter 9, people listened to prose passages with the shadowed ear and said them aloud along with the speaker. At the same time, the unshadowed ear heard random words, which the subjects were supposed to ignore. Creative people remembered more of the random words than did uncreative people, indicating that in creative people attention is less focused. If this is so, creative people are aware of more stimuli at any one time, thus increasing their chances of associating dissimilar elements. Colin Martindale (1981) argues that short-term memory is, therefore, a key to creativity and that because of unfocused attention, more elements in the semantic network are aroused at any one time, allowing creative people to engage in a continuous combination of elements outside the focus of attention.

This difference in arousal could account for another difference between creative and uncreative people: their performance on word-association tests. Asked to respond to a word with all the words that come to mind, uncreative people produce the same few responses, then stop. But creative people go on to produce many more words that are less commonly associated with the stimulus word. For example, given the word "cat," both creative and uncreative people might respond with "milk," "dog," "mouse," "purr," but a creative person like poet Carl Sandburg might also respond with "fog." And indeed one of his poems was based on exactly that unlikely combination, beginning: "The fog comes/on little cat feet." When poet Emily Dickinson took a word-association test, it was said that she responded with a higher proportion of unique responses than was ever encountered outside a mental hospital (Bingham, 1953).

Putting together all the research on creativity, Martindale (1981) proposes that the major difference between creative and uncreative people can be traced to differences in their arousal systems. In uncreative people, the more intense a stimulus, the more aroused they become; but in creative people, there is a more complicated arousal system with a dip in arousal coming in response to fairly intense stimuli. As a result, says Martindale, all people react to neutral stimuli ($2 + 2 = 4$) with indifference and to bizarre ideas or extremely intense stimuli (the sound of a subway train) with displeasure, but they react differently to other stimuli. Uncreative people find conventional ideas and moderately intense stimuli pleasant and dislike novel ideas and somewhat more intense stimuli. But creative people actively dislike conventional ideas and moderately intense stimuli; they react with excitement and enthusiasm to the novel ideas and somewhat more intense stimuli that make uncreative people uncomfortable. At this level, there is a dip in arousal and a lack of focused attention that coincides with the illumination phase of the creative process.

Practical Approaches to Problem Solving

Although an uncreative person is unlikely to write an enduring poem or produce a scientific breakthrough, all of us can learn to improve our problem-solving abilities. If a person is likely to face numerous problems in a particular area, amassing knowledge in that area diminishes the need for creative problem solving (Anderson, 1980). Just as the chimpanzee with a large store of knowledge relating to sticks had no need to await inspiration before getting the distant food, so human beings with an expertise in an area routinely solve problems that appear insurmountable to the novice. As we saw in Chapter 9, the chess master remembers not individual pieces on the board but visual chunks, each containing four or five pieces, that correspond to positions normally encountered in games. After spending years developing such knowledge, chess masters have a store of about 50,000 chess positions and have learned what to do in the presence of each (Simon and Gilmartin, 1973). The possession of a vast store of knowledge in any subject radically changes the nature of most problem solving in that area from seeking creative solutions to retrieving stored answers, leaving the expert free to devise solutions to complicated problems (Anderson, 1980).

Since people can become experts in only a few areas, the challenge is to become better at creative problem solving. Some psychologists believe that the application of the sort of research we have been discussing can make us better at solving creative problems and have suggested a number of recommendations (Anderson, 1980):

1. In problems where past experience is no guide, become aware of all the allowable ways of getting from the initial state to the goal and the way to get from one intermediate state to another.
2. Become aware of the various strategies that can be used to attack problems, such as hypothesis testing, algorithms, and heuristics.
3. Plan ahead.
4. Become aware of the limitations of heuristics so that decisions are as unbiased as possible.
5. Become aware of various ways of framing problems and consider personal reactions to end states instead of relying on current wishes.
6. Become aware of the role that fixation and functional fixedness play in problem solving and make a conscious effort to change mental set.

Memorizing these suggestions will not help anyone to become better at devising creative solutions, but practice in applying the techniques to hypothetical problems can lead to the transfer of these strategies to problems in daily life. Problems for practice in creative solutions can be found in such books as *How to Solve Problems* by W. A. Wickelgren (1974).

Figure 10.10 Answer to the problem shown in Figure 10.3: "Having recognized . . . that the symbols stood for letters, and having applied the rules which guide us in all forms of writing, the solution was easy enough. The first message was so short that it was impossible to do more than say that the symbol 𝄇 stood for E. As you are aware, E is the most common letter in the English Alphabet . . . [so] it was reasonable to set this down as E . . . in some cases, [this] figure was bearing a flag, but it was probable, from the way in which distributed, that they were used to break the sentence up into words. I accepted this as a hypothesis. . . . I waited for fresh material. . . . [Now] I got the two E's coming second and fourth in a word of five letters. It might be 'sever' or 'level' or 'never'. . . . The latter as a reply to an appeal is far the most probable. . . . Accepting it as correct, we are now able to say that the symbols 𝄇 ⼅ 𝄇 stand respectively for N, V and R." And so on. The last fragment was a threat of murder against Mrs. Cubitt: ELSIE. PREPARE TO MEET THY GOD." (A. Conan Doyle. *The Return of Sherlock Holmes*, "The Adventure of the Dancing Men." New York: Ballantine Books, © 1975.) The **photograph** offers the solution of the problem posed in Figure 10.8.

SUMMARY

1. **Cognition** is the process of knowing, and it encompasses all higher mental processes, which are based on learning and memory. During the nineteenth century, psychologists studied cognition through **introspection**, the self-report of mental activities under controlled conditions. When the subjective nature of introspection led to its discreditation, psychologists stopped studying cognition on the grounds that its objective study was impossible. Behaviorists confined their study to observable behavior, which could be studied objectively. When the information-processing approach to knowledge developed, it became possible to think of human beings in terms of gathering, processing, and storing information. This approach, together with the development of

computers, allowed psychologists to return to the study of cognition, using objective methods to reveal human thought processes.

2. Problems vary in their complexity, but in all problems an individual is prevented from reaching a goal and must devise a way to circumvent or surmount the barrier that stands in the way. Problem solving depends on past experience, and the problem serves as a retrieval cue that brings relevant information out of storage. Using imagination, an individual decides whether the retrieved information will lead to a solution. When old rules can be applied to a new problem, the solution is reached by **reproductive thinking**. But when familiar rules cannot be used, new rules based on other information must be generated, and the solution is reached by **creative thinking**.

3. Among the strategies used to solve problems is **hypothesis testing**, in which various ways a goal can be reached are formulated and tested. Hypothesis testing involves the generation of a hypothesis; the construction of a test of the hypothesis; evaluation of its outcome; and if the hypothesis is incorrect, a return to the beginning and the generation of a new hypothesis. Hypothesis testing can take an algorithmic or a heuristic approach. **Algorithms**, precisely stated sets of rules that specify each step in the problem-solving process, provide a strategy that speeds the solution of problems. However, algorithms cannot be used in situations that have more possible solutions than can be tested. **Heuristics**, or rules of thumb that provide a general direction for the solution of problems, can often lead to quick solutions. One common heuristic is **subgoal analysis**, in which a difficult problem is divided into a series of smaller problems, or subgoals, that are relatively easy to solve.

4. To solve problems, human beings rely on their knowledge of concepts through which they categorize the world. Category membership appears to depend upon family resemblance, and learning which objects belong to a category may be accomplished by forming a **prototype**, a typical example of the category, which is produced by averaging specific examples of it. Another way in which people form categories may be by noticing what sets of features tend to accompany category membership and developing the category around these features.

5. In **computer simulation**, psychologists attempt to construct computer programs that reproduce human thought processes. The General Problem Solver (GPS) is a computer simulation program that relies on heuristics and that closely resembles the thinking of human beings as they approach abstract problems. Later computer programs have given computers an elaborate set of concepts that correspond to elements of human experience, along with a set of rules that cover the possible relationship of these concepts. Despite advances in computer simulation, an enormous gulf remains between the computer and human cognition.

6. Among the impediments to problem solving are **fixation**, the automatic application of an inappropriate strategy to a problem and then rigidly clinging to that ineffectual approach, and **functional fixedness**, the inability to use a familiar object in an unfamiliar way. Both fixation and functional fixedness are examples of **mental set**, or a tendency to keep repeating solutions that worked in other situations, caused by the inappropriate transfer of knowledge.

7. Emotional and motivational states of the problem solver (the level of arousal) can cause a temporary impediment to the solution of problems. At low levels of arousal, performance is poor. As arousal increases (whether due to motivation or stress), performance improves until the **optimal arousal level** is reached. After that point, further increases in motivation or stress lead to a deterioration in performance, a relationship called the **Yerkes-Dodson law**.

8. Human decisions are based on heuristics, but their inappropriate application can lead to errors in judgment. When using the heuristic of **representativeness**, people base their predictions on resemblances between the predicted event and a typical example. In some cases, reliance on representativeness leads people to discard other information in their possession, to ignore the size of the

sample they are considering, and to make the gambler's fallacy, basing estimates of probability on fallacious premises. When using the heuristic of **availability**, people base predictions on a comparison of the current situation with similar situations in the past. The vividness of information helps determine its availability, for availability uses the most easily retrieved, hence the most memorable, examples from the past. When this past information is biased, errors in judgment result.

9. The starting point from which decisions are made can also bias judgment, an effect called **anchoring**. Anchoring focuses attention on the starting point, causing the person to neglect other information. Looking back on events after they have occurred, or the application of **hindsight**, also leads to biased judgments. This comes about because after people hear of an event, they tend to regard its occurrence as inevitable and to maintain that their knowledge of the event had no effect on their belief that it would occur.

10. Most problems can be posed in more than one way, and a problem's **frame**, or the way in which it is phrased, can affect the decision. When choices involve possible gains, people tend to be risk averse, but when choices involve possible losses, people tend to take risks—whether the decision affects lives, money, or time. By manipulating the anchoring point of a decision, its outcome can be changed from a potential gain to a loss—or vice versa—altering the final decision.

11. In **creativity**, two previously unconnected elements are combined in a new and useful way, whether the result is an original solution to a practical problem or the creation of a poem. Creativity requires **insight**, or the sudden perception of a new relationship that leads to an innovative solution. Although creative people report that their solutions simply "appear," the creative process requires four stages: preparation, incubation, illumination (or insight), and verification. Highly creative people show different patterns of attention and arousal from those customarily found in uncreative people. It has been speculated that this difference leads creative people to respond differently to the world; they react with enthusiasm and excitement to novel ideas and to stimuli at a level of intensity that makes uncreative people uncomfortable. At this level, creative people experience a dip in arousal and a lack of focused attention that corresponds with the illumination phase of creativity.

12. The creative solutions of experts are based on the possession of a vast store of knowledge that changes the nature of most problem solving in the area of expertise to the retrieval of stored answers, thereby leaving the expert free to devise solutions to complicated problems. Since people can become experts in only a few areas, they can improve their performance in creative problem solving by practice—applying techniques based on psychological research to hypothetical problems.

KEY TERMS

algorithm	frame	mental set
anchoring	functional fixedness	optimal arousal level
availability	heuristic	prototype
cognition	hindsight	representativeness
computer simulation	hypothesis testing	reproductive thinking
creative thinking	insight	subgoal analysis
creativity	introspection	transfer of training
fixation	learning set	Yerkes-Dodson law

RECOMMENDED READINGS

ADAMS, J. L. *Conceptual Blockbusting: A Guide to Better Ideas*. 2nd ed. New York: Norton, 1979. Describes strategies of problem solving that teach people how to select the most attractive path from many ideas or concepts. Provides exercises to limber up your mental muscles.

DODD, D. H., and R. M. WHITE. *Cognition: Mental Structures and Processes*. Boston: Allyn & Bacon, 1980. A textbook that presents the state of the art of the scientific field of cognition. It is written for someone with a continuing interest and some background in psychology.

HUNT, M. *The Universe Within: A New Science Explores the Human Mind*. New York: Simon & Schuster, 1982. A wonderfully readable, lucid, first hand account of the latest discoveries and theories of cognitive science—the study of how our minds work. The author draws upon two years of interviews with scientists at the cutting edge of this new discipline.

PAPERT, S. *Mindstorms*. New York: Basic Books, 1980. This book presents an exciting vision of education for the future—the collaboration of computers and children. It describes the new computer language, LOGO, that is now enabling children to program the computer.

REED, S. K. *Cognition: Theory and Applications*. Monterey, Calif.: Brooks/Cole, 1982. A textbook on cognition covering a wide range of topics including problem solving and decision making. It places a greater emphasis on the application of cognitive psychology than is typically found in an undergraduate text.

PART FOUR

Human Development

Development can take place in mysterious ways. There can be extraordinary gaps in the most sophisticated of us, and surprising areas of success in the most disregarded.

For instance, I am incredibly educated. Throughout my life I have been immersed in books and intellectual experiences, and I have been blessed with a most retentive memory and with instant recall. I have always reacted with indignation to any event that served to show me to be ignorant.

My son, on the other hand, when he was young, seemed to show no signs of following in my footsteps. (And, as a matter of fact, he didn't.) He found other pleasures in life, those that did not include being a bookworm. Nor did he seem to be attracted to a course of mental achievement and adventure. In fact, he seemed to be most interested in watching television programs of what I considered minimal intellectual value.

Well, then, twenty years ago I was doing a job for the *World Book Encyclopedia* and as part of my reward I received a gift from them. My wife and I unwrapped it, and were instantly flabbergasted.

It was a metal cylinder (probably aluminum, I guessed from its weight) and I hadn't the faintest idea of what use it could be put to. It didn't seem to be the right shape or material for a vase or a flower pot or an umbrella stand or a wastepaper basket or anything else that I could think of.

What could we do? The logical thing was to call up the *World Book* people and ask them what on earth it might be. But that was impossible. How could I own up to such ignorance and how could I so denigrate a gift that must have been given to me with the thought that I would at once recognize and cherish it. The only other alternatives were to pass it on as a gift to someone else, hoping he would casually identify it; or just place it on the mantelpiece, hoping someone would see it and say, "What a nice aspidistra!" or whatever.

And then, in walked my son, who was at that time, ten years old. He cast a rather casual look at the arcane object and said, "Hey, who sent you the champagne bucket?"

That solved the mystery at once. Neither my wife nor myself drank anything stronger than ginger ale. We had never owned a bottle of champagne and had very rarely been anywhere where anyone was drinking champagne. We just barely knew that champagne buckets existed and had certainly never seen anything that anyone had specifically identified as a champagne bucket.

But if one mystery was solved, another greater mystery was set up. How was it that our ten-year-old son, who also never drank, and who certainly did not move in any circles more sophisticated than those we frequented, and who had frequently showed many signs of not having any clear indication of what 8 x 7 might be, should be so familiarly acquainted with champagne buckets?

"David," I said, curiously, "how do you know that thing is a champagne bucket?"

He shrugged and said, "Easy. I saw one on the *Three Stooges* program."

Which shows that no human experience lacks the capacity to promote development. Who knows what stage of sophistication I might have attained if *I* had more frequently watched the *Three Stooges*.

ISAAC ASIMOV

CHAPTER 11

Early Development

The competent adult who solves problems, makes decisions, works at a job, and develops relationships with other people was once a newborn infant with fleeting memories, whose activities depended primarily upon biological states and inborn dispositions and whose survival depended upon the care of other people. The transition from infancy to adulthood is common to all normal members of the human species. William Shakespeare, Pablo Picasso, Albert Einstein, and your psychology instructor all followed the same general course that characterized your own development: a familiar path that is governed by the combined action of heredity and environment.

This chapter describes what psychologists know about the way heredity and environment work together during the earliest months of life. As we shall see, the process of human development is an orderly sequence of events from childhood to old age, directed by heredity but constantly influenced by the environment. An examination of prenatal development will show the crucial role environmental factors play in a baby's development before it is born. Finally, we shall focus on the human newborn, noting what abilities human beings have at birth, and how quickly they begin to acquire the cognitive and social traits characteristic of their species. Research suggests that the world of the newborn infant is less confusing than we might suspect and that a baby begins acquiring knowledge almost immediately after birth.

The Process of Development

The psychologist who studies the process of human development is faced with two key questions: How do people change—physically, mentally, and socially—as they grow older? And why do these particular patterns of change occur as they do? These two basic questions—the how and the why of human development—are explored by assessing the contributions of heredity and environment and the possibility of sensitive periods in human beings.

Developmental Sequences: The Question of How

Anyone who has watched children grow knows that many changes in their behavior are neither accidental nor random. There is an orderly sequence to the development of a young person's behavior in every area of functioning. This development does not cease when an individual reaches adulthood. In all human beings, sequential patterns of development and change continue into old age.

An obvious example of a developmental sequence is that associated with motor development during infancy. By the time babies are about two months old, they can raise the head and chest while lying on the stomach—a feat that enables them to scan a world beyond the crib. Between the fourth and seventh months, hand–eye coordination has improved enough to enable them to reach out and grasp almost any object within range—mother's glasses, father's nose, the mobile dangling overhead. By seven months, they usually can sit up without support, and a few months later they are able to hoist themselves into a standing position while holding on to furniture. At ten months, most babies are accomplished crawlers, capable of wreaking havoc on all low-lying areas of the house. And finally, around the first birthday most infants take their first step—an event that opens a whole new realm of experience. Such orderly sequences appear in the development of language, cognition, and social and emotional development as well, as we shall see in Chapters 12, 13, and 14.

Although all children pass through these sequences of development, each child's timing and style are likely to vary from established timetables. These individual differences arise because any sequence of development consists of averages or **norms**, established after observing a large number of babies. Such descriptions do not describe the ideal behavior; they simply report the behavior of the mathematically "average" baby. The age at which normal infants master different skills varies widely. Some perfectly normal babies, for example, never crawl, but go directly from sitting and standing to taking their first steps. Walking may begin as early as eight months or as late as twenty. Some babies are talking about everything they see months before other babies have uttered their first word. Yet the concept of developmental sequences remains useful, because it emphasizes the important fact that human development is not random: the progression through the sequences is orderly and predictable.

Determinants of Development: The Question of Why

Although each person goes through similar developmental sequences, individual rates of development differ. What accounts for these similarities and differences among individuals?

The answer lies in two interrelated factors: heredity and environment.

Hereditary Factors   Every person begins life as a single cell that is formed when a male germ cell, or sperm, penetrates a female germ cell, or egg. Unlike all other cells in the human body, which contain paired chromosomes, these germ cells contain twenty-three *single* **chromosomes**—coiled, threadlike structures that carry **genes**, the units of hereditary information. The germ cell is formed in a process called **meiosis**, in which the twenty-three chromosome pairs of a single cell are split apart, rearranged, and distributed to two germ cells having twenty-three single chromosomes each. At conception, the twenty-three chromosomes from the mother's germ cell pair with the twenty-three from the father's to make a complete set of genetic instructions for a new human being. Meiosis and fertilization guarantee variety. During meiosis, segments of chromosomes break apart and rejoin, so that instead of producing germ cells with various combinations of twenty-three chromosomes, each person produces germ cells in which the twenty-three chromosomes are composed of combinations of anywhere from sixty-five to eighty chromosome segments (Scarr and Grajek, 1982). As a result, there are so many millions of possible chromosome combinations for each united egg and sperm (from 2^{65} to 2^{80}) that each individual (with the exception of identical twins, who come from the same egg and sperm) is genetically unique.

Only within the last several decades have scientists discovered how the genes carried by the chromosomes influence development. Chromosomes are composed primarily of long strands of a complex substance called DNA (deoxyribonucleic acid). Each of the beadlike genes that make up a chromosome carries the chemical instructions for the development and maintenance of a living organism. These small portions of a DNA molecule may contain the code for producing one of the many proteins from which the body is built or they may specify how those proteins will combine to form the organism's body and dispose it toward certain behavioral patterns.

Genes affect development throughout life, and every organism has, to some extent, a genetically programed timetable for its physical maturation. Under normal circumstances, the physical development of an individual's muscles, organs, and nervous system will unfold at a certain pace. Since we are all human, we share similar (though not identical) maturational timetables. At different phases of development, some genes become active and others cease to act. Puberty is a clear example of a genetically timed event, and it appears that genes also affect longevity and the rate at which a person ages (Jarvik et al., 1972). Heredity, then, has a three-fold influence on human development: it influences physical form, behavioral capacities, and the rate of physical maturation.

Does this mean that genes *determine* the rate and pattern of certain developmental sequences? To answer this question, researchers have turned to studies of identical twins. Identical twins are born when a single fertilized egg divides in two, each half having a full complement of the same genetic instructions. (Fraternal twins, in contrast, develop from two separately fertilized eggs and are no more alike than other brothers and sisters.) Because identical twins are genetically identical, researchers have believed that differences between them that emerged during their development could be taken as evidence of the influence of environmental factors. Conversely, if one twin received a certain kind of stimulation from its environment that the other did not, but the twins nevertheless developed at the same rate, then this could be taken as evidence of strong genetic influence on the development of a certain behavior sequence.

Research with identical twins has generally supported the supposition that genes affect many aspects of development. For example, case studies of identical twins who were adopted into very different environments found that their rates of maturation, their hobbies, food preferences, choice of friends, and academic achievement were quite similar (Bouchard, 1981). Another way to look for genetic influences on development is to compare similarities and differences in adopted siblings with those of biological siblings. In one such study of adolescents, intelligence-test scores of the adopted siblings showed no correlation at all, but test scores of biological siblings showed a correlation of .35, indicating that genes have some influence on the development of cognitive processes (Scarr and Weinberg, 1978). Such studies have also found a slight genetic influence on interests and personality differences (Grotevant, Scarr, and Weinberg, 1977; Scarr et al., 1981).

Early studies of twins (e.g., McGraw, 1935; 1939a) indicated that motor development in infancy was heavily influenced by heredity, and studies of children in different cultures have tended to confirm this finding. Although different societies give babies different opportunities and encouragement to practice motor skills, records from five of Europe's largest cities showed that most infants took their first steps within a few months of one another. Even Hopi Indian infants, who spent their first year bound to cradle boards that severely restricted their movements, walked at about the same age as infants in other cultures who had had far more practice in muscular coordination (Dennis and Dennis, 1940), although later studies have found that cradle-boarded Native American babies consistently begin to walk about a month later than Anglo babies. On the basis of such studies, the assumption was made that environmental differences had little influence on when basic motor skills emerged. Later research was to suggest a somewhat different conclusion.

Environmental Factors   Scientists now know that heredity is never the sole influence on development. Environment is necessarily an important factor in any developmental process, including that of the prenatal period. An organism cannot grow without material from the environment (food) to build its cells and tissues, and the environment continues to influence its development throughout life. In the case of motor skills, development can be accelerated or retarded by the presence or absence of environmental stimulation. Apparently, the ranges of the environmental variations in the earlier studies, mentioned above, had been too limited to reveal this.

We now know that a severe lack of social and intellectual stimulation accompanied by little opportunity for physical activity can retard development. In a foundling home in Lebanon, for example, where children spent most of their first year lying on their backs in bare cribs, virtually ignored by adults, motor skills were so retarded that some infants over a year old could not sit up, let alone walk (Dennis and Sayegh, 1965). However, a simple change of program produced dramatic results among these foundlings. When they were propped into sitting positions and allowed to play for as little as an hour each day with such ordinary objects as fresh flowers, pieces of colored sponge, and colored plastic disks strung

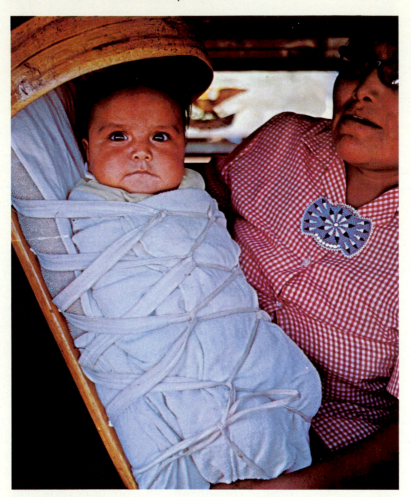

Infants around the world develop motor skills at approximately the same age, regardless of the practices of their culture. Even Hopi babies, who spend much of their time bound to cradleboards, walk at about the same age as babies who have extensive practice in crawling and standing.

on a chain, the babies' rate of motor development accelerated enormously. In fact, foundlings who receive visual and aural enrichment, along with human attention, develop as rapidly —both physically and cognitively—as infants in middle-class homes (Hunt, 1980).

While an impoverished environment retards development, extra experience and stimulation can encourage some motor skills—provided the stimulation is appropriate to the baby's age. For example, all normal infants have a "walking reflex": when held upright, with the feet just touching a flat surface, a newborn infant will march along as if walking, although babies this young cannot support their own weight. Normally, this reflexive stepping motion disappears by the second month. But one study has shown that when babies are trained to use their walking reflex regularly, they not only do not lose the behavior in later infancy, but they also begin to

walk about one to two months earlier than most other infants (Zelazo et al., 1972). There are, however, limits to this enhancement of motor development; no matter how much exercise young infants are given, none will walk at six months. In addition, although the age at which the babies in the experiment walked was significantly earlier than average, the difference is well within the normal range of individual differences. Moreover, we do not know whether the acceleration was caused by rapid development of muscle strength or by rapid learning. The important point is that—within limits—developmental sequences respond to environmental manipulation.

Like the repeated practice of specific skills, generalized stimulation can also lead to accelerated development. This has been demonstrated with premature infants. Nurses and parents tend to regard premature babies as especially fragile and so avoid fondling them as they do normal babies. But physical stimulation may be exactly what these infants need. One researcher (Rice, 1975) encouraged a group of mothers to stroke and gently massage their premature babies for fifteen minutes, then to rock and cuddle them for five minutes, four times a day. At the end of four months, the stimulated babies had shown significant gains in weight, motor reflexes, and mental functioning over a control group of premature babies who did not receive extra handling. In another study (Rose et al., 1980), premature infants who had been massaged, rocked, and talked to while in the hospital nursery showed better recognition memory at the age of six months than premature babies who had not been so stimulated.

These studies suggest that stimulation from the environment not only enhances muscle strength but also facilitates the development of the nervous system. Most infants receive adequate stimulation in their natural surroundings, but infants who grow up under grossly abnormal conditions, such as those in the foundling home in Lebanon, may not get enough stimulation for normal development. A number of experiments with animals have found that lack of stimulation has marked effects on brain development. For example, rats raised in an impoverished environment (isolated from litter mates and with no ob-

jects in the cage) had thinner and lighter cerebral cortexes, fewer glial cells, smaller neurons, and reduced neurotransmitter activity than rats raised in an enriched environment (in group cages with objects to explore and manipulate; Rosenzweig et al., 1972). In another study, rats placed in bare cages within larger enriched environments—where they could see other rats climbing on equipment and manipulating objects but were unable to participate themselves—showed no more brain change than did isolated rats (Ferchmin et al. 1975). Clearly, an organism must participate in the environment for stimulation to have its effects; mere exposure is not enough. However, the "enriched" environments of these studies did not accelerate brain development but maintained it at a relatively normal rate. Rats raised in natural environments showed greater brain development than their litter mates who grew up in the "enriched" laboratory environment (Rosenzweig et al., 1972).

It appears, therefore, that although severely abnormal environments clearly have deleterious effects on development (see Figure 11.1), healthy development can proceed in many different environments (Kagan, 1978). Infant intelligence, for example, shows little variation; although some babies reach various developmental levels sooner than others, all normal babies acquire all the cognitive skills of infancy

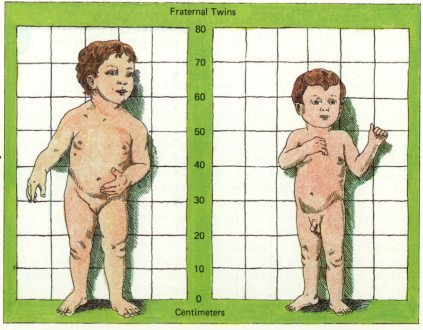

Figure 11.1 Deprivation dwarfism. In one study, the effects of emotional deprivation were observed in a pair of fraternal twins. This drawing, based on photos taken when the children were almost thirteen months old, shows that the female was normal, in weight and stature, but her brother was the size of a seven-month-old. Shortly after the twins were born, the father lost his job and left home. Hurt and angry, the mother displaced her hostility toward the father to the son and soon the boy's growth rate began to decline. It is thought that emotional stress affects the pituitary gland, depressing the secretion of growth hormone and thus stunting growth. When the father eventually returned home and the emotional climate of the household improved, the boy began to grow again. (After Gardner, 1972.)

Fraternal Twins

Centimeters

(Scarr-Salapatek, 1976). When infants experience normal freedom of movement and the opportunity to interact with the environment found in most homes, they seem to be only modestly affected by extra enrichment. Thus, there may be an optimal amount of stimulation for optimal development, but it must be appropriate to the baby's age and abilities (White, 1967; 1971). Overwhelming young infants with a profuse display of toys and mobiles and showering them with constant attention does not guarantee the development of precocious children. Instead, an overload of stimulation before the baby is ready for it may be merely irritating or confusing.

Sensitive Periods of Development   The relationship between hereditary and environmental determinants of behavior can be seen in the sensitive periods of development, discussed in Chapter 7. During such periods, an organism is especially susceptible to certain kinds of environmental influences. The same experience before or after this period may have little or no impact. An organism's "readiness" depends on genetically guided maturation; the outcome depends on the environment. As noted in Chapter 7, some baby birds appear to establish permanent social bonds with members of their own species only if they are exposed to them during a critical time span. And dogs can be socialized to human beings only during a sensitive period that lasts from three to twelve weeks after birth. If puppies are not exposed to people during this period, they are unlikely to become attached to a human master later in life (Scott et al., 1974).

Some psychologists (e.g., Klaus and Kennell, 1976; Hess, 1970) believe that there are sensitive periods in human development. For example, John Bowlby (1958) has suggested that human social and emotional development is marked by sensitive periods. He argues that babies seem to have an innate drive to establish a bond with a parent or caretaker, that love objects selected later in life resemble that person, and that early disruption of the bond can have severe effects on later development. Similarly, the optimal period for language acquisition seems to be between two and thirteen years, and after that time it is extremely difficult to learn a first language.

Many psychologists reject the idea of sensitive periods in human beings. Although most agree that children must reach a level of maturational readiness before they can profit from certain

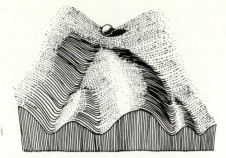

Figure 11.2   Geneticist Conrad Waddington's graphic analogy for the interaction of heredity and environment in development. The landscape represents the possibilities determined by genetic factors, and the path of the rolling ball represents the actual course of development. Such forces on the ball as cross-winds represent environmental factors. The ball can roll down different valleys, depending on the forces that are brought to bear on it, but it cannot easily change from one valley to another once it has started. The analogy is useful in helping us understand how genetic and environmental factors interact to produce different personality traits or different degrees of intellectual ability. (After Waddington, 1957.)

kinds of experiences, they point out that human beings are extremely resilient and can generally overcome the effects of harmful early experiences. Children who have suffered years of neglect, shut away in attics, basements, and closets, often recover and become normal adults when they are given adequate environments (Clarke and Clarke, 1979). Negative influences that persist into adulthood appear to be the result of continuing bad experiences, not the effect of deprivation during an early sensitive period. The effects of early experience, if the experience is not repeated, appear to fade with time. A human child is like a piece of magic plastic with a "memory"; the child can be bent out of shape by severe environmental pressures, but when the pressure is removed, she or he tends to resume a normal shape, functioning without any deep dents (Scarr, 1981).

The basic point of this section—indeed, of this entire chapter—is that hereditary and environmental influences are two sides of the same coin. Although it is useful to distinguish between them, they can never be entirely separated, as the graphic analogy in Figure 11.2 shows. Despite our inability to separate these determinants, individual differences in development can depend upon genes, upon environment, or upon the combined action of both. Genes can determine the kind of response an individual makes to a particular situation, and environment can provide or deny certain types of experiences and can determine the way a genetic influence is expressed. The close collaboration between nature and nurture also applies to developmental disorders that have specific genetic causes (see the accompanying box). As later sections indicate, the typical course of human development is a combination of heredity and environment.

Prenatal Development

Development begins as soon as a sperm and egg unite, and in approximately thirty-eight weeks this single cell is transformed into a newborn baby. Since this is a period of remarkable growth and change, it has been studied in great detail.

Prenatal Growth and Behavior

Development, during the nine months of pregnancy, is more rapid than during any postnatal period. This first major developmental sequence unfolds in a predictable manner, initiated and guided by both genetic and environmental factors. Behavioral potential, as well as structural complexity, increases during this phase, which is divided into three basic periods: germinal, embryonic, and fetal.

The Germinal Period   Almost immediately after fertilization, the egg begins the process of cell division that eventually produces a human body. At first the multiplying cells are all identical: nerve, muscle, bone, and blood cells cannot be distinguished from one another. But by the end of the first two weeks, the cells have begun to differentiate into three primary layers that will form the various tissues and organs, each layer producing different body systems. Exactly what triggers this process is still a mystery, but scientists believe that the answer may lie in subtle differences in the chemical environments to which different cells are exposed as the cell mass increases in size.

The Embryonic Period   Within four weeks after conception, the organism, called an **embryo**, is about one-fifth of an inch long, 10,000 times

larger than the original fertilized egg. In appearance it is nearly all head and it has developed a spinal cord and a two-lobe brain. Many of the major organs have formed, as well as indentations in the head region that will eventually become jaws, eyes, and ears. At about six weeks, the embryo responds reflexively, moving its upper trunk and neck when the mouth area is stroked with a fine hair (Humphrey, 1970). By the end of this period, about the eighth week, the embryo is almost an inch long.

The Fetal Period   For the next thirty weeks, until its birth, the developing organism is known as a **fetus**. At nine weeks, it bends its fingers and curls or straightens its toes in response to touches on the palm of the hand or the sole of the foot. Gradually, during the fetal period, diffuse responses narrow, so that when the mouth is touched only reflexes about the mouth—instead of the entire upper body—appear. By sixteen weeks, when the fetus is about six inches long, hair may appear on the head and facial features approximate their finished appearance. The major internal organs have attained their typical shape and plan, although they could not keep the fetus alive outside the uterus. By this time, the cortex has grown back over the lower parts of the brain, and at between sixteen and twenty weeks all 100 billion neurons have developed, although the brain is immature in other respects. At this stage, a mother may first feel the fetus move.

By twenty-three weeks, the fetus has become quite active, sleeping and waking and taking a favorite position for naps. Studies of prematurely delivered fetuses have shown that by twenty-four weeks a fetus can cry, open and close its eyes, and look up, down, and sideways (Hooker, 1952). It has developed a grasping reflex and it may even hiccup. During the final weeks in the uterus, fat forms over the entire body, smoothing out the wrinkled skin and rounding out contours. The fetus usually gains about a half pound a week during the last eight or nine weeks, so that at birth the average baby is about twenty inches long and weighs a little more than seven pounds.

Environmental Influences

Although prenatal growth proceeds on a solid genetic foundation, even within the uterus the

Controlling Genetic Damage Through Environmental Change

Scientists have made significant advances in the prevention and alleviation of certain developmental disorders, including some once thought to be impervious to environmental control because they were the result of genetic defects. Since 5 out of every 100 children born have a genetic defect or malformation of some kind, this sort of research is immensely important (Etzioni, 1973). By considering phenylketonuria and Down's syndrome, two disorders with effects that until recently were believed impossible to prevent or control, we can see the progress that has been made.

Phenylketonuria

One of the hundreds of rare abnormalities caused by a single gene is **phenylketonuria,** or **PKU,** which afflicts approximately one in every 10,000 to 15,000

children. PKU is caused by a defect in the gene that controls the body's use of phenylalanine, a protein present in food. The defective gene causes phenylalanine to build up in the body, where it changes to a toxin that attacks the nervous system and causes progressive mental retardation.

Children with PKU appear normal at birth, but their intelligence soon stops developing. Without treatment, one-third of PKU victims never learn to walk, and two-thirds never learn to talk. Children with PKU have lighter pigmentation of skin and hair, shorter stature, and greater irritability than normal children.

Fortunately, in the case of PKU, scientists have been able to circumvent the effects of the defective gene. Since the mid-1960s, babies born in the United States have been tested for the presence of phenylalanine. An abnormally high level indicates the presence of the defective gene, and the baby is immediately started on a diet low in phenylalanine. Although hospitals test for PKU in the delivery room, some affected babies may not have ingested and metabolized enough milk to show an ex-

---

fetus is not immune from external influences. Perhaps the most important developmental influence is the diet of the mother, from whom the fetus receives its nourishment. Diets deficient in calcium, phosphorus, iodine, and vitamins B, C, and D are associated with high frequencies of malformed fetuses. Studies with animals suggest that a maternal protein deficiency may cause an irreversible reduction in brain weight, number of brain cells, and learning ability in offspring (Winick and Noble, 1966). More disturbing still is the finding that female rats born to protein-deficient mothers may bear learning-disabled offspring even if the second-generation females receive well-balanced diets during their own pregnancies (Bresler et al., 1975). The disability, described as the "grandmother effect," apparently results from the second-generation mothers' inability to form a normal placenta, the network of blood vessels through which their de-

veloping young are nourished. If these findings apply to human beings, then malnutrition during pregnancy may have negative influences not only on a woman's children but on her grandchildren as well.

Fetal development is also adversely affected by various drugs. A golden rule of obstetric practice is to advise women to take as little medication during pregnancy as possible. The thalidomide tragedies of the early 1960s, when many European women who took the sedative thalidomide during the early weeks of pregnancy produced babies with severely deformed arms and legs, vividly illustrates the consequences of using certain drugs. More recently, cancer has been found in many young women whose mothers had taken the drug diethylstilbestrol (DES) early in pregnancy to prevent miscarriage.

Alcohol's effects on the fetus have been established only during the past few years. Babies

cess of phenylalanine. Infants are therefore routinely retested at their six-week check-up. Simply by adjusting the infant's diet, doctors can prevent the devastating effects of PKU.

Down's Syndrome

Another genetic disorder that responds somewhat to environmental intervention—but in this case intervention with the external environment—is **Down's syndrome** (or "mongolism"). Afflicting one child out of every 600 born, Down's syndrome is usually associated with severe retardation. Victims also have poor muscle tone, short stature, protruding tongues, small ears, stubby fingers, and a fold of skin at the inner corners of the eyes that gives them a vaguely Asiatic appearance. Down's syndrome results from a chromosomal abnormality. Instead of having the normal twenty-three pairs of chromosomes, children born with the syndrome have an extra chromosome in the twenty-first pair.

As yet, nothing can be done to prevent the formation of the extra chromosome, but its presence can be detected early in pregnancy. In the course of development the fetus normally sloughs off cells, and by analyzing cultures grown from these cells, physicians can diagnose many abnormalities. Between the fourteenth and sixteenth week of pregnancy, the physician uses a technique called **amniocentesis,** in which a hollow needle is inserted into the maternal abdomen and some of the amniotic fluid, containing fetal cells, is withdrawn. The cells can then be tested for the presence of abnormal chromosomes.

The effects of Down's syndrome cannot be prevented, but research indicates that environmental therapy may lessen some of its effects. In one study, a group of two-year-olds with Down's syndrome were given eighteen months of intensive practice in a number of the motor skills of infancy. By the time they were three and a half, these children were performing as well on simple tasks as normal children of the same age (Rynders, 1975). It is too soon to evaluate any lasting effects of this program, but other studies (e.g., Cornwell, 1974) have indicated that the worst impairment among children with Down's syndrome is in the area of language and abstract conceptualization, with simple tasks and rote skills least affected. Although children with Down's syndrome rarely achieve normal intelligence, environmental intervention may help lessen their impairment.

born to alcoholic mothers may have low birth weights and be mentally retarded. Some may also have cleft palates, heart murmurs, kidney damage, and eye or skeletal defects (Streissguth et al., 1980). Not all of these results may be directly caused by alcohol, because heavy drinkers tend to use both prescription and nonprescription drugs, to eat unwisely, and to smoke.

Cigarette smoking is known to affect the fetus. Women who smoke during pregnancy tend to miscarry more often than nonsmokers and to produce babies who are, on the average, lighter and smaller than normal (Babson et al., 1980). The reasons for this are not clear. Tar and nicotine in cigarettes may have direct effects on fetal development, and carbon monoxide may also play a role. Smoking appears to reduce the capacity of the blood to carry oxygen; in addition, when pregnant women who are nonsmokers inhale cigarette smoke, the fetal heart rate increases. However, smokers may not eat properly and a dietary deficiency may also retard fetal development.

Timing is often a crucial factor in determining whether an environmental influence will produce abnormality in a developing fetus. The first **trimester**, or third, of pregnancy appears to be an especially sensitive period for the development of certain kinds of birth defects because most of the basic organ systems are forming at this time. If organs are already formed—or have not yet developed—a destructive agent may have less serious effects, or none at all. The effect of timing is especially apparent in the case of rubella, or German measles, which can cause blindness, deafness, or mental retardation. Forty-seven percent of the babies born to women who contracted this seemingly minor disease during the first month of pregnancy were seriously affected; 22 percent of the babies born to women who contracted the disease in the second month were seriously affected; and 7 percent of the babies of those who contracted it during the third month were seriously affected (Michaels and Mellin, 1960). Generally, however, the fetus is most vulnerable during the second and third months, because more structures develop during these two months than during any other period of pregnancy.

The Competency of the Newborn

Among the mammals, sensory and motor development varies widely at birth. Some mammals are born with impressive motor coordination and highly acute sensory capabilities. Newborn horses, calves, and guinea pigs are extremely precocious in the sense that they can see, hear, stand, walk, even run within a few hours after birth. Because of this, they are classified as **precocial** species. Others are born almost completely helpless. Kittens, mice, and puppies come into the world blind and physically feeble, totally dependent on their parents for survival. They are classified as **altricial** species.

Like other primates, newborn human babies are both altricial and precocial—a peculiar mixture of incapacity and competence. And among the primates, none of whom can creep or walk at birth, human babies are the most helpless and immature. Most human newborns are physically weak and helpless; few can hold up their own heads. Yet when we look at the sensory development of the human infant, we find remarkably mature and well-integrated systems. All the human senses, in fact, are capable of functioning even before birth (Gottlieb, 1976). Thus, human infants many not be able to navigate in their environment at birth, but they can both perceive and be influenced by that environment from the moment they are born.

Reflexes and Motor Skills

Because of their limited motor capacity, most babies appear quite helpless at birth. Relatively weak for many months, they are completely dependent on their care givers. Yet newborns quickly master such essential motor skills as feeding, which requires the coordination of three separate activities: sucking, swallowing, and breathing. Newborns also come equipped with a set of reflexes that can be elicited by specific stimuli. Some of these reflexes are adaptive and may help babies survive in their new surroundings, as when they close their eyes to a bright light or jerk their limbs away from sources of pain. Others are simply manifestations of neurological pathways in the baby that will later come under voluntary control or will be integrated into more mature patterns of behavior, such as stepping movements of the legs (Minkowski, 1967). Still others may be remnants of traits possessed by prehuman ancestors.

One of the most familiar reflexes is the rooting reflex, a baby's tendency to turn the head in the direction of any object that gently stimulates the cheek or the corner of the mouth. This reflex has obvious adaptive significance for feeding: it helps the baby locate the nipple with her or his mouth.

In the first few weeks of life, babies also have a strong grasping reflex. If one places a week-old baby on her or his back and inserts a finger into the hand, the infant usually grasps the finger firmly. Sometimes a newborn's grasp is so tight that the infant can hang by one hand. Although the meaning of this reflex is not entirely clear, it could be a remnant of our prehuman past. Our early ancestors may have carried their offspring on their backs or stomachs as many other primates do today. Thus, the ability to grasp the mother's fur or skin would keep an infant from falling and increase the chances of survival (Prechtl, 1965).

Reaching also appears among newborns. During the first few weeks of life, babies reach out for objects they see, at times successfully grasping them. At about four weeks, this eye-hand coordination is lost, not to reappear for nearly four months (Bower, 1976).

Another reflex of newborns that follows a similar course is the "swimming" reflex. If a baby only a few weeks old is placed face down in a pool of water, the infant moves both arms and legs in a coordinated pattern that resembles crawling and that can propel the baby through the water. Moreover, if the infant's head is submerged, another reflex inhibits breathing, preventing water from entering the lungs. The swimming reflex soon disappears, and four-month-old babies who are placed in water thrash about, coughing and gasping if their heads slip under the water.

At about the beginning of the second year babies again show a tendency to make rhythmic swimming motions. However, these motions are quite different from the early, reflexive movements and appear deliberate and purposeful (McGraw, 1939b). Yet these, too, disappear. If children lack experience with water in the preschool years, at age six they will struggle vainly to hold themselves up in the water and will have to be "taught" to swim—a skill they once performed easily.

Why do swimming, reaching, and stepping appear, disappear, then reappear in a different form? It may be that the initial reflexes are controlled by subcortical brain structures, and that when control shifts to the developing cortex, the behavior becomes voluntary and must be learned. The fact that many infant response patterns take this repetitive course of appearance, loss, and reappearance supports this view. In addition, babies born without any cortex at all behave much like normal newborns for the first three months (Kessen, 1967). Then, because they have no cortex and hence cannot develop cortical control, their behavior diverges rapidly from that of normal babies. However, Thomas Bower (1976) has pointed out that these reflexive patterns must be connected with later behavior, because when newborns are given practice in either stepping or reaching, the behavior may reappear earlier than expected or, when it does reappear, take a more skillful form.

Sensory and Perceptual Abilities

Do newborn infants perceive a world made up of stable objects and distinct sounds? Or is the sensory world of newborns a chaos of meaningless shapes and noises—as William James (1890) put it, "one great blooming, buzzing confusion"?

These questions are difficult to answer because babies cannot tell us what they see or hear. Therefore researchers study the sensory and perceptual capabilities of infants by carefully watching their responses to various stimuli, noting changes in their rate of sucking, their patterns of eye movement, and their expressions of pleasure or displeasure. From these observations, researchers infer how the infant perceives the world. For example, infants look away, fidget, or cry when shown a movie that is out of focus. Moreover, five-week-old babies quickly learn to suck vigorously on a pacifier attached to

the focusing mechanism of a movie projector to bring a blurred picture into focus (Kalnins and Bruner, 1973). This study suggests that babies are attuned to distinct edges; if their visual world were simply a blurry confusion, babies would not care that a movie was out of focus.

In recent years a great amount of research has been devoted to assessing the newborn infant's perceptions. These investigations have refuted the notion that a baby's world is essentially disorganized and chaotic.

Vision The visual world of the newborn infant is less confusing than we might suppose because of the infant's limited visual capacities. An inability to change focus and limited peripheral vision sharply reduce the amount of stimulation that newborns receive, thereby greatly lessening possible confusion. Although newborns are not blind, they can see only objects about nine inches from the eyes, and those objects probably appear blurred to them. Vision improves rapidly and by six months, babies can see as clearly as the average adult; however, it takes from seven months to a year before visual capacities are fully developed (Cohen et al., 1979).

Newborns apparently have some sense of depth perception, because when they are held upright and an object is moved rapidly toward the face, they protect themselves by raising their hands and pulling back their heads (Bower et al., 1971). Newborns also seem to distinguish between an approaching object that is likely to hit them and one that will sail harmlessly past (Ball and Tronick, 1971). Babies who are slightly older, however, have lost this response. For example, when researchers project the image of a solid object that approaches babies as if to strike them, all infants look intently at the image, but until they are five months old babies neither reach toward the object nor blink and withdraw their heads as the image appears ready to strike them (Yonas et al., 1978).

It may be that the perception of depth is like stepping, reaching, and swimming: a reflexive response that appears only as long as control over the behavior is subcortical and that must later develop anew under cortical control. The reemergence of depth perception has been traced in recent studies using paired computer-generated displays made up of red and green dots that work in the same way as the three-dimensional effects in the Hollywood movies of thirty years ago and the recent series of films that began in 1981 with *Comin' At Ya*. The audience at these Hollywood films used cardboard glasses with one lens of red cellophane and the other of green to turn a blurred image into a sharp scene with depth. Similarly, when these computer-generated displays are viewed through lenses—a green lens over one eye and a red lens over the other—the two images are fused and a single, three-dimensional image appears. In the first experiment (Fox et al., 1980), babies from two and a half to six months old watched a series of such displays, in which solid forms changed position and appeared to move across the screen. The youngest babies paid little attention to the changing shapes, following the movement with their eyes no more often than chance. But the older the baby, the more likely she or he was to watch the changing shapes, and by six months most of the babies tracked the shifting display most of the time. When investigators showed the older babies displays that could not be fused to make a solid image, their attention lagged and they behaved just as the youngest babies had done when shown the three-dimensional images.

In the second experiment (Petrig et al., 1981), researchers again used the computer-generated dot displays, but this time they relied on evoked potentials, which were discussed in Chapter 3, as a measure of vision. As a result, they were able to trace the emergence of depth perception. After establishing the visually evoked potentials of adults and older children when watching two-dimensional and three-dimensional displays, researchers tested babies between the age of seven and forty-eight weeks old. No baby under the age of ten weeks showed any visually evoked potentials that indicated three-dimensional perception, although all showed evoked potentials typical of two-dimensional perception. Beginning at the age of ten weeks, however, some babies showed evidence of three-dimensional perception, and among the older babies, all who were more than nineteen weeks old (approximately four and a half months) showed such evidence. In addition, when five two-month-olds who had shown no signs of depth perception were retested at the age of six months, all of them had developed the evoked potentials that accompany three-dimensional vision. These researchers believe that the cortical mechanisms required for three-dimensional vision are not fully developed at birth and that they begin functioning some time between ten and nineteen weeks. Apparently, both maturation (heredity)

and environment (experience) are necessary for true depth perception, and as we saw in Chapter 5, unless there is a coordinated use of both eyes in early childhood, true depth perception will not develop (Lema and Blake, 1977).

Experience is also necessary before babies can transfer the perception of depth into a warning of danger when placed on precarious heights. The importance of this experience became clear in a series of studies (Gibson and Walk, 1960; Scarr and Salapatek, 1970; Campos et al., 1978) involving the "visual cliff," a platform covered with plexiglass, but patterned and lighted so that it appears to have a "deep" and a "shallow" side (see Figure 11.3). Investigators placed babies on

Figure 11.3 The visual cliff apparatus. An infant who can crawl may cross the glass surface over the "shallow" side but is unlikely to venture out over an edge that appears to be a sudden drop or to cross the surface over the "deep" side.

the cliff and carefully observed their reactions. Babies who could crawl would not cross the "deep" side of the cliff even to reach their mothers, who beckoned to them and showed them attractive toys. In addition, the babies' hearts sped up, indicating their fear of the drop. Babies who could not crawl indicated their awareness of depth, both by the way they explored the plexiglass surface and by a slowed heartbeat. Yet they showed no uneasiness when they were placed on the deep side, directly over the apparent drop. It appears that human babies develop a fear of heights at about the time they become able to move about, a characteristic they share with the young of other species. When young animals are placed on the visual cliff, they show fear as soon as they can walk surely, with chickens and goats avoiding the deep side in the first day of life and rats and kittens avoiding it at three or four weeks. This fear has survival value, for cues of depth can warn an animal that it is in danger of falling.

Babies who learn to crawl quite early—by the time they are six months old—do not seem to develop this fear of the cliff, and investigators speculate that these infants have learned to crawl before the perceptual-motor program that normally controls crawling has matured (Richards and Rader, 1981). These babies look around as they crawl, whereas babies who crawl after they are six months old look at the surface ahead of them. Thus, early crawlers depend less on visual input to guide them than do other babies, relying instead on touch.

How soon babies perceive color has provoked a good deal of debate, primarily because babies are quite sensitive to brightness and until recently, researchers had trouble separating brightness and hue in such a way as to test babies' color vision (Maurer, 1975). As we shall see in Chapter 13, such color categories are universal, and people in every culture appear to perceive the visual spectrum in the same way.

Hearing   All normal newborns can hear, although they may have trouble telling one sound from another. They can also tell whether a sound comes from the left or right, behind or in front. This is a simple task for a normal adult, who locates sounds in space by noting which ear the sound hits first. A sound on the left, for example, is heard by the left ear a fraction of a second before it is heard by the right. This split-second difference in timing is the major clue to a sound's

location. One experiment suggests that infants enter the world with such a capacity for locating sounds in space (Wertheimer, 1961). The researcher used a toy cricket to make a soft, clicking sound near the right ear of a baby girl who was only a few minutes old. The baby stopped crying, opened her eyes, and looked in the direction of the sound. Then the investigator clicked the cricket near the infant's left ear. This time she turned her head and looked to the left. This newborn could not only locate sounds in space but could coordinate her eyes and ears as well. Such coordination is probably reflexive, for in another study (Field et al., 1980), which followed babies from three days to three months of age, the coordination dropped out and then reappeared. Newborns turned their heads when researchers shook a bottle filled with popcorn, but at two months few of these same babies turned their heads toward the source of the sound. By the time they were three months old, however, all the babies were again responding, searching with their eyes for the source of the sound.

In another experiment on auditory discrimination, three-week-old babies had no trouble distinguishing the familiar sound of their mother's voice from the voice of another woman (Mills and Melhuish, 1974). Babies were placed behind a screen and given a pacifier wired to measure the strength of their sucking. To hear a voice, a baby had to suck vigorously on the pacifier. The babies sucked much harder to hear the familiar sound of her or his mother's voice than to hear the voice of a stranger. Thus, before they are a month old, infants can tell a familiar voice from an unfamiliar one.

It also appears that newborn babies perceive the sounds of speech in the way that they are used to make phonetic distinctions in natural languages, so that the perception of language— like that of color—is based upon capacities common to the species. Using what we know about the behavior of young babies, researchers have devised experiments that support this conclusion. Babies suck at a constant rate as long as no new sight or sound strikes their attention, but when stimulation suddenly changes, they suck rapidly. In one study (Eimas, 1975) babies were given pacifiers attached to tape recorders in such a way that rapid sucking increased the volume of the sounds, but slow sucking allowed them to fade into inaudibility. First the babies heard the same sound, "pa," over and over until they habituated and their sucking fell to the steady, slow

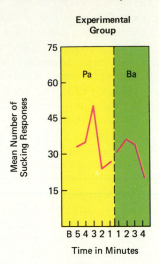

Experimental Group

Figure 11.4 Discrimination of speech sounds in one-month-old infants. Infants were given a pacifier, which was attached to a tape recorder. Every time an infant sucked, it would hear the sound "Pa." When infants in the experimental group habituated to this sound, a new one, "Ba," was introduced. Where sucking responses just prior to the change in sound were low, sucking increased after the change. This would indicate that these infants perceived the "Ba" sound as new and found it interesting enough to keep sucking in order to hear it (until they again became habituated). This and similar research approaches have yielded information on other aspects of infant auditory abilities involving differentiation of sounds. (Adapted from Eimas et al., 1971.)

rate. Suddenly, the sound the babies heard switched from "pa" to "ba," and the babies immediately sucked faster (see Figure 11.4). Using similar techniques, researchers have found that young infants are sensitive to differences between vowel and consonant sounds, as well as to differences in speech intonation (Morse, 1972; Trehub and Rabinovitch, 1972; Trehub, 1973).

Taste, Smell, and Touch Infants' perceptions of taste, smell, and touch have not been studied extensively, but the conclusion about these senses is basically the same as for vision and hearing: newborns can detect and discriminate basic sensory information through taste, smell, and touch.

In a study of seventy-five babies less than a day old, sweet, sour, and bitter fluids were dripped onto their tongues before they had their first feeding (Steiner, 1979). The infants responded

with the expressions we associate with these tastes. A sweet fluid made them smile, then suck eagerly and lick their upper lips. A sour taste led them to purse their lips, wrinkle their noses, and blink their eyes. A bitter taste caused them to stick out their tongues and spit, with more than half of them trying to vomit. The consistency of the babies' facial expressions led the researcher to conclude not only that newborns can discriminate among tastes, but that their responses to certain basic tastes are essentially reflexive. That is, the expressions elicited by sweet, sour, and bitter are properties of the organization of the human nervous system.

Other research supports the idea of an innate human sweet tooth. When newborn babies are given sweet solutions to drink, they drink more but it takes them longer to do it. Their sucking slows and their heart rate increases, leading the researcher to speculate that babies find the taste so delicious that they slow down to enjoy it, and the resulting pleasure excites them, speeding up their hearts (Lipsitt, 1977).

The Roots of Cognitive and Social Development

The cognitive and social characteristics that define the baby as distinctly human develop from rudimentary capacities for vocalization, movement, and perception. From babbling to language ability, from mysterious smiles to mirth, from an interest in faces to strong social attachments, infants display the progressive development of complex psychological processes. Cognitive and social development will be discussed in detail in subsequent chapters; here, a look at the roots of these most human aspects of development will provide a basis for later discussion.

Looking at Faces By the time a baby is six weeks old, a smiling adult face generally elicits a smile in return. But is this a social gesture by the baby, an intentional smile at another human being, or simply pleasure at the high-contrast image of eyes, nose, and mouth?

Some research (Fantz, 1961) suggests that babies show an early visual preference for faces or facelike stimuli over other kinds of stimuli. Infants of various ages were shown a set of six flat disks. Three of the disks were patterned, one with a facelike image; the others were plain but brightly colored. Babies two to three months old spent about 50 percent more time gazing at the face than they did looking at any of the other five disks. Although the researchers originally suggested that this reflected an inborn preference for faces, later research showed that infants prefer simple, high-contrast patterns of many sorts (Bond, 1972). However, at about two months, babies do show a distinct preference for faces, perhaps indicating that cortical maturation allows the infant to attend to whole faces instead of being captured by specific features (Salapatek, 1975), or perhaps indicating that as babies interact with people and discover the social rewards of that interaction, the infants develop an affinity for the human face.

Since babies cannot say whether they can tell the difference between two colors, researchers test their discrimination by using a technique called **habituation**, in which babies are shown a stimulus until they stop looking at it, as if they had become bored with the sight. Then the babies are shown a new stimulus, generally accompanied by the old one. If the babies look at the new stimulus in preference to the old one, researchers assume that they are paying attention to the new stimulus because they realize that they have never seen it before. In one study (Bornstein et al., 1976), four-month-old infants were shown a particular color—say, a shade of blue—for a number of fifteen-second trials until they became habituated to it. Then the color was changed. If the babies perceived the new color as similar to the old one, they would have paid little attention to it, but if they perceived the new color as different, they would have gazed at it for some time. When the second color was chosen from what adults would consider a different category (say, green), the babies showed renewed attention. But they did not gaze long at a different shade of the original color (say, a lighter blue). Repeated tests using different colors indicated that by the time they are four months old, babies seem to perceive the visual spectrum as divided into the primary adult color categories of red, yellow, green, and blue (Bornstein, 1981).

Other investigators (Haith et al., 1977) used a special apparatus to discover exactly what babies look at in faces. In testing babies from three to eleven weeks old, they found that very young infants looked most at the edges of the face. This corresponded to earlier findings that newborns spend a great deal of time looking at the places where contrast is great (e.g., the hairline). By the time they are two months old, however, babies show a striking increase in eye contact, especially when adults are talking to them.

Why does a baby's attention focus on the eyes rather than on the moving lips? The answer may lie in the importance of eye contact to the development of social bonds, particularly between mother and child. A mother usually derives pleasure from gazing into her baby's eyes, and she usually accompanies her gaze with words, touches, and smiles. The infant, in turn, seems to enjoy this heightened attention, and when she or he returns the look, the mother tends to prolong the interaction. Thus, eye contact is reinforced, and the social bond between mother and child may be strengthened. In the process, the baby's interest in all faces increases, as the accompanying photo indicates.

Imitation Children are great imitators, and imitation plays an important role in human development. Most psychologists believe that babies begin imitating the facial expressions of others when they are about eight months old; before that time, babies can imitate only actions that they have performed themselves, such as movements of the hands or legs. About five years ago, however, a great controversy was stirred up by research indicating that two-week-old babies could imitate adults' expressions and movements. Andrew Meltzoff and Keith Moore (1977) reported that babies this young would stick out their tongues, protrude their lips, open their mouths, or open and close their fists in imitation of an adult.

In the study, adults repeated these gestures several times to make sure that a baby had seen them. After each display, the experimenters kept their faces expressionless so as not to encourage or reward the baby for any response. The baby's reactions were videotaped; when these tapes were watched by people who were unaware of which behavior the baby had just been shown, their judgments of the gestures indicated that the infants were indeed imitating the adult model.

Meltzoff and Moore believe that babies have an innate ability to imitate. They argue that when newborns stick out their tongues in response to an adult's protruding tongue, they are somehow mentally representing visual information and sensory information from their mouths, lips, and tongues, matching the two, then imitating the gesture they have seen.

This interpretation of the babies' actions has been challenged by other investigators, who suggest that this early imitation is a response to a sign stimulus, such as those discussed in Chapter 7, and that imitation is an unconditioned, automatic response that babies make to specific stimuli, just as baby blackbirds, who automatically thrust up their heads and open their beaks whenever a parent bird lands on the nest, will do the same when any object is thrust toward them (Tinbergen, 1973). In a study by Sandra Jacobson (1979), young babies indeed stuck out their tongues in response to a protruding adult tongue, but they also stuck out their tongues when a small ball or a felt-tip pen was moved toward their mouths, held there momentarily, and then moved away. And babies opened and closed their hands in response to Jacobson's hand movements, but they did the same whenever an orange plastic ring was placed near their hands. Jacobson suggests that sticking out the tongue has an adaptive function related to feeding.

Meltzoff and Moore (1977) have dismissed the idea that these imitative responses are reflexive on the grounds that the babies' actions were not stereotyped; that is, babies showed individual differences in the way that they stuck out their tongues, protruded their lips, and so forth. However, a reflexive response need not be stereotyped; it must only fall within a behavioral range common to the species.

The human smile provides another example of such behavior. Although smiles appear in the first week of birth, they are not reflexive, for the smile is not elicited by a stimulus. Instead, babies smile as they are drifting off to sleep after a feeding. As we have seen, by six weeks babies smile in response to the human face, and it is this smile that is believed to strengthen the bond between infant and care giver. Such an explantion was suggested long ago by Charles Darwin (1872), who proposed that the smile has survival value for the infant because it evokes a feeling of joy in the care giver. Thus this early smile, which is triggered by the sight of the human face, does not have to be seen as intentional on the part of the infant, just as early "imitation" need not have any intent. It would appear that such imitation among newborns is related to such behavior as stepping, swimming, and reaching—an auto-matic response that drops out as soon as control passes to the developing cortex.

Self-Awareness   If the baby's first imitations are essentially reflexive, when do babies develop self-awareness—an essential human trait? It has long been suggested that self-awareness emerges only when a person has opportunities to observe others through social interaction (Cooley, 1912; Mead, 1934). According to this assumption, a person reared in isolation would fail to develop a true sense of self. This conclusion is tentatively supported by an experiment with humanity's closest relative, the chimpanzee (Gallup, 1977). Each chimpanzee was placed in a cage with a full-length mirror for ten days. Some of the animals had been raised with other chimpanzees; the rest had been rasied in isolation. At first, both groups responded to the reflection in the glass as if it were another animal. They made threatening displays, chattered at the creature, and engaged in other behavior typical of social interaction among chimpanzees. On the second or third day, however, the group-raised chimpanzees began to act as if they recognized the reflection as their own image. Now they used the mirror to gain information about parts of their body that they normally could not see. Looking at their reflection, they picked bits of food from their teeth, blew bubbles, and made faces at themselves. The chimpanzees raised in isolation, in contrast, continued to act as if the reflection were another animal.

The chimpanzees were then anesthetized and while they were unconscious, researchers painted bright red odorless marks above their eyebrows and on the tops of their ears. When placed before the mirror, the chimpanzees that had previously shown signs of self-recognition touched the painted areas on their heads and faces. Some even touched a red mark, then sniffed their fingers, as if trying to identify the substance. The chimpanzees raised in isolation, which had always acted as if the image were another animal, paid no special attention to the red spots and made no attempt to inspect them. It appears then, that chimpanzees do develop some form of self-awareness and that its emergence depends upon social interaction.

If self-awareness among human beings also depends on social contact, a search for its emergence must begin early, for normal babies interact with others from the moment of birth. Following reports from people who work in hospital nurseries that when one baby starts to cry, the entire nursery is soon wailing, researchers took their tape recorders into the hospital. They played recordings of a newborn's cries and found that the claims were correct; babies did start crying when they heard the cries of a peer (Sagi and Hoffman, 1976).

Recently, researchers have found that babies only a day old not only cry in response to the recorded wails of another newborn, but recognize their own recorded cries and respond to them by ceasing to cry and turning their heads to listen (Martin and Clark, 1982). Moreover, the newborns in this study did not cry when they heard the cries of an infant chimpanzee or an eleven-month-old baby. As yet we do not know how newborns can tell when recorded cries are their own and not those of another baby or why the cries of their peers distress them, although it has been suggested that the distress is inborn and an early precursor of human empathy (Sagi and Hoffman, 1976).

As we saw in the discussion of imitation, intent is not a necessary component of such newborn behavior. Yet there is some kind of rudimentary self-recognition involved when newborns lapse into silence at the sound of their own voices. Research with older babies has shown that the sort of self-awareness shown by chimpanzees does not begin to develop in human beings until the latter part of the first year, and most babies are at least a year and a half old before they recognize their own mirror images (Lewis, 1977). In a study like that with the chimpanzees, babies ranging in age from nine months to twenty-four months were exposed to a mirror. Each infant's mother then surreptitiously placed a spot of red dye on her baby's nose. When returned to the mirror, no baby less than nine months old showed any awareness that the smudged nose in the mirror was her or his own, but one-fourth of the fifteen- to eighteen-month-olds and three-fourths of the twenty-four-month-olds knew immediately, grabbing for their noses as soon as they looked into the mirror. That this self-awareness depends upon cognitive development is suggested by a similar study of children with Down's syndrome; among these retarded children, most showed no recognition of their mirror images until they were nearly three years old (Mans et al., 1978).

This baby shows unmistakable signs of self-recognition.

Several other tests have revealed that self-recognition is a gradual development. Babies as young as nine months responded more to videotapes of themselves than they did to tapes of strange babies. When they saw themselves, they smiled and imitated their own behavior on the screen twice as much as they imitated strange babies. By the time babies were twelve months old, when they saw themselves on tape with an adult approaching from behind, some turned and looked over their shoulders (Lewis, 1977).

Perhaps the most convincing evidence of early self-recognition comes from experiments on the effects of delayed-action videotapes. Babies between the ages of nine and twelve months looked at tapes of themselves that had been made just three seconds previously. Most adults find similar situations disconcerting: they cannot continue to talk, for example, when they hear their voices played back with only a fraction of a second's delay. Presumably, if babies recognized the image on the screen as their own, the delayed replay would confuse them. When shown these delayed-action tapes of themselves, infants stopped what they were doing and stared intently at their own images on the screen. Tapes of strange babies did not have such a pronounced effect. The researcher concluded that between the ages of nine and twelve months, infants seem to develop some sense of self (Lewis, 1977).

Although infants' self-awareness may be rudimentary, psychologists believe that the roots of these important capacities may develop very early in life. Newborn infants notice and react to the world about them, seeking some kinds of stimulation and avoiding others. Their sensory and motor skills serve as the foundation for the development of complex cognitive and social abilities. The studies reviewed here suggest that the foundation of many complex skills may emerge along with sensory and motor coordination. The young infant's abilities to interact with the environment are far greater than was once thought, and babies begin processing information and interacting with others almost as soon as they are born.

SUMMARY

1. Human development consists of the physical, cognitive, and social changes from birth until the end of life. The infant's motor skills, language, cognition, and social behavior emerge in orderly developmental sequences, which can be described in terms of **norms**, averages derived from observing many individuals. The age at which a particular baby masters any skill may vary widely from the norm. Variations in the rate of development depend on the hereditary and environmental influences that combine to affect all aspects of development.

2. Germ cells (the sperm and ovum) are formed by the process of **meiosis,** in which each cell has twenty-three single chromosomes instead of twenty-three pairs of chromosomes like the rest of body cells. When the ovum and sperm unite, a unique combination of genes is established that will influence physique, behavior, and the rate of development. Genetic influences can be established by studying identical twins or adopted children. The environment also affects all aspects of development. Extreme deprivation can retard development, but most homes provide a reasonable level of stimulation so that enrichment is likely to have only small effects. Although the existence of sensitive periods in human development has been proposed, human beings are resilient and negative environmental effects appear to be the result of continuing bad experiences, not simply bad experience during early development.

3. The thirty-eight-week period of prenatal development begins at conception and ends at birth. Prenatal development can be divided into three periods: the *germinal period* (from conception to the fourth week of pregnanacy), when cells multiply rapidly and begin to differentiate; the *embryonic period* (from four to eight weeks), when the organism develops a two-lobed brain and responds to stimulation with movements over large body areas; and the *fetal period* (from eight weeks to birth). By sixteen weeks, all neurons have formed, and by twenty-four weeks the fetus cries and moves its eyes. Environmental agents can affect the developing fetus, especially during the first **trimester** (or third) of pregnancy, when basic organ systems are developing. Disease, deficient maternal diet, certain drugs, and cigarette smoking can all have negative effects on the fetus.

4. A newborn infant is both **precocial** (competent) in sensory skills and **altricial** (helpless) in motor skills. Babies are born with reflexes, such as rooting and grasping, that can be elicited by specific stimuli. Some, such as swimming, grasping, and stepping, show a repetitive pattern: they appear, disappear, and reappear. Initial reflexes are controlled by subcortical brain structures; when control shifts to the cortex, they disappear and must be relearned. Newborn infants are probably not confused by the environment because of their limited visual abilities, but vision devel-

ops rapidly and by six months, babies see as clearly as adults do. Newborns can perceive depth but this ability disappears, only to reappear by nineteen weeks. After babies can move around, they use cues of depth to warn them of danger and are frightened by heights. By using **habituation**, in which a stimulus is presented until it becomes boring, researchers have established that by the time babies are four months old they perceive colors, dividing the spectrum as adults do. Newborns can locate sounds in space, turning their heads in the direction of a sound, although this ability is lost, reappearing at about three months. Newborns perceive the sounds of speech in the way they are used to make phonetic distinctions in language, discriminating between closely related sounds. Newborns respond to tastes with expressions that resemble adults' responses.

5. From an early age, babies seem to prefer faces and other high-contrast stimuli. At first they scan the outlines of faces; later they seek eye contact, reinforcing the social bond. Newborn babies appear to imitate adults, but the ability is probably reflexive and without intent, as the early social smile may also be. Some kind of self-recognition is present at birth, for newborns, who cry when they hear the wail of another newborn, fall silent at the sound of their own cries. Self-awareness (as measured by self-recognition in a mirror) may be in part a product of social interaction; such self-awareness develops slowly during the second year of life.

KEY TERMS

altricial	embryo	norms
amniocentesis	fetus	phenylketonuria (PKU)
chromosome	gene	precocial
Down's syndrome	habituation	trimester
	meiosis	

RECOMMENDED READINGS

ACHENBACH, T. M. *Developmental Psychopathology.* New York: Ronald, 1974. A basic presentation of developmental problems—descriptions, foundations, and treatments—from a broad range of perspectives.

BOWER, T. G. R. *A Primer of Infant Development.* San Francisco: Freeman, 1977. A lucid account of emerging motor, sensory, and cognitive skills of the infant.

BRONFENBRENNER, U. *Influences on Human Development.* Hinsdale, Ill.: Dryden, 1972. An excellent collection of scientific articles dealing with critical issues in developmental pychology from infancy to adolescence.

GESELL, A. L., F. L. ILG, L. B. AMES, and J. L. RODELL. *Infant and Child in the Culture of Today: The Guidance of Development in Home and Nursery School.* Rev. ed. New York: Harper & Row, 1974. The classic presentation of developmental norms and their use in assessing developmental readiness.

MCCLEARN, G. E., and J. C. DEFRIES. *Introduction to Behavioral Genetics.* San Francisco: Freeman, 1973. A clearly written, comprehensive review of most of the issues in the inheritance of behavior.

CHAPTER 12

Cognitive Development

Most kindergartners believe that they can make the clouds move by walking and that the sun and moon follow them around. The mental activity of a young child is obviously different from the mental activity of a thirty-year-old adult. But exactly how does it differ? And why? Is the change that occurs simply **quantitative**: the result of nearly thirty years' experience, the piling up of memories and practice so that new information is processed more swiftly in the context of increased knowledge? Or is adult cognition the result of **qualitative changes**: the radical restructuring of the mind, so that the thinking processes of children and adults are different in kind as well as degree?

There is no agreement on this issue among psychologists. Although today no one suggests that children are simply miniature adults, as most people believed during the Middle Ages (Ariès, 1962), some psychologists believe that what looks like radical change in the child's thought is the result of slow, cumulative learning, in which the learning of associations and discriminations lead children to develop concepts and rules (Gagné, 1968). In the process, children's cognitive skills expand and they can apply them to a wider and wider range of tasks (Fodor, 1972). Cognitive development, in this view, is a gradual, continuous process, resembling the growth of a seedling into a flowering plant.

Other psychologists believe that children pass through a series of cognitive **stages**, in which thought at each period is radically different from thought at an earlier period— although each stage of development builds on previous stages. As children's nervous and endocrine systems mature and they have increased experience with the world, their mental functions are reorganized and they pass into a more advanced cognitive stage (Piaget and Inhelder, 1969). Cognitive development, in this view, is a discontinuous process, with each stage as different from the one that preceded it as a caterpillar is from a butterfly.

There is also a third way of looking at the development of cognition, which sees learning as leading to a primarily quantitative change in thought, but which does not rule out the possibility of qualitative change. In this view, the child learns about the world within the bounds of biological **constraints** on thought (Keil, 1981). These constraints, which are tailored to various cognitive domains (such as number, language, deductive reasoning), guide the ways in which thought develops and limit the rules the child can discover from experience with the world. The child is seen as a little scientist who generates rules about the world, uses them for a time, then either keeps them or discards them in favor of better rules. Since the constraints operate on adults as well as on children, there are—despite wide differences in their performance on intellectual tasks—remarkable similarities between the thought of young and old.

Thus, in the major views of cognitive development, mental activity either changes gradually as the result of learning, goes through radical reorganizations as maturation and experience combine, or is primarily the result of learning—learning that at any age is limited by the child's biological immaturity. Whichever view of cognitive development is correct, there is no doubt that Jean Piaget (1896–1980), a Swiss psychologist, has done much to broaden our understanding of the child's mind. His careful observations of infants and children have given us a comprehensive account of mental development that has had wide influence on psychologists and educators. It must be kept in mind that when Piaget spoke of children, he was referring to average individuals.

The Process of Cognitive Development: Piaget's Framework

Early in his career, Piaget spent two years in the Paris laboratory of Alfred Binet, the father of intelligence tests (see Chapter 20), where Piaget worked with schoolchildren to standardize tests. Finding himself more interested in the reasons behind children's wrong answers than in the answers themselves, Piaget soon turned to investigating the development of thought, a project that would occupy him for the rest of his life.

For nearly sixty years, Piaget devoted himself to understanding how the child's intelligence is transformed into the intelligence of the adult, becoming increasingly complex, abstract, and subtle (Piaget, 1952b, 1954, 1978; Inhelder and Piaget, 1958). Piaget saw children as passing through a series of stages in which they develop new ways of thinking, so that thought in each of these stages is qualitatively different. He characterized intelligence as a process by which people actively construct an understanding of reality. This understanding—indeed, all knowledge—grows out of interactions between children and objects in the world. In the course of such interactions, children encounter discrepancies between what they already understand and what the environment presents to them. The resolution of these discrepancies transforms their view of how objects and events are related into a new, and more mature, understanding.

Some Basic Concepts

Vital to this process of intellectual growth are three psychological concepts: scheme, assimilation, and accommodation.

Scheme Babies begin life unable to distinguish between their own bodies and objects and people in the world around them. Therefore, they have neither an understanding of the objects that make up their world nor any idea of how their own actions affect those objects. This knowledge is gradually acquired through a process of exploration and experimentation, using recurrent action patterns, such as grasping or throwing. These action patterns, which Piaget called **schemes**, are the infant's form of thought, and they consist of whatever in an action can be repeated and generalized to other situations (Gallagher and Reid, 1981). Infants begin life with a few simple, innately organized schemes, among them grasping and sucking. By using these schemes, infants come to understand and appreciate much of their world in terms of things that can be grasped and sucked. A baby girl learns, for instance, that she can grasp a toy duck and lift

According to Piaget, infants learn the world by using simple action patterns, called schemes, such as grasping and sucking.

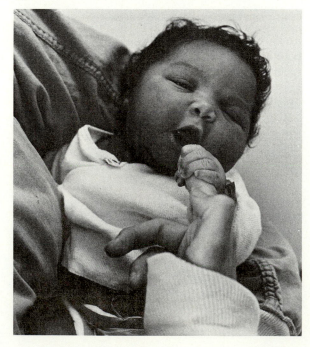

it in her hand, but that a wall cannot be grasped. Moreover, when she puts the duck in her mouth and sucks on it, she discovers its body is soft and pliable, very different from the texture of the crib bar, which she has also tried to suck. From simple actions such as these, infants gradually learn the effects their own movements have on objects, as well as some of the properties of those objects.

As children grow older, their schemes for understanding the world become more complicated and less dependent on overt action. They become internalized, and children can carry them out mentally without physical action. Mental arithmetic replaces counting on the fingers; logical reasoning replaces physical experimentation with cause-and-effect relationships. Thus a ten-month-old baby may explore gravity by dropping peas from the highchair tray and watching intently as each one hits the floor. But an older child, who has come to understand the way gravity operates, knows that if any object is released from an elevated position, it will always fall. The scheme of the older child is internalized; that of the infant is not.

Assimilation and Accommodation   According to Piaget, children's thinking develops through the processes of assimilation and accommodation, which work together in a complementary fashion. **Assimilation** refers to the incorporation of new knowledge through the use of existing schemes. **Accommodation** refers to the modification of existing schemes to incorporate new knowledge that does not fit them. Consider a baby boy who has been bottle fed for several months and sucks very competently on a nipple. One day he is given milk in a cup. At first the infant tries assimilation, sucking on the cup exactly as he has always sucked on his bottle. But the strategy does not work and more milk runs down his chin than enters his mouth. He therefore modifies, or accommodates, his oral skills to this new element. Within a few days, he will be using his sucking skills to drain milk from the cup (assimilation), but he will also have modified these skills so that they are more effective for cup drinking (accommodation) (see Figure 12.1). This new way of sucking represents a temporary balance between the two processes.

In Piaget's view, cognitive development consists of a continual search for such a balance, or equilibrium, between assimilation and accommodation. This process of **equilibration** takes

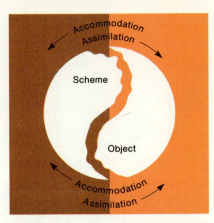

Figure 12.1   Piaget's "knowing circle." Assimilation and accommodation are reciprocal processes that continue until a fit is achieved between a scheme and an object. The entire process of cognitive development is regulated by the continuous interaction of assimilation and accommodation and the shifting balance or equilibrium between them.

the form of progressive approximations toward an ideal equilibrium that is never reached. Infants start life with relatively simple schemes. As they apply those schemes to the world, they meet new information that cannot be readily assimilated. At other times, through maturation they become ready to accommodate information they could not previously handle. Either situation upsets children's equilibrium; when it is restored through accommodation, they advance to a higher level of cognitive organization. Their intelligence grows. The photos on page 274 show how a child applies a grasping and pulling scheme to a toy and how she accommodates that scheme by assimilating features of the environment—the shape of the toy and the space between the bars of the crib. Through this sort of activity, the child matures in both her knowledge about the world and her competence in it.

Stages of Intellectual Development

Much of the power of Piaget's view comes from his careful documentation of how children construct their understandings of reality. In his description of intellectual development, Piaget proposed four increasingly complex stages that always follow in the same order. We shall explore each of the periods separately, but the sharp characteristics that distinguish them pro-

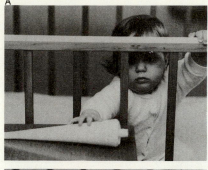

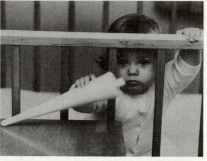

A
B
C
D

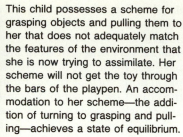

This child possesses a scheme for grasping objects and pulling them to her that does not adequately match the features of the environment that she is now trying to assimilate. Her scheme will not get the toy through the bars of the playpen. An accommodation to her scheme—the addition of turning to grasping and pulling—achieves a state of equilibrium.

vide an overview of intellectual development. Through most of the **sensorimotor period**, which encompasses the first two years of life, infants rely on action schemes. After they internalize these schemes, they move into the **preoperational period**, which covers the preschool years; during this period, which is characterized by the development of language and elaborate symbolic play, thought is not logical. The **concrete-operational period**, which begins to appear about the time children start school, is characterized by logical thought—but only in regard to concrete objects. The **formal-operational period**, which begins around adolescence and may continue to develop throughout adulthood, represents the culmination of cognitive development, and it is characterized by abstract reasoning and the ability to assume artificial premises that are known to be false.

The rate at which individual children progress through each of the four stages varies widely, depending upon their genetic make-up and environment. In a suitably rich environment, children gradually acquire the cognitive capabilities that will carry their thinking to a new, more mature stage of intellectual development. Yet the thought processes of the earlier periods are not entirely lost—they are simply reduced in importance. For example, an adult who has mastered formal-operational thinking does not always use

it and at times functions at the level of an earlier period.

Psychologists other than Piaget have attempted to describe the various periods of human intellectual development. Whatever labels are attached to them, these periods represent roughly the same stages of cognitive growth: infancy, the preschool years, later childhood, adolescence, and adulthood. The remainder of this chapter, therefore, is devoted to the cognitive changes that occur during these five basic periods. The presentation draws heavily on the work of Piaget, but includes the research of psychologists who see development as continuous or as bounded by constraints as well.

Infancy

During the first two years of life, there is an enormous growth in cognitive skills, a growth based on the interaction of biological maturation and cumulative experience. Reflexive actions give way to deliberate movement guided by thought, as mind begins to control muscle (Kopp, 1979). Memory develops, and the infant who seemed to forget an object as soon as it was removed from sight becomes the toddler who imitates actions seen days, or even weeks, earlier. From a very early age, infants process complex information, and by the time they are two years old, have established basic concepts and categories of thought (Nelson, 1981). These achievements can be traced by examining learning, memory, and the development of the object concept during infancy.

The Infant's Capacity for Learning

As mentioned in Chapter 7, babies are capable of learning from the moment of birth, and perhaps even earlier. Babies less than six months old have learned to suck on a pacifier in order to clear up a television picture (Siqueland and Delucia, 1969) and to babble in order to get tickled (Rheingold, Gewirtz, and Ross, 1959).

Conditioning and the Newborn Conditioning techniques are fairly effective, even with newborn infants. In one operant conditioning experiment (DeCasper and Carstens, 1981), babies only a few days old learned to turn on music by pacing their sucking on a pacifier. Babies suck at nipples in bursts separated by pauses of several seconds. To hear a woman singing lullabies and light opera, the newborns had to change their sucking patterns; unless they waited for a prescribed minimum interval before beginning a new burst, their sucking would not start the music. The infants quickly learned to pace their sucking in order to hear the music. When the contingency was removed, so that no matter how the babies adjusted their sucking pattern they could not control the music, they began to grimace, cry, and move about in an apparent display of distress. It seems clear that human newborns have the capacity to learn simple connections between their actions and events, but those contingencies cannot be arbitrary. The most successful conditioning of young infants relies on responses connected with survival, such as head turning and sucking (Sameroff and Cavanaugh, 1979).

Learning for the Fun of It Once they are past the neonatal period, babies seem to learn readily, although the reward involved may be as minor as

Television—How Early Does Its Influence Begin?

Television brings the outside world into the home from the baby's first days and before long, most babies are exposed to its stimulation for about two hours each day (Anderson and Levin, 1976). But until infants attain a certain level of cognitive development, the medium has little influence on them. By the time they are six months old, babies will watch television for short stretches of time (Hollanbeck and Slaby, 1979); but, when toys are available and "Sesame Street" is on the screen, year-old children spent nearly 90 percent of their time ignoring the program (Anderson et al., 1979).

There appears to be little systematic television watching by children until they are about two and a half years old (Anderson et al., 1979), yet before that time children *can* learn from the flickering screen. It depends upon whether the content of the program is simple, captures the child's attention, and has some relevance to the child's natural behavior (McCall, Parke, and Kavanaugh, 1978).

When eighteen-month-olds were placed before a television screen on which a woman demonstrated attractive toys, they watched 68 percent of the time. Two-year-olds watched 78 percent of the time, and three-year-olds were captivated; they watched 95 percent of the time. These youngsters also imitated the televised model, but until they were three, they were more likely to imitate a live model than the model on the screen (McCall, Parke, and Kavanaugh, 1978).

The influence of television appears to become important when children are about two and a half. By the time they are three years old, children are clearly capable of learning a great deal from the medium. Three-year-olds who watched "Sesame Street" regularly made much higher scores on tests of cognitive skills than did five-year-olds who were nonviewers (Ball and Bogatz, 1972). Indeed, one researcher (Reese, 1977) has suggested that today's preschoolers are in some ways more advanced cognitively than were preschoolers twenty years ago, and he believes that television may be responsible for the change.

the flash of a light bulb (Papousek, 1969). Apparently, solving a problem or learning the relationship between their own actions and an event in the external world has its own rewards for infants. The pleasure involved in such an experience seemed obvious among a group of nine-month-old infants who were given a chance to control a mobile. A mobile was suspended above each infant, who lay in a crib with a string attached to each wrist and ankle. Only the string tied to the left ankle was connected with the mobile. As the infants waved their arms and kicked their legs, a curious thing happened. An infant would freeze, eyes fixed on the fluttering objects. Then slowly, the infant would move one arm and then the other, one leg and then the other, until the infant discovered the connection between the kicking of the left leg and the bobbing of the mobile. A wide smile would spread across the infant's face and with delighted gurgles, the infant would kick the appropriate leg and watch the moving mobile. When the contingency was changed, so that one of the infant's arms controlled the toy, the infant would again search for the solution and show the same apparent joy in discovering it (Monnier, Boehmer, and Scholer, 1976).

This delighted response to learning suggests that babies derive pleasure from discovering their power over the environment or simply from solving a problem (J. S. Watson, 1972). Nor is this pleasure limited to infancy. In an experiment with fifth- and sixth-graders (Harter, 1974), subjects were asked to solve some word puzzles that varied in difficulty. The children smiled more and reported far more pleasure when they solved a difficult puzzle than an easy one. The implication is that humans of all ages, from infants to adults, derive pleasure from intellectual mastery.

Infant Memory

Unless babies remember what they have seen or heard, they cannot learn, but the study of infant memory presents certain problems. Babies cannot tell researchers whether they remember sounds or objects, so most studies of infant memory rely on **habituation**, in which babies are shown a stimulus until they stop looking at it, a sign that is taken to indicate the babies' boredom with the stimulus. Then the babies are shown the same stimulus again, along with a new stimulus. If the babies look at the new stimulus in prefer-

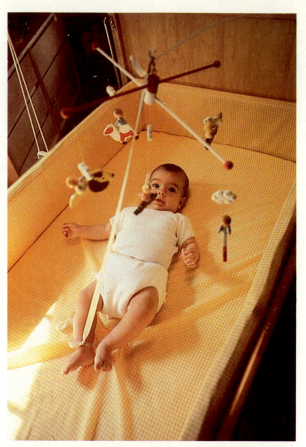

Babies can make their own fun. Several investigators have found that if a mobile is attached to an infant in such a way that the infant's own movements activate the mobile, the infant soon discovers this relationship and coos, smiles, and seems to delight in making the appropriate kick to set the mobile in motion.

ence to the old one, researchers assume that they are paying attention to the new stimulus because of its novelty. Recognition time shortens as babies mature, but allowed to look at something until losing interest, a two-month-old baby remembers a stimulus as well as older babies do. Apparently, older babies can encode information in memory much faster than younger babies do, but once the information has been processed, there is no difference in the babies' ability to retain it (Werner and Perlmutter, 1979).

Recognition and Recall   From studies using the habituation technique, we can conclude that even a newborn can form a memory of a stimulus, retain that memory for five to ten seconds, then compare it with a new stimulus. In short, newborns show clear evidence of the form of retrieval called recognition. Studies have shown that babies recognize sounds, three-dimensional objects, patterns, and photographs, and these memories can be quite durable. For example, four- to six-month-olds were shown the photograph of a human face for several minutes. Two weeks later, the babies were brought back into the laboratory and shown the same photograph they had seen before, along with the photograph of a different person. They consistently looked longer at the new photograph than at the old one, demonstrating that they recognized the original photograph (Olson, 1976).

Recognition seems almost automatic, but recall requires babies to make an active search of their memories in the absence of whatever they are to remember. Because babies cannot talk, there is little experimental evidence to show the existence of recall in infants. However, when parents of seven- to eleven-month-old infants were asked to observe their babies carefully and to record instances of recall, many such incidents turned up. Babies seemed surprised when a household item, such as a bottle of baby lotion, was not in its accustomed place; they searched for people or objects; and they recalled the routines of games (Ashmead and Perlmutter, 1980). In another study (DeLoache, 1980), eighteen-month-old infants who had watched their mothers hide a toy later recalled its hiding place and immediately found the toy although there had been a lengthy delay between the hiding and the search.

Infant Amnesia Anecdotal evidence suggests that much of what babies see and hear is not permanently retained. Few people claim to remember specific events from the first two years of life, although infancy is a time when an impressive amount of information about the world is learned. Since permanent memory and language ability tend to emerge at about the same time, it has been suggested that we cannot remember specifics unless they are labeled. Or perhaps Freud was right, and events from infancy are repressed. A third possibility is that the failure to lay down permanent memories is related to the immaturity of neurons in the infant brain (Campbell et al., 1974).

In an experiment supporting this idea, baby rats eleven to sixteen days old were conditioned to fear a tone by associating the sound with a brief shock (Coulter, Collier, and Campbell, 1976). Six weeks later when the rats heard the tone again, they showed little evidence of fear. Yet rats who had learned to fear the tone when they were seventeen days old were still afraid of it after a lapse of six weeks. This abrupt change in a rat's apparent capacity for long-term memory occurs during an important period of brain development, suggesting that infantile amnesia in young rats may be due to the immaturity of brain structures. Like rats, human infants are born with immature neurons and incompletely developed neural circuits. Thus, neural maturation may underlie the emergence of an ability to store information so that it can be retrieved from long-term memory.

Obviously, babies do not forget everything they learn; the problem is to explain why some things are recalled and others forgotten. A study with human infants similar to the experiment with young rats suggests that repeated environmental cues may be as important as neural maturation in establishing memories (Rovee-Collier et al., 1980). Three-month-old babies learned to operate a mobile by kicking their feet. After a lapse of several weeks they were given another chance to work the mobile, but under different conditions. Half of the babies had had no glimpse of the toy since they had learned to work it; the rest of them were allowed to see—but not to operate—the mobile for three minutes the day before they had their second chance. Babies who had been reminded of the toy by the three-minute reencounter immediately began kicking to set the mobile in motion, but just as the very young rats had forgotten the shock, babies who had had no reminder seemed to have forgotten the toy and had to learn to operate it all over again. The investigators suggest that reencounter with the mobile made access to the earlier memory of play with it available and that when babies seem to forget, it is not because an event has been wiped from memory but because it has become inaccessible, as was suggested for adult memory in Chapter 9.

Sensorimotor Intelligence and the Object Concept

Simple relationships between objects in the world and between their own behavior and those objects make up most of what babies learn during their first few months. Such learning, which is the result of the baby's spontaneous activity, is part of what Piaget calls sensorimotor intelligence. By repeating actions that give them pleasure, babies learn to act in the world. Toward the end of the first year, they coordinate their action schemes into larger schemes, using them to attain a goal, perhaps tugging a cloth toward them to reach an attractive toy that is lying on it. However, infants do not appear to contemplate their own behavior—to think about what they are doing and why they are doing it.

An important aspect of the development of sensorimotor intelligence is the development of the **object concept**, which involves the concept of **object permanence**, or the awareness that objects continue to exist when out of sight. According to Piaget, very young infants do not seem to understand that their bodies are separate objects in a world of objects, some animate like themselves, others inanimate. Nor do they appear to recognize that objects have a permanent existence apart from their own interactions with them. The ability to conceive of objects as having an existence of their own emerges gradually during the first two years of life.

Until babies are about four months old, they have no object concept at all. Babies follow a toy with their eyes and if it is within their reach grasp it. But when the object is moved out of sight, babies act as if it had never been there. They neither search for it nor show any other sign that they are aware of its continued existence.

The first signs of the object concept appear around the fourth month, although some researchers (Bower, 1974) believe it may develop earlier. If only part of a familiar object is visible —if, for example, the handle of a rattle sticks out from beneath a blanket—babies of this age often reach for the toy, suggesting that they realize the rest of it is attached to the exposed part. At an earlier stage, infants would not have reached for the rattle unless it were fully visible. Now, however, babies begin to understand that a disappearing object may still exist. If an object moves across their visual field, infants between four and eight months turn their heads to follow it; they also keep following the object's path after it has vanished from sight. They seem to make a visual search for the missing object.

At this stage, if the object is suddenly covered by a piece of paper or a pillow, babies will neither search for the object, nor pull it back if they are holding it. When a cloth is dropped over something in their hand, infants seem unaware that the object is within their grasp and often let go of it, withdrawing the empty hand. At this age their object concept is clearly rudimentary.

At the next stage in the development of the object concept, from about eight to twelve months, infants will make a manual search for an object that disappears. Suppose a baby girl is shown a desirable toy and while she watches, the toy is put under a pillow. At this stage, she will pull away the pillow and grab the toy. But if, while the baby watches, a toy that has earlier been placed under one pillow is moved under a second pillow, the baby keeps looking for the toy under the first pillow. This consistent reaction has been explained in several ways. Either the baby cannot separate the object from its place, or the baby remembers not the place but the response that earlier gained her the toy, or the baby knows where the toy is but cannot inhibit the earlier learned response (Bremner and Bryant, 1977).

During the next stage, from about twelve to eighteen months, children can follow all visible movements of an object and find it in the last place it was hidden. When an object is hidden under one pillow and then under a second, a third, or even a fourth pillow, the child can find it. Yet at this age, babies cannot cope with transformations they do not see. Suppose a small toy is hidden in a matchbox and the box is placed under a pillow. Then the object is surreptitiously slipped from the box and left under the pillow. If the empty box is placed in front of a little girl, she will look inside it for the toy. But she will not search under the pillow, because she cannot consider the possibility that something she did not see might have happened. Not until the last half of the second year do children understand that an object can be moved from place to place even when they do not see it being moved. This development is significant because it indicates that children can now hold the image of an object in short-term memory long enough to make a search for it. They have developed the object concept. At the same time, they also develop **deferred imitation**, the ability to mimic in play on one occasion actions they have observed at an earlier time. The sensorimotor period now rapidly ends and children move into the preoperational period of early childhood.

Early Childhood

Preschoolers have left the cognitive world of infancy behind them. They have discovered that symbols can stand for objects and words, and they are rapidly acquiring language. Once a child can talk, the ability to think and to communicate expands enormously. Clearly, the intelligence of young children is very different from the action-bound intelligence of infants, but it is also different from the "sensible" thought of later childhood when children begin to think about concrete objects in logical ways.

Now children begin to acquire many cognitive skills that will be important to them in adult life. They learn to count, for example, and to classify objects into general categories. They know that mashed potatoes are "food" and so is hamburger, and that a parakeet is a "bird" and so is a robin. But young children's grasp of these concepts may be deceptive. Their intelligence during what Piaget calls the preoperational stage is based on intuition, not logic.

Advances in the Young Child's Thinking

The development of the object concept in infancy marked the beginning of **representational thought**, in which children mentally represent objects that are not directly in front of them. This important cognitive skill underlies the intelligence of the preschool child, for it breaks the boundaries of immediate perception, allowing children to imagine things that might happen and to recall things that have already happened.

The ability to think in this way engenders a number of accomplishments. Language is the most obvious example of this new thought. In addition, deferred imitation, which also developed toward the end of infancy, expands into the rich, symbolic play of childhood. Finally, children show insight learning, in which they confront a problem, think about it for a moment, and then solve it.

The glimmerings of a concept of "number" appear as early as the third year of life. Two-year-olds count, although they may count only as far as two and may invent their own sequence of number words, which they use consistently. As they count objects, they point to them or touch them, and say their number words aloud. Four- and five-year-olds can count a group of objects in many ways, starting with a different object each time, indicating that they are developing an understanding of the principles that govern counting. They can add and subtract, and they can figure out whether one group of objects has the same number of items as a second group. If one object is taken from the second group, they will notice it. But young children can do all these things only if the number of objects they must deal with is small, and they must always count them (Gelman and Gallistel, 1978).

Immature Features of the Young Child's Thinking

Through representational thought, preschool children develop an intuitive understanding of many complex tasks, but their intellectual capacities are in many ways still immature. For one thing, their thought is egocentric. This term does not mean that children are selfish, but that they are prisoners of their own viewpoint. Because of their **egocentrism**, preschool children seem to believe that other people see things just as they see them and react in exactly the same way in all situations. For example, in one study (Piaget and Inhelder, 1956), children were shown a scale model of three mountains in a triangular arrangement (see Figure 12.2). After children walked around it and looked at it from all sides, each child sat in a chair facing one of the mountains. Then the child looked at a series of photographs and chose the one that showed what a doll sitting on the opposite side of the model would see. Repeatedly, the child chose the picture showing her or his own view of the landscape. Even when the child was allowed to get up and look at the mountains from the doll's position, the youngster still came back and chose the picture that showed the display from her or his own seat. Some investigators have pointed out that children's errors when faced with a situation like the mountain landscape may not always be the result of egocentrism. When the experiment is redesigned so that it places less demand on developing cognitive skills, such as language or memory, and more closely parallels incidents in children's daily lives, their performance improves sharply (Donaldson, 1979; Flavell et al., 1978).

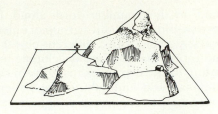

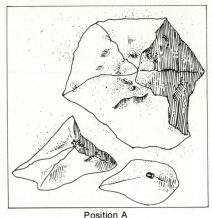

Position A

Figure 12.2 A model used to demonstrate egocentrism. Piaget and Inhelder first had children walk all around the model and look at it from all sides. Then they seated children of various ages at position A and asked them how the scene would appear to observers at other positions. Preoperational children regularly indicated that the scene would appear as it did from position A, no matter where the observer was located. Their thinking did not allow them to mentally reconstruct the scene from a point of view other than their own. (After Piaget and Inhelder, 1956.)

A second immature feature of the young child's thought is known as **complexive thinking** (Vygotsky, 1962), in which the child's thought jumps from one idea to the next instead of unifying a number of ideas around a single theme. This kind of thought is illustrated in the following poem written by Hilary Anne Farley, age five:

I LOVE ANIMALS AND DOGS

I love animals and dogs and everything
But how can I do it when dogs are dead and a
    hundred?
But here's the reason: If you put a golden egg
    on them
They'll get better. But not if you put a star or
    moon.
But the star-moon goes up
And the star-moon I love.   (Lewis, 1966)

Although the thought in this poem frequently shows connections between adjacent ideas, it has no overall integration. Some element in one idea made Hilary-Anne think of another idea. Some element in the second idea made her think of a third, and so on. Although every idea is related to some other, the various ideas are not coordinated into a meaningful whole. Complexive thinking like Hilary-Anne's is common in preschool children.

Finally, the inability to carry out tasks that require self-directed thinking is also common among preschoolers. Young children need external cues to guide and sustain their behavior. For example, a four-year-old may prefer to play with building blocks that have projections and indentations because they show the child how the blocks fit together. Ordinary blocks, without such guides, are less likely to hold his or her interest. The young child lacks the skill to coordinate the building of a pyramid in the absence of clear external cues.

These limitations of preschool children's thought form a unified picture. On the one hand, the children's capacity for representation allows them to carry on new, complex kinds of mental activity. On the other hand, because they lack the ability to organize their thinking into coordinated systems, young children's thought is egocentric, complexive, and controlled by prominent cues in the environment.

Middle Childhood

Although some of the thinking of older children is similar to the intuitive thought of preschoolers, older children can think in ways that younger children cannot. About the time they begin school, children enter what Piaget called the stage of concrete operations, in which they can think logically about concrete objects and understand simple transformations of them. It takes several years for this capacity to become fully developed, and the gradual development of concrete-operational thought can be traced in children's understanding of conservation.

The Concept of Conservation

Children's understanding of **conservation**, or the principle that irrelevant changes in the external appearance of objects have no effect on the

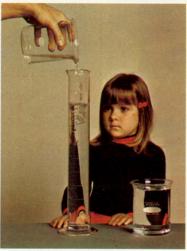

The girl taking part in this demonstration has not yet acquired the ability to understand the concept of conservation of quantity of liquid. She agrees that there is an equal amount of water in the two shorter beakers on the right, but when the water from one of them is poured into the taller beaker on the left, she incorrectly asserts that there is more water in the taller beaker than in the shorter. To develop an understanding of the principle of conservation, the child must be able to coordinate her thoughts about the length and width of the first container, the length and width of the second container, and the change or transformation brought about by pouring the liquid from the shorter beaker into the taller. Preoperational children cannot do this: they consider the state of each container separately, and consequently point to the beaker that "looks like more" as the one that actually "is more."

object's quantity, can be tested in a simple manner. First, a child is shown two identical containers filled to the same level with water, as shown in the accompanying photographs. After the child agrees that there is an equal amount of water in the two squat containers, the experimenter—calling attention to her or his actions—pours the liquid from one container into a tall, narrow container and asks the child whether the containers now hold the same amount of water. A child who understands the conservation of quantity will say that the water in both the tall and squat containers remains equal, but a child who lacks the concept will assert that the tall, narrow glass has more water.

A child who has mastered this aspect of conservation also understands the conservation of number, and is certain that when two equal rows of marbles are lined up, spreading out the marbles in one row does not increase the number, nor does bunching up the marbles decrease their number. Other similar concepts that are grasped early in the concrete-operational period are the conservation of length and the conservation of mass, illustrated in Figure 12.3. All these transformations involve the conservation of quantity.

It will be several years before the child understands less obvious transformations, such as the conservation of weight and the conservation of volume, in the sense that the change in an object's shape does not change the amount of water the object displaces (Piaget and Inhelder, 1941). Although older children understand a growing number of specific concrete operations, they cannot yet understand the similarities among them.

Piaget maintained that the four-year-old's inability to grasp conservation compared with the eight-year-old's understanding of the concept indicated that the two children were in qualitatively different stages of cognitive development. Yet simple changes in the circumstances of a test, such as allowing children to pour the water themselves, failing to indicate that the experimenter's actions are important, or not asking the children about the quantity of water before its appearance is manipulated, increase the number of five- and six-year-olds who answer the critical question correctly (Donaldson, 1979; Rose and Blank, 1974).

In Piaget's eyes, however, it is not the answer given on a conservation test that is important but

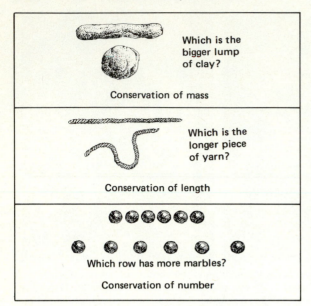

Which is the
bigger lump
of clay?

Conservation of mass

Which is the
longer piece
of yarn?

Conservation of length

Which row has more marbles?

Conservation of number

Figure 12.3 Examples of problems for which a child must acquire the concept of conservation. Concrete-operational children interiorize the possibility of making and unmaking the transformations for each task shown here. Thus, they come to see the lengths and quantities as unchanged in each case. Preoperational children, who are not able to imagine the transformations required, respond to perceptually striking but irrelevant aspects of the objects in attempting to answer the questions. For example, preoperational children will answer that there are more marbles in the bottom row than in the top one.

the reason the child gives for it. If a child says that pouring the water back into the squat container will bring the level just where it was before, the youngster has demonstrated a firm grasp of conservation, because she or he can mentally reverse the transformation. Younger children who pass the test often say that the water is simply the same water as it was before, demonstrating a grasp of the water's identity (Acredolo and Acredolo, 1979). That is, they understand that changes in the water's appearance are irrelevant, just as they understand that putting a boy into a dress does not change him into a girl—a concept that gradually develops during the preschool years. However, they do not necessarily understand that the process can be reversed.

Taken together, these findings indicate that it is impossible to say with assurance that there are qualitative differences in the cognitive skills of preschoolers and schoolchildren. Tests of conservation and other concepts generally test more

than one cognitive skill, so that the preschooler's perception, attention, and grasp of language can affect the results—as can a simple desire to give the researcher the answer she or he seems to want. In addition, older children have greater experience with liquids under various conditions and greater experience in the combined use of their cognitive skills, which lead to quantitative differences between the two groups.

Memory Strategies in Children

Older children also do much better than preschoolers on tasks that involve memory. This improved performance is largely the result of the older children's use of memory strategies, or techniques for storing and retrieving information. The use of deliberate strategies at the time information is stored begins to develop at about the same time children grasp the concept of conservation and continues to improve throughout childhood. Although preschoolers can use obvious external cues, such as depending on a landmark to remember where an item has been hidden (Ritter et al., 1973), children as old as six fail to use less blatant cues, such as categories, to retrieve information.

Children's increasing tendency to use such cues was demonstrated in a study in which six-, eight-, and eleven-year-olds looked at twenty-four pictures of objects that fell into eight categories, along with a card to help them remember each grup (Kobasigawa, 1974). One group of pictures, for example, consisted of a bear, a monkey, and a camel, while the cue card showed a zoo with three empty cages. The experimenter explicitly related the card to the pictures, saying such things as, "In the zoo you find the bear." Later, the children were asked to recall the pictures and told they could look at the cue cards if that would help them remember.

Two-thirds of the six-year-olds ignored the cards, but eight-year-olds had begun to use them, although not in an efficient manner. For example, they would look at a cue card, recall one object, then move to the next card. Eleven-year-olds, in contrast, used the cards effectively, often recalling all three items associated with a card before moving on to the next one. However, the younger children knew more than they had recalled: when the children were specifically asked to recall the three items associated with each cue card, age differences in recall disappeared.

It seems that much of the improvement that appears in the memory of older children is due not to an increase in memory capacity, but to increased skill in the use of strategies. Indeed, some psychologists (Chi, 1976; Brown, 1975) believe that there is no increase in memory capacity after children are about five, and that the improvement that occurs over the course of childhood is the result of increased knowledge and the conscious and practiced use of strategies. Children's knowledge of the world is limited, but when they know more about a subject than adults do, it is the adults' performance that is inferior. For example, children who are skilled chess players can recall chess positions much better than adults who are indifferent chess players (Chi, 1978). Asked to reproduce eight middle-game positions that had an average of twenty-two pieces, not only did children whose average age was ten recall more chunks of information than did the adults, but the first chunks they recalled also tended to contain more chess pieces.

The use of strategies appears to develop as children learn more about how the memory system works. Young children are simply unaware that such strategies as rehearsal or grouping will help them to remember, and even when they are shown how to use a strategy, they drop it as soon as its use no longer is required (Keeney, Canizzo, and Flavell, 1967). Older children who are taught a new strategy continue to use it. When mentally retarded children between the ages of ten and thirteen were taught a few simple memory aids, those children with a mental age of eight were still using the strategies a year later, but children with a mental age of six were not (Brown, Campione, and Barclay, 1979). As children come to understand the process of remembering and forgetting, they begin to *plan* to remember, setting a memory goal and using strategies to help them reach it (Flavell, 1977).

Organizing Concepts

Another way to contrast the thinking capacities of older children with those of preschoolers is to compare the way they organize their concepts about the world. Preschoolers have developed a wide range of concepts, in which they apply symbols, such as "dog," "poodle," or "fox terrier," to many related examples of the concept. These concepts are based on the perceptual qualities and the function of objects, and as children gain experience, their concepts increasingly resemble those of adults (Anglin, 1977).

After they learn concepts, children face the task of organizing them into the hierarchical system that adults use, understanding, for example, that poodles, terriers, and spaniels are all subclasses of the more general class, "dogs," and that dogs, cats, and cows are all subclasses of the even more general class, "animals." This sort of knowledge requires children to analyze objects on more than one level and to coordinate their thinking about them.

As with conservation, preschool children can grasp some of the concepts needed to understand the hierarchy of classes, but they cannot coordinate their thinking. Children as young as two can sort a pile of objects (say, dolls and rings) into separate piles, but a child this young is likely to put all the dolls in one pile before moving the rings into another. Such a young child appears to keep only one thing in mind at a time. By the time children are three years old, they can keep both classes in their mind and sort the toys by separating first a doll, then a ring from the pile of objects (Sugarman, 1982).

A late preschool child who has sorted a group of small toys (eight poodles, two terriers, and three cats) can answer a number of questions about the classification. Asked which toys are dogs, the child points to the poodles and to the terriers. Asked which are animals, the child points to all three groups. The child will also say that there are more poodles than terriers. Such a child seems to understand the hierarchy of classes, but another question will reveal that the understanding is incomplete. Given eight toy poodles and two toy terriers and asked whether there are more dogs or more poodles, the preschool child will say "more poodles." Piaget (1952a) explained this response by saying that preoperational children cannot think of both a class and a subclass at the same time, therefore they cannot compare them. But concrete-operational children, said Piaget, have mastered the hierarchy of classes and understand that one class includes another. Despite the distinction drawn by Piaget, many eight- and nine-year-olds fail such tests and, like the preschooler, insist that there are more poodles than dogs (Winer, 1980).

As with conservation, the way the problem is posed affects the number of children who understand it. When investigators use collective nouns

A

B

C

Color

Shape

Photographs A and B show a problem that requires multiplication of classes and the partial solution that a preoperational child might be able to achieve. The diagram (C) shows how the concrete-operational child can "multiply" two bases for classification (shape and color) to produce a complete classification.

(forest, band, army) to describe the general class instead of class nouns *(trees, musicians, soldiers)*, the number of children who can answer such questions jumps dramatically (Markman and Seibert, 1976), so it is clear that the way the child thinks about the problem affects her or his understanding of it. The key to understanding the relationship between classes and subclasses appears to go back to Piaget's notion of thinking simultaneously about the class and the subclass. When children look at the poodles and terriers, they can encode information about them in three different ways: as dogs (the entire class), as poodles and terriers (the subclasses), or both as dogs and as poodles and terriers (hierarchically). Only children who can code the toy dogs hierarchically (thus thinking of the objects as both class and subclass members) will say that there are more dogs than poodles (Trabasso et al., 1978).

The capacity of older children to coordinate their thoughts into systems extends beyond experimental situations devised by psychologists. Older children have mastered the rules of complicated games, such as Monopoly and baseball. They are also less egocentric, in the sense that they are better able to understand that their viewpoints are not the only possible ones, to comprehend the fact that other people's viewpoints may disagree with theirs, and to coordi-

nate other people's viewpoints with their own. Thus, the thinking of children in the concrete-operational stage has taken on many of the characteristics of adult thought.

Just as advances in memory depend upon increased understanding of the way memory works, so other cognitive advances in childhood depend upon **metacognition**, an understanding of the cognitive processes. Indeed, the understanding of memory is an example of metacognition. Because they lack this understanding of cognition, young children neither monitor nor evaluate their own cognitive processes, and this passive approach to comprehension results in their inability to realize that they do not understand an instruction, a process, or a game. When six-year-olds were given deliberately incomprehensible instructions concerning the rules of a card game or how to perform a magic trick, they failed to notice when essential information had been omitted—despite the fact that they understood that they were helping establish a set of instructions that other children could understand. Eight-year-olds, on the other hand, detected the absence of essential information right away and complained about it (Markman, 1977). The sort of passive information processing that appeared among younger children in this study helps explain their lack of comprehension in many situations, and the active processing used by older children helps explain their obviously increased understanding of the world.

However, there are limitations to older children's capacity to coordinate their thinking. They are still unable to understand abstract principles or to apply logic to hypothetical situations. This further advance in cognition does not develop until adolescence.

Gender Differences in Cognitive Development

As children go through school, gender differences in their cognitive abilities become increasingly obvious. As we saw in Chapter 3, these differences are also present in adults, with women displaying superior language-based skills and men showing superiority in tasks that require the visualization of three-dimensional objects (Springer and Deutsch, 1981). Some researchers believe that the disparity is primarily the result of biology, and others believe it arises from the way children are socialized. Each side can point to evidence supporting its views.

Studies of gender differences in cognitive functioning have recently concentrated on mathematical ability, since aptitude tests consistently show a substantial disparity between boys and girls. Twelve-year-old girls do much better than boys in arithmetic, but boys show superior mathematical reasoning (Fox, 1976). For the past eight years, talented junior-high-school students have been given the Scholastic Aptitude Test customarily reserved for high-school juniors and seniors in an attempt to discover and encourage mathematical talent. Although both sexes, on average, do equally well on the verbal section of the test, each year boys tend to outperform girls on the mathematical section, and among the top-scoring students the boys' superiority is impressive. Since there is no difference in the formal mathematics education of elementary school girls and boys, the disparity has led some researchers to conclude that the differences uncovered are the result of superior mathematical ability among males, which may be based on their greater visual-spatial ability (Benbow and Stanley, 1980). However, other researchers (Tomizuka and Tobias, 1981) have pointed out that while the content of classroom math courses may be identical, the experiences of girls and boys outside the classroom is vastly different, with boys' recreational interests (such as science, sailing, billiards) often requiring mathematical reasoning; in addition, young adolescents tend to draw into prescribed sex roles, which leads girls to shy away from mathematics, a subject generally considered "masculine." Further, girls are often actively discouraged from pursuing mathematical interests (Luchins and Luchins, 1981), and from the age of twelve, boys—but not girls—predict that science and mathematics will be relevant to their adult careers (Harris, 1979).

The question of sex-based differences in cognitive abilities is far from settled. They may be the result of socialization pressures, or it may be that a small biological difference leads boys and girls to use different cognitive strategies. In one study, three-month-old infants were trained to gaze at translucent circles set into a black ceiling. Baby boys learned fastest when given a visual reward (a red light) and baby girls learned fastest

Boys' and girls' recreational experiences differ throughout childhood. This may be one contributing factor to differences in visual-spatial ability or mathematical ability.

when rewarded with a sound (a low tone). However, the difference appeared only at the beginning of the study; after several periods of conditioning, boys and girls did equally well, whether the reward was a sight or a sound (L. A. Watson et al., 1980). If the initial difference in learning ability was not a chance finding, the researchers may have uncovered a predisposition on the part of males to respond to sights and on the part of females to respond to sounds, a difference that could lead each gender to seek out the kind of stimuli it found most rewarding. When we carry the speculation further, we could suppose that girls' resulting early superiority in language ability might lead them to code visual-spatial information in linguistic terms, a strategy that would leave them at a disadvantage with boys, who use a more efficient spatial coding (Harris, 1979). But despite the fascinating differences, the overlap of the sexes in all cognitive areas is far greater than the differences between them, so that there is little reason to consider the cognitive development of boys and girls separately.

Adolescence

As children move into adolescence, a new set of cognitive capabilities, which Piaget called formal-operational intelligence, starts to emerge. Adolescents who have developed this capacity can use scientific reasoning, testing possible explanations in attempts to prove or disprove hypotheses. They can also consider hypotheses that they know to be false and reason in abstract terms. As a result, their thinking is far superior to that of the concrete-operational child, and they can solve problems that they could not have handled only a few years before.

However, some people never develop formal thought, and most studies find that from 40 to 60 percent of college students and adults have attained this final level of cognitive development, which Piaget regarded as the highest form of intelligence (Keating, 1980). In some cultures, the ability to reason about hypotheses may not appear at all (Piaget, 1976), and some investigators believe that its development is the direct result of living in a highly technological Western society that stresses formal education (Super, 1980).

Systematic Experimentation

One of the most important new skills of adolescents is the ability to reason scientifically, considering all possible combinations of factors that may have caused an event and, through systematic testing, to eliminate irrelevant ones. A task Piaget used to investigate this skill shows the difference between concrete-operational and formal-operational thought. Children are given four beakers of colorless, odorless liquids labeled 1, 2, 3, and 4, as well as a smaller bottle labeled g that also contains a colorless, odorless liquid. Using empty glasses, the children are to find the liquid or combination of liquids that will turn yellow when a few drops from bottle g are added (see Figure 12.4). The yellow color is produced when g (potassium iodide) is added to a mixture of 1 (diluted sulfuric acid) and 3 (oxygenated water). The liquid in beaker 2 is plain water and has no effect on the reaction; the liquid in 4 (thiosulfate) prevents the yellow from appearing. Since children are to discover all the combinations that produce a yellow liquid, they must try every possible mixture, even if their first or second try should result in a glass of yellow fluid.

Faced with this problem, elementary school children often begin in a systematic manner, trying out all the single possibilities. They may test 4 plus g, then 2 plus g, then 1 plus g, then 3 plus g. When they fail to produce yellow, they generally say, "I tried them all and none of them works." A few hints from the experimenter may make them realize that they can combine more than one liquid with g, but they then drop the systematic approach and begin mixing the liquids haphazardly. But adolescents can systematically consider all possible combinations of the four liquids. Although they may need paper and pencil to keep track of their combinations, they understand how to generate the full set. Since they are capable of conducting systematic experiments, they can also go on to make general statements about their findings and to construct theories.

Hypothetical Ideas and Abstract Thinking

Adolescents also develop the capacity to consider the hypothetical, reasoning from premises that they know are fanciful. Suppose, for example, that an adolescent and a younger child are asked, "If a man can climb a ladder at 2 miles per

Figure 12.4 A problem that requires the systematic examination of hypotheses for its solution. The chemicals selected by Piaget and Inhelder for this problem have unexpected interactions. It is virtually impossible to determine how the color yellow is produced without trying every possible combination of the liquids, as shown here, and keeping track of the results. Not until children reach the formal-operational period can they conceive of such a procedure. (After Piaget and Inhelder, 1969.)

pothesis and reason out the answer, because the cognitive processes of adolescents are no longer bound by physical reality.

With the ability to think hypothetically comes the ability to understand general principles. Adolescents can, for example, understand the abstract principles of law, whereas a younger child can understand only their concrete applications, as exemplified by the judge, the jail, or the policeman (Adelson, 1975). This new capacity is extremely important, for it allows adolescents to study such fields as mathematics, science, economics, and language on an abstract level and it brings about dramatic changes in their daily concerns. Adolescents may become preoccupied with such notions as ethical ideals, conformity, and phoniness, and they often apply their new abilities to their own thoughts and motives. It is no accident that adolescence is the first phase of life in which individuals begin to think carefully about themselves, their role in life, their plans, and the validity and integrity of their beliefs. Unlike younger children, who deal largely with the present, adolescents are often concerned with the meaning of their past and the direction of their future.

Adolescents who have reached the stage of formal operations do not apply their new reasoning abilities successfully in all appropriate situations. At times they misunderstand the demands of a particular task; on other occasions they find the problem too difficult. In a study of adolescents, only 2 percent of those who showed formal-operational thought in solving one problem applied formal thought to the entire series of ten tasks, which included such problems as figuring out what factors affect the speed of a pendulum's swing (Martorano, 1977). Other studies have found that even well-educated adults commit all sorts of errors on problems of formal reasoning (Henle, 1962; Wason and Johnson-Laird, 1972). Piaget himself felt that most adults probably use formal thinking only in their own areas of experience and expertise. Astronomers, for example, apply formal hypothesis testing to the calculation of planetary motion, but they may not be able use it when trying to repair their cars. Thus specific knowledge and training are as important to cognitive performance as is the general level of intellectual development. Both scientists and auto mechanics may use highly logical, deductive reasoning to solve problems; the major difference between them is the subject matter to which they apply those processes.

hour, how long will it take him to reach the moon, which is 240,000 miles away?" The younger child is likely to dismiss the question, assume a patronizing look, and declare, "You can't climb to the moon on a ladder." The adolescent, in contrast, can accept the absurd hy-

Adulthood

There is no fixed line between adolescence and adulthood, no single age at which all people are considered mature. Instead, adolescence fades gradually into adulthood as people begin to take on adult responsibilities, building on the decisions they have made in late adolescence. Adults continue to learn and to understand increasingly complex material, and their cognitive development follows a predictable pattern. Although individuals vary, most people proceed through a similar cycle of intellectual growth and productivity from early to middle to later adulthood.

Cognitive Skills in Early and Middle Adulthood

Since it is impossible to specify the exact age at which a person passes from adolescence to early adulthood and from early adulthood to middle age, we will define early adulthood as the years from twenty to forty, and middle adulthood as the years from forty to sixty. These forty years are a time of peak intellectual accomplishment. A study of intellectual performance that followed people for thirty-eight years found that IQ generally increases into the middle years (Kangas and Bradway, 1971), and other longitudinal studies have found additional increases in IQ scores among fifty-year-olds (Bayley, 1955).

Young adults usually perform better on any learning or memory task than they ever have before, and if success at a task depends on how fast it is completed, they probably do a little better than they ever will again. During early adulthood, people are intellectually flexible. They find it easy to accept new ideas, and they can readily shift their strategies for solving problems. However, age itself is a poor predictor of learning, memory, and thinking ability. These cognitive processes are heavily determined by intelligence, education, and physical health.

Provided individuals remain healthy, their verbal and reasoning skills are likely to improve during middle adulthood. Middle-aged adults continue to learn and to store new information just as they always have. Consequently, they are often more knowledgeable than they were in their younger years. The ability to organize and to process visual information, as in finding a simple figure in a complex one, also improves in middle adulthood. In addition, the ability to think flexibly, shifting the set of one's mind to solve a problem, is likely to be as good as it was in early adulthood. Only when asked to complete a task that involves coordinated hand-eye movements do people tend to perform less well than they used to, because motor skills often decline in middle age (Baltes and Schaie, 1974). In all other ways, however, adults in their middle years are in their intellectual prime.

Cognitive Skills in Later Adulthood

The group of Americans who are more than sixty-five years old has been growing twice as fast as the population as a whole. In 1900, 4 percent of the population was sixty-five or older; today 11 percent has reached that age (New York Times News Service, 1981). Although many Americans who are past sixty-five are unable to do hard physical labor, they do not necessarily show any significant impairment of intellectual performance. Some physical and cognitive decline does generally accompany the aging process, but healthy older adults make as capable workers as do younger people.

Two problems plague our studies of intellectual performance in later life. First, it is almost impossible to separate the effects of aging from the effects of social change (Neugarten, 1977). That is, the group of people born in 1910, for example, has less education than the group born in 1960, and the content of their education, because of scientific and social changes, was very different from that received by students a half century later. Second, although **senility**, the loss of physical and mental ability that sometimes accompanies old age, is not an inevitable accompaniment of aging, it has been estimated that one in every six older adults suffers from some loss of mental ability, most of them victims of organic disease that is marked by deficiency in a neurotransmitter and by physical changes in the brain (Kolata, 1981). It is very possible that individuals with mild cases of senility are included in most studies of older adults, thereby accounting for part of whatever cognitive impairment is found and resulting in assessments that do not apply to adults who remain healthy. Keeping such problems in mind, we can explore the changes associated with aging and ways to avert cognitive decline in later years.

Changes Associated with Aging Of all the changes that accompany aging, perhaps the most characteristic is the tendency to "slow down." This slowness begins with perception, for it appears that with age, sensory input is reduced. Physical changes in the eye curtail the amount of light that reaches the retina, and hearing loss often develops, particularly for high tones; thus the absolute threshold (see Chapter 4) for visual and aural stimuli rises. In addition, older people with good visual acuity may nevertheless require more contrast than younger adults do to recognize important features of the visual environment (Sekuler, Hutman, and Owsley, 1980). Finally, older adults seem to require more time to process any single perceptual event (Hoyer and Plude, 1980). Since the central nervous system processes all information more slowly with age, the older individual reacts more slowly.

Along with slowness, memory impairment is the cognitive change most frequently assumed to accompany aging. But in many respects, the memory of an older person is no worse than that of a younger adult—or at least not significantly so. A number of memory changes, however, do tend to appear with age.

Some of these changes are related to sensory memory. Although some investigators (Botwinick, 1978) have suggested that sensory memory operates as efficiently in the elderly as in the young, recent research (Fozard, 1980) has questioned this proposal. Aging appears to slow down the rate at which information is assimilated from sensory memory, so that more information decays before it can be processed. As noted in Chapter 9, when people are given a brief glimpse of seven unrelated letters, they can recall no more than four of them before the letters fade from sensory memory. Older adults consistently do worse than younger adults in this situation, recalling three letters at exposures that allow younger people to recall four, and two letters at exposures that allow younger people to recall three (Fozard, 1980). The same effect is found in echoic memory. In dichotic listening tasks, older people are as accurate as younger adults in remembering information heard by the shadowed ear, but recall less than do younger people from the unshadowed message. Since information fed to the unshadowed ear must be held longer in sensory memory than shadowed information before it is reported, the message heard by the unshadowed ear decays before it can be reported (Inglis and Caird, 1963).

When it comes to short-term memory, older people can hold as much information in awareness as younger people do, so that they can remember the name of a person they have just met or a phone number they have looked up as well as they ever did (Fozard, 1980). But when older people must reorganize information in short-term memory—for example, if they must repeat a list of letters, numbers, or words backward—they tend to perform somewhat more poorly than younger adults (Bromley, 1958). In addition, an older person's short-term memory is more likely to be hindered by a task that requires a division of attention. In a typical task of this nature, people are seated in front of a panel consisting of twelve light bulbs and twelve keys, and each time a bulb lights up, the person presses the key directly below it. This extinguishes the first bulb and turns on another one. Young and old perform this task with equal ease. But if the task is changed so that the requirement shifts from pressing the key beneath the lighted bulb to the key beneath the bulb that has just been extinguished, older adults do worse than younger ones. This task requires a division of attention; in addition to storing the position of the lighted bulb, people must retrieve the position of the bulb they have just turned off (Kay, 1953; Kirchner, 1958). Such short-term memory deficits are small, however, and they do not affect a person's ability to function effectively. Outside the laboratory, most differences between the short-term memory performance of young and old escape notice. When carrying out processes that have become automatic, older adults are efficient in allocating attention, and it has been suggested that practiced skills, such as those used by air-traffic controllers, computer technicians, surgeons, and trial lawyers, do not suffer as people age (Hoyer and Plude, 1980).

Long-term memory in older adults is much different from the stereotypical picture of the elderly person with perfect recall of events from youth coupled with forgetfulness about things that happened yesterday or last week. Like everyone else, older people have the greatest difficulty remembering information from the distant past, while their recall is best for events that happened most recently. For example, in one study (Warrington and Sanders, 1971), adults of different ages were questioned for their retention of major news events that had occurred from one month to two years earlier. For all age groups, the amount of information recalled declined with the number of months that had elapsed since the event. Memory fades with time, regardless of whether a person is twenty-six or sixty-six.

In another study, adults of all ages were asked questions about movies, sports, and current events. Investigators found that total knowledge increased with age and that older people were as efficient at recalling the answers to such questions as "What was the former name of Muhammad Ali?" as were young adults (Lachman and Lachman, 1980). In fact, older people are faster at retrieving information when they are more familiar with it than younger people are, and just as fast when both groups know the material equally well. It appears that when older people show any slowness in recalling information, the delay is due to slowed perceptual-motor skills and not to a sluggish search of long-term memory (Fozard, 1980).

However, information is not simply recalled; it must be used. Tests of problem solving show that older adults can solve anagrams as well as younger adults; in fact, not age, but education and measures of nonverbal intelligence are the best predictors of an adult's problem-solving ability (Giambra and Arenberg, 1980). Intelligence remains high among the aged; when older adults were given IQ tests every four years, their scores showed little meaningful decline between the ages of sixty-seven and seventy-nine (Botwinick and Siegler, 1980). It is when older adults have to reorganize material that declines appear. Asked simple questions about information they have heard, older people do as well as younger adults. But when asked to draw inferences about the material, they do significantly worse, presumably because slowed information processing makes it difficult both to register surface meaning and to reorganize the information so that inferences can be made (Cohen, 1979).

Minimizing Cognitive Decline   Although certain cognitive changes tend to be associated with aging, research shows that none of them are inevitable. A small percentage of elderly people suffer no decline in cognitive functioning, and some elderly people, such as Pablo Casals, Pablo Picasso, Grandma Moses, Bertrand Russell, and Eleanor Roosevelt, have been known for the sharpness of their intellects. Exceptional elderly subjects have also been found in laboratory experiments. Yet other people are senile by sixty. The one indisputable fact about aging is that its

effects are widely varied and that age is a poor way to rate a person's cognitive skills (Fozard, 1980). The best explanation for these large variations is the interaction of biological, environmental, and emotional factors.

One contributing factor is biological. Some forty years after finishing school identical twins are more alike in their cognitive functioning than are unrelated individuals or fraternal twins (Jarvik, 1975). These similarities do not mean that genetic programming inevitably sets a person's timetable for aging. However, identical twins may share a predisposition toward—or resistance to—degenerative diseases that affect cognitive functioning. Whatever the causal link, some of the variation in cognitive decline among the elderly is biologically based.

Equally important are environmental factors —especially the degree to which an older person is physically active and intellectually stimulated (De Carlo, 1971; Spirduso, 1975). If older people continue to use their minds, there is a strong likelihood that their intellectual powers will not be blunted. Expectations and opportunities have as much to do with intellectual performance in old age as they do in any other stage of development.

Finally, a person's emotional state has a profound effect on the aging process. Motivation is known to affect memory, and older people may simply have fewer natural incentives—such as a pending promotion—that would motivate them to remember. When nursing-home residents were given material or social incentives to remember, both men and women showed sharp improvements in their memory (Langer et al., 1979). Perhaps more important than motivation is the toll that depression, despair, a sense of worthlessness, and a lack of hope can take on physical and mental well-being. The resulting degeneration often results in deepened depression, and a cycle of premature decline sets in. But when people are optimistic, secure, and generally content with their lives, they stand a better than average chance of remaining physically healthy and intellectually adept throughout their later years.

Since biological, environmental, and emotional factors all affect the speed and course of the aging process, some researchers have been attempting to change environmental factors and are looking for ways to avert the cognitive decline that too often accompanies the aging process. It has been found, for example, that many older people do not automatically use strategies to help them encode information or retrieve it from storage, and that training in such strategies increases their performance on memory tasks (Poon et al., 1980). In problem-solving situations, training has been effective in getting older people to use systematic testing of possible solutions, as has simple opportunity for practice. It appears that, given time to develop their own strategies, older people can develop their own cognitive skills and improve their own performance (Giambra and Arenberg, 1980). As studies have repeatedly demonstrated, a person who is seventy-five can often look, act, and feel far younger than a person who is only sixty (Birren and Renner, 1977).

SUMMARY

1. Researchers are divided over whether cognitive development is **quantitative**, the result of accumulated knowledge; **qualitative**, involving a radical restructuring of mind; or guided by biological **constraints**, which limit the ways in which thought can develop. The foremost exponent of the qualitative view was Piaget, who saw intelligence as a process by which a person actively constructs an understanding of reality. Central to Piaget's theory are the concepts of scheme, assimilation, and accommodation. A **scheme** is an action pattern, which consists of whatever in an action (such as sucking) can be repeated and generalized to other situations. As children grow older, their schemes are internalized and they can carry them out mentally. **Assimilation** is the incorporation of new knowledge through the use of existing schemes. **Accommodation** is the modification of existing schemes to incorporate knowledge that does not fit them. Piaget saw cognitive development in terms of **equilibration**, or a continual search for a balance between the two processes. In Piaget's theory, intellectual development moves through four main stages that do not vary, each involving a qualitative change in thought. The periods roughly correspond to customary divisions of development: the **sensorimotor period** (infancy, or the first two years of life); the **preoperational period** (the preschool years); the **concrete-operational period** (childhood); and the **formal-operational period** (adolescence and beyond). The speed with which children move through these periods depends upon genetic make-up, maturation, and environment.

2. Babies only two to four days old can learn, unlearn, and relearn simple contingencies through conditioning, and the learning is most successful when responses related to survival are used. Babies seem to derive pleasure from solving problems and from discovering their own power over the environment. Studies of infant memory use **habituation**, in which a stimulus is presented until it becomes boring, to demonstrate the existence of recognition. Although there are no laboratory studies of infant recall, babies from seven to eleven months old show instances of such memory in daily life. Infants in the sensorimotor period learn through spontaneous activity and apparently do not reflect on what they are doing. During the first two years, the **object concept**, or the understanding that objects have an existence of their own, develops gradually. The full development of this concept indicates that babies can represent objects in short-term memory while they search for them.

3. A child's intelligence during the preschool years is based on intuition, and during this preoperational period, **representational thought** (which enables children to think about objects that are not physically present) expands rapidly. A concept of number begins to develop during the third year, and by the time children are five, they can add and subtract and figure out whether two groups are equal—but only if the numbers are small and only if they are allowed to count them. The immaturity of preoperational thought shows in **egocentrism** (or the belief that others literally see things as they do), **complexive thinking** (jumping from one idea to another without coordinating them), and the inability to carry out tasks that provide no external cues and that require self-directed thinking.

4. Older children who have reached the stage of

concrete operations can use logical thought about concrete objects. Between the ages of five and seven, children begin to understand the concept of **conservation**, which involves the understanding that simple transformations do not alter an object's quantity and that they may be reversed. During the school years, children show increasing memory skills, which result from their deliberate use of strategies for storing and retrieving information. Another concrete operation that develops during childhood is the organization of concepts into the hierarchical system that adults use. Advances in cognitive skills depend upon **metacognition**, an understanding of cognitive processes.

5. Although cognitive abilities in adults show gender differences, researchers have not established whether these differences are biological or the result of socialization. Male superiority in mathematical ability may be based on the wide disparity in the experiences of boys and girls outside the classroom and the active discouragement given girls who pursue mathematical interests. However, a small biological difference between the genders may lead boys and girls to use different cognitive strategies, leading to differences in male and female abilities. Yet the overlap in cognitive ability is enormous.

6. Formal-operational thought emerges around the beginning of adolescence and involves the ability to think hypothetically and in abstract terms. With formal thought comes the ability to carry out systematic experiments, considering all possible factors and eliminating the irrelevant ones. The capacity to think hypothetically and to understand abstract principles allows adolescents to think about their own thoughts, actions, and motives, to consider the past and the future.

7. Cognitive development during adulthood generally follows a predictable pattern. Early adulthood (from age twenty to forty) and middle adulthood (from age forty to sixty) are a time of peak intellectual achievement, and IQ generally increases into the middle years. Young adults usually perform better than

they ever have before on memory and learning tasks and faster than they ever will again. They are also most intellectually flexible. When people remain healthy, verbal and reasoning skills generally improve during middle adulthood. An adult in the middle years is in his or her intellectual prime; the only decline may be in motor skills.

8. Many people experience little significant impairment of intellectual performance in later adulthood. Because it is difficult to separate the effects of aging from the effects of social change or to be certain that people with mild cases of **senility** (the loss of physical and mental ability) are not included in studies of older adults, studies of cognitive functioning in later life must be interpreted cautiously. The most characteristic change of old age is the tendency to "slow down." Older adults show increased absolute thresholds for visual and aural stimuli and require more time to process a perceptual event. Information is assimilated more slowly from sensory memory, so that more information decays before it can be processed. Older people can hold as much information in short-term memory as younger people do, but when they must reorganize the information, they perform less well than younger adults. In addition, short-term memory among the elderly is generally hindered by tasks that require a division of attention, although they allocate attention well in tasks that have become almost automatic. Long-term memory remains strong, and any slowness in recalling information from storage among old people is probably due to slowed perceptual-motor skills—not to sluggish searches of memory. Intelligence remains high among older people, but when they are asked to draw inferences, their performance suffers. When cognitive declines appear, they seem to be the result of biological, environmental, and emotional factors. When older people are trained in the use of memory strategies, their performance on memory tasks improves, and training has also been successful in getting older people to use systematic testing of possible solutions to problems.

KEY TERMS

accommodation
assimilation
complexive thinking
concrete-operational period
conservation
constraints
deferred imitation
egocentrism

equilibration
formal-operational period
habituation
metacognition
object concept
object permanence
preoperational period
qualitative change

quantitative change
representational thought
schemes
senility
sensorimotor period
stages

RECOMMENDED READINGS

FLAVELL, J. H. *Cognitive Development.* Englewood Cliffs, N.J.: Prentice-Hall, 1977. This book is written by one of the great researchers in cognitive development. It provides an especially clear introduction to the work of Piaget.

HALL, E., M. PERLMUTTER, and M. LAMB. *Child Psychology Today.* New York: Random House, 1982. A topically organized introduction to child development. It offers a balanced view of social and cognitive theories as it covers developmental processes from conception through early adolescence.

LESSER, G. S. *Children and Television: Lessons from Sesame Street.* New York: Random House, 1974. One of the originators of *Sesame Street,* the innovative educational TV program for children based on cognitive-developmental theory, discusses some of the effects it has had on elementary education.

PIAGET, J. *Biology and Knowledge.* Chicago: University of Chicago Press, 1971. Piaget describes the significance of his lifetime work for understanding the human ability to know and the relationship of that ability to human biological heritage.

POON, L. W. (ed.). *Aging in the 1980's.* Washington, D.C.: American Psychological Association, 1980. A book of contributed chapters on all aspects of aging. Includes chapters not only on cognitive aspects of aging, but also on clinical, neuropsychological, pharmacological, and other issues.

REESE, H. W., and L. P. LIPSITT (eds.). *Advances in Child Development and Behavior.* New York: Academic Press, 1982. A series of chapters by well-known researchers. Each reviews the literature and presents some new data. Some of the topics are concept development, perception of facial expressions, and the development of numerical understanding.

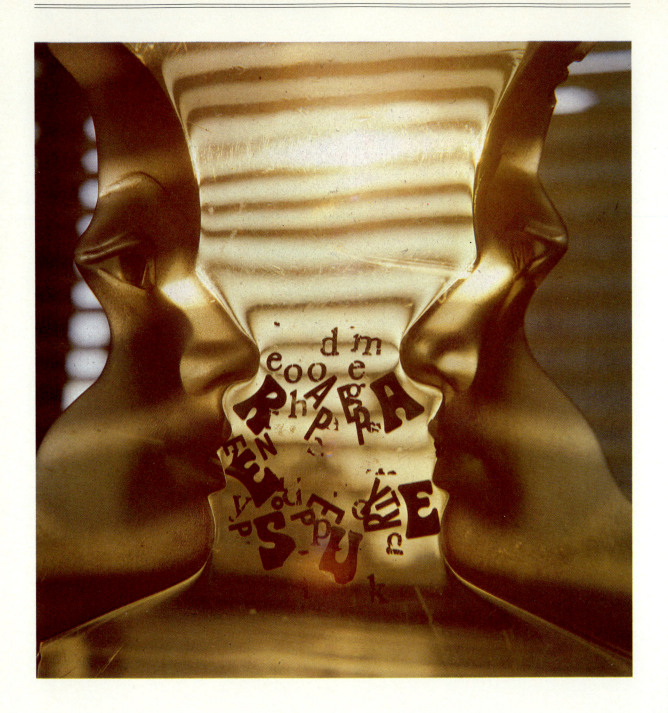

CHAPTER 13

Acquiring and Using Language

Walking seems as natural to us as breathing. We do it without any conscious effort and with little concern—unless we make a slip of the tongue that gets us into trouble. A newscaster whose report of a crime includes the statement, "His body was found lying on the floor by a cleaning woman," might even be sued for slander on the grounds that the cleaning woman's character had been injured by the implication that she had been lying on the floor with a man. If the newscaster's statement had been made at the scene of the crime, as the cleaning woman was telling investigators how she entered the apartment and discovered a body, there would have been no doubt as to the meaning of the sentence. But because the words were heard in isolation—stripped of their context—and because the English language is ambiguous (one meaning of "by" is "close to"), listeners are more likely to interpret the statement as placing the cleaning woman on the floor.

Sometimes our slips of the tongue go undetected by us but utterly confuse a listener. Consider the driver who notices that the rear-view mirror on the passenger side of the car needs adjustment. The driver turns to the passenger and says, "Please adjust the window." With a blank look, the passenger says, "What do you want me to do?" "Adjust the window for me," the driver replies. Since the driver still does not notice that he has pulled the word "window" instead of

"mirror" from long-term storage, this exchange is repeated several times, with voices and frustration levels rising on both sides. The misunderstanding will not be cleared up until the driver realizes, first, that he has made an error and second, just what the error is (Norman, 1980). If the passenger says, "Do you want the 'window' opened?" the driver may say, "What do you mean, 'window'?" and then suddenly realize that he has been using the wrong word for several minutes.

If that situation seems unlikely, try responding with a solution to this problem:

A chartered airline flying from Houston to Montreal crashed exactly on the border between the United States and Canada. A major political issue developed over the following question: In which country should the survivors be buried? (Norman, 1980, p. 46).

If your reply involved a burial site, your confusion was as deep as that of the automobile driver. No one should be concerned with burying survivors—only with the disposition of casualties.

At times language confusion is amusing, as when people lard their language with garbled clichés ("My kids are going to drive me to an early drink"); mangled metaphors ("a tidal wave of avalanche proportions"); and malapropisms ("a radioactive pay raise" or the "postmortem depression" suffered by some new mothers; Longworth, 1981). Although psychologists are amused by this kind of language confusion, they also see it as important. Scientific studies of the misuse of language can deepen our understanding of the way human beings process information. Psychologists would point out, however, that although these examples represent a confusion of meaning, in none of them was the original user of language an incompetent speaker. As we shall see, each normal speaker of a language has a sophisticated grasp of the language's basic structure. But before we can follow the developmental process of language acquisition, we should attempt to discover just what language is.

The Nature of Language

Suppose you overheard a four-year-old girl say to her friend, "Mary, do you want a cookie?" You might infer that the preschooler who asked the question understood something about language. But suppose that as you walked into the next room, a parrot called from its cage, "Polly wanna cracker?" This time you would not infer that the bird understood anything about language despite the similarity between the two utterances. Clearly, speech, or linguistic performance, is not synonymous with language. **Performance** is simply one aspect of language; it is the way we use our knowledge of language in listening or in speaking. Equally important is linguistic **competence**: our abstract knowledge of a language's rules and principles (Chomsky, 1978). As we have just seen, the performance of competent speakers of a language may be full of mistakes, because they have misunderstood the speech of others; because they have momentarily forgotten a word they intend to use; or because they hesitate, stutter, repeat themselves, or make slips of the tongue. In fact, a person who can hear but cannot speak because of a physical handicap may still be competent in a language. In one study (Lenneberg, 1967), a child who could not speak was told a short story and asked questions about its content using grammatically complex sentences. The boy responded by pointing to things, nodding, or shaking his head, showing by his responses that he clearly understood the language (i.e., had linguistic competence) despite his inability to speak.

Since we cannot define language as speech, a better way to arrive at a definition is to look at the way we use language. We use language to communicate—to get our ideas across to other people and to discover what they have in mind themselves. Without such communication, societies could not exist, culture could not be transmitted from one generation to the next, and human interaction would be virtually impossible.

Communication is thus the basic function of language, and each sentence we utter is designed to serve a specific function, whether to obtain a loan, offer a cup of coffee to a guest, warn an intruder to leave, thank a friend for a gift, or order a child not to touch a fragile vase. The study of linguistic function is known as **pragmatics**, which attempts to describe how a speaker uses the signal system of language to accomplish some goal that depends upon a listener's comprehension.

Yet a language's function cannot be separated from its structure, or **grammar**, which relates the sounds of speech to meaning and determines how ideas can be expressed. Grammar is the complex system of rules that deal with three major aspects of language: phonology, syntax, and semantics. Rules of **phonology** identify the particular sounds that are linguistically meaningful and prescribe how they should be ordered to form words. **Syntax** refers to the rules that govern how words should be combined to form sentences. **Semantics** refers to the rules that prescribe the meaning of words and sentences (Clark and Clark, 1977). The way that function and structure are intertwined becomes clear when we look at the acts of speaking (producing language) and comprehension (understanding it).

Producing Language

Producing a simple utterance, such as "Please pass the butter" or "I'm voting for Rebecca Simpson," involves an intricate series of cognitive processes, in which a speaker determines the idea to be communicated, selects the form and precise words to be used, holds the string of words in memory, and finally expresses them in a series of sounds. During the initial stages of this process, the speaker may also be listening to the utterance of another and planning an elaboration of her or his own utterance. Despite this complexity, the process of producing an utterance occurs without visible effort (Dodd and White, 1980).

Context and Intention

An utterance begins in a physical and social context, which consists of the setting (a courtroom, an automobile, the dinner table, a football game), the relationship of the people involved, and the content of conversation that precedes the utterance. This context places constraints on what is expressed and what words are used to express it. For example, an utterance made in a courtroom would take an entirely different form from an utterance made during a football game, and speech to a judge would take a different form from speech to a lover or a child. Similarly, if the previous conversation has been about politics, a reference to last night's movie would sound inane unless certain words were used to weave a connection. Finally, rules regulating conversations further constrain the form of an utterance. If, for example, the preceding utterance was a question, the next utterance should first take the form of an answer, even if the speaker wants to shift the conversation to a different topic.

Pragmatic goals, that is, what the speaker hopes to accomplish through the effects of her or his words on the listener, also play a major role in planning an utterance, or **speech act** (Searle, 1969). The hoped-for effect could be to persuade, to warn, to frighten, to enlighten, to get information, and so forth. Not all speech acts are direct. In getting a person who has just come in from the cold to shut the door, the question, "Haven't you forgotten something?" can be an indirect speech act that is generally as effective as the direct order, "Close the door." Intention and context work together in the planning of each utterance.

Choice of Form

The structure of a language generally allows the speaker a choice of possible forms in which to express an intention. Planning an utterance may be regarded as solving a problem in pragmatics; the problem is solved when the speaker chooses the form that will have the desired effect on a specific listener in a specific context. The speaker must choose the appropriate code (English, French, Spanish or some other language; formal or informal); a structure that emphasizes the content appropriately; and the precise words that fit into the structure. In choosing a structure, a speaker may select a command, a question, an active assertion, or a passive statement. For example, if the conversation takes place just after an automobile has been seen to strike a pedestrian, the speaker probably would say, "The car hit Charles!" (active assertion), but if the conversation concerns a friend who is in the hospital, the speaker probably would say, "Charles was hit by a car." If the speaker wants information, the utterance would

How we speak depends on where we are and whom we are speaking to. With friends in a restaurant, for example, we may be gregarious and animated.

take the form of a question, "Was Charles hit by a car?" In selecting the precise words, a speaker will be guided by pragmatic intent, information about the listener's knowledge of the situation, and any assumptions or wishes the listener may have. First content words (nouns, verbs, adjectives, adverbs) are selected, then words such as articles, conjunctions, and prepositions, as well as the prefixes and suffixes that clarify meaning (-s for plural, -ed for past tense, and so forth). Finally, the speaker must build the exact utterance, syllable by syllable (Garrett, 1975).

Production The utterance apparently is not planned in its entirety before the speaker begins to produce it; instead it is planned over stretches no longer than a phrase or clause (Dodd and White, 1980). Evidence that this sectional planning occurs has come from studies of speech errors in production (e.g., Fromkin, 1973), since slips of the tongue reveal which words or sounds the speaker has planned. Because slips almost invariably occur within six or seven words of each other, investigators have concluded that speech is planned no farther than six or seven words in advance (Clark and Clark, 1977).

Slips of the tongue occur because a word other than the desired word has been called up from long-term memory and is available. Slips confined to single sounds (such as "bake my bike" for "take my bike") indicate that the three-word phrase had been planned, because the "b" of "bike" was available, but that the process of production itself progresses at the level of **phonemes**, or the smallest sound units in the language (Fromkin, 1973). "Bake my bike" is a slip known as an **anticipation**, because the produced sound ("b") was scheduled to appear later in the utterance. Anticipations are the commonest form of slips. Other slips that involve sounds include **perseverations**, in which a produced sound is erroneously repeated later in the utterance ("pulled a pantrum" for "pulled a tantrum"), and **reversals**, in which sounds are exchanged ("food the peech" for "feed the pooch"). Such reversals gained fame for William Spooner, an English clergyman whose probably deliberate sound reversals customarily produced real words, such as "insanitary spectre" for "sanitary inspector" or "our queer old dean" for "our dear old queen."

Slips of the tongue also occur at the semantic level. If a speaker has called up two possible words but has not yet decided between them, the word actually produced may be a blend of both words, as in "grastly," used to describe a scene that was "grisly" and "ghastly," or "stummy" from "stomach" and "tummy." Sometimes slips take the form of another word that apparently is stored close to the planned word in semantic memory and has been called up in error. Slips in this category include words from related classes ("blond eyes" for "blond hair") and antonyms ("my dissertation is too short—long").

Comprehending Language

Understanding the utterances of others requires us to make meaningful a string of sounds that strikes our ears. The process of comprehension invokes memory and requires us to make inferences, using our knowledge of the situation and of language itself—its sounds, syntax, and semantics.

Speech Perception The first stage in language comprehension is the recognition of sounds as individual words. The task is more difficult than it seems, because although the speaker knows beforehand what words are uttered, the listener has no access to that information. For more than forty years, researchers have been trying to build computers that can change human sounds into meaning and have had only limited success. Today, some commercial computers can recognize isolated words or short phrases from a vocabulary of up to thirty words, and some research computers can recognize as many as a thousand words—if the speaker pronounces words carefully, pauses between them, and uses simple sentences (Levinson and Liberman, 1981). Two major problems affect word recognition, whether by computer or human brain: sound and context. The sound of a word varies, depending upon the speaker and the sentence in which the word is embedded. Emotion changes sounds as does informality and the variability of human speech itself. For example, the word "cat," spoken on two occasions, may differ in sound more than the words "cat" and "pat," uttered by the same speaker. Human beings find this variation easier to deal with than computers do. The context in which an utterance is made is also an important aid in word recognition, as is knowledge about the world. This sort of information, which aids the human task of decoding sound, is not available to computers, whose only context is that provided by a program.

Human sound decoding appears to be carried out at the level of syllables, so that instead of processing individual phonemes, we process sound patterns. Apparently, sounds are first analyzed in auditory memory (see Chapter 9), where they are categorized and transferred to working memory. The original analysis, which is made on the basis of the listener's knowledge of the language and expectations as to what might be said in the given situation, may be changed as further sounds are processed (Dodd and White, 1980). In fact, when isolated words taped during a normal conversation are replayed, they cannot be understood by a listener; it requires up to five connected words before such recordings are comprehensible (Pollack and Pickett, 1963).

When words have more than one meaning, it appears that all meanings are retrieved from semantic memory; then, as context makes the speaker's meaning clear, the unwanted meanings slip from working memory and are lost. For that reason, a sentence in which context leads to the wrong meaning are difficult to process. If a speaker says, "The punch at the party gave Betty a concussion," the context of the sentence leads the listener to hold only "beverage" as the meaning of "punch" in working memory, so that as the last word is heard, a complete reprocessing of the sentence is required (Dodd and White, 1980).

Comprehending Syntax   While the speaker is uttering the string of words, the listener is predicting what will come next, using those predictions to help decode the sentence. For example, when an utterance begins with "is" or "are," it is safe to predict that a question is coming and that the decoded words will adhere to that structure. Other syntactic features such as word order, which generally follows the form subject-verb-object in English, also aid the listener in the task of decoding. In addition, when an article, conjunction, or preposition is heard, the listener assumes that a new major subdivision of the sentence is on the way (Kimball, 1973). Such divisions, which consist of noun phrases ("the next morning"), prepositional phrases ("off our starboard bow"), and the like, are called **constituents**, and they are held in working memory as the utterance progresses. The end of one sen-

tence constituent is signaled by the beginning of another, and unless the sentence is quite short, working memory is cleared at the end of each constituent. As a result, the listener retains the meaning of a sentence but not its exact wording (Clark and Clark, 1977).

When sentences are ambiguous, because of multiple word meaning or because the structure could relate constituents in different ways, the listener appears to consider all possible meanings until the speaker reaches the end of a clause. At that time only a single meaning remains and the alternate meanings are wiped from working memory (Dodd and White, 1980).

Meaning and Intention   If a speech act is successful, the listener translates the sounds of speech into the meaning intended by the speaker and reacts as the speaker had hoped. If the speech act was an assertion, the listener registers the information; if it was a question, the listener provides an answer; if it was an instruction, the listener complies—or else generates a speech act of her or his own explaining why compliance is impossible. These pragmatic goals will be accomplished only if the listener uses inference and problem solving throughout the decoding process. As we have seen, the listener relies in part on syntactic cues, such as constituents and sentence structure, to infer meaning. Another major cue is context. Suppose someone says, "Get it off!" Stripped of context, the statement makes little sense. But if the topic of conversation has been a dead bug on the kitchen counter, or if a tree has just fallen on a woman's leg, or a small boy has just appeared in a muddy shirt, there will be no doubt about the meaning (Dodd and White, 1980).

A third important decoding technique that is essential to comprehending speech is the **given-new strategy**, in which the listener takes the new information in the utterance and integrates it with old information already stored in memory (Clark and Haviland, 1977; Haviland and Clark, 1974). Since utterances take place in context, the old information should be available and in most cases will have either been indicated in the utterance itself or mentioned recently.

In English, a speaker tags old information for the listener by using the definite article, "the," and reserves the indefinite article, "a," for new information. In the statement, "A dog barked," nothing is given; all the information is new. But

The Psycholinguistics of Violence

In addition to conveying a speaker's intentions, language can also reveal the person's needs, motives, and possible behavior. This fact has made it possible for psycholinguist Murray S. Miron to help law-enforcement agencies analyze the written and spoken threats and demands of extortionists, highjackers, and terrorists (Rice, 1981). Although most of the psycholinguists whose work is discussed in this chapter focus on the relationship between language and the characteristics of the group (children, adults, speakers of English, among others), Miron's psycholinguistic specialty is the discovery of the individual speaker's characteristics as revealed by her or his language.

From content analyses of hundreds of threat messages, Miron has created a computerized "threat-analysis dictionary," which breaks down messages according to eighty-five categories, such as humiliation, subjugation, powerlessness, authority, submission, and isolation. Based on the context of each word and phrase in the message, the computer analyzes the message into these categories. By examining the frequency of the various categories, Miron identifies the themes of the message. He is then often able to predict the behavior of the person who sent the message.

For example, in 1974 Miron was asked to assist authorities in the Patty Hearst kidnapping case. His analysis of the tapes made by the Symbionese Liberation Army (SLA) led him to predict that the group intended "to commit suicide by establishing the conditions in which their destruction at the hands of someone else is inevitable" (Rice, 1981). When the SLA fought to the death in a televised shootout with the police, Miron's prediction came true. Computer analysis of Patty Hearst's own recorded messages indicated that she would come to identify with her kidnappers and probably would join

in the statement, "The dog barked," the use of "the" indicates that either the listener already knows about the dog or the animal has just been discussed (Dodd and White, 1980). The given-new strategy can be clearly seen in a pair of statements: "Shady Brook Farm bought a new cow. The cow was white." Information about the cow's purchase in the first sentence is new, indicated by the use of "a." When the listener decodes the second statement, the problem is to decide which cow is being referred to. The use of "the" tells the listener that the cow is one that she or he has knowledge of; that is, the cow is old information. Therefore, it must be the cow referred to in the first utterance, and the new information in the second utterance is the color of the cow.

Sometimes, however, the old and new information are not related so clearly. For example, "Mary got some picnic supplies out of the car. The beer was warm." The use of "the" in the second statement signals the listener that the beer has previously been referred to, yet it does not appear in the previous statement. When listeners face this kind of situation, they build assumptions that bridge the two statements. In this case, they assume that the beer was part of the picnic supplies Mary took from the car. Making a bridging assumption takes extra processing time. When people read pairs of sentences, it took them longer to read and comprehend those two sentences about the beer and the picnic supplies than it did to read and comprehend the sentences, "Mary got some beer out of the car. The beer was warm" (Haviland and Clark, 1974).

We are so accustomed to using "a" and "the" to mark new and old information that when someones asserts that new information is old by marking it with the definite article, we tend to accept it as such. Later we will remember it as if it were a fact we had always known instead of an assertion of new information, and we will reconstruct our memories to include it, as discussed in Chapter 9. In one study (Loftus, 1979), people watched a film and afterward were asked questions about it. Some were asked, "Did you see a broken headlight?" Others were asked, "Did you see the broken headlight?" There was no broken headlight in the film, but a week later, when asked whether there had been a broken headlight on a truck in the film, people who heard the question about "the broken headlight" were

them in committing some criminal act. Again Miron was correct; Hearst carried a gun and stood as lookout while the SLA robbed a bank.

Miron is not always right. His analyses do not predict what a writer *will* do, but what a person driven by the categories that pervade the message is *likely* to do. Yet Miron is correct often enough to keep the police and the FBI consulting him. He examines threatening messages to judge whether the threats are serious, to detect the writer's personality and motives, and to suggest ways of handling the threat that will lessen the chance of violence (Rice, 1981). A message that

says "You will be killed" is less dangerous than one saying "I will kill you," since the latter message reveals a writer who is committed to carry out the threat.

Sometimes Miron reports that the message is a hoax. For example, a small-town mayor once received a hand-printed message demanding $30,000; if the mayor did not pay up, both he and his wife would be killed. Because the language in the message revealed a steady diet of televised police drama and youthful bluster and because the demand was for a ridiculously small sum, Miron proposed that the message was merely juvenile fantasy—the work of an adolescent. He advised ignoring the threat. The

mayor complied and nothing happened. The message had indeed been a fake.

Although Miron believes that "threat analysis" is not reliable enough to be used as evidence of guilt, he sees it as a way to understand the nature of people who use violence against society. He has found that the language of terrorists is filled with the need for attention, respect, success, belonging, affection, and dignity (Rice, 1981). If such needs were met, perhaps the need to lash out with resentment and violence against society would dissipate.

much more likely to recall seeing a broken headlight than were people who heard the question about "a broken headlight."

Comprehending human speech requires knowledge, attention to the speaker, and skills. The difficulties involved in this complicated task that we accomplish without any apparent effort help to explain why computers find it almost impossible and why our words are so often misunderstood.

Human Language and Animal Communication

The members of almost every animal species—from the simplest to the most complex—communicate in some fashion. For example, the tiny yellow flashes that fill the evening air in spring and summer are communications: male fireflies are signaling their location to females. The chemical odors that ants emit are a means of communication; they mark trails, induce mating, signal alarm, and attract other ants to food

sources. Some animals combine sound and movement to convey messages: Bees dance on the floor of the hive to tell other workers where nectar can be found. Call systems are common in the animal world: Sea gulls use distinct cries to communicate the location of food or the presence of danger.

These systems of communication are species-specific, which means that the behavior is characteristic of all members of the species and results from neural specialization and certain anatomical traits, as we saw in Chapter 7. Environmental influences also affect species-specific behavior, but they tend to have an impact only during sensitive periods in the animal's development, as in the case of the baby chaffinch, which must hear adult chaffinches singing during the early months of its life if it is to develop a normal song. Although learning is involved in the emergence of species-specific behavior, the readiness to learn is biologically controlled and often dependent upon brain maturation.

Some psychologists regard human language as a species-specific behavior that is radically different in kind from animal communication. To be classified as species-specific, language must be a

These animals at play are having little difficulty communicating with each other, though they lack the capacity for language in the human sense.

distinctive feature of the entire human species—which it is; it must be based on human anatomical features and human brain organization; further, it is likely to emerge during a sensitive period. Experience with language before or after this period would have less impact on language development than the same amount of experience during the period. And if human language is radically different from animal communication, requiring neural capacities not found in other species, then no other animal will be able to acquire human language.

The Uniqueness of Human Language

To decide whether language is unique to human beings, we must first determine what characteristics define it. The major qualities of human language, which will be discussed in this section, are (1) semanticity and arbitrariness of units, (2) discreteness, (3) displacement, (4) productivity, and (5) iteration and recursion (Anderson, 1980). **Semanticity** refers to meaningfulness. Language achieves semanticity by attaching an arbitrary meaning to each separate word. A word's meaning has no connection to a concept except that the speakers of the language have agreed on the link. Thus, shown the same object, Americans say "hat," the French, "chapeau," and Spaniards, "sombrero." Some animal communications also have this arbitrary quality. For

example, the waggles in the dance of a honeybee indicate the distance of a nectar source from the hive (von Frisch, 1967), and the warning calls of some monkeys differ depending upon the predator (Marler, 1967).

Language also possesses **discreteness**; that is, the units that compose it are distinct. In human language, the units are the separate words. Warning calls of monkeys are also distinct; for example, the "chutter" call used to signal the presence of snakes is a discrete unit, as is the "chirp" call that signals the presence of leopards. The dance of the honeybee has no such discrete units.

Language must also permit **displacement**, the transmission of information about distant objects or events, such as the record player in the next room, dragons, or the future of common stocks. This characteristic of language allows us to communicate about things that are not present or things that may not exist. Since the source of nectar is distant from the hive, the honeybee's dance permits displacement; but because monkeys give their specific calls only in the presence of predators, their communication does not.

Productivity, the capacity for allowing individual units to be combined into an unlimited number of messages, is another characteristic of language. The syntax of language allows us to combine words into phrases and sentences, thus expressing an almost infinite number of meanings from a limited number of words. No system of animal communication possesses this sort of productivity, although the dance of the honeybees comes close. Bees have strict rules governing their dance of sound and movement, and researchers have identified six separate rules (Brines and Gould, 1979). By following these rules, bees can communicate an enormous number of messages about the direction and location of a nectar source. Since their conversation is limited to one subject, however, their productivity is limited.

Finally, language permits **iteration**, or adding constituents to old sentences in order to form new statements, and **recursion**, or the capacity to embed one structure of meaning within another. An example of iteration is the adding of phrases or clauses, as in "The president mounted the rostrum. The president mounted the rostrum and began to speak. The president mounted the rostrum and began to speak and urged the people to support the proposed civil rights bill." An example of recursion is the placing of successive constituents within a statement, as in "The girl played the piano. The girl whom the critic applauded played the piano. The girl whom the critic who wrote for *The New Yorker* applauded played the piano." No system of animal communication possesses this characteristic of language.

It appears, then, that human language is a unique form of communication. Notably absent from this list of essential characteristic is speech. Earlier we noted that people can be competent in a language without speaking; it is also possible for a language to lack any sounds at all.

Silent Language: ASL   Most of the deaf people in this country use American Sign Language (ASL), a manual-visual language, to communicate. This communication system possesses all the essential characteristics of spoken human language we have just described, but uses movement in space instead of sound to carry its message (Klima and Bellugi, 1978). Signs are composed of hand configurations (e.g., position of the fingers); the relationship between the two hands; the orientation of the hands (e.g., facing the body); the place of articulation (e.g., beginning from the chest); and movement (e.g., upward). The eyes are used to indicate the beginning and ending of a statement and also to mark the presence of a relative clause (introduced by the pronouns "who," "which," or "that") within an utterance (Padden, 1976). Deaf children who grow up in a signing home acquire ASL as easily and naturally as hearing children acquire spoken language (Conrad, 1979).

Although the vocabulary of ASL is much smaller than English vocabulary, shades of meaning are easily expressed. ASL has, for ex-

Sign language, used by many deaf persons, is a means of communicating with a range of expression all its own.

ample, only one word to indicate beauty, whereas English has many; when signing "beauty," however, changes in the way the sign is made and the signer's facial expression modify the meaning so that any of the English variations of "beautiful," from pretty to gorgeous, are easy to convey (Benderly, 1980). In fact, the language is so flexible that rhythmic song and signed poetry are common (Klima and Bellugi, 1978).

The resemblance between ASL and spoken language seems close in all aspects except the medium it uses to convey meaning. For that reason, some psychologists who believe that the difference between human and animal cognition is quantitative instead of qualitative have used ASL in attempts to teach language to other primates.

Chimpanzee Talk   If chimpanzees ever acquired language, the distance between human and animal cognition would be sharply reduced. Since these primates lack the vocal apparatus for speech, every attempt to teach them spoken language has failed (Hayes and Hayes, 1951; Kellogg and Kellogg, (1933). Noting the resemblance between spoken language and ASL, Beatrice and Allen Gardner (1969) took advantage of chimpanzees' dexterity and began teaching ASL to Washoe, a female chimpanzee.

Washoe's training began when she was about a year old, and after four years she had acquired 132 signs. Washoe's progress in some ways resembled that of a young child learning a spoken language. As soon as she had learned a sign, she used it in other appropriate situations. For example, she learned the sign "open" to request the opening of a particular door, then used the same gesture when she wanted someone to open the refrigerator, a cupboard, a drawer, a jar, and a bottle of soda, or to turn on a water faucet. Some of her mistakes resembled those children commonly make, as when she applied the sign for bruises and scratches to red stains, a tattoo, and her first sight of the human navel—a case of overgeneralizing the meaning. By the time Washoe had learned ten signs, she began to use them in combination, forming such sentences as "Hurry open," "Please sweet drink," and "Gimme key." However, Washoe paid little attention to word order, which meant that she lacked a grasp of syntax. For example, if she wanted to be tickled, she would sign either "you tickle" or "tickle you" (Klima and Bellugi, 1973).

Not all psychologists who attempt to teach language to chimpanzees use ASL. In Chapter 2 we met a chimpanzee named Sarah who learned to use small plastic symbols of varying colors and shapes to represent words (Premack, 1971a;

Washoe, a chimpanzee, was taught to communicate in sign language. Eventually she was able to learn more than a hundred signs, but she never mastered grammar.

1971b). Sarah learned to construct sentences by arranging symbols on a special magnetized board. She learned to understand compound sentences, putting an apple in a pail and a banana in a dish after "reading" the symbols "Sarah insert apple pail banana dish." Her language also included displacement. For example, she had learned the symbol for "brown," and when her trainer arranged the symbols "Take brown," Sarah picked up a brown object from a group of other articles.

A third method of teaching chimpanzees language involved a special typewriter controlled by a computer, which a chimpanzee named Lana learned to operate (Rumbaugh, Gill, and von Glasersfeld, 1963). The fifty keys on the machine each displayed a geometric design that represented a word in Yerkish, a system named after the primatologist Robert Yerkes. When Lana pressed a key, the design appeared on a screen in front of her. She learned to correct herself by checking the sequence of designs on the screen, "reading" what she had written. Lana replied to people who conversed with her through the computer, and she began conversations, typing such sequences as "Please machine give apple."

For a while it appeared that chimpanzees were well on their way to language. They had mastered semanticity, discreteness, and displacement, and seemed to show limited signs of productivity. Then, psychologist Herbert Terrace and his associates (1979) analyzed several hours of videotaped conversations involving the chimpanzee Nim and decided that researchers had been deluding themselves. Nim had learned 125 signs and regularly combined them in utterances, but on close inspection of the films, Terrace discovered that Nim's progress in acquiring ASL bore little resemblance to the child's acquisition of language—either signed or spoken. When repeated signs were eliminated, the length of Nim's utterances averaged only 1.6 signs. Sometimes the chimpanzee put together as many as nineteen signs, but such combinations seemed a grab bag of every sign that could apply to a situation and they showed no increase in either syntactic or semantic competence. Most of Nim's signs were imitations of his teachers' statements, and the chimpanzee rarely expanded on a teacher's utterance, as children generally do. Further, Nim continually interrupted his teachers, showing no evidence that he understood turn taking, a basic rule that children master before they begin to talk. When Terrace then examined film of other "talking" primates, he found the same pattern of imitative signing that Nim displayed.

Terrace's announcement was followed by other reexaminations of the evidence. An analysis of Lana's typewritten utterances showed that almost everything the chimpanzee wrote would fit six stock sentences, into which nouns or verbs could be plugged, depending on the situation (Thompson and Church, 1980). Lana's instructors had already come to similar conclusions. They decided that Lana—and other "talking" chimpanzees as well—had gone no farther in language acquisition than the average nine-month-old child and that Lana used symbols simply as replacements for the chimpanzee's natural gestural system. It appeared, they said, that Lana had done no more than a pigeon that has learned to peck keys in the correct order to get corn (Savage-Rumbaugh, Rumbaugh, and Boysen, 1980).

Such realizations on the part of psychologists opened the floodgates of criticism. Since the question of linguistic competence on the part of apes opens up basic questions about the nature of human beings and the nature of language, the new criticism was often heated (Marx, 1980; Wade, 1980). Researchers who worked with chimpanzees were even accused of naïveté or fraud, yet neither Terrace nor Lana's instructors had said that chimpanzees *could* not learn language, only that they *had* not.

Perhaps the best response from the researchers has come from Lana's instructors in the form of new research. Lana had not learned to use symbols in the context of natural interaction with objects as children do; instead she learned to name objects and then to put the symbols she learned into a sequence that would bring her food, toys, company, or a chance to look out the window. So Lana's instructors taught symbols to a new pair of chimpanzees, Sherman and Austin, in a way that required the animals to learn to ask for tools they needed to solve problems. After the animals were trained to use tools, they were placed in adjoining rooms and had to use the computer to ask each other for whatever tool one of them needed, such as a key to unlock a padlock on a box containing food. Later, all three chimpanzees were taught to sort six objects as either "food" or "tools." All succeeded. But when the chimpanzees were asked to categorize new objects, labeling each as "food" or "tool," Sherman and Austin had no trouble with the task but Lana failed miserably. Apparently, by using symbols in natural situations, Sherman and Austin had learned the concepts involved and could apply those concepts to new objects (Savage-Rumbaugh, Rumbaugh, Smith, and Lawson, 1980). This feat represents a much higher cognitive achievement than learning which typewriter keys bring bananas and indicates that the question of whether chimpanzees can learn a true language is still open.

Biological Adaptation for Human Language

Just as there is no doubt that chimpanzees lack the biological structure that would allow them to use spoken language, there is no doubt that human language ability is closely related to our own biological structure. The human vocal organs, breathing apparatus, auditory system, and brain are highly specialized for spoken communication (see Figure 13.1).

Figure 13.1 The human speech apparatus, including the larynx (which houses the vocal cords), areas of the brain associated with speech, and other such essential physical structures as the tongue and lips. Below are the configurations of these structures necessary for the production of three vowel sounds.

● Areas of the brain associated with speech

⬤ Larynx

"oo"   "aw"   "ee"

Vocal and Auditory Specialization   In human speech, the lungs expel air through the throat and mouth; the vocal cords vibrate to create sound; the tongue, palate, lips, teeth, and facial muscles work together to pronounce vowels and consonants. Stop a moment and feel these structures move as you read this sentence aloud and you will see that their flexibility makes it seem as if they were designed to produce speech.

Human beings can make a far greater diversity of vocal sounds than any other animal. As we have seen, not even chimpanzees can reproduce human speech sounds, yet we observe that human babies begin babbling spontaneously at a very early age.

Just as the human vocal apparatus is well adapted to the production of widely varied speech sounds, so the human sense of hearing is well adapted to perceiving those sounds. As noted in Chapter 11 (Eimas and Tartter, 1979), infants only a few weeks old can detect the difference between "ba" and "pa," sounds so similar that in some languages they are not considered distinct. Further, babies only a few days old prefer human voices over other sounds and will suck more to hear voices singing with music than to hear music alone (Butterfield and Siperstein, 1974). Thus, human beings may be born prepared to discriminate among speech sounds.

Brain Specialization   Specialized vocal and auditory systems are essential for normal human speech; these systems are controlled by the brain. In human beings, the cortex is much larger than it is in other animals, and the large areas called the association cortex (see Chapter 3) are certainly involved in language, although they are involved in other cognitive processes as well. The question is whether language must be considered separately, with a distinct neural basis, or whether language is simply another aspect of human cognition and information processing (Clark and Clark, 1977).

Arguments for the special nature of language focus on the functional asymmetry of the brain, called hemispheric lateralization, which was discussed in Chapter 3. As we saw in that discussion, when the left hemisphere is injured, language ability is often impaired, and an individual finds it difficult to communicate with others and to understand them. Observations that have been made of patients undergoing neurosurgery indicate that when the left hemisphere is anesthetized, the person cannot sing the words of a familiar song but has no trouble carrying the melody. The effect is reversed when only the right hemisphere is anesthetized: the patient loses the melody but can recite the words (Gorden and Bogen, 1974).

This hemispheric dominance for language has been said to represent a biological foundation for language abilities in human beings, since such relatively clear localization is found only in the human species (Lenneberg, 1967). Signs of lateralization have been detected in infants less than ten months old for speech as against musical notes (Glanville, Best, and Levenson, 1977), or for speech as against nonspeech stimuli (Molfese, Freeman, and Palermo, 1975), suggesting that special brain mechanisms in children may serve as a foundation for learning language.

Should a child's brain be injured, however, the plasticity of the immature brain allows the right hemisphere to take over the language function. Children whose left hemispheres have been surgically removed (because they were the focus for debilitating seizures) appear to develop near-normal language abilities (Lenneberg, 1967; Smith and Sugar, 1975). Yet one study (Dennis and Whitaker, 1976) has found a deficit in such right-hemisphere language. Nine- and ten-year-olds whose left hemispheres had been removed before they were five months old could not understand passive sentences (e.g., "I was paid the money by the boy"), indicating that some aspects of language structure—but not semantics—may be limited to the left hemisphere.

In dealing with the problem of whether language and cognition are closely related, a second look at chimpanzees may be helpful. Some researchers have argued that chimpanzee cognition differs from human cognition only in degree and that an adult chimpanzee is as clever as a three-year-old child (Bever, Fodor, and Garrett, 1974). Yet no chimpanzee has gone farther in linguistic competence than a nine- or ten-month-old child (Savage-Rumbaugh, Rumbaugh, and Boysen, 1980), a finding that argues for the special nature of language. However, retarded children generally show a similar retardation in language acquisition, whereas highly intelligent children develop language quite early, findings that argue for the notion that language is dependent on cognition in general and that language ability rests on the human capacity for information processing (Anderson, 1980; Clark and Clark, 1977). Thus, we can maintain that there is something special about the human brain that makes language possible and that the left hemisphere is more involved in language ability than the right. However, the claim that whatever brain organization is responsible for human language is somehow different from other cognitive abilities has not been definitely established.

Sensitive Periods

Human language ability emerges at about age two, which may signal the beginning of a sensitive period for language acquisition, a period that ends at puberty. This period, argued Lenneberg (1967), is related to the development of hemispheric lateralization, which he believed takes place gradually between birth and puberty. Some evidence supports this position. Children who lose their speech as a result of brain damage during this period are more likely than adults to recover completely, presumably because lateralization is complete in adults but not in children. Yet as we have seen, studies have found some evidence of lateralization in babies too young to speak.

One test for the existence of a sensitive period is whether people can learn a second language easily after puberty. If a true sensitive period exists, then during that period a new language would be acquired without an accent, no formal instruction would be needed, the child would develop native competence in both syntax and semantics, and the course of acquisition would be similar to that found among children learning their native language. After puberty, however, a new language would be acquired with an accent, formal instruction would be required, the speaker would not acquire native competence, and the course of acquisition would differ from that found among children learning their native language. Although in one review of second-language studies each of these predictions was borne out, the differences between language acquisition before and after puberty were not as dramatic as would be expected if a sensitive period existed (Krashen, 1975). Another review of similar studies that controlled for such factors as the amount of exposure to the new language, the type of exposure, and the speaker's willingness to learn the language, found no evidence of a sensitive period (Ervin-Tripp, 1974). In fact, the older the individual, the faster she or he learned the new language. Only in regard to phonology did the idea of a sensitive period have any validity: younger children were less likely to have an accent in the new language. Finally, among English-speaking families that moved to the Netherlands, adolescents learned Dutch fastest and preschoolers were the slowest to learn, acquiring the language much more slowly than their parents and even losing much of their fluency in English (Snow and Hoefnagel-Höhle, 1978).

Although there seems to be no true sensitive period for second-language acquisition, the concept may hold good when applied only to the acquisition of a first language. If that is the case, it would be difficult or impossible to learn a first language after the sensitive period. The case of Genie, a California girl who grew up in almost total isolation, indicates that acquiring a first language in adolescence may present special problems (Curtiss, 1977). Genie was nearly fourteen when she was rescued from an almost total isolation (see Chapter 2). She had spent her days strapped to an infant's potty chair, her nights harnessed in a sleeping bag that acted like a strait jacket. Her only social contact came when her silent, almost blind mother spooned baby food into her. No one spoke to the girl, although her father often growled or barked like a dog at her. She had never fed herself; she could neither talk nor stand. By the time Genie was eighteen, she could understand normal language but could not produce some of its basic structures. Her speech was rule-governed and productive, she used some prepositions, and she spoke of people and objects that were not present. But her language lacked the rich fluency found in the speech of the average schoolchild. Although Genie's case seems to indicate that acquiring a first language after the sensitive period is extremely difficult, her special circumstances make it impossible to draw a definite conclusion. The severe sensory and social deprivation Genie endured, her malnutrition, and the brutal treatment meted out by her father may have combined to affect cognitive as well as linguistic development.

How Children Acquire Language

At birth, human babies are speechless. Indeed, the word "infant" comes from the Latin word for "without language." Slowly, the infant progresses from meaningless babbling to one- and two-word utterances and, in time, to complete grammatical sentences. By the age of four or five, children around the world have a command of their native tongues. As we shall see, several theories have been advanced to explain this acquisition of language.

The Stages of Language Acquisition

Despite the wide variation in human cultures, children in every society appear to acquire language in the same way (Brown and Fraser, 1963; Bloom, 1970; Brown and Hanlon, 1970; Brown, 1973). Although one child may begin to use words earlier than another or to talk more fluently, all normal children master the basic features of whatever language they hear spoken.

Prespeech Communication From the earliest weeks of life, the sounds that babies make attract the attention of others and although they are not meant to communicate, the noises succeed in informing parents about the baby's needs. Each infant has three patterns of crying: the basic rhythmical pattern (often called the hunger cry); the anger cry, and the pain cry. A mother quickly learns to detect these differences in her baby's cries and responds to them appropriately. For example, in response to the pain cry, she immediately rushes into the baby's room (Wolff, 1969).

Other sounds soon appear, and by three months babies are cooing. By five or six months, they babble, chanting sequences of sounds that resemble syllables. Much early babbling is apparently motor play, because deaf babies babble just as hearing babies do. Soon after six months, however, deaf babies stop babbling, probably because they have not been stimulated by hearing human speech. In early babbling, infants make sounds from all languages, and the babbling of Chinese babies is indistinguishable from the babbling of American babies. Gradually, children develop control over the sounds that they make and begin to imitate the sounds made by others.

Infants are not limited to sounds, but also use gestures to communicate. At about ten months, babies begin to seek help from adults, looking at a toy that is out of reach, looking at a nearby adult, stretching their hand toward the toy, looking again at the adult and making a regular fussing sound that increases in volume if the adult does not respond. Now the infant has demonstrated both an intent to communicate and a realization that agreed-upon signals can be used for the purpose (Bates, 1979).

Babies also communicate through intonation, expressing their intentions by the patterns of pitch changes in their sounds. One investigator (Tonkova-Yampol'skaya, 1973) found that babies in the first year of life learn intonations that signal happiness, commands, requests, and questions, using patterns that correspond closely to typical adult patterns. When they are about seven to ten months old, for example, babies express commands with a sharply rising then falling pitch that adults use in phrases such as "Stop that!" Toward the end of the first year, the intonation patterns of babies begin to resemble the patterns in the speech they hear around them. Now Chinese babies babble in Chinese cadences, and American babies babble long sequences of sound with the pitch contour of adult sentences. This early acquisition of pitch and emphasis is important in the development of language, because intonation is a grammatical device that changes the meaning of utterances—even reversing their meanings.

First Words Around their first birthdays, children understand the names that stand for a few people or objects, and many have produced their first words. Generally, these words are the names of objects and indicate that the baby now realizes that objects are worth talking about and that they have names (Nelson and Nelson, 1978). First words refer to the immediately tangible and visible; the child's language does not yet exhibit displacement.

During this one-word stage, infants often use a single word for many purposes, relying on intonation to supply meaning. For example, an infant who has learned the word "door" can, by changing the intonation, make a declaration ("That's a door"); ask a question ("Is that a door?"); or state a demand ("Open the door!") (Menyuk and Bernholtz, 1969). Such one-word utterances can be understood only in context. If a toddler reaches for a doorknob, it is safe to assume that the emphatic "Door!" means "Open the door." Thus, the success of these one-word utterances depends upon the ability of other people to use context, intonation, and gestures to interpret the child's pragmatic intentions. These clues will remain important as the child's command of language grows. Even in adulthood, tone of voice and body language often provide essential clues to the meaning of spoken language.

Children in this early stage of language acquisition often extend the meaning of a word to cover objects or actions for which they have no words, a process called **overextension**. Up to a third of a child's early words are extended in this fashion (Nelson et al., 1978). For example, a small girl who has learned the word "bow-wow" may overextend it from dogs to all four-legged animals. When she learns a new word, say "moo" for cows, she has two animals' names in her vocabulary, "moo" for cows and "bow-wow" for all other animals. As the youngster learns new words she attends to other features of animals, such as size and sound, and her concept of "bow-wow" becomes narrower; eventually she will have separate names for all animals (Clark, 1973). This also works the other way: as children develop an increasing ability to perceive distinctions among things in the world, the stage is set for them to learn a new label. Overextension does not always indicate a confusion of meaning, because children who overextend a word in speaking rarely confuse it in comprehension. A child who calls all animals "bow-wow," when asked to find the "bow-wow" in a picture of animals will always point to the dog and never to the sheep (Gruendel, 1977).

The possession of a basic vocabulary is not the same as the acquisition of language. Language requires the words to be combined according to certain rules, but grammar cannot emerge until the child has reached a certain level of neurological maturation. However, just as crawling prepared infants to walk, one-word utterances prepare them to speak in a truly human way.

First Sentences About the time children reach their second birthday, they begin to put two words together, with no pause between the word and a falling intonation that spreads over the entire utterance. They are now speaking in sentences, and this new capability indicates an improvement in short-term memory: they can now plan and produce a statement before the first word is forgotten. Because of the two-word limit, utterances are stripped to essentials, and articles, prepositions, and conjunctions are omitted. Such utterances resemble telegrams, so they are known as **telegraphic speech** (Brown and Bellugi, 1964). For example, if a little girl in the two-word stage wants her mother to read her a book, she can say "Mommy book," or "Read book," or "Mommy read," but she cannot say "Mommy read book." Thus, the girl means more than she can say. She can, however, string together a pair of two-word utterances to express her thoughts, such as "Kitty book. Read it" (Scollan, 1979).

At this two-word stage, the rudiments of grammar have appeared in the child's speech. Children do not merely juxtapose any two words in an utterance. Instead, they generally follow a basic syntactic rule concerning **word order**, which in English prescribes the sequence subject-verb-object to indicate meaning. Thus, the two-year-old will say "eat cake" (verb-object) but not "cake eat" (object-verb) (Brown, 1973). Two-year-olds also use some **inflections**, such as the "–s" that is added to nouns to indicate the plural form. Finally, they use **intonation**, indicating a statement by ending their utterance with a falling tone, or a question by ending it on a rising tone. Another way for intonation to indicate meaning is through stress, and children in the two-word stage say, for example, "DADDY coat," with emphasis on the first word to indicate possession ("This is Daddy's coat"); or "Daddy COAT," with emphasis on the last word to indicate location ("There is Daddy's coat) or action ("Daddy, put on your coat").

Yet these childish sentences are not simply shorthand versions of sentences heard from adults. The utterances are governed by basic rules—even unique sentences, such as 'All-gone sticky" from a little boy who has just washed his hands. Children's sentences are so predictable that psycholinguists have been able to compile formal rules, describing what is acceptable in the child's system and what is not.

Two-word utterances can express an impressive range of meanings. Although the basic categories of meanings shown in Table 13.1 are based on data from children around the world, the entire list could be compiled from the speech of two-year-olds in any language. Regardless of the culture in which they are reared, two-year-

Table 13.1   Categories of Meanings Expressed in the Two-Word Stage

Category of Meaning	Description
Identification	Utterances such as "See doggy" and "That car" are elaborations on pointing, which emerged in the preverbal stage, and naming, which began in the one-word stage.
Location	In addition to pointing, children may use words such as "here" and "there" to signal location—as in "Doggy here" or "Teddy down." To say that something is in, on, or under something else, children juxtapose words, omitting the preposition—as in "Ball [under] chair" or "Lady [at] home."
Recurrence	One of the first things that children do with words is call attention to, and request, repetition—as in "More cookie" or "Tickle again."
Nonexistence	Children who pay attention to the repetition of experiences also notice when an activity ceases or an object disappears. Utterances such as "Ball all gone" and "No more milk" are common at this stage.
Negation	At about age two, children discover that they can use words to contradict adults (pointing to a picture of a cow and saying, "Not horsie") and to reject adults' plans (saying, "No milk" when offered milk to drink).
Possession	In the one-word stage children may point to an object and name the owner; in the two-word stage they can signal possession by juxtaposing words—as in "Baby chair" or "Daddy coat."
Agent, Object, Action	Two-word sentences indicate that children know that agents act on objects. But children at this stage cannot express three-term relationships. Thus, "Daddy throw ball" may be expressed as "Daddy throw" (agent-action), "Throw ball" (action-object), or "Daddy ball" (agent-object). Children may also talk of the recipient of an action by using similar constructions—saying, "Cookie me" or simply "Give me" instead of "Give me a cookie."
Attribution	Children begin to modify nouns by stating their attributes, as in "Red ball" or "Little dog." Some two-word sentences indicate that children know the functions as well as the attributes of some objects—for example, "Go car."
Question	Children can turn types of sentences described here into questions by speaking them with a rising intonation. They may also know question words, such as "where," to combine with others—as in "Where kitty?" or "What that?"

Source: Adapted from R. Brown, *A First Language: The Early Stages.* Cambridge, Mass.: Harvard University Press, 1973.

olds express the same universal range of concepts in their two-word sentences. These basic concepts form the core of all human language, and much later language development is a matter of elaborating and refining these basic ideas.

Acquiring Complex Rules   Like one-word utterances, two-word sentences are virtually impossible to interpret out of context. For example, "Mommy shoe" could mean "This is Mommy's shoe" or "Mommy is wearing her shoe" or "There's mud on Mommy's shoe" or "Mommy, put on your shoe!" Although as we have seen, context remains important in adult conversation, children's language becomes less context bound as sentences lengthen and they begin to use prepositions, conjunctions, verb inflections, and the like. As they master complex grammatical rules, children are able to communicate about what happened yesterday and what might happen tomorrow.

Most of these rules are acquired between the ages of two and five, so that the child who enters school has a good grasp of grammar. However, children do not memorize a set of rules ("To form the possessive, add 's"). Indeed, many adults have trouble stating these rules, although they apply them correctly. Instead, children approach language with expectations and a set of strategies that they apply to the words they hear (Slobin, 1973). These strategies determine what sort of linguistic constructions will be easiest for children to learn.

One of these strategies is "Pay attention to the end of words." Children appear to learn suffixes ("–ed," "–ing," "–s") more easily than they learn prefixes. In one study (Kuczaj, 1979), preschoolers heard a series of sentences, in which the same nonsense syllable ("–ip") was always placed either at the beginning or the end of words. For example, some children heard "The boy drove the ip-car" while others heard "The boy drove the car-ip." With some children, "ip" always meant "big"; with other children it always meant "red." But whether "ip" meant "big" or "red," children who heard the syllable used as a suffix found its meaning much easier to learn than children who heard it used as a prefix.

A more specific rule that children discover by paying attention to the end of words is the rule for forming plurals in English: add an "s" or "z" sound to the singular form of the noun ("dog/dogs"). Children's knowledge of this rule can be tested by showing them a large stuffed toy for which there is no name. Then the investigator names the toy, handing it to the child and saying, "Here is a wug." Next the investigator places a second identical toy beside the first and says "Now there is another wug. There are two_____?" If the child knows the rule for forming plurals, she or he will says "wugs," pronouncing it "wugz." (Berko, 1958).

In mastering grammatical rules, children may go through several strategies. In one study (Bever, 1970), two-, three-, and four-year-olds used a toy horse and a toy cow to act out the following sentences:

1. The cow kisses the horse.
2. It's the cow that kisses the horse.
3. It's the horse that the cow kisses.
4. The horse is kissed by the cow.

Two-year-olds acted out the first three sentences correctly, but on sentence 4, they were as likely to have the horse kiss the cow as to have the cow kiss the horse. According to the researcher, two-year-olds assume that when a noun is followed by a verb, the noun is the actor. But if other words interrupt the sequence, as in sentence 4, two-year-olds simply guess. Four-year-olds also act out the first two sentences correctly, but in sentence 4, they reverse the interpretation, consistently making the horse kiss the cow. What is more, they also pick the horse as the actor in sentence 3, which two-year-olds interpreted correctly. Four-year-olds are led astray, says the investigator, because they have adopted a different strategy. They hear the first noun in a sentence as the actor and the noun following the verb as the object of the action. Such a strategy leads them to misinterpret sentences like 3 and 4. Apparently, children construct and discard a variety of temporary grammars as they acquire language.

The acquisition of grammar demands not only that children gradually grasp the underlying rules for combining words into sentences, but also that they understand when to apply the rules. Because there are exceptions to many grammatical rules, this second task can be very difficult. One basic strategy appears to be "Avoid exceptions," and it leads three- to six-year-olds to commit errors of **overregularization**—that is, they extend a grammatical rule to cases in which it does not apply (Bellugi, 1970; Slobin, 1973). Overregularizations show that children have

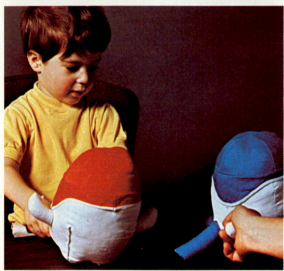

How can a researcher know for sure how a young child is interpreting adult sentences? One way is to have the child act the sentences out. This boy has been handed two dolls and a washcloth and asked by an experimenter to "Show me 'The boy is washed by the girl.'" The boy treats this sentence as though it were "The boy washes the girl." The grammatical rules that he has acquired so far are inadequate to process correctly a sentence in the passive voice.

In this singular-plural test, (top) the child is handed an object for which he has no name and is told, "Here is a wug." (middle) Then another is put down, and the child is asked to finish the sentence, "Now there are two _____." (bottom) If the child knows the rule for forming plurals, he responds with "wugs."

control of certain language rules and that they are systematically applying them.

Overregularization is extremely common when children apply the rule governing the past tense in English. Very young children learn as separate items the common but irregular past verb forms, such as "broke" and "went." But once they learn the rule for forming the past tense (add "-ed," as in "asked" or "climbed"), they apply it to the irregular verbs they have already learned and begin saying such things as "Daddy goed to work" and "It breaked." Children of five or six may apply the rule to the correct irregular past forms and say such things as "wented" or "ated," but by the time they are seven most no longer overregularize verbs (Kuczaj, 1978).

Children go through a similar sequence with plural nouns. After they learn to add the "s" or "z" sound to the singular form, such incorrect plurals as "foots," "mans," and "mouses" creep into their conversation. Often these forms are followed by a double plural—"mens" and "mices" before children return to the original correct form.

Such behavior represents progress in children's analysis of language, as they construct forms to conform to the regularities they have noticed in the speech of others. Children seem predisposed to look for regularities and to impose order on their language.

Explaining Language Acquisition

Most empirical evidence indicates that children are neurologically equipped to figure out the structure of any particular human language. Children readily acquire language, provided that they live in an environment in which language is used as a means of communication. Beyond this general requirement, psychologists have been unable to agree on the exact nature of the factors that influence children's acquisition of language.

According to the biological view put forth by linguist Noam Chomsky (1972; 1975; 1979), the acquisition of language is primarily a matter of maturation. All languages of the world share a common underlying deep structure, which he calls a universal grammar, a structure that is based on special faculties of the human brain. As we have seen, all languages make similar distinctions relating to combining sounds into words (phonology) and words into sentences (syntax).

Chomsky maintains that these distinctions reflect special cognitive abilities built into the human brain. Thus, in acquiring their native tongues, Chomsky argues, children are aided by an inborn knowledge of this universal grammar, and this ability is different from general cognitive abilities.

Some behaviorists, especially B. F. Skinner (1957), sharply disagree with Chomsky and see language acquisition as simply "verbal behavior" —another example of operant conditioning. Because mothers use words to express affection as they care for their babies, the mother's speech becomes reinforcing. Eventually, babies reinforce themselves by listening to their own vocalizations. In addition, parents and other adults reinforce youngsters with attention and approval when they begin to label objects in the world (Bijou and Baer, 1965). When children learn to say things that other people can understand, this accomplishment is reinforcing because it provides the child with a way to communicate needs and desires. Gramatically correct constructions tend to be repeated because they get desired results.

Other behaviorists agree that language is learned, but those who are social-learning theorists would say that imitation plays a major role in the process. Parents act as models for their children, who imitate both the words and the structures they hear (Bandura, 1977). Two-year-olds' acquisition of certain grammatical forms has been accelerated through modeling (Nelson, 1977). For example, when a child asked, "Where it go?," the experimenter responded to the question by modeling the future-tense form, "It will go there" and "We will find it." Soon the children began using the new form in their own sentences.

Many psychologists believe that simple reinforcement and imitation cannot fully account for children's acquisition of language. They point out that most parents reinforce children for intelligibility, not for correct grammar. When a child asks for a cookie or a game of peek-a-boo, a parent's compliance reinforces the form of the communication, even when it is ungrammatical. For example, when a little girl wanted to indicate that her mother was also female, she said, "He's a girl." Her mother replied, "That's right" (Brown, Cazden, and Bellugi-Klima, 1968). But a child who says "Friday is my birthday" will be corrected if the birthday falls on Saturday. Thus, as long as parents can understand a child and as

Children learn language in part by imitating their parents. When a mother scolds her daughter, the child may in turn scold her doll.

long as the child's statements are true, grammar receives little attention.

Imitation also seems to fall short as an explanation for language acquisition. Children learn more than words, they learn rules, producing sentences they have never heard. When a child says, "I seed two mouses," the youngster is applying the rules for forming the past tense of verbs and plurals—but applying them incorrectly. No parent explains such grammatical rules to young children. In fact, there is abundant evidence that children do not simply repeat what adults say to them. Efforts to correct a child's speech often seem hopeless, as in the following conversation:

CHILD: My teacher holded the baby rabbits and we patted them.
MOTHER: Did you say your teacher held the baby rabbits?

CHILD: Yes.
MOTHER: What did you say she did?
CHILD: She holded the baby rabbits and we patted them.
MOTHER: Did you say she held them tightly?
CHILD: No, she holded them loosely (Gleason, 1967).

In this exchange, the little boy clings to his over-regularization despite hearing the correct form modeled twice by his mother.

In recent years, a number of researchers have begun to explain language acquisition by looking at social interaction in infancy (Gleason and Weintraub, 1978). They believe that pragmatics is the key to language development and contend that nonlinguistic aspects of language provide the basis, sending children a long way toward acquiring language before they say their first words. Early exchanges between infant and parent, in which the parent at first supplies both sides of the conversation, teach babies something about the nature of human conversation. Infants begin to acquire language by using the context of a situation to figure out a speaker's intentions, eventually learning the pragmatic rules that govern languages. In early interactions and the games of infancy, children learn to take turns, to make eye contact, and to indicate that they are paying attention (Bruner, 1980). In addition, parents speak in special ways to their infants, talking slowly and using simple sentences, replacing difficult consonants with easy ones, substituting nouns for pronouns, and repeating words, phrases, or whole sentences. This special way of talking to children, which simplifies the child's task of figuring out the language, has been found in at least fifteen cultures, and it is used with infants, parents, strangers, and older children (Ferguson, 1977). It has been suggested that interaction with adults who speak in this special way cues a biologically adapted *process* within the child instead of priming a universal *grammar* as has been proposed by Chomsky (Bruner, 1980).

Language and Thought

As children's mastery of language grows, they are able to express complex thoughts, not only about the here and now, but about things removed in time and space, events that exist only in imagination, and abstract ideas. Certainly, language and thought interact and it is difficult to study one without involving the other. If we ask someone what she or he is thinking about, the information comes to us in the form of words. But which is more influential: thought or language? Some psychologists say that our language determines the way we think and others that thought determines the language we use.

How Language Affects Thought

It has been proposed that language sets the boundaries of what we are able to think about, determining how we can think about objects and events. George Orwell (1949) spelled out some ominous implications of this view in his novel *Nineteen Eighty-Four,* in which a tyrannical government controls thought by removing words from the language, coining new ones, and redefining others in such a way that it is impossible even to think subversive thoughts.

The idea that language determines thought was expounded eloquently by Benjamin Lee Whorf (1897–1941). Whorf's **linguistic relativity hypothesis** is based on the notion that language determines our ideas, thoughts, and perceptions. When a child acquires language, she or he simultaneously acquires a "world view," because language determines the way in which a person sees the world. According to Whorf (1956), different languages influence thinking in different ways; therefore, people with different languages have different views of the world. Language accomplishes this effect through vocabulary and through grammar.

Vocabulary Language may affect cognition through vocabulary because the words we learn determine the categories we use to perceive and understand our world. For example, English has a single word for snow, but Eskimos—who live in an environment where snow is very important—have more than twenty specific words for different types of snow. If language determines our perception of the world, then when Eskimos look out on a fresh snowfall, their perception of the white substance on the ground should differ from that of speakers of English.

We can say that the Eskimo's vocabulary forces

an Eskimo to notice the condition of the snow—whether it is slushy, powdery, crusty, and so forth—and that vocabulary encourages the English speaker to overlook the snow's condition. Yet when snow condition is important, as it is for the subgroup of English speakers who ski, a specialized vocabulary develops and many words for snow exist (Brown, 1958). Thus, the vocabulary of a particular language does not make it impossible for us to perceive such differences.

Vocabulary is important, however, although not in the way that Whorf proposed. It is impossible to master certain fields without learning their special vocabularies (Clark and Clark, 1977). For example, surgeons could not learn the anatomical facts that guide every operation if there were no vocabulary to enable them to make precise distinctions among muscles, nerves, and organs of the body and their various parts. Vocabulary enables us to pass along essential human experience in every field and to open up knowledge.

Having new words for novel information affects learning and memory (Dodd and White, 1980). In Chapter 9, we saw that labeling an ambiguous figure as "eyeglasses" caused it to be remembered differently than when it was labeled as "dumbbell" (Carmichael, Hogan, and Walter, 1932), so that words seem to determine how information is encoded in memory. Other research has shown that attaching a common category label to different stimuli makes them seem related, perhaps because the common label encourages people to notice their similarities instead of their differences (Dodd and White, 1980). In addition, as we saw earlier in this chapter, simply using a definite article instead of an indefinite article changes the way people reconstruct their memories of events (Loftus, 1979). Finally, labels can affect a person's self-concept and thus change her or his behavior. In one study (Kraut, 1973), in which all other conditions remained the same, people who heard themselves called "charitable" were more likely to contribute to future charity appeals, and people who heard themselves called "uncharitable" were much less likely to contribute.

Grammar Whorf (1956) also believed that language affects the way people think about time, space, and matter, because languages differ in the grammatical categories that they express (such as number, gender, tense, voice). Whorf called Hopi a "timeless language" because, although its grammar recognizes duration, it does not distinguish among the present, past, and future of an event. English compels us to do so, either by verb inflection ("He talks"; "He talked") or by use of certain words and expressions ("Tomorrow I talk"). Hopi verbs, instead, distinguish between various kinds of validity. They are inflected to indicate whether the speaker is reporting an event, expecting an event, or making a generalization about events. If these very different ways of grammatically classifying events affect thought, a Hopi-based physics should be very different from an English-based one.

Research with English speakers has failed to confirm this sort of claim. For example, either verbs or nouns can be used to express certain ideas in English, as in "The attack of the army was swift" or "The army attacked swiftly." If Whorf's claim is correct, when "attack" is a noun, the English speaker mentally represents it as a permanent object, but when "attack" is a verb, it is represented as an action with temporal limits. Yet these aspects of English play so small a role in shaping thought that, a few minutes after having heard one of the two sentences, a person cannot recall which of the two has been heard (Iannucci and Dodd, 1975).

Apparently, then, language does not determine thought in the way that Whorf proposed. Although language can make things easier to think about and although the way we label objects can affect how we perceive and remember things, the linguistic differences Whorf stressed are not nearly so significant as he believed.

How Thought Affects Language

Most psychologists and linguists now believe that language limits thought only to a small extent, and evidence exists that some types of thought are completely independent of language (Furth, 1966). Interest has shifted to the opposite proposition: that universal characteristics of human thought processes create universal linguistic structures.

If the biological foundations of language are also the biological foundations of thought, and if language is simply another aspect of human cognition, then thought would be expected to influence language. Among developmental psychologists, the strongest champion of this view is Jean Piaget, who agreed that language could increase the power and speed of thought, but that language was structured by thought and evolved under its guidance (Piaget and Inhelder, 1969).

The search for linguistic universals that depend upon human perceptual and cognitive capacities has focused on color terms. Various cultures use different systems for naming colors, with some cultures having many different words that distinguish hues and other cultures having few (Berlin and Kay, 1969). English uses eleven basic color categories: black, white, red, green, yellow, blue, brown, purple, pink, orange, and gray. But speakers of Ibibio in Nigeria have only four basic color terms; speakers of Jalé in New Guinea only two. If Whorf was correct, these different ways of describing colors should lead people whose language has only a few color terms to see color differently from people whose language has many terms. Speakers of Ibibio or Jalé should be unable to perceive the same color distinctions as speakers of English.

However, research has shown that people in various cultures do not arbitrarily carve up the color spectrum, and that the structure of the human visual system, not a culture's language, determines the way we perceive color (Miller, 1978). Despite the diversity of color terms in different languages, all languages apparently select color terms from the list of eleven basic color categories used in English (Berlin and Kay, 1969). If a language has fewer than the eleven terms, it lacks terms for the categories lower down in the list. Thus Jalé, with its two terms, names only the first two basic categories (black and white); Ibibio, with its four terms, names the first four general categories (black, white, red, green); and so on, down through the eleven terms shown. The fewer the terms, of course, the wider the range of colors they apply to. Thus, the Ibibio green would encompass the English green, yellow, and blue.

The similarity of human color perception was demonstrated by preparing a color chart like the one in Figure 13.2, which contains 320 hues—virtually all the hues that the human eye is capable of distinguishing. When native speakers of dozens of languages were shown a similar chart and asked to point out the best example of each color term in their language, the choices were virtually the same from language to language. The Navaho *lichi* is the same as the Japanese *aka*, the Eskimo *anpaluktak*, the English *red*. Basic colors correspond across languages. However, the

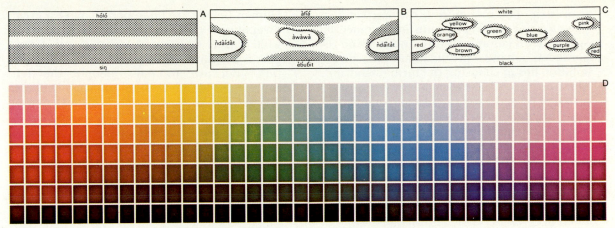

Figure 13.2 Some of Berlin and Kay's evidence that there is a universal cognitive basis for the naming of colors. The large color chart (D) shows most of the color chips Berlin and Kay presented to members of various cultures. (They also presented a black chip, a white chip, and several shades of gray chips.) The three small diagrams correspond to the large color chart, with the bands at the top and bottom of each diagram corresponding to the black and white not shown in the large chart. (Grays are not shown at all.) Each diagram shows the names that members of a particular culture applied to various chips. A name inside an outlined area indicates that it was applied to all the chips that correspond to that area in the large chart. The surrounding gray areas indicate chips to which that name was applied with less certainty. Thus, English speakers (C) designate as "green" a small set of chips that are included in a somewhat larger set of chips called "awawa" by speakers of Ibibio, a language of South Nigeria (B). These chips in turn are among an even larger set of chips for which the people of New Guinea who speak Jalé have no name at all (A). (After Berlin and Kay, 1969.)

boundaries of basic color categories—whether pink is included in red, for example, or is given a separate label—vary according to the number of color terms that a language has (Berlin and Kay, 1969).

Certain basic colors are more conspicuous than others to all people, and these hues are called "focal colors." When a language lacks a term for a focal color, speakers of that language can still distinguish the hues, and find it easy to borrow terms for them from other languages, indicating that there are natural, universal color categories. Indeed, as noted in Chapter 12, infants apparently perceive differences between focal colors long before they learn labels for them (Bornstein, Kessen, and Weiskopf, 1976). Thus, color categories, like many other linguistic connections, seem to reflect both physiological and cognitive characteristics of people. Although human beings in different cultures apply different labels to things, they nonetheless seem to perceive these things in much the same way.

SUMMARY

1. Speech, or linguistic **performance**, is only one aspect of language; equally important is linguistic **competence**, our abstract knowledge of a language's rules and principles. Communication is the basic function of language, and each sentence is designed to serve a specific purpose. **Pragmatics**, which refers to the function of language, describes how a speaker uses language to accomplish a goal. **Grammar**, or the structure of a language, is divided into **phonology**, the ordering of meaningful sounds to form words; **syntax**, the rules for combining words to form sentences; and **semantics**, the rules that prescribe the meaning of words and sentences.

2. Producing an utterance involves a series of cognitive processes, in which a speaker determines the ideas to be communicated, selects the form and words to be used, holds the string of words in memory, and finally expresses them in a series of sounds. The context of an utterance places constraints on what is expressed and what words are used to

express it. The intention of the speaker also plays a major role in planning an utterance, or speech act. Planning an utterance may be regarded as solving a problem, and the correct solution lies in choosing the form (command, question, assertion) that will have the desired effect. Slips of the tongue reveal that an utterance is planned over stretches no longer than a phrase or clause in length. Among the commonest slips of the tongue are **anticipations**, **perseverations**, and **reversals**.

3. Understanding the utterances of others requires the listener to use memory and to make inferences based on the knowledge of context and of the language itself. Human sound decoding is carried out at the level of syllables, processing sound patterns instead of individual **phonemes**, or the smallest units of sound. When words have more than one meaning, all meanings are retrieved from semantic memory and held until context makes the speaker's meaning clear. Syntactic features allow the listener to predict what will come next in the utterance; for example, a word that generally introduces a **constituent**, or sentence subdivision, alerts the listener to the new feature. An important technique in comprehending speech is the **given-new strategy**, in which the listener integrates the new information in an utterance with old information already stored in memory. When the old and new information are not clearly specified, the listener builds assumptions that bridge statements.

4. The major qualities of human language are **semanticity** and arbitrariness of units ("arbitrary" meaning attached to each word), **displacement** (referral to distant objects and events), **productivity** (capacity to combine units into an infinite number of statements), **iteration** (adding new constituents to old statements) and **recursion** (embedding one meaning structure within another). No form of animal communication has all these features, making human language unique. Language does not require sound, for American Sign Language (ASL), the manual-visual language of the deaf, has all these features. Although chimpanzees have learned to communicate using signs, plastic tokens, and computer terminals, none has yet demonstrated a grasp of language more advanced than that shown by a ten-month-old child.

5. Human beings are equipped to make a great diversity of vocal sounds and to perceive a wide variety of sounds, indicating that language is related to human biological structure. Because in most people the left hemisphere dominates for language abilities, it has been suggested that a distinct neural basis for language exists. Many psychologists believe that language is simply one aspect of general human cognitive abilities. Researchers disagree as to whether there is a sensitive period for language development in human beings, and evidence exists on both side of the argument.

6. Children acquire language rapidly, mastering their native tongues by the age of four or five. They do so in a series of stages that are associated with brain maturation. Babies make sounds from the earliest weeks of life and quickly develop three patterns of crying: the basic rhythmical pattern, the anger cry, and the pain cry. As infants grow, they communicate through gestures and intonation, as well as through sounds, and at about ten months, they appear to realize that agreed-upon signals can be used to accomplish their intentions. The first true words refer to immediate objects and events. During this one-word stage, infants rely on intonation and context, and they tend to *overextend* the meanings of words. Around the age of two, children begin to use **telegraphic speech**, making two-word utterances whose interpretation depends upon context. This simple language is highly structured, showing the use of **word order**, **inflection**, and **intonation**. Regardless of culture, two-word utterances express the same universal range of concepts. Between the ages of two and five, children seem to acquire grammatical rules in a fairly stable order; they do not progress directly toward adult grammar, but construct and discard a variety of temporary grammars as they go along. In the progress, they tend to **overregularize** words, extending a grammatical rule to instances in which it should not apply.

7. The debate over exactly how to explain the acquisition of language continues. In the biological view of Noam Chomsky, the acquisition of language is primarily a matter of maturation, based on special cognitive abilities built into the human brain. Behaviorists

believe that language acquisition is a matter of learning, with B. F. Skinner viewing it as the result of operant conditioning, in which the child's attempts at language are reinforced. Social-learning theorists believe that reinforcement plays some part, but that imitation is the key to language acquisition, with parents serving the children as models. A more recent view of language acquisition, which is based on pragmatics, sees language as emerging out of social interaction between infant and care giver, with the acquisition made easier by the special language all adults adopt when talking to infants.

8. The idea that language may determine the way in which we think about objects and events and may limit the matters we are able to think about is at the basis of Benjamin Lee Whorf's **linguistic relativity hypothesis**. If this hypothesis holds true, vocabulary may affect cognition because words determine the categories we use to perceive the world. However, although vocabulary may make it easier or harder to perceive certain distinctions, it does not make the perception of these differences impossible. If vocabulary affects thought, it does so by affecting the way information is encoded in memory or by encouraging us to notice similarities or by changing our self-concepts. If the linguistic relativity hypothesis holds up, grammar affects the way people think about time, space, and matter. Yet research has failed to confirm such claims. Some types of thought appear to be independent of language, and it is believed that universal characteristics of human thought processes may create universal linguistic structures. Studies of color terms illustrate this proposal, since no matter how few color terms a language possesses, its speakers can make small distinctions in hue. Color categories seem to reflect human physiological and cognitive characteristics.

KEY TERMS

anticipation
competence
constituent
discreteness
displacement
given-new strategy
grammar
inflection
intonation

iteration
linguistic relativity hypothesis
overextension
overregularization
performance
perseverations
phonemes
phonology
pragmatics

productivity
recursion
reversals
semanticity
semantics
speech act
syntax
telegraphic speech
word order

RECOMMENDED READINGS

CLARK, H. H., and E. V. CLAR. *Psychology and Language: An Introduction to Psycholinguistics.* New York: Harcourt Brace Jovanovich, 1977. Surveys the field of language and psychology. It reads very well and is illustrated nicely. Emphasis is given to the mental processes involved in the comprehension of language.

DAVIS, F. *Eloquent Animals: A Study in Animal Communication.* New York: Coward, McCann and Geoghegan, 1978. This book is about communication in animals, including apes, birds, and whales. It is a personal account of animal research provided by someone who visited various research sites.

FOSS, D. J., and D. T. HAKES. *Psycholinguistics: An Introduction to the Psychology of Language.* Englewood Cliffs, N.J.: Prentice-Hall, 1978. This book covers a great deal of research on language and language comprehension.

LLOYD, P., and M. BEVERIDGE. *Information and Meaning in Child Communication.* New York: Academic Press, 1981. Concerned with the problem of how children use language to convey information to others and to influence the actions of others. A body of empirical research on the ability of normal preschool and older retarded children of similar mental age is reported for the first time.

CHAPTER 14

Personality and Social Development

Differences among human beings appear in the first hours of life, and throughout development the differences steadily increase. Despite the obvious disparity in the behavior of newborn infants, they are more alike than three-year-olds; three-year-olds show more similarity than adolescents; and adolescents are much more alike than a group of seventy-year-olds. Divergent experiences combined with each person's heredity heighten individual differences. Yet, despite our differences, we develop in strikingly similar ways, passing through the same sequence of developmental events. To understand the development of personality and social behavior, we must both grasp these common processes and account for the wide diversity among people. Only the careful study of an individual life can show how any particular person becomes a unique individual, but general principles of personality and social development can be discerned. As we trace this aspect of development from infancy through later adulthood, we shall explore such general principles as they apply to human bonds, sex roles, friendship, aggression, and moral development, as well as examining the changing personal concerns of adults.

Perspectives on Personality and Social Development

Personality has been defined in many ways, and a great many theories of personality

structure and functioning have arisen to explain it, as we shall see in Chapters 18 and 19. Psychologists use the concept of personality to search for the factors that make individuals unique as well as for those that make any one individual seem to behave consistently in a variety of situations over long periods. According to one team of psychologists, **personality** is "those enduring characteristics of the person that are significant for interpersonal behavior" (Goodstein and Lanyon, 1975). How do personal patterns of aggressiveness, friendliness, or other "enduring characteristics" develop? What processes shape each person's personality and social behavior? In attempting to answer these questions, psychologists have taken various viewpoints; among the major approaches to personality are the biological perspective, Freud's psychosexual theory, the cognitive-developmental perspective, and the behavioral perspective.

The Biological Perspective

A biological basis for personality development has not been as firmly established as has the biological basis for other human capacities. However, some aspects of personality show clear traces of biological influence.

One aspect of personality that is influenced by biology is **temperament**, the individual's pattern of activity, susceptibility to emotional stimulation, response to stimuli, and general mood (Buss, Plomin, and Willerman, 1973). Differences in temperament can be seen among newborn infants, and heredity has been confirmed as a component of emotionality, activity, sociability, and impulsivity. One study (Buss, Plomin, and Willerman, 1973) showed that identical twins are much more similar in temperament than are fraternal twins, a resemblance that has been attributed to the twins' common genetic endowment. Researchers have not been able to conclude that specific personality traits such as self-confidence are inherited, but other studies of twins suggest a hereditary element in personality structure (Dworkin et al., 1976). Research also indicates that heredity may be involved in such aspects of personality as vocational interests and authoritarian attitudes: the members of biological families resemble one another in their attitudes and interests much more closely than do members of families in which the children were adopted at a very early age (Scarr and Weinberg, 1978).

Perhaps the most valuable contribution of the biological perspective is its reminder that our biologically determined characteristics interact with our experiences. For instance, a baby's temperament has a significant effect on the treatment the baby receives from parents and others (Thomas and Chess, 1977). An active, responsive baby will probably be given much more attention and receive much more social stimulation than an inactive, quiet baby. From this perspective, our individual uniqueness results from the complex interplay of biology and experience. The exact nature of these complex relationships, however, has not yet been determined.

Freud's Theory of Psychosexual Development

Sigmund Freud's concept of psychosexual stages has had a dominant influence on research into personality and social development. Freud (1933) maintained that from earliest infancy we are motivated by powerful biological instincts to seek pleasure and that at different ages, different parts of the body, called **erogenous zones**, become the focus of this pleasure. As these instinctive demands clash with the demands others make on us, we gradually learn to control our instincts and develop socially acceptable behavior.

According to Freud, from birth to adolescence children pass through five stages of psychosexual development: the oral stage, the anal stage, the phallic stage, a latency period, and the genital stage. In each stage, the child's interest is focused on the erotic pleasure that is derived from a different part of the body, and the shifts from one erogenous zone to another are directed by biological mechanisms. Freud argued that the adult personality results from the ways in which pleasurable impulses are channeled at each stage of development. At any stage, failure to resolve the conflict between the need to gratify impulses and the demand of parents for self-control can lead to **fixation** at that stage; as an adult such a person would show maladaptive behavior patterns dominated by the distinct traits of the critical stage (an oral personality or an anal personality).

During the **oral stage**, which occupies the first year of life, the baby's mouth is the primary source of sensual pleasure. In their active search for oral stimulation, babies suck, mouth, and chew on whatever they can find. During the **anal stage**, in the second and third years of life, the child's attention shifts to the anus and the pleasures of holding in and pushing out feces. These pleasures are barely established, however, before the child encounters the social demands of toilet training. Freudian theorists regard toilet training as a crucial event, a systematic attempt to impose social requirements on the child's natural impulses just as she or he has begun to gain some bodily control.

The **phallic stage** of psychosexual development covers the years from about three until five or so, when the child's attention is focused on the genitals and the pleasures of fondling them. It is at this stage that the child finds out about genital differences between the sexes. This discovery precipitates the **Oedipal conflict**, which Freud saw as the most important conflict in the child's psychological development. Children perceive themselves as rivals of their same-sex parents for the affection of the parent of the opposite sex. A boy's wish to win his mother for himself puts him in conflict with his father. A girl's desire for her father's love makes her long to shut out her mother. As we shall see, the resolution of the Oedipal conflict has important consequences for the development of sexual identity and morality.

From the phallic stage, children move into the fourth stage, a **latency period**. Until puberty, children's sexual impulses remain in the background, and they busy themselves exploring the world and learning new things. With the hormonal changes of puberty, sexual feelings reemerge and the **genital stage** begins. The focus in this final stage of psychosexual development is on the pleasures of sexual intercourse.

Although Freud's ideas have had a profound effect on psychological thought, they have been difficult to test. For example, his notions of "oral" and "anal" personality types have been supported, but there is no evidence that shows their origin in the oral or anal stages of development (Fisher and Greenberg, 1977). However, some aspects of Freud's thought, such as his belief that early childhood experiences have a crucial impact on adult personality and his notion that different stages of an individual's life present different, predictable problems in social and personality growth, have been widely accepted even by some psychologists who adhere to differing developmental perspectives. And another important theorist, Erik Erikson (1963), has expanded Freud's stages of personality development to cover the entire life span. However, Erikson places primary emphasis on the social rather than the sexual aspects of development (see Chapter 18).

The Cognitive-Developmental Perspective

Like Freudian theory, the cognitive perspective on the development of personality and social behavior is based on the concept of developmental stages. Instead of emphasizing the conflict between demands for gratification and the requirements of society, however, cognitive theorists emphasize thinking, reasoning, and role taking in the development of social behavior and personality.

In this view, which was heavily influenced by the approach of Jean Piaget, social behavior depends in part on the child's level of cognitive maturity. For example, the baby's sense of self has been shown to be closely connected with the development of the object concept, which was discussed in Chapter 12 (Bertenthal and Fischer, 1978). As cognitive skills develop, children are able to construct social schemes (conceptual frameworks) about social situations; these are analogous to schemes about the physical world, and they enable children to know the social world and act within it. Initially, people and objects are treated similarly, but as babies begin to differentiate themselves from the environment,

they construct schemes for social interaction. Each person's unique schemes then contribute to the development of enduring personal characteristics—that is, of personality.

As children advance through the stages of cognitive development, they develop increasingly complex schemes for social interaction. In the first sensorimotor stage, social behavior is primitive. It begins with a simple recognition of familiar persons and an early attachment to the mother or other person who cares for the child. To develop a sense of autonomy (independence), the child must develop a sense of the self as a being who is able to act on the environment in a planned and voluntary manner (Lee, 1976). This capacity for planning requires the child to engage in representational thinking and to use symbolic representations of objects and events. For example, a two-year-old may pick up a toy hammer to imitate Mother hanging a picture or Father repairing a chair. Such imitative role playing is essential for social and personality development.

Another cognitive ability seen as important in social and personality development is **role taking**. The infant is egocentric, seeing the world only from her or his own perspective. But the concrete-operational child is capable of taking the perspective of another person and can imagine what that person might be feeling. This operational capacity allows the child to develop elaborate social schemes that include the active roles of other people and the reciprocal nature of social interaction.

During adolescence, further connections between cognitive ability and social and personality development appear. As young people move into their teens and become capable of abstract reasoning, they begin to question the beliefs and teachings of their parents and to formulate their own system of values. It is no accident, then, that identity crises occur not during the elementary school years, but during adolescence and young adulthood, when we become able to analyze the meaning of our past and the direction of our future.

The Behavioral Perspective

Psychologists have also tried to explain the development of personality and social behavior on the basis of the principles of learning that were presented in Chapter 8. Such behavioral psy-

The Effects of Day Care

Nearly a million American children spend a good part of their waking hours in day-care centers (Connell, Layzer, and Goodson, 1979). This time is spent away from parents and under the influence of peers and substitute care givers. Some psychologists (Blehar, 1974) have worried about the effects of this separation, but others believe that attending a good day-care center helps children develop socially, intellectually, and emotionally (Bruner, 1980). Although not much can be said about the effects of commercial day-care centers in the United States (Belsky and Steinberg, 1978), children who attend high-quality day-care centers connected with American universities have been thoroughly studied, as have most children in day-care centers in Bermuda.

High-quality day care seems to have virtually no effect—either good or bad—on the general intellectual development of middle-class American children. Their scores on standardized tests are indistinguishable from those of, children who spend their preschool years at home. Among disadvantaged children, whose scores generally begin to drop during the preschool years, good day care appears to stave off the decline for several years. Such children seem less likely to repeat grades or to be placed in special education programs than disadvantaged children who have never been in day care (Belsky and Steinberg, 1978). In Bermuda, language development was affected by day care. Children attending high-quality centers were more advanced in language development than children at centers where there was little verbal interaction between adults and children (McCartney et al., 1982).

A child's bond with the mother seems impervious to the separation involved in good day care. Studies of children ranging in age from ten to forty-five months found no difference in reactions of day-care and home-reared children when the youngsters were separated from their mothers and placed with a stranger (Brookhart and Hock, 1976; Roopnarine and Lamb, 1978; Portnoy and Simmon, 1978). However, Bermudan children who entered day care in early infancy tended to be more emotionally maladjusted than children who spent the first year of life at home or in the care of a sitter (McCartney et al., 1982).

Day care places children among their peers at a much earlier age than was the custom a generation ago. This early interaction seems to make the youngsters more peer oriented and in later school years more sociable than home-reared children (Moore, 1975). There are two sides to social development, however, and good day care also seems to make children more aggressive, impulsive, and self-assertive. Among Bermudan children, those in centers with little verbal interaction between adults and children tended to be more aggressive, anxious, and hyperactive than children in day-care centers where adults and children did a good deal of talking (McCartney et al., 1982).

It seems clear that the verdict on day care is still out, and even clearer that the quality of the day-care center is extremely important, with the care givers having a greater influence than the level of physical equipment in the centers (McCartney et al., 1982).

chologists regard the unique qualities and enduring characteristics of each person as patterns of behavior that have been learned through reinforcement, punishment, or imitation. In this view, development is continuous, not broken into discrete stages. Specific characteristics are acquired in two ways: on the basis of direct experience, in which the person receives reinforcement or punishment connected with particular behavior; or, according to social-learning theory, through vicarious experience, in which the person observes and imitates a model's behavior.

An example of behavior acquired through direct experience is the infant's attachment to her or his care giver, which behavioral theorists believe is based on the warmth, comfort, and reduction of hunger that the infant associates with the care giver. This example is an instance of classical conditioning, but behavioral patterns are also acquired through operant conditioning.

Like grandpa, like grandson: according to social-learning theorists, we learn much of our behavior by imitating that of our parents or other adult models.

For example, a preschool boy who is big for his age may learn to achieve his goals by using physical aggression, because threatening or hurting smaller children often allows him to get what he seeks (Patterson, Littman, and Bricker, 1967). Much attention-seeking behavior in children, such as whining, is thought to be acquired in this way—that is, it achieves a desired end, and thus is reinforced.

Social-learning theorists argue that complex forms of social behavior and the enduring characteristics of personality are probably based on observational learning (Bandura, 1977). Imitating parents and peers allows a child to develop complex patterns of behavior without having to be directly reinforced. For example, children learn male or female roles at least in part by imitating the parent of the same sex. That is, the child observes the parent and rehearses behavior that will become appropriate as she or he matures. Children also observe the consequences of a model's behavior; when the model is reinforced, children are likely to imitate her or his behavior because they anticipate receiving the same reinforcement themselves (Bandura, 1965).

Thus, the behavioral perspective emphasizes the impact of the environment on the child. The child acquires behavioral patterns when specific behavior is reinforced—either directly or vicariously. Although social-learning theory stresses the central importance of cognitive activities in personality development (Mischel, 1973; Bandura, 1977), the focus is still on two factors: (1) the impact the environment has on the individual and (2) the continuous development of behavioral patterns rather than development through a series of discrete stages.

None of these perspectives by itself provides a satisfactory account of personality and social development. Each, however, has led to important advances in our understanding of the processes by which each human being develops into a unique individual. In the following discussions, each of these perspectives—and in some cases all of them—will be used to explain particular aspects of development.

Infancy

Infancy usually refers to approximately the first two years of life, or the period that begins at birth and ends when the child begins to use language (Bower, 1977). During this period, important social and personality development centers on the phenomenon of **attachment**, the emotional bond formed between the infant and her or his primary care giver. In later infancy, social relationships with peers develop and become increasingly important.

Attachment

Both Freudian and social-learning approaches to attachment explain the emotional bond of infant to care giver as a tie based on nurturance. That is, as the infant learns that the mother is the primary source of food, warmth, and comfort, an attachment to her develops as a positive response to a person who satisfies these needs. Attachment is also viewed as having adaptive significance, a concept discussed in Chapter 7. According to John Bowlby (1969), attachment helps babies to survive by keeping them near adults who provide them with necessary care and protection.

Although attachment applies to the infant's bond with her or his care giver, the parent also forms an emotional attachment to the infant. It has been proposed that the baby's "cute" appearance, typical of all immature mammals, naturally evokes positive emotional responses from adults (Lorenz, 1943; Alley, 1981). In addition, babies soon develop coos, smiles, and eye contact, which seem designed to promote parental affection. Some research suggests that interaction between infant and parents during the hours immediately after birth increases the strength of the parents' attachment to the baby (Klaus and Kennell, 1976), although later research has been unable to demonstrate any lasting effect on the relationship (Lamb, 1982).

According to Bowlby (1969), attachment does more than keep a baby alive. It helps infants develop essential social and cognitive skills by providing the emotional security that allows the infant to interact freely with people outside the family (promoting social development) and to explore the world (promoting competence).

The development of attachment has been extensively studied and appears to go through four phases (Bowlby, 1969; Ainsworth et al., 1978). In the first two or three months, babies respond to anyone and display no special behavior toward their mothers. Then, in the second phase, babies begin to discriminate among people and to respond to their mothers in special ways. At this age, however, babies will not protest if they are left with a sitter. At six or seven months, true attachment develops, and babies actively seek to remain close to their mothers, clinging to them

or crawling after them. Now babies show **separation distress**, protesting when they are parted from their mothers and expressing joy at the mother's return. A month or two after this third stage of attachment develops, babies also show **wariness of strangers**, perhaps responding to strangers with fear or withdrawal, looking away, frowning, or even crying at a stranger's approach. The reactions are intense when the baby's care giver is absent, but much milder when she or he is present. Indeed, if a stranger approaches slowly, pausing before coming near, the baby may smile and show no distress at all (Trause, 1977). Finally, when children are between two and three years old and their developing cognitive abilities allow them to interpret their mothers' behavior, the attachment relationship becomes more flexible and separation distress vanishes. In this final and lasting stage of attachment, children develop a "partnership" with their mothers.

Although most research on attachment has focused on the bond between infant and mother, Bowlby (1969) has suggested that attachment also develops to fathers and other care givers. When researchers finally looked at babies and fathers, they discovered that babies become attached to their fathers at about the same time they develop an attachment to their mothers, and to the same degree (Lamb, 1977; 1978).

Despite the deep attachment between infants and their parents, infants do not have to have a parent in constant attendance to thrive. As long as they have a stable relationship with a central care giver, they show normal social and emotional development (Rutter, 1971). Children have been reared successfully in Israeli kibbutzim, where they lived in residential nurseries and saw their parents for only a few hours a day. In these cases, the parents provided not the child's basic needs but emotional gratification (Beit-Hallahmi and Rabin, 1977).

The *nature* of the interaction between child and principal care giver, not the *amount* of time spent together, appears to be the important factor. When children who were placed in an experimental day-care center at three months were followed for more than two years, it became obvious that neither attachment to their mothers nor the children's cognitive development was any different from development among a control group of children reared within their own homes. Nor did a relationship with the two care givers at the day-care center affect the relation-

14.1 In Harlow's experiments, infant monkeys were presented with a new and frightening object (the mechanical bear) and were given a choice of two surrogate mothers to flee to. Infant monkeys of all ages greatly preferred the terrycloth mother to the wire mother, even though some of the infant monkeys received food only from the wire mother. (After Harlow, 1959.)

ship between the children and their mothers. Apparently children from homes that provide supportive relationships develop normally when most of their day is spent in a high-quality day-care center (Kagan et al., 1978).

Attachment in human beings appears to develop in ways that are similar to the attachment between baby rhesus monkeys and their mothers. Since it is impossible to experiment with human babies in order to search for the important factors in the development of the infant-mother bond, these young monkeys have been the subjects of experiments aimed at separating the various factors. Infant monkeys have been taken from their mothers and raised with two surrogate "mothers," one made of bare wire mesh and the other covered with soft terrycloth (Harlow and Harlow, 1966; 1969). Although the bare wire "mother" was equipped with a feeding mechanism and dispensed all the monkeys' nourishment, the monkeys became attached to the soft, cuddly, terrycloth "mother," clinging to it, running to it when frightened, and using it as a base from which to explore the world (see Figure 14.1). These studies seem to indicate that comfortable contact is more important than food in establishing attachment—at least among rhesus monkeys.

Attachment Deprivation

Opportunities to form emotional bonds are among the crucial learning experiences of the first few years of life. The importance of such emotional bonds is shown by children's responses to their temporary rupture. When young children are temporarily separated from their parents, as when they are admitted to a hospital, many show intense distress. They go through a period of active protest, then undergo a period of withdrawal and sadness, and finally become detached. When parents and child are reunited, the child may seem distant, although the aloofness may alternate with periods of excessive clinging (Bowlby, 1973; Schaffer, 1977). However, such separations rarely have lasting effects on the bond between children and their parents or on the children's later personality (Rutter, 1971).

When the opportunity to form an attachment is completely denied, the effects can be devastating and difficult to cure. Rhesus monkeys raised in total isolation behave in profoundly abnormal ways, clutching themselves and rocking, and later becoming apathetic and inactive or else acting in a bizarre manner that resembles schizophrenia. As adults both their sexual and social behavior is severely disturbed (Harlow, Harlow, and Suomi, 1971). However, other species of monkeys react to isolation differently (Sackett et al., 1981). Crab-eating macaques show abnormal individual behavior but are interested in exploring the world and behave almost normally when introduced to other monkeys. Pigtailed macaques show near-normal individual behavior and explore the world freely, but behave abnormally with other monkeys. Since social isolation and the lack of an emotional bond affect three closely related species of monkeys in such different ways, we should be cautious in applying specific effects found in rhesus monkeys to human beings.

Rhesus monkeys do recover from most of the effects of isolation if they are placed with younger normal monkeys (Suomi and Harlow, 1972). The younger monkeys gradually draw the isolates into social interaction and play. The nonthreatening behavior of young monkeys helps the isolates make up the developmental deficit caused by their earlier lack of attachment.

Few human infants are reared in social isolation, but when such children are discovered and restored to a supportive environment, they make great strides and can develop normal social functioning (Clarke and Clarke, 1977). A secure attachment is extremely important and undoubtedly gives a child a head start, for it provides a firm foundation on which social competence can be built. In fact, studies have found that two- and three-year-olds with secure attachments, who come from stable homes, are more competent and independent, more likely to be peer-group leaders, to be empathic, and to enjoy learning new skills than are two- and three-year-olds with insecure attachments (Matas, Arend, and Sroufe, 1978; Waters, Wippman, and Sroufe, 1979). Yet an insecure attachment does not doom a child to failure. The experiences of infancy can be reversed, and what happens during later childhood appears to be as influential as the events of infancy, as has been shown by the successful development of homeless children from war-torn areas of Greece and Korea who were adopted into American families (Kagan, 1978). If a child never has an opportunity to develop a secure attachment, some traces of early deprivation may remain. For example, a child who passes through a series of foster homes and forms only shallow, rapidly changing attachments may develop into a facile person who finds it difficult to form deep relationships (Bower, 1977).

The Beginnings of Social Interaction

Although babies depend upon adults for food, shelter, protection, and affection, they also show the beginnings of autonomy and a striving for competence. Babies appear to find satisfaction in exploring new aspects of their social world. They are attracted to novel situations and people, especially when the presence of a care giver provides security. For example, infants in a strange room did not cling to their mothers, but explored the area and readily approached unfamiliar toys and people (Rheingold and Eckerman, 1970; Eckerman and Rheingold, 1974).

Interactions with other babies and toddlers are not necessary for the development of social competence, but infants and toddlers do notice one another and find others like themselves attractive social objects. Familiarity seems especially important to peer interaction in infancy. Among pairs of nine-month-old babies, familiar peers played with each other much more than did peers who were strangers, and the play was more complex (Becker, 1977). Older infants certainly learn about the social world from peers, and a child's attitude—positive or negative—toward other children may be affected by experiences in the second year of life. Although the ability to sustain social interactions with another child increases throughout the second year, peer relationships probably do not become a major influence until a child acquires language and can begin to understand another child's intent (Bronson, 1981).

Childhood

Parents exert the greatest influence on development during childhood, but other adults, children, and television also affect the child. Once children start school, the influence of these other figures becomes progressively stronger.

As other influences increase, the role of the parent changes. During the child's infancy, the parent is primarily a nurturing, loving care giver. During childhood, the emphasis changes and parents switch their efforts from physical care to controlling the child's behavior and teaching the child to act in ways that society considers good or acceptable. This process of absorbing society's attitudes, values, and customs is called **socialization**, and it has a profound effect on the child's social and personality development. The goal of socialization is **internalization**—the child's incorporation of society's values to such an extent that violation of these standards produces a sense of guilt. Socialization plays an important part in the development of gender roles and peer relationships, in the control of aggression, and in the fostering of prosocial behavior.

Acquiring Gender Roles

Sex differences in behavior appear at a very early age, and these differences become magnified during childhood. As children grow, they acquire **gender roles**, adopting attitudes and patterns of behavior that society considers acceptable for their own gender. Some aspects of gender roles are determined by biology (bearing children or impregnating others); other aspects are arbitrary and vary from culture to culture (planting crops and marketing goods). Biology and socialization both play important parts in the development of gender roles, with socialization exaggerating whatever differences exist between the sexes at birth.

The Impact of Biology   There is no way to assess exactly how biology affects the behavior of boys and girls. We may get an idea of innate factors that could be responsible, however, if we observe the differences between male and female infants at and soon after birth, before they have had much chance to be affected by their environment.

Temperamental differences between boys and girls appear to exist at birth, and to center on activity, sensitivity to stimuli, and social interaction (McGuinness and Pribram, 1979). For example, when newborn infants were studied in a hospital nursery, boys were awake more than girls and showed more general activity—screwing up their faces, turning their heads, waving their hands, twitching, and jerking (Phillips, King, and Dubois, 1978). In addition, three-month-old baby boys fuss considerably more than girls (Moss, 1974); year-old boys tend to play more vigorously than girls (Maccoby and Jacklin, 1974); and year-old boys tend to prefer toys that require gross motor activity.

Such differences in temperament could underlie the consistently observed gender differences in style of play and in aggression. In most studies, preschool boys are more aggressive than preschool girls (Maccoby and Jacklin, 1980), and boys are much more likely to engage in rough-and-tumble play than girls (Blurton-Jones and Konner, 1973). These differences hold true in studies that have been done in various cultures.

Researchers believe that biology affects behavior through the action of male and female hormones on the fetal brain. For example, compared with their sisters, girls who were exposed before birth to male hormones showed much higher levels of rough, outdoor play and a lack of interest in play that involved dolls, babies, and traditional feminine roles (Erhardt and Meyer-Bahlburg, 1981). In another study, prenatal exposure to male hormones was linked with increased feelings of aggression in both boys and girls. Boys who were exposed to additional male hormones before birth had significantly higher scores than their brothers on tests designed to measure a person's potential for aggressive behavior, and girls who were similarly exposed had significantly higher scores than their sisters (Reinisch, 1981).

Yet biology does not work alone; instead, a child's predispositions interact with the way parents, siblings, peers, and other adults respond to them and with the physical environment. Thus, initial differences in their levels of activity may cause male and female babies to experience different kinds of care and social interaction. Active babies may elicit more attention than passive babies. In addition, the greater activity of infant boys may lead them to see and do more than girls, and at an earlier age. These differences in stimulation could influence both cognitive and personality development. In this way, innate temperamental differences between the sexes could produce a variety of differences in behavior linked with gender roles.

The Power of Socialization   Despite these possible biological influences, many aspects of gender roles have no relation to biology. If gender differences were primarily genetic in origin, then gender roles would be similar at all times and in all the world's societies. Although masculinity and femininity are always attached to opposite traits and jobs, the attributes of personality and occupations vary from culture to culture (Tavris and Offir, 1977). In the United States, for example, women are considered the emotional and irrational sex, but in Iran women are seen as cold and logical. In the United States, women are supposed to be gossips, but members of one Philippine tribe believe that it is men who cannot keep a secret.

Obviously, socialization is a powerful force in the development of gender roles. It is of primary importance in social-learning theory, which sees environmental factors as responsible for the development of **sex-typed behavior**, behavior that is regarded as appropriate for only one sex (Mischel, 1966). The process works through reinforcement, punishment, and observational learning, and the agents of socialization are parents, siblings, peers, teachers, other adults, and the media.

Parents are the primary influence on infants, and by the time they can walk, boys and girls get different treatment. For example, in one study (Fagot, 1978), toddler boys and girls reaped different rewards and punishments for the same behavior. Boys were encouraged for playing with blocks; girls were not. Girls were discouraged when they manipulated objects; boys were not. Girls were encouraged to ask for assistance and to "help"; boys were not. Thus, before their second birthdays, girls were learning to be dependent and boys were learning independence.

Fathers appear to be more concerned than mothers with gender roles. A study (Langlois and Downs, 1980) of preschoolers with their parents indicated that fathers tend to ridicule their young sons when they play with girls' toys, but mothers tend to reward them for such play. In addition, fathers' disapproving reactions toward both sons and daughters who play with toys "belonging" to the opposite sex is vigorous, whereas mothers react mildly to such play, disapproving it only in their daughters.

Parents are also viewed as important socializing agents in gender-role development by psychoanalytic theorists, but the process is seen as the outcome of the Oedipal conflict. In resolving the conflict, boys identify with their fathers and girls with their mothers; in **identification**, the child wants to be like the parent and so adopts whatever behavior the parent consistently displays. Cognitive-developmental theorists also believe that children identify with the same-sex parent, but believe that the identification is not the result of an Oedipal conflict but a consequence of **gender identity**, the child's understanding that she or he is female or male and will always remain so (Kohlberg, 1966). Once gender identity develops, children want to think, talk, and act as do others of their gender and identify with the parent in part to fulfill this goal. Social-learning theorists, in contrast, believe that children imitate all sorts of models—children, adults, television personalities—but that they are especially likely to imitate models who are warm and nurturant, as most parents are (Bandura and Walter, 1963). In one study (Perry and Bussey, 1979), eight- and nine-year-olds who watched a series of adult models later imitated those who showed sex-typed behavior, indicating that children do look for appropriate models and that such models need not be parents.

Peers also push children into their prescribed gender roles. In nursery school, boys who play with dolls or play dress-up are loudly criticized by other boys and girls; girls who play with boys' toys are mostly ignored (Fagot, 1977). When young children are punished by peers for such cross-sex play, they respond by stopping it almost immediately, although when punished for gender-appropriate play, they tend to keep on playing with the toy (Lamb, Easterbrooks, and Holden, 1980). Apparently three- and four-year-olds already know the gender-linked rules for toys and need only be reminded of them.

Teachers also unobtrusively steer children into traditional gender roles. They reinforce independence in boys and dependence in girls. In one study (Serbin et al., 1973), children were making paper party baskets; when it came time for the handle to be stapled to the basket, boys were routinely handed the stapler and told how to use it while girls watched as their teacher took their baskets and stapled on the handles for them. Teachers also serve as models, and their actions—indeed their very presence—leads children to enter activities. When investigators observed the effects of a nursery-school teacher on her or his pupils, girls responded to the teacher's presence or actions whether or not the activity was gender-appropriate, but boys responded only when the activity was appropriate for them (Serbin, Connor and Citron, 1981). Perhaps the fact that boys receive more criticism and ridicule than girls for cross-sex play is responsible for the difference in reactions.

The media—books, magazines, newspapers, movies, and television—also shape gender roles. Movies and television are especially likely to provide a predominance of stereotypical gender models. In fact, one study (Frueh and McGhee, 1975) that examined the link between gender roles and television viewing found that children who watched television more than twenty-five hours each week had significantly more stereotyped views of appropriate male and female behavior than did children who watched for ten hours or less.

Peer Relationships

In all cultures, children begin to have extensive contact with their peers during the preschool years. Such relationships are important because they are between equals. In relationships with adults, the power runs one way; the child is dependent and the adult has the responsibility of controlling and nurturing the youngster (Hartup, in press). Through equal interactions with their peers, children learn social skills, developing independence, cooperation, and ways to handle aggression; learn to evaluate themselves in comparison with others, developing a sense of their own identity; and develop a sense of belonging to a group (Rubin, 1980). The importance of peer relationships is shown by the repeated findings that children who are rejected by their peers are more likely than other children to drop out of school, to have later emotional and behavioral problems, and—among middle-class and upper-lower-class boys—to become delinquent (Ullman, 1957; Cowen et al., 1973; Roff, Sells, and Golden, 1972). The role that peers play in socialization can be seen by examining children at play, in individual friendships, and in groups.

Play   Peers and play are closely intertwined. Although play can be solitary, much of it is social and it encompasses a bewildering array of activities. To be considered play, an activity must meet four conditions: (1) it must be pleasurable; (2) it must be an end in itself, not a means to some goal; (3) it must be spontaneous and freely chosen by the player; and (4) it must involve some active engagement on the part of the player (Garvey, 1977).

Play is more than just a pleasant pastime, and its essential role in development has been spelled out by Jerome Bruner (1972). During play, the consequences of a child's actions are minimized, so that learning takes place in less risky circumstances. A four-year-old can practice such adult social roles as pilot, doctor, automobile driver, cook, warrior, parent, or spouse without suffering any of the economic, physical, or emotional consequences that accompany mistakes made in the actual performance of these roles. In the process, children learn about the conventions of society and about the importance of convention itself—both the conventions of language that allow us to communicate and the procedural conventions that, for example, keep us all driving on the right side of the road. Play also gives children a chance to experiment, trying out combinations of behavior that would never be attempted under the pressures of daily life. Such opportunities allow children to develop a flexible approach to problems and to

Play is more than fun. In it, a child can practice adult roles in a safe, scaled-down way.

anticipate new ways of using objects or putting together various subskills to accomplish a goal. Finally, play can serve a very personal function, in which the child works out problems or fulfills wishes through fantasy.

The symbolic play of childhood builds on the play of infancy, and the year-old infant's first symbolic actions, such as pretending to drink from a cup, rapidly develop into adept flights of imagination. Toward the end of the second year, a child can pretend that a spoon is a doll and use Mother's handkerchief as a "blanket" (Belsky and Most, 1981). By this time children have become so skilled at make-believe that they can use dissimilar objects in imaginative play, pretending that a toy car is a cup of tea. When one little boy at this age was asked to imitate a researcher who drank tea from a cup, he picked up a piece of lint from the carpet and pretended to drink from it (Jackowitz and Watson, 1980).

Symbolic play thrives during the preschool years, as children act out roles they see around them, pretend to be television characters, or develop imaginary playmates. More than half the preschoolers in one study had imaginary playmates, with only children being most likely to imagine a companion (Singer and Singer, 1981).

As children grow, play becomes increasingly social. One sort of social play, rough-and-tumble play, is concentrated among boys. In **rough-and-tumble play**, children run, chase and flee, wrestle, jump up and down, beat at each other without landing blows, laugh, and fall down, smiling all the while (Blurton-Jones, 1976). Although rough-and-tumble play sometimes develops into aggressive play, usually it does not. The gender difference in such play does not seem to be solely a matter of boys' desire for vigorous activity since, given an opportunity, many girls play as vigorously as boys. Among one group of preschoolers, girls were as active on a trampoline as boys, but shunned the rough-and-tumble play that often followed boys' interactions. The investigator speculates that an action that boys interpret as an invitation to roughhouse is seen by girls as a threatening bid for dominance (DiPietro, 1981).

After the flowering of make-believe in the preschool years, informal make-believe eventually goes underground and takes the form of fantasy and daydreams; it is transformed into play without action (Vygotsky, 1978). In its place develop games, which center on shared rules. Among younger elementary schoolchildren, the rules are binding, but as children get older, they understand that game rules are another convention that can be modified if all agree (Piaget, 1932).

Researchers have used games to explore the effect of cooperation upon subsequent activities. In one study (Orlick, 1981), kindergarten children were taught either games that required cooperation or traditional games that centered on individual effort. Afterward, children who played cooperative games were more likely than children who played traditional games to share their candy with others.

Friendship   Most children have special relationships with one or more of their peers. These friendships change in meaning, depth, and complexity as children grow, and the changes are linked to cognitive development, with friendships becoming increasingly reciprocal.

According to Robert Selman (1980; Selman and Jacquette, 1977), among preschoolers friends are important as playmates and in most cases, children's friends are whomever they happen to be playing with. In the early school years, friendship becomes one-way assistance; a child's friends are valued because they do what the child likes to do. During late childhood comes fair-weather cooperation, in which a child and her or his friend adapt to each other's needs but loyalty, sensitivity, and intimacy play little part in the relationship. Only in adolescence do intimacy and mutual sharing characterize friendship; friendships change from the cooperation of two individuals to a sense of shared identity (Youniss, 1980).

Friends generally resemble each other; a pair of friends are usually the same age, the same sex, the same race, and enjoy the same things (Hartup, in press). If the friendship endures, the resemblance increases (Duck and Craig, 1978; Kandel, 1978). Although personality differences between friends remain, their behavior, attitudes, and values become more similar, indicating that friends apparently socialize each other.

Groups   Children also socialize one another within the peer group, where some children are inevitably more popular than others. Popular children seem to have all the valued qualities. They tend to have attractive names; to be physically attractive, friendly, sociable, intelligent, achieving; to have moderately positive self-con-

In children's play groups, there is normally a hierarchical structure, with clearly acknowledged leaders and followers.

cepts; and to have older siblings. They also praise other children freely, help and protect them, give them gifts, pay attention to them, and initiate conversations (Masters and Furman, 1981). Although most aggressive children are not excluded, a child who disrupts the group with inappropriate blows, verbal abuse, or aggressive acts may indeed be kept out of the group. In middle childhood, rejected children are often described as dishonest, irritating, or immature (Hartup, in press). Isolated children, who are simply ignored by the group, either lack social skills or do not use the ones they have.

Children inevitably develop a hierarchical structure in their groups. Popularity does not, however, guarantee that a child will be a leader. The child leader tends to direct, coordinate, and sanction the actions of other children, and each group selects its leaders in terms of specific characteristics (Sherif and Sherif, 1964). Studies of nursery-school play groups (Strayer and Strayer, 1976) indicate that dominance is established by physical attack, threats, and struggles over objects. Despite the role of aggression in establishing dominance, the most dominant child is rarely the most aggressive (Strayer, 1977). As children grow, the dominant child changes from one who knows how to hang onto and use possessions to the child who is good at directing play and games. As children reach adolescence, the basis for dominance will shift again (Hartup, in press).

Although some psychologists (e.g., Bronfenbrenner, 1970) believe that the segregation of children into age-graded groups (which is encouraged by the structure of the educational system) can erode the power of parental and social value systems, studies indicate that serious conflict between child and adult values is mostly illusory. Research (e.g., Costanza and Shaw, 1966) has indeed shown that a child's susceptibility to peer influence increases with age, but it also shows that the power of the peer group reaches a peak and then gradually declines during adolescence. In one study (Berndt, 1979), children's tendencies to conform to their parents' wishes concerning neutral activities (such as going for a walk when they wanted to play cards) decreased between the third and ninth grades, while their tendencies to conform to antisocial pressure from their peers (cheating or stealing) increased sharply. Third graders who found peer and parental values in conflict generally adhered to parental values; sixth graders seemed to live in two worlds, each with its own sphere of influence that did not conflict; but ninth graders found antisocial peer pressure hard to resist. Despite this increased peer pressure, however, ninth graders continued to conform to parental values in matters with positive social implications: achievement, academic performance, career aspirations, and fundamental moral principles. Within a few years, antisocial peer pressure loses its power;

among eleventh and twelfth graders, adolescents no longer felt compelled to conform to the anti-social wishes of their peers.

Prosocial Development

Although peer pressure toward antisocial behavior becomes stronger during the school years, children often behave in altruistic ways, sharing their toys or coming to the rescue of another child. Such actions are examples of **prosocial behavior**—action intended to benefit another person, taken without expectation of external reward, and generally involving some cost to the individual (Mussen and Eisenberg-Berg, 1977). When prosocial behavior springs from a combination of emotional distress at another's plight and understanding of her or his needs, it is referred to as **altruism**. As children grow, their concepts of altruism, justice, and morality change, as do the reasons they give for their moral and ethical acts. These changes are the result of cognitive and social development.

Moral Behavior Preschoolers are reluctant to share their toys or to give away candy or money. Although spontaneous acts of altruism can be seen in nursery school, prosocial behavior increases only slightly during these years (Hartup, in press). During the early school years, children steadily become more generous, with prosocial behavior increasing until children are about ten years old, then leveling off (Mussen and Eisenberg-Berg, 1977).

The effects of specific situations on such behavior have been studied. For example, children often behave generously after observing an adult act in an unselfish manner (Bryan, 1975). In addition, reinforcement for altruistic acts is effective. Children who are praised for their generosity often behave more generously, but the form of praise affects children of different ages in a different way. In one study (Grusec and Redler, 1980), eight-year-olds who were praised for themselves ("You are a very nice and helpful person") transferred their generosity to other situations several weeks later, but eight-year-olds who were praised for their acts ("That was a helpful thing to do") did not. However, ten-year-olds were generous in later situations whether they had earlier been praised for their acts or for themselves, perhaps reflecting the older children's greater flexibility in interpreting rules.

Altruism and friendship interact in a complex manner. Despite the importance of friends to children, they are not more altruistic with friends than with acquaintances. When kindergartners, second-graders, and fourth-graders were paired either with best friends or with acquantances on tasks in which altruism would cost the children money but increase their friends' take, girls and kindergarten boys treated friends and acquaintances alike. Second- and fourth-grade boys, however, were more likely to show altruism toward acquaintances than toward friends (Berndt, 1981b). Although in many situations the informality that accompanies friendship results in greater cooperation (Newcomb et al., 1979), when cooperation means that boys will lose a competition, informality apparently allows them to be less altruistic.

In a similar study (Berndt, 1981a) of competition among friends, children could arrange to win, to lose, or to share nickels equally with a friend. Now fourth-graders were more altruistic than first-graders, and there were no sex differences. When the same children who had been tested in the fall were tested again the following spring, the deeper friendships among the fourth-graders became apparent; altruism between fourth-grade friends increased while it decreased between first-grade friends.

Moral Judgment Various attempts have been made to explain children's increasing inclination toward prosocial behavior. Psychoanalytic theorists believe that moral behavior depends upon the establishment of guilt. When children identify with a parent, they internalize the parent's moral code. Thereafter, each time a child is tempted to violate the parent's standards, the child feels guilty. Social learning theorists believe that moral behavior is a matter of learning, the result of reinforcements, punishments, and delayed imitation.

Such analyses of behavior have little interest for cognitive-developmental theorists, who believe that the study of moral development should focus on changes in the way children think about moral choices and how they justify their decisions. According to Lawrence Kohlberg (1969), children pass through six developmental stages of moral reasoning, with each stage in the invariable sequence developing out of its predecessor, so that children must understand the reasoning involved in one stage before they can progress to the next. These stages are said to be universal—to characterize the development of moral reasoning in all societies.

Kohlberg's six stages form three basic levels of moral judgment. In the first, **preconventional level** (stages 1 and 2), the child judges moral issues in terms of pain or pleasure or of the physical power of authority. At the second, **conventional level** (stages 3 and 4), the child—or adult, because most adults reason on the conventional level—decides moral issues in terms of maintaining the social order and meeting the expectations of others. At the highest, **principled level** (stages 5 and 6), the person judges moral issues in terms of self-chosen principles and standards based on universal ethical principles and on the ideals of reciprocity and human equality. In Kohlberg's view, a moral decision always involves a conflict in values; hence, the decision itself is not important, but the justification given for it. In any moral dilemma, a person at any stage may decide either way.

Although Kohlberg's theory is appealing, it has been criticized on several counts, including a lack of clear distinction between stages at any level, the lack of any correlation between the particular stages and behavior (Kurtines and Greif, 1974), the fact that it can be applied only to constitutional democracies (Harkness, 1980), and its apparent sexist bias (Gilligan, 1977). The charge of sexism comes from Kohlberg's relegation of compassion, responsibility, and obligation—qualities stressed in the socialization of girls—to the conventional level of reasoning. Despite this placement, Kohlberg (1971) insists that all moral rules are interpreted by taking the role of another. Studies (Hoffman, 1977) have consistently shown girls to be more empathic (if not more altruistic) than boys and a tendency for boys (who are socialized to be independent) to respond to problems with a problem-solving approach instead of with empathy.

A child's gender also affected the results in other research (Leahy, 1981), which found that child-rearing practices were linked to adolescents' levels of moral reasoning. Boys and girls sometimes responded differently to similar practices by their parents. Among boys, authoritarian methods of child rearing resulted in reasoning at lower levels, whereas less punitive practices and the encouragement of autonomy led to principled reasoning. Among girls, however, while encouragement of autonomy encouraged principled reasoning, so did a high degree of control and supervision on the part of the father. Nurturance (acceptance, encouragement, and warmth) was linked to principled reasoning in both sexes.

No gender differences have been found in children's ideas of equity, or fairness, another aspect of prosocial behavior. The concept of equity is connected to the development of logical reasoning, and children's allocation of rewards for work could be predicted by their scores on tests of mathematical reasoning (Hook, 1978). Preschoolers either operated on self-interest, taking the lion's share no matter how little labor they contributed, or else gave everybody equal shares, no matter how the labor was divided. Between the ages of six and twelve, children gave more rewards to people who worked more and less to people who worked less, but no attempt was made to see that rewards were proportional to effort. (A child who did 80 percent of the work might get only 55 percent of the rewards.) Not until children were thirteen did the idea of equity as reward proportional to effort appear.

Cognitive development and moral development are related. Other studies have found a connection between a child's level of cognitive development—judged by the ability to perform Piagetian logical tasks—and her or his level of moral reasoning (Selman, 1976; Kuhn et al., 1977); between a child's level of cognitive development and her or his concept of justice (Damon, 1975); and between the ability to understand another's thoughts and feelings and moral reasoning (Moir, 1974). Yet similar conduct can result from great disparities in moral reasoning, and precisely how these factors interact in the process of moral development is not clear.

Control of Aggression

Children are expected to become increasingly altruistic as they get older, but they are expected to gain control over their aggressive impulses early. Parents begin imposing restraints on their children's behavior at the first signs of temper tantrums, blows, or the hurling of toys in anger. As they grow, children learn that aggression must be restrained at home and in the classroom, but that it is applauded on the football field. Thus, they must learn where, when, and how to express their aggressiveness.

Parents often try to channel children's aggressive impulses into socially acceptable activities—boxing, for example.

Children—and adults—show two major forms of aggression: **hostile aggression**, which aims at hurting another person, and **instrumental aggression**, which aims at acquiring or retrieving objects, territory, or privileges (Feshbach, 1964). Because very young children find it difficult to understand that another person might not react to an incident as they do, they rarely believe that other people have negative intentions toward them. Nor do they interpret their own frustration as a threat to their self-esteem. Thus, their aggression is predominantly instrumental. In a study (Hartup, 1974) that followed children for ten weeks, four- to six-year-olds showed more aggression than six- to eight-year-olds, and the difference was primarily due to a decline in instrumental aggression among the older children. As children get older, they also tend to switch from physical to verbal aggression, which is considerably safer.

Reinforcement, punishment, and observational learning affect the amount of aggression children display. Negative reinforcement is ap-

parently quite important in the encouragement of aggression. Much childish aggression comes about because a child's past outbursts of violence have stopped teasing, put a halt to parental nagging, or ended the child's being ignored by a parent or teacher (Patterson, 1980). There are also positive reinforcements connected with aggression, and the immediate consequences of a child's blow affect whether the child will hit again in the same situation (Patterson and Cobb, 1973). In many cases, a young child who successfully counterattacks an aggressive bully will later become an aggressor and attack a third child (Patterson, Littman, and Bricker, 1967). When aversive stimuli arouse a child's emotions, whether the child will respond with aggression depends upon how she or he has learned to cope with stress and how effective these methods have been (Bandura, 1973). One child might seek help, another might try harder, a third might give up, a fourth might hit. Although anger or frustration might increase the likelihood of an aggressive response, neither is necessary.

From models children learn both aggressive responses and the probable consequences of their use. A parent who spanks a child for fighting is modeling aggression and teaching the child that in some circumstances it is appropriate to hit. However, parents are not the only models for aggression. Older siblings, peers, other adults, and television and film characters also serve as models.

Television brings aggressive models into the home, and as soon as infants attend to the glowing tube, they see aggression modeled in cartoons, dramatic shows, sporting events, and the nightly news. The long-term effects of televised violence are uncertain, since children do not imitate every action they observe. In a nine-month study of nursery-school children (Singer and Singer, 1981), researchers found a connection between the regular watching of action-adventure television programs and aggressive behavior. The effect was especially strong among boys; regular television viewers who were low in aggression at the beginning of the study showed consistent increases in aggression over the months; those who were low in aggression but watched little television showed no such increase.

In the only study (Eron et al., 1972) that has followed the same children as long as a decade, boys who watched the most televised violence as nine-year-olds were also the most aggressive nineteen-year-olds. These investigators believe that a preference for watching violence contributes to the development of aggressive behavior.

Not all research finds the same connection between violence on the screen and violence in life (e.g., Feshbach and Singer, 1971), and some investigators believe that television instead teaches children to become passive in the face of aggression (Gerbner and Gross, 1976). Since behavior results from a combination of the child's predispositions and experience, the piling up of different experiences over the years means that no two children will respond to the same situation in precisely the same manner.

Adolescence

Adolescence is the period between reproductive maturity and the assumption of adult responsibilities. Its beginning is marked by **puberty**, the period of sexual maturation that transforms a child into a physical adult. A major concern during this phase of life is the need to establish an independent identity, and decisions made at this time can have lasting effects on the task. Individual decisions, such as whom to date, whether to have intercourse, take drugs, select a certain major, work part-time, or become politically active, combine to form a more or less consistent core that shapes personality and the course of an individual life (Marcia, 1980). In time, these early decisions influence the major decisions (occupation and marriage, among others) each adolescent eventually faces.

Physical Maturation

Long before the emotional and social conflicts that are associated with adolescence erupt, hormonal changes begin to have their effects on a young person's body. These changes trigger the maturation of the reproductive organs and the development of secondary sex characteristics, such as facial hair in males and breasts in females, a process that generally takes about four years to complete (Peterson and Taylor, 1980). Although the timing of these changes varies considerably with the individual, puberty usually begins between the ages of ten and twelve in girls and twelve and fourteen in boys (Muuss, 1975).

With physical maturation, the urges associated with sexual maturity arise. Changing sexual behavior will be discussed in Chapter 17, but the first forays into dating are not associated with sexual maturation itself but with peer pressure. Adolescents who fail to date are dropped by their peer group, and studies have found that chronological age (which is related to the peer group) is a better predictor of the onset of dating than is sexual maturation (Dornbusch et al., 1981).

Social Maturation

The sexual maturation heralded by puberty transforms the child physically into an adult. But whether the child is assigned the social status of adulthood after puberty depends on the culture in which she or he lives. In some societies, children who have attained reproductive maturity are considered working members of the adult community and may start their own families. For them there is no adolescence, no transitional period between childhood and adulthood (Knepler, 1969; Muuss, 1975). In Western societies, however, the child who has passed through puberty is not yet considered an adult. Instead, she or he enters a transitional period that lasts until the individual is at least seventeen or eighteen years old.

Although the adolescent has not yet assumed adult responsibilities, many have begun to work at part-time jobs. The proportion of adolescents who are gainfully employed rises from 42 percent among high-school sophomores to 63 percent among seniors (National Center for Educational Statistics, 1981). How does the dual responsibility of school and job affect adolescents? A recent study (Greenberger, Steinberg, and Vaux, 1981) indicates that working adolescents report fewer symptoms of physical ailments than those who have no jobs, and that among boys, there are also fewer reports of psychological distress. However, other indications of stress do appear among adolescents who work. Even after controlling for extra income, time spent working is linked with increased use of cigarettes, alcohol, and marijuana.

Establishing an Identity

Although many of them would never admit it, young adolescents are still dependent on their parents for security, guidance, and support.

Within a decade, however, most generally provide for their own needs. Along with the outward signs of independence, such as making their own decisions and becoming financially responsible, most young adults have gained a sense of themselves as separate, autonomous people. The establishment of this separate identity is the major developmental task of adolescence. A person who manages this transition successfully is ready to meet the challenges of adulthood. One who fails to do so is severely handicapped as a young adult.

As Erik Erikson (1963) has pointed out, developmental change in adolescence often disrupts the concept of self. The physical, sexual, and social demands on the adolescent may produce internal conflict, an **identity crisis**, that requires the adolescent to develop a new self-concept. To resolve this crisis, adolescents must incorporate their new physical and sexual attributes, developing a sense of continuity between what they were in the past and what they will become. This is what is meant by **identity**: an individual's sense of personal sameness and continuity.

According to Erikson, adolescents often try out different roles in the process of establishing an identity. An adolescent might try her hand at the school paper, become absorbed in the study of philosophy, and be drawn into a political movement. Such experimentation allows adolescents to form some idea of possible adult lives without irrevocably committing themselves to any one. Such experiments are possible only in societies, like the United States, which provide a lengthy period of adolescence and do not force young people into permanent adult roles soon after puberty.

In the United States, many youths do not develop a stable identity until the college years, or even later. Interviews with college students suggest that young people are at one of four levels in the achievement of an independent identity (Marcia, 1980). At one extreme are those who have experienced a period of conflict and indecision concerning their values and choice of career, but who have successfully resolved that crisis and are now strongly committed to an occupation and an ideology. They have established an identity. At the other extreme are the drifters —those who are uncommitted to any occupation or ideology and who seem unconcerned. Somewhere between these extremes are two other types: those in the midst of resolving an identity crisis and those so strongly committed to their parents' values and choice of a career for them

that it is difficult to tell where the parents end and the young person begins. When students were interviewed first as freshmen and later as seniors, 2 percent had already established a firm sense of both occupational and ideological identity when they entered college, and 19 percent had done so by the end of their college careers (Waterman, Geary, and Waterman, 1974).

The common assumption is that all adolescents go through a stormy period as they struggle to establish an identity. But such turmoil and conflict do not commonly accompany adolescence, which is generally more peaceful and less racked by conflict than people suppose. Most adolescents cope well with their developmental tasks and move smoothly into adulthood (Offer, Ostrov, and Howard, 1981). The fabled generation gap has also been vastly oversold. By the time adolescents are sixteen or seventeen years old, they have begun to accept conventional adult standards (Berndt, 1979). Further, studies of political attitudes have shown that parents and adolescents agree closely on most matters, falling out only over such topics as sex and drugs (Gallatin, 1980).

Adult Development

Adulthood has sometimes been described as the period of life that begins when we stop growing up and start growing old. It has also been characterized as a period of little change in personality, and many theorists have claimed that among normal adults personality remains quite stable. For example, Freud believed that many of a person's characteristics are established during childhood and that identity is fixed early in adulthood. But society has changed greatly since Freud's day, and for the first time a significant portion of the population is middle-aged or older. In earlier times life expectancy was shorter, and few people survived past the age of forty. Today, there are more than 50 million men and women in the United States—one-fourth of the total population—who are in the midlife period from age forty to sixty. Furthermore, in the year 2010, when members of the post-World War II baby boom join the aging, 16 of every 1,000 Americans will have passed their sixty-fifth birthday. As the population has grown older, developments and changes in personality and behavior during adulthood have received increased attention. As a result, the awareness has grown that adulthood is as complex, as dynamic, and as liable to change in important ways as is childhood or youth (Neugarten, 1979).

Changes in Personal Concerns

People's personal concerns change across the life span; even their gender-related attitudes and behavior alter. In one study (Feldman, Beringer, and Nash, 1981), their stage of family life affected people's feelings of compassion, tenderness, and autonomy. Single men and women were less compassionate, less tender, and more socially inhibited than were the married. Becoming parents appeared to make people more traditional; women's feelings of tenderness increased, as did men's feelings of leadership and autonomy. But becoming grandparents made grandmothers more autonomous and grandfathers more compassionate and tender.

Shifts in the attitudes and orientations of men and women have also been explored by Roger Gould (1972). In one study Gould interviewed all the patients in group therapy at a psychiatric outpatient clinic. In a second study he gave questionnaires to 524 white, middle-class men and women who were not psychiatric patients. Among both groups, the same clear differences in the major concerns and key attitudes appeared at various ages. Young adults (ages twenty-two to twenty-eight) felt autonomous and focused their energy on attaining the goals they had set. But members of the next age group (twenty-nine to thirty-four) had begun to question their goals, wondering, "What is life all about now that I have done what I am supposed to do?" Those between thirty-five and forty-three continued to question the values they had lived by, but they had also developed a new awareness of the passage of time, asking, "Is it too late for me to change?" With the onset of middle age (forty-three to fifty), adults entered a period of greater stability, of acceptance of the structure of life and of greater satisfaction with their spouses. This last trend continued after age fifty. As people gained awareness of mortality, they came to value personal relationships more highly and to develop a desire to contribute something meaningful to society.

From interviews with more than 2,000 adults, Bernice Neugarten (1976) has also found characteristic psychological changes in adulthood. Among the middle-aged, she found a greater concern with inner life, with introspection, and conscious reappraisal of themselves. They also showed a change in time perspective and looked at life in terms of time left to live instead of the time since birth. This changed perspective led them to an awareness of personal mortality and the recognition of death as a real possibility.

Ways of Aging

Making the transition from one phase of adulthood to the next is not always easy. But most people cope with major life transitions—such as the departure of children from the home, retirement from a career, the death of a parent, and the approach of death—without undue stress (Neugarten, 1976). These events become traumatic only when they are not anticipated or when they occur at an unexpected time in the life cycle. Thus, the death of a child is much more stressful than the death of a parent, and divorce when a

Most old people are not frail and sick, contrary to the common stereotype. Many are still active and vigorous, even into advanced old age.

woman is forty is more difficult to accept than widowhood when she is sixty-five. A study of men who had retired from their life's work (Barfield and Morgan, 1970) found that nearly 70 percent of those who retired as planned were content with their new status, as compared with less than 20 percent of those who retired unexpectedly due to layoffs or poor health.

Older people are often seen by the young in terms of stereotypes that apply only to a minority of the aged—the frail, the sick, the isolated, and the needy. But old people are not a homogeneous group, and their lives differ more than do the lives of the young. People are vigorous for so much longer than they used to be that some seventy-year-olds still consider themselves "middle-aged," and Neugarten (1980) has proposed calling the healthy, active majority of old people the "young-old," reserving the term "old-old" for those who fit the stereotype. Most old people are not lonely; a national survey found a steady decline in loneliness with age, and people who

were more than seventy were the least lonely of all (Rubenstein, Shaver, and Peplau, 1979). The elderly were more satisfied with their friendships than the young, had higher self-esteem, and felt more independent than did young adults.

As long as the expected rhythm of the life cycle is not disrupted, most adults cope successfully even with the final stage of life. For example, a study (Lieberman and Coplan, 1970) of elderly people showed that those who were living in familiar and stable surroundings were not afraid of dying, but that those who were about to be admitted to a home for the aged and thus were living in an abnormal, uncertain situation were afraid of death. An older person's attitude toward life and death depends upon previous experience as well as upon present status. Those who feel they have achieved their goals, who have good incomes, and are well-educated have the most positive attitudes toward their own deaths (Keith, 1979) and have successfully dealt with life's last developmental task: death.

SUMMARY

1. Various views exist concerning the way that **personality**, or one's enduring personal characteristics, develops. According to the biological perspective, some aspects of personality are biologically determined. Differences in **temperament** (individual patterns of activity, susceptibility to stimulation, and general mood) exist from birth, and these biologically determined characteristics interact with experience. According to Freud, human beings are motivated to seek pleasure, and during **psychosexual development** the focus of this erotic pleasure shifts from one **erogenous zone** of the body to another. Consequently, he called the psychosexual stages the **oral stage**, the **anal stage**, the **phallic stage**, a **latency period**, and the **genital stage**. If the conflict between impulse and control at any stage is not resolved, the personality will remain **fixated** at that stage. According to the cognitive-developmental perspective, social behavior depends in part on the child's level of cognitive maturity. **Role taking**, or being able to imagine oneself in another's place, plays an important part in social and personality development. According to the behavioral perspective, personality and social behavior follow the principles of learning.

"Enduring characteristics" are patterns of behavior that have been learned through reinforcement, punishment, and imitation.

2. During infancy, social and personality development center around **attachment**, the bond between an infant and her or his main care givers. A secure attachment not only helps babies survive, but also encourages the development of social and cognitive skills by providing the emotional security that allows the baby to interact freely with others and to explore the world. Once attachment has developed, babies show **separation distress**, protesting at separation from a care giver and showing joy at the care giver's return, and then **wariness of strangers**. The nature of the interaction between infant and care giver, not the amount of time spent together, is the important aspect of the bond. Although a secure attachment provides a firm foundation for social competence, the experiences of infancy can be reversed. What happens during later childhood appears to be as influential as the events of infancy.

3. As children grow, the parents' primary role switches from physical care to **socialization**,

in which children absorb society's attitudes, values, and customs. With **internalization**, the child incorporates these standards so that their violation produces a sense of guilt. Children soon acquire **gender roles**, attitudes and behavior considered gender appropriate in their society. Biology apparently has some effect on gender-related behavior, because temperamental differences between boys and girls exist at birth. These gender-based predispositions interact with the way people respond to children and with the physical environment to produce behavioral differences. Socialization also has a powerful impact on **sex-typed behavior**, behavior that is considered appropriate for only one sex. According to social-learning theorists, parents, peers and other adults use rewards and punishment to steer children toward sex-typed behavior; these people also serve as models of such behavior. Psychoanalytic theorists believe that sex-typed behavior appears when children **identify** with the parent of the same sex and adopt the parent's behavior patterns. Cognitive-developmental theorists believe that identification must follow **gender identity**, the child's understanding that she or he will always be male or female.

4. Peer relationships are important because they are between equals. Through interactions with their peers, children learn social skills, learn to evaluate themselves in comparison with others, develop a sense of their own identity, and develop a sense of belonging to a group. Children's play has an essential role in development because it minimizes the consequences of a child's actions and gives children a chance to try out behavior that would never be attempted under the pressure of daily life. Children's friendships change in meaning, depth, and complexity as children grow; these changes are linked with cognitive development and the relationships become increasingly reciprocal. Popularity does not guarantee group leadership, for each group selects its leaders in terms of specific characteristics. A child's susceptibility to peer influence increases with age, peaking in early adolescence and then declining.

5. **Prosocial behavior**, action intended to benefit another person, taken without expectation of external reward, and generally involving some cost, is the result of cognitive and social development. Although spontaneous acts of **altruism** appear among children in nursery school, prosocial behavior increases very little until children enter elementary school. At that time it begins to increase steadily, leveling off when children are about ten years old. Psychoanalytic theorists believe that prosocial behavior depends upon guilt, which is established when children internalize parental moral codes. Social-learning theorists believe that prosocial behavior results from reinforcements, punishment, and delayed imitation. Cognitive-developmental theorists focus not on prosocial behavior, but on children's reasoning about moral problems. According to Kohlberg, children pass through three levels of moral development: the **preconventional level**, in which they judge moral issues in terms of pain, pleasure, or the physical power of authority; the **conventional level**, in which they judge moral issues in terms of maintaining the social order and meeting the expectations of others; and the **principled level**, in which they judge moral issues in terms of self-chosen principles based on universal ethical principles, on reciprocity, and on human equality. Although cognitive development and moral judgment are related, similar conduct can result from great disparities in moral reasoning, hence the way these factors interact in moral development is not clear.

6. Children must learn how to control their aggressive impulses and where they may be expressed. Aggression among young children is primarily **instrumental aggression**, in which the aim is to retrieve or acquire objects, territory, or privileges. As children get older, they show less aggressive behavior and when it appears, it is likely to be **hostile aggression**, in which the aim is to hurt another person. Reinforcement, punishment, and observational learning affect the amount of aggression children display. Television provides aggressive models, and some studies have shown that children (especially boys) who watch a good deal of violent television may become more aggressive as a result. However, some psychologists believe that televised aggression can teach passivity in the face of aggression.

7. Adolescence begins with the onset of **puberty**, the period of sexual maturation. Although some cultures equate adulthood and repro-

ductive maturity, Western societies provide the transitional period of adolescence, which lasts until the individual is seventeen or eighteen years old. The major developmental task of adolescence is the establishment of **identity**: the individual's sense of personal sameness and continuity. According to Erik Erikson, the physical, sexual, and social demands on the adolescent often produce internal conflict, an **identity crisis**, which is resolved by developing an inner sense of continuity. During this period, adolescents often temporarily try out different roles.

8. Adulthood is as complex, as dynamic, and as liable to change in important ways as is childhood or youth. People's personal concerns change across the life span, and gender-related attitudes and behavior appear to be affected by the stages of family life. As people become middle-aged, there develops a concern with inner life, with introspection, with conscious self-reappraisal, as well as a shift in time perspective that brings an awareness of personal mortality. Most people cope with major life transitions without undue stress, and they become traumatic only when they are not anticipated or when they occur at an unexpected time in the life cycle. Most old people do not fit the stereotype of the aged, and people are now vigorous for such an extended period that it has been suggested we call the healthy, active old people the "young-old," reserving "old-old" for the stereotypic minority.

KEY TERMS

altruism	hostile aggression	oral stage	rough-and-tumble play
anal stage	identification	personality	separation distress
attachment	identity	phallic stage	sex-typed behavior
conventional level	identity crisis	preconventional level	socialization
erogenous zones	instrumental aggression	principled level	temperament
fixation	internalization	prosocial behavior	theory of psychosexual
gender identity	latency period	puberty	development
gender roles	Oedipal conflict	role taking	wariness of strangers
genital stage			

RECOMMENDED READINGS

DAMON, W. *The Social World of the Child*. San Francisco: Jossey-Bass, 1977. Children, play, friendships, relationships with parents, moral reasoning, and ideas about justice are topics in this interesting review of the social world of childhood.

ERIKSON, E. H. *Childhood and Society*. New York: Norton, 1950. This classic book is Erikson's penetrating analysis of the concept of ego identity.

KAGAN, J., R. KEARSLEY, and P. ZELAZO. *Infancy: Its Place in Human Development*. Cambridge: Harvard University Press, 1978. The early chapters describe the changing nature of ideas about infancy, historically and cross-culturally. Later chapters report one of the best studies of infant day care yet done.

LEVINSON, D. J. *The Seasons of a Man's Life*. New York: Knopf, 1978. A study of transitions in the lives of adult men from the establishment of careers and relationships in the early twenties through major turning points in the fifties and beyond to retirement. Original research that reads like a novel.

MACCOBY, E. *Social Development*. New York: Harcourt Brace Jovanovich, 1980. A readable account of social and personality development from infancy to adolescence. The influences of parents, peers, television, and schools are all considered.

MUSSEN, P., and N. EISENBERG-BERG. *Roots of Caring, Sharing, and Helping: The Development of Prosocial Behavior in Children*. San Francisco: W. H. Freeman, 1977. A nicely integrative review of research and theory in a very active and important field.

TAVRIS, C., and C. OFFIR. *The Longest War: Sex Differences in Perspective*. New York: Harcourt Brace Jovanovich, 1977. The battle of the sexes and the war over *why* there are sex differences in human behavior are featured in this delightfully funny and scholarly review. Advocates of both biological and social bases of sex differences will find this book informative.

PART FIVE

Feeling and Activation

A young lady once asked permission to interview me in connection with a book she was writing on "workaholics." A workaholic, I presume, is a person who is addicted to work, and who finds it impossible to stay away from it long. The word is derived through analogy with "alcoholic."

I found the word offensive, however, and refused the interview.

I suppose it is only reasonable to consider me a workaholic, since I do work every day, including Sundays and holidays, and never take a vacation of any kind voluntarily; and I *have* published 258 books so far with no signs, yet, of slowing up.

Just the same, I don't consider myself "addicted," or "compulsive," or any of the other words one uses in connection with an alcoholic, or junkie, or tobacco fiend who finds himself unable to shake the habit. In the case of the true addicts, there are actual physiological and biochemical changes that take place when the drug is withdrawn, and there is therefore a *physical* need to continue.

I don't think there are actual physical changes in my body if I goof off for a while. I don't sit at my typewriter or word processor because of any physical hunger; I do so merely because I enjoy it. Dedicated golfers are not called "golfaholics," nor are people who love to fish called "fishaholics," nor are people who love to stretch out in the sun called "sunaholics."

In fact, if I made no money out of writing, but simply worked away at it as a "hobby," or as an "amateur activity," no one would remark on it, any more than if I had a shop in my basement and turned out gimcracks and oddments for my own amusement.

It is the "work" that bothers people. Because most people don't like the work they are forced to do to earn money to live on, and therefore abandon it as soon as they can and for as long as they can, the assumption is that no one can do his work longer than he absolutely has to, unless he is physically addicted.

Well, I deny that. I did not decide to write in order to "make a living" at it. It was my belief, until I approached middle age, that I was going to make a living by being a professor of biochemistry. I wrote only for the pleasure of it. I was paid for my writing, to be sure, and that was something to be welcomed, but it seemed only a side effect.

When, to my considerable surprise and delight, my spare-time writing began to earn me more money than my stint as professor did, I eventually came to the decision that I might as well spend all my time at my pleasurable hobby, and so I stopped actively professing. My writing is no more work, and has become no less fun, just because I am now making many times more money than I was making as a professor. In fact, the chief value I place on the money making is that it forces people to let me stay at my typewriter or word processor. No one can say to me, "Why don't you stop that, you lazy bum, and go out and find a job and support your family?"

So call me a "hedonist," if you wish. Call me "pleasure-mad." Call me "playboy." But *don't* call me a "workaholic." Please get my motivation right!

ISAAC ASIMOV

CHAPTER 15

Emotions

Imagine a world suddenly bereft of emotion—a world in which human beings are abruptly deprived of the capacity to experience emotions. Events in the environment can evoke neither pleasure nor pain. In this bizarre world, there is no joy but there is no despair; there is neither sadness nor regret, but neither is there happiness or satisfaction. People are incapable of feeling love or hate, compassion or contempt. Above all, it is a world without fear.

Try to imagine the consequences of such a transformation. Society would soon disappear. Because there is neither joy nor pleasure, pain nor fear, an individual is as likely to repeat an act that results in deprivation or injury as one that is useful or rewarding. Indeed, there *is* no reward. Because this emotionless world lacks rewards or punishments, there is no learning. People cannot benefit from experience. They are as likely to harm one another as to provide help and support. In a world without friends or enemies, there can be no marriage, no affection, and no love. Because there is no enjoyment of beauty, there is no art. Because people cannot be amused, diverted, or entertained, there is no music, no theater, no books, no television or movies. Because consumers' tastes are unpredictable, the production of goods is haphazard. A superb meal is no more satisfying than a raw turnip. Because earning $10 million is no better than earning $10, there is no incentive to work. In

fact, there are no incentives of any kind, for as we will see in the discussion of motivation (see Chapter 16), incentives imply a capacity to enjoy them.

The chances that such a species would survive is near zero. Emotions are the basic instruments of survival and adaptation. They are essential in individual survival, in the maintenance of community, and in the development of civilization. Without basic emotions, groups could not form, because no bonds of attachment would hold them together. The species would procreate only at random and offspring would be left unattended and uncared for. Individuals would have no concept of crime, morality, loyalty, pride, shame, or guilt. A person's death would evoke no more distress than the loss of a dime.

As we explore the nature of emotions, we will first focus on the ways in which people manifest emotional states: their physiological reactions, their behavior, and their feelings. Once these aspects of emotion have been discussed separately, we will examine the interplay among them.

The Nature of Emotions

Most people can vividly remember or at least imagine the joy of falling in love, the anguish of a loved one's death, the embarrassment of being called on in class when completely unprepared, or the frustration of discovering a dead car battery when late for an important appointment. Emotional experiences are so much a part of our life that we can easily empathize with others who are in emotion-arousing situations. But as familiar as emotions are, it is not easy to formulate a general definition of them—to describe exactly the essential elements that are common to love, grief, embarrassment, and frustration.

Like other reactions of the human organism, emotions can arise from three sources: biological, sensory, and cognitive. Thus the injection of heroin produces temporary euphoria—a biological source; the sight of a rattlesnake elicits fear—a sensory source; and the remembrance of a child's death reawakens a parent's grief—a cognitive source. Some stimuli and some properties of a stimulus seem to elicit an emotional state that does not depend on learning. For example, stimulation of high intensity, such as loud sounds, bright lights, and pungent odors, generally elicits unpleasant emotional reactions. Other kinds of experiences, such as the sudden loss of physical support or the confrontation with a novel or strange event, also bring on nearly universal emotional states, and sexual excitation can occur without previous learning or experience. However, many emotions require prior knowledge and must develop out of previous experience. Thus many people who lack experience with gasoline are more afraid of full gasoline drums than of empty ones, although the empty drums are far more liable to explode and should evoke greater fear and caution. Similarly, some people fear all snakes while others with more knowledge fear only the poisonous varieties. Other emotions that require previous experience and considerable cognitive appraisal include pride—such as the pride derived from the success of a relative or friend, and shame—such as the shame of being caught in a transgression or betraying a friend.

Whatever the emotion—whether learned or unlearned, whether fear, love, grief, shame, or pride—it has the same three aspects: arousal, expression, and experience. Arousal consists of the physiological changes that occur, primarily in the autonomic nervous system. Expression consists of the behavioral acts that are uniquely elicited by an emotion, such as baring the teeth in a moment of rage. The experience of emotion is its subjective feeling—the perception and realization of an emotional state.

Physiological Correlates of Emotion: Arousal

Strong emotions are associated with internal changes resulting from the activation of the autonomic nervous system. As discussed in Chapter 3, the autonomic nervous system usually functions without our awareness or conscious control. Its two divisions, the sympathetic and the parasympathetic, both exert some control over glands and visceral muscles. This dual control generally works in an antagonistic manner, with sympathetic activity dominating parasympathetic activity, or vice versa. The sympathetic division, which promotes energy expenditure, dominates during situations of emergency or stress; the parasympathetic division, which promotes energy conservation, dominates under conditions of relaxation. Most of the internal changes that accompany such emotions as intense fear or anger are associated with action of the sympathetic division.

When the sympathetic nervous system is activated, certain predictable changes occur. Suppose, for example, you are crossing the street and the sudden loud blast of a car horn startles you. As a result of this emotion-arousing situation, several physiological changes will take place:

1. The heart rate increases, sometimes more than doubling.
2. Movement in the gastrointestinal tract nearly stops as blood vessels leading to the stomach and intestine constrict. At the same time, vessels leading to the larger skeletal muscles expand, diverting blood to where it may be needed for fighting or, as in this case, fleeing.
3. The endocrine glands stimulate the liver to release sugar into the bloodstream so that needed energy can be supplied to skeletal muscles.
4. Breathing deepens and becomes rapid. The bronchioles (the small branches of the bronchi, the air passages that lead into the lungs) expand, and mucus secretion in the bronchi decreases. These changes increase the supply of oxygen in the blood-

In a situation of fear or threat, our sympathetic nervous system is activated; our heart pounds, our stomach constricts, and our breathing becomes rapid. These bodily changes prepare us to cope with danger.

stream, which helps to burn the sugar being sent to the skeletal muscles.

5. The pupils of the eyes dilate, and visual sensitivity increases.

6. The salivary glands may stop working, causing dryness of the mouth, while the sweat glands increase their activity, resulting in a decrease in the resistance of the skin to electrical conduction (commonly called the **galvanic skin response, or GSR**).

7. The muscles just beneath the surface of the skin contract, causing hairs to stand erect, a condition called "goose bumps" (Lang, Rice, and Sternbach, 1972).

As you leap to safety and the car passes, the opposing effects of the parasympathetic division of the autonomic nervous system reassert themselves. Heartbeat, respiration, glandular secretions, and muscular tension return to normal, and the physiological experience of the emotion subsides.

Measuring Physiological Correlates of Emotion: The Polygraph   With the proper equipment, the physiological changes associated with emotions can be measured. Although the polygraph is often called a "lie detector," it is essentially an "emotion detector," for it measures some of the physiological activities related to emotional states. Its use as a lie detector depends upon the tendency of a person who lies to feel guilt or anxiety. These emotions bring on changes in blood pressure, respiration rate, and the GSR. Electrodes attached to a subject's hand measure changes in the GSR, a rubber tube around his chest measures respiration, and a cuff on his left arm records changes in heart rate and blood pressure. The polygraph records these physiological responses while the subject is questioned. Typically, the interrogator begins with a series of routine questions ("How old are you?" "Where do you live?") to establish a baseline against which reactions to emotionally charged questions can be evaluated. A person suspected of, say, robbing a bank on the previous Thursday may next be asked, "Where were you between 2 and 3 P.M. last Thursday?" If the verbal response is "At home, reading," but autonomic responses show noticeable changes, the interrogator suspects that the statement may be untrue.

Several problems connected with such tests make the use of lie detectors controversial, and in some areas their findings are inadmissible as evidence in court. First, there is no distinctive, involuntary physiological response that invariably follows a lie (Lykken, 1981). Changes in GSR and other responses are not always reliable indicators of lying. Because skin resistance changes in reaction to many events and not just to events an individual is trying to conceal, the results of lie-detection tests must be interpreted with caution. For example, the mention of rape generally conjures anxiety-provoking images or sexual fantasies, so that any male who is questioned about a specific rape may show elevated GSR—not because he was connected with the offense but because the subject of rape heightens his emotional arousal. An innocent suspect's anxiety at being connected with a crime may also produce polygraph tracings that resemble those of a guilty person.

Second, a person can alter the results of the baseline condition, making subsequent comparisons meaningless. For example, if a man suspected of robbing a bank thinks about the robbery when asked for his current address, the resulting baseline will show responses as strong as those that follow questions associated with the crime. In this case, lies concerning the crime will reveal no special physiological change. Habitual liars may experience no emotion when telling a lie and show only slight physiological changes—or none at all. Knowledgeable suspects may practice lying to gain control over their "involuntary" responses.

Because arousal in general and GSR in particular can be affected by many conditions besides lying, caution in their use is well advised. For example, suspects who have forgotten information relevant to an event in question may become aroused when asked about the matter, because they think that the failure to remember pertinent information might cast doubt on their innocence. Their GSRs will show corresponding changes.

Emotion and the Brain   Although the physiological changes that accompany emotion are triggered by the autonomic nervous system, that system is coordinated by the brain. Research with cats has shown that stimulating certain areas of the hypothalamus can cause intense activation of the sympathetic nervous system followed by an emotional display that can be interpreted as feline rage. The cat's pupils dilate, the fur along its back and tail stands up, its ears flatten, its spine arches, its claws are unsheathed, and it hisses and snarls. Stimulating other portions of the brain leads to behavior associated with other sorts of emotion, such as the "quiet, stalking movements" characteristic of cats in pursuit of prey (Flynn et al., 1970). Thus, there is a clear connection among brain stimulation, sympathetic nervous system activation, and emotional arousal.

Animals may be programed with the potential for displaying emotional behavior that they do not normally exhibit, for a cat that has never before shown rage can be induced to do so by stimulation of the lateral hypothalamus. It has been suggested that human beings also possess unused emotional potential. This speculation is supported by cases in which exaggerated emotional behavior followed damage to certain areas of the limbic system (an area closely connected to the hypothalamus, as noted in Chapter 3). Children with such brain damage may exhibit impulsive hyperactivity, indiscriminate aggression, and violence. Brain tumors have also been found in cases of exaggerated emotional behavior (Mark and Ervin, 1970). In one instance, Donald L., a peaceable family man, became increasingly violent over a six-month period. After attempting to murder his family with a butcher knife, he was taken to a hospital, where he had to be restrained by heavy fish netting. Whenever anyone approached, he snarled, bared his teeth, and lashed out with his hands and feet. Finally, he was subdued by drugs and examined, whereupon a brain tumor was found to be pressing directly on the limbic system. After the tumor was removed, Mr. L. returned to his old peaceable self.

The cortex also plays a role in emotion, and there is now a good deal of evidence that cortical involvement is primarily a function of the right cerebral hemisphere. Patients with lesions in their right cerebral hemispheres, directly opposite the area in the left cerebral hemisphere that controls speech (see Chapter 3), speak intelligibly, but their utterances lack all emotional quality, sounding as if they had been produced by a computer (Ross and Mesulam, 1979). It appears that the modulations in voice that lend an emotional quality to human speech might be controlled by the right cerebral hemisphere, while language content and structure are processed primarily by the left cerebral hemisphere.

This emotional dominance of the right cerebral hemisphere is also evident in the facial expression of emotion. The left side of the face (which is controlled by the right cerebral hemisphere) seems more expressive and communicates emotion better than the right. Researchers photographed faces expressing six primary emotions: happiness, sadness, anger, surprise, fear, and disgust. After making two negatives of each photograph, they cut them in half and constructed two composite faces for each emotion. The resulting prints looked like intact faces, with two composites for each emotion, one made up of two left sides and the other of two right sides. Without knowing the nature of the photographs, people judged them for emotional expression and generally said that the left-side composites (controlled by the right side of the brain) expressed the emotion more clearly than did the right-side composites (Sackheim and Gur, 1978). In fact, right-hemisphere damage impairs the display of emotion, for in such patients the facial expression of joy, sorrow, fear, anger, and other emotions is weaker than in patients with left-hemisphere damage or in normal people (Buck and Duffy, 1980).

The highly organized emotional responses of human beings, with their characteristic patterns of sympathetic and parasympathetic arousal, thus appear to be coordinated by the brain and involve hypothalamus, limbic system, and cerebral cortex. Although emotional reactions can be elicited by brain dysfunction, they are normally responses to environmental situations.

Behavioral Correlates of Emotion: Expression

Although feelings are often imprecise and difficult to measure, the behavior that accompanies strong emotion can be observed directly. Moreover, there is general agreement on the meaning of such behavior. Silent movies, for example, depend for their effect on this general agreement. When the villain bares his teeth and clenches his fists, the audience assumes that he is angry; when the heroine furrows her brow and wrings her hands, the audience assumes that she is worried. We learn to recognize such nonverbal behavioral cues very early in life, and this learning serves as a basis for identifying the states that go with various emotional labels.

A great deal of painstaking research has been done on the nonverbal expression of emotion (e.g., Ekman, 1972; Izard, 1971), and many forms of emotional expression have been identified and classified. The degree of similarity across various cultures is so strong that the role of prominent facial features has been precisely described for at least six emotions, which are expressed by the positions of the muscles in the brow and forehead, eyelids, and lower face (see Table 15.1). The differences in brow and forehead formation for surprise, fear, and anger are illustrated in Figure 15.1. As we shall see, various investigators have speculated that these typical expressions have an evolutionary significance.

Figure 15.1 Examples of the Facial Affect Scoring Technique (FAST) scoring definitions: the brows-forehead items for surprise (B9), fear (B10), and anger (B12). (Copyright © 1972 by Paul Ekman.)

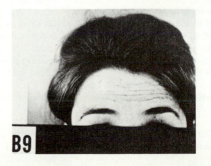

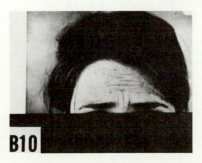

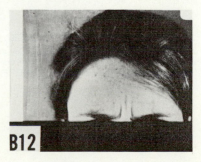

Table 15.1 Appearance of the Face for Six Emotions

	Brows-Forehead	Eyes-Lids	Lower Face
Surprise	Raised curved eyebrows; long horizontal forehead wrinkles	Wide opened eyes with schlera showing above and often below the iris; signs of skin stretched above the eyelids and to a lesser extent below	Dropped-open mouth; no stretch or tension in the corners of the lips, but lips parted; opening of the mouth may vary
Fear	Raised and drawn together brows; flattened raised appearance rather than curved; short horizontal and/or short vertical forehead wrinkles	Eyes opened, tension apparent in lower lids, which are raised more than in surprise; schlera may show above but not below iris; hard stare quality	Mouth corners drawn back, but not up or down; lips stretched; mouth may or may not be open
Anger	Brows pulled down and inward, appear to thrust forward; strong vertical, sometimes curved forehead wrinkles centered above the eyes	No schlera shows in eyes; upper lids appear lowered, tense and squared; lower lids also tensed and raised, may produce an arched appearance under eye; lid tightening may be sufficient to appear squinting	Either the lips tightly pressed together or an open, squared mouth with lips raised and/or forward; teeth may or may not show
Disgust	Brows drawn down but not together; short vertical creases may be shown in forehead and nose; horizontal and/or vertical wrinkles on bridge of nose and sides of upper nose	Lower eyelids pushed up and raised, but not tensed	Deep nasolabial fold and raising of cheeks; mouth either open with upper lip raised and lower lip forward and/or out, or closed with upper lip pushed up by raised lower lip; tongue may be visible forward in mouth near the lips, or closed with outer corners pulled slightly down
Sadness	Brows drawn together with inner corners raised and outer corners lowered or level, or brows drawn down in the middle and slightly raised at inner corners; forehead shows small horizontal or lateral curved and short vertical wrinkles in center area, or shows bulge of muscular contraction above center of brow area	Eyes either glazed with drooping upper lids and lax lower lids, or upper lids are tense and pulled up at inner corner, down at outer corner with or without lower lids tensed; eyes may be looking downward or eyes may show tears	Mouth either open with partially stretched, trembling lips, or closed with outer corners pulled slightly down
Happiness	No distinctive brow-forehead appearance	Eyes may be relaxed or neutral in appearance, or lower lids may be pushed up by lower face action, bagging the lower lids and causing eyes to be narrowed; with the latter, crow feet apparent, reaching from outer corner of eyes toward the hairline	Outer corners of lips raised, usually also drawn back; may or may not have pronounced nasolabial fold; may or may not have opening of lips and appearance of teeth

Source: P. Ekman. "Universals and Cultural Differences in Facial Expression of Emotion," in J. K. Cole (ed.), *Nebraska Symposium on Motivation*. Lincoln: University of Nebraska Press, 1972, 207–283. Copyright © 1972 by Paul Ekman.

The Universe of Emotion

Everyone feels emotion, and we all talk glibly about anger, hate, jealousy, love, joy, sorrow, and grief. But when Jennifer says she feels sad, is she having the same subjective experience that Mike calls sadness? And how does elation differ from joy, or depression from disappointment, or apprehension from fear? Considering the multitude of emotional words we use, how many basic emotions are there?

In an attempt to answer some of these questions, Robert Plutchik (1980a) turned to a rating scale called the **semantic differential.** This scale presents pairs of polar adjectives (good/-bad, nice/nasty, quick/slow, active/passive, strong/weak, sweet/sour, hot/cold) and each concept is rated on a seven-point scale between the two adjectives (Osgood, Suci, and Tannenbaum, 1957). Since most ratings are covered by three dimensions—evaluation (good/bad); potency (strong/weak); and activity (active/passive)—a specially devised analysis can locate the meaning of each word in a three-dimensional semantic space. Similarities and differences in meaning are thus represented spatially, so that the greater the distance between words, the less similar their meaning.

By subjecting emotional words, such as joyful, angry, and frightened, to the semantic differential, Plutchik hoped to discover how people organize the subjective feelings that correspond to emotions. He asked a large group of people to rate twenty-two different emotional terms on semantic differential scales for thirty-four pairs of adjectives. When the answers were plotted in semantic space, Plutchik found that there were eight primary emotions (fear, surprise, sadness, disgust, anger, anticipation, joy, and acceptance) and that they fell in a circle that resembled the color wheel in Chapter 4. Emotions resembled colors in other ways. Each primary emotion had its opposite, with joy falling directly opposite sadness in semantic space and acceptance opposite from disgust, as shown in Figure 15.2. Each emotion also blended into the next, forming a secondary emotion, so that love turned out to be a mixture of joy and acceptance, contempt a mixture of anger and disgust.

Any one person's verbal reports of emotion are likely to be highly idiosyncratic. For example, when students at Columbia University were asked to describe their associations to various emotional words, their answers varied wildly. One student might associate sadness with physiological change (loss of appetite), another with self-esteem (a feeling of insignificance), another with behavior (an impulse to cry; Plutchik, 1980b). However, by forcing many people to think metaphorically ("Anger is extremely sour"), judging the emotions in terms of the same qualities, it is possible to get a general agreement of affective meaning. In this way, Plutchik has produced an objective measure of a subjective experience.

Figure 15.2 Plutchik's emotion "wheel," showing the eight primary emotions and "dyads" resulting from mixtures of adjacent primaries. The wheel plots the similarities among emotions—and what they produce when mixed—as described by lab subjects. Thus, the primaries fear and surprise, when combined, yield the dyad awe, and joy mixed with acceptance leads to love. (From Plutchik, 1980b. Reprinted from *Psychology Today Magazine.* Copyright © 1980. Ziff-Davis Publishing Company.)

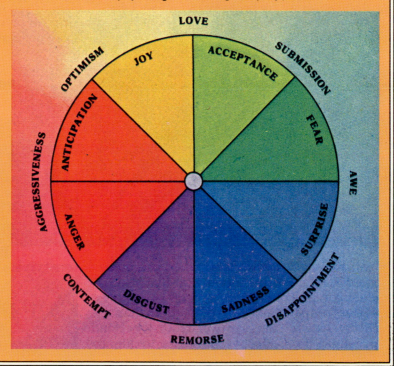

Cognitive Correlates of Emotion: Subjective Experience

Every emotion is accompanied by an awareness of the feelings associated with it, even though those feelings may be difficult to put into words. When we are happy, for example, we sometimes say that there is a special lift in everything we do, a bouncy feeling. If we are humiliated, we may say that we feel as if we would like to shrink or disappear. Many psychologists who investigate emotions have relied on such subjective reports, despite their imprecise quality. Because a specific emotion sometimes does not reveal itself in either facial expressions or overt actions, a subjective report may be the only way to discover if someone is experiencing the emotion at all.

Psychologists have devised special rating scales and measurement techniques to help them record these subjective reports in a systematic way. General agreement among people in rating common experiences (a movie, perhaps) as "hilarious," "disgusting," "sad," or "happy" indicates that our personal emotional reactions to things are shared by many others. Such ratings contribute to an understanding of the degree to which emotional reactions are consistent—or vary—from one individual to the next. After exploring the ways in which we perceive and interpret the emotional communications of others, we shall return to the problem of how we label our emotions and the role of physiology and cognition in that process.

Perceiving and Understanding the Emotions of Others

We are all familiar with the figure of Charlie Chaplin as he appeared in silent movies. A master of body language, Chaplin clearly expresses every emotion without words. Happiness? He does a little dance. Despair? His shoulders slump; the corners of his mouth turn down; he grows smaller before our very eyes. But one does not have to be a talented actor to convey emotion without words. We do it ourselves and respond to it in others, every day, in countless situations. For example, the facial expression of a friend as you describe your problems is likely to betray sympathy, annoyance, impatience, or indifference. The decision to continue or to cut short a tale of personal woe depends in most cases upon the nonverbal reactions of the listener.

Interpreting Nonverbal Communication of Emotion

The way in which people express their emotions through facial expression, body movement, gesture, posture, and tone of voice is one aspect of nonverbal communication. The other aspect, which is required to make communication complete, is the observer's ability to interpret such cues correctly. The range of emotions successfully communicated through body language is

People's posture and facial expressions often send a powerful nonverbal message.

The human face is an eloquent communicator of emotions, from grief to joy, with many fine gradations in between.

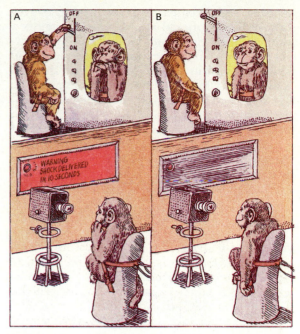

Figure 15.3 In Miller, Caul, and Mirsky's experiment, the warning light was followed by shock to monkey A in ten seconds, unless monkey B pressed the OFF switch within the interval. The experimenters reported that monkey B often pressed the switch at the correct time, even though the only communication between the two monkeys was by means of the televised image of the expression on monkey A's face.

diverse (Duncan, 1969), and can be expressed by smiles, stares, frowns, winces, grimaces, yawns, grunts, laughs, slumps, and shrugs.

Considering the often subtle differences in the expression of similar emotions, the human capacity for nonverbal communication is impressive. Facial expressions of surprise, for example, can be conveyed with many different overtones. There are various qualities of surprise—questioning, dumbfounded, startled, dazed—as well as various intensities—slight, moderate, or extreme (Ekman and Friesen, 1975). Moreover, facial expressions frequently display blends of such diverse emotions as surprise and joy, anger and fear, amusement and annoyance. If we could not see the faces and gestures of the people around us, we would lose an important vehicle of human communication.

Monkeys, apes, and other animals also communicate by means of facial expression and body language. Such communication has been observed in the laboratory as well as in the wild. In one experiment (Miller, Caul, and Mirsky, 1967), rhesus monkeys learned to avoid shock by pressing a bar whenever a panel lit up. Two of the monkeys were then placed in separate rooms, as shown in Figure 15.3. One room contained the shock apparatus and signal light, but no bar that would halt the shock. The other room contained only the bar and a television screen on which the monkey in the first room could be observed. When the panel in the first room lit up, a look of anguish crossed the face of the monkey hooked up to the shock apparatus; it had no way of preventing the impending pain. The second monkey could not see the warning light, but the first monkey's facial expressions on the television screen apparently told it when the shock was about to be delivered. In most cases, the watching monkey pressed the bar in its own room to keep both monkeys from suffering the shock.

The Role of Biology and Learning

Both the expression of emotion and the interpretation of those expressions by others appear to be based on a combination of innate and learned factors. People from widely diverse cultures show a great deal of similarity in the postures, gestures, and facial expressions used to convey comparable emotional states, which suggests a common biological foundation. However, certain differences in expression and interpretation are also found in various cultural groups. For example, in Chinese literature the expression, "He scratched his ears and cheeks," was a signal that a character was happy (Klineberg, 1938). In Western culture this action might be interpreted as indicating that the character was anxious, even distraught. Thus learning as well as biology plays an important role in both the expression and interpretation of emotion.

Biological Universals   In his classic work *The Expression of the Emotions in Man and Animals* (1872), Charles Darwin asserted that many of our patterns of emotional expression are inherited—that they evolved because they had survival value. Since there are no fossils of behavior, such conjectures cannot be proved, but the possible evolutionary significance of some expressions is easy to see. For example, when eyebrows are raised in surprise or fear, the individual increases visual perception, and raising the upper lip in rage, thereby baring our teeth, readies us to bite. Other animals also bare their teeth as a threat or

when preparing to fight, as shown in Figure 15.4, giving their enemies a warning that may in itself prevent a violent and damaging encounter. According to Darwin, the baring of teeth served a similar function among our ancestors, and this expression that communicates a threat is still characteristic of our species.

Even though emotional expression is not entirely innate, there is evidence that some of its aspects are biologically based. In a study of heredity (Allerand, 1967), identical twins, fraternal twins, and nontwin siblings described their experiences of affection, anger, delight, disgust, excitement, fear, sadness, and worry. The reports of identical twins (who have exactly the same genetic make-up) were more nearly alike than the reports of either fraternal twins or nontwin siblings, suggesting the possibility of a hereditary factor in emotions.

The capacity for emotional expression develops early. Although the first social smile appears at about two months, some researchers have found that infants as young as twelve days old will imitate emotional expressions quite accurately, sticking out their tongues or opening their mouths in response to an adult's actions (Meltzoff and Moore, 1977), as seen in Figure 15.5. Whether the response is a true imitation or a fixed action pattern like those described in

Figure 15.4   Innate patterns of emotional expression in dogs. In the top row anger increases from left to right. In the bottom row fear increases from left to right. This illustration is based on sketches by Charles Darwin.

Figure 15.5 Sample photographs from videotape recordings of two- to three-week-old infants imitating (A) tongue protrusion, (B) mouth opening, and (C) lip protrusion demonstrated by an adult experimenter. (From Meltzoff and Moore, 1977.)

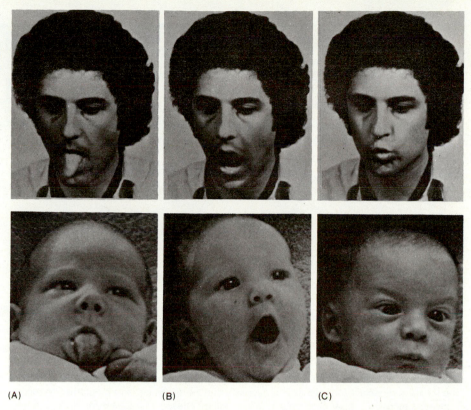

(A)   (B)   (C)

Chapter 7 and part of the species' inheritance (Jacobson, 1979), the response suggests a biological basis for human emotional expression.

Another piece of evidence that is frequently cited in support of the biological underpinnings of emotional expression is the study of a ten-year-old girl who was born deaf and blind (Goodenough, 1932). Obviously the little girl could not have learned emotional expressions by observation, so her behavior was presumed to reflect innate tendencies. When the girl displayed her pleasure upon finding a doll hidden in her clothing, she "threw herself back in her chair. . . . Both the hand containing the doll and the empty hand were raised in an attitude of delight, which was further attested by peals of hearty laughter. . . . Her laughter was clear and musical, in no way distinguishable from that of a normal child." The girl also showed anger in characteristic ways, indicating mild resentment by turning away her head, pouting her lips, or frowning, and expressing more intense resentment by throwing back her head and shaking it from side to side, while exposing her clenched teeth.

The way this child expressed her emotions was remarkably similar to the emotional expression found in most normal ten-year-olds. There were, however, enough differences to lead the researcher to conclude that human emotional expressions are built on innate tendencies that have been altered by a "social veneer." Later studies of handicapped children have supported this conclusion.

Moods appear to be as universal as emotions. Moods are different from sudden surges of emotion, because they last longer and their bodily expression is diffuse. For example, depression is accompanied by changes in movement, muscle tone, reaction speed and intensity, and the contraction of particular facial muscles. Darwin believed that the corrugator muscle, which draws down the eyebrow and makes vertical wrinkles in the forehead, was involved in the expression of grief. The universality of the muscle's role in grief was supported by a study with depressed patients, who were first put on an antidepressant drug and two weeks later had changes in the muscle's activity measured. **Electromyographic recordings (EMGs)**, which measure electrical currents caused by slight muscle movements, showed that among patients who had improved

Photograph Judged						
Judgment	Happiness	Disgust	Surprise	Sadness	Anger	Fear
Culture			**Percent Who Agreed with Judgment**			
99 Americans	97	92	95	84	67	85
40 Brazilians	95	97	87	59	90	67
119 Chileans	95	92	93	88	94	68
168 Argentinians	98	92	95	78	90	54
29 Japanese	100	90	100	62	90	66

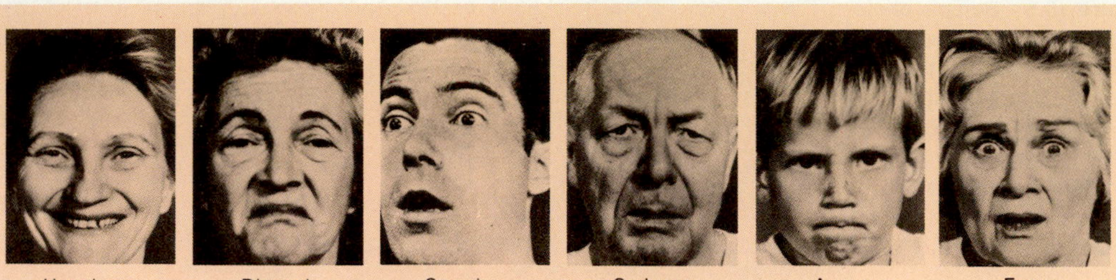

Figure 15.6   As this table indicates, there is a great deal of agreement among the members of different cultures about the meaning of facial expressions. This suggests that we are biologically programed to recognize and produce the emotions conveyed by certain facial expressions. (After Ekman, Friesen, and Ellsworth, 1972.)

while on the drug there was considerably less activity in the muscle, indicating that as depression lifts, the corrugator muscle relaxes (Schwartz et al., 1978).

Finally, additional evidence that biological factors play an important role in the expression and interpretation of emotion comes from cross-cultural research. When people in different societies were asked to identify the emotions expressed in a series of photographs of faces (see Figure 15.6), they consistently recognized anger, fear, disgust, surprise, and happiness, regardless of the culture in which they lived (Ekman and Friesen, 1971). Even members of New Guinea tribes, who had little previous contact with Westerners and their characteristic patterns of expression, promptly labeled these basic emotions and, as shown in Figure 15.7, had little trouble in displaying them (Ekman, 1980). Apparently there is a universal basis in the human display and interpretation of certain feelings, which suggests a strong biological component.

Cultural Differences   Learning also plays an important role in the expression and interpretation

of emotion, especially in establishing the occasions on which certain feelings are seen as appropriate. For example, on hearing a subtle verbal insult, different people may express resentment, fear, disdain, or embarrassment, depending on such matters as their relationship to the speaker (a relative, a teacher, a peer, a stranger); whether they interpret the remark as an insult; and their cultural background. Some cultures encourage the expression of emotions like affection or fear, but others teach their members to suppress such displays.

Cultural differences in the sort of situation that produces a particular emotion turned up in a study that compared Ugandan adolescents with American adolescents (Davitz, 1969). Sixty students from each country wrote descriptions of emotional states and described a personal experience with each emotion. In describing happiness, Ugandans tended to associate it with academic success, whereas the Americans most often mentioned social success, although nonacademic success in such efforts as learning to drive was a close second. The researcher explained this difference by pointing out that academic success provides most adolescents in

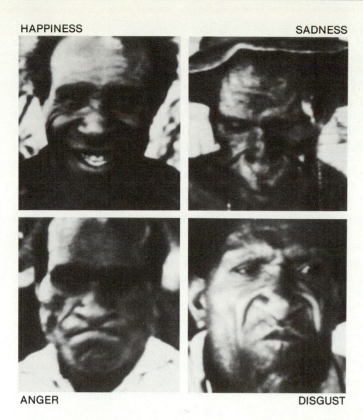

HAPPINESS SADNESS

ANGER DISGUST

Figure 15.7 Video frames of attempts to pose emotion by subjects from the Fore of New Guinea. (Copyright © 1972 by Paul Ekman.)

urban Uganda with the only escape from poverty, and that most of the Americans were not poor. In their descriptions of sadness, most Ugandan students wrote about the death of a friend or relative, while the Americans usually mentioned social difficulties. Again, these differences could be explained by differences in cultural experience. Early death is more common in Uganda than in the United States, and the Ugandan extended-family system emphasizes the importance of relatives significantly more than does the American nuclear-family arrangement.

But how do people learn to express their own emotions and to interpret the emotions of others in the first place? Although we noted the early development of emotional expression, we have also seen (in Chapter 8 and Chapter 14) that social isolation in early life can have damaging effects on later social behavior. It has been suggested that this impairment may occur when there is no opportunity for proper social communication to develop (Mason, 1961). Experiments with socially isolated monkeys support this interpretation. In an extension of the research described earlier, in which monkeys communicated fear through their facial expressions (Miller, Caul, and Mirsky, 1967), it was found that monkeys raised in isolation were significantly retarded in their ability both to display facial expressions of fear that other monkeys could interpret and to respond properly to the facial expressions of normal monkeys threatened by electric shock. The study also indicated that there might be a period in early life that is critical for the proper development of emotional expression. Although the isolated monkeys had been deprived of social contact with other monkeys during the first year of life, they had subsequently spent several years with other monkeys. This social experience evidently came too late to permit the monkeys to learn how to communicate their emotions, despite the fact that they must have feared the shock as much as did the normal monkeys.

Perceiving and Understanding Our Own Emotions

Emotions are not only communicated, they are experienced; that is, they are also perceived by the person in whom they are evoked. The relation between the bodily changes that characterize emotions and our perceptions both of these changes and of the arousing situation presents psychologists with a major problem. Do we experience fear because our hearts pound and our hands tremble? Or does our cognitive appraisal of a particular circumstance induce the feeling we call fear, which is then followed by the physiological changes that prepare us for fight or flight? Over the years, psychologists have proposed different answers to these questions, and their experiements have led to a better understanding of the issues involved.

The James-Lange Theory

Our language suggests that the physiological changes accompanying emotions differ in some ways for different emotions. When we are frightened, for example, we say we feel a "knot" in the stomach; when we are nervous, we say we experience "butterflies"; during intense anger, we sometimes refer to a "pounding" in the temples; and when we feel shame, we often describe it as a "blush." This raises the possibility that the emotion experienced at a given moment is simply the result of particular bodily changes.

One of the first psychologists to propose that the ability to identify and label our own emotional states was based on the ability to interpret these bodily changes was William James. His proposal directly contradicted many of the theories of emotion popular in the late nineteenth century. Most other writers argued, quite logically, that events in the environment trigger a psychological state—the emotion—which in turn gives rise to responses by the body. James disagreed:

> My theory, on the contrary, is that *the bodily changes follow directly the perception of the exciting fact, and that our feeling of the same changes as they occur IS the emotion.* Common-sense says, we lose our fortune, are sorry and weep; we meet a bear, are frightened and run; we are insulted by a rival, are angry and strike. The hypothesis here to be defended says that this order of sequence is incorrect . . . and that the more rational statement is that we feel sorry because we cry, angry because we strike, afraid because we tremble. . . . Without the bodily states following on the perception, the latter would be purely cognitive in form, pale, colorless, destitute of emotional warmth. We might then see the bear, and judge it best to run, receive the insult and deem it right to strike, but we should not actually *feel* afraid or angry. (James, 1890)

According to James, then, our perception of a stimulus triggers a pattern of changes in the body. These changes cause sensory messages to be sent to the brain, which produce the experience of emotion. Each emotional state is signaled by a unique pattern. James emphasized visceral reactions (that is, "gut reactions") as central to emotional states. Writing at about the same time, a Dane named Carl Lange proposed a similar theory that specifically emphasized vascular changes (changes in blood pressure). Ever since, the view that emotion is simply the perception of bodily changes has been called the **James-Lange theory of emotion** (Lange and James, 1922).

The James-Lange theory stimulated a great deal of research, much of it designed to disprove that theory's claims. In 1927 Walter B. Cannon presented a powerful critique of the theory based on several arguments. First, he pointed to evidence that physiological changes do not necessarily produce emotions, as the James-Lange theory might predict: When a person exercises vigorously or is injected with adrenaline, she or he experiences the bodily changes typical of strong emotions but does not necessarily *feel* a particular emotion. Physiological change alone, Cannon argued, cannot produce emotion.

Second, the idea that bodily reactions cause us to experience emotion is questionable because emotions are often felt rapidly. We see a bridge collapsing and immediately feel panic; we see an old friend and instantaneously feel joy. How could the viscera, which react sluggishly, be the source of such sudden emotion, as James suggested?

Finally, said Cannon, if the James-Lange theory is correct and our emotions come from interpreting our bodily sensations, it would stand to reason that each emotion would be characterized by a somewhat different set of physiological changes. But, as Cannon's research showed, this does not appear to be the case; many of the same bodily changes occur in conjunction with differing emotional states.

Later investigations tend to confirm Cannon's argument. Although it is possible to make physiological distinctions between certain emotions—anger, for instance, is generally associated with an increase in gastric activity; fear is generally associated with an inhibition of gastric functions (Wolff and Wolff, 1947)—efforts to find clear-cut physiological differences between some of the more subtle emotions have not been successful.

The James-Lange theory of emotion holds that our emotions result from bodily change. This idea has been questioned by many, who point out that our emotional reactions to frightening events occur far more quickly than do changes in our bodies.

Moreover, even the general patterns of bodily response that have been identified for emotions such as anger and fear vary among individuals and from situation to situation for the same individual (Lang, Rice, and Sternbach, 1972). For most emotions, then, unique physiological changes have been difficult to identify.

Although the James-Lange theory appears to be wrong on several counts, we cannot conclude that the perception of physiological change plays only a minor role in the experience of emotions. A number of studies have shown a relationship between a person's bodily responses and perceived emotional state (Fehr and Stern, 1970). For example, among twenty-five men who as adults had suffered spinal cord lesions, damage to the autonomic nervous system had caused significant changes in the nature and intensity of certain emotions, especially anger and fear (Hohmann, 1966). Generally speaking, the higher on the spinal cord the lesion occurred, the more extensive was the disruption of visceral responses, and the greater the change in these emotions. Although the men continued to perceive the significance of emotion-arousing situations and also displayed the sort of behavior associated with strong emotions, the quality of their emotional experiences had altered. As one man remarked about his feelings of anger: "Sometimes I get angry when I see some injustice. I yell and cuss and raise hell, because if you don't do it sometimes I've learned people will take advantage of you. But it just doesn't have

the heat to it that it used to. It's a mental kind of anger." Apparently the physical correlates of anger—pounding heart, trembling hands, the sensation of being "heated up"—contribute to the full experience of anger.

An approach to emotion that has much in common with the James-Lange theory is the **facial-feedback hypothesis**, which holds that our subjective experience of emotion comes from an awareness of our facial expressions (Izard, 1977). Thus, we feel angry because we scowl, happy because we smile. This approach to emotion has been studied by inducing people to smile or frown or look sad and measuring their physiological arousal and subjective experience.

In one study (Tourangeau and Ellsworth, 1979), researchers told college students that they were interested in measuring physiological responses to subliminal stimuli that had been spliced into a film. The students were attached to a polygraph and told that any movement of their facial muscles during the film would disturb EMG recordings from facial electrodes. Each student was then instructed to extend some muscles and contract others and to hold the muscles in that position during the two-minute film. Although the students were unaware of it, the instructions led them to produce an expression of fear or of sadness. While the students watched either a neutral, a sad, or a frightening film, their heart rate and GSR were recorded, and they reported their subjective responses. This study failed to support the facial-feedback hypothesis.

When there was a conflict between the facial expression and the film, the students' subjective reports corresponded with the emotional tone of the film, not with the assumed facial expression. However, the requirement that facial muscles be frozen for as long as two minutes may have affected the students' responses. Perhaps the effort of controlling a particular set of muscles for a long period produces "noisy" feedback that disrupts the emotional response.

Others studies (Laird, 1974; Laird and Crosby, 1974; McArthur, Solomon, and Jaffe, 1980; Rhodewalt and Comer, 1979) using a similar approach have supported the facial-feedback hypothesis. One researcher (Laird, 1974) reported that a subject who had unwittingly frowned said, "When my jaw was clenched and my brows down, I tried not to be angry but it just fit the position" (p. 480). In addition, when people are asked to deceive an observer by exaggerating or concealing an emotional reaction, their physiological responses (i.e., heart rate, GSR changes) and their subjective experience follow the false patterns they try to communicate to the observers (Kleck et al., 1977; Lanzetta, Cartwright-Smith, and Kleck, 1976; Zuckerman et al., 1981).

The Schachter-Singer Theory

Although physiological arousal may be important in experiencing full-blown emotions, it cannot completely explain their cause. Awareness of an emotion-provoking situation is also an essential component. This was demonstrated in an early study in which 210 people were injected with adrenaline and asked to report the effects (Marañon, 1924). Nearly three-quarters said that they experienced only physical symptoms—a rapidly beating heart, a tightness in the throat—with no emotional overtones whatsoever. The remainder reported emotional responses of some kind, but their descriptions were of what the investigator called "as if" emotions. These people said, "I feel *as if* I were afraid" or "I feel *as if* I were happy." Thus, their feelings resembled emotions but clearly were not what we could consider true emotions. In the few cases in which a genuine emotion followed the injection, the experience seemed to be produced when a person's thoughts combined with the physiological changes. Memories with strong emotional content, such as a father's recollection of a time when his child was seriously ill, were especially

effective. In other words, people did not interpret the physiological state produced by adrenaline as "emotional" unless they imagined an emotion-arousing situation.

Studies like the one just described led Stanley Schachter to propose a **two-factor theory of emotion**. According to this theory, the experience of an emotion is based on a physiological change plus a cognitive interpretation of that change. In experiments that explored this point of view (Schachter and Singer, 1962), people received what they thought was a vitamin injection. They believed that they were participating in a study to assess the effects of the "vitamin" on vision. The injection was actually adrenaline, and the real purpose of the study was to see whether people in different situations would assign different labels to the physiological sensations produced by the adrenaline. Those in one group were told that the "vitamin" produced certain side effects, such as heart palpitations and tremors (which are real side effects of adrenaline). People in another group were led to expect side effects not usually associated with adrenaline, such as itching and headache. Those in a third group were told that the injection had no side effects. The situation faced by the first group was similar to that in the earlier study, in which subjects knew that they were receiving adrenaline. Since the other two groups were given no explanation for their physiological arousal, the researchers expected them to attribute their arousal to "emotional" factors.

While waiting for the "vision test," each subject sat in a room with another person, who was a confederate of the experimenters. In some cases, this "stooge" acted in a happy and frivolous manner, throwing paper airplanes, laughing, and playing with a hula hoop. In other cases, the stooge acted annoyed and angry, finally tearing up a questionnaire he was supposed to fill out.

The researchers' suspicions were borne out. People in the two groups that did not expect any physiological arousal, and thus had no way of explaining the sensations they were experiencing, tended to use the emotion shown by the confederate as a label for their own feelings. They expressed euphoria or anger, depending on the emotion displayed by the stooge (see Figure 15.8). In contrast, people who had expected heart palpitations and tremors were less likely to share the confederate's feelings.

Subsequent studies have supported this two-

Figure 15.8 Two of the conditions in Schachter and Singer's experiment on emotion. (A) A subject is misled about the effects he should expect from the adrenalin injection he is receiving. Placed with a companion who joyfully flies paper airplanes around the waiting room, he attributes his state of arousal to a similar mood in himself and joins in. (B) A subject is told exactly what to expect from the injection. Although placed in the same situation as the first subject, he recognizes his physical sensations as the product of the injection and is unmoved by the euphoria of the experimenter's confederate.

factor theory. In one experiment, for example, subjects who had been injected with adrenaline laughed more and harder while watching a slapstick comedy film than did people in a control group who received injections of salt water, a placebo that causes no physiological change. Further, people who were injected with chlorpromazine, a drug that inhibits physiological arousal, laughed less than the control group did (Schachter and Wheeler, 1962). A similar study showed that people behave more aggressively toward a person they dislike (the cognitive factor) if they have been physiologically aroused by exercise (the physiological factor; Zillman, 1971). Speculative extensions of Schachter's theory have also been suggested, such as the possibility that "falling in love" may be an incorrect label given to sexual arousal or to feelings of frustration or jealousy.

If Schachter's theory is correct, it ought to explain why, as James originally noticed, there is such a wide variety of emotional experiences. It could be that there are as many differences in the emotions we experience as there are in the *situations* associated with physiological arousal. This argument fits very well with James's observation that synonym dictionaries distinguish feelings more by the stimuli that evoke them than by the tone of their subjective experience (James, 1890).

Yet the Schachter-Singer theory is not entirely correct, as recent studies (Maslach, 1979; Marshall and Zimbardo, 1979) have shown. The proposal that physiological change and its cognitive interpretation are both required to produce an emotion is violated by the fact that several depressants produce physiological and behavioral manifestations of depression. These chemical depressants affect all three aspects of emotion: internal physiological response (heart rate, muscle tone, blood pressure decrease); behavior (movements become sluggish, facial muscles droop in a sad expression); and subjective feelings (the individual feels depressed). The action of the depressant on the autonomic nervous system produces the emotion of depression without any "labeling" or other cognitive interpretation on the part of the individual. In fact, many drugs prescribed for patients with hypertension produce depression as a side effect. There is little doubt, however, that when the origin of the emotional arousal is ambiguous, information that is supplied by the environment can have the sort of effects that the Schachter-Singer theory predicts.

The Effect of Cognitive Factors on Arousal and Experience of Emotion

As we have seen, some theorists propose that emotion produces physiological response, some that emotion is the perception of bodily changes, and others that emotion is the interpretation of arousal. Another possibility has also been emphasized. Both the emotional experience and the bodily changes may follow the perception and appraisal of a potentially harmful or beneficial situation (Arnold, 1960). For example, a caged lion causes no emotional reaction among visitors to a zoo, but a lion wandering loose in the park provokes terror. The important difference may be registered during the individual's initial appraisal of the situation.

Other researchers have studied the cognitive processes involved in the initial appraisal of a situation. For example, in one study people watched emotion-arousing films, such as a graphic portrayal of adolescent circumcision rites of a primitive tribe (Lazarus and Alfert, 1964). While they watched, subjects' heart rates and galvanic skin responses were measured to provide indicators of physiological arousal. Cognition was manipulated by playing special sound tracks designed to encourage various reactions to the film. A "denial" sound track, for example, explained that the participants were actors or that the incidents portrayed were not painful, thus denying the stressful aspects of the movie. Such denial was effective, as Figure 15.9 shows. Galvanic skin response was lower when the denial sound track was played during the film

than when the film was shown without a sound track. What is more, the denial sound track lowered GSR even further when it was played before the film was shown. Cognitive appraisal apparently plays a role not only in placing an emotional label on a state of physiological arousal but also in determining the intensity with which the emotion is expressed.

The Effects of Expression on Arousal and Experience of Emotion

Most people are accustomed to thinking that whatever behavior accompanies their emotions is a result of their feelings. In other words, they smile because they are happy, clench their fists because they are angry, pace up and down because they are tense. But the relationship between feelings and overt behavior is as tangled as the relationship between physiological response and feelings. Studies have shown that at times emotion-related behavior may be as much a cause as an effect; in certain instances overt behavior may actually help to bring on feelings. If you are tense, then relax your muscles intentionally, you may suddenly discover that you feel less anxious. If you walk with a shuffling, stooped-over posture, you may begin to feel somewhat

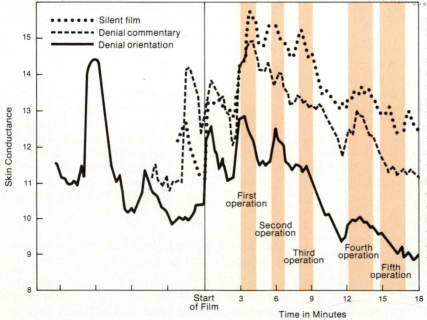

Figure 15.9 The results of an experiment on emotion and cognition by Lazarus and Alfert. They used an anthropological film about puberty rites involving subincision (the cutting open of the urethra along the underside of the penis) as the emotion-provoking stimulus. Changes in galvanic skin response (GSR) were measured as an index of anxiety. All the subjects saw the film. One group (Denial Commentary) heard a sound track with the film saying that the people in the film were actors and the operations were causing no pain. Another group (Denial Orientation) heard the same sound track before they were shown the film. A third group (Silent Film) heard no commentary at all. (After Lazarus and Alfert, 1964.)

depressed regardless of your previous mood. Perhaps the behavior gives rise to physiological sensations that we label according to learned categories. That is, we have learned to connect muscle tension with anxiety and the sensation of a stooped shuffle with depression.

Whatever the explanation, the influence of behavior on subjective feelings has been tested in a variety of ways. In a recent study, people listened to a tape played over a set of earphones, with the understanding that the purpose of the experiment was to assess the quality of the earphones under conditions of movement. People in one group were to move their heads up and down and those in another group, from side to side. After listening to the tape, people were asked about the quality of the earphones as well as about their feelings on the issues that were discussed on the tape. People who "nodded" as they listened to the tape more often agreed with the statements they heard than did people who shook their heads (Wells and Petty, 1980). Thus, to some degree, overt behavior can serve as a cause as well as a result of our feelings.

Given the findings discussed in this chapter, how much of our behavior is controlled by emotion and how much by cold rational processes? Clearly, what earlier philosophers called "passions" continue to dominate much of the violent action that occurs today, and a "crime of passion" is still classified as second-degree murder. But the question of how much either emotion or cognition controls behavior is as meaningless as the question of how much behavior is influenced by heredity or environment. Some tasks demand greater cognitive effort, others demand greater emotional capacities. Different people may approach the same situations with varying degrees of emotion, and the same person may approach the same event differently on different occasions.

In many aspects of behavior that we believe are dominated by cognition, emotional factors are often basic and come first. This is especially true of our preferences. We prefer familiar stimuli to novel and strange ones (Zajonc, 1968). In fact, one theory of music appreciation holds that familiarity is the essential factor in determining whether we like or dislike a particular piece of music (Mull, 1957). Western listeners dislike Japanese music when they first hear it, for example. The theory states that we like the familiar music because of our subjective feelings of recognition. We listen to a composition, recognize a particular musical phrase, and correctly antici-

pate its development. The resulting feeling of familiarity makes the piece attractive. If this is the case—if familiarity is the basis for our liking—then our judgments of familiarity should be more accurate than our judgments of preference. This is not always so. In laboratory studies, people preferred geometric figures they had previously seen in glimpses so brief that they could not discriminate them from similar figures they had never seen (Kunst-Wilson and Zajonc, 1980). Apparently, we like the familiar even when we cannot recognize it as such.

A somewhat similar study showed that the same process that has been observed in the laboratory works in daily life. Smokers of Camels, Chesterfields, and Lucky Strikes smoked cigarettes without being allowed to see what brands they were smoking (Littman and Manning, 1954). A paper label covered the upper half of each cigarette, obscuring its brand name. Half the smokers were asked whether the cigarette was the brand they customarily smoked or another brand. The rest were asked how much they liked the cigarette they were smoking. Smokers were more likely to say they liked their own brand than to identify it accurately. That is, smokers could not tell whether they were smoking their customary cigarette, but their preferences for their own brand clearly indicated that at some level of emotional involvement they could make the distinction.

Relationship Among the Correlates of Emotion

As we have seen, emotions are not simple reactions. All emotions derive from some stimulus in the environment and ultimately result in some action on the part of individuals that enables them to respond adaptively to threats or opportunities. One way to view the relationship among the correlates of emotion is in terms of the entire sequence of action from the initial stimulus to the adaptive function of the behavioral response. Emotions can be distinguished according to the type of event that elicits them. The initiating events are interpreted by a person as having a definite meaning, and it is the meaning that evokes a particular feeling, not the event itself. For example, the stimulus "person entering our

Table 15.2 The Complex, Probabilistic Sequence of Events Involved in the Development of an Emotion

Stimulus Event	Inferred Cognition	Feeling	Behavior	Effect
Threat	"Danger"	Fear, terror	Running, or flying away	Protection
Obstacle	"Enemy"	Anger, rage	Biting, hitting	Destruction
Potential mate	"Possess"	Joy, ecstasy	Courting, mating	Reproduction
Loss of valued person	"Isolation"	Sadness, grief	Crying for help	Reintegration
Group member	"Friend"	Acceptance, trust	Grooming, sharing	Affiliation
Gruesome object	"Poison"	Disgust, loathing	Vomiting, pushing away	Rejection
New territory	"What's out there?"	Anticipation	Examining, mapping	Exploration
Sudden novel object	"What is it?"	Surprise	Stopping, alerting	Orientation

Source: From R. Plutchik, "A General Psychoevolutionary Theory of Emotion," in R. Plutchik and H. Kellerman (eds.), *Emotion: Theory, Research, and Experience.* Vol. 1. New York: Academic Press, 1980, p. 16.

house" could be interpreted as "friend," "neighbor," "stranger," "son," or "burglar," with each interpretation eliciting a different emotional response. This feeling is followed by some action in the service of some goal. If "person entering our house" is interpreted as "burglar," the interpretation is danger, the feeling is fear, the behavior is to flee, and the goal is safety. This sequence of events, shown for eight basic emotions in Table 15.2, illustrates the various aspects of

emotion, the role of emotion in human life, and the way emotions help us to manage the environment to survive (Plutchik, 1980c).

Emotions, moods, and preferences are thus the result of a complex interaction among physiology, behavior, and cognition. And emotion—the result of the interaction—can in turn affect the way we think and act. Nowhere is this interplay more evident than in the area of human sexuality, the subject of Chapter 17.

SUMMARY

1. Emotions are essential to individual survival, to the maintenance of community, and to the development of civilization. Emotions can arise from biological, sensory, or cognitive sources, and all emotions consist of arousal, expression, and experience. Arousal consists of physiological changes; expression consists of overt behavior; and experience consists of the subjective feelings that accompany emotion.

2. Strong emotions are associated with internal changes resulting from activation of the autonomic nervous system. The sympathetic division dominates during emotion-arousing situations, and when it is activated, heart rate, respiration, glandular secretion, and muscular tension increase. Some of the physiological activities related to emotional states can be measured by a polygraph. The use of the polygraph as a lie detector is controversial because a subject's physiological responses

when lying are not always reliable and because a person can alter the baseline condition, making subsequent comparisons meaningless. The brain coordinates the activation of the autonomic nervous system as it triggers emotional arousal, and the hypothalamus, the limbic system, and the right hemisphere of the cortex are involved in the expression of emotion.

3. Much of the behavior accompanying strong emotion can be observed directly, and there is general agreement concerning its meaning, with the role of prominent facial features charted for at least six basic emotions. The extent to which people agree in rating a common experience helps establish the degree of consistency in our subjective emotional experiences.

4. Both the expression and interpretation of emotions seem to be based on a combination

of inherited and learned factors. A biological basis to emotion is suggested by the fact that identical twins report emotional experiences that are more alike than the experiences of other siblings and by the typical emotional displays of a ten-year-old girl who had been born deaf and blind. Some researchers contend that the expression of emotions is built on innate tendencies, which are altered by experience. The role of learning is suggested by the fact that the occasions on which certain feelings are regarded as appropriate vary across cultures and from person to person.

5. A debate continues over the relationship between the bodily changes that characterize emotions and a person's perception of those changes and of the situation that produced them. The **James-Lange theory of emotion** postulates that the perception of bodily changes is emotion. This theory has been challenged because (1) physiological changes do not necessarily produce emotions; (2) the speed with which emotions are felt makes it doubtful that the visceral organs could be their source; (3) similar bodily changes occur in conjunction with differing emotional states. However, the perception of physiological changes does play a significant role in the experience of emotions. The **facial-feedback hypothesis**, which links the perception of emotion to an awareness of our own facial expressions, has had some experimental support. Cognitive awareness of an emotion-provoking situation is an important component of emotional experience. Schachter's **two-factor theory of emotion** postulates that the labeling of an emotion is based on a physiological change plus a cognitive interpretation of that change. However, the importance of a person's initial appraisal of a situation may precede both the emotional experience and the bodily changes. The behavior associated with emotions is not always a result of the emotions; behavior may sometimes bring on the feelings.

6. It is impossible to say how much either cognition or emotion controls behavior. However, in the matter of our preferences, emotional factors seem to predominate. It has been suggested that we like what we are familiar with, even when we cannot recognize it.

7. Most emotions seem to progress through the same sequence of events: eliciting stimulus, interpretation of the stimulus, feeling, behavior, and goal. The common sequence shows the role of emotions in human survival.

KEY TERMS

electromyographic recording (EMG)
facial-feedback hypothesis

galvanic skin response (GSR)
James-Lange theory of emotion

semantic differential
two-factor theory of emotion

RECOMMENDED READINGS

BUCK, R. *Human Motivation and Emotion*. New York: Wiley, 1976. A broad introduction to the psychological literature on emotion and motivation.

DARWIN, C. *The Expression of the Emotions in Man and Animals* (1872). Chicago: University of Chicago Press, 1965. This classic work describes emotion and interprets them in terms of evolution and natural selection.

EKMAN, P., and W. V. FRIESEN. *Unmasking the Face*. Englewood Cliffs, N.J.: Prentice-Hall, 1975. A thoroughly illustrated treatment of facial expressions that are associated with a wide variety of emotional states.

JAMES W. "The Emotions," in *The Principles of Psychology*. Vol. II. New York: Holt, 1890. A fascinating classic that reviews basic issues and presents and defends what is now called the James-Lange theory of emotions.

SCHACHTER, S. *Emotion, Obesity, and Crime*. New York: Academic Press, 1971. A compilation of previously published papers related to Schachter's theory of emotion.

SELYE, H. *The Stress of Life*. New York: McGraw-Hill, 1956. Pioneering work on stress, emphasizing the common physiological changes that accompany a wide variety of stresses.

CHAPTER 16

Motivation

Anyone who has ever watched a detective program on television or read a mystery story knows that the way to find out who killed the rich widow is to discover who had the best motive for doing her in. Was it her son, who stood to inherit her $3 million estate; her attorney, who was afraid she had discovered that he had been embezzling from her for years; or her step-daughter, who blamed her for a car accident that had left the young woman crippled?

We all seek explanations for behavior in people's motives, but discovering motivation would be impossible unless behavior was organized. Organization is one of the most important properties of behavior. That is, when viewed over time, an individual's actions seem to make sense and some theme emerges. Once we detect the theme, we can interpret a given act as more likely, more appropriate, and more efficient than another. Unless we had some standard against which to evaluate these separate actions, we could not understand why any particular behavior is more likely than another, nor could we speak of its appropriateness or efficiency. Thus, the appropriateness of Ruth's decision to stay home and study while the rest of us go to the basketball game becomes apparent only if we also know that she wants to go to law school. And if we examine what she is studying and note how its content might help her pass the law school entrance exam, we can determine whether it is also efficient.

To understand the way a person's behavior is organized, we must infer that behavior is guided by some purpose and that it leads to some **end state**, which may be a goal or the satisfaction of some need. End states cannot be observed directly but must be inferred. Thus an act, such as the refusal to eat dinner, can be understood only if we know the context of the behavior, especially what preceded it. For example, Michael may have refused to eat dinner because he ate a heavy meal only a short time ago, because he customarily fasts one day each week, or because he has joined a political hunger strike. This dynamic property of behavior that gives it organization over time and that defines its end states is called a **motive**, and the corresponding process is called **motivation**.

Since motivation cannot be observed directly, psychologists focus their attention on behavior, formulating theories of motivation to account for the initiation, direction, and persistence of goal-directed behavior. Initiation and direction have to do with why one activity is chosen over another at a particular time. Why does one student work as a waiter after school while another plays football? Why does one student study harder after receiving a poor grade while another decides to drop the course? Persistence of behavior is an important aspect of motivation, because the study of persistence reveals the conditions under which one goal is abandoned and another chosen, why some actions cease while others continue unabated, and what properties of behavior are oriented toward long-term goals.

The initiation and direction of some behavior is largely determined by the physiological state of the organism. The nervous system is constructed in such a way that deficits in blood, sugar, water, oxygen, salt, or essential vitamins lead to changes in behavior designed to return the body to a condition of chemical balance. This internally motivated behavior, which is found in human beings as well as in other animals, helps the organism to survive.

Many human motives, such as Ruth's desire to get into law school, do not have a simple physiological basis. Although not all psychologists would agree on the explanation of such behavior, none would say that it was the result of physiological deficits. As we shall see, various explanations have been advanced to account for human activities.

Motivational Bases of Behavior

Motivation and emotion are studied as if they were distinct psychological processes. Motivational analysis looks at the future and sees behavior as primarily goal directed; that is, it seeks to explain the actions of the organism as directed toward some future end state. The hungry animal seeks food, the ambitious lawyer waits for the case that will make her famous. The analysis of emotion, in contrast, looks mainly at the past —at the stimulus situation that generated the emotional state. If we wish to know why a man is blushing, we must know just what has happened to make him feel ashamed or embarrassed.

There is, however, a great deal of overlap between motives and emotions. Emotions can initiate a chain of motivated behavior. For example, to gain self-esteem, the embarrassed man may insist on giving lengthy explanations to account for his action. Conversely, motivation can produce emotion. An individual whose path to a goal is blocked feels frustrated. A child whose sand castle was destroyed by a careless sunbather may show anger, grief, or rage.

The most basic goal-directed behavior serves two vital functions: survival and reproduction. In satisfying these functions, organisms respond to certain cues in the environment, as noted in

Chapter 7. Frogs flick out their tongues at moving black spots; gulls sit on the eggs in their nest, whether the eggs belong to them or not. But these responses occur only in certain circumstances. Frogs do not always strike at flies. Gulls do not sit on eggs they encounter outside the breeding season.

Something more than the specific stimulus is needed to evoke goal-directed behavior. It is here that the concept of motivation comes in. For a stimulus to elicit a particular response, a certain internal state must also be present. Thus, before the frog flicks its tongue at moving black spots, it must be hungry. The psychological concept of motivation is based on a combination of external motivational stimuli, called **incentives**, and internal motivational factors, called **drives**. In other words, motives have two components: the internal drive state that activates and orients the animal toward some goal, and the external incentive that is the goal itself.

However, explaining eating or any other behavior merely by labeling it with an appropriate motivational state has serious shortcomings. First, the reasoning is circular. If we say that an animal drinks because it is "thirsty," we are merely inferring a cause from the behavior we have observed and then using that hypothetical cause to explain the behavior we started with. We are implying that thirst is the cause of the animal's behavior and at the same time we are using the observation of that behavior to prove the presence of thirst.

Second, explaining behavior by labeling it with a motive does not tell us why the same motive can give rise to different responses. For example, the desire for a new car might lead one person to get a part-time job, another to coax a rich uncle for a gift, and yet another to steal.

Third, a motivational label does not explain how individuals identify their own motivational states. How do you know that you are hungry, thirsty, lustful, or acquisitive? It is therefore necessary to look more deeply into what constitutes a basic motivational state.

Motivation as a Regulatory Process: Primary Drives

Basic motivational processes are best understood in terms of the functions they serve for the organism. As noted in Chapter 7, behavior often has adaptive significance and contributes to the organism's survival. When motivational processes are expressed in behavior, such as the frog's tongue flicking, they have obvious adaptive significance associated with the regulation of basic physiological needs. An organism's **primary drives** are produced by emotional and physiological conditions that stimulate the animal to seek fulfillment of basic needs. Eating, drinking, breathing, and maintaining a stable body temperature are all examples of behavior based on primary drives, and such behavior regulates basic physiological requirements for a particular organism. As we saw in Chapter 3, this kind of regulation is called homeostasis, and describes the organism's tendency to maintain an optimal level of a physiological requirement by attempting to restore any deviation from the optimal condition (Cannon, 1929). Put simply, you are seeking homeostasis when you take off your jacket because you are too hot and put it back on because you are too cold.

Not all behavior fits this homeostatic model of motivation. Sexual behavior, which will be discussed in Chapter 17, is an example of highly motivated behavior that contributes to the survival of the species, but that is neither related to the organism's specific physiological requirements nor characterized by an optimal physiological state to be maintained. By examining such regulatory behavior as drinking, however, we will have a basis for a better understanding of motivation that is not connected with homeostasis.

Thirst and Water Balance

Most research on regulatory motives has attempted to answer two basic questions: How does an organism know when an adjustment is necessary? And what mechanism is used to make the adjustment? Thirst provides a good example of the way in which these questions can be answered.

Water is the principal constituent of all living cells and is essential to all physiological processes. Since water continually leaves the body in sweat, urine, and exhaled air, the organism must take in fluids to maintain its water balance. Certain stimuli produce sensations of thirst, telling us to drink, and other stimuli tell us when to stop.

Inducing Thirst   The stimuli that induce drinking come from three different sources. The first is an increased salt concentration in the fluid compartments of the body—inside cells, around cells, and in the blood. Specialized cells in the hypothalamus (see Chapter 3) are sensitive to this change in salt concentration and their activation results in the sensation of thirst, followed by drinking. The location of these cells was discovered by implanting small tubes into various areas of the brains of animals and then stimulating the areas with very small amounts of salt solutions injected through the tubes (Andersson, 1953). Only in certain areas do such injections induce an animal to drink.

Another stimulus for drinking is a decrease in the volume of fluid in the circulatory system (Fitzsimons, 1961). This stimulus involves no change in chemical concentration, but simply a decrease in volume, such as that which results from hemorrhage. Thus, severe bleeding causes intense thirst.

The discovery that the brain can recognize a change in blood volume illustrates how physiological mechanisms are involved in drive states (Fitzsimons, 1969). All blood is filtered through the kidneys. If a kidney senses a reduction in blood volume, it releases a chemical that alters the structure of a substance in the blood. This altered substance then acts directly on the hypothalamus to elicit drinking.

The third major stimulus for drinking is produced by the expenditure of energy or by an increase in body temperature. The mechanism involved is probably identical to that involved when cells in the hypothalamus sense a change in salt concentration. Both energy expenditure and increased body temperature result in sweating, which takes water from the blood as it cools the body. With less water, the concentration of salt in the blood rises, stimulating the salt-sensing cells and resulting in the drive to drink.

Satiating Thirst   Long before the body has absorbed water from the stomach and before the blood's salt concentration has returned to normal, thirst disappears and animals stop drinking. Drinking ceases despite a lack of homeostasis because other stimuli report that it is time to stop. One of these stimuli is stomach distention, the feeling of fullness. It has been suggested that cold water satisfies thirst more quickly than warm water because cold water moves out of the stomach much more slowly and thus provides clearer stomach-distention signals to the brain (Deaux, 1973).

Stomach-distention signals are not the only stimuli involved in satiety. If a dog is allowed to drink freely but the water it drinks is prevented from reaching its stomach (diverted through an incision made in its neck for experimental purposes), the dog does not drink indefinitely. It takes in some water, then stops drinking. Soon the dog begins to drink again, but once more it stops. Some "mouth-metering" mechanism appears to gauge the amount of fluid that is ingested and compares it with the amount needed to restore the water balance. If the internal need is not fulfilled, internal stimuli override the mouth messages, and the animal again begins to drink (Bellows, 1939).

But the mouth meter is not essential to maintaining a correct water balance. Animals can learn to press a bar that causes spurts of water to be delivered directly into their stomachs and still regulate their water balance although no fluid passes through their mouths (Epstein, 1960). Clearly, several physiological mechanisms monitor and control thirst. These mechanisms provide animals with a number of ways to sense the need for water, thus increasing the likelihood that the proper homeostatic condition will be maintained.

Hunger and Weight Regulation

As we have seen, a variety of stimuli, both external and internal, contribute to drive regulation. This is especially true in regard to eating. If you have ever eaten a hot fudge sundae after finishing a large meal, you know that internal hunger signals (such as stomach contractions) had little to do with your actions. The sundae looked and tasted delicious, and these external factors were enough to persuade you to eat it. Exactly how the internal and external factors relate to one another in the control of eating has received a great deal of attention.

As we saw in Chapter 3, major control of hunger and satiety resides in the hypothalamus, and lesions in this area have pronounced effects on food consumption. Receptors in the hypothalamus seem to monitor substances in the blood that increase or decrease with food intake or deprivation. Using this information, the hypothalamus regulates food intake and body weight.

In addition to internal physiological factors, much eating is determined by external factors:

social customs; the look, smell, and taste of food; and the amount of effort required to obtain it. In view of all these potential influences on the regulation of eating, it is remarkable that human beings and other animals regulate their weights so precisely. Most people who do not continually monitor their weight manage to keep it within a range of a few pounds, despite great variations in their physical activity and in the caloric value of the foods they eat (Keesey and Powley, 1975).

Similarly, laboratory animals with unrestricted access to food regulate their body weights within a narrow range. Anyone who has a cat has observed that the cat often eats only part of its food, leaving the rest for the next meal. Cats seem to be more successful at food regulation than some people, and research has provided insight into why these people have such difficulty regulating their weight.

If we look at the ways obese and normal individuals eat and compare their responses to internal and external signals, we find some differences in sensitivity. For example, people of normal weight respond to the internal cue of stomach distention by refusing food, but obese people tend to go on eating. Internal cues from the stomach, which signal hunger and satiety, seem to have little relation to the eating patterns of these individuals. In one study (Schachter, Goldman, and Gordon, 1968), normal-weight and obese people were deprived of a meal. Half of each group were then given a roast-beef sandwich and the other half were left hungry. Everyone was then allowed to eat as many crackers as she or he wished. Although the announced purpose of the study was to rate the flavor of the crackers, the goal of the experimenters was to see how many crackers each person ate. Among individuals of normal weight, those who had eaten the roast-beef sandwiches and were presumably no longer hungry ate only a few crackers, as expected. But having eaten a sandwich made no difference to the obese individuals. They ate more crackers than the others, whether or not they had eaten a sandwich at the start of the experiment.

Although obese people are relatively insensitive to internal cues that regulate eating, they seem especially responsive to external cues such as the sight, taste, or availability of food. The importance of the sight of food was demonstrated in a study in which hungry people were given sandwiches (Nisbett, 1968). In one group, people received one sandwich each but were told they could get more sandwiches from a nearby refrigerator. People in the other group had three sandwiches placed before each one of them. Among the people who were given three sandwiches, obese individuals ate more than did people of normal weight. Among people who had to go to the refrigerator to get another sandwich, however, obese individuals ate less than people of normal weight. It seems that obese people tend to keep eating as long as food is in sight, regardless of whether their physiological need for food has been satisfied; normal-weight people, by contrast, will forage for more food if visible food has been consumed but their physiological need for food has not yet been satisfied.

It has been suggested by Stanley Schachter (1970; 1971) that this tendency to be highly responsive to external cues related to food and relatively insensitive to internal cues is the reason some people have difficulty controlling their body weight. Insensitivity to stomach distention reduces the ability of obese individuals to detect when they have eaten enough. When that insensitivity is coupled with their high sensitivity to the taste, smell, and sight of food, obese people tend to overeat—especially in a society like ours, in which tempting foods are readily available.

However, the relationship between obesity and responsiveness to internal and external cues may be more complex than was originally thought (Rodin, 1981). Some people who are highly responsive to external cues never become obese. It seems that a multitude of factors contribute to the eating patterns of obese people, and to a degree obesity is self-perpetuating. For example, as fat cells increase in size, their capacity to store fat increases, they can become still larger, and so on. In addition, obese people generally have higher levels of insulin, which enhances the conversion of sugar into fat, than do people of normal weight; therefore, they can store fat better. Patients with very high levels of insulin often report feeling hungry whether or not they have eaten recently (Williams, 1960). Finally, external and internal cues interact. An external stimulus, such as the sight of food, can activate an internal state of arousal that leads the individual to eat great quantities of food. For example, a chicken that has been allowed to eat to its heart's content will consume two-thirds again as much food when placed next to a hungry chicken that eats in its presence (Bayer, 1929). Since the final effect of external cues is mediated by internal states, it appears that obese people cannot be said to rely primarily on external cues. Conversely, internal states affect our responsiveness to external cues, making some of them more powerful. As we saw in Chapter 5, a hungry individual tends to perceive food qualities in ambiguous objects much more readily than does a person who has just eaten (Sanford, 1937).

Needs Without Specific Drives: Learning What to Eat

Whether we are obese or of normal weight, we need certain nutrients to satisfy physiological requirements. With so many kinds of foods available, how do we know which ones to eat for a nutritionally balanced diet?

When a person is unable to fulfill a basic need for a period of time, the deprivation activates the person to seek ways of supplying whatever is missing. Generally speaking, the greater the biological need, the stronger and more single-minded the accompanying drive to seek satisfaction. With persistent deprivation, the resulting drive can come to dominate all aspects of a person's behavior. The all-consuming nature of such a drive became evident in a study of people who volunteered to spend six months in a state of semistarvation, restricted to less than half their normal caloric intake (Keys et al., 1950). Before long, the thoughts, dreams, and conversation of these volunteers centered on food, and their oral behavior, such as gum chewing, coffee drinking, and smoking, increased markedly. As the study continued, they spent more time collecting "pinups" of recipes and cooking utensils and devising elaborate menus. The desire for food had come to dominate their thoughts and behavior.

In the case of these food-deprived people, the drive to obtain food and the physiological need for nourishment were so highly correlated that it is hardly worthwhile to distinguish them. But in many instances, the connection between biological needs and specific drives is not so evident. For one thing, there are specific biological needs that do not appear to be accompanied by specific drives.

Vitamin and mineral requirements provide good examples of this. Although we all need vitamin C, for instance, we do not actively seek it out when we are deprived of it, nor, if we did search for it, do we have any senses that would detect it in the foods we eat.

Because of this inability to detect needed nutrients, early Arctic explorers sometimes died of scurvy—a severe vitamin C deficiency—in areas where the native Eskimos were thriving (Stefán-son, 1938). It was later found that the Eskimos ate a good deal of animal fat and other animal parts that contain large amounts of vitamin C. The explorers, however, tended to eat only lean meat. Although their basic need for vitamin C was not being met, the explorers felt no drive to obtain it. Moreover, the explorers never experimented with different foods in the area, some of which were abundant sources of the missing nutrient, but instead clung to habitual eating patterns despite their novel environment. The health of the Eskimos demonstrates that eating habits can satisfy basic needs although no accompanying specific drives exist; the fate of the explorers shows that learned eating habits can interfere with adjustment to the demands of a new feeding situation.

Yet people and other animals do come to meet basic biological needs that are not accompanied by specific drives. In laboratory experiments (Rozin, 1968), rats fed a well-balanced diet distinctly preferred their familiar diet to other foods. But when the diet was made deficient in certain essential vitamins or minerals, the rats developed an aversion to their customary food and a corresponding preference for new food. What is more, if a particular diet had been made deficient, rats continued to avoid it even after the deficiency had been corrected. Through their experience with various foods, animals seem to learn to use taste and odor cues to identify the diets that best satisfy their biological needs. If their diets become deficient, the animals seek new food sources that will correct the deficiency and then continue to favor the diet associated with their recovery from the effects of the deficiency.

Thus, although many animals are born without specific drives for every biological need, they manage to learn, often by trial and error, which available foods provide the most satisfactory diets (Barker, Best, and Domjan, 1977). Presumably, people are capable of doing the same thing, and through centuries of cultural evolution have learned to select a balanced diet from among the alternatives available in their particular environment. It has been suggested, for example, that people with diets low in calcium discovered, probably through learning processes like those described above, ways of preparing foods to increase available calcium. In Mexico, corn is ground in limestone mortars, which adds small amounts of lime to the meal; in China, spareribs

are cooked with vinegar. Both of these practices increase the amount of calcium ingested (Rozin, 1977). When people move to a new environment with new food sources, as the Arctic explorers did, they must learn new eating patterns that supply basic biological needs. This process might well take more than one generation, however, for people show a strong tendency to stay with a familiar diet even when more nutritious alternatives are available (Rozin, 1977; Katz, 1982).

Motives Without Specific Primary Needs

Fortunately, most needs *are* related to drives and thus can be more readily recognized and satisfied. Activities directed toward satisfying thirst and hunger are obviously related to basic biological needs for water and food. However, people and other animals engage in many activities that seem unrelated to specific biological needs. Some human behavior, such as sky diving and mountain climbing, actually threatens life instead of increasing the probability of survival (see the box on pages 374–375). Such seemingly "unnecessary" behavior, though seldom so hazardous, can be observed throughout the animal kingdom. For example, one group of researchers (Harlow, Harlow, and Meyer, 1950) found that rhesus monkeys became highly competent in solving various mechanical puzzles (such as undoing a chain, lifting a hook, opening a clasp) that required several steps for solution—despite the fact that they received no reward for their actions. Observing this, the researchers proposed that the monkeys were displaying a "manipulative drive." Other studies led to similar hypotheses about drives, such as a "curiosity drive" (Butler, 1954) and an "exploratory drive" (Montgomery, 1954) for which an activity seems to be its own reward. In Chapter 11 we saw that infants and children have a similar propensity to manipulate, explore, and learn about new things in the environment apparently just "for the fun of it." Whether we look at hamsters running in an activity wheel or people riding bicycles, we find an apparent drive for activity that is intrinsically rewarding.

In all these drives for activity, however, internal conditions that help give rise to them are not

An example of behavior that cannot readily be explained by a drive-reduction model of motivation. A monkey will work hard for the privilege of viewing an electric train, but it would be difficult to say what drive is reduced as a result.

apparent as they are in physiological drives (Bolles, 1967). Yet these activities undoubtedly have adaptive significance for individual animals, and ultimately for the species, because investigating and manipulating the environment lead to knowledge that can be used in times of stress or danger. But the activities fulfill no immediate biological needs.

It has been suggested that behavior of this sort is based on a built-in tendency to seek a certain optimal level of stimulation and activity. Theories stressing this idea, such as the Yerkes-Dodson law discussed in Chapter 10, are called **optimal-level theories**. Optimal-level theories are similar to the homeostatic model of physiological drive regulation (Arkes and Garske, 1977). According to these theories, each individual becomes accustomed to a certain level of stimulation and activity, and each desires experiences that are somewhat different from what she or he is used to, but not extremely different. If, for example, people are asked to rate the pleasantness of various temperatures of water after they have adapted to some moderate temperature, they show a preference for temperatures slightly above or below the temperature to which they have adapted, as shown in Figure 16.1 (Haber, 1958). More extreme temperatures, although they do not cause pain or discomfort, are rated as relatively unpleasant. A person's optimal level is apparently based on what that person has become accustomed to. Thus an experienced musician tends to prefer complex sequences of tones over relatively predictable sequences,

whereas a nonmusician prefers the opposite (Vitz, 1966). Once a person attains a new optimum, she or he adapts to it and yet another optimum emerges.

Optimal-level theories are valid only within certain limits. New experiences that are quite different, but positive, are more tolerable than new experiences that are quite different, but negative. A student who expects a D on an exam will be surprised at receiving an A, but not unhappy. However, the student who expects an A and receives a D will be miserable. Events that are extremely different from expectations are evaluated less on their magnitude than on their direction (Brickman, 1972).

Nor is all behavior explained by optimal-level theories. An explanation put forth by Richard Solomon (1980), called opponent-process theory, seems to clarify such phenomena as taste aversion, food cravings, attachment, and addiction. In **opponent-process theory**, there are always two processes involved in acquired motivation—a primary process and a secondary process that opposes the first. The secondary

Figure 16.1 The results of an experiment in adaptation. Subjects became adapted to water of the same temperature as their skin and rated the experience as emotionally "indifferent" (represented by the intersection of the vertical and horizontal lines in the center of this diagram). Then they were asked to place their hands in water that was either cooler or warmer than skin temperature and to rate their emotional response to the experience as "pleasant" or "unpleasant." They rated as most pleasant those temperatures that were either slightly warmer or slightly cooler (represented by the two peaks in the diagram) than the temperature to which they had adapted earlier. (After Haber, 1958.)

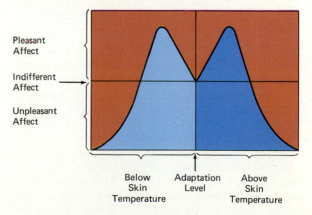

What Motivates People to Take Unnecessary Risks?

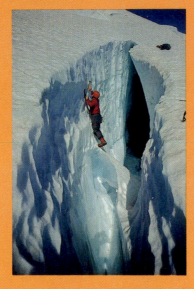

It was nearing noon that Sunday when a stiff, warm breeze suddenly materialized. Brent Hansen, a 29-year-old student . . . had been waiting for it most of the morning. Helmetless, he picked up the control bar of his multicolored hangglider, fastened his harness and ran 10 yards along the top of a 600-foot cliff above "Escape Country" near El Toro, California. But no sooner was he aloft than he got into serious trouble.

Somehow he had become tangled in his harness. "I'm caught, I'm caught," he screamed. But his friends below could only watch as he dove nosefirst into the ground at roughly 40 mph. After three days in the intensive-care unit . . . he recovered, only to hangglide again.
(Greenberg, 1977, p. 17)

What makes Brent Hansen and others like him return to a sport that nearly killed him? Whatever it is, it is the same force that sends race-car drivers back to the track and parachutists back to the sky.

When Danger Feels Good
The drawing power of danger has been explained in terms of oppo-nent-process theory, with a pre-dictable sequence of emotional states appearing in people who court danger. During a parachu-tist's first jump, the novice is terri-fied. On landing, terror is re-placed by a stunned feeling, which lasts for several minutes, to be followed by normal compo-sure. With experience, the emo-tions change, but the pattern re-mains. Although the terror is gone, parachutists may be anx-ious before a jump. On landing, they are exhilarated and the emo-tion may last for hours. Parachu-tists give this feeling as their rea-son for jumping (Epstein, 1967).

Presumably, other dangerous activities elicit the same pattern of emotional responses: After many experiences, fright is re-placed by eagerness, and a re-lieved daze gives way to jubila-tion. Just as the dog slowly comes to take pleasure in the cessation of shock, a gradual ad-aptation to intense emotion ena-bles people to take risks that the uninitiated find overwhelming.

Risk Takers:
A Personality Profile
The opponent-process theory ex-plains the changes that make dangerous sports attractive to so many people, but it does not ex-plain why some people are drawn to risks in the first place. When a psychologist looked at the per-sonality profiles of an interna-tional group of top athletes, he found that an interest in high-risk sports was accompanied by cer-tain personality traits: a strong need for success and recogni-tion; high autonomy and a strong need to dominate; self-assertive-ness and forthrightness; a prefer-

process is a reaction of the central nervous sys-tem automatically triggered by the primary proc-ess that reduces intense feeling—whether the feeling is pleasant or aversive. For example, when a dog is first exposed to electric shock, it is terrorized: it crouches, whines, urinates, defe-cates, and shows signs of behavioral disorganiza-tion. When the shock stops, the dog acts confused. If the dog is shocked several times, the pattern of behavior changes. The animal shows less terror, does not urinate or defecate, and often passively accepts the shock. When the shock terminates, the dog seems not confused, but joyful: wagging its tail, jumping, and show-ing signs of extreme pleasure.

According to the opponent-process theory, the primary emotional reaction begins with the onset of stimulus and ends with its termination —starting and stopping sharply. The secondary opponent process is more sluggish. It starts some time after the stimulus onset and builds slowly, taking time to dissipate. After several ex-periences, the pattern changes: the primary proc-ess (a) remains unaltered but the opponent pro-cess (b) is strengthened. Thus, as Figure 16.2 indicates, after a few shocks the dog is not as

ence for transitory emotional relationships; a low level of anxiety; a strong sense of reality; and a high degree of emotional control (Ogilvie, 1974). These risk-taking athletes were "stimulus-addictive," for they had developed a need to extend themselves to their physical, emotional, and intellectual limits as a way of escaping from the lack of tension in their daily lives.

A Social-Psychological View: Risk Taking in the Technological Society

Other psychologists maintain that the appeal of risk-taking stems from certain conditions within American society. In a culture that stresses competition and aggression, few jobs provide outlets for these strong drives. Assembly-line workers are drawn to high-risk recreation to distinguish themselves, and as more jobs become routine, members of the middle class are also drawn to high-risk sports (Klein, cited in Greenberg, 1977).

The Biological Side: High Risks and Brain Chemistry

Finally, an explanation that is more biological than psychological has also been suggested. The results of personality tests administered to more than 10,000 people showed that those who like risky sports also like other intense experiences. Those who seek high sensation are likely to have a number of similar tastes, ranging from sky diving to a variety in sexual partners (Zuckerman, 1978). It may be that physiology helps determine whether a person seeks sensation or security. Researchers have found that people respond differently to various levels of stimulation. For example, the brain reacts to stimulation with bursts of electrical activity called evoked potentials (see Chapter 3). According to Marvin Zuckerman (1978), among some people, the more intense a stimulus, the stronger the evoked potential. Among others, intense stimuli actually diminish the evoked potential. Zuckerman calls the first group "augmenters" and the second group "reducers," and found that high-sensation seekers tend to be augmenters. He believes that sensation seekers are neither following their peers nor driven by neurotic needs to master anxiety or to reduce sexual tension. Instead, they aim to increase the tension in their lives and need constant variety to reach their optimal level of arousal. Once accustomed to a high level, they may go on to seek even higher degrees of stimulation.

Thus, sensation seeking does not contradict optimal-level theory. It is probable that the difference between augmenters' optimal level and their level of adaptation is not greater than that of others. Augmenters' optimum is simply higher than that of other people. Augmenters continually subject themselves to higher levels of stimulation and excitation than the rest of us. A sky diver is more likely to commute to work on a fast motorcycle than is an accountant. Since augmenters live at a high level of excitation, to achieve an optimal departure from that level, they must attain levels of excitation that would be unpleasant to many people.

alarmed as it was at first, because the opponent process (b) has grown until it subtracts from the primary fear reaction. When the stimulus terminates, the pleasure is greater. As the box indicates, the same pattern appears among parachute jumpers, in which the novice's terror is replaced by the veteran's exhilaration.

Opponent-process theory can also explain addiction. A novice's reaction to an opiate is a potent "rush," which is succeeded by a less intense but pleasurable state. When the effects of the drug dissipate, the new user may experience a runny nose and eyes, sweaty hands, abdominal pressure, and muscle pains. The discomfort is equivalent to "craving" and it disappears when another dose of the opiate is taken. However, the second dose produces a diminished rush and less euphoria, and the aftereffects are more aversive. Abstinence may eventually result in agony. The rush represents a positive primary process and the aversive state that grows with experience represents a negative opponent process. In an attempt to remove the aversive state, the person again uses the drug, administers higher doses, and becomes increasingly fearful of the time when the effects wear off.

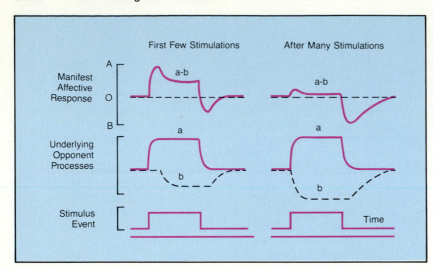

Figure 16.2 The comparison of the combined effects of the primary process (a) and the secondary process (b). The bottom panel shows the stimulus duration; the middle panel shows the component processes separately; the upper panel shows the difference between the primary (a) and the secondary opponent process (b). Note that the change which results from several repetitions of a given experience (good or bad) is entirely due to the changes which occur in the opponent process. The primary process remains unchanged with repeated experiences. (Adapted from Solomon, 1980.)

Human Motivation

Beyond the needs that human beings share with other animals for the necessities of life, and beyond the portion of our behavior that is determined by drives to obtain these necessities, unraveling the special nature of human motivation becomes a complex endeavor. One reason for this complexity is the tremendous variation in behavior, goals, and preferences among human beings. For one person, jogging is the road to physical health; for another, it is the way to aching muscles and sore feet. One person's favorite activities are reading books and deciphering ancient manuscripts; another likes nothing better than to play football. Psychologists have sought some way to include such individual differences in accounts of human motivation, and the problem has been approached in several ways.

Achievement Motivation

One method of studying human motivation is based on work done by Henry Murray and his colleagues in the late 1930s. Murray emphasized the role of "psychogenic," or nonphysiological needs in determining human behavior and accepted Sigmund Freud's idea that people express their motives more clearly when free-associating, saying whatever comes to mind, than when giving direct reports (see Chapter 18). Guided by clinical evidence, Murray and his colleagues devised the Thematic Apperception Test (TAT), in which people write or tell brief stories about pictures that show ambiguous situations (see Chapter 20). The stories are then analyzed for signs of particular motives.

Using the TAT, Murray and his colleagues (1938) identified a list of human motives, among which "achievement," "affiliation," and "dominance" have been most frequently studied. By concentrating on the study of the **achievement motive**, or the capacity to derive satisfaction by attaining some standard of excellence, we can see how these motives are measured and analyzed, and how knowledge gained from studying them might have practical benefits.

Measuring Achievement Motivation   To measure the achievement motive, David McClelland, his colleagues, and John Atkinson (McClelland et al., 1953; Atkinson, 1958a) showed people pictures from the TAT. Each person spent about four minutes writing a story that answered the following questions: (1) What is happening? Who are the people? (2) What has led up to the situation—that is, what has happened in the past? (3) What is being thought? What is wanted? By whom? (4) What will happen? What will be done? Typically, each person wrote stories for three or four different pictures to provide a sample of fantasy large enough to score. The scoring system was devised by comparing stories written under achievement-oriented conditions (when each person also took a competitive intelligence test) with stories written under relaxed, noncompetitive conditions. In the accompanying box, several sample stories are presented in the order in which they were scored, as revealing high- to low-achievement motivation.

Measuring the Achievement Motive

Shown here is a picture of the sort that might be used in measures of achievement motivation. Examples of stories that would be scored from fairly high to low are shown with the picture. The portions of the stories printed in italics are the kinds of themes considered to reflect a need for achievement.

This guy is just getting off work. These are all working guys and they don't like their work too much either. The younger guy over on the right knows the guy with the jacket.

Something bad happened today at work—*a nasty accident that shouldn't have happened.* These two guys don't trust each other *but* they are going to talk about it. *They mean to put things to rights.* No one else much cares it seems.

The guy with the jacket is *worried.* He feels that *something has to be done. He wouldn't ordinarily talk* to the younger man but now *he feels he must.* The young guy is ready. He's *concerned* too but doesn't know what to expect.

They'll both realize after talking that you never know where your friends are. *They'll both feel better* afterward because they'll feel they have someone they can rely on next time there's trouble.

Harry O'Silverfish has been working on the Ford assembly line for thirteen years. Every morning he gets up, eats a doughnut and cup of coffee, takes his lunch pail, gets in the car, and drives to the plant. It is during this morning drive that his mind gets filled *with fantasies of what he'd like to be doing* with his life. Then, about the same time that he parks his car and turns off his ignition, he also *turns off his mind*—and it remains turned off during the whole working day. In the evenings, he is *too tired and discouraged to do much* more than drink a few beers and watch TV.

But this morning Harry's mind didn't turn off with the car. He had witnessed a car accident on the road—in which two people were killed—soon after leaving home. Just as he reaches the plant gate, Harry suddenly turns. Surprised, he discovers that he has made a *firm decision* never to enter that plant again. He knows that he *must try* another way to live before he dies.

These are hard-hats. It's the end of the shift. There is a demonstration outside the plant and the men coming out are looking at it. Everyone is just walking by. They are not much interested. One person is *angry* and *wants* to go on strike, but this does not make sense to anyone else. He is out of place. Actually he is not really angry, he is just bored. He looks as though he might do a little dance to amuse himself, which is more than the rest of them do. *Nothing will happen* at this time till *more people join* this one man in his needs.

TAT stories are said to reflect the individual's needs, fears, and wants, feelings that may not be conscious and that normally would not be expressed. To assess individual differences in the achievement motive, people are given the TAT under neutral conditions, and their stories are numerically scored for achievement imagery (Atkinson, 1958b). In stories that score high on achievement, the main character is concerned with standards of excellence and with a high level of performance; with unique accomplishments, such as inventions and winning awards; and with the pursuit of a long-term goal or career. High-achievement stories also deal with persistent attempts to accomplish something and with good or bad feelings (pride or shame) aroused by the success or failure of achievement-related activity. In fact, fear of failure is a major negative component of the achievement motive: the greater the fear of failure, the lower the achievement motive. When scoring a story, independent scorers (people who do not know the hypothesis of the experimenter) trained in the use of this method generally reach close agreement.

Comparison of People with High- and Low-Achievement Motivation   Early studies of achievement found that people who showed high-achievement motivation on TAT stories performed better on such tasks as anagram puzzles and addition problems than did people who made low scores. The high scorers also persisted longer at difficult tasks, were more likely than low scorers to recall interrupted tasks (indicating a continuing desire to complete the tasks), and chose "expert" work partners more often than "friendly" ones (because experts were more likely to contribute to success).

In one study that followed from Atkinson's theory (Weiner, 1972), people who scored high in achievement motivation, and who also showed low test anxiety, chose to stand at an intermediate distance from the target in a ring-toss game, thus making the game challenging but not impossible. Subjects with low-achievement motivation and high test anxiety, however, were more likely to stand either very close to the target, where success was assured, or far away from the target, where they seemed to feel that no one could blame them for failing. In daily life, people with high-achievement motivation tend to pursue careers that are difficult enough to be challenging but not so difficult that they will end in failure. People with low-achievement motivation are less realistic. They tend to choose either very easy jobs, where success is certain but the rewards are small, or very difficult jobs, at which they cannot be blamed for failing.

Achievement motivation also affected the way people attempted to explain their successes and failures (Weiner, 1972). People high in achievement motivation usually attributed their performance to internal factors—their successes to high ability and high effort and their failures to lack of effort. People low in achievement motivation were more likely to attribute success to external factors (ease of task and good luck) and failure to an internal factor—the lack of ability. From such results, it is possible to predict how much success a person will anticipate when confronted again with a particular task. For example, a person who attributes her or his success to

stable factors (ability and task difficulty) will expect to succeed the next time the task is undertaken. If unstable causes are believed to be responsible, the person is less certain of succeeding at a task again (especially if luck is emphasized).

These differences in the way people view the causes of their successes and failures help to explain behavioral differences that have been found. For example, people who choose achievement-related activities may do so because in the past they have experienced strong positive emotion after success (having attributed it to their own ability and effort). They persist longer in the face of failure than do their counterparts with low motivation, perhaps because highly motivated people think that failure is the result of insufficient effort and that increased effort will lead to success. People low in achievement motivation give up easily because they attribute failure to their own low ability and feel that nothing can be done about it.

Applications: Managing Achievement Motivation
If the achievement motive is essentially learned, it may be possible to train people to be achievement oriented. Indeed, in one study (McClelland and Winter, 1969), a group of college students were encouraged and instructed to create fantasies of successful achievement, and the training led to greater academic success and higher grades.

In a comprehensive project, D.C. McClelland and David Winter (1969) succeeded in raising achievement-motivation levels among businessmen in a village in India. Their program, called the Kakinada Project, consisted of encouraging the businessmen to create high-achievement fantasies, to make plans that would help them realize the goals of a successful entrepreneur, and to communicate with one another about their goals and their methods of reaching them. McClelland approached the project pragmatically; his aim was to raise the achievement-motivation level among the businessmen, rather than to identify the best techniques for doing so. For that reason, he does not know exactly why his program succeeded—whether one technique worked and the others did not or whether all of them helped—but succeed it did. The businessmen became more productive as entrepreneurs, starting several large industries, enlarging their businesses, and hiring more than 5,000 of their neighbors. Although the scope of the Kakinada Project was small, its success indicates that larger efforts of the same kind could be a major force in economic development. In a subsequent assessment of this study, McClelland (1978) compared it with a more complicated project that had the immediate purpose of improving the standard of living in another village in India and the long-range goal of teaching the people to help themselves.

The Barpali Village Project, as it was called, was conducted by the American Friends Service Committee. Training and technical aid were provided for digging wells and building latrines, establishing better schools and health facilities, providing information on family planning, improving methods of farming, starting village industries, and teaching the villagers how to repair equipment and to maintain the programs.

Ten years after all American personnel had returned to the United States, the village was revisited and the project evaluated. There was little sign that the Americans had ever visited the village. Most of the wells were unused; the advanced agricultural procedures had been abandoned; the villagers' health was as poor as ever; and the birth-control program was an utter failure (population had, in fact, increased more than in a neighboring village).

In terms of time, money, and enduring effects, McClelland's achievement-training project was far more successful. The Barpali Village Project cost $1 million, lasted ten years, and failed to have any permanent effect on the population. The Kakinada Project, however, cost $25,000, lasted only six months, and resulted in long-term improvement in the villagers' standard of living through self-sustaining programs and expanded employment. While the Barpali Village Project was based on the common-sense idea that people will do things if they are taught how to do them, the Kakinada Project was based on the psychological concept that without motivation, knowledge is unlikely to alter people's behavior.

Sex Differences in Achievement Motivation: The Fear of Success

Studies based on theories of achievement motivation often failed to predict the behavior of women as well as they predicted the behavior of men (Mednick, 1979; Sherif, 1976). Scientists wondered why.

Since girls and women often have higher test-anxiety scores than men do, some psychologists suggested that females were inherently more anxious than males. However, others proposed that socialization was responsible for the difference. As Eleanor Maccoby (1963) pointed out, girls who maintain the qualities of dominance, independence, and striving for success are defying cultural sex-role standards, and if they are successful in their efforts, they are likely to suffer negative consequences. Since women traditionally are not supposed to compete in certain kinds of activity, attempts to succeed in these areas may lead to anxiety.

Studies by Matina Horner (1970; 1972) support this suggestion, for they indicate that sex differences in performance may indeed be the result of culturally imposed sex differences in motivation. Horner proposed that women are motivated to avoid success, and that they fear success because negative consequences often befall women who succeed in traditionally male areas. Horner devised a way to measure the motive to avoid success, or **fear of success**. Using a variation of the TAT, she gave college students the opening sentence of a story that they were to complete. Women received the sentence, ''After first-term finals, Anne finds herself at the top of her medical school class''; for men, the name ''John'' was substituted for ''Anne.''

A story was scored as showing fear of success if Anne or John met with negative consequences as a result of their high grades. As with Atkinson's scoring system for achievement imagery, well-trained independent raters agreed on the appropriate scoring category for over 90 percent of the stories.

In Horner's study, women showed a significantly higher motive to avoid success than did men, with more than 65 percent of the women writing stories containing fear-of-success imagery, but fewer than 10 percent of the men doing so. Typical stories are shown in the accompanying box on page 380.

Horner speculated that the motive to avoid success would affect performance only in situations in which that specific motive was aroused and suggested that it was aroused when people were anxious about competition and its aggressive overtones. In a second experiment, Horner gave people several achievement tasks to perform in a large, competitive group of both men and women. Afterward, some of the subjects worked alone, solving an additional task in a completely noncompetitive situation.

Most men did better in the competitive situation than in the noncompetitive one, but less than a third of the women did so. Most of the

Motivation in Women: The Avoidance of Success

These stories were written by subjects in Matina Horner's research on the motive to avoid success. The first three stories, written by women, show such a motive. The last two, which were written by men, do not.

Anne has a boyfriend Carl in the same class and they are quite serious. Anne met Carl at college and they started dating around their sophomore years in undergraduate school. Anne is rather upset and so is Carl. She wants him to be higher scholastically than she is. Anne will deliberately lower her academic standing the next term, while she does all she subtly can to help Carl. . . . His grades come up and Anne soon drops out of med school. They marry and he goes on in school while she raises their family.

Aggressive, unmarried, wearing Oxford shoes and hair pulled back in a bun, she wears glasses and is terribly bright. Anne is really happy she's on top, though Tom is higher than she—though that's as it should be. . . . Anne doesn't mind Tom winning.

Congrats to her! Anne is quite a lady—not only is she tops academically, but she is liked and admired by her fellow students. Quite a trick in a man-dominated field. She is brilliant—but she is also a lady. A lot of hard work. She is pleased—yet humble and her fellow students (with the exception of a couple of sour pusses) are equally pleased. That's the kind of girl she is— you are always pleased when she is—never envious. She will continue to be at or near the top. She will be as fine practicing her field as she is studying it. And—always a lady.

John is a conscientious young man who worked hard. He is pleased with himself. John has always wanted to go into medicine and is very dedicated. His hard work has paid off. He is thinking that he must not let up now, but must work even harder than he did before. His good marks have encouraged him. (He may even consider going into research now.) While others with good first term marks sluff off, John continues working hard and eventually graduates at the top of his class. (Specializing in neurology.)

John is very pleased with himself and he realizes that all his efforts have been rewarded, he has finally made the top of his class. John has worked very hard, and his long hours of study have paid off. He spent hour after hour in preparation for finals. He is thinking about his girl Cheri whom he will marry at the end of med school. He realizes he can give her all the things she desires after he becomes established. He will go on in med school making good grades and be successful in the long run.

From Matina Horner, in *Feminine Personality and Conflict.* Monterey, Calif.: Brooks/Cole, 1970.

women who had shown a strong motive to avoid success in the competitive situation did much better in the noncompetitive setting. But women with a weak motive to avoid success behaved just like men and performed much better in the competitive situation than in the noncompetitive one (see Figure 16.3).

From such results, it appeared that women who show a fear of success believe that success threatens close relationships with men, and by traditional standards it thus signifies their failure as women. Such women might be expected to marry and have children sooner than women scoring low on the measure, for having a baby can confirm a woman's femininity, remove her from the competitive arena, and reestablish her dependent relationship with her husband. A follow-up study of the same women Horner had assessed found this to be the case (Hoffman, 1977). Indeed, many of these women seemed to

have become pregnant when faced with the possibility of success in some area that would put them in competition with their husbands.

Figure 16.3 Data from Horner's experiment on the motive to avoid success in women. (After Horner, 1970.)

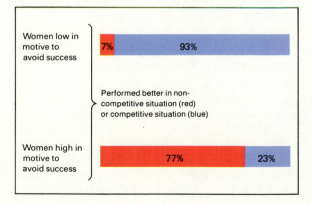

Women low in motive to avoid success: 7% / 93%

Performed better in non-competitive situation (red) or competitive situation (blue)

Women high in motive to avoid success: 77% / 23%

Although fear of success provides an intuitively appealing explanation of some sex differences in motivation, the findings do not apply in all situations. Fear of success is not universal among females, and it appears to differ from task to task (Stein and Bailey, 1973). For example, in situations that depend on social skills, women do not fear success as they seem to do when intellectual or athletic skills are critical. Various investigators (Tresemer, 1974; Zuckerman and Wheeler, 1975) have criticized the TAT stories as a measure of the motive to avoid success. Some psychologists (Condry and Dyer, 1976) have suggested that many women write stories saturated with a fear of success because cultural standards lead them to attribute to other women a fear that they do not feel for themselves. However, a different and more objective measure also supports the idea that there are gender differences in the motive to avoid success among undergraduate college students, and that women score higher on the measure (Zuckerman and Wheeler, 1975).

Cognitive Consistency

The environment can either provide us with a means of satisfying our goals and needs or generate barriers that frustrate their attainment. However, the environment also creates conditions that lead to the arousal of powerful motivational states. Thus, a second approach to understanding human motivation is based on the proposition that, just as we seek physiological homeostasis, we also seek equilibrium in cognitive states.

Our cognitive processes are affected by information, and information inundates us from every possible source—from the environment, from other people, and from our thoughts, dreams, plans, and achievements. Since the information we collect expands at a rapid rate, we must find an efficient way to store it. By storing information in the form of categories, or concepts, and rules (see Chapter 10), we can process it more efficiently.

The information that comes our way usually fits some of our categories and some of our rules. If it fits none—if it is inconsistent—we are surprised and disturbed. We are thrown into a state of cognitive imbalance and we ask ourselves why this item does not fit with anything else we know. To restore equilibrium, we try to resolve inconsistencies in our rules and categories. One way to do this is to find an explanation in the form of a new category or a new rule. If Ann discovers that Jeanne, her best friend, voted for the "wrong" presidential candidate, she will be surprised and feel uncomfortable. Generally people who like each other like similar things and have similar views (Duck and Craig, 1978)—a rule that we have learned through contact with others. Ann's state of cognitive discomfort will lead her to seek explanations for Jeanne's vote until she finds some consistency. Under some circumstances, Ann may change her own mind about the presidential candidates, so as to restore balance. Thus, the state of disequilibrium that is created by the conflict among three cognitions ("I like Jeanne"; "I like my presidential candidate"; "Jeanne doesn't like my presidential candidate") has motivational consequences. It makes Ann tense, propels her to seek new information about Jeanne and the two candidates, and puts pressure on Ann's political preferences.

These tendencies were incorporated by Fritz Heider (1958) into a theory of cognitive consistency called **cognitive balance theory**. Since the information we receive about people or objects is often inconsistent, contradictory, and leads to opposing inferences, our cognitive processes can be thrown out of balance. According to cognitive balance theory, the resulting conflict causes us to feel a tension that we seek to resolve. Thus, motivational pressures from the environment impose on the individual a need to attain a consistent view of the world.

Cognitive Dissonance

Heider's theory of cognitive balance considered a person's attitude toward other people and objects. A more general approach to cognitive consistency is that of **cognitive dissonance theory**, which is also based on the attempt to avoid cognitive inconsistency but which considers the tendency to restore consistency among any attitudes, thoughts, beliefs, or perceptions. According to Leon Festinger (1957), who first proposed the theory, holding two contradictory cognitions about our own attitudes, beliefs, or behavior throws us into a state of psychological distress known as dissonance. Because this state is uncomfortable, even painful, we naturally attempt to rid ourselves of it and reestablish internal harmony (see Figure 16.4).

The situations in which dissonance can arise—and the methods used to reduce it—are varied. Suppose, for example, that you need a car to commute to campus. You go to a used-car lot

Figure 16.4 Attitudes are frequently modified in order to resolve contradictions. This motivation for attitude change is called cognitive dissonance. In this figure Mary has expressed two attitudes that are now brought into conflict by Bill's behavior: She cannot "love that man" and "hate those clothes" without experiencing the discomfort of dissonance. A resolution can be accomplished in a number of ways. Mary can start wondering if she really loves Bill after all, or she can broaden her tastes, or she can make such mental rearrangements as "Good taste isn't really what I'm looking for in a man anyway."

and find two automobiles that you like, a Volkswagen Rabbit and a Datsun. The two cars have about the same number of miles on them and are the same price, the same age, and in equally good condition. You find it difficult to decide between them because both cars seem equally attractive. At last you settle on the Rabbit. Immediately you are cast into an unpleasant state of dissonance. You liked the Datsun a great deal,

but you bought the Rabbit instead and you wonder if you made the right decision. According to cognitive dissonance theory, you would attempt to reduce your distress by adjusting your attitudes toward the two cars. You would try to develop both a more favorable attitude toward the Rabbit, playing up its good qualities and playing down its negative ones, and a less favorable feeling toward the Datsun, focusing on its undesirable features and ignoring its positive ones. Research confirms that this process of rationalization is common. In one early study, people who had just purchased a new car were more inclined to read advertisements for the model they had bought than for those they had considered but rejected, presumably with the goal of reducing the dissonance created by their decision (Ehrlich et al., 1957).

Cognitive dissonance theory has wide applications in the fields of psychotherapy, religion, buying and selling, and politics (Wicklund and Brehm, 1976). For instance, it has been used to explain why people who publicly say or do something contrary to their private beliefs often shift their attitudes to make them conform to their public stance. In fact, the less incentive people have to express the contradictory view, the *more* likely they are to change their original attitudes. Apparently, the lower the incentive, the greater the dissonance created—and therefore the greater the need to restore a state of cognitive consistency.

A classic early experiment (Festinger and Carlsmith, 1959) illustrated this point. People were given the boring task of putting round pegs in round holes and square pegs in square holes for two hours. Then the experimenter asked each person to tell the next person who was to perform the task that the experiment had been fun and exciting. He promised half the subjects one dollar for telling this lie and the other half twenty dollars. After passing on the erroneous information, the original subjects evaluated the degree to which they had enjoyed the experimental task. Those who had been paid one dollar for telling the lie said they enjoyed the task more than did people who had received twenty dollars.

Why did the people who were paid one dollar rate the boring job more favorably than those who were paid twenty dollars? According to dissonance theory, to say something you do not believe ordinarily causes psychological discomfort, but when you have a good reason for lying, you experience little or no dissonance. Therefore, people who received only one dollar and could not justify the lie to themselves "decided" that the task had not been so boring after all, so they had not really lied. People who were paid twenty dollars had a good reason for saying something they did not believe, because in 1959 twenty dollars was a substantial sum. The behavior of the second group created little dissonance and they could readily admit that the task had been dull.

Other explanations have been offered for the apparent motivational effects of lying for pay in this experiment. One researcher (Bem, 1965) has argued that people tend to interpret their own behavior as they interpret the behavior of others. Seeing someone else get a small reward and hearing the person say that the task was enjoyable leads to the conclusion that the person enjoyed the task. Subjects view their own feelings in the same way. After hearing themselves say that the task was enjoyable and seeing themselves pocket a meager reward, they conclude that they must have enjoyed the task.

Both the cognitive dissonance theory and Bem's self-perception theory have been challenged on the grounds that, in many cases, people can easily accommodate contradictory and conflicting information (Tedeschi, Schlenker, and Bonoma, 1971). But they do not like to *appear* inconsistent. Claiming to like a boring task after receiving a small reward makes a person appear inconsistent—unless that person gives some evidence that she or he does like the task. In such situations, people resort to impression management, in which they manage the impressions others may get of them to appear consistent. Thus, they claim to have enjoyed the task. **Impression management theory** maintains that a person's attitudes remain impervious to the effects of dissonance and that the insufficient reward affects only the expression of attitudes to others.

Other motivational consequences of cognitive states were investigated in an experiment that required college students to learn a list of words under painful conditions—they received two shocks on each trial until they learned the entire list (Zimbardo et al., 1969). Although the experiment was ostensibly over once the list had been learned, the students were asked to continue for another session. Half of them were given considerable justification for continuing (the experiment was important to science, to the space program, and so forth). The rest were given poor

reasons for participating (nothing might come out of the experiment). When the students who agreed to continue learned the next list, those who had been given little justification learned faster, perceived the shocks as less painful, and showed lower physiological reactions to pain, such as a galvanic skin response (GSR), than students who had been given high justification. The differences in justification manipulated cognitive dissonance among the students in the same way as did paying subjects to lie in the earlier experiment.

In this case, the cognitions in conflict were "I have agreed to suffer considerable pain" and "There will be nothing in it for me, nor will either science or society benefit." Students in the high-justification group felt no such conflict because they believed that there were good reasons for enduring the pain. Apparently, cognitive dissonance can have powerful motivational effects on perception (feeling the shock as less painful), on behavior (learning faster), and on physiological reactions (lower GSRs). According to the researchers, the resolution of dissonance leads people to deny and suppress pain, and this suppression affects behavior and physiology.

Intrinsic and Extrinsic Motivation

The experiment on pain and cognitive dissonance focuses on a distinction between two classes of motivation: intrinsic and extrinsic. Behavior that is undertaken because of some external reward is considered to be **extrinsically motivated**, and behavior that is undertaken because of long-term goals or an individual's established preferences is considered to be **intrinsically motivated** (Deci, 1975). In the pain experiment, students in the low-dissonance group were given external justification for their behavior, thus their motivation was extrinsic. Students in the high-dissonance group had to create their own reasons for enduring pain, thus their motivation was intrinsic.

Behavior that is extrinsically motivated depends upon the external conditions that support it: it persists only as long as external rewards and punishments continue, and it varies with their magnitude. Intrinsic behavior persists despite setbacks and frustrations. Most of our daily behavior is a mixture of both kinds of motivation. Going to college may be mostly a matter of intrinsic motivation, for the goal (a degree) can be reached only after a long period and substantial concentrated effort. But the effort given to daily assignments may be partly motivated by extrinsic factors: praise from the instructor, admiration from peers, and the like.

In some cases, intrinsic motivation may be weakened when extrinsic motivation is also present. The presence of external rewards may lead individuals to revise their conceptions about their real goal, thereby lowering their intrinsic motivation (DeCharms, 1968). For example, someone who looks forward to the crossword puzzle in the daily newspaper may begin working it less often if he or she is paid several times for solving it. In this example, solving the puzzle has moved from intrinsic motivation (pleasure) to extrinsic motivation (money); payment has made work out of play.

Although the assertion that extrinsic motivation can weaken intrinsic motivation has not been fully substantiated (Scott, 1975), the effect of punishment on motivation is becoming clear, with mild admonitions shown to be a more effective means of prohibition than the prospect of severe punishment, apparently because mild punishment leads to the development of intrinsic motivation. The finding has been especially strong in studies of children (Lepper, 1981). In typical experiments, children are told not to play with an attractive toy, and the admonition is ei-

ther severe (the threat of punishment) or mild (a simple request not to play with the toy). The children are then left alone in the presence of the toy, and in most cases none of them plays with it. When later asked about the toy, children who were threatened with punishment still think it is a nice toy, but those who were merely requested not to play with it now have a low opinion of it. By derogating its value, they find an internal justification for complying with the request, thus resolving any dissonance. What is more, six weeks later these children are more likely to avoid the toy than children who earlier had been threatened with punishment. Children in the latter group had been given a good external justification for not playing with the toy, and it still seemed attractive to them.

A Hierarchical Conception of Human Motives

The discussion of motivation indicates that to be complete theories must account for motives based on physiological needs similar to those of other animals, for drives that are akin to physiological needs, and for motives that cannot be characterized without reference to human cognitive processes. One way to organize these di-

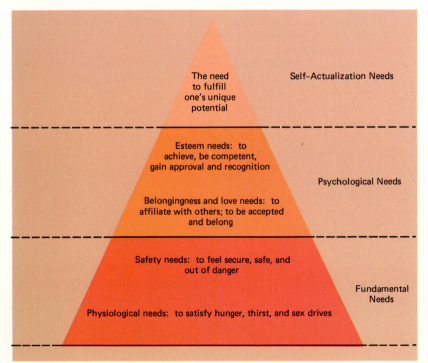

Figure 16.5 This pyramid represents Maslow's hierarchy of needs. According to Maslow, fundamental needs must be satisfied before a person is free to progress to psychological needs, and these in turn must be satisfied before a person can turn to self-actualization needs. More recently, Maslow (1970) has added a need for transcendance that is even higher than the need for self-actualization. (After Maslow, 1971.)

The need to fulfill one's unique potential

Self-Actualization Needs

Esteem needs: to achieve, be competent, gain approval and recognition

Psychological Needs

Belongingness and love needs: to affiliate with others; to be accepted and belong

Safety needs: to feel secure, safe, and out of danger

Fundamental Needs

Physiological needs: to satisfy hunger, thirst, and sex drives

verse motives conceptually has been suggested by Abraham Maslow (1954), a personality theorist whose work is discussed in Chapter 19.

Maslow believed that human needs, or motives, are organized in a hierarchy. The **basic needs** include fundamental physiological needs (for food, water, and so on) and intermediate psychological needs (for safety, affection, self-esteem, and so on). These needs are also "deficiency needs" because if they are not met, people seek to make them up in some way. Failure to attain a feeling of basic security, social acceptance, or self-esteem can produce pathological discomfort and maladjustment that may be almost as debilitating as physical starvation. The highest motives, called **metaneeds**, have to do with creativity, justice, and what Maslow called "self-actualization" (see Figure 16.5).

According to Maslow, the lower needs take precedence: extreme hunger or thirst is so urgent that severely deficient individuals have no opportunity to worry about social acceptance and psychological security, let alone the creative exercise of their talents. Similarly, people who continually seek social acceptance are not free to create scholarly or artistic works.

Although little research has been done to test Maslow's hierarchical concept of motivation, it does draw attention to the complexity of human motivational processes. In addition, it emphasizes aspects of human motivation extending beyond basic survival needs and economic accomplishments.

However, the need for self-actualization is easily misunderstood, a misunderstanding that arises from the belief that each individual has a unique potential that can and should be attained. If people believe that only one occupation, one particular environment, one set of relationships, and one mate will lead to self-actualization, they may become filled with doubt, because no one can ever know whether her or his unique potential has been attained. Nor is there any objective way to establish that a person's potential has been actualized.

It is possible that each individual has a unique potential, but it is more probable that the difference between actualizations is small, and that the very best actualization is not far removed from the next best actualization, and so on. People adapt to all kinds of novel situations, but the human tendency to exaggerate the consequences of our decisions—what courses to take, whom to go out with, what car to buy, what job to accept—overlooks the species' enormous adaptability and our ability to make changes in our environment after the decision has been made.

SUMMARY

1. Human behavior is organized and best understood by inferring that it is guided by a purpose and that it leads to an **end state**—a goal or the satisfaction of some need. The property that organizes behavior and defines its end states is called a **motive**. **Motivation** cannot be observed directly, but must be inferred from behavior.

2. The most basic goal-directed behavior serves the vital functions of survival and reproduction. A motive has two components: an **incentive** (an external motivational stimulus) and a **drive** (an internal motivational factor). Applying motivational labels to behavior does not explain behavior because the reasoning is circular, because labeling fails to explain why the same motive can lead to different responses, and because it does not explain how individuals identify their own motivational states.

3. **Primary drives** are produced by emotional and physiological conditions that stimulate the organism to seek fulfillment of basic needs, thereby restoring homeostasis. Thirst shows how an organism knows when an adjustment is necessary and which mechanisms make the adjustment. Thirst and drinking are induced by increased salt concentration in body fluids, decreased amount of fluid in the circulatory system, and increased energy expenditure or body temperature. Thirst can be satiated by stomach distention and other physiological mechanisms that maintain the body's water balance. Hunger and weight regulation show the contribution of internal and external stimuli to drive regulation. The hypothalamus helps regulate food intake, but much eating is determined by external factors: social customs; the look, taste, and smell of food; and the effort required to obtain it. Obese individuals often eat in response to external cues; however, a number of other factors (insulin levels, size of fat cells, and the

interaction of internal and external cues) also contribute to obesity.

4. When a biological need increases, the drive to seek its satisfaction becomes stronger. Some biological needs do not appear to be accompanied by specific drives, as in the case of vitamin and mineral requirements. People and other animals engage in many activities that seem to be unrelated to specific primary needs, such as investigating and manipulating the environment. This behavior has adaptive significance, for it leads to knowledge that can be used in stress or danger. **Optimal-level theories** propose that such behavior is based on a built-in tendency to maintain a certain level of stimulation, and that people desire experiences that are somewhat different from what they are used to, but not extremely different. The **opponent-process theory** explains acquired motivations as the result of two opposing processes, with the second (opposing) process being a central nervous system response that reduces intense feeling—whether pleasant or aversive.

5. Human motivation is complex and distinguished by great variation in behavior, goals, and preferences. Human motives can be measured by using the Thematic Apperception Test (TAT); and the **achievement motive**, or the capacity to derive satisfaction by attaining some standard of excellence, has been studied extensively in this manner. People who show high-achievement motive generally perform better than low scorers on various tasks and tend to persist longer on difficult tasks. High scorers tend to choose challenging but not impossible careers, while low scorers tend to make unrealistic choices. High scorers attribute success or failure to internal factors, while low scorers tend to attribute success to external factors and failure to lack of ability. People have been trained to be achievement oriented, and a variety of techniques, including the encouragement of high-achievement fantasies, appear to be effective.

6. Human beings seek cognitive equilibrium in the form of cognitive consistency. According to Heider's theory of **cognitive balance**, we try to resolve any inconsistencies in our concepts by discovering new concepts or by changing our thoughts. According to Festinger's **cognitive dissonance theory**, contradictory thoughts throw us into a distressful state of dissonance, which we may resolve by seeking new information or changing our attitudes. Cognitive dissonance can affect perception, behavior, and physiological reactions. Motivation can be **intrinsic** (undertaken because of long-term goals or preferences) or **extrinsic** (undertaken because of external reward). The introduction of extrinsic motivation may weaken intrinsic motivation, turning play into work. Punishment can affect motivation, with mild punishment being most effective because it leads to the development of intrinsic motivation.

7. The level of achievement motivation does not predict female behavior as well as it does male behavior. Women often obtain higher test-anxiety scores than men, and an inherent higher level of anxiety has been suggested as the cause. However, socialization may be responsible for differences in behavior. **Fear of success**, or the motive to avoid success, appears to be more common among women than among men and may be due to culturally imposed sex differences in motivation. Fear of success is not universal among women and does not appear in situations that depend on social skills.

8. Maslow proposed a theory of motivation that accounts for motives based on physiological needs, for drives that are akin to physiological needs, and for motives that cannot be characterized without reference to human cognitive processes. Maslow believed that these various kinds of motives are organized hierarchically and that the lower needs take precedence over the higher needs. **Basic needs** include fundamental physiological needs and intermediate psychological needs (safety and self-esteem, among others). **Metaneeds** are the highest motives, having to do with creativity and self-actualization.

KEY TERMS

achievement motive
basic needs
cognitive balance theory
cognitive dissonance theory
drive
end state

extrinsic motivation
fear of success
impression management
   theory
incentive
intrinsic motivation

metaneeds
motivation
motive
opponent-process theory
optimal-level theories
primary drive

RECOMMENDED READINGS

ARKES, H. R., and J. P. GARSKE. *Psychological Theories of Motivation.* Monterey, Calif.: Brooks/Cole, 1977. A broad, basic introductory survey of dominant approaches to motivation in psychology, ranging from instinct through psychoanalysis to attribution theory.

ATKINSON, J. W. (ed.). *Motives in Fantasy, Action, and Society.* New York: Van Nostrand Reinhold, 1958. An important book that pulls together work done by many investigators on the various methods used to assess and study individual differences in motivational dispositions such as achievement, affiliation, and power. Scoring manuals and self-teaching materials are also included.

ATKINSON, J. W., and N. T. FEATHER. *A Theory of Achievement Motivation.* New York: Wiley, 1966. Focuses on the contemporaneous determinants of achievement-oriented behavior and the marked advances made in psychologists' understanding of the problem.

JUNG, J. *Understanding Human Motivation: A Cognitive Approach.* New York: Macmillan, 1978. A well-written basic textbook emphasizing individual differences and cognitive factors in human motivation.

McCLELLAND, D. *The Achieving Society.* New York: Van Nostrand Reinhold, 1961. Addresses the question of the social origins and consequences for society of achievement motivation.

WEINER, B. *Theories of Motivation: From Mechanism to Cognition.* Chicago: Markham, 1973. A textbook covering, among other topics, drive theory, achievement theory, and—most important—the author's attribution-theory approach to achievement motivation. Presents clearly the differences between mechanistic (for example, drive) and cognitive (for example, attribution) theories.

CHAPTER 17

Human Sexuality

"It's funny because all your life all that stuff is wrong and you're not supposed to let a boy touch you, and then the priest says something and all of a sudden everything is supposed to be all right. But my wedding night was terrible and I cried and cried because I didn't know what I was supposed to do and it did not seem right" (in DeLora and Warren, 1977, p. 197).

Despite the openness about sexuality in this society, the young woman who gave this description of her wedding night to a marriage counselor is not an isolated case. Most of us have learned more about avoiding sex than about enjoying it. We learn the rules our culture has established concerning when and how it is acceptable to express sexual feelings. We even learn what is sexy. In the United States, a small-breasted woman might wish to increase her breast size, but she would never think of stretching her lower lip to appear desirable. Yet among some peoples of South Africa, a pendulous lower lip is an attractive feature (Katchadourian and Lunde, 1975). As a result, although the nature of the physiological response to "effective sexual stimulation" is essentially the same for all human beings, the nature of that stimulation varies greatly from culture to culture. And within a single culture, different learning experiences produce different sexual attitudes.

Because each of us is a sexual being, human sexual behavior fascinates us all. As we explore human sexuality, we shall investigate the factors that influence gender, ways of studying sexual behavior, the nature of the sexual response, some major sexual problems, sex therapy, and the wide variations in sexual behavior. Because many factors that have nothing to do with sexuality influence the nature of our emotionally intense sexual relationships, we shall reserve a discussion of falling in love for Chapter 26.

Influences on Gender

The concept of gender—maleness or femaleness—is composed of many factors, including heredity, anatomy, hormones, and the psychological determination of gender identity. The ability to sort out the respective contributions of these influences on gender is a recent addition to our knowledge of human sexuality.

Genetic and Hormonal Influences

An individual's genetic sex is determined at conception by information carried on one of the twenty-three chromosomes (see Chapter 11) in the father's sperm, which may be either X (female) or Y (male). Since all female germ cells (eggs) contain an X chromosome, an egg that is fertilized by a sperm bearing the X chromosome will be female (genotype

XX), but an egg that is fertilized by a sperm bearing the Y chromosome will be male (genotype XY).

In the first six weeks after conception, the sexual development of males and females follows an identical course. Gender first becomes apparent in genetically male embryos (XY), when the gonad begins to develop into testes at about six weeks. In genetically female embryos (XX), ovaries begin to appear some weeks later.

Hormones produced by the tiny gonads determine the way the reproductive organs develop. But the effect of hormones on the fetal brain is equally important. Without male sex hormones (**androgens**), the hypothalamus (see Chapter 3) will develop in a female pattern, set to maintain hormone production in the cyclical pattern that maintains the female reproductive system. When androgens are present, the hypothalamus develops in a male pattern, set to maintain a continual production of hormones.

Yet ovarian hormones are not required for the development of a female. If an embryo receives only a single X chromosome and no Y (a condition known as **Turner's syndrome**), the fetus will develop into an anatomical female, but will have no ovaries and thus will never develop secondary sex characteristics. If an embryo receives a Y but no X chromosome, it will not survive because the X chromosome apparently contains genetic information vital to the development of every fetus. Should the body cells of a genetically male (XY) fetus fail to respond to androgen, the baby will be born genetically male but with the external anatomy of a female (Money, 1963; Money and Ehrhardt, 1972). These children, who have an **androgen insensitivity syndrome**, are reared as girls, and the condition is not generally discovered until late in adolescence when the failure to menstruate leads to a medical examination. From a biological standpoint, the male pattern appears to be an elaboration of the female pattern.

Social Influences: Gender Identity and Gender Roles

With rare exceptions, the child's biological sex, as determined by genes and hormones, is immediately apparent at birth. Up to this point there have been no social influences on sexual development. Following birth, social and cultural forces help to shape a person's gender identity and sexual behavior. They affect how that person relates to other people emotionally and sexually, the things that arouse the individual sexually, and much more.

In Chapter 14 we saw how minor gender differences in behavior are magnified by socialization, and the part played by the environment in the development of gender roles. As a child grows, the child also develops a gender identity, the understanding that he or she is male or female and the inner feelings that accompany the outward behavior of gender role.

Studies of children reared in gender roles that are partially or completely incompatible with their anatomical or genetic sex provide clues as to the influence of upbringing on gender identity. Because upbringing is a powerful force on the development of identity, it has been proposed that when medical reasons make it necessary to change a child's sex, the switch may be done without harm to gender identity up to the age of eighteen months (Money and Ehrhardt, 1972). Yet the major case upon which this theory was built does not appear to be clear-cut. An infant boy's genitals were accidentally mutilated so that he would never be able to function sexually as a normal male. When the child was seventeen months old, surgery was performed to change the child's anatomical sex to female, and the parents reared the child as a girl. At the age of four, the child had adopted a female gender role: "she" played with dolls, was proud of ruffled dresses, and behaved like a typical girl. The child seemed to be developing a female gender identity, while her identical twin brother was developing into a typical boy. It appeared that upbringing, when combined with a surgical sex change, had overcome the influence of genes and prenatal hormones on gender (Money and Ehrhardt, 1972).

By the age of thirteen, however, the child had developed a masculine gait, was called the "cave woman" by other children, wanted to become a mechanic, and her fantasies showed some discomfort with her female role. Psychiatrists treating her reported that she was not a happy child and at the age of sixteen, she was having considerable difficulty in adjusting to life as a female (Diamond, in press).

On the basis of this case, we cannot say that social and cultural influences, powerful as they are, can completely eradicate the combined effect of genes and prenatal hormones. Yet upbringing appears to be extremely powerful. Nine out of ten genetic boys with androgen insensitivity syndrome who were reared as girls developed secure female gender identities (Green, in press).

A great deal of interest has focused on the effect of prenatal hormones in the establishment of gender roles and gender identity. Among girls who were exposed to abnormal levels of prenatal androgens (either because the girls' own adrenal glands overproduced androgens or because their mothers were treated during pregnancy with drugs that raised fetal androgen levels), the exposure appeared to leave lingering traces on gender role but not on gender identity. The girls were born with clear signs of masculinization— for example, a greatly enlarged clitoris that resembled a penis. They received corrective surgery and all were reared as girls. The girls preferred male playmates, dressing in pants to wearing dresses, outdoor games and sports to playing with dolls, and fantasized about future careers instead of about marriage or motherhood. However, the girls' behavior was within acceptable "tomboy" bounds, most did expect to marry males, and they appeared to have developed female gender identities (Ehrhardt and Meyer-Bahlburg, 1981).

A relatively rare condition called **transsexualism**, in which people develop a gender identity that is inconsistent with their genetic and anatomical sex, provides further evidence of the separation between biological sex and gender identity. Transsexuals feel they are trapped in the body of the wrong sex. Male transsexuals (and most are male) think of themselves as women, want heterosexual relations with men, and sometimes request surgery to "correct" their anatomy. For them, the surgery involves removing the testes and most of the penis and constructing a vagina from the remaining tissue. A series of hormone treatments reduces body hair and enlarges breasts. For female transsexu-

Renée Richards, ex-tennis pro and coach of Martina Navratilova, is a well-known and successful transsexual. However, many transsexuals continue to have adjustment problems after their gender change.

als, surgery involves mastectomy, hysterectomy, and the construction of an artificial penis, accompanied by hormonal treatments.

The advisability of such surgery has recently been called into question, and Johns Hopkins University, which has a major program for transsexuals, has stopped the practice. Some psychiatrists argue that transsexuals are no better adjusted after surgery than transsexuals who do not receive surgery, but others insist that when transsexual candidates for surgery are carefully selected, they adjust well to their new anatomical sex.

Male transsexuals show feminine behavior at an early age—although most feminine boys do not become transsexuals. They like to dress in girls' clothes, play with girls, and avoid rough-and-tumble play and sports in favor of Barbie dolls and similar toys. When female transsexuals were compared with lesbians, researchers found a similar childhood behavior and play patterns, characterized by tomboyism, a preference for male playmates, and a disdain for dolls or motherhood. They were distinguished only by cross-dressing, which appeared after puberty only among the transsexuals. Psychological differences between the two groups were sharp: only lesbians had developed female gender identities and only transsexuals had a highly negative reaction to breast development and menstruation (Ehrhardt, Grisanti, and McCauley, 1979).

Richard Green (in press), who has studied transsexuals extensively, indicates that both early socialization and prenatal hormones may well be involved in the development of transsexuality. Despite the influence of early socialization, life with a transsexual parent appears to have little effect in pushing a child toward transsexuality. Studies of children reared by transsexual and homosexual parents show that such children develop gender identities like those of children reared by conventional parents (Green, 1978).

As research on transsexualism shows, social influences on the development of gender are strong, but interact with genes and hormones in a complex and not always predictable way.

Methods of Studying Sexual Behavior

For the first half of this century, most of the data psychologists had about sexual behavior came from the memories and reports of people who had undergone psychotherapy. Today there is a wealth of data on sexual behavior, and it comes from a variety of sources.

Cross-Cultural Studies

The ways in which people learn about, experience, and express adult sexuality also vary widely from individual to individual and from culture to culture. There are cultures that approve homosexual relationships and even encourage them as a sexual outlet before marriage (Davenport, 1965). Other cultures permit masturbation among children, in polygamous marriages, and as an extramarital sexual activity. The average amount of sexual contact engaged in by members of our culture would be considered very low in some societies and very high in others (Ford and Beach, 1951).

Mangaia, a small Polynesian island in the South Pacific, is a good example of a culture in which sexual standards differ radically from our own. Childhood masturbation is considered a normal part of sexual development in Mangaia. Since families live in one-room huts, children are free to watch their parents' sexual activities. Adolescent boys and girls are expected to form sexual relationships so that they can practice their sexual skills and find a suitable marriage partner. Mangaians believe that frequent sexual contact is necessary to health, that female orgasm is a learned skill, and that it is the male's duty to bring his partner to orgasm. As adults, Mangaians have sexual intercourse more often than do the people of Western cultures, and female orgasm is almost universal (Marshall, 1971).

In comparison, sexual activity among the 350 inhabitants of Inis Beag, an island off the western coast of Ireland, is meager. An anthropologist (Messenger, 1971) who spent more than a year on the island considered it one of the "most sexually naive" societies in the world. Sexuality is heavily repressed, and children are severely punished for sexual expression of any kind—talk, masturbation, bodily explorations. Nudity is abhorred, boys and girls are kept apart, and courting is considered sinful. Celibacy is common, marriages are late and arranged without considering the couple's feelings. Misconceptions about sex are rampant: female orgasm is extremely rare and considered deviant; sexual intercourse is believed to be debilitating. Foreplay is limited, and apparently only the "missionary" (man on top) position is used in intercourse.

Cross-cultural studies have forced a reconsideration of the kind of sexual practices that should be considered "abnormal," "unnatural," or "pathological." The wealth of information that has been gathered makes it harder for us to call many sexual practices that are unusual to us pathological. In general, only two sorts of sexual acts are now considered pathological: those that upset people who feel compelled to practice them (e.g., father-daughter incest) and those that are forced on an unwilling participant (such as rape). Clearly, what is abnormal is relative to the culture in which it is observed, and few practices are considered abnormal in every society.

Nevertheless, cross-cultural studies have also shown that every society imposes some restrictions on sexual behavior. Nowhere in the world are men and women free to do whatever they like, whenever, wherever, and with whomever they please.

Surveys

The first widespread sex surveys were done by Alfred C. Kinsey, a biologist and expert on gall wasps who in 1930 was asked to teach a course on sex education. Unable to find reliable information on sexual behavior, Kinsey decided to collect data himself (Pomeroy, 1966). He and his associates spent the next eighteen years talking to people of different ages, backgrounds, and marital status about their sex lives. The results of interviews with 5,300 American men, *Sexual Behavior in the Human Male* (1948), and with 5,940 women, *Sexual Behavior in the Human Female* (1953), made history—and headlines.

Kinsey's goal was to substitute facts about the sexual behavior of Americans for cultural myths and to gather data on the population as a whole. His method was to collect sexual histories in detailed, confidential interviews, concentrating on Americans' "sexual outlets" (the number and kinds of sexual experiences they had). Kinsey's most controversial findings concerned premarital and extramarital sex (most men and many women reported such experiences) and homosexual experiences (which he found were far more common than anyone cared to believe).

The Kinsey study relied on volunteers—"self-selected" subjects who may have had ulterior motives for participating. It did not include major segments of the population—in particular black, rural, and poorly educated Americans. It did report on what white, well-educated volunteers *said* they did or did not do sexually in America in the 1940s. Until the mid-1960s, Kinsey's were the only comprehensive data on American sexual behavior, and they provided the foundation for most contemporary research on human sexuality.

Observational Studies

Shortly after the Kinsey studies were released, William Masters and Virginia Johnson launched the first observational study of human sexual behavior. Their goal was to concentrate "quite literally upon what men and women do in response to effective sexual stimulation . . . rather than on what people say they do or even think their sexual reactions and experiences might be" (Masters and Johnson, 1966, p. 20). Volunteers were recruited to masturbate and have intercourse in a laboratory where their physiological responses to sexual stimulation could be observed closely. Women, for example, masturbated with an artificial penis equipped with a light and camera. Over twelve years, 694 men and women participated, most of them married couples, allowing the Masters and Johnson team to observe some 10,000 sexual episodes.

The value of these observational studies was limited in that the volunteers, as in the Kinsey survey, may have been atypical. Sexual experiences in a laboratory may be quite different from similar experiences at home in private; and the presence of observers no doubt influenced some aspects of the subjects' behavior. Nevertheless, Masters and Johnson's research has led to a fuller understanding of of the human sexual response and of human sexual problems.

Controlled Experimentation

The studies of human sexual behavior we have been describing are essentially descriptive: from them we learn *what* occurs, but not *why*. The influence of various factors on sexual behavior can be examined only through controlled experiments in which specific hypotheses can be tested and discarded.

A study by Julia Heiman (1975) comparing the sexual arousal of men and women in response to pornography illustrates this kind of research. Kinsey et al. (1953) had speculated that men and women are sexually aroused by different kinds of stimuli. He wrote that although the two sexes seem equally aroused by tactile (touch) stimulation, men seem clearly more aroused by "psychosexual stimuli." That is, more men than women reported that they were aroused by pornography and the sight of the opposite sex. Men also talked more about sexual matters and seemed to have more sexual thoughts, fantasies, and dreams than did women. But from Kinsey's data there was no way to tell whether women were less responsive than men to erotic stimuli or whether the women Kinsey interviewed were simply more reluctant than men to talk about such things. To test Kinsey's speculation, Heiman directly measured physiological signs of arousal.

The subjects in Heiman's study were male and female college students, most of whom were sexually experienced. Male sexual response was measured using a device shaped like a rubber band, which was placed around the penis to record the size of the erection. Female arousal was more difficult to measure. From Masters and Johnson's research, it was known that an unmistakable sign of female arousal is an increase in the flow of blood through the vaginal blood vessels. So Heiman measured female arousal levels by using a small, tamponlike device that was sensitive to color changes in the vaginal walls—the darker the color, the higher the arousal level.

Students were divided into four groups: group 1 listened to *erotic* tapes that contained explicitly sexual material; group 2 heard *romantic* tapes that described a tender and affectionate episode in which there was no sexual contact; group 3 listened to an *erotic-romantic* tape that conveyed both explicit sexuality and affection; and group 4 heard a *control* tape in which there was neither sex nor romance.

The physiological measures indicated a clear difference in arousal levels among the four groups. The men and women who heard explicitly sexual material—those in groups 1 and 3—showed high levels of arousal. In contrast, little sexual arousal was recorded among groups 2 and 4.

The results refuted the stereotypical notion that women find romance and affection more arousing than nonemotional sex. Females and males alike showed the same low-level response to the romantic tape as to the control tape. Nor did adding romance to explicit sex (group 3) heighten arousal in women. Thus, by using a controlled experiment, the researcher was able to show that both men and women are aroused by the same kind of erotic material.

As we have seen, there are limitations to every method of studying human sexual behavior. Such studies raise both practical and ethical questions. From a practical standpoint, sexual behavior is so complex that designing an experiment that mirrors sexual response in the world is extremely difficult. From an ethical standpoint, sexual experiments—unless they are part of a therapy program—often evoke intense community reaction and could have unknown effects upon the subjects. For example, showing children pornography in an attempt to assess the effects of childhood experiences on later sexual responses as an adult would clearly be unethical. Because of such problems, few experimental studies have been done on human beings. Experimental studies with animals have provided some information, but such data have limited value because of the difficulty of relating the results to human beings.

The Human Sexual Response

All healthy men and women are physiologically equipped to respond to sexual stimulation—both physical stimulation (touching and being touched by the hands, lips, body, and perhaps objects) and psychological stimulation (provocative sights, sounds, and behavior, and erotic fantasies). Furthermore, as we shall see, men and women experience similar physiological reactions to sexual stimulation.

The Physiology of Arousal and Orgasm

Although no two people react to stimulation in exactly the same way, Masters and Johnson (1966) found that the sexual response in both men and women can be divided into four phases: excitement, plateau, orgasm, and resolution.

During the **excitement phase**, the heart begins to beat faster and the respiration rate increases. Blood flows into the genitals, causing the penis to become erect and the clitoris to swell. Drops of moisture form on the vaginal walls. Women's (and some men's) nipples may become erect, and women may develop a "sex flush" (a reddening, usually beginning on the chest, caused by the dilation of small blood vessels in the skin) over the body.

In the **plateau phase**, the genitals become fully

engorged with blood. The clitoris retracts into its hood, though it remains highly sensitive. The entrance to the vagina contracts by as much as 50 percent; the uterus rises slightly, causing the inside of the vagina to balloon. The glans of the penis enlarges and deepens in color. Some fluid (which can contain live sperm) may seep out the opening of the penis as this happens. The testes swell and pull up higher within the scrotum. As excitement reaches a peak, the feeling that orgasm is inevitable sweeps over the individual.

During **orgasm**, muscular contractions force the blood that has been collecting in the genitals back into the bloodstream. The muscles around the vagina push the vaginal walls in and out and the uterus pulsates. The muscles in and around the penis contract rhythmically, causing **ejaculation**—the discharge of fluid. In males the discharged fluid, called **semen**, contains sperm. Although researchers have long believed that women do not ejaculate, recent studies have shown that some women do expel a clear liquid from the genital opening during orgasm and that these women tend to produce stronger uterine and pelvic muscle contractions than do other women (Addiego et al., 1981; Perry and Whipple, 1981). For both men and women, the first five or six orgasmic contractions are the strongest and most pleasurable. In both sexes, the anus also contracts during orgasm, and experiments indicate that by monitoring anal blood flow and anal contractions, researchers will be able to compare the physiological orgasmic responses of men and women (Bohlen, Held, and Sanderson, 1980). Some people also experience intense muscle spasms in their faces and limbs during orgasm, and some cry out uncontrollably; others show few obvious signs of orgasm.

The body gradually returns to its normal state during the **resolution phase**. Muscle tension dissipates and the genitals return to their usual size and shape.

Masters and Johnson found that the sexual response cycle is physiologically the same for all orgasms, whether produced by intercourse or masturbation. Masturbatory orgasms are often more intense physically, probably because the individual has precise control over the kind and intensity of stimulation. Masturbation may be less emotionally satisfying than intercourse, however (Masters and Johnson, 1966).

The subjective experience of sexual arousal, like the physiology of arousal, appears to be basically the same in men and women. A group of gynecologists, psychologists, and medical students who were asked to read descriptions of orgasm written by twenty-four male and twenty-four female subjects guessed the writer's sex in some cases, but no more often than would be expected by chance (Vance and Wagner, 1976).

Figure 17.1 Graphs summarizing Masters and Johnson's description of coitus in the human male and female. The four phases are defined in terms of measurable physiological changes. In both sexes excitement leads to a plateau phase that may be maintained for considerable periods without orgasm. The male has only one pattern of response after this: he ejaculates quickly in orgasm, and his arousal decreases rapidly. There is a period after his ejaculation, the refractory period, in which he is incapable of another ejaculation. He may repeat the orgasmic phase several times before returning to an unaroused state. The female may variously have one orgasm or several orgasms in succession (line A), not achieve orgasm at all and return relatively slowly to an unaroused state (line B), or, rarely, have a single prolonged orgasm followed by rapid resolution (line C).

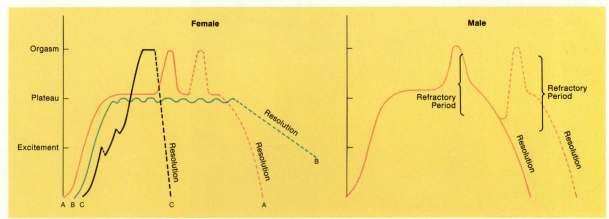

Although the pattern of sexual response is the same, there are some physiological differences between the sexes. First, as noted earlier, most women apparently do not ejaculate at orgasm. Second, men experience a **refractory period**—a period of time (ranging from minutes to hours or even days) that must pass after an orgasm before they can become sexually aroused again. In contrast, women may experience **multiple orgasms**, one after another, without going through the resolution phase in between (see Figure 17.1). Although some men have reported multiple orgasms, a close analysis of the reports indicates that their response differs sharply from that of women who have several orgasms within a few minutes (Robbins and Jensen, 1978). In males who report multiple orgasms, the orgasms are spaced over an hour or more, and it appears that these men either have an extremely short refractory period or that they stop an orgasm each time it begins—before semen is ejaculated—allowing the orgasm to proceed to completion only at the final climax.

Stimulation and Arousal

As we have seen, both men and women respond consistently to effective sexual stimulation whether the source is psychological or physical (Masters and Johnson, 1962). Physiological arousal in response to erotic materials, such as sexually explicit pictures or stories, takes the same form as the arousal that occurs in the initial stages of intercourse (Byrne and Byrne, 1978). But since learning plays a significant role in determining sexual responsiveness, effective sexual stimulation is not the same for everyone.

Touch is the most obvious source of sexual arousal. Certain areas of the body, called **erogenous zones**, are particularly sensitive to touch (the glans of the penis, the clitoris, the mouth, the nipples, the inside of the thighs). Other less obvious areas (the palms, the lower back) also may be highly sensitive. The degree of sensitivity depends on the individual, with one person being almost totally insensitive in an erogenous zone where another is so sensitive that touch is somewhat painful.

Odors exert a powerful influence on mating activity in most animals—even to the extent that placing urine from the receptive female mouse onto the back of a male mouse will incite other male mice to sexually assault the fragrant male (Connor, 1972). Although studies indicate that women are more sensitive than men to odors emitted by the opposite sex, experiments have been unable to establish any clear effects of such olfactory stimuli among human beings (Rogel, 1978). However, the increasingly popular belief that odors do influence human sexual behavior is reflected in the marketing of odorous substances as aphrodisiacs and in the way perfumes are advertised.

The popularity of erotic films, magazines, and books testifies to the effectiveness of visual stimulation, with both women and men responding

Research indicates that visual erotic stimulation—films, photographs, and live shows, for example—can cause sexual arousal in both men and women. Our own sexual fantasies, however, may be even stronger stimulants.

to such materials (Heiman, 1975). Fantasies—the pictures in our own minds—may be the most powerful stimulant of all. Males in two studies were able to either decrease (Laws and Rubin, 1969) or increase (Rubin and Henson, 1975) the vigor of their erections through fantasy. In another study, adults who were instructed to imagine sexually exciting situations became more aroused than others who saw explicit slides or read explicit stories (Byrne and Lambreth, 1971). Sexual fantasies frequently accompany intercourse, even among people who are sexually well adjusted and find their partners sexually attractive. For example, 65 percent of suburban housewives reported that they sometimes had erotic fantasies during sexual intercourse with their husbands; 37 percent had fantasies most of the time. Fantasies about imaginary lovers and submission to a dominating male were common. Interviews with these women indicated that their fantasies enhanced their sexual responsiveness (Hariton and Singer, 1974).

Sexual Responsiveness and Aging

Most of us think of sexuality as something that emerges at puberty, reaches full strength in early adulthood, gradually fades with increasing age, and eventually stops. The "sex symbols" of our culture are almost invariably young, attractive men and women, and we often have difficulty imagining that children and older adults are also sexual beings. But surveys and observations have found sexual activity throughout the life span. In the studies of Kinsey and his associates (1948; 1953), men sixty-five and older generally reported having sexual activity about four times a month, typically with their wives. Of the older married men and women in the Kinsey samples, 25 to 30 percent said they supplemented intercourse with another sexual outlet, masturbation. Subsequent studies have found essentially the same thing: most old people who have an available partner maintain relatively vigorous sex lives. Those who are most sexually active tend to be those who also were most sexually active in their youth (Newman and Nichols, 1960).

Some physiological changes do occur with aging; hormone production generally decreases in both sexes and gradual changes in sexual functioning follow. As women and men become older, it takes more intense physical stimulation for a longer period of time to produce adequate vaginal lubrication and penile erection. Elderly men who have sexual intercourse several times a week find that although sex is satisfactory, they do not ejaculate on every occasion. With age less semen is emitted in any single ejaculation, and the intensity of orgasmic contractions decrease. None of these changes diminishes the pleasure of sexual activity; in fact, their effect is to make sexual intercourse last longer than it once did. By showing that there is no physiological reason for stopping sexual activity with advancing age (Masters and Johnson, 1970), modern sex research may have encouraged more people to enjoy sexual activity throughout life.

Sexual Problems and Therapy

There are times when a person cannot be aroused or satisfied sexually. The individual may be tired, preoccupied, drunk, angry at the partner, anxious about "performing" well, or simply uninterested in sex at the time. This happens to everyone on occasion. However, for some individuals it is a recurring experience that can become very upsetting. Any problem that prevents an individual from engaging in sexual relations or from reaching orgasm during sex is known as a **sexual dysfunction**. It is important to recognize that this term applies only to problems in sexual *response*, not to sexual preferences or what are sometimes called, inappropriately in many cases, "deviations" (the choice of unusual sex objects or modes of gratification). For example, a couple who prefers oral-genital sex or mutual masturbation to intercourse is not dysfunctional, so long as both partners are satisfied with their activities.

Sexual Dysfunctions in Men and Women   In everyday conversation the term "impotence" is often used to describe all forms of male sexual dysfunction. Similarly, the term "frigidity" is applied to all manner of female sexual problems, with the implication that the woman is totally unresponsive, cold emotionally as well as sexually. As popularly used, neither term tells us what precisely the problem is. And they incorrectly suggest an invariably permanent rejection of sexuality. One of the goals of sex researchers has been to replace these overgeneralized, pejorative labels with more precise definitions of specific dysfunctions.

Psychologists now reject the term "impotence" and instead use the term **erectile failure** to describe a man's inability to achieve or maintain an erection. Some men have never been able to achieve or maintain an erection (a rare condition known as **primary erectile failure**). Much more common is **secondary erectile failure**, in which men who have experienced no erectile failure with a partner in the past are unable to achieve or maintain an erection in some or all sexual situations. For other men arousal is not the problem. Some acquire an erection easily but ejaculate before they or their partners would like. This is called **premature ejaculation**, and it appears to be the most prevalent complaint among male college students (Werner, 1975). Other men can achieve and maintain an erection but are unable to ejaculate during sex with a partner—a problem called **inhibited ejaculation**. Secondary erectile failure, premature ejaculation, and inhibited ejaculation afflict most males at one time or another. Only when they are extremely persistent and are upsetting to the individual should they be considered dysfunctional.

Some women suffer from **vaginismus**, involuntary muscle spasms that cause the vagina to shut tightly so that penetration by the male partner's penis is extremely painful. In many cases, the vaginal spasms are so severe that sexual intercourse is impossible, and the couple eventually seeks sexual therapy so that their marriage can be consummated. Other women engage in, and often enjoy, sexual intercourse but do not experience orgasms. The term **primary orgasmic dysfunction** refers to the situation of women who have never experienced an orgasm through any means. The expression **secondary** (or **situational**) **orgasmic dysfunction** refers to the situation of women who experience orgasms sometimes, through certain kinds of stimulation (such as masturbation), but not with their primary sexual partner or not during sexual intercourse. Secondary orgasmic dysfunction is a common complaint among female college students (Werner, 1975). As with most of the male problems, difficulties women may have in experiencing orgasm can be viewed as part of normal human variation and are not necessarily considered dysfunctional. Most research (e.g., Kinsey et al., 1953; Hunt, 1974) indicates that about a third of all women do not regularly have orgasms during intercourse. If these women enjoy intercourse, find it pleasurable and arousing, and can reach orgasm through oral or manual manipulation, they are considered sexually normal by most sex therapists (LoPiccolo, 1978).

It is not clear why some people respond freely to sexual stimulation but others do not. Research has revealed that most sexual problems have no physiological basis (Masters and Johnson, 1970). Instead, for some psychological reason, people are unable to abandon themselves to sexual pleasure. Some of these problems may be related to conflicts within the individual experiencing them, while others may be related to conflicts between partners. Therapists often find that many people who seek help for sexual problems were brought up with rigid religious, moral, or social standards concerning sex. Intellectually they may have rejected the belief that sex is wrong, but emotionally or psychologically they have not.

Other psychological sources of sexual problems range from having been the victim of "innocent" ridicule of one's anatomy in childhood to having suffered outright sexual abuse. Fear of failure may also cause sexual dysfunction. An individual may have one disappointing experience, then begin to wonder about his or her sexual adequacy. This anxiety can interfere with free response during the next sexual encounter, and the next, confirming the person's self-doubt. Thus, fear of sexual failure sometimes becomes a self-fulfilling prophecy.

At times, however, physiological factors are responsible for sexual dysfunction. Hormonal deficits, an insufficient blood supply to the penis, medication, and other medical conditions can all result in erectile failure. In fact, complaints of erectile failure sometimes lead to the discovery of diabetes, which can cause damage to the vessels that supply blood to the penis (Karacan et al., 1978). It is often possible to distinguish between physiologically and psychologically based erectile failure by monitoring bodily activity during sleep. Approximately every ninety minutes during sleep, healthy males have periods of erection that are associated with REM sleep (see Chapter 6), and these nocturnal erections can be detected by the use of devices that record changes in the diameter of the penis. Males whose erectile failure is due to psychological factors will have regular erections during sleep; those whose erectile failure is due to physiological factors will not.

Sex Therapy   In the approach to sex therapy developed by Masters and Johnson (1970), the couple is always treated as a unit by a pair of sex therapists, one male and one female. The focus is on the sexual relationship, on education, on the reduction of sexual anxiety, and on changing sexual behavior. Usually, to lessen the fear of failure, the couple is told not to engage in sexual intercourse for the time being and is assigned "nondemanding" sensual exercises, such as massaging each other. Gradually, more sexual activities are introduced, until at last the couple is permitted to engage in sexual intercourse.

Although many of the techniques developed by Masters and Johnson are still used, both the philosophy and methods of sex therapy have broadened during the past decade. Today sex therapists believe that sex is not always an isolated problem; thus they look at the couple's entire relationship, considering cognitive and emotional factors that affect it and applying techniques from various therapeutic approaches. The couple is helped to resolve conflicts, so that the division of household chores as well as sexual techniques can come within the scope of sex therapy (Heiman, LoPiccolo, and LoPiccolo, 1980).

The conditions of therapy have also changed. There may be only a single therapist, and people may be treated individually or in groups. Educational films and books may be used, and self-help techniques are sometimes prescribed in the treatment of premature ejaculation or orgasmic dysfunctions. Training in directed masturbation is often a part of the treatment for primary orgasmic dysfunction (Heiman, LoPiccolo, and LoPiccolo, 1980).

The fact that the couple is "given permission" to try out new activities by an authority figure (the therapist) may be therapeutic in itself. In most cases, sex therapy is brief (ten to fifteen sessions) but intensive. When the therapy is successful, a couple will find increased pleasure and satisfaction in sexual intercourse. Both partners will also develop a greater acceptance of themselves and of their individual differences.

Sexual Behavior

As with other drive-related behavior, such as eating, sexual activities vary with cultural and personal characteristics: just as we develop specific tastes in food, so do we develop specific tastes in

sexual partners and in the occasions on which we desire them. Furthermore, what we ourselves do, or refuse to do, often defines for us the bizarre or deviant: although some people consider oral-genital sex natural and pleasurable, others find it disgusting. The line between what one person considers "variations" and another considers "deviations" is a fine and difficult one to draw, and often depends on who is doing the drawing. In sexual preferences and practices, the range of human variability is wide.

Celibacy

Celibacy, or complete abstinence from sexual activity, seems unusual to most people, although some religious orders, such as the Catholic clergy, have idealized it as a preferred way of life. Until recently, coaches imposed pledges of temporary chastity on athletes in training, in the belief that regular sexual activity saps a person's strength. (There is no evidence for this belief.)

The percentage of people who choose permanent celibacy as a way of life is small. Most people go through periods of temporary chastity—in youth, after the breakup of a marriage or romance, and after the death of a spouse. Since surveys and studies of sexual activity have told us little about sexual inactivity, we know little about how people who have become accustomed to regular sex adjust to life without sex.

Masturbation

Attitudes toward masturbation have changed during the last two decades. Forty or fifty years ago physicians regularly warned youngsters that self-stimulation (or "self-abuse," as masturbation was then called) would cause acne, fever, blindness, even insanity. Today most people know that this is nonsense. According to a survey of more than 2,000 Americans, masturbation is thought to be wrong by only 15 percent of males and 14 percent of females eighteen to twenty-four years old and by 29 percent of males and 36 percent of females over fifty-five (Hunt, 1974). However, most adults are somewhat ashamed and secretive about masturbating. Few admit to their mates or friends that they occasionally stimulate themselves. Apparently the idea lingers that "playing with oneself" is immature behavior, symptomatic of personal inadequacies or of dissatisfaction with one's spouse as a sexual partner.

Yet surveys indicate that masturbation is common. In a survey by Morton Hunt (1974), 65 percent of the men said they had begun masturbating by age thirteen, compared with 45 percent in the sample of Kinsey and his associates (1948). The percentage of women who said that they had masturbated by age thirteen jumped from 15 percent in 1953 (Kinsey, 1953) to 40 percent in 1974. Masturbation rates increased most among women, with 82 percent of the women in Hunt's sample reporting that they masturbated regularly. The average rate was about every ten days—twice as often as in Kinsey's report. However, since the sample in the Hunt survey is *not* representative—especially among the youngest age group—its findings may somewhat inflate the incidence of sexual behavior.

Some theorists believe that early experiences with masturbation help to establish the foundation for adult sexuality. According to this view, self-stimulation is an important part of self-discovery.

Heterosexuality

Undoubtedly the most common sexual activity is heterosexuality, a man and a woman stimulating each other sexually. But what couples do together varies from day to day, year to year, and couple to couple. Standard sexual intercourse (penis in vagina) is only one possibility. Many heterosexual couples enjoy petting to orgasm, oral-genital stimulation, anal intercourse, intercourse between the thighs, dressing in fantasy costumes, and other forms of sex play. There is no "normal" position for intercourse itself, which may take place in as many positions as imagination and agility allow.

Premarital Sex   In Kinsey's day, most Americans claimed that they strongly disapproved of premarital sex. Yet 98 percent of men with a grade-school education, 85 percent of male high-school graduates, and 68 percent of men with a college education told investigators they had had sexual intercourse before getting married (Kinsey, Pomeroy, and Martin, 1948). Nearly half the women in the sample of Kinsey and his associates (1953) had also had premarital sexual experience, and over half of these had had intercourse only with their future husbands.

Since the time of the Kinsey reports, the incidence of premarital sex for men appears to have increased somewhat, particularly among college men. By age seventeen, half the college men in the Hunt sample (1974) were no longer virgins, compared with 23 percent in Kinsey's sample (1948). The biggest change for college men may

In recent years, the incidence of premarital sex has increased. One result of this trend is a rise in the number of teenage pregnancies, leading to conflicting points of view on whether to make birth control information and devices easily available to teens.

be in the women they choose as partners. In Kinsey's day, sex partners for most single young men were prostitutes or casual pickups. Today most college men have sex with women they care deeply for and with whom they have a continuing relationship (McCary, 1978). Even so, men's attitudes have not changed as much as one might expect. According to one survey (Pietropinto and Simmenauer, 1977), 33 percent of American men still want to marry virgins. Another 25 percent want to marry a woman who has had only one previous sexual partner.

Among women, the incidence of premarital sex has increased dramatically. In the Hunt sample (1974), 81 percent of the women aged eighteen to twenty-four had sexual intercourse before they were married—compared with only 31 percent of the women fifty-five and older. However, the majority of the women in the Hunt survey were no more casual about sex than their mothers had been. Over half had had sex with only one partner. In contrast, the median number of premarital sex partners for men was six.

The double standard persists, with one code of acceptable sexual behavior for men, another for women. In the Hunt sample, 60 percent of the men and 37 percent of the women thought it was all right for men to have sex with someone for whom they felt no strong affection; only 44 percent of the men and 20 percent of the women thought it was all right for women to do so—with men granting women more sexual freedom than women allowed themselves.

Extramarital Sex   About half the husbands and a quarter of the wives in the sample of Kinsey and his associates (1948; 1953) had had sexual intercourse with someone other than their spouse while they were married. To judge from the Hunt survey (1974), the percentage of married men who "play around" has not changed much since the 1940s, but the percentage of married women who do—especially young wives—has. Twenty-four percent of the wives under age twenty-five in the Hunt sample claimed to have had extramarital sexual experiences, compared to 8 percent in the Kinsey sample. But again, women are more conservative. Twice as many husbands as wives have had sex with six or more extramarital partners. According to the Hunt survey, it seems that men are more likely than women to seek extramarital sex without emotional involvement. Women are less likely to sep-

arate sexual desire from affection; they tend to embark on affairs only when they are dissatisfied with their marriages (Tavris and Offir, 1977).

Although the proportion of people who have extramarital sex is rising, attitudes toward the practice have not changed. More than 80 percent of the couples in the Hunt survey (1974) regarded it as wrong.

Homosexuality

Who is a homosexual? In the United States the tendency has been to label anyone who has had any homosexual experience, however infrequent, as homosexual. However, surveys have shown that sexual experimentation between members of the same sex is relatively common during adolescence (Kinsey, Pomeroy, and Martin, 1948). In the view of most psychologists, a

Homosexuality is a sexual preference for members of one's own gender. No longer classified as a disorder by the American Psychiatric Association, its causes remain unclear despite extensive research.

homosexual is a person whose primary source of sexual gratification is members of the same sex.

This definition was reflected in a seven-point scale created by Kinsey and his associates (1948; 1953) for their surveys. At one extreme (category 0) were people who were exclusively heterosexual; at the other (category 6) were people who were exclusively homosexual. Individuals who were predominantly heterosexual or homosexual but had a passing interest in the other sex were assigned to categories 2 and 4, respectively. Category 3 was for bisexuals, who had about equal interest in members of their own and the opposite sex. In this way, Kinsey set up a continuum of sexual preferences and avoided dividing the world into two opposing camps, one exclusively heterosexual and the other exclusively homosexual. Since the Kinsey scale is based upon counting sexual acts, it may categorize people in a way that does not accord with their self-image. For example, people in category 3 may not feel equally drawn to men and women despite the similarity shown in their behavior.

In gathering statistics on homosexuality, the Kinsey team included reports of both psychological and physical arousal, as well as any erotic contact, whether or not it led to orgasm. The results are shown in Table 17.1. These figures are dated, but they are still the only comprehensive estimates we have of the incidence of homosexual behavior in the general population.

It is likely, however, that the results overrepresent the degree of homosexuality in the male population. Among the men the researchers interviewed were a large minority with no higher education, many of whom had prison experience. In addition, they interviewed groups of men from homosexual organizations. A more accurate estimate of the proportion of exclusively homosexual men is between 3 and 4 percent. The estimate of Kinsey and his associates that between 2 and 3 percent of women are exclusively homosexual is probably accurate, for those interviews contained no biased groups (Gagnon, 1977). Since the Kinsey researchers classified adolescent sexual explorations between people of the same sex as homosexual and since their male sample was biased, their estimates concerning people with varying degrees of homosexual preferences are also too high.

Psychologists have advanced two basic hypotheses to explain why some people choose sex partners of the same biological sex; one hypothesis is biochemical and the other stresses social learning. According to the biochemical hypothesis, the level of sex hormones helps to determine sexual preference. Although one team of researchers (Kolodny et al., 1971) found that homosexual males had lower levels of the male hormone testosterone and lower sperm counts than did a comparable group of heterosexuals, other studies have found no difference between such groups, and some studies have found higher testosterone levels among homosexuals (Meyer-Bahlburg, 1977). Studies with women have found normal levels of sex hormones in most female homosexuals, but elevated levels of male hormones in about a third of them (Meyer-Bahlburg, 1979). However, because female hormone levels fluctuate with the menstrual cycle, with the use of oral contraceptives, and with

Table 17.1 Heterosexual–Homosexual Ratings (Ages 20–35)

Category		In Females (Percent)	In Males (Percent)
0	Entirely heterosexual experience		
	Single	61–72	53–78
	Married	89–90	90–92
	Previously married	75–80	
1–6	At least some homosexual experience	11–20	18–42
2–6	More than incidental homosexual experience	6–14	13–38
3–6	As much homosexual experience as heterosexual experience, or more	4–11	9–32
4–6	Mostly homosexual experience	3–8	7–26
5–6	Almost exclusively homosexual experience	2–6	5–22
6	Exclusively homosexual experience	1–3	3–16

Source: From data in Kinsey *et al. Sexual Behavior in the Human Female.* Philadelphia: W. B. Saunders, 1953, p. 488.

menopause, these findings do not demonstrate a link between male hormones and female homosexuality.

According to the second hypothesis, homosexuality is the product of early learning. One group of researchers (McGuire, Carlise, and Young, 1965) suggested the following developmental sequence:

Step 1. A "homosexual event" occurs. The individual engages in homosexual play, is approached by an older homosexual, or observes homosexual behavior.

Step 2. The individual fantasizes about this event while masturbating. Orgasm during masturbation reinforces the homosexual fantasy.

Step 3. When homosexual fantasies have been reinforced with orgasm, the individual is more likely to engage in overt homosexual behavior should the opportunity arise.

The peer group may play an important role in the development of homosexuality. Homosexuals of both sexes tend to report a preference for the company and the activities of the opposite sex during childhood. The resulting socialization within a peer group of the opposite sex may lead children to adopt the group's sexual orientation (Green, 1980).

Psychoanalytic hypotheses have also been advanced. It has been suggested that many male homosexuals had harsh fathers who did not allow their sons to be close to them. Hence, the sons did not identify with the fathers and did not learn the male role (Saghir and Robins, 1973). Others argue that male homosexuals had aggressive, domineering mothers and passive fathers (Bieber et al., 1962). In this case, too, a son might not form a strong masculine identity.

None of these hypotheses has been adequately documented. There is no more clear agreement on a single explanation of homosexual development than there is on a single theory of overall psychosexual development.

An interactive explanation that combines biochemistry with social learning has been advanced by Richard Green (1980), who suggests that inborn temperamental differences and behavioral predispositions (which may be linked with prenatal hormones) combine with the effects of parents and peer group to produce a child who develops in ways that are typical of the opposite sex. Early in the child's life, the parents make no attempt to discourage behavior that is typical of the opposite sex, the child gravitates to the opposite peer group, and the pattern of homosexual preference develops.

Traditionally, homosexuality has been considered a psychological disorder, but several years ago the American Psychiatric Association rejected the idea that homosexuality is a "disease" or that homosexuals are "sick." However, a number of psychiatrists continue to argue that homosexuality is necessarily a symptom of neurosis, immaturity, personality disorders, or faulty upbringing. The controversy is likely to continue.

The goals for homosexuals in therapy have shifted over the years. In the past therapists assumed that same-sex orientation was the root or symptom of other problems, and they concentrated on transforming homosexuals into heterosexuals despite the general agreement that this sort of conversion was extremely difficult to bring about. Today some therapists let their homosexual clients choose whether they want to change their sexual orientation or to become more comfortable with it. The problem is that, given this choice, many individuals may feel subtly pressured into saying that they want to change. Gerald Davison (1976), for one, argues that a therapist should never try to change a person's sexual orientation. The goal of therapy, he says, should be to enhance interpersonal relationships and perhaps sexual technique, with no reference to sexual preferences.

Deviant Sexual Behavior

Some forms of sexual behavior so strongly violate community norms that they are regarded with abhorrence and punished with lengthy prison sentences. In many societies, including the United States, rape and incest fall into the class of deviant sexual behavior, although both have at times been permitted in some cultures. In ancient Egypt, for example, the incestuous marriage of brother and sister was customary, while in wartime the rape of women has historically been considered the right of invading warriors (Brownmiller, 1975). Either rape or incest can result in physical or emotional harm to the victim.

Rape

When sexual intercourse with another person is the result of physical force, threat, or intimidation, it is called **rape**, and most psychologists feel that the primary motive for rape is not sex at all but anger or the assertion of power. In a study of 133 convicted rapists (Groth and Burgess, 1977), just over a third of the attacks were the result of anger; these rapes, which were unpremeditated, were characterized by violent physical assault, insults, and acts considered degrading by the rapist. The rest of the rapes were an assertion of power; these rapes were planned in advance, fantasized about beforehand, and the rapist stalked the victim, using threats but no more force than was necessary to succeed. According to these investigators, rape—whether motivated by anger or power—can serve many purposes. It compensates for the rapist's feelings of helplessness, reassures the rapist about his sexual adequacy, asserts his identity, defends him against homosexual impulses, bolsters his status among peers, and discharges frustration as well as supplying sexual gratification.

The relative unimportance of sexual gratification in rape is shown by the characteristics of rapists. Most rapists are young, married or dating women with whom they have sex on a voluntary basis, but either lack or believe they lack the ability to establish a satisfying, loving relationship with a woman (Rada, 1978). In studies (Abel, Blanchard, and Becker, 1978) similar to those used by Heiman (1975) to test male and female arousal to pornography, rapists and a control group of normal men both responded with erections to audio tape descriptions of mutually enjoyable intercourse, but only the rapists responded to descriptions of rape. In addition, a small group of rapists—presumably those who raped as a result of anger—responded sexually to tapes of aggression that had no sexual component. In these studies, normal men's reports of their own sexual arousal corresponded closely to their measured physical responses, but rapists consistently underestimated their own sexual arousal.

Although most rapists are male and most victims are female, such is not always the case. Men who rape other men are generally not homosexuals and are motivated not by sexual gratification but by power, revenge, sadism, status, or affiliation (Groth and Birnbaum, 1978). Their victims generally suffer greater physical injury than do female rape victims, and they are more likely than females to be subjected to gang rapes (Kaufman et al., 1980). Although women have been known to rape men, such cases are extremely rare and most women involved as aggressors in rapes are helping men rape another women.

Victims of rape at first show acute disorganization, characterized by shock, disbelief, fear, and anxiety. They may lose their appetite, startle at minor noises, develop headaches, insomnia, or fatigue; many have trouble maintaining normal family or occupational life. Some rape victims are plagued by frightening dreams or develop irrational fears (Burgess and Holstrom, 1974). In one study (Feldman-Summers et al., 1979), rape victims experienced a marked decrease in sexual satisfaction from petting or sexual intercourse, although masturbation and heterosexual signs of affection (talking, holding hands, simply being held) were as satisfying as they had always been. About two months after the rape, victims began to find petting or sexual intercourse more satisfying.

Incest

When sexual activity takes place between closely related persons, it is called **incest**. Although some authorities apply the term "incest" only to genital intercourse, the term is generally expanded to include oral-genital contact, fondling of the genitals, and mutual masturbation to include sexual activity with very young girls (with whom genital intercourse is extremely difficult) and homosexual incest (Meiselman, 1978). Cases of incest are rarely reported; the average incidence is one to two cases per million Americans each year (Weinberg, 1955). Most authorities agree, however, that the rate is much higher and that people are reluctant to bring cases to the attention of authorities because the consequences of a conviction are so severe—long prison terms, loss of job, and public ostracism. Among a group of adolescent girls in a state school for delinquents, for example, 15 percent had been involved in incestuous affairs with their fathers or stepfathers (Halleck, 1962).

Because so few cases of incest are reported and fewer are studied and because incest covers such a variety of relationships (father-daughter, mother-son, brother-sister, aunt-nephew, uncle-

Does Pornography Cause Sex Crimes?

Pornography is intended to create sexual arousal, and nearly 80 percent of Americans have seen some kind of pornography—written material, photographs, or film displaying explicit sexual activity (Abelson et al., 1970). Most adolescents are exposed to such material, generally among groups of peers at school, at home, or in the neighborhood.

The availability of pornography is an emotionally charged issue, and the failure of research to demonstrate that pornography has any harmful effects has had no influence on public attitudes. Indeed, the number of Americans who support some sort of government control to limit pornography has risen from 42 percent in 1974 to 74 percent in 1977 (Yankelovich et al., 1977).

A study (Donnerstein, 1980) with college men indicates that explicit sex films involving the coercion of women do make men more likely to behave aggressively toward women than toward men. Yet free access to pornography in Denmark was followed by a drop in sexual offenses, with the number of offenses steadily declining from 85 per 100,000 people in 1967 to just over 50 per 100,000 in 1971 (Kutchinsky, 1973).

More than a decade ago, the Commission on Obscenity and Pornography (1970) was created by Congress to study the effects of pornography on people. Among the 3,000 psychologists and psychiatrists they surveyed, 80 percent said they had never seen a case in which pornography contributed to a sex offense or a crime of violence, and 77 percent saw no connection between pornography and juvenile delinquency. But only 31 percent of the police chiefs surveyed for the commission believed there was no connection between juvenile delinquency and pornography. These responses were purely subjective judgments.

In an attempt to search out connections between pornography and sex crimes, other investigators (Goldstein and Kant, 1970) interviewed sixty convicted sex criminals and sixty-three normal men whose ages and educational backgrounds matched that of the sex offenders. They found that men convicted of rape and child molestation had seen much less pornography as adolescents than had the control group of normal men. In addition, the sex offenders had also seen less pornography in their last year of freedom than had the normal males. Thus the commission was unable to establish any connection between pornography and either rape or child molestation.

Nor do the people who purchase pornographic material seem to be out of the ordinary. In a series of studies (Massey, 1970; Finkelstein, 1970; Nawy, 1970; Winick, 1970), customers of adult bookstores were observed in Denver, Boston, San Francisco, Manhattan, Los Angeles, Chicago, Detroit, Atlanta, and Kansas City. In every city the typical pornography buyers were the same: white, middle-aged, middle-class, neatly dressed married men. The same pattern appeared when these investigators observed patrons of theaters showing explicit sex films. At only one theater did the audience differ: at a theater located in a town with several colleges, the patrons were younger, tended to be casually dressed, and included a number of male-female couples.

The commission concluded that they could discover no reason for interfering with the rights of adults to have access to sexually explicit material (Abelson et al., 1970). Indeed, the long-term effect of pornography may be boredom. When college men were paid to view explicit films for ninety minutes each day over a two-week period, their initial measured arousal to the films disappeared. Many of the men said they became so bored by the films that only a commitment to research and the hundred dollars they had been promised for their participation kept them returning to the laboratory (Howard et al., 1973).

niece, grandparent-grandchild), it is not possible to generalize about the motives involved. It has been suggested that father-daughter incest develops when a cold woman rears a sexually unresponsive daughter who later cannot fulfill her role as wife and who, as a consequence, encourages her own daughter to take over the role

(Kaufman, Peck, and Taguiri, 1954). However, the causes of father-daughter incest are probably more complex than this explanation of cold grandmother–unresponsive mother would indicate.

There is no general agreement about the long-term effects of such incest on girls (LaBarbera,

Dozier, and Martin, 1979). Some studies find that girls develop anxiety, guilt, or depression; other studies find that they seem uncertain about their sexual identification, that they later become promiscuous, or that they find it difficult to respond sexually as women. But some studies can find no adverse effects. It appears that a girl's age, the nature of the incestuous contact, its duration and frequency, the quality of the relationship between father and daughter, and the family's socioeconomic status affect the likelihood and the degree of disorder.

Changing Attitudes Toward Sexuality

American attitudes toward sexuality have undergone a radical shift in recent years. Among the effects of the "sexual revolution" is a new openness about sex. There are more books about sex in the stores, more chapters about sex in textbooks, more X-rated movies, more songs with explicit references to sex. This new willingness to discuss sex has been accompanied by increased knowledge about the physiology and psychology of sexuality, an increased acceptance of those whose sexual behavior diverges from the traditional code, and the provision of therapy for sexual dysfunction.

Another change that seems to be gaining momentum is the trend toward a single sexual standard. It has been suggested that male sexuality has traditionally been "body centered," concerned primarily with the physical aspects of sex, and that female sexuality has traditionally been "person centered," concerned primarily with tender and loving relationships (Reiss, 1973). Some of this difference may be biological, but a good deal of it comes from socialization. Whether the shifts in gender roles that have been taking place in social areas will result in a single sexual standard for both men and women remains to be seen.

SUMMARY

1. Gender is influenced by genetic, hormonal, and social factors. Genetic sex is determined at conception, when an ovum (which always has an X chromosome) is fertilized by a sperm having either an X chromosome (which produces a female) or a Y chromosome (which produces a male). When the testes or ovaries emerge, they produce hormones that complete the process of biological sex differentiation. Social influences on sexual development begin to operate as soon as a baby is born and affect both gender identity and gender role. Social factors seem able to override either genes or hormones, but may not always be able to overcome their combined effect. **Transsexualism**, in which gender identity is inconsistent with anatomical sex, confirms the need to consider gender identity and biological sex separately.

2. The major methods of studying sexual behavior are cross-cultural studies, sexual surveys, observational studies, and controlled experiments. Cross-cultural studies disclose the wide variations in sexual behavior in different cultures and have forced a redefinition of which sexual practices should be considered abnormal. The most important surveys of sexual activity were conducted by Alfred C. Kinsey in the 1940s, and despite some methodological shortcomings, these surveys have provided the foundation for later research on human sexuality. The first observational study of human sexual behavior was conducted by William Masters and Virginia Johnson in the 1960s. Although this study also had shortcomings, it provided some understanding of human sexual response. Controlled experiments can isolate the influences of various factors on sexual behavior, although practical and ethical considerations limit their use with human beings.

3. Men and women respond physiologically to sexual stimulation in parallel ways, and their response can be divided into four basic phases: the **excitement phase**, the **plateau phase**, **orgasm**, and the **resolution phase**. The subjective experience of orgasm is similar for men and women, but there are some gender differences in orgasm: not all women **ejaculate**, and men experience a **refractory**

period after orgasm, while women may experience **multiple orgasms**. Either psychological or physical stimulation can arouse both men and women, but effective sexual stimulation varies from person to person. Touch is one form of arousal, and the sensitivity of **erogenous zones** varies with the individual. Visual stimulation is very effective, but the role of odor in human sexual response has not been established. Fantasies may be the most powerful erotic stimulant of all. Despite the physiological changes that accompany aging, enjoyable sexual activity can continue throughout life.

4. Any problem that prevents an individual from engaging in sexual relations or from reaching orgasm is known as a **sexual dysfunction**. **Erectile failure** refers to a man's inability to achieve or maintain an erection with a partner. In **primary erectile failure**, a man has never achieved or maintained an erection; in **secondary erectile failure**, a man has reached orgasm in the past but is unable to acquire or maintain an erection at present or in certain situations. **Premature ejaculation** means that a man ejaculates before he or his partner would like. **Inhibited ejaculation** refers to a man's inability to ejaculate during sex with a partner. **Vaginismus** is a condition in which a woman's vagina involuntarily clamps shut so that penetration by her partner's penis is impossible or extremely painful. In **primary orgasmic dysfunction**, a woman has never experienced an orgasm by any means; in **secondary orgasmic dysfunction**, a woman sometimes experiences orgasm but not with her present partner or not during intercourse. Most sexual dysfunction has a psychological basis, but physiological factors—such as hormonal deficits, an insufficient blood supply to the penis, and other medical conditions, can result in erectile failure.

5. People's sexual activities vary with their cultural and personal characteristics. Although few people choose **celibacy** as a permanent way of life, most people go through periods of temporarity chastity. Masturbation is common among both men and women, and relatively few people consider it wrong. Early experiences with masturbation may help to establish the foundation for adult sexuality. Hetereosexual interaction, which can take a great number of forms, is the most common sexual activity. Since the 1940s, premarital sex appears to have increased a little among men and a great deal among women. The proportion of women engaging in extramarital sex is rising, although a majority of people consider such affairs as wrong. A **homosexual** is a person whose primary source of gratification is members of the same sex. Psychologists have advanced a variety of hypotheses—biochemical, learning, and psychoanalytic—to explain homosexual development, but have not reached agreement on any single explanation. As attitudes toward homosexuality have changed, therapy goals for homosexuals have shifted. All therapists once attempted to transform homosexuals into heterosexuals, but many now let their clients decide whether to change their sexual orientation or to strive for greater acceptance of their homosexuality.

6. **Rape** is sexual intercourse with another person as the result of physical force, threat, or intimidation, and its primary motive is not sexual gratification but anger or the assertion of power. Rape can compensate for a rapist's feelings of helplessness, assert his identity, defend him against homosexual impulses, bolster his status among his peers, or discharge his frustration. Victims of rape may show shock, disbelief, fear, or anxiety; they may have trouble maintaining a normal family or occupational life, and most experience a marked decrease in satisfaction from sexual intercourse. **Incest** is sexual activity between two closely related persons, and cases are rarely reported because the consequences of conviction are so severe. Because incest covers such a variety of relationships, it is not possible to generalize about the motives involved. Father-daughter incest appears to have varying effects, depending on the girl's age, the nature of the incestuous contact, its duration and frequency, the quality of the relationship between father and daughter, and the family's socioeconomic status.

7. Surveys suggest that the sexual revolution is more accurately described as a change in sexual attitudes than a change in sexual behavior.

KEY TERMS

androgen insensitivity
   syndrome
androgens
celibacy
ejaculation
erectile failure
erogenous zones
excitement phase
homosexual
incest

inhibited ejaculation
multiple orgasms
orgasm
plateau phase
premature ejaculation
primary erectile failure
primary orgasmic dysfunction
rape
refractory period

resolution phase
secondary erectile failure
secondary (or situational)
   orgasmic dysfunction
semen
sexual dysfunction
transsexualism
Turner's syndrome
vaginismus

RECOMMENDED READINGS

CROOKS, R., and K. BAUR. *Our Sexuality.* Menlo Park, Calif.: Benjamin Cummings, 1980. A personalized approach to the study of human sexuality, with an emphasis on common problems.

FORISHA, B. L. *Sex Roles and Personal Awareness.* Glenview, Ill.: Scott, Foresman, 1978. An up-to-date, lucid presentation of the complex issue of gender role development.

KINSEY, A. C., W. B. POMEROY, and C. E. MARTIN. *Sexual Behavior in the Human Male.* Philadelphia: Saunders, 1948.

KINSEY, A. C., W. B. POMEROY, C. E. MARTIN, and P. H. GEBHARDT. *Sexual Behavior in the Human Female.* Philadelphia: Saunders, 1953. The classic "Kinsey studies" of sexual behavior, which provided the first broad survey and comprehensive statistics concerning the sexual behaviors of Americans.

LOPICCOLO, J., and L. LOPICCOLO (eds.). *Handbook of Sex Therapy.* New York: Plenum Press, 1978. A comprehensive and mature presentation of the principles and techniques of modern sex therapy.

LURIA, Z., and M. D. ROSE. *Psychology of Human Sexuality.* New York: Wiley, 1979. A well-written basic text which surveys the psychological literature on sexuality.

MASTERS, W. H., and V. E. JOHNSON. *Human Sexual Response.* Boston: Little, Brown, 1966. Based on observational studies, this was the first thoroughly detailed account of the physiological changes that accompany sexual arousal and orgasm.

MONEY, J., and H. MUSAPH (eds.). *The Handbook of Sexology.* Amsterdam: Elsevier/North Holland Biomedical Press, 1977. Containing over a hundred chapters, this is a very comprehensive and sophisticated presentation of scientific and theoretical approaches to the study of sexual behavior.

MORRISON, E. (ed.). *Human Sexuality.* 2nd ed. Palo Alto, Calif.: Mayfield, 1977. A book of light but interesting readings, many from popular magazines, covering a broad range of issues in sexuality.

PART SIX

Personality and Individual Differences

My wife, Janet, has many endearing traits. She is, for instance, a lover of plants and animals. I, myself, don't dislike them, you understand, but if they'll leave me alone, I'll be delighted to leave them alone. (It's an example of our own individual personality differences.)

Just to show you, Janet even loves pigeons, those not very bright birds that seem to be more at home in Manhattan than people are.

Once she noted that a pigeon had discovered our balcony (thirty-three stories above ground level) and she found it impossible not to feed it. Naturally, it came back the next day, and the next, and after a while, it brought its mate. Other pigeons, noting that old Joe was getting fat, followed it, and also located our balcony, which came to look like something out of Hitchcock's, *The Birds.*

Janet now buys bird seed and various other types of avian comestibles, in huge fifty-pound bags or something and is, I believe, feeding every pigeon in New York (and cleaning the balcony of its accumulation of guano, periodically, with a pick and shovel.)

All these pigeons look alike to me, but Janet can tell them apart at a glance. To her they have distinct colors, personalities, and patterns of behavior. She talks to them, worries about them in bad weather, and, I think, has grown unaware that they are non-people.

My daughter, Robyn (Janet's stepdaughter), is also fond of plants and animals. Her specialty is cats. She has two of them. There is no difficulty telling them apart. One is solid black ("Satan") and the other looks like an animated patchwork quilt in predominantly light colors ("Angel"). There's no difficulty telling the personalities apart, either. Satan talks to everyone; Angel talks only to Robyn.

My son, David, is allergic to cats—literally. That is too bad for if he could endure being in the same room with one, he would love them. In fact, the way we discovered his allergy was by observing him stroking an alley cat lovingly, and then walking into the house a few minutes later a bloated travesty of himself.

I like cats, too, but I'm suspicious of dogs. It's not hatred, mind you, but merely an inner feeling that unless I avoid them carefully, they'll slobber over me. Dogs sense this uneasiness in me and react appropriately—by their standards.

They love me.

I will never forget the doom-ridden evening when our dinner hosts turned out to have a huge canine beast (an elephant-hound, I believe), which was the size of a large calf. It walked into the dining room, stared at all of us in turn, assessing the situation, then, without a scrap of hesitation came to me, as I shrank, large-eyed, back in my chair, and plopped down on my feet. It then uncorked about a yard of tongue and panted at me. I'm sure it meant well.

The point I am making is that you can take any odd corner of human affairs—the interaction of people and animals—and have no trouble in discovering that no two people are entirely alike.

But, then, why should they be?

ISAAC ASIMOV

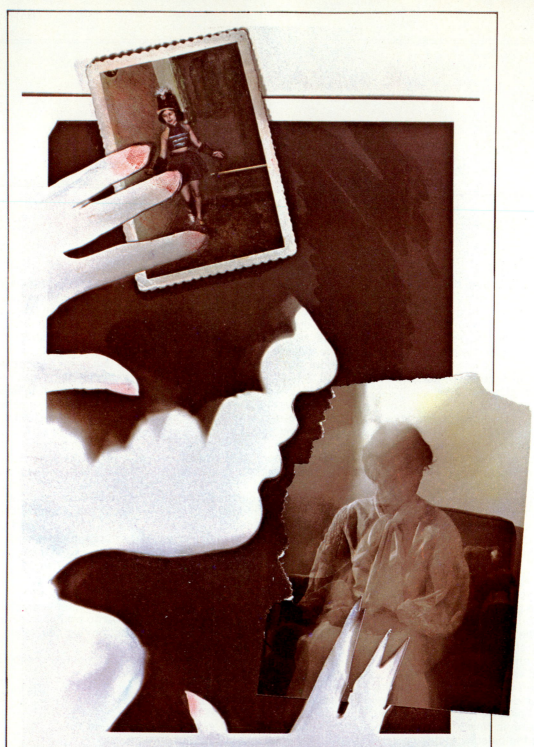

"Midway in life's journey I was made aware, that I had strayed into a dark forest and the right path appeared not anywhere. —"

CHAPTER 18

Psychoanalytic Theories of Personality

Like the man who was surprised to learn that he had been speaking "prose" all his life, you may be unaware that you already know a great deal about the psychology of personality. You know, for example, that if you tell two friends a joke, one is likely to find it hilarious, while the other is likely to miss the point. Ask three people their opinion of the same movie, and their reports are likely to vary, attributing different motivations to the characters, recalling different episodes as important, and stating different themes. Introduced to a young woman, one young man will smile politely and go back to watching the football game; another will shuffle his feet and lower his eyes; and a third will tell her she is beautiful and ask for her phone number. Thus, everyday experiences show that each person is unique, with her or his own responses to the world. Moreover, these unique characteristics seem to be stable and enduring. The friend who laughs easily at a joke is almost always ready for a good time; the foot shuffler is nearly always shy and uncomfortable around women.

Such differences among people and the stability of any individual's behavior over long periods is the essence of **personality**. Regardless of their approach, all personality theorists address two key questions: When several people confront the same situation, why do they not all behave the same? What accounts for the relative consistency of a person's behavior from one situation to the next? These questions inevitably lead to others. Is there something inside that makes people think, feel, and act in distinctive and characteristic ways? Are people driven by biological forces? Do we inherit personality traits from our parents? How do outside forces—our experiences, our relationships, our culture, and the times in which we live—shape us? Are we motivated by unconscious forces, or do we act as we do simply out of habit? Can we—do we—change over time?

Faced with the extraordinary complexity of human behavior and the wide range of individual differences in personality, theorists have developed radically different explanations in their attempts to answer these questions. The resulting theories, discussed in this chapter and in Chapter 19, are best regarded as complementary—not contradictory—explanations of human diversity. Each theory sheds light on certain aspects of personality and none can satisfactorily account for all aspects. The approaches discussed in this chapter have developed from psychoanalytic theory and research; they emphasize the significance of childhood experience and the power of mental events to determine human behavior.

Freud's Psychoanalytic Theory

The most influential theorist in the field of personality has been Sigmund Freud (1856–1939). He conceived the first formal theory of personality, and after nearly a century, his theory remains the most detailed and original yet formulated. Critics of Freud—and there have been some vociferous ones—admit that the range of phenomena he identified and explored stands as a challenge and an inspiration to personality theorists. Freud drew on a number of assets to make the rich observations he set down on paper: his remarkable skill as an observer of human behavior; his training in medical science; his background in literature and history, including an extensive knowledge of such materials as jokes and folk tales; and his unusually fine writing ability. A reader needs no particular training in psychology to be excited, entertained, and educated by some of Freud's major works, such as *The Interpretation of Dreams* (1900), *Civilization and Its Discontents* (1930), and *New Introductory Lectures on Psychoanalysis* (1933).

Freud first became interested in personality when he tried to account for his patients' strange physical problems. Many of them suffered from what seemed to be a neurological defect—for example, paralysis of an arm, loss of sensation in a hand, deterioration of hearing or vision. But Freud, trained as a neurologist, knew that in many cases the defect had no physical origin. When a patient lost feeling in a hand, for instance, the affected region might be confined to an area that is covered when wearing a glove ("glove anesthesia")—a pattern that does not correspond to any known grouping of nerves.

Freud speculated that such symptoms could be caused by emotional stress. He had been treating these "hysterical" disorders, as he called them, with hypnosis. He soon began a collaboration with Josef Breuer, who had discovered that the symptoms sometimes disappeared if the patient was asked to recall critical events from early childhood while hypnotized (Breuer and Freud, 1937). One of Breuer's patients was a young woman he called Anna O. While caring for her dying father, she had become exhausted and developed a nervous cough, severe headaches, abnormal vision, and other physical problems. When Breuer visited Anna, she often passed into a trancelike state that she called "clouds." In this state she recounted past experiences, a process she called "chimney sweeping." If she recalled an experience related in some way to one of her symptoms—especially if she seemed to relive the emotions connected with it—the symptoms often disappeared for several hours. Breuer sometimes hypnotized Anna and encouraged her to talk about emotional events that seemed to be related to her physical symptoms. This technique, too, was often effective in relieving her symptoms.

After using hypnosis for a time, Freud concluded that it was not an ideal therapeutic procedure. Many patients could not be hypnotized, and although hypnosis offered others relief, their symptoms often recurred. Moreover, hypnotized patients did not seem to understand their underlying difficulties.

As a result, Freud turned to another technique he called **free association**, in which the patient lay down on a couch and said whatever came to mind. In the course of these apparently aimless statements, themes centering on the patient's important emotional conflicts often emerged. As these conflicts were talked about, the patient began to understand them and to find them less frightening; when this happened, the symptoms disappeared, just as Anna O's symptoms had vanished under hypnosis.

Freud found that although Anna O. and the other patients with "hysterical" disorders at first could not remember childhood experiences, especially the wishes and fears that seemed to produce their symptoms, free association, sometimes assisted by hypnosis, brought back the memories. From such evidence, Freud theorized the existence of an aspect of personality, unknown to the mind of the subject, that he called the **unconscious**.

The concept of the unconscious is Freud's major contribution to the understanding of human behavior and personality. In attempting to explain his view that the contents of the conscious mind are only a part of personality, Freud drew an analogy between the mind and an iceberg: people's conscious thoughts resemble the small tip of an iceberg; beneath the surface—out of the person's awareness—lies the massive unconscious. The unconscious—which is a process, not a thing—represents instinctual drives and infantile goals, hopes, wishes, and needs that have been repressed, or concealed from conscious awareness, because they cause internal conflict. Freud coined the term **psychoanalysis** to describe the process by which he attempted to bring unconscious material into the patient's awareness, where it could be examined rationally.

Free association turned out to be only one method of reaching the unconscious. Freud later discovered that dreams, jokes, and even accidents—all instances in which normal conscious controls over behavior have been suspended—are keys that help unlock unconscious emotional conflicts. Freud believed that such conflicts are common and that they arise when social or moral constraints clash with impulses to engage in sexual or aggressive actions. People are generally not completely aware of either side of the conflict, which results in an unconscious or semiconscious compromise whose nature is often revealed in dreams, jokes, accidents, and physical symptoms. For instance, the "glove anesthesia" referred to earlier may be the result of a compromise between a desire to engage in a forbidden action—perhaps to masturbate or to strike someone—and the requirement that sexuality or hostility be expressed only in socially acceptable ways.

Dreams, in Freud's view, may be seen as expressing unacceptable impulses, disguised from one's conscious self by their apparent incoherence. Dreams have both manifest and latent content. The **manifest content** is the surface meaning of the dream, the events the dreamer relates—perhaps a terrifying elevator ride with an old man to the top of a tower. The **latent content** is the underlying meaning of the dream, which may be uncovered through free association and analysis—in this example, perhaps an unconscious wish to have sexual relations with one's father. A dream's manifest content had no interest for Freud except as it provided clues to its latent content.

As Freud pointed out, jokes also serve as an outlet for sexual or aggressive impulses that society can accept when they are disguised as harmless humor. And accidents, such as forgetting an appointment, spilling a drink on a friend's best suit, or mispronouncing the name of a disliked person, are additional signs of unconscious conflicts. Suppose a woman is scheduled to visit her parents and anticipates that the meeting may be unpleasant. She does not want to go home, yet she cannot admit this to herself. An unconscious compromise may be to miss the last bus home and then, in genuine distress, to call her parents with an apology.

Through psychoanalytic treatment, the sources of such compromises can be made conscious. The procedure can help people to understand themselves better, to express formerly unconscious and forbidden impulses in an acceptable way, and to reduce the unwanted side effects caused by emotional conflicts.

Psychoanalysis was introduced to the world in 1900 with the publication of Freud's book entitled *The Interpretation of Dreams*. Although Freud's ideas were not accepted at first—especially the idea that sexual drives and conflicts originate in childhood and are involved in most emotional problems of adults—psychoanalysis gradually came to be recognized as a major breakthrough in self-understanding. Many people came to Vienna to study Freud's methods, and soon psychoanalysts were practicing in many countries, including the United States. Until his death in 1939, Freud continually revised and supplemented his theory, but never completely finished his work. His writings grew voluminous and as he developed new insights, a number of contradictions appeared.

Freud's Conceptualization of Personality Structure

Although Freud's view of unconscious conflicts emerged from his work with troubled patients, the idea was based on a coherent theory of personality that he believed explained the behavior of everyone. Freud divided personality into three separate but interacting agencies: the id, the ego, and the superego. Each of these agencies has its own highly specific role in maintaining normal personality functioning. It may help our understanding of this concept of personality to know that the German word that Freud used for id is *es*, which means "it," implying an alien force, something in a person that is not recognized as part of the self. The ego he called *Ich*, which means "I," the part of the personality recognized and accepted as oneself. "Superego" (*überich*) thus means "over the I"; as we shall see, it refers to the moral component that is imposed on the self by society.

Freud sometimes referred to the three agencies as if they had wills of their own—as if the ego were a rational, self-controlled person at war with an irrational and impulsive person (the id) and a harsh, moralistic person (the superego). This manner of reference, while dramatic and

Freud on the Id, Ego, and Superego

We are warned by a proverb against serving two masters at the same time. The poor ego has things even worse: it serves three severe masters and does what it can to bring their claims and demands into harmony with one another. These claims are always divergent and often seem incompatible. No wonder that the ego so often fails in its task. Its three tyrannical masters are the external world, the superego and id. . . . Owing to its origin from the experiences of the perceptual system, it is earmarked for representing the demands of the external world, but it strives too to be a loyal servant of the id, to remain on good terms with it, to recommend itself to it as an object and to attract its libido to itself. In its attempts to mediate between the id and reality, it is often obliged to cloak the *Ucs.* [unconscious] commands of the id with its own *Pcs.* [preconscious] rationalizations, to conceal the id's conflicts with reality, to profess, with diplomatic disingenuousness, to be taking notice of reality even when the id has remained rigid and unyielding. On the other hand it is observed at every step it takes by the strict super-ego, which lays down definite standards for its conduct, without taking any account of its difficulties from the direction of the id and the external world, and which, if those standards are not obeyed, punishes it with tense feelings of inferiority and of guilt. Thus the ego, driven by the id, confined by the superego, repulsed by reality, struggles to master its economic task of bringing about harmony among the forces and influences working in and upon it; and we can understand how it is that so often we cannot suppress a cry: "Life is not easy!" If the ego is obliged to admit its weakness, it breaks out in anxiety—realistic anxiety regarding the external world, moral anxiety regarding the super-ego and neurotic anxiety regarding the strength of the passions in the id.

From Sigmund Freud, *New Introductory Lectures on Psychoanalysis* (1933). James Strachey (ed. and tr.). New York: W. W. Norton, 1965.

---

engaging, has received much criticism from psychologists who believe that such descriptions border on mysticism. It will avoid confusion if we take the terms in the sense actually intended by Freud—as metaphorical names for the functional (not physical) divisions of the personality. The id, ego, and superego are not persons, places, or physical things; they are the names given to certain motivational forces whose existence is inferred from the way people behave. If they sometimes seem to be more places or entities than abstract forces, this is only a result of Freud's literary style. The accompanying quotation is both a good example of that vibrant style and a clear explanation of Freud's view of the relationships among the three components of adult personality.

The Id   Freud characterized the **id** as a reservoir of psychic energy that can be neither increased nor decreased. Although it is not a place, it may be seen metaphorically as a pool of instinctual biological drives present in every individual at birth, so that the personality of a newborn baby is all id. In Freud's terms, an **instinct** is the psychological expression of a biologically based physical need, such as food, sex, elimination of waste, or any other bodily requirement. To satisfy a need that has been aroused, human beings develop "wishes" that motivate and direct behavior. The instincts provide the psychic energy that powers the entire personality. Thus the id—that is, all the instincts together—is the energy source for the ego and the superego, which develop later in childhood.

Freud distinguished between two broad types of instincts in the id. The first type is **Eros** (the Greek word for "love"), the constructive life instinct responsible for survival, self-propagation, and creativity. In Eros are included the need for food, warmth, and, above all, sex. Freud used the term "sex" broadly, to cover a wide range of life-giving and life-sustaining activities, from genital intercourse to artistic creation. The energy of Eros is generated by what Freud called the **libido**, a driving force permeating the entire personality and propelling it through life.

The second type of instinct, **Thanatos** (from the Greek word for "death"), or the death instinct, is opposed to Eros. Freud's discussion of the death instinct came late in his writings, and the concept remains vague. While studying aggression, he concluded that the human organism is instinctively drawn back to the original inanimate state from which it arose, a state in which all tension would be dissipated—in short, the state of death (Freud, 1920). This instinctive attraction to death gives rise in each individual to aggressive tendencies directed at the self. However, since self-destruction is opposed by the life-preserving energy of the libido, aggression against the self usually is redirected outward, against the world, motivating human beings to compete, to conquer, and to kill. Although sex and aggression can be seen as two opposing forces, they are also closely related. Both have their origin in the id; both seek the release of tension.

Because the instincts that make up the id are biological, they take no account of logic or reason, reality or morality. The id is concerned only with reducing the tensions generated by the organism's needs: the need for warmth, food, tactile stimulation, and so forth. This tendency of the id to devote itself exclusively to the immediate reduction of tension is called the **pleasure principle**.

The Ego Although the id instinctively desires the satisfaction of biological needs, it has no way to satisfy them, other than by activating reflex actions such as sucking. Nor does it have any way to determine which means of tension reduction are safe and which bring danger to the organism. To do these things, a new psychic component, the **ego**, develops after an infant is approximately six months old. The ego takes for itself part of the energy of the id and proceeds to serve as the mediator between the id and reality (Freud, 1920; 1923). Unlike the id, much of the ego is conscious. Building on the basis of the child's previous contacts with reality, the ego uses memory, reason, and judgment in attempts to satisfy the desires of the id, to anticipate the consequences of a particular means of gratification, and sometimes to delay gratification in order to achieve long-range goals.

Suppose a three-year-old boy is playing in his room. The id signals that aggressive impulses seek release, and the boy reaches for his toy hammer. The ego then goes into action, scanning the environment for an appropriate outlet. The boy's baby sister is playing nearby. Should he hit her in the head with his hammer? The ego, which

Freud believed that aggressive behavior is a product of a self-destructive instinct, which he termed Thanatos. Because self-destruction conflicts with the constructive impulses of the libido, it is deflected outward, leading to competition and violence.

knows from experience that such an action will result in the painful consequence of a spanking, says no and continues the scanning process. A wooden block lies on the carpet. The ego determines that no harm will come from pounding the block, and so the boy proceeds to bang away at it.

Thus, in contrast to the pleasure principle of the id, the ego operates on what is called the **reality principle**, the foundation of which is the concern for safety. The ego is often called the executive agency of personality, because it controls the individual's actions and manipulates the environment. Through this basic ego function of finding realistic means to satisfy the id, the mind develops and refines its higher cognitive functions: perception, learning, discrimination, memory, judgment, and planning.

The Superego   The third psychic component, the **superego**, is that part of the personality that represents the moral standards of the society as conveyed to the child by the parents. Suppose that three years have passed since the little boy banged the wooden block, and the same child once again sits with hammer in hand looking for something to pound. Again he considers his sister's head, but this time he rejects that outlet not just to avoid being punished, but because hitting her would be "wrong." This reaction indicates that the boy has developed a superego—the approximate equivalent of a conscience.

In Freud's view, the superego emerges from the resolution of the Oedipus complex (see Chapter 14), when children repress their desire for the parent of the opposite sex and identify with the parent of the same sex. In this way, a boy can share vicariously his father's special relation with his mother, and a girl can share vicariously her mother's special relation to her father. Children **internalize** the moral standards they learn from the parent of the same sex—that is, they incorporate these standards into their own personality.

Like the ego, the superego receives its energy from the id. Unlike the ego, however, the superego takes no more account of reality than the id does. Instead of considering what actions are realistic or possible, the superego embraces both an **ego ideal**—our values and abstract moral ideals—and a conscience that constantly commands the individual to stifle the id's sexual and aggressive impulses that conflict with moral goals. The function of the superego, then, is to prohibit what is morally wrong and to promote what is morally right. Thus it is up to the ego to find a way to satisfy the id without giving pain to the superego—pain experienced as remorse or guilt. After the superego develops, doing something "wrong" can result in a double punishment: chastisement from someone else, and headaches, dreams of being arrested for an unknown crime, or such self-punishment as losing vital notes the night before final exams.

Thus in the fully developed psychic structure, the ego has to deal with three irrational forces: the id, which seeks only the satisfaction of its irrational and amoral demands; the superego, which seeks only the satisfaction of its ideals; and reality, which offers only a limited range of objects for satisfying the id and which delivers stern punishment for unwise choices (Blum, 1953).

Freud's Theory of Personality Dynamics

As the description of personality structure makes clear, Freud's theory concerning the motivating or driving forces behind personality, or the **dynamics** of personality, is based on conflict between opposing energies. Intrapsychically—that is, within the person—there are conflicts between the life instinct and the death instinct, between love and hate, between creativity and destructiveness. In addition, within each of us the urge to satisfy our inborn instincts conflicts with the urge to obey the rules of society, which insist that our instinctual desires be restrained and rechanneled in socially acceptable ways.

Freud believed that most human behavior is directed toward resolving these conflicts, reducing tension, and restoring **homeostasis**—or a state of equilibrium. A bodily source of excitation, or a need, arouses an instinct; the aroused instinct activates behavior. If the behavior is effective, the person returns to the state that existed before the instinct was aroused.

Of course, Freud recognized that many acts are responses to events in the external world. A threatening gesture from another person, a sudden thunderstorm, or a ringing telephone elicit behavior, but such events are relatively easy to handle. A person need only flee from a threat, come in from the rain, or answer the phone. However, a "threat" from the superego, a "thunderstorm" in the id, or a "ring" of anxiety is another matter. Such intrapsychic events activate all parts of the personality, and the ego must cope with the contending demands of the id and the superego, as well as with the reality of the situation. For this reason, Freud emphasized internal sources of excitation over stimulation from the external world. In Freud's view, instincts were the driving force behind behavior.

Displacement of Instinctual Energy   In some cases it is obvious that instinct is the force behind behavior—as when a man responds to seductive behavior by a sexually attractive woman. In other cases the instinctual basis of behavior is less obvious. What instinct motivates a person to compose a symphony, for example?

To understand the way Freud would answer this question, we must reexamine his concept of instincts. According to Freud, an instinct has four characteristic features: (1) a **source**, which is a bodily condition or need, such as the need for sexual release; (2) an **aim**, which is to satisfy the need and stop the excitation; (3) an **object**, which is the means the person uses to satisfy the need; and (4) a force called **impetus**, whose strength is determined by the intensity of the need. The source and aim of an instinct remain constant throughout life. However, the means a person uses to satisfy the same need (its object) vary considerably. Psychic energy can be **displaced**, or transferred from the original object to a variety of substitute objects. A person who wants to express hostility, for example, but fears the consequences of an aggressive act, can redirect the energy to another object—as when a man who is afraid to assert himself at the office comes home and blows up at his wife. This capacity for displacing instinctual energy from one object to another is a key concept in Freud's theory of personality dynamics.

Many human habits, characteristics, and interests develop when energy is displaced from the objects originally chosen by our instincts. For example, smoking may be considered the displacement of energy that was originally directed toward sucking the mother's breast. Similarly, a woman's need to keep her apartment spotless may be a displacement of energy originally directed toward anal pleasure. The substitute object is, however, seldom as satisfying as the original object. Thus tension accumulates and acts as a permanent motivating force behind each person's behavior.

Sometimes displacement can be positive and produce high cultural achievement. In *Civilization and Its Discontents* (1930), Freud pointed out that the development of civilization was made possible by the inhibition of original object choices and the diversion of instinctual energy from them to social organization and cultural development, a mechanism he called **sublimation**. Freud suggested, for example, that Leonardo da Vinci's urge to paint Madonnas was a sublimated expression of his longing for reunion with his mother, from whom he had been separated at an early age. But for most of us, sublimation fails to bring complete satisfaction, and

residual tension may discharge itself in the form of nervousness or restlessness. This dissatisfaction, Freud noted in one of his characteristically pessimistic passages, is the price human beings pay for civilization, and it may be a cause of periodic wars and other lapses into violent behavior.

Anxiety   **Anxiety** is a state of psychic pain that alerts the ego to danger; it is akin to fear. Freud distinguished three types of anxiety, each based on a different source of danger. In **reality anxiety**, which is the closest to what we call "fear," the danger comes from the outside world. A person who sees a rattlesnake a foot away experiences reality anxiety. In **moral anxiety**, danger comes from the superego, which threatens to overwhelm the person with guilt or shame over some act that has been committed or merely contemplated. In **neurotic anxiety**, the danger comes from the id, when impulses threaten to burst through ego controls and cause the individual to do things that will bring punishment or shame.

Defense Mechanisms   When anxiety is acute and there appears to be no reasonable way of dealing with it, the ego resorts to what are called **defense mechanisms**. Defense mechanisms are intrapsychic schemes to conceal the source of anxiety from the self and the world. For example, a young woman who fears that her application to law school will be rejected may "forget" to take her birth control pills, "accidentally" become pregnant, and convince herself and others that the demands of motherhood prevent her from continuing her legal education. Her pregnancy allows her to avoid the problem, because the prospect of caring for an infant makes a law school application unlikely, and if she does not apply, she cannot be rejected. There are a number of common defense mechanisms, and they all share two characteristics: (1) they deny, falsify, or distort reality; and (2) they usually operate unconsciously, so that the person is not aware of what is taking place.

The fundamental defense mechanism, one that keeps threatening thoughts and memories from consciousness and pushes them back into the unconscious, is called **repression**. Repression was one of Freud's earliest discoveries. He observed that without considerable probing, his patients were unable to recall **traumatic**, or psychologically damaging, childhood events. These traumatic memories are concealed from conscious awareness and kept in the unconscious by strong forces. According to Freud, the threats from these unpleasant memories, the expenditures of energy needed to conceal them, and the anxiety generated in the process are at the basis of neurosis (see Chapter 22).

Fixation, another common defense mechanism, is a temporary halt in development, and it is a response to the anxiety associated with the next stage of psychosexual development. (Freud's concept of developmental stages is reviewed in the following section.) For example, a little girl entering the phallic stage may experience anxiety if her parents disapprove of her interest in genital organs. This anxiety may make the child afraid to move into the phallic stage, in which attention and energy are focused on the genital organs. Instead, the child may become temporarily fixated at the previous, anal, stage.

The defense mechanism of **regression** is a return to an earlier stage of development in response to some perceived threat. Regression is related to fixation in that a person usually regresses to a stage at which she or he was previously fixated: the child fixated at the oral stage can grow into the adult who regresses by overeating, as when a middle-aged man who is having difficulties with his wife overeats, because eating had given him pleasure in childhood.

Reaction formation, another common defense mechanism, is the replacement of an anxiety-producing impulse or feeling by its opposite; its function is to make a person unaware of the original source of distress. Instead of acknowledging that she hates her child, a mother may shower the child with expressions of love. A man who really wants to start fires may become a firefighter and spend his time putting them out. Generally, the stronger the impulse toward socially unacceptable behavior, the stronger the defense against it, so that crusaders who "protest too much" against what they consider reprehensible behavior may be displaying reaction formation.

The defense mechanism of **projection** involves the unknowing attribution of a person's instinctual impulses or threats from conscience to other people or to the external world. Such a process eases the anxiety that arises from these internal impulses and threats. A woman who is growing tired of a lover but who hesitates to break off the relationship, because subconsciously she feels it would be an aggressive move, may project her feelings onto her lover and begin to believe he is growing tired of her. If she expresses this belief, repeatedly stating that the man no longer loves her, she may induce him to break off the relationship—at once confirming her assertion and achieving her real goal. Another example of projection is the man who continually complains about being short-changed by clerks, perhaps because he wishes to cheat *them*. Similarly, people who keep fretting about the sexual promiscuity of the younger generation may be projecting fears concerning their own sexual impulses onto others.

Freud's Psychosexual Stages of Development

Freud was the first psychological theorist to emphasize the developmental aspects of personality and to stress the decisive role of infancy and childhood in establishing the basic character structure of an individual. Indeed, Freud believed that personality is formed by the time a child enters school and that later growth consists of elaborating this basic structure. The discussion in Chapter 14 noted Freud's belief that the child passes through a series of psychosexual stages during the first five years of life, with each stage originating in the sexual instincts of the personality and organized around one of the erogenous zones of the body. The three early stages, collectively called the **pregenital stage**, are the **oral** (birth to one year), the **anal** (one to two years), and the **phallic** (three to five years) stages. The possible relationships between a child's behavior in each of these stages and adult personality characteristics are shown in Figure 18.1. Following the pregenital stage, the child enters a period of **latency** (from about six to eleven years), in which libidinal dynamics are more or less stabilized. With adolescence, another eruption of libidinal forces upsets the stabilization of the latency period, and the adolescent enters the final stage of psychosexual development, the **genital stage**. As the adolescent attains mature sexuality and moves into adulthood, these libidinal forces gradually come under control. Although Freud believed that these stages of personality growth are distinct, he did not assume that children shift abruptly from one stage to another; instead, the transitions are gradual and the ages approximate. The

Figure 18.1 The relationship between a child's behavior at each of Freud's pregenital psychosexual stages and the adult personality that Freud predicted could result from becoming fixated at each stage. (A) A baby girl obtains oral gratification by putting just about anything she can find into her mouth; as an adult, she shows a similar lack of discrimination about what she takes into herself. (B) A two-year-old in the anal stage thwarts his mother by refusing to release his feces; as an adult he obtains satisfaction by hoarding money. (C) A four-year-old girl in the phallic stage, observing that she lacks a penis, gives up her hopes of being like a man in any way. As an adult, she adopts a traditionally passive female sex role.

organization of the adult personality includes contributions from all stages, and is a consequence of the way the child meets the demands of the id during each stage.

Development of Neo-Freudian Theories

Condensing Freud's rich and difficult theory into a few pages makes it seem terribly abstract, but his ideas came from concrete case studies of real people. Freud's psychoanalytic theory was painstakingly constructed and revised by checking and rechecking each interpretation until he was convinced that his observations and the theory fit together coherently. New data that could not be accounted for led him to revise his ideas until he was certain his theory was internally consistent and amply supported by case studies.

However, Freud's observations were made behind a closed office door—either while listening to patients pour out their dreams, feelings, and free associations or while scrutinizing himself (as he did in astonishing detail, reserving the final half-hour of each day for self-analysis). It is not surprising, therefore, that other investigators of personality failed to agree with everything Freud said. Even if we assume that Freud was a completely unbiased observer, we can question his particular sample of cases and his reliance on himself as a source of data. For example, Freud's strong attachment to his mother, an attractive woman half the age of Freud's father who was quite close to her son, may not be at all typical. It is possible—some would say likely—that other people's experiences are very different from those of Freud and his patients.

Little wonder, then, that before Freud had worked out his own ideas clearly, two of his close associates, Carl Jung and Alfred Adler, broke away from him. Throughout Freud's career, other students did the same. The positions of these **neo-Freudians**, who have retained some of Freud's insights, are worth considering, for they have challenged Freud's insistence on the primacy of the instincts.

Jung's Analytic Psychology

Carl Jung (1875–1961), who in 1913 founded his own school of psychoanalysis called **analytic psychology**, had a view of personality vastly different from Freud's. Though he adopted many of Freud's concepts, Jung strongly disagreed with him on two important issues: the importance of

the future and the nature of the unconscious (Jung, 1967). Jung believed that personality development is characterized by a forward movement: people are guided by their future aims as well as by their past experiences. Human beings continually try to realize their full potential and to achieve unity among all aspects of their personality. A person begins this effort by developing all parts of her or his personality, a process Jung called **individuation**. After achieving individuation, a person attempts to unite the contradictory aspects of personality into a fully realized self. Although Jung realized that no one can attain perfect unity, he held that this goal was the great driving force of all human behavior. Jung's theory, therefore, casts human beings in a more favorable light than Freud's, since Jung sees people as capable of doing more than simply adapting to and displacing their instinctual urges. In addition, they can act to develop their potential. Jung also proposed that there are two major personality orientations: **introversion**, in which the person withdraws interest from the external world and consequently is quiet, reserved, and cautious, and **extraversion**, in which the person is primarily oriented to the external world and thus is outgoing, sociable, and excitement-seeking.

In regard to the unconscious, Jung agreed with Freud on the great importance of unconscious influences on behavior, but Jung distinguished two levels of the unconscious. One level,

This young woman appears to be an example of the personality orientation Jung called introversion—a tendency to withdraw from the external world and to be cautious and reserved.

the **personal unconscious**, is similar to the unconscious as depicted by Freud; it contains experiences the individual has repressed or forgotten. According to Jung, the contents of the personal unconscious can be returned to consciousness.

The other level, which Jung called the **collective unconscious**, is a storehouse of memories and behavior patterns inherited from humanity's ancestral past. It is almost entirely detached from anything personal in the life of the individual. The collective unconscious consists of **archetypes**, ancient ideas or images common to all human beings in all eras and all regions of the world. For example, because our ancestors were in close contact with wild animals and had evolved from lower animal forms, all human minds contain an inborn animal archetype (Jung called it "the shadow"), which predisposes us to fear animals. Jung observed these archetypes, or "primordial images," coming to the surface in many different situations—in fables and myths, in dreams, in religious writings, in literature and art, and in the delusions of psychotics (Jung, 1972).

Jung's theory of personality, then, leads to a view of the human condition that differs quite sharply from that implied by Freud's theory. From Freud's perspective, adult life becomes a repetitious pattern of excitation and reduction of tension in which the person's needs and the means of satisfying them have been determined in the course of psychosexual development. Jung's theory is more positive, for it emphasizes continual growth and change. The ability to develop selfhood is the adult personality's lifelong task; it requires continual growth and change and an assimilation of unconscious material by the conscious ego.

Social Determinants of Personality

Both Freud and Jung emphasized biological factors in the development of personality, stressing that personality is chiefly a product of physical and biological needs and genetic endowment. Both asserted that environmental influences—even the family—are of secondary importance.

Just about the time Freud and Jung were proclaiming their theories, in the late nineteenth and early twentieth centuries, two new disciplines, sociology and anthropology, were revealing the enormous impact that social conditions can have on human behavior. Social scientists studying remote tribes and ancient civilizations discovered wide variations in behavior. They began to realize that environmental forces—such as economic conditions, education, religious beliefs, political ideas, and, most of all, other people—have great effects on individual behavior. A number of Freudian theorists responded to this intellectual and scientific challenge by modifying psychoanalytic theories so that they acknowledged social as well as biological determinants of personality. Prominent in this group were Alfred Adler, Karen Horney, and Erich Fromm.

Adler's Individual Psychology Alfred Adler (1870–1937), like Jung, was an intimate associate of Freud. In 1911 he broke away and founded his own school of **individual psychology**, incorporating social-psychological ideas.

Adler did not share Freud's belief that human beings are motivated primarily by sexual instincts. Instead, Adler at first claimed that the aggressive drive is responsible for most human behavior. Gradually, however, he came to believe that not the aggressive impulse, but the "will to power" motivates human beings. Finally, Adler abandoned the notion of the "will to power" in favor of the idea of "the striving for superiority," making this striving the basis of his theory (Adler, 1930). By "superiority" Adler did not mean social distinction or dominance, but a quest for perfection. His theory has a strongly idealistic quality, for it asserts that "the great upward drive" is the moving force in human life. This conscious striving toward "completion" of the self carries the human being—indeed, the human species—from one stage of development to the next.

A sense of incompleteness or imperfection in any aspect of life gives rise to feelings of inferiority, according to Adler. These feelings are normal and originate in the childhood realization that adults can do things that children cannot. In their efforts to overcome feelings of inferiority, some individuals succeed in conveying to themselves, and perhaps to others, only the *appearance* of strength and competence. Because they have not improved their actual circumstances, their underlying feelings of inferiority remain. To describe this situation, Adler coined the term **inferiority complex** (Adler, 1931), distinguishing between universal feelings of inferiority and the feelings and actions that characterize a person with an inferiority complex. Adler also placed greater emphasis on conscious motivation than Freud did.

Another of Adler's basic concepts is the idea of **social interest** (1931). He claimed that in addition to seeking individual perfection, each of us is born with a desire to strive for the public good. As we mature, our personal ambition changes to social commitment—provided we received proper guidance and education along the way. We can compensate for feelings of inferiority and incompleteness by working toward the common good. The ultimate goal of each person thus becomes the perfection of society, and normal people strive to achieve goals that are primarily social in character. The neurotic person, therefore, is one who continues striving toward selfish goals such as self-esteem, power, and self-aggrandizement.

Horney's Theory of Basic Anxiety and Basic Hostility Karen Horney (1885–1952), a German-born psychoanalyst, sought to modify basic psychoanalytic theory. She accepted such concepts as the importance of early experience, unconscious motivation, and unconscious defenses, but she challenged Freud's biological or instinctive approach to personality development. For Horney (1945), motivation and conflict, even though unconscious, are based on social factors, not on the interplay between biologically based needs and the environment. She attempted to make psychoanalysis a richer and more workable interpretation of human behavior by focusing on the social determinants of conflict and on how neurotic behavior affects social relationships.

While Freud based his theory of human personality on sexual and aggressive instincts, and Adler on the innate striving for perfection, Horney's theory revolved around what she called "basic anxiety and basic hostility." **Basic anxiety** develops because the child feels isolated and helpless in a potentially hostile world. Young children, discovering that they are weak and small in a land of giants, soon learn that they are utterly dependent on parents for all their needs and safety. Warm, loving, and dependable parents create a sense of security that reassures the child and produces normal development. If the parents severely disturb a child's sense of security—for example, by indifference, erratic behav-

ior, or disparaging attitudes—the child's feeling of helplessness increases, giving rise to basic anxiety. So, unlike Freud and Adler, who based their views of personality development on inborn instincts, Horney constructed a theory based on social and environmental factors.

In Horney's view, basic anxiety is generally accompanied by **basic hostility**, which arises from resentment over parental indifference, inconsistency, and interference. This hostility cannot be expressed directly, because the child needs and fears the parents and must have their love. The resulting repression of this hostility increases feelings of unworthiness and anxiety, and the child is torn between hostility toward the parents and dependence upon them. This conflict between anxiety and hostility leads to the development of three modes of behavior and social interaction: (1) moving toward others, (2) moving against others, and (3) moving away from others.

In the normal personality, Horney believed, these three modes of behavior are integrated and each used in appropriate circumstances. An individual sometimes moves toward other people to gain nurturance and affection; sometimes moves against them to establish dominance and attain goals; and sometimes withdraws to attain integrity and serenity. Neurosis develops when one of these three ways of relating to other people becomes the *only* framework for an individual's social relationships.

For example, someone who only moves toward other people becomes compliant, a kind of doormat, always anxious to please. Such a person seeks security by subjugating himself or herself to gain affection and approval. This self-effacing behavior buys security by totally repressing basic hostility, thereby leading to psychological martyrdom and intense unhappiness.

The individual who only moves against others attempts to find security through domination, assuming that the establishment of power over others safeguards the self. Resolving the conflict this way vents some basic hostility, but it also suppresses the acknowledgment of basic anxiety. Such a person avoids anything that connotes helplessness or loss of control.

The person who only moves away from others tries to find security by becoming aloof and withdrawn, never allowing close relationships to develop. People who adopt this solution protect themselves from harm, but in the process they give up the possibility of growth and change.

Thus, in each case the neurotic personality is characterized by compulsive rigidity—the repetition of a single mode of behavior no matter what the situation (Horney, 1937). The neurotic behavior described by Horney is often identical to that observed by Freud: rigid, obsessional actions, unconscious hostility toward parents, jealousy of siblings. Horney differed radically from Freud, however, in explaining the motivation for this behavior, seeing it as a product of social relationships rather than as an expression of innate sexual and aggressive instincts. For example, she stripped away the sexual interpretation of the Oedipus complex and replaced it with an explanation based on interpersonal relations. A typical Oedipus situation, in which a child passionately clings to one parent and expresses jealousy or covert aggression against the other parent, becomes, in Horney's view, the result of the interplay between the child's anxiety and hostility (see the accompanying box). To achieve security and to cope with basic anxiety and hostility, a little boy may turn to his mother for comfort, especially if his father arouses the boy's hostility by dominating him or by denying the gratification of his wishes. If the boy finds relief from anxiety, the relationship with his mother is strengthened. Anything that threatens it or competes for the mother's attention (primarily the father) becomes an object of jealousy or covert aggression.

In another area of personality, Horney rejected Freud's analysis of female personality. Freud (1974) believed that women were culturally inferior because they lacked a strong, mature

Members of groups such as the Nazis, who seek security for themselves by oppressing others, are likely to have personalities that stress the mode of behavior that Horney called moving against others.

Horney on Basic Anxiety and Hostility

The typical conflict leading to anxiety in a child is that between dependency on the parents . . . and hostile impulses against the parents. Hostility may be aroused in a child in many ways: by the parents' lack of respect for him; by unreasonable demands and prohibitions; by injustice; by unreliability; by suppression of criticism; by the parents dominating him and ascribing these tendencies to love. . . . If a child, in addition to being dependent on his parents, is grossly or subtly intimidated by them and hence feels that any expression of hostile impulses against them endangers his security, then the existence of such hostile impulses is bound to create anxiety. . . . The resulting picture may look exactly like what Freud describes as the Oedipus complex: passionate clinging to one parent and jealousy toward the other or toward anyone interfering with the claim of exclusive possession. . . . *But the dynamic structure of these attachments is entirely different from what Freud conceives as the Oedipus complex. They are an early manifestation of neurotic conflicts rather than a primarily sexual phenomenon.*

From Karen Horney, *The Neurotic Personality in Our Time.* New York: Norton, 1939.

superego. This deficiency, Freud believed, was the result of the little girl's perception of herself as castrated and her consequent "penis envy." Horney retorted that Freud was in a poor position to know what little girls think. According to Horney (1967), it is not little girls who perceive their condition as degraded. Rather, it is little boys—and the men they eventually become—who see females as woefully mutilated and deficient and who have created the self-fulfilling prophecy that has doomed women to inferiority. Any feelings of inferiority in women, believed Horney, arise from their social experiences, which can lead to dependency and a lack of confidence.

Fromm's "Escape from Freedom"   Erich Fromm (1900–1980) based his theory of personality on interpersonal relationships set in a historical context. Taking his fundamental ideas from Karl Marx as well as from Freud, Fromm distinguished between animal nature, consisting of the biochemical mechanisms for physical survival, and human nature, consisting of our ability to reason and to know ourselves. Reason and self-knowledge inevitably set human beings apart from the rest of the animal kingdom and lead to a freedom that permits great creative accomplishment. But fear of isolation and loneliness that accompanies our freedom may lead people to shrink from it.

On the social level, shrinking from freedom leads to mindless conformity and a tendency to submit to dictators and totalitarian governments. On a personal level, it leads to psychotic withdrawal and self-defeating behavior. According to Fromm (1941), we must instead utilize freedom, fulfilling our human nature by uniting with others in an egalitarian spirit of love and shared work.

In Fromm's view, the conditions of human existence produce five basic needs: (1) a need for relatedness, which arises from the fact that, in becoming human, we were torn from the animal's primary union with nature; (2) a need for transcendence, or an urge to overcome animal nature and to become creative; (3) a need for rootedness, or for a sense of belonging to the human family; (4) a need for personal identity, or for being distinctive and unique; and (5), a need for a frame of reference, or a stable and consistent world.

Fromm believed that the ways in which these needs express themselves are determined by society, which can change. Personality develops in accordance with whatever opportunities a particular society offers. In a capitalist society, for example, a person may gain a sense of personal identity by becoming rich or may develop a feeling of rootedness by becoming a dependable employee in a large company. For a society to function properly, Fromm points out, it is essential that children's characters be shaped to fit the needs of that society. Thus, in a capitalist system, the desire to save money must be instilled early so that capital will always be available to enable the economy to expand.

By making demands upon human beings that are contrary to their nature, however, society often prevents them from fulfilling the basic conditions of their existence. For example, when a society changes in any important respect—as when the factory system displaced the individual artisan during the Industrial Revolution—the prevailing social character no longer fits the demands of the new society. As a result, although people are free to move in new directions, many feel a sense of alienation and despair.

One of the great dangers inherent in such a situation is that attempts to escape alienation and despair also involve an escape from freedom (Fromm, 1941). Fromm's warning not to let our fear of freedom lead us to abandon the opportunities of freedom is basic to his view of personality. For this reason he is called a humanitarian socialist. Optimistic about the possibility of developing a society that does not inhibit personal freedom, he asserted that taking an active role in determining the future is an essential part of human nature. He thus differed strongly from Freud, who saw human beings primarily as subject to biological laws that determine a destiny they passively accept.

Erikson's Psychosocial View of Personality

Not all psychoanalytic thought is considered neo-Freudian. Some psychoanalytic investigators, who are called **ego-psychologists**, consider themselves Freudians who are elaborating his theory. Although they agree with Freud on the existence of the unconscious and the personality structure of id, ego, and superego, they believe that Freud devalued the ego by making the id all-important. These ego-psychologists take a more optimistic course than Freud did, focusing

Figure 18.2 Erikson views life as a succession of biological stages, each having its own developmental conflict whose resolution has lasting effects on personality. Erikson's psychosocial stages represent an extension and expansion of Freud's psychosexual stages, with parallels between the first four stages of each theory. (After Erikson, 1950.)

Stage	1	2	3	4	5	6	7	8
Maturity								Ego Integrity vs. Despair
Adulthood							Generativity vs. Stagnation	
Young Adulthood						Intimacy vs. Isolation		
Puberty and Adolescence					Identity vs. Role Confusion			
Latency				Industry vs. Inferiority				
Locomotor-Genital			Initiative vs. Guilt					
Muscular-Anal		Autonomy vs. Shame, Doubt						
Oral Sensory	Basic Trust vs. Mistrust							

on the importance of the ego and insisting that it has its own energy and its own functions. Among the ego-psychologists, Erik Erikson (b. 1902) has had a powerful influence on theories of personality development.

In line with the emphasis on ego instead of id, Erikson conceives of personality development in **psychosocial** terms. He agrees with Freud that the early years, when a child learns to reconcile biological drives with social demands, establish the individual's basic orientation to the world, but stresses the social rather than the instinctual sexual aspects of development. According to Erikson, a child develops a basic sense of trust during what Freud called the oral period, autonomy during the anal period, and initiative during what Freud called the phallic period. Failure to meet the developmental tasks of these periods leads, respectively, to mistrust, shame and doubt, and guilt. However, Erikson does not adhere to the Freudian belief that personality is unalterably determined in the first five years of life. He sees personality as continuing to develop throughout the life span, placing equal emphasis on the child's efforts to master the skills valued by society, on the adolescent's striving to achieve a sense of identity in that society, on the young adult's quest for intimacy, and on the mature person's desire to guide younger generations and thus contribute to society. Depending on how an individual negotiates these challenges, old age may bring a sense of integrity or despair.

In working out these "eight ages of man" (see Figure 18.2), Erikson expands Freud's concept of identification. He argues that the ego is not content simply to assimilate the values of a parent or other admired person, but strives to form an integrated, autonomous, unique "self," which Erikson calls the **ego identity**. He has suggested that establishing an ego identity may be especially difficult in complex societies such as our own, which present the individual with a staggering array of choices in styles of living. In some societies, tradition prescribes the roles the individual will play as an adult. A young person can count on living much as his father or her mother did, among relatives and neighbors known since childhood. By contrast, the intense struggle waged by adolescents in Western societies to achieve individuality and coherence led Erikson to describe the process as an **identity crisis**.

As this concept suggests, Erikson believes, as Fromm did, that the culture and times into which a person is born have a crucial effect on personality development. Psychosocial conflicts are universal and inevitable. However, at some point a society either eases its members' transition from one stage to another or exploits their fears and doubts. In other words, a society can reinforce growth or discourage it. A person's ego identity, Erikson (1950) argues, is grounded in the identity of the culture.

The effort to create a bridge between the study of individuals and the study of societies led Erikson in unorthodox directions. He worked among America's Sioux Indians to learn how historical circumstances and cultural differences affect child-rearing practices and the development of personality. And he was a pioneer in the field of **psychohistory**, the application of psychoanalytic

Erikson on Gandhi

. . . I must now confess that a few times in your work (and often in the literature inspired by you) I have come across passages which almost brought *me* to the point where I felt unable to continue writing *this* book because I seemed to sense the presence of a kind of untruth in the very protestation of truth; of something unclean when all the words spelled out an unreal purity; and above all, of displaced violence where nonviolence was the professed issue.

. . . you seem either unaware of— or want to wish or pray away—an ambivalence, a coexistence of love and hate, which must become conscious in those who work for peace.

It is not enough any more—not after the appearance of your Western contemporary Freud— to be a watchful moralist. For we now have detailed insights into our inner ambiguities, ambivalences, and instinctual conflicts; and only an additional leverage of truth based on self-knowledge promises to give us freedom in the full light of conscious day, whereas in the past, moralist terrorism succeeded only in driving our worst proclivities underground, to remain there until riotous conditions of uncertainty or chaos would permit them to emerge redoubled.

You, Mahatmaji, love the story of that boy prince who would not accept the claim of his father, the Demon King, to a power greater than God's, not even after the boy had been exposed to terrible tortures. At the end he was made to embrace a red-hot metal pillar; but out of this suggestive object stepped God, half lion and half man, and tore the king to pieces.

. . . we must admit that you could not possibly have known of the power of that ambivalence which we have now learned to understand in case histories and life histories. . . . It is, therefore, not without compassion that I must point out that your lifelong insistence on the "innocence" (meaning sexlessness) of children is matched only by your inability to recognize the Demon King in yourself.

Source: From Erik H. Erikson, *Gandhi's Truth: On the Origins of Militant Nonviolence.* New York: W. W. Norton, 1969.

---

principles to the study of historical figures. His biography of Martin Luther (1968), for example, focuses on the Protestant reformer's identity crisis. His admiring biography of India's great nonviolent political leader, Mahatma Gandhi, is a psychoanalytic interpretation not only of the man but also of his culture and times. The accompanying quotations from Erikson's book *Gandhi's Truth: On the Origins of Militant Nonviolence* (1969) appear in a section titled "A Personal Word," which Erikson wrote when he discovered that his insight as a psychoanalyst made it impossible to ignore certain flaws in Gandhi's character that might otherwise have been overlooked.

Evaluating Psychoanalytic Theories

Freud's thought has influenced all later attempts to explain personality, but psychoanalytic theories have been controversial since they were first enunciated. The feminist attack on Freud's analysis of female personality represents only one of the areas in which his and other psychoanalytic theories have been criticized.

Criticisms of Psychoanalytic Theory

A basic criticism of psychoanalytic theory has been the difficulty of testing its essential concepts. Some of them are vague and metaphorical and do not lend themselves to an objective formulation. Other concepts are stated as universals, such as Freud's pronouncement that all males must resolve an Oedipus conflict or Adler's dictum that everyone has a drive for superiority. Since the male Oedipal conflict can show itself either by a boy's displaying great love for his mother or by its opposite, when he represses that love and ignores her, the proposition as a whole simply cannot be tested. One portion of the male Oedipal conflict that has been examined—the expectation that the male identifies with his father's masculinity out of fear of him—has failed to pass the test (Fisher and Greenberg, 1977). Instead, it appears that a positive, nurturant father eases both the boy's identification with his father and the internalization of the father's moral standards.

As a matter of fact, psychoanalytic theories are much better at hindsight than at foresight, and in Chapter 10 we explored the biases of hindsight. A look at the concept of instinct shows how hindsight is employed to explain behavior. We can say, for example, that a person who is continually involved in fights or arguments has a strong aggressive instinct, but only *after* the fact. Before an "instinct" is expressed, it is invisible and hence unpredictable, so that although psychoanalysis can provide logical explanations for the causes of behavior, it seems unable to predict future behavior.

Another criticism of psychoanalytic theories has focused on their heavy dependence on inference. In the psychoanalytic view, a person who *never* shows aggression has repressed a basic instinct. Yet an unexpressed instinct cannot be observed; it can only be inferred. In the same way, the meaning of dreams, habits, or slips of the

Freud, His Father, and Oedipus

When Freud adopted the myth of Oedipus as a parable of psychosexual development, he changed the way people regarded early childhood. Oedipus unwittingly slew his father and married his mother, and Freud proposed that all little boys similarly harbor an incestuous love for their mothers and a hostility toward their fathers, which they overcome by identifying with the father.

Some scholars have questioned not only the validity of the Oedipal struggle but Freud's motives in proposing it. Originally Freud believed that the roots of his patients' disorders lay in childhood episodes of sexual abuse. Patient after patient told him tales of early seduction and, in every case, the blame was placed on the father. Freud finally decided that sexual abuse could not be as widespread as his patients claimed. He rejected the seduction theory, which saw the child as passive victim, and proposed in its place the Oedipal conflict, in which the sexual incidents were imagined—the expression of his patients' childhood sexual desires toward a parent.

This transformation of childhood sexuality may have come about because Freud could not bring himself to apply the seduction theory to his own family. Freud had been analyzing himself, which may have been one source of his resistance. In addition, he had discovered symptoms in his brothers and sisters indicating that his father had sexually abused his children. In a letter to Wilhelm Fliess, he included his own father among the ranks of the accused.

Such a situation was clearly unthinkable. In fact, when Freud first presented his theory to the Viennese Society, he never mentioned fathers as sexual aggressors. Despite the fact that in every case his patients had charged their fathers with seducing them, Freud portrayed the seducers of young children as "nurses, maids, governesses, teachers, and near relations" (Rush, 1980).

It was after his father's death that Freud abandoned the seduction theory, perhaps because he was unable to handle sexual guilt on the part of his father. The night after his father's funeral, Freud dreamt that he visited the local barbershop and discovered a sign: "You are requested to close the eyes." According to Freud, his dream meant that he wanted to be forgiven for arranging such a modest funeral for his father. However, other analysts have suggested that the sign commanded him to shut his eyes to his father's guilt—not his own (Gelman, 1981).

Whatever the actual motivation, the result was a reversal of Freud's original theory. The child, not the parent, became the focus, and Oedipal feelings were at the basis of adult disorders. The choice of Oedipus as symbol for childish sexuality is ironic. In transferring the guilt from father to child, Freud "omitted" the incident upon which the entire Oedipal myth turns: the guilt of Oedipus' father, who abandoned his infant son on a mountainside to die. Had the father not been guilty of attempted infanticide, the son could not have killed his father by mistake.

tongue can only be inferred. Does a man smoke a pipe because he is fixated at the oral stage or because during his childhood all the males he admired smoked pipes?

In fact, Freud's description of how personality is formed has not been supported. Studies have not demonstrated that oral or anal personalities are formed because of critical events in those stages of development. Nor has any consistent support been found for Freud's proposal that depression in adulthood is a reaction to the loss of a parent or other loved object in childhood (Crook and Eliot, 1980). His description of female personality development has simply not held up. Studies consistently indicate a much smaller difference between male and female personality development and organization than Freud supposed (Fisher and Greenberg, 1977). Freud's notion that women are culturally inferior was based on his supposition that male biology and male psychology constitute the norm for the species and on his observation of the role of women in European society at the turn of the century. Thus, his views of female personality development were bound to the culture of his time.

Psychoanalysis has also been criticized for the small size of the sample on which the theories are based. Most of Freud's published cases were upper-middle-class Viennese women, and on the statements of these adult females with emotional problems, Freud built a universal theory of personality development. Some investigators are uncomfortable with a theory of normal personality development that is based on retrospective childhood accounts of people with emotional problems.

Finally, Freud's metaphorical use of language has led to a reification of his concepts, so that they seem to lead a material existence. Although Freud stressed that he was speaking, not of places or things, but of states of mind, the continued use of metaphor has led to the impression that within each human mind three little creatures—the id, the ego, and the superego—wage a continual battle. Such use of language, though effective in fixing concepts, leads to a gross oversimplification of personality dynamics.

Contributions of Psychoanalytic Theory

Despite these criticisms, Freud has made a lasting contribution to our understanding of human beings. Although he was not a rigorous scientist, Freud was "a patient, meticulous, penetrating observer and a tenacious, disciplined, courageous, original thinker" (Hall and Lindzey, 1978). In fact, psychoanalytic theory has withstood a number of tests. When thousands of studies of psychoanalytic concepts were evaluated, many of Freud's concepts were supported (Fisher and Greenberg, 1977). As Freud proposed, male homosexuals do seem to have a disturbed relationship with their fathers, who tend to be unfriendly or unapproachable. Children do seem to have an early erotic interest in the parent of the opposite sex; dreams do seem to provide a release for emotional tensions. People who focus on oral activities do tend to be dependent and passive—traits Freud considered "oral" (Masling et al., 1981; Masling, Johnson, and Saturansky, 1974); those who are preoccupied with anal functions do tend to be parsimonious, compulsive, and orderly—traits Freud considered "anal."

Many basic psychoanalytic concepts, such as anxiety and defense mechanisms, have extended our understanding of human personality. The framework they provide for the explanation of abnormal behavior shows that bizarre and adaptive behavior result from the same developmental processes. As a result, we no longer divide the world into the "sick" and the "healthy," the "sane" and the "insane," but instead see people as falling somewhere on a continuum that shades imperceptibly from adaptive to maladaptive.

Psychoanalytic theory has also expanded our concept of motivation to include impulses, conflicts, or past experiences that have slipped from awareness. Even psychologists who do not accept the concept of an "unconscious" do accept the idea that we have stored much more information about the past than we are aware of. This general acceptance of the notion that much of our thought is unconscious has changed the way we look at art, at literature, and at life itself.

Finally, Freud's methods of psychoanalysis revolutionized the treatment of emotional problems. To Freud we owe the idea that individual psychotherapy (the "talking cure") can, through the relationship of patient and therapist, develop self-knowledge and thus increase the patient's control over her or his actions. Forms of therapy that reject much or all of Freud's basic theory rely on variations of his technique.

Psychoanalysis has had an enormous influence

on the thought of psychologists, psychiatrists, and ordinary citizens. Our tendency to see human behavior as richly determined by our past experiences and as reflecting irrational inner forces is in part the result of Freud's emphasis on both factors.

SUMMARY

1. **Personality** theorists, no matter what their approach, address two key issues: the consistency of an individual's behavior from one situation to the next and the differences in the behavior of individuals confronted with the same situation.

2. Sigmund Freud's psychoanalytic theory was the first formal theory of personality, and it has been the most influential. His concept of the **unconscious** is based on his study of the memories, wishes, and fears that were revealed through **free association**, in which patients talked about their emotional conflicts; this process of bringing material from the unconscious into the conscious mind he called **psychoanalysis**. Freud found that dreams, jokes, and accidents also reveal unconscious conflicts. Dreams have both a manifest content (what the dreamer relates) and a **latent content** (the dream's underlying meaning).

3. According to Freud, personality consists of three interacting aspects: the id, the ego, and the superego. The **id** consists of the biological drives with which the infant is born, and its energy is divided between **Eros**, the life instinct generated by the **libido**, and **Thanatos**, the death instinct. The id's tendency to devote itself to the immediate reduction of tension is called the **pleasure principle**. The **ego**, which develops at about the age of six months, controls the individual's actions and manipulates the environment according to the **reality principle**, which is based on the organism's concern for safety. The **superego**, which impels the individual toward an **ego ideal** of moral perfection, is also an approximate equivalent of conscience. It emerges from the resolution of the Oedipus complex, as the child **internalizes** the moral standards of the parent of the same sex.

4. Freud believed that nearly all human behavior is directed toward resolving inner conflicts and restoring **homeostasis**, or equilibrium. He conceived of instincts as having four characteristic features: a source, an aim, an object, and an impetus. According to Freud, psychic energy can be **displaced**, or transferred, from the original object to a variety of substitute objects. **Sublimation** is a displacement that produces high cultural achievement. **Anxiety** is a state of psychic pain akin to fear, and can take the form of reality anxiety, moral anxiety, and neurotic anxiety. Through **defense mechanisms**, we conceal sources of anxiety from ourselves and from the world. **Repression** is a defense mechanism that keeps threatening thoughts and memories in the unconscious. **Fixation** is a temporary halt in development—a response to anxiety associated with the next developmental stage. **Regression** is a return to an earlier stage of development in response to a perceived threat. **Reaction formation** is the replacement in consciousness of an anxiety-provoking feeling with its opposite. **Projection** is the unknowing attribution of one's own impulses or fears onto others.

5. Freud stressed the decisive role of infancy and childhood in determining basic personality structure. He believed that a child passes through a series of psychosexual stages, starting with the **pregenital stage**, which is divided into **oral**, **anal**, and **phallic** stages. After a period of **latency** comes the adolescent eruption of libidinal forces, which stabilize in the **genital** stage.

6. Carl Jung was one of the first **neo-Freudians** to break with Freud over theory. Jung's **analytic psychology** diverged from Freud's theory in two ways. Jung believed that the future as well as the past is important to personality development and that people try to realize their potential through **individuation**. He also conceived of a two-level unconscious: the **personal unconscious**, which is similar

to Freud's concept; and the **collective unconscious**, consisting of **archetypes** (universal themes and images common to all human beings).

7. When sociology and anthropology challenged the psychoanalytic emphasis on biological factors in personality development, a number of neo-Freudian theorists modified psychoanalytic theory to acknowledge social as well as biological determinants. Alfred Adler's **individual psychology** emphasized the drive toward perfection as the highest human motivation. He believed that the inability to overcome a childhood sense of incompleteness results in an **inferiority complex**. According to Adler, as people mature they naturally work for social interest.

8. Karen Horney's theory of personality is based on the concepts of **basic anxiety**, which arises out of a child's sense of helplessness, and **basic hostility**, which arises from resentment against one's parents. Unexpressed hostility leads to three ways of behaving: moving toward others, moving against others, and moving away from others. In a normal person, these modes are integrated and each used when appropriate.

9. Erich Fromm's theory of personality is based on interpersonal relationships set in a historical context. He believed that there are five basic human needs: for relatedness, for transcendence, for rootedness, for personal identity, and for a frame of reference. Society—which can change—determines the ways in which these needs are expressed. When the social structure gives rise to alienation and despair, attempts to escape them can also lead to an escape from freedom.

10. Erik Erikson, an **ego-psychologist**, conceives of personality in **psychosocial terms** and sees personality development as a life-long process through eight stages. He believes that the ego strives to form an integrated, autonomous, unique "self" or **ego identity**. The struggle of Western adolescents to achieve individuality was described by Erikson as an **identity crisis**. Erikson pioneered in the field of **psychohistory**, trying to bridge the study of individuals and the study of societies.

11. Psychoanalytic theory has been criticized because its essential concepts are impossible to disconfirm, because it is better at explaining behavior than at predicting it, because it relies on inference, because it is based on an inadequate sample, and because its concepts have been reified. Some aspects of psychoanalytic theory have withstood testing, however, and the theory has contributed to our understanding of personality. Concepts such as anxiety and defense mechanisms have shown that bizarre and abnormal behavior result from the same developmental processes. Psychoanalytic theory has expanded our concepts of motivation to include unconscious conflicts. Freud originated the method of individual psychotherapy that revolutionized the treatment of the emotionally disturbed.

KEY TERMS

aim	ego ideal	individual psychology	neurotic anxiety
anal stage	ego identity	individuation	object
analytic psychology	ego-psychologist	inferiority complex	oral stage
anxiety	Eros	instinct	personality
archetypes	extraversion	internalize	personal unconscious
basic anxiety	fixation	introversion	phallic stage
basic hostility	free association	latency stage	pleasure principle
collective unconscious	genital stage	latent content	pregenital stage
defense mechanism	homeostasis	libido	projection
displacement	id	manifest content	psychoanalysis
dynamics	identity crisis	moral anxiety	psychohistory
ego	impetus	neo-Freudians	psychosocial

reaction formation	regression	source	Thanatos
reality anxiety	repression	sublimation	traumatic
reality principle	social interest	superego	unconscious

RECOMMENDED READINGS

FISHER, S., and R. P. GREENBERG. *The Scientific Credibility of Freud's Theories and Therapy.* New York: Basic Books, 1977. This book provides a detailed review of research on Freudian theory.

FREUD, S. *New Introductory Lectures on Psychoanalysis* (1933). J. Strachey (ed. and tr.). New York: Norton, 1965. A readable overview of psychoanalysis by Freud himself.

HALL, C. S., and G. LINDZEY. *Theories of Personality.* 3rd ed. New York: Wiley, 1978. This edition of the classic secondary source on theories of personality includes a chapter on contemporary psychoanalytic theory, with an excellent presentation of Erik Erikson's work, and a chapter on Eastern psychology and personality theory.

MADDI, S. R. *Personality Theories: A Comparative Analysis.* 3rd ed. Homewood, Ill.: Dorsey Press, 1976. Classifies personality theorists according to whether their basic assumption relates to *conflict*, *fulfillment*, or *consistency*. Examines what the theorists have to say about the core and periphery of personality. Presents research on each position and draws conclusions about their strengths and weaknesses.

SMITH, B. D., and H. J. VETTER. *Theoretical Approaches to Personality.* Englewood Cliffs, N.J.: Prentice-Hall, 1982. This book emphasizes individual theorists and presents each person's theory in detail.

CHAPTER 19

Humanistic, Behavioristic, and Trait Theories of Personality

Last night you observed Karen at a party. She was laughing, talking, and seemed the center of a small group who hung on her every word. Last week she was given the job of meeting an author who was visiting campus, and by the time she had driven the distinguished visitor back to campus, they were talking like old friends. Today she dominated the discussion at lunch and seemed at ease despite the fact that Cathy, with whom she had just had a bitter disagreement, was sitting at the same table. What kind of statement can you make about Karen's personality? You might say that she was an outgoing, sociable, optimistic person who was always poised in social situations. Or you might say that her behavior depended upon the situation, and that her behavior on all three occasions was a response to the immediate circumstances and not a revelation of any personality traits. Her sociability at the party may have been a response to a small amount of alcohol. Her friendship with the visiting author may have been a response to the fact that they were both scuba divers and had inadvertently discovered a common interest. Her poise at lunch may have been a conscious performance, as she tried to show Cathy that she was not upset about their quarrel.

Although any dissection of Karen's personality would require much more information than those three incidents provide, most nonpsychoanalytic theories of personality would take one of the two approaches; that is, these theories are either person centered or situation based. No matter what approach these nonpsychoanalytic theories take, however, each is concerned with the same key questions that occupy psychoanalytic theory. Why do different individuals behave differently in the same situation? And why does an individual's behavior remain fairly consistent in different situations? In terms of their responses to these questions, most nonpsychoanalytic theories can be classified into one of three groups: humanistic theories, behavioristic theories, and trait theories.

Briefly, **humanistic theories** are person-centered theories that emphasize the potential of human beings for growth, creativity, and spontaneity. Although humanists recognize biological needs and needs for safety, they reject the behaviorist's idea that people are primarily influenced by rewards and punishments. **Behavioristic theories** are situational theories that are primarily based on the principles of learning and reinforcement discussed in Chapter 8. Behaviorism views the development and functioning of the personality as a set of learned responses instead of as resulting from conflicts among the forces of id, ego, and superego. Instead of making sweeping claims about human nature, **trait theories** simply state that human behavior can be organized according to enduring characteristics that are called traits—

for example, aggression, friendliness, and honesty. People differ from one another in the amount of each trait they show. Thus, a person who is always honest has more of this particular trait than one who sometimes cheats on an income-tax return.

As we shall see, all of these approaches deemphasize unconscious, destructive, and sexual forces as determinants of human behavior. They also give much more importance to observable behavior, learning, and conscious cognitive processes than do psychoanalytic theories.

Humanistic Theories

Humanistic psychologists emphasize the potential of human beings for growth, creativity, and spontaneity. They stress the uniqueness of the individual and her or his freedom to make choices. The most influential humanistic psychologists have been Abraham Maslow and Carl Rogers.

Maslow's Humanistic Psychology

The guiding spirit behind humanistic psychology has generally been identified as the American psychologist Abraham Maslow (1908–1970). He deliberately set out to create what he called a "third force" in psychology as an alternative to psychoanalysis and behaviorism. Maslow based his theory of personality on the characteristics of healthy, creative people who used all their talents, potential, and capabilities, rather than on studies of disturbed individuals as Freud had done. These healthy people, according to Maslow (1971a; 1971b), strive for and achieve **self-actualization**. They develop their own potential to its fullest, yet instead of competing with others, each strives to be "the best me I can be." Maslow (1966; 1968) criticized other psychologists for their pessimistic, negative, and limited conceptions of human beings. As a result, he noted, there was no psychology that took account of gaiety, exuberance, love, and expressive art to the same extent that it dealt with misery, conflict, shame, hostility, and habit. There is an active drive toward health in every person, Maslow believed, an impulse toward the actualization of one's potentialities. But because human instincts are so weak in comparison with those of animals, a person's impulses toward self-actualization can be distorted by society, habit, or faulty education.

Maslow (1955) identified two groups of human needs: basic needs and metaneeds. The basic needs are physiological (food, water, sleep, and so on) and psychological (affection, security, and self-esteem, for example). These basic needs are also called **deficiency needs** because if they are not met, a person, lacking something, will seek to make up for the deficiency. The basic needs are

According to Abraham Maslow, the drive for love, joy, and fulfillment exists in us all. This striving to reach our potential culminates in self-actualization.

Table 19.1 Characteristics of Self-Actualized Persons

They are realistically oriented.	They identify with mankind.
They accept themselves, other people, and the natural world for what they are.	Their intimate relationships with a few specially loved people tend to be profound and deeply emotional rather than superficial.
They have a great deal of spontaneity.	Their values and attitudes are democratic.
They are problem-centered rather than self-centered.	They do not confuse means with ends.
They have an air of detachment and a need for privacy.	Their sense of humor is philosophical rather than hostile.
They are autonomous and independent.	They have a great fund of creativeness.
Their appreciation of people and things is fresh rather than stereotyped.	They resist conformity to the culture.
Most of them have had profound mystical or spiritual experiences although not necessarily religious in character.	They transcend the environment rather than just coping with it.

Source: A. Maslow, *Motivation and Personality*. New York: Harper & Row, 1954.

hierarchically organized, meaning that some (such as the need for food) take precedence over others.

The higher needs Maslow called **metaneeds**, or **growth needs**. They include the need for justice, goodness, beauty, order, and unity. In most instances, deficiency needs take priority over growth needs. People who lack food or water cannot attend to justice or beauty. Nor, according to Maslow, can those who lack basic security and self-esteem feel free to consider fairness; to feel deep, reciprocal love; to be democratic; or to resist restrictive conformity. Since metaneeds are not hierarchically organized, one metaneed can be pursued instead of another, depending on a person's circumstances. The metaneeds are real, and when they are not met, **metapathologies**, such as alienation, anguish, apathy, and cynicism, can develop.

By studying a group of historical figures whom he considered to be self-actualized—among them Abraham Lincoln, Henry David Thoreau, Ludwig van Beethoven, Thomas Jefferson, William James, Eleanor Roosevelt, and Albert Einstein—Maslow (1954) developed a portrait of the self-actualized person, who shows the personality characteristics listed in Table 19.1. Included in Maslow's studies of self-actualized people were college students and some of his own friends.

Maslow also investigated what he called **peak experiences**—those profound moments when a person feels in complete harmony with the world: highly autonomous, spontaneous, perceptive, yet relatively unaware of space and time. During a peak experience any person temporar-ily becomes self-actualized (Maslow, 1968). Some women report peak experiences at the moment of childbirth, and in one study (Tanzer, 1968), such women were most likely to be those whose husbands were present at delivery. Some of the words women used to describe how they felt about the world and about themselves during this peak experience are listed in Figure 19.1.

Maslow has had a wide influence on American psychology. He has inspired many researchers to pay attention to healthy, productive people and has led many group leaders, clinicians, and psychologists working in organizations to seek ways of promoting the growth and self-actualization of workers, students, and people in therapy.

How the World Seemed	Women's Feelings About Themselves
truth	queenly
goodness	receptive
beauty	victorious
wholeness	trusting
connectedness	joyous
aliveness	blissful
uniqueness	rapturous
perfection	supreme
inevitability	in ecstasy
completeness	integrated
justice	
order	
simplicity	
richness	
effortlessness	
playfulness	
self–sufficiency	

Figure 19.1 Natural childbirth is a "peak experience" for many women. Maslow believed that such experiences are rare in the majority of people's lives. (After Tanzer, 1968.)

The Self Theory of Rogers

Also closely identified with humanistic psychology is the American clinical psychologist Carl Rogers. Like Maslow, Rogers believes that people are governed by an innate impulse toward positive growth. In contrast to Maslow, however, Rogers developed his theory from observations made while practicing psychotherapy, not from studying self-actualized people. He noticed that his clients (a term he prefers to "patients" because the latter implies illness) typically had trouble accepting their own feelings and experiences. They seemed to have learned during childhood that to obtain the regard of others, they had to feel and act in distorted or dishonest ways; they had to deny certain feelings in order to be accepted by parents, relatives, or peers.

Rogers (1971) summarized his observations about the denial or distortion of feelings by saying that almost every child is the victim of **conditional positive regard**. That is, love and praise are withheld when a child does not conform to parental or social standards. If a little boy comes to dinner with a dirty face, he may be told that he is "disgusting" and sent away from the table. If he hits his little sister, he may be called "naughty" and sent to his room. On the other hand, his cleanliness and brotherly affection often are rewarded by smiles, compliments, and kisses. These conditions placed on positive regard initiate a process in which the child learns to act and feel in ways that earn approval from others rather than in ways that may be more intrinsically satisfying. The process continues into adulthood, and to maintain positive regard, adults suppress actions and feelings that are unacceptable to important people in their lives, rather than guiding their behavior by their own spontaneous perceptions and feelings. Thus, what Rogers calls **conditions of worth** develop —extraneous standards whose attainment assures positive regard. Any experiences that do not meet conditions of worth are misperceived, distorted, or denied.

This denial and distortion of experiences leads to the distinction that Rogers makes between the concepts of the organism and the self. The **organism** he defines as the total range of a person's possible experiences; the **self** is the parts of those experiences that the individual recognizes and accepts. Ideally, the organism and the self are identical because a person can, in principle, recognize and accept all experience. In practice, however, the organism and the self often oppose each other (see Figure 19.2). For example, the self can deny consciousness to certain sensory and emotional experiences simply by refusing to symbolize or conceptualize them. This idea is similar to the psychoanalytic concept of repression and to its neo-Freudian reformulations. Ac-

This little girl is gaining more than a knowledge of music when she plays the recorder. She is learning that her parents respond warmly to her when she performs well.

This, as we see it, is the basic estrangement in man. He has not been true to himself, to his own natural organismic valuing of experience, but for the sake of preserving the positive regard of others has now come to falsify some of the values he experiences and to perceive them only in terms based upon their value to others. Yet this has not been a conscious choice, but a natural—and tragic—development in infancy. The path of development toward psychological maturity, the path of therapy, is the undoing of this estrangement in man's functioning, the dissolving of conditions of worth, the achievement of a self which is congruent with experience, and the restoration of a unified organismic valuing process as the regulator of behavior.

Figure 19.2 Carl Rogers believes that the fundamental problem of personality is how to make the self more congruent with the total experience of the organism. It is through the therapeutic relationship, in which the therapist creates an atmosphere of total acceptance, or "unconditional positive regard," that the client may achieve closer—or even complete—congruence. (From Rogers, 1971.)

client's feelings by restating what has been said ("You seem to have been disappointed whenever your father failed to approve of one of your boy friends"), but does not offer divergent interpretations or tell the client what to do or how to act. For this reason, Rogers' therapeutic method is called **nondirective,** or **client centered**. In this therapeutic context, the client learns to reintegrate self and organism, to accept all experiences as genuine, and to establish an unconditional positive self-regard.

It may be asked whether a person who receives unconditional positive regard will become selfish, cruel, and destructive. After all, it is to prevent this kind of behavior that children are punished and police forces are maintained. And what of Freud's assertion that human beings have aggressive or destructive instincts? Rogers maintains that in years of therapeutic experience, he has seen little evidence for this pessimistic view. Instead, he has come to believe that the human organism naturally seeks growth, self-actualization, and pleasant, productive relations with others. When not restricted by social forces, a person wants to become what most of us would recognize as healthier and happier.

cording to Rogers, denial is likely to occur if a feeling or experience is incompatible with the self-concept. Even an action can be disowned by saying, "I don't know why I did it" or "I must have been carried away."

According to Rogers (1971), psychological adjustment "exists when the concept of the self is such that all sensory and visceral experiences of the organism are, or may be, assimilated on a symbolic level into a consistent relationship with the concept of self." The characteristics of psychologically adjusted, or **fully functioning**, people are openness to experience, absence of defensiveness, accurate awareness, unconditional positive self-regard, and generally harmonious relations with other people.

If the breach between self and organism grows too wide, the person may become defensive, tense, conflicted, and unable to relate well to others. Such people are often argumentative and hostile, and they may project their denied feelings onto others. The split between self and organism can be healed, according to Rogers, if people describe their experiences and express their feelings freely in a nonthreatening therapeutic context. The therapist, should, unlike most other people in the client's life, maintain an attitude of **unconditional positive regard**, continuing to support the client regardless of what she or he says or does. The therapist clarifies the

Evaluation of Humanistic Theories

Humanistic theories of personality have been criticized for being unscientific and subjective. They are considered unscientific because they are based on scientifically unverifiable inferences that are stated in a vague and imprecise manner. For example, how can the various metaneeds be shown to be essential to full human development? And how do we know when a basic need has been gratified? Further, how does one go about testing a person's habit of "transcending the environment," one of the characteristics of self-actualization set forth by Maslow? Or determine the "conditions of worth" that Rogers asserts that each of us develops as a standard of conduct? By recording therapy sessions and analyzing their content, Rogers systematically tested inferences drawn from his theory; for example, he compared self-concept before and after therapy. However, his theory of personality is less open to test. Giving unconditional positive regard to children from birth, for example, might have very different—and less positive—effects than providing unconditional positive regard to people who have become unable to accept many of their feelings and actions.

The second charge against humanistic approaches is that they lack neutrality. For example, Maslow's claim that human nature is "good" has been called an intrusion of subjective values into what should be a neutral science. His study of self-actualized people has been criticized because the sample was chosen on the basis of Maslow's own subjective criteria. How can self-actualized people be identified without knowing the characteristics of such people? But if we already know their characteristics, why list them as if they were the results of an empirical study? Finally, self-actualized people are supposed to be fully developed in all areas of personality, yet some of the people Maslow considered self-actualized are reported to have had severe personal problems.

Despite such criticism, the work of Maslow and Rogers has had a significant impact on research, therapy, and counseling. For example, it has led many psychologists to concentrate on their patients' or clients' personal growth and to adopt Rogers' concept of unconditional positive regard, letting clients know that they are still accepted even if they behave in self-destructive ways. Along with the concentration on personal growth has come an interest in exploring the limits of human potential through altered states of consciousness (Tart, 1975). As we saw in Chapter 6, a Western interest in meditation, yoga, hypnosis, and hallucinogenic drugs has increased in recent years, heightened by the impact of humanistic approaches to personality.

In fact, the group-therapy movement, which has grown rapidly in the past twenty-five years, can trace its strength and impetus to humanistic psychology. Group therapy is generally characterized by a focus on growth and on personal interaction freed from conventional restraints. The humanistic approach has also been responsible for the establishment of personal-growth centers throughout the United States; perhaps the most famous of these is the Esalen Institute in California, where Maslow worked until his death in 1970. Carl Rogers has for a number of years been a fellow at the Center for the Study of the Person in La Jolla, California, which is also widely known for its humanistic emphasis.

Behavioristic Theories

Since the beginning of this century, American psychology has been concerned with animal and human learning. Some of the most famous American psychologists—among them Edward L. Thorndike, John B. Watson, Edward Tolman, Clark Hull, and B.F. Skinner—are known for their research on learning. Naturally, when Freud's ideas became known in American universities, learning theorists took notice and tried to assimilate his work into their own.

Dollard and Miller's Behavior Theory

The most ambitious attempt at assimilation of Freud's ideas was made during the 1940s at Yale University by John Dollard and Neal Miller. Their behavior theory represents an effort to translate the psychodynamic phenomena identified by Freud into the concepts developed by behavioristic learning theorists.

The terms used by Dollard and Miller (1950), such as *drive, cue,* and *reinforcement,* have no direct equivalents in Freud's concepts, but in combination they can be used to explain some of the same phenomena that Freud described. These theorists regarded defense mechanisms as anxiety-reducing responses. For example, repression, which Freud saw as a means of pushing threatening thoughts into the unconscious, was called "learned not-thinking" by Dollard and Miller. Suppose a young man who feels anxious whenever he thinks about having sexual intercourse with his girl friend is rewarded (by a reduction of anxiety) for shifting his thoughts to something less threatening, such as rearranging his apartment. In terms of learning theory, his habit of "not-thinking" about a particular topic is reinforced because it relieves an unpleasant state—his anxiety (Miller, 1948; 1959).

In Dollard and Miller's theory, personality is composed of habits that are made up of learned associations between various stimuli and responses. Neurotic behavior is learned in the same way as any other behavior and is simply an extreme instance of ordinary conflict, in which two motives clash, so that satisfying one motive frustrates the other. Such a situation is called an **approach-avoidance conflict**, and the analysis of it is based on several assumptions (Dollard and Miller, 1950). First, the nearer an organism comes to a goal, the stronger the tendency to approach it. Second, the nearer an organism comes to a feared object or situation, the stronger the tendency to avoid it. Third, as an organism nears an object, the tendency to avoid something that is feared increases more rapidly

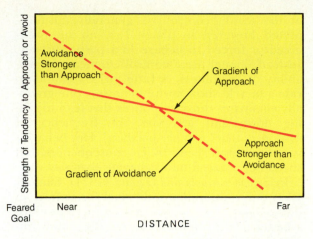

Figure 19.3 Simple graphic representation of an approach-avoidance conflict. The tendency to approach is the stronger of the two tendencies far from the goal, while the tendency to avoid is the stronger of the two near to the goal. Therefore, when far from the goal, the subject should tend to approach part way and then stop; when near to it, he should tend to retreat part way and then stop. In other words, he should tend to remain in the region where the two gradients intersect. (Adapted from Dollard and Miller, 1950.)

than does the tendency to approach something that is desired. Fourth, the stronger the drive that is behind an organism's tendency to approach or avoid something, the stronger the tendency will be. The typical approach-avoidance conflict is represented in Figure 19.3, which graphically translates these tendencies into gradients.

Using rats, Miller (1944) set up an approach-avoidance conflict by allowing a hungry rat to run down an alley to get food. While the rat was eating, it received a brief but painful electric shock. Later, when the rat was again placed in the alley, it began running toward the food but suddenly stopped, then started toward the food, retreated, started toward the food once more, and again retreated, since each step toward the food was also a step toward electric shock. The animal vacillated, as if torn between the desire to approach the food (approach) and the desire to avoid the painful shock (avoidance). Finally, the rat stayed in one spot, drawn equally by the pull of food and the fear of shock. In rats, as in human beings, conflict occurs when avoidance and approach tendencies have equal strength. Like rats, human beings caught in an approach-avoidance conflict vacillate and can be trapped in a situation that both attracts and repels them. For example, after breaking up, a couple often try to

patch up their differences. While they are living apart, the tendency to approach is strong, and they reunite. But living together allows the negative aspects of their relationship to resurface and again they break up, retreating because the tendency to avoid unpleasantness becomes strongest near the goal.

Dollard and Miller's approach was important for two reasons. First, it showed that psychoanalytic concepts were accessible to American researchers. Second, it helped pave the way for behavior therapy—a set of procedures, based on learning principles, for changing neurotic and psychotic behavior. (Behavior therapy is discussed in detail in Chapter 24.) Some psychologists have criticized Dollard and Miller for drawing analogies between rats and human beings, because these critics believe that animal research is unlikely to shed much light on human cognitive processes. Yet Dollard and Miller's behavior theory has had an important effect on the research techniques used to study personality. The experiments they conducted made it clear to other theorists that theories of personality based on invisible dynamic processes can be subjected to experimental tests. And they demonstrated convincingly that quite simple concepts from learning theory can be combined to explain complex human behavior.

Skinner's Radical Behaviorism

Although his radical behaviorism is not a theory of personality, through his general influence B. F. Skinner has had a great impact on personality theory. Unlike Dollard and Miller, Skinner rejects such concepts as drive because they cannot be directly observed and thus do not lend themselves to scientific examination (Skinner, 1975). Moreover, Skinner sees no need for a general concept of personality structure. He focuses instead on a *functional* analysis of behavior—that is, an analysis of the relationships between environmental events and a particular response. This exclusive focus on the environment is known as radical behaviorism, because it makes no allowance for cognitive or symbolic processes.

In his analysis of behavior, Skinner (1971) says that internal events, such as thoughts and feelings, can be ignored because they are by-products of external observable events, such as words and deeds. Notice that Skinner does not deny the existence of internal events, only their importance in understanding behavior. A good

"After all, it's a simple and sensible program. .We set up a system of gradually increasing annoyances and frustrations against a background of complete serenity. An easy environment is made more and more difficult as the children acquire the capacity to adjust."

"But why?. . .What do (the children) get out of it?"

"What do they get out of it! . . .what they get is escape from the petty emotions which eat the heart out of the unprepared. They get the satisfaction of pleasant and profitable social relations. .They get new horizons, for they are spared the emotions characteristic of frustration and failure."

Figure 19.4   Can that green-eyed monster of jealousy—as well as other destructive or antisocial emotions—be eliminated, or will such emotions always haunt us? This dialogue from *Walden Two,* Skinner's novel about a utopian society, gives us his answer. Traits and emotions are seen not as inherent biological qualities or essences, but as learned and therefore *controllable* or *extinguishable* behaviors. Through principles of operant conditioning and reinforcement, Skinner argues, we can engineer a perfect society. Do you agree? (Skinner, 1949.)

illustration of this point is the typical answer to the question, "Why are you going to the theater?" Usually the theatergoer says that she or he "feels" like going. For Skinner, this feeling is a by-product of previous reinforcement. Thus, it would be more to the point to ask what happened during past theater visits and what the person has heard or read about the play. Since it is possible to explain a person's behavior by reinforcing events in the past, Skinner believes that internal events can safely be ignored.

Arguing that all behavior is controlled by rewards and punishments, Skinner describes, in his novel *Walden Two* (1949), how these principles might be applied to produce a utopian society (see Figure 19.4). The idea of controlling people with systematic rewards is a frightening concept to many who find it more reminiscent of Aldous Huxley's totalitarian *Brave New World* than of Thoreau's individualistic *Walden*. Skinner's use

of the word "control" is generally misinterpreted, however. In *Walden Two,* no one is coerced or forced to behave in a particular way. Instead Skinner uses "control" to mean predictability or lawfulness. A little girl's attempts to ride a bicycle show lawful behavior. She gradually eliminates those responses that lead to falling down and increases the frequency of responses that keep her balanced. Her behavior is being "controlled" by its consequences, but she is not coerced into behaving that way.

In *Beyond Freedom and Dignity* (1971), Skinner takes the position that individual freedom is an illusion and maintains that if we want to produce a better world, we must change the contingencies of reinforcement. Today's society, for example, often rewards people for acting immorally: the slumlord gets more profit by letting property run down than by spending money to maintain it. Skinner suggests that we should not complain about personality characteristics such as the slumlord's greed. Instead we should change the contingencies that reinforce the slumlord's behavior, perhaps through the provision of tax breaks so that taking care of buildings brings greater rewards than letting them decay.

Although Skinner has been extremely influential, most behaviorists do not ignore internal events. Social-learning theorists, whose work was discussed in Chapter 8, acknowledge that cognitive or symbolic activities are important determinants of behavior, and their approach to personality has been influential.

Social-Learning Theory

Views of personality based on social learning theory differ most sharply from Skinner's radical behaviorism in their emphasis on the cognitive capabilities of human beings—on the ability to reason, to remember, and to think abstractly.

This conceptualization gives rise to different images of human existence. From the radical behaviorist's view, there are two components, environment and behavior, with the latter being a relatively passive response to the former. In the social learning view, there are three components —environment, behavior, and person—each influencing and being influenced by the others (Bandura, 1977; 1978). Although behavior is partly determined by events in the environment, it is also determined by cognitive events. This means that the environment is not autonomous. We actively transform it both by perceiving the environment in the light of our own memories and expectations and by altering it to suit our desires.

The Acquisition of Behavior Social-learning theorists maintain that most new behavior is acquired through observational learning, in which we watch the actions of models and vicariously experience their rewards and punishments. As noted in Chapter 8, we can acquire attitudes, emotions, and social styles as well as practical information in this way. The cognitive processes that ensure the retention of observed behavior can involve describing or naming the model's behavior, representing it visually, or acting it out physically. For example, suppose that you get a summer job waiting on tables in a restaurant. You carefully watch the most experienced waiter, who is always attentive and friendly with the customers. You mentally rehearse his procedures, from the smile with which he greets each diner to the way in which he presents the check. Then, when you wait on tables yourself, you imitate his attentive, friendly manner and find that your tips increase.

Social-learning theorists do not believe that reinforcement is needed for people to learn by observing models, although reinforcement can make such learning easier. Reinforcement is much more important in getting people to repeat newly learned behavior than in teaching it to them initially (Rosenthal and Bandura, 1978). In other words, you may learn the mechanics of taking orders and serving food without receiving any reward yourself, but you will not be likely to volunteer to handle extra tables unless you anticipate that your behavior will earn the reinforcement of a raise, greatly increased tips, or the approval of the other waiters.

Although social-learning theory emphasizes observing models, it also acknowledges the role of direct experience in learning. However, in this view, direct experience does not automatically strengthen a given response, as radical behaviorists maintain: rather, it provides information and motivation that in turn strengthen the response. For example, Eric finds it difficult to assert himself, and others often take advantage of him. In the past month, he has spent a good many hours working on a fund-raising event for a campus organization. A friend calls and asks

Eric to fill in for her by taking tickets at the door so she can go skiing. Eric has already spent more time than anyone else on the project and, suddenly angry, he hears himself saying that he is simply too busy. To his surprise, his friend is neither upset nor angry and simply says she'll ask someone else. The experience gives Eric information: he does not have to accede to every request in order to keep his friends. The experience of asserting himself motivates Eric to be less submissive. The next time someone asks an unreasonable favor, Eric will be less likely to agree.

The Regulation and Maintenance of Behavior According to social-learning theory, once behavior has been acquired it is regulated and maintained by three kinds of control: stimulus control, reinforcement control (both seen as controls in radical behaviorism as well), and cognitive control.

Stimulus control means that some particular behavior takes place only when a particular stimulus in the environment evokes it at the appropriate time. In this case, behavior is under the control of the situation, and stimuli in the environment determine whether we are friendly or withdrawn in a specific situation. Stimuli that occur in social situations may be indirect and their message may not always be clear. A person who asks, "How are you?" may only be expressing politeness, not concern, and is not interested in the details of your recent fight with your roommate. The stimuli of facial expressions and gestures often must be interpreted to determine whether certain behavior will be rewarded.

Reinforcement control is a way of regulating and maintaining behavior by rewarding an individual after she or he has behaved in a particular way. If Jill has frequently been rewarded for aggressiveness, she will tend to react aggressively in most situations in which it is a possible option. Intermittent schedules of reinforcement, in which rewards come only after a varying number of responses, are effective at maintaining behavior long after reinforcement has ceased. That this kind of reinforcement control is effective in maintaining high "addictive" rates of behavior can be confirmed by looking down the rows of slot machines in any casino, where people stuff coins into slots as fast as they can, many of them playing two or more machines at the same time.

Cognitive control refers to the guidance and maintenance of behavior through self-reinforce-

Even shadows such as these may be seen as stimuli that are subject to various interpretations by onlookers.

ment. An individual compares her or his own behavior to an internalized standard and then provides either reinforcement or punishment. Cheryl, who has an image of herself as an honest person, buys a movie ticket and receives change for a $20 bill instead of a $10 bill. She returns the extra $10 and reinforces herself with congratulations for her honesty. If she had said nothing and pocketed the $10, she would have mentally castigated herself.

All three types of controls—stimulus, reinforcement, and cognitive—work together. Stimuli that are physically present trigger cognitive representations (images or symbols) of other stimuli, which lead to expectations of reinforcement, which in turn lead to behavior that can lead to direct reward.

Social-Learning Theory as a Theory of Personality

How does social-learning theory account for the fact that each person reacts to a situation in a unique manner and the fact that each person's behavior is relatively stable and consistent over time? According to Walter Mischel (1973; 1979),

social-learning theory can explain both uniqueness and consistency by means of five overlapping and interlocking concepts:

1. *Competencies:* People are unique and fairly consistent in the sequences of behavior that they construct, on the basis of past learning, to respond to various situations.
2. *Encodings:* Each person has a unique way of perceiving and categorizing experience; one person may see a situation as threatening while another person sees it as challenging, and each responds accordingly.
3. *Expectancies:* Through learning, people have different expectations of being rewarded or punished for various kinds of behavior.
4. *Values:* The value a person places on various stimuli—such as money, social approval, and good grades—influences the person's behavior.
5. *Plans:* Each person has a set of plans or rules for her or his own behavior in a given situation—for example, self-control, courage, or brilliance.

These components of personality are seen by Mischel as products of past learning and at the same time as guides for future learning. Thus, a continuous interaction takes place between individuals and the situations they confront, an interaction that leads to new learning and to further development of personality.

Social-learning theory has developed into a complex system of concepts that attempt to account for the variety and complexity of human behavior. It has a distinct behavioristic flavor because of its emphasis on observable phenomena and its avoidance of psychoanalytic concepts such as instinct and unconscious motivation. Yet it has moved far beyond the radical behaviorist position to emphasize characteristically human abilities, such as cognition, the use of symbols, reasoning, and language.

Evaluation of Behavioristic Theories

Like psychoanalytic and humanistic theories of personality, behavioristic theories have been criticized. Despite the criticisms that have been leveled against them, behaviorist theories of personality have had major impact on the way we think about people as well as on other theories of personality.

Criticisms of Behavioristic Theories   The quarrels of other theorists with behaviorism center on charges that it oversimplifies life, that it is deterministic, and that it can lead to totalitarianism. Because it reduces human action to small, measurable units of behavior and ignores thought and feeling, the behavioristic approach has been criticized as a naïve *oversimplification* of human existence that distorts whatever behavior it measures (London, 1969). The exclusion of thought and feeling by radical behaviorists, it is charged, means that behaviorists refuse to study anything that distinguishes the human species from other animals, hence their principles are simply not applicable to human beings. By giving a major role to cognitive processes, social-learning theory appears to meet these criticisms, but some critics argue that this new behaviorism is still oversimplified. They maintain that a person's personality is determined by more than the easily accessible self-statements upon which social-learning theorists have focused.

Behavioristic theories are also criticized because they are *deterministic,* a charge that arises because behaviorists see most human behavior as the product of conditioning. Not free will, they say, but the stimuli that surround us determine what we will do. Social-learning theory, although it considers cognitive processes, is also deterministic because it regards thoughts and plans as the products of learning; self-reinforcement is thus the product of external reinforcement. Such a position makes many psychologists and philosophers uneasy, because they see law, religion, and morality as based on the principle that we can choose between right and wrong and believe that if people cannot be held responsible,

A social-learning theorist would explain the extreme prejudice of the Ku Klux Klansman as a form of learned behavior. Critics argue that even if people are conditioned to behave in a certain way, or are brought up with a set of beliefs, they must still be held accountable for their behavior.

then there is no foundation for legal systems, religion, or moral codes.

Finally, behavioristic approaches have been seen as *totalitarian* because they regard behavior as "controlled" by contingencies in the environment. In fact, one critic called Skinner's plan for using the techniques of behavior modification to restructure society a blueprint for the "theory and practice of hell" (Rubenstein, 1971). Skinner has acknowledged that the principles of behavior modification could be used by totalitarian governments (Hall, 1972). However, he points out that he opposes the aversive techniques used by such regimes and stresses instead the use of positive reinforcement so that people will "feel free" and enjoy what they do.

Contributions of Behavioristic Theories   The contributions of behavioristic theories to the study of personality have been twofold: they have contributed mightily to the treatment of personality disorders, and their focus on objective aspects of personality has changed psychology. The application of behavior modification to personal problems has resulted in treatments that are faster, cheaper, and often more effective than treatments that have come out of other theoretical approaches to personality. As we noted in Chapter 8 and as we shall see in detail in Chapter 24, behavior modification has been used to end smoking and bed-wetting, to help alcoholics control their drinking, to assist mentally retarded people become more nearly self-sufficient, to end phobias such as intense fear of snakes, and to draw children out of the isolation of autism (Leitenberg, 1976).

The objectivity of behavioristic theories of personality stands in sharp contrast to the vague, inferential statements that come from other theories of personality. Because behaviorists use clearly defined language and study behavior that can be measured, their claims can be tested and retested. Today almost all research in psychology uses behavioristic methods, which are based on experimentation, objective measurement, and operational definitions of inferred constructs (Bootzin and Acocella, 1980).

Trait Theories

Trait theories are—at least on the surface—similar to the kinds of assessments we make about people every day. For example, Betsy spends hours talking to other people, circulates freely at parties, and strikes up conversations while she waits in the dentist's office. Carl, however, spends more time with books than with people and seldom goes to parties. Their acquaintances say that Betsy is friendly and Carl is not. Friendliness is considered a personality trait, and some theorists have argued that studying such consistencies in human behavior is the best approach to solving the puzzle of personality.

A **trait** has been defined as "any relatively enduring way in which one individual differs from another" (Guilford, 1959). Thus, a trait is an inferred predisposition to respond in a consistent way in many different situations—in a dentist's office, at a party, or in a classroom. More than other personality theorists, trait theorists emphasize and try to explain the consistency of human behavior.

Trait theorists generally make two key assumptions about these underlying sources of consistency: they assume that every trait applies to all people (for example, everyone can be classified as more or less dependent); and they assume that these descriptions can be quantified (for example, we could establish a scale on which an extremely dependent person scores 1 while a very independent person scores 10).

Thus, people can be classified on a continuum for any trait. For example, a few people are extremely aggressive and others rarely show a trace of aggression, but most of us fall somewhere in the middle. Specifying an individual's traits allows us to understand that person and to predict her or his behavior in the future. If you were hiring someone to sell vacuum cleaners, you would probably choose outgoing Betsy over bookish Carl. This choice would be based on two assumptions: that friendliness is a useful trait for salespeople and that friendliness in the dentist's office and at parties predicts similar behavior in other situations.

In searching for the underlying sources of consistency in human behavior, trait theorists go beyond this kind of common-sense analysis. They look for the best way to describe the common features of Betsy's behavior, trying to discover whether she is friendly, extraverted, socially aggressive, interested in people, sure of herself, or something else. In other words, they ask, What is the underlying structure that organizes her behavior?

Most (but not all) trait theorists believe that a few basic traits are central for all people. An underlying trait of self-confidence, for example, might explain superficial characteristics such as social aggressiveness and dependency. If personality does arise primarily from basic traits, then a person would be dependent because she or he lacked self-confidence. Psychologists who accept this approach set out on the theoretical search for basic traits with few assumptions about the exact nature of the traits they will find.

This approach is very different from that of other personality theorists we have considered. Freud, for example, started out with a well-defined theory of instincts. When he observed that some people were stingy, he explained their stinginess in terms of his theory, suggesting that it was a displaced form of anal retentiveness. Trait theorists would not begin by trying to understand stinginess; instead they would try to find out if stinginess was indeed a trait. That is, they would want to know whether people who were stingy in one situation were also stingy in others. Then they might ask whether stinginess is one aspect of a more basic trait, such as possessiveness, and whether a stingy person is also possessive in relationships. Thus, the first question for trait theorists is, What kinds of behavior seem to go together?

Instead of relying on powerful theories telling them *where* to look, trait theorists use complex and sophisticated methods that tell them *how* to look. These methods begin with the statistical technique of correlation (discussed in Chapter 2), which uses one set of scores to predict another. For example, does knowing that a person talks to strangers in line at the supermarket predict that she or he will tend to strike up conversations in a singles bar? Such predictions are never perfect. Perhaps Betsy's outgoing behavior in the dentist's office is not friendliness but fear, and she jabbers to strangers in order to forget her terror. Sometimes actions that look like manifestations of one trait may reflect something entirely different.

Some psychologists, among them Gordon Allport, regard traits as real entities that exist in the mind. Most other theorists consider traits to be no more than useful devices for answering the two key questions about the uniqueness and consistency of human behavior. To the question, "Why don't all people respond to the same situation in the same way?" the trait theorist would answer, "Because they don't all have the same traits, or they don't have them to the same degree." To the question, "Why does each person respond to different situations in a relatively con-sistent manner?" the trait theorist would answer, "Because a person's basic traits do not change easily or quickly."

However, when we use traits to explain behavior, we must be careful to avoid circular reasoning, in which we predict that Susan gets so little done because she is lazy—and then establish her laziness by the fact that she gets so little done. This kind of circularity can be avoided, at least in part, if a trait predicts several kinds of behavior that form a consistent pattern.

Allport's Classification of Traits

For almost forty years, Gordon W. Allport was a leading trait theorist who continually developed and refined his theory (Allport, 1937; 1961; 1966). Allport believed that traits accounted for the consistency of human behavior and that a trait made a wide range of situations "functionally equivalent"—that is, a person could interpret different situations as calling for a similar or identical response. For example, an aggressive person would see aggressive behavior as the appropriate response in many situations.

The English language provides a vast array of specific explanations for a countless number of behavioral responses. In 1936 Allport (Allport and Odbert, 1936) searched an unabridged dictionary, noting all the terms that could be used to describe people, and found about 18,000 different words. Even after omitting clearly evaluative terms (like "disgusting") and terms describing transient states (like "abashed"), between 4,000 and 5,000 items remained. Surely, Allport thought, this multitude of descriptions could be reduced to a few essentials.

In his attempt to clarify and simplify these descriptions, Allport described behavior as characterized by three kinds of traits: cardinal, central, and secondary. A **cardinal trait** is a single trait that directs a major portion of a person's behavior. Thus, a person consumed by ambition or by greed would be characterized by a cardinal trait. Famous historical and mythical figures have given their names to cardinal traits, such as Machiavellian, after the sixteenth-century Italian political theorist Niccolo Macchiavelli, which describes a person who persistently manipulates others; and narcissistic, after the Greek youth Narcissus who fell in love with his own reflection, which describes a person who is inordinately preoccupied with himself or herself. Actually, Allport believed that cardinal traits are rare, and

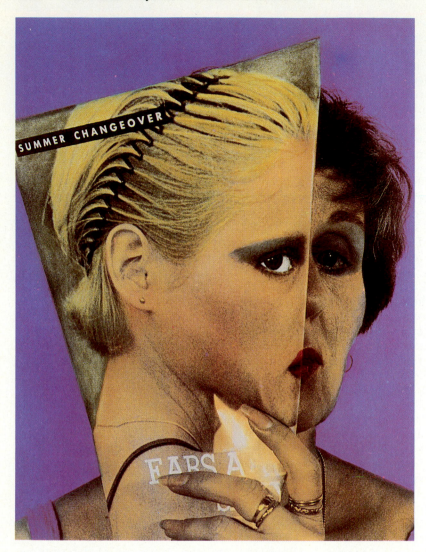

Magazine Makeover
by Judith Golden.

that most individuals do not have one predominant trait. Instead, on the basis of life experiences, people develop a few **central traits**, or characteristic ways of dealing with the world that can be captured by a trait name, such as honest, loving, gregarious, and so on. Less influential are **secondary traits**, or characteristic modes of behavior that are less prominent than central traits and are seen in fewer situations. Secondary traits, though subject to fluctuation and change, might be described as generalized tastes and preferences, such as preferences for certain foods or styles of music.

Allport believed that all people could be described in terms of cardinal, central, and secondary traits, but he distinguished between common traits and individual traits. **Common traits**, such as aggression, are basic modes of adjustment that are approximately the same for different individuals. Because we must all interact in a competitive world, each of us develops our own level of aggression, and each of us can be placed somewhere on a scale of aggressiveness. But since each person is unique, Allport argued, most traits are **individual traits**, which are unique ways of organizing the world and cannot be applied to all people. Allport (1961) later renamed individual traits, calling them **personal dispositions**, since he believed that the uniqueness of individual experience led each person to develop a unique set of dispositions to behave in certain ways. A personal disposition cannot be measured by a standardized test, but can be discerned only by careful study of the individual.

Factor Analysis: Cattell and Eysenck

More recent theorists have concentrated on what Allport called common traits, trying to quantify them in a precise, scientific manner. Their primary tool in this task has been factor analysis, a statistical method for identifying underlying factors that will be discussed in Chapter 20. In applying factor analysis to personality, as shown in Figure 19.5, researchers look for underlying sources of consistency in behavior. Factor analysis is a powerful tool that has the same superiority over simpler statistical techniques as a three-dimensional model of a chemical molecule has over a two-dimensional blackboard diagram.

Factor analysis has been used extensively to study personality traits by Raymond B. Cattell, who identifies a trait as a tendency to react to related situations in a way that remains fairly stable. Cattell distinguishes between two kinds of tendencies: surface traits and source traits. **Surface traits** describe clusters of behavior that tend to go together. An example of a surface trait is altruism, which involves such related behavior as helping a neighbor who has a problem and contributing to an annual blood drive. Other examples of surface traits are integrity, curiosity, realism, and foolishness. **Source traits** are the underlying roots or causes of these behavior clusters, and they are the focus of Cattell's research. Examples of source traits are ego weakness or strength, submissiveness or dominance, and timidity or venturesomeness. Surface traits generally correspond to common-sense descriptions of behavior and can often be measured by simple observation. But since surface traits are the result of interactions among source traits,

Figure 19.5 An example of the technique of factor analysis. Imagine that the five items on the left have been presented to a number of different people, and, from the resulting data, correlations between the various items have been computed. These correlations are shown in the matrix on the right. As you can see, they reveal that items 1 and 5, for example, are closely related; people tend to answer these two items in the same way. Items 1 and 2 appear not to be related; the way a person responds to one has little to do with how he responds to the other. By rearranging the order of the items in the matrix as shown here, it is possible to see that two distinct and independent personality factors are being measured. Items 1, 3, and 5 seem to have something to do with confidence in working ability, and items 2 and 4 seem to describe sociability.

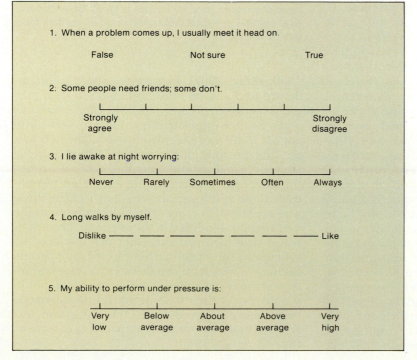

explanations of behavior are not valid unless they are based on source traits, which are the stable, structural factors that determine personality. Cattell believes that by identifying both kinds of traits and learning to measure them, we will be able to specify the common characteristics that are shared by all people as well as the individual characteristics that distinguish one person from another.

Cattell (1965) discovered these traits by using data from life records, questionnaires, and objective tests to study large numbers of people. Life records of an individual include everything from descriptions by the person's friends and acquaintances to school report cards and records of automobile accidents. Questionnaire data are the answers a person gives to a series of questions, whether or not they are truthful. (The fact that an individual underrates herself or himself or tries to create a highly favorable impression may be significant.) Objective test data are a person's responses to tests specifically designed to detect or prevent this type of distortion.

Similar mathematical techniques have led Hans Eysenck to somewhat different conclusions about personality. According to Eysenck (1970), two major dimensions are critical for understanding normal human behavior: extraversion-introversion and neuroticism-stability. For example, Figure 19.6, which shows the way several kinds of people typically score on these dimensions, indicates that depressives tend to be slightly neurotic and slightly introverted.

Eysenck proposes that these traits have a biological basis. He suggests, for example, that people who are extraverted have a low level of cortical arousal. That is, the extravert's cerebral cortex is naturally rather quiet, so that she or he seeks stimulating environments, such as loud parties, intense social interactions, and risky situations, to increase arousal. The introvert, however, has a naturally high level of cortical arousal, so she or he seeks situations that minimize stimulation, such as sitting quietly alone.

Many different observations support this basic split. Introverts, for example, take longer to fall asleep and are more sensitive to pain than extraverts, suggesting that they are more aroused. In addition, as the Yerkes-Dodson law (discussed in Chapter 10) indicates, arousal and performance are related in such a way that moderate levels of arousal lead to optimal performance and performance deteriorates when arousal is too low or too high (Yerkes and Dodson, 1908; Broadhurst,

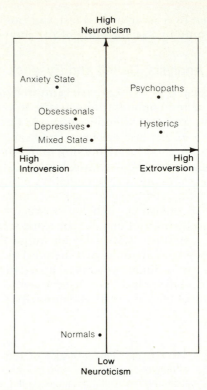

Figure 19.6   Two dimensions in Eysenck's classification system and the locations of people with various psychological disorders within space the dimensions describe. This space (with the addition of a third dimension, psychoticism) is the result of a factor analysis of many personality tests. After these dimensions emerged from his analysis, Eysenck postulated possible biological factors that could account for them. (After Eysenck, 1970.)

1959; Duffy, 1962). Extraverts appear to be underaroused and do better on ability tests if they are under time pressure or if they have had caffeine. Just the opposite is true for introverts, who appear to be more highly aroused. They do better with no time pressure and without caffeine (Revelle, Amaral, and Turriff, 1976). However, the time of day when people are tested complicates these results. Extraverts, particularly those who are impulsive, are helped by caffeine in the morning but hindered in the evening. The opposite is true for introverts; they are hindered by caffeine in the morning but helped by it in the evening. Thus, it appears that extraverts and introverts may not differ in general arousal, but in the rhythm of their daily arousal, with introverts being more aroused in the morning and less aroused in the evening as compared to extraverts (Revelle et al., 1980).

Whether or not Eysenck's theory is correct, he has shown that once basic traits have been identified by factor analysis, it is possible to develop sophisticated theories to account for human behavior.

Evaluation of Trait Theories

Although researchers have developed sophisticated trait theories, other theorists have questioned their usefulness in understanding human behavior. Trait theories have been criticized on the grounds that providing a label does not provide an explanation. If we say that one of the characteristics of "friendliness" is smiling, we have learned nothing when we are told that John smiles because he is friendly. This is the same sort of circular reasoning that we explored in regard to motivation (see Chapter 16). A related criticism is that once a trait has been labeled, it tends to be reified and seen as a "thing" rather than as a short-hand description for the prevalence of a certain kind of behavior. A trait is no more than a theoretical construct and has no independent existence.

Some critics are concerned that assigning traits to people obscures individual differences. Once a person has been labeled "shy" or "aggressive," the pattern of that person's behavior is lost. For example, calling a woman "assertive" is much less helpful than noting that she is assertive with her friends but not with her sister, or is assertive only when provoked, but never in the presence of her lover. By lumping all this behavior under a single trait name, valuable information about the way the woman behaves in the various contexts of her life are lost (Mischel and Peake, in press). Finally, there is little evidence that traits persist across situations. A person who is anxious in one situation may not be anxious under other circumstances, and the label "anxious" does not specify when or with whom a person is anxious. However, as we shall see in the next section, people do tend to show similar traits in similar situations over a long period.

Despite these criticisms, trait theories have contributed to our understanding of personality. They have led to the development of sophisticated analytical techniques that can be used to describe the structure of personality, and they have generated an enormous amount of research that documents the stability and generality of personality.

A Current Controversy: Personality Versus Situational Factors

We have spent two chapters summarizing different approaches to the questions, What makes people different from one another? and What makes each person behave in a relatively consistent way in diverse situations? A third question has not yet been raised: How do we know whether personality traits exist or whether personality consists of varying responses to external situations? This question is the basis of the box on page 450.

For a number of years, researchers used tests to measure personality traits and then correlated the test scores with measures of behavior in various situations. For convenience, the situations were often constructed in laboratories, where researchers measured everything from ego strength to extraversion and correlated their results with such diverse indexes of behavior as career aspirations and tolerance of pain. Because interesting relationships between variables were being discovered and documented, it seemed that scientific progress was being made, and the value of the procedures was seldom questioned.

The Critique

Then in 1968, social-learning theorist Walter Mischel cast a shadow across this entire enterprise. Reviewing one study after another, Mischel showed that correlations between personality trait measures and behavior rarely exceeded .30. Such relationships may be genuine, and may even have theoretical significance, but they are too weak to have much practical value, as Figure 19.7 shows. On the basis of such correlations, a teacher, employer, or clinical psychologist cannot make valid decisions concerning specific students, potential employees, or clients.

Mischel thought he had seen enough evidence to conclude that broad personality trait measures are of little value in predicting behavior outside of test situations. Moreover, he thought he knew why. If people behave the way they do because they have been reinforced for particular responses in particular situations, it is not surprising to find that they act differently in different situations. A person might act consistently in

"You're Dishonest, but I Need the Money"

The debate over the role of personality traits and the demands of a situation may have been obscured by the way in which our perceptions of ourselves differ from our perceptions of others. Suppose you are rushing to make an important appointment and push someone aside to catch a bus. You might well say, "He was being obstinate, so I had to shove him out of the way because I was in a terrific hurry." You would be unlikely to say, "He was being obstinate, so I was rude."

This difference in perception appeared in a study (Nisbett et al., 1973) in which male college students were asked why they had chosen their girl friends as well as why their best friend had chosen his girl friend. When talking about themselves, the men pointed out the qualities in the woman that attracted them—relying on the situation. But when explaining their friend's choice, they talked only about the friend's personality and made no mention of anything about the woman that might have attracted him.

This widespread tendency to emphasize personality traits in others and situational aspects in ourselves may be based on the kind of information that is available (Jones and Nisbett, 1972). We have extensive knowledge of our own experiences and feelings, and we are aware of the way that a situation can affect our intentions. When we judge others, however, we have only behavior as our guide: how the other person looks and sounds and acts.

This difference in perceptual perspective, according to whether a person is an observer or an actor, may have profound effects (Jones and Nisbett, 1971). When you watch someone else, she or he is at the center of your attention and therefore seems to "cause" whatever happens; you fail to notice the environmental forces acting on the person. But when you are the actor, the environment tends to hold your attention; you are more aware of outside pressures than of your own role in the process. Thus, if you see the woman ahead of you at the supermarket counter quietly pocket an extra $10 in change, you say to yourself, "She is dishonest." But if you should similarly pocket an extra $10, you might recall that your next check is four days away and you have only $7 in your billfold and say, "I need the money." Thus you ascribe the other person's action to personality traits and your own to the pressing needs of the situation.

---

the same situation (John might always be aggressive on the football field and Martha might always be arrogant with younger co-workers) but her or his behavior would show little consistency across situations. Thus John is aggressive on the football field but very shy and retiring at a party; Martha is arrogant toward younger co-workers

but deferential to superiors. There is no reason, said Mischel, to expect people to have general traits or to be classifiable along the same trait dimension, such as introverion-extraversion.

The Response

Mischel's argument generated a heated debate. It focused on the lack of consistency in behavior across situations and the inability of trait theory

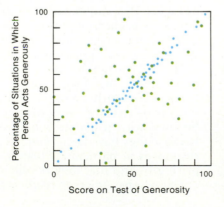

Figure 19.7 Two possible results of an attempt to validate an imaginary pencil-and-paper test of generosity against some measure of generous behavior in everyday situations. The small blue dots represent a correlation near 1.0; the large green dots represent a correlation of 0.25 between the two measures. The second correlation is of the magnitude usually observed when such attempts at validation are made. To be useful in predicting individual behavior, the test would have to have a correlation with generous behavior in daily life that is much closer to that represented by the small blue dots.

to handle it. His critique has evoked several different responses.

One group of researchers (Green, 1978; Epstein, 1980) suggested that Mischel's findings primarily reflected problems in the measurement of behavior and pointed out that each situation is like one item of a test. To get a reliable measure of how a person behaves, that person's behavior would have to be averaged across many situations. Indeed, when people's behavior was measured over a twelve-day period, the consistency of their actions increased substantially (Epstein, 1979).

However, Mischel and Philip Peake (in press) replied that most of the behavior rated in the Epstein (1979) study related to a consistency Mischel had never denied: temporal stability, or a person's tendency to act consistently in the same situation. Mischel and Peake (in press) showed that when a group of sixty-three students at Carleton College were rated on conscientiousness by themselves, their friends, and their parents, the students' behavior on nineteen different measures related to conscientiousness showed an impressive stability over time on many of the measures, but little consistency across situations. A student who attended class regularly was not necessarily on time nor were her or his assignments neatly prepared.

A second type of response came from researchers who took an interactionist position. Neither personality traits nor situations are of primary importance, they said, and neither allows us to predict behavior. Instead, a person's actions are determined by an interaction between personality and situation (Magnusson and Endler, 1977). Yet this explanation has never been questioned, and at some level every theorist agrees that person and situation interact. As we saw earlier, Mischel discusses how the characteristics of a person interact with each situation. Even by applying an interactionist interpretation, however, critics have not been able to improve predictions of behavior across situations.

Finally, Daryl Bem and Andrea Allen (1974) pointed out that some people are more consistent than others. They proposed that by starting with a group of subjects who are known to be consistent in a particular trait, it is possible to show consistency across situations. Bem and Allen asked students to rate themselves on their consistency of "friendliness" and "conscientiousness," then observed their behavior. Students who had rated themselves as consistent in friendliness later showed a correlation of .73 between their behavior in a group discussion and their spontaneous friendliness as measured by how long it took them to strike up a conversation with a confederate in a waiting room. Among students who had rated themselves as variable, the correlation was .30—about what Mischel had found in his review. Students who were consistently friendly were generally not consistently conscientious, and vice versa. It appeared that for any given trait, some people will behave consistently; for others, the trait is irrelevant and thus has no usefulness in predicting behavior.

Yet the students studied by Bem and Allen showed no consistency on conscientiousness and only displayed consistency in friendliness on one measure: between spontaneous friendliness and friendliness in group discussion (Mischel and Peake, in press). When Mischel and Peake replicated Bem and Allen's research with the Carleton College students, they found that students who were highly consistent in conscientiousness showed much greater stability over time than students whose ratings were inconsistent, but there was no difference between the two groups across situations. In an apparent paradox, those who claimed to be consistently conscientious, and were rated that way by parents and peers, showed no generalization of conscientiousness from one situation to another.

In an attempt to resolve the paradox, Mischel and Peake propose that the college students, their parents, and their friends were all judging the students in the same way: by the temporal stability of some behavior that is highly typical of conscientiousness. Because the student consistently behaved the same way in a situation that is seen as a prototype of conscientiousness (perhaps always being on time), the student is seen as conscientious in all situations. However this "conscientious" student may not behave conscientiously in other areas, because Mischel and Peake found little consistency across situations, even on behavior that is considered highly typical of conscientiousness.

Earlier, Mischel (1973) had pointed out that we tend to be biased in the way we perceive actions, maintaining our first impression of a person even if she or he later acts quite differently. For example, if we see a woman act cruelly toward someone and later see her act with compassion—even if she is compassionate on several occasions—we are likely to say to ourselves, "She certainly hides her vicious nature well."

Thus the fact that we perceive consistency in behavior may have more to do with the way we organize information than with how consistently a person behaves.

This selective perception and the related cognitive processes by which the individual perceives situations and plans behavior are now being explored systematically (e.g., Cantor and Kihlstrom, 1981). It may be possible to predict behavior by paying close attention to the situations being studied. As we have seen, people whose behavior seems unpredictable in relation to a given trait are often quite predictable in relation to a given situation.

No matter what theoretical approach to personality we adopt, it seems clear that the convolutions of human behavior can be explained only by the complicated interaction of internal forces —whether they are instincts, needs, traits, or constructs—and such external forces as environment, family, and situation.

SUMMARY

1. Most nonpsychoanalytic theories of personality can be classified as either behavioristic approaches, humanistic approaches, or trait theories. These approaches deemphasize unconscious forces as determinants of personality and emphasize observable behavior, learning, and cognitive processes.

2. **Humanistic theories** emphasize human constructive and creative potential and stress personal growth. Abraham Maslow based his theory on people who had achieved **self-actualization**, those who find fulfillment in doing their best. He believed that there is an active impulse toward the actualization of one's potentialities and identified two groups of human needs: basic, or **deficiency needs** (physiological and psychological needs) and **metaneeds** or growth needs (that include justice, goodness, beauty, order, and unity). Unfulfilled growth needs can lead to **metapathologies**, such as alienation. Carl Rogers' self theory suggests that people have an innate impulse toward becoming **fully functioning**, or psychologically adjusted. Rogers believed that **conditional positive regard** in childhood leads to the denial and distortion of feelings so that we develop **conditions of worth** under which we know we will receive positive regard. Rogers distinguished between the **organism**, or the total range of possible experiences, and the **self**, or the recognized and accepted parts of experience. In Rogers' **nondirective**, or **client-centered**, **therapy**, the therapist maintains an attitude of **unconditional positive regard** toward the client. Humanistic theories of personality have been criticized for being unscientific and subjective. The contributions of humanistic approaches include the emphasis psychologists now place on their clients' personal growth, the recent interest in exploring altered states of consciousness, and the strength of the group-therapy movement.

3. **Behavioristic theories** view personality as a set of learned responses. Dollard and Miller's behavior theory seeks to translate psychoanalytic phenomena into behavioristic terms. In this theory, neurotic conflicts are learned; they are characterized as extreme **approach-avoidance conflicts**, in which two motives clash so that satisfying one frustrates the other. B. F. Skinner's radical behaviorism analyzes behavior in terms of the external conditions that control it, paying no attention to internal events such as thoughts and feelings. Social-learning theorists believe that most new behavior is acquired through observational learning, but emphasize human cognitive capabilities. Once acquired, behavior is regulated and maintained by **stimulus control** (a particular behavior takes place only when a stimulus evokes it at an appropriate time); **reinforcement control** (previously rewarded behavior is maintained by intermittent reinforcement); and **cognitive control** (the ability to guide and maintain behavior by providing self-reinforcement). According to Walter Mischel, social-learning theory accounts for both the uniqueness and the consistency of human personality. Behavioristic approaches to personality have been criticized on the grounds that they oversimplify life, that they are deterministic, and that they can lead to totalitarianism. The contributions of behavioristic approaches have been their methods of treating personality disorders (behavior modification) and their focus on the objective aspects of personality.

4. According to **trait theories** of personality, the extent to which an individual possesses various **traits** (or enduring ways in which individuals vary) accounts for the uniqueness and consistency of behavior. Gordon Allport believed that traits can render different situations "functionally equivalent." He classified three kinds of traits: **cardinal traits** (a single trait that dominates behavior), **central traits** (several basic and characteristic ways of dealing with the world); and **secondary traits** (tastes and preferences). Any of these traits may be either **common traits**, which are approximately the same for different individuals, or **individual traits** (also called **personal dispositions**), which make each individual's behavior unique. Some trait theorists have used factor analysis to develop measures of personality's fundamental dimensions. Raymond Cattell obtained a number of **surface traits**, which he further analyzed to yield **source traits**, the underlying dimensions of personality. Hans Eysenck concluded that there are two major trait dimensions underlying personality: introversion-extraversion and neuroticism-stability. Eysenck related personality differences to biological factors.

5. A current controversy concerns whether fixed personality traits exist or whether personality consists of varying responses to external situations. Walter Mischel believes that people act differently in different situations because of the way they have been reinforced for particular responses. Despite objections to Mischel's critique on various grounds, it appears that people behave differently across situations but consistently in the same situation over time. Yet people are often perceived as being more consistent than they are. This perception may be the result of perceptual biases. The first impression of a person tends to be lasting, so that later behavior is interpreted as if the initial behavior were typical.

Key Terms

approach-avoidance conflict	fully functioning	reinforcement control
behavioristic theories	growth needs	self
cardinal trait	humanistic theories	self-actualization
central trait	individual traits	secondary trait
client-centered therapy	metaneeds	source trait
cognitive control	metapathologies	stimulus control
common trait	nondirective therapy	surface trait
conditional positive regard	organism	trait
conditions of worth	peak experiences	trait theories
deficiency needs	personal disposition	unconditional positive regard

RECOMMENDED READINGS

MADDI, SALVATORE R. *Personality Theories: A Comparative Analysis*. 3rd. ed. Homewood, Ill.: Dorsey Press, 1976. This recent textbook classifies personality theorists according to whether their basic assumption relates to *conflict, fulfillment, or consistency*. Examines what the theorists have to say about the core and periphery of personality. Also presents research on each position and draws conclusions about its strengths and weaknesses.

MISCHEL, WALTER. *Introduction to Personality*. 3rd ed. New York: Holt, Rinehart and Winston, 1981. This recent textbook by a well-known social-learning theorist divides theories into five categories: type and trait, psychoanalytic, psychodynamic behaviorist, social learning, and phenomenological. The book covers theory, assessment techniques, and personality development and change (including therapy). Because of the author's orientation, behavior theories and behavior modification techniques receive more emphasis than usual, and a great deal of attention is paid to empirical evidence, especially from laboratory experiments.

SMITH, B. D., and H. J. VETTER. *Theoretical Approaches to Personality*. Englewood Cliffs, N.J.: Prentice-Hall, 1982. This book emphasizes individual theorists and presents each person's theory in detail.

CHAPTER 20

Psychological Assessment

Every year since 1972 a mathematical talent search has been conducted in the United States in the hope of finding students whose mathematical reasoning is far advanced and helping them to develop their talent. We might expect that the surest way to find such youth would be to ask seventh-grade mathematics teachers in schools across the country to recommend their best students. From that group, it should be easy to pick the best and the brightest mathematical talent in the nation. An incident that took place in 1975 indicates, however, that teachers are not always aware of talent under their noses. It revealed that limiting talent searches to students whose ability has drawn the teacher's attention may cause us to overlook some of the most gifted young people.

That year the Department of Mathematics of Johns Hopkins University held a contest for eleventh-grade math students in the Baltimore area. Following what seemed to be obvious logic, the department asked teachers to nominate their most promising students to participate. As a special favor, Julian C. Stanley, who directs the annual talent search among the nation's seventh graders, asked that he be allowed to nominate ten students himself. The students he selected has been tested several years earlier as part of Stanley's Study of Mathematically Precocious Youth, and their scores on the mathematical part of the College Entrance Examination Board's Scholastic Aptitude Test (SAT-M) had been impressive.

After the Johns Hopkins math department had finished testing the nominated students, they discovered that three of Stanley's nominations had finished 1, 2, 3 in the group of fifty-one students, and that only one of them had also been nominated by a teacher. Further, the rest of Stanley's nominations ranked 5.5, 7, 8, 12, 16.5, 19, and 23.5 in the group, and among these students only two had been nominated by their teachers (ranks 5.5 and 19; Stanley, 1976). Thus, a standardized objective test of mathematical aptitude was better at predicting mathematical performance than the judgment of mathematics teachers who had spent almost an entire school year working with the students in the classroom.

Although psychological tests are by no means perfect instruments, as we shall see, they are efficient when used properly. Aptitude tests, such as the SAT-M, do a good job of selecting students who are academically gifted; personality tests can identify specific problems that require treatment in the mentally disturbed; intelligence tests can discover children with previously unrevealed gifts or needs. With all their flaws, psychological tests are still important tools for evaluation.

Requirements of a Test

A **psychological test** is an objective and standardized measure of a sample of behavior (Anastasi, 1982), which provides a systematic basis for making inferences about people (London and Bray, 1980). Unless a test is reliable and valid, it cannot measure behavior accurately, and unless it has been standardized, there is no way to determine the meaning of an individual's score. Therefore, reliability and validity are important criteria for judging a test's value, and standardization is essential in judging its utility.

Reliability

A test is **reliable** if it measures something consistently. We trust a yardstick; it can be expected to produce the same measurements whether it is used today or next week and whether it is used by a carpenter or a plumber. Like a yardstick, a psychological assessment technique is reliable only if it yields the same results with repeated measurements. When a test is reliable, a group of people can take the test on two separate occasions and their scores will fall in approximately the same order each time (see Figure 20.1).

Different sorts of tests require different measures of reliability. In psychological assessment, three types of reliability are used: **internal consistency reliability**, the extent to which different parts of the test produce the same results; **test-retest reliability**, the extent to which repeated administration of the test to the same group of people produces the same results; and **interjudge reliability**, the extent to which scoring or interpretation by different judges will produce the same results.

A test's internal consistency is important if the test uses many items to measure a certain characteristic. For example, if a test constructed to measure anxiety consists of sixty items, its internal consistency can be assessed by randomly dividing the test in half and comparing people's scores on one half of the test with their scores on the other half. If the test is internally consistent,

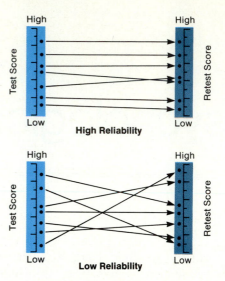

Figure 20.1 The concept of test reliability. On the left in each diagram the test scores of seven individuals are ordered on a scale. On the right the corresponding scores on a second version of the same test, or on the same test given at a later time, are ordered. In the upper diagram the two sets of scores correspond very closely. This pattern of scores means that the test is highly reliable. In the lower diagram, there is little relationship between the two sets of scores. This scrambled pattern means that the test has a low reliability: Two different administrations of the same test gave quite different results.

people's scores on the two sections will be highly correlated. The test must be divided at random, because such factors as boredom, fatigue, or practice can progressively affect the way a person answers the items, so that comparing scores on the first thirty items with scores on the second thirty will not assess the test's reliability.

Test-retest reliability is the extent to which repeated administrations of a test to the same group of people produce the same result. It is especially applicable if the test measures a stable characteristic, such as intelligence or ability. When test-retest reliability is high, taking the test on two different occasions yields similar scores, indicating that the test is not particularly susceptible to such temporary influences as stress, illness, or distractions at the time of testing. For example, students who score high on the SAT-M in February should also score high on the test in November, since mathematical aptitude can be expected to remain constant. Not all measures are expected to have high test-retest reliability. For example, a test that measures an unstable attribute, such as attitude or mood, would not be likely to produce similar results each time it is taken. Similar scores on the same test are not always an indication of test-retest reliability. Suppose a woman takes an intelligence test on Friday and on the following Monday takes the test again. With such a short interval between the tests, her similar scores may be the result of her recalling on Monday a good many answers from the test's first administration.

Not all tests are scored objectively; some require the scorer to interpret a person's answers, as in psychiatric diagnoses, the grading of essay examinations, or ratings of observed behavior. In such tests interjudge reliability is extremely important, for if two people cannot judge a test and arrive at similar scores, a person's score would fluctuate wildly, depending upon who scored the answers. Therefore, before subjectively scored tests can be considered reliable, there must be evidence that any appropriately trained persons can administer, score, and interpret them with similar results.

Validity

A test is **valid** when it measures what it purports to measure, and the way its validity is established depends upon the purpose of the test. **Content validity** refers to whether the test actually covers a representative sample of the measured attribute. Unless tests given in school situations, such as a final exam or the Advanced Test portion of the Graduate Record Examination (GRE), have content validity, they are not accurate yardsticks of a student's knowledge of the field. For example, if a GRE exam in literature contained only items about French poetry, it would lack content validity.

Content validity is sometimes confused with **face validity**, which refers to whether the test *appears* valid to the people taking it. For example, a law school admission test would lack face validity if questions testing knowledge of algebra were included. When tests lack face validity (although they may be valid), people who are expected to take them may become hostile and refuse to cooperate.

If the purpose of the test is to predict future performance, content validity is not enough. Suppose a city asks applicants for the job of firefighter to take a civil service examination and fills vacancies on the basis of test results. A test for prospective firefighters must have **predictive validity**; that is, scores on the test must show a relationship to future performance on the job. If people who make low scores on the test do as well at preventing and fighting fires as those who make high scores, the test lacks predictive validity and is not a good yardstick for personnel selection.

Predictive validity is often difficult to establish, because it may require years to determine, but once a test has been shown to have predictive validity, it becomes extremely valuable. Exactly what test givers want to predict, however, must be clear. The SAT-M accurately predicted performance on a math test devised by the Johns Hopkins mathematics department, but that correlation does not necessarily demonstrate the SAT-M's validity in predicting success in a mathematical career, which can only be established by showing a relationship between this subsequent success and SAT-M scores.

A test is also considered to be a valid predictor if it has **concurrent validity**; that is, if scores on the test correlate highly with other existing measures or standards. Concurrent validity is especially useful when a simple test, such as a quickly answered pencil-and-paper test of depression, can be shown to correlate with a time-consuming, expensive interview by trained clinicians.

Finally, **construct validity** refers to whether the test actually measures the trait or theoretical construct it claims to measure (Anastasi, 1982). Since that definition encompasses almost everything that interests a psychologist, including intelligence, anxiety, shyness, leadership, mechanical ability, mathematical ability, fatigue, and anger, construct validity is essential in psychological testing. For example, if a test of shyness has construct validity, scores on the test should be related to the number of parties a person attends, talkativeness in groups, and ratings of shyness obtained from parents and friends. But it should not be related to other measures such as intelligence. Construct validity is thus the unifying concept of validity because it integrates external standards and internal test content into a framework for testing hypotheses about important relationships (Messick, 1980).

A valid test is reliable, but reliable tests are not always valid. For example, astrological horoscopes are highly reliable, because they will always produce the same prediction for the same person. But horoscopes are not valid, because they neither describe personality nor predict future events accurately. Similarly, measuring head size as an indicator of intelligence is highly reliable. Using the same tape measure in the same way will always produce the same head measurement. But head size is not a valid indicator of intelligence because there is no relationship between head size and academic success or scores on intelligence tests. Head size, however, is both a reliable and a valid indicator of hat size.

Standardization

An individual test score tells us very little unless we also know what kind of scores other people have attained. If a person has answered correctly fifty-three of the eighty-eight questions on a test, it is impossible to say whether the subject has done well or poorly unless we know that most people can answer only forty-four questions correctly. Before a test is put into general use, testers develop normative distributions, or **norms**, which show the frequency with which particular scores on the test are made. Norms are established by giving the test to a large and well-defined group of people, called a

standardization group. The arithmetical average of the standardization group becomes a reference point, and norms indicate how far above or below this average any given score is.

The most common methods of translating "raw" scores (that is, the scores individuals actually make) into scores that are relative to the scores of others are the percentile system and the standard score system.

The **percentile system** divides a group of scores into one hundred equal parts. Since each percentile then contains 1/100 of the scores, a percentile number shows the proportion of the standardization group that is above and below a person's score. For example, a score at the eightieth percentile would be higher than the scores of 79 percent of the rest of the people who took the test and lower than the scores of 19 percent.

The **standard score system** is more complex. Standard scores represent points on a bell-shaped curve that reflects the normal pattern of distribution of scores on almost any test. (The concept of normal distribution was discussed in Chapter 2.) As Figure 20.2 shows, in a normal distribution the majority of people obtain scores

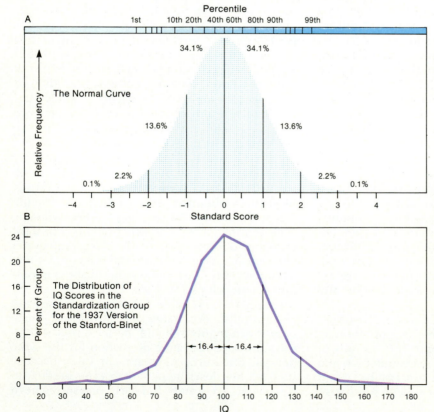

Figure 20.2 The theoretical normal curve (A) and a practical application of it (B). The curves show the proportions of a group or population that fall at various points on a scale. The theoretical curve is useful because it has precise mathematical characteristics from which such relative measures as standard and percentile scores can be calculated. A standard score describes the position of an individual's score in terms of the variance of the group's scores. A percentile score describes the position of an individual's score in terms of the percentage of scores in the group that his or her score exceeds. A single standard-score unit corresponds to about 16.4 IQ points on the 1937 Stanford-Binet test. Knowing this correspondence and knowing the average IQ (approximately 100), one can convert any IQ into a standard score or a percentile score by reading the theoretical curve. (Bottom graph after Terman and Merrill, 1973.)

within a narrow range lying somewhere in the middle of the distribution of all test scores. The farther a score is from the middle, or average, the fewer the people who obtain it.

On most intelligence tests (discussed in the following section), raw scores of people within the same age group are converted to standard scores with a mean of 100 and a standard deviation (see Chapter 2) of 15. As a result, about 68 percent of the population achieves scores between 85 and 115; more than 95 percent achieves scores between 70 and 130; and more than 99.7 percent achieves scores between 55 and 145.

If a test is to provide accurate information about the relative standing of a score, the standardization group must represent the population that takes the test. Different standardization groups are needed for different purposes. Thus, when we want to know how an eleventh-grade student's achievement-test score compares with the scores of other eleventh-graders in the same high school, the standardization group is different from that used to compare the student's score with those of eleventh-graders across the country. Under some circumstances, it is useful to develop separate norms for different groups. For example, a physical fitness test generally has separate norms for males and females, and most intelligence tests have separate norms for various age groups. But in both cases, the normative group must represent the population with which the individual is compared.

The Measurement of Intelligence, Aptitude, and Achievement

The most frequently administered test measuring mental characteristics is the intelligence test. Alfred Binet (1857–1911), a French psychologist, was the first to develop a reliable test of this kind. In the late nineteenth century, mental ability was assessed by simple tests of sensory discrimination and reaction time, which could be measured with precision. Such tests were used because it was considered impossible to measure complex intellectual functions objectively. However, Binet believed that by finding tasks on which performance improved with age, psychologists could directly measure complex intellectual functions. He reasoned that if older children did better on these tasks than younger

children, then children who performed better than others of their own age must be mentally older—more intelligent than their age mates.

In 1904 Binet began to develop a test that could identify mentally defective children in the Paris schools, so that these children could be taught separately. In collaboration with Theodor Simon, a psychiatrist, Binet devised thirty simple tests, covering such tasks as word meaning, recognition of familiar objects, and understanding commands. The tests were arranged in order of difficulty and incorporated into a scale. By 1908, Binet's tests were being used to predict school performance among normal children (Binet and Simon, 1916).

On the basis of their scores, children were assigned a mental age, which corresponded with the average age of children who obtained that score on the intelligence test. Binet originally defined as retarded those children whose mental age was two years or more below their chronological age. One problem with this definition was that children aged fourteen who were two years behind their age group were considered to be as retarded as children of six who were also two years behind their age group. To solve the problem, a German psychologist, William Stern (1914), suggested that instead of using the *difference* between mental age and chronological age, examiners should use the *ratio* of mental age to chronological age. His idea resulted in the **intelligence quotient (IQ)**, which is computed by dividing mental age by chronological age and multiplying by 100 (to get rid of the decimals).

In modern intelligence tests, a person's IQ no longer represents the quotient of mental age to chronological age. Instead, it is a standard score with a mean of 100 and a standard deviation of 15, in relation to the person's own age group. Although the scores are still called IQ scores, they are more accurately called "deviation IQs" because they show how far a person's score deviates from the mean of her or his own age group.

Tests take various forms. Some intelligence tests are designed to be administered to individuals, some to groups; other tests measure aptitude or achievement rather than IQ. The purpose for which the test is given generally determines the kind that is used.

Individual Intelligence Tests

Individual intelligence tests are administered by one examiner to one subject. Two individual intelligence tests in wide use today are a version of

Binet's test and the intelligence scales developed by David Wechsler.

The Stanford-Binet Test Since Binet developed his test of intelligence, it has been revised many times. The most successful revision, which was developed at Stanford University under the direction of Lewis Terman (1916; Terman and Merrill, 1937; 1960) and is called the **Stanford-Binet Test**, is widely used in the United States. This test contains a number of subtests—some of verbal ability and some of performance—that are grouped by age. Performance subtests include such activities as picture completion, block design, picture arrangement, and object assembly (see photo). They are arranged in an order designed to hold the interest of the person being tested. To ensure that the scores do not reflect factors other than ability, the examiner is trained to carry out the standardized instructions exactly, but at the same time to try to put the subject at ease and keep him or her motivated.

The examiner first asks the subject some questions—often from the vocabulary test—to locate the proper level at which to start. For example, if a nine-year-old who seems reasonably bright is being tested, the examiner will probably begin with the tests for an eight-year-old. If the child misses some of the questions, the examiner drops back to tests for year seven. After locating the basal age—the highest age at which the child can pass all items—the examiner proceeds with tests at later year levels. When the child reaches the level at which he or she can pass no items, the testing session ends.

The original Binet tests were designed for school-age children, but successive revisions of the Stanford-Binet tests have extended the scale to both preschool and adult levels.

The Wais and the Wisc During the 1930s, David Wechsler became dissatisfied with the Stanford-Binet Test because it was a poor measure for testing adults and because it was primarily a test of verbal ability. To overcome these problems, he developed a test to be used with adults that measured both performance and verbal ability. This test eventually became the **Wechsler Adult Intelligence Scale (WAIS)**, and after its revision in 1981 it became known as the WAIS-R. Wechsler also developed the **Wechsler Intelligence Scale for Children (WISC)**, which he revised in 1974 as the WISC-R. In the 1960s, he developed the **Wechsler Preschool and Primary Scale of Intelligence (WPPSI)** to be used with children from four to six and a half years old. Its form is similar to the WISC, although some easier items have been added to it.

The WAIS, the WISC, and the WPPSI are among the most frequently used individual intelligence tests. In all of these tests, items of the same kind are grouped together into a subtest

Two tests of the Stanford-Binet Intelligence Scale being administered to a little boy. Both these tests are ones that would be easily passed by him unless he were severely retarded. (left) The examiner has built a tower of four blocks and has told the child, "You make one like this." The average two-year-old is able to build the tower. Three-year-olds are asked to copy a three-block bridge. (right) The examiner shows the child the card with six small objects attached to it and says, "See all these things? Show me the dog," and so on. The average two-year-old can point to the correct objects as they are named.

and arranged in order of difficulty. The examiner administers each of the subtests, starting with a very easy item and continuing until the end or until the person has missed a predetermined number of items in succession (Wechsler, 1955; 1958).

The Wechsler tests differ from the Stanford-Binet in several ways. For one thing, the Wechsler tests have more performance tasks and are therefore less biased toward verbal skills. For another, the Wechsler tests do not have different items for different ages; the WISC items are the same for children of all ages, and the WAIS items are the same for all adults. Finally, the Stanford-Binet Test yields a single IQ score; the Wechsler tests give separate scores for each kind of subtest —vocabulary, information, arithmetic, picture arrangement, block design, and so on. The subtest scores are in turn combined into separate IQ scores for verbal and performance abilities. This method of scoring helps the examiner make a qualitative sketch of how an individual reacts to different kinds of items (see Figure 20.3). Most important, it encourages the treatment of intelligence as a number of related abilities rather than simply as a single generalized ability.

Group Intelligence Tests

Group intelligence tests are strictly paper-and-pencil measures; there is no person-to-person interchange, as with individual tests. The convenience and economy of group tests have led to their use in schools, employment offices, and many other mass testing situations. The Army Alpha and Army Beta tests, for example, were developed during World War I for classifying soldiers.

Clinicians and school personnel generally prefer individually administered intelligence tests to group tests, because individual tests provide the examiner with a rich sample of the person's behavior in addition to the standardized information about intelligence. The behavioral information is often useful in understanding the basis of a child's difficulty or in deciding among alternative programs.

Group testing, however, has become routine because of its convenience, and most children in school are repeatedly given group achievement and aptitude tests.

Figure 20.3 A simplified version of a WISC profile for a thirteen-year-old male. (The optional digit span and mazes subscales were not administered.) Scores from each of the subscales within the verbal and performance groupings are first converted into special scaled scores and plotted accordingly on the chart. Then individual subtest scores are added together, yielding a total verbal and a total performance score. In turn, these scores are summed to reflect the full-scale score. Lastly, the full-scale score is converted into the full-scale IQ score—in this case 103, or about average. The separability of scores on the subscales is sometimes useful in determining specific talents or deficits that might not have been apparent if only the overall IQ score were reported. (Adapted from WISC-R record form, © 1971, 1974, The Psychological Corporation.)

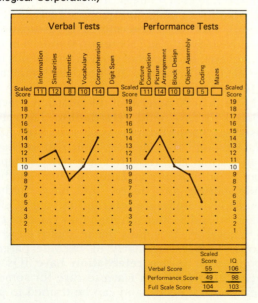

Achievement and Aptitude Tests

Achievement tests were originally constructed to assess the extent of an individual's knowledge about subjects taught in school; **aptitude tests** were designed to find out about an individual's talent or capacity for particular lines of work. As time passed, however, the distinction between the two types of tests blurred. What psychologists first thought were tests of aptitude— defined as innate ability or talent—turned out partly to measure different kinds of experience, so that they had to be regarded in some sense as achievement tests as well. Because achievement tests often turned out to be good predictors of many kinds of occupational abilities, they were also in some sense aptitude tests. Thus the distinction has come to rest more on purpose than on content. When a test is used to evaluate what a person knows, it is an achievement test; when the same test is used to predict how successful the person will be, it is an aptitude test.

The Scholastic Aptitude Test   The College Entrance Examination Board's **Scholastic Aptitude Test (SAT)** has probably been taken by almost every student who reads this book. The test is a direct descendant of the Army Alpha Test and was first administered in 1926. Designed to measure "aptitude for college studies" rather than school achievement or general intelligence, the test has been continually and meticulously revised and updated. It yields two scores, SAT-V for verbal aptitude and SAT-M for mathematical aptitude. The reliability of both scores is very high: .89 for SAT-V and .88 for SAT-M (Wallace, 1972)—quite close to a perfect correlation, which, as we saw in Chapter 2, would be 1.00. The validity for predicting college grades is .39 for SAT-V and .33 for SAT-M. High-school records, which show a validity of .55, are more valid than the two SAT scores as a predictor of college grades. But when all three measures are combined into one index, the correlation with college grades is .62 (DuBois, 1972). These validities are high enough to make the SAT useful in predicting college performance, but low enough to make it clear that other factors, such as motivation, are also important determinants of academic success.

Until recently, students who took the SAT received their scores but no information as to the correctness of specific answers. Since 1980, however, students in New York State have been able to get copies of the tests, their marked answer sheets, and the correct answers. Almost immediately, it became clear that a valid, reliable test can contain some wrong answers (see accompanying box). As a result, in 1981 the practice was voluntarily extended to the entire country.

Variations in Intelligence

Although nearly 70 percent of the population make scores on intelligence tests that fall within a narrow range of 30 IQ points (85 to 115), a few people show extreme variations in intelligence, being either mentally retarded or gifted. At present we know more about the causes of mental retardation than about the causes of giftedness, but many aspects of extremely low or high intelligence continue to be baffling. Just as baffling is the basis of creativity and its link with intelligence.

Mental Retardation   Approximately 6.5 million people in the United States are mentally retarded, as are nearly 70 percent of the permanently disabled population (Robinson and Robinson, 1976). Such a large pool of retarded individuals presents a serious social problem, since mental retardation refers to a person's adaptive behavior as well as to her or his intellectual functioning. These twin aspects of retardation are the basis of the accepted definition of **mental retardation**, drawn up by the American Association on Mental Deficiency (1977):

Mental retardation refers to significantly subaverage general intellectual functioning existing concurrently with deficits in adaptive behavior, and manifested during the developmental period (p.11).

Despite the fact that all people whose functioning fits this definition are considered mentally retarded, mentally retarded people vary greatly in the degree of their limitations. Some are able to live productive lives with a minimum of assistance; others may be unable to speak or to take care of themselves. Because of this wide variation, mental retardation is generally divided into four levels (mild, moderate, severe, and profound), each level determined by estimates of adaptive behavior and scores on standard intelligence tests. Each level of retardation blends into the next, so that there are no clear boundaries between the categories.

More than 90 percent of the retarded are considered to have **mild retardation**. Their IQs, based on Stanford-Binet scores, are from 52 to 67. Although they develop much more slowly than normal children, they are fairly independent by adolescence and most of them can hold undemanding jobs, marry, and have children. People with **moderate retardation** have IQs between 36 and 51 and although they can take care of themselves, they must live in sheltered workshops. They rarely marry or become parents. People with **severe retardation** have IQs between 20 and 35, can learn to care for some of their physical needs, and can be trained to per-

Errors in the SAT

When New York State enacted a truth-in-testing law in 1980, which required the return of tests, their answers, and a student's marked answer sheet to any student who requested them, test makers objected on the grounds that the practice would make tests more expensive and lead to a deterioration in their quality. The first part of the objection proved true: students now pay more to take the SAT and must pay an additional fee to see their answers. The reason is simple. When tests are revealed, they cannot be reused, so an organization like Educational Testing Service (ETS), which publishes the SAT, now must make up ten different tests each year instead of the four or five they used to prepare. The second part of the objection, a prediction that quality would deteriorate, was based on the belief that having to write and screen so many more questions would inevitably lead to a decline in their quality.

The first fallout from test disclosure, however, could result in an improvement—not a decline —in test quality. After students found two errors in ETS's own answers, ETS announced that in the future they would either use computer simulation or build physical models to verify answers to SAT-M questions involving solid geometry. The practice may further increase test costs, but it may also lead to fewer bad questions.

The defective solid geometry question was spotted by Daniel Lowen, a student in Cocoa Bay, Florida, who took the PSAT, a preliminary SAT used to screen applicants for National Merit Scholarships. Asked to answer the question in Figure A concerning the exposed faces of two juxtaposed pyramids, Lowen decided that four of the seven faces would be merged into two when

FIGURE A

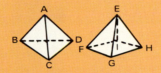

In pyramids ABCD and EFGHI shown above, all faces except base FGHI are equilateral triangles of equal size. If face ABC were placed on face EFG so that the vertices of the triangles coincide, how many exposed faces would the resulting solid have?

(A) Five   (B) Six   (C) Seven
(D) Eight   (E) Nine

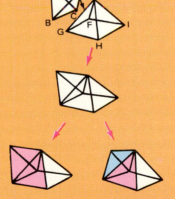

Five-Sided Figure   Seven-Sided Figure

the pyramids were connected, resulting in five exposed faces instead of the seven decreed by ETS. Lowen was right, and as a result ETS raised the scores of students who answered as Lowen did, adding 200 additional semifinalists to the scholarship competition.

The second error, found in the regular SAT by Michael Galligan, a student in New York City, concerned cubes and squares of integers (see Figure B). Asked to choose from among five rows of numbers the row containing "both the square of an integer and the cube of a different integer," Galligan gave the "correct" answer but raised an objection. He pointed out that the question has two correct responses: Row B, which included 9 (the square of 3) and 8 (the cube of 2); and Row C, which contained 8 (the cube of 2) and 4 (the square of minus 2). Again the student was right; the test makers had forgotten to consider negative integers when they made up the question. And again the test scores of thousands of students were raised.

FIGURE B				
Row A	7	2	5	4	6
Row B	3	8	6	9	7
Row C	5	4	3	8	2
Row D	9	5	7	3	6
Row E	5	6	3	7	4

Which row in the list above contains both the square of an integer and the cube of a *different* integer?

(A) Row A   (B) Row B   (C) Row C
(D) Row D   (E) Row E

form simple work in sheltered workshops or to do household tasks. They require considerable supervision. People with **profound retardation** have IQs below 20. Although many remain in institutions, they can sometimes carry out a few tasks under close supervision. Some cannot speak, although they may understand simple communication.

The causes of mental retardation are as varied as the differences in the ability of the retarded to function effectively. Among the causes of mental retardation are abnormal chromosomes, inherited metabolic disturbances, infections contracted during the fetal period, toxins, brain damage, severely disadvantaged home environments, and severely deprived institutional environments.

The Mentally Gifted   At the other end of the scale from the mentally retarded are the mentally gifted. Although the causes of extremely high intelligence are not known, a classic study of people with high IQs supervised by Lewis Terman (1916) has given us a great deal of information about the characteristics of the gifted. In 1921, Terman selected 1,500 children with IQs of 140 or more, who have been followed and tested periodically during the next sixty years (Terman and Oden, 1947; Terman and Oden, 1959; Oden, 1968; Sears, 1977). Terman found a significant positive correlation between IQ and physical, academic, social, and moral development. As children, the gifted were above average in height, weight, and the age at which they walked and talked. As they developed, compared with other people they were generally taller, heavier, stronger, more advanced in social and personal maturity, and more successful in school and other social situations. People with high IQs were also less likely to show lethal behavior (fatal accidents, suicide), delinquency and criminality, alcoholism, drug dependency, and severe mental illnesses. And, finally, Terman found that highly intelligent people received more degrees, distinctions, awards, professional licenses and certifications, and income; they made more artistic and literary contributions and reported more satisfaction in life. But the degree of achievement varied within the group, and not every one of these gifted individuals was successful, indicating that a high IQ does not guarantee success. In addition, the relationships Terman found may result not from IQ alone. His sample

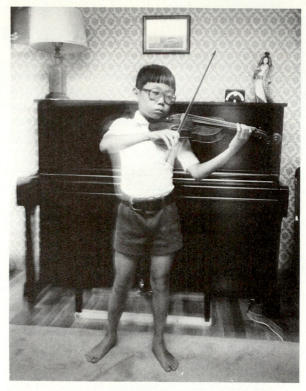

Gifted children are likely to grow into successful adults who make their mark in the professions and in academics, as well as in the arts.

may have omitted some of the most intellectually talented children because he relied on teacher nominations for the initial pool of children from which his subjects were drawn. As we saw at the beginning of the chapter, talent sometimes escapes the attention of a teacher, and these teachers may have been impressed by social presence or cooperation, thus overlooking bright children who were less likeable or less well adjusted.

Enriched education experiences have been the key in the encouragement of mathematically gifted young people discovered by the Study of Mathematically Precocious Youth (SMPY) discussed in the opening of this chapter. In this program, the mathematically talented are discovered while in the seventh grade by administration of the SAT. They are then counseled and given fast-paced summer math classes that will carry them through the first two college semesters of calculus (Stanley and George, 1980). In addition, the program has provided instruction in chemistry, physics, and languages with the intention of later obtaining advanced placement for these youths in college. SMPY has been searching for the mathematically gifted since 1972 and by 1978 had identified about 7,000 of these youths. The highest combined SAT-M and SAT-V score earned to date was made by a seventh-grade boy who later graduated from high school at age twelve and by his fourteenth birthday was a junior at a university, where he majored in chemistry and physics.

IQ Scores: Nature or Nurture?

Many people have tried to use intelligence tests to obtain answers to the age-old question about whether there are innate intellectual differences among groups, but the quest has not led to reliable conclusions. People whose childhood environment has been quite different from that of the majority of American and European children tend to have lower scores on tests developed in the United States and Europe. This difference, even when statistically significant, is not evidence that various groups differ in innate potential, because a person's score reflects not only her or his genetic potential for intellectual development (nature) but also what she or he has learned from experience (nurture).

Cultural Bias in Testing   If a test is developed for people with a specific cultural background, it cannot legitimately be used for people with a markedly different background. For example, vocabulary items provide the best single estimate of IQ scores, yet vocabulary clearly depends upon cultural background. A person who has never heard words like "sonata" or "ingenuous" will perform poorly on verbal intelligence tests. And a person who has grown up in a community where the primary language is not English will be handicapped even further.

It is very difficult to eliminate cultural bias from intelligence tests, but easy to incorporate it. The Counterbalance Intelligence Test, deliberately devised by Adrian Dove, a black, to be culturally biased against whites, demonstrates through exaggeration the effect a person's background can have on intelligence test scores (see Figure 20.4). Obviously, any test that relies heavily on vocabulary terms like these is culturally biased. It would not be fair to judge the intelligence of white middle-class youngsters by their ability to define expressions they have never

The Dove Counterbalance Intelligence Test
by Adrian Dove

If they throw the dice and "7" is showing on the top, what is facing down?
(a) "Seven"   (b) "Snake eyes"
(c) "Boxcars"   (d) "Little Joes"
(e) "Eleven".

Jazz pianist Ahmad Jamal took an Arabic name after becoming really famous. Previously he had some fame with what he called his "slave name." What was his previous name?
(a) Willie Lee Jackson
(b) LeRoi Jones
(c) Wilbur McDougal
(d) Fritz Jones   (e) Andy Johnson

In "C. C. Rider," what does "C. C." stand for?
(a) Civil Service
(b) Church Council
(c) County Circuit, preacher of an old-time rambler
(d) Country Club
(e) "Cheating Charley" (the "Boxcar Gunsel")

Cheap "chitlings" (not the kind you purchase at the frozen-food counter) will taste rubbery unless they are cooked long enough. How soon can you quit cooking them to eat and enjoy them?
(a) 15 minutes   (b) 2 hours
(c) 24 hours
(d) 1 week (on a low flame)
(e) 1 hour

If a judge finds you guilty of "holding weed" (in California), what's the most he can give you?
(a) Indeterminate (life)   (b) A nickel
(c) A dime   (d) A year in county
(e) $100.00.

A "Handkerchief Head" is
(a) A cool cat   (b) A porter
(c) An "Uncle Tom"   (d) A hoddi
(e) A "preacher"

Figure 20.4 An extreme example of how an intelligence test may depend on knowledge specific to one culture. A population of urban blacks would score high on this test, and a population of suburban whites would score low. Even when a test's items do not show this kind of obvious culture loading, a test may have validity problems. For example, many subcultures within Western society place great emphasis on competence in test taking. In a subculture where such emphasis is lacking, the validity of almost any test is likely to suffer. (Copyright 1968 by Newsweek, Inc. All rights reserved. Reprinted by permission.)

heard. Yet the makers of IQ tests often include words that are undoubtedly more familiar to white middle-class children than to their minority-group peers.

The issue of cultural bias in IQ tests has been reviewed by George Albee (1978), who pointed out that the tests are generally used to predict academic performance—performance in schools largely run by and for the white middle class, schools that embrace and promote the dominant values of our society. In fact, Terman, who brought Binet's test to the United States and adapted it to American use, limited his selection of items to material from the prevailing school curriculum (Garcia, 1972). Of course, the original purpose of these tests was to predict school performance, and that is exactly what they do best. IQ tests are the best single predictor of school success for children of all socioeconomic levels (McCall, Appelbaum, and Hogarty, 1973).

However, the scoring of IQ tests also seems biased in favor of white middle-class standards of behavior. For example, to the question, "What would you do if another child grabbed your hat and ran with it?" most white middle-class children answer that they would report the problem to an adult. Many black inner-city youngsters, however, answer that they would chase the offender and fight to get the hat back. The first response would be scored as "correct," the second as "incorrect," although neither solution is right for all children under all conditions (Albee, 1978). In addition, the standardization groups for IQ tests are generally composed of white urban children from English-speaking families.

The most obvious victims of cultural bias in IQ tests are the poor and the nonwhite, particularly blacks and Hispanics. However, about a half century ago newly arrived immigrant groups from southern and eastern Europe faced the same cultural bias and made low average IQ scores. In fact, one tester reported that 83 percent of Jews, 80 percent of Hungarians, 79 percent of Italians, and 87 percent of Russians were "feeble-minded" (Kamin, 1976). Today, after roughly fifty years of upward mobility, Americans from these groups attain scores that equal or surpass the national average. But groups that have not risen economically have not shown a similar improvement in average IQ scores (Sowell, 1977).

Differences among the *average* IQ scores of different races and nationalities do exist. However, it has proved to be impossible to conceive of the differences as resulting primarily from either differences in heredity or differences in upbringing and environment. Still, the relationship between the factors continues to fascinate social scientists.

Racial Differences in IQ: The Debate In 1969, Arthur Jensen, an educational psychologist, as-

serted that genetic factors might prove to be "strongly implicated" in the fact that the IQ scores of black people are, on the average, 11 to 15 points lower than the scores of white people. Jensen's thesis, that IQ is highly heritable and that therefore racial differences in IQ are due largely to differences in the gene distributions of the populations studied, caused an uproar that has not yet died down.

To understand the arguments for and against Jensen's view, it is necessary to understand two concepts: reaction range and heritability. **Reaction range** refers to the unique range of responses to the environment possible for the genetic make-up of each person. In the case of height, good nutrition will make each of us taller than poor nutrition will, but under both conditions genetic make-up will dictate that some of us will be taller than others. Genes do not specify a particular height for anyone. What they do specify is a *pattern* of growth that varies in response to nutrition and other environmental factors. Thus, the height a person reaches is a result of both heredity and environment.

The development of the intellectual skills measured by IQ tests also has a reaction range. No matter how stimulating their environments, few people become Albert Einsteins or Leonardo da Vincis. And in other than extremely deprived circumstances, most people do not become mentally retarded. Each person who is not subjected to severe deprivation (which can make anyone mentally retarded) has a range of perhaps 20 to 25 points in which her or his IQ score can vary, depending on that person's environment (Scarr-Salapatek, 1971).

The second concept, **heritability**, which was discussed in Chapter 7, refers to the extent to which observed variation of a trait (such as IQ) can be attributed to genetic differences. The fact that a trait has high heritability does not mean that genes "cause" it, nor does low heritability mean that the environment is responsible. Heritability is an estimate that is specific to a given population in a given environment. For that reason, the environment is highly implicated in heritability, and the heritability of a trait can change as the group's environment changes.

Heritability may be different among blacks and whites, and among middle- and lower-class groups. Because many blacks live in an environment that is characterized by poor nutrition, poor medical care, and other factors that constrict the development of intelligence, the influence of these factors decreases the heritability of intelligence among them. Many whites, on the other hand, live in favorable environments that increase the heritability of intelligence and allow its development nearer the upper end of the reaction range.

However, the conclusion that there is high heritability for intelligence within populations is based on many studies in many different countries. When all the studies done up to 1981 were summarized and correlations obtained between people of different degrees of relatedness, the overwhelming conclusion was that the results reflected a genetic component (Bouchard and McGue, 1981).

When Jensen made his original assertion regarding heritability, his work was based on data from a series of studies by the English psychologist Sir Cyril Burt (1966; 1972). Burt compared the IQs of identical and fraternal twins and showed, for example, that when identical twins—who have the same genetic make-up—were separated early in life and brought up in different environments, their IQs as adults were similar. This suggested that environment played only a minor role in the development of IQ. Jensen's side of the controversy, presented first in his 1969 article and later expanded in two books (1973; 1980), can be phrased as follows: If individual differences in intelligence *within* the black and the white populations taken separately have a high heritability, it is possible that the average differences *between* these racial groups likewise reflect genetic differences.

In making his argument, Jensen ruled out a number of environmental factors that have been proposed to explain black-white IQ differences. He made four major points:

1. Even when socioeconomic class of the two races is equated, blacks score well below whites on the average.
2. Environmental deprivation affects Native Americans (Indians) more than blacks, yet Native Americans score higher on IQ tests than blacks on the average.
3. The absence of the father in many lower-class black homes has not been found to account for the lower intelligence level.
4. Characteristics of the test and testing situation, such as cultural bias and the race of the examiner, do not appear to account for the differences in the IQ scores of black children. The same difference occurs on nonverbal tests and on tests administered by black examiners.

Jensen's argument began to founder when his basic data were called into question by Leon Kamin (1974; 1976), who found that no matter how many sets of twins Burt presented, the correlations between IQ and relatedness for each set were the same to three decimal places—a coincidence that seemed virtually impossible. Burt's data have been rejected by most psychologists, and his research has come to be seen variously as careless (Jensen, 1978), as an example of experimenter bias, and as fraudulent (Hearnshaw, 1979).

But even without Burt's data, the conclusion that there is high heritability within populations (at least white populations) remained strong, and those opposed to Jensen's position have provided a rebuttal based on other grounds:

1. High heritability within populations tells us nothing about the cause of differences between populations. A crop grown in rich soil, loaded with nutrients, will produce a heavier yeild than the same crop grown in deficient soil. And all crops, no matter what their genetic differences, grow better in good soil. Differences between populations could be due primarily to the environment even though differences within populations are due primarily to heredity.
2. Blacks and whites differ in numerous ways besides genetic make-up, such as their living conditions and the degree to which they experience discrimination. Blacks and whites supposedly in the same socioeconomic class actually differ considerably in income, education, and quality of housing.
3. Jensen's assertion that black-white IQ differences are not explained by the environmental factors that he dismisses does not rule out an explanation due to other, as yet unspecified factors. For example, young children commonly eat the lead paint chips that peel from the walls of many slum dwellings; the lead in the paint can cause brain damage, which results in sharp decreases in intelligence. Moreover, pregnant women sometimes develop a craving for paint chips, and research has shown that lead can be transmitted from a pregnant woman to her unborn child (Barltrop, 1969; Scanlon and Chisolm, 1972). Partly because of this transmission and because lead poisoning is common among urban blacks, its effects may be erroneously seen as genetic (Needleman, 1973; 1974). In addition, blacks

IQ tests are not a fully reliable measure of differences in intelligence among racial groups. Motivation, anxiety, and test-taking skills all influence a child's score, even though they are not related to his or her intelligence.

are more likely than whites to be members of large families, and family size can have a subtle effect on intelligence. Robert Zajonc (1976; Zajonc and Markus, 1975) has found that IQ scores are generally lower for children from large families than for children from small families, and lower for later-borns than for first-borns. This birth-order effect is particularly noticeable among children who are close in age to their siblings. Zajonc proposes that with the arrival of each additional child, the intellectual environment of the family is diluted.

4. IQ tests are affected by such nonintellectual influences as motivation, anxiety, and test-taking skills. These nonintellectual influences lessen the value of the IQ score as a reliable measure of the differences in intelligence among racial groups.

5. Jensen's critics say that he seems to imply that heredity "fixes" intelligence-test scores within limits and that he does not take reaction range into account. Data from adoption studies (Skodak and Skeels, 1949; Schiff et al., 1978) suggest that when children are adopted into a higher social class than the one into which they were born, they can develop significantly higher IQs than would be expected if they had been reared by their natural parents. The broad reaction range of IQ and the fact that it can be dramatically affected by changes in the environment was confirmed in a study by

Sandra Scarr and Richard Weinberg (1976). These researchers measured the IQ scores of black children who had been adopted by white couples of higher than average socioeconomic status and of above average intelligence. The adopted children had an average IQ of 106, well above the average for the entire population and about 15 points above the average IQ of black children reared in their own homes in the part of the country in which the study was conducted.

After reviewing all the research, Scarr (1981) wrote that she could "see no evidence for the hypothesis that the average difference in intellectual performance between U.S. whites and blacks results primarily from genetic racial differences" (p. 528). After an earlier review, J. C. Loehlin, Gardner Lindzey, and J. N. Spuhler (1975) concluded that on tests of intellectual ability, differences in the scores of members of different American racial and ethnic groups reflect in part the inadequacies and biases in the tests, in part environmental differences, and in part genetic differences. The three factors interact, and "differences among individuals within racial-ethnic and socieconomic groups greatly exceed in magnitude the average differences between such groups" (p. 239). Thus, conclusions about hereditary racial differences are difficult to evaluate and of little value in making predictions about a person's behavior. Since there is far more intellectual variability within populations than between them, people should be treated as individuals instead of as stereotypical members of a group.

The Measurement of Personality

Intelligence tests attempt to assess abilities, but a yardstick that measures only cognitive functioning deals with only part of the person. Personality tests, which explore emotions, motives, interests, attitudes, and values, are widely used in counseling, clinical practice, and screening for employment. Various methods have been devised to assess personality, including observations, self-report inventories, projective tests, and physiological measures.

Self-Report Inventories

One of the quickest and least expensive methods of measuring personality is the self-report inventory, which shares the assumption and method of intelligence tests. First, personality inventories assume that people possess varying amounts of the trait being measured. Second, many items are used to obtain a reliable assessment, because no single item is applicable to everyone.

One type of personality inventory is constructed by **factor analysis**, a statistical method that analyzes responses to a host of possible scale items and reduces them to highly correlated items that reflect a few underlying factors. For example, Julian Rotter (1966) used factor analysis to develop a scale that measures an individual's locus of control, or the degree to which people believe that they are personally responsible for what happens to them: People with an internal locus of control believe that their own behavior primarily determines their fate, whereas people with an external locus of control believe that what they do makes little difference and that their fate is determined by luck, fate, or powerful people. The items finally placed in the scale were chosen after many administrations of separate scales pertaining to various goals, such as achievement or social recognition. By factor analysis, Rotter discovered that all the scales re-

flected a single general factor, which could be measured with twenty-nine items that forced a person to choose either an external or an internal explanation for such events as promotions, grades, or divorce. With further testing and refinement, the scale was finally reduced to twenty-three items (Lefcourt, 1981).

Another type of personality test is constructed and developed using the empirical method. In such a test items are first selected without regard to their relationship to a certain trait. The items are then administered to an experimental group of people who are known to have various psychological disorders and to another group of people who are known to be "normal," or free of the disorder being measured. Those items that differentiate between the two groups—items that receive one answer from most of the disturbed subjects and a different answer from most of the normal subjects—are retained; the others are discarded. This refinement and selection process is repeated several times until the test is as reliable and valid as possible. Not all empirical tests are developed by using people with psychological disorders. For example, tests used to discover occupational interests are developed by using groups from different occupations.

The validity of both factor-analytic and empirical tests can be questioned. Tests developed by factor analysis have no outside yardsticks by which the relationship of various items to a particular trait can be validated. We cannot tell, for example, if an item tests for shyness or locus of control unless we have some independent measure of the construct. Thus, factor analysis, which is used in the construction of tests, does not substitute for validity studies. Tests developed by this method are, however, useful tools for research on the structure of personality.

Tests developed empirically depend on the reliability of the diagnosis that divided people into various groups during the test construction. If the experimental groups upon which the test depends are not well differentiated, the test will make no useful distinctions. However, if the original diagnostic groups are reliable, the test will identify other people who have similar psychological characteristics.

The Minnesota Multiphasic Personality Inventory The most widely used personality inventory, the **Minnesota Multiphasic Personality Inventory (MMPI)**, was developed empirically, using

133 I have never indulged in unusual sex practices.

151 Someone has been trying to poison me.

182 I am afraid of losing my mind.

234 I get mad easily and then I get over it soon.

244 My way of doing things is apt to be misunderstood by others.

288 I am troubled by attacks of nausea and vomiting.

A

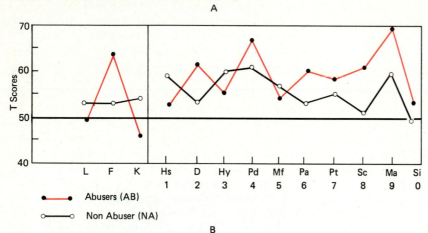

Abusers (AB)

Non Abuser (NA)

B

Figure 20.5 (A) Sample MMPI items. (B) MMPI profiles for abusive and nonabusive fathers. The letters along the bottom of the graph correspond to the scales described in Table 20.1. Note that the two groups obtained different profiles: fathers who abused their children scored much higher than nonabusive fathers on the Depression (D), Psychopathic Deviate (Pd) and Mania (Ma) scales. While it appears that the MMPI can differentiate between abusive and nonabusive parents, further study would be necessary before a more conclusive profile of an abusive parent could be drawn. This research does offer some tentative hypotheses about important personality differences between abusers and nonabusers. (Adapted from Paulson, Afifi, Thomason, and Chaleff, 1974.)

groups of psychiatric patients and groups of normal people. Items that distinguished between the two groups were then combined into separate scales that were used originally to aid in the diagnosis or evaluation of mental illness (see Figure 20.5).

The authors of the test (Hathaway and McKinley, 1940) began with a set of 550 true-false statements. Many of these items dealt directly with psychiatric symptoms—including delusions, hallucinations, obsessive and compulsive states, and sadistic and masochistic tendencies—but the other items ranged widely over areas such as physical health, general habits, family and marital status, occupational and educational problems, and attitudes toward religion, sex, politics, and social problems.

By following the development of the depression scale, we can see exactly how MMPI scales were constructed. The original set of 550 items was administered to patients with depressive disorders and to normal people. About 53 items distinguished significantly between the two groups. Later, a few items were added to sharpen the differentiation between patients with severe depressive reactions and those with other psychiatric diagnoses. The MMPI-D (for Depression) scale has been found to be a highly sensitive indicator not only of psychotic depression but also of less severe forms of depression, of varying mood states, and even of reactions to various methods of psychological treatments. In a similar way, eight additional clinical scales were developed for the original MMPI, as well as a masculinity-and-femininity scale. These clinical scales, as well as the three validity scales that determine whether the person taking the test is answering honestly, are described in Table 20.1.

The MMPI is best used for its original purposes: the identification and diagnosis of psychopathology (Butcher and Owen, 1978). It is a valuable tool in the hands of a skilled clinician who has been trained to interpret the profile of the clinical scores. Some of the clinical scores are also useful in determining the effectiveness of psychotherapy. The depression scale, for example, has been used in studies that evaluate different therapies. But the MMPI is not a useful tool for measuring normal personality or for screening job applicants and it was not developed for these purposes.

Projective Tests

Unlike self-report inventories, **projective tests** have not been rigidly standardized and although they can be scored objectively, the overall assessment depends upon clinical interpretation. In these tests, personality characteristics are re-

Table 20.1   Scales of the MMPI

VALIDITY SCALES

Lie Scale (L)	Items that reflect socially desirable but unlikely behavior and are therefore likely to be marked true by a naive faker.
Infrequency Scale (F)	Items that are rarely marked true except by people who either are trying deliberately to give an exaggerated impression of their problems or are in fact highly deviant.
Correction Scale (K)	Items that reflect how defensive or how frank the person is being. The scale is sensitive to attitudes more subtle than those that affect the Lie Scale.

CLINICAL SCALES

1. Hypochondriasis (Hs)	Items selected to discriminate people who persist in worrying about their bodily functions despite strong evidence that they have no physical illness.
2. Depression (D)	Items selected to discriminate people who are pessimistic about the future, feel hopeless or worthless, are slow in thought and action, and think a lot about death and suicide.
3. Hysteria (Hy)	Items selected to discriminate people who use physical symptoms to solve difficult problems or avoid mature responsibilities, particularly under severe psychological stress.
4. Psychopathic Deviate (Pd)	Items selected to discriminate people who show a pronounced disregard for social customs and mores, an inability to profit from punishing experiences, and emotional shallowness with others, particularly in sex and love.
5. Masculinity-Femininity (Mf)	Items selected to discriminate men who prefer homosexual relations to heterosexual ones, either overtly, or covertly because of inhibitions or conflicts. Women tend to score low on this scale, but the scale cannot be interpreted simply "upside-down" for women.
6. Paranoia (Pa)	Items selected to discriminate people who have delusions about how influential and how victimized they are or how much attention is paid them by other people.
7. Psychasthenia (Pt)	Items selected to discriminate people with obsessive thoughts, compulsive actions, extreme fear or guilt feelings, insecurity, and high anxiety.
8. Schizophrenia (Sc)	Items selected to discriminate people who are constrained, cold, aloof, apathetic, inaccessible to others, and who may have delusions or hallucinations.
9. Hypomania (Ma)	Items selected to discriminate people who are physically overactive, emotionally excited, and have rapid flights of disconnected, fragmentary ideas; these activities may lead to accomplishment but more frequently are inefficient and unproductive.
10. Social Introversion (Si)	Items selected to discriminate people who are withdrawn from social contacts and responsibilities and display little real interest in people.

Source: Based on W. G. Dahlstrom, G. S. Welsh, and L. E. Dahlstrom, *An MMPI Handbook,* Vol. 1 (Minneapolis: University of Minnesota Press, 1972).

vealed in the way people respond to and interpret ambiguous material. There are no right or wrong answers. Because there is no established meaning to the test materials, it is hoped that whatever meaning people put into their responses will reveal something about their personalities. Some of the ambiguous test materials are highly abstract, like inkblots; others are more concrete, like pictures of actual social situations.

The Rorschach Inkblot Test   Perhaps the best-known projective test is the one developed in 1921 by Hermann Rorschach, a Swiss psychiatrist (Rorschach, 1942). In the **Rorschach Inkblot Test** a person is handed a series of symmetrical inkblots, one at a time, and asked to report what she or he sees, using free association. Then the examiner asks certain general questions in an attempt to discover what quality of the inkblots prompted the person's responses (e.g., Beck, 1961). A sample inkblot like those used in the Rorschach Inkblot Test and a sample response are presented in the box which appears on page 472.

In scoring the test, three general categories

"It Looks Like a Monster with Big Feet"

Rorschach inkblots are used in a projective test of personality. In interpreting a person's response to the ten inkblots in the series, examiners pay at least as much attention to the style of the responses as to their content. For example, a person's tendency to see white or shaded areas as meaningful, or to see the blot as a whole rather than as a collection of parts, is deemed significant in scoring and interpretation.

When presented with the inkblot shown here, a young female outpatient free-associated that "it sort of looks like a monster with big feet. A cute little thing. Really a dashing little monster. Such a friendly little guy." Further probing by the examiner showed that the woman was responding to the blot as a whole instead of to only a portion of it, and was concerned primarily with its shape or form, which, while human-like, was not distinctly human. Interpreting the meaning of Rorschach responses is a complicated task. Despite the fact that formal attempts to establish its reliability and validity have failed, the test remains widely used.

Source: Richard I. Lanyon and Leonard D. Goodstein. *Personality Assessment,* © 1971, p. 50. Reprinted by permission of John Wiley and Sons, Inc., New York.

---

are involved. The first category indicates how much of the inkblot the person responds to, ranging from small or even minute detail to the whole blot. The second relates to the determinants of the response—whether the person responds primarily to form, color, shading, or level of activity. The third category concerns the content of the responses. The specific content is less important than the way the individual *uses* it. For example, mixing indiscriminately parts belonging to different animals and human beings may indicate a serious psychological disorder, and so may talking about things that go far beyond the test materials at hand.

It would be a mistake to place too much emphasis on the scoring techniques used by Rorschach examiners. The Rorschach method is highly impressionistic and has been greatly influenced by Freudian personality theory, which was discussed in Chapter 18. The interpretation of responses is largely based upon the examiner's insight, capacity for careful observation, and awareness of the manner in which psychopathology is revealed. In the assessment procedure, the examiner will incorporate not only the individual's Rorschach responses but also her or his reaction to the test situation itself. Some people, for example, are extremely defensive and wary in the test situation. Others define it in authoritarian terms, seeing the examiner as a "boss" whose orders they must follow. Still others view the situation as competitive, expecting their performance to be evaluated against some standard and judged for its quality (Schachtel, 1966).

The lack of structure involved in the Rorschach technique, as in many other projective tests, is both a strength and a weakness. Its strength lies in its broad sampling of behavior and the fact that it permits certain patterns to emerge that might otherwise remain hidden. Its weakness is that because the procedure is individualistic and subjective, it is extremely difficult to establish the test's validity and reliability. This weakness makes the test's interpretation vulnerable to the examiner's biases.

The Thematic Apperception Test   The **Thematic Apperception Test (TAT)**, developed by Henry Murray in 1935, consists of a series of cards depicting ambiguous scenes involving one, two, or three people. A person is shown up to thirty cards, chosen for their appropriateness to her or his age and sex. The person is asked to tell a story about each picture including what led up to the situation, what the characters are thinking and feeling, and how the situation will end.

The stories are usually analyzed on an individual basis; that is, one person's stories are not compared with another's. Originally, Murray suggested that the TAT be interpreted in terms of a person's ''internal needs'' and ''environmental presses''—concepts in Murray's own theory of personality (Murray et al., 1938). Now a variety of other systems, including some based on psychoanalytic theory, are also employed. Clinical psychologists agree only moderately well about interpretations of the TAT and predictions based on it. In fact, agreement among professionals often does not exceed that among psychology students who have not been trained in TAT interpretation.

All the methods of interpreting the TAT depend on certain assumptions regarding the sort of fantasy that is tapped by the test. Common assumptions are that the subject will identify with the hero or heroine of the story, that the stories will reveal the subject's motives, and that unusual responses are more likely than typical ones to reveal important aspects of personality.

Physiological Measures

Because emotion and physiological functioning are so closely related, physiological measures are sometimes used to establish individual differences in personality. Rising blood pressure is connected with levels of hostility; anger is ac-

companied by rapid heart rate, increased skin conductance, and high blood pressure; anxiety, by a rapid heart rate, rapid breathing, perspiration, and muscle tension. As we saw in Chapter 15, the polygraph is useful in detecting physiological states connected with emotion, and by monitoring changes in blood pressure, EEG, GSR, and EMG (or electromyograph, which records changes in the electrical activity of muscles), examiners can establish individual differences in arousal. For example, when studying the way people cope with stress, examiners often measure autonomic levels of arousal in addition to obtaining self-report inventories (e.g., Coyne and Lazarus, 1980).

Since physiological measures indicate emotional responses to stimuli, they can be useful in linking environmental events to physiological or emotional problems. For example, patients with high blood pressure are sometimes asked to monitor their own blood pressure at regular intervals, recording their activities at the time of each measurement. When sharp rises in blood pressure regularly accompany certain activities, such as discussions with a child about homework or arrival at the office, the physiological measure has provided a clue to a major source of stress for that person.

The Ethics of Testing

We have seen that tests can be effective tools when properly used. However, like other tools, tests are not always used properly. Although their results are not always accurate, they may change the course of people's lives. A high score on a mathematics examination may result in an accelerated program in math for one student, but a low score on the same exam may mean the denial of admission to college for another. Because tests are so powerful, being used widely to place children in school, to admit students to college, and to screen job applicants, several ethical issues have been raised concerning their use.

One issue has to do with the appropriate interpretation of test results. Many people draw sweeping conclusions from personality and intelligence test scores, forgetting that the tests often measure much less than we think they do and that their results are always a matter of probability. At best, tests provide a good estimate of what they are designed to measure. For these reasons, it is important that a given test be valid for the specific purpose for which it is being used.

A second ethical issue concerns the proper use of test information. Even if test results are valid, the question of how widely the scores should be available is unanswered. Employers, college admission boards, parents of schoolchildren, and the subjects themselves have either demanded, been given, or been denied test results in various situations.

These issues have attracted widespread attention in connection with the placement of children in special education classes, personnel decisions, and truth-in-testing legislation.

IQ Tests and Special Education

Children who are labeled "mentally retarded" on the basis of intelligence tests are often placed in special classes for the "educable mentally retarded." The proportions of blacks and Hispanics in such classes are far higher than their respective percentages of the population; the proportion of white middle-class students in special classes is far lower. A few years ago, for example, there were four times as many blacks and three times as many Hispanics, proportionately, as there were white English-speaking children in California's special education classes (Albee, 1978).

For the most part, it is schools who label children as retarded, and they do it primarily on the basis of IQ scores. Judging subjects on their adaptive behavior (their ability to function in society) as well as on their IQs, Jane Mercer (1972) concluded that a vast number of "retarded" adults should not have been so labeled.

IQ tests and the institutions that administer them are increasingly being challenged in the courts. In one case, a young man sued the New York City Board of Education, claiming that the board had been negligent in denying him an adequate education. At the age of four he had scored one point below normal on an IQ test and had then been put into a special class for the mentally retarded. He was not tested again until he was eighteen, and at that point his score was within the normal range. The jury awarded him the sum of $750,000 (Fiske, 1977).

In a pair of cases, black children in special classes for the educable mentally retarded brought class-action suits that have had opposite implications for the future use of intelligence testing. In the first case, *Larry P.* v. *Wilson Riles* (1979), the court found IQ tests to be racially and culturally biased and banned the use of intelligence tests for placing children in classes for the educable mentally retarded. In addition to finding the tests biased against blacks, the judge stated that because the tests were standardized on white, middle-class groups, they had not been shown to be valid for blacks. Validation for blacks had been "assumed, not established." In the second case, *PASE* v. *Hannon* (1980), the court found that the tests were *not* culturally biased and said that they could be used to help place children in special-education classes. The judge examined the tests and proclaimed "all but a few of the items on their face appear racially neutral." This judge refused to rule on the issue of validity, saying that the question was not involved in the case. Both cases have been appealed and the question will probably not be settled until both the Appeals Court and the Supreme Court issue rulings.

Psychologists themselves cannot agree on the issues involved in these cases. In each instance, they have testified for both sides, and the American Psychological Association, because its membership is so divided, refused to enter either case (Armstrong, 1980). However, both judges have been widely criticized by psychologists. The judge in the first case was reproached for defining an unbiased test as one that yields "the same pattern of scores when administered to different groups of people," because tests are fair when they predict with equal accuracy for all groups— not when they provide equal results (Bersoff, 1979). The judge in the second case came under fire for declaring a test valid on the basis of his subjective opinion of the questions, since validity cannot be established so casually (Armstrong, 1980).

Personnel Selection

School-related cases are not the only controversies over tests reaching the courts; personality, intelligence, and aptitude tests used to select or to promote employees have also been at the center of litigation. In most instances, the charge is discrimination, with the plaintiff asserting that the test is used to keep people of a particular race, color, religion, sex, or nationality out of jobs or to deny them promotion. If tests are used to discriminate against any of these groups, they are in violation of the Civil Rights Act of 1964.

The discrimination need not be intentional; if the plaintiff can show statistically that the effect of the test is to discriminate, the discrimination has been proved to the court's satisfaction. However, tests that discriminate against a particular group have been allowed in some instances. For example, if a test has predictive validity, it may be used if the plaintiff cannot show that an alternative, but nondiscriminatory, test exists (Griffin, 1980). In this case, the issue is whether the test accurately predicts performance on the job. Even that requirement has been softened since the Supreme Court established it in 1971. In separate cases, the court has ruled that predictive validity need apply only to a training program, not to performance on the job itself (*Washington* v. *Davis,* 1976) and that in some instances content validity is sufficient proof of job-relatedness (*National Education Association* v. *State of South Carolina,* 1978).

Although the courts have relied on predictive or content validity in their rulings, some psychologists have suggested that tests with predictive validity are useful only in simple, repetitive jobs and that in jobs involving complex tasks the criterion should be construct validity (Lerner, 1977). However, the courts are not interested in the issue of validity unless its absence leads to discrimination. Presumably, a test based on the casting of horoscopes would be acceptable in the courts' eyes as long as it did not discriminate against any group specified in the Civil Rights Act.

Truth-in-Testing Laws

It has customarily been difficult for individuals to find out exactly how they scored on intelligence, achievement, aptitude, or personality tests. A guide to test use, *Standards for Educational and Psychological Tests* (APA, 1974), advises that test scores be reported only to people who are qualified to interpret them, a standard that rules out most of the people who take the tests. However, the *Standards* also states that when test results are used in making career decisions affecting people's future, those people have the right to know their scores. This position is similar to the one behind legislation regulating credit bureaus, which gives individuals the right to see information in their credit files. But under this arrangement, only test scores—not copies of the tests themselves or the answers—are available.

New York State's truth-in-testing law (discussed earlier) goes much further, however, stipulating that people who take college admission exams like the SAT may later get copies of the test and its answers. Some psychologists are uneasy about truth-in-testing laws, because they worry that widespread publication of tests could decrease their validity. Indeed, on the assumption that revealed tests may become less valid, ETS has increased the number of SAT forms it constructs each year.

There is another aspect of test confidentiality that truth-in-testing laws fail to consider. One reason for test confidentiality has been the protection of the person who takes the test. Keeping test scores confidential was meant to protect people from ridicule and harassment and to prevent the misuse of test results. One problem is the dissemination of test scores outside a company personnel staff, so that information gathered for one purpose is used for another, as when hiring tests are used in considering promotions, changes in work assignment, or selection for training programs. Unless an employee has been informed of the way test results may be used in the future, such multiple usage presents an ethical problem. One way to prevent misuse of information is to destroy old scores as they become obsolete, so that outdated information cannot be used when considering an employee's promotion or termination. However, decisions to clear files are often difficult to make. First, some ratings still have predictive validity as long as sixteen years after they are collected; and second, material that has been used to make personnel decisions in the past may be needed in the future should the company ever become involved in a lawsuit concerning the employee (London and Bray, 1980).

Psychologists are aware that personality and intelligence tests can be used with desirable or undesirable results. In the case of intelligence tests, the undesirable results include the excusing of bad education for minority groups and the labeling of children who lack exposure to the dominant culture as "retarded." Intelligence tests have also had desirable results: they have kept other children *out* of classes for the retarded; they have indicated whether a child's problem was intellectual or behavioral; they have selected gifted children for educational opportunities; and they have given children from disadvantaged families a way out of poverty (Hyman, 1979). And they have done this in a manner that keeps the attitudes of teachers from affecting the decisions. Similarly, tests used to screen employees allow people to be hired or promoted on their own merits and help eliminate disqualification because of employer biases. By providing realistic information about capabilities and dispositions, tests can also help people make appropriate social and occupational choices.

But as the debate over ethical issues indicates, knowledge about people entails power over their lives, and tests can be used as potent weapons as well as helpful instruments. If tests are to be used for the benefit of the individual and society, the ethical issues raised by their use will require careful, continuing attention.

SUMMARY

1. A **psychological test** is an objective and standardized measure of a sample of behavior, which provides a systematic basis for making inferences about people. When used properly, psychological tests are efficient tools for selecting students who are academically gifted, for identifying specific problems that require treatment in the mentally disturbed, and for discovering children with previously unrevealed gifts or needs. If a test is to be useful, it must be reliable, valid, and standardized.

2. A test is **reliable** if it yields the same results with repeated measurement. Psychological tests used to measure a certain characteristic or a possibly unstable attitude or mood should have **internal consistency reliability**: different parts of the test must produce the same result. Tests that measure a stable characteristic, such as intelligence, must have **test-retest reliability**, so that repeated administrations of the same test to the same group of people produce the same results. Tests that require the scorer to interpret a person's answers should have **interjudge reliability**, so that scoring by different judges produces the same results.

3. A test is **valid** if it measures what it purports to measure. A test with **content validity** covers a representative sample of the measured attribute. A test with **predictive validity** produces scores that show a relationship to future performance. A test with **concurrent validity** produces scores that correlate highly with other existing measures or standards. A test with **construct validity** actually measures the hypothetical construct, such as dominance, it claims to measure. Valid tests are reliable, but reliable tests are not always valid.

4. Unless a test has been standardized, so people's scores can be compared with those of others, it is of little use. To standardize tests, **norms**, or normative distributions, are established by giving the test to a **standardization group** of people. Raw scores are converted into standardized scores either by the **percentile system**, which shows the proportion of the standardization group that is above and below a person's score, or by the **standard score system**, which locates a score on a bell-shaped curve that reflects the normal pattern of score distribution. Unless the standardization group represents the population taking the test, standardized scores will not be accurate.

5. Intelligence tests are the most frequently administered tests measuring mental characteristics. On the basis of their test scores, children are given a mental age, which is converted into an **intelligence quotient (IQ)**, which represents the ratio of mental age to chronological age. Individual intelligence tests are administered by one examiner to one subject at a time. The **Stanford-Binet Test**, an individual test based on Binet's original test, contains both verbal and performance subtests that are grouped by age level. The **Wechsler Adult Intelligence Scale (WAIS)** and the **Wechsler Intelligence Scale for Children (WISC)**, also individual tests, treat intelligence as a number of abilities rather than as one overriding ability. Group intelligence tests, which are paper-and-pencil measures, are convenient to administer, but clinicians prefer individual

tests because they provide a sample of behavior in addition to standardized information about intelligence. Achievement tests and aptitude tests are distinguished from one another primarily by their purpose. An **achievement test** evaluates what a person knows; an **aptitude test** predicts how successful a person will be in a certain situation. The **Scholastic Aptitude Test (SAT)** is a reliable, valid test that measures a student's likelihood of succeeding in college by assessing verbal and mathematical aptitude.

6. **Mental retardation** refers to deficiencies in a person's adaptive behavior as well as to deficiencies in intellectual functioning. Most mentally retarded people have **mild retardation**, in which IQ is between 52 and 67; they are able to hold undemanding jobs, marry, and have children. **Moderate retardation** indicates an IQ between 36 and 51; **severe retardation** indicates an IQ between 20 and 35; and **profound retardation** indicates an IQ below 20. The causes of mental retardation include abnormal chromosomes, inherited metabolic disturbances, congenital infections, toxins, brain damage, cultural-familial deprivation, and institutional deprivation.

7. Mentally gifted people tend to be above average in physical, academic, social, and moral development, to be more successful than most, and to show less alcoholism, drug dependency, or severe mental illness. Although many gifted people are creative, creativity does not require brilliance, but divergent abilities—the ability to come up with many answers to a problem.

8. IQ scores reflect not only a person's genetic potential (nature) but also what the person has learned from experience (nurture). IQ tests predict school performance according to white, middle-class standards so that they appear to be biased against the poor and nonwhite. Although differences do exist between the average IQ scores of different races and nationalities, the differences may be due primarily to environmental causes. **Heritability** depends as much on environment as on genes, and the environment determines in what part of the **reaction range** genetic influences will be expressed.

9. **Self-report inventories** assume that subjects have varying amounts of the trait being measured, and many items are used to measure each trait. Some personality inventories are constructed by **factor analysis**, a statistical method that reduces responses to highly correlated items that reflect a few underlying factors; such tests are useful for research on the structure of personality. Empirically constructed personality inventories, such as the **Minnesota Multiphasic Personality Inventory (MMPI)**, are most valuable for diagnostic purposes.

10. **Projective tests** attempt to measure personality through the responses of people to ambiguous material. In the **Rorschach Inkblot Test**, a person uses free association to report what she or he sees in a series of inkblots. In the **Thematic Apperception Test**, a person tells a story about each of a number of ambiguous pictures. Because emotion and physiological functioning are so closely related, physiological measures, such as changes in blood pressure, EEG, GRS, and EMG, are sometimes used to establish individual differences in personality.

11. A number of ethical questions have arisen in regard to psychological testing, including the proper interpretation of test results and the proper use of test information. The labeling of children as mentally retarded can have a powerful influence on the course of their lives, and a number of legal suits have been brought in an attempt to stop the practice. Tests used for personnel selection have also been challenged in court on the grounds that they discriminate against certain groups. However, if the tests have predictive validity—or in some cases content validity—the court will allow their use even if they do discriminate. Finally, truth-in-testing laws have been enacted that force institutions to give people who take college admission tests copies of the test, the answers, and their own marked answer sheets. The opposite problem of privacy exists in business, where test information can be used in many ways, and where psychologists attempt to keep test results confidential in order to protect employees.

KEY TERMS

achievement tests
aptitude tests
concurrent validity
construct validity
content validity
face validity
factor analysis
heritability
intelligence quotient (IQ)
interjudge reliability
internal consistency reliability
mental retardation
Minnesota Multiphasic
    Personality Inventory
    (MMPI)

mild retardation
moderate retardation
norm
percentile system
predictive validity
profound retardation
projective tests
psychological test
reaction range
reliable
Rorschach Inkblot Test
Scholastic Aptitude Test
    (SAT)
severe retardation
standard score system

standardization group
Stanford-Binet Test
test-retest reliability
Thematic Apperception Test
    (TAT)
valid
Wechsler Adult Intelligence
    Scale (WAIS)
Wechsler Intelligence Scale
    for Children (WISC)
Wechsler Preschool and
    Primary Scale of
    Intelligence (WPPSI)

RECOMMENDED READINGS

AMERICAN PSYCHOLOGICAL ASSOCIATION. *Standards for Educational and Psychological Tests*. Washington, D.C.: American Psychological Association, 1974. The latest revision of the Association's guidelines for test construction and use.

ANASTASI, A. *Psychological Testing*. 4th ed. New York: Macmillan, 1982. This is an outstanding text which covers reliability and validity and surveys tests of intellectual development and personality.

LOEHLIN, J. C., GARDNER LINDZEY, and J. N. SPUHLER. *Race Differences in Intelligence*. San Francisco: Freeman, 1975. A careful, balanced examination of the research evidence relevant to the issue of genetic and environmental determinants of IQ differences between racial groups.

WECHSLER, DAVID. *The Measurement and Appraisal of Adult Intelligence*. 4th ed. Baltimore: Williams & Wilkins, 1958. A classic discussion of intelligence and intelligence testing.

PART SEVEN

Behavior Disorders and Therapy

If there are individual differences, then each of us is bound to find that every person he or she meets is going to do things, view things, or say things in ways that he or she does not. Sometimes this may grate on us. Some very little difference may bother us to the point where our reaction becomes extreme. We react so indignantly to somebody else's "crazy" behavior that the reaction may itself seem "crazy" to an observer who happens to be relatively unmoved by the particular oddity in question.

Television's Archie Bunker, a notoriously inflexible individual, was routinely chafed by anything his son-in-law, Michael Stivic, did that in any way departed from his own standards. This was by no means limited to Michael's liberal views, or to his penchant for sex in the afternoon. Major arguments (hilarious ones) would arise, for instance, over the fact that Michael would put on a left sock, a left shoe, a right sock and a right shoe in that order, whereas to Archie it was a law of nature that one should put on a left sock, a right sock, a left shoe, and a right shoe, in *that* order.

Janet and I laugh heartily over the inability to tolerate such nonsignificant variations in behavior—but are we any better? No.

It took a while for Janet to get used to the fact that faced with a variety of items on a dish, I will eat all of one, then all of another, then all of a third, and so on; doing it in what was to me the order of increasing gustatory delight. She lectured me frequently on the superior morality and godliness of taking some of each item on the fork each time.

I, on the other hand, find it inconceivable that she should persist in buttering her bread when preparing a sandwich of corned beef or other cold cut. I have explained to her at length that the only truly civilized spread in such cases is mustard.

It is only our deep love for each other that keeps us from arranging a divorce over such world-shaking differences.

In two different ways do such individual differences in behavior and the reaction thereto cease being funny.

First, might not such differences, as they become greater and greater, cease to be idiosyncracies to be treated with an each-to-his-taste shrug, and come to be abnormalities that interfere with the well-being or safety of the person concerned or of those about him?

This is a problem a psychiatrist must face in his everyday professional routine and I do not envy him the task. It is no surprise, really, that when a law court is the scene of a not-guilty-by-reason-of-insanity defense, one side can find a number of psychiatrists who will support the plea, and the other side an equal number who will deny it.

Secondly, differences that are certainly within the realm of normality, *do* bring about the kind of friction, that, building up and building up, will cause divorce, lifelong enmity, murder, and, in larger context, tribal feuds, civil wars and, one can imagine, even a nuclear holocaust.

And how does one stop that?

ISAAC ASIMOV

CHAPTER 21

Adjustment to Stresses

On Monday Karen, a college student, got an A on a chemistry test. On Tuesday she got a D on a paper in political science. On Wednesday the law student she had met three weeks before finally asked her out. On Thursday her father called to tell her that her beloved Irish setter had been run over and seriously injured. On Friday her car broke down and had to be towed ten miles to a garage. On Saturday she was chosen to play the lead in the college production of *A Doll's House.*

How Karen reacts to these events is one aspect of the process called adjustment. **Adjustment** is a continuous and ever-changing process of interacting with the people, events, and forces that affect our lives—such as our friends and families, physical growth and aging, and the environment. These factors continue to change as long as we live, and most of us adjust successfully to changing situations. Successful adjustment allows continued functioning in society, performance of tasks, maintenance of family and social relationships, and a subjective feeling of comfort and contentment. But adjusting to situations like those Karen faced in a single week is sometimes accompanied by stress and physical and psychological dysfunction. The challenges of life, both those that bring pleasure and those that cause pain, often tax our power to cope with them.

Although everyone has a vague notion of what is meant by **stress,** psychologists have not been able to agree on a precise definition of it. Some locate stress in the external world—any stimulus that places a strain on a person's physical or psychological capacity to adjust (Martin, 1981). Others place it within the person—an internal response to some disruptive or disquieting situation (Coleman, Butcher, and Carson, 1980). In our daily language we use both meanings, and both are used in this chapter. Whether stress is seen as a stimulus or a response, it demands that we adjust.

The process of adjustment usually proceeds while we continue to meet our ordinary responsibilities. Although it is at times painful and difficult, we find ways to resolve the problems of life without succumbing to severe forms of psychological dysfunction. Severe, disabling psychological disorders and their treatment are discussed in Chapters 22, 23, and 24. In this chapter our concern is with the problems of adjustment that confront almost everyone at some time and that are most often resolved with little or no professional help.

Attempts to cope with difficult situations tend to fall into three major categories: problem solving, acceptance, and defense mechanisms. Problem solving is what most people consider coping. For example, Karen must deal with the problems of getting her car fixed and paying for the towing and repair work. The development of problem-solving skills to meet a wide variety of situations is a useful aid to adjustment.

The second category, acceptance of the situation, can also be an effective tool in the process of adjustment. Karen can do little to help her injured dog, and despite her sorrow, acceptance of the event and its consequences—rather than frantic, undirected activity—is the best approach to the accident. Unconsidered acceptance can sometimes be dangerous, however, because it can lead us to accept consequences that we could have avoided. It is important to distinguish between situations that call for active problem solving and those that require acceptance.

The third category of coping is the use of the defense mechanisms described in Chapter 18. Most difficult situations produce stress, and defense mechanisms such as repression and denial can help to alleviate them. Karen may worry about her upcoming date with the law student because although she is strongly attracted to him, she recently overheard him arguing against affirmative action programs for women and ethnic minorities—something Karen feels strongly about—and she wonders whether their conflicting attitudes will make any kind of relationship impossible. One way for Karen to deal with her stress is to deny that she finds the young man attractive and to assert that she does not really care whether or not he likes her. Such a defense mechanism may help to reduce the stress. But there is a danger that continual use of this defense will have undesirable long-term consequences. If Karen makes a habit of denying that she finds men attractive, she may not be able to maintain successful social or sexual relationships with them. In other words, *occasional* use of defense mechanisms as a means of coping with stress is a tool for adjustment; *overuse* can lead to severe disturbances.

Useful methods of coping do not always reflect the values of society. For example, society would probably favor a direct approach to Karen's problem of the D on her political science paper. If Karen accepts that view, she can schedule a meeting with her instructor to analyze the paper and work out a way of improving her course grade. But Karen may decide that her other activities are more important than getting a good grade in the course. If she plans to become an actress, devoting her free time to rehearsals may be a much more important step toward her goal than raising her political science grade, although

Karen is aware of the consequences of simply accepting a D. Neither of these modes of coping is good or bad in itself; which approach is more useful for Karen depends on many factors in her life.

Specific strategies for coping and adapting, then, can be evaluated only in relation to the situation the person confronts—and only in terms of the effectiveness of the strategy for that person. There is no single formula for successful adjustment.

In this chapter we shall examine the physical and psychological impact of stressful events, then go on to consider some of the situational factors that make adjustment to such events easier or more difficult—especially the factor of the control a person feels able to exert over events. The issue of control will come into focus as we consider ways of controlling our own behavior to cope with stress. Since adjustment is a process rather than a product, it is a lifelong concern; therefore, the final section of the chapter will describe the kinds of changes and stressful events that await us as we go through life.

Stress and Physical Functioning

Stress like that faced by Karen can scarcely be avoided, but stress is not always undesirable because it can involve the body's response to pleasure as well as to pain. According to Hans Selye (Selye and Cherry, 1978), who first detailed the specific physiological reactions to stress, enjoying a passionate kiss with a lover can be as stressful as sitting in a dentist's chair. In both instances, the pulse races, breathing quickens, and heartbeat soars. Thus, our aim should not be to avoid stress but to learn to recognize our typical responses to it and to govern our lives so as to live with it.

The Body's Response to Stress

In similar situations people experience different amounts of stress. Giving a public lecture may be a terror to a student, a tonic to a politician, a bore to an ambassador. But under any kind of stress —emotional or physical—all bodies seem to show a common set of reactions. If the stress is severe or prolonged, it can take a harsh toll on the body.

Selye's Three Stages   Selye (1956) observed that when assaulted by viruses, starvation, frostbite, anger, fear, or any other attack, the body can pass through a three-stage reaction: alarm, resistance, and exhaustion. The moment a man leaps into icy water, he is shocked; then his body begins to adapt, resisting the initial numbness. If he stays in the water too long, his body becomes unable to react and he succumbs to exhaustion. This pattern describes the human body's reaction to all kinds of stress. First comes the alarm, consisting of an initial shock and a subsequent countershock. In this initial phase, the autonomic nervous system triggers an increased secretion of hormones by the adrenal glands. If stress in this first phase is overwhelming, death can follow. More commonly, the countershock sets in, as the body responds to continuing stress. The autonomic and endocrine systems step up their general resistance, while appropriate local defenses come into play. During this phase, the **stress syndrome** appears: enlarged adrenal glands, shrunken thymus gland and lymph nodes, and ulcerated stomach.

As the body moves into the resistance phase, its local, specific defenses take over the battle, eliminating the need for generalized activities of the nervous system and glands. Resistance can last for days, weeks, or even months. Hormone production falls to near normal levels, and the physical symptoms of the countershock phase disappear.

Often local defenses win the war at this stage, but if stress continues too long or increases, the body's resistance fails and exhaustion sets in. Once more the endocrine system is aroused, hormone levels rise, and the physical symptoms of countershock recur. Now the body's systems of defense can be its own worst enemies: the increased flow of hormones in the exhaustion stage may overwork the systems that these hormones activate, producing additional stress. According to Selye (1956), if stress remains unchecked during this stage, the only possible outcome is death.

Stress-Related Disease and Death   Some people thrive on stress, working hard and racing the clock with no ill effects, but prolonged stress can contribute to disease. It is difficult to separate the physical from the psychological causes of stress, but several studies (e.g., Weiss, 1972; Lubrosky, Docherty, and Penick, 1973) suggest that

Continual stress, such as these pilots experience, often leads to physical illness.

anxiety, frustration, helplessness, resentment, and depression contribute heavily to stress. For some unknown reason, psychological stress is more likely than muscular overload to lead to disease. Emotional stress is known to relate to such illnesses as peptic ulcers, hypertension, certain kinds of arthritis, asthma, and heart disease. People who work in high-stress occupations may pay a high price. Air traffic controllers, for example, who spend their days juggling the flights of giant airliners and whose minor errors can mean mass death, are said to suffer from the highest incidence of peptic ulcers of any occupational group (Grayson, 1972; Cobb and Rose, 1973).

Other studies (e.g., Schmale, 1972) suggest that emotional factors are implicated in the onset of most diseases, including diabetes and cancer. Whether stress is actually a contributing factor in disease has not been established, because these relationships are all correlational. As we saw in Chapter 2, correlations do not say anything about causes. The link between stress and disease could reflect the fact that people respond to the early stages of a disease in ways that produce stress.

Nevertheless, the idea of psychosomatic disease is familiar, and no one is surprised that mind and body are so intimately connected that the mind's distress can lead to the body's suffering. A student may come down with flu on the day before an important exam, or a director may have an attack of asthma on the opening night of his play. In these cases, stress may not have caused the illness but instead may have affected the body's ability to respond to attacks by bacteria, viruses, or allergens, perhaps by depleting resources that could otherwise have warded off disease. The speed of recovery from diseases may be affected by stress in a similar manner. However, prolonged stress may be serious when it is accompanied by a feeling of helplessness, which often arises from a deep personal loss. In one study, helpless, hopeless feelings correlated highly with the onset of cervical cancer (Schmale, 1972). In another study, the mortality rate among 4,500 British widowers was 40 percent higher during the first six months of widowerhood than among other men the same age (Parkes, Benjamin, and Fitzgerald, 1969).

Sudden, acute stress can be followed by immediate death, although such instances are rare and probably require a preexisting condition like heart disease. Among the publicized cases is the death of the fifty-one-year-old president of CBS on the way to his father's funeral. In another instance, a fifty-six-year-old woman saw the wreckage of her husband's truck, ran to the scene, collapsed, and died (her husband had escaped uninjured). An elderly man was accidentally locked in a public lavatory and died while struggling to get out. Even joy can be so intense as to overwhelm the body: a seventy-five-year-old man collapsed at the race track as he was about to cash in his winning $2 ticket for $1,683, and a fifty-six-year-old minister who had been "elated" to talk to President Carter on a radio phone-in show had a fatal heart attack soon after hanging up (all cited in Engel, 1977).

In terms of Selye's stages, these deaths occurred during the shock phase of the alarm reaction, when adrenal hormone level, heart rate, and blood pressure had risen abruptly. Although there is ample evidence that emotional stress—even the stress of triumph—can kill, it would be a mistake to try to eliminate stress from our lives. Stress is like food: too much is damaging, but we cannot live without some of it. Stress is the body's nonspecific response to any demand made upon it, and mild stress occurs even during sleep and dreaming. As Selye (1974) has pointed out, "Complete freedom from stress is death."

The relationship between *specific* stressful events and *immediate* physical effects seems obvious, as when extreme excitement and agitation in a cardiac patient are followed by a heart attack. But precise knowledge about the relationship between stress and physical illness would be useful. Apparently major events precipitate illness, but some have suggested that the combined stress from a number of minor events can also affect physical functioning. This association between the number and severity of stressful events in a person's life and the probability of physical illness has been studied extensively by physicians and psychologists since the early 1960s.

The Measurement of Stress

A way of measuring the amount of stress a person may experience from various sources over a given period was devised by Thomas Holmes and Richard Rahe (1967). Their Social Readjustment Rating Scale (SRRS) was constructed by first identifying a number of events that can cause changes in a person's life, then asking large groups of people to rate the importance of each event according to the amount of change or adaptation needed to adjust to it, and finally assigning each event a numerical value, as shown in Table 21.1. Not the desirability or the undesirability of the event, but the intensity and duration of change accompanying it determined its rank value. When using the SRRS, individuals indicate whether each event has occurred in their lives and, if so, when. Then for any given time span a score, expressed in Life Change Units (LCUs), can be calculated.

Work based on the SRRS showed that clusters of life events help to account for the time at which an illness appears (Holmes and Masuda, 1974). When life changes added up to 150 or more LCUs in a single year, a person was judged to have experienced a "life crisis." Among people studied, as LCUs increased, so did the incidence of illness, and 79 percent of those whose scores were 300 LCUs or more had experienced physical illness or a change of health within one or two years of amassing the score. The discovered correlation between life stress and heart disease is not unexpected (Rahe and Lind, 1971; DeFaire, 1975); but an unexpected, similar association has been found between life stress and broken bones (Tollefson, 1972) and the onset of cancer in children (Jacobs and Charles, 1980).

Table 21.1   Social Readjustment Rating Scale
The amount of life stress a person has experienced in a given period of time, say one year, is measured by the total number of life change units (LCUs). These units result from the addition of the values (shown in the right column) associated with events that the person has experienced during the target time period.

Rank	Life Event	Mean Value
1	Death of spouse	100
2	Divorce	73
3	Marital separation	65
4	Jail term	63
5	Death of close family member	63
6	Personal injury or illness	53
7	Marriage	50
8	Fired at work	47
9	Marital reconciliation	45
10	Retirement	45
11	Change in health of family member	44
12	Pregnancy	40
13	Sex difficulties	39
14	Gain of new family member	39
15	Business readjustment	39
16	Change in financial state	38
17	Death of close friend	37
18	Change to different line of work	36
19	Change in number of arguments with spouse	35
20	Mortgage over $10,000	31
21	Foreclosure of mortgage or loan	30
22	Change in responsibilities at work	29
23	Son or daughter leaving home	29
24	Trouble with in-laws	29
25	Outstanding personal achievement	28
26	Spouse begin or stop work	26
27	Begin or end school	26
28	Change in living conditions	25
29	Revision of personal habits	24
30	Trouble with boss	23
31	Change in work hours or conditions	20
32	Change in residence	20
33	Change in schools	20
34	Change in recreation	19
35	Change in church activities	19
36	Change in social activities	18
37	Mortgage or loan less than $10,000	17
38	Change in sleeping habits	16
39	Change in number of family get-togethers	15
40	Change in eating habits	15
41	Vacation	13
42	Christmas	12
43	Minor violations of the law	11

Source: T. H. Holmes and R. H. Rahe. "The Social Readjustment Rating Scale," *Journal of Psychosomatic Research,* II (1967), 213–218.

All these studies were retrospective analyses: the scale was administered after the onset of illness, so that subjects' memories of life events might have been affected by their illnesses. Such retrospective studies cannot demonstrate that stress caused the illness. Although no prospective studies, in which LCUs are measured first and subjects are then watched for symptoms of illness, have been done on cancer, such relationships have been found for minor diseases. For example, in studies of the armed services, recent life change levels predicted the symptoms of minor illness within a year (Rahe and Arthur, 1978). And in a well-controlled study of streptococcal throat infections, throat cultures were taken from each family member in the study at least every three weeks for one year. Families were interviewed periodically to complete ratings of stress on each person. Investigators found that respiratory infections were four times as likely to follow a family crisis as to precede it (Meyer and Haggerty, 1962).

Social Support and Physical Illness

Many of the most stressful events in our lives are connected with close personal relationships—a fact reflected in the SRRS, where four of the top five items involve the loss of a family relationship (see Table 21.1). Changes in these relationships are often followed by physical illness; for example, many children who developed cancer had recently lost a person with whom they had an important emotional relationship (Jacobs and Charles, 1980).

Perhaps the absence of such relationships is nearly as important as their loss, for the negative consequences of isolation and loneliness appear to be substantial. Premature death—defined as death before the age of sixty-five—is consistently higher among people who are single, widowed, or divorced than among people who are married. This connection appears among males and females, whites and nonwhites, and is true for almost every cause of death, including heart attacks, cancer, strokes, cirrhosis of the liver, hypertension, pneumonia, suicide, and even automobile accidents (Lynch, 1977).

The most likely explanation for the dramatic effect of loneliness is that the presence of others can reduce stress. In a series of laboratory experiments, people sought out others when they found themselves in stressful situations, and the presence of others seemed to reduce anxiety (Schachter, 1959). If the findings of another study (Back and Bogdonoff, 1964) are true of most people, the effect is heightened when our companions are people who care about us. People undergoing a highly stressful interrogation showed an increase of free fatty acids in the bloodstream, a factor that has been linked to heart disease. But when the questioning took place in the presence of strangers, the jump in fatty acid levels was significantly higher than when friends were present. The presence of someone who cares about us may tend to neutralize stress, reducing its detrimental effects on the body.

Social support in stressful situations also reassures animals. In one study, dogs were shocked ten seconds after they heard a warning tone. Whenever the warning tone sounded, a dog's heart rate usually accelerated about 50 to 100 beats per minute. However, if the dog was petted throughout the entire experience—during the period of tone and the subsequent shock—its heart rate showed no change (Lynch and

At times of loss or stress, the company of others reduces anxiety and makes unhappy situations more bearable.

McCarthy, 1967). Finally, there is considerable evidence that social support helps an individual adapt to undesirable events of all kinds, including spinal cord injury, surgery, and cancer (e.g., Meyerowitz, 1980; Sklar and Anisman, 1981; Silver and Wortman, 1980).

Although marriage and family life appear to help protect people against the stresses of everyday life, the disruption of a marriage appears to be a particularly potent form of stress, as indicated by the high position of divorce and separation on the SRRS. Separation or divorce is strongly associated with a wide range of physical and emotional disorders (Bloom, Asher, and White, 1978), especially among people under psychiatric care. Those who are separated or divorced are much more likely to receive psychiatric care than those who are married, are widowed, or who have remained single. Such correlations, however, cannot show whether mental disorder was the result of a marital break-up, whether the break-up was caused by mental disorder, or whether some other factor such as financial problems contributed to both.

Personality and Physical Illness

People differ considerably in the way they respond to the stresses of their lives. Some are relaxed and calm, others are impatient and tense. Some find it easy to express anger, while others are quite inhibited and find it almost impossible to voice their feelings, even when they are furious. Evidence is accumulating to show that these different personality patterns can affect the amount of stress that a person experiences and that they may also influence the course of physical illness.

Although different personality patterns have been implicated in the development of various disorders, perhaps the most heavily researched relationship is that between heart disease and what has been called **Type A behavior.** People who fit the Type A pattern are highly competitive, hostile when thwarted, and their behavior shows the urgency of working against the pressure of time (Friedman and Rosenman, 1974). The Type A pattern seems to be associated with a strong need to exert control in stressful situations (Glass, 1977). In situations where this is not possible, Type A people may become frustrated and blame themselves for their inability to control events (Brunson and Matthews, 1981). Type B people, in contrast, are relaxed and show little

or no sense of being under any pressure of time. In an impressive longitudinal study that followed more than 2,000 male executives between the ages of thirty-nine and fifty-nine for nine years (Rosenman et al., 1975), the connection between Type A responses and heart disease was clear. Although the executives were almost equally divided between Type As and Type Bs, among the 257 men who had heart attacks 178 were Type A and only 79 were Type B. The Type-A behavior pattern strongly predicted heart disease, even after the traditional predictors of family history, smoking, high blood pressure, and high cholesterol level were controlled for.

This sort of evidence has led to a series of projects in which Type A people are taught to cope with stress and anger in a fashion more typical of the Type B pattern (e.g., Roskies, 1982). It is still too early to tell whether such programs will significantly reduce the incidence of heart disease.

Stress and Physical Illness: A Model

The disparity in the incidence of heart disease between Type As and Type Bs makes it clear that some people can tolerate a level of stress that produces physical illness in others. An explanation for the relationship between stressful life events and physical illness has been proposed by Gary Schwartz (1977), whose **disregulation model** suggests that physical disorders arise when the body's internal regulatory systems fail to operate properly. In Schwartz's model, these bodily systems are regulated by negative feedback, which means that information from a part of a system that is turned on leads to the turning off of another part—just as the thermometer's information that room temperature has reached 68 degrees tells the thermostat to turn off the furnace. Within the body, negative feedback can be seen in the digestive system. At the sight of a sizzling steak the nervous system turns on the flow of gastric juices (positive feedback). Once the steak is eaten and the stomach is full, that news reaches the nervous system and the gastric juices are then turned off (negative feedback). Schwartz believes that the body's regulatory systems can go awry, thus failing in their regulatory functions, at one or more of four stages: (1) environmental demands, (2) information processing in the central nervous system, (3) a peripheral organ, or (4) in the negative feedback process itself.

This woman copes with her highly stressful job by smoking. This may ease her stress, but it adds another unhealthy element to her life.

The initial stage, environmental demands, can lead to illness if the demands placed upon a person are so great that she or he is forced to ignore negative feedback from the body. For example, a person who ignores negative feedback from the body because of the inescapable stress of her or his occupation will probably develop stress-related illness.

At the second stage, illness can develop because of faulty information processing by the brain. Either heredity or learning can lead to the mishandling of environmental demands or of the body's negative feedback. For example, children who have learned—through parental example or admonishment—to continue eating after the stomach's negative feedback signals that it is full often become obese.

The third stage, at which a bodily organ responds to central nervous system commands, can also be a source of disregulation. In this case, either heredity or disease can be the cause of an inappropriate response to signals from the brain, as when a weak heart fails to respond to signals from the brain to increase blood flow in response to stress.

At the fourth stage, the negative feedback process itself can lead to disregulation, because the message turning off a system just does not get through. For example, when blood pressure rises in response to environmental stress, pressure-sensitive cells surrounding the blood vessels normally signal the brain that pressure is high so that the brain can lower it. But some people are born with defective pressure-sensitive cells so that notice of rising blood pressure is not transmitted to the brain and they develop hypertension.

When things go wrong at any of the four stages, the process is disregulated for the entire bodily system. When heart rate is disrupted, the entire cardiovascular system goes awry; when the flow of gastric juices is disrupted, the entire gastrointestinal system malfunctions. This disregulation model attempts to account for the specific stimulus, for differences in individual responses, and for the physical disorder—whether its source is organic or psychological stress. Thus, the model provides a comprehensive explanation for the translation of stress into physical illness.

Stress and Psychological Functioning

While some researchers were studying the relationship between stressful events and physical illness, others were looking at the relationship between stressful events and psychological or emotional disturbances. Although *physical* illness often follows considerable stress—whether that stress is associated with pleasant or unpleasant events—*psychological* dysfunction seems to be associated primarily with the stress caused by undesirable events. Again, such associations do not establish stress as a cause of psychological dysfunction. Although such a connection is possible, it is just as likely that psychological disturbance can produce indications of stress or that some unknown third factor produces the relationship.

A link between undesirable stress and psychological functioning appeared in a study of men who showed no psychological disturbance (Vinokur and Selzer, 1975). The men filled out questionnaires rating events of the previous year in terms of the pressure they evoked and their desirability or undesirability. They also answered questions and rated themselves on scales pertaining to aggression, paranoid thinking, depression, and tendency toward suicide; and they answered questions about such indications of stress and anxiety as headaches, insomnia, and drinking, as well as direct questions about tension and distress in their lives. In their reports, all these factors were primarily associated with situations involving undesirable stress. In contrast, situations involving desirable stress, such as that linked with personal achievement, marriage, promotions, or vacations, showed no substantial correlation with these factors.

Undesirable life events have also been associated with severe forms of psychological disorder. In one study (Paykel, 1974), 185 depressed patients were matched with nonpatients by sex, age, marital status, race, and social class. The depressed patients reported three times as many stressful events of all kinds during the preceding six months as their matched controls. Situations involving undesirable stress—such as increased arguments with a spouse, marital separation, or the death of a family member—were reported much more frequently by the depressed people, a finding that concurs with studies showing a close connection between marital separation or divorce and psychiatric care (Bloom, Asher, and White, 1978). Undesirable stress has also been found among schizophrenics and people who had attempted suicide (Paykel, 1974). Although stress is not the only factor that contributes to such reactions, stressful experiences seem to be closely related to the rehospitalization of schizophrenics. It seems that schizophrenics already have a high stress level, so that the addition of a highly stressful event can affect the timing—and perhaps the probability—of schizophrenia's onset (Rabkin, 1980).

These studies suggest that it may be the undesirable nature of an event that contributes to psychological dysfunction. In other words, desirable events may stress the body, but they are not associated with signs of psychological disturbance.

Life in a Stressful Environment

At some time in our lives, each of us must cope with a situation involving extreme stress, such as death, divorce, or the loss of a job, but all of us must also cope with the annoyances and problems inherent in daily life. Rural environments have their own kinds of stress: for example, people in the country must learn to cope with the effects of isolation and bad weather. Urban stress is more obvious and more dramatic: city dwellers live amid high levels of noise, crowding, traffic, street crime, and a hectic pace of life.

Environmental stress almost always takes the form of aversive events—noise, heat, crowds, earthquakes, floods—and the more intense the event, the more stress we would expect people to feel. But another aspect of environmental stress is that such events are usually unpredictable or uncontrollable—or both. The U.S. Weather Service often accurately predicts a hurricane, but there is no way to control the storm when it does hit. Urban noise—traffic, airplanes, jackhammers, loud parties in the next apartment—is usually both unpredictable and uncontrollable. There is no way to know when it will start or stop, and it can be controlled only by soundproofing buildings or plugging the ears—seldom by making the noise itself stop.

Researchers have wondered whether such events would produce similar levels of stress if we had some way to predict or control them. In seeking to clarify the problem, some researchers have investigated the link between adjustment to stress and our belief in both its predictability and our power to control it.

Predictability of Events Predictable aversive events are experienced as less stressful than

The stress caused by the loss of a home after a violent storm may be heightened by the uncontrollable nature of the disaster and by its suddenness.

those that are unpredictable. This is as true for animals as it is for human beings. Laboratory animals, when given the chance, consistently choose to receive electric shocks that are preceded by a signal rather than shocks that occur at unpredictable intervals (Badia, Harsh, and Abbott, 1979). Predictability has parallel effects on the consequences of stress. In other experiments, rats that received shocks preceded by a signal were much less likely to develop ulcers than rats that received unpredictable shocks (Weiss, 1977). The reactions of the British to the Blitz during World War II may have been related to this phenomenon. Londoners, who were bombed with considerable regularity, showed few signs of anxiety, but residents of the surrounding villages, where bombing was infrequent but unpredictable, showed considerable anxiety and apprehension (Vernon, 1941).

Predictable events may be less stressful because they allow preparation and signal safety. When we are forewarned we can prepare for the stress, thereby lessening its effects. If we know when an aversive event will occur, we also know when it will *not* occur and thus we know when it is safe to resume normal activities. In research with animals, the safety function of predictability seems to be more important than its preparation function (e.g., Weiss, 1977). With predictable stress, there are long periods of relief, while with unpredictable aversive events anticipatory stress and anxiety remain at a constant high.

The effects of predictability have been evaluated in a series of experiments on noise, an important source of environmental stress (Glass and Singer, 1972). The researchers were primarily concerned with the effects of predictable and unpredictable noise on task performance after the noise had ceased. If unpredictable noise is experienced as more stressful than predictable noise, then people should use more resources adjusting to it; as a result, their subsequent task performance will be affected more severely.

In one experiment, these researchers asked female college students to spend twenty-three minutes working at verbal and numerical tasks. During the work period, the women were subjected to intermittent tape-recorded noise, half of them at fixed (predictable) intervals and half at random (unpredictable) intervals. In addition, half the women in both groups heard the noise amplified to an unpleasant 110 decibels (the sound level of a motorcycle engine), while the other half heard the same noise amplified to only

56 decibels (the level of ordinary conversation). A control group heard no recorded noise while they worked. Before, during, and after the exposure to noise, measures were taken of all the subjects' levels of physiological tension (as indicated by GSR). These measurements, together with the subjects' successful completion of the assigned tasks, showed that they had adapted to the noise, both physiologically and psychologically.

Next, the researchers set out to discover what effects the intensity of the noise and its predictability or unpredictability would have on the subjects' tolerance for frustration and performance on tasks in the future. They gave the subjects two complex tasks, the first requiring the solution of four picture puzzles—two of which were insoluble—and the second requiring them to proofread seven pages of written material, correcting errors in spelling, punctuation, and the like. Although they were not subjected to noise while working at these new tasks, the subjects who had been exposed to loud, random noise did a significantly poorer job than those in the other experimental conditions or those in the control group: they gave up sooner on the insoluble puzzles and they overlooked more errors in the proofreading task.

Thus, the subjects did adapt to unpredictable, unpleasant noise, but the cost of their adaptation was high. The energy they spent to overcome the distraction and irritation caused by the noise was energy they could not apply toward the subsequent tasks. And the louder and less predictable the noise had been, the higher the price they had to pay.

Control Over Events Why should enduring an unpredictable, loud noise affect a person's subsequent tolerance for frustration and ability to perform a task? Another experiment (Glass, Reim, and Singer, 1971) provided some clues (see Figure 21.1). This time the subjects were male college students, all of whom were exposed to random bursts of the same 110-decibel noise used in the study described above. Men in one group were told that they could stop the noise by signaling another subject to press a button, but understood that the researchers preferred that no signal be given. Each man in the second group was told that another subject had a control button, but was given no means of communicating with that subject. In the third group, neither

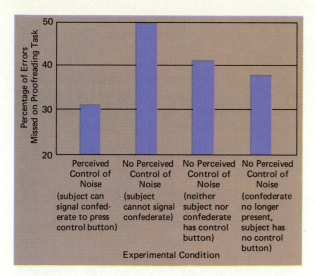

Figure 21.1 Coping with a stressful environment. In two experiments David Glass and colleagues have shown that exposure to uncontrollable and unpredictable noise had a much greater effect on performance of a subsequent task in a quiet environment than did exposure to controllable and unpredictable noise. More effort is required to adapt to the unpredictable and uncontrollable noise, which leaves the person less able to deal effectively with future tasks.

Surgeons may suffer somewhat less anxiety and stress than might be thought. Their high level of training and skill provides the control they need when performing an operation.

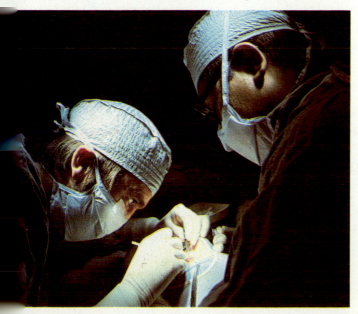

of the subjects in a pair could control the noise. In the fourth group, each subject was alone in the room with no way of controlling the noise. Thus, for all men the noise was unpredictable, but only those in the first group believed that they could stop it when it did come.

After twenty-four minutes of intermittent exposure to the random noise, each man was taken to another room and given a proofreading task. Men who had believed that they had had some control over the noise did significantly better on this task—and showed significantly less tension —than men who had believed that they had had no control over the noise.

These findings suggest that the effect of environmental stress on our adjustment may be due to our inability to control or avoid the stress, rather than to the intensity of the stress itself. Like predictable stress, controllable stress is usually experienced as less aversive than uncontrollable stress. For example, rats who escaped or avoided shock developed fewer ulcers than rats who received the same number of shocks but whose behavior had no effect on the shock (Weiss, 1977). Control also seems to have been a factor in the development of anxiety among air crews during World War II. Pilots of heavy bombers reported less fear than their gun crews. Although casualties were much higher for fighter planes than for bombers, fighter pilots experienced the least fear of any air crew members (Rachman, 1978). Pilots have more control over disastrous consequences than their crew members, and fighter pilots have more flexibility and thus more control than bomber pilots. Bomber pilots, for example, must fly in formation and have little opportunity to engage in evasive actions. As this example indicates, it is perceived control—not actual control—that determines anxiety. Fighter pilots have the highest degree of perceived control, even though their casualty rates are higher than those of bomber crews. If a feeling of control allows us to adjust more effectively to stress, and a feeling of helplessness leads to anxiety and a diminished ability to adjust, then the conditions that create a feeling of helplessness are an important aspect of adjustment.

Learned Helplessness

The belief that we are helpless to relieve certain types of unpleasant stress is rooted in folk wisdom, and most of us have repeated such familiar sayings as "You can't fight city hall" or "Better the devil you know than the devil you don't." In addition, our own experiences lead us to express similar sentiments, such as "I can't learn to dance—I have two left feet" or "I'll never get more than a C in this course no matter what I do." Since feelings of helplessness impaired performance in the noise experiment and led to anxiety among flight crews, there is the possibility that feeling helpless in one situation might teach us to be helpless in other kinds of situations.

Experiments with dogs indicate that this may indeed be the case. In an already classic experiment (Overmier and Seligman, 1967), each dog was placed in a sling, where it received a series of shocks. Nothing a dog did had any effect on the shocks, and the animal could not escape. Later each dog was placed in a shuttlebox, consisting of two compartments separated by a low barrier that the dog could easily jump. A series of electrical shocks was then delivered to the dog's feet through a grid on the floor of the box. Instead of leaping into the safe compartment, the dog simply sat and endured the shock. Some dogs never learned to escape, even after they were lifted from one compartment to the other to show them the way. A control group of dogs, which had not been subjected to inescapable shock, learned to escape after the first or second shock. Martin Seligman and his associates propose that the dogs were victims of **learned helplessness**, and that a similar mechanism underlies human depression, a disorder we shall consider in Chapter 22. However, the concept of learned helplessness also provides a way to understand the effects of uncontrollable environmental stress.

Research has demonstrated that learned helplessness can be an important factor in the failure to adjust to stressful events. In one study (Hiroto and Seligman, 1975), groups of college students were subjected to an inescapable loud tone. On subsequent tasks, when the students could escape from the unpleasant, distracting noise, they made fewer attempts to get away from it and performed the new task poorly compared with students who had earlier experienced a tone from which they could escape. Inescapable noise was not the only means of inducing such helplessness. Students who faced a series of unpredictable failures at a problem-solving task also learned to be helpless. Furthermore, helplessness learned in one situation carried over to the

other, so that students who could not escape a tone were also helpless in the problem-solving task.

Helpness may also affect the body's ability to fight disease. Visintainer, Volpicelli, and Seligman (1982) injected three groups of rats with cancer cells. One group received electric shocks they could terminate by pressing a bar, another group received shocks they could neither escape nor terminate, and the final group received no shocks. The results were dramatic. The helplessness group, those receiving inescapable shock, rejected the tumors only half as often as those in the other two groups.

Although the concept of learned helplessness seems to apply to many situations, it is incomplete. As Seligman and his colleagues (Abramson, Seligman, and Teasdale, 1978) point out, the concept does not explain why some people become helpless when confronted with an aversive event and others who face the identical event do not. Nor does it account for the fact that people generally feel sad or guilty after enduring aversive events that cannot be avoided.

To fill these gaps in the theory, Seligman and his associates have revised their explanation of learned helplessness. According to the new formulation, learned helplessness is not simply the result of a person's belief that she or he lacks control over a situation but depends upon the person's explanations for this lack of control. People are likely to become helpless only when they see their lack of control as due to causes that are (1) permanent rather than temporary; (2) internal (located within themselves) rather than external (located within the environment); and (3) applicable to many areas of their life rather than limited to a single area of functioning. Although this revision seems intuitively correct, it fails to answer some important questions about the development of learned helplessness. For example, the revised theory cannot explain why some people who are confronted with an inescapable aversive event attribute it to a factor in the environment, whereas others blame themselves for the situation (Wortman and Dintzer, 1978).

Gaining Control Over the Environment

The other side of the coin of learned helplessness is the problem of control. An important question is whether restoring control to people who believe they have none will reduce feelings of helplessness and make adjustment to the stresses of life easier. One experiment (Langer and Rodin, 1976) indicates that leading people to perceive that they control various aspects of their lives has positive effects. Researchers worked with ninety-one residents in a nursing home for the aged, whose ages ranged from sixty-five to ninety. After dividing these people into two groups, the investigators encouraged people in the first group to take responsibility for their belongings and to make decisions about how they spent their time. Those in the second group were encouraged to leave decisions and responsibility to the staff. People in the first group, for example, were allowed to choose a plant and care for it themselves, and to decide which night they would like to see a movie. Those in the other group were given plants that the staff chose and cared for, and were assigned a movie night.

Three weeks later, according to ratings by the residents themselves and observations by the staff, 93 percent of the group that had been encouraged to take more control of their environment showed overall improvement; they were more active and felt happier. Only 21 percent of the group that had been encouraged to rely on the staff were judged to have improved.

Eighteen months after they had rearranged conditions in the nursing home, the researchers returned and assessed the health and well-being of the people in both groups (Rodin and Langer, 1977). The old people who had been encouraged to take responsibility were still more vigorous and active than those who had been encouraged to leave decisions to the staff. Furthermore, there had been a lower death rate in the first group: 15 percent, in contrast to 30 percent for the other group.

These findings are of great potential importance in shaping our policies and practices regarding the care of the elderly. It may be that preserving a feeling of control and responsibility among the elderly will add years of happy, more vigorous activity to their lives—and, in due course, to our own.

The results of the experiment in the home for the aged are in accord with the earlier discussions of stress and physical functioning. Adjustment is a process that goes on throughout our lives. Events we face can lead to physical illness and psychological dysfunction, and stress can lower our tolerance for frustration and impair our performance. When stress appears beyond

Old people who are responsible for themselves remain healthy and happy longer than those whose lives are controlled by others.

our control, its effects are multiplied, and when the outcome is clearly beyond our control, learned helplessness results, which may prevent our coping in new situations that are actually under our control.

Although helplessness increases stress by increasing anxiety and impairing performance, helplessness is not always a maladaptive force. On the contrary, when a situation is truly uncontrollable—as when someone has a fatal illness or loves a person who does not return the affection —the most adaptive behavior is to stop struggling and accept the situation (Wortman and Brehm, 1975). In experiments with animals, continued attempts to gain control of situations that are impossible to control result in greater stress than simply giving up and becoming passive. However, since it is often difficult to determine which situations we can change and which we cannot, in most cases attempts at control lead to both an improvement in the situation and better psychological adjustment.

Coping With Stress

Although we cannot always control our environment, there are steps we can take to cope with the inevitable stresses of life. A number of techniques have been developed that make it possible to modify our physiological and cognitive responses to stress, thereby lessening its toll on our body and mind.

Relaxation

Perhaps the most frequently used technique for coping with stress is relaxation, a method that is commonly prescribed for the relief of chronic anxiety, insomnia, headaches, ulcers, cardiovascular problems, and other consequences of stress. Strong popular interest in relaxation has created large followings for transcendental meditation, yoga, progressive relaxation, and autogenic training.

Opinion is divided as to whether the various relaxation techniques affect different physiological systems or whether they all produce the same pattern of physiological response. Those who advocate the latter position maintain that all relaxation techniques lower rates of metabolism (as indicated by diminished oxygen consumption), lessen muscle tension, alter respiration, lower heart rate and blood pressure, and lower GSR. One advocate of relaxation, Herbert Benson (1975), describes what he calls the "relaxation response," which he believes is elicited by all techniques for producing relaxation. Other researchers (Davidson and Schwartz, 1976) maintain that different relaxation techniques produce different physiological patterns. For example, meditation procedures are more cognitive in nature than conscious muscle relaxation, therefore meditation would be likely to have a stronger effect on cognitive arousal than on muscle tension.

Relaxation, like stress, is complex and to some extent both sides are correct. The different components of the relaxation response are loosely related, so that many physiological responses are similar. But there are large differences among people in the way their bodies respond in relaxation, and some of this difference is probably due to the techniques used to relax. As we saw in Chapter 6, brain-wave patterns in meditation are different from those that accompany relaxation. However, most physiological differences among relaxation techniques are neither large nor specific.

Meditation techniques were described in Chapter 6. Two other common procedures that use relaxation to help cope with stress are progressive relaxation and autogenic training.

In **progressive relaxation,** which was developed by Edmund Jacobson (1938; 1964), the individual tenses and then releases different muscle groups in sequence. During this process, the individual learns to relax deeply the muscles of the body. For example, the first step might be to bend the left hand as far back as possible and to notice the pattern of strain in the back of the hand and up the arm. After maintaining that position for about ten seconds, the person is told to let the hand relax completely (a procedure Jacobson called "going negative") and to notice the difference in sensation at the points where the strain had been felt. The object of this training program is to teach the individual how each muscle group feels when relaxed and to provide practice in achieving further relaxation. Once a person can discriminate patterns of muscle tension from those of relaxation, she or he no longer is required to tense the muscles before

Tension and anxiety are reduced by exercises that relax the muscles.

Jogging as an Aid to Adjustment

In the first paragraph of his best-selling book *The Complete Book of Running* (1977), James Fixx recalls a run through a Boston suburb. As Fixx ran by, an old man called out to him, "Say, what do you gain by running?" Fixx shouted back, "It makes you feel good!" Millions of people would agree. In just a few years running has gone from an activity pursued only by track stars and a few eccentrics to a national craze.

When Fixx said that running makes you feel good, he was not referring only to the physical benefits of running, such as firmer muscles and greater cardiovascular endurance. Jogging—long, slow, regular running—also contributes to psychological well-being. Olympic runner Ted Corbitt put it this way: "People get relief of tension from running. It's like having your own psychiatrist. . . . One thing that almost always happens is that your sense of self-worth improves. You accept yourself a little better" (quoted in Fixx, 1977, p. 15).

In interview after interview, Fixx found that runners and those who have studied them invariably began talking about the psychological benefits of the sport. In addition to increasing self-acceptance, running seems to reduce feelings of depression and anxiety. Dr. Frederick D. Harper of Howard University described a study aimed at understanding the psychological changes that occurred in students who gradually increased their running from one-quarter mile to several miles per day. Many reported feeling less anxious and generally feeling better about themselves (cited in Fixx, 1977, p. 16).

That running reduces anxiety is not really surprising. Physicians have found that the deepest muscular relaxation follows a period of *increased* muscular tension (Henderson, 1976, p. 57). And, since it is hard to feel anxious and relaxed at the same time, running seems an obvious antidote to anxiety.

A number of psychiatrists think that jogging is so effective an anxiety reducer that they recommend it as an adjunct to psychotherapy. California psychiatrist Thaddeus Kostubala, a marathon runner himself, runs with his clients. He reports that depression almost always disappears after thirty minutes of running, and is replaced by a "runner's high" (Henderson, 1976, p. 62). After they run, clients meet for group therapy in which they discuss the thoughts and feelings that came to them while running.

For many people, looking not for psychotherapy but for an enjoyable way of relieving tension and distracting themselves temporarily from the stresses and strains of their lives, running (under medical supervision) may be the answer. To Joe Henderson, author of *The Long-Run Solution,* running is not a cure-all for life's problems; but though there are no guarantees, running is extremely worthwhile as "a pursuit of happiness" (1976, p. 55).

relaxing them. Instead the muscles are relaxed from whatever level of tension they have reached.

An abbreviated form of progressive relaxation is an important part of a procedure used in behavior therapy, called systematic desensitization, which will be described in Chapter 24. By itself, progressive relaxation is an effective treatment for a variety of stress-related disorders. For example, studies have found that progressive relaxation effectively reduces general tension and anxiety (Borkovec, Grayson, and Cooper, 1978); relieves insomnia (Borkovec et al., 1979); and reduces high blood pressure (Jacob, Kraemer, and Agras, 1977).

A second relaxation procedure, called **autogenic training,** which depends upon self-suggestion and imagery, was developed by Johannes Schultz and Wolfgang Luthe (1959). They devised this technique after observing that during hypnosis people seemed to be able to induce physiological changes in themselves. A suggestion to a hypnotized person that an arm is getting heavy often elicits changes in the arm's muscle potential, indicating that the arm is becoming very relaxed. Schultz and Luthe speculated that a person did not need hypnosis to elicit physiological changes, but could achieve the same effects with language. To accomplish this, the individual repeats suggestions, such as "My arm is heavy. I am at peace. My arm is heavy." Each attempt to relax lasts from thirty to sixty seconds. After an individual has learned to make the whole body "heavy," she or he follows similar procedures to induce warmth, control heart rate, respiration, and abdominal warmth, and cool the forehead.

When the use of progressive relaxation and the heaviness and warmth suggestions of autogenic training were compared in their effects on insomniacs, both were found to be effective treatments (Nicassio and Bootzin, 1974). Because autogenic training relies primarily on imagery and self-suggestion, it is often used in combination with biofeedback. Progressive relaxation is difficult to use with biofeedback, because the tensing of muscles interferes with the measurements of brain waves, muscle tension, heart rate, or blood flow needed for biofeedback control.

Biofeedback

As described in Chapter 6, biofeedback is a method that gives a person a continuous flow of information about the functioning of a physiological system. Lights, clicks, changes in sound volume, or displays on a cathode ray tube inform the person of any fluctuation in the monitored system. Earlier we described various biofeedback techniques and noted that, with such training, people can learn to control such biological responses as blood pressure, heart rate, skin temperature, and muscle tension. In addition to the potential therapeutic use of biofeedback to reduce high blood pressure, learning to control the secretion of stomach acid might help people avoid ulcers and learning to control brain waves might reduce the frequency and intensity of epileptic seizures (Sterman, 1978). Although biofeedback is still in its experimental stage for many of these stress-related ailments, it can often be used as one part of a more comprehensive medical treatment.

In the case of tension headaches, migraine headaches, and muscle reeducation, biofeedback has been considerably effective in clinical practice (Olton and Noonberg, 1980). Biofeedback may also be the only effective treatment for the paralysis of nerves and muscles that often follows strokes and injuries to the spinal cord. In such cases, the present level of muscular activity is first measured, then the patient begins a sequence of treatment (DeBacher, 1979). First the patient learns to relax those muscles that are excessively tight. The next step is learning to contract weak or flaccid muscles while keeping the previously tight muscles relaxed. A patient at this stage of treatment gets feedback from two sets of muscles and must increase activity in the weak muscle while decreasing activity in the strong muscle. Finally, the patient learns to coordinate muscle movements, a process that often requires feedback from several muscles and careful changes in muscle activity. At this point, the sight of the moving joint may be the most effective form of feedback (Olton and Noonberg, 1980).

Relaxation and biofeedback are not the only methods for dealing with stress. Several cognitive restructuring procedures have been developed, in which the way an individual thinks about a stressful situation changes her or his perception of the stress. For example, the pain that accompanies some stress-related disorders can be reduced if a person's attention is distracted (in one experiment, by the tape-recorded details of an actor's erotic escapades); if the person uses self-suggestion (imagining, perhaps, that an aching body part is insensitive to pain); or if the person uses imagery (imagining pleasant events; Chaves and Barber, 1976). In one technique called "stress-inoculation," people learn to combat thoughts that increase stress by substituting positive self-statements for self-defeating thoughts. A common use of the various stress-control procedures discussed in this chapter is found in the Lamaze method of childbirth, in which relaxation, social support, the focusing of attention, and positive self-statements are used instead of medication to ease the tension and pain that often accompany childbirth.

Adjustment: A Lifelong Process

Adjustment to life's stresses continues as long as life itself. At each stage of life, certain predictable events produce stress in many people. The developmental stresses encountered by an adolescent are different from those faced by men and women in midlife, but each requires adjustment.

Crises of Adjustment for Adolescents and Young Adults

Adjustment problems that occur during adolescence are the result of a combination of biological changes and personality development. Adolescents seek to separate themselves psychologically from their parents and to establish their own identity, and they become physically and sexually mature. Looking and feeling like an adult intensifies the desire to act like an adult, to make one's own decisions and to assert one's own individuality. Often this desire takes the form of open rebelliousness—wearing sloppy clothing because Mom and Dad value neatness, or playing rock music because Mom and Dad value Beethoven. Because adolescents have a foot in each world—the world of children and the world of adults—their problems of adjustment are compounded by ambivalent feelings. They want to leave their parents behind, but they are not yet ready to be alone. They want to be financially independent, but they do not want to give up their allowance. However, research has shown that such ambivalence is not necessarily accompanied by unhappiness or emotional troubles, that adolescents generally like and respect their parents, and that serious adolescent rebellion is rare (Offer, Ostrov, and Howard, 1981).

Although adolescence is a time for psychological separation from one's parents, during early adulthood the separation generally becomes physical as well. Early adulthood is a time when most people first live away from home, establishing a life style that is completely separate and perhaps quite different from that of their parents. This is a major life event and one that inevitably generates stress. Whether the stress is positive or negative depends on how well young adults cope with the changes in themselves and their environment.

Until the early twenties, as they go through the phase of separating from parents and searching for identity, the lives of males and females are quite similar. Some stresses in adult life are also similar. Both men and women must decide whether to marry and have children, and both may face adjustment to divorce or life as a single parent. Single parents must adjust to handling all the responsibilities ordinarily shared by two people, to loneliness, to sexual need, and to economic demands (Weiss, 1979).

In other ways, however, the lives of most men and women diverge. Although some men are now deciding to participate more directly in child rearing and the running of the household, most men are primarily caught up in career decisions. Similarly, although more women are remaining single or are focusing their lives on their careers, the majority of women must decide how to juggle career and homemaker patterns or whether to focus on the latter. These decisions result in different crises of adjustment for the two sexes.

Crises of Adjustment for the Adult Man

The developmental crises faced by many men were illustrated when researchers at Yale University, led by Daniel Levinson (1978), interviewed men between the ages of thirty-five and forty-five. These men included executives, blue-collar workers, white-collar workers, writers of varying degrees of fame, and biologists at various stages in their careers. From these interviews, a **life structure** was developed for each man in the sample. Each life structure was an account of the major periods of the man's life, as determined by his activities, his associations, and his parental, marital, and family relationships. A careful analysis of these life structures revealed a pattern that seemed to characterize almost all of the men sampled. The pattern is a combination of the

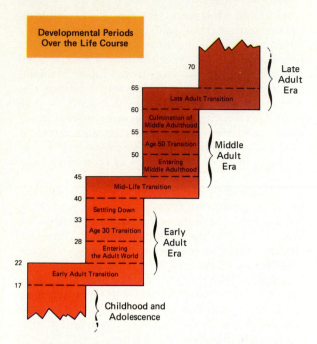

Figure 21.2 A model of the developmental sequence of a man's life developed by Daniel Levinson. The major life eras are childhood and adolescence, early adulthood, middle adulthood, and later adulthood; within each era there are distinctive stages, and between eras a major transition occurs. This model emphasizes that development is a continuing process that requires continual adjustment. (Levinson, 1978.)

major eras in the adult life of a man and the transitions from one era to another.

The model of adult development for men that Levinson and his colleagues proposed (see Figure 21.2) is composed of three major eras: early adulthood (from about age seventeen to about age forty); middle adulthood (forty to sixty); and late adulthood (beginning at about sixty). Between these eras are important transition periods, each lasting approximately five years. In Levinson's research on the early adult era and the midlife transition, four major aspects of male development became clear.

Entering the Adult World From about age twenty-two to age twenty-eight, a young man is considered, both by himself and by society, to be a novice in the adult world—not fully established as a man, but no longer an adolescent. During this time he must attempt to resolve the conflict between the need to explore the options of the adult world and the need to establish a stable life

structure. He needs to sample different kinds of relationships, to keep choices about career and employment open, to explore the nature of the world accessible to him as an adult. But he also needs to begin a career and to establish a home and family of his own. The first life structure, then, may have a tentative quality. The young man may select a career or a job but not be committed to it. Although he may form romantic attachments or even marry during this period of early adulthood, his life structure often lacks a sense of stability or permanence.

The Age Thirty Crisis The years between twenty-eight and thirty-three are often a major transition period for men. The thirtieth birthday is often a turning point, and for most men in Levinson's sample, it could be called the "age thirty crisis." During this transitional period, the tentative commitments that were made in early adulthood are reexamined, and many questions about the choices of marriage partners, career, and life goals are reopened, often in a painful way. A man feels that any parts of his life that are unsatisfying or incomplete must now receive urgent attention because it will soon be too late for him to make major changes.

Settling Down The questioning and searching that are part of the age thirty crisis begin to be resolved as the second adult life structure develops. Having made some firm choices about their careers, family, and relationships, most men now begin actively carving out a niche in society, concentrating on what Levinson calls "making it" in the adult world. A man attempts to move up the ladder of prestige and achievement in his career or profession and shifts from novice to full-fledged member of adult society.

Near the end of the settling-down period, approximately between the ages of thirty-six and forty, Levinson found a distinctive phase that he has labeled "becoming one's own man." Whereas a man in early adulthood looks to an older, more experienced man as a mentor, someone who will share his experience and wisdom, as a man moves into his late thirties the relationship with the mentor often undergoes a fundamental change or is broken off. Once a man is fully independent, he strives to attain the seniority and position in the world that he identified as his ultimate goal at the beginning of this period.

A Man at Midlife

What kinds of adjustment does a man face in the course of his life? This autobiographical passage, written by a man of forty-four, documents a few of his personal difficulties and adjustments. How would you compare the adjustment process between this man and the woman quoted in the box on p. 500? What positive and negative changes, irreversible losses, and kinds of compromise characterize each life? And what kinds of movement and new life choices would you expect from each?

After I graduated from law school I took the bar examination [and] . . . flunked . . . [and] learned a pretty good lesson regarding ego. Defeats and losses have never had as great an impact upon me. While studying for the bar for the second round, I obtained employment with an attorney . . . and I spent one of the most fascinating years of my life doing really what amounted to political work, rather than legal work, in helping to prepare defense and testimony for the Committee [for lawyers who had been subpoenaed by the House Committee on Un-American Activities]. . . .

[Shortly afterward] I went into the general practice of law where I struggled for five years building a practice completely on my own . . . but I received no satisfaction from the practice or from the struggle to establish one. I knew few lawyers who would undertake a civil rights case, and I felt that this was what I wanted to do as well as establish myself economically. So I formed a partnership with . . . [another lawyer] who felt exactly the same as I. . . . We did build a successful general practice with heavy emphasis on free work and civil liberties.

For the first few years each of us . . . received a great deal of satisfaction from what we felt we were accomplishing for ourselves [and] for our community. . . . [But] I slowly began to develop more of a practice in representing injured persons in personal injury cases, and my income increased [and] so did my guilt. . . . [Now] I no longer have any feelings of guilt about the type of legal practice in which I am engaged, but neither do I receive any satisfaction from my work as I did in the earlier years, even though then I had economic problems which I no longer face.

• • •

. . . Concerning beliefs and values, . . . I no longer feel I am the idealist I was some twenty years ago. . . . Whereas in the past I would have been the writer of a petition, or the petition circulator, I now might be the petition signer. . . .

• • •

My personal life has not been such as I would have anticipated when I was a student. I married shortly after graduation from law school, and can't even now explain why I did. . . . The hardest decision of my life was to leave [my wife], in view of the fact that we had three children . . . [but] I remarried shortly after my divorce and am very happily married now. . . .

• • •

. . . I would advise any young man today to do what he feels he wants to do and to make his own decisions in that regard. . . . It took me quite a while to see the wisdom [of this].

Source: R. W. White, M. M. Riggs, and D. C. Gilbert. *Case Workbook in Personality.* New York: Holt, Rinehart and Winston, 1976. Abridged from pages 56–60.

The Midlife Transition   At about age forty the period of early adulthood comes to an end and the midlife transition begins (see accompanying box). From about age forty to age forty-five, a man once again questions his life, but the questioning probes the past as well as the future. He may ask: "What have I done with my life?" "What have I accomplished?" "What do I still want to accomplish?" At thirty, a man primarily looks ahead toward goals, but when he enters the midlife transition, he is in a position to assess his accomplishments and to determine whether or not they have been satisfying. During this transition he begins to develop yet another life structure that will predominate during the period of middle adulthood.

The midlife transition has been the most-discussed aspect of Levinson's work. About 80 percent of the men in his sample experienced the midlife transition as a moderate to severe crisis, characterized by the questioning of virtually every aspect of their lives. But from this period of questioning a new life structure emerges. Often a successful midlife transition is accom-

A Woman at Midlife

What kinds of adjustment does a woman face in the course of her life? This autobiographical passage, written by a forty-eight-year-old woman, outlines her particular process of life adjustment. However, there is not yet enough data on the life histories of women in general to produce a developmental scheme that might apply to most or all women.

20s

I worked for eight years before I married [mostly] in an advertising agency. I liked the field, but my job was menial and not satisfying in any way. . . . I couldn't break out of the secretarial mold. . . . I was confident that if someone could pick me up and put me in an important position I could do it, but I just couldn't seem to get there on my own.

About the age of 27 I began to get depressed—when I would visit married friends with children I would come away with the keen realization that I was not the center of anyone's life—that I was not important to anyone or ones. . . .

About this time I met my husband, Don. . . . We became engaged in three weeks and married within three months. [We] share the same attitudes, interests and intensity of feeling toward these attitudes. . . . Our first marital years were stormy—problems from without and those of our own making. . . .

30s

We had three children in the first five years. . . . I guess life would have gone along as usual . . . if something tragic had not occurred to make us stop and think. Our oldest child, Paul, died suddenly at the age of seven. . . . We went through a period of grieving. [It] was the beginning of a turning point in our marital relationship, parental handling of children, outlook and actions as human beings as part of a larger society.

. . . My religious beliefs were challenged. . . . My whole faith began to shatter [but it] was slowly rebuilt, and this time had new strength because I was more mature. . . .

40s

I always knew I would go back to work. . . . I made up my mind that I would do something that was interesting. . . . I realized I would need further education. [I enrolled in] a program in community psychology. This seemed to be the direction I should go in because of my desire to work in the field of social action. I enjoyed being back in the academic atmosphere. . . . I landed a good [job]. I am project director of a senior citizens' volunteer program, and I enjoy this very much. . . .

I believe that I have more confidence in myself now [at 48]. . . . I am much crankier and more argumentative . . . [but] I think I am a happier person now than I was in college.

Source: R. W. White, M. M. Riggs, and D. C. Gilbert. *Case Workbook in Personality.* New York: Holt, Rinehart and Winston, 1976, pp. 90–103.

---

panied by the man's becoming a mentor for a younger man, which signals the attainment, in Erik Erikson's terms, of generativity rather than stagnation.

Levinson's analysis of the life structures of adult males emphasizes that development is a continuing process that requires continual adjustment. These eras and transitions can be viewed as major life events, in which the individual must adjust to the new forces that enter his life.

Crises of Adjustment for the Adult Woman

The stages of a woman's life used to be marked primarily by her capacity to reproduce. One critical stage came at puberty, marked by the onset of menstruation, and the other at menopause, marked by the end of menstruation and the capacity to bear children. Women today confront a much more complex set of possibilities and expectations. (For one woman's self-evaluation in relation to these adjustments, see the accompanying box.)

As work becomes central for more women, their crises of adjustment may come more closely to resemble those of men. However, most women now in midlife have been socialized into traditional patterns.

Career Versus Family Until recently, both men and women in industrialized societies felt that a woman's identity necessitated an either-or decision: either she was a homemaker, or she had a career outside the home. However, now that half of all women work, many are combining the roles, either simultaneously, or by moving back and forth from home to the workplace. A woman may marry young and have children, while vicariously enjoying her husband's career. Ten years later, with her children no longer demanding so much of her time and attention, she may go back to school or begin her own career. Conversely, the woman who chooses to go directly into a career may postpone marriage and children until her mid-thirties, when she may feel the desire to emphasize the nurturing side of her personality, which has been secondary up to this time. Some women do both at once, entering a career and marriage early, and taking off only a few weeks or months when a child is born. If a woman tries to do both of these things as superbly as the woman who takes on only one role at a time, she may find herself so overloaded that she takes no pleasure in either role (Sales, 1978). However, the woman who switches from one role to another must make new adjustments each time she renegotiates her decision.

Physical Attractiveness in Midlife   As we shall see in Chapter 26, the selection of a partner for courtship and marriage depends to a great extent on physical attractiveness, which is also an important factor in other aspects of social interaction. Although men in midlife are also concerned with fading attractiveness, in this culture, youth is more important to female beauty than to male beauty. Thus, as a woman ages she may need to adjust to a different image of herself. It has been shown that physical attractiveness, which eased social adjustment for college women, actually made adjustment more difficult for them twenty years later (Berscheid and Wal-

ster, 1974). This later difficulty in adjustment may not be entirely the result of lost youth; the contrast between their socially active college years and the unexciting routine of family life may have led these women to feel more dissatisfied than their less attractive schoolmates, who were neither spoiled by previous pleasures nor misled by great expectations.

The "Empty Nest" Syndrome   For some women whose lives have centered on their families, a crisis may occur as children grow up and leave home. Sometimes, when a woman finds that her role as mother has diminished, she may think, "Nobody needs me any more." When coupled with the physical changes associated with menopause, the psychological effects of the empty nest syndrome are occasionally experienced as intense depression. However, studies have shown that for most women, neither menopause nor the empty nest is experienced as a crisis, because both events are seen as normal and natural (Neugarten, 1970, 1974; Rubin, 1979). To adjust to midlife changes in herself and to changes in her family, a woman who has remained at home may search for satisfying work outside the home, possibly returning to an interrupted career or starting a new one. A warm relationship with her husband can provide important support as a woman adjusts to her changing situation.

As this discussion has made clear, the life cycle creates stress that requires adjustment among both men and women. Yet once an adjustment to developmental stress has been made—whether "good" or "bad"—no one has achieved a steady state that will continue throughout life. Adjustment is a process that never ceases and that is more or less successful at various times as we develop new ways of coping with the stress of life in today's world.

SUMMARY

1. **Adjustment** is a continuous and ever-changing process of interacting with the people, events, and forces that create stress in our lives. **Stress** can be either any stimulus that places a strain on our capacity to adjust or the internal response to a disruptive situation. Attempts to cope with difficult situations tend to fall into three major categories: problem-solving skills, acceptance, and defense mechanisms.

2. Stress is not always undesirable, because it involves the body's response to pleasure as well as to pain. However, if stress is severe or prolonged, it can take a harsh toll on the body. According to Selye, the body's reac-

tions to stress pass through three stages: alarm, resistance, and exhaustion. If the initial phase of alarm is overwhelming, death can follow, although this is not common. In the second stage of resistance, the **stress syndrome** appears: enlarged adrenal glands, shrunken thymus and lymph nodes, and ulcerated stomach. If the body's defenses do not conquer stress at this stage, the third stage of exhaustion can set in and unchecked stress can lead to death.

3. Prolonged stress is associated with most diseases, and psychological stress is more likely than muscular overload to lead to disease. Although major life events seem to precipitate illness, the combined effect of numerous minor events may have a similar effect. Holmes and Rahe's Social Readjustment Rating Scale indicates a correlation between cumulative stress and many disorders, including heart disease, fractures, and the onset of cancer in children. Loneliness appears to increase the effects of stress, and social support can help individuals adapt to stressful events. Personality patterns can affect both the amount of stress a person experiences and the course of physical illness. People who show **Type A behavior** are highly competitive, hostile when thwarted, and seem always to be working against time; they also are more likely to develop heart disease than the relaxed, unpressured Type Bs. The relationship between stressful events and physical illness may be explained by Schwartz's **disregulation model,** which suggests that physical disorders arise when the body's internal systems, which are regulated by negative feedback, fail to operate properly. The regulatory systems can go awry at one or more of four stages: environmental demands, information processing in the central nervous system, a peripheral organ, or in the negative feedback process itself.

4. Environmental stress nearly always takes the form of aversive events, and research has shown that such unpleasant events produce less stress when they can be predicted and controlled. **Learned helplessness** is the acquired belief that one cannot exert any control over the environment. Helplessness learned in one situation can be carried to another. People are likely to become helpless when they see their lack of control as due to

causes that are (a) permanent rather than temporary; (b) internal rather than external; and (c) applicable to many areas of their life. However, learned helplessness cannot explain why some people attribute inescapable aversive events to an environmental factor whereas others blame themselves. Leading older people to perceive that they had control over their lives resulted in increased activity and happiness and to significantly lower death rates among residents of a nursing home for the aged. When a situation is truly uncontrollable, the most adaptive behavior is acceptance.

5. A number of techniques have been developed that make it possible to modify physiological and cognitive responses to stress, thereby lessening its effects. In **progressive relaxation,** developed by Jacobson, people tense and then relax muscle groups in sequence, thereby learning to discriminate patterns of muscle tension from those of relaxation. Progressive relaxation effectively reduces tension and anxiety, relieves insomnia, and reduces high blood pressure. **Autogenic training,** developed by Schultz and Luthe, induces relaxation by self-suggestion and imagery. Like progressive relaxation, autogenic training is effective in treating insomnia. It is also used in conjunction with biofeedback, in which a continuous flow of information about bodily processes allows people to learn how to control them. Biofeedback has been used to reduce high blood pressure, control the development of ulcers, reduce the frequency and intensity of epileptic seizures, control tension and migraine headaches, and restore functioning to paralyzed muscles. Other effective means of reducing response to stress involve cognitive restructuring, which changes a person's perception of stress.

6. Adjustment is a lifelong process, and each stage of life has its own particular demands. In adolescence, problems result from biological changes and personality development, and adolescents face the task of separating themselves psychologically from their parents and establishing their own identities. As more women focus on careers, stress patterns in the two sexes may become more nearly alike. Today, however, according to Levinson the **life structures** of men are composed of three major eras: early adulthood, middle adult-

hood, and late adulthood, with transition points between each of these eras. Early adulthood is characterized by the conflict between a need to explore options and a need to establish a stable life structure. Later male patterns include a reexamination of many choices made during the twenties, a settling-down period, and a midlife questioning of past activities and future plans that leads to a new life structure in middle adulthood.

Women must decide whether to go immediately into a career, to begin with marriage and a family, or to attempt both roles simultaneously. Diminished youthful attractiveness in midlife may require more adjustment in women than in men. Some women whose lives have been exclusively devoted to their families may experience the "empty nest syndrome" when their children grow up and leave home.

KEY TERMS

adjustment
autogenic training
disregulation model

learned helplessness
life structure
progressive relaxation

stress
stress syndrome
Type A behavior

RECOMMENDED READINGS

CALHOUN, J. F., and J. R. ACOCELLA. *Psychology of Adjustment and Human Relationships*. 2nd ed. New York: Random House, 1983. This is a textbook, but it is also a very practical guide to problem solving. The authors present psychological principles relevant to the process of adjustment, and they provide clear illustrations of how the principles may be applied.

GLASS, D. C., and J. E. SINGER. *Urban Stress: Experiments on Noise and Social Stressors*. New York: Academic, 1972. Glass and Singer devised a number of incisive laboratory studies designed to explore the psychological impact of urban stress. This book is a summary of those studies.

HENDERSON, J. *The Long Run Solution*. Mountain View, Calif.: World Publications, 1976. Henderson describes the psychological benefits of long, slow running and offers the reader very practical advice about how to start a program of running and stay with it.

KUTASH, I. L., L. B. SCHLESINGER, and ASSOCIATES (eds.). *Handbook on Stress and Anxiety*. New York: Jossey-Bass, 1980. This book contains contributed chapters from the major theorists and researchers in stress and anxiety.

LEVINSON, D. J. *The Seasons of a Man's Life*. New York: Knopf, 1978. This is the long-awaited report of Levinson's research on stages of development in adult males. On the basis of intensive interviews with forty men from four different occupational groups, Levinson proposes a model of the stages, crises, and transitions experienced by most men.

SELIGMAN, M. E. P. *Helplessness*. San Francisco: Freeman, 1975. Seligman has done pioneering work in the area of learned helplessness. This is his summary of the determinants and consequences of learned helplessness in a variety of species, including humans.

SELYE, H. *Stress Without Distress*. Philadelphia: Lippincott, 1974. This is a highly readable book by one of the pioneers in stress research. It contains his suggestions for how to live in a pressure-ridden society.

ZIMBARDO, P. G. *Shyness: What It Is, What to Do About It*. Reading, Mass.: Addison-Wesley, 1977. In this engagingly written, nontechnical examination of the causes and possible cures of shyness, Zimbardo documents the prevalence of shyness and offers suggestions for overcoming it.

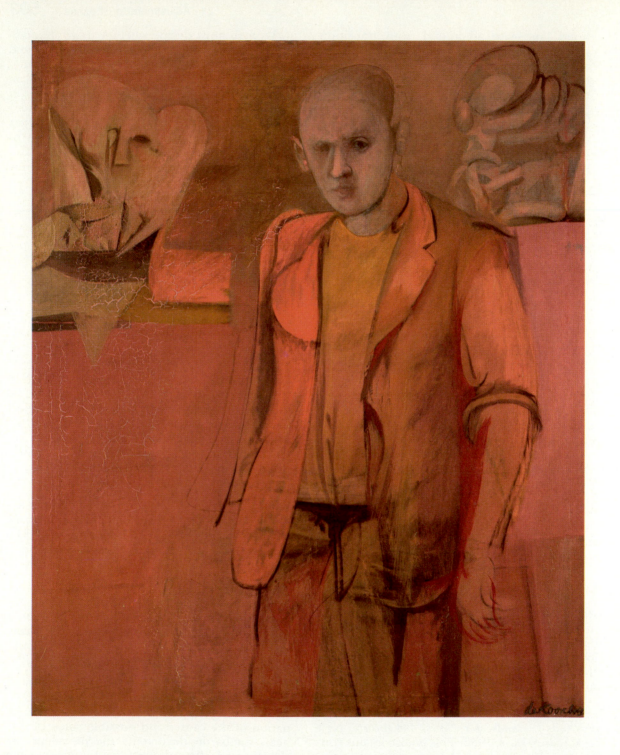

CHAPTER 22

Psychological Disorders

A scantily clad woman staggers toward you. She is soaked with perspiration, her lips are flecked with foam, her face is contorted, and she can barely speak. If you met this woman in an art gallery, you might think her mad. But if you were standing at the finish line of the Boston marathon, you would probably applaud her courage and endurance. A man invites his friends and neighbors to a party, where he gives them all of his possessions, thus making himself a pauper. Most of us would consider him demented, yet when this same behavior takes place at a ceremony called the potlatch, it elicits respect and admiration among the members of Native American tribes in the Pacific Northwest. Behavior that appears abnormal in one context can seem perfectly ordinary in another situation. Given such widely different interpretations of the same actions, can we say with any confidence when behavior is abnormal?

Definitions of Abnormality

In medicine "abnormality" generally refers to a lack of integrity in any organ's structure or function. A broken bone, an excess of certain sugars in the blood, an ulcer on the wall of the stomach—all are abnormal. For physicians, the line between normality and abnormality is relatively easy to draw. For psychologists and psychiatrists, however, the criteria that divide normal behavior from abnormal behavior are not easily specified, and several definitions of abnormality are used, each based on a different theoretical orientation. As we shall see, there are several ways of defining psychological abnormality, and some of these definitions may change from one society to another and from time to time in the same society.

Norm Violation

Each society has a set of **norms**—rules that prescribe "right" and "wrong" behavior—by which its members live. These norms cover every aspect of life, from whom one may marry and when to what food may be eaten and where. In American society, scantily clad, sweat-soaked women who attend art galleries and men who give away all their possessions have violated cultural norms.

Since norms are absorbed in childhood during the process of socialization, people take them for granted. Although nearly every one of their actions is governed by some norm, people notice a norm only when it is broken—and if the violation is bizarre, they label the violator as abnormal. Thus, the man without a jacket who enters an expensive restaurant will be loaned one by the management, the barefooted person who enters will be turned away, but the person who comes in naked will be arrested and will probably receive a psychiatric examination.

Norms change over the years, sometimes gradually and almost imperceptibly, but at other times the change is accompanied by friction. For example, one aim of the Gay Liberation Movement is to convince society to change its norms so that homosexuality is regarded as normal behavior. Despite loud resistance from certain sections of society, these attempts have had some success and reflect the fact that American definitions of normality have broadened over the past few decades—especially in regard to sexual conduct. As a result, the range of behavior that is considered abnormal has shrunk somewhat.

Since norms can change drastically, they may seem an inappropriate basis for the definition of normality. Yet they remain the dominant standard because they have been so deeply absorbed that they seem natural, right, and proper and violations automatically seem abnormal. Norms may even be grounded in the evolutionary history of the species. Since a social group cannot exist without some kind of norms, their development may have some survival value. A danger in using only norms to define abnormality is that they may enforce conformity as "good" and mark the nonconformist as automatically "bad."

Statistical Abnormality

A related, but somewhat different, way of defining abnormality is to call it any substantial deviation from a statistically calculated average. People whose behavior conforms with that of the majority are considered normal; those whose behavior differs greatly are abnormal. This statistical definition automatically encompasses norm violators, because the majority of people follow cultural norms.

The greatest attraction of the statistical definition of abnormality is its simplicity, and it continues to be used in some areas of psychological functioning. For example, the diagnosis of mental retardation is in large part statistical: people whose scores on intelligence tests fall below the range established as average are considered retarded.

Although a statistical definition of abnormality does make such diagnoses simple, this view of psychological functioning also has problems. Using statistics to define the bounds of normality leaves us without any way to distinguish between the desirable differences of genius and creativity and the undesirable difference of psychological disorder. Indeed, "average" human behavior may not be the sort that society would like to encourage. In one study of New Yorkers, 75 percent were considered psychologically disturbed (Srole et al., 1962). If we were to apply a statistical yardstick, people without symptoms of psychological disturbance would be considered abnormal.

Personal Discomfort

A less restrictive approach to the definition of abnormality than either norm violation or statistical rarity is that of personal discomfort, in which people judge their own normality and only those who are distressed by their own thoughts or behavior are considered abnormal. This approach is now being used by many psychologists and psychiatrists in regard to homosexuality, and the diagnosis of psychological disorder is reserved for homosexuals who are seriously unhappy with their sexual preference (American Psychiatric Association, 1980).

This approach allows genius to flourish, encourages harmless eccentricities, and gives no problem in the case of homosexuals. However, like other definitions of abnormality, the criterion of personal discomfort has its problems. Identical behavior patterns can make one person miserable and bother another only a little—or not at all, so that limiting the definition to personal discomfort leaves us no yardstick for evaluating that behavior. In addition, when behavior harms other people or disrupts society, personal contentment is not a sufficient measure of normality. For example, some rapists and murderers may be perfectly content with their way of life, and a man's delusion that he has an enormous fortune might make him happy but is likely to disrupt the lives of the people with whom he transacts business.

Impairment of Functioning

An approach to abnormality that overlaps somewhat with personal discomfort is impairment of functioning. If a person cannot keep a job, maintain relationships with family or friends, or get out of bed, most people would agree that she or he shows some psychological disturbance. In

Unable to cope with the demands of a job and the tasks of life, severely disturbed people may live in the streets, as this "bag lady" does.

most instances, the accompanying personal distress may lead the individual to seek professional help. This is not always the case, and a severely impaired person may not recognize the problem. When people cannot hold a coherent conversation or handle the simple tasks of living, however, the diagnosis of abnormality can be made by an outsider. Although this approach may work fairly well with people who are completely out of touch with reality, many people who might be considered disordered by themselves or others may show only a slight impairment in their social or occupational functioning.

Deviation from an Ideal

A fourth way of defining abnormality is to set up a description of the ideal well-adjusted personal-

ity—such as that proposed by Carl Rogers (see Chapter 19)—and to regard as abnormal people who deviate from that ideal in any serious way. This sort of definition leaves most of us in the abnormal category, for few people ever achieve this ideal adjustment, no matter how hard they try.

Deviation from the ideal is also an imperfect guideline in our search for a definition of abnormality. This approach leads people who seem to be functioning adequately and who show no serious symptoms of disorder to regard themselves as disturbed and in need of therapy. For example, a woman with many friends and a bright career may seek psychotherapy because she lacks an intense, intimate relationship or because she feels that she is not self-actualized—both standards of adjustment in various theories. Such pursuit of ideal adjustment can make people feel seriously inadequate, when they are only imperfect human beings. In addition, since the definition of the ideal personality is as culture bound and relative as social norms, it is just as weak a foundation as norms for the diagnosis of abnormality.

Thus, although we have five ways of defining abnormal behavior, no one of them encompasses all behavior that might be termed abnormal. Depending upon the type of disorder, different standards may be applied by the legal system, by therapists, and by ordinary citizens. Although we can reach high levels of agreement about clearly abnormal behavior, strong disagreements still exist. One instance of the problems inherent in applying the label of abnormality is shown in the box on the following page.

Classification of Abnormal Behavior

Attempts to understand abnormal behavior have led to its classification into various categories. The generally accepted classification is that provided by the American Psychiatric Association: the third (1980) revision of the *Diagnostic and Statistical Manual of Mental Disorders,* commonly called *DSM-III,* which consists of highly detailed descriptions of virtually all known forms of psychological disturbances. The *DSM-III* is meant to assist psychiatrists, psychologists, counselors, and psychiatric social workers in diagnosing pa-

On Being Sane in Insane Places

The problem of separating the sane from the insane was brought into sharp focus by David Rosenhan (1973), a psychologist who tested the adequacy of our diagnostic methods by getting psychologically stable people with no history of mental disorder admitted to mental hospitals. As Rosenhan has pointed out, normal people often lose their tempers for no good reason, become anxious at times, are temporarily depressed, or find it difficult to get along with certain people. Similarly, "insane" people often have long periods of lucidity when they behave in an apparently normal fashion.

In Rosenhan's study, three psychologists, a psychiatrist, a graduate student in psychology, a pediatrician, a painter, and a housewife presented themselves at mental hospitals in five different states. Except for lying about any connections they had with the mental health establishment and adopting fictitious names, all gave accurate histories. However, each added one false detail, claiming that she or he heard voices that seemed to say something like "hollow," "empty," or "thud."

All eight people were promptly admitted as patients, and all except one were diagnosed as schizophrenic. Once they were admitted, the pseudo-patients never again referred to the phantom voices and behaved in a completely normal fashion. Yet not one of them was exposed as a fraud. Although nurses, doctors, and attendants were easy to fool, the other patients were not. They accused the pseudo-patients of being sane and charged them with being journalists or professionals who were investigating the hospital.

Each of the patients was discharged after stays of seven to fifty-two days, with an average stay of nineteen days. Upon discharge, they were classified as having psychosis "in remission"; in other words, they were still insane and their psychotic symptoms might reappear.

In evaluating his study, Rosenhan concludes that we are unable to distinguish between sanity and insanity with any sort of accuracy. He charges that the pseudo-patients' normality was not detected because a psychiatric diagnosis distorts all future evaluations of a patient, making it impossible for mental health professionals to see the person except in the role of "schizophrenic" or whatever label she or he has received. Since in this study the pseudo-patients had been admitted to the hospital, the staff simply assumed that they were indeed disturbed. As a result, Rosenhan believes that we do not know how to distinguish the sane from the insane.

His conclusion has been contested by other researchers. For example, Robert Spitzer (1976), a psychiatrist who participated in the development of DSM-III, argues that neither the pseudo-patients' ability to get themselves admitted nor the inability of the staff to detect their normality after admission proves that the diagnostic system is invalid. Hallucination is ordinarily a sign of severe psychological disturbance, and the admitting staff had no reason to question the pseudo-patients' original statements. In addition, the subsequent absence of hallucination gave the staff no reason to assume that their pseudo-patients were "sane." People are diagnosed on the basis of past as well as present behavior, and to discount a symptom because it had not appeared for a few weeks would be extremely careless. As Spitzer points out, the short hospital stays of these pseudo-patients shows that the staff responded rapidly to the "patients'" failure to produce further symptoms. And their release "in remission" is a rare diagnosis that suggests that their insanity was recognized as atypical, if not faked.

One conclusion from the Rosenhan study is clear: psychiatric diagnoses are powerful and should be applied with the greatest care.

tients' disorders so that they can be effectively treated. The *DSM-III* is tied to the **medical model** of abnormal behavior, which views psychological problems in the same way as it views physical problems—as diseases with specific symptoms, causes, predictable courses, and treatments. However, *DSM-III* does not assume that these disorders have a biological cause. Instead, it merely describes mental disorders as fully as possible, without speculating about causes. As we shall see, there is widespread disagreement over the idea of assessing and categorizing abnormal behavior, and the use of the medical model is especially controversial.

Advantages of Classification

By enabling us to communicate about mental disorders, the classification of abnormal behavior has major advantages in both treatment and the advancement of knowledge. To treat a disorder, we have to be able to talk about it, hence the importance of *DSM-III*'s provision of a special language for behavioral disorders. This classification system sorts abnormal behavior into various categories, describing each in detail and giving it a label, such as "schizophrenia" or "bipolar disorder" or "phobia." After comparing a patient's behavior with the various descriptions, a psychologist or psychiatrist names the patient's problem by attaching the label that most closely describes it. If we can describe an individual's problem accurately, we are more likely to be able to predict the future course of her or his behavior and to decide on the appropriate treatment.

In addition, a classification system makes advancement of knowledge about various disorders possible. Indeed, without it research would be well-nigh impossible since researchers would have no way of sorting out the vast array of disordered behavior. By having an agreed-upon label for each distinguishable disorder, researchers and clinicians can exchange information about research findings and clinical experience. An accurate system of diagnosis greatly increases the chances of identifying the causes of various disorders and designing appropriate treatments for them.

Criticisms of Psychiatric Diagnosis

Some theorists feel that the use of terminology based on the medical model is a serious error, because it labels people as "sick," removes them from normal life for treatment in a "hospital," and often maintains or even creates bizarre behavior. Call people "sick" and treat them accordingly, say some social scientists, and they will act out the role that is expected of them. In the view of some critics, abnormal behavior is not an illness but a "problem in living" (Szasz, 1961).

A second criticism of the practice of classifying abnormal behavior is that our labels give the illusion of explanation. To say that a man is highly suspicious because he is paranoid leads us to believe that we understand the cause of his actions. In reality, all the label does is to describe a pattern of behavior—a collection of symptoms whose cause is unknown.

A third criticism of such labels is that they stigmatize people. The label itself can intensify a person's problems by disrupting personal relationships, leading to the termination of employment or making it impossible to get a job, and depriving the person of civil rights. As noted in the criticism of the medical model, the patient may also accept the label and adopt the role of mental patient. In addition, the label creates expectations on the part of mental health professionals, as the accompanying box indicates.

Finally, diagnosis has been criticized because of its unreliability. When examined by two different professionals, a patient may receive two different diagnoses, being called schizophrenic by one and depressive by the other. With the publication of *DSM-III*, this criticism is no longer as valid as it once was. *DSM-III* has provided a highly specific set of criteria for each disorder—something that was missing from earlier editions of the manual—and makes no attempt to ascribe causes of disorders unless they have been definitely established.

Despite the difficulty of defining abnormality and the problems involved in psychiatric diagnosis, some sort of classification system is necessary, and the *DSM-III* is the most practical system yet devised. In fact, our classification system is not so far off the mark as some critics indicate, for some of the same patterns of psychopathology occur around the world, in both highly industrialized and extremely isolated cultures (Murphy, 1976; Draguns, 1980).

This chapter follows the classification system used in *DSM-III*. One notable consequence of doing so is that the term "neurosis" has been discarded as a diagnostic label. In the view of psychoanalytic theorists, **neurosis** is any condition in which a person develops some maladaptive behavior as a protection against unconscious anxiety. **Psychosis** is reserved for conditions in which the person's perceptions of reality are highly distorted. As a result, psychoanalysts grouped all disorders they saw as characterized by anxiety—whether the anxiety was apparent or not—into the single category of neurotic disorders. However, the diagnostic manual is intended for use by mental health professionals of all theoretical persuasions, so the use of a term that has come to imply a psychoanalytic interpretation is not appropriate. Moreover, a number of criticisms have been leveled at the assertion that anxiety is the chief characteristic by which neurotic disorders might be classified together: (1) anxiety has actually been observed in only a few of the so-called neuroses; (2) anxiety is difficult to measure accurately and thus is an unreliable standard for diagnosis; and (3) anxiety is a universal emotion, experienced to some degree not only by neurotics but also by normal people, psychotics, depressives, and sexual deviants (Nathan et al., 1969).

In this chapter, following the format of *DSM-III*, we will discuss anxiety disorders, somatoform disorders, and dissociative disorders as independent categories.

Anxiety Disorders

Anxiety is a feeling of dread, apprehension, or fear. It is accompanied by physiological arousal, manifested as increased heart rate, perspiration, muscle tension, and rapid breathing. Anxiety also affects cognition, throwing the individual into a state of confusion and making it difficult to think clearly or to solve problems.

As we noted above, virtually everyone experiences anxiety at one time or another. Without mild anxiety, bills would not get paid on time, term papers would not get written, drivers would not slow down on foggy mornings, and people would not get medical checkups. In addition, most people have difficulty in coping with some area of their lives. One person may worry about getting cancer at the first symptoms of a sore throat; another may be afraid to make decisions; a third may become tongue-tied in social situations; a fourth may have difficulty spending money. For most of us, such hang-ups do not severely limit activities or interfere with daily life. If we wish, we can adjust our routines to avoid situations that we find difficult. We can turn down a high-pressure job that would make us anxious or take the bus if flying makes us nervous. While some inconvenience is involved in these evasions, life is still livable.

For some people, however, one situation—or many—becomes a major source of anxiety, taking up more and more time and attention. Anxiety becomes so severe or so persistent that it interferes with everyday functioning—family life, social activities, and work or school. This condition is classified as an **anxiety disorder**.

Generalized Anxiety Disorder and Panic Disorder

Generalized anxiety disorder is characterized by diffuse and generalized anxiety that is impossible to manage by avoiding specific situations. The whole personality may be engulfed by anxiety, and the person is jumpy, irritable, and frequently upset. Although the person with a generalized anxiety disorder expresses a great many fears and worries, she or he cannot specify what is generating these fears—a condition that Freud called **free-floating anxiety.**

Individuals in this condition often show motor tension: they may be jumpy, complain of aching muscles, tire easily, and find it impossible to relax. Their autonomic nervous system is overactive, and they often complain of cold, clammy hands, a racing heart, dizziness, indigestion or diarrhea, and a frequent need to urinate. Such people also expect the worst to happen. They may fear that they will faint or lose control of themselves or worry that members of their family will develop some disease or be hit by a car. Because they are so apprehensive about the future, they become extremely attentive. This eternal vigilance may make them irritable or impatient, and they may find it difficult to concentrate or to fall asleep. In the morning they feel tired rather than relaxed.

From time to time people suffering from generalized anxiety may have **panic attacks,** episodes in which the already heightened state of tension mounts to an acute and overwhelming level. Usually these attacks last anywhere from fifteen minutes to an hour. Individuals may report a shivering sensation. The heart begins to pound loudly, perspiration flows, and breathing becomes difficult. A feeling of inescapable disaster overcomes them. They try to escape, but no place offers safety. When the attack subsides, they are exhausted. When no specific stimulus precedes the panic attack, it is called a **panic disorder.** Sometimes, however, panic attacks come in response to a specific stimulus, in which case they are classified as phobias.

Phobic Disorder

When anxiety is irrationally centered on a particular object or situation, it is called a **phobia.** The focus of anxiety may be a stimulus that is slightly dangerous, such as snakes, dogs, elevators, or high places, or it may be some situation that car-

People with a generalized anxiety disorder may feel threatened by environmental stimuli that would not bother other people. Being surrounded by mirrors, for example, may prove so disorienting that a panic attack results.

ries no danger at all, such as a fear of being alone or of being in public places where escape might be difficult (see Figure 22.1). This fear, called agoraphobia, is the most common phobia among people seeking treatment and can utterly disrupt an individual's life. A person who suffers from agoraphobia is likely to have a panic attack in any public place, so that she or he may become a virtual prisoner, afraid to leave the safety of home.

Phobias sometimes develop after an initial association of fear with some stimulus. For example, one woman developed an automobile phobia after being a passenger in a car that was struck broadside by a truck that ran a red light (Wolpe, 1973). After spending a week in the hospital with knee and neck injuries, the woman felt frightened while being driven home. Within a few weeks, she became extremely anxious in a car whenever another vehicle approached from either side, and her panic became severe when the car she was in made a left turn in front of approaching traffic. She was also anxious when walking across streets, even when the traffic light was in her favor and the nearest car was a block away.

Phobias have two somewhat distinct effects. First, there is the anxiety associated with the

Figure 22.1 An artist's representation of three phobias: (A) fear of heights, called acrophobia; (B) fear of enclosed spaces, called claustrophobia; and (C) fear of dirt, called mysophobia. (After Vassos, 1931.)

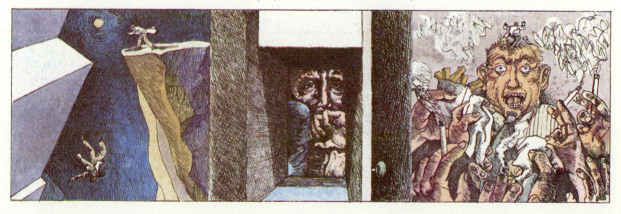

phobia and the consequent avoidance of situations in which the feared object will be present. Second, there are the complications in a person's daily life, which must be rearranged to accommodate the phobia—a maneuver that requires time and trouble. If the person feels guilty or ashamed of the phobia, as some do, there is the additional effort of hiding the phobia from others, so that the anxiety connected with the feared object is compounded by the fear of being found out.

Obsessive-Compulsive Disorder

An **obsession** is an involuntary, irrational thought that occurs repeatedly. An obsession may be mild, as in those instances when we cannot stop wondering whether we remembered to turn off a faucet or lock a door before leaving home. In some cases, however, an obsession becomes so persistent that it markedly interferes with daily life. Severe obsessions often have a violent or sexual quality to them, such as the desire to burn down the house or rape a neighbor, which makes the person feel guilty and horrified as much by the content of the thought as by its persistence.

A **compulsion** is an action that a person uncontrollably performs again and again, although she or he has no conscious desire to do so. The act is often senseless, such as looking under the bed several times before going to sleep or locking and unlocking the door several times before going out. There are two general categories of compulsions: checking rituals, such as looking under the bed; and contamination compulsions, such as hand washing (Rachman et al., 1973). A person may show little anxiety when carrying out a compulsion. However, if she or he is prevented from carrying out the compulsive ritual, the person becomes extremely anxious.

Such ritual behavior is often both obsessive and compulsive. Constant hand washing, for example, may be caused by an obsessive preoccupation with germs. Although we all can remember times when a song lyric ran persistently through our minds, no matter what we did to get rid of it, or when we checked several times to make sure that the alarm clock was set, these minor obsessions and compulsions pass. A pathological obsession or compulsion continues—day after day, year after year.

Somatoform Disorders

The distinguishing feature of **somatoform disorders** is the persistence of symptoms that have a somatic or physical form, but in which there is no physiological malfunction. Somatoform disorders are quite different from psychosomatic ailments like those discussed in Chapter 21, in which psychological factors, such as stress, cause or complicate actual physiological disease. Thus, a person in a stressful situation who develops ulcers does not suffer from a somatoform disorder. Two typical somatoform disorders are hypchondriasis and conversion disorders.

Hypochondriasis

Hypochondriasis is the preoccupation with bodily symptoms as possible signs of serious illness. Although the hypochondriac is perfect healthy, she or he lives with the conviction that cancer, heart disease, diabetes, or some other particular disorder is about to develop. Hypochondriacs do not imagine their symptoms, but each vagrant twinge or cramp, each headache, each skipped heartbeat, is taken as a sign that major disease has struck. The hypochondriac is likely to read everything in the popular press concerning health, to adopt strenuous health routines, or to consume vast quantities of vitamins and other medicines. Since physicians generally give them a clean bill of health, hypochondriacs change doctors frequently, looking for one who will confirm their own dire diagnoses.

Conversion Disorders

In **conversion disorders**, which were mentioned in Chapter 18, an individual develops some physical dysfunction—such as blindness, deafness, paralysis, or loss of sensation in some part of the body—that has no organic basis and apparently expresses some psychological conflict. Although no medical evidence supports these afflictions, they are not under a person's voluntary control. For example, a hand might become completely numb, as in "glove anesthesia," but sensation might be clearly felt in an area directly above the wrist (see Figure 22.2). If the numbness were actually a result of neurological dysfunction, the line between sensitivity and

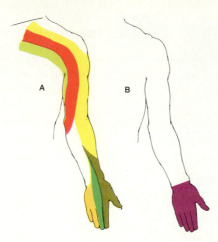

Figure 22.2 A patient who complained to a doctor that his right hand had become numb might be diagnosed either as suffering from damage to the nervous system or as a neurotic suffering from hysteria, depending on the exact pattern of his numbness. The skin areas served by different nerves in the arm are shown in A. The "glove anesthesia" shown in B could not result from damage to these nerves.

numbness would not be so clear-cut. Such symptoms often appear or disappear suddenly. Many "miraculous cures" in which patients who have been paralyzed suddenly leave their wheelchairs and walk, or people who have been blind suddenly are able to see again, come about because the original dysfunction was the result of a conversion disorder.

There is, however, a major diagnostic problem in distinguishing between some conversion disorders and the early stages of actual neurological disease. In fact, many people who are diagnosed as having a conversion disorder are later found to have developed neurological disorders. For example, a group of 122 patients were followed, half of them diagnosed as having conversion disorders and the other half as having anxiety or depression disorders. At the subsequent examination, more than 60 percent of the patients diagnosed as having conversion disorders had developed signs of organic brain disorder, as compared with only 5 percent of the patients with anxiety or depression (Whitlock, 1967).

Dissociative Disorders

As the name implies, **dissociative disorders** designate the dissociation, or splitting off, of certain kinds of behavior that are normally integrated. Among the dissociative disorders are amnesia, fugue, and multiple personality.

Amnesia is the partial or total loss of memory concerning past experiences, such as an automobile accident or a battle. Psychogenic amnesia can be differentiated from organic amnesia in several ways. It appears suddenly, often following severe stress, and disappears just as suddenly. It is selective in nature. And the forgotten material can often be recovered under hypnosis.

The dissociative disorder called **fugue** ("flight") is related to amnesia. Individuals in a fugue state flee from the home as well as the self. They may be absent for days or months or years and may take up a totally new life, later recalling nothing of what happened while they were in the fugue state.

A rare and extreme form of dissociation is **multiple personality,** a division into two or more complete behavior organizations, each as well-defined and highly distinct from the others as the two personalities of the main character in Robert Louis Stevenson's story *The Strange Case of Dr. Jekyll and Mr. Hyde.* Two actual cases of multiple personality, *The Three Faces of Eve* and *Sybil,* have been widely publicized in films and books, but the disorder is so rare that fewer than 100 cases have been reported (Rycroft, 1978). Cases of multiple personality often seem to involve personalities that take extreme forms: one personality may be conformist and "nice," while the other is rebellious and "naughty." Multiple personalities seem to be exaggerations of the normal conflicts we all have. Since multiple personality is sometimes called "split personality," it is often erroneously confused with schizophrenia, because the word "schizophrenia" comes from Greek words for "to split" and "mind." Schizophrenia, as we shall see, refers to a separation of ideas, emotions, and perceptions within a single person—not to the development of separate personalities.

Major Affective Disorders

Affective disorders are characterized by disturbances of mood. Everyone is subject to mood

In dreams, we often experience physical states that are impossible to achieve while awake. Severely disturbed people may experience delusions or hallucinations which they believe are real.

changes, and emotional response, or **affect**, is usually influenced by a change in the environment. A promotion on the job or the resolution of a difficult love affair can bring elation; the death of a close relative or a letter of rejection from graduate school can induce depression. Occasionally feelings of unhappiness or extreme pleasure arise for no apparent reason. These variations in mood are normal, but—depending on their intensity and duration—moods can become abnormal. Depression is a matter of concern when it is so exaggerated as to interrupt normal functioning and to cause psychic discomfort. Fluctuation of mood is labeled "psychotic" when emotional responses are exaggerated and inappropriate, often including **delusions**, irrational beliefs that are maintained despite overwhelming evidence that they have no basis in reality, or **hallucinations**, spontaneous sensory perceptions—usually of sounds—that are unrelated to external stimuli. In such cases the disturbance of mood may severely interfere with functioning and cause an individual to lose touch with reality. Two major affective disorders are major depression and bipolar disorder.

Major Depression

All of us have had periods of sadness or disappointment, and perhaps have suffered from feelings of guilt, loss of appetite, and lack of sexual interest. Usually such feelings are experienced in response to a negative situation in our lives: the loss of a job, an argument with a friend, a poor mark on an exam. Sometimes the upset comes for no apparent reason; it seems as if we just "got up on the wrong side of the bed." These symptoms of normal depression do not differ in kind from abnormal, or major depression, but they do differ drastically in degree.

Major depression consists of one or more major depressive episodes with no intervening episodes in which people feel extremely elated or unnaturally euphoric. The course of a major depressive episode often follows a fairly smooth curve with a gradual onset, taking weeks or months to appear, lasting for several months, then ending as it began, slowly and gradually.

A person in a major depressive episode shows radical changes in mood, motivation, thinking, and physical and motor functioning. During such an episode a person's behavior shows the following characteristics: *depressed mood,* which may be described as utter despair, loneliness, or simply boredom; *feelings of worthlessness and guilt,* in which the individual sees her- or himself as lacking intelligence, physical attractiveness, health, or social skills—whatever attributes the person values most; *reduced motivation,* in which interest and pleasure vanish from formerly valued activities;

disturbances of appetite, sleep, and sex drive, in which a person either cannot eat or sleep or else eats and sleeps to excess, and almost invariably loses interest in sex; *psychomotor retardation or agitation,* in which people commonly seem overcome by fatigue and move slowly and deliberately or else become agitated, wring the hands, pace, fidget, or moan incessantly; *reduced energy,* so that the person feels exhausted all the time; *difficulties in thinking,* in which cognitive processes slow and there is difficulty in thinking, concentrating, and remembering; and *recurrent thoughts of death or suicide,* which sometimes do culminate in suicide.

Some of these characteristics of major depression are illustrated in the following patient's description:

I began not to be able to manage as far as doing the kinds of things that I really had always been able to do easily, such as cook, wash, take care of the children, play games, that kind of thing. One of the most . . . I think one of the most frightening aspects at the beginning was that time went so slowly. It would seem sometimes that at least an hour had gone by and I would look at my watch and it would only have been three minutes. And I began not to be able to concentrate. Another thing that was very frightening to me was that I couldn't read any more. And if awakened early . . . earlier than I needed to, I sometimes would lie in bed two hours trying to make myself get up because I just couldn't put my feet on the floor. Then when I did, I just felt that I couldn't get dressed. And then, whatever the next step was, I felt I couldn't do that. (Educational Broadcasting Corporation, 1975)

Such severe depression is a major health problem, with about 20 percent of women and 10 percent of men having at least one major depressive episode during their lives. In 6 percent of women and 3 percent of men, the episode is severe enough to require hospitalization (American Psychiatric Association, 1980). Depression is also the most frequent problem seen in outpatient psychiatric clinics, where it accounts for one-third of all patients (Woodruff et al., 1975).

Bipolar Disorder

Although patients with bipolar disorder have depressive episodes, they also have manic epi-

sodes, periods of intense, unrealistic elation. **Bipolar disorder** is characterized by the episodic nature of these extreme moods. The first sign of bipolar disorder is almost always a manic episode of intense euphoria, excitement, and activity; this is followed by a depressive episode. A person in a manic episode shows an *elevated mood,* composed of euphoria mixed with irritability; *hyperactivity,* in physical, social, occupational, and often sexual functioning; *sleeplessness,* without any decrease in energy; *talkativeness,* with loud, rapid, and continual speech; *flight of ideas and distractibility,* with racing thoughts that abruptly switch from one topic to another; *inflated self-esteem,* in which people see themselves as extremely attractive, important, and powerful; *reckless behavior,* including buying sprees, reckless driving, careless business investments, and sexual indiscretions; and *irritability,* which in some cases overcomes the euphoria. Episodes in bipolar disorder are generally briefer and more frequent than the major depressive episodes of depressive disorders.

Bipolar disorders are much less common than major depression. When bipolar disorder develops, the onset usually takes place before the person is thirty years old. This disorder affects both

Major depression leaves a person feeling unable to do tasks as simple as washing dishes or clearing a table.

sexes equally, unlike depression, which is twice as common among women. There appears to be a genetic link in both these affective disorders. Patients with bipolar disorders often have relatives with bipolar disorders, and patients with major depression often have relatives who have suffered depression (Winokur, 1973).

Schizophrenia

Schizophrenia is a group of disorders characterized by thought disturbance that may be accompanied by delusions, hallucinations, attention deficits, and bizarre motor activity. It is a **psychotic disorder**, one that is characterized by a generalized failure of functioning in all areas of a person's life. Schizophrenia was originally called *dementia praecox,* or "premature mental deterioration" by Emil Kraepelin (1902), who devised the first comprehensive classification system for mental disorder. Kraepelin believed that such behavior was due to a disease of mental deterioration that began in adolescence. Ten years later, however, the Swiss psychiatrist Eugen Bleuler pointed out that many patients displaying these symptoms do not continue to deteriorate and that the illness itself often starts after adolescence has passed. Bleuler believed that Kraepelin's term only made diagnosis confusing, so he substituted the term "schizophrenia" to indicate a "psychic split," or the dissociation of various psychic functions within a single personality. Emotions may be split from perception and be inappropriate to the situation; words may be split from their usual meanings; motor activity may be dissociated from reason. In Bleuler's words, "The personality loses its unity" (1911, p. 9). However, schizophrenia should not be confused with multiple personality, which is a dissociative disorder. Although depression is the most prevalent mental disorder, schizophrenia is the most common cause of hospitalization for mental illness in the United States.

Symptoms of Schizophrenia

Although thought disorders are often the predominant symptom, the schizophrenic person generally displays a variety of other abnormalities, including disorders of perception, emotion, and motor behavior. All schizophrenics display some of these symptoms some of the time, but no schizophrenic displays all the symptoms all the time.

Disorders of Thought   In most schizophrenics, there is a split among various ideas or between ideas and emotions. Normal people mentally link concepts and symbols and establish logical connections with a main idea that they wish to express. They might think, for example, that they are hungry and would like to eat a steak. The concept of hunger is joined to the concept of steak, and a relationship is set up between the two: namely, steak satisfies hunger. The incoherence or dissociation in the thought processes of the schizophrenic, however, interrupts such relationships. Concepts, ideas, symbols are sometimes thrown together merely because they rhyme. Such a series of rhyming or similar-sounding words is called a **clang association**. The following transcript of a conversation between a doctor and a schizophrenic patient, who produced rhymes in about half his daily speech, illustrates clang associations.

DOCTOR: How are things going today, Ernest?
PATIENT: Okay for a flump.
DR.: What is a flump?
PT.: A flump is a gump.
DR.: That doesn't make any sense.
PT.: Well, when you go to the next planet from the planet beyond the planet that landed on the danded and planded on the slanded.
DR.: Wait a minute. I didn't follow any of that.
PT.: Well, when we was first bit on the slip on the rit and the man on the ran or the pan on the ban and the sand on the man and the pan on the ban on the can on the man on the fan on the pan.
[All spoken very rhythmically, beginning slowly and building up to such a rapid pace that the words could no longer be understood.]

In addition to showing interruptions in the logical connections of words, schizophrenic thought sometimes is characterized by a tendency to dwell on the primary association to a given stimulus (called **perseveration**). More often, there is a loosening of associations, so that each sentence is generated from some mental stimulus in the preceding sentence, thus wandering further and further from the central idea (called **overinclusion**). This tendency to slip from one track of thought to another can lead to syntactically correct communication that conveys almost no information, as in the following letter, written by one of Bleuler's patients:

Dear Mother,
I am writing on paper. The pen which I am using is from a factory called "Perry & Co." This factory is in England. I assume this. Behind the name of Perry Co. the city of London is inscribed; but not the city. The city of London is in England. I know this from my school days. Then, I always liked geography. My last teacher in that subject was Professor August A. He was a man with black eyes. I also like black eyes. There are also blue and gray eyes and other sorts, too. I have heard it said that snakes have green eyes. All people have eyes. There are some, too, who are blind. These blind people are led about by a boy. It must be very terrible not to be able to see. There are people who can't see and, in addition can't hear. I know some who hear too much. One can hear too much. (Bleuler, 1911, p. 17)

The dissociation of concepts also produces delusions, one of the most common thought disorders among schizophrenics. Delusions take several forms. Some are delusions of grandeur, in which an individual believes that she or he is some famous person like Napoleon or Jesus Christ. Some are delusions of persecution, in which the individual believes that others, often extraterrestrial beings or secret agents, are plotting against her or him, controlling that person's thoughts and actions. Some are delusions of sin and guilt, in which the person believes that she or he has committed some terrible deed or brought evil into the world. The speech of a young woman whose long battle with schizophrenia began when she was fifteen is filled with delusions:

Mick Jagger wants to marry me, I don't have to covet Geraldo Rivera. Mick Jagger is Saint Nicholas and the Maharishi is Santa Claus. . . . Teddy Kennedy cured me of my ugliness. I'm pregnant with the Son of God. I'm going to marry David Berkowitz and get it over with.

Creedmoor [a mental hospital] is the headquarters of the American Nazi Party. They're eating the patients here. Archie Bunker wants me to play his niece on his TV show. . . . I'm Joan of Arc. I'm Florence Nightingale. . . . Divorce isn't a piece of paper, it's a feeling. Forget about zip codes. I need shock treatments. The body is run by electricity. My wiring is all faulty. A fly is a teenage wasp. . . . Israel is the promised land, but New Jersey is heaven (Sheehan, 1982).

Disorders of Perception   A distinguishing characteristic of schizophrenia is a distorted view of reality. Although this distortion is in part the result of disturbed thought processes, it is directly related to the fact that schizophrenics seem to perceive the external world in an altered manner. They consistently report distortions of sensory perception—auditory, somatic, and tactile hallucinations. Auditory hallucinations may take the form of insulting comments on the schizophrenic's behavior; tactile hallucinations may be felt as tingling or burning sensations; and somatic hallucinations may be reported as the sensation of snakes crawling under the abdomen (American Psychiatric Association, 1980). Visual, gustatory, and olfactory hallucinations are less common; in fact, visual hallucinations may be a symptom of drug poisoning (as in alcoholism), and olfactory hallucinations are often experienced by epileptics.

The hallucinations of schizophrenia differ from the imagery of normal people in two ways: they are spontaneous and apparently uncontrollable, and the schizophrenic perceives them as real. The pattern of tactile hallucinations experienced by one woman during a schizophrenic episode is shown in Figure 22.3. This woman felt that patches of her flesh were being stretched, sometimes as far as twelve inches from her head, and at other time times contracting into her head. The sensations varied in intensity and occasionally caused acute pain. She was so frightened by these strange sensations that her personality, thought, and actions were affected in a devastating manner (Pfeifer, 1970).

Perception in schizophrenia is also disturbed in additional ways, including an inability to focus attention, difficulty in identifying people and understanding their speech, and exaggerated sensitivity to certain stimuli, such as odors. Standard

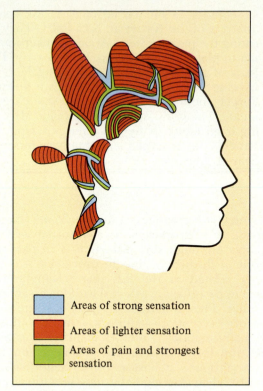

Areas of strong sensation

Areas of lighter sensation

Areas of pain and strongest sensation

Figure 22.3 A schizophrenic woman's drawing of her own tactile hallucinations, showing the areas of sensation and their associated strengths. (After Pfeifer, 1970.)

laboratory tests of perception confirm perceptual disturbance, indicating that schizophrenics do poorly on attempts to estimate size (Strauss, Foureman, and Parwatikar, 1974), time, and the positioning of their own hands and feet. The elements of perception are all there, but they seem somehow to have "gone off the track" or become "short-circuited," so the usual external stimulus does not produce the corresponding perceptual observation.

Disorders of Affect   Like other aspects of functioning, the emotional responses of schizophrenics are disturbed. Schizophrenics frequently show inappropriate emotional responses, or none at all. A schizophrenic might laugh when told of the death of a favorite relative, get angry when given a present, or show no emotion on any such occasion. In the last case, the schizophrenic's face remains immobile and the voice becomes a monotone. Again, the external situation or stimulus fails to trigger an appropriate response.

Disorders of Motor Behavior   The schizophrenic may behave in bizarre ways, or, more often, may perform repetitive and inappropriate acts. One patient might spend hours rubbing his forehead; another spend hours slapping her leg; still another might sit all day on a couch tracing the pattern of the fabric. In some cases, there is no physical activity at all; the patient is said to be in a catatonic stupor, remaining in one position for hours at a time, responding to neither persons nor things.

Disorders of Identity   In schizophrenia, the sense of individuality is often so disturbed that individuals seem uncertain as to who they are, and they become preoccupied with the question of their identity.

Disorders of Volition   Schizophrenics nearly always display a lack of interest in self-directed activity and are unable to initiate or to complete a project. When volition disappears, a schizophrenic's resulting inability to make decisions or choices may lead to almost complete inactivity.

Disorders of Relationship to the World   Schizophrenics often withdraw from involvement in the world's activity, becoming preoccupied with their own thoughts (see Figure 22.4). Interaction with other people is almost totally absent, and schizophrenics may act as if other people did not exist. To the observer, schizophrenics may seem to be living in their own world.

The Course of Schizophrenia

Schizophrenia does not manifest itself in the same way in all people, and no one patient shows all the disorders described in the preceding section. The disorder has been divided into five major subtypes, which are described in Table 22.1. However, schizophrenia generally follows a regular course that moves through three distinct phases: prodromal, active, and residual.

The Prodromal Phase   Before schizophrenia becomes active, the person may go through a phase of deterioration called the **prodromal phase**, in which she or he becomes increasingly

Figure 22.4 These paintings were done by a male schizophrenic with paranoid tendencies. Both illustrations are characterized by the consistent symbolism of watchful eyes, grasping hands, and the self as subject matter. In the first painting, which reflects a subdued emotional state, there is a strong emphasis on the eyes, with a figure watching over the shoulder. The torso of the central figure is surrounded by hands, and the figure in the background is reaching out. The second painting, elaborate in composition and vivid in color, reflects a more active emotional state. Again there is an emphasis on the eyes and on the hands, represented by tentacles and claws.

withdrawn, eccentric in behavior, and unable to carry out daily functions. Emotions slowly become inappropriate or nearly absent, and those close to the person notice a distinct change in personality. The prodromal phase may be brief, or it may last for years, in which case the deterioration in behavior is so gradual that the person may be entering the active phase before the family notices the severity of the disorder. Just such a slow deterioration was attributed to John W. Hinckley, Jr., the man who wounded President Ronald Reagan in an assassination attempt. Testifying in Hinckley's defense, one psychiatrist said that Hinckley had gradually withdrawn during his adolescent years and was schizophrenic.

The Active Phase During the **active phase**, the person shows some of the psychotic symptoms discussed in the preceding section. Delusions, hallucinations, disorganized speech, catatonic stupor, or any of the other symptoms mentioned may appear. The active phase often begins when a person in the prodromal phase encounters a particularly stressful situation (American Psychiatric Association, 1980).

The Residual Phase After a period in the active phase, most schizophrenics enter the **residual phase**, in which behavior is much as it was during the prodromal phase. The person may continue

Table 22.1 Five Types of Schizophrenia

Disorganized (hebephrenic) schizophrenia	Individuals live in private worlds dominated by hallucination, delusions, and fantasy. Behavior is almost completely unpredictable, and speech may be unintelligible. Most severe disintegration of personality.
Catatonic schizophrenia	Individuals show either excessive, sometimes violent, motor activity or a mute, unmoving, stuporous state. Some catatonic schizophrenics alternate between these two extremes, but often one or the other behavior pattern predominates.
Paranoid schizophrenia	Individuals have delusions of persecution, grandeur, or both. Paranoid schizophrenics trust no one and are constantly watchful, convinced that others are plotting against them. May seek to retaliate against supposed tormentors.
Undifferentiated schizophrenia	Individuals are schizophrenic but do not meet the above criteria, or else they show symptoms of several subtypes.
Residual schizophrenia	Individuals are not in an active phase of schizophrenia, but show residual symptoms.

to show diminished emotions and be unable to hold a job, but behavior is far less bizarre. Should any delusions or hallucinations persist, they are weakened and have less power to disturb the individual. Some schizophrenics pass through the residual phase and go on to complete recovery, but many lapse back into the active phase. A longitudinal study that followed more than a thousand schizophrenics indicated that 25 percent became able to function normally; 10 percent remained permanently in the psychotic, or active, phase; and between 50 and 65 percent alternated between the residual and active phases (M. Bleuler, 1978).

Social Disorders

The disturbances described thus far include some of the major mental disorders. Although it is impossible to encompass all disorders in a single chapter, several additional classes of disturbance are important enough to warrant a brief description. Because they often create social complications and involve longstanding habits of thought and behavior, personality disorders, sexual deviance, and disorders of substance use might be considered together as social disorders.

Personality Disorders

When personality traits become so inflexible and maladaptive that they impair a person's functioning, they are known as **personality disorders**. The individual with a personality disorder often does not recognize that it exists or that her or his behavior is at all deviant or disturbed. This inability to recognize the disorder comes about because the problem behavior is part of the person's personality, so deeply ingrained as to be second nature and accepted as familiar character traits. Often adopted at an early age to cope with specific stress in the environment, the pattern of deviant behavior is difficult to change. Frequently these individuals have little motivation to change their behavior, since their actions generally cause more discomfort to others than to themselves. Although *DSM-III* outlines eleven different types of personality disorders—none of which are considered psychotic—we shall focus on only one—the antisocial personality.

The **antisocial personality**, or **sociopath**, is one who is indifferent to the rights of others. Such people appear to be blind to moral considerations, to have no conscience, and to be untouched by a whole range of emotions shared by the "normal" population. Yet the intellectual faculties of sociopaths are intact, and their abilities to reason and to perform tasks are unimpaired. Sociopaths show antisocial behavior by early adolescence, and this antisocial quality pervades most behavior. To be diagnosed as a sociopath, a person must display at least four of the following nine qualities: aggressiveness, impulsiveness, recklessness, deceptiveness, involvement in criminal activities, inability to hold down a job, inability to maintain a lasting sexual attachment, failure to act as a responsible parent, and failure to honor financial obligations (American Psychiatric Association, 1980).

The most striking characteristic of this disorder is the absence of emotion in social relationships. The sociopath is simply indifferent to other people and preys upon them with no more feeling than if she or he were picking an apple from a tree. Thus, the sociopath shows no guilt over the most callous murder and no sadness at the death of a parent or friend. The remarks of one such person, Dan F., show this absence of normal emotions (McNeil, 1967). Thinking over the death of his best friend from leukemia, Dan decided that he felt nothing about the loss of his friend, that he wouldn't miss his mother or father if they died, and that he "wasn't too nuts" about his brothers and sisters either. Despite such a lack of emotion, the sociopaths' impulses are at times positive: they may buy presents for a friend or give money to charity; but the motivation for these acts has as little feeling behind it as their casual shoplifting or embezzling. Although usually intelligent, cunning, and clever, sociopaths seem to have little insight into the disorder and are slow to learn from experience. No matter how often they face prison terms, social sanctions, expulsions from school, and loss of jobs, sociopaths tend to repeat the very behavior patterns that have brought punishment down upon them.

Sexual Deviance

Definitions of sexually deviant behavior have changed over the past few years. *DSM-II*, the previous edition of *DSM-III*, was published in

1968, and it defined as sexually deviant any "individuals whose sexual interests are directed primarily toward objects other than people of the opposite sex, toward sexual acts not usually associated with coitus [sexual intercourse], or toward coitus performed under bizarre circumstances" (American Psychiatric Association, 1968, p. 44). Just twelve years later, the only kinds of sexual behavior classified as disorders in *DSM-III* are "those deviations from standard sexual behavior that involve gross impairments in the capacity for affectionate sexual activity between adult human partners" (American Psychiatric Association, 1980).

The change shows a recognition by the American Psychiatric Association that social attitudes vary, and so do sexual practices. Nevertheless, there is still some sexual behavior that psychologists and psychiatrists consider "abnormal" in our society and in others. The most common are:

Fetishism: sexual gratification that is dependent on an inanimate object or some part of the body other than the genitals.

Transvestism: sexual gratification obtained through dressing in clothing of the opposite sex.

Transsexualism: gender identification with the opposite sex.

Exhibitionism: sexual gratification obtained through exhibiting the genitals to an involuntary observer.

Voyeurism: sexual gratification obtained through secret observations of another person's sexual activities or genitals.

Pedophilia: sexual gratification obtained through sexual contacts with children.

Incest: sexual relations among members of the immediate family.

Rape: sexual relations achieved by threatening or using force on another person.

Sadism: sexual gratification obtained through inflicting pain on another person.

Masochism: sexual gratification obtained through having pain inflicted on oneself.

Mild forms of such "abnormal" behavior can appear among sexually "normal" individuals without being diagnosed as deviant. For example, many people become sexually aroused by the sight of lacy underwear or by swimming in the nude, and both the woman who is aroused by displaying her breasts in a low-cut dress and the man who is aroused by the display are behaving in a normal fashion. Such behavior is considered a serious disorder only when it is a person's sole or primary means of achieving sexual gratification.

Substance Abuse

As long as a person's use of a drug, whether tobacco, alcohol, marijuana, cocaine, or any other consciousness-altering substance, remains within reasonable bounds—when the drug is used and not abused—the practice does not fall under the category of psychological disorders. But when a person comes to depend upon one of these substances, so that her or his life is primarily devoted to getting and using the drug, the condition fits all the definitions of abnormality discussed in this chapter. Although there are as many varieties of substance abuse as there are drugs, we shall focus on only one—alcohol abuse.

Alcoholism is the most serious drug problem in the United States, and alcoholism is a major subcategory of mental disorder. According to one estimate, 5.75 million Americans are alcoholics and another 5.75 million are "problem drinkers"—a total of more than 10 percent of the population (Keller and Gurioli, 1976).

Alcohol abuse carries a high social and personal cost. The social damage of alcohol abuse takes many forms: family disruption; decreased job productivity due to inefficiency, accidents, absence, and low morale; death, injury, and property damage from alcohol-related automobile accidents; and increased medical care for alcoholics. The American Hospital Association estimates that approximately half of all occupied beds in United States' hospitals are filled by people with ailments linked to the consumption of alcohol (United States Department of Health and Human Services, 1981). In the economic area alone, alcoholism cost the American economy almost $43 billion in 1975. The personal costs of alcoholism are severe psychological and physiological deterioration.

As we saw in Chapter 6, alcohol is a depressant, suppressing inhibitions and allowing people to do or say things they ordinarily would not. Some people feel good when they drink, others become depressed, and others lose all anxiety or guilt over their past, present, or future behavior. In large quantities, alcohol causes disorders of sensation and perception, can lead to dangerous, self-destructive behavior, and is capable of producing coma and death.

Alcoholics build up a tolerance for alcohol; to experience the original feeling of well-being, or freedom from anxiety, they must increase their intake of alcohol. Often drinkers develop such a psychological dependence on alcohol that they feel normal only when they have been drinking and experience severe, painful symptoms if they stop. The slide into alcoholism generally follows the same sequence of behavior. A study of 2,000 alcoholic men showed that the sequence begins with periodic excessive drinking, then progresses through blackouts, sneaking drinks, losing control over the amount of alcohol drunk, remorse over drinking and rationalization of excess alcohol consumption, enforcing a change in drinking patterns in an attempt to solve the problem, morning drinking, alcoholic binges lasting for several days, and the onset of alcohol-related physical ailments, the centering of life around alcohol, and the admission of defeat (Jellinek, 1946).

Because of the toxic effects of alcohol on the body and the malnutrition that so often accompanies chronic alcoholism, alcoholics are likely to develop diseases affecting the liver, brain, and nervous system. Prolonged alcoholism leads to degenerative brain disease.

Organic Disorders

Various explanations have been offered for the development of psychological disorders, and Chapter 23 will present them in some detail. From Kraepelin on, many theorists have believed that mental disorders such as schizophrenia or depression are due to organic dysfunction of the brain. Much evidence supports this idea. But many social scientists feel that such mental disorders are due to psychological factors, emotional disturbances, and environmental stress. About certain disorders, however, there is little argument; they are directly traceable to the destruction of brain tissue or to biochemical imbalance in the brain. These disorders are known as **organic brain syndromes** and are classified as a separate category in *DSM-III.* Included in the list are: presenile and senile dementia; alcoholic psychoses such as delirium tremens; intracranial infections such as encephalitis and tertiary syphilis;

other cerebral conditions such as epilepsy, cerebral arteriosclerosis, and brain trauma; endocrine disorders; metabolic and nutritional disorders; systemic infections; and drug or poison intoxication.

Because physical and mental health are so closely related, it is often difficult to determine whether a particular behavioral disturbance is due to organic dysfunction or to emotional factors. Most organic brain disorders are accompanied by five major symptoms: impairment of orientation (awareness of who and where one is); impairment of memory; impairment of other intellectual functions, such as comprehension, calculation, knowledge, and learning; impairment of judgment; inappropriate affect. However, the majority of these symptoms are also present in schizophrenic patients, in patients with conversion disorder, and even in depressed patients. Thus an accurate diagnosis of organic brain syndrome is not easy.

Epidemiology of Mental Disorder

Epidemiology is the study of the range of occurrence, distribution, and control of illness in a population. In the case of mental disorder, the range of occurrence is difficult to estimate, since the number of people admitted to hospitals for mental disorder is much smaller than the number of people who actually experience it. On the basis of admission and residence rates for clinics and state and county hospitals, it is estimated that from 6 to 10 percent of the population of the United States will be treated for mental disorder at some point in their lives and that a sizable proportion of the remaining population will suffer symptoms of disorder but will go untreated.

Demographic Variability

Not all segments of the population show the same incidence of mental disorders. Such factors as sex, marital status, and social class appear to affect a person's chances of developing some psychological disturbance.

Sex   Although there is considerable variability among samples, most researchers have found a higher incidence of organic brain syndromes among males, but a higher incidence of psychological disorders among females. Alcoholism, drug dependence, and sexual deviation are more likely to appear in men than in women, but studies have consistently found that women are more prone to depression.

Marital Status Marital status appears to have an effect upon the likelihood of psychological disturbance. People who are married are less likely than others to have psychological disorders, but people whose marriages break up are the most likely to have disorders. The highest rate of mental disorder is reported among separated and divorced persons; the next highest among single persons; the next highest among widows and widowers; and the lowest among married men and women. Yet marriage itself may not be the important factor. It may be that disturbed people are more likely than others to stay single or to fail at marriage.

Social Class Social class is a broad category that encompasses such variables as ethnic group, occupation, marital status, and religion. Most studies have found a clear relationship between social class and reported mental disorder. In nineteen of twenty-four studies, the lower the social class, the higher the incidence of serious mental disorder (Kolb, Bernard, and Dohrenwend, 1969). Two major explanations have been advanced to account for this difference: first, life in lower social classes is more stressful than life in the middle and upper classes and thus produces more mental illness; and second, as people develop serious mental disorders they tend to withdraw from others and their ability to function in society deteriorates. As this happens to people in the middle and upper classes, they drift downward into lower social classes. Both stress and the downward drift are probably involved in this relationship between social class and psychological disorders.

Cross-Cultural Variability

Earlier we noted the role of social norms in defining abnormal behavior. A comparison of the symptoms of mental disorder in various cultures is of great interest to psychologists because it can help them to differentiate between changing environmental factors and unchanging basic elements of mental disorder. Other cultures also report disorders similar to schizophrenia, bipolar disorder, and anxiety disorders. In fact, some form of most disorders appears in most cultures, but the symptoms appear to vary across cultures. For example, although in many cultures schizophrenia is characterized by social and emotional withdrawal, auditory hallucinations, general delusions, and inability to react, the style of the symptoms varies from one culture to another (Murphy et al., 1961). Among schizophrenic Christians and Moslems, religious delusions and delusions of destructiveness are common, but Asians are most likely to develop delusions that involve jealousy.

It is clear that cultures may supply the material for delusions, but the extent to which differences in symptoms directly reflect differences in culture is difficult to measure. It is probably safe to conclude that no disorder is completely immune to cultural influence, and that no serious disorder is entirely a creation of cultural and social forces. It also appears that psychoses are less influenced by culture than are other disorders, and that symptoms involving thought, perception, and emotion show less variation across cultures than do symptoms involving a person's role and social behavior (Draguns, 1980). Yet the complexity of human behavior continues to confound and confuse even those who study it most closely.

SUMMARY

1. Several definitions of abnormality are used within the field of psychology: **norm** violation; substantial deviation from a statistically calculated average; personal discomfort arising from thoughts or behavior; impairment of functioning; and deviation from the ideal, well-adjusted personality. None of these definitions encompasses all abnormalities.

2. The generally accepted classification of abnormal behavior is that provided by the American Psychiatric Association in its *Diagnostic and Statistical Manual of Mental Disorders (DSM-III)*. *DSM-III* is tied to the **medical model**, which views psychological problems as diseases with specific symptoms, causes, predictable courses, and treatments, but *DSM-III* does not assume that these disorders have a biological cause. By enabling us to communicate about mental disorders, such classification has major advantages in both treatment and the advancement of knowledge. The disadvantages are the medical model's labeling of people as "sick," the illusion that naming a disorder explains it, the stigmatizing of people by attaching labels to their behavior, and the unreliability of diagnoses. However, *DSM-III* provides the most practical classification system yet devised.

3. **Anxiety** is a feeling of dread, apprehension or fear, and when severe and persistent anxiety interferes with daily functioning, the condition is classified as an **anxiety disorder. Generalized anxiety disorder** is characterized by generalized anxiety that cannot be managed through avoidance and by **free-floating anxiety**—an inability to specify the source of the fear. In **panic attacks**, tension mounts to an acute and overwhelming level. When no specific stimulus precedes the attack, it is called a **panic disorder**. Anxiety that is irrationally focused on a particular object or situation is called a **phobia**. An **obsession** is a recurring irrational thought; a **compulsion** is the repeated performance of a particular irrational act. Much ritual behavior is both obsessive and compulsive. In **somatoform disorders**, physical symptoms are unaccompanied by physiological malfunction. **Hypochondriasis** is the preoccupation with bodily symptoms as possible signs of serious illness. In **conversion disorders**, a person develops a physical dysfunction that has no organic basis. In **dissociative disorders**, the dysfunction is psychological and certain normally integrated behavior is split. The major dissociative disorders are **amnesia**, **somnambulism**, **fugue**, and **multiple personality**.

4. **Affective disorders** are characterized by disturbances of mood. **Major depression** consists of one or more major depressive episodes with no intervening episodes of euphoria. In a major depressive episode, a person shows radical changes in mood, motivation, thinking, and physical and motor functioning. **Bipolar disorder** is characterized by extreme moods, beginning with a manic episode of euphoria, excitement, and activity, followed by a depressive episode.

5. **Schizophrenia** is characterized by disordered thought accompanied by other abnormalities such as disordered perception, emotion, and motor behavior. Most schizophrenics show a lack of association among various ideas or between ideas and emotion, as shown in a **clang association** in which speech becomes a series of rhyming or similar-sounding words. Some schizophrenics show **perseveration**—a tendency to dwell upon the primary association of a stimulus—but more common is a loosening of associations in which each sentence is generated from some mental stimulus in the preceding sentence. Another common thought disorder is **delusion**, an irrational belief held in the face of overwhelming disproof. Disordered perception generally appears as **hallucinations**, spontaneous sensory perceptions that are unrelated to external stimuli. Schizophrenics also display disorders of **affect**, or emotional response, of motor behavior, of identity and volition, and of their relationship to the world. The course of schizophrenia often begins with a **prodromal phase** of gradual deterioration, followed by an **active phase**, in which psychotic symptoms dominate, then a **residual phase**, in which behavior resembles that of the prodromal phase. From the residual phase, schizophrenics either recover or lapse back into an active phase.

6. **Personality disorders** involve inflexible and maladaptive personality traits that impair functioning. The deviant behavior is completely integrated into the individual's life and she or he may be unaware of any disturbance. The **antisocial personality**, or **sociopath**, violates the rights of others without feeling any guilt, lacks all conscience or emotion in relationships, and seems unable to learn from experience. Although definitions of sexual deviance vary with time and place, certain sexual behavior is considered abnormal, including **fetishism**, **transvestism**, **transsexualism**,

exhibitionism, **voyeurism**, **pedophilia**, **incest**, **rape**, **sadism**, and **masochism**. Among disorders of substance abuse, alcoholism is a major subcategory of mental disorder and is the country's most serious drug problem.

7. Certain psychological disorders, the **organic brain syndromes**, can be traced to the destruction of brain tissue or to biochemical imbalance in the brain. The most common form of organic brain disease is cerebral arteriosclerosis and other forms of senility.

8. **Epidemiology** is the study of the range of occurrence, distribution, and control of illness in a population. Establishing the epidemiology of mental disorder is difficult because far fewer people are admitted to treatment than suffer mental disorder. The incidence of mental disorder varies with such factors as sex, age, marital status, and social class. Comparison of mental disorders across cultures helps to distinguish between changing environmental factors and unchanging basic elements of psychological disturbances.

KEY TERMS

active phase
affect
affective disorders
amnesia
antisocial personality
anxiety
anxiety disorders
bipolar disorder
clang association
compulsion
conversion disorders
delusions
dissociative disorders
epidemiology
exhibitionism
fetishism
free-floating anxiety

fugue
generalized anxiety disorder
hallucinations
hypochondriasis
incest
major depression
masochism
medical model
multiple personality
neurosis
norms
obsession
organic brain syndromes
overinclusion
panic attacks
panic disorder
pedophilia

perseveration
personality disorders
phobia
prodromal phase
psychosis
psychotic disorder
rape
residual phase
sadism
schizophrenia
sociopath
somatoform disorders
transsexualism
transvestism
voyeurism

RECOMMENDED READINGS

AMERICAN PSYCHIATRIC ASSOCIATION. *Diagnostic and Statistical Manual of Mental Disorders.* 3rd ed. (DSM III) Washington, D.C.: American Psychiatric Association, 1980. The generally accepted classification system which contains detailed descriptions and criteria for psychological disturbance.

BOOTZIN, R. R., and J. R. ACOCELLA. *Abnormal Psychology: Current Perspectives.* 3rd ed. New York: Random House, 1980. A comprehensive textbook that describes the major categories of psychological disorder and presents a variety of theoretical perspectives.

LANDIS, C. *Varieties of Psychopathological Experience.* F. A. Mettler (ed.). New York: Holt, Rinehart and Winston, 1964. A collection of autobiographical reports that provide a glimpse into the experience of disorder. A valuable complement to theoretical discussions.

SZASZ, T. S. *The Myth of Mental Illness. Foundations of a Theory of Personal Conduct.* New York: Dell, 1967. A highly original, stimulating discussion of mental illness. Szasz argues that what is called mental illness really involves "problems in living."

ZILBOORG, G., and G.W. HENRY. *A History of Medical Psychology.* New York: Norton, 1941. A fascinating discussion of the history of madness; a classic in the field.

CHAPTER 23

Theories of Abnormality

A thirty-two-year-old man complained that his thoughts were being repeated in public and that he was being "tortured by rays." He claimed that people who lived on the other floors of his apartment building were transmitting abusive messages to him through the central heating system. At times he would stare into the mirror, grimacing at his reflection. On occasion he broke a silence or interrupted a conversation by speaking or singing words that bore no relation to the situation, such as "Emperor Napoleon." He often laughed boisterously and for no apparent reason. He complained about odd sensations in his hair and scalp, saying that they felt "as if they were congealed." Finally, he began to pound on the walls in the middle of the night, waking his family and people in the neighboring apartments (Bleuler, 1978). Such irrational behavior, delusional thinking, disordered perceptions, and inappropriate emotional responses are signs of psychological abnormality.

What made this man, who was diagnosed as schizophrenic, behave in such a manner? What causes any psychological disorder? The causes of mental abnormality are complex, and psychologists and psychiatrists have developed many theories concerning the causes of behavior that a society considers abnormal. As we shall see, each perspective stresses a different aspect of abnormality, with some centering on the way the environment can encourage and maintain deviant behavior and others focusing on possible physiological bases of disorders. To understand present theories of disorder, it is helpful to consider the way people in past centuries have viewed abnormality.

Some Theories from the Past*

All through history, deviant behavior—behavior that is strikingly different from that of most people—has been explained and defined according to the philosophical and religous outlook of a particular society. Most societies attribute psychological disturbance to gods, demons, disease, or emotional stress.

Demonology

During the Stone Age, people believed that all the movements of nature are governed by supernatural forces. Unusual behavior must, therefore, be caused by gods or demons. Their method of dealing with unfriendly spirits was to poke a hole in the skull of the person considered possessed. This treatment, called trephining, was supposed to allow the evil spirit to escape.

---

*This section is loosely based on Zilboorg and Henry, 1941.

The trial of George Jacobs, Salem, Massachusetts, 1692. Jacobs was hanged on the testimony of his granddaughter, who later admitted her accusations were false.

Similar ideas of possession endured for many centuries among the ancient Chinese, Egyptians, Hebrews, and Greeks. In some instances, possession was considered a desirable state; in Greece, for example, the priestess at Delphi was revered, and the cryptic prophecies she delivered were thought to come from a god who was inhabiting her body.

It was the Greeks, a people with a strong belief in reason, who eventually developed a nonreligious explanation of abnormal behavior. More than two thousand years ago, Hippocrates (c. 460–c. 360 B.C.), applying the scientific method to the study of deviant behavior, observed that it was a natural, not a supernatural, phenomenon. He developed the first organic (physiological as opposed to psychological) theory of abnormal behavior. Believing the body to be composed of four liquids, or "humours"—blood, phlegm, yellow bile and black bile—each with special characteristics, Hippocrates proposed that too much or too little of any humour could lead to changes in personality and disturbances in behavior. For example, melancholy (depression) was thought to be caused by an excess of black bile.

Religious influences again became prevalent during the Middle Ages. Some deviant behavior was explained in terms of demonic forces, a connection that prevailed for centuries. During the same period, much abnormal behavior continued to be explained in terms of common-sense naturalistic causes such as the death of a spouse or a blow to the head. These people were often treated humanely (Neugebauer, 1978). However, those who were considered to be voluntarily in league with the Devil were strangled, beheaded, or burned to death. The most notorious American example occurred in 1692, when a group of eight girls in Salem, Massachusetts, began spouting gibberish, throwing fits, and claiming that the Devil and his witches were afflicting them. The community believed the girls were under the spell of witches and, after the famous series of trials, nineteen people were executed as witches (Deutsch, 1949). According to conservative estimates, more than 100,000 people (about 85 percent of them women) were executed as witches in Western Europe from the middle of the fifteenth century to the end of the seventeenth century (Deutsch, 1949).

Biogenic Theory and the Medical Model

A few lonely voices were raised in protest against witch hunts. One was that of Johann Weyer (1515–1588), a German physician who stated that abnormal behavior is an illness and should be treated by a physician rather than a priest. Another was St. Vincent de Paul (1576–1660), a French priest who placed himself in great danger by declaring openly that the possessed were simply ill and that it was the duty of Christians to help rather than to persecute them. Thus, it was in the seventeenth century, in the midst of the witch hunts, that illness began to be put forth as an explanation for deviant behavior. Not until the eighteenth century, however, during the period known as the Enlightenment, did demonology finally die out. Despite sporadic claims of demonic possession, deviant behavior was once again widely viewed as a result of natural forces.

The view of mental disorder as having a physical, or organic, cause is known as **biogenic theory**. Although an organic explanation had been put forward by various physicians since Hippocrates first proposed it, the biogenic theory was not firmly established among psychiatrists until the German physician, Emil Kraepelin, (1856–1926) brought out his *Textbook of Psychiatry* in 1883. In that book Kraepelin argued cogently for the central role of brain pathology in mental disturbances. He applied the medical model to mental disturbances, adopting the same scientific standards of observation and classification used in studying physical diseases. As noted in Chapter 22, he furnished psychiatry with its first comprehensive classification system, based on distinctions among different types of mental disorders and their clusters of symptoms. Kraepelin's classification system provided the basis for the American Psychiatric Association's first *Diagnostic and Statistical Manual of Mental Disorders* (*DSM-I*, 1952), and the current edition, *DSM-III*, is a descendant of Kraepelin's system.

By the turn of this century, neurological research was progressing rapidly, and one mysterious mental disorder after another yielded to biogenic explanations. Senile psychoses, toxic psychoses, cerebral arteriosclerosis, and some forms of mental retardation were shown to be caused by brain pathology. Most stunning of all, general paresis, a puzzling disorder marked by the gradual breakdown of physical and mental functioning, was shown to be advanced syphilis.

The successes of the biogenic approach led researchers to treat all abnormal behavior as if it had an organic cause. The influence of the medical model's early success can be seen in the terms we apply to psychological disorders and those who have them: "patient," "symptom," "syndrome," "pathology," "therapy," "cure," and "mental illness" (Price, 1978).

In the past few decades, many psychiatrists have criticized the pervasive influence of the medical model, and perhaps the most eloquent and relentless of the critics has been the American psychiatrist Thomas Szasz. In *The Myth of Mental Illness* (1961), Szasz asserts that most of the disorders that are called mental illnesses are not organic illnesses at all; instead, they are "problems in living" that manifest themselves in behavior that deviates from arbitrary social norms. Szasz argues that by labeling abnormal behavior as "illness," we not only describe the problem inaccurately but we deprive individuals of responsibility for their own behavior as well. Although Szasz's arguments have had some influence, the biogenic approach to understanding and treating abnormal behavior continues to thrive. For example, recent research has implicated neurotransmitters in abnormal behavior, and these exciting advances will be described in the section on the biological perspective.

Psychogenic Theory

As biogenic theory was making great strides, **psychogenic theory**, which holds that mental disturbances result primarily from emotional stress, was also rapidly gaining ground. It began with the colorful figure of Franz Anton Mesmer (1733–1815), an Austrian physician who thought that the heavens influenced people's mental states. Mesmer held that the movements of the planets control the distribution of a universal magnetic fluid, and that the shifting of this fluid is responsible for the health or sickness of mind and body. In accordance with his principle of "animal magnetism," Mesmer believed that by touching various parts of a person's body with colored rods and a special wand, he could adjust the distribution of magnetic body liquids. His treatment seems to have brought about improvement in many cases, a recovery due to the power of suggestion in curing mental disorders. The discovery of this power was Mesmer's major contribution to psychotherapy. In treating his patients, he used "mesmerism," an artificially induced, sleeplike state in which the subject is highly susceptible to suggestion.

Mesmerism eventually developed into the technique of hypnosis (see Chapter 6), which was adopted and used systematically by two French physicians, Ambroise-Auguste Liébault (1823–1904) and Hippolyte Bernheim (1837–1919), who in turn influenced the famous Parisian neurologist Jean-Martin Charcot (1825–1893). Charcot found hypnosis to be a highly successful treatment for hysteria, the original term for conversion disorders, in which physical symptoms have no corresponding organic causes. It was Charcot's example that influenced Josef Breuer and Sigmund Freud to use hypnosis in treating psychological disorders.

The steps by which Freud progressed from the use of hypnosis to the techniques of psychoanalysis, free association, and dream analysis have been described in Chapter 18. Although Freud's psychoanalytic theory is a general theory of personality, it is also a detailed theory of abnormal behavior (as we shall see in the next section). Other dominant views of abnormal behavior that are based on psychogenic theory are behavioral, humanistic-existential, family, and sociocultural perspectives. As we shall see, psychogenic views have broadened to include the role played by society in the development of disorders. Biogenic views of mental disorders remain strong, focusing on genetic and biochemical factors. Psychogenic and biogenic approaches are presented separately here, but an understanding of mental disorder clearly requires attention to both psychological and organic factors.

The Psychoanalytic Perspective

Psychoanalytic theory holds that mental disorders arise when the balance among id, ego, and superego has been disturbed by a failure to resolve conflicts and the person encounters additional stress or conflict. As we saw in the detailed discussion of Freud's theory of personality (see Chapter 18), conflicts among the id, the ego, and the superego may produce anxiety. Freud identified three kinds of anxiety (see Figure 23.1). The first is **reality anxiety**, the result of an external danger: A man points a gun at you and says, "Your money or your life!" and you become frightened. The second is **moral anxiety**, caused by the superego's demands for moral behavior and self-punishment for moral transgression:

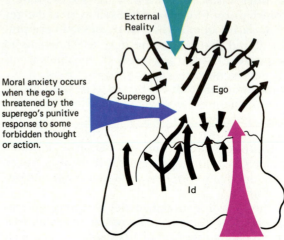

Reality anxiety occurs when the ego feels overwhelmed by threats from the external environment.

Moral anxiety occurs when the ego is threatened by the superego's punitive response to some forbidden thought or action.

Neurotic anxiety occurs when the id threatens to overwhelm ego constraints, leading to unacceptable or impulsive behavior.

Figure 23.1 According to psychoanalytic theory, the rigid and excessive use of ego defense mechanisms to relieve anxiety leads to the various forms of neurosis.

You copy someone else's answers on a test and feel guilty. The third is **neurotic anxiety**, produced when impulses generated by the id threaten to overwhelm the ego and interfere with its functioning: In a noisy quarrel with your roommate you feel a sudden sense of panic arising from aggressive impulses that threaten to break loose and cause you to strike out uncontrollably. To deal with neurotic anxiety, the weak ego begins to use defense mechanisms in an increasingly rigid manner.

The particular defense mechanism that is employed determines the form of abnormal behavior a person displays. The panic attacks that characterize anxiety disorders (see Chapter 22) are seen as the result of desperate attempts by the ego to control the impulses of the id, using repression of those impulses as the major defense. The ego succeeds in pushing down (repressing) the impulse, and, although the anxiety is directly experienced, the true nature of the conflict remains hidden in the recesses of the unconscious.

The defenses employed in other disorders are considerably more complex, and the level of anxiety that is experienced is somewhat less severe. **Obsessive-compulsive disorders** that are characterized by rituals of orderliness or cleanliness,

According to psychoanalytic theory, anxiety may be directly experienced by an individual, but the conflict that causes the anxiety may remain unconscious. Through dream interpretation and free association in psychoanalysis, the true nature of the conflict may be revealed.

such as continual hand washing, are seen as the product of reaction formation, another defense mechanism. The ego responds to unacceptable impulses to soil oneself, to be dirty and destructive, by outwardly abhorring dirtiness and practicing fastidious cleanliness. Conversion disorders are also seen as a defense against unacceptable impulses. For example, glove anesthesia, as we have seen in Chapter 18, can be interpreted as a defense against an aggressive impulse to strike someone or a sexual impulse to masturbate.

Defense mechanisms are not implicated in psychotic disorders, which according to psychoanalytic theory are caused by severely deficient ego functioning. In contrast to the anxiety, somatoform, and dissociative disorders that Freud called "neuroses,"* psychoses occur when the ego is unable to use defense mechanisms as a shield against unacceptable impulses: the person loses contact with reality and regresses to an early phase of the oral psychosexual stage. The psychotic person suffers from deficient ego functioning in perception, verbalization, and problem solving. In the psychoanalytic framework, a psychosis is not just a severe form of neurosis, but a disorder of a different kind. Neurosis is associated with the overuse of defense mechanisms; in psychosis the ego

is so weakened or deficient that it has no effective defenses against the id's impulses. A normal or adequately functioning person, in contrast, has an ego that effectively mediates the conflicting demands of id and superego without resorting excessively to defense mechanisms.

Psychoanalytic theory developed out of the clinical experience of Freud and his students, and it has led to many insightful observations. For example, the psychoanalytic view of depression, first put forth by Freud's student Karl Abraham (1911; 1916), is that depression arises when a person loses a love object toward whom she or he had both positive and negative feelings. The loss can be a real or a perceived loss or rejection. In the face of desertion by the love object, a person's negative feelings turn to intense anger. At the same time, the positive feelings give rise to guilt based on the feeling that the person failed to behave properly toward the lost love object. The rage and reproach remain unconscious and are turned inward, becoming depression. Athough theorists from other perspectives might disagree as to whether anger turned inward causes depression, the early psychoanalytic observation that depression includes elements of anger is now widely accepted.

In Chapter 18, we saw how other psychoanalytic theorists have expanded Freud's theory to emphasize social factors and the role of the ego. Psychoanalytic theory is not static, but continues to grow and change in response to the contributions of many psychoanalytic theorists.

---

*Although *DMS-III* discarded the term "neurosis" because it represented a theory about the cause of mental disorders, some theories still use the term.

The Behavioral Perspective

Although behavioral theories of personality, which are described in Chapter 19, also see a psychogenic basis to emotional disorders, adherents of the behavioral perspective reject most Freudian concepts. They believe that the learning principles of modeling, classical conditioning, and operant conditioning can explain the development of abnormal behavior. These theorists assume that abnormal behavior is learned in the same way as other behavior. The person with a psychological disorder differs from others because she or he either has learned inappropriate behavior or has never learned the adaptive behavior that most people acquire.

Maladaptive behavior is sometimes the result of modeling, and many people learn to be fearful and anxious in particular situations by observing the anxiety of others (Rosenthal and Bandura, 1978). For example, a boy may develop a fear of dogs because he observes his mother's fearful reactions to the animal and he is rewarded with her comfort when he acts in the same way. In addition, some people learn fears through classical conditioning, developing anxiety and phobias following traumatic events, natural disasters, and accidents. For example, all but one of the thirty-five survivors of a gasoline tanker explosion on the Delaware River reported severe symptoms of nervousness, depression, and phobic reactions when at sea as long as four years after the accident (Leopold and Dillon, 1963).

Direct reinforcement can teach behavior that allows people to avoid something unpleasant. For example, a girl who hates going to school may learn either to develop a stomach ache every morning or to behave so disruptively in class that she is repeatedly suspended. Both types of behavior are reinforced, because both allow her to miss school.

Reinforcement and extinction may work together in the development of maladaptive behavior. It has been suggested that one cause of depression may be the reinforcement of depressed behavior with attention, kindness, and sympathy from family, friends, and therapists (Ullmann and Krasner, 1975). At the same time, any active, "nondepressed" behavior by the person may be undergoing extinction from lack of reinforcement. The reduction in reinforcement may be the result of changes in a person's environment. The amount of positive reinforcement any person receives depends on three broad factors: (1) the number and range of stimuli that the person finds reinforcing; (2) the availability of such reinforcers in the environment; and (3) the person's skill in obtaining reinforcement (Lewinsohn, 1974). If a person retires or loses a spouse through divorce or death, for example, one or more of these factors may be suddenly and dramatically affected, leaving the person inactive, withdrawn, and distressed. To treat depression, the therapist adds possible sources of reinforcement to the depressed person's environment and helps the person acquire skills that will increase the chances of obtaining it (Lewinsohn, 1975).

In recent years, behaviorally oriented theorists have been paying more attention to the role of cognitive events in the development and treatment of abnormal behavior. The cognitive approach emphasizes that the way we interpret events may be almost as important as the events themselves. Thus a poor grade on an essay might produce self-blame and a feeling of failure in one person, the determination to try harder in another, and the conviction that the instructor misgraded the essay in a third. The interpretation placed on the event influences how the person feels about it and how she or he behaves in the future. In this view, depression is a behavioral response that develops when a person consistently interprets events as hopeless through the exaggeration of disappointments, the overgeneralization of criticisms, and the recall of only their unpleasant aspects (Beck et al., 1979).

From the behavioral perspective, maladaptive behavior is neither symptomatic of illness, as the medical model would have it, nor a sign of underlying psychic conflict, as the psychoanalytic framework interprets it. Instead, the maladaptive behavior itself is the problem. A behavioral analysis attempts to identify the stimuli that elicit the behavior and the reinforcing consequences that maintain it. In many ways, the behavioral perspective is primarily a perspective of treatment, and behavioral theories have contributed successful treatment procedures for a wide range of clinical problems, which will be discussed in detail in Chapter 24.

The Humanistic-Existential Perspective

Another psychogenic approach to psychological

disorder is that of the **humanistic-existential perspective**, which includes both humanistic and existential theorists. Humanistic personality theories, like those of Abraham Maslow and Carl Rogers (see Chapter 19), emphasize the potential of human beings for growth and self-actualization. Although humanistic and existential theorists differ somewhat in their view of disorders, they share a number of basic assumptions: (1) both insist on a **phenomenological approach**—an approach that stresses the individual's own perception of events as opposed to a therapist's interpretation of hidden causes; (2) both stress the uniqueness of each individual; (3) both place great emphasis on human potential; and (4) both stress the individual freedom to make choices, a freedom that makes each person responsible for her or his own behavior.

Humanistic theorists believe that maladjustment develops when a hostile and rejecting family and society thwart the individual's natural drive for self-actualization, thus leading to a negative self-concept. Existential theorists emphasize the establishment of personal values and **authenticity**—living by those values—over self-actualization. For example, Viktor Frankl (1962), an existential psychiatrist, considers the need to find meaning in life the primary human motive. When people are unable to find meaning, they experience **existential frustration**, a major source of abnormal behavior. While acknowledging the biological and psychological components of behavioral disorders, Frankl distinguishes between two major categories of psychological disturbance: anxiety neurosis and obsessional neurosis. He interprets anxiety neurosis as stemming from the neurotic person's guilt over not having pursued any values. In contrast, obsessional neurosis is caused by the inability of a person with values to endure the discrepancy between the real and the ideal. As we shall see in Chapter 24, the role of the existential therapist is to help patients live life as it is (the real) and to help them discover values inherent in life (Frankl, 1975).

A more radical view of abnormal behavior, particularly schizophrenia, is presented by another existential psychiatrist, R. D. Laing (1967). According to Laing, modern society and the modern nuclear family are psychologically destructive environments. By surrounding us with "double messages" and by demanding that we stifle our feelings and pursue meaningless goals, both family and society consistently discourage authentic behavior in favor of inane conventional behavior. Although all of us are subjected to this destructive environment, the demands of the schizophrenic's family are even worse. Within the family schizophrenics develop their particular ways of experiencing, understanding, and behaving in the world. These ways may seem incomprehensible to outsiders, but within the family they are appropriate and can be seen as adaptive in that context. Because members of a schizophrenic's family are not honest with one another, their interaction forces each of them to deny parts of their experiences and to invalidate important feelings (Laing and Esterson, 1971).

Laing came to believe that emotional disturbance is inherent in contemporary Western society and that schizophrenics are victims not only of their families but also of society itself. In fact, he believes that the abnormal behavior of psychotics reflects their attempts to reconcile the self that existed before socialization (the "true" self) with the self created by cultural demands and social sanctions. In this view, schizophrenia is not insanity but "hypersanity," a voyage from our own mad reality into another reality in the existential search for an authentic identity.

Many of the positions of the humanistic-existential perspective are emphatically rejected by proponents of other perspectives, even those who agree that society plays a role in the development of disorders. Nevertheless, the humanistic-existential perspective has made an important contribution to our understanding of abnormality by stressing the validity of each individual's experience.

The Family Perspective

Adherents of the psychogenic perspectives discussed—psychoanalytic, behavioral, and humanistic-existential—are convinced that an individual's family has an important role in the development of abnormal behavior. From the psychoanalytic perspective, early childhood events are particularly critical in the psychosexual development of the child and in laying the foundation of the person's personality. From the behavioral perspective, family members are the major models for behavior and important sources of reinforcement. As a result of family interactions, maladaptive behavior can be learned in the same way as adaptive behavior. From the humanistic-existential perspective, the family is the primary vehicle for transmitting society's values, and within the family the individual learns to conform by suppressing individuality, self-actualization, and authenticity. Although all three perspectives affirm the importance of the family, their primary emphasis is on the psychological processes of the individual. Other psychogenic perspectives, in contrast, focus more directly on the processes of family interaction as the primary determinant of abnormal behavior.

One group of investigators, headed by Theodore Lidz (Lidz et al., 1957; Lidz, 1973) explored the role of family interaction in the development of schizophrenia. After studying schizophrenics and their families for several years, these researchers suggest that two basic family patterns can produce schizophrenics: marital schism and marital skew.

In stable environments, families seem able to avoid the conflicts and confusions caused by marital schism and marital skew.

In the **marital schism** pattern, the parents of the schizophrenic were bitterly divided, and the marital relationship aggravated the personality difficulties of each parent. The parents were continually on the verge of separation, and communication between them was reduced to coercion and defiance—both open and carefully masked to avoid a fight. The parents carried their hostility toward each other into their children's lives, with each partner habitually telling the children about the faults and worthlessness of her or his spouse.

In the **marital skew** pattern, the family was calmer but one parent totally dominated the other. The marriage consisted of one extremely dependent or masochistic partner and one strong partner who acted as a parental figure to the weak partner but who generally appeared to be the disturbed member of the pair. The dependent parent accepted or even supported any weakness or psychopathology displayed by the dominant parent. As a result, although the family atmosphere was abnormal, the other spouse's acceptance of the abnormality probably made the environment seem normal to the children (Lidz et al., 1957).

Lidz and his associates concluded that the child faced with the conflict and confusion found in either of these family situations would develop ways of coping that led to problems later in life.

Another theorist, Frieda Fromm-Reichmann, placed most of the blame on the mother instead of on the marital relationship. She believed that the influence of the mother is so crucial in the development of schizophrenia that in 1948 she coined the term "schizophrenogenic mother" to describe a cold, domineering mother who simultaneously rejects and overprotects her child (Fromm-Reichmann, 1974). Such a mother, in conjunction with a passive father who exerts little influence in the family, seems to Fromm-Reichmann to be capable of inducing schizophrenia in her offspring.

A third group of investigators, headed by Gregory Bateson and Don Jackson, examined the family environments of schizophrenics and decided that faulty communication lay at the root of schizophrenia. According to their **double-bind hypothesis**, parents in these families habitually send conflicting messages to their children so that no matter what a child does, the action is wrong (Bateson, Jackson, et al., 1956). An obvious double bind is reflected in the familiar joke in which a mother gives her child two shirts for his birthday and he immediately puts on one of them. His mother looks at him and says, "What's the matter? Didn't you like the other one?"

In the family of the schizophrenic, the double bind works in the following manner. Suppose a mother has great difficulty accepting her child's affection for her, but at the same time finds it hard to deal with any anxiety or hostility she feels toward her child. As a result she *talks* in a loving manner, perhaps telling the child to give her a kiss, but then stiffens her body when the child approaches. The child, perceiving the discrepancy between the mother's speech and her actions, receives contradictory messages. If such occasions are common, the child never learns to distinguish among the meanings expressed in normal language and behavior. She or he develops the bizarre language and social ineptness characteristic of schizophrenics.

Recent studies have gone beyond the communication between mother and child to focus on communication patterns among all family members. Considerable research indicates that families of schizophrenics typically have deviant communication patterns, which have been described as blurred, muddled, vague, confused, fragmented, or incomplete (Hassan, 1974; Lewis et al., 1981; Wynne et al., 1975). In one study (Doane et al., 1981), deviant communication by the parents predicted whether their adolescent children would be diagnosed as schizophrenic five years later. Despite these findings, we cannot say with certainty that schizophrenia results when a "normal" child grows up surrounded by abnormal communication, for some studies have found that anyone who attempts to communicate with schizophrenics ends up sounding confused (Liem, 1974). In other words, it may be the presence of a disturbed child that produces abnormal communication from other family members.

The Sociocultural Perspective

Instead of confining the social causes of abnormal behavior to family interaction, the sociocultural perspective, a final psychogenic view, places the primary blame on the entire society. The sociocultural perspective embraces two interrelated views, social stress and social labeling. In the social stress view, abnormal behavior can be caused by the stresses of living in modern society. As noted in Chapter 22, psychological disturbance is linked with social class, so that the lower the socioeconomic class, the higher the prevalence of mental disorder. From the sociocultural perspective, this relationship is caused by such stresses as poverty, discrimination, and the lack of valued roles for people in certain segments of our society, such as the elderly.

In the social labeling view, which follows naturally from the social stress view, the link between social class and disorder arises because people from the lower socioeconomic classes are more likely than members of higher socioeconomic classes to be labeled as mentally disordered.

It has been proposed that the "mentally ill" are simply people who have had the label attached to them because of behavior that violates social norms (Scheff, 1975). Although much deviant behavior is ignored by society, if such behavior comes to the attention of the mental health establishment, the individual may be labeled as disordered. Attaching the label to an individual places her or him in the social role of the mentally ill person, and it is probable that she or he will accept it. So labeled, the person is discriminated against for attempting to behave in a normal fashion, perhaps being fired, refused employment, or shunned by others. But the same person is rewarded with attention, sympathy, and removal of all responsibility if she or he will only accept the role.

The label of mentally ill is more likely to be attached to people in lower socioeconomic classes for several reasons that were discovered in a series of studies (Hollingshead and Redlich, 1958; Myers and Bean, 1968). First, the label automatically accompanies admission to mental hospitals, and disturbed people without money for private care frequently find themselves in state mental hospitals. The middle-class person with the same degree of disturbance is likely to be seeing a private psychiatrist regularly and so escape the label. Second, lower-class people tend to display deep unhappiness by becoming aggressive or rebelling against social norms. Although such behavior is regarded as a "normal" sign of frustration in the lower class, it appears aberrant to mental health professionals, since in their own middle class the appropriate response to such unhappiness is withdrawal and self-deprecation. Therefore, the person from a lower socioeconomic class who goes to a mental health clinic has a good chance of being labeled as psychotic and being hospitalized, whereas the

Admission to a psychiatric hospital automatically labels one as "mentally ill." A middle-class person with the same symptoms as a lower-class person may avoid both the hospital and the label.

middle-class person is likely to be considered neurotic, a status that is not regarded as "sick." In addition, the psychotic is given small chance for improvement and usually meets those expectations, whereas the neurotic, who is supposed to improve with regular therapy and resume daily responsibilities, is likely to do just that. Thus, socioeconomic class may affect not only a person's diagnosis but the chances of eventual improvement as well.

The Biological Perspective

Ever since Hippocrates suggested that abnormal behavior is a result of too much phlegm or bile circulating through the body, scientists have attempted to find biogenic explanations for psychological disorder. Like psychogenic theories, biogenic theories are varied and stress different aspects of organic functioning. Genes, biochemistry, and neurological impairment have all been the focus of biogenic explanations. In many cases, organic causation is clear and undeniable, as when impairment results from brain injury, infection, or tumor. The effects of alcoholism and untreated syphilis, for example, have been mentioned earlier. For a number of other disorders, primarily anxiety disorders, most research has focused on psychogenic explanations. In the case of psychoses, a good deal of research has been directed at establishing some organic basis. Schizophrenia, the most prevalent psychosis, has been the subject of both genetic and biochemical research.

Genetic Theories of Disorder

A direct connection between genes and behavior is difficult to document, as noted in Chapter 11, and only a few disorders have been traced directly to specific genetic defects. Chromosomal abnormality has been established as the cause of Down's syndrome and Turner's syndrome, both of which result in mental retardation. But establishing a link between defective gene combinations and a complex disorder like schizophrenia is an extremely difficult task. The main obstacle is the virtual impossibility of eliminating environmental factors—the influence of family and society. In schizophrenia, as in most other situations, there is no simple way to separate genes from environment.

Nevertheless, fragmentary evidence that schizophrenia may be hereditary has come from studies that explore the incidence of schizophrenia in families. It has been discovered, for instance, that the brother or sister of a schizophrenic, with whom she or he shares many genes, is more likely to be schizophrenic than is, say, the schizophrenic's first cousin (Slater, 1968). Studies of identical and fraternal twins also seem to affirm the role of heredity in schizophrenia. In about 40 to 50 percent of the cases, when one identical twin had schizophrenia, the other twin also had it; the frequency among fraternal twins was much lower but still significant —10 to 15 percent, as shown in Figure 23.2 (Gottesman, 1978).

The problem with studies of twins is that most pairs are reared under the same conditions, making it difficult to rule out environmental factors. To overcome the environmental obstacle, researchers have studied children adopted in infancy. Using adoption and hospitalization records in Denmark, one group of investigators identified schizophrenics who had been adopted as children. After establishing a control group of nonschizophrenic adults who also had been adopted as children, the researchers traced the adoptive and biological relatives of both groups. Adoptive relatives of the schizophrenics, who had shared their environment, showed no greater incidence of schizophrenia than did adoptive relatives of adults in the control group. But among biological relatives of the schizophrenics, who shared their genes but not their environment, the incidence of schizophrenia was significantly higher than among biological relatives of the control group (Kety et al., 1971).

Other studies have looked at children born to mothers hospitalized with schizophrenia who gave their infants up for adoption. In one study that compared fifty-eight adopted children of schizophrenic mothers with a control group of adopted children, more than 15 percent of the children born to schizophrenic mothers, but none of the children in the control group, developed schizophrenia (Heston, 1966).

Finally, researchers identified seventy-six cases in which parents had given up their children for adoption before the parents themselves

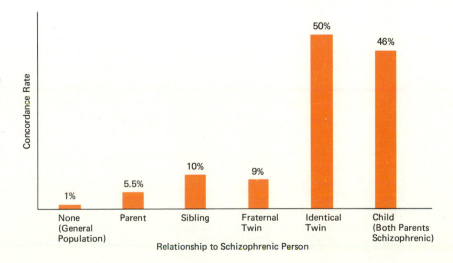

Figure 23.2 The concordance rates that accompany various degrees of relationship to a schizophrenic person. A concordance rate of 100 percent would mean that if one member of the related pair is schizophrenic, the other person will be too. Note that if a fraternal twin is schizophrenic, the concordance rate is about the same as that for any other sibling, but that the concordance rate for an identical twin is far higher. (After Gottessman and Shields, 1972.)

At Risk for Schizophrenia

Studying schizophrenics to explain the development of their disorder presents problems. The behavioral and biochemical differences that distinguish schizophrenics from nonschizophrenics could be the result of drug therapy or institutional living. Differences in family communication patterns could be the response of family members to a disturbed child. Recollections from parents, grandparents, or mental health professionals could be colored by their present knowledge of the person's condition.

For these reasons, the ideal way to trace the development of schizophrenia is to follow children from birth, keeping track of their physiological, psychological, and social histories, and then —after the disorder develops—to look for connections between environmental conditions and eventual schizophrenia.

Since few people become schizophrenic, the best place to look for future cases is among the children of schizophrenic mothers. About 15 percent of these children eventually develop the disorder, compared with less than 1 percent of the general population.

In the early 1960s, Sarnoff Mednick (1970) and Fini Schulsinger set up just such a longitudinal study among Danish children. The investigators found 200 normally functioning children of schizophrenic mothers and matched them with a control group of children whose mothers were not schizophrenic.

This study had several notable points. First, none of the children had ever been institutionalized, had drug therapy, or experienced any of the other environmental aspects of schizophrenic treatment. Second, bias could be

eliminated from the testing and diagnosis because no one knew which children would become schizophrenic. Third, no one's colored recollections were part of the record; all information was current. Fourth, in addition to the formal control group, the investigators had built in a second control group consisting of high-risk children who did not develop schizophrenia (Mednick, 1971).

By 1971, twenty-seven of the two hundred high-risk children had been diagnosed as emotionally disturbed. When these children were compared with children in the control group and with high-risk children who were not deviant, investigators found five critical differences:

1. The mothers of deviant children were hospitalized earlier in their children's lives and were more severely

were hospitalized for schizophrenia, thereby eliminating the possibility that a parent's abnormal condition during the active phase of the disorder might have affected the child. When the children were traced, 33 percent of them showed some symptoms of schizophrenia, although only one child had been hospitalized for the disorder. In a control group of adopted children with non-schizophrenic parents, only 15 percent showed any symptoms of schizophrenia (Rosenthal et al., 1971).

Although these adoption studies support the view that heredity plays a role in schizophrenia, they do not rule out environmental influences. First, adoption is not random. Children with the worst prospects may be given to the worst adoptive parents. Second, these schizophrenics may have inherited a vulnerability to schizophrenia, but unless certain environmental factors are present, the disorder will not develop. Thus, most

researchers believe that, whatever combination of genes is involved, genes alone will not produce the disorder. If schizophrenia were primarily a matter of heredity, the incidence of schizophrenia would be far higher than has been found. According to the most widely held view, which is known as the **diathesis-stress model**, genes establish a diathesis, or predisposition, to schizophrenia, but the disorder will not develop unless the predisposition is combined with certain stressful environmental factors.

Biochemical Theories of Disorder

If genes are involved in the transmission of some psychological disorders, the problem is to establish how they operate to produce abnormal behavior in some environments. Converging evidence indicates that an important influence

schizophrenic than the mothers of children who were not deviant.

2. The deviant children were aggressive and disruptive in school.

3. On a word-association test, the deviant children quickly drifted from the stimulus word, so that, given the word "table," a deviant child might reply, "chair, top, leg, girl, pretty, shy."

4. The deviant children showed quite different GSRs; when they heard a series of irritating noises, for example, their GSRs did not eventually habituate as did the responses of other children.

5. Complications during the mother's pregnancy or the child's birth had occurred among 70 percent of the deviant children, but among only 15 percent of the healthy high-risk group and 33 percent of the control group (Mednick, 1971).

Later reports from this and other projects have found additional differences. Children in the high-risk group:

1. commit more criminal offenses (Kirkegaard-Sorenson and Mednick, 1975);

2. show more adjustment problems (Hanson et al., 1976);

3. have difficulty focusing their attention (Asarnow et al., 1977);

4. show maturational lags in the processing of visual stimuli (Herman et al., 1977);

5. have different EEG patterns (Ital, 1977).

Between 1972 and 1974, all the children in the study went through an intensive diagnostic assessment. Among the high-risk group, seventeen were diagnosed as schizophrenic, but only one low-risk child was diagnosed as schizophrenic. However, one difference that had earlier distinguished deviant children in the high-risk group had disappeared. Those in the high-risk group who were diagnosed as schizophrenic did not show more drift on the word-association task than did those who did not become schizophrenic (Griffith et al., 1980).

It will be another ten years before all the data from this project are collected and analyzed. Once the findings are complete, we may have a better idea of how schizophrenia develops.

---

may be the body's chemistry. As we saw in Chapter 11, genes are the transmitters of all hereditary information. A single defective gene can disrupt the program for a sequence of necessary biochemical transformations; such a disruption can result in physical or mental disorder. For example, Chapter 11 described how a single defective gene, by upsetting the body's metabolism of phenylalanine, produces phenylketonuria (PKU), with its severe mental retardation.

The hypothesis that mental disorder is caused by some biochemical abnormality can be explored by searching for some biochemical difference between people with a particular disorder and a control group of nondisturbed people. Although this procedure seems straightforward, it is often difficult to carry out. Complications can arise in finding an appropriate control group. The perfect control group would have to live in an environment identical to that of the people who suffer from the disorder, so that the only difference between the subjects and the control group would be the disorder.

However, the biochemistry of human beings is extremely complex, and our understanding of it is far from complete. The medical and life histories, and even the diets, of psychiatric patients are markedly different from those of the members of control groups. Most hospitalized schizophrenics, for example, eat an institutional diet, smoke heavily, get little exercise, and have long histories of drug therapy. Any of these factors can alter a person's biochemistry. Moreover, the extreme emotional and physical stresses associated with having a mental disorder can also cause changes in biochemical functioning (Kety, 1969). When researchers find that the body chemistry of disturbed persons differs from that of nondisturbed people, they must then find ways of determining whether these differences

Sometimes the environment contributes to feelings of stress and depression, as evoked in this photograph, in which a boy stands in an empty school playground, surrounded by ominous-looking apartment buildings.

are related to the causes of the disorder or to its effects.

Some progress has been made in distinguishing causes from effects, especially in the biochemistry of schizophrenic disorders. The most promising biochemical approach involves neurotransmitters and is called the **dopamine hypothesis**. According to this view, schizophrenia is associated with excessive activity in those parts of the brain that use dopamine to transmit neural impulses. The major impetus for this hypothesis comes from research on "antipsychotic" drugs (the phenothiazines and butyrophenones), which effectively reduce the primary symptoms of schizophrenia, including thought disorder, blunted emotional responses, withdrawal, and autistic behavior. The drugs work by blocking the absorption of dopamine by the dopamine receptors in the neurons, thereby reducing neural activity in those areas of the brain that use dopamine to transmit neural impulses (Creese, Burt, and Snyder, 1975; Snyder, 1981).

This evidence has been supported by research into the effects of amphetamine and methylphenidate, two stimulants that are known to increase dopamine activity in the brain. As we saw in the discussion of amphetamine psychosis in Chapter 6, these substances can produce temporary psychotic states remarkably similar to schizophrenia (Snyder, 1972; 1976). Furthermore, when either drug is given to schizophrenic patients, their symptoms become even more pronounced (Van Kammen, 1977).

The focus on dopamine has revealed a possible link between schizophrenia and Parkinson's disease, an organic brain disorder that produces uncontrollable body tremors. As noted in Chapter 3, Parkinson's disease is caused in part by a gradual destruction of the pathways that normally carry dopamine, and the drug L-dopa, which increases dopamine activity, effectively reduces tremors in patients with the disease. However, L-dopa can also produce symptoms like those of schizophrenia, and antipsychotic drugs often produce a Parkinson's-like movement disorder as a side effect (Paul, 1977).

Although many lines of evidence converge to support the dopamine hypothesis, there is also evidence against it. For example, not all schizophrenics respond to drugs that block the absorption of dopamine; from 50 to 75 percent of patients who receive the drugs during an acute episode show improvement, but the rest do not respond (Gelder and Kolakowska, 1979). In addition, schizophrenics who do respond to these drugs improve gradually, over a period of about six weeks. Yet it takes only a few hours for the drugs to block dopamine receptors in the brain. If schizophrenia were merely the result of activity in these neural tracts, it should improve dramatically within a few hours (Davis, 1978). It is apparent that dopamine's involvement in the development of schizophrenia is not simple and that we are far from establishing a clear-cut cause-and-effect relationship.

A similar approach to the causes of depression has resulted in the **catecholamine hypothesis**. Again, neurotransmitters are involved, and this time the focus is on norepinephrine. (Norepinephrine is one of the catecholamines.) According to this hypothesis, depression results from low levels of norepinephrine in the brain, while high levels of norepinephrine can produce mania. As with the dopamine hypothesis, the supporting evidence is indirect and based primarily on drug effects. Drugs that increase norepinephrine levels relieve depression or produce mania, whereas drugs that reduce norepinephrine levels produce depression or alleviate mania (Schildkraut, 1965; 1972). More recently, it has been suggested that norepinephrine levels by themselves may not produce depression. Instead, an interaction between norepinephrine and excess hormones produced by the thyroid gland may be responsible for depression and mania (Whybrow and Prange, 1981).

Although evidence relating schizophrenia and depression to neurotransmitters continues to grow, psychogenic factors cannot be dismissed. As noted earlier, the social and psychological bases of schizophrenia and depression—as well as other mental disorders—must be taken into account in any complete explanation of the disorder.

One noteworthy attempt at synthesizing psychogenic and biogenic explanations has been the proposal that many factors increase the likelihood of a person's developing schizophrenia, including genes, social class, and family communication patterns (Zubin and Spring, 1977). In this view, a person's vulnerability to schizophrenia depends upon the cumulative total of such factors. In addition, the degree of vulnerability might be reduced by improving a person's competence and ability to cope with stressful events.

Such a synthesis reminds us that physical and mental functioning cannot realistically be separated, as we saw in the discussion of stress (see Chapter 21). Since mind is a function of the nervous system, psychogenic and biogenic theories of abnormal behavior are probably complementary rather than mutually exclusive. Although some biological theorists claim that all mental disorders are organically based, and some behaviorists argue that all abnormal behavior is the consequence of learning, it is extremely unlikely that any one perspective or any one theory will ever be able to account for all abnormal behavior.

SUMMARY

1. Societies have always explained and defined deviant behavior according to their own particular philosophical and religious outlooks. Typical explanations for psychological disturbances have been gods, demons, disease, and emotional stress. Theorists today tend to draw on both biogenic and psychogenic explanations. **Biogenic theory**, which views mental disorder as having a physiological cause, was established among psychiatrists in the late nineteenth century by Kraepelin. The biogenic approach led to the rise of the medical model, which has received a good deal of criticism. **Psychogenic theory**, which holds that mental disturbances result from emo-

tional stress, began with Mesmer, whose major contribution to psychotherapy was the discovery of the power of suggestion in curing mental disorders.

2. Psychoanalytic theory holds that mental disorders arise when id, ego, and superego are out of balance because of unresolved conflicts, and the person encounters additional stress. Conflicts among the id, ego, and superego can lead to **reality anxiety**, when an external danger triggers fear; to **moral anxiety**, when the superego demands moral behavior and self-punishment for transgressions, or to **neurotic anxiety**, when

impulses generated by the id threaten to overwhelm the ego. To relieve neurotic anxiety, the ego may use defense mechanisms in an increasingly rigid manner; the defense mechanism chosen determines the form of abnormal behavior that appears. "Neuroses" are associated with the overuse of defense mechanisms to control the id; psychoses occur when the ego is so weak that it has no defenses against the id.

3. Behavioral theorists believe that abnormal behavior is learned in the same way as is all other behavior. The person with a psychological disorder has either learned inappropriate behavior or failed to learn adaptive behavior. Maladaptive behavior can result from modeling, from direct reinforcement, or from a combination of reinforcement and extinction. Behaviorally oriented theorists who take a cognitive approach believe that the way people interpret events determines their feelings and behavior. Since maladaptive behavior is seen as neither an illness nor a symptom of psychic conflict, the task is to identify what stimuli elicit the behavior and what reinforces it; thus, the major emphasis of the behavioral approach is treatment.

4. The **humanistic-existential perspective**, which includes both humanistic and existential theorists, makes four basic assumptions: (a) a **phenomenological approach**—which stresses the individual's perception of the world—is necessary; (b) each individual is unique; (c) human potential must be emphasized; (d) the individual is free to make choices and is responsible for her or his own behavior. Humanistic theorists believe that maladjustment is the result of a thwarted drive for self-actualization. Frankl, an existential theorist, divides psychological disorders into anxiety neuroses, the result of guilt over not having pursued personal values, and obsessional neuroses, the result of a person's inability to endure the discrepancy between the real and the ideal. Laing, another existential theorist, believes that disorders are caused by modern society and the modern nuclear family; he believes most people are mad and the schizophrenic is "hypersane" and searching for an authentic identity.

5. The family perspective goes beyond the psychological processes of the individual to focus on the family's role in the development of abnormal behavior. According to Lidz, families of schizophrenics show one of two family patterns: (a) the **marital schism** pattern, in which the parents are bitterly divided; and (b) the **marital skew** pattern, in which a strong but disturbed parent totally dominates a dependent or masochistic parent who supports the dominant parent's actions. Other theorists believe that faulty family communication is at the root of schizophrenia. According to the **double-bind hypothesis**, parents in these families habitually send conflicting messages to their children so that a child never learns to distinguish among the meanings expressed in normal language and behavior.

6. The sociocultural perspective, which places the primary blame for disorders on society, stresses two interrelated views: social stress, in which the stresses of modern society cause abnormal behavior; and social labeling, in which having a "mentally ill" label attached to oneself leads to the adoption of a "sick" role. In both views, compared to people in the middle class, people in lower socioeconomic classes are more likely to show mental disorder, because they face more stress, and are more likely to be labeled as disordered.

7. In the biological perspective, mental disorders have biogenic causes: genes, biochemistry, or neurological impairment. Genetic studies of schizophrenia, in which the disorder is traced in families and which uses studies of twins and of children adopted in infancy, indicate that heredity plays some role in schizophrenia. According to the **diathesis-stress model**, genes establish a predisposition to schizophrenia and environmental stress allows it to develop. Biochemical studies indicate that neurotransmitters are involved in schizophrenia and in depression. According to the **dopamine hypothesis**, schizophrenia is associated with excessive activity in those parts of the brain that use dopamine to transmit neural impulses. According to the **catecholamine hypothesis**, **depression** is associated with low levels of norepinephrine in the brain.

8. Physical and mental functioning cannot be separated, and psychogenic and biogenic theories of abnormal behavior are probably complementary rather than mutually exclusive. Neither perspective, by itself, is likely to account for all psychological disturbances.

KEY TERMS

authenticity	existential frustration	neurotic anxiety
biogenic theory	humanistic-existential	obsessive-compulsive
catecholamine hypothesis	perspective	disorders
diathesis-stress model	marital schism	phenomenological approach
dopamine hypothesis	marital skew	psychogenic theory
double-bind hypothesis	moral anxiety	reality anxiety

RECOMMENDED READINGS

Bootzin, R. R., and J. R. Acocella. *Abnormal Psychology: Current Perspectives.* 3rd ed. New York: Random House, 1980. A comprehensive textbook that describes the major categories of psychological disorders and presents the major theoretical perspectives.

Maser, J. D., and M. E. P. Seligman. *Psychopathology: Experimental Models.* San Francisco: Freeman, 1977. A collection of papers in which each author explores the fundamental nature of a different disorder through experimental research.

Snyder, S. H. *Madness and the Brain.* New York: McGraw-Hill, 1974. A highly readable account of the biological bases of mental disorder by one of the leading researchers in the field.

Wynne, L. C., R. L. Cromwell, and S. Matthysse (eds.). *The Nature of Schizophrenia: New Approaches to Research and Treatment.* New York: Wiley, 1978. A collection of papers on the latest findings and theories regarding schizophrenia.

CHAPTER 24

Approaches to Treatment

A person who claims to hear voices might be venerated as a saint in one age, burned as a witch in a second, and hospitalized as a psychotic in a third. Just as the supposed cause of abnormal behavior varies with each society's notions about mental disorders, so does the treatment. When people were thought to be possessed by evil spirits, the spirits were allowed to escape through holes drilled in the skull or were driven out by exorcism. For many centuries the church was the agency of treatment for all disorders. During other periods, families kept strangely behaving individuals at home, hiding them away in attics or caring for them as children. In the last half century, in line with current notions about abnormal behavior, mental health professionals have assumed many of the therapeutic functions once served by family and church.

This chapter will examine the ways these professionals use psychotherapy to treat mental disorders, both individually and in groups. We will also look at various organic modes of treatment, which range from drugs to psychosurgery.

The Nature of Psychotherapy

Psychotherapy may be defined as a systematic series of interactions between a thera-

pist trained to aid in solving psychological problems and a person who is troubled or is troubling others. In contrast to the advice of family and clergy, psychotherapy is a relatively formal arrangement in which the therapist is a paid professional. Psychotherapists may have had any of several kinds of professional training. A **psychiatrist** is a physician (MD) who specializes in the diagnosis and treatment of mental illness. Usually she or he has completed a three-year residency in psychiatry. A **clinical psychologist** has earned a doctorate (PhD or PsyD) in clinical psychology and has completed a one-year clinical internship. A **psychoanalyst** is usually a psychiatrist (although she or he can be a psychologist or a lay person) who has had special training in the technique of psychoanalysis and who has been psychoanalyzed as part of the training. A **psychiatric social worker** has earned a master's degree in social work and has specialized in psychiatric social work. A **psychiatric nurse** is a registered nurse who has specialized in psychiatric nursing.

Psychotherapists may use any of a wide variety of therapeutic approaches, depending upon their training, their view of the therapist's role, and their own style. The goal of some psychotherapies is the patient's understanding of her or his motives for behaving in a particular way; the goal of other psychotherapies is to change the patient's behavior directly, paying little or no attention to motives. There are more than 100 different varieties of psychotherapy, each with its own specific program. Although the distinctions among different therapies are not always clear-cut, most therapists adhere to one of the major perspectives described in Chapter 23. Thus, the simplest and most accessible way to examine the various psychotherapies is in terms of those perspectives. Each perspective has its own notion of who should be treated, the focus of the treatment, the client's role, and the role of the therapist.

Psychodynamic Therapies

The psychodynamic therapies, particularly psychoanalysis, are closely identified with Sigmund Freud. Psychoanalysis is at once a general theory of personality, a theory of psychopathology, and a form of psychotherapy. All therapies that focus on a dynamic interplay of conscious and unconscious elements are derived from psychoanalysis. For a variety of reasons, including economic ones, few practioners today use standard Freudian psychoanalysis (Korchin, 1976). Although it can be effective, it is a long and expensive process.

Freudian Psychoanalysis

Freud's experiences with his patients led him to conclude that the source of neurosis was the anxiety experienced when unacceptable unconscious impulses threatened to break through the constraints established by the ego. To deal with this threat, the patient would resort to defense mechanisms, the most important of which was repression—the "forgetting" of thoughts and impulses that the conscious mind considered shameful or forbidden. Although such impulses could be hidden for a while, they remained alive in the unconscious, provoking anxiety and draining strength from the ego, which expended energy in keeping them hidden. According to

During psychoanalysis, patients must resolve childhood conflicts that originated in their relationship with their parents.

Freud, the proper treatment for these anxiety-based disorders was to allow the unacceptable unconscious thoughts to emerge fully into the consciousness, where they could be confronted and "worked through," thus eliminating anxiety and liberating psychic energy for more constructive endeavors.

The aim of psychoanalysis is to uncover these long-buried impulses, putting the patient in touch with her or his unconscious, where past traumas and childhood conflicts still live. Various techniques are used to unlock the doors of memory. The client lies on a couch, a relaxing position that helps to loosen the restraints on the unconscious. Once relaxed, she or he free-associates, putting into words whatever thoughts come to mind in whatever order, without imposing self-censorship or logical structure and without interruption from the therapist, whose remarks are kept at a minimum and who sits out of the patient's view.

The therapist and the patient look for clues to present anxiety in dreams, in which the usual restraints on the unconscious are loosened. But because the unconscious is censored even in sleep, forbidden material appears only in symbolic form. Thus every dream has its manifest content, its plot or story line, and its latent content, the symbolic meaning of the dream, which exposes unconscious conflicts (see Chapter 18). For example, a client who has just had a baby might dream that she had given birth to two boys and that one had died (manifest content). The latent content of the dream, however, may indicate the new mother's ambivalent feelings toward her son, whom she both wants and does not want.

The conscious confrontation and recognition of forbidden thoughts are not pleasant. Often at this stage in the therapy clients begin to show signs of **resistance,** or attempts to block treatment. They may pick an argument with the therapist, make jokes, even miss appointments rather than squarely face the unpleasant material. The therapist's interpretation of resistance is an important part of treatment, for it enables the client to learn to confront and analyze painful conflicts that would otherwise be avoided.

As the psychoanalysis progresses, the client may respond to the analyst with strong feelings —sometimes love and at other times hostility. Freud interpreted this phenomenon as **transference,** a transfer to him of his clients' childhood feelings toward important people in their lives, particularly their parents. It has become a basic assumption of traditional psychoanalysis that therapy will not be effective unless each client goes through this stage, called **transference neurosis**, in which the client reenacts with the analyst childhood conflicts with the parents. In the process, the client can bring out repressed emotions, unsatisfied needs, and misconceptions, and can begin to deal with them realistically.

The client attends one-hour psychoanalytic sessions three, four, or five times a week, for several years. In successful psychoanalysis the client eventually breaks through resistance, confronts unconscious conflicts, and resolves the transference neurosis, thereby eliminating anxiety and self-defeating responses to it.

Other Psychodynamic Therapies

Some of Freud's earliest associates, among them Carl Jung and Alfred Adler, began to modify psychoanalytic theory while Freud was still formulating it. As a result of their theoretical disagreements, which were discussed in Chapter 18, they developed variations on Freud's therapeutic techniques. Later psychoanalysts also made important revisions in both theory and therapy. One group, of whom the most prominent is Erik Erikson, formed a loosely knit band called ego psychologists. Although they accept a major portion of Freudian theory, ego psychologists reject Freud's assertion that all energy originates in the id and argue that the ego has substantial energy of its own, controlling such important functions as memory, judgment, perception, and planning. Thus, instead of concentrating on conflicts produced by uncontrollable impulses of the id, ego psychologists, in therapy, tend to focus on ego mechanisms and on how the person learns to cope with stress. Working primarily within the theoretical tradition founded by Freud, ego psychologists use free association, dream interpretation, and the analysis of resistance and transference to lead the client to insight. This adherence to Freudian tradition is not found among neo-Freudians, a group of psychodynamic theorists including Erich Fromm, Karen Horney, and Harry Stack Sullivan, who emphasize social influences and interpersonal relationships.

The many variations on psychoanalysis have been called, collectively, psychoanalytically ori-

BOXED IN by GIL SPITZER

HE HAD PROBLEMS WITH HIS PARENTS — SO WE TALKED ABOUT IT.

HE HAD PROBLEMS WITH HIS WIFE, — SO WE TALKED ABOUT IT.

HE HAD PROBLEMS WITH HIS KIDS — WE TALKED ABOUT THAT TOO.

HE HAD PROBLEMS PAYING ME FOR TREATMENT, WE'RE NOT TALKING ANYMORE!

© GIL SPITZER '78

Although some forms of therapy such as psychoanalysis may sometimes be expensive, other kinds of treatment such as group therapy and services offered by clinics may be quite inexpensive.

ented psychotherapy (Korchin, 1976). Although the therapists who practice such psychotherapy believe that training in psychoanalytic theory and techniques enhances their effectiveness, only a small percentage of them rigorously follow Freud's techniques. Many retain the general psychoanalytic framework, uncovering unconscious motivation, breaking down defenses, and dealing with resistance, but they practice a greatly modified form of psychoanalysis. The couch is generally dispensed with in favor of a situation in which clients sit up and face their therapists and the therapists take a more active role, advising, interpreting, and directing. Moreover, these modern psychotherapists tend to emphasize situations in the present, especially personal relationships, rather than events from the distant past. Therapy is briefer and less intensive, and its aim is usually more modest than the Freudian goal of completely restructuring the client's personality. Little research has been done on the effectiveness of traditional psychoanalysis (Luborsky and Spence, 1978), but evaluations of modified forms of psychoanalysis will be discussed later in the chapter.

ical principles to problem behavior (Bootzin, 1975). Basic to the approach of behavior therapy is the belief that the same principles govern all behavior, normal or deviant. Behavior therapists regard psychological problems as learned responses and view problem behavior not as a symptom of unconscious conflicts that must be uncovered but as the primary and legitimate target of therapy.

Behavior therapists also believe that the environment plays a crucial role in determining behavior and that problem behavior is specific to particular types of situations. Consequently, behavioral assessment requires accurate descriptions of observed behavior and the environmental events that accompany it.

Behavior therapists differ from other therapists such as psychoanalysts in the way they deal with the person's inner life. Psychoanalysts tend to regard a person's statements about thoughts and feelings as clues to deep-seated conflicts; but to behavior therapists, emotions and cognitions are simply hidden responses, subject to the same laws of learning as observable responses and equally open to change (e.g., Wolpe, 1978).

Behavior Therapies

In behavior therapy, the therapist applies learning and other experimentally derived psycholog-

Therapies Based on Classical Conditioning and Extinction

Techniques that use classical conditioning and extinction are meant to change behavior by changing emotion—the extent to which certain stimuli elicit feelings of joy, fear, liking, and disliking. In behavior therapy, the client's task is often to unlearn the connection between particular stimuli and her or his maladaptive emotional responses, as in the case of a student who is debilitated by anxiety during every examination. Behavior therapy can also be directed at developing aversions to stimuli that we might like too much—such as alcohol, cigarettes, and fattening foods. The most common techniques include systematic desensitization, flooding, and aversive conditioning.

Systematic Desensitization Perhaps the earliest example of the therapeutic use of classical conditioning was the experiment discussed in Chapter 8, in which a little boy named Peter was cured of his fear of rabbits by being given candy and other snacks as a rabbit was gradually brought closer and closer (Jones, 1924). **Systematic desensitization**, which was developed by Joseph Wolpe (1958), is a similar procedure in which the client is gradually exposed to anxiety-producing stimuli while relaxed.

Systematic desensitization aims at the gradual extinction of anxiety, and it involves three steps. First, the therapist trains the client in deep-muscle relaxation, generally using Jacobson's progressive relaxation, which was described in Chapter 21. In the second step, the therapist and patient construct a hierarchy of fears—that is, a list of anxiety-producing situations, ranked from the least to the most feared, as shown in Table 24.1. Third, in the actual desensitization, after the client relaxes, the therapist describes the least anxiety-producing scene in the hierarchy and asks the client to imagine it. Once the client can imagine the scene without any anxiety, the therapist moves to the next scene in the hierarchy and again asks the client to imagine it. This procedure is repeated over a series of sessions until the client is able to imagine the scene that formerly produced the most anxiety without experiencing any rise in anxiety at all.

Systematic desensitization is not confined to imaginary stimuli; it can be used with real stimuli as well. The method appears to work because it indirectly encourages people to expose themselves to actual situations that they fear (Leitenberg, 1976). The technique has been extensively evaluated and has been found to be effective with phobias, recurrent nightmares, and complex interpersonal problems, such as fear of rejection and fear of behaving aggressively (Kazdin and Wilson, 1978; Rimm and Masters, 1979).

Flooding Flooding might be described as cold-turkey extinction therapy. It has been used to treat many of the same anxieties as systematic desensitization, but **flooding** involves real, not imaginary, situations, although imagination may be used in conjunction with actual exposure. The technique has been particularly useful in the elimination of obsessive-compulsive rituals (Rachman, Marks, and Hodgson, 1973). For example, if hand-washing rituals are based on the fear of contamination, flooding would require the clients actually to contaminate themselves by touching and handling dirt or whatever substance they are trying to avoid, and afterward to be prevented from carrying out their cleansing ritual. Over repeated trials, the intense anxiety elicited by "contamination" without hand washing would be extinguished. However, this treatment is intensive and requires that someone be with the client twenty-four hours a day to prevent the ritual. Thus, it is customarily used with patients who have been admitted to a hospital, where they are under constant supervision.

Aversive Conditioning When **aversive conditioning** is used to change emotional responses, the client is exposed to stimuli that elicit maladaptive responses, accompanied by aversive stimuli such as electric shock or nausea-produc-

Table 24.1 A graduated hierarchy of situations that elicited increasing amounts of anxiety from a client being systematically desensitized to the fear of death. A rating of 100 means "as tense as you ever are"; a rating of zero means "totally relaxed."

Ratings	Items
5	1. Seeing an ambulance
10	2. Seeing a hospital
20	3. Being inside a hospital
25	4. Reading the obituary notice of an old person
30–40	5. Passing a funeral home (the nearer, the worse)
40–55	6. Seeing a funeral (the nearer, the worse)
55–65	7. Driving past a cemetery (the nearer, the worse)
70	8. Reading the obituary notice of a young person who died of a heart attack
80	9. Seeing a burial assemblage from a distance
90	10. Being at a burial
100	11. Seeing a dead man in a coffin

Source: J. Wolpe and D. Wolpe. *Our Useless Fears.* Boston: Houghton Mifflin, 1981.

ing drugs. Through classical conditioning, the formerly attractive stimuli become repellent. Aversive conditioning has been used effectively in the treatment of sexual deviations and alcoholism (Rachman and Wilson, 1980). For example, a pedophiliac is given electric shocks while being shown slides of young children, or an alcoholic is given a drug that produces nausea and is then asked to sip an alcoholic beverage. Such therapy, particularly when it involves electric shock, has been controversial, even among behavior therapists.

One alternative to the use of painful shock is a technique called **covert sensitization**, in which clients are asked to visualize the behavior they are trying to eliminate and then to conjure up the image of an extremely painful or revolting stimulus (Cautela, 1966; 1967). For example, a therapist may instruct a smoker to close her eyes, relax, and picture herself taking out a cigarette. As she imagines lighting up and taking a puff, she is told to imagine that she feels nauseated, starts gagging, and vomits all over the floor, the cigarettes, and finally herself. The details of this scene are imagined with excruciating vividness and in minute detail. The client also practices visualizing an alternative, "relief" scene in which the decision not to smoke is accompanied by pleasurable sensations.

Aversive conditioning is most successful when combined with techniques aimed at teaching the client adaptive responses to replace the maladaptive responses. Thus, a problem drinker may need to learn not only how to avoid alcohol but also how to control stress more effectively and how to be more effective in relations with other people. Some of the techniques for controlling stress were discussed in Chapter 21; in the next sections we will see how therapists help clients to acquire new skills.

Therapies Based on Operant Conditioning

Therapies based on classical conditioning are extremely useful in extinguishing maladaptive responses and substituting adaptive ones. But often a client's behavior is not so much maladaptive as it is deficient or missing altogether (Goldfried and Davison, 1976). The person has never learned the appropriate response, or has been so seldom reinforced for it that it rarely occurs.

In treatments based on operant conditioning, desirable behavior is increased by reinforcement and undesirable behavior is decreased by punishment and extinction. Operant conditioning has been used effectively with many different problems to teach new skills and to increase the frequency of people's adaptive behavior in a wide variety of settings. The technique has been successfully applied in teaching retarded children to care for themselves, teaching language to autistic children, increasing the adaptive behavior of schizophrenics, increasing hyperactive children's ability to attend to schoolwork, and helping individuals who overeat, cannot sleep, or have difficulty studying. The effectiveness of operant conditioning can be enhanced within a framework of behavioral contracts or token economies.

Behavioral Contracts Often therapists find it helpful to write a contract that specifies exactly what behavior will earn reinforcement. This is particularly useful in the solution of marital and family conflicts. All parties agree on exactly what behavior each desires from the other. The behavior, along with rewards and sanctions, is stipulated in the contract, which all parties sign. A behavioral contract drawn up between a sixteen-year-old girl, Candy, and her parents is shown in Figure 24.1 (Stuart, 1971). Candy had a long record of drug abuse, promiscuity, truancy, and running away from home. Her parents, who felt they could no longer control her, wanted her hospitalized by the state. Instead, they were persuaded to try living by the terms of a behavioral contract. As the contract shows, both parties had much to gain from the agreement. Candy got an allowance and time to herself; the parents got compliance with household rules. In this case, the contract worked. Candy kept her side of the bargain most of the time, and the family remained together.

Contracts can also be used by individuals for personal goals involving self-control. The effectiveness of individual behavioral contracts was shown by the long-term results of a weight-loss program (Craighead, Stunkard, and O'Brien, 1981). Dieters kept a diary of all the food they ate over a preliminary period. On the basis of this diary, behavior therapists worked out individual contracts aimed at changing the dieters' eating habits. For example, the contract of one dieter might require that the dinner plate be filled at the stove so that dishes of food would not sit temptingly on the table, inviting second help-

PRIVILEGES	RESPONSIBILITIES
	GENERAL
In exchange for the privilege of remaining together and preserving some semblance of family integrity	Mr. and Mrs. Bremer and Candy all agree to concentrate on positively reinforcing each other's behavior while diminishing the present overemphasis upon the faults of the others.
	SPECIFIC
In exchange for the privilege of riding the bus directly from school into town after school on school days	Candy agrees to phone her father by 4 P.M. to tell him that she is all right and to return home by 5:15 P.M.
In exchange for the privilege of going out at 7 P.M. on one weekend evening without having to account for her whereabouts	Candy must maintain a weekly average of B in the academic ratings of all of her classes and must return home by 11:30 P.M.
In exchange for the privilege of going out a second weekend night	Candy must tell her parents by 6 P.M. of her destination and her companion and must return home by 11:30 P.M.
In exchange for the privilege of going out between 11 A.M. and 5:15 P.M. Saturdays, Sundays, and holidays	Candy agrees to have completed all household chores before leaving and to telephone her parents once during the time she is out to tell them that she is all right.
In exchange for the privilege of having Candy complete household chores and maintain her curfew	Mr. and Mrs. Bremer agree to pay Candy $1.50 on the morning following days on which the money is earned.
	BONUSES AND SANCTIONS
If Candy is 1–10 minutes late	she must come in the same amount of time earlier the following day, but she does not forfeit her money for the day.
If Candy is 11–30 minutes late	she must come in 22–60 minutes earlier the following day and does forfeit her money for the day.
If Candy is 31–60 minutes late	she loses the privilege of going out the following day and does forfeit her money for the day.
For each half hour of tardiness over one hour	Candy loses her privilege of going out and her money for one additional day.
Candy may go out on Sunday evenings from 7 to 9:30 P.M. and either Monday or Thursday evening	if she abides by all the terms of this contract from Sunday through Saturday with a total tardiness not exceeding 30 minutes, which must have been made up as above.
Candy may add a total of two hours divided among one to three curfews	if she abides by all the terms of this contract for two weeks with a total tardiness not exceeding 30 minutes, which must have been made up as above, and if she requests permission to use this additional time by 9 P.M.
	MONITORING

Mr. and Mrs. Bremer agree to keep written records of the hours of Candy's leaving and coming home and of the completion of her chores.

Candy agrees to furnish her parents with a school monitoring card each Friday at dinner.

_____

_____

_____

Figure 24.1 A contingency contract between a delinquent girl, Candy, and her parents. Such a contract states clearly what is expected of both parties to it. Contracts have been found useful with troubled families, especially when there has been a great deal of conflict, and family members have become hostile to one another. This procedure encourages all parties involved to develop positive behaviors (please one another) and at the same time reach their own goals (please themselves). (Adapted from Stuart, 1971.)

ings, while the contract of another dieter who customarily snacked on cookies might require confining snacks to popcorn. The terms of the contracts had to be followed five out of every seven days, which allowed the dieters to backslide occasionally without feeling like failures. The contract specified punishments for breaking its terms and rewards for following them; a typical reward might be a mid-week movie for adhering to the contract for a full week.

Dieters who used the behavioral contracts lost an average of twenty-four pounds; when checked up on a year later, the average dieter had gained back only four of those pounds, maintaining a twenty-pound weight loss for an entire year and indicating that adhering to the contract had had a lasting effect on eating habits. The power of the behavioral contract was made clear when these dieters were compared with another group who used commonly prescribed drugs as an aid to a typical restricted diet. The drug-assisted group lost more weight at first (thirty-two pounds), but when they stopped using drugs they tended to regain weight. A year later, the average drug-assisted dieter had regained twenty pounds, so that their net loss was only twelve pounds.

Token Economies Since reinforcement can so effectively change behavior, attempts have been made to structure a person's environment so that appropriate behavior in many areas of life is reinforced while inappropriate behavior is extinguished. The result is the **token economy**, used primarily in institutions, in which a wide range of appropriate behavior is rewarded with tangible conditioned reinforcers, or tokens, that patients can use to "buy" back-up reinforcers. In the typical token economy ward, a board lists various kinds of desirable behavior and the token reward for each. Within the institution is a canteen where patients can exchange their tokens for back-up reinforcers, such as candy, toiletries, or cigarettes. In many cases, tokens can also be spent on privileges—television time, access to the telephone, overnight passes, and so forth (Kazdin, 1977).

In one study (Paul and Lentz, 1977), highly dysfunctional mental patients, with an average of seventeen years of hospitalization, were placed in a strict token economy. The patients were severely disturbed; at any moment, at least 90 percent of them were behaving in a bizarre fashion—repetitive movements, blank staring, delu-

sions, hallucinations, incoherent speech, and sometimes assaulting staff members. When the token economy was instituted, the patients' lives changed drastically. Instead of living in custodial care, the patients spent 85 percent of their waking hours learning how to produce appropriate behavior, for which they were reinforced with prompt, courteous, and friendly attention. Maladaptive behavior was ignored, in an attempt to extinguish it. Adaptive behavior was reinforced; praise was handed out along with tokens, which could be earned in almost every aspect of hospital life: personal care, bed making, bathing, behavior at meals, classroom participation, and social behavior during free periods.

In this hospital, tokens were spent not only on luxuries but also on necessities. Patients without tokens to spend for their meals were turned away from the dining room. If lack of food appeared to create a health problem, the patients were given a "medical meal" that cost no tokens but that consisted of all the food served in a regular meal thrown into a blender and dyed purple-gray. The program eventually produced so much improvement that 98 percent of the patients could either be released into shelter-care arrangements or launched on an independent life. During the same period, only 45 percent of patients in the regular hospital program were released. Once released, all patients participated in a behaviorally oriented after-care program. As a result, few patients needed to be rehospitalized during the eighteen-month follow-up.

Therapies Based on Modeling and Cognitive Restructuring

Not all behavior therapists rely on the techniques of classical and operant conditioning. Those who have been influenced by the social-learning perspective place great emphasis on cognition. They believe that modeling has a powerful effect on behavioral change and that the way people interpret events in their lives is as important as what actually happens to them.

Modeling **Modeling** is the process by which a person learns some new behavior by watching another person perform it; as we saw in Chapter 8, in this observational learning the model's actions are considered stimuli that act as information. Modeling has been particularly effective in the treatment of phobias (Rosenthal and Bandura, 1978). For example, researchers have been able to eliminate dog phobia in children by having them, in a number of successive sessions, watch another child (called "Fearless Peer") approach a dog, touch it, pet it, and eventually play actively with it. After observing the Fearless Peer, 67 percent of the children had overcome their fear of dogs to such an extent that they could climb into a playpen with a dog, pet it, and remain alone with the animal (Bandura, Grusec, and Menlove, 1967).

More effective than modeling alone is **participant modeling**, in which the therapist models the feared activity and then helps the client to confront and master a graduated series of threatening activities (Bandura, Jeffery, and Wright, 1974). This procedure is one we all use to learn many skills in everyday life—not simply from observing another but by practicing our imitation of the model until we have mastered the activity. When applied to social behavior, a similar procedure has been called **behavior rehearsal**. It has been included in programs for social skills training and assertiveness training, in which people learn how to assert themselves, overcoming their passivity yet not becoming aggressive (e.g., Sarason, 1976).

Recently, Albert Bandura (1977) has proposed a comprehensive theory of behavior change. He suggests that the mechanisms by which behavior is regulated are primarily cognitive. Particularly important in his view are **efficacy expectations**—people's beliefs that they can successfully execute whatever behavior is required to produced a desired outcome. Efficacy expectations determine how hard people will try, how long they will persist, and whether they will attempt an act at all. Since success raises expectations and failure lowers them, expectations can be increased either by experiencing the sense of mastery that follows one's own successful performance or by observing the success of another. Thus, participant modeling and behavior rehearsal are likely to be effective treatments because they are powerful means of changing efficacy expectations.

Cognitive Restructuring   The process of **cognitive restructuring** focuses on the client's ways of perceiving the world and regards self-defeating behavior as a result of the client's false assumptions. Consequently, therapy aims at identifying these irrational assumptions and subjecting them to the cold light of reason. Albert Ellis (1962), for example, argues that thousands of people lead unhappy lives because of certain irrational beliefs that they hold, such as "I must be loved and approved of by everyone whose love and approval I seek" or "I must be utterly competent in everything I do." In Ellis' **rational-emotive therapy**, clients are first led to recognize the irrational nature of these previously unexamined beliefs, then are aided in establishing a more realistic cognitive framework so that they interpret events in their lives in the light of different assumptions.

An effective way to change a person's erroneous assumptions and patterns of thought has been developed by Donald Meichenbaum (1977). Meichenbaum calls his method of cognitive restructuring **self-instructional training**, and it works directly on maladaptive mental processes. Meichenbaum gives clients new ways of thinking and talking about their problems, and in concentrating on this positive "self-talk," people give up their old self-defeating ways of thought that have become self-fulfilling prophecies. In self-instructional training, the therapist first helps the client to identify the defeating self-talk that leads to maladaptive behavior (e.g., "I can't control myself"). Then the therapist models constructive self-talk (e.g., "If I take my time and attend to each part of the problem, I can perform much better") that the client can use in stressful situations such as an examination or a job interview. Self-instructional training has been successful at improving the problem-solving skills of hyperactive children, at improving the rationality of schizophrenics' speech, at reducing the anxiety and increasing the effectiveness of college students when they must speak in public or take examinations, and at increasing tolerance for pain (Meichenbaum, 1977).

A third method of cognitive restructuring is **cognitive therapy**, a treatment devised by Aaron Beck (1976). Beck also believes that irrational thoughts and faulty assumptions can lead to emotional disorders, and he has been especially successful in treating depression. When treating depressed people with cognitive therapy, the therapist's first task is to show them that what they think determines how they feel. In the process, the therapist questions clients in such a way that they examine the connection between their own interpretations of events and their subsequent feelings. Gradually, they discover that the negative conclusions they have made about themselves and the world are not based on fact; when this point is reached, the therapist helps the clients to substitute appropriate interpretations of events and to correct the unreasonable assumptions that have led them to distort reality and are thus central to their depression (Beck et al., 1979).

Humanistic Therapies

In humanistic therapies, the concepts of illness, doctor, and patient are deemphasized. Instead, psychological treatment is viewed as a growth experience, and the therapist's task is to help clients fulfill their individual human potential. Unlike behavior therapy and psychodynamic therapies, humanistic therapies emphasize the clients' sense of freedom and their ability to choose their own future rather than their enslavement to the past. A close client-therapist relationship is encouraged as the therapist attempts to share the client's experience while providing an uncritical atmosphere in which the client's inner strength can emerge.

Client-Centered Therapy

The best-known of the humanistic therapies is Carl Rogers' system of **client-centered therapy**, which is also referred to as **nondirective counseling**. Rogers (1951) believes that people are innately motivated to fulfill their own individual potentials; thus, the role of the therapist is to help clients clarify their feelings and come to value their own experience in the world, thus healing the split between self and organism discussed in Chapter 19.

In order to accomplish this, the therapist must be empathic, warm, and sincere. Thus, the therapist must have **congruence**, or genuineness, the ability to share her or his own feelings with the client in an open and spontaneous manner. In addition, the therapist must have **empathic understanding**, the ability to see the world through the eyes of the client. The therapist offers the client **unconditional positive regard**, supporting the client regardless of what she or he says or does. Instead of interpreting or instructing, the therapist clarifies the client's feelings by restating what has been said ("You seem to have been disappointed whenever your father failed to approve of one of your boy friends"), but does

not offer divergent interpretations or tell the client what to do or how to act. According to Rogers, as clients become more aware of their own emotions and learn to accept them, they can make constructive choices that fit in with their goals. In this nonthreatening therapeutic context, the client learns to reintegrate self and oganism, to accept all exeriences as genuine, and to establish an unconditional positive self-regard.

Rogers and his followers have been pioneers in investigating the process and outcome of therapy. Rogers was one of the first therapists to tape-record his sessions with clients in an attempt to encourage analysis of the therapeutic process. His efforts led to extensive studies of the therapeutic process, in which all types of therapy have been examined (e.g., Garfield, 1978; Orlinsky and Howard, 1978). Despite Rogers' assertion, however, the qualities of empathy, warmth, and sincerity do not seem to be strongly related to the outcome of therapy (Lambert, de Julio, and Stein, 1978).

Gestalt Therapy

In **Gestalt therapy**, Freudian concepts are blended with humanistic philosophy and radically different therapeutic techniques. Frederick (Fritz) S. Perls (1970; Perls, Hefferline, and Goodman, 1951), who developed Gestalt therapy, depended heavily on Freudian ideas concerning motivation, dream interpretation, and the influence of old, unresolved conflicts on present psychological disorder, but he rejected Freud's determinism. Gestalt (meaning "whole," "form," "pattern," or "image") therapy attempts to take all life into consideration. The organism is seen as having an inherent capacity for growth, which is accomplished through insights and interactions with the environment. The ultimate goal is "organismic self-regulation," or balance and integration of the individual. Through awareness, imbalances can be corrected and successful integration of the different aspects of personality can be achieved and maintained.

The role of the therapist is to help the client dispense with defenses, unfold potential, increase awareness, and release pent-up feelings. The three major values of Gestalt therapy are emphasis on the *now*, rather than the past or the future; focus on the *spatial*, what is present rather than what is absent; and concentration on the *substantial,* the act rather than the fantasy (Korchin, 1976).

Gestalt therapists use a variety of techniques to achieve these goals. Therapy takes place within the framework of explicit rules governing communication and language. All communication between therapist and client is focused on the present and on the client's present awareness, and it is an exchange between equals. Clients are expected to use the first-person singular ("I am," "I do," "I feel") to show that they take responsibility for their own actions and feelings (saying, for example, "I am angry," rather than "Don't you think I have a right to be annoyed?"). Some exercises are designed to heighten the client's awareness of past conflicts. As clients act out their conflicts, they assume different aspects of their personality, shifting from one role to another to experience conflicting needs and demands. The reenactment of these conflicts often becomes violent and highly emotional. Other exercises develop clients' awareness of their own movements, tone of voice, and feelings. Once clients have focused awareness on various aspects of self, they can take responsibility for their own feelings, thoughts, and actions. When dreams are analyzed, the different characters and objects in the dream are seen as fragments of the self, and the client is encouraged to imagine that she or he is each character and object and to express the feelings that accompany these roles. Such reenactments lead to acceptance and reintegration of these aspects of the self.

Group and Family Approaches

Individual therapy is both expensive and time-consuming. In addition, the therapist sees the client alone, plucked out of her or his normal environment and stripped of the human relationships that may be affecting the client's disorder. The goal of making therapy cheaper, quicker, and more relevant to the patient's daily problems has led to the increasing popularity of treating people in couples, families, or groups.

Group Therapy

The concept of group therapy can be traced to Joseph Hershey Pratt, a Boston internist who worked with tubercular patients at the turn of the century. In an attempt to relieve the debilitating effects of depression and isolation experienced by the severely ill patients, he began to arrange regular group sessions, instructing his patients to keep diaries of their weight gains and losses, everyday events of their lives, and their general emotional state (Korchin, 1976). During the next thirty years, a number of psychiatrists independently experimented with group methods. In the 1930s and 1940s, group methods applying psychological principles began to evolve. And after World War II, the group-therapy movement gained impetus when it became necessary to treat large numbers of people, both veterans and civilians, who had suffered from the social, political, and economic upheavals of the period.

Group therapy lessens the economic problem that other therapies pose by allowing more patients to be treated at lower fees. But its chief advantage is that it concentrates on and promotes better interpersonal relationships. Moreover, clients who are extremely resistant to individual therapy seem to respond to the emotional support of the group. This is particularly true when all members of the group have a common problem, such as drug addiction, alcoholism, or obesity.

The variety of groups is endless. There are awareness groups for women, men, homosexuals, and divorced people; self-help groups for ex-convicts, chain smokers, and gamblers; and other kinds of groups for a variety of people with a variety of problems, needs, and goals. Each approach to psychotherapy that has been discussed in this chapter has been developed into a form of group psychotherapy. There are psychoanalytic therapy groups, behavior therapy groups, and humanistic therapy groups (especially Gestalt groups). In each of these groups, therapy is based on the extension of psychotherapeutic principles into a group setting. There are also some forms of group therapy that are not so easily recognized as outgrowths of individual therapy approaches: for example, transactional analysis and encounter groups (see the box on page 556).

Psychodynamic theory provides the basis for **transactional analysis**, a therapy originated by Eric Berne and often used with groups of couples. According to Berne, personality is made up of three ego states that are similar to Freud's view of personality structure: the parent, which corresponds to the superego; the child, which

Encounter Groups

One form of group therapy is not meant to help people overcome psychological problems. Instead, encounter groups aim at personal growth and increased openness in personal relations. Although group members sometimes talk about daily problems in a session, the emphasis is often on the members' emotional reaction to one another. Members voice whatever emotion—love, anger, jealousy, warmth, suspicion—they feel toward other members, who respond in kind. Emotional outbursts are encouraged: people may yell, weep, touch one another. The interpersonal encounters are instant, brief, and intense. Such exchanges give people practice in expressing their emotions and perhaps provide insight into the way they affect others. Eventually, the experience may teach them how to work out conflicts in personal relationships.

In encounter groups, the leader is not supposed to play "expert," as in other therapies. However, she or he must make sure that each person is allowed a chance to express feelings and that the group does not make any member a scapegoat. Thus, the leader swerves between direction and participation, and is considered fair game for the members.

The format of the group varies. Some are conducted as marathons, lasting as long as an entire weekend—day and night. Constant exposure in the group "pressure cooker" builds up emotional intensity, speeding the process of self-revelation. Other group techniques involve the setting (all members nude or in a swimming pool) or the exercises used to initiate group interaction. (**eyeball-to-eyeball**, in which pairs of participants stare into each other's eyes, or **blind mill**, in which participants close their

eyes and wander around the room, communicating only by touch). The aim of all such maneuvers is to force members to interact honestly and spontaneously.

Although encounter groups are popular, they are not always harmless. In one study of seventeen different encounter groups, the experience turned nearly a tenth of the members into "casualties"—people whose psychological distress increased because of their group experience and who remained seriously distressed for six to eight months after the group disbanded. Yet about the same number of participants reported great benefits that lasted for at least six months (Lieberman, Yalom, and Miles, 1973a; see table).

Changes in Encounter Group Members

		Negative			Neutral	Positive		Total
		Casualty	Negative Change	Dropout	Unchanged	Moderate Change	High Change	
Immediately after Group	Group Members	8%	8%	13%	38%	20%	14%	206
	Control Group	—	23%	—	60%	13%	4%	69
Six to Eight Months after Group	Group Members	10%	8%	17%	33%	23%	9%	160*
	Control Group	—	15%	—	68%	11%	6%	47*

*Data not available on total sample

Source: M. A. Lieberman, I. D. Yalom, and M. B. Miles, "Encounter: The Leader Makes the Difference," *Psychology Today,* 6 (1973), 74.

corresponds to the id; and the adult, which corresponds to the ego. People can operate out of any of these ego states, so that interactions become transactions between two ego states, as shown in Figure 24.2. In Berne's view, marriages are often parent-child relationships, with one partner playing the admonitory parent and the

other being the rebellious child. In psychological disturbance, one of the ego states dominates the entire personality, and the goal of transactional analysis is to help people identify the pattern of their transactions and to realize when they are operating out of the various ego states.

Books written for the general public, such as

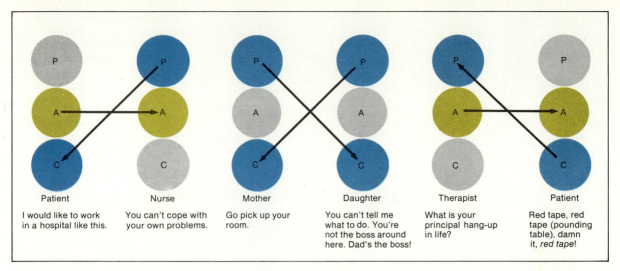

Figure 24.2 Three examples of what Eric Berne describes as "crossed transactions." Drawing an analogy between human relations and economic exchanges, Berne refers to interactions between people as transactions. He considers each personality to be capable of expressing itself as a child (C), an adult (A), or a parent (P) (compare Freud's id, ego, and superego). Berne maintains that normal, or healthy, transactions can be represented in diagrams like these with arrows that run horizontally: adult to adult, parent to parent, child to child. It is not difficult to see that the transactions illustrated here, with their diagonal lines, are ones that lead to trouble. (After Berne, 1964.)

Berne's *Games People Play* (1964) and Thomas Harris' *I'm OK—You're OK* (1967) have increased the popularity of transactional analysis. In *Games People Play*, Berne describes how partners set up rules for each other that may satisfy their own neurotic needs but undermine mutual comfort. For example, in the game "Now I've Got You, You Son of a Bitch," one partner provokes or invites exploitative behavior in the other and then complains bitterly of being exploited. Through transactional analysis, people try to uncover these counterproductive interactions and change the rules of the game to promote mutual satisfaction.

Family and Marital Therapy

In marital and family therapy, the group is a natural one, formed by the bonds of kinship. Although the symptoms of one member may have brought the couple or family into therapy, the entire group is viewed as the treatment unit, and the assumption is that the group as a whole is disturbed.

There are several types of family therapy. In behavioral family therapy, family interactions are stressed, and members are made aware of the way their actions reinforce one another's behavior. Some therapists see family distress as the result of "coercion," in which each member uses aversive acts or words to influence the others' behavior (Patterson and Hops, 1972). In marital behavior therapy, for example, it is assumed that the couple have been locked into frustrating behavior exchanges for so long that they have lost sight of the effect of their behavior on each other and are unaware of the sources of their unhappiness. The therapist's aim is to shift the couple's behavior toward positive, mutually reinforcing interactions, to improve communication between them, and to shift the power in the relationship toward an equal balance (Papajohn, 1977).

In the communications approach (Satir, 1967; Watzlawick, Beavin, and Jackson, 1967), it is assumed that subtle nonverbal signals that directly contradict family members' verbal signals are involved in the disorder. This approach developed out of the double-bind theory of schizophrenia, which was discussed in Chapter 23. Therapists uncover such signals, show what is being communicated, and point out how this negates what members profess to be saying. The therapist tries to get family members to talk openly, telling one another about their feelings and the kind of family relationship they would like.

In the systems approach, the assumption is that people are members of a family social system and that all members influence one an-

Family therapists believe that, although one member may take the role of "symptom bearer," all members of the family are involved in the disturbance.

other's behavior (Minuchin, 1977). The emphasis is on the interactions of the members and the role each member takes in the relationship. In the course of living together, each couple or family, consciously or unconsciously, sets up expectations for one another and assigns roles for each person to fill. Thus there may be a "weak" member, a "strong" member, a "caretaker," a "scapegoat." When roles are inappropriate or unduly restrictive, the most fragile member of the unit may show symptoms of mental disturbance, but all members are believed to contribute to the breakdown. Indeed, some therapists contend that the role system of the nuclear family requires a sick member (Minuchin, 1974). In therapy, role expectations and patterns of communication are examined to readjust restrictive roles and promote mutual reinforcement.

The Effectiveness of Psychotherapy

In 1952 Hans Eysenck reviewed twenty-four studies of the outcome of psychotherapy, five concentrating on psychoanalytic treatment and nineteen on "eclectic" treatment, in which several different therapeutic approaches are combined. He concluded that psychotherapy was no more effective than no treatment at all. According to his interpretation of these studies, only 41 percent of the psychoanalytic patients improved, while 64 percent of those given eclectic psychotherapy were "cured" or had improved. But Eysenck argued that even this 64 percent improvement rate was no indication that psychotherapy had any effect, since it had been reported that 72 percent of a group of hospitalized neurotics improved without treatment (Landis, 1937). If no treatment at all produces as much improvement as psychotherapy, the obvious conclusion is that psychotherapy is ineffective. Eysenck (1966; 1967) has vigorously defended this controversial position and believes that only behavioral therapy is at all effective.

Many additional reviews and studies have been generated by Eysenck's charges. In a thoughtful review, Allen Bergin (1971; Bergin and Lambert, 1978) replied to Eysenck. First, Bergin demonstrated that when different but equally defensible assumptions about the classification of patients were made, the effectiveness of psychoanalytic treatment was much greater than Eysenck had reported; perhaps as many as 83 percent of the patients improved or recovered. Second, when Bergin and Lambert reviewed seventeen studies with untreated control groups, the rate of improvement without treatment was only about 43 percent.

Bergin's reviews question the validity of Eysenck's sweeping generalization that psychotherapy is no more effective than no treatment at all. But much of Bergin's argument is based on differences of opinion about how patients should be classified. Precise criteria for "improvement" are difficult to define and to apply. The nature of "spontaneous remission" (sudden disappearance) of symptoms in persons who have not received formal psychotherapy is difficult to assess, for these people may have received help from unacknowledged sources—friends, relatives, religious advisers, family physicians.

In an attempt to surmount some of these problems, Mary Lee Smith, Gene V. Glass, and Thomas I. Miller (1980) analyzed 475 controlled studies of psychotherapy (see Figure 24.3). They devised a statistical technique for summarizing the findings of the studies and found strong evidence for the effectiveness of psychotherapy. The average client who had received therapy scored more favorably on the outcome measures than 80 percent of the persons in untreated control groups. Smith, Glass, and Miller also assessed the effectiveness of different types of psychotherapy and found that all types of individual therapy were more effective than no treatment. In addition, group therapy was found to be as effective as individual therapy. From this evaluation, it could be concluded that psychotherapy is more effective than no treatment, and that differences in effectiveness between various forms of therapy are small.

However, many of the studies included in Smith, Glass, and Miller's review were flawed by methodological problems. In most of them, the client's improvement was measured by the therapist's overall impression, which in turn was based on the client's own reports. Both sources of information—the therapist's opinion and the client's opinion—are extremely indirect measures of the client's actual functioning.

In a review of sixteen methodologically strong outcome studies that evaluated various therapies for "neurotic" disorders, nine showed that behavior therapy was the most effective treatment and seven showed no difference in effectiveness between behavioral and other treatments. However, none found any other type of treatment to be more effective than behavior therapy. In addition, behavior therapy was superior for many problems not included in the review of 475 studies by Smith, Glass, and Miller. Behavior therapy was more effective than other therapies for the treatment of addiction, the institutional management of psychotic disorders, and childhood disorders such as bed-wetting and hyperactivity (Kazdin and Wilson, 1978).

Although many types of psychotherapy can be of substantial benefit, there is still much to be learned about the development of effective therapies for specific disorders.

Organic Approaches to Therapy

The various psychotherapies described in this chapter are based on psychogenic approaches to

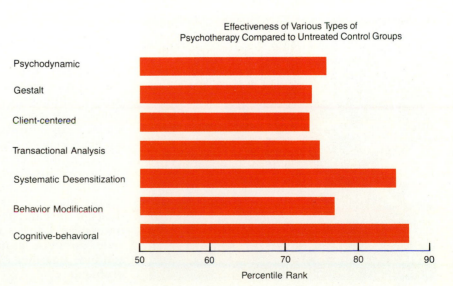

Figure 24.3 Is psychotherapy effective? Researchers who reviewed 475 studies think the answer is yes. Clients receiving each of the types of psychotherapy shown in this graph were compared with untreated control groups. The bars indicate the percentile rank that the average treated client attained on outcome measures when compared with control subjects for each type of therapy. Thus the average client receiving psychodynamic therapy scored more favorably on outcome measures than 75 percent of the untreated controls. (Adapted from Smith, Glass, and Miller, 1980.)

Effectiveness of Various Types of Psychotherapy Compared to Untreated Control Groups

Psychodynamic
Gestalt
Client-centered
Transactional Analysis
Systematic Desensitization
Behavior Modification
Cognitive-behavioral

50   60   70   80   90
Percentile Rank

mental disorders. Instead of restricting themselves to changing behavior, emotions, or cognition, therapies based on biogenic theories aim at altering the workings of the central nervous system. This is most commonly done with drugs, although intervention by means of electroconvulsive therapy or psychosurgery is also possible. Drug therapies are often used in conjunction with psychotherapy.

Antianxiety Drugs

Commonly known as "minor" tranquilizers, antianxiety drugs are used to reduce anxiety, apprehension, and tension. Since most people have experienced anxiety at one time or another, these drugs are in wide use. The most popular tranquilizers are Tranxene (clorazepate); Librium (chlordiazepoxide hydrochloride); and Valium (diazepam). In fact, tranquilizers have become so popular that Valium is now the most frequently prescribed drug in the world (Ray, 1978).

One reason for the popularity of these drugs is their presumed effectiveness in helping normal people cope with difficult periods in their lives, but they are also prescribed for the alleviation of various anxiety disorders, for stress-related physical disorders, and for symptoms of

Antipsychotic drugs such as Thorazine and Stelazine help to ease the symptoms of psychotic patients.

alcohol withdrawal. The major effect of Tranxene, Librium, and Valium is to depress the activity of the central nervous system. If the drugs are taken properly, the side effects are few and consist mainly of drowsiness. However, prolonged use may lead to dependency, and since depressants are synergistic (see Chapter 6), heavy doses taken along with alcohol can result in death.

Antipsychotic Drugs

Antipsychotic drugs, known as "major" tranquilizers, dramatically affect the symptoms of psychosis—agitation, withdrawal, thought disorder, hallucinations, and delusions. They do not affect anxiety.

Among these drugs, the most widely prescribed are the phenothiazines, including Thorazine (chlorpromazine), Stelazine (trifluoperazine), and Mellaril (thioridazine). When Thorazine was introduced in the United States in the mid-1950s, it was an immediate success. Within eight months of its appearance, it had been used by approximately 2 million patients (*Hospital and Community Psychiatry,* 1976). Because patients improved so dramatically, Thorazine led to an opening up of the mental hospitals. Fewer wards were locked, and more and more patients were returned to the community. Thus, the introduction of phenothiazines contributed considerably to the community mental health movement, which will be discussed later in the chapter. Phenothiazines have also advanced our knowledge of schizophrenia, because the effort to discover how these drugs worked led researchers to the dopamine hypothesis, which was discussed in Chapter 23.

Although antipsychotic drugs are effective, there are several drawbacks to their use. Their calming influence is accompanied by side effects that include constipation, blurred vision, dry mouth, and muscle rigidity and tremors. An additional side effect that is resistant to treatment is **tardive dyskinesia**, a muscle disorder in which patients grimace and smack their lips uncontrollably. Tardive dyskinesia usually appears in patients over forty years old after six months or more of continuous treatment with antipsychotic drugs. Since the vast majority of psychotic patients in the United States take one of the major tranquilizers on a daily basis and since the disorder does not disappear when the drug is discontinued, tardive dyskinesia presents a serious problem.

Despite their effectiveness in returning people to society, antipsychotic drugs are limited in their power. They do not cure schizophrenia, and if released patients stop taking the drugs, their symptoms generally return. Thus for many patients, chronic hospitalization has been changed to a "revolving-door" existence of releases, relapses, returns to the hospital, and rereleases after the drugs again take effect. In addition, patients who are taking phenothiazines usually make only a marginal adjustment to life in society.

Antidepressant Drugs

The antidepressant drugs, which are used to lift the mood of depressed patients, were discovered by accident in 1952 when Irving Selikof and his colleagues, treating patients for tuberculosis with a drug called Iproniazid, noticed that it made them cheerful and optimistic. Iproniazid interferes with the action of monoamime oxydase (MAO), an enzyme that degrades neurotransmitters, including norepinephrine and serotonin. Iproniazid was later found to cause liver damage and is no longer prescribed, but other MAO inhibitors are occasionally used. When taking a MAO inhibitor, a person must follow a highly restricted diet because the drugs interact with tyramine and can cause death. Thus, foods high in tyramine—including aromatic cheese, avocado, beer, chicken liver, cream, lox, and yeast extracts—must be eliminated from the diet.

More effective and less dangerous than MAO inhibitors are the tricyclics, so named because their molecular structure is arranged in three rings. The major tricyclics are Tofranil (imipramine) and Elavil (amitriptyline), and their effectiveness was also discovered by accident. Since they are similar in structure to the phenothiazines, the tricyclics were tried on schizophrenics, who showed an unexpected elevation of mood. Tricyclics increase the availability of serotonin and norepinephrine at receptor sites in the brain and MAO inhibitors decrease transmitter availability; thus both classes of drug support the norepinephrine hypothesis of depression discussed in Chapter 23 (Berger, 1978).

Lithium, relatively new to the psychiatric community in the United States, is administered as a simple mineral salt, lithium carbonate. This substance was discovered to have sedative qualities by John Cade, an Australian physician, in 1949. It is used to treat manic episodes and bipolar disorders, because it effectively returns patients to a state of emotional equilibrium in which extreme swings of mood do not occur (Prien, Klett, and Caffrey, 1974; Stallone et al., 1973). It is sometimes effective in cases of major depression as well. Lithium was not introduced into the United States until the late 1960s, because it can be toxic and it has caused death. Its riskiness lies in the fact that the effective dosage is quite close to the toxic dosage. Therefore, its level in the patient's bloodstream must be closely monitored. Among the possible side effects of lithium are kidney damage, stomach upsets, and weight gain (Mendels, 1976).

Electroconvulsive Therapy

"Shock treatment," as **electroconvulsive therapy (ECT)** is commonly called, has proved extremely effective in the treatment of severe depression and usually works faster than antidepressant drugs. It involves administering a series of brief electrical shocks of approximately 70 to 130 volts, spaced over a period of several weeks. The shock induces a convulsion similar to an epileptic seizure. Although no one understands exactly how ECT works (Greenblatt, 1977), it is the convulsion that seems to produce the therapeutic effect; shock at levels too low to induce convulsion is ineffective.

As it is now applied, ECT entails very little discomfort for the patient. Before treatment, the patient is given a sedative and injected with a muscle relaxant to alleviate involuntary muscular contractions and to prevent physical injury. Even with these improvements, however, ECT is a drastic treatment and must be used with great caution. Common side effects include temporary loss of memory, which in some instances can persist for several years.

Psychosurgery

Psychosurgery is the most extreme of all organic treatments. It involves high risks for the patient and irreversible surgical effects. Modern psychosurgery began in 1935, when Egas Moniz and Almeida Lima developed the procedure known as **prefrontal lobotomy**, in which a surgical instrument is inserted into the brain and rotated to sever nerve fibers connecting the frontal lobe (thought center) and the thalamus (emotional center). It was expected that, in cases of severe metal disorder, this interruption in communication would help reduce the impact of disturbing stimuli on mood and behavior. During the next twenty years other methods of psychosurgery evolved, and thousands of operations were performed. Although some severely disturbed patients were helped by these procedures, many were left in childlike and lethargic states, and others died on the operating table. In the 1950s the discovery of antipsychotic drugs brought a halt to most psychosurgery.

Today the surgical techniques of the 1940s and 1950s have been abandoned in favor of "fractional operations," which destroy very small amounts of brain tissue in precise locations (Valenstein, 1973). Such operations are sometimes performed in the United States, but only after all other modes of treatment have been exhausted. In 1976, the National Commission for the Protection of Human Subjects in Biomedical and Behavioral Research concluded that these limited procedures have been beneficial in cases of depression associated with intractable pain. Furthermore, the serious side effects and risks associated with lobotomy appear not to accompany the new techniques. The commission encouraged further research, and recommended that psychosurgery be considered an experimental procedure to be used only under stringent safeguards of the patient's rights and welfare. As the discussion in Chapter 3 indicated, the procedure remains highly controversial.

Community Mental Health

It is seldom easy for a person who has been hospitalized for a mental disorder to reenter society. Often released patients find themselves too far from the hospital for any supplementary care and too fragile to cope independently with the pressures of the outside world. Without community support, these patients may not be able to make a successful return to society. Some community assistance is available through community mental health centers, halfway houses, and hot lines, but the ultimate goal is the prevention of disorder.

Community Mental Health Centers

The Community Mental Health Centers Act of 1963 was designed to solve some of the problems faced by patients trying to reenter society. It mandated one mental health center for every 50,000 members of the U.S. population, to supply needed psychological services for the former patient attempting to function within the community. Other purposes of these centers were to educate community workers such as police, teachers, and clergy in the principles of preventive mental health, to train paraprofessionals, and to carry out research. Although funding for centers has recently been cut back, those that are in operation supply such important supports as outpatient, inpatient, and emergency services as well as community consultation.

When outpatient services are provided, people can walk into a clinic and receive therapy once, twice, or several times a week, without leaving school, job, or family, and without feeling stigmatized as institutionalized mental patients. The centers also serve as a bridge between hospitalization and complete independence by giving aftercare and supplementary services to patients released from hospitals.

When inpatient services are available, severely disturbed people can be hospitalized within the community. Friends and family have easy access to them, and the patients feel less isolated and more accepted. Many centers have arrangements for day hospitals, in which patients take advantage of the support systems and therapy offered by a hospital during the day and go home at night. Night hospitals work in a similar manner: patients may work or go to school during the day and spend the night at the hospital.

When community mental health centers provide emergency services, they often take the form of storefront clinics that are open around the clock to deal with such sudden crises as acute anxiety attacks, suicide attempts, and severe drug reactions. The centers may have teams of psychologically trained personnel on call, ready to go to city hospital emergency rooms and deal with psychological traumas.

When community consultation services are provided, mental health centers have qualified personnel available to advise other community workers, such as teachers, police, and clergy, on the handling of psychological problems in the classroom and within the community. Sensitivity workshops give instruction on such matters as how to intervene in potentially violent family quarrels, how to talk potential suicides out of jumping off a bridge, and how to keep truants from dropping out of school.

Halfway Houses

Halfway houses, which provide an intermediate step between the hospital and the community, are houses in which individuals with common problems live together. The residents provide support for one another and use whatever supplementary services they need until they are able to function entirely on their own. These houses have proliferated in recent years and have been quite useful in easing the transition from hospital care to community life. Halfway houses have been successful in the rehabilitation of drug addicts, newly released mental patients, former convicts, and alcoholics. Reports indicate that residents of small halfway houses are less likely to be rehospitalized than patients who have been returned to the community without any supplementary support system (Cannon, 1975).

In large urban centers, few true halfway houses exist. Instead former mental patients are often sent to nursing homes or large, converted

This woman, being cared for in a battered woman's shelter, is the victim of abuse. Others like her can find help by using telephone hotlines.

hotels, where no supplementary support systems are provided. Such facilities may be little more than "back wards" located within the community (Jones, 1975). To be successful, community-based care must have adequate financial support. In the absence of funds for small, high-quality facilities, the alternative method of housing former mental patients in nursing homes and hotels may simply constitute dumping them into our urban centers to survive as best they can.

Crisis Intervention: The Hot Line

Community services that involve clinics, hospitals, or halfway houses are costly and complicated to set up, but the crisis hot line provides an instant, economical, and effective way to deal with emergency situations. People who are in trouble can telephone at any time and receive immediate counseling, sympathy, and comfort. The best known of these systems is the Los Angeles Suicide Prevention Center, established in 1958. Similar hot lines have been set up for alcoholics, rape victims, battered women, runaway children, gamblers, and people who just need a shoulder to cry on. In addition to providing sympathy, hotline volunteers give information on

Living in a halfway house after leaving a mental hospital gives former mental patients a chance to gain the skills and confidence they will need to live independently.

the community services available to deal with each kind of problem.

Prevention

The basic goals of community psychology are to prevent the development of disorder (primary prevention); to prevent the worsening of disorder (secondary prevention); and to prevent the severe effects of major disorder on the victim and on society (tertiary prevention). Primary prevention of mental disorder is desirable but difficult to accomplish. It requires changing those aspects of society and the environment that lead to psychological disturbance, and we have seen in Chapter 23 how complex the causes of disorder can be. Nevertheless, nutritional counseling, teaching effective coping skills, and designing less stressful school environments are all potentially important methods of reducing the incidence of disorder.

Secondary prevention, the early detection and treatment of problems before they become severe, is somewhat less complex, but is still no easy task. Outpatient clinics, emergency services, hot lines, and some paraprofessional programs are examples of secondary prevention. Early detection of problems usually requires a trained professional, but consultation programs with schools and law enforcement agencies are one way to expand secondary prevention.

Tertiary prevention programs include the day hospitals and night hospitals and the halfway houses described above. These programs are designed to help those who have suffered a serious disorder to resume useful roles in society and to prevent the recurrence of disorder.

The prevention of disorder is the goal of both the community mental health movement and community psychology, but some psychologists maintain that they have become preoccupied with the delivery of individual services, whereas their major effort should be to improve social conditions. Community psychologists have been urged to focus on the design of social systems that foster health and growth, thus turning their efforts to primary prevention in its broadest sense (Goodstein and Sandler, 1978). If that goal is achieved, the incidence of psychological disorder will be significantly reduced. But society cannot be changed quickly, and in the meantime those individuals affected by psychological disorder must be treated with the best methods available.

SUMMARY

1. **Psychotherapy** is a systematic series of interactions between a therapist trained to solve psychological problems and a person who is troubled or is troubling others. Its goal is to alleviate the problem, either through the patients' understanding of their motives or through directly changing behavior. Professionals who treat mental disorders may be **psychiatrists**, **psychoanalysts**, **clinical psychologists**, **psychiatric social workers**, or **psychiatric nurses**.

2. Psychodynamic therapies are closely identified with Freud and focus on a dynamic interplay of conscious and unconscious elements. During therapy, **resistance**, or attempts by the client to block treatment, must often be dealt with. **Transference neurosis**, often regarded as necessary to effective therapy, occurs when the client transfers to the analyst emotions originally directed toward the parents and reenacts early conflicts. Ego psychologists and neo-Freudians are among the psychoanalytically oriented psychotherapists. Most psychodynamic therapy tends to emphasize present situations, and is briefer and less intensive than traditional psychoanalysis.

3. Behavioral therapies that use classical conditioning and extinction are meant to change behavior by changing emotions. The techniques include **systematic desensitization**, in which a relaxed client is gradually exposed to imaginative or real re-creations of anxiety-producing stimuli; **flooding**, in which the client is exposed to real situations that produce intense anxiety; and **aversive conditioning**, in which the client's exposure to stimuli that elicit maladaptive responses is accompanied by aversive stimuli (electric shock or drugs). In **covert sensitization**, a variation of aversive conditioning, the aversive stimuli are imagined. Therapies based on operant conditioning generally punish or extinguish maladaptive responses while reinforcing adaptive

ones. Sometimes used in such therapies are behavioral contracts, written contracts that specify behavior, reinforcements, and punishments, and **token economies**, in which behavior is rewarded with tangible objects that can be exchanged for secondary reinforcers. Therapies based on **modeling**, which can take the form of **participant modeling** or **behavioral rehearsal**, place great emphasis on cognition. Bandura has proposed that cognition is responsible for behavior change and that **efficacy expectations**, the belief that one can successfully execute a behavior, are important in the process. **Cognitive restructuring**, including **rational-emotive therapy**, **self-instructional training**, and **cognitive therapy**, attempts to change a client's false perceptions and assumptions to more rational beliefs.

4. Humanistic therapies view psychological treatment as a growth experience, and the therapist helps clients to fulfill their individual potential by emphasizing a sense of freedom and the ability to choose their own future. In **client-centered therapy**, the therapist helps clients clarify feelings and come to value their own experience of the world. Therapists must have **congruence**, the ability to share their own feelings with the client, and communicate **unconditional positive regard**, nonjudgmental acceptance of the client. **Gestalt therapy** combines Freudian concepts with humanistic philosophy. Always concentrating on the present, the therapist helps the client give up defenses, expand potential, increase awareness, and release pent-up feelings. Clients follow rules of communication that help them take responsibility for their thoughts and actions, act out conflicts, and express feelings.

5. Group therapy was developed as a cheap, quick treatment that was relevant to a patient's daily problems. Each psychotherapeutic approach has developed a form of group therapy. **Transactional analysis**, which is based on psychodynamic theory, works with groups of married couples and focuses on ego states (parent, child, adult) that correspond to Freudian personality structure (superego, id, ego). In family and marital therapy, the group is a natural one and the entire group is the treatment unit. In behavioral family therapy, the stress is on family interactions and an awareness of how members reinforce one another's behavior. In the communications approach, based on the double-bind theory, contradictory family communications are uncovered. In the systems approach, the role each member takes in the relationship is emphasized.

6. Based on studies of therapy, it has been contended that psychotherapy has no effect at all and that people do as well without therapy as with it. Later, more extensive reviews have found strong evidence for the effectiveness of psychotherapy; some reviews have found little difference among the various therapies in their effectiveness and others have found behavioral therapy to be most effective. As yet researchers have not identified the most effective method of treatment for various disorders.

7. Organic therapies aim at altering the central nervous system. Antianxiety drugs (such as Valium) are mild tranquilizers that are prescribed for anxiety disorders, stress-related physical disorders, and withdrawal from alcohol. Antipsychotic drugs (such as Thorazine) are major tranquilizers used to alleviate extreme agitation and hyperactivity in psychotic patients. They have allowed many chronic patients to return to society but have serious side effects, such as **tardive dyskinesia**, a muscle disorder. Antidepressant drugs (such as imipramine) are used to regulate mood, and they have been helpful in treating depression. **Electroconvulsive therapy**, or shock treatment, is effective in the treatment of depression; it is a drastic treatment that may be followed by loss of memory. Psychosurgery, including the procedure known as **prefrontal lobotomy**, is an extreme treatment. Lobotomies were halted by the discovery of antipsychotic drugs, but a more localized procedure, known as a "fractional operation," is still sometimes used after all other treatments have failed.

8. Community mental health programs provide transitional support for discharged mental patients, help people stay within the community, and educate community workers. They often provide outpatient, inpatient, and emergency services as well as community consultation. Halfway houses, in which people with a common problem live together, ease

the transition from hospital care to community life. The crisis hotline is an instant, economical, and effective means of dealing with emergencies by telephone. The basic goals of community psychology are to prevent the development of disorder (primary prevention); to prevent the worsening of disorder (secondary prevention); and to prevent the severe effects of major disorder on the victim and on society (tertiary prevention).

KEY TERMS

aversive conditioning
behavior rehearsal
blind mill
client-centered therapy
clinical psychologist
cognitive restructuring
cognitive therapy
congruence
covert sensitization
efficacy expectations
electroconvulsive therapy
empathic understanding

eyeball-to-eyeball
flooding
Gestalt therapy
modeling
nondirective counseling
participant modeling
prefrontal lobotomy
psychiatric nurse
psychiatric social worker
psychiatrist
psychoanalyst
psychotherapy

rational-emotive therapy
resistance
self-instructional training
systematic desensitization
tardive dyskinesia
token economy
transactional analysis
transference
transference neurosis
unconditional positive regard

RECOMMENDED READINGS

BERNSTEIN, D. A., and M. T. NIETZEL. *Introduction to Clinical Psychology.* New York: McGraw-Hill, 1980. A textbook on clinical psychology including chapters on community psychology and clinical interventions from various perspectives.

CORSINI, R. J. (ed.) *Current Psychotherapies.* Itasca, Ill.: Peacock Publishers, 1973. Most of the chapters were written by distinguished leaders of the various approaches, and major current therapies are covered. Each author follows the same format and outline, which makes comparison of therapies easier.

GARFIELD, S. L., and A. E. BERGIN. *Handbook of Psychotherapy and Behavior Change: An Empirical Analysis.* 2nd ed. New York: Wiley, 1978. The most comprehensive collection of readings on psychotherapy. It contains sections on experimentation in psychotherapy, analysis of therapies, and discussions of a variety of therapeutic approaches.

GURMAN, A. S., and A. M. RAZIN (eds.). *Effective Psychotherapy: A Handbook of Research.* Elmsford, N.Y.: Pergamon, 1977. A collection of research articles on all aspects of psychotherapy by leaders in the field; an excellent overview.

HERINK, R. (ed.). *The Psychotherapy Handbook.* New York: New American Library, 1980. Brief descriptions and bibliographies for 250 different psychotherapies.

KORCHIN, S. J. *Modern Clinical Psychology.* New York: Basic Books, 1976. A comprehensive survey of all aspects of clinical practice, with clear presentations and comparisons of various therapeutic approaches.

WILSON, G. T., and K. D. O'LEARY. *Principles of Behavior Therapy.* Englewood Cliffs, N.J.: Prentice-Hall, 1980. An introductory textbook by two leading behavior therapists.

PART EIGHT

Social Psychology

To a scientist, the most irritating and frustrating social psychological aberration of the day (and perhaps the most dangerous in the long run) is the current tendency for people, supposedly educated, to be antiscientific.

This tendency is perhaps more noticeable in the United States than in any other industrialized nation (and, I suspect, than in many nonindustrialized nations). Why should it be that the nation that leads the world in science and technology and that has benefited from them in terms of national power, international influence, and high standard of living, should be so intensely antiscientific?

There are a number of reasons, I think.

First, there is a confusion between science and technology. Science is a methodology, an organized system for squeezing information out of the universe and gaining knowledge and understanding. Technology is the application of the knowledge gained by science toward the solution of problems of life.

It is quite possible that such solutions create other problems that can be viewed as worse than the problems that have been "solved." Insecticides may produce resistant strains of pests; food additives may cause cancer; new sources of energy may produce risks of death by radiation; factories producing useful products may also produce chemical wastes and air pollution that may help destroy the biosphere, and so on.

In that case is it the knowledge itself that is the danger, even the method of gaining that knowledge; or is it the unwise application of the knowledge? Is it the scientist who makes discoveries who is responsible for evil; or the generals and politicians, who apply them with only military or political advantages in mind, and the industrialists who do so with only profits in mind? Shall we learn to apply knowledge wisely, or shall we cut the Gordian knot by decreeing perpetual ignorance as the only safe way of avoiding harm (ignoring the fact that ignorance is sure to be the cause of still greater harm)?

I think the answer is obvious.

To be sure, there are people who are openly and specifically antiscience; who claim that there are other methodologies for gaining knowledge, and that the scientific method has no monopoly on truth; or who strenuously object to scientific "orthodoxy" and claim all sorts of fringe beliefs, or outright idiocies, to be "scientific"; or who object to specific conclusions of science and who want the whole structure destroyed rather than be asked to accept what they don't want to accept.

There is no easy way to deal with this. The scientific method is an austere discipline that offers no royal road to knowledge. It requires training and thought, and there are bound to be those who feel that it is just as good to "feel" or to be "intuitive" or to "dream" or to do whatever it is that these antiscientific types would rather do. None of these things are "just as good," but they *are* easier.

Fantasies and dramatic heresies and childhood myths may have a stronger hold on the emotions than science can have on the intellect but that makes none of the former true or useful. Indeed, if the American people amuse themselves by destroying science, they will make it certain that other nations, more respectful of scientific knowledge, will lead the world instead. And if all humanity discards science, then all humanity will be destroyed.

Civilization *may* be destroyed, and we with it, even with science, but it *will* be destroyed without it. You may make your choice between a chance for survival, and no chance. I have made mine.

ISAAC ASIMOV

CHAPTER 25

Attitudes and Attitude Change

Most behavior, whether human or animal, is the product of social factors. In the previous chapters of this book we explored such aspects of behavior as learning, memory, thinking, perceiving, and feeling, and to simplify our analysis, we considered them in their "pure" form. Hence, we ignored the fact that in daily life these processes—which we viewed as abstracted from society—are primarily social in nature. Most learning takes place under the control of reinforcement which is administered by parents, teachers, superiors, and friends. Our thoughts and their organization are dominated by social events: we think about our friends, our relatives, people we like, people we wish to avoid, people with whom we go to school, or must invite to dinner. Our perceptions of the world around us are mostly of people and their products.

Our emotions are social as well. If someone singles us out for praise, we feel happy. If we are caught in an embarrassing situation, we are ashamed. If we fail to meet someone's expectations, we feel guilty. Most of our emotions are reactions to others, and our expression of them is regulated by rules that have social origins. It is, for example, quite improper to express sexual desires in public or to display rage. In this chapter we shall focus on the individual in the social environment and examine some psychological processes such as perception, cognition, and emotion in the social context and in terms of the way they combine to shape attitudes.

The Nature of Attitudes

When you make a new acquaintance, some of the first things you tell each other are the things you like and dislike. You may talk about the movie you liked, or a teacher you hate, a lecture she found interesting, how you hate to diet, and love to jog. We want to know the attitudes of our new acquaintances and we want them to know ours because they will determine the course of our relationship with them. Imagine that you—a liberal feminist—discovered that your new acquaintance strongly opposes abortion. And if the new acquaintance does not like your favorite movies, and loves the teacher you hate, dislikes jogging and has very few of the same attitudes as you, chances are that the relationship does not have much chance to go very far.

We have attitudes about an enormous number of subjects: political candidates, remedies for inflation, the value of a college education, shrimp, New York champagne, roommates, friends, and countless other objects and events, concrete or abstract. Because our attitudes may influence our behavior, public-opinion polling has become part and parcel of our political, economic, and social life. Large survey-research firms like the Gallup and Harris organizations devote their time to compiling thousands of responses to questions about everything from presidents to pollution. And almost every major corporation conducts consumer surveys to collect information on people's attitudes about subjects as diverse as toothpaste preferences and banking needs. The nature of attitudes, then, is a topic of wide public interest.

Although it is easy to compile a list of various attitudes, the concept of **attitude** is difficult to define with any precision. For purposes of analysis, attitudes can be viewed as having two components: the cognitive and the affective. The cognitions we have about a particular senator— that is, what we know about her or him—for example, are part of our attitude toward that person. Does the senator support or oppose school

War brings out our deepest feelings. People's attitudes toward the Vietnam War, both for and against, were extremely intense.

busing? Increased defense spending? An increase in taxes? Is the senator susceptible to special interests? Cognitions, however, are simply collections of facts and beliefs; they are not in themselves attitudes. An attitude results from the affective response that we associate with our cognitions. If we *like* the senator's stand on busing or defense spending or tax increases, our attitude toward her or him will be favorable. It has been suggested that our attitude toward an object—a person, a situation, a behavior—is based on the extent to which we believe the object has attributes or consequences that we evaluate as pertinent. We integrate our various beliefs to arrive at an evaluation of the object— and hence at an attitude toward the object (Fishbein and Ajzen, 1975).

The *affective* component of attitudes represents only the attraction or the aversion that the person feels toward the attitude object. The same *cognition* about an object may promote attraction in one individual and aversion in another. Learning that a new acquaintance is a homosexual may make the new acquaintance attractive or unattractive depending on our affective reaction to homosexuality.

Our tendency to approach or avoid objects can be expressed in a variety of ways. Remaining near an object or escaping from it are obvious manifestations, as is praising or derogating the object. The range of behavior that may derive from an attitude extends from a faint smile of approval or a response to a survey question to the sacrifice of one's life.

It is important to understand, however, that not all attitudes are based on collections of facts and beliefs. Sometimes the affective component is primary. For example, attitudes such as preferences for particular foods arise before we know much about what we are eating. Early in life, Mexican children develop a fondness for chili pepper, a food that produces a burning sensation, severely irritates the mouth, and can make the nose run and bring tears to the eyes. Mothers give their toddlers food that contains small amounts of chili pepper and gradually increase the concentration until the five-year-old is voluntarily eating chili pepper at its full strength (Rozin and Rozin, 1981; Rozin and Schiller, 1980). These children like chili pepper not because they know it contains vitamins A and C, nor do they like it because they know that it might accelerate heat loss in a warm climate or stimulate digestion.

Although cognitive factors need not provide the basis of attitude formation, they are integral parts of attitude structures. However, the cognitive component has less stability than the affective component. Much of our knowledge about a given object, say some food, may change profoundly. We may learn the chemical structure of chili pepper, we may discover what is involved in its digestion, we may acquire sophisticated knowledge about the numerous varieties of chili pepper, about how it is raised and cured, and about its many uses. But our preference or aversion for chili pepper may not be greatly influenced by this knowledge.

In fact, once our relationship to the object has been established, we may forget or reject the fact or belief that may have been crucial in establishing the relationship (Zajonc and Markus, 1982). Think about a close friend you may have originally sought out for a specific reason, perhaps the ability to help you with a particular computer-programing problem. As the course of friendship progresses, the person's programing skills cease to form the cognitive basis of your attitude toward your friend. The affect that has built up over months of positive interaction has become autonomous and independent of the original cognitions. If asked why you liked this person, programing skills would not be among your reasons.

Explaining Attitude Formation and Change

If what we know about an object is not always central to our attitudes, how do we form an attraction or an aversion—and what can change it? Asked to present your own attitudes toward pornography, marijuana, the military draft, or your roommate, your statements would indicate your belief that your attitude toward each of these things has its origins in the objects themselves. You are for or against marijuana because of what you believe the effects of the drug to be. You like or dislike your roommate because you believe her or him to be a certain kind of person.

Research suggests, however, that this simple, very rational explanation of how attitudes are formed is only part of the actual process. Obviously attitudes do not have their origin in the objects themselves because our attitudes can change while their objects remain constant. Thus if you start with a strong aversion toward snails or chili pepper and eventually grow to like them, it is not the objects that have changed, but you.

The development of an attitude is influenced by many factors: emotional associations, expectations of reward or punishment, a desire to emulate the attitudes of people we respect and admire, a need to establish some degree of consistency between what we say we believe and what we do. In other words, attitudes about everything from breakfast cereals to nuclear weapons are subject to any number of influences. To complicate matters, we are only vaguely aware of some of these influences.

The Effects of Repeated Exposure

The most elementary basis of attitude formation is simple experience. If a person encounters an object on repeated occasions, she or he will develop a positive attitude toward it. Repeated experience with the object is *in itself* enough to enhance the person's attitude. No reward, no reason, no belief, no goal of any sort need be connected with the object. Simple repeated encounter is all that is needed to produce a positive attitude—a phenomenon called the **exposure effect**. On the other hand, no such simple mechanism exists that can produce negative attitudes. If a person is to acquire a negative attitude toward some object, the encounter must be accompanied by aversive consequences. There must be disgust, fear, or pain connected with the object for an individual to become negatively disposed toward it. Often only one negative experience is necessary for an aversion to develop, but for positive attitudes to develop from mere exposure, repeated neutral encounters are sufficient.

The effect of exposure is not limited to human beings. Rats raised to the continual strains of Mozart will, given a choice between Mozart and Schonberg, choose Mozart. And rats raised to the sound of Schonberg prefer that composer to Mozart (Cross, Holcomb, and Matter, 1967). (The choice is accomplished by placing the animals in a cage with a hinged floor suspended over two switches, so that the rat controls the sound by moving from one side of the cage to the other.)

The exposure effect is not peculiar to animals. In one study, researchers showed college stu-

Familiarity seems to breed acceptance. This couple still prefers the sounds of band music to other rhythms because that is what they are used to.

We do not know why repeated exposure generates a positive attitude, although we do know that some explanations that seem plausible do not account for the effect. At one time, for example, it was thought that recognition was a valid explanation of the exposure effect, and that familiar objects are liked better than unfamiliar ones because the feeling of recognition is pleasurable. The individual who is confronted with a recognizable stimulus, say a piece of music, is able to detect familiar themes in the composition, can anticipate correctly how they are developed and, when those expectations are confirmed, experiences pleasure. E. B. Titchener (1910), an American psychologist who was influential early in this century, described the effect of recognition as giving us "a glow of warmth, and a feeling of ownership." However, a number of experiments have shown conclusively that exposure can generate liking even when people do not recognize the stimuli they have previously seen and even when they are unaware that the stimuli have been presented.

For example, in one study (Kunst-Wilson and Zajonc, 1980), polygons were flashed so briefly

Figure 25.1 Average rated affective connotation of nonsense words and Chinese-like characters as a function of frequency exposure. (After Zajonc, 1968.)

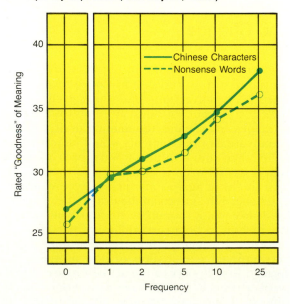

dents various innocuous items, such as Chinese ideographs, nonsense words, or photographs of faces, a number of times. No other event that might affect attitudes accompanied the presentations. Some items were shown twenty-five times, others ten times, five times, or only once. Following the series of exposures, the students were asked how much they liked each of the items they had previously seen. Included with the more-or-less familiar items were other similar items the students had never seen. The unfamiliar items were liked the least, and the more often the students had seen the other items in the series, the better they liked them (see Figure 25.1).

(only one millisecond) that people could not possibly recognize them. In fact it was not clear to the viewers that any stimulus at all had been presented. Later, when these viewers were shown pairs of stimuli (one that had been flashed and one they had never seen) and asked which of the two they preferred, they chose the flashed stimuli in a majority of cases—stimuli that were objectively familiar despite the absence of any subjective feeling of recognition. Apparently, the subjective feeling of recognition is not responsible for the effects of exposure.

Reinforcement Theories

The repeated exposure of the object is the most elementary process underlying attitude acquisition. There are more complex processes whereby attitudes are formed, and one of these involves rewards and punishments. Attitudes can be acquired by the administration of rewards and punishments that are contingent upon the expression of the attitude responses, in very much the same way as other habits and behavioral dispositions. When we want to know why a person is a lifelong liberal or conservative, a committed capitalist or a revolutionary, a staunch Catholic or an avowed atheist, we can find part of the explanation in the principles of learning discussed in Chapter 8—classical and operant conditioning. According to these theories, many attitudes are formed because of the rewards or punishments associated with them.

Note that when attitudes are acquired through mere exposure, no response—attitudinal or otherwise—is required. In reinforcement, however, the person must make some response to the attitude object, and this attitudinal response is either rewarded or punished. It is the contingency of the reinforcement on the subject's response that establishes her or his future tendency to react in the same way to the attitude object.

Classical Conditioning Psychologists have demonstrated that attitudes can be formed by the same conditioning process through which Ivan Pavlov's dogs learned to salivate at the sound of a bell. When a previously neutral object is repeatedly encountered along with either a pleasant or an unpleasant stimulus, the object itself eventually elicits the response originally associated with the stimulus. In one experiment

(Zanna, Kiesler, and Pilkonis, 1970), fifty women were told that they would receive electric shocks at intervals and that a signal would announce the beginning and ending of each interval. For one group, the onset of shock was signaled by the word "light" and its termination by the word "dark"; for the other group, the signal words were reversed. Before the experiment all the women evaluated "light" more favorably than "dark," but their preference was influenced by the nature of the stimulus with which each word was paired in the experiment. When "light" signaled shock and "dark" signaled relief from shock, for example, "light" was evaluated much less favorably and "dark" much more so. Thus by associating words with emotionally charged stimuli, the women developed attitudes toward those words that reflected the nature of the stimuli. In addition, the women generalized what they had learned to other, related words. Those who had been shocked on the word "light," for instance, also evaluated the word "white" less favorably, while those who had been shocked on the word "dark" also developed more negative attitudes toward "black."

Findings such as these suggest that attitudes can be formed simply by associating objects with emotion-arousing circumstances. We might, for example, learn to dislike people whom we encounter only in hot, crowded subways, or be particularly drawn to ideas put forth by attractive, entertaining teachers. Through classical conditioning, we attach a positive or negative emotional reaction to some object without a corresponding set of cognitive beliefs. This process suggests that many of our most emotionally laden attitudes might be acquired, at least in part, through this basic mechanism of learning.

Operant Conditioning In contrast with the "involuntary" reflex responses (such as fear or pleasure) involved in classical conditioning, operant conditioning involves voluntary behavior. Operant conditioning is based on the assumption that people tend to repeat behavior that has a desirable result and tend not to repeat behavior that has an undersirable result. The person is attempting to obtain some reward or avoid some punishment. By manipulating rewards and punishments, psychologists have shown that almost any organism can be conditioned to perform a variety of behavior.

Research confirms that attitudes, too, can be learned through operant conditioning. Consider a situation in which you are verbally reinforced for expressing certain attitudes. Every time you mention to your friends that you believe people should make a greater effort to convert to solar energy, they respond by saying, "That's an excellent idea" or "I agree completely." Would these responses tend to make you a more ardent supporter of solar energy? Apparently so.

An experiment at the University of Hawaii (Insko, 1965) demonstrated the strength of verbal reinforcent on attitude formation. During an interview, students were complimented for expressing a favorable attitude toward Aloha Week, a celebration held by the university every autumn. About a week after these "conditioning" interviews, the students filled out a questionnaire about local issues. Included in the list of items was a question about the possibility of adding a second Aloha Week to the university's spring schedule. Students whose positive attitudes toward the festival had previously been verbally reinforced expressed more favorable attitudes toward a springtime celebration than did a control group that had not been previously conditioned.

If our attitudes can be shaped by an unknown experimenter who simply repeats "good" every time we express a certain opinion, imagine how easily attitudes can be shaped when the rewards are highly valued, such as approval and affection of family and friends. In fact, the principle of reinforcement may be one of the reasons young children so often parrot their parents' attitudes long before the children understand what they are saying. Youngsters of five or six enthusiastically support the Democratic or Republican candidate during every presidential election campaign, although they cannot understand either their candidate's platform or the election process. Similarly, seven- or eight-year-olds who shout racial slurs in the playground or scribble them on the schoolyard wall seldom grasp the full significance of their words. It is very likely that these children have at some time been positively reinforced for expressing the attitudes that their parents hold.

There is some debate among psychologists about what is actually learned through conditioning. Does an organism simply acquire a stereotyped chain of responses that it performs almost mechanically? Or does it acquire an expectation that some reward or punishment will follow a certain kind of behavior? If it is expectations that are acquired, the organism is clearly a more active decision maker in the response sequence. It can substitute one behavior for another as long as the outcome is the same, or it can pursue an entirely different goal that holds out the promise of an even greater reward. Many social psychologists who have investigated reinforcement theories of attitude formation and change argue that acquiring expectations about outcomes is central to the learning process (Hovland, Janis, and Kelley, 1953). We adopt those attitudes that we believe will gain us some desired end and reject those that we feel will have some unfavorable result. Moreover, we weight the value of the various anticipated rewards and select those attitudes that we perceive will yield the greatest benefit. In other words, the greater the reward, the greater the likelihood that a corresponding attitude will be formed.

Reinforcement and Attitude Change   The discussion of cognitive consistency in Chapter 16 indicated that when we hold two conflicting cognitions we are thrown into a state of dissonance and that we will seek some way of resolving the dissonance and restoring internal harmony. In that discussion, an experiment (Festinger and Carlsmith, 1959) was described in which people who were rewarded with only one dollar if they lied about the nature of their task developed more positive attitudes toward that task than people who were given twenty dollars to lie about it. In this study, people seemed to act in a manner exactly contrary to what we might expect from a reinforcement model of attitude change: the lower their reward, the greater their shift in attitude. It is possible, however, that subjects in this experiment may really have had little knowledge about their own feelings and attitudes, and that they discovered these feelings and attitudes in very much the same way as they discover the feelings and attitudes of others—by observing behavior. In the case of learning about our own feelings and attitudes, Bem (1967) claims that in ambiguous cases, we observe our *own* behavior and thus we discover how we feel about something. Thus, the subjects in the twenty-dollar group saw themselves saying that they liked the task and at the same time they saw themselves receiving a substantial amount of money for communicating to others that they liked the task. They saw themselves, therefore, extolling for money the virtues of previous task performance. Their own attitudes could not have been faithfully reflected in their statements because they were simply responding to a "bribe." However, the one-dollar subjects had no outside reason to praise the task and had to attribute their statement to an underlying disposition—to their attitudes. Thus, they took their own behavior—their own statement together with the size of the reward—to make an inference about their "true" attitudes to the task.

Subsequent investigations suggest that both cognitive dissonance and reinforcement principles influence behavior, but under different circumstances. One factor that seems to affect whether dissonance theory or reinforcement theory is better at predicting behavior is the extent to which people have freedom of choice (Linder, Cooper, and Jones, 1967). Students were asked to write a forceful, persuasive essay supporting a very unpopular bill that would ban Communists and people who took the Fifth Amendment from speaking at state-supported institutions, such as state colleges and universities. The experimenters told some students that the decision to write the essay was entirely up to them; with others, the experimenters acted as if compliance with this request were naturally expected. The amount of money offered the students also varied—a low monetary incentive for some and a high one for others. After completing the essay, each student was asked to indicate her or his real opinion about the speaker-ban legislation. Students who had written the essay under the "free choice" condition behaved as predicted by dissonance theory: they were more likely to change their attitudes in the direction of the proposed ban when the reward they received was low. Students who had written under the "no choice" condition, however, tended to behave as would be predicted by reinforcement theory: those who received the greater reward were more likely to change their attitudes. Thus rather than being contradictory, reinforcement and cognitive consistency models both contribute to our understanding of how people form and change their attitudes.

Persuasive Communication

Repeated exposure and reinforcement are the basic and most prevalent processes that are im-

plicated in attitude *formation.* Once formed, however, attitudes are very resistant to *change.* A multimillion-dollar industry exists in the United States to discover better ways of changing attitudes and to employ these ways in the service of business and politics. Advertisements, sales pitches, political campaigns, lobbying efforts, and newspaper editorials are all examples of **persuasive communication**—that is, direct, overt attempts to change people's attitudes. Many discussions between parents and children, employers and employees, salespeople and customers, contain arguments meant to change another's attitudes. Persuaders hope, of course, that a change in attitude will be followed by a change in behavior.

An advertiser tries to convince consumers of the superiority of a certain brand of cigarette so that they will buy it; parents try to convince their daughter of the evils of smoking so that she will stop. Persuasion, in its form and effects, is one of the most thoroughly studied topics in social psychology.

Persuasive communications that try to change attitudes are mainly directed at the cognitive components of attitudes—they work directly on the person's knowledge about the attitude object. They try to reach the knowledge that is the basis of the subject's positive or negative predisposition toward it.

Influences on Persuasiveness

There is no magic formula that will enable a wily persuader to control people's attitudes toward candidates, political issues, or consumer products. The effectiveness of any effort at persuasion depends on a number of factors, including the characteristics of the source, the content and style of the message, and the nature of the audience.

The Characteristics of the Source The extent to which a person's attitudes are changed by persuasive communication depends as much on who delivers the message as on what that person says. People tend to be more persuaded by a communicator who they believe is knowledgeable about the issues involved. In a classic study, conducted more than thirty years ago (Hovland and Weiss, 1951), people who were given a statement about the practicality of atomic submarines were more convinced of its truth when the source was said to be an American physicist than when it was said to be the Russian newspaper *Pravda*. Similarly, more people were convinced by an article about antihistamine drugs when they thought it had appeared in the prestigious *New England Journal of Medicine* than when they thought it had been published in a mass-circulation pictorial magazine.

The degree to which any persuader is influential depends not only on her or his prestige but also on whether the audience thinks she or he is trustworthy. The audience may decide that the persuader has some ulterior motive for making the appeal and therefore is not completely believable. This is why voters, knowing that a political candidate is specifically trying to persuade them of her or his own merits, are likely to look to another person or organization to verify the candidate's qualifications. One manifestation of the importance of trustworthiness is the tendency for people to be more persuaded by a message if they overhear it than if it is addressed directly to them (Walster and Festinger, 1962). Apparently, when people overhear a communication, they are less likely to call the source's motives into question, perhaps because they assume from the situation that the message is candid.

Another factor that can affect the persuasiveness of a particular communicator is simply how attractive and likable the listeners find her or him. Football players are probably not especially knowledgeable about the relative merits of deodorants and hair tonics. Moreover, when a football star endorses a particular brand of deodorant or hair tonic on television, everyone knows that he is doing so for an ulterior motive: he is being handsomely paid for his efforts. Yet such testimonials are quite effective in persuading thousands of fans to use the product. An attractive, likable source, then, is especially persuasive. An unattractive, unlikable source may produce a "boomerang" effect: the audience may respond by adopting attitudes contrary to those advocated by the source. In conformity with cognitive consistency theory, the listeners adapt their attitudes about the message to their attitudes about the person who delivers it.

The nonverbal behavior of a persuader can affect the audience's perception of her or his trustworthiness and likability. In a face-to-face

Sponsors prefer to use attractive models in their TV commercials, because viewers' positive feelings toward the model are transferred to the product as well.

setting, such as a public speech or interview, a person's actions, posture, and position can either enhance or detract from the impact of the message. Someone who smiles, makes eye contact with the listeners, and faces them directly is perceived as friendly and honest and will be more effective as a communicator than someone who does not look at the audience. A case in point is the series of televised debates between presidential candidates Richard M. Nixon and John F. Kennedy during the 1960 campaign. Nixon's unconscious nonverbal communication decidedly worked against him. He appeared awkward and ill at ease, shifted his position frequently, stood stiffly, and avoided looking into the camera. After losing that election by a narrow margin, Nixon made an effort to change his style when he ran for president again in 1968. He appeared more relaxed, sat rather than stood for most of his interviews, established eye contact, was less formal in appearance and tone, and thereby inspired greater confidence than before. This time he was elected, possibly helped by his improved image.

The physical distance between speaker and audience is another aspect of nonverbal behavior that can affect the impact of a message. In one study (Albert and Dabbs, 1970), researchers found that a message produced most attitude change when the speaker's distance from the audience was great (fourteen to fifteen feet) and least when the distance was small (one to two feet). They speculated that the subjects may have regarded extreme closeness of a speaker as an invasion of their privacy and therefore resisted the speaker's message. In a manual written for volunteers campaigning for peace candidates in the 1972 election, two social psychologists advised door-to-door canvassers to maintain an informal conversational distance of four to five feet (Abelson and Zimbardo, 1970). There is probably no single best distance for delivering a successful message; it is more likely that the most effective physical distance varies with the nature of the message and the relationship between the speaker and the audience.

No matter how prestigious, trustworthy, or attractive the source, the amount of attitude change that occurs will also depend upon the gap between the listener's original attitude and the attitude advocated in the communication. The larger the discrepancy between the two attitudes, the easier it is to dismiss the effort at persuasion. As Figure 25.2 indicates, it would be much easier

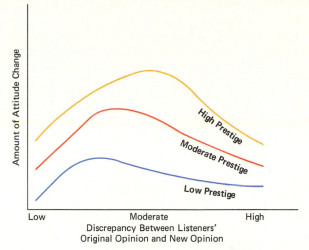

Figure 25.2 Attitude change may be affected both by the discrepancy and by the prestige of the source of a communication. Discrepancy refers to the difference between the listener's original attitude and the attitude implied by the communication. If the discrepancy is too high (in trying to persuade a Republican to vote Communist, for example) or too low (in which case there is little room for change), the amount of attitude change will be less than for moderate discrepancies. As the figure shows, the amount of discrepancy that will produce the maximum change depends on the prestige of the persuader. A high-prestige source coupled with a low degree of discrepancy produces the greatest amount of attitude change in the audience. (Adapted from Freedman, et al., 1970.)

for a prestigious source to convince a Republican to vote for a Democrat than to get the Republican to support a candidate who was an avowed Communist.

The Characteristics of the Message   We are all familiar with the kind of television commercial in which a certain brand of toothpaste, aspirin, or paper towel is declared to be superior to "other leading brands" or to "the product you're currently using." Most advertisers avoid naming competing brands because they fear giving free, even if unfavorable, exposure to a rival product. These companies want to make sure that the name the viewer remembers is that of their brand, not their competitor's. In the past few years, however, some brave manufacturers of soft drinks, cold remedies, pain relievers, automobiles, cigarettes, and other products have stopped referring to Brand X and begun naming the competition.

Which approach is more effective? When trying to influence attitudes, is it better to avoid mentioning the other side or to discuss the weaknesses of the opponent while extolling our own strengths? Whether a one-sided or two-sided argument is more effective appears to depend on the audience for whom the message is intended.

In an early experiment conducted during World War II (Hovland, Lumsdaine, and Sheffield, 1949), more than 200 men received a series of radio transcripts arguing that, even after Germany surrendered, it would take at least two years to end the war with Japan. However, half the men received a one-sided message that pointed only to obstacles, such as distance, plentiful Japanese resources, and a large Japanese army. The rest of the men received a two-sided message. It contained all the information in the one-sided message along with opposing evidence that pointed to such factors as the superiority of the U.S. Navy and the improved chance of Allied success when all resources could be devoted to a one-front war. Overall, the one-sided and two-sided communications produced substantially the same net change in attitudes, but important differences emerged when the men's initial opinions and education were taken into account. Those who initially believed that the war would probably continue for another two years were more influenced by the one-sided message, while those who initially thought that the war would end sooner were more influenced by the two-sided argument. Also, men who were better educated, and who would be expected to view the communications fairly critically, were more impressed with the two-sided communication, while the reverse was true for less-educated men. Thus, a one-sided argument is more effective than a two-sided one if the audience initially favors the communicator's position and is relatively poorly educated. Conversely, an audience composed of people who are initially opposed to the communicator's viewpoint and who are relatively well educated will be more influenced by a two-sided argument.

Linking the message with a pleasant emotional state is another successful method of persuasion. When a television commercial shows a new car being admired by a beautiful woman or a handsome, sophisticated man, the advertisers are using this technique. So are corporate executives when they talk business with prospective clients over dinner at an elegant restaurant. Research confirms that associating a point of view with positive emotions can help change the attitudes of an audience. For example, in one study (Janis, Kaye, and Kirschner, 1965) subjects who were given peanuts and Pepsi while reading a persuasive communication were more inclined than people in a control group to be convinced by the arguments they encountered. Apparently, the pleasant emotional state created by snacking on desirable food can make a message seem more agreeable.

Negative emotions can also be used to change attitudes. Fear has frequently been used as a technique of persuasion, especially in campaigns to reduce cigarette smoking, traffic fatalities, and drug abuse. A critical factor in the success of scare tactics is the amount of fear induced. A classic study (Janis and Feshbach, 1953) that compared the effectiveness of three different levels of fear found that an appeal that aroused a small amount of fear was the most persuasive. High-school students watched a film on oral hygiene that stressed the importance of regular tooth brushing. A high-fear group saw the consequences of dental neglect in graphic detail, including close-ups of severely decaying teeth and unpleasant mouth infections. A second group saw more moderate cases of tooth decay. A third, low-fear group saw only diagrams and all photographs were of completely healthy teeth. Later, 36 percent of the students exposed to the low-fear condition reported favorable changes in their dental hygiene practices as compared with 22 percent exposed to the high-fear condition. It seems that if the fear induced by a message is too great, people attempt to reduce their anxiety by pushing the information to the back of their minds—in short, by ignoring it. This is especially true when the audience is not told how to prevent the feared consequences, feels incapable of taking the necessary steps, or believes that their actions will be ineffective (Leventhal, Singer, and Jones, 1965).

However, if the audience is told how to avoid undesirable consequences and believes that the preventive action is possible and effective, then high levels of fear will lead to substantial attitude change, demonstrated in a study in which high levels of fear were most effective in persuading university students to get tetanus inoculations (Dabbs and Leventhal, 1966). In addition, the more specific the recommendations presented for action, the greater will be the extent of change in behavior (Leventhal, Singer, and Jones, 1965). Thus, in assessing the effectiveness of fear, we must distinguish between avoidable outcomes and unavoidable outcomes: Regardless of our level of fear, if we believe that a recommended change in our attitudes or behavior or both will help us avoid an unfavorable outcome, we are likely to make the change; if we think the change is useless, we are not likely to make it.

The Characteristics of the Audience   The source and the message do not work in isolation; as we have already seen, the educational level and prior attitudes of the audience help to determine the effectiveness of persuasion. Other characteristics of the audience are equally important.

Sometimes deep psychological needs and motives affect a person's readiness to be persuaded. There is evidence, for example, that people with a strong need for social approval tend to be susceptible to social influence (Marlowe and Gergen, 1969). Some psychological reasons for persuasibility are less obvious. Ernest Dichter (1964), a motivational researcher who has engineered many commercial advertising campaigns, once lent his talents to a Red Cross drive for blood donations. He suggested that men might be reluctant to give blood because it aroused unconscious anxieties associated with the draining of their strength and virility. So he recommended that the campaign focus on masculinity, implying that each man in the audience had so much virility that he could afford to give away a little. Dichter also proposed that each man be made to feel personally proud of any suffering connected with the process. One of Dichter's strategies was to give each blood donor a pin in the shape of a drop of blood—the equivalent of a wounded soldier's Purple Heart. These tactics did in fact produce a sharp increase in blood donations by men.

Susceptibility to persuasion is also related to a person's knowledge about or interest in the issue at hand. For example, the fact that in past studies women appeared more persuasible than men may simply have been the result of researchers' choice of traditionally "male-oriented" issues, such as political and economic affairs (Aronson, 1976). This hypothesis is supported by studies such as an experiment (Sistrunk and McDavid, 1971) in which men were found to be easier to influence about traditionally "female-oriented" issues, such as home management or family relations, while women were more open to persua-

sion about traditionally "male-oriented" topics. On the whole, neither gender was found to be more susceptible to persuasion than the other.

Resistance to Persuasion

Even the most compelling persuasive communication may fail because of resistance on the part of the audience. People are not passive. While they listen to a communication, they evaluate the points the speaker makes and may draw up counterarguments of their own. Research indicates that resistance to persuasion is strongest when counterarguments are available and weakest when there are none. Thus factors that increase the availability of counterarguments will in turn increase resistance to persuasion.

Inoculation   Some attitudes are taken so much for granted that when they are strongly attacked, people find it difficult to muster effective counterarguments. How would you react, for example, if you read an extremely persuasive article arguing that monthly self-examinations have no effect on the incidence of death from breast cancer or that regular brushing is useless in preventing tooth decay? Despite your surprise that these widely held beliefs had been attacked, you might very well end up accepting the new points of view simply because you were unprepared to defend the old ones (although they are true).

William McGuire and his colleagues have argued that people can be "inoculated" against such persuasive assaults in much the same way that we are inoculated against tetanus or diptheria (McGuire and Papageorgis, 1961). In medical inoculation a person who has never been exposed to a disease is given a weakened form of the disease-causing agent, which stimulates the body to manufacture defenses against it. If a virulent form of the disease should later attack, these defenses make the person immune to infection. An analogous principle underlies inoculation against persuasion. The person who has never before heard a particular point of view attacked is exposed to opposition and then given a dose of the counterarguments needed to defend that viewpoint.

For inoculation against persuasion, McGuire first exposed people to challenging arguments against a formerly unquestioned proposition (that regular brushing prevents tooth decay),

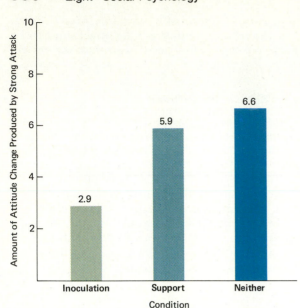

Figure 25.3 This graph shows the amount of attitude change in three groups of subjects, measured in response to a strong attack on a commonly held belief (that brushing the teeth three times daily is a good thing to do). The "inoculation" subjects were previously exposed to a weak form of the attack and were helped to defend their initial belief against the weak argument. The "support" group was given some prior support for the initial belief without any kind of attack on it. The "neither" group received no prior treatment. The "inoculation" group showed much more resistance to change in their attitudes on the subject than the other two groups. Attitude change was measured on an arbitrary scale of 1 to 10, with 10 representing a complete change of attitude. (After McGuire and Papageorgis, 1961.)

then to a statement that refuted those arguments and reinforced the initial belief. A week later the same people read another communication that challenged the same initial belief. Far fewer of the people who had received the inoculation were persuaded by the challenge than those who had not been inoculated. The inoculation had effectively stimulated their psychological defenses against a challenge and made their initial attitude more resistant to change, as shown in Figure 25.3.

Forewarning   People cannot always be armed with arguments to refute an opposing point of view, but they can sometimes be warned that their own beliefs will be challenged. Evidence on the effectiveness of such warnings is mixed. In one study (Freedman and Sears, 1965), a group of teenagers who had been warned ten minutes in advance that they would hear a speech on why young people should not be allowed to drive were more resistant to persuasion than a group who had not been forewarned. But other researchers have obtained different results. For example, people who were forewarned that they would hear arguments against their own view on the likelihood of an economic recession were the ones who displayed the greatest change in their attitudes (Hass and Mann, 1976).

One way to reconcile these seemingly contradictory findings is to take into account the level of the subjects' commitment to their initial attitude. When people are firmly committed to a particular belief, as most teenagers are about their right to drive, they become more likely to resist an opposing point of view after they are warned. However, when people are somewhat ambivalent toward a belief, as those who believed in the likelihood of a recession may have been, they become more inclined to succumb to a persuasive challenge (Kiesler and Jones, 1971).

A person's level of knowledge about the issues involved may also help explain the varying results of forewarning experiments. When people are not particularly well-informed about a subject, anticipation of an opposing argument may cause them to modify their own position in that direction. The strategy is basically taken to save face: people want to avoid being caught in a situation that would force them to defend a view they cannot intelligently support (Hass and Mann, 1976).

Can Attitudes Predict Behavior?

It should follow from the discussions in this chapter that knowing a person's attitudes will not allow us to predict how she or he will behave in a particular situation. Indeed, the distinction between cognition and affect suggests that the person may say one thing and actually feel another. Thus, a person's verbal behavior may give no clue to actual attitudes or how they will be expressed in such other behavior as voting, giving to charity, or eating liver. Since most attitude measures tap primarily the cognitive component of attitudes, it would be unwise to expect these measures to predict behavior with any precision.

In fact, attitudes are sometimes seemingly quite inconsistent with behavior.

This inconsistency was demonstrated by a classic study conducted a half century ago by Richard LaPiere (1934), who traveled around the United States with a Chinese couple, expecting to encounter anti-Oriental attitudes that would make it difficult for them to find places to sleep and eat. But this was not the case. "In something like ten thousand miles of motor travel," wrote LaPiere, "twice across the United States, up and down the Pacific Coast, we met definite rejection from those asked to serve us just once" (p. 232). Judging by the friendly behavior of the innkeepers and tradespeople they encountered, we might conclude that Americans in the 1930s were almost entirely free of prejudice against Orientals. Our conclusion would be wrong. LaPiere followed up his travels by writing a letter to each of the 251 establishments he and his Chinese friends had visited, asking whether they would provide food or lodging to members of the Chinese race. Of the 128 who responded (who, it must be noted, were not necessarily the same people the travelers had encountered), over 90 percent answered with a flat No. Only one said Yes, and the rest said their decision would depend on the circumstances. People's attitudes toward serving Chinese, then, seemed to be extremely inconsistent with the behavior they had already shown.

This discrepancy between attitudes and behavior has since been confirmed. In one study (Wicker, 1971), the attitudes of people toward their church were measured against three kinds of church-related behavior: the frequency of church attendance, the amount of church contributions, and the degree of participation in church activities. It seems reasonable to expect that people who expressed the strongest, most positive attitudes toward their church would be most inclined to attend services, make contributions, and participate in church activities. There was a slight tendency in this direction, but in general, the correlation between attitudes and behavior was very weak. In fact, knowledge of a person's attitude toward the church was practically useless in predicting that person's church-related behavior.

Because the relationship between attitudes and behavior can be inconsistent, one might be tempted to abandon the concept of attitudes entirely. After all, if the concept provides no indication of behavior it has little practical use. Social psychologists argue that it is unrealistic to expect attitudes to correspond perfectly to behavior. Behavior is seldom—if ever—the product of a single influence. Thus, these social psychologists argue that an evaluation of attitudes must take into account factors that may weaken the relationship between attitudes and behavior. Attitudes do determine some variation in behavior, and it is equally true that behavior has an influence on attitudes, as the box at the end of the chapter illustrates.

First, situational factors can weaken this relationship, prompting a person to act in a manner inconsistent with her or his predispositions. LaPiere concluded that his friends were received and well treated by establishments that did not ordinarily accept Chinese because of such situational factors as the high quality of their clothing and luggage and their friendly manner, which inspired courtesy.

Second, a discrepancy between attitudes and behavior may result from conflicts among attitudes. For instance, a man may hold the attitude that one should avoid trouble by minding one's own business, but he may also hold the attitude that one should help the defenseless. What does this Good Samaritan do when he sees an old man being assaulted on the street and can help the victim only by attacking the aggressor? If he stands idly by, his behavior is inconsistent with the attitude that he should help; if he attacks, his behavior is inconsistent with the attitude that he should not get involved. It is inevitable that attitudes will sometimes come into conflict with one another, resulting in at least partial inconsistency between attitudes and behavior.

Third, a single attitude can be expressed through a variety of behaviors. For instance, in the study on church-related attitudes and behavior (Wicker, 1971), the researcher concluded that a person can express devotion to the church in many ways. A person who does not attend services regularly, contribute money weekly, or participate in most church activities may nevertheless be the first person to offer help when the church is damaged by fire or when it needs to be defended from the criticism of others.

Finally, the strength and importance of an attitude, the impact it has on an individual's life, helps to determine the extent to which it governs behavior. Two people may share the attitude that public education should be improved, but a parent is far more likely than a nonparent to act on that attitude by voting for school bond issues,

Attitudes that have a strong impact on our lives are likely to influence our behaviors. People who feel that they and their children are threatened by nuclear weapons are likely to join a demonstration opposing such weapons.

attending hearings on education, and visiting schools.

It would be naïve to expect to be able always to predict behavior from a particular attitude. However, when significant factors are taken into account, consistency between attitudes and behavior emerges. M. Snyder and D. Kendzierski (1982) have clarified the attitude-consistency controversy by considering three additional factors. First, they argued that if attitudes are to be used by individuals as guides to action, the individuals must have access to their attitudes—*they must know how they feel.* Secondly, people must perceive that the attitudes they hold are *relevant*

to the action they are about to take. Thirdly, Snyder and Kendzierski observed that attitudes serve as important guides to action for some individuals, whereas for others, they are less crucial. Because action is determined not only by attitudes but also by the immediate and transitory requirements of the situation, we need to take into account the *extent to which individuals submit* to these requirements and the extent to which they ignore them. In an earlier exploration in individuals' awareness of their attitudes, Snyder (1979) appealed to a difference between individuals in self-monitoring. The self-monitoring scale developed by Snyder contains such items as "My behavior is usually an expression of my true inner feelings, attitudes, and beliefs" and "I can only argue for ideas which I already believe," both of which are endorsed more frequently by persons who are low self-monitors and rejected by high self-monitors. In contrast, items such as "I sometimes appear to others to be experiencing deeper emotions than I actually am" is endorsed by high self-monitors and rejected by low self-monitors.

In all conditions the subjects had to consider a court case involving allegations about sex discrimination. Their attitudes toward sex discrimination were measured two weeks prior to the actual experiment, and during the experiment, their decisions and recommendations for the case were the behavior that Snyder and Kendzierski (1982) examined for correspondence with attitudes.

Snyder and Kendzierski varied the relevance of attitude to behavior by having one group of subjects simply read résumés of two biologists, MR. Sullivan and MS. Harrison, and making attitudes on sex discrimination *available* by asking the subjects to "organize [their] own thoughts and [their] own views on the issue of affirmative action" or making the attitudes fully relevant to the behavior by telling the subjects that "Not only will your decision have implications for the parties involved, but it may also have implications for affirmative action programs."

The results were quite interesting. For the low self-monitors the correspondence between attitude and behavior was 0.18 in the minimal case, 0.47 in the "attitudes available" group, and 0.45 in the "attitudes relevant" group. However, the high self-monitors were much more influenced by the availability and the relevance of the attitude for behavior. When the attitudes were not

Can Behavior Affect Attitudes?

Emotions, rewards, punishments, exposure, and persuasion can have powerful effects on our attitudes. Until recently, however, the proposition that body movements can affect our attractions or aversions was not taken seriously. In the early days of psychology, the motor components involved in attitudes received considerable emphasis—so much, in fact, that attitudes were understood primarily as motor phenomena. Sir Francis Galton (Fleming, 1967) observed that an easy way to measure interpersonal attitudes was to place pressure gauges under the legs of chairs at dinner parties. The gauges would indicate what inclinations the guests had toward each other—inclinations in the physical sense of the word.

An experiment by two social psychologists (Wells and Petty, 1980) has dramatized the effect of body movements on attitudes. Students were asked to assist in testing the quality of headphones while the listener was in motion. Three groups of students put on the headphones and listened to music and an editorial about tuition. One group, told that they were acting as controls, made no movements at all while listening. The second group moved their heads up and down, while the third group shook their heads from side to side. Afterward, the students rated the quality of the headphones and judged the material they had heard. Among the questions was one about tuition. Half the students had heard an editorial suggesting that tuition be raised to $750 and half that it be dropped to $400. The editorials by themselves were persuasive; they influenced students who listened to them without moving their heads. However, movements made by the students as they listened had a strong effect on their opinions.

When asked what tuition would be fair, those who heard the editorial that suggested raising tuition to $750 thought, on the average, that tuition should be $582. Those who heard the editorial suggesting that tuition be lowered to $400 thought that a fair tuition would be $412. The involvement of body movements had a striking effect. Students who nodded their heads as they heard the $750 editorial thought that a fair tuition would be $646, but students who shook their heads while hearing the same editorial thought that no more than $467 was fair. Thus performing of habitual motor responses that signal agreement or disagreement apparently had a pronounced effect on attitudes—effects that are not trivial. Test yourself by trying to say, "I agree with you perfectly!" while shaking your head, or, "You are absolutely wrong!" while nodding. These habitual gestures are not easy to overcome.

involved at all and the subjects dealt only with the résumés, the correlation between their attitudes and case decision was −0.17 for high self-monitors. It was 0.18 for high self-monitors in the "attitude available" situation and as much as 0.60 in the "attitude relevant" situation. Note, therefore, that whether there is a correspondence between attitudes and behavior depends on a multiplicity of factors.

Accurate predictions are of great value because attitudes play such an important role in behavior. They help determine where we live, what we eat, how we dress, where we work, how we spend our leisure time, and whom we marry. Because attitudes have such a pervasive influence on behavior, social psychologists have devoted considerable effort to trying to understand how attitudes are formed and how they change.

SUMMARY

1. An **attitude** is an attraction or aversion toward an object, together with what we know about that object. The attraction or aversion is the *affective* component of an attitude, and our knowledge structure (facts and beliefs) is the *cognitive* component. The affective component is more enduring than the cognitive component, and once an attitude has been established, the cognitions that were its original basis may be abandoned.

2. Many factors influence the development of an attitude. The **exposure effect**, repeated neutral encounters with an object, can produce a positive attitude. A negative attitude will not develop unless aversive consequences are connected with the encounter, but a single negative experience can lead to an aversion. Exposure affects attitudes even when people do not recognize the objects they have previously encountered, indicating that the feeling of recognition is not responsible for the effects of exposure.

3. According to reinforcement theories, attitudes can be formed through classical conditioning (in which a positive or negative emotional reaction becomes associated with some object) or through operant conditioning (in which people tend to repeat behavior that results in something desirable and fail to repeat acts that result in something undesirable). Cognitive consistency theories of attitude formation assume that attitudes are often formed or changed when people in a state of cognitive dissonance try to reestablish internal harmony by shifting their attitudes. Both theories explain attitude formation and change; dissonance theory seems to predict attitudes better when people have freedom of choice, and reinforcement theory seems to predict better when people feel they have little freedom to choose.

4. **Persuasive communication** is a direct, overt attempt to change attitudes. Its effectiveness depends upon various factors, including the characteristics of the source, of the message, and of the audience. The prestige, trustworthiness, and attractiveness of the source all affect the extent to which the message changes attitudes. Nonverbal behavior and the distance between the source and the audience both affect the audience's perceptions of the source's trustworthiness and attractiveness. In regard to the message, a one-sided argument is more effective than a two-sided argument if the audience initially favors the communicator's position and is relatively poorly educated; a two-sided argument is more effective with a relatively well-educated audience that is initially opposed to the communicator's viewpoint. Linking the message with a pleasant emotional state or arousing fear in the audience are also successful means of persuasion. Low amounts of fear often seem to be most successful at changing attitudes, although when people are given explicit ways to combat the fear and believe their actions will be effective, high levels of fear are also effective. In regard to the audience, a person's susceptibility to persuasion is determined by psychological needs and motives and decreased by knowledge about or interest in the issue.

5. Resistance to persuasion is greatest when counterarguments are available and weakest when they are unavailable. Factors that enhance the availability of counterarguments will increase resistance to persuasion. People can sometimes be "inoculated" against persuasion by being given counterarguments needed to defend their viewpoint. Forewarning is effective in making people resistant to persuasion when they have a high level of commitment to their initial attitude.

6. Attitudes and behavior are sometimes quite inconsistent. The relationship between attitudes and behavior may be weakened by situational factors, conflicts among attitudes, the possibility of expressing a single attitude in a variety of ways, or the relative unimportance of the attitude in a person's life. The *self-monitoring* scale developed by Snyder provides a basis for predicting the degree of consistency between attitudes and behavior. It assumes that individuals need to know how they feel to use attitudes as guides to action, that they must perceive that their attitudes are relevant to the action under consideration, and that individuals' tendency to submit to the immediate and transitory requirements of the situation or to ignore them affects the strength of the correlation between attitudes and behavior.

KEY TERMS

attitude   exposure effect   persuasive communication

RECOMMENDED READINGS

FESTINGER, LEON. *A Theory of Cognitive Dissonance.* Stanford, Calif.: Stanford University Press, 1957. The original systematic statement of a theory that has had a major impact on attitude-change research

FESTINGER, LEON, HAROLD RIECKEN, and STANLEY SCHACHTER. *When Prophecy Fails.* Minneapolis: University of Minnesota Press, 1956. A fascinating account of the development of a doomsday religious cult and its members' attitudes and behavior when their prophecy of the end of the world did not come true.

FISHBEIN, MARTIN, and ICEK AJZEN. *Belief, Attitude, Intention and Behavior: An Introduction to Theory and Research.* Reading, Mass.: Addison-Wesley, 1975. The authors present their own, rather attractive theory of attitude formation and change.

HOVLAND, CARL S., IRVING L. JANIS, and HAROLD H. KELLEY. *Communication and Persuasion: Psychological Studies of Opinion Change.* New Haven, Conn.: Yale University Press, 1953. A classic book, reporting the early work of the Yale Communication Research Program.

MATLIN, M. W., and D. J. STANG. *The Pollyanna Principle.* Cambridge, Mass.: Schenkman, 1978. This is a very clearly written book presenting most of the research on exposure effects and other related attitude issues.

McGUIRE, WILLIAM J. "The Nature of Attitudes and Attitude Change," in Gardner Lindzey and Elliot Aronson (eds.), *The Handbook of Social Psychology.* 2nd ed. Vol. 3. Reading, Mass.: Addison-Wesley, 1969, pp. 136-314. An excellent, comprehensive review of the field. The best single source for an overview.

ZIMBARDO, PHILIP G., EBBE B. EBBESEN, and CHRISTINA MASLACH. *Influencing Attitudes and Changing Behavior.* 2nd ed. Reading, Mass.: Addison-Wesley, 1977. An informative and easy-to-read introduction to principles of attitude change.

CHAPTER 26

Interpersonal Perception and Attitudes

The social world is so important that most of our attention is focused on it. We pay more attention to the way we look than to the way we feel, because we believe that the way we look is more likely to influence the way we are treated by others than the way we feel. And we pay much more attention to our friends than to our health. Even as young children, we learn to make countless distinctions and how to act upon them. We must know how to vary our behavior depending on whether we are interacting with a young person or an old one, a male or a female, an acquaintance or a stranger, a student or a professor, a Catholic or a Christian Scientist. But to tune our social behavior so finely, we must learn the small distinctions among the people we meet and the situations in which we meet them. As we shall see in this chapter, there is a constant interplay among our perceptions of others, our attitudes, and our behavior, and the result has a strong effect upon the friends we make.

Interpersonal Perception

Since it would be impossible to base our interactions with each person and our behavior in each social situation on a special rule, we learn to group people and situations into classes and categories. By assigning a given person to a category we automatically gain extra information. If all we know about a man is that he is a lawyer from Philadelphia, we can guess many other things about him. For example, it would probably be safe to say that he is quite clever, very likely to be wealthy, over thirty years old, highly verbal, wears dark suits and ties, is in fair control of his emotions, speaks without a Southern accent, and works long, hard hours.

As we saw in Chapter 8, categories enable us to organize our knowledge about the world so that we can think about it more efficiently. Once a physical object, a person, or an imaginary idol is assigned to a grouping, the properties that distinguish the members of the category from nonmembers provide more information. Once you assign a person to the category of "Philadelphia lawyer" or "Harvard freshman," you know a lot about the person. In this sense categorization is good, because it frees us from the burden of attending to all the particular properties of each object we meet—or of the same object slightly changed, or under slightly different circumstances. But at the same time categorization may cause us to jump to premature conclusions that give way to prejudice. To prejudge a person is to relegate her or him to a category blindly, assigning to that person all the attributes of the category without first making sure that

Sexism and Racism

The words racism, prejudice, and discrimination are often used interchangeably, but there are clear distinctions among them. **Racism** and **sexism** are terms denoting a specific pattern of attitudes and behavior, whereas prejudice and discrimination are the two general components that make up these patterns.

Prejudice and Discrimination: Attitude and Behavior
Prejudice refers to negatively toned attitudes and opinions about an entire group, such as a racial minority or women. In most instances, however, the beliefs on which prejudice is based are either exaggerated or untrue, and the evaluations associated with those beliefs are usually very negative.

Discrimination is the behavioral expression of prejudice and refers to specific practices, such as excluding women or members of racial minorities from certain kinds of activities, jobs, organizations, or educational opportunities. As we noted in Chapter 25, however, attitudes and behavior are not always closely linked. A person may be prejudiced without showing discriminatory behavior, and conversely, a person may exhibit discriminatory behavior in response to group pressure without holding an attitude of prejudice.

Racial and sexual prejudice are almost always based on **stereotypes**, or standardized beliefs about a certain group. Once an individual has been categorized as a member of that group, all the characteristics associated with the stereotype are believed to apply to that person. Thus, if a man considers women to be passive and helpless, he will regard an individual woman as passive and helpless, no matter how aggressively and competently she behaves. The evaluation associated with stereotypic beliefs forms the generally negative attitude known as prejudice.

Negative attitudes about racial and ethnic groups may also be the result of intergroup conflict and economic competition. As a racial or ethnic minority attempts to establish a more favorable position for itself in the economy and in society in general, members of that minority come into conflict with the dominant group, and the conflict leads to the development of hostility.

A series of field experiments conducted by Muzafer Sherif and his colleagues (1961) provides a good illustration of this process. Groups of young boys at summer camp were placed in situations of intergroup conflict. Residents of each cabin sat at their own table

---

they apply. As we saw in Chapter 8, category boundaries are fuzzy, many members of a category have some distinguishing features but not others, and many categories are extremely vague. In the case of prime numbers, for example, it has not always been clear how to handle zero. If you mistake zero for a prime number, the error will not affect any "zeros," since they have no real existence. But if you mistake a poisonous mushroom for an edible one, there are consequences both for the mushroom and for you. If you eat the mushroom, it will die and you may die as well.

The Consequences of Social Categorization

Categories are created in the minds of people, and once created, they can have profound consequences—social, political, religious, economic. At times a category may mean the difference between life and death.

With only a little imagination, we can see that innumerable disasters—at the individual, social, and national levels—could have been averted if the perceptions and beliefs existing at the moment had been different. Think of the international conflicts that could have been averted if political leaders had had a more charitable, less stereotypical view of each other. Would Adolf Hitler have attacked the Soviet Union in 1941 if he thought the Russian army and the Russian people would put up such stiff resistance? He obviously attributed to the category of "Russians" characteristics that underestimated that people's courage and dedication to their native land.

Social psychologists are especially interested in the categories that we have for other people. How are these categories formed? How do they emerge? Why is there a category of redheads, of paraplegics, of geniuses, of punks, of teen-agers, of strangers, of people who are shy or meek or

for meals and encountered the residents of other cabins only in competitive situations, such as intercabin races and tugs-of-war. Before long, negative stereotypes of the other groups developed in each group. Overt hostility, in the form of raids and fights, arose from the climate of competition and conflict.

Racial and ethnic discrimination may be manifest through suppression or violence, or both, and avoidance of contact with members of minority groups (Jones, 1972). Discrimination against women in our culture does not really fit either of those categories, however. The behavior of men toward women seems to be closely tied to the gender role stereotype; that is, men view —and treat—women as less competent, less aggressive, and more emotional and in need of their protection.

Eliminating Sexism and Racism
Discriminatory behavior is common in the United States, although it is less pervasive than it once was and it no longer has the force of law behind it. One way of lessening prejudice and discrimination may be to promote cooperation between groups. Sherif's research team (1961) found, for example, that intergroup cooperation effectively bridged the gap that had been created between the competitive groups of young campers. Subsequent research (Aronson et al., 1975) showed that the racial tensions created by forced busing of schoolchildren for the purpose of integrating schools can be reduced by structuring classroom activities to foster cooperation between racial groups.

The long-term solution, of course, is to change the beliefs that support prejudicial attitude

and discriminatory behavior. As a first step toward changing existing stereotypes, agents of socialization—parents, media, teachers—would have to change their own behavior to reduce the extent to which children develop racial and sexual stereotypes through social learning. There is some evidence that this process has begun and is spreading, but stereotypes persist (Karlins, Coffman, and Walter, 1969).

Racism and sexism will not easily be rooted out of American life. Nevertheless, there is hope that as more and more of us become aware of the terrible costs of racism and sexism, we will become more careful in our language and behavior in order to keep stereotypes from being transmitted so widely and effectively to each new generation.

These young people, made up in the "punk" style, form a category. The way others react to this group will be influenced by the traits they perceive "punks" to possess.

boring, of groups that are cliquish or rowdy or stingy or industrious? Some of these categorizations have an objective basis. After all, redheads do have hair that contains some semblance of the color red, and teen-agers can be distinguished by their age. However, each of these categories implies other properties besides the distinguishing objective features. Redheads are generally thought of as hot-tempered and teenagers as tactless. Since people behave toward the members of a category according to the characteristics they associate with it, people who include "hot-tempered" among the properties of redheads might not entrust a redhead with serious responsibility, and those whose category of teenager includes "tactless" would not send a teenager to resolve a touchy conflict between a newly married couple.

The fact that our reactions to other people are based on the way we categorize them may eventually be reflected in our behavior. For instance, as we saw in Chapter 14, popular children tend to be attractive and sociable, and to praise other children and help them (Masters and Furman, 1981). Such a combination of traits is unlikely to be innate; there are no known "genetic clusters," in which attractiveness, sensitivity, and kindness occur together. Instead, sensitivity and kindness may develop as a consequence of others' responses to attractive youngsters.

In a study of the stereotypical expectations associated with attractiveness (Snyder, Tanke, and Berscheid, 1977), a group of college men were asked to get acquainted with college women over the phone. The men were given fictitious biographical information about the women, and each biography was accompanied by a snapshot, presumably of the woman described. The women in the snapshots had been previously rated for attractiveness by independent judges, and the photographs of the women who had been rated most and least attractive were used in the study. Although all the men received the same biographical information, half of them were given the snapshot of an attractive woman and the other half a snapshot of an unattractive woman. The conversations were taped and judges rated the behavior of both parties.

The men's impressions of the women's beauty indirectly affected the women's behavior. Women who talked with men holding photographs of an attractive woman were friendlier, more confident, and more sociable than women talking with men holding photographs of an unattractive woman. The difference in the women's behavior was a reaction to the men, for the judges rated the men who thought they were talking to attractive women as more sociable, sexually warm, interesting, outgoing, humorous, attractive, confident, and socially adept than men who thought they were talking to unattractive women. Thus, stereotypical views of attractiveness affected a man's behavior, which in turn drew friendlier behavior from the women. It appears that our behavior depends very much on how we are perceived by others and how these perceptions and beliefs form the basis of their actions toward us.

It is probably fair to say that social categorization is in some ways based on the objective properties of category members. However, the social and affiliative networks through which people relate to one another also play important roles in determining categories. The basis of categorization often has nothing to do with the object itself; instead it depends on the person making the attribution. The same individual, say a Bulgarian, will be classified as "one of us" or "one of them," depending on whether the Bulgarian is interacting with another Bulgarian or with an American.

Although the requirements for social categorization are often trivial, they can have fatal consequences. The segregation of untouchables into special quarters, of Jews and blacks into ghettos, and of the mentally ill during the Middle Ages had fatal consequences for these populations.

A dramatic illustration of the divisive effects of segregation is found in research with bees. Bees that live in adjacent hives do not mingle, nor do inhabitants of one hive enter the other. If a strange bee enters a hive, the guard bees gather around the entrance and attack the alien viciously. In one experiment by Jean Lecomte, cited by Chauvin (1968), about 100 bees who lived harmoniously together were taken from the hive and placed in a new cage, which had a glass partition in the middle. Half the bees were placed on one side of the partition and the rest on the other. When the partition was removed twenty-four hours later, the bees from the two halves of the cage interacted in an amicable fashion. When the partition was left in place for four days, however, its removal led to severe conflict, with each group trying to exterminate the other. These bees were half-sisters, but fratricidal behavior developed because each group of bees has a distinctive odor that arises from continual food exchanges among its members. In only four days, the passing of food led to distinct odors in the divided populations so that each subgroup classified the other as "strangers."

In an analogous situation, the boys in the summer camp experiment described in the box on sexism and racism developed into hostile groups. At the camp, negative attitudes arose only after the boys competed as groups in relays and similar activities. The results of another experiment (Rabbie and Horwitz, 1969) indicate that organized competition is unnecessary for the development of negative social categorization; the chance bestowal of a gift will have the same effect. Groups of Dutch adolescents were invited to a laboratory, eight at a time, and divided into teams of four on a random basis. The adolescents understood that the division was made for convenience and had no meaning. Both groups were then given a few simple tasks; afterward the researcher announced that transistor radios would be given to the members of one group and that the award would be based on the flip of a coin. The radios were distributed and the adolescents asked to rate the members of their own and the other group. Both the outgroup as a whole (the category) and its individual members received negative ratings, with the adolescents seeing the other group as more hostile and less desirable than their own and members of the other group as less open, less responsible, and less desirable as friends. Subsequent experiments (Tajfel, 1981) have replicated these results and shown that categorizing people on trivial grounds that involve neither competition nor prizes can also produce distinctions between "us" and "them." In such cases, substantially less favorable attitudes are felt toward the outgroup.

Despite its pitfalls and dangers, categorization keeps us from being overwhelmed by the masses of information that confront us every day. Categorization allows us to go beyond the information given, to make decisions and act on inferences that do not have to be validated on each new occasion.

People seem to need to organize their perceptions about others. An accurate assessment of other people lends a measure of security to our interpersonal relationships. In sizing up your new history instructor, for example, it is not enough to observe that he is smoking in a no-smoking area. You attach some meaning to his actions in an attempt to figure out what this behavior says about his personality. You try to decide whether he is so nervous he has to smoke or is simply indifferent to rules and authority. The ability to judge another's personality helps you predict what she or he may do in other circumstances; this knowledge gives you some control over your future dealings with that person. If you conclude that your instructor is indifferent to rules, you can risk missing an assignment or coming late to class without the fear that it will hurt your grade.

Clues to the Personalities of Others

We are all detectives who gather clues about the personalities of others from a variety of sources: speech, posture, dress, walk, facial expression, even whether a person wears glasses. The musical *My Fair Lady* makes the point that changing outward characteristics, especially voice and dress, can change the way others perceive a person's inner nature. When Liza Doolittle was raggedly dressed and dropped her "h's," she was thought to be dishonest, immoral, and lazy. But clad in fancy clothes and speaking with an upper-class accent, she was considered honest, virtuous and clever. Thus appearance and behavior are the two major categories we use to judge a person's nature.

Expectations Based on Appearance   At times we know something about people before we meet them; a teacher's reputation as a disciplinarian or harsh grader, for example, generally is known to students before the first meeting of the class. But in most cases we have little or no prior knowledge about someone we are encountering for the first time. Appearance plays a large part in forming a first impression. We tend to categorize strangers by the way they look, drawing upon preconceived notions or stereotypes to fill in the details. Thus, the girl without a bra is thought to be sexually liberated, the muscular football player a "jock," the man in the three-piece suit a conservative Republican.

Some stereotyped expectations that have received a great deal of attention are those associated with physical attractiveness. Although we have always heard that "beauty is only skin deep," research indicates that we act as if attractiveness permeates the entire personality. In one study (Dion, Berscheid, and Walster, 1972), people looked at pictures of men and women and

Attractive people impress others as having a host of positive traits.

rated their personality traits. Those who were physically attractive were consistently viewed more positively than those who were less attractive. Attractive people were seen as more sensitive, kind, interesting, strong, poised, modest, and sociable, as well as more sexually responsive. Moreover, the power of beauty to create the illusion of desirable personality traits seems to begin at an early age. Children as young as three years old have been found to prefer physically attractive youngsters as friends (Dion, 1973), and adults respond more favorably to attractive children, judging them smarter and better behaved than unattractive children (Clifford and Walster, 1973).

Homely people, however, are generally viewed in an unfavorable light. Research has shown that obese adults, who in our culture are considered unattractive, are often discriminated against and stigmatized (Allon, 1975). Homely children are often targets of prejudice. An unattractive child who misbehaves is more likely to be judged "bad" or "cruel" than is an attractive child who commits the same act. When women were shown pictures of attractive and unattractive children who were misbehaving, the unattractive children were seen as chronically antisocial, whereas the attractive children were seen as "having a bad day" (Dion, 1972).

Inferring Traits from Behavior: Attribution Theory
Although the first opinion of someone's personality is generally based on physical appearance, we can alter this impression by observing a person's actions. In fact, some of the most important information about others comes from clues in their behavior. In the 1940s Fritz Heider examined the process by which the actions of others cause us to infer that they have stable dispositions. Twenty years later, other psychologists elaborated on Heider's work by advancing **attribution theories**—theories that propose to explain how people attribute personality traits to others on the basis of their behavior.

In one such theory (Jones and Davis, 1965), a person's motive or intention provides the link between behavior and personality traits. We observe the behavior and ask ourselves what the person intends to accomplish by acting in that way. If, for example, a new friend says that you look terrible in your new red sweater, you could regard the comment as an attempt to be helpful or as an act of hostility. Depending upon the motive you assign to the statement, you would attribute different personality traits to the same behavior.

Not all behavior is equally informative. Some acts are so common that they reveal little about personality. Observing a professor lecturing to students in an Elizabethan drama class and then conferring with students during office hours would enable you to deduce virtually nothing about this professor's personality, because these same activities are performed by almost all teachers. But if you observed the same professor arriving a half-hour late for class every morning and refusing to set aside office hours for students, you might be able to infer a great deal about her or his personality. It is behavior that seems unexpected or unusual and that can most plausibly be explained by only one motive that provides important clues to a person's real nature (Jones and Davis, 1965).

In an experiment designed to test attribution theory (Jones, Davis, and Gergen, 1961), subjects listened to what they believed were tape-recorded interviews with applicants for training as astronauts or submariners. Beforehand, the investigator described the ideal astronaut candidate as "inner-directed"—independent, resourceful, and self-reliant—and the ideal submariner candidate in the opposite manner, as "other-directed"—obedient, cooperative, and friendly. Half of the subjects who listened to an astronaut candidate heard the applicant present himself as highly inner-directed, whereas the other half heard the candidate present himself as other-directed. Similarly, half of the subjects heard the submariner applicant present himself as closely conforming to the ideal other-directed type, while the rest heard the applicant present himself as inner-directed.

After listening to the interviews, the subjects rated the applicants according to their perceptions of the applicants' actual personalities. Consistently, applicants whose answers were contrary to what would be expected from an ideal candidate received higher ratings for credibility. The people listening to the interviews assumed that a candidate would not have given a "wrong" answer unless it was true. In contrast, they reasoned that an applicant who painted himself as conforming to expectations may have been telling the truth, but it was just as likely that he was saying what would get him admitted to the training program. In the latter case, there was no way to discover the applicant's real motives. These findings support attribution theory, since unusual behavior (giving an unexpected response) that could reasonably be explained by only one motive was seen as most revealing.

Biased Inferences   Our inferences about other people and their motives do not always follow the rules of logic. The same biases in judgment that affect problem solving affect our perceptions of people, since figuring out a person's personality and probable behavior is a form of problem solving. As we saw in Chapter 10, a variety of biases affect our conclusions and guesses, including biases in representativeness, availability, anchoring, and hindsight.

When making judgments about other people, we tend to be so thrown off by a resemblance to a stereotypical example that we discard any other information we might have (Kahneman and Tversky, 1973). For example, graduate students in psychology were asked to predict another graduate student's specialty on the basis of the following personality sketch:

Tom W. is of high intelligence, although lacking in true creativity. He has a need for order and clarity, and for neat and tidy systems in which every detail finds its appropriate place. His writing is rather dull and mechanical, occasionally enlivened by somewhat corny puns and by flashes of imagination of the sci-fi type. He has a strong drive for competence. He seems to have little feel and little sympathy for other people and does not enjoy interacting with others. Self-centered, he nonetheless has a deep moral sense (Kahneman and Tversky, 1973, p. 238).

The graduate psychology students were told that the sketch was written while Tom was a senior in high school on the basis of projective tests, which were described in Chapter 20. Despite the fact that the students held projective tests in low esteem (rating them as accurate less than a quarter of the time), the fact that the sketch was at least five years old, and the fact that the students had some idea of the relative proportion of graduate enrollment in the nine fields that were presented as possibilities, 95 percent of the students said that Tom's specialty was computer science. At the time of this study, computer science had an extremely small enrollment and the other possible fields included two with large enrollments—education and humanities. Yet the students ignored numerical information on enrollments and judged on the basis of specific evidence that they regarded as unreliable.

Why did the students zero in on computer science? There must, after all, be quite a few education and humanities students who are orderly, tidy, competent, dull, self-centered, moral, and reluctant to interact with others. It appears that descriptive traits tilted the balance in favor of computer science, overpowering information that would have given them a better chance at an accurate prediction. As with other examples of the representativeness bias, the cluster of characteristics has a compelling pattern that resembles the computer scientist more than the educator, and it forces itself upon our belief in the manner of a perceptual illusion. Like other biases of judgment, the bias of representativeness is widespread and is found even among people trained in statistics and acquainted with probability (Kahneman and Tversky, 1973; Nisbett and Ross, 1980).

Integrating Impressions of Others

Once we infer that a person possesses certain traits, our perceptions become more integrated and we form a lasting impression. In the process of fitting together the pieces of personality, some traits seem more important than others to the final impression.

Central Traits   Certain traits apparently have a disproportionate impact on our evaluation of people. In one experiment (Kelley, 1950), students at the Massachusetts Institute of Technology (MIT) were told that their class would be taught that day by a new instructor, whom they would be asked to evaluate at the end of the period. Before the instructor was introduced, the students were given a biographical note about him. The students did not know that two versions of the note had been distributed. Half the students read the description in Figure 26.1A, and the rest read the one in Figure 26.1B. The two sketches differed by only a single word, with the first describing the instructor as "warm" and the second calling him "cold." This simple change created differing sets of expectations and thus had great impact on how the students perceived the instructor. In the evaluations they filled out at the end of class, students who had read the biography that included the word "warm" rated the instructor as substantially more considerate, informal, sociable, popular, goodnatured, and humorous than did students who had read the word "cold." The instructor's description as "warm" or "cold" also affected the students' response to him during a class discussion: 56 percent of the students who expected "warmth" participated in the discussion, whereas only 32 percent of those who expected "coldness" did so. (The instructor's appearance is shown in the accompanying photo.)

Your regular instructor is out of town today, and since we of Economics 70 are interested in the general problem of how various classes react to different instructors, we're going to have an instructor today you've never had before, Mr. Blank. Then, at the end of the period, I want you to fill out some forms about him. In order to give you some idea of what he's like, we've had a person who knows him write up a little biographical note about him. I'll pass this out to you now and you can read it before he arrives. *Please read these to yourselves and don't talk about this among yourselves until the class is over so that he won't get wind of what's going on.*

Mr. Blank is a graduate student in the Department of Economics and Social Science here at M.I.T. He has had three semesters of teaching experience in psychology at another college. This is his first semester teaching Ec. 70. He is 26 years old, a veteran, and married. People who know him consider him to be a very warm person, industrious, critical, practical, and determined.

Figure 26.1A   This is the introduction read to the class in Kelley's experiment on person perception and one of the notes that was then handed out. Read the note and try to imagine yourself in the situation. Then look at the accompanying photo. Form an impression of the instructor and note your reactions to him. When you have done so, look at Figure 26.1B. (After Kelley, 1950.)

A re-creation of the classroom scene in Kelley's experiment on person perception (see Figures 26.1A and 26.1B). Kelley was able to demonstrate in this study how strongly our impressions of people can be influenced by our expectations about them.

Solomon Asch, who conducted similar pioneering experiments in the late 1940s and early 1950s, called such traits as "warm" and "cold" **central traits** because they have such marked effects on the way other, related traits are perceived (Asch, 1946). Apparently, when we think we have detected a central trait, we build around it a cluster of expectations of additional traits the person will possess and of how she or he will behave toward other people.

The Primacy Effect   The order in which traits are perceived can also affect the impression of personality. There is evidence that the traits that are detected first influence subsequent information about the person, a process called the **primacy effect**. If, for example, your first meeting with a classmate is at a football game where the young man impresses you with his knowledge of game strategy and team standings, it may be difficult to see him as an intellectual when you later learn he is an "A" student with a major in philosophy. In your mind he will remain more the sports enthusiast than the student of Plato.

The primacy effect is so powerful because, as we saw in Chapter 19, we consider the behavior observed during a first meeting typical, and as information comes in successive chunks, it is absorbed in the context of that initial knowledge. If you discover that a woman is calm after you have learned that she is intelligent, you have a different image of her than if you had discovered that she is calm after you have learned that she is shrewd.

In one experiment (Luchins, 1957) people were given the conflicting sets of information about Jim shown in the box on page 596. In the first paragraph Jim is portrayed as extroverted and friendly; in the second paragraph he is seen as introverted and shy. Some people read paragraph A first; others read paragraph B first. As expected, the order of presentation affected impressions of Jim's personality. Most of the students who read paragraph A first labeled Jim a basically outgoing person, and most of those

who read paragraph B first considered Jim to be essentially a loner. First impressions do tend to shape our assessment of people. Apparently we screen out, reinterpret, or assign less importance to information we receive after the first impression of a person is formed.

Primacy is in part a form of another inference bias—availability. As noted in Chapter 10, biases of availability lead people to give more weight to information that is most available in memory. Things that first come to mind have more impact on judgment than information that is dredged up later (Kahneman, Slovic, and Tversky, 1982).

Self-Perception

Of all the people we encounter, the one that is always available for our own examination but extremely difficult for psychologists to study is the self. How do we perceive ourselves? How do we gather information about and evaluate ourselves? When we evaluate others, we tend to make inferences from their appearance and behavior and often resort to stereotypes in an effort to manage the information we receive. Some psychologists argue that our perception of others and our self-perception are similar processes. We observe our own behavior, assign motives to our acts, and sometimes infer corresponding personality traits (Bem, 1972).

As we do this, we appear to build up rich and important cognitive structures about the self called **self-schemata**—clusters of generalizations about the self based on past experiences that organize, summarize, and explain our behavior in specific domains (Markus, 1977). These self-schemata derive from specific incidents in the past ("I was fifteen minutes late for my dental appointment yesterday") and from generalizations about behavior made by the self and others ("Sally says I'm not very dependable but I never stand anyone up"). Once a schema is established, it helps us deal with information that is related to a particular aspect of behavior, such as whether we are masculine, feminine, creative, dependable, independent, or obese. Studies (Markus, 1977) indicate that we develop numerous schemata and not all of us have the same ones. Some people have a schema about their masculinity while others do not, so that with respect to masculinity they are "aschematic." A person with a masculinity schema is like an ex-

Mr. Blank is a graduate student in the Department of Economics and Social Science here at M.I.T. He has had three semesters of teaching experience in psychology at another college. This is his first semester teaching Ec. 70. He is 26 years old, a veteran, and married. People who know him consider him to be a rather cold person, industrious, critical, practical, and determined.

Figure 26.1B   The other note in Kelley's experiment on person perception. (If you have not looked at Figure 26.1A, do so first.) Read this description, let it sink in, and then look at the accompanying photo again, noting your reactions as before.

Is Jim an Introvert or an Extrovert?

(A) Jim is an extrovert

Jim left the house to get some stationery. He walked out into the sun-filled street with two of his friends, basking in the sun as he walked. Jim entered the stationery store which was full of people. Jim talked with an acquaintance while he waited for the clerk to catch his eye. On his way out, he stopped to chat with a school friend who was just coming into the store. Leaving the store, he walked toward school. On his way out he met the girl to whom he had been introduced the night before. They talked for a short while, and then Jim left for school.

(B) Jim is an introvert

After school Jim left the classroom alone. Leaving the school, he started on his long walk home. The street was brilliantly filled with sunshine. Jim walked down the street on the shady side. Coming down the street toward him, he saw the pretty girl whom he had met on the previous evening. Jim crossed the street and entered a candy store. The store was crowded with students, and he noticed a few familiar faces. Jim waited quietly until the counterman caught his eye and then gave his order. Taking his drink, he sat down at a side table. When he had finished his drink he went home.

How do first impressions strike us? Quite powerfully, suggests the Luchins experiment. How did you picture Jim after reading A, then B? Can you visualize him differently by rereading the paragraphs in reverse order?

Source: A. S. Luchins, "Primacy-recency in impression formation," in C. I. Hovland (ed.), *The Order of Presentation in Persuasion.* New Haven: Yale University Press, 1957. Pp. 34–35.

pert in this area; she or he knows a great deal about what other traits go with masculinity, what masculine people would tend to do under a given circumstance, how others behave toward masculine people, and what they think of them. Once a schema is developed, a person uses it to decide what information to attend to and how important it is, to understand intentions and feelings, and to identify appropriate or probable behavior. The person with a schema for mascu-

linity absorbs other information about the area more rapidly, retains it better, will make judgments and predictions in situations that contain a masculinity element more quickly, and will be more confident about them than a person who lacks a masculinity schema.

Other psychologists point out that although we do come to know our feelings, attitudes, and traits by observing our own behavior, there are differences between the ways we perceive our-

The way we perceive ourselves strongly affects the way we behave. The boys flexing their muscles probably think of themselves as fine physical specimens. The girls seem to be viewing their images a bit less seriously.

Figure 26.2 The different interpretations of behavior made by self and others showed clearly in this experiment. Actors A and B conversed while Observers C and D looked on. Later, when both actors and observers rated the actors' behavior, Actors A and B tended to attribute their behavior to situational factors, whereas Observers C and D tended to see the actors' behavior in terms of personal dispositions. (Adapted from Storms, 1973.)

selves and the ways we perceive others. For one thing, we usually explain another person's behavior in terms of enduring traits, but we tend to explain our own behavior in terms of situational demands, a point that was touched on in Chapter 19. For example, in a conference with her faculty advisor, a student would probably attribute her failing marks to external factors—emotional stress over a sick relative, financial problems that forced her to work after school instead of studying, a particularly heavy program of courses. The advisor, however, while probably appearing to be sympathetic, would be likely to attribute the student's poor academic performance to underlying traits—lack of intelligence, laziness.

This tendency appeared among students participating in a study of differences in perception (Nisbett et al., 1973). The students explained why they had chosen their own major and why they thought a friend had chosen her or his major. When they answered for themselves, the students frequently linked their behavior to an external cause ("Chemistry is a high-paying field"), but when they answered for a friend, they generally offered explanations based on personality traits ("He has a very logical, scientific mind"). Figure 26.2 portrays an experiment with similar results.

There is, however, an important exception to our tendency to ascribe our own actions to external causes. When our behavior leads to success or achievement of some kind, we tend to attribute the favorable outcome to our own inherent

traits—a practice that boosts our self-esteem. If the outcome is unfavorable we blame it on the situation or on others. A study (Snyder, Stephan, and Rosenfield, 1976) in which people played a series of games confirmed this tendency. Without the players' knowledge, the experimenters controlled who won or lost most of the games. Afterward, each player was asked to account for the results. The losers tended to attribute their performance to bad luck (external causes), while the winners tended to attribute their performance to skill (personal causes). Moreover, losers were less likely than winners to attribute the winners' success to skill, and winners were more likely than losers to attribute the losers' defeat to a lack of skill. In each case, the interpretation favored the self over others.

Interpersonal Attitudes

Perception of others is seldom a dispassionate and objective activity in which details of social information are quietly examined. When we meet a man who is famous, we immediately experience a positive feeling toward him. When we are confronted by a woman who has just won the Boston marathon, we experience admiration. We respond to intelligence, wealth, and beauty with positive emotions, whereas ugliness, fraud, and stupidity evoke the opposite reactions. Thus social perception and social categorization are highly evaluative processes that are accompanied by strong attitudes.

Our attitudes toward religious symbols, economic policies, or political candidates are important, but for most of us, they play a minor role in our daily lives compared with our attitudes toward the people around us. Hardly an hour passes without our having occasion to respond to someone, and our attitudes color our responses. What we say or do is in part determined by our attitude toward the person, and the manner of her or his response will either change or reinforce that attitude. Casual conversations are full of attitudinal statements and declarations: "I like Jack. He is a nice guy"; "Judy stood me up last night. You can't depend on her"; "Did you hear that lecture? The instructor is terrible."

Because of their importance, interpersonal attitudes have been extensively investigated by social psychologists and constitute one of the oldest fields of inquiry in this discipline. The range of interest of social psychologists working on attitudes covers questions of first impressions on the one hand and the permanence of marriage at the other extreme. How are friendships formed? How are they maintained? What are the factors implicated in interpersonal relationships? These are the main questions we shall examine in the remainder of this chapter.

Interpersonal Attitudes and Friendship Formation

At the first session of a new class, what makes you decide that you would rather sit next to one person than another? At a party full of strangers, what triggers the decision to talk to one person instead of another? The answers to these questions depend upon a number of factors that determine whether a new acquaintance becomes a friend or remains distant. Although first impressions certainly affect the development of our attitudes toward others, two factors that influence the development of friendship are proximity and similarity.

The Effects of Proximity

Think of your own friends. If you live in San Francisco, chances are your best friends are San Franciscans, probably people who live in your neighborhood or go to your school. You may believe that many interesting people live in Philadelphia or Atlanta, but unless you met some of them, you could not become their friends. In fact, the single most important factor in friendship is physical **proximity**—how close together people live and work.

The powerful effects of proximity were demonstrated in a study (Segal, 1974) of a police academy in which male cadets were alphabetically assigned to dormitory rooms and classroom seats. Upon entry, a cadet whose name began with A was likely to room with another cadet whose name also began with A, or with B or C, and sit near him in class. After six weeks, the researcher asked cadets about their choices of friends among their classmates. As Figure 26.3 indicates, there was a remarkable tendency for cadets to choose as friends classmates whose names began with letters near their own in the alphabet. Among the sixty-five friendships formed among the cadets, twenty-nine (45 percent) were between men next to each other in alphabetical order, and such choices were more likely to be reciprocated than were choices made out of alphabetical order. The accident of names predisposed Smith to become friends with Simmons rather than with Adkins, and Adkins to become friends with Abelson, indicating that physical proximity often leads to the development of friendship.

Proximity is a powerful factor in friendship because the exposure effect, which was discussed in Chapter 25, depends on proximity. But proximity has other effects. People who live close to each other tend to be similar in many ways: socioeconomic status, school background, educational attainment, ethnic background, political leanings, clothing style, family structure, and so forth. Since similarity is another powerful factor in friendship formation, as we shall see in the following section, geographic proximity promotes a host of processes that combine to generate and maintain friendships. It is no accident that many people marry the person next door.

The Effects of Similarity

There is apparently a good deal of truth to the old saying, "Birds of a feather flock together." People do tend to form relationships with others who are like them in a number of ways. As we saw

Figure 26.3 Matrix of friendship choices. Numbers across the top of the matrix indicate place in alphabetical order of *chosen*. Numbers down the left of the matrix indicate place in alphabetical order of *chooser*. (Adapted from Segal, 1974.)

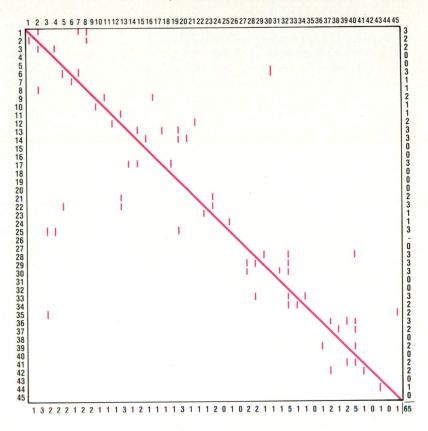

in Chapter 14, this is as true of children as it is of adults (Hartup, 1982). One way to examine the effects of similarity is to look at the way it affects attraction between the sexes.

Similarity in Appearance In romantic novels and movies, the handsome hero almost always ends up with the beautiful heroine. Life apparently follows fiction in most cases, with beauty attracting beauty. Studies (Murstein, 1972) of dating relationships indicate that people of similar physical attractiveness tend to pair off.

One possible explanation for this pattern is that when choosing a date, people consider not only the attractiveness of the other person but also the probability of being rejected by that person. Dating, in other words, follows the rules of the marketplace: a man calculates risks and rewards before he approaches a woman for a date. If a man considers himself to be fairly unattractive, he considers it probable that an attractive woman will reject him, so he lowers his sights to

a somewhat less attractive date. Some evidence of this "matching process" has been supplied by research in which it was found that when there was no possibility of refusal, men tended to choose more attractive women for dates than they would have chosen under ordinary conditions (Berscheid et al., 1971).

Other studies, however, have produced somewhat contradictory results. In one experiment (Huston, 1973), men who rated themselves low in physical attractiveness seemed to select dates as attractive as those selected by men who rated themselves high in physical attractiveness. This held true although men who gave themselves low ratings also believed they had a poorer than average chance of being accepted by the most attractive females. It is possible that men with a low evaluation of themselves were less sensitive to rejection than those who considered themselves to be attractive. Unattractive men may become accustomed to being turned down, and the chance of a highly rewarding partner may encourage them to risk refusal.

Another possible interpretation is that people will try to develop dating relationships with the most attractive partner available, regardless of the probability of rejection. But since they are rejected by those who think they can find more attractive dates, people of similar attractiveness end up paired. According to this explanation, such a "sorting process" can explain the finding that dating couples tend to be similar in physical attractiveness.

Similarity in Social Background   Not only do most couples tend to be similar in physical attractiveness, they also tend to share the same race, religion, economic status, and educational level. Young people often encounter strong social pressures, especially from parents, to marry someone with a similar social history. Such a sorting process is encouraged by proximity. As noted earlier, people of similar income levels and ethnic backgrounds generally live in the same areas and send their children to the same schools. When children and adolescents encounter only people who share their race, religion, and economic level, their friends and potential dating partners will inevitably be similar to them in social background.

Similarity versus Exposure

The proverb about birds that flock together raises a question about the relative strength of these two mechanisms of attitude formation. Is mere exposure to people like us the stronger force on our liking for others, or is a person's similarity to us more important in the development of attraction? We have no data from human research that can provide an answer, but the situation has been explored among newly hatched chicks (Zajonc, Wilson, and Rajecki, 1975). When food coloring is injected into an egg between the eleventh and thirteenth days of incubation, the hatchling emerges with plumage of the injected color. Shortly after hatching, pairs of chicks dyed either green or red were placed together in otherwise isolated compartments for sixteen to eighteen hours. Members of some pairs were of the same color (birds of a feather) and other pairs were mixed (one red and one green chick). Afterward, the chicks were observed in interaction with their cagemate, with a strange bird of their own color, and with a strange bird of the other color. As a test of affiliation, researchers used pecking, because chicks peck strangers much more than they peck companions. The results were clear: exposure was more important than similarity. Chicks of both colors liked their cagemates most—whether or not the cagemates resembled them—and birds unlike their cagemates least. That is, red chicks raised with green chicks preferred strange green chicks to strange chicks with feathers like their own, and green chicks raised with red chicks preferred strange red chicks.

There is a rich interplay among friendship, proximity, and similarity. Proximity can promote the formation of friendships. But it also predisposes people to become similar to each other—in language, in culture, in dress, in likes and dislikes, in political opinions, and in income. At the same time a reciprocal influence exists between friendship and proximity. Proximity determines the range of people with whom it is possible to make friends and it ensures repeated exposure.

Similarity can be very comforting in interpersonal relations.

Figure 26.4 The set of relationships among proximity, similarity, and friendship.

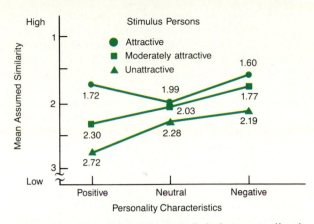

Figure 26.5 Mean assumed trait similarity between self and target persons. The numbers beside each data point are mean responses. Lower numbers reflect greater assumed trait similarity. (Adapted from Marks, Miller, and Maruyama, 1981.)

But once friendships are formed, friends tend to remain close to each other and to maintain contact. Thus, friendship promotes proximity.

Similarity also affects the development of friendships. Like the relationship between friendship and proximity, the relationship between similarity and friendship is also reciprocal: We want our friends to share our views, our tastes, and we want them to be like us in many ways. Similarity may also promote proximity. For example, people tend to move into neighborhoods occupied by others more or less like themselves. They seek out ethnic and religious affinity, and similarity of socioeconomic level. No one likes to be among people who are "different" and to risk the danger of being considered an "outsider." Thus, proximity, similarity, and friendship all enhance and reinforce each other (see Figure 26.4).

Attraction and Attribution of Similarity

Since attractive people make desirable friends and since one avenue of friendship formation is through similarity, we might ask just how far we would go out of our way to seek out similarities between us and an attractive stranger. Perhaps we simply hope that our behavior, tastes, and attitudes resemble those of attractive people. Or perhaps we perceive ourselves as already having the qualities we see in an attractive stranger. Or perhaps we impute our own qualities—whether good or bad—to attractive people who might become our friends.

A recent study indicated that the last possibility may best describe the situation and that people will go some distance in imputing their own qualities to an attractive stranger (Marks, Miller, and Maruyama, 1981). College students who judged both themselves and strangers on a number of personality traits assumed that physically attractive strangers were more like themselves than were unattractive strangers. The assumption was so strong that the students declared that they were similar to attractive strangers even on such undesirable traits as greed, conceit, phoniness, selfishness, and hostility (see Figure 26.5). In contrast, the students denied their close resemblance to unattractive strangers on such positive traits as thoughtfulness, intelligence, openmindedness, dependability, and honesty.

Despite our wishful assumptions of similarity, we do look for other qualities in friendship. The course of friendship is strongly affected by such rewarding aspects as approval and the compatibility of needs.

The Effects of Approval

The promise of approval from others weighs heavily in the formation of friendships. People who approve of us and show that they like us bolster our sense of self-worth.

It might be expected, then, that showering someone with praise would be the surest path to friendship. Yet some studies have shown that unquestioning approval does not produce the most favorable attitudes toward the approving person. In one study (Aronson and Linder, 1965), women overheard a series of remarks about themselves made by the researchers' confederate. Women in one group heard only complimentary remarks, and those in a second group heard only derogatory remarks. A third group heard very derogatory remarks, which gradually became positive and at last were highly complimentary (this was called the gain condition). A fourth group heard comments that were at first very positive but became less favorable and finally very disparaging (this was called the loss condition). When each woman was asked how much she liked the confederate, the one who began by saying negative things and ended by being laudatory was liked the best. The confederate who was uniformly positive was liked—but not as much as the one who switched from criticism to approval. The confederate who said consistently negative things was also preferred to the one who began with compliments and ended with disapproval.

As noted in Chapter 25, attitudes are influenced by many factors. In this case, the early disparaging remarks made in the gain condition may have established the genuineness and credibility of the confederate. The subject may have thought the change revealed that the confederate was a discriminating person and not easy to impress. As a result, the eventual approval may have seemed especially rewarding. When the confederate's remarks were uniformly positive, the subject may have thought that the confederate praised everyone. The remarks, therefore, were less gratifying, and the confederate was liked somewhat less. In the loss condition, the subjects who heard positive comments followed by negative ones may have experienced such a surprising and disappointing loss of self-esteem that they felt cooler toward that confederate than they would have felt toward someone who had been critical all along.

The Effects of Complementary Needs

Important as approval is, the ways in which the personalities of people mesh may be more important than the need for unstinted praise. Attempting to explain bonds of mutual interdependence between lovers, Carl Jung (whose theories were discussed in Chapter 18) suggested that people have unconscious "archetypes," or ideals, of the sort of persons who would best complement them. When someone encounters a person who corresponds to this archetype, she or he immediately becomes aware of the match and falls in love.

Other theorists (e.g., Winch, 1958) have suggested that complementary needs are a basis for attraction between friends as well as lovers. Thus, a person with the need to dominate is attracted to one with the need to be dominated; a person with a need to care for others is drawn to one with a need to be cared for. In describing a friendship between two teen-aged boys, psychologist Robert White (1972) provided a good example of how two personalities complemented one another:

> Ben, whose school experience had been so unstimulating that he never read a book beyond those assigned, discovered in Jamie a lively spirit of intellectual inquiry and an exciting knowledge of politics and history: Here was a whole world to which his friend opened the door and provided guidance. Jamie discovered in Ben a world previously closed to him, that of confident interaction with other people. Each admired the other, each copied the other, each used the other for practice.

Later research suggests, however, that friendships may depend more on a compatibility of needs than on a simple complementarity. An example of compatible needs in a pair of friends is a high level of dominance in one person and a low need for autonomy in the other. A high need for dominance in one partner and a low need for dominance in the other would be complementary, but would not necessarily be compatible. The importance of compatibility appeared in an assessment of camp counselors who had worked together for at least a month and had formed friendships. There was strong evidence that counselors with compatible need structures tended to become friends (Wagner, 1975).

Compatibility of needs may be important for a harmonious marriage. When the need structures of married couples were studied, there was no evidence of any relationship between marital adjustment and simple complementarity. But couples who scored high on a scale of marriage adjustment had similar needs for affiliation, aggression, autonomy, and nurturance. Apparently, similarity in these needs makes for a harmonious marriage. A couple with similarly high needs for affiliation, for example, can socialize a great deal, while a couple who are both low in the need for affiliation can be stay-at-homes. Sharply different levels of need for affiliation would be expected to produce tension between marriage partners.

Although a knowledge of needs may be a reliable guide to friendship patterns and marital adjustment, the principles for determining need compatibility are complex and subtle. They are complicated by the fact that the social context of a relationship affects the compatibility of need structures (Wagner, 1975). Because of these complexities, the relationships of compatibility and complementarity must be examined on a trait-by-trait basis.

The Effects of Birth Order

Given the influences on friendship formation discussed so far, the fact remains that no matter what the situation, some people are obviously shy and have difficulty making friends and others are just as obviously popular and become friendly with a stranger in minutes. These inclinations affect all our social relationships, and we have little control over them. Although the precise circumstances that help to shape such traits as sociability and shyness are unknown, research suggests that family experiences may be of major importance in their development. Specifically, **birth order**, or the sequence in which children are born into a family, appears to give later-born children a social advantage, so that they tend to make friends more easily than do first-born children.

The greater sociability of later-born children develops because of what seem like disadvantages in childhood. The first-born have their parents to themselves until they acquire their first sibling, so that their first and most frequent contact as infants and young children is with adults. The later-born, however, never have their parents to themselves in early childhood, and much of their growth is dominated by interaction with an older sibling. Thus, first-born children, in contrast with those born later, acquire different conceptions about what sorts of people might be friends with them, how to get other people to do things for them, and what sorts of people have power and what sorts do not. Later-born children, on the other hand, are likely to feel powerless, because they must learn to work with—and around—other family members to achieve their

goals. As a result of their birth order, the later-born develop social skills that contribute to their popularity outside the family (Markus, 1981). In fact, when researchers (Miller and Maruyama, 1976) asked a large number of children to choose from among their classmates the child they would like to play ball with during recess, the later-born were picked more often than the first-born.

The contribution of birth order to personality is the basis for a theory that predicts the probable success of adult heterosexual relationships. This **duplication hypothesis**, which was developed by Walter Toman (1976), applies the influence of similarity on attraction to experiences that accompany a person's birth order. According to Toman, marriage partners seek to duplicate their childhood sibling relationships and are happiest when they do so. Thus, a first-born woman who grew up with a younger brother would be happiest if she married a man who had an older sister. Toman used his hypothesis to predict the probability of divorce and separation, with some success, although subsequent research has failed to support his predictions.

However, if younger siblings are indeed more sociable and outgoing than first-born children, it would follow that couples made up of the later-born should have especially satisfactory relationships. Besides developing strong social skills, the later-born learn to settle for second-best (as they often had to do at home), an ability that should lend their relationships more give-and-take and therefore greater stability. To test this idea, researchers (Ickes and Turner, in press) observed forty male-female pairs during informal, face-to-face interaction. Both men and women with an older sibling of the opposite sex were likely to have rewarding interactions with strangers of the opposite sex. Last-born men talked more than first-born men, asked more questions, and were better liked by their female partners. Last-born women were more likely to start a conversation than were first-born women, and they smiled more at their partners. First-born women tended to be rated as strong, vain, or sensitive by their male partners, and first-born men as unassertive, unexciting, and unfriendly by their female partners. Although a five-minute conversation between a pair of strangers cannot be used to predict the stability—or even the likelihood—of marriage, the study does support the notion that the later-born have an edge in social situations.

Interpersonal Attraction and Love

Every American grows up in a culture that is suffused with the notion of romantic love. It is our constant companion in books and movies, on the television screen, in songs, in advertisements. Growing up in this romantic atmosphere leads most adolescents to believe that falling in love is inevitable.

Social psychologists have begun to probe the nature of romantic love, and the questions that instigated their research are similar to the ones that people have been asking for centuries. What is love, and how does it differ from liking? What causes two people to fall in love? Some of the answers that have come from this research may lead us to look at romantic love differently.

Romantic love, long the province of poets, has also become a subject for psychologists.

Love is a subjective experience. Thus it is exceedingly difficult to define scientifically. Some psychologists have tried to distinguish it from liking by asking people to describe their feelings toward a lover, compared to their feelings toward a friend. For example, the individuals who comprised more than 200 dating couples from colleges in the Boston area answered a lengthy questionnaire concerning their feelings toward their boyfriend or girl friend (Rubin, 1970). Their answers fell into two groups, with one set describing feelings that reflected what is commonly regarded as "liking" and the other describing "loving." Some of the relationships were predominately loving, and others were predominately liking.

Feelings are often expressed in behavior, and researchers have also attempted to identify behavior that is related to love. In the Boston college study, "loving" couples—couples who scored high on statements reflecting love—spent more time gazing into each other's eyes than did "liking" couples (Rubin, 1973). As we shall see in Chapter 28, eye contact within extremely short distances is reserved for the expression of deep emotion. Therefore sustained eye contact reflects the strong, positive feelings that are assumed to characterize love and the intimate communication that is common among lovers.

The emotions that accompany love are complex and far from being clearly understood. They involve sexual excitement (see Chapter 17), dependency needs, joy, anxiety, jealousy, sometimes a desire for control, and many other feelings. Especially in the early stages of a relationship, people find it difficult to label these emotions and may mistake one for another. For example, when a man first met an attractive woman, he might have confused whatever emotions he was feeling with sexual excitement and sexual attraction, even though his arousal had little to do with sexuality.

Evidence for such "misattribution" of emotion comes from a study (Dutton and Aron, 1974) testing the hypothesis that arousal from a source unconnected with sexual excitement might be mistaken for sexual excitement if environmental cues about sexuality are present. In this study, men met an attractive female stranger, either under fear-provoking conditions or in safety. In the fear-arousing condition, the men had just crossed an unsteady, decrepit bridge that swayed in the wind high above a rocky gorge. As they stepped from the bridge, the woman—who was a confederate of the experimenter—asked them to write a brief story for a project. The stories these men wrote contained more sexual imagery than did stories written by men in a control group who had been approached by the same woman as they crossed a solid bridge that spanned a shallow stream. The men who crossed the unsteady bridge were also more likely to telephone the attractive confederate later to be told more about the project. According to the two-factor theory of emotion, discussed in Chapter 15, crossing the shaky, dangerous bridge frightened (and thus physically aroused) the men; at the sight of the woman, they relabeled their arousal as sexual attraction. If this interpretation is correct, perhaps other strong emotions could be appraised as love if the situation makes that appraisal possible.

Romantic attraction, then, may be based on physiological arousal, perhaps coupled with the operation of learning principles. But these explanations need not detract from the pleasures of intimate friendship and love. The sun is no less enjoyable on a warm summer day when we know that the rays are part of the electromagnetic spectrum produced by the fusion of hydrogen atoms into helium. In the same way, the pleasures of friendship and love need not be diminished by our increased understanding of them.

SUMMARY

1. Categories enable us to organize our information about the world, freeing us from the burden of attending to all the properties of each object we meet. But categories also cause us to jump to premature conclusions so that *social categorization* can result in stereotyping and prejudice with extremely serious consequences for the stereotyped group. Although social categorization has some basis in objective properties of the category members, a category generally implies additional properties that the member may not possess. In addition, categorization often depends on the person who assigns the object to a category and not at all on the object itself. Categorizing people into groups, even on trivial grounds, can produce distinctions and lead to unfavorable attitudes toward the outgroup.

2. Assessing another's personality helps to predict that person's behavior and provides some control in future dealings with her or him. Appearance and behavior are two major categories often used in judging a person's nature. First impressions of strangers are often formed on appearance, with stereotypes connected with their appearance used to infer personality. Physically attractive people are generally viewed positively and physically unattractive people are generally viewed negatively. It may be that the kindness, sociability, and sensitivity ascribed to attractive people is the result of others' behavior toward them—behavior based on the stereotypical notion that they indeed possess these qualities.

3. According to **attribution theories**, which explain how people ascribe personality traits to others on the basis of their behavior, a person's apparent motive provides the link between behavior and action. Important clues to personality are found in unexpected behavior that can be plausibly explained by only one motive. However, attributions are sometimes wrong, because the same biases in judgment that affect problem solving also affect our inferences about people's personality.

4. After we infer another's traits, we integrate those perceptions to form a lasting impression of that person. **Central traits** have marked effects on the way other, related traits are perceived, and the detection of a central trait creates expectations about other traits and probable behavior. According to the **primacy effect**, the traits that are first perceived influence further impressions of a person. People tend to screen out, reinterpret, or assign less importance to information received after a first impression has been formed.

5. Some psychologists believe that our perception of others and self-perception are similar processes. As a perception of the self develops, cognitive structures are formed called

self-schemata—clusters of generalizations about the self based on past experiences that organize, summarize, and explain our behavior in specific domains. An established schema helps in dealing with information related to that aspect of behavior. Other psychologists point out that a person usually explains another's behavior in terms of enduring traits and her or his own behavior in terms of situational demands. An exception to this rule is the tendency for people to ascribe their own successes to inherent traits because it boosts their self-esteem.

6. **Proximity**, or how close together people live and work, influences the development of attitudes and plays a major role in the development of friendships. Similarity is another factor in the development of attitudes, and people tend to form friendships and romantic attachments with others like themselves in level of attractiveness, race, religion, economic status, and educational level. Although the relative strengths of exposure and similarity are unknown, exposure seems to be the stronger force among newly hatched chicks.

7. The promise of approval from others affects the development of friendship, yet constant approval seems to produce less favorable attitudes than does approval that follows criticism. However, the context in which approval or criticism is received determines its effects in daily life. Need structures also play a role in attraction, with complementary and compatible needs both affecting friendships. Again, context is important; in marriage, unless certain needs are compatible, marital tension is likely to develop. Another factor that influences friendship is **birth order**, or the sequence in which children are born into a family. Later-born children develop social skills that contribute to their popularity. According to the **duplication hypothesis**, people are happiest when they re-create their birth-order position in their marital relationship.

8. Psychologists who have studied romantic love have distinguished between "liking" and "loving," and found that "loving" is sometimes reflected in such behavior as prolonged eye contact. It has been suggested that falling in love can be explained by the two-factor theory of emotion, in which physiological arousal is attributed to the presence of another and interpreted as love.

KEY TERMS

attribution theories	duplication hypothesis	racism
birth order	prejudice	self-schemata
central traits	primacy effect	sexism
discrimination	proximity	stereotypes

RECOMMENDED READINGS

BERSCHEID, ELLEN, and ELAINE WALSTER. *Interpersonal Attraction.* 2nd ed. Reading, Mass.: Addison-Wesley, 1978. A well-organized and valuable review of research in this area.

DUCK, STEVE W. (ed.). *Theory and Practice in Interpersonal Attraction.* London: Academic Press, 1976. A collection of chapters by leading researchers and theoreticians, focused on interpersonal attraction.

HARVEY, JOHN H., WILLIAM Y. ICKES, and R. F. KIDD (eds.). *New Directions in Attribution Research.* Hillsdale, N.J.: Erlbaum, 1976. A collection of provocative papers—the frontiers of research on person perception—by leading researchers and theoreticians.

HUSTON, TED L. (ed.). *Foundations of Interpersonal Attraction.* New York: Academic Press, 1974. An excellent collection of papers by leading researchers in the field.

RAJECKI, D. W. *Attitudes: Themes and Advances.* Sunderland, Mass.: Sinauer, 1982. This is the most recent book on attitudes. It presents a lucid review of theory and research on attitudes. It concludes with a review of application of attitude research to the notions of self, prosocial behavior, and social stereotypes.

SCHNEIDER, D. J., A. H. HASTORF, and P. C. ELLSWORTH. *Person Perception.* 2nd ed. Reading, Mass.: Addison-Wesley, 1979. Extensive survey of issues in person perception, including impression formation and the interpersonal perception of nonverbal cues.

TVERSKY, A., and D. KAHNEMAN. "Judgment Under Uncertainty: Heuristics and Biases," *Science,* 185 (1974), 1124–1131. A review of biases and errors people make in drawing inferences about others and about social events.

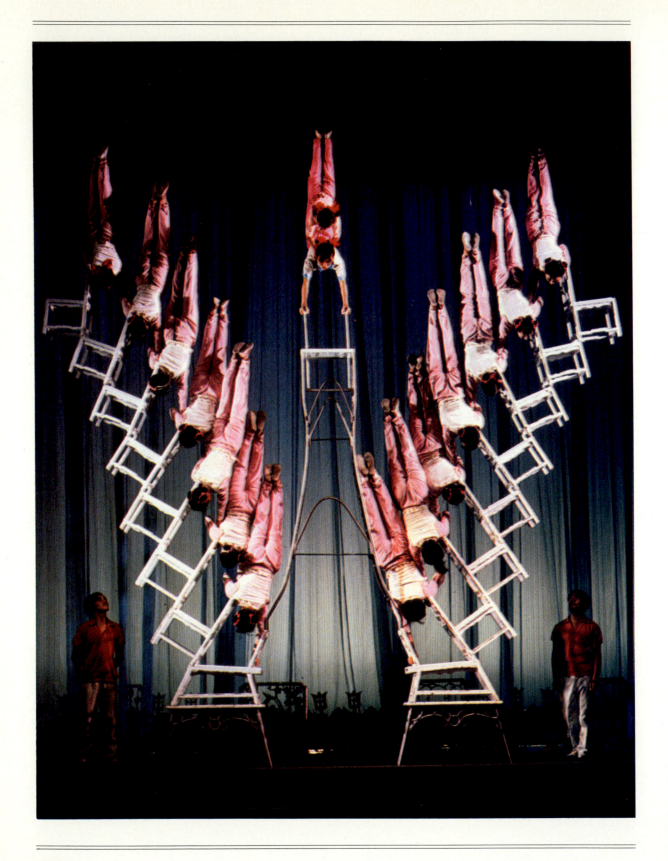

CHAPTER 27

Social Influence and Group Processes

By now it is clear that human behavior has many causes. Much of our behavior depends on internal states—our needs, our memories, or our beliefs. Much of it depends on external conditions—the stimuli around us and the information that can be gleaned from them. But our behavior changes most significantly in response to other people, so social influences are an important force in determining behavior. Social influence ranges from the primitive influence exerted by the mere presence of others to the complex effects of brainwashing. In this chapter, we shall investigate various forms of social influence. After exploring the influences of others on a single individual, we shall turn to an examination of mutual influence as it occurs in such group processes as cooperation and competition.

Social Facilitation

The simplest form of social influence was studied by the earliest social psychologists. At the turn of the century, investigators became interested in the way the mere presence of others affected human performance. For example, an early researcher (Triplett, 1897) noted that bicycle racers do much better in competitive races than when racing alone against the clock. He decided that the presence of others performing the same task increases a person's motivation and thus improves performance. At first it appeared that Triplett's explanation was correct. **Social facilitation**, or enhanced performance in the presence of others, was supported by a number of subsequent studies (Dashiell, 1930; Travis, 1925).

But psychologists began to doubt the phenomenon when conflicting evidence appeared. People took longer to solve complex problems and made more mistakes when they worked on the same task in the presence of one another (Allport, 1920), and it took people longer to learn a complex maze when other people were around (Pessin and Husband, 1933). Similar experiments with animals also were ambiguous. Social facilitation appeared among animals who ate or drank in the presence of others. For example, a chicken allowed to eat grain until it would eat no more began eating again when it was joined by a hungry chicken (Bayer, 1929). But animals became slow at learning mazes when in groups. Furthermore, a solitary cockroach found its way though a maze much more rapidly than did pairs or groups of three cockroaches (Gates and Allee, 1933).

Yet there was a consistency in these results that explained the seeming chaos. Social facilitation occurred when people or other animals worked on simple tasks or on tasks they had already mastered, whereas performance worsened on complex tasks or those that required them to learn new skills. Human beings and animals alike showed an increase in **dominant responses**, or those responses that are best learned and therefore most likely to be made by an organism in a given situation. Thus, eating might be the dominant response when food is placed before a hungry or greedy animal and escape may be the dominant response when an animal is threatened. In simple tasks, the dominant responses are mainly correct, but when learning a new skill, such as riding a bicycle, the dominant responses are mainly wrong.

Why should the presence of others facilitate dominant responses? According to behaviorist Kenneth Spence, there is a connection between motivation and performance. Spence (1956) noted that when motivation increases, performance on simple tasks increases and performance on complex tasks deteriorates; he proposed that drives, the internal motivational factors discussed in Chapter 16, increase dominant responses. On simple tasks, dominant responses are largely correct; on complex tasks, they are largely incorrect. The presence of another person apparently has this sort of motivational effect. When we are in the presence of another, our arousal increases and dominant responses are enhanced. They will be more likely to occur and to occur more often, and each response will be more intense than when our arousal ebbs and our motivation decreases.

Most research on social facilitation has supported this explanation (Zajonc, 1965). For example, when people work at tasks in the presence of observers, their palms begin to sweat, a sign of arousal (Martens, 1969). Further, although the presence of others interferes with performance when a person is just beginning to learn to trace the path through a maze with the finger, once the individual has mastered the maze, the presence of others improves speed and proficiency (Hunt and Hillery, 1973). In addition, when the maze is complex, the presence of others leads to many errors, but when a simple maze is used, fewer errors appear (see Table 27.1).

What is the nature of the drive underlying social facilitation? Perhaps the presence of spectators or other individuals working on the same task leads to apprehension, with people becoming concerned about the way others might evaluate them (Cottrell, 1972)? The results from a study (Markus, 1978) indicate that apprehension over evaluation may not be a necessary factor in social facilitation. In this study, students supposedly waiting to take part in an experiment were asked to change clothes in order to resemble other subjects in the group. Students changed their outer garments either in a room by themselves or in a room occupied by a technician, who sat with his back to the students and appeared to be absorbed in repairing a piece of electronic apparatus. When students were taking off or putting on their own clothes (a well-learned task with correct dominant responses),

Learning to play tennis with a group may make things more difficult at first, but once skills have been learned, the presence of other people may improve performance.

Table 27.1 Social facilitation has similar effects on people and on animals. The presence of others leads to improved performance in a simple maze and causes performance in a complex maze to deteriorate.

Subjects	Simple Maze		Complex Maze	
	Alone	*Together*	*Alone*	*Together*
Cockroaches (running time in seconds)	40.48	32.96	110.45	129.46
Human Beings (number of errors)	44.67	36.19	184.91	220.33

Sources: R. B. Zajonc, A. Heingartner, and E. M. Herman. "Social Enhancement and Impairment of Performance in the Cockroach," *Journal of Personality and Social Psychology*, 13 (1969), 83–92. P. J. Hunt and J. M. Hillery. "Social Facilitation in a Coaction Setting: An Examination of the Effects over Learning Trials," *Journal of Experimental Social Psychology*, 9 (1973), 563–571.

the presence of the technician speeded their responses. But when the students were putting on the unfamiliar coats and shoes (a relatively unfamiliar task), the presence of the technician slowed their responses. The simple task of changing clothes in the presence of an uninterested worker of the same sex is unlikely to arouse any evaluation apprehension, yet both social facilitation and interference from the presence of others affected the students.

Conformity

Social facilitation is the simplest form of social influence, but its effects are primitive in that behavior is merely slowed down or speeded up. The *direction* of behavior does not change, and the mere presence of others does not lead to the acquisition of new habits or to the extinction of old ones. Other forms of social influence that we hardly notice have powerful effects on us.

It is difficult to imagine much behavior that is not affected by social influence—the food we eat, the clothes we wear, the books we read, the movies we see, the music we listen to, the religious and political beliefs we hold, the people we like and dislike, and the way we work. If you wrote down all your behavior that is not influenced by social factors, you would produce a tiny list, limited mostly to physiological function, although

even these are socially influenced. For example, cultural influences determine how wastes are eliminated, where this is done, and the hygienic rules governing the process. In some cultures elimination is a more shameful act than in others, but all cultures have norms about its conduct and train children to comply with them.

The norms of a culture are social forces that exert a powerful, although often unrecognized, influence toward conformity. For example, most Americans insist that they would never have supported Adolf Hitler if they had lived in Germany during World War II. Yet millions of Germans did, and these people were not unusual in any significant respect—not particularly weak or especially open to suggestion. They were simply ordinary people responding to extraordinary circumstances in what was apparently a very ordinary way.

Social influence has received a great deal of attention from social psychologists, and two areas have been of special interest. One is the way in which social pressure can induce a person to conform to a prevailing attitude or perception, and the other is the process that leads people to obey commands from authoritative sources even when it means violating their own moral standards.

Individual Conformity to Norms

Conformity is the result of implicit or explicit social pressure and can be defined as the tendency to shift one's views or behavior closer to the norms expressed by other people. When you conform, it is not necessarily because you are convinced that what you are saying or doing is right. You may simply take a particular public stance because you believe that others prefer, or even demand, that you do so.

Although the word "conformity" often has a negative connotation, acceptance of prevailing norms is generally constructive, and in some cultures (for example, China or Japan), it has a more positive connotation than in the United States. Common standards make it possible for us to predict the behavior of others with some accuracy and to communicate with them without misunderstanding. In addition, conformity to norms can provide the necessary emotional support that enables a person to accomplish important goals—giving up drugs, for example, or resisting tyrannical authority.

Yet some instances of conformity have little to recommend them (Allen, 1965). People may at times renounce a belief they know to be right simply to avoid being out of step with the majority. Voting against a potential club member because other members do not like the candidate's religion and refusing to speak out against a politician because she or he is a local favorite are examples of this kind of conformity.

Sherif's Experiments Individual conformity can go beyond matters of belief and custom; social influence can lead people to question the information received by their senses. A classical demonstration of visual conformity was provided by Muzafer Sherif (1936), who exploited a visual illusion to study the effects of norms. Sherif used the "autokinetic effect," in which a stationary pinpoint of light, when viewed in total darkness, appears to move. People viewed such lights by themselves and, over the course of many judgments, each arrived at a stable—but different—range of judgments on the distance the light "moved." Afterward, several individuals, each with a different pattern of judgment, viewed the light together and judged aloud the distance the light "traveled." In the course of making these judgments, their widely divergent estimates converged until they resembled one another closely.

The situation in this experiment differs substantially from that found in social facilitation. In social facilitation, the effect is caused by the mere presence of others—their behavior provides no reinforcement and furnishes no cues as to appropriate responses. In the conformity experiment, however, the person does receive information from others. Although she or he is not required to use this information as a guide to behavior, it is available. If the person feels any compulsion to follow it, social influence has exerted an effect. In Sherif's experiments, people who viewed the light together from the beginning made similar judgments during the first session. And people who started by making their judgments in groups and then watched the light by themselves had adopted the social norm as their own—they persisted in giving approximately the same estimates that had been developed within the group.

Asch's Experiments Some psychologists doubted that Sherif's experiments had demonstrated the power of conformity, because the situation was so ambiguous and each viewer so uncertain of her or his judgments that they eagerly accepted the only available information—the judgments of other subjects. One of those who doubted the significance of Sherif's results was Solomon Asch, who thought that if people could judge unambiguous stimuli under optimal conditions, the sort of convergence Sherif found would not appear. Individuals who shifted their opinions when the facts are uncertain would not be moved when faced with reality. When Asch (1951) tested his proposal with male college students, the results surprised him.

Each student was told that he was participating in an experiment on visual judgment in which he would compare the lengths of lines. He would be shown two large white cards: one card with a single vertical line, and another with three vertical lines of different lengths (see Figure 27.1). The alleged experimental task was to determine which of the three lines on the second card was the same length as the standard.

The student was seated in a room with seven other apparent subjects who were actually Asch's confederates. After unanimous judgments on the first two sets of cards, the third set was shown. Although the correct response was obviously line 2, the first confederate declared that line 1 matched the standard. In turn, the other six confederates agreed—and with great certainty. Now the true subject was faced with a dilemma. His eyes told him that line 2 was the correct choice, but six other people had unani-

Figure 27.1 The stimuli in a single trial in Asch's experiment. The subject must state which of the comparison lines he judges to be the same length as the standard. The discrimination is an easy one to make: Control subjects (those who made the judgments without any group pressure) chose line 2 as correct over 99 percent of the time.

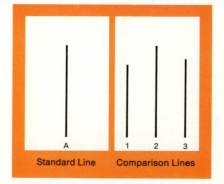

Standard Line   Comparison Lines

mously and confidently selected line 1. Confronted with a solid—but obviously wrong—majority, almost one-third of the fifty people Asch tested bowed to social influence and conformed with the obviously incorrect choice at least half the time.

Factors Influencing Conformity What accounts for the conformity found in Asch's research? Part of the answer may lie in situational factors built into the experimental design. For one thing, the judgments of the confederates were unanimous; not one of them hinted that another answer might be possible. By varying the basic experiment, Asch found that the extent of agreement was an important influence. When only one confederate gave the correct answer, the proportion of subjects who conformed dropped dramatically—from 32 percent to 5 percent. It appears that a single voice raised in opposition to an otherwise unanimous judgment can have a remarkable effect. Others who may be leaning toward a dissenting view but are not sure that they should express it may decide to assert themselves against the majority.

Another situational factor that influenced the conformity Asch found was the requirement that his subjects interact face-to-face with the confederates. Later research showed that when people can respond anonymously, they conform less often (Deutsch and Gerard, 1955).

However, the Asch experiments included situational factors that might have lowered the pressure to conform. The confederates were complete strangers to the subject, with no special claim on her or his loyalty or affection. The subject had never seen them before and probably would never see them again. Consequently, she or he had little reason to fear that nonconformity would have social repercussions. The existence of this situational factor, which would logically reduce the pressure to conform, has led some psychologists to conclude that Asch's work revealed only the tip of the conformity iceberg. If the pressure to conform among strangers is so strong, it seems likely that the pressure to conform among friends is far stronger.

Social pressure to conform with inaccurate visual judgments has some limits. To assess the relative influence of social and perceptual factors, investigators (Jacobs and Campbell, 1961) subjected several "generations" to the autokinetic effect and observed the transfer of norms from one generation to the next. The first subject was led into a dark room where there were two confederates instructed to announce that the pinpoint of light moved 15 or 16 inches. (When there were no other cues and no other individuals making judgments, the average distance of the light's apparent movement was about 3½ inches.) The confederates made their judgments first. After the two confederates and the subject had judged the movement, one of the confederates was thanked for participating and replaced by a new subject. Now there were two true sub-

Figure 27.2 In a study using the autokinetic effect, social influences were gradually overcome by perceptual factors, but it required ten "generations" of subjects before judgments of a light's apparent motion were the same as those of a control group who had never come under social pressure to conform. (After Jacobs and Campbell, 1961.)

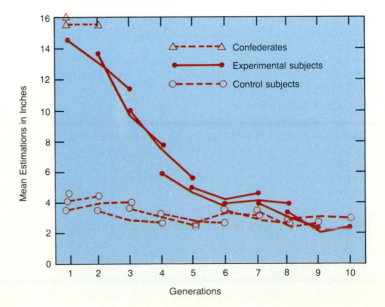

jects and only one confederate. After the second set of judgments, the last confederate was replaced by a third subject, leaving no one with instructions to make obviously false judgments. On the fourth set of judgments the first naive subject was replaced by a new subject and this procedure was continued for ten generations of subjects. As shown in Figure 27.2, in the presence of confederates, subjects judged the light to make large movements, but as the confederates were replaced by true subjects, perceptual influences became increasingly powerful, and the judgments of the final generation were the same as those of subjects in a control group who had never been exposed to erroneous judgments.

Zimbardo's Prison Experiment   Social conformity of a different sort was studied when Philip Zimbardo and Craig Haney (1977) advertised in newspapers for volunteers to take part in a mock prison experiment. The volunteers were randomly assigned roles as "prisoners" and "guards." Both groups were placed in the basement of the Stanford University psychology building and given minimal instructions; they were told to assume their assigned roles and that the guards' job was to "maintain law and order." In only a few hours, the behavior of one group became sharply differentiated from the behavior of the other group. The guards adopted the behavior patterns and attitudes that are typical of guards in maximum security prisons, with most of them becoming abusive and aggressive. Most of the prisoners became passive, dependent, and depressed, although some became enraged at the guards. Suffering among the prisoners was so great that one had to be released in less than thirty-six hours; several other prisoners also had to be released before the intended two-week experiment was ended after six days.

Stereotypical social norms controlled the behavior of both groups. The guards adopted a manner they believed was necessary to simulate their role and maintain order. The prisoners, who were the targets of the guards' abuse, assumed attitudes that accorded with their image of prison life. As the groups became antagonistic, each reinforced the other's behavior. The prisoners expected the guards to be mean and vicious and treated them accordingly. The guards expected the prisoners to be rebellious and acted so as to prevent unruly behavior. A situation of pretense, by virtue of the partici-

pants' perceptions, had real effects on the feelings and behavior of everyone involved. As this experiment shows, conformity to social norms is not simply the result of social pressures from one's own group; the influence of other groups in society magnifies the pressure to conform.

Obedience to Authority

The key conflicts that emerged between the prisoners and guards in Zimbardo's experiment concerned obedience, behavior that can in some circumstances be destructive. "When you think of the long and gloomy history of man," wrote C. P. Snow (1961), "you will find more hideous crimes have been committed in the name of obedience than have been committed in the name of rebellion." **Obedience** is any behavior that complies with the explicit commands of a person in authority. The Spanish Inquisition, the Salem witch hunts, the Nazi war crimes, the massacre of Vietnamese civilians at My Lai, are historical examples of inhumane behavior resulting from obedience to authority.

Obedience does not always have destructive results. Compliance with the demands of parents and teachers, for example, is an important part of developing into a mature, responsible adult. And compliance with the law is essential if any society is to function successfully. Nevertheless, most of the research on obedience has focused on the negative consequences of unquestioning compliance, in the hope of discovering how such destructive acts as atrocities committed during wartime could have come to pass.

Milgram's Experiments   The most dramatic and extensive investigation of obedience was conducted by Stanley Milgram (1974), who studied men of all ages and from a wide range of occupations. Each subject was paid to take part in what he was told was a study of the effects of punishment on learning. The experimenter, dressed in a white laboratory coat, instructed each subject to read a list of word pairs to a "learner" (really a confederate of the experimenter) whose task it was to memorize them. The learner was taken into an adjacent room, out of the subject's sight, for the duration of the experiment. Every time the learner made a mistake, the subject was to punish him by administering a shock from an impressive-looking shock generator (which, of

Obedience is not necessarily a negative trait. In many situations, smooth performance requires uniform behavior.

course, was not connected). The generator had thirty clearly marked voltage levels, with switches ranging from 15 to 450 volts and labels ranging from "Slight Shock" to "Danger: Severe Shock." Whenever the learner made a mistake, the subject was to increase the voltage by one level and administer the shock.

Acting under instructions, the learners made many errors, necessitating increasingly severe shocks. When the shock level reached 300 volts,

the learner pounded on the wall in protest and then fell silent. At this point, the experimenter instructed the subject to treat the silence as a wrong answer and to raise the voltage. If the subject ever asked to stop the experiment, the researcher sternly told him to go on.

Our obedience to authority is greater than most people believe. Psychiatrists, college students, and middle-class adults consulted by Milgram believed that virtually all subjects would

Figure 27.3 Results of Stanley Milgram's classic experiment on obedience. Subjects were told to administer increasing amounts of shock to a "learner" on the pretext that scientists were studying the effects of punishment on learning. Of forty experimental subjects, all administered shocks scaled "intense" or higher, and only fourteen refused to go all the way to the most severe, "XXX" shock level. (After Milgram, 1963.)

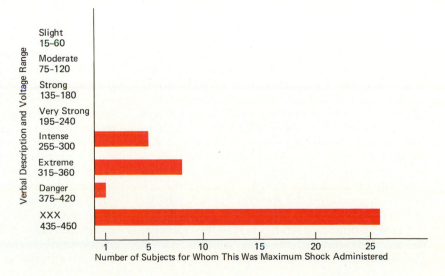

Two Responses to Milgram's Obedience Experiment

The excerpts which follow show the responses of a yielder and an independent. The yielder's response is described by an experimenter; the independent's response is described by the subject.

Yielder
"I observed a mature and initially poised businessman enter the laboratory smiling and confident. Within 20 minutes he was reduced to a twitching, stuttering wreck, who was rapidly approaching a point of nervous collapse. He constantly pulled on his earlobe, and twisted his hands. At one point he pushed his fist into his forehead and muttered: 'Oh, God, let's stop.' And yet he continued to respond to every word of the experimenter and obeyed to the end."

Independent
"I think he's trying to communicate, he's knocking. . . . Well it's not fair to shock the guy. . . . These are terrific volts. I don't think this is very humane. . . . Oh, I can't go on with this; no, this isn't right. It's a hell of an experiment. The guy is suffering in there. No, I don't want to go on. This is crazy." (Subject refused to administer more shocks.)

Source: S. Milgram. "Behavioral Study of obedience," *Journal of Abnormal and Social Psychology,* 67 (1963), 371–438. Copyright 1963 by American Psychological Association.

---

break off the experiment before the dangerous shock levels were reached. Yet among forty subjects, twenty-six, or 65 percent, continued to obey the experimenter to the very end (see Figure 27.3). These subjects were not sadists. Many of them showed signs of extreme anxiety during the session, and they frequently told the experimenter that they wanted to stop (see the accompanying box). But despite their distress, most of them continued to obey the experiment's commands. (At the time these experiments were conducted the present strict guidelines for the protection of human subjects did not exist.)

Factors Influencing Obedience   Many factors influence the extent to which people will obey authority, especially when obedience means acting against their own moral standards. Of first importance is whether the person giving instructions is viewed as a legitimate authority. From the time we are children, we are taught that certain people can, by virtue of their social position, legitimately expect compliance with their wishes. When a police officer orders a driver to pull over to the side of the road or a physician requests that a patient undress, people usually do as they are told. Indeed, the sight of a person in uniform is often enough to prompt compliance. In one experiment (Bickman, 1974), researchers approached people on the streets of New York City and ordered them either to pick up a paper bag or to give a dime to a stranger. Half the researchers were dressed in neat street clothes, half in guard uniforms. Less than 40 percent of the sub-

jects obeyed the "civilian," but more than 80 percent obeyed the "guard," even when he walked away after delivering the order and could not see whether they complied.

Another situational factor that affects obedience is the degree of face-to-face contact. In Milgram's original experiment (1963), the experimenter's presence encouraged compliance. Obedience dropped sharply (from 65 percent to 22 percent) in an experimental variation (1965) in which the experimenter did not remain in the room with the subject, but left the laboratory after issuing instructions and gave subsequent orders by telephone. As in the defiance of group norms, disobedience to authority seems easier when people do not have to confront authority directly.

Milgram also found that increasing the proximity of the subject to the victim increased the likelihood that the subject would defy authority. In his original study, Milgram's subjects did not see their victim and the only audible protest was the pounding on the wall. However, when subjects were placed closer and closer to the victim, compliance dropped. In one condition, although the victim was in another room, the subject could hear the groans escalate to screams as the shocks were increased. In another arrangement, the victim and subject were in the same room—seated only eighteen inches apart. In the final condition, the subject was required to force the victim's hand onto the shock plate to administer punishment. As Figure 27.4 indicates, the maximum shock delivered by subjects decreased steadily as contact with the victim increased. When the vic-

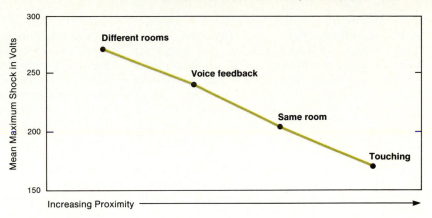

Figure 27.4 This graph of the results of some of Milgram's studies on obedience shows that the closer the subject was to the victim, the less the amount of shock he was willing to administer, despite the experimenter's demands that he continue. With increased proximity, there was a decrease in compliance. (After Milgram, 1974.)

tim was remote, subjects apparently found it easier to deny the pain they were inflicting. As such denial became less possible, the victim's suffering exerted greater influence in the struggle between individual conscience and authority.

Social support for defiance is another factor that increases people's resistance to authority. In a test of this factor (Milgram, 1965), the subject was teamed with two other "subjects" who were actually the experimenter's confederates. After the shock level had reached 150 volts, one of the confederates announced that he would not continue and took a seat in another part of the room. After 210 volts, the second confederate refused to go any farther. Although the experimenter ordered the true subjects to continue, only 10 percent of them did so.

In this last condition, people were forced to choose between obedience to authority and conformity to their peers. The fact that 90 percent chose to conform to the more socially acceptable actions of their peers should not lead us to be complacent about resistance to authority. Some one person must always be first to resist, and in life, no confederates will lead the way. Also, penalties inflicted in the world for disobedience may be far more severe than the disapproval of an unknown experimenter.

The tendency toward conformity and obedience so dramatically demonstrated in the laboratory and in natural settings may strike some people as alarming. But conformity and obedience are neither good nor bad in and of themselves. They are facts of social behavior and can lead to either desirable or undesirable outcomes. As Milgram points out, for every person who performs an immoral act in obedience to authority, another is restrained from doing so (Milgram and Tavris, 1974). He believes that as we come

to understand such submission better, we may learn to resist it when necessary.

Aggression

In both the Milgram and the Zimbardo experiments, one human being inflicted suffering on another. Moreover, the suffering was caused needlessly—or at least for trivial reasons. Any act that is intended to cause pain, damage, or suffering to another is an act of interpersonal **aggression**. The key attributes of an aggressive act are the intention and the target. To be considered aggressive, an act must be both deliberate and directed against a person, a definition that encompasses verbal attacks, such as insult and slander. Accidental injuries are not aggression.

Aggression is a common feature of contemporary life. News broadcasts invariably mention some aggressive act—murder, rape, muggings, vandalism, political terrorism, or war. The broadcasts reveal alarming facts. In 1980, for example, 1,309,000 Americans were victims of reported violent crime (FBI *Uniform Crime Reports,* 1981), an increase of 11.1 percent over the previous year. Every twenty-four seconds one violent crime is committed in the United States. Attempts to explain the high levels of abusive behavior among human beings fall into three categories: biological explanations, social-learning explanations, and situational explanations.

Biological Influences

The idea that human aggression has a biological basis has a long history and many advocates. Sigmund Freud, for example, postulated that we are driven to self-destructive and aggressive behavior by a death instinct (*Thanatos*) that is at least as powerful as the life instinct (*Eros*) that impels us toward growth and self-fulfillment. According to Freud, the urge to conquer and kill is never very far beneath the surface, and the balance between our destructive and procreative impulses is, at best, uneasy. Today, psychologists generally consider Freud's concept of a death instinct highly speculative. But the underlying idea—that human aggression has a biological basis—lives on. As yet no evidence for a genetic basis of human aggression has been found. However, such evidence does exist for several animal species, including the mouse, on whose chromosomes specific gene locations for aggression have been isolated (Eleftheriou, Bailley, and Denenberg, 1974).

A number of researchers believe that biological abnormalities can explain why some individuals are especially hot-tempered and violent. For example, instead of the normal forty-six chromosomes, some men convicted of violent crimes have been found to have forty-seven, the extra chromosome being a second Y (male) chromosome (Jarvik, Klodin, and Matsuyama, 1973). Yet genetic abnormalities do not seem to account for the high levels of human aggression. The XYY chromosome pattern is exceedingly rare (it occurs at most once or twice in a thousand births), and many XYY males are upstanding citizens. A study of more than 4,000 Danish men turned up no connection between an XYY chromosome pattern and violent behavior (Witkin et al., 1976).

In other cases, violent behavior has been linked to various types of brain damage, such as an interruption in the flow of blood to the brain (which kills brain cells), injuries to the frontal or temporal lobes from falls or blows to the head, viral infections of the brain, and brain tumors (Mark and Ervin, 1970). As we saw in Chapter 3, some research has linked certain parts of the brain, shown in Figure 27.5, with human aggression. However, even granted the possibility that some damage escapes detection, brain damage cannot explain the incidence of human aggression. An estimated 10 to 15 million Americans suffer from some form of brain injury, but the majority of these people are no more aggressive than anyone else. Of greater importance is the fact that the majority of people with a history of violent behavior have no brain injury at all.

The shortcomings of biological abnormalities as a sufficient explanation of aggression become clear when we examine the case of Paul M. (Mark and Ervin, 1970). Paul admitted himself to Boston City Hospital because he was afraid he was losing his mind and could not control his violent impulses. He had, in fact, "gone wild," pulling plaster off the walls of his apartment, smashing a mirror, and badly gashing his body with a piece of the glass. Examination revealed that Paul was suffering from mild brain damage. An antiseizure drug was prescribed for him, and his rages stopped. On the surface, Paul's disorder appears purely biological, but a look at his history suggests other causes. One of eight children, Paul was reared in severe poverty. His father and brothers were all hot-tempered, and he was frequently beaten as a child. An older brother who had been arrested three times for armed robbery and aggravated assault was his childhood idol.

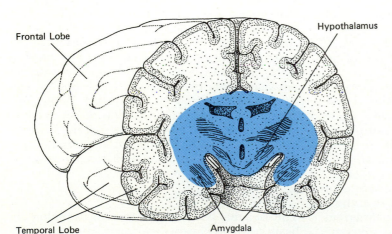

Frontal Lobe

Hypothalamus

Temporal Lobe

Amygdala

Figure 27.5 Some researchers suggest that there is a biological origin of aggression in the oldest and most primitive parts of the human brain. Evidence from animal and human studies suggests that the hypothalamus and other structures in the temporal lobe (shown in blue) play an important role in mediating aggressive behavior. In some cases, surgical removal of the hypothalamus and amygdala has resulted in complete loss of emotional reactivity. (After Scherer, Abeles, and Fischer, 1975.)

Clearly, social learning was partly responsible for Paul's explosive behavior.

Social-Learning Mechanisms

Most aggressive behavior—whether slashing with a knife, throwing a blow to the chin, setting off a pipe bomb, pulling a trigger, or shouting verbal insults—requires intricate, learned skills (Bandura, 1976). According to social-learning theory, exposure to models of violent behavior and reinforcement for aggressive acts explain why people attack one another.

The Importance of Models By observing others, we learn how and when to perform specific aggressive acts (such as how to fire a gun) as well as general strategies of aggression (such as "Stay on the offensive"). In the American culture, two of the most influential models are family members and the characters portrayed on television and in films.

Parents frequently provide powerful models of aggression for their children. Every year, several hundred thousand American children are abused by adults, and many of these children grow up to become child abusers themselves (Kempe and Kempe, 1978). But violent modeling is unnecessary, and most aggressive children do not have criminally violent parents. In subtle ways, law-abiding parents who resort to "acceptable" forms of aggression to solve problems, favor coercive methods of child rearing, and are hostile toward the world in general promote aggressive behavior in their children. Such parents serve as models of aggression, not by their deeds, but by their words and attitudes (Bandura, 1976).

After watching aggressive models, children are most likely to imitate the aggression if the model has been live, as Figure 27.6 shows. Nevertheless, as we saw in Chapter 14, films and television are also pervasive influences on behavior, and steady exposure to violence on the screen can lead to increased aggression. In one study (Parke et al., 1977), researchers observed a group of sixty delinquent boys in a minimum-security detention facility over a period of three weeks. The boys living in one cottage were shown aggressive movies every night for five nights, while the boys in another cottage were shown neutral, nonaggressive movies. The vio-

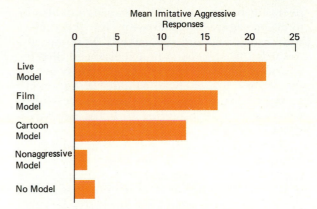

Mean Imitative Aggressive Responses

Figure 27.6 Bandura and his colleagues found that live models were more effective than either film models or cartoon characters in eliciting imitative aggressive behavior in children. (After Bandura, 1973.)

lent films had a definite impact on behavior: the boys who watched them showed clear increases in verbal and physical aggression. These findings are not limited to delinquent boys; studies of delinquent girls and of nondelinquent college students have yielded similar results. However, the media are not responsible for all the violence in contemporary society. People beat, raped, and murdered one another for thousands of years before the invention of television and movies. As we saw in Chapter 8, people do not automatically perform all the behavior they learn through observation. In most cases, the behavior appears when there is some form of inducement or some expectation of reward.

The Importance of Reinforcement According to social-learning theory, people do not behave aggressively unless such behavior has "paid off" for them in the past or unless they expect it to pay off in the future. There is ample evidence that aggression *does* pay off. In one study of children, close to 80 percent of physical and verbal assaults on others produced highly rewarding results for the aggressor (Patterson, Littman, and Bricker, 1967).

Sometimes the rewards for aggression are tangible—new territory can be acquired when one nation invades another or a seat on a crowded bus can be the reward for an individual who elbows other passengers aside. At other times the rewards are social, as when soldiers are given medals and treated as heroes for their skill in killing or adolescent boys are admired by their peers for being tough. The rewards can also be internal: aggressive behavior can become a source of pride and self-esteem. Nor must the rewards for aggression be experienced directly; vicarious reinforcement can be extremely powerful. People are likely to imitate an aggressive model whose behavior has been successful or who has not been punished for behaving aggressively.

Thus modeling and reinforcement interact to promote aggression. We learn aggressive behavior by watching others and refine our aggressive skills through the reinforcements that follow their practice (Bandura, 1976).

Situational Factors

The social-learning explanation of aggression makes good sense. But certain situations seem so unbearable, so frustrating, that we would expect anyone to explode in anger, regardless of the consequences. Moreover, accounts abound of ordinary people being carried away and, protected by the anonymity of a crowd, engaging in behavior they otherwise might never have considered. The urban riots of the 1960s and the looting that occurred in New York City during the blackout of 1977 testify to the destructive potential of mob action. Both frustration and anonymity seem to promote aggressive behavior.

According to the **frustration-aggression hypothesis** put forward by John Dollard and his colleagues, "aggression is always a consequence of frustration" and, conversely, "frustration always leads to some form of aggression" (1939, p. 1). Dollard defined **frustration** as interference with any form of goal-directed behavior. When people are thwarted in their attempts to obtain food or water, sex or sleep, love or recognition, he and his colleagues argued, they may become aggressive.

To test this hypothesis, a team of researchers (Barker, Dembo, and Lewin, 1941) created a frustrating situation for a group of children. The children were taken to a room, showed a collection of attractive toys, and told that they could look but not touch. Later, when the children were allowed to play with the toys, they were extremely hostile—smashing them against the walls and floor. Another group of children who had not been frustrated in advance played happily and peacefully with identical toys.

One possible consequence of frustration is displaced aggression, which may take many forms. Since aggressive responses often bring punishment to the aggressor, a frustrated person can express aggression safely by displacing it. Thus the angry employee who has been reprimanded by his boss might kick his dog when he returns home or insult his golf partner. In dreams, aggression may be displaced to another target, especially if violence against the original target might provoke feelings of guilt. A child who has been spanked by her mother might displace an aggressive impulse against her parent by dreaming that she has harmed another authority figure, perhaps a teacher. Men may be more likely to displace aggression in this way than are women; men's dreams contain much more aggression and hostility than do the dreams of women (Winget, Kramer, and Whitman, 1972).

Aggression is only one of many possible responses to frustration, however. Some people withdraw when frustrated and others intensify their efforts to reach a goal by nonaggressive means. Nor is aggression always preceded by frustration. Most people hit back when they are attacked physically and attempt to "get even" when they are insulted or slandered. To say that a verbal or physical assault is a form of frustration is stretching the term considerably.

According to some psychologists (e.g., Berkowitz, 1962), the key to predicting aggression is not the frustration but the level of anger it arouses. In this view, frustration is neither necessary nor sufficient to provoke aggression. Anger, which may be provoked by frustration or by other experiences, such as verbal attacks, is the crucial factor (Rule and Nesdale, 1976). This proposal has been confirmed by a study (Gentry, 1970), in which student volunteers were given a timed intelligence test. The members of one group were frustrated: they were repeatedly interrupted with irrelevant questions, stopped before the time had elapsed, and then told they had failed. Another group was insulted: the experimenter made derogatory remarks about their appearance, general behavior, and immature attitudes, but the students were told they had passed the test. A control group completed the test without interruption or insult. Afterward, each student monitored the experimenter's performance on a test and had the choice of either flashing a light or delivering a shock whenever the experimenter made a mistake.

Throughout the monitoring phase of the experiment, the students' blood pressure—a physiological correlate of emotional arousal—was recorded. Frustration failed to increase the students' arousal or aggression, but insults did. Only the insulted students' blood pressure rose, and only they responded aggressively by administering simulated shocks to the experimenter. Thus frustration does not always lead to aggression, nor is aggression always the result of frustration.

Among other factors that contribute to aggression is uncontrollable stress. In one study (Donnerstein and Wilson, 1976), noise over which a person had no control increased aggressive behavior. In another study (Baron and Bell, 1976), heat was found to be a significant factor in aggression. When experiments were conducted in rooms heated to 93°, people administered more shocks to a confederate and their aggression was more intense than when the room temperature was normal. When people working in these hot rooms were given cool drinks, they gave fewer shocks. Such findings are in accord with the fact that riots are more likely to break out during hot weather.

Helping

The opposite of aggression is an act that is intended to benefit another individual. As we saw in Chapter 14, altruistic acts offer no obvious rewards, so that making an anonymous donation to charity is altruistic, but making the same donation to secure a tax deduction is not. Risking one's life to rescue a child from a burning building is altruistic; risking one's life to earn applause from the crowd on the street is not. Although the altruistic person may experience internal satisfaction, the motive is to help someone else in need. In addition, an act must be intentional to be considered altruistic. Accidentally frightening a mugger away from a victim is not altruistic behavior.

Both animals and human beings behave in altruistic ways, and altruism appears to have both social and biological bases. According to the sociobiological view, which was discussed in Chapter 7, human beings are genetically programed to help one another (Dawkins, 1975;

True altruism is motivated by the wish to help another person. Here, two policemen with little regard for extreme danger risk their lives to keep a 92-year-old woman from ending hers.

Wilson, 1975). According to the concept of inclusive fitness, by giving up its own life (or chance to have offspring) to increase the chances of survival among its relatives, the individual allows part of its own genes to survive.

Some forms of dangerous altruistic behavior can be explained by the concept of inclusive fitness but its validity among human beings has not been established. Indeed, many social scientists reject the proposition for the same reason that they reject the instinct theory of human aggression: it is based on questionable analogies between human and animal behavior, it ignores the role that learning plays in human social interaction, and it cannot explain variations in behavior between and within people. Whether or not altruism has a genetic base, there is little doubt that human beings acquire specific altruistic behavior through modeling and reinforcement. The problem for social psychologists is to explain the circumstances that evoke such behavior.

Bystander Intervention in Emergencies

Nearly twenty years ago, a young woman named Kitty Genovese was savagely attacked outside her apartment building in Queens, a borough of New York City, at 3:00 A.M. She screamed for help, and although thirty-eight neighbors came to their windows, not one offered assistance. No one even called the police. The attack lasted more than thirty minutes while Kitty Genovese was attacked, stabbed, and finally killed.

The murder caused a sensation, and press accounts wondered how people could be so indifferent to the fate of another human being. Many saw it as an example of the city dweller's reluctance to "get involved." Yet investigation revealed that the witnesses to the woman's murder had been far from indifferent. Her neighbors watched her ordeal transfixed, "unable to act but unwilling to turn away" (Latané and Darley, 1976, pp. 309–310). Research on bystander intervention indicates that a number of powerful social forces worked to prevent them from acting.

The Presence of Other Bystanders   After staging a number of "emergencies" and recording the response of bystanders, Bibb Latané and John Darley (1976) concluded that the presence of other bystanders inhibits would-be altruistic bystanders from intervening to help. Latané and Darley offer three possible explanations for the failure of bystanders to respond.

The first is **audience inhibition**. When other people are present, we think twice because we are concerned about their evaluation of our behavior. Emergencies are often ambiguous. Smoke pouring from a building might signal a fire or it might be normal incinerator fumes; cries of help from the next apartment might be genuine or they might be coming from the neighbor's television set. Offering aid when none is wanted or needed places the altruistic bystander in an embarrassing situation, and the embarrassment is compounded by the presence of others who have realized that no emergency exists.

Social influence, the second factor, also prevents individuals from intervening because when others are present, each person waits for the others to define the situation as an emergency by their actions. While searching for a clue as to whether the situation is serious or not, everyone tries to appear calm and collected. The result is that each bystander is taken in by the others' nonchalance and led—or misled—to define the situation as a nonemergency.

When other people are present, the need for any one individual to act seems lessened and there is a **diffusion of responsibility**. An onlooker assumes that there may be a doctor or police officer or friend or relative of the victim among the bystanders who is qualified to give aid, the sense of personal responsibility is diminished, and the onlooker can leave the scene without feeling guilty.

Latané and Darley's findings suggest that bystanders are least likely to act if all three forces —audience inhibition, social influence, and diffusion of responsibility—are operating (see Figure 27.7). One of their experiments confirms this belief. Men who thought they were participating in a study of repression sat in cubicles equipped with television monitors and cameras; while the experimenter ostensibly went to check some equipment, they filled out a questionnaire.

As the men worked on their questionnaires, the experimenter staged an elaborate performance. He entered the room with the equipment and innocently picked up two wires. Immediately he screamed, threw himself in the air, hit a wall, and crashed to the floor. A few seconds later he began to moan softly. As Latané and Darley pre-

Figure 27.7 As this "decision tree" indicates, in an emergency a bystander must: (1) notice that something is happening; (2) interpret it as an emergency; and (3) decide that he or she has a personal responsibility to intervene. But the presence of others complicates this process: the presence of strangers may prevent us from concluding that the situation is an emergency; group behavior may lead us to define the situation as one which does not require action; and when other people are there to share the burden of responsibility, we may not feel obligated to aid. Thus the more witnesses to an emergency, the less aid the victim is likely to receive. This combination of factors was what inhibited Kitty Genovese's neighbors from helping her. (After Darley and Latané, 1968.)

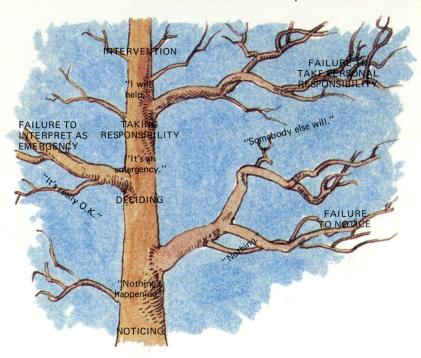

dicted, the willingness of the subjects' to help the experimenter seemed to depend on the number of social forces at work.

Among those subjects who believed they were alone in the situation, 95 percent intervened almost immediately, but among those who thought that an unseen person in another cubicle had also witnessed the accident, altruism dropped to 84 percent. In this case, the difference can be attributed to diffusion of responsibility. When other factors were added to the experimental situation, the rate of intervention decreased further. If subjects could see another person (a confederate of the experimenter) defining the situation by failing to respond (social influence), or if they thought that a confederate was watching them (social inhibition), 73 percent offered to help. When the subject could see the confederate and believed that the confederate could also see the subject, so that all three factors affected the subject's behavior, only 50 percent of the subjects came to the experimenter's assistance.

Studies such as this are very persuasive, but under certain conditions the presence of others does not prevent bystanders from offering assistance. When bystanders have clear evidence of an emergency, the inhibiting effects of others are weakened. For example, if bystanders can gauge one another's reactions through nonverbal cues,

they are likely to come to the aid of an apparent accident victim. In one experiment (Darley, Teger, and Lewis, 1973), half the subjects were seated directly opposite a second subject and so could see that person's startled reaction to the sound of a heavy object falling, followed by a nearby worker's groans. In this situation, nonverbal behavior defined the event as an emergency, and subjects responded as often and as quickly as those who were alone when they heard the accident occur.

The Assessment of Costs   The presence of others is only one influence on bystanders' decisions to intervene in an emergency. Bystanders also assess the costs involved—both the costs of intervening (inconvenience, unpleasantness, personal danger) and the costs of *not* intervening (principally feelings of guilt and scorn from others). Rewards, such as heightened self-esteem, praise, and thanks, are also taken into account. People are most likely to help when the costs of intervening are low and the costs of not intervening are high (see Figure 27.9). But as the cost of helping rises, individuals must decide whether it is worse to step in and risk injury or turn away and face self-recrimination.

Although individual traits may make one bystander more likely to intervene than another,

Social-Impact Theory and Loafing

The same factors that affect bystander intervention enter into social behavior that requires the participation of several people. According to **social-impact theory** (Latané, 1973), when social forces affect a situation, the larger the group, the less pressure on any one member because the impact of the forces is spread over the entire group. The credit for social endeavor is diffused among an entire group just as responsibility is diffused among bystanders at an emergency. Thus the presence of several participants in a joint endeavor reduces the individual contribution of each. For example, the force exerted by two people pulling on a rope is less than the sum of two individuals pulling separately.

More than fifty years ago, it was found that the more individuals who pull on the rope, the less effort each puts forth (Moede, 1927). Working alone, each student pulled nearly 63 kg, but two students working together pulled, not 126 kg, but 118 kg. And three pulled only 160 kg, which is about 2 1/2 times what a single individual pulls. This diminished effort has two possible explanations. The first possibility is that energy is lost in a coordinated pull because individual efforts are not exerted at exactly the same instant—a factor required for maximum power. The second possibility is that individuals slacken their efforts when there are many contributors to a common task—in effect, they loaf.

Although some effort may be lost due to poor coordination, studies (Latané, Williams, and Harkins, 1979) have found a defi-

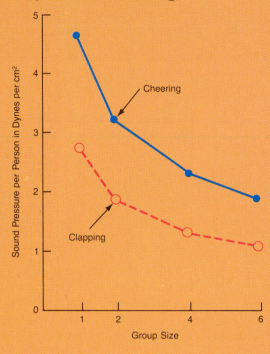

Figure 27.8 As group size increased, the intensity of each student's clapping and cheering diminished. This result can be explained by social-impact theory, which proposes that credit for joint endeavor is spread over the entire group, diminishing the credit given each individual and leading each to expend less effort. (After Latané, Williams, and Harkins, 1979.)

nite decrease in individual effort as well. Students clapped and cheered by themselves and in groups of different sizes. Measures of sound pressure indicated that the average sound pressure per person dropped steadily as the size of the group increased from one to six (see Figure 27.8). Even with the loss of pressure due to poor coordination controlled, individual contributions decreased substantially as the group size increased, with the largest drop in effort appearing between solitary individuals and groups of two. The effect remained when students wore earphones that shut out the sound of other group members. When they believed that one other student was cheering along with them, their shouts were 82 percent as intense as their individual cheers,

and when they thought they were cheering in a group of six, their shouts were only 72 percent as loud.

Note that in social-impact experiments there is a joint product, such as amount lifted or loudness of applause. In social facilitation there is no question of such a joint product, and each individual works "for himself." Thus, comparisons of social-facilitation and social-impact experiments must take this difference into account because the expectations of members to achieve a common goal change their motivation and orientation quite radically.

A Model to Predict Bystander Intervention

Cost of No Help to Victim	Cost of Direct Help	
	Low	High
High	(A) Direct intervention	(C) Indirect intervention or Redefinition of situation, disparagement of victim, etc.
Low	(B) Variable (largely a function of perceived norms in situation)	(D) Leaving scene, ignoring, denial, etc.

Figure 27.9 Their work on bystander intervention in emergency situations led Piliavin and his colleagues to propose a model for predicting intervention by coordinating the cost of helping with the cost of not helping the victim. The cost to the bystander of direct help would include variables such as lost time, danger, exposure to disgusting experiences; the cost to the bystander of not helping would include self-blame, blame from others, and loss of potential rewards (such as honor, fame, praise). Thus if the cost of direct help is low—the bystander perceives no danger—and the cost of not helping is high—the bystander would feel guilty for not aiding—then it can be predicted that he or she is almost certain to intervene. (After Piliavin, Piliavin, and Rodin, 1975.)

helping in emergencies appears to be heavily influenced by the surrounding situation. A study of bystander response to a staged emergency in New York City illustrates how the situation can affect decisions to help (Piliavin, Rodin, and Piliavin, 1969). In the experiment a young man feigned collapse in the subway. Sometimes he carried a cane: other times he carried a bottle of liquor in a brown paper bag and acted as if he had been drinking. Bystanders were quicker to aid the man with the cane than the apparent drunk. The costs of helping the man with the cane were low (he was not likely to hurt anyone), and the costs of not helping were high (guilt because he might be seriously injured). The costs of helping the "drunk" were higher (disgust as well as the possibility that he would become abusive), and the costs of not helping were lower (less self-blame and minimal social disapproval because a drunk can be held responsible for his condition).

In a follow-up study (Piliavin, Piliavin, and Rodin, 1975) the researchers introduced another condition: they planted a man dressed in a white hospital uniform near the scene of the accident. Help from bystanders decreased, whether the apparent victim carried a cane or a bottle. The presence of someone who seemed qualified to give professional help reduced the cost of not intervening, probably by absolving bystanders of responsibility.

Giving and Sharing

Every year at Christmas time *The New York Times* publishes a series of profiles describing the neediest families in the metropolitan area. The articles are designed not to solicit aid for particular families, but to remind people to contribute to various charities.

Like helping in emergencies, giving to charity is an altruistic act because the giver expects nothing in return. There are differences between the two situations, however. In emergencies, the needs of the victim and the appropriate response are often ambiguous. In requests for charity, the needs of the recipients are usually well defined and the traditional, appropriate response is well known. Moreover, giving poses no risks for the donor, so that some of the costs involved in emergency aid do not apply. The two factors that seem to have the greatest impact on giving and sharing are social norms and individual mood.

The Influence of Norms Most Americans feel some social responsibility to help others who are less fortunate than themselves (Staub, 1972). This is one of the social norms, or expectations for behavior, that we learn in the process of socialization (see Chapters 14 and 25). Because human behavior is influenced by so many factors, it is difficult to establish just how extensively the norm of social responsibility affects our actions. But research shows that when people recognize a worthwhile need, and are reminded of the norm of giving, their tendency to donate increases.

An experiment (Macaulay, 1970) conducted at Christmas demonstrated this relationship. Observers stationed near a chimney-shaped donation box placed outside a department store discovered the impact of the "Santa effect." On days when the box was unattended, passers-by donated a total of $1 to $3, but on days when a costumed Santa Claus was present for only two hours, total donations increased to $16 to $25. People must notice the existence of a need before they can respond to it, and the red-suited

Santa commanded attention from busy shoppers that an unattended donation box could not.

Next a behavioral model was introduced. A middle-aged woman, dressed like other shoppers, walked up to the chimney, put down her shopping bag, and started to open her purse. Sometimes she announced, "Well, I guess I can give something," and did, with a smile. On other occasions, she decided, "No, I don't want to give anything here," and walked away. Regardless of whether she made a donation, the presence of the model increased donations from others, leading the researcher to speculate that even when the model turned away, her action reminded people of the norm of giving. Making people aware of a social responsibility, then, increases the likelihood that the responsibility will be met.

This study does not show why the mere reminder of a norm spurs action. It may be that we conform to the norm because we are concerned about how other people will evaluate our behavior. Or perhaps our conformity meets self-expectations, enhancing our self-image by action in accord with internalized values. In many situations both forces undoubtedly are at work. We are motivated by the expectations of other people as well as by our own personal standards.

The Influence of Moods   It is not difficult to understand that mood might influence the willingness to give and that our generosity may increase when our spirits are high. There is abundant evidence that people are likely to give or share when they are in a good mood. Humor, success, the receipt of a gift or money, and simply thinking happy thoughts all increase the tendency to give (Cialdini and Kenrick, 1976). This effect was demonstrated in an experiment (Rosenhan, Underwood, and Moore, 1974) with children who were paid with candy and pennies for taking a simple hearing test (see Figure 27.10). Before each child left the laboratory, half the youngsters were asked to describe something that made them sad; the other half described something that made them happy. Then each child was given an opportunity to share her or his candy and pennies with other children. Those in a happy mood were twice as likely to donate some of their earnings as those who left feeling sad.

However, research exploring the proposition that a bad mood depresses the tendency to share has had contradictory results. In one experiment

(Isen, Horn, and Rosenhan, 1973), fourth-graders who had received a failing mark on a test gave less to charity than those who had received no mark. In other studies (Cialdini and Kenrick, 1976), however, negative moods, failure, embarrassment, receipt of an insult, and the sight of another person in trouble or pain have all been linked to increased willingness to help.

It has been suggested that the apparent contradiction is due to the age of the subjects involved (Cialdini and Kenrick, 1976). Many of the experiments on mood and altruism have used children as subjects, and negative feelings may not be related to increased altruism among young children. In one experiment (Cialdini and Kenrick, 1976), a negative mood slightly suppressed generosity among first-graders, slightly enhanced it among fifth-graders, and substantially increased it among tenth- to twelfth-graders. Socialization may create a link between altruism and social approval, because part of the process includes praising children who help others and scolding, if not actually punishing, those who withhold help. As children become older, the link becomes stronger. In time, benevolence becomes its own reward. Empathy, which also increases with age, also enhances the internal rewards of altruistic behavior. When we help someone, we vicariously experience their relief

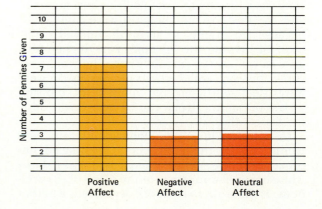

Figure 27.10   Mood affects altruistic behavior, and youngsters give most when they feel good. Second- and third-graders who had earned pennies were randomly divided into three groups. One group was induced to recall a sad experience, the second group recalled a happy experience, and the third spent the time counting numbers. When given the opportunity to share with other children the pennies they had just earned, youngsters who had experienced positive emotions shared the most. (After Rosenhan, Underwood, and Moore, 1974.)

As we mature, helping others becomes intrinsically rewarding. Here, a grandson helps his feeble grandfather.

and happiness. Thus being helpful becomes one way of making ourselves feel better. These relationships, however, require time and experience, and small children have not learned to consider virtue its own reward.

The Human Dilemma: Cooperation Versus Competition

Each day does not bring a stranger in distress, an appeal for charity, or a situation that evokes naked aggression. Yet every day choices are made between aid and antagonism. Do you share your lecture notes with a classmate or keep them to yourself? Do you tell a prospective buyer about your car's faulty transmission or keep quiet to get a higher price for the car? Do you

visit an elderly aunt to please your parents or flatly refuse to change your plans? The choice between fullfilling only one's own needs and considering those of others underlies everything from such trivial decisions as whether to grab a seat on a crowded bus to such vital issues as deciding how the earth's limited resources will be distributed. Because so many of life's prizes—and indeed necessities—are scarce, people cannot always act in ways that maximize both their own immediate goals and those of others. The necessary choice between self-interest and cooperation is a persistent human dilemma.

Studying the Human Dilemma

Suppose that you and a friend are arrested for a petty theft. The district attorney believes that the two of you have committed a far more serious crime, but does not have enough evidence to take you to court. In an attempt to get a confession for the serious crime, she has you and your friend questioned in separate rooms. If neither you nor your friend confesses, the court will send both of you to prison for one year on the petty theft charge. If both of you confess to the serious crime, the DA will recommend leniency—eight years instead of ten. If only one of you confesses to the serious crime, that person will be sentenced to only three months for turning state's evidence, but the other will go to prison for the full ten years. The dilemma is obvious. The best strategy for both of you is to stick to your alibis and refuse to confess; you'll both get one year in prison, but no more. However, if you follow this strategy, but your friend betrays you by confessing, you will go to prison for ten years. And if you confess but your friend does not, you will get off with a three-month sentence. The Prisoner's Dilemma Game (see Figure 27.11), as this situation is called, has proved a valuable tool for discovering the conditions under which people are most likely to cooperate with each other. The experimenters explain the rules of this game, or some variation of it, to pairs of subjects. Then the game begins. Typically the experimenter runs fifteen to twenty trials. Over the long run, cooperation promises the best reward in every case. Yet blind self-interest is the most commonly chosen strategy. In most studies, between 60 and 70 percent of subjects behave selfishly despite the costs involved in doing so (Oskamp and Kleinke, 1970).

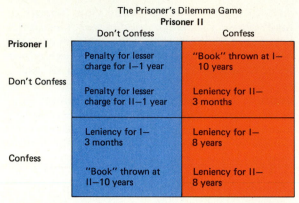

The Prisoner's Dilemma Game
Prisoner II

	Don't Confess	Confess
Prisoner I **Don't Confess**	Penalty for lesser charge for I—1 year Penalty for lesser charge for II—1 year	"Book" thrown at I— 10 years Leniency for II— 3 months
Confess	Leniency for I— 3 months "Book" thrown at II—10 years	Leniency for I— 8 years Leniency for II— 8 years

Figure 27.11 The prisoner's dilemma can be diagrammed as a 2 × 2 matrix. Each person must choose one of two options, prisoner I controlling the horizontal rows and prisoner II the vertical columns; the outcomes of a joint decision are given by the intersection between the row and column chosen. The best outcome is obtained by both partners cooperating with each other—in this case, by cooperating *not* to confess—but studies show that a selfish strategy is chosen more often than a cooperative one.

The Prisoner's Dilemma Game can also be used to illustrate the way various motives affect a pair of individuals in a situation involving gains and losses. As we saw, if both prisoners seek to advance their individual interests, both will get a one-year sentence. Under these conditions, the most profitable outcome for both players is "to stick to their alibis," that is, to cooperate with each other, although few choose it.

Yet self-interest is not the only possible motive for the game. People also harbor additional motives such as altruism, envy, or the common good. The motives of altruism or the common good make a cooperative strategy even more rewarding because of the psychological benefits each player reaps from the other's good fortune. Only when envy is added to the motive of self-interest, so that each player derives pleasure from the other's misfortunes, does self-interest become the preferred strategy (Zajonc, 1982).

Choices are clear when both players harbor the same motive. This is not always the case, however, and other factors also influence the likelihood of cooperation in the game.

Factors Influencing Two-Person Cooperation

Although altruism, the common good, and simple self-interest all favor a cooperative strategy,

cooperation among the subjects in the Prisoner's Dilemma Game is rare. By varying the conditions under which these games are played, researchers can isolate factors that tend to promote or discourage self-interest. Two of the most important factors are threats and experience.

The Use of Threats   At the bargaining table, roommates or members of a family—like nations or labor and management—often resort to threats in an attempt to extort cooperation. Yet according to one experiment (Deutsch and Krauss, 1960), threats are not very effective.

In pairs, people played a game that is similar in structure to the Prisoner's Dilemma Game. In this game, each player is in charge of a trucking company that ships goods over the routes shown in Figure 27.12. The company earns 60 cents, minus 1 cent per second in "operating expenses," for every completed trip. Hence the object of the game is to get from the starting point to the destination in the shortest possible time. Only one truck at a time can travel over the middle portion of the main route, and players can either share this road or use winding, time-consuming alternative routes. The best strategy for both players is to take turns using the main route.

To test the effects of threats, the investigators introduced two conditions. In the first, one player was given a gate that could be locked to prevent the other player from using the main route (the unilateral threat condition). In the second, both players controlled gates (the bilateral threat condition). Cooperation, which was difficult to achieve in the no-threat condition, became even more difficult in the unilateral threat condition, and almost impossible in the bilateral threat condition. Players attempted to gain access to the main route by threatening to lock their gates. When neither player yielded, both would close their gates, use the alternative route, and incur heavy penalties. Once this pattern began, the gates were no longer simply signals or warnings, but became a means of punishment and retaliation.

Whether these results can be generalized to real life, in which the stakes are often high and the consequences serious, is debatable (Pruitt and Kimmel, 1977). For example, some argue that the fact that the United States and the Soviet Union are capable of destroying each other serves to deter each from the use of force against

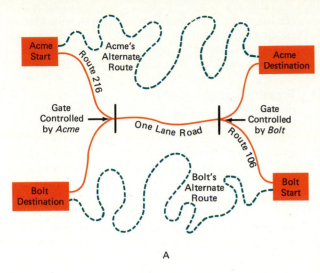

A

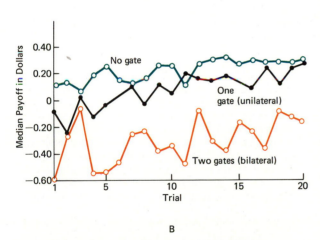

B

Figure 27.12 (A) The game used to study the effects of threat on cooperation. Each of two players (called Acme and Bolt) was told that the aim was to maximize individual profit by reaching their respective destinations as quickly as possible. The quickest route involved a shared one-lane road, and the best strategy dictated that they cooperate, taking turns using it. (B) When the variable of threat was introduced by giving only one player access to a gate which could block the road for the opponent (one gate, unilateral threat) or by giving both players access to a controlling gate (two gates, bilateral threat), cooperation was impeded. Threat was detrimental to reaching agreement, especially in the bilateral threat condition. (After Deutsch and Krauss, 1960.)

the other. Because of the consequences, both nations are reluctant to issue a direct threat, much less to launch an attack.

Observation and Experience   The object of nearly all games is to win, so it is not surprising that players in games like those described at first follow self-interest. Later they may realize that cooperation is the best strategy, but by then it may be too late. The players may be locked into a competitive struggle. Or they may be too involved in the conflict to see the benefits of cooperation. But what if they watch other games before they themselves play?

Since observational learning is an important aspect of socialization, investigators (Braver and Barnett, 1976) explored its effects on cooperation in such games by allowing people to observe games in progress. Some potential players watched games in which one player used a cooperative strategy and was rewarded with the other player's cooperation; others watched games in which one player tried to cooperate but the other chose to compete; and a third group watched games in which both players pursued a competitive strategy throughout. Afterward, each observer played the game with a new opponent. The natural assumption is that regardless of the sort of strategy they had watched, people would have learned that cooperation was most effective and so would pursue that strategy. They did not. Only those who had watched a highly competitive game chose to cooperate. Apparently, observing conflict "inoculates" observers against becoming embroiled in conflict themselves.

The explanation for this selective learning may lie in attribution theory. As noted in Chapter 26, people tend to attribute another person's failures to his or her own behavior, but to attribute another person's successes to external factors such as luck or the help of others. Hence when they watch a model playing a competitive game, they attribute a low score to that player's behavior and learn to avoid that strategy. But when they observe a cooperative game, they attribute the model's success to the luck of having a cooperative partner. Since they may not have the same luck themselves, they are not willing to risk cooperation (Braver and Rohrer, 1978).

Promoting Social Cooperation

So far we have focused on choices between cooperation and competition faced by two individuals and the personal consequences of those decisions. But many individual choices between cooperation and self-interest have consequences for communities, societies, and ultimately for all humanity.

The Tragedy of the Commons

Consider what Garrett Hardin (1968) calls "the tragedy of the commons." A commons is an open pasture where anyone can graze cattle. People naturally take advantage of the free grazing by adding more animals to their herds whenever they can. Disease, poaching, and war may keep the animal and human populations low so that, for a time, the system works. But eventually the day of reckoning comes: the population grows beyond the capacity of the commons to sustain it and the overgrazed grass becomes sparse. It is only a matter of time before the once lush pasture is barren.

Each individual herder may have some sense of this. But when she or he weighs the personal benefits of acquiring another animal against the cost of damage to the common pasture, there is no comparison. When the extra animal is sold, the herder gets all the money, but the cost of overgrazing is shared by all herders, in the form of a slight decrease in the weight of each animal. The logical course for the herder to pursue in order to maximize personal gain is to add another animal—and another, and another. Every herder comes to the same conclusion. This is the "tragedy of the commons": in pursuing individual interest, people move steadily toward eventual ruin for all.

The tragedy of the commons is an example of a **social trap,** in which as the result of personal decisions, people, organizations, or societies start moving in some direction or initiate relationships that later prove to be unpleasant or lethal but that seem virtually impossible to stop (Platt, 1973).

It is easy to see how social traps develop. Behaviorists have demonstrated over and over that the immediate consequences of an action—what happens in a few seconds, hours, or days—have more impact on behavior than do long-term outcomes—what happens in a few days, weeks, a year, or a decade. Short-term rewards are seductive. The herder is quickly rewarded for buying and selling another animal. The punishment for overgrazing lies years in the future and has little effect on the herder's daily behavior. Thus, in the

commons and in a number of structurally similar situations, powerful psychological and social forces steadily work against cooperation.

Breaking Out of Social Traps

According to Hardin (1968), the tragedy of the commons cannot be solved by appeals to conscience, because the participants hear two conflicting messages: the value of behaving as a responsible citizen (exercising restraint) and the value of behaving according to one's immediate self-interest (maximizing short-term personal gains). Only mutually agreed-upon coercion will get people out of social traps. By coercion, Hardin does not mean depriving people of all freedom, but simply making it so difficult or expensive to exploit the commons that few will do it.

Research suggests that there may be other ways to break out of social traps. Improving communication seems to be a promising approach, and it has been effective in the prisoner's dilemma (see Figure 27.13A). Communication

Figure 27.13A The standard Prisoner's Dilemma Game does not permit communication between partners, but when the game is altered so that communication is allowed, strategies change. For example, Wichman varied the amount of communication possible in four ways: in one condition, (I) isolated subjects could neither see nor hear each other; in a second condition they could hear each other (HO); in a third they could see each other (SO); and in a fourth they could both see and hear each other (S&H). As this graph shows, the more extensive the communication, the higher the rate of cooperation. (After Wichman, 1970.)

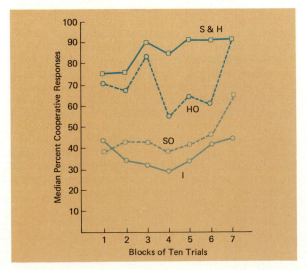

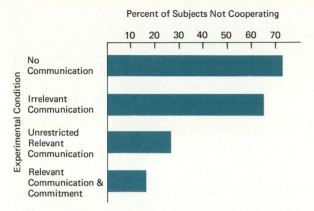

Percent of Subjects Not Cooperating

Figure 27.13B The effects of communication on behavior were examined in an eight-person "commons" dilemma that pitted individual financial gain against group financial gain. The researchers hypothesized that greater amounts of communication among group members would decrease behavior motivated by individual self-interest and promote behavior motivated by the collective interest. Four different communication conditions were possible: no communication, communication irrelevant to the task, relevant communication, and relevant communication plus public commitment to a position. As expected, there were fewer defectors, or noncooperators, in those conditions where communication was greatest. (After Dawes, McTavish, and Shaklee, 1977.)

may increase cooperation for three reasons: First, communication allows individuals to become acquainted, thus increasing their concern for one another. Second, communication permits people to exchange information relevant to a cooperative decision. And third, communication allows people to state their intentions and to assure others that those intentions are honest (Dawes, McTavish, and Shaklee, 1977).

The impact of these three factors was examined by means of a game that replicated the commons dilemma (Dawes, McTavish, and Shaklee, 1977). People were divided into small groups of six to eight strangers, and each person was asked to choose between a cooperative and a competitive strategy. After the players got acquainted their choice of a cooperative strategy increased slightly, but their exchange of information about the choice's consequences and their open declaration of intentions significantly boosted the choice of cooperation. When all three factors were at work, only 16 percent of the players—or about one person in each group—adopted a competitive tactic (see Figure 27.13 B).

Research on the factors that encourage or discourage cooperation is not an academic exercise. In 1970, futurist John Platt identified the most serious threats to humankind as nuclear annihilation, ecological imbalance, and the population explosion. He estimated that we had at most twenty to fifty years to reverse current trends. Since these threats are social problems, they will not be ended by technological advances; instead they can be solved only by changes in human behavior.

Recent events show that human behavior can change. At the time Platt wrote, most experts believed that the 1970s would be a time of rising birth rates in the United States; instead the rates plunged dramatically. Tight job markets, women's liberation, effective birth control, and public awareness of the population problem combined to reduce population growth with amazing rapidity (Ehrlich and Ehrlich, 1979). Although birth rates in less developed countries are still alarming, the experience of the United States shows that there is a way out of social traps. By 1982, widespread support for nuclear disarmament in Europe and the United States indicated that public awareness of the nuclear threat was growing, and the reduction in American oil consumption showed that some progress was being made in regard to energy problems.

Although such signs are hopeful, we still need a better understanding of the human dilemma and ways to resolve it. The kind of social-psychological research discussed in this chapter holds out some hope of providing such understanding.

SUMMARY

1. **Social facilitation**, or enhanced performance in the presence of others, occurs whenever people or animals work on simple tasks or on tasks they have already mastered. This appears to come about because the presence of others increases arousal and leads to an increase in **dominant responses**, which are the responses most likely to be made by an organism in a particular situation. On easy tasks, dominant responses are usually correct, but on difficult or new tasks, they are likely to be wrong. For this reason, the presence of others leads to poor performance on complex tasks or in the learning of new skills.

2. **Conformity** is the tendency to shift views or behavior closer to the norms followed by other people. It is the result of social pressure and can lead people to question perceptual information received by their senses. If a single person objects to the majority view or when people can remain anonymous, deviation from group norms becomes easier. **Obedience** is any behavior that complies with the explicit commands of a person in authority. In studies of obedience, people have been willing to deliver what they believed were serious or lethal shocks when ordered to do so by an authority figure. Many factors can lead to disobedience, however, including a lack of direct confrontation with authority and nearness to the victim (which makes it more difficult to deny the infliction of pain). Conformity to peers can also override the demands of authority.

3. Any act that is intended to cause pain, damage, or suffering to another is an act of interpersonal **aggression**. No evidence of a genetic basis for aggression has been found in humans, and biological abnormalities (such as an extra Y [male] chromosome or brain damage) cannot explain the prevalence of human aggression. Even in cases where a biological factor has been found, the expression of aggression is influenced by the environment. According to social-learning theorists, exposure to violent models and reinforcement for aggressive acts explain why people so often attack one another. Situational factors also appear to play a role in aggression. According to the **frustration-aggression hypothesis**, aggression is always a consequence of **frustration** (the interference with goal-directed behavior) and frustration always leads to aggression. Frustration can also lead to displaced aggression, but aggression is not the only response to frustration. It appears that not frustration, but level of anger (which may be produced by frustration) is a necessary factor in most aggression. Uncontrollable stress also contributes to aggression.

4. Both animals and human beings behave in altruistic ways, and altruism appears to have both social and biological bases. According to sociobiologists, organisms are motivated to protect their genes, not their lives, so that inclusive fitness explains why animals sacrifice themselves to protect others. The application of this concept to human beings has not been established. In emergencies, the presence of bystanders appears to inhibit people from giving aid. The explanation of this inhibiting effect includes **audience inhibition** (concern about others' evaluation of our behavior); **social influence** (waiting for others to define the situation as an emergency); and **diffusion of responsibility** (spreading the responsibility for intervening over all the bystanders). When the situation is unambiguous, however, people often intervene in emergencies. Bystanders also assess the costs of intervening and intervene when costs of intervening are low and the costs of not intervening are high. Reminding people of the norm of social responsibility increases donations to charity, because it reminds them of the expectation of others and of their own personal standards. A happy mood also increases the likelihood that a person will donate to charity, and a mood of unhappiness increases donations among adults but not among young children. Apparently the vicarious experience of another's happiness leads adults, but not children (who have not learned this vicarious happiness), to be generous.

5. The choice between cooperation and self-interest in daily life has been studied by using the Prisoner's Dilemma Game. Despite the fact that a cooperative strategy helps both players, most people choose self-interest. Although threats are not very effective in games based on the prisoner's dilemma, people use them when they are available, and cooperation goes down in a unilateral threat condition and almost disappears in a bilateral threat condition. If people observe a game played using competitive strategy, they are more likely to cooperate when they play the game themselves, but observation of cooperative strategies (despite their success) does not increase cooperation—a finding which is in line with attribution theory.

6. Individual choices can have serious social consequences, as in "the tragedy of the commons," which results when individual herders keep adding animals until the common pasture is destroyed by overgrazing. The tragedy of the commons is an example of a **social trap**, in which as the result of personal decisions, people, organizations, or societies start moving in some direction that later proves to be

unpleasant or lethal but that seems virtually impossible to stop. Social traps develop because the immediate consequences of an action (personal gain) outweigh long-term outcomes (social harm). It has been suggested by some social psychologists that only mutu-ally agreed-upon coercion, which makes anti-social action difficult or expensive, will get people out of social traps. However, improved communication in instances when people see the possibility of long-term gain may also open social traps.

KEY TERMS

aggression	dominant responses	obedience	social influence
audience inhibition	frustration	social facilitation	social trap
conformity	frustration-aggression	social-impact theory	
diffusion of responsibility	hypothesis		

RECOMMENDED READINGS

BARON, ROBERT A. *Human Aggression.* New York: Plenum Press, 1977. An excellent, up-to-date textbook that analyzes social, environmental, and individual determinants of aggression.

BERKOWITZ, LEONARD. *Aggression: A Social-Psychological Analysis.* New York: McGraw-Hill, 1962. The successor to *Frustration and Aggression* (see below), in which the frustration-aggression hypothesis is refined and expanded.

DERLEGA, V., and J. GRZELAK (eds.). *Cooperation and Helping Behavior: Theories and Research.* New York: Academic Press, 1982. The most recent and extensive review of the current thinking about altruism, self-interest, competition, and cooperation.

DOLLARD, JOHN, LEONARD W. DOOB, NEAL E. MILLER, O. H. MOWRER, and ROBERT R. SEARS. *Frustration and Aggression.* New Haven, Conn.: Yale University Press, 1939. The classic monograph that stimulated a research effort to understand aggression that continues even today.

HARDIN, GARRETT, and JOHN BADEN (eds.). *Managing the Commons.* San Francisco: W. H. Freeman, 1977. Hardin popularized the tragedy of the commons as a model of resource mismanagement. In this collection of papers a variety of perspectives are brought to bear on the problem of avoiding the tragedy of resource depletion.

JANIS, IRVING L. *Victims of Groupthink: A Psychological Study of Foreign-Policy Decisions and Fiascos.* Boston: Houghton Mifflin, 1973. With great insight, Janis applies social-psychological theory to a series of historic decisions made by groups in such situations as the Bay of Pigs invasion, the Cuban missile crisis, and the escalation of the Vietnam war.

LATANÉ, BIBB, and JOHN M. DARLEY. *The Unresponsive Bystander: Why Doesn't He Help?* New York: Appleton-Century-Crofts, 1970. The prizewinning report of the authors' fascinating series of experiments on the behavior of bystanders in emergencies.

MACAULAY, JACQUELINE, and LEONARD BERKOWITZ (eds.). *Altruism and Helping Behavior: Social Psychological Studies of Some Antecedents and Consequences.* New York: Academic Press, 1970. A collection of research reports that provide useful insights into the determinants of sharing, giving, and helping.

MILGRAM, STANLEY. *The Individual in a Social World: Essays and Experiments.* Reading, Mass.: Addison-Wesley, 1977. A stimulating excursion through Milgram's work on such varied topics as obedience, the urban experience, and the effects of television on antisocial behavior, in all of which Milgram finds similar social forces affecting behavior.

RAPOPORT, ANATOL. *Experimental Games and Their Uses in Psychology.* Morristown, N.J.: General Learning Press, University Modular Publications, 1973. A clear and concise introduction to games (like the Prisoner's Dilemma Game) that are used to study competition and cooperation.

SHAW, MARVIN E. *Group Dynamics: The Psychology of Small Group Behavior.* New York: McGraw-Hill, 1976. An exellent text in which the author reviews the field, summarizes what is known, and points to problems for future research.

CHAPTER 28

Environmental Psychology

"First we shape our buildings," said Winston Churchill, "and afterwards our buildings shape us." Churchill's statement overlooks the continuing interaction between human beings and their surroundings, yet it acknowledges the importance of the environment in human affairs. Think for a moment of the way the physical environment affects the way you study, sleep, socialize, shop, attend class, play tennis, use the library, or watch a film. The noise level, the amount of light, the quality of the air, the number of people around you, the temperature, the furnishings, the view—or the lack of it—all affect you in some way. An environment that is conducive to studying—room to spread out your books, a good light, a chair that is neither uncomfortably hard nor so soft as to make you drowsy, and perhaps soft music in the background—is important if you are to attend to your textbook. On the other hand, if you arrived at a party, planning to spend the evening dancing and socializing, you would be dismayed to be greeted by a nearly empty, quiet, brightly lighted room when you opened the door.

The environment can affect the way we feel and what we do; it influences our moods, our emotions, our attention, and our ability to process information. As we saw in Chapter 21, elements of the environment such as the noise level can place us under extreme stress. There is no escape from the effects of the environment, for it is always about us; it touches every aspect of our lives. Despite the power of the environment, most of us remain unaware of its influence most of the time.

The Nature of Environmental Psychology

During the past two decades, a heightened interest in environmental influences has led to the emergence of a relatively new field: environmental psychology. The concerns of **environmental psychology** are extremely broad; the field encompasses the investigation of the interrelationships between the physical environment and people's experience and behavior, specifically such topics as the effects of the environment on cognition, perception, and the performance of tasks. Some of the effects of the environment on individual behavior were examined in Chapter 21. In this chapter the emphasis will be upon social behavior. We shall explore some of the ways that social behavior is shaped by, and in turn shapes, the physical environment. In the process we shall find that the environment influences both our interpersonal behavior and our behavior within a group—the areas covered by social psychology. As we shall see, the field of environmental psychology is one important area

Our attempts to study and shape our environment require the efforts of experts in many fields, including psychology, sociology, and city planning.

where knowledge derived from social psychology has been applied to life, in areas as diverse as making college dormitories more satisfactory living environments and reducing the stress of urban life.

Yet environmental psychology is not simply a branch of applied social psychology. It is a collaborative effort involving psychologists, sociologists, anthropologists, geographers, physicians, architects, and city planners. The stress on both investigating problems and seeking basic knowledge has led to a reliance on naturalistic observation and studies conducted in the world as well as tightly controlled laboratory studies. As the interdisciplinary nature of the field indicates, the range of environmental psychology is immense; in this chapter we shall explore four of its basic concepts: personal space, territoriality, privacy, and crowding. After examining these concepts separately and considering the way they combine to affect behavior, we shall see how they can be used to solve problems in the world.

Personal Space

Suppose that the police have arrested a suspect in a robbery and are interrogating him. The suspect sits in one chair, with an officer about three feet away in another chair. As the questioning continues, the officer gradually edges his chair closer until the wooden seats touch and one of the suspect's knees is almost between the officer's knees. During the interrogation, the officer has established his authority and intimidated the suspect by deliberately invading the suspect's **personal space**, the zone around each individual into which other people may not trespass uninvited. This zone, which is like an invisible bubble that surrounds each of us, creates a boundary between a person and potential intruders.

Each of us relies on the integrity of our personal space; it is an essential but subtle aspect of our interactions with others, and violations of its boundaries make us uncomfortable. As we go about our daily business, we maintain our personal space with a variety of nonverbal signals, including eye contact, head gestures, and facial expressions—especially around the mouth (Efran and Cheyne, 1974). Although personal space has an important role in social behavior, we are rarely conscious of the actions we take to maintain it and, if asked, would probably attribute them to custom or politeness. Yet our language incorporates some awareness of the concept, for we speak of keeping people "at arm's length" or say with obvious dismay, "He shook his fist in my face."

Studies of personal space have found that the invisible bubble expands and contracts, depending upon gender, age, culture, and degree of familiarity. For example, two males generally stand farther apart when interacting than two females, and proximity is generally closest between a male-female pair (Evans and Howard, 1973).

Interaction Distances

Social circumstances appear to dictate the size of an individual's surrounding bubble. This expansion and contraction of personal space has been studied by Edward T. Hall (1966), an anthropologist who has found that social interactions among most Americans are regulated by four distinct zones: intimate, personal, social, and public distance. Although this pattern of regulation accurately describes the interactions of most Americans, it would have to be altered to reflect interactions of another cultural or ethnic group, as the box on page 638 indicates.

Intimate Distance   Within the **intimate distance**, which extends from physical contact to eighteen inches, interaction is reserved for the expression of deep emotion. It is the distance that encompasses the embracing lovers, the parent comforting a child, or a baseball manager with his jaw thrust angrily into an umpire's face.

Personal Distance   **Personal distance**, which extends from one and a half to four feet, is considered appropriate spacing for close friends and for conversations among acquaintances that concern personal matters. At this distance, the other person is "at arm's length." It is possible to reach out and touch her or him, although at the outer boundaries both parties must reach to make contact.

Social Distance   The space that extends from four to twelve feet around an individual is the **social distance**. Most business contacts take

We can assume that these men are friends by the close contact they maintain while speaking. Strangers would not be likely to be so close together as they conversed.

Personal Space in Other Cultures

Cultural differences in the use of personal space can make the members of one culture regard persons from another culture as rude, inept, or uninterested. Edward T. Hall (1966; 1976) has applied his view of personal space to observations in other cultures to explain radically different uses of space in England, Germany, France, and the Arab world.

Personal Space in England

Many of the differences in the use of space between English and Americans can be traced to the tendency of Americans to rely on space (home and business address, the locations of an office within a building) to define status, whereas the English rely on the social system. Nor do the English feel the need for a private office or a room of their own, since middle- and upper-class English children share a nursery and at about the age of ten, go off to boarding schools. The lack of spatial privacy in England has led to customs that seem reserved and formal to Americans. For example, the English obtain privacy for conversations by lowering their voices. The English speaking voice is kept at a level that is just discernible, yet conversing Englishmen remain about eight feet apart, in the middle of the social distance zone.

Personal Space in Germany

Germans tend to be more formal and distant than Americans in their use of space, and they are more offended by violations of their spatial norms. They demand visual privacy and interpret the gaze of another person as intrusive, even when the gazer is in the public distance of twelve to twenty-five feet. Aural privacy is also prized in Germany. Germans in conversation feel they have been intruded upon if anyone approaches within seven feet. In German homes and offices heavy, often double, doors shut out sound. Noise that comes through doors or walls is sensed as an intrusion on personal space.

Personal Space in France

Among the French who live south and east of Paris, individuals partition space in a way that is typical of most Mediterranean cultures. People interact closely with a high level of sensory involvement, an arrangement Americans interpret as "crowded." The French use their eyes in a way that is consonant with such involvement. In speaking they gaze directly at their partner, leaving no doubt as to their intent. Staring at a person on the street is both common and accepted.

Personal Space in the Arab World

The use of space in the Arab world is dramatically different from American and European patterns. The Arab carries no invisible bubble of personal space into public areas and recognizes no such phenomenon as intrusion in a public place. A seat on a public bench belongs to no one. An Arab who would like an occupied place considers it perfectly acceptable to squeeze in and attempt to usurp it. Yet when an Arab is moving, the situation is reversed. A bubble of privacy then surrounds the body and to cut in front of an Arab who is driving a car is a gross violation. Most conversations in the Arab world occur on the border between the intimate and personal distance zones, for Arabs feel it is essential to breathe upon their conversational partner. To deny the partner your breath is to behave as if you are ashamed, and to inhale a friend's breath is desirable. During their conversation, Arabs stare intently into their partner's eye, a custom that seems hostile or challenging to most American males.

place in this zone, with people who customarily work together and people at casual social gatherings clustering in the four- to seven-foot range, and formal business and social dealings transacted at the farther range. A business desk effectively keeps people in the far end of the social distance, where sensory contact is limited to eye and ear.

Public Distance   People who are separated by twelve to twenty-five feet or more are operating within **public distance**. Individuals interacting at this range are neither personally nor socially involved; it is the area of the actor or politician addressing an audience. The voice must be raised and language must be carefully chosen and words enunciated clearly to ensure comprehension. Once people are more than twenty-five feet apart, nonverbal communication takes the form of exaggerated gestures and body stance.

The Protective Function of Personal Space

Many environmental psychologists believe that personal space serves the function of self-protection and that this space acts as a buffer against possible physical or emotional threats from others. For this reason, the invisible bubble of personal space has been called a "body-buffer zone" (Horowitz, Duff, and Stratton, 1964). It has been found that violent individuals maintain a larger body-buffer zone than do people who are relatively nonviolent (Kinzel, 1970) and that when people are placed under stress they maintain an increased zone of personal space (Dosey and Meisels, 1969).

The self-protective nature of personal space has been investigated primarily by experiments that deliberately violate another person's space. In one study, Robert Sommer (1969) located male patients sitting alone on benches in the parklike grounds of a California mental hospital. When Sommer found such a person, he walked over and silently sat down about six inches from him. In most cases, the patient indicated his stress by turning his body away from Sommer, pulling in his shoulders, and placing his elbows at his sides. Within two minutes a third of the patients had fled; within nine minutes, half had departed.

Students in a college library were as uncomfortable as mental patients when their personal space was violated. In this study (Sommer, 1969), a female investigator invaded the personal space of women sitting alone at tables and studying. The investigator sometimes sat directly across from the student and sometimes sat next to her. Reactions varied: some students shifted their posture, others made defensive gestures or edged their chairs away. When the investigator continued to sit close to them, most students left their seats; 70 percent had fled within thirty minutes.

When two people are interacting, the zone of personal space encompasses the pair, and a person forced to invade this space feels awkward, embarrassed, and uncomfortable. This reaction was demonstrated in a study that required each subject to walk between a pair of people who were deep in conversation (Efran and Cheyne, 1974). A hidden camera photographed the subject's reactions, which included a slightly protruding tongue and tight lips, or pursed or twisted lips. The stressful, unpleasant nature of the invasion was confirmed by the subjects' answers on a mood scale after they had passed between the talking pair.

The stress involved in such an encounter is affected by the size and status of the group whose personal space must be violated. In a similar study conducted on a university campus (Knowles, 1973), the size of the group increased the amount of stress felt by the intruder: more people chose to squeeze by on the side when four people were talking than when only two were conversing. Status also increased stress and the proportion of sidlers: a pair of talkers who appeared to be faculty members blocked as many passersby as did four students in conversation.

Personal Space and Interpersonal Attraction

The interaction that takes place in the zone of intimate distance indicates that when people are emotionally involved with one another, the buffer zone shrinks and personal space may be entered. Thus the free penetration of personal space is an expression of interpersonal attraction, whether between friends, lovers, or family members.

The friendlier the relations between two people, the smaller the zone of personal space between them. Naturalistic observations of spontaneous interactions have confirmed such tendencies. In one study (Heslin and Boss, 1980), investigators watched greetings and departures at the Indianapolis Airport and found that the more intimate the relation between the travelers and those who had come to meet them or send them off, the more intimate and lingering their encounters. In each male-female pair observed, the older person was more likely to initiate touch, but in the interactions of same-sex pairs age seemed to have no effect on who touched first. There was more intimate physical contact between pairs of women than between pairs of men. However, the ritual of greeting and leave-taking may allow Americans to engage in intimate touching without customary discomfort: there were fewer handshakes and more kisses on the mouth than the degree of intimacy of the relationships involved would have predicted.

In an effort to analyze the use of personal space to express attraction, one investigator (Mehrabian, 1968) used a simulation study in which fifty college students pretended to be interacting with men and women whom they disliked intensely or moderately, had no special feelings about, or liked intensely or moderately. The students assumed a consistent range of postures that communicated their attitudes in the various situations. As might be expected, increased liking narrowed the distance between the student and her or his imaginary partner, accompanied by increased eye contact and a body turned toward the partner. Women communicated intense dislike by increased relaxation, indicated by leaning sideways in the chair. Men also showed intense dislike of women by a similar relaxed posture, but their dislike of other men was communicated by tension and an upright posture, perhaps indicating that they found disliked males to be threatening.

The bubble of personal space serves important human functions. It can be used to express affection or to establish distance. By reducing stress, it may help to control aggression (Evans and Howard, 1973). Yet personal space does not exist in a void, but in a world where it must interact with the concept of territoriality.

Territoriality

Among the residents of seventeen homes for the aged in England, most had a favorite chair that

was considered "mine," a designation that both staff and other residents respected. If a new resident inadvertently sat in a chair that "belonged" to someone, she or he was quickly told to move on (Lipman, 1968). This assertion of ownership, as well as clashes of larger dimension over a backyard, a corner office, or an entire country, can be regarded as a demonstration of what environmental psychologists call territoriality. Among human beings, **territoriality** refers to behavior that is displayed in connection with the ownership of a place or a geographic area by an individual or a group. The behavior may include personalization of the area and defense against any intrusion into it (Altman, 1975).

The Nature of Territoriality

Territoriality links behavior to geographical places, which helps to distinguish it from personal space. Territory is stationary, whereas personal space accompanies an individual wherever she or he goes. Territoriality and personal space also differ in other ways. The boundaries of a territory are often visible, whereas the boundaries of personal space are always invisible. The body need not be near the territory, whereas it is always at the center of personal space.

After reviewing the research, Irwin Altman (1975) identified three types of territory: primary, secondary, and public. This division reflects how closely the territory impinges on the daily life of an individual or group as well as the permanence of the assertion of control over the territory.

The ownership of **primary territories** is clearly recognized; they are controlled by their users for long periods of time, and they are central to their occupants' daily lives. Primary territories, such as homes, help to regulate privacy. It is understood that no one enters them without permission, and their violation—especially if successful—threatens the owner's identity.

The ownership of **secondary territories**, which are semipublic places where acquaintances and neighbors regularly interact, is neither permanent nor exclusive. Regular users enter freely and may exert some sort of control over the territory's use by others, but it is less central to the lives of those who dominate it than is a primary territory. Typical secondary territories are country clubs, backyards, and neighborhood bars. The users of a secondary territory tend to change, the area is not always clearly identified to

This man's office is his primary territory. In it, he can organize things in his own way—even if it is messy—as long as he gets his work done.

outsiders, and others often have access to it; as a result, conflict frequently arises over its possession and boundaries. For example, outsiders who wander into a neighborhood bar may be met with hostile glances and remarks meant to drive them away.

As the name implies, there is free access to **public territories**. They are not central to their users' lives, and they may be occupied temporarily by anyone as long as minimal rules are observed. Public territories range from streets, parks, and playgrounds to tables in a restaurant, seats in a bus or theater, and telephone booths. Public territories are governed by cultural norms and customs, and their design can make temporary occupancy comfortable (as when restaurant tables are not crowded together) or difficult (as when telephone booths have poor sound shielding).

Interviews with urban and suburban residents have supported Altman's classification of territory (Taylor and Stough, 1978), and indicate that such secondary territories as backyards and sidewalks are used heavily for socializing by suburbanites but not by urban residents, primarily because suburban residents feel that they have control over such areas and feel safe and comfortable in them, and urban residents do not.

Territoriality is a complex phenomenon, and researchers have used various approaches to study its function. The aspects that have been most extensively studied include defense, social organization, and identity.

Territoriality and Defense

When the concept of territoriality was first developed by ethologists (Howard, 1920), active defense played a major part in the notion. Ethologists continued to stress this aspect for decades, with Konrad Lorenz (1969) defining territorial behavior as "the defense of a given area." As the concept spread from the field of animal behavior to the study of human beings, other characteristics were added to the definition until finally, environmental psychologists began avoiding the term altogether (Edney, 1974).

Sociobiologists also see defense as an important aspect of territoriality, and Edward O. Wilson (1978), the founder of sociobiology, proposes that although human territoriality has a biological basis, its expression is heavily affected by the environment. Human beings do not, he says, defend group territory unless it is economically defensible. For example, hunter-gatherers who live a nomadic existence on a sparsely populated range with unpredictable food supplies have no concept of land ownership, but hunter-gatherers who live on land that has reliable food resources tend to defend their territory aggressively.

In contrast to ethological and sociobiological theories of territoriality, sociocultural theories view territorial behavior as a function of social learning and cultural influences. Sociocultural theorists recognize that human beings engage in territorial behavior but as we saw in Chapter 7, they maintain that human territoriality is very different from the territoriality displayed by other species. Julian Edney (1974) has listed a number of ways in which they diverge: (1) human beings use space in highly varied ways—as group territory, family territory, or individual territory —indicating learning, whereas animals use space in a stereotypical, fixed fashion indicating innate behavior; (2) the connection between territory and aggression is not as clear-cut in human beings as it is in animals; (3) human beings often maintain territories in several locations (home, office, vacation condominium) whereas animals maintain only a single territory at any time; (4) human beings use territories (such as a seat in a theater) for a brief time, surrendering them at the end of the period, whereas such time-sharing is rare among animals; (5) human beings are the only species that amicably entertains occupants of another territory on home ground.

For these reasons, sociocultural theorists contend that human territoriality can be understood only in the context of the complex social organization and cultural diversity of human societies. Edney (1974) speculates that socialization is extremely important in the development and expression of territoriality because of the specific environmental contexts that often accompany social roles. For example, the exclusive use of certain territories often accompanies particular social roles, as when access to the executive dining room is part of being a corporate executive. In addition, territory often receives meaning in connection with its use, as when a room is endowed with meaning through its exclusive use by a physician to examine patients. Thus territoriality is seen not as genetically determined behavior, but as learned behavior that supports social roles.

Extreme biological views of territoriality are no longer generally accepted. Most investigators emphasize the sociocultural position, but many feel that a complete view of territoriality includes some biological influence that is greatly moderated by social and cultural factors.

Territoriality and Social Organization

The link between culture and territoriality becomes apparent when we examine the way territory helps develop and maintain a stable social organization. Social groups are generally organized in terms of the status of group members, whose position is generally determined by their relative **dominance,** or ability to influence others. One function of territoriality is to help establish and maintain dominance hierarchies among human beings and animals.

Whenever human beings are thrown into continual contact, some sort of dominance structure generally emerges. As we saw in Chapter 14, dominance hierarchies exist in preschool play groups, with youngsters using physical attack, threat, or struggles over objects to establish their positions in the group (Strayer and Strayer, 1976). Territoriality has been found among five-year-olds, who established their own areas in a playroom and when they revisited the room after an absence of nearly two years, immediately tried to reclaim their old territories (Paluck and Esser, 1971).

The connection between dominance and territoriality was clear in a study of adolescent boys in a home for juvenile offenders (Sundstrom and Altman, 1974). Among these youngsters, highly dominant boys were the most territorial and used the desirable spaces in the building most frequently. When the two most dominant boys were released, conflicts arose and the remaining boys tended to use all the spaces indiscriminately until new territories were established. It appeared that territoriality helped maintain the social order by distributing space among group members in an effective manner—a function that became apparent only when dominant group members left and the system broke down.

Territoriality and Identity

Territoriality can also help to foster and maintain a person's sense of identity, both as an individual and as a member of a social group. Part of our sense of identity is derived from the territory we occupy, whether it is our home, our neighborhood, our city, our state, or our country.

A house is more than a place of security and shelter from the elements. It has been suggested that a person's home functions as a symbol of the self. For example, a study of California suburbanites indicated that people tended to buy homes that bolstered their self-image as individuals and as persons with a certain social status (Werthman, 1968). This function of housing may be at the basis of many people's distaste for high-rise apartment living, since the hivelike arrangement of similar rooms could threaten the apartment dweller's self-image (Cooper, 1974).

If a home is indeed a symbol of the owner's self, it should proclaim that image to others, and one study (Sadalla, Burroughs, and Quaid, 1980) indicates that our houses do communicate something about our personalities. Working on the assumption that homeowners send messages about themselves through their choice of homes, investigators asked upper-middle-class homeowners to rate themselves on such personality dimensions as interesting/bland, formal/informal, energetic/lazy, optimistic/pessimistic, and artistic/nonartistic. The ratings fell into four stereotypical personality clusters: individualism, an individual who is an artistic nonconformist; self-discipline, an organized, efficient, formal individual; graciousness, a social individual who prefers formal interaction; and warm-cold, a highly relaxed, social individual. Afterward, college students looked at color photographs of the houses' living rooms and rated their owners on the same personality dimensions. The students' ratings agreed significantly with the self-ratings of the homeowners despite the fact that the two groups differed in age and socioeconomic level.

Identity is also demonstrated in regard to territory by the way space is personalized. Altman (1975) describes the way his sons gradually personalized their own rooms so that by the time they reached adolescence, the decorations installed by their parents had been replaced by items that marked the rooms as personal territory. Such personal observations were supported by a study of students' rooms at a western university (Hansen and Altman, 1976). Within two weeks of their arrival at the university, 88 percent of the freshmen men in the study had decorated the wall over their beds, and by the end of the quarter, 98 percent of them had done so. Over the weeks, the amount of wall devoted to decoration increased, and the posters, pictures, photographs, calendars, maps, and sports equipment that hung there identified the students' personal interests and values. Students who failed to decorate their walls, who decorated sparsely, or who decorated primarily with items that indicated personal relationships (such as photographs of family or girlfriends) tended to drop out of school before the end of the year. The investigators suggest that by personalizing their territory, students reveal their social and psychological states and reflect their degree of commitment to the environment.

Territoriality appears to have several functions in human society. Once seen only as defensive in nature, territoriality is now recognized as supporting social roles, maintaining dominance hierarchies, and fostering a sense of personal identity.

Privacy

Although we rarely think about our privacy unless someone intrudes upon it, the concept is intimately bound up with our social lives. When we need a quiet place to study, a restful corner where we can become lost in a good book, or a secluded spot for intimacy with a special person, privacy is essential.

The Nature of Privacy

Privacy has a number of connotations to ordinary citizens, behavioral scientists, and lawmakers. Some definitions are vague and ambiguous, but they all connote withdrawal from others and control over personal information. The withdrawal aspect of privacy involves seclusion and an avoidance of interaction with others, whereas the control aspect involves the ability to open or close access to the self or group, depending upon one's relationship to others and the characteristics of the situation.

Research aimed at establishing the meaning of privacy in the context of daily interaction has affirmed that withdrawal and control over personal information are basic elements of privacy. In a study (Marshall, 1970) of college sophomores and their parents, six distinct attitudes toward privacy were found, but all reflected either withdrawal or the control of information. Withdrawal covered the attitudes of solitude, seclusion, and intimacy. The solitary person values time away from family and friends, prefers solitary activities, does not enjoy interacting in small groups, and generally feels a lack of sufficient privacy. The seclusive person prefers a house that is out of the sight and earshot of others, does not want to know the neighbors, finds being alone comfortable, and neither visits without an invitation nor expects others to do so. The intimate person expands the circle of privacy to include a close friend, a lover, or the family: she or he prefers activities that involve a few people and wants friends and acquaintances to call before dropping in.

A private spot along a mountain trail allows this hiker to have a quiet moment, away from the company of others.

Control of information comprises the attitudes of anonymity, reserve, and "not neighborly." The anonymous person has little physical privacy and must find it in the anonymity of city living, keeping interactions on a casual level and losing herself or himself in a crowd. People who seek anonymity dislike casual visiting and do not choose neighbors as friends, but they also dislike solitary activities. The reserved person likes visual privacy, is unwilling to disclose much personal information to acquaintances, and prefers interacting in large groups. The person who is not neighborly tends to live with few people, dislikes casual visits, avoids neighbors as friends, and entertains only a handful of guests. However, she or he prefers the anonymity of attending a ball game to interacting in small groups.

For our purposes, the best definition of **privacy** is the selective control of access to the self or to the social group (Altman, 1975). Although this definition emphasizes the control aspect of privacy, it also encompasses the concept of withdrawal since one way to restrict access is by withdrawing. In addition this definition assumes that privacy is a process and allows us to consider its changing nature in relations between individuals, between groups, and between individuals and groups.

Development of the Individual's Concept of Privacy

The notion of privacy begins to develop early through the social interactions of childhood. The first experiences may come when the young child, who has no personal privacy, is cast as an intruder into adult affairs ("don't come in"; "get out of here") and is in turn freely intruded upon by adults. Not until the child lies successfully or manages to hide some forbidden behavior does an awareness grow that she or he has the ability to control others' access to personal information (Laufer, Wolfe, and Proshansky, 1976).

In a study with Robert Laufer, Maxine Wolfe (1978) interviewed 900 children between the ages of five and seventeen about their concept of privacy. Even the youngest children had some notion of privacy, and those who could not define the concept for themselves had no trouble describing how their parents and older siblings demanded and used privacy. Changes in the concept with age paralleled children's experiences. For example, although the ideas of withdrawal and control are found at all age levels, children under seven are most likely to mention being alone (withdrawal) as a feature of privacy. Controlling access to a place is most often mentioned by children between the ages of seven and twelve, and when they describe how their parents act when they want privacy, these youngsters nearly always say the cue is "going into the bedroom." The concept of privacy is more complex among adolescents, who are most likely to mention both being alone and controlling access to information and who tend to add such qualifiers as "when I want to" to their definitions.

In another study (Parke and Sawin, 1979), investigators traced the development of privacy as withdrawal among more than 100 middle-class children. As children grew, they were more likely to use physical markers to indicate their own need for privacy (shutting a bedroom or bathroom door) and the need of others (knocking on a sibling's closed bedroom door).

Privacy and Self-Disclosure

One method of controlling the invasion of privacy is to regulate **self-disclosure**—what we tell another person about ourselves. In disclosing information about the self, we open the boundary between ourselves and another person, generally by providing verbal information, although such nonverbal methods as eye contact and special smiles may also be used. Most self-disclosure is intentional, but sometimes a temporary loss of control can lead to inadvertent self-disclosure, as when we bang a fist on the table in frustration or stomp out of the room in anger (Derlega and Chaikin, 1977).

Most theorists agree that self-disclosure performs a major function in the regulation of privacy. For example, Sidney Jourard (1966) discussed privacy as the outcome of the wish to withhold from others knowledge of personal experience, actions, and intentions and said that lack of self-disclosure represents an attempt to control another's perceptions and beliefs concerning the reticent person. Since privacy is the selective control of access to the self, the freedom to decide whether to disclose personal information is essential to the concept of privacy, and privacy in this sense enlarges our freedom of choice, giving us increased control over our activities (Laufer, Proshansky, and Wolfe, 1976).

Self-disclosure is also central to Alan Westin's (1967) analysis of privacy. He defines the concept as "the claim of individuals, groups or institutions to determine for themselves when, how, and to what extent information about them is communicated to others." Thus privacy gives us intimacy in which to disclose personal information and the right to select what information—if any—we shall reveal.

Self-disclosure involves the management of two kinds of personal boundaries. In addition to opening the barrier between the self and the person who is receiving information, there is the boundary around the self and the confidant. Unless a person is certain that this barrier will not be breached by the leakage of personal information to third parties, self-disclosure will be considered dangerous and will not take place (Derlega and Chaikin, 1977).

The effect of the physical environment on disclosures was demonstrated in a study that simulated a counseling situation (Holahan and Slaikeu, 1977). Students who volunteered to act as subjects in the development of scales for psychological interviews were asked questions that included probes into intimate areas ("Do you ever worry about how attractive you are to the opposite sex?"). In this situation, verbal self-disclosure was reduced when a third person was in the room.

Sometimes we find ourselves telling people a good deal more about ourselves than we intend to reveal. This can happen in the "stranger on the train" situation, in which our confidant will never see us again and has no connection with any of our friends or acquaintances. In such a situation we are guaranteed anonymity, because the boundary around self and confidant cannot be broken. Unintended revelations can also occur simply because self-disclosure tends to be reciprocal; that is, people tend to match openness in a conversational partner with their own openness. When someone's self-disclosure threatens our own privacy but we do not wish to disrupt the relationship, one solution is to increase the breadth of our personal remarks (including more topic areas) without increasing their depth (refusing to disclose intimate information on any topic; Derlega and Chaikin, 1977).

Privacy's importance in human life is shown by the fact that all human societies provide ways to attain it. Environmental barriers, words, and nonverbal signs help to establish privacy and social norms regulate it.

A crowded Tokyo public beach is not necessarily unpleasant. The sight and sounds of many other people enjoying themselves can increase one's own fun.

Crowding

Life in the twentieth century makes us particularly aware of crowding. None of us has escaped some of its unpleasant consequences, whether on the highway, stuck in bumper-to-bumper traffic; in line for the next performance of a popular film; or in the housing market, attempting to find a vacant apartment. Yet a crowd is not always unpleasant. A camaraderie and rising excitement build among the crowd at a hotly contested football game, a political rally, or a rock concert, and most of its members feel exhilarated, not crowded.

The Nature of Crowding

When researchers first began to study crowding, they generally measured it in terms of **density**—the physical conditions of the setting expressed in terms of the number of people in a given space. But situations such as a football game or a rock concert make it clear that density is not a good measure of crowding. Today most researchers define **crowding** as the perception of restricted space and the limits it places on action. According to this definition, crowding is a motivational state in which the goal is to alleviate infringements on action either by acquiring more space or adjusting one's cognitions so that the restriction of space is perceived as less unpleasant (Stokols, 1972). In this view, density becomes a necessary precondition for crowding, but is not by itself sufficient to cause the experience.

Crowding requires that density be accompanied by certain social and personal factors: with an inability to coordinate actions with others because of spatial constraints, an arousal of competitive feelings, or the presence of impatient or aggressive people (Stokols, 1972). Further, people who are used to living and working under high-density conditions, such as the residents of Hong Kong, will feel less crowded in a situation that a resident of an American suburb would find oppressive.

The effects of crowding and how people cope with them have been investigated using correlational studies, laboratory experiments, and field studies. All have contributed to our understanding of crowding. Experiments and field studies show how crowding affects individual behavior and social processes, while a correlational study can tell us something about the long-term effects of crowding on people's lives (Altman, 1975). For example, researchers (Galle, Gove, and McPherson, 1972) have established correlations between the number of people per room and juvenile delinquency, enrollment on welfare rolls, and death rates. The experience of high-density living is eloquently portrayed in *The Children of Sanchez* (Lewis, 1961), in which a young woman who lived in one room with eight relatives describes the quality of her life primarily in terms of lack of privacy: her inability to control her bedtime and to select a radio program; her embarrassment over sharing the room's semi-public toilet; and her shame at being scolded in front of the entire family. Recent research has concentrated on social processes, such as the effect of density on aggression among children.

Crowding and Information Overload

Since urban residents live, work, and play amid throngs of other people, the experience of living in cities has become a model for understanding how people cope with crowding. American cities are characterized by great masses of people from disparate ethnic backgrounds packed into a relatively small area. Stanley Milgram (1970) has speculated that these three factors—numbers, density, and heterogeneity—produce a constant flood of information that confronts the city dweller with inputs (bits of information) at a rate that exceeds the human ability to process them. This **information overload** is obvious to the visitor from a small town who steps onto a New York or London street for the first time.

In Milgram's view, urban residents handle this information overload by developing social norms that curtail social contacts and diminish their intensity. Urban social norms are the result of a series of adaptations: each input receives less time. Low-priority inputs, such as the derelict curled up on the sidewalk, are disregarded. Whenever possible, the boundaries of a social transaction are redrawn to shift responsibility to the other person; for example, bus drivers will not make change for passengers. Reception of inputs is often blocked off, whether by unlisted phone numbers or forbidding facial expressions. Inputs are filtered to diminish the intensity of personal involvement. And specialized institutions, such as welfare departments, absorb many of the inputs. The result of these adaptations, says Milgram, is a restriction on moral and social involvement with others.

To see whether information overload would develop when many people were crowded together, investigators (Mackintosh, West, and Saegert, 1975) sent people into a Manhattan department store, half of them during peak shopping hours and the other half when the store was uncrowded. Afterward, both groups remembered descriptions of merchandise and store layout that they had written down while in the store. But the people who had been crowded learned much less about other aspects of the store's environment and drew less complete and less accurate maps of the store than did people who visited it when it was uncrowded. Apparently, they coped with information overload by processing and encoding less of the environment.

After analyzing numerous experiments on crowding, other researchers (Schmidt and Keat-

Riders on crowded subways try to maintain a feeling of privacy despite the close contact they must have with strangers. Avoiding eye contact is one way people block out unwanted inputs.

ing, 1979) proposed that the underlying cause of these negative psychological effects is loss of personal control. The individual who is placed in a high density situation and feels unable to control the level of informational input will feel crowded—a description that fits the first-time visitor to a large city.

A study that took place in Manhattan supermarkets supports this interpretation. Researchers (Langer and Saegert, 1977) sent eighty women with identical shopping lists into supermarkets. Their task was to comparison shop, jotting down the most economical brand and size of each item on the list. Women who were told beforehand about the physiological and psychological reactions that often arise in crowded settings found items on the list more readily, thought it was easier to make decisions, were more comfortable, and felt that the market was less crowded than did women who were not briefed ahead of time. Thus cognitive awareness —knowing what to expect—can confer a sense of personal control that relieves some of the unpleasant behavioral and psychological effects of crowding.

Crowding and Social Withdrawal

One way to deal with information overload is to withdraw, and a number of studies (e.g., Schmidt, Goldman, and Feimer, 1979) have found that as density increases, people tend to withdraw by avoiding social interactions. Withdrawal in a short-term situation appeared among male college students who had agreed to interact with five other men to develop impressions of the men's personalities (Sundstrom, 1975). Students placed in a small, crowded room withdrew by becoming much more reluctant to talk about intimate topics than did students in a large room.

The simple knowledge that you will soon find yourself in a crowd can trigger social withdrawal —even when the crowd never materializes. Investigators (Baum and Greenberg, 1975) told college students who agreed to take part in a study of groups that they would be playing a bargaining game. Half of the students believed they would be joined in the small room by three other students; the rest believed that nine others would be taking part in the game. Students awaiting nine people took seats in a corner of the room and tended to look away from people who joined them—a habit that reduces eye contact

and the possibilities of social interaction. Students awaiting only three people generally sat in the middle of the room or along a wall, and they looked in others' faces much more often than did the students who expected to be crowded. Compared with students who had no reason to believe they would be crowded, students who expected to experience crowding said that they were more uncomfortable, that the room was smaller and stuffier, that they felt more crowded, and that they disliked the students more who did join them, rating them as pushy and aggressive. Apparently, past experiences with crowding create expectations that alter our perceptions of our surroundings and affect our behavior.

Long-term exposure to crowded living conditions may lead people to find most social interaction stressful. Students who lived in dormitories in which all the rooms opened off a corridor (seventeen double-occupancy rooms, one lounge, and one bathroom per floor) behaved quite differently in social situations than did students who lived in dormitories with a suite design (three double-occupancy rooms surrounding one lounge and one bathroom; Valins and Baum, 1973; Baum, Harpin, and Valins, 1975). When placed in a situation that promised to involve social interaction with another person of the same sex, students from the corridor-style dormitory sat farther away, talked less, and looked less at the other person than did students from the suite-style dormitory. In addition, students from the corridor-style dormitory were less able to reach agreement after group discussion of a topic and were less likely to develop social groups among the students with whom they shared bath and lounge facilities. The investigators believe that the corridor-style dormitory provided the same sort of information overload that Milgram found in cities and that the students' social withdrawal resulted from their attempts to cope with the resulting stress.

Crowded college dormitories seemed to produce overload in another study of male undergraduates (Baron et al., 1976). In this case, a sudden influx of students had led the college to assign three men to a number of rooms designed for two students. Compared with students who were housed in double rooms, students in triple-occupancy rooms said they got less cooperation from their roommates, were more dissatisfied with them, and felt less control over almost every aspect of their situation, including privacy, noise, study, and sleep.

Crowding and Altruism

If social withdrawal is a common reaction to crowding, then we might predict that altruism declines when people feel crowded. Indeed, Milgram (1970) has suggested that the restricted social involvement of city dwellers inevitably leads to deficiencies in social responsibility. The prediction of declining altruism has been supported by experiments and field studies, which have consistently found that as density increases, people become less willing to help.

The most striking deficiencies in the city dweller's social responsibility are seen in situations of crisis, such as the instance described in Chapter 27, when thirty-eight people watched from their apartments as a young woman in the street below was stabbed to death (Milgram, 1970). As the earlier discussion indicated, when an individual believes that others are also aware of the crisis, the feeling of personal responsibility is reduced and the individual becomes less likely to help (Darley and Latané, 1968). Thus, had the stabbing victim been in a place where only one person witnessed her plight, she might have had some sort of aid.

This diffusion of responsibility is not the only factor that lessens altruism in the city. People who live in a crowded city are often less friendly and tend to be more suspicious of strangers than are people in small towns, as studies reported by Milgram (1970) indicate. In one of them, students rang doorbells and, saying they had misplaced the address of a friend who lived nearby, asked to enter and use the telephone. People living in small towns often complied with the request; city residents were much less likely to do so. Since women gained entry much more often than men, the reluctance of city dwellers to be helpful in this case seems related to a heightened perception of the dangers of city life and their suspicions that the intruder might have criminal intentions.

However, this explanation cannot be applied to a second study reported by Milgram, in which a telephone caller asked for a favor that required time but no risk. Explaining that they were calling long-distance and had reached the resident in error, the callers asked for information about the weather and for the phone number of a suitable hotel or motel in the area. Again, city dwellers were less helpful and less informative than residents of small towns. Thus no matter what your need, the less dense the population, the more likely you are to be helped.

Lessened altruism in densely populated environments is not confined to the city/small-town division. Researchers (Bickman et al., 1973) have found that students living in high-density, high-rise dormitories are less altruistic than students living in low-density dormitories. The researchers dropped sealed, addressed, and stamped letters without return addresses in dormitory corridors. As the density of dormitories increased, the percentage of letters that were picked up and mailed decreased, dropping from 100 percent in low-density residences to 63 percent in high-density dormitories. What is more, students in the high-rise dorms trusted the other residents in their house less than students in low-density dorms did, more of them locked their doors, and fewer of them said they would report a broken dorm window. The investigators believe that the diminished altruism they found was the ultimate result of information overload. Students in densely populated dormitories meet so many other students that they stop dealing with them as individuals and withdraw in a manner similar to that found among many urban residents.

Research has had few positive things to say about crowding. Indeed, as we shall see, crowding itself is the result of a failure in the other aspects of environmentally related behavior.

Microinterpersonal Behavior

Thus far we have emphasized the differences among personal space, territoriality, privacy, and crowding. Yet these concepts do not affect human action in isolation. Territoriality and personal space are both linked to the concept of privacy, for maintaining control of territory is one means people use to attain privacy, and violation of personal space is considered an invasion of privacy. Crowding is linked to the other three concepts, because the conditions generally referred to as "crowded" reduce both the amount of control we have over territory and the possibilities of physical privacy—although as we have seen, a degree of privacy can be obtained in a crowd through anonymity.

All four concepts have been integrated by Irwin Altman (1975) into the broader concept of microinterpersonal behavior. **Microinterpersonal behavior** refers to face-to-face interaction

The moveable chairs in this small New York City park allow people to achieve intimacy or privacy within a very confined space.

orchestra blend their sounds into a symphony. When these mechanisms fail to function effectively and a person experiences undesired social contact, the social-psychological condition known as crowding develops. Altman thus sees crowding as a "breakdown in privacy regulation."

At present our knowledge of privacy, the key concept in Altman's system, is primarily speculative. Privacy has been the focus of less research than any of the other concepts in the system. What we know of microinterpersonal behavior, however, already has applications in environmental planning and design.

Design Applications

Environmental psychologists are concerned with the application of empirical knowledge to environmental planning and design. With their help, architects, urban planners, and interior design specialists can make our lives more pleasant and comfortable and even safer.

Our knowledge of personal space, for example, can lead to the design of interior spaces that promote social interaction. Take the apparently simple matter of chair placement. When Edward Hall's view of interaction distances was applied in a field study set in a mental health center, it became clear that the placement of chairs clearly changed the quality of the initial psychological interview (Lassen, 1973). When patients were separated from the therapist by nine feet (far social distance), they felt they did not get their point across as well as when they sat either three feet from the therapist (personal distance) or six feet away (close social distance). However, the personal distance was too close for successful communication; patients talked most openly about their fears and anxieties at six feet, indicating that close social distance probably creates the most favorable conditions for self-disclosure.

Our knowledge of territoriality can be used to design residential environments that more effectively meet the needs of their residents. For example, can the design of city public housing projects reduce crime in their vicinity? When Oscar Newman (1972) applied knowledge of territoriality to the question, he found that some designs seemed to encourage crime by making spaces such as lobbies, elevators, and grounds

between people that is affected by the physical environment itself and by people's active use of that environment. Altman believes that privacy is the central concept in microinterpersonal behavior and that it provides the glue holding personal space, territoriality, crowding, and privacy together.

As noted earlier, privacy is a regulatory process through which a person or group makes itself more or less open to other people. From this perspective, personal space and territoriality are both behavioral mechanisms people can use to attain a desired degree of privacy. Manipulating the bubble of personal space controls interpersonal boundaries so that communication increases or decreases. Possession, marking, and the defense of objects and areas—all territorial behavior—also increase or decrease privacy, limiting or expanding social contact.

When privacy-sustaining behaviors operate efficiently, they function together smoothly in a single system, much as the various sections of an

indefensible. He proposed that crime could be reduced by incorporating zones of potential territorial influence in designs of building clusters and interiors and establishing natural opportunities for surveillance. Although Newman's approach has been criticized (Kaplan, 1973), his efforts to change public perception of community areas from "nobody's territory" to "our territory" seem to be a step in the right direction.

Our knowledge of privacy can be applied to the design of occupational environments so as to increase job satisfaction and job performance. How much privacy do office employees need? Studies of three office environments found that when office design gave workers visual and acoustic isolation, employees had increased feelings of privacy (Sundstrom, Burt, and Kamp, 1980). Employees preferred privacy to accessibility, and those who had privacy were more satisfied with their jobs. It may be that placing room dividers and sound-absorbent partitions in open-plan offices would improve employee morale and performance.

Our knowledge about crowding can be applied to the design of high-density residential environments to make life in such surroundings more pleasant. How, for example, might the stress and social withdrawal found in crowded college dormitories be reduced? In a field experiment in a university dormitory, researchers (Baum and Davis, 1980) found that a simple modification in dormitory design could reduce crowding. They converted three central bedrooms on a long dormitory corridor to lounge space, creating two small groups of residents on the dormitory floor. The modification in design increased social interaction on the floor and reduced levels of stress from crowding.

Thus, although the field of environmental psychology is new, its application of social-psychological principles to the environment holds great promise. The physical environment continuously influences our behavior, but by putting research to use, we can also influence the environment so that it does a better job of meeting human needs.

SUMMARY

1. **Environmental psychology** encompasses the investigation of interrelationships between the physical environment and people's behavior. Environmental psychology has always been an interdisciplinary field, which developed when psychologists, sociologists, architects, and city planners became interested in the effects of the environment and when changes in society were making serious consideration of the environment imperative. Since environmental psychology stresses the investigation of problems, it has emphasized naturalistic observations and studies conducted in the world as well as in the laboratory.

2. **Personal space** is the invisible bubble that surrounds each individual into which other people may not trespass, and any violation of its boundaries makes the individual uncomfortable. Personal space expands and contracts, depending on gender, age, culture, and degree of familiarity. Social interactions among most Americans are regulated by four zones: **intimate distance** (up to 18 inches), which is reserved for the expression of deep emotion; **personal distance** (1½ to 4 feet), which is used by close friends; **social distance** (4 to 12 feet), which is used for business and casual social gatherings; and **public distance** (12 to 25 or more feet), which is used to address an audience. Cultural differences in the use of personal space often give rise to misunderstandings, but some form of personal space appears in every society. Personal space protects the individual and acts as a buffer against emotional or physical threat. It may reduce the stress caused by the proximity of others and thus help to control aggression within the species. When people are emotionally involved with each other, personal space may be entered, so that its free penetration expresses interpersonal attraction.

3. Among human beings, **territoriality** refers to behavior that is displayed in connection with the ownership of a place; the area may be personalized and its owners may defend against any intrusion into it. There are three kinds of territory: **primary territory**, in which ownership is clearly recognized, users control it for long periods, and the space is central to

the occupants' daily lives; **secondary territory**, which is a semipublic place, is less central to its users' lives, and is neither permanent nor exclusive; and **public territory**, which may be occupied temporarily by anyone and is not central to its users' lives. In the ethological and sociobiological views of territoriality, defense against any encroachment is a central aspect of the concept, and territoriality is seen as having a biological basis. In the sociocultural view of territoriality, territorial behavior is a function of social learning and cultural influence. Social groups are generally organized according to the relative dominance of their members, and through the dominant members' control of desirable places, territoriality helps in the ordering of social groups. Territoriality can also help to foster and maintain a person's sense of identity as an individual and as a member of a social group. By personalizing space, people increase the contribution of territoriality to identity.

4. **Privacy** is the selective control of access to the self or to the social group. One way to restrict access is by withdrawing. Concepts of privacy change through the interaction of stage of life, social roles, cultural norms, and past experiences. Children have some idea of privacy by the time they are five years old, and changes in their understanding parallel their experiences. One way to control the invasion of privacy is by regulating **self-disclosure**, what we tell another person about ourselves. The freedom to decide whether to disclose personal information is essential to privacy, and in this sense privacy enlarges our freedom of choice. The level of self-disclosure depends upon the content of the information, social relationships, personality characteristics, and the physical environment.

5. **Density**, the physical condition of the situation expressed in terms of the number of people in a given space, is not generally considered a good definition of crowding. In-

stead, **crowding** is regarded as the perception of restricted space and the limits it places on action. However, density is a necessary precondition for crowding. The great numbers of people in a city, their density, and their heterogeneity confront the urban resident with **information overload**, a flood of informational inputs at a rate that exceeds the human ability to process them. Urban residents handle this overload by devising norms that curtail social contact and diminish their intensity. The inability to control the level of informational input leads individuals to feel crowded. However, cognitive control can ameliorate some of the behavioral and psychological effects of crowding. As density increases, people tend to withdraw by avoiding social interactions. The expectation that one will be in a crowded situation alters perceptions so that a person who expects to be crowded will withdraw socially. As a result of long-term exposure to crowded living conditions, people may find most social interaction stressful. As density increases, people become less altruistic. This decline in altruism is due partly to the diffusion of responsibility created when many people are present and partly to the increased suspicion and unfriendliness that often characterize life in the city.

6. **Microinterpersonal behavior** refers to face-to-face interaction between people that is affected by the physical environment and by people's use of that environment. Privacy is proposed as the central concept in microinterpersonal behavior, with personal space and territoriality seen as behavioral mechanisms people use to obtain privacy. When these mechanisms fail to function effectively, crowding develops.

7. Knowledge of personal space, territoriality, privacy, and crowding derived from environmental psychology can be used to make the environment more responsive to human needs.

KEY TERMS

crowding

density

dominance

environmental psychology

information overload

intimate distance

microinterpersonal behavior

personal distance

personal space

primary territory

privacy

public distance

public territory

secondary territory

self-disclosure

social distance

territoriality

RECOMMENDED READINGS

ALTMAN, I. *The Environment and Social Behavior.* Monterey, Calif.: Brooks/Cole, 1975. A thorough and integrative analysis of research on personal space, territoriality, privacy, and crowding.

ALTMAN, I., and M. CHEMERS. *Environment and Culture.* Monterey, Calif.: Brooks/Cole, 1980. A discussion of environmental psychology from a cross-cultural perspective.

HOLAHAN, C. J. *Environmental Psychology.* New York: Random House, 1982. A comprehensive introduction to research, theory, and practice in environmental psychology.

PROSHANSKY, H. M., W. H. ITTELSON, and L. G. RIVLIN (eds.). *Environmental Psychology: People and Their Physical Settings.* New York: Holt, Rinehart, and Winston, 1976. An anthology bringing together many of the major writings in environmental psychology.

SOMMER, R. *Tight Spaces: Hard Architecture and How to Humanize It.* Englewood Cliffs, N.J.: Prentice-Hall, 1974. A discussion of how environmental psychology may be applied to humanizing a variety of architectural settings.

References

The number in brackets after each entry refers to the chapter in this book in which that work is cited.

Abel, G. G., Blanchard, E. B., and **Becker, J. V.** An integrated treatment program for rapists. In R. T. Rada (Ed.), *Clinical aspects of the rapist.* New York: Grune & Stratton, 1978. Pp. 161–214. [17]

Abelson, H., Cohen, R., Heaton, E., and **Suder, C.** Public attitudes toward and experience with erotic materials. In Commission on Obscenity and Pornography, *Technical reports of the Commission on Obscenity and Pornography* (Vol. 6). Washington, D.C.: U.S. Government Printing Office, 1970. [17]

Abelson, R. P., and **Zimbardo, P. G.** *Canvassing for peace: A manual for volunteers.* Ann Arbor, Mich.: Society for the Psychological Study of Social Issues, 1970. [25]

Abraham, K. Notes on psychoanalytic investigation and treatment of manic-depressive insanity and allied conditions (1911). In *Selected papers of Karl Abraham,* M.D. London: The Hogarth Press, 1948. [23]

———. The first pregenital stage of the libido (1916). In *Selected papers of Karl Abraham,* M.D. London: The Hogarth Press, 1948. [23]

Abramson, L. Y., Seligman, M. E. P., and **Teasdale, J. D.** Learned helplessness in humans: Critique and reformulation. *Journal of Abnormal Psychology,* 1978, *87,* 49–74. [21]

Acredolo, C., and **Acredolo, L. P.** Identity, compensation, and conservation. *Child Development,* 1979, *50,* 524–535. [12]

Adams, R. An account of a peculiar optical phenomenon seen after having looked at a moving body. *London and Edinburgh Philosophical Magazine and Journal of Science,* 1834, *5,* 373–374. [5]

Addiego, F., Belzer, Jr., E. G., Comolli, J., Moger, W., Perry, J. D., and **Whipple, B.** Female ejaculation: a case study. *The Journal of Sex Research,* February 1981, *17,* 13–21. [17]

Adelson, J. The development of ideology in adolescence. In S. Dragastin and G. H. Elder (Eds.), *Adolescence in the Life Cycle.* Washington, D.C.: Hemisphere, 1975, 63–78. [12]

Adler, A. Individual psychology. In C. A. Murchison (Ed.), *Psychologies of 1930.* Worcester, Mass.: Clark University Press, 1930. Pp. 394–405. [18]

———. *What life should mean to you.* Boston: Little, Brown, 1931. [18]

Agnew, H. W., Jr., Webb, W. B., and **Williams, R. L.** Comparison of stage four and REM sleep deprivation. *Perceptual and Motor Skills,* 1967, *24,* 851–858. [6]

Ainsworth, M. D. S., Blehar, M. C., Waters, E., and **Wall, S.** *Patterns of attachment.* Hillsdale, N.J.: Erlbaum, 1978. [14]

Ajzen, I., and **Fishbein, M.** Attitude-behavior relations: A theoretical analysis and review of empirical research. *Psychological Bulletin,* 1977, *84,* 888–918. [25]

Albee, G. W. I.Q. tests on trial. *The New York Times,* February 12, 1978, E = 13. [20]

Albert, S. M., and **Dabbs, J. M., Jr.** Physical distance and persuasion. *Journal of Personality and Social Psychology,* 1970, *15,* 265–270. [25]

Allen, V. L. Situational factors in conformity. In L. Berkowitz (Ed.), *Advances in experimental social psychology* (Vol. 2). New York: Academic Press, 1965. Pp. 133–170. [27]

Allerand, A. M. *Remembrance of feelings past: A study of phenomenological genetics.* Ph.D. dissertation, Columbia University, 1967. [15]

Alley, T. R. Headshape and the perception of cuteness. *Developmental Psychology,* 1981, *17,* 650–654. [14]

Allon, N. The stigma of overweight in everyday life. In G. A. Bray (Ed.), *Obesity in perspective.* Washington, D.C.: U.S. Government Printing Office, 1975. [26]

Allport, F. H. The influence of the group upon association and thought. *Journal of Experimental Psychology,* 1920, *3,* 159–182. [27]

Allport, G. W. *Personality: A psychological interpretation.* New York: Holt, Rinehart & Winston, 1937. [19]

———. *Pattern and growth in personality.* New York: Holt, Rinehart & Winston, 1961. [19]

———. Traits revisited. *American Psychologist,* 1966, *21,* 1–10. [19]

———. and **Odbert, H. S.** Trait-names: A psycho-lexical study. *Psychological Monographs,* 1936, *47,* Whole No. 211. [19]

Altman, I. *The environmental and social behavior.* Monterey, Calif.: Brooks/Cole, 1975. [28]

American Association on Mental Deficiency. *Manual on terminology and classification in mental retardation* (1977 revision). Washington, D.C.: American Association on Mental Deficiency, 1977. [20]

American Psychiatric Association. *Diagnostic and statistical manual of mental disorders (DSM-I).* Washington, D.C.: American Psychiatric Association, 1952. [23]

———. *Diagnostic and statistical manual of mental disorders* (2nd ed.). Washington, D.C.: American Psychiatric Association, 1968. [22]

———. *Diagnostic and statistical manual of mental disorders.* (3rd ed.). Washington, D.C.: American Psychiatric Association, 1980. [22]

American Psychological Association. *Directory of the American Psychological Association.* Washington, D.C.: American Psychological Association, 1981. [1]

———.*Ethical principles of psychologists.* Washington, D.C.: American Psychological Association, 1981. [2]

———, **American Educational Research Association** and **National Council on Measurement in Education.** *Standards for educational and psychological tests.* Washington, D.C.: American Psychological Association, 1974. [20]

Ames, A., Jr. Visual perception and the rotating trapezoidal window. *Psychological Monographs,* 1951, *65,* 7, Whole No. 234. [5]

Amoore, J. E., and **Venstrom, D.** Correlations between stereochemical assessments and organoleptic analysis of odorous compounds. In T. Hayashi (Ed.), *Olfaction and taste.* Oxford: Pergamon, 1967. Pp. 3–17. [4]

Anand, B. K., and **Brobeck, J. R.** Localization of a feeding center in the hypothalamus of the rat. *Proceedings for the Society of Experimental Biological Medicine,* 1951, *77,* 323–324. [3]

———. **Chhina, G. S.,** and **Singh, B.** Some aspects of electroencephalographic studies in yogis. *Electroencephalography and Clinical Neurophysiology,* 1961, *13,* 452–456. [6]

Anastasi, A. *Psychological testing* (5th ed.). New York: Macmillan, 1982. [20]

Anders, T. F., and **Roffwarg, H. P.** The effects of selective interruption and deprivation of sleep in the human newborn. *Developmental Psychobiology,* January 1973, *6,*1, 77–89. [6]

Anderson, B. F. *The psychology experiment.* Belmont, Calif.: Brooks/Cole, 1971. [2]

Anderson, D. R., Alwitt, L. F., Lorch, E. P., and **Levin, S. R.** Watching children watch television. In G. A. Hale and M. Lewis (Eds.), *Attention and cognitive development.* New York: Plenum, 1979. Pp. 331–362. [12]

———. and **Levin, S. R.** Young children's attention to 'Sesame Street.' *Child Development,* 1976, *47,* 806–811. [12]

Anderson, J. P., Kline, P. J., and **Beasley, C. M.** A general learning theory and its application to schema abstraction. In G. H. Bower (Ed.), *The psychology of learning and motivation* (Vol. 13). New York: Academic Press, 1979. [10]

Anderson, J. R. Arguments concerning representations for mental imagery. *Psychological Review,* 1978, *85,* 249–277. [9]

———. *Cognitive psychology and its implications.* San Francisco: W. H. Freeman, 1980. [9,10,13]

———, and **Bower, G. H.** *Human associative memory.* Washington, D.C.: Winston, 1973. [9]

Andersson, B. The effect of injections of hypertonic NaCl solutions into different parts of the hypothalamus of goats. *Acta Physiologica Scandinavica*, 1953, *28*, 188–201. [16]

Andrews E. A., and **Braveman, N. S.** The combined effects of dosage level and interstimulus interval on the formation of one-trial poison-based aversions in rats. *Animal Learning and Behavior*, 1975, *3*, 287–289. [8]

Anglin, J. *Word, object, and concept development*. New York: Norton, 1977. [12]

Aries, P. *Centuries of childhood: A social history of family life*. New York: Vintage, 1962. [12]

Arkes, H. R., and **Garske, J. P.** *Psychological theories of motivation*. Monterey, Calif.: Brooks/Cole, 1977. [16]

Armstrong, B. Illinois judge upholds IQ test use: Departs from *Larry P. APA Monitor*, November 1980, 6–7. [20]

Armstrong, R. H., et al. Gastric secretion during sleep and dreaming. Paper presented at the annual meeting of the Association for the Psychophysiological Study of Sleep, March 1965. [6]

Arnold, M. B. *Emotion and personality*. New York: Columbia University Press, 1960. [15]

Aronson, E. *The social animal* (2nd ed.). San Francisco: Freeman, 1976. [25]

_____, **Blaney, N., Sikes, J., Stephan, C.,** and Snapp, M. Busing and racial tension: The jigsaw route to learning and liking. *Psychology Today*, February 1975, *9*, 43–50. [25,26]

_____, and **Linder, D. E.** Gain and loss of esteem as determinants of interpersonal attractiveness. *Journal of Experimental Psychology*, 1965, *1*, 156–172. [26]

Asarnow, R. F., Steffy, R. A., MacCrimmon, and **Cleghorn, J. M.** An attentional assessment of foster children at risk for schizophrenia. *Journal of Abnormal Psychology*, 1977, *86*, 267–275. [23]

Asch, S. E. Forming impressions of personality. *Journal of Abnormal and Social Psychology*, 1946 *41*, 258–290. [26]

_____. Effects of group pressure upon the modification and distortion of judgments. In H. Guetzkow (Ed.), *Groups, leadership, and men*. Pittsburgh: Carnegie Press, 1951. [27]

Ashmead, D. H., and **Perlmutter, M.** Infant memory in everyday life. In M. Perlmutter (Ed.), *New directions in child development* (No. 10). *Children's memory*. San Francisco: Jossey-Bass, 1980. Pp. 1–16. [12]

Athanasiou, R., Shaver, P., and **Tavris, C. A.** Sex. *Psychology Today*, July 1970, *4*, 37–52. [2]

Atkinson, J. W. (Ed.). *Motives in fantasy, action and society*. New York: Van Nostrand Reinhold, 1958a. [16]

_____. Thematic apperceptive measurement of motives within a context of motivation. In J. W. Atkinson (Ed.), *Motives in fantasy, action, and society*. New York: Van Nostrand Reinhold, 1958b [16]

Atkinson, R. C., and **Shiffrin, R. M.** Human memory: A proposed system and its control

processes. In K. W. Spence and J. T. Spence (Eds.), *The Psychology of Learning and Motivation: Advances in Research and Theory* (Vol. 2) New York: Academic Press, 1968. Pp. 80–195. [9]

Attneave, F. Some informational aspects of visual perception. *Psychological Review*, 1954, *61*, 183–193. [5]

Azrin, N. H., and **Foxx, R. B.** *Toilet training in less than a day*. New York: Simon & Schuster, 1974. [8]

Babson, S. G., Pernoll, M. L., Benda, G. I., and **Simpson, K.** *Diagnosis and management of the fetus and neonate at risk: a guide for team care* (4th ed.). St. Louis: C. V. Mosby, 1980. [11]

Back, K. W., and **Bogdanoff, M.** Plasma lipid responses to leadership, conformity, and deviation. In P. H. Leiderman and D. Shapiro (Eds.), *Psychological approaches to social behavior*. Stanford, Calif.: Stanford University Press, 1964. [21]

Baddeley, A. D. Selective attention and performance in dangerous environments. *British Journal of Psychology*, 1972, *63*, 537–546. [10]

Badia, P., Harsh, J., and **Abbott, B.** Choosing between predictable and unpredictable shock conditions: Data and theory. *Psychological Bulletin*, 1979, *86*, 1107–1131. [10]

_____, and **Runyon, R. P.** *Fundamentals of behavioral research*. Reading, Mass.: Addison-Wesley, 1982. [2]

Baer, D. M. Laboratory control of thumbsucking by withdrawal and representation of reinforcement. *Journal of the Experimental Analysis of Behavior*, 1962, *5*, 525–528. [8]

Bakan, P. The eyes have it. *Psychology Today*, April 1971, *4*, 64–67 passim. [2]

Baker, M. C., Spitler-Nabors, K. J., and **Bradley, D. C.** Early experience determines song dialect responsiveness of female sparrows. *Science*, *1981, 214*, 819–821. [7]

Baker, R. R. Goal orientation by blindfolded humans after long-distance displacement: Possible involvement of a magnetic sense. *Science*, 1980, *210*, 555–557. [4]

Ball, S., and **Bogatz, G. A.** Summative research of "Sesame Street": Implications for the study of preschool children." In A. D. Pick (Ed.), *Minnesota Symposia on Child Psychology* (Vol. 6). Minneapolis: University of Minnesota Press, 1972. Pp. 3–17. [12]

Ball, W., and **Tronick, E.** Infant responses to impending collision: Optical and real. *Science*, 1971, *171*, 818. [11]

Baltes, P. B., and **Schaie, K. W.** Aging and IQ: The myth of the twilight years. *Psychology Today*, March 1974, *7*, 35–40. [12]

Bandura, A. Influence of models' reinforcement contingencies on the acquisition of imitative responses. *Journal of Personality and Social Psychology*, 1965, *1*, 589–595. [14]

_____. *Aggression: A social-learning analysis*.

Englewood Cliffs, N.J.: Prentice-Hall, 1973. [14,27]

_____. Social learning analysis of aggression. In E. Ribes-Inesta and A. Bandura (Eds.), *Analysis of delinquency and aggression*. Hillsdale, N.J.: Erlbaum, 1976. Pp. 203–323. [27]

_____. *Social learning theory*. Englewood Cliffs, N.J.: Prentice-Hall, 1977. [8,3,14,19]

_____. Self-efficacy: Toward a unifying theory of behavioral change. *Psychological Review*, 1977, *84*, 191–215. [24]

_____. The self system in reciprocal determinism. *American Psychologist*, 1978, *33*, 344–358. [19]

_____, **Grusec, J. E.,** and *Menlove, F. L.* Vicarious extinction of avoidance behavior. *Journal of Personality and Social Psychology*, *1967, 5*, 16–23. [24]

_____, **Jeffery, R. W.,** and **Wright, C. L.** Efficacy of participant modeling as a function of response induction aids. *Journal of Abnormal Psychology*, 1974, *83*, 56–64. [24]

_____, and **Walters, R. H.** *Social learning and personality development*. New York: Holt, Rinehart & Winston, 1963. [8]

_____, and _____. *Social learning and personality development*. New York: Holt, Rinehart & Winston, 1963. [14]

Barber, T. X. Measuring 'hypnotic-like' suggestibility with and without 'hypnotic induction': Psychometric properties, norms, and variables influencing response to the Barber Suggestibility Scale (BSS). *Psychological Reports*, 1965, *16*, 809–844. [6]

_____. Responding to 'hypnotic' suggestions: An introspective report. *American Journal of Clinical Hypnosis*, 1975, *18*, 6–22. [6]

Barfield, R. A., and **Morgan, J. N.** *Early retirement: The decision and the experience*. Ann Arbor, Mich.: Institute of Social Research, University of Michigan, 1970. [14]

Barker, L. M., Best, M. R., and **Domjan, M. (Eds.).** *Learning mechanisms in food selection*. Waco, Tex.: Baylor University Press, 1977. [16]

Barker, R. G., Dembo, T., and **Lewin, K.** *Frustration and regression: an experiment with young children*. University of Iowa Studies in Child Welfare, 1941, *18*, 386. [27]

_____, and **Wright, H. F.** *Midwest and its children*. Evanston, Ill.: Row, Peterson, 1955. [20].

Barlow, H. B., Narasimhan, R., and **Rosenfeld, A.** Visual pattern analysis in machines and animals. *Science*, 1972, *177*, 251. [4]

Barltrop, D. Transfer to lead to the human foetus. In D. Barltrop (Ed.), *Mineral metabolism in pediatrics*. Oxford: Blackwell Scientific Publications, 1969. [20]

Baron, R. A., and **Bell, P. A.** Aggression and heat: The influence of ambient temperature, negative affect, and a cooling drink on physical aggression. *Journal of Personality and Social Psychology*, 1976, *33*, 245–255. [27]

Baron, R. M., Mandel, D. R., Adams, C. A., and **Griffen, L. M.** Effects of social density in university residential environments. *Journal of Personality and Social Psychology*, 1976, *34*, 434-446. [28]

Barron, F. H. Behavioral decision theory: A topical bibliography for management scientists. *Interfaces*, 1974, *5*, 56-62. [10]

Bartel, G. D. Group sex among the mid-americans. In L. G. Smith and J. R. Smith (Eds.), *Beyond monogamy*. Baltimore: Johns Hopkins University Press, 1974. Pp. 185-201. [17]

Bartlett, J. C., and **Santrock, J. W.** Affect-dependent episodic memory in young children. *Child Development*, 1979, *50*, 513-518. [9]

Bartoshuk, L. The chemical senses, I: Taste. In J. W. Kling and L. A. Riggs (Eds.), *Woodworth and Schlosberg's Experimental Psychology* (3rd ed.) New York: Holt, Rinehart & Winston, 1971. [4]

_____, **Dateo, G., Vandenbelt, D., Buttrick, R.,** and **Long, L.** Effects of *Gymnema Sylvestre* and *Synsepalum Dulficum* on taste in man. In C. Pfaffman (Ed.), *Olfaction and taste* (Vol. 3.). New York: Rockefeller University Press, 1969. [4]

Bates, E. *The emergence of symbols: cognition and communication in infancy*. New York: Academic Press, 1979. [13]

Bateson, G., Jackson, D., Haley, J., and **Weakland, J.** Toward a theory of schizophrenia. *Behavioral Science*, 1956, *1*, 251-264. [23]

Baum, A., and **Davis, G. E.** Reducing the stress of high-density living: An architectural intervention. *Journal of Personality and Social Psychology*, 1980, *38*, 471-481. [28]

_____, and **Greenberg, C. I.** Waiting for a crowd: The behavioral and perceptual effects of anticipated crowding. *Journal of Personality and Social Psychology*, 1975, *32*, 671-679. [28]

_____, **Harpin, R. E.,** and **Valins, S.** The role of group phenomena in the experience of crowding. *Environment and Behavior*, 1975, *7*, 185-197. [28]

Bayer, E. Beitrage zur Zweikomponententheorie des Hungers. *Zeitschrift fur Psychologie*, 1929, *112*, 1-54. [16, 27]

Bayley, N. On the growth of intelligence. *American Psychologist*, 1955, 10, 805-818. [12]

Beach, F. A. The descent of instinct. *Psychological Review*, 1955, *62*, 401-410. [7]

Beck, A. T. *Cognitive therapy and the emotional disorders*. New York: International Universities Press, 1976. [24]

_____, **Rush, A. J., Shaw, B. F.,** and **Emery, G.** *Cognitive theory of depression*. New York: Guilford Press, 1979. [23,24]

Beck, S. J. *Rorschach's test*. (Vol. 1.) *Basic processes* (3rd ed.). New York: Grune & Stratton, 1961. [20]

Becker, J. M. A learning analysis of the development of peer-oriented behavior in nine-month-old infants. *Developmental Psychology*, 1977, *13*, 481-491. [14]

Beit-Hallahmi, B., and **Rabin, A. I.** The kibbutz as a social experiment and a child-rearing laboratory. *American Psychologist*, 1977, *32*, 532-541. [14]

Bekesy, G. von. Current status of theories of hearing. *Science*, 1956, *123*, 779-783. [4]

Bellows, R. T. Time factors in water drinking in dogs. *American Journal of Physiology*, 1939, *125*, 87-97. [16]

Bellugi, U. Learning the language. *Psychology Today*, December 1970, *4*, 32-35 *passim*. [13]

Belsky, J., and **Most, R. K.** From exploration to play: A cross-sectional study of infant free play behavior. *Developmental Psychology*, 1981, *17*, 630-639. [14]

_____, and **Steinberg, L. D.** The effects of day care: A critical review. *Child Development*, 1978, *49*, 929-949. [14]

Bem, D. J. An experimental analysis of self-persuasion. *Journal of Experimental Social Psychology*, 1965, *1*, 199-218. [16]

_____. Self-perception: An alternative interpretation of cognitive dissonance phenomena. *Psychological Review*, 1967, *74*, 183-200. [25]

_____.Self-perception theory. In L. Berkowitz (Ed.), *Advances in experimental social psychology* (Vol. 6.). New York: Academic Press, 1972. Pp. 1-62. [26]

_____, and **Allen, A.** On predicting some of the people some of the time: The search for cross-situational consistencies in Behavior. *Psychological Review*, 1974, *81*, 506-520. [19]

Benbow, C. P., and **Stanley, J. C.** Sex differences in mathematical ability: Fact or artifact? *Science*, 1980, *210*, 1262-1264. [12]

Benderly, B. L. Dancing without music. *Science '80*, December 1980, *1*, 54-59. [13]

_____. Flashbulb memory. *Psychology Today*, June 1981, *15*, 71-74. [9]

Benson, H. *Relaxation response*. New York: Morrow, 1975. [21]

Berger, P. A. Medical treatment of mental illness. *Science*, 1978, *200*,974-981. [24]

Bergin, A. E. The evaluation of therapeutic outcomes. In A. E. Bergin and S. L. Garfield (Eds.), *Handbook of psychotherapy and behavior change: An empirical analysis*. New York: Wiley, 1971. [24]

_____, and **Lambert, M. J.** The evaluation of therapeutic outcomes. In S. L. Garfield and A. E. Bergin (Eds.), *Handbook of psychotherapy and behavior change: An empirical analysis* (2nd ed.). New York: Wiley, 1978. [24]

Berko, J. The child's learning of English morphology. *Word*, 1958, *14*, 150-177. [13]

Berkowitz, L. *Aggression: A social psychological analysis*. New York: McGraw-Hill, 1962. [27]

Berkun, M. M., Bialek, H. M., Kern, R. P., and **Yagi, K.** Experimental studies of psychological stress in man. *Psychological Monographs*, 1962, *76*,15. [10]

Berlin, B., and **Kay, P.** *Basic color terms: Their universality and evolution*. Berkeley: University of California Press, 1969. [13]

Berndt, T. J. Developmental changes in conformity to peers and parents. *Developmental Psychology*, 1979, *15*, 608-616. [14]

_____. Age changes and changes over time in prosocial intentions and behavior between friends. *Developmental Psychology*, 1981a, *17*, 408-416. [14]

_____. Effects of friendship on prosocial intentions and behavior. *Child Development*, 1981b, *52*, 636-643. [14]

Berne, E. *Games people play*. New York: Grove Press, 1964. [24]

Bernstein, I. Learned taste aversions in children receiving chemotherapy. *Science*, 1978, *200*, 1302-1303. [8]

Berntson, G. G., Hughes, H. C., and **Beattie, M. S.** A comparison of hypothalamically induced biting attack with natural predatory behavior in the cat. *Journal of Comparative and Physiological Psychology*, 1976, *90*, 167-178. [7]

Berscheid, E., Dion, K., Walster, E., and **Walster, G. M.** Physical attractiveness and dating choice: A test of the matching hypothesis. *Journal of Experimental Social Psychology*, 1971, *7*, 173-189. [25,26]

_____, and **Walster, E.** Physical attractiveness. In L. Berkowitz (Ed.), *Advances in experimental Psychology* (Vol. 7.). New York: Academic Press, 1974. [21]

Bersoff, D. N. Regarding psychologists testing: Legal regulation of psychological assessment in the public schools. *Maryland Law Review*, 1979, *39*, 27-120. [20]

Bertenthal, B. I., and **Fischer, K. W.** Development of self-recognition in the infant. *Developmental Psychology*, 1978, *14*, 44-50. [14]

Bever, T. G. The cognitive basis for linguistic structures. In J. R. Hayes (Ed.), *Cognition and the development of language*. New York: Wiley, 1970. Pp. 279-362. [13]

Bexton, W. H., Heron, W., and **Scott, T. H.** Effects of decreased variation in the sensory environment. *Canadian Journal of Psychology*, 1954, *8*, 70-76. [5,6]

Bickman, L. The social power of a uniform. *Journal of Applied Social Psychology*, 1974, *4*, 47-61. [27]

_____, **Teger, A., Gabriele, T., McLaughlin, C., Berger, M.,** and **Sunaday, E.** Dormitory density and helping behavior. *Environment and Behavior*, 1973, *5*, 465-490. [28]

Bieber, I., et al. *Homosexuality: A psychoanalytic study*. New York: Basic Books, 1962. [17]

Bijou, S. W., and **Baer, D. M.** *Child development* (Vol. 2). *Universal stage of infancy*. New York: Appleton-Century, 1965. [13]

Binet, A., and **Simon, T.** *The development of*

intelligence in children (The Binet-Simon Scale). Baltimore: Williams & Wilkins, 1916. [20]

Bingham, M. T. Beyond psychology. In *Homo sapiens auduboniensis: A tribute to Walter Van Dyke Bingham.* New York: National Audubon Society, 1953. Pp. 5–29. [10]

Birch, H. G. The role of motivation factors in insightful problem-solving. *Journal of Comparative Psychology,* 1945, *38,* 295–317. [10]

————, and **Rabinowitz, H. S.** The negative effect of previous experience on productive thinking. *Journal of Experimental Psychology,* 1951, *41,* 121–125. [10]

Birren, J. E., and **Renner, V. J.** Research on the psychology of aging: Principles and experimentation. In J. E. Birren and K. W. Schaie (Eds.), *Handbook of the Psychology of Aging.* New York: Van Nostrand Reinhold, 1977. Pp. 3–41. [12]

Blakemore, C. The baffled brain. In R. Gregory and E. H. Gombrich (Eds.), *Illusion in nature and art.* New York: Charles Scribner's Sons, 1973. Figure 27, p. 35. [5]

Blehar, M. Anxious attachment and defensive reactions associated with day care. *Child Development,* 1974, *45,* 683–692. [14]

Blest, A. D. The function of eyespot patterns in Lepidoptera. *Behavior,* 1957a, *11,* 209–256. [7]

————. The evolution of protective displays in the *Saturnioidea* and *Sphingidae* (Lepidoptera). *Behavior,* 1957b, *11,* 257–309. [7]

Bleuler, E. *Dementia Praecox or the group of schizophrenias* (1911). New York: International Universities Press, 1950. [22]

Bleuler, M. E. The long term course of schizophrenic psychoses. In L. C. Wynne, R. L. Cromwell, and S. Matthyse (Eds.), *The nature of schizophrenia: New approaches to research and treatment.* New York: Wiley, 1978. [22]

Bleuler, M. *The schizophrenic disorders.* New Haven, Conn.: Yale University Press, 1978. [23]

Bliss, J. C., et al. Optical-to-tactile image conversion for the blind. *IEEE Transaction on Man-Machine Systems,* 1970, MMS-*11,* 58–65. [4]

Bloom, B. L., Asher, S. J. and **White, S. W.** Marital disruption as a stressor: A review and analysis. *Psychological Bulletin,* 1978, *85,* 867–894. [21]

Bloom, L. M. *Language development: Form and function in emerging grammars.* Cambridge, Mass.: MIT Press, 1970. [13]

Blum, G. S. *Psychoanalytic theories of personality.* New York: McGraw-Hill, 1953. [18]

Blurton-Jones, N. Rough-and-tumble play among nursery school children. In J. Bruner, A. Jolly, and K. Sylva (Eds.), *Play.* New York: Basic Books, 1976. Pp. 352–363. [14]

————, and **Konner, M. J.** Sex differences in behaviour of London and Bushmen children. In R. P. Michael and J. H. Crook

(Eds.), *Comparative ecology and behavior of primates.* London: Academic Press, 1973. P. 689. [14]

Boals, G. F., Peterson, D. R. Farmer, L., Mann, D. F., and **Robinson, D. L.** The reliability, validity, and utility of three data modes in assessing marital relationships. *Journal of Personality Assessment,* 1982, *46,* 85–96. [20]

Bohlen, J. G., Held, J. P., and **Sanderson, M. O.** The male orgasm: Pelvic contractions measured by anal probe. *Archives of Sexual Behavior,* 1980, *9,* 503–521. [7]

Bolles, R. C. *Theory of motivation.* New York: Harper & Row, 1967. [16]

Bond, E. K. Perception of form by the human infant. *Psychological Bulletin, 1972, 77,* 225–245. [11]

Bootzin, R. R. *Behavior modification and therapy: and introduction.* Cambridge, Mass.: Winthrop Press, 1975. [24]

————, and **Acocella, J. R.** *Abnormal psychology: Current perspectives* (3rd ed.). New York: Random House, 1980. [19]

Boring, E. G. *A history of experimental psychology* (2nd ed.). New York: Appleton-Century-Crofts, 1957. [1]

————. A new ambiguous figure. *American Journal of Psychology,* 1930, *42,* 444–445. [5]

Borkovec, T. D., Grayson, J. B., and **Cooper, K. M.** Treatment of general tension: Subjective and physiological effects of progressive relaxation. *Journal of Consulting and Clinical Psychology,* 1978, *46,* 518–528. [21]

————, ————, **O'Brien, G. T.,** and **Weerts, T. C.** Relaxation treatment of pseudoinsomnia and ideiopathic Insomnia: An electroencephalographic evaluation. *Journal of Applied Behavior Analysis,* 1979, *12,* 37–54. [21]

Bornstein, M. H. "Human infant color vision and color perception" reviewed and reassessed: A critique of Werner and Wooten (1979a). *Infant Behavior and Development,* 1981, *4,* 119–150. [11]

————, **Kessen, W.,** and **Weiskopf, S.** The categories of hue in infancy. *Science,* 1976, *191,* 201–202. [11,13]

Botwinick, J. *Aging and behavior* (2nd ed.) New York: Springer, 1978. [12]

————, and **Siegler, I. C.** Intellectual ability among the elderly: Simultaneous cross-sectional and longitudinal comparisons. *Developmental Psychology,* 1980, *16,* 49–53. [12]

Bouchard, T. J. *Separated identical twins: preliminary findings.* Invited address, annual meeting of the American Psychological Association, Los Angeles, Calif., August 1981. [11]

Bouchard, T. J., Jr., and **McGue, M.** Familial studies of intelligence: A review. *Science,* 1981, *212,* 1055–1059. [20]

Bower, G. H. Mental imagery and associative learning. In L. Gregg (Ed.), *Cognition in learning and memory.* New York: Wiley, 1973. [9]

————. Improving memory. *Human Nature,* February 1978, *1,* 64–72. [9]

————. Mood and memory. *American Psychologist,* 1981, *36,* 129–148. [9]

————, **Karlin, M. B.,** and **Dueck, A.** Comprehension and memory for pictures. *Memory and Cognition,* 1975, *3,* 216–229. In J. R. Anderson, *Cognitive psychology and its implications.* San Francisco: Freeman, 1980. [9]

Bower, T. G. R. *Development in infancy.* San Francisco: Freeman, 1974. [12]

————. Repetitive processes in child development. *Scientific American,* November 1976, *235,* 38–47. [11]

————. *A primer of infant development.* San Francisco: Freeman, 1977. [14]

————, **Broughton, J.,** and **Moore, K. M.** The development of the object concept as manifested by changes in the tracking behavior of infants. *Journal of Experimental Child Psychology,* 1971, *12,* 182–193. [11]

Bowers, K. S. *Hypnosis for the seriously curious.* Monterey, Calif.: Brooks/Cole, 1976. [6]

Bowers, P. Hypnosis and creativity: The search for the missing link. *Journal of Abnormal Psychology,* 1979, *88,* 564–572. [6]

Bowlby, J. The nature of the child's tie to his mother. *International Journal of Psychoanalysis,* 1958, *39,* 350–373. [14]

————. *Attachment and loss* (Vol. 1). *Attachment.* New York: Basic Books, 1969. [14]

————. *Attachment and loss* (Vol. 2). *Separation.* New York: Basic Books, 1973. [14]

Brackbill, Y. Cumulative effects of continuous stimulation of arousal level in infants. *Child Development,* 1971, *42,* 17–26. [2]

————, **Adams, G., Crowell, D.,** and **Gray, L.** Arousal level in neonates and preschool children under continuous auditory stimulation. *Journal of Experimental Child Psychology,* 1966, *4,* 178–188. [2]

Braun, J. J. Neocortex and feeding behavior in the rat. *Journal of Comparative and Physiological Psychology,* 1975, *89,* 507–522. [3]

————, and **McIntosh, H., Jr.** Learned taste aversions induced by rotational stimulation. *Physiological Psychology,* 1973, *1,* 4, 301–304. [7]

Braver, S. L., and **Barnett, B.** Effects of modeling on cooperation in a prisoner's dilemma game. *Journal of Personality and Social Psychology,* 1976, *33,* 161–169. [27]

————, and **Rohrer, V.** Superiority of vicarious over direct experience in interpersonal conflict resolution. *Journal of Conflict Resolution,* 1978, *22,* 1. [27]

Bremner, J. G., and **Bryant, P. E.** Place versus response as the basis of spatial errors made by young infants. *Journal of Experimental Child Psychology*, 1977, *23*, 162–171. [12]

Bresler, D. E., Ellison, G., and Zamenhof, S. Learning deficits in rats with malnourished grandmothers. *Developmental Psychobiology*, 1975, *8*, 315–323. [11]

Breuer, J., and Freud, S. *Studies of hysteria*. (1937). New York: Basic Books, 1957. [18]

Brickman, P. Rational and nonrational elements in reactions to disconfirmation of performance expectations. *Journal of Experimental Social Psychology*, 1972, *8*, 112–123. [16]

Brines, M. L., and Gould, J. L. Bees have rules. *Science*, 1979, *202*, 571–573. [13]

Bringmann, W. Wundt's lab: "Humble . . . but functioning." *APA Monitor*, September/October 1979, *10*, 13. [1]

Broadhurst, P. L. The interaction of task difficulty and motivation: The Yerkes-Dodson Law revived. *Acta Psychologica*, 1959, *16*, 321–338. [19]

Bromley, D. B. Some effects of age on short-term learning and memory. *Journal of Gerontology*, 1958, *13*, 393–406. [12]

Bronfenbrenner, U. *Two worlds of childhood*. New York: Russell Sage, 1970. [14]

Bronson, W. C. *Toddlers' behaviors with agemates: Issues of interaction, cognition, and affect*. Norwood, N.J.: Ablex, 1981. [14]

Brookhart, J., and Hock, E. The effects of experimental context and experiential background on infants' behavior toward their mothers and a stranger. *Child Development*, 1976, *47*, 333–340. [14]

Brooks, L. R. Spatial and verbal components of the act of recall. *Canadian Journal of Psychology*, 1968, *22*, 349–350. [9]

Brown, A. L. The development of memory: Knowing, knowing about knowing, and knowing how to know. In H. W. Reese (Ed.), *Advances in child development and behavior* (Vol. 10). New York: Academic Press, 1975. Pp. 104–153. [12]

_____, Campione, J. C., and Barclay, C. R. Training self-checking routines for estimating test readiness: Generalization from list learning to prose recall. *Child Development*, 1979, *50*, 501–512. [12]

Brown, B. B. *New mind, new body*. New York: Harper & Row, 1974. [6]

_____. *Super mind: The ultimate energy*. New York: Harper & Row, 1980. [6]

Brown, R. *Words and things: An introduction to language*. New York: Free Press, 1958. [13]

_____. *A first language: The early stages*. Cambridge, Mass.: Harvard University Press, 1973. [13]

_____, and Bellugi, U. Three processes in the child's acquisition of syntax. *Harvard Educational Review*, 1964, *34*, 133–151. [13]

_____, Cazden, C., and Bellugi-Klima, U.

The child's grammar from I to III. In J. P. Hill (Ed.), *Minnesota Symposia on Child Development* (Vol. 2). Minneapolis: University of Minnesota Press, 1968. Pp. 28–73. [13]

_____, and Fraser, C. The acquisition of syntax. In C. N. Cofer and B. S. Musgrave (Eds.), *Verbal behavior and learning problems and processes*. New York: McGraw-Hill, 1963. Pp. 158–209. [13]

_____, and Hanlon, C. Derivational complexity and order of acquisition in child speech. In J. R. Hayes (Ed.), *Cognition and the development of language*. New York: Wiley, 1970. [13]

_____, and Kulik, J. Flashbulb memories. *Cognition*, 1977, *5*, 73–99. [9]

_____, and McNeill, D. The 'tip-of-the-tongue' phenomenon. *Journal of Verbal Learning and Verbal Behavior*, August 1966, *5*, 325–337. [9]

Brownmiller, S. *Against our will*. New York: Simon & Schuster, 1975. [17]

Brozoski, T. J., Brown, R. M., Rosvald, H. E. and Goldman, P. S. Cognitive deficit caused by regional depletion of dopamine in the prefrontal cortex of Rhesus monkey. *Science*, 1979, *205*, 929–932. [3]

Bruner, J. *Under five in Britain*. London: Grant McIntyre, 1980. [14]

Bruner, J. S. Nature and uses of immaturity. *American Psychologist*, 1972, *27*, 687–708. [14]

_____. *The social context of language acquisition*. The Witkin Memorial Lecture, presented at Educational Testing Service, Princeton, N.J., May 1980. [13]

Brunson, B. I., and Matthews, K. A. The Type A coronary-prone behavior pattern and reactions to uncontrollable stress: An analysis of performance strategies, affect, and attributions during failure. *Journal of Personality and Social Psychology*, 1981, *40*, 906–918. [1,21]

Bryan, J. H. Children's cooperation and helping behaviors. In E. M. Hetherington (Ed.), *Review of child development research* (Vol. 5). Chicago: University of Chicago Press, 1975. Pp. 127–182. [14]

Buck, R., and Duffy, R. Nonverbal communication of affect in brain-damaged patients. *Cortex*, 1980. [15]

Budzynski, T. Biofeedback and the twilight states of consciousness. In D. Goleman and R. J. Davidson (Eds.), *Consciousness: Brain, States of Awareness, and Mysticism*. New York: Harper & Row, 1979. Pp. 161–165. [6]

Burgess, A. W., and Holstrom, C. L. *Rape: Victims of crisis*. Bowie, Md.: R. J. Brady, 1974. [17]

Burt, C. The genetic determination of differences in intelligence: A study of monozygotic twins reared together and apart. *British Journal of Psychology*, 1966,

57, 137–153. [20]

_____. Inheritance of general intelligence. *American Psychologist*, 1972, *27*, 174–190. [20]

Buss, A. H., Plomin, R., and Willerman, L. The inheritance of temperament. *Journal of Personality*, 1973, *41*, 513–524. [14]

Butcher, J. N., and Owen, P. L. Objective personality inventories: Recent research and some contemporary issues. In B. B. Wolman (Ed.), *Clinical diagnosis of mental disorders: A handbook*. New York: Plenum Press, 1978. [20]

Butler, R. A. Curiosity in monkeys. *Scientific American*, February 1954, *190*, 70–75. [16]

Butterfield, E. C., and Siperstein, G. N. Influence of contingent auditory stimulation upon non-nutritional suckle. In *Proceedings of the Third Symposium on Oral Sensation and Perception: The Mouth of the Infant*. Springfield, Ill.: Thomas, 1974. [13]

Bvotzin, R. Insomnia. *Arts and Sciences*, Northwestern University, Spring 1981, 2–6. [6]

Byrne, D., and Byrne, L. A. (Eds.). *Exploring human sexuality*. New York: Crowell, 1978. [17]

_____, and Lambreth, J. The effects of erotic stimuli on sex arousal, evaluative responses, and subsequent behavior. Technical report of the commission on obscenity and pornography (Vol. 8). Washington, D.C.: U.S. Government Printing Office, 1971. [17]

Campbell, B. A., Misanin, J. P., White, B. C., and Lytle, L. D. Species differences in ontogeny of memory: Support for neural maturation as a determinant of forgetting. *Journal of Comparative and Physiological Psychology*, 1974, *87*, 193–202. [12]

Campos, J. J. Heart rate: A sensitive tool for the study of infant emotional expression. In L. P. Lipsitt (Ed.), *Developmental psychobiology: The significance of infancy*. New York: Halstead Press, 1976. [2]

_____, Hiatt, S., Ramsay, D. Henderson, C., and Svejda, M. The emergence of fear on the visual cliff. In M. Lewis and L. Rosenblum (Eds.), *The origins of affect*. New York: Plenum, 1978. [11]

Cannon, M. S. The halfway house as an alternative to hospitalization. In J. Zusman and E. Bertsch (Eds.), *The future role of the state hospital*. Lexington, Mass.: Lexington Books, 1975. [24]

Cannon, W. B. The James-Lange theory of emotions: A critical examination and an alternative theory. *American Journal of Psychology*, 1927, *39*, 106–124. [15]

_____. Organization for physiological homeostatics. *Physiological Reviews*, 1929, *9*, 280–289. [16]

_____. "Voodoo" Death. *American Anthropologist*, 1942, *44*, 169–181. [3]

Cantor, N., and Kihlstrom, J. F. (Eds.). *Personality, cognition, and social interaction*.

Hillsdale, N.J.: Erlbaum, 1981. [19]

Carlson, N. R. *Physiology of behavior* (2nd ed.). Boston: Allyn & Bacon, 1980. [3]

Carmichael, L., Hogan, H. P., and **Walter, A. A.** An experimental study of the effect of language on the reproduction of visually perceived form. *Journal of Experimental Psychology,* 1932, *15,* 73-86. [9,13]

Carrier, J. K., Jr. and **Peak, T.** *NON-SLIP: Non speech language imitation program.* Lawrence, Kansas: H. & H. Enterprises, 1975. [2]

Casswell, S., and **Marks, D. F.** Cannabis and temporal disintegration in experienced and naive subjects. *Science,* 1978, *179,* 803-805. [6]

Cattell, R. B. *The scientific analysis of personality.* Baltimore: Penguin, 1965. [19]

Cautela, J. R. Treatment of compulsive behavior by covert sensitization. *Psychological Record,* 1966, *16,* 33-41. [24]

———. Covert sensitization. *Psychological Reports,* 1967, *20,* 459-468. [24]

Cermak, L. S., and **Craik, F. I. M.** (Eds.). *Levels of processing in human memory.* Hillsdale, N.J.: Erlbaum, 1979. [9]

Chauvin, R. *Animal societies.* New York: Hill and Wang, 1968. P. 63. [26]

Chaves, J. F., and **Barber, T. X.** Hypnotism and surgical pain. In D. I. Mostofsky (Ed.), *Behavior control and modification of physiological activity.* Englewood Cliffs, N.J.: Prentice-Hall, 1976, 443-465. [21]

Cherry, E. C. Some experiments on the recognition of speech with one and two ears. *Journal of the Acoustical Society of America,* 1953, *25,* 975-979. [9]

Chi, M. T. H. Short-term memory limitations in children: Capacity or processing deficits? *Memory and Cognition,* 1976, *4,* 559-572. [12]

———. Knowledge structures and memory development. In R. S. Siegler (Ed.), *Children's thinking: What develops?* Hillsdale, N.J.: Erlbaum, 1978. Pp. 73-96. [12]

Chomsky, N. *Language and mind.* New York: Harcourt Brace Jovanovich, 1972. [13]

———. *Reflections on language.* New York: Pantheon, 1975. [13]

———. On the biological basis of language capacities. In G. A. Miller and E. Lenneberg (Eds.), *Psychology and biology of language and thought.* New York: Academic Press, 1978. Pp. 199-220. [13]

———. *Language and responsibility.* New York: Pantheon, 1979. [13]

Chorover, S. L. *From genesis to genocide: The meaning of human nature and the power of behavior control.* Cambridge, Mass.: MIT Press, 1979. [3]

Cialdini, R. B., and **Kenrick, D. T.** Altruism as hedonism: A social developmental perspective on the relationship of negative mood state and helping. *Journal of Personality and Social Psychology,* 1976, *34,* 907-914. [27]

Clark, E. V. What's in a word? On the child's

acquisition of semantics in his first language. In T. E. Moore (Ed.), *Cognitive development and the acquisition of language.* New York: Academic Press, 1973. Pp. 65-110. [13]

Clark, H. H., and **Clark, E. V.** *Psychology and language: An introduction to psycholinguistics.* New York: Harcourt Brace Jovanovich, 1977. [13]

———, and **Haviland, S. E.** Comprehension and the given-new contract. In R. O. Freedle (Ed.), *Discourse production and comprehension.* Norwood, N.J.: Ablex, 1977. Pp. 1-40. [13]

Clarke, A. M., and **Clarke, A. D. B.** *Early experience: Myth and evidence.* New York: The Free Press, 1979. [11,14]

Clifford, M., and **Walster, E.** The effect of physical attractiveness on teacher expectations. *Sociology of Education,* 1973, *46,* 248-258. [26]

Cobb, S., and **Rose, R.** Hypertension, peptic ulcers, and diabetes in air traffic controllers. *Journal of the American Medical Association,* April 23, 1973. [21]

Cohen D. B. Remembering and forgetting dreaming. In J. F. Kihlstrom and F. J. Evans (Eds.), *Functional Disorders of Memory.* Hillsdale, N.J.: Erlbaum, 1979. Pp. 239-274. [6]

Cohen, G. Language comprehension in old age. *Cognitive Psychology,* 1979, *11,* 412-429. [12]

Cohen, L. B., DeLoache, J. S., and **Strauss, M. S.** Infant visual perception. In J. D. Osofsky (Ed.), *Handbook of infant development.* New York: Wiley-Interscience, 1979, Pp. 393-438. [11]

Coleman, J. C., Butcher, J. N., and **Carson, R. C.** *Abnormal psychology and modern life* (6th ed.). Glenview, Ill.: Scott Foresman, 1980. [21]

Combs, B. J., Hales, D. R., and **Williams, B. K.** *An invitation to health: Your personal responsibility.* Menlo Park, Calif.: Benjamin/Cummings, 1980. [6]

Commission on Obscenity and Pornography. *Report.* Washington, D.C.: U.S. Government Printing Office, 1970. [17]

Condry, J. C., and **Dyer, S. L.** Fear of success: Attribution of cause to the victim. *Journal of Social Issues,* 1976, *32,*3, 63-83. [16]

Connell, D. B., Layzer, J. I., and **Goodson, D. B.** National study of day care centers for infants: Findings and implications. Paper presented at the annual meeting of the American Psychological Association, New York, September 1979. [14]

Connor, J. Olfactory control of aggressive and sexual behavior in the mouse (Mus musclus L.). *Psychonomic Science,* 1972, *27,* 1-3. [17]

Conrad, R. *The deaf schoolchild: Language and cognitive function.* London: Harper & Row, 1979. [13]

Cook, S. W. A comment on the ethical issues involved in West, Gunn and Chernicky's

"Ubiquitous Watergate: An attributional analysis." *Journal of Personality and Social Psychology,* 1975, *32,* 66-68. [2]

Cooley, C. H. *Human nature and the social order.* New York: Scribners, 1912. [11]

Cooper, C. The house as a symbol of self. In J. Lang et al. (Eds.), *Architecture and human behavior.* Stroudberg, Penn.: Dowden, Hutchinson & Ross, 1974. [28]

Coren, S., Porac, C., and **Ward, L. M.** *Sensation and perception.* New York: Academic Press, 1979. Pp. 65, 71. [4]

Cornwall, A. C. Development of language, abstraction, and numerical concept formation in Down's syndrome children. *American Journal of Mental Deficiency,* 1974, *79,* 179-190. [11]

Costanza, P. R., and **Shaw, M. E.** Conformity as function of age level. *Child Development,* 1966, *37,* 967-975. [14]

Cottrell, N. B. Social facilitation. In C. G. McClintock (Ed.), *Experimental social psychology.* New York: Holt, Rinehart & Winston, 1972. [27]

Coulter, X., Collier, A. C., and **Campbell, B. A.** Long-term retention of early Pavlovian fear conditioning in infant rats. *Journal of Experimental Psychology: Animal Behavior Processes,* 1976, *2,* 48-56. [12]

Cowen, E. L., Pederson, A, Babijian, H., Izzo, L. D., and **Trost, M. A.** Long-term follow-up of early detected vulnerable children. *Journal of Consulting and Clinical Psychology,* 1973, *41,* 438-446. [14]

Coyne, J.C., and **Lazarus, R. S.** Cognitive style, stress perception, and coping. In I. L. Kutash and L. B. Schlesinger (Eds.), *Handbook on stress and anxiety.* San Francisco: Jossey-Bass, 1980. [20]

Craighead, L. W., Stunkard, A. J., and **O'Brien, R. M.** Behavior therapy and pharmacotherapy for obesity. *Archives of General Psychiatry,* 1981, *38,* 763-768. [24]

Craik, F. I. M., and **Lockhart, R. S.** Levels of processing: A framework for memory research. *Journal of Verbal Learning and Verbal Behavior,* 1972, *11,* 671-684. [9]

Creese, I., Burt, D. R., and **Snyder, S. H.** Brain's dopamine receptor—Labeling with [dopamine—H-3] and [H21 operidol—H3]. *Psychopharmacology Communications,* 1975, *1,* 663-673. [23]

Crook, T. and **Eliot, J.** Parental death during childhood and adult depression: A critical review of the literature. *Psychological Bulletin,* 1980, *87,* 252-259. [18]

Cross, H., Holcomb, A., and **Matter, C. G.** Imprinting or exposure learning in rats given early auditory stimulation. *Psychonomic Science,* 1967, *7,* 233-234. [25]

Crowe, S. J., Guild, S. R., and **Polvogt, L. M.** Observations on the pathology of high-tone deafness. *Bulletin of John Hopkins Hospital,* 1934, *54,* 315-379. [4]

Curtiss, S. R. *Genie: A psycholinguistic study*

of a modern-day 'wild child.' New York: Academic Press, 1977. [2, 13]

Dabbs, J. M., Jr., and **Leventhal, H.** Effects of varying the recommendations in a fear-arousing communication. *Journal of Personality and Social Psychology,* 1966, *4,* 525-531. [25]

Damon, W. Early conceptions of positive justice as related to the development of logical operations. *Child Development,* 1975, *46,* 301-312. [14]

Daniel, R. S. *Notes for a course in professional problems.* Unpublished manuscript, 1975. [1]

Darley, C. F. Tinklenberg, J. R., Roth, W. T., Hollister, L. E., and **Atkinson, R. C.** Influence of marihuana on storage and retrieval processes in memory. *Memory and Cognition,* April 1973, *1, 2,* 196-200. [6]

Darley, J. M., and **Latane, B.** When will people help? *Psychology Today,* 1968, *2,* 54. [27]

_____, and _____. Bystander intervention in emergencies: Diffusion of responsibility. *Journal of Personality and Social Psychology,* 1968, *8,* 377-383. [28]

_____, **Teger, A. I.,** and **Lewis, L. D.** Do groups always inhibit individuals' responses to potential emergencies? *Journal of Personality and Social Psychology,* 1973, *26,* 295-399. [27]

Darwin, C. *On the origin of the species by means of natural selection.* (1859). Cambridge, Mass.: Harvard University Press, 1964. [7]

_____. *The expression of the emotions in man and animals* (1872). Chicago: University of Chicago Press, 1967. [7, 15]

_____. *The expression of the emotions in man and animals* (1872). New York: The Philosophical Library, 1955. [11]

Darwin, C. J., Turvey, M. T., and **Crowder, R. G.** An auditory analogue of the Sperling partial-report procedure: Evidence for brief auditory storage. *Cognitive Psychology,* 1972, *3,* 255-267. [9]

Dashiell, J. F. An experimental analysis of some group effects. *Journal of Abnormal and Social Psychology,* 1930, *25,* 190-199. [27]

Davenport, W. Sexual patterns and their regulation in a society of the southwest pacific. In F. A. Beach (Ed.), *Sex and Behavior.* New York: Wiley, 1965. [17]

Davidson, R. J., and **Schwartz, G. E.** The psychobiology of relaxation and related states: A multi-process theory. In D. I. Mostofsky (Ed.), *Behavior control and modification of physiological activity.* Englewood Cliffs, N.J.: Prentice-Hall, 1976. [21]

Davies, I. K. Algorithms. *Psychology Today,* April 1970, *3,* 53-55 *passim.* [10]

Davis, J. M. Dopamine theory of schizophrenia: A two-factor theory. In L. C. Wynne, R. L. Cromwell, and S. Matthysse (Eds.), *The nature of schizophrenia: New*

approaches to research and treatment. New York: Wiley, 1978. [23]

Davis, P. G., McEwen, B. S., and **Pfaff, D. W.** Localized behavioral effects of titrated estradiol implants in the ventromedial hypothalamus of female rats. *Endocrinology,* 1979, *104,* 898-903. [3]

Davison, G. C. Homosexuality: The ethical challenge. *Journal of Consulting and Clinical Psychology,* 1976, *44,* 157-162. [17]

Davitz, J. R. *The language of emotion.* New York: Academic Press, 1969. [15]

Dawes, R. M., McTavish, J., and **Shaklee, H.** Behavior, communication, and assumptions about other people's behavior in a common dilemma situation. *Journal of Personality and Social Psychology,* 1977, *35,* 1-11. [27]

Dawkins, R. *The selfish gene.* New York: Oxford University Press, 1975. [7, 27]

Deaux, E. Thirst satiation and the temperature of ingested water. *Science,* 1973, *181,* 1166-1167. [16]

DeBacher, G. Biofeedback in spasticity control. In J. V. Basmajian (Ed.), *Biofeedback—Principles and practices for clinicians.* Baltimore: Williams & Wilkins, 1979. [21]

De Carlo, T. J. Recreational participation patterns and successful aging: A twin study. Doctoral dissertation, Columbia University, 1971. [12]

Decasper, A. J., and **Carstens, A. A.** Contingencies of stimulation: Effects on learning and emotion in neonates. *Infant Behavior and Development,* 1981, *4,* 1-17. [12]

DeCharms, R. *Personal causation: The internal affective determinants of behavior.* New York: Academic Press, 1968. [16]

Deci, E. L. *Intrinsic motivation.* New York: Plenum, 1975. [16]

DeFaire, U. Life change patterns prior to death in ischaemic heart disease: A study on death-discordant twins. *Journal of Psychosomatic Research,* 1975, *19,* 273-278. [21]

Deich, R. F. and **Hodges, P. M.** *Language without speech.* New York: Brunner/Mazel, 1977. [2]

DeLoache, J. S. Naturalistic study of memory for object location in very young children. In M. Perlmutter (Ed.), *New directions in child development.* (No. 10). *Children's memory.* San Francisco: Jossey-Bass, 1980. pp. 17-32. [12]

DeLora, J. S., and **Warren, C. A.** *Understanding sexual interaction.* Boston: Houghton Mifflin, 1977. [17]

Dement, W. C. *Some must watch while some must sleep.* San Francisco: Freeman, 1974. [6]

_____. Two kinds of sleep. In D. Goleman and R. J. Davisdon (Eds.), *Consciousness: Brain, states of awareness, and mysticism.* New York: Harper & Row, 1979. pp. 72-75. [6]

_____, and **Wolpert, E. A.** The relation of eye movements, body mobility, and external

stimuli to dream content. *Journal of Experimental Psychology,* 1958, *55,* 543-553. [6]

Democrat and **Chronicle.** Hinckley ill, took assassins' traits, psychiatrist says. *Democrat and Chronicle,* Rochester, N. Y., May 15, 1982, 5-a. [22]

Dennenberg, V. H., Hudgens, G. A., and **Zarrow, M. X.** Mice reared with rats: Modification of behavior by early experience with another species. *Science,* 1964, *143,* 380-381. [7]

Dennis, M., and **Whitaker, H. A.** Language acquisition following hemidecortication: Linguistic superiority of the left over the right hemisphere. *Brain and Language,* 1976, *3,* 404-433. [13]

Dennis, W. *Children of the creche.* New York: Appleton-Century-Crofts, 1973. [20]

_____, and **Dennis, M. G.** The effect of cradling practices upon the onset of walking in Hopi children. *Journal of Genetic Psychology,* 1940, *56,* 77-86. [11]

_____, and **Sayegh, J.** The effect of supplementary experiences upon the behavioral development of infants in institutions. *Child Development,* 1965, *36,* 81-90. [11]

Derlega, V. J., and **Chaikin, A. L.** Privacy and self-disclosure in social relationships. *Journal of Social Issues,* 1977, *33,* 102-115. [28]

Deutsch, A. *The mentally ill in America* (2nd ed.). New York: Columbia University Press, 1949. [23]

Deutsch, M., and **Gerard, H. B.** A study of normative and informational influences on social judgment. *Journal of Abnormal and Social Psychology,* 1955, *51,* 629-636. [27]

_____, and **Krauss, R. M.** The effect of threat upon interpersonal bargaining. *Journal of Abnormal and Social Psychology,* 1960, *61,* 181-189. [27]

DeValois, R. L. Analysis and coding of color vision in the primate visual system. *Cold Spring Harbor Symposia on Quantitative Biology,* 1965, *30,* 567-579. [4]

Diaconis, P. Statistical problems in ESP research. *Science,* 1978, *201,* 131-136. [6]

Diamond, M. Sexual identity, monozygotic twins reared in discordant sex roles and a BBC follow-up. *Archives of Sexual Behavior* (in press). [17]

Diamond, S. Pigeon pilots. *Learning,* November 1979, 37. [8]

Dichter, E. *Handbook of consumer motivations.* New York: McGraw-Hill, 1964. [25]

Dion, K. Physical attractiveness and evaluations of children's transgressions. *Journal of Personality and Social Psychology,* 1972, *24,* 207-213. [26]

_____. Young children's stereotyping of facial attractiveness. *Developmental Psychology,* 1973, *9,* 183-188. [26]

_____, **Berscheid, E.,** and **Walster, E.** What is beautiful is good. *Journal of Personality and Social Psychology,* 1972, *34,* 285-290. [26]

DiPietro, J. A. Rough-and-tumble play: A

function of gender. *Developmental Psychology*, 1981, *17*, 50–58. [14]

DiVesta, F. J. *Language, learning, and cognitive processes*. Monterey, Calif.: Brooks/Cole, 1974. [8]

Doane, J., West, K., Goldstein, M. J., Rodnick, E., and Jones, J. Parental communication deviance and affective style as predictors of subsequent schizophrenia spectrum disorders in vulnerable adolescents. *Archives of General Psychiatry*, 1981, *38*, 679–685. [23]

Dodd, D. H., and White, R. M., Jr. *Cognition: Mental structures and processes*. Boston: Allyn & Bacon, 1980. [10, 13]

Dollard, J., Doob, L. W., Miller, N. E., Mowrer, O. H., and Sears, R. R. *Frustration and aggression*. New Haven, Conn.: Yale University Press, 1939. [19]

———, and Miller, N. E. *Personality and psychotherapy: An analysis in terms of learning, thinking, and culture*. New York: McGraw-Hill, 1950. [19]

Donaldson, M. *Children's minds*. New York: Norton, 1979. [12]

Donnerstein, E. Aggressive erotica and violence against women. *Journal of Personality and Social Psychology*, 1980, *39*, 269–277. [17]

———, and Wilson, D. W. Effects of noise and perceived control on ongoing and subsequent aggressive behavior. *Journal of Personality and Social Psychology*, 1976, *34*, 744–781. [27]

Dornbush, R. L. The long-term effects of Cannabis use. In L. L. Miller (Ed.), *Marijuana: Effects on human behavior*. New York: Academic Press, 1974. pp. 221–232. [6]

Dornbusch, S. M., Carlsmith, J. M., Gross, R. T., Martin, J. A., Jennings, D., Rosenberg, A., and Drake, P. Sexual development, age, and dating: A comparison of biological and social influences upon one set of behaviors. *Child Development*, 1981, *52*, 179–185. [14]

Dosey, M. A., and Meisels, M. Personal space and self-protection. *Journal of Personality and Social Psychology*, 1969, *11*, 93–97. [28]

Draguns, J. G. Psychological disorders of clinical severity. In H. C. Triandis and J. G. Draguns (Eds.), *Handbook of cross-cultural psychology* (Vol. 6). *Psychopathology*. Boston: Allyn & Bacon, 1980. [22]

DuBois, Philip H. Review of the Scholastic Aptitude Test. In Oscar K. Buros (Ed.), *The seventh mental measurements yearbook*. Highland Park, N.J.: Gryphon Press, 1972. pp. 646–648. [20]

Duck, S. W., and Craig, G. Personality similarity and the development of friendship: A longitudinal study. *British Journal of Social and Clinical Psychology*, 1978, *17*, 237–242. [14, 16]

Duffy, E. *Activation and behavior*. New York: Wiley, 1962. [19]

Duncan, S., Jr. Nonverbal communication. *Psychological Bulletin*, 1969, *72*, 118–137. [15]

Duncker, K. On problem solving (1935). L. S. Lees (Trans.). *Psychological Monographs*, 1945, *58*, Whole No. 270. [10]

Dutton, D., and Aron, A. Some evidence for heightened sexual attraction under conditions of high anxiety. *Journal of Personality and Social Psychology*, 1974, *30*, 510–517. [26]

Dworkin, R. H., Burke, B. W., Maher, B. A., and Gottesman, I. I. A longitudinal study of the genetics of personality. *Journal of Personality and Social Psychology*, 1976, *34*, 510–518. [14]

Dykes, M., and McGhie, A. A comparative study of attentional strategies of schizophrenic and highly creative normal subjects. *British Journal of Psychiatry*, 1976, *128*, 50–56. [10]

Ebbinghaus, H. *Memory: A contribution to experimental psychology* (1885). H. A. Roper and C. E. Bussenius (Trans.). New York: Teachers College, Columbia University, 1913. [9]

Eccles, J. C., Ito, M., and Szentagotnaik, J. *The cerebellum as a neuronal machine*. New York: Springer, 1976. [3]

Eckerman, C. O., and Rheingold, H. L. Infants' exploratory responses to toys and people. *Developmental Psychology*, 1974, *10*, 255–259. [14]

Edney, J. J. Human territoriality. *Psychological Bulletin*, 1974, *81*, 959–975. [7, 28]

Educational Broadcasting Company. Depression: The shadowed valley. From the series *The thin edge*. Educational Broadcasting Corporation, 1975. [22]

Efran, M. G., and Cheyne, J. A. Affective concomitants of the invasion of shared space: Behavioral, physiological, and verbal indicators. *Journal of Personality and Social Psychology*, 1974, *29*, 219–226. [28]

Ehrenwald, J. Parapsychology and the seven dragons: A neuropsychiatric model of Psi phenomena. In G. R. Schmeidler (Ed.), *Parapsychology: Its relation to physics, biology, psychology, and psychiatry*. Metuchen, N.J.: Scarecrow Press, 1976. pp. 246–263. [6]

Ehrhardt, A. A., Grisanti, G., and McCauley, E. A. Female-to-male transsexuals compared to lesbians: Behavioral patterns of childhood and adolescent development. *Archives of Sexual Behavior*, 1979, *8*, 481–490. [17]

Ehrlich, D., Guttman, I., Schonbach, P. and Mills, J. Postdecision exposure to relevant information. *Journal of Abnormal and Social Psychology*, 1957, *54*, 98–102. [16]

Ehrlich, P. R., and Ehrlich, A. H. What happened to the population bomb? *Human Nature*, January 1979, *2*, 88–92. [27]

Eich, J. E., Weingartner, H., Stillman, R. C., and Gillin, J. C. State-dependent accessibility of retrieval clues in the retention of a categorized list. *Journal of Verbal Learning and Verbal Behavior* 1975, *14*, 408–417. [9]

Eimas, P. D. Speech perception in early infancy. In L. B. Cohen and P. Salapatek (Eds.), *Infant perception: From sensation to cognition* (Vol. 2) *Perception of space, speech, and sound*. New York: Academic Press, 1975. Pp. 193–231. [11]

———, Siqueland, E. R., Jusczyk, P., and Virogito, J. Speech perception in infants. *Science*, 1971 *171*, 303–306. [11]

———, and Tartter, V. C. On the development of speech perception: Mechanisms and analogies. In H. W. Reese and L. P. Lipsitt (Eds.), *Advances in child development and behavior*. (Vol. 13). New York: Academic Press, 1979. Pp. 155–193. [2,13]

Einhorn and Hogarth. *Uncertainty and causality in practical inference*. Lecture Syllabus, April 1981. [10]

Ekman, P. Universals and cultural differences in facial expression of emotion. In J. K. Cole (Ed.), *Nebraska Symposium on Motivation*. Lincoln: University of Nebraska Press, 1972. Pp. 207–283. [15]

———. *The face of man: Expressions of universal emotions in a New Guinea village*. New York: Garland STPM Press, 1980. [15]

———, and Friesen, W. V. Constants across culture in the face and emotion. *Journal of Personality and Social Psychology*, 1971, *17*, 124–129. [15]

———, and ———, *Unmasking the face: A guide to recognizing emotions from facial expressions*. Englewood Cliffs, N.J.: Prentice-Hall/Spectrum, 1975. [15]

———, ———, and Ellsworth, P. *Emotion in the human face: Guidelines for research and an integration of findings*. Elmsford, N.Y.: Pergamon, 1972. [15]

Eleftheriou, B. E., Bailley, D. V., and Denenberg, V. H. Genetic analysis of fighting behavior in mice. *Physiology and Behavior*, 1974, *13*, 773–777. [27]

Ellis, A. *Reason and emotion in psychotherapy*. Secaucus, N.J.: Lyle Stuart, 1962. [24]

Ellis, H. C. *Fundamentals of human learning, memory, and cognition* (2nd ed.). Dubuque, Iowa: Wm. C. Brown, 1978. [8]

Elms, A. C. *Social psychology and social relevance*. Boston: Little-Brown, 1972. [5]

Engel, G. Emotional stress and sudden death. *Psychology Today*, November 1977, *11*, 114–118. *passim*. [21]

Epstein, A. N. Water intake without the act of drinking. *Science*, 1960, *131*, 497–498. [16]

Epstein, S. M. Toward a unified theory of anxiety. In B. A. Maher (Ed.), *Progress in experimental personality research* (Vol. 4). New York: Academic Press, 1967. [16]

Epstein, S. The stability of behavior: I. On predicting most of the people much of the time. *Journal of Personality and Social Psychology*, 1979, *37*, 1097–1126. [19]

_____. The stability of behavior. II. Implications for psychological research. *American Psychologist*, 1980, *35*, 790-806. [19]

Erhardt, A. A., and Meyer-Bahlburg, H. F. L. Effects of prenatal sex hormones on gender-related behavior. *Science*, 1981, *211*, 1312-1318. [14,17]

Ericsson, K. A., Chase, W. G., and Faloon, S. Acquisition of a memory Skill, *Science*, 1980, *208*, 1181-1182. [9]

Erikson, E. H. *Childhood and society*. New York: Norton, 1950. [18]

_____. *Childhood and society* (2nd ed.). New York: Norton, 1963. [14]

_____. *Young man Luther: A study in psychoanalysis and history*. New York: Norton, 1968. [18]

_____. *Gandhi's truth: On the origins of militant nonviolence*. New York: Norton, 1969. [18]

Eron, L. D., Huesmann, L. R., Lefkowitz, M. M., and Walden, L. O. Does television cause aggression? *American Psychologist*, 1972, *27*, 253-263. [14]

Ervin-Tripps. Is second language learning like the first? *TESOL Quarterly*, 1974, *8*, 111-127. [13]

Etzioni, A. Doctors know more than they're telling you about genetic effects. *Psychology Today*, November 1973, *7*, 26-36 *passim*. [11]

Evans, E. F. Neural processes for the detection of acoustic patterns and for sound localization. In F. O. Schmitt and F. G. Worden (Eds.), *The Neurosciences, third study program*. Cambridge, Mass.: MIT Press, 1974. Pp. 133-146. [4]

Evans, G. W., and Howard, R. B. Personal space. *Psychological Bulletin*, 1973, *80*, 334-344. [28]

Eysenck, H. J. The effects of psychotherapy: An evaluation. *Journal of Consulting Psychology*, 1952, *16*, 319-324. [24]

_____. *The effects of psychotherapy*. New York: International Science Press, 1966. [24]

_____. New ways in psychotherapy. *Psychology Today*, June 1967, *1*, 39-47. [24]

_____. *The structure of human personality*. London: Methuen, 1970. [19]

Fagot, B. I. Consequences of moderate cross-gender behavior in children. *Child Development*, 1977, *48*, 902-907. [14]

_____. The influence of sex of child on parental reactions to toddler children. *Child Development*, 1978, *49*, 459-465. [14]

Fantz, R. L. The origin of form perception. *Scientific American*, May 1961, *204*, 66-72. [11]

Fechner, G. T. *Elemente der Psychophysik*. Leipzig: Breitkopf un Hartel, 1860. [4]

Fehr, F. S., and Stern, J. A. Peripheral physiological variables and emotion: The James-Lange theory revisited. *Psychological Bulletin*, 1970, *74*, 411-424. [15]

Feldman, S. S., Beringen, Z. C., and Nash, S. C. Fluctuations of sex-related self-attributions as a function of state of family life cycle. *Developmental Psychology*, 1981, *17*, 24-35. [14]

Ferchmin, P. A., Bennett, E. L. and Rosenzweig, M. R. Direct contact with enriched environment is required to alter cerebral weight in rats. *Journal of Comparative and Physiological Psychology*, 1975, *88*, 360-367. [11]

Ferguson, C. A. Baby talk as a simplified register. In C. E. Snow and C. A. Ferguson (Eds.), *Talking to children: Language input and acquisition*. New York: Cambridge University Press, 1977. Pp. 219-236. [13]

Feshbach, S. The function of aggression and the regulation of aggressive drive. *Psychological Review*, 1964, *71*, 257-272. [14]

_____, and Singer, R. D. *Television and aggression*. San Francisco: Jossey-Bass, 1971. [14]

Festinger, L. *A theory of cognitive dissonance*. Stanford, Calif.: Stanford University Press, 1957. [16]

_____, and Carlsmith, J. M. Cognitive consequences of forced compliance. *Journal of Abnormal and Social Psychology*, 1959, *58*, 203-210. [16,25]

_____, Riecken, H. W., Jr., and Schachter, S. *When prophecy fails*. Minneapolis: University of Minnesota Press, 1956. [2]

Field, J., Muir, D., Pilon, R., Sinclair, M., and Dodwell, P. Infants' orientation to lateral sounds from birth to three months. *Child development*, 1980, *51*, 295-298. [11]

Finkelstein, M. M. Traffic in sex-oriented materials, part I: Adult bookstores in Boston, Massachusetts. In *Technical reports of the Commission on Obscenity and Pornography* (Vol. 4). Washington, D. C.: U. S. Government Printing Office, 1970. [17]

Fischer, R. A cartography of the ecstatic and meditative states. *Science*, 1971, *174*, 898. Copyright © 1971 by the American Association for the Advancement of Science. [6]

Fischoff, B. Perceived informativeness on facts." *Journal of Experimental Psychology: Human Perception and Performance*, 1977, *3*, 349-358. [10]

Fishbein, H. D. *Evolution, development, and children's learning*. Santa Monica, Calif.: Goodyear, 1976. [3]

Fishbein, M., and Ajzen, I. *Belief, attitude, intention and behavior: An introduction to theory and research*. Reading, Mass.: Addison-Wesley, 1975. [25]

Fisher, S., and Greenberg, R. P. *The scientific credibility of Freud's theories and therapy*. New York: Basic Books, 1977. [14,18]

Fiske, E. B. An issue that won't go away. *The New York Times Magazine*, March 27, 1977, 58. [20]

Fitzsimons, J. T. Drinking by rats depleted of body fluid without increase in osmotic pressure. *Journal of Physiology*, 1961, *159*, 297-309. [16]

_____. The role of renal thirst in drinking induced by extracellular stimuli. *Journal of Physiology*, 1969, *201*, 349-368. [16]

Fixx, J. *The complete book of running*. New York: Random House, 1977. [21]

Flavell, J. H. *Cognitive development*. Englewood Cliffs, N.J.: Prentice-Hall, 1977. [12]

_____, Shipstead, S. G., and Croft, K. Young children's knowledge about visual perception: Hiding objects from others. *Child Development*, 1978, *49*, 1208-1211. [12]

Fleming, D. Attitude: The history of a concept. In D. Fleming and B. Bailyn (Eds.), *Perspectives in american history*. Cambridge, Mass.: Harvard University Press, 1967. [25]

Flynn, J. P., Vanegas, H., Foote, W., and Edwards, S. Neural mechanisms involved in a cat's attack on a rat. In R. E. Whalen et al. (Eds.), *Neural control of behavior*. New York: Academic Press, 1970. Pp. 135-173. [7,15]

Fodor, J. A. Some reflections on L. S. Vygotsky's *Thought and Language*. *Cognition*, 1972, *1*, 83-95. [12]

Ford, C. S., and Beach, F. A. *Pattern of sexual behavior*. New York: Harper & Row, 1951. [17]

Foulkes, D. Theories of dream formation and recent studies of sleep consciousness. *Psychological Bulletin*, 1964, *62*, 236-247. [6]

Fowler, C. A., Wolford, G., Slade, R., and Tassinary, L. Lexical access with and without awareness. *Journal of Experimental Psychology: General*, 1981, *110*, 341-362. [5]

Fox, R., Aslin, R. N., Shea, S. L., and Dumais, S. T. Steropsis in human infant. *Science*, 1980, *207*, 323-324. [11]

Fozard, J. L. The time for remembering. In L. Poon (Ed.), *Aging in the 1980's*. Washington, D.C.: American Psychological Association, 1980. Pp. 273-287. [12]

Frankl, V. E. *Man's search for meaning*. Boston: Beacon Press, 1962. [23]

_____. *The unconscious god: Psychotherapy and theology*. New York: Simon & Schuster, 1975. [23]

Freedman, D. G. *Human sociobiology: A holistic approach*. New York: Free Press, 1979. [7]

Freedman, J. L., Carlsmith, J. M., and Sears, D. O. *Social psychology*. Englewood Cliffs, N.J.: Prentice-Hall, 1970. [25]

_____, and Fraser, S. C. Compliance without pressure: The foot-in-the-door technique. *Journal of Personality and Social Psychology*, 1966, *4*, 195—202. [25]

_____, and Sears, D. O. Warning, distraction and resistance to influence. *Journal of Personality and Social Psychology*, 1965, *1*, 262-266. [25]

Freud, S. *The ego and the id* (1923). London: Hogarth Press, 1947. [18]

———. *An outline of psycho-analysis* (1940). New York: Norton, 1949. [1]

———. Beyond the pleasure principle. In J. Strachey (Ed.), *The standard edition of the complete psychological works of Sigmund Freud* (Vol. 18, 1920). London: Hogarth Press, 1953. [18]

———. *The Interpretation of Dreams* (1900). New York: Basic Books, 1955. [6,18]

———. *Civilization and its discontents* (1930). J. Strachey (Ed. and trans.). New York: Norton, 1962 [18]

———. *New introductory lectures on Psycho-analysis* (1933). New York: Norton, 1965. [14,18]

———. Femininity. In J. Strouse (Ed.), *Women and analysis: Dialogues on psychoanalytic views of femininity*. New York: Dell, 1974. [18]

Fried, I., Ojemann, G. A., and **Fetz, E. E.** Language-related potentials specific to the human language cortex. *Science*, 1981, *212*, 353–356. [3]

Friedman, M., and **Rosenman, R. H.** *Type A behavior and your heart*. New York: Knopf, 1974. [21]

Friedman, M. I., and **Stricker, E. M.** The physiological psychology of hunger: A physiological persepective. *Psychological Review*, 1976, *83*, 409–431. [3]

Frisby, J. *Seeing: Illusion, brain and mind.* Oxford: Oxford University Press, 1980. [4]

Fromkin, V., (Ed.). *Speech errors as linguistic evidence*. The Hague: Mouton Publishers, 1973. [13]

Fromm, E. *Escape from freedom.* New York: Holt, Rinehart & Winston, 1941. [18]

Fromm-Reichmann, F. *Psychoanalysis and psychotherapy: Selected papers.* Chicago: University of Chicago Press, 1974. [23]

Frueh, T., and **McGhee, P. E.** Traditional sex role development and amount of time spent watching television. *Developmental Psychology*, 1975, *11*, 109. [17]

Furth, H. *Thinking without language.* New York: Free Press, 1966. [13]

Gagne, R. M. Contributions of learning to human development. *Psychological Review*, 1968, *75*, 177–191. [12]

Gagnon, J. H. *Human sexualities.* Glenview, Ill.: Scott, Foresman, 1977. [17]

———, and **Simon, W.** *Sexual conduct: The social sources of human sexuality.* Chicago: Aldine, 1973 [17]

Galanter, E. Contemporary psychophysics. In R. Brown, E. Galanter, E. H. Hess, and G. Mandler, *New directions in psychology.* New York: Holt, Rinehart & Winston, 1962. [4]

Gallagher, J. M., and **Reid, D. K.** *The Learning theory of Piaget and Inhelder.* Monterey, Calif.: Brooks/Cole, 1981. [12]

Gallatin, J. Political thinking in adolescence. In J. Adelson (Ed.), *Handbook of adolescent psychology.* New York: Wiley-Interscience, 1980. Pp. 344–382. [14]

Galle, O. R., Gove, W. R., and **McPherson, J. M.,** Population density and pathology: What are the relationships for man? *Science*, 1972, *176*, 23–30. [28]

Gallup, G. G., Jr. Self-recognition in primates: A comparative approach to the bidirectional properties of consciousness. *American Psychologist*, May 1977, *32*, 329–338. [11]

Galton, Sir F. *Hereditary genius: An inquiry into its laws and consequences.* London: Macmillan, 1869. [1]

———. *Inquiries into human faculty.* London: Macmillan, 1883. [1]

Garcia, J. I.Q.: The conspiracy. *Psychology Today*, September 1972, *6*, 40–43 *passim*. [20]

———, **Ervin, F. R.,** and **Koelling, R. A.** Learning with prolonged delay of reinforcement. *Psychonomic Science*, 1966, *5*, 121–122.. [8]

———, **Hawkins, W. G.,** and **Rusiniak, K. W.** Behavioral regulation of the *milieu interne* in man and rat. *Science*, 1974, *185*, 824–831. [7]

———, and **Koelling, R. A.** Relation of cue to consequence in avoidance learning. *Psychonomic Science*, 1966, *4*, 123–124. [1,7,8]

———, **McGowan, B. K.,** and **Green, K. F.** Biological constraints on conditioning. In M. E. P. Seligman and J. L. Hager (Eds.) *Biological boundaries of learning.* New York: Appleton-Century-Crofts, 1972. Pp. 21–43. [7]

———, and **Rusiniak, K. W.** What the nose learns from the mouth. In D. Mueller Schwarze and B. M. Silverstein (Eds.), *Chemical senses.* New York: Plenum, 1980. [7]

Gardner, B. T., and **Gardner, R. A.** Evidence for sentence constituents in the early utterances of child and chimpanzee. *Journal of Experimental Psychology: General*, 1975, *104*, 244–267. [13]

Gardner, E., *Fundamentals of neurology.* Philadelphia: Saunders, 1975. Copyright 1975 by Scientific American, Inc. All rights reserved. [3]

Gardner, L. I. Deprivation dwarfism. *Scientific American*, July 1972, *227*,1, 76–82. [11]

Garfield, S. L. Research on client variables in psychotherapy. In S. L. Garfield and A. E. Bergin, (Eds.) *Handbook of psychotherapy and behavior change: An empirical analysis* (2nd ed.). New York: Wiley, 1978. [24]

Garrett, M. F. The analysis of sentence production. In G. H. Bower (Ed.), *The psychology of learning and motivation* (Vol. 9). New York: Academic Press, 1975. Pp. 133–177. [13]

Garvey, C. *Play.* Cambridge: Mass.: Harvard University Press, 1977. [14]

Gary, J. A., and **Wedderburn, A. A.** Grouping strategies with simultaneous stimuli. *Quarterly Journal of Experimental Psychology*, 1960, *12*, 180–184. [9]

Gates, M., and **Allee, W. C.** Conditioned behavior of isolated and grouped cockroaches on a simple maze. *Journal of Comparative Psychology*, 1933, *13*, 331–358. [27]

Gazzaniga, M. S. The split brain in man. *Scientific American*, August 1967, *217*, 24–29. [3]

———. *The bisected brain.* New York: Appleton-Century-Crofts, 1970. [3]

———. One brain—two minds? *American Scientist*, 1972, *60*, 311–317. [3]

———. One brain—two minds? In I. Janis (ed.), *Current trends in psychology.* Los Altos, Calif.: William Kaufmann, 1977. Pp. 7–13. [3]

———. 1981 Nobel Prize for Physiology or Medicine. *Science*, 1981, *214*, 517–518. [3]

Geldard, F. A. *The human senses* (2nd ed.). New York: Wiley, 1972. [4]

Gelder, M., and **Kolakowska, T.** Variability of response to neuroleptics in schizophrenia: Clinical, pharmacological, and neuroendocrine correlates. *Comprehensive Psychiatry*, 1979, *20*, 397–408. [23]

Gelman, D. Finding the hidden Freud. *Newsweek*, November 30, 1981, 64–70. [18]

Gelman, R., and **Gallistel, C. R.** *The child's understanding of number.* Cambridge, Mass.: Harvard University Press, 1978. [12]

Gentry, W. D. Effects of frustration, attack and prior aggressive training on overt aggression and vascular processes. *Journal of Personality and Social Psychology*, 1970, *16*, 718–725. [27]

Gerbner, G., and **Gross, L.** The scary world of TV's heavy viewer. *Psychology Today*, April 1976, *9*, 41–45. [14]

Geschwind, N. Specialization of the human brain. *Scientific American*, September 1979, *241*, 180–201. [3]

Ghiselin, B. (Ed.). *The creative process.* Berkeley, Calif.: University of California Press, 1952. [10]

Giambra, L. M., and **Arenberg, D.** Problem solving, concept learning, and aging. In L. Poon (Ed.), *Aging in the 1980's.* Washington, D.C.: American Psychological Association, 1980. Pp. 253–259. [12]

Gibson, E. J., and **Walk, R. D.** The effect of prolonged exposure to visually presented patterns on learning to discriminate them. *Journal of Comparative and Physiological Psychology*, 1956, *49*, 239–242. [5]

———, and ———. The Visual Cliff. *Scientific American*, April 1960, *202*, 64–71. [11]

Gibson, J. J. *The senses considered as perceptual systems.* Boston: Houghton Mifflin, 1966. [5]

Gilligan, C. In a different voice: Women's conceptions of self and of morality. *Harvard Educational Review*, 1977, *47*, 481–517. [14]

Glanville, B. G., Best, C. T., and **Levenson,**

R. A cardiac measure of cerebral asymmetries in infant auditory perception. *Developmental Psychology*, 1977, *13*, 54–59. [13]

Glass, A., Gazzaniga, M., and **Premack, D.** Artificial language training in global aphasia. *Neuropsychologia*, 1973, *11*, 95–103. [2]

Glass, D. C. *Behavior patterns, stress, and coronary disease.* Hillsdale, N.J.: Erlbaum, 1977. [1,21]

———, **Reim, B.,** and **Singer, J. E.** Behavioral consequences of adaptation to controllable and uncontrollable noise. *Journal of Experimental Social Psychology*, 1971, *7*, 244–257. [21]

———, and **Singer, J. E.** *Urban stress: Experiments on noise and social stressors.* New York: Academic Press, 1972. [21]

Glaze, J. A. The association value of nonsense syllables. *Journal of Genetic Psychology*, 1928, *35*, 255–269. [8]

Gleason, J. B. Do children imitate? *Proceedings of the International Conference on Oral Education of the Deaf*, 1967, *2*, 1441–1448. [13]

———, and **Weintraub, S.** Input language and the acquisition of communicative competence. In K. E. Nelson (Ed.), *Children's language* (Vol. 1). New York: Gardner Press, 1978. Pp. 171–222. [13]

Golden, C. J., Graber, B., Blose, I., Berg, R., Coffman, J., and **Bloch, S.** Difference in brain densities between chronic alcoholic and normal control patients. *Science*, January 1981. *211*, 508–510. [3]

Goldfried, M. R., and **Davison, G. C.** *Clinical behavior therapy.* New York: Holt, Rinehart & Winston, 1976. [24]

Goldman, P. S. The role of experience in recovery of function following orbital prefrontal lesions in infant monkeys. *Neuropsychologia*, 1976, *14*, [3]

Goldstein, M. J., and **Kant, H.** Exposure to pornography and sexual behavior in deviant and normal groups. In *Technical reports of the Commission on Obscenity and Pornography* (Vol. 2). Washington, D.C.: U.S. Government Printing Office, 1970. [17]

Goleman, D. *The varieties of the meditative experience.* New York: Dutton, 1977. [6]

———, and **Davidson, R. J.,** (Eds.). *Consciousness: Brain, states of awareness, and mysticism.* New York: Harper & Row, 1979. [6]

Goodenough, F. L. Expression of the emotions in a blind-deaf child. *Journal of Abnormal and Social Psychology*, 1932, *27*, 328–333. [15]

Goodstein, L., and **Sandler, I.** Using psychology to promote human welfare: A conceptual analysis of the role of community psychology. *American Psychologist*, 1978, *33*, 888–891. [24]

Goodstein, L. D., and **Lanyon, R. I.** *Adjustment, behavior and personality.* Reading,

Mass.: Addison-Wesley, 1975. [14]

Gorden, H. W., and **Bogen, G. E.** Hemispheric lateralization of singing after intracarotid sodium amylbarbitone. *Journal of Neurology, Neurosurgery, and Psychiatry*, 1974, *37*, 727–738. [13]

Gottesman, I. I. Schizophrenia and genetics: Where are we? Are you sure? In L. C. Wynne, R. L. Cromwell, and S. Matthysse (Eds.), *The nature of schizophrenia: New approaches to research and treatment.* New York: Wiley, 1978. [23]

———, and **Shields, J.** *Schizophrenia and genetics—a study vantage point.* New York: Academic Press, 1972. [23]

Gottlieb, G. Conceptions of prenatal development: Behavioral embryology. *Psychological Review*, 1976, *83*, 215–234. [11]

Gould, J. L., and **Able. K. P.,** Human homing: An elusive phenomenon. *Science*, 1981, *212*, 1061–1063. [4]

Gould, R. L. The phases of adult life: A study in developmental psychology. *American Journal of Psychiatry*, 1972, *129*, 521–531. [14]

Goulet, L. R., and **Baltes, P. B.** *Life-span developmental psychology: Research and theory.* New York: Academic Press, 1970. [1]

Graubard, P. S., and **Rosenberg, H.** *Classrooms that work: Prescriptions of change.* New York: Dutton, 1974. [8]

Gray, F., Graubard, P. S., and **Rosenberg, H.** Little brother is changing you. *Psychology Today*, March 1974, *7*, 42–46. [8]

Grayson, R. Air controllers syndrome: Peptic ulcers in air traffic controllers. *Illinois Medical Journal*, August, 1972. [21]

Green, D. M., and **Swets, J. A.** *Signal detection theory and psychophysics.* New York: Wiley, 1966. [4]

Green, R. Sexual identity of 37 children raised by homosexual or transsexual parents. *American Journal of Psychiatry*, 1978, *135*, 692–697. [14]

———. Patterns of sexual identity in childhood: Relationship to subsequent sexual partner preference. In J. Marmor (Ed.), *Homosexual Behavior.* New York: Basic Books, 1980. Pp. 255–266.

———. Prenatal androgens and postnatal socialization: Influences on psychosexual development. *Annals of Internal Medicine* (in press). [17]

Greenberg, P. F. The thrill seekers. *Human Behavior*, April 1977, *6*,4, 17–21. [16]

Greenberger, E., Steinberg, L. D., and **Vaux, A.** Adolescents who work: Health and behavioral consequences of job stress. *Developmental Psychology*, 1981, *17*, 691–703. [14]

Greenblatt, M. Efficacy of ECT in affective and schizophrenic illness. *American Journal of Psychiatry*, 1977, *134*, 1001–1005. [24]

Gregory, R. L. *The intelligent eye.* New York:

McGraw-Hill, 1970. [5]

———. Visual illusions. *Scientific American*, 1968, *219*:5, 66–76. [5]

Grier, J. B., Counter, S. A. Y., and **Shearer, W. M.** Prenatal auditory imprinting in chickens. *Science*, 1967, *155*, 1692–1693. [7]

Griffin, G. *Legal Views of Test Validity.* Unpublished paper. Northwestern University, November, 1980. [20]

Griffith, J. J. Mednick, S. A., Schulsinger, F., and **Diderichsen, B.** Verbal associative disturbances in children at high risk for schizophrenia. *Journal of Abnormal Psychology*, 1980, *89*, 125–131. [23]

Grinspoon, L. *Marihuana reconsidered* (2nd ed.). Cambridge, Mass.: Harvard University Press, 1977. [6]

———, and **Bakalar, J. G.** *Cocaine: A drug and its social evolution.* New York: Basic Books, 1976. [6]

Groth, A. N., and **Burgess, A. W.** Rape: A sexual deviation. *American Journal of Orthopsychiatry*, 1977, *47*, 400–406. [17]

Grossman, S. P. Eating or drinking elicited by direct adrenergic, or cholinergic stimulation of hypothalamus. *Science*, 1960, *132*, 301–302. [3]

Grotevant, H. D., Scarr, S., and **Weinberg, R. A.,** Patterns of interest similarity in adoptive and biological families. *Journal of Personal and Social Psychology*, 1977, *35*, 667–676. [11]

Groth, A. N., and **Birnbaum, H. J.** Adult sexual orientation and attraction to underaged persons. *Archives of Sexual Behavior*, 1978, *7*, 175–181. [17]

Gruendel, J. M. Referential overextension in early language development. *Child Development*, 1977, *48*, 1567–1576. [13]

Grusec, J. E., and **Redler, E.** Attribution, reinforcement, and altruism: A development analysis. *Developmental Psychology*, 1980, *16*, 525–534. [14]

Guilford, J. P. *Personality.* New York: McGraw-Hill, 1959. [19]

———. Varieties of creative giftedness: Their measurement and development. *Gifted Child Quarterly*, 1975, *19*, 107–122. [20]

———. *Way beyond the IQ.* Buffalo, N.Y.: Creative Education Foundation, 1977. [20]

Gur, R. E., Gur, R. C., and **Harris, L. J.** Cerebral activation, as measured by subjects' lateral eye movements, is influenced by experimenter's location. *Neuropsychologia* 1975, *13*, 35–44. [2]

———, **Packer, I. K., Hungerbuhler, J. P., Reivich, M., Obrist, W. D., Amarnek, W. S.** and **Sackeim, H. A.** Differences in the distribution of gray and white matter in human cerebral hemispheres. *Science*, 1980, *207*, 1226–1228. [3]

Gurin, J. Chemical feelings. *Science 80*, November/December, 1979, *1*, 28–33. [3,4]

Haber, R. N. Discrepancy from adaptation level

as a source of affect. *Journal of Experimental Psychology,* 1958, *56,* 370–375. [16]

_____. Eidetic images. *Scientific American,* April 1969, *220,* 36–44. [9]

_____, and **Standing, L. G.** Direct measures of short-term visual storage. *Quarterly Journal of Experimental Psychology,* 1969, *21,* 43–45. [9]

Hailman, J. P. How an instinct is learned. *Scientific American,*1969, *221,* 98–106. [7]

Haith, M. M., Bergman, T., and **Moore, M. J.** Eye contact and face scanning in early infancy. *Science,* 1977, *198,* 853–854. [11]

Hall, C. S. The meaning of dreams. In D. Goleman and R. J. Davidson (Eds.), *Consciousness: Brain, states of awareness, and mysticism.* New York: Harper & Row, 1979, Pp. 79–82. [6]

_____, and **Lindzey, G.** *Theories of personality* (3rd ed.). New York: Wiley, 1978. [1,18]

Hall, E. Will success spoil B. F. Skinner? An interview with B. F. Skinner. *Psychology Today,* November 1972, *6,* 65–72 *passim.* [19]

_____. *Possible impossibilities: A look at parapsychology.* Boston: Houghton Mifflin, 1977. [6]

Hall, E. T. *The hidden dimension.* New York: Doubleday, 1966. [28]

_____. *Beyond culture.* New York: Anchor/ Doubleday, 1976. [28]

Halleck, S. L. The physician's role in management of victims of sex offenders. *Journal of the American Medical Association,* 1962, *180,* 273–278. [17]

Hamilton, W. D. The evolution of altruistic behavior. *American Naturalist,* 1963, *97,* 354–356. [7]

Haney, C., and **Zimbardo, P. G.** The socialization into criminality: On becoming a prisoner and a guard. In J. L. Tapp and F. L. Levine (Eds.), *Law, justice and the individual in society: Psychological and legal issues.* New York: Holt, Rinehart, & Winston, 1977. Pp. 198–223. [27]

Hansen, W. B., and **Altman, I.** Decorating personal places: A descriptive analysis. *Environment and Behavior,* 1976, *8,* 491–504. [28]

Hanson, D. R., Gottesman, I. I., and **Heston, L. L.** Some possible childhood indicators of adult schizophrenia inferred from children of schizophrenics. *British Journal of Psychiatry,* 1976, *129,* 142–154. [23]

Hardin, G. The tragedy of the commons. Science, 1968, *162,* 1243–1248. [27]

Hare-Mustin, R. T. and **Hall, J. E.** Procedures for responding to ethics complaints against psychologists. *American Psychologist,* 1981, *36,* 1494–1505. [2]

Hariton, E. B., and **Singer, J. L.** Women's fantasies during sexual intercourse: Normative and theoretical implications. *Journal of Consulting and Clinical Psychology,* 1974, *42,* 313–322. [17]

Harkness, S. The cultural context of child

development. In C. M. Super and S. Harkness (Eds.). *New directions for child development.* (No. 8). *Anthropological perspectives on child development.* San Francisco: Jossey-Bass, 1980. pp. 7–13. [14]

Harlow, H. F. The formation of learning sets. *Psychological Review,* 1949, *56,* 51–65. [10]

_____. Love in infant monkeys. *Scientific American,* June 1959, *200,* 6, 68–74. [14]

_____, and **Harlow, M. K.** Learning to think. *Scientific American,* August 1949, *181,* 36–39. [10]

_____, and _____. Learning to love. *American Scientist,* 1966, *54,* 244–272. [1, 14]

_____, and _____. Effects of various mother-infant relationships on Rhesus monkey behaviors. In B. M. Foss (Ed.), *Determinants of infant behavior.* (Vol. 4). London: Methuen, 1969, pp. 15–36. [14]

_____, _____, and **Meyer, D. R.** Learning motivated by a manipulation drive. *Journal of Experimental Psychology,* 1950, *40,* 228–234. [16]

_____, _____, and **Suomi, S. J.** From thought to therapy: Lessons from a private library. *American Scientist,* 1971, *59,* 538–549. [14]

Harmon, L. D. The recognition of faces. *Scientific American,* May 1973, *229,* 70–82. [5]

Harris, B. Whatever happened to little Albert? *American Psychologist,* 1979, *34,* 151–160. [8]

Harris, L. J. Variances and anomalies. *Science,* 1979, *206,* 50–52. [12]

Harris, T. *I'm OK—You're OK: A practical guide to Transactional Analysis.* New York: Harper & Row, 1969. [24]

Harter, S. Pleasure derived by children from cognitive challenge and mastery. *Child Development,* 1974, *45,* 661–669. [12]

Hartmann, E. The strangest sleep disorder. *Psychology Today,* April 1981, *15,* 14–18. [6]

_____. The psychology of tiredness. In D. Goleman and R. J. Davidson (Eds.), *Consciousness: Brain, states of awareness, and mysticism.* New York: Harper & Row, 1979. Pp. 69–71. [6]

Hartup. W. W. Aggression in childhood: Developmental perspectives. *American Psychologist,* 1974, *29,* 336–341. [14]

_____. The peer system. In P. H. Mussen and E. M. Hetherington (Eds.), *Carmichael's manual of child psychology.* (4th ed.). New York: Wiley, 1982. [14, 25, 26]

Hasler, A. D., and **Larsen, J. A.** The homing salmon. *Scientific American,* 1955, *193,* 2, 72–76. [7]

Hass, R. G., and **Mann, R. W.** Anticipatory belief change—Persuasion or impression management. *Journal of Personality and Social Psychology,* 1976, *23,* 219–233. [25]

Hassan, S. A. Transactional and contextual invalidation between the parents of disturbed

families: A comparative study. *Family Process,* 1974, *13,* 53–76. [23]

Hathaway, S. R. and **McKinley, J. C.** A multiphasic personality schedule (Minnesota): I. Construction of the schedule. *Journal of Psychology,* 1940, *10,* 249–254. [20]

Hauser, P. M. The census of 1980. *Scientific American,* November 1981, *245,* 53–61. [2]

Haviland, S. E., and **Clark, H. H.** What's new? Acquiring new information as a process in comprehension. *Journal of Verbal Learning and Verbal Behavior,* 1974, *13,* 512–521. [13]

Hayes, K. J., and **Hayes, C.** The intellectual development of a home-raised chimpanzee. *Proceedings of the American Philosophical Society,* 1951, *95,* 105–109. [13]

Hearnshaw, L. S. *Cyril Burt, psychologist.* Ithaca,N.Y.: Cornell University Press, 1979. [20]

Heath, R. G. Electrical self-stimulation of the brain in man. *The American Journal of Psychiatry,* 1963, *120,* 571–577. [3]

Hebb, D. O. The mind's eye. *Psychology Today,* May 1969, *2,* 54–57. *passim.* [6]

_____. What psychology is about. *American Psychologist,* February 1974, *29,* 2, 71–79. [6]

Heckel, R. B., Wiggins, S. L. and **Salzberg, H. C.** Conditioning against silences in group therapy. *Journal of Clinical Psychology,* 1962, *18,* 216–217. [8]

Heider, F. *The psychology of interpersonal relations.* New York: Wiley, 1958. [16]

Heilman, M. E. and **Saruwatari, L. R.** When beauty is beastly: The effects of appearance and sex on evaluations of job applicants for managerial and nonmanagerial jobs. *Organizational Behavior and Human Performance,* 1979, *23,* 360–372. [1]

Heiman, J. R. The physiology of erotica: Women's sexual arousal. *Psychology Today,* April, 1975, *8,* 90–94. [17]

_____, **LoPiccolo, L.,** and **LoPiccolo, J.** The treatment of sexual dysfunction. In A. Gurman and D. Kniskern (Eds.), *Handbook of family therapy.* New York: Bruner-Mazel, 1980. Pp. 592–627. [17]

Held, R. Development of visual resolution. *Canadian Journal of Psychology,* 1979, *33,* 213–221. [5]

_____, and **Hein, A.** Movement-produced stimulation in the development of visually guided behavior. *Journal of Comparative and Physiological Psychology,* 1963, *56,* 872–876. [5, 7]

Helson, H. *Adaptation-level theory.* New York: Harper & Row, 1964. [4]

Henderson, J. *The long-run solution.* Mountain View, Calif.: World Publications, 1976. [21]

Henle, M. On the relation between logic and thinking. *Psychological Review,* 1962, *69,* 366–378. [12]

Henning, H. Die Qualitatenreihe des Geschmacks. *Zeitschrift fur Psychologie,* 1916, *74,* 203–319. [4]

Herrnstein, R. J. The evolution of behaviorism. *American Psychologist*, August 1977, *32*, 593-603. [1]

Herron, J. (Ed.). *Neuropsychology of left-handedness*. New York: Academic Press, 1979. [3]

Heslin, R., and Boss, D. Nonverbal intimacy in airport arrival and departure. *Personality and Social Psychology Bulletin*, 1980, *6*, 248-252. [28]

Hess, R. D. Social class and ethnic influences on socialization. In P. H. Mussen (Ed.), *Carmichael's manual of child psychology*. (3rd ed.). (Vol. 2). New York: Wiley, 1970. Pp. 457-557. [11]

Heston, L. L. Psychiatric disorders in foster home reared children of schizophrenic mothers. *British Journal of Psychiatry*, 1966, *112*, 819-825. [23]

Hetherington, A. W., and Ranson, S. W. Hypothalamic lesions and adiposity in the rat. *The Anatomical Record*, 1942, *78*, 149-172. [3]

Higbee, K. L. *Your memory*. Englewood Cliffs, N.J.: Prentice-Hall, 1977. [9]

Hilgard, E. R. *Hyponotic susceptibility*. New York: Harcourt Brace Jovanovich, 1965. [6]

_____. A neodissociation interpretation of pain reduction in hypnosis. *Psychological Review*, 1973, *80*, 396-411. [6]

_____. Hypnosis. Annual Review of Psychology, 1975, *26*, 19-44. [6]

_____. *Divided consciousness: Multiple controls on human thought and action*. New York: Wiley, 1977. [6]

_____. Hypnosis and consciousness. *Human Nature*, January 1978, *1*, 42-49. [6]

Hilgard, J. R. *Personality and hypnosis: A study of imaginative involvement*. Chicago: University of Chicago Press, 1970. [6]

_____. Imaginative involvement: Some characteristics of the highly hypnotizable and the nonhypnotizable. *International Journal of Clinical and Experimental Hypnosis*, 1974, *22*, 138-156. [6]

Hiroto, D. S., and Seligman, M. E. P. Generality of learned helplessness in man. *Journal of Personality and Social Psychology*, 1975, *31*, 311-327. [21]

Hirsch, J., and Boudreau, J. C. Studies in experimental behavior genetics: I. The heritability of phototaxis in a population of drosophila melanogaster. *Journal of Comparative and Physiological Psychology*, 1958, *51*, 647-651. [7]

_____, Lindley, R. H. and Tolman, E. D. An experimental study of an alleged innate sign stimulus. *Journal of Comparative and Physiological Psychology*, 1955, *48*, 278-280. [7]

Hirst, W., Neisser, U., and Spelke, E. Divided attention. *Human Nature*, June 1978, *1*, 54-61. [1]

Hochberg, J. *Perception* (2nd ed.). Englewood Cliffs, N.J.: Prentice-Hall, 1978. [4, 5]

Hoffman, M. L. Personality and social development. Annual review of psychology, 1977,

28, 295-321. [16]

_____. Sex differences in empathy and related behaviors. *Psychology Bulletin*, 1977, *84*, 712-722. [14]

Hohmann, G. W. Some effects of spinal cord lesion on experienced emotional feelings. *Psychophysiology*, 1966, *3*, 143-156. [15]

Holahan, C. J. *Environmental psychology*. New York: Random House, 1982. [1]

_____, and Slaikeu, K. A. Effects of contrasting degrees of privacy on client self-disclosure in a counseling setting. *Journal of Counseling Psychology*, 1977, *24*, 55-59. [28]

Holden, C. Psychosurgery: Legitimate therapy or laundered lobotomy? *Science*, 1973, *179*, 1109-1112. [3]

_____. Scientist convicted for monkey neglect. *Science*, 1981, *214*, 1218-1220. [2]

Hollanbeck, A. R., and Slaby, R. G. Infant visual and vocal responses to television. *Child Development*, 1979, *50*, 41-45. [12]

Hollingshead, A. B., and Redlich, F. C. *Social class and mental illness*. New York: Wiley, 1958. [23]

Holmes, T. H., and Rahe, R. H. The social readjustment rating scale. *Journal of Psychosomatic Research*, 1967, *11*, 213-218. [21]

_____, and Masuda, M. Life change and illness susceptibility. In B. S. Dohrenwend and B. P. Dohrenwend (Eds.), *Stressful life events: Their nature and effects*. New York: Wiley, 1974. Pp. 45-72. [21]

Hook, J. The development of equity and logico-mathematical thinking. *Child Development*, 1978, *49*, 1035-1044. [14]

Hooker, D. *The prenatal origin of behavior*. Lawrence: University of Kansas Press, 1952. [11]

Horner, M. S. Femininity and successful achievement: A basic inconsistency. In J. Bardwick, E. M. Douvan, M. S. Horner, and D. Gutmann (Eds.), *Feminine personality and conflict*. Monterey, Calif.: Brooks/Cole, 1970. [16]

_____. Toward an understanding of achievement-related conflicts in women. *Journal of Social Issues*, 1972, *28*, 157-175. [16]

Horney, K. *The neurotic personality of our times*. New York: Norton, 1937. [18]

_____. *Our inner conflicts*. New York: Norton, 1945. [18]

_____. *Feminine psychology*. New York: Norton, 1967. [18]

Horowitz, M. J., Duff, D. F. and Stratton, L. O. Body-buffer zone. *General Psychiatry*, 1964, *11*, 651-656. [28]

Hovland, C. I., Janis, I. L., and Kelly, H. H. *Communication and persuasion: Psychological studies of opinion change*. New Haven, Conn.: Yale University Press, 1953. [25]

_____, Lumsdaine, A., and Sheffield, F. *Experiments on mass communication*. Princeton, N.J.: Princeton University Press, 1949. [25]

_____, and Weiss, W. The influence of source credibility on communication effectiveness. *Public Opinion Quarterly*, 1951, *15*, 636-650. [25]

Howard, E. *Territory in bird life*. (1920). New York: Atheneum, 1964. [28]

Howard, J. L., Liptzin, M. B., and Reifler, C. B. Is pornography a problem? *Journal of Social Issues*, 1973, *29*, 133-146. [17]

Hoyer, W. J., and Plude, D. J. Attentional and perceptual processes in the study of cognitive aging. In L. Poon (Ed.), *Aging in the 1980's*. Washington, D.C.: American Psychological Association, 1980. Pp. 227-238. [12]

Hoyt, J. L. Effect of media violence "justification" on aggression. *Journal of Broadcasting*, 1970, *14*, 455-464. [1]

Hubel, D. H. The brain. *Scientific American*, September 1979, *241*, 45-53. [3]

_____, and Wiesel, T. N. Receptive fields, binocular interaction and functional architecture in the cat's visual cortex. *Journal of Physiology*, *160*, 1962, 106-154. [3]

_____, and _____. Brain mechanisms of vision. *Scientific American*, September 1979, *241*, 150-163. [4]

Humphrey, T. The development of human fetal activity and its relation to postnatal behavior. In H. W. Reese and L. P. Lipsitt (Eds.), *Advances in child development and behavior*. (Vol. 5). New York: Academic Press, 1970. Pp. 2-59. [11]

Hunt, J. McV. *Early psychological development*. Worcester, Mass.: Clark University Press, 1980. [11]

Hunt, M. *Sexual behavior in the 1970's*. New York: Dell, 1974. [17]

Hunt, P. J., and Hillery, J. M. Social Facilitation in a coaction setting: An examination of the effects over learning trials. *Journal of Experimental Social Psychology*, 1973, *2*, 563-571. [27]

Huston, T. L. Ambiguity of acceptance, social desirability, and dating choice. *Journal of Experimental Social Psychology*, 1973, *9*, 32-42. [25, 26]

Huxley, A. The Doors of perception. In D. Goleman and R. J. Davidson (Eds.), *Consciousness: Brain, states of awareness, and mysticism*. New York: Harper & Row, 1979. Pp. 102-104. [6]

Hyman, I. A. Psychology, education, and schooling. *American Psychologist*, 1979, *34*, 1024-1029. [20]

Iannuci, D. and Dodd, D. H. Surface syntactic structures in linguistic memory: Some experimental evidence. *San Jose State Occasional Papers in Linguistics*, 1975, *1*. [13]

Ickes, W., and Turner, M. On the social advantages of having an older opposite-sex sibling: Birth order influences in mixed-sex dyads (in press). [26]

Inglis, J., and Caird, W. K. Age differences in successive responses to simultaneous stimulation. *Canadian Journal of Psychology*, 1963, *17*, 98–105. [12]

Inhelder, B., and **Piaget, J.** *The growth of logical thinking from childhood to adolescence.* New York: Basic Books, 1958. [12]

Insko, C. A. Verbal reinforcement of attitude. *Journal of Personality and Social Psychology*, 1965, *2*, 621–623. [25]

Institute of Medicine. *Marijuana and health.* Washington, D.C.: National Academy Press, 1982. [6]

Isen, A. M., Horn, N., and **Rosenhan, D. L.** Effects of success and failure on children's generosity. *Journal of Personality and Social Psychology*, 1973, *27*, 239–247. [27]

Ital, T. M. Qualitative and quantitative EEG findings in schizophrenia. *Schizophrenia Bulletin*, 1977, *3*, 61–79. [23]

Iverson, L. I. The Chemistry of the Brain. *Scientific American*, September 1979, *241*, 134–149. [3, 6]

Iversen, S. D., and **Iversen, L. L.** *Behavioral pharmacology.* New York: Oxford University Press, 1975. [6]

Izard, C. E. *The face of emotion.* New York: Appleton-Century-Crofts, 1971. [15]

———. *Human emotions.* New York: Plenum, 1977. [15]

Jackowitz, E. R., and **Watson, M. W.** Development of object transformation in early pretend play. *Developmental Psychology*, 1980, *16*, 543–549. [14]

Jacob, R., Kraemer, H., and **Agras, W. S.** Relaxation therapy in the treatment of hypertension. *Archives of General Psychiatry*, 1977, *34*, 1417–1427. [21]

Jacobs, R. C., and **Campbell, D. T.** The Perpetuation of an arbitrary tradition through several generations of a laboratory microculture. *Journal of Abnormal and Social Psychology*, 1961, *62*, 649–658. [27]

Jacobs, T. J., and **Charles, E.** Life events and the occurence of cancer in children. *Psychosomatic Medicine*, 1980, *42*, 11–24. [21]

Jacobson, E. *Progressive relaxation.* Chicago: University of Chicago Press, 1938. [21]

———. *Anxiety and tension control.* Philadelphia: Lippincott, 1964. [21]

Jacobson, S. W. Matching behavior in the young infant. *Child Development*, 1979, *50*, 425–430. [11, 15]

James, W. *The principles of psychology.* New York: Holt, 1890. [9, 11, 15]

———. *The varieties of religious experience* (1902). New York: New American Library, 1958. [6]

Janis, I. L., and **Fesbach, S.** Effects of fear-arousing communications. *Journal of Abnormal and Social Psychology*, 1953, *48*, 78–92. [25]

———, **Kaye, D.,** and **Kirschner, P.** Facilitating effects of "eating-while-reading" on responsiveness to persuasive communica-

tions. *Journal of Personality and Social Psychology*, 1965, *1*, 181–186. [25]

Jarvik, L. F. Thoughts on the psychobiology of aging. *American Psychologist*, May 1975, 576–583. [12]

———, **Blum, J. E.,** and **Varma, A. O.** Genetic components and intellectual functioning during senescence: A 20-year study of aging twins. *Behavior Genetics*, 1972, *2*, 159–170. [11]

———, **Klodin, V.,** and **Matsuyama, S. S.** Human aggression and the extra Y chromosome: Fact or fantasy? *American Psychologist*, 1973, *28*, 674–682. [27]

Jellinek, E. M. *Phases in the drinking history of alcoholics.* New Haven, Conn. Hillhouse Press, 1946. [22]

Jenkins, J. G., and **Dallenbach, K. M.** Oblivescence during sleep and waking. *American Journal of Psychology*, 1924, *35*, 605–612. [9]

Jensen, A. R. How much can we boost I. Q. and scholastic achievement? *Harvard Educational Review*, 1969, *39*, 1–123. [20]

———. *Educability and group differences.* New York: Harper & Row, 1973. [20]

———. Sir Cyril Burt in perspective. *American Psychologist*, 1978, *33*, 499–503. [20]

———. *Bias in mental testing.* New York: Free Press, 1980. [20]

Johnson, P. J. and **Davidson, J. M.** Intracerebral androgens and sexual behavior in the male rat. *Hormones and Behavior*, 1972, *3*, 345–357. [3]

Jones, E. E., and **Davis, K. E.** From acts to dispositions: The attribution process in person perception. In L. Berkowitz (Ed.), *Advances in experimental social psychology* (Vol. 2). New York: Academic Press, 1965. Pp. 219–266. [26]

———, **Davis, K. E.,** and **Gergen, K. J.** Role playing variations and their informational value for person perception. *Journal of Abnormal and Social Psychology*, 1961, *63*, 302–310. [26]

———, and **Nisbett, R. E.** *The actor and the observer: Perceptions of the causes of behavior.* Morristown, N.J.: General Learning Press, 1971. [19]

———, and ———. The actor and the observer: Divergent perceptions of the causes of behavior. In E. E. Jones et al. (Eds.) *Attribution: Perceiving the causes of behavior.* Morristown, N.J.: General Learning Press, 1972. [10, 19]

Jones, J. M. *Prejudice and racism.* Reading, Mass.: Addison-Wesley, 1972. [25, 26]

Jones, M. C. A laboratory study of fear: The case of Peter. *Pedagogical Seminary*, 1924, *31*, 308–315. [8, 24]

Jones, M. Community care for chronic mental patients: The need for a reassessment. *Hospital and Community Psychiatry*, 1975, *26*, 94–98. [24]

Jonides, J., Kahn, R., and **Rozin, P.** Imagery

instructions improve memory in blind subjects. *Bulletin of the Psychonomic Society*, 1975, *5*, 5, 424–426. [9]

Jourard, S. M. Some psychological aspects of privacy. *Law and Contemporary Problems*, 1966, *31*, 307–318. [28]

Jouvet, M. The function of dreaming: A neurophysiologist's point of view. In M. S. Gazzaniga and C. Blakemore (Eds.), *Handbook of psychobiology.* New York: Academic Press, 1975. Pp. 500–528. [6]

Judd, C. M., and **Kulik, J. A.** Schematic effects of social attitudes on information processing and recall. *Journal of Personality and Social Psychology*, 1980, *38*, 569–578. [1]

Jung, C. G. *Collected works.* Princeton, N.J.: Princeton University Press, 1967. [18]

———. *Psychological reflections.* Princeton, N.J.: Princeton University Press, 1972. [18]

Kagan, J. The baby's elastic mind. *Human Nature*, January 1978, *1*, 66–73. [11]

———. *The growth of the child.* New York: Norton, 1978. [14]

———, **Kearsley, R. B., Zelazo, P. R.,** and **Minton, C.** *Infancy: Its place in human development.* Cambridge, Mass.: Harvard University Press, 1978. [14]

Kahneman, D., Slovic, P. and **Tversky, A.** *Judgment under uncertainty: Heuristics and biases.* Cambridge, Engl.: Cambridge University Press, 1982. [26]

———, and **Tversky, A.** Subjective Probability: A judgment of representativeness. *Cognitive Psychology*, 1972, *3*, 430–454. [10]

———, and ———. On the psychology of prediction. *Psychological Review*, 1973, *80*, 237–251. [10, 26]

Kalnins, I. V., and **Bruner, J. S.** The coordination of visual observation and instrumental behavior in early infancy. *Perception*, 1973, *2*, 307–314. [11]

Kamin, L. G. *The science and politics of IQ.* New York: Wiley, 1974. [20]

———. Heredity, intelligence, politics, and psychology: I. In N. J. Block and G. Dworkin (Eds.), Pantheon, 1976. Pp. 242–264. [20]

Kandel, D. B. Homophily, selection, and socialization in adolescent friendships. *American Journal of Sociology*, 1978, *84*, 427–436. [14]

Kangas, J., and **Bradway, K.** Intelligence at middle age: A thirty-eight-year follow-up. *Developmental Psychology*, 1971, *5*, 333–337. [12]

Kanizsa, G. Subjective contours. *Scientific American*, April 1976, *234*, 48–52. [5] Copyright 1976 by Scientific American, Inc. All rights reserved.

Kaplan, S. Review of *Defensible Space. Architectural Forum*, 1973, *138*, (4), 8. [28]

Karacan, I., Ware, J. C., Dervent, B.,

Altinel, A., Thornby, J. I., Williams, R. L., Kaya, N., and **Scott, F. B.** Impotence and blood pressure in the flaccid penis: Relationship to nocturnal penile tumescence. *Sleep*, 1978, *1*, 125-132. [17]

Karlins, M., Coffman, T. L., and **Walter, G.** On the fading of social stereotypes: Studies in three generations of college students. *Journal of Personality and Social Psychology*, 1969, *13*, 1-16. [25,26]

Kasamatsu, A., and **Hirai, T.** An electroencephalographic study on the zen meditation (zazen). *Folia Psychiatrica et Neurologica Japonica*, 1966, *20*, 315-366. [6]

Katchadourian, H. A., and **Lunde, D. T.** *Fundamentals of human sexuality* (2nd ed.). New York: Holt, Rinehart & Winston, 1975. [17]

Katz, S. Food, behavior, and biocultural evolution. In L. M. Barker (Ed.), *Psychobiology of human food selection*. Westport, CT.: Avi Publishing Co., 1982 [16]

Kaufman, A., Baron, A., and **Kopp, R. E.** Some effects of instructions on human operant behavior. *Psychonomic Monograph Supplements*, 1966, *1*, 243-250. [8]

Kaufman, I., Peck, A. L., and **Tagiuri, C. K.** The family constellation and overt incestuous relations between father and daughter. *American Journal of Orthopsychiatry*, 1954, *24*, 266-277. [17]

Kazdin, A. E. *Behavior modification in applied settings*. Homewood, Ill.: Dorsey Press, 1975. [8]

———. *The token economy: A review and evaluation.* New York: Plenum, 1977. [24]

———. *History of behavior modification: Experimental foundations of contemporary research.* Baltimore: University Park Press, 1978. [1]

———, and **Wilson, G. T.** *Evaluation of behavior therapy: Issues, evidence and research strategies.* Cambridge, Mass.: Ballenger, 1978. [24]

Keating, D. P. Thinking processes in adolescence. In J. Adelson (Ed.), *Handbook of adolescent psychology.* New York: Wiley-Interscience, 1980. Pp. 211-246. [12]

Keegan, J. *The face of battle.* New York: Viking, 1976. [10]

Keeney, T. J., Cannizzo, S. F., and **Flavell, J. H.** Spontaneous and induced verbal rehearsal in a recall task. *Child Development*, 1967, *38*, 953-966. [12]

Keesey, R. E., and **Powley, T. L.** Hypothalamic regulation of body weight. *American Scientist*, September-October 1975, *63*, 558-565. [16]

Keil, F. C. Constraints on knowledge and cognitive development. *Psychological Review*, 1981, *88*, 197-227. [12]

Keith, P. M. Life changes and perceptions of life and death among older men and women. *Journal of Gerontology*, 1979, *34*, 870-878. [14]

Keller, M., and **Gurioli, C.** *Statistics on consumption of alcohol and alcoholism.* New Brunswick, N.J.: Rutgers Center of Alcohol Studies, 1976. [22]

Kelley, H. H. The warm-cold variable in first impressions of persons. *Journal of Personality*, 1950, *18*, 431-439. [27]

Kellogg, W. N., and **Kellogg, L. A.** *The ape and the child.* New York: McGraw-Hill, 1933. [13]

Kempe, R. S., and **Kempe, C. H.** *Child abuse.* Cambridge, Mass.: Harvard University Press, 1978. [27]

Kenrick, D. T., and **Gutierres, S. E.** Contrast effects and judgments of physical attractiveness: When beauty becomes a social problem. *Journal of Personality and Social Psychology*, 1980, *38*, 131-140. [2]

Kessen, W. Sucking and looking: Two organized congenital patterns of behavior in the human newborn. In H. W. Stevenson, E. H. Hess, and H. L. Rheingold (Eds.), *Early behavior: Comparative and developmental approaches.* New York: Wiley, 1967. Pp. 147-180. [11]

Kety, S. S. Biochemical hypotheses and studies. In L. Bellak and L. Loeb (Eds.), *The schizophrenic syndrome.* New York: Grune & Stratton, 1969. Pp. 155-171. [23]

———. Disorders of the human brain. *Scientific American*, September 1979, *241*, 202-214. [3]

———, **Rosenthal, D., Wender, P. H.,** and **Schulsinger, F.** Mental illness in the biological and adoptive families of adopted schizophrenics. *American Journal of Psychiatry*, 1971, *128*, 302-306. [23]

Keys, A., Brozek, J., Henschel, A., Michelson, O., and **Taylor, H. L.** *The biology of human starvation.* Minneapolis: University of Minnesota Press, 1950. [16]

Kiesler, C. A., and **Jones, J.** The interactive effects of commitment and forewarning: Three experiments. In C. A. Kiesler (Ed.), *The psychology of commitment: Experiments linking behavior to belief.* New York: Academic Press, 1971. Pp. 94-108. [25]

Kimball, J. P. Seven principles of surface structure parsing in natural language. *Cognition*, 1973, *2*, 15-47. [13]

Kimura, D. The Asymmetry of the Human Brain. *Scientific American*, 1975,, *232*, 70-78. [3]

Kinsey, A. C., Pomeroy, W. B., and **Martin, C. E.** *Sexual behavior in the human male.* Philadelphia: Saunders, 1948. [17]

———, ———. ———, and **Gebhard, P. H.** *Sexual behavior in the human female.* Philadelphia: Saunders, 1953. [17]

Kinzel, A. S. Body buffer zone in violent prisoners. *American Journal of Psychiatry*, 1970,, *127*, 59-64. [28]

Kirchner, W. K. Age differences in short-term retention of rapidly changing information. *Journal of Experimental Psychology*, 1958, *55*, 352-358. [12]

Kirkegaard-Sorenson, L., and **Mednick, S. A.** Registered criminality in families with children at high risk for schizophrenia. *Journal of Abnormal Psychology*, 1975, *84*, 197-204. [23]

Klatzky, R. L. *Human memory* (2nd ed.) San Francisco: Freeman, 1980. [9]

Klaus, M. H., and **Kennell, J. H.** *Maternal-infant bonding.* St. Louis: C. V. Mosby, 1976. [11,14]

Kleck, R. E., Vaughn, R. C., Cartwright-Smith, J., Vaughan, K. B., Colby, C. Z., and **Lanzetta, J. T.** Effects of being observed on expressive, subjective, and physiological responses to painful stimuli. *Journal of Personality and Social Psychology*, 1977, *34*, 1211-1218. [15]

Klein, D. B. *A history of scientific psychology: Its origins and philosophical backgrounds.* New York: Basic Books, 1970. [1]

Kleiter, G. D., Gachowetz, H., and **Huber, D.** *Bibliography: Decision making.* Salzburg: Psychology Institute, University of Salzburg, 1976. [10]

Klima, E. S., and **Bellugi, U.** Teaching apes to communicate. In G. A. Miller (Ed.), *Communication, language, and meaning: Psychological perspectives.* New York: Basic Books, 1973. Pp. 96-106. [13]

———, and ———. Poetry without sound. *Human Nature*, October 1978, *1*, 74-83. [13]

Klineberg, O. Emotional expression in Chinese literature. *Journal of Abnormal and Social Psychology*, 1938, *33*, 517-520. [15]

Kluver, H., and **Bucy, P. C.** Preliminary analysis of functions of the temporal lobes in monkeys. *Archives of Neurology and Psychiatry*, 1939, *42*, 979-1000. [3]

Knepler, A. E. Adolescence: An anthropological approach. In G. D. Winter and E. M. Nuss (Eds.), *The young adult: Identity and awareness.* Glenview, Ill.: Scott, Foresman, 1969. [14]

Knowles, E. S. Boundaries around group interaction: The effect of group size and member status on boundary permeability. *Journal of Personality and Social Psychology*, 1973, *26*, 327-331. [28]

Kobasigawa, A. Utilization of retrieval cues by children in recall. *Child Development*, 1974, *45*, 127-134. [12]

Koch, R., Costa, P. B., and **Dobson, J. C.,** Two metabolic factors in causation. In R. Koch and J. C. Dobson, *The mentally retarded child and his family.* New York: Brunner/Mazel, 1971. [20]

Kohlberg, L. A cognitive-developmental analysis of children's sex-role concepts and attitudes. In E. E. Maccoby (Ed.), *The development of sex differences.* Stanford, Calif.: Stanford University Press, 1966. Pp. 82-173. [14]

———. Stage and sequence: The cognitive-developmental approach to socialization. In D. A. Goslin (Ed.), *Handbook of socialization theory and research.* Chicago: Rand McNally, 1969. Pp. 347–480. [14]

_____. Stages of moral development as a basis for moral education. In C. M. Beck, B. S. Crittenden, and E. V. Sullivan (Eds.), *Moral education: Interdisciplinary approaches.* Toronto: University of Toronto Press, 1971. [14]

Kohler, I. Experiment with goggles. *Scientific American,* May 1962, *206,* 62–72. [5]

Kohler, W. *The mentality of apes.* New York: Harcourt, Brace, 1925.[10]

Kolata, G. B. Clues to the cause of senile dementia. *Science,* 1981, *211,* 1032–1033. [12]

Kolb, L. C., Bernard, V. W., and Dohrenwend, B. P., (Eds.). *Urban challenges to psychiatry: The case history of a response.* Boston: Little, Brown, 1969. [22]

Kolodny, R. C., Masters, W. H., Hendry, B. F., and Toro, G. Plasma testosterone and semen analysis in male homosexuals. *New England Journal of Medicine,* 1971, *285,* 1170–1174. [17]

Kopp, C. B. Perspectives on infant motor system development. In M. H. Bornstein and W. Kessen (Eds.), *Psychological development from infancy: Image to intention.* Hillsdale, N.J.: Erlbaum, 1979 Pp. 9–36. [12]

Korchin, S. J. *Modern clinical psychology.* New York: Basic Books, 1976. [24]

Koriat, A., and Lieblich, I. What does a person in a "TOT" state know that a person in a "don't know" state doesn't know? *Memory and Cognition,* 1974, *2,*4, 647–655. [9]

Kraepelin, E. *Clinical psychiatry: A textbook for physicians.* New York: Macmillan, 1902. [22]

_____. *Textbook of psychiatry* (1883). (8th ed.). New York: Macmillan, 1923. [23]

Krashen, S. D. The critical period for language acquisition and its possible basis. In D. Aaronson and R. W. Rieber (Eds.), *Developmental psycholinguistics and communication disorders.* Annals of the New York Academy of Sciences, 1975, Vol. 263. Pp. 211–224. [13]

Kraut, R. E. Effects of social labeling on giving to charity. *Journal of Experimental and Social Psychology,* 1973, *9,* 551–562. [13]

Kuczaj, S. A., II. Children's judgments of grammatical and ungrammatical irregular past-tense verbs. *Child Development,* 1978, *49,* 319–326. [13]

_____. Evidence of a language learning strategy; On the relative ease of acquisition of prefixes and suffixes. *Child Development,* 1979, *50,* 1–13. [13]

Kuhn, D., Langer, J., Kohlberg, L., and Haan, N. S. The development of formal operations in logical and moral judgment. *Genetic Psychology Monographs,* February 1977, *95L,* 97–188. [14]

Kulik, J. A., and McKeachie, W. J. The evaluation of teachers in higher education. In F. N. Kerlinger (Ed.), *Review of research in education.* Itasca, Ill.: Peacock, 1975 [1]

Kunst-Wilson, W. R., and Zajonc, R. B. Affective discrimination of stimuli that cannot be recognized. *Science,* 1980, *207,* 557–558. [5,15,25]

Kuo, Z. Y. The genesis of the cat's responses to the rat. *Journal of Comparative Psychology,* 1930, *11,* 1–35. [7]

Kurtines, W., and Greif, E. B. The development of moral thought: Review and evaluation of Kohlberg's approach. *Psychological Bulletin,* 1974, *81,* 453–470. [14]

Kutchinsky, B. The effect of easy availability of pornography on the incidence of sex crimes. *Journal of Social Issues,* 1973, *29,* 163–180. [17]

LaBarbera, J. D., Dozier, J. E., and Martin, J. E. Research on father-daughter incest: Current status and problems. Paper presented at annual meeting of American Psychological Association, New York, 1979. [17]

Lachman, J. L., and Lachman, R. Age and the actualization of world knowledge. In L. W. Poon, J. L. Fozard, L. S. Cermak, D. Arenberg, and L. W. Thompson (Eds.), *New directions in memory and aging: Proceedings of the George A. Talland Memorial Conference.* Hillsdale, N.J.: Erlbaum, 1980. [12]

Laing, R. D. *The politics of experience.* New York: Pantheon, 1967. [23]

_____, and Esterson, A. *Sanity, madness, and the family* (2nd ed.). New York: Basic Books, 1971. [23]

Laird, J. D. Self-attribution of emotion: The effects of expressive behavior on the quality of emotional experience. *Journal of Personality and Social Psychology,* 1974, *24,* 475–486. [15]

_____, and Crosby, M. Individual differences in the self-attribution of emotion. In H. London and R. Nisbett (Eds.), *Thinking and feeling: The cognitive alteration of feeling states.* Chicago: Aldine, 1974 [15]

Lamb, M. E. The development of mother-infant and father-infant attachments in the second year of life. *Developmental Psychology,* 1977, *13,* 637–648. [14]

_____. Social interaction in infancy and the development of personality. In M. E. Lamb (Ed.), *Social and personality development.* New York: Holt, Rinehart & Winston, 1978. Pp. 26–49. [14]

_____. Maternal attachment and mother-neonate bonding: A critical review. In M. E. Lamb and A. L. Brown (Eds.), *Advances in developmental psychology* (Vol. 2). Hillsdale, N.J.: Erlbaum, 1982. [14]

_____, Easterbrooks, M. E., and Holden, G. W. Reinforcement and punishment among preschoolers: Characteristics, effects, and correlates. *Child Development,* 1980, *51,* 1203–1236. [14]

Lambert, M., de Julio, S., and Stein, D. Therapists interpersonal skills.

Psychological Bulletin, 1978, *83,* 467–489. [24]

Landis, C. A. A statistical evaluation of psychotherapeutic methods. In L. E. Hinsie (Ed.), *Concepts and Problems of psychotherapy.* New York: Columbia University Press, 1937. Pp. 155–165. [24]

Lane, H. *The wild boy of Aveyron.* Cambridge, Mass.: Harvard University Press, 1976. [2]

Lang, P. J., Rice, D. G., and Sternbach, R. A. The psychophysiology of emotion. In N. S. Greenfield and R. A. Sternbach (Eds.), *Handbook of psychophysiology.* New York: Holt, Rinehart & Winston, 1972. [15]

Lange, C. G., and James, W. *The emotions.* Baltimore: Williams & Wilkins, 1922. [15]

Langer, E. J., and Rodin, J. The effects of choice and enhanced personal responsibility for the aged: A field experiment in an institutional setting. *Journal of Personality and Social Psychology,* 1976, *34,* 191–198. [21]

_____, _____, Beck, P., Weinman, C., and Spitzer, L. Environmental determinants of memory improvement in late adulthood. *Journal of Personality and Social Psychology,* 1979, *37,* 2003–2013. [12]

_____, and Saegert, S. Crowding and cognitive control. *Journal of Personality and Social Psychology,* 1977, *35,* 175–182. [28]

Langlois, J. H., and Downs, A. C. Mothers, fathers, and peers as socialization agents of sex-typed play behaviors in young children. *Child Development,* 1980, *51,* 1237–1247. [14]

Lanners, E. (Ed.). *Illusions.* New York: Holt, Rinehart, and Winston, 1977. [5]

Lansdell, H. A sex difference in effect of temporal lobe neurosurgery on design preference. *Nature,* 1962, *194,* 852–854. [3]

Lanyon, R. I., and Lanyon, B. *Behavior therapy: A clinical introduction.* Reading, Mass.: Addison-Wesley, 1978. [8]

Lanzetta, J. T., Cartwright-Smith, J., and Kleck, R. E. Effects of nonverbal dissimulation on emotional experience. *Journal of Personality and Social Psychology,* 1976, *33,* 354–370. [15]

LaPiere, T. R. Attitudes vs. actions. *Social Forces,* 1934, *13,* 230–237. [25]

Larry P. v. Wilson Riles 495 F. Supp. 926 (N.D. Cal. 1979). [20]

Lassen, C. L. Effect of proximity on anxiety communication in the initial psychiatric interview. *Journal of Abnormal Psychology,* 1973, *81,* 226–232. [28]

Latane, B. *A theory of social impact.* St. Louis, Mo.: Psychonomic Society, 1973. [27]

_____, and Darley, J. M. Help in a crisis: Bystander response to an emergency. In J. W. Thibaut, J. T. Spence, and R. C. Carson (Eds.), *Contemporary topics in social psychology.* Morristown, N.J.: General Learning Press, 1976. Pp. 309–322. [27]

_____, and Elman, D. The bystander and the thief. In B. Latane and J. M. Darley (Eds.), *The unresponsive bystander: Why doesn't he help?* New York: Appleton-Century-Crofts, 1970. [2]

———, Williams K., and Harkins, S. Many hands make light the work: The causes and consequences of social loafing. *Journal of Personality and Social Psychology,* 1979, *37,* Pp. 822-832. [27]

Laufer, R.S., Proshansky, H. M., and Wolfe, M. Some analytic dimensions of privacy. In H. M. Proshansky, W. H. Ittelson, and L. G. Rivlin (Eds.), *Environmental psychology: People and their physical settings* (2nd ed.). New York: Holt, Rinehart & Winston, 1976. Pp. 206-217. [28]

Lazarus, R. S., and Alfert, E. The short-circuiting of threat by experimentally altering cognitive appraisal. *Journal of Abnormal and Social Psychology,* 1964, *69,* 195-205. [15]

Leahy, R. L. Parental practices and the development of moral judgment and self-image disparity during adolescence. *Developmental Psychology,* 1981, *17,* 580-594. [14]

Lecomte, J. L'interattraction chez l'Abeille. *Compte Rendus de l'Academie de Sciences,* 1956, *229,* 857-858. [26]

Lee, L. C. *Personality development in childhood.* Monterey, Calif.: Brooks/Cole, 1976. [14]

Lefcourt, H. M. Overview. In H. M. Lefcourt (Ed.), *Research with the locus of control construct* (Vol. 1). *Assessment methods.* New York: Academic Press, 1981. [20]

Lehrman, D. S. Problems raised by instinct theories. *Quarterly Review of Biology,* 1953, *28,* 337-365. [7]

———. The reproductive behavior of ring doves (1964). In R. F. Thompson (Ed.), *Progress in Psychobiology: Readings from Scientific American.* San Francisco: Freeman, 1976. Pp. 62-68. [7]

Leibowitz, H. W., and Pick, H. A., Jr. Cross-cultural and educational aspects of the Ponzo perspective illusion. *Perception & Psychophysics,* 1972, *12,* 430-432. [5]

Leitenberg, H. (Ed.). *Handbook of behavior modification and behavior therapy.* Englewood Cliffs, N.J.: Prentice-Hall, 1976. [19]

———. Behavioral approaches to treatment of neuroses. In H. Leitenberg (Ed.), *Handbook of behavior modification and behavior therapy.* Englewood Cliffs, N.J.: Prentice-Hall, 1976. Pp. 124-167. [24]

Lema, S. A., and Blake, R. Binocular summation in normal and stereoblind humans. *Vision Research* (Vol. 17). London: Pergamon Press, 1977. Pp. 691-695. [5,11]

Lenneberg, E. H. *The biological foundations of language.* New York: Wiley, 1967. [7,13]

Leopold, R. L., and Dillon, H. Psychoanatomy of a disaster: A long-term study of post-traumatic neuroses in survivors of a marine explosion. *American Journal of Psychiatry,* 1963, *119,* 913-921. [23]

Lepper, M. R. Intrinsic and extrinsic motivation in children: Detrimental effects of superfluous social controls. In W. A. Collins (Ed.), *The Minnesota symposia on child psychology* (Vol. 14). *Aspects of the development of competence.* Hillsdale, N.J.: Erlbaum, 1981. Pp. 155-214. [16]

Lerner, B. *Washington* v. *Davis:* Quantity, quality, and equality in employment testing. In P. Kurland (Ed.), *The Supreme Court Review* (1976 vol.). Chicago: University of Chicago Press, 1977. [20]

Leventhal, H., Singer, R., and Jones, S. Effects of fear and specificity of recommendation upon attitudes and behavior. *Journal of Personality and Social Psychology,* 1965, *2,* 20-29. [25]

Levinson, D. J., with Darrow, C. N., Klien, E. B., Levinson, M. H., and McKee, B. *The seasons of a man's life.* New York: Knopf, 1978. [21]

Levinson, S. E., and Liberman, M. Y. Speech Recognition by Computer. *Scientific American,* April 1981, *244,* 64-76. [13]

Lewin, R. Is your brain really necessary? *Science,* 1980, *210,* 1232-1234. [3,13]

Lewinsohn, P. M. Clinical and theoretical aspects of depression. In K. S. Calhoun, H. E. Adams, and K. M. Mitchell (Eds.), *Innovative treatment methods of psychopathology.* New York: Wiley, 1974. [23]

———. The behavioral study and treatment of depression. In M. Hersen, R. M. Eisler, and P. M. Miller (Eds.), *Progress in behavior modification* (Vol. 1). New York: Academic Press, 1975. [23]

Lewis, B. N., Horabin, I. S., and Gane, C. P. *Case studies in the use of algorithms.* New York: Pergamon, 1967. [10]

Lewis, H. R., and Papadimitriou, C. H. The efficiency of algorithms, *Scientific American,* 1978, *238,* 96-109. [10]

Lewis, J. M., Rodnick, E. H., and Goldstein, M. J. Intrafamilial interactive behavior, parental communication deviance, and risk for schizophrenia. *Journal of Abnormal Psychology,* 1981, *90,* 448-457. [23]

Lewis, M. The busy, purposeful world of a baby. *Psychology Today,* February 1977, *10,* 53-56. [11]

Lewis, O. *The children of sanchez.* New York: Random House, 1961 [28]

Lewis, R. *Miracles: Poems by children of the English-speaking world.* New York: Simon & Schuster, 1966. [12]

Liben, L. S. Perspective taking skills in young children: Seeing the world through rose-colored glasses. *Developmental Psychology,* 1978, *14,* 87-92. [1]

Lichtenstein, P. E. Studies of Anxiety. The production of feeding inhibition in dogs. *Journal of Comparative and Physiological Psychology,* 1950, *43,* 16-29. [8]

Lidz, T. *The origin and treatment of schizophrenic disorders.* New York: Basic Books, 1973. [23]

———, et al. The intrafamilial environment of schizophrenic patients: Marital schism and marital skew. *American Journal of Psychiatry,* 1957, *114,* 241-248. [23]

Lieberman, M. A., Yalom, I. D., and Miles, M. B. *Encounter groups: First facts.* New York: Basic Books, 1973a. [24]

———, ———, and ———. Encounter: The leader makes the difference. *Psychology Today,* 1973b, *6,* 74. [24]

———, and Coplan, A. S. Distance from death as a variable in the study of aging. *Developmental Psychology,* 1970, *6,* 71-84. [14]

Liebeskind, J. C., and Paul, L. A. Psychological and physiological mechanisms of pain. *Annual Review of Psychology,* 1977, *28,* 41-60. [4]

Liem, J. H. Effects of verbal communications of parents and children: A comparison of normal and schizophrenic families. *Journal of Consulting and Clinical Psychology,* 1974, *42,* 438-450. [23]

Linder, D. E., Cooper, J., and Jones, E. E. Decision freedom as a determinant of the role of incentive magnitude in attitude change. *Journal of Personality and Social Psychology,* 1967, *6,* 245-254. [25]

Lindholm, E., and Lowry, S. Alpha production in humans under conditions of false feedback. *Bulletin of the Psychonomic Society,* 1978, *11;2,* 106-108. [6]

Lindsay, P. H., and Norman, D. A. Human information processing. New York: Academic Press, 1972. [5]

Lipman, A. Building design and social interaction. *The Architects Journal,* 1968, *147,* 23-30. [28]

Lipsitt, L. P. The study of sensory and learning processes of the newborn. *Clinics in Perinatology,* March 1977, *4.* [11]

Littman, R. A., and Manning, H. M. A methodological study of cigarette brand discrimination. *Journal of Applied Psychology,* 1954, *38,* 185-190. [15]

Loehlin, J. C., Lindzey, G. and Spuhler, J. N. *Racial differences in intelligence.* San Francisco: Freeman, 1975. [20]

Loftus, E. F. *Eyewitness testimony.* Cambridge, Mass.: Harvard University Press, 1979. [1,9,13]

———. *Memory.* Reading, Mass.: Addison-Wesley, 1980. [6,9]

———, and Fries, J. F. Informed consent may be hazardous to health. *Science,* 1979, *204,* 11. [2]

———, and Loftus, G. R. On the permanence of stored information in the human brain. *American Psychologist,* 1980, *35,* 409-420. [3,9]

———, Miller, D. G., and Burns, H. J. Semantic integration of verbal information into a visual memory. *Journal of Experimental Psychology,* 1978, *4,* 19-31. [9]

———, and Marburger, W. Since the eruption of Mt. St. Helens, did anyone beat you up?: Improving the accuracy of retrospective reports with landmark events. Unpublished manuscript, University of Washington, 1982. [2]

_____, and **Palmer, J. C.** Reconstruction of automobile destruction: An example of the interaction between language and memory. *Journal of Verbal Learning and Verbal Behavior,* 1974, *13,* 585-589. [9]

Loftus, G. R., and **Loftus, E. F.** *Human memory: The processing of information.* Hillsdale, N.J.: Erlbaum, 1976. [9]

London, M., and **Bray, D. W.** Ethical issues in testing and evaluation for personnel decision. *American Psychologist,* 1980, *35,* 890-901. [20]

London, P. *Behavior control.* New York: Harper & Row, 1969. [19]

Longworth, R. C. Hello, Mrs. Malaprop, grief-stricken woman in widow's tweeds. *Seattle Times,* March 12, 1981, A-15. [13]

LoPiccolo, J. Direct treatment of sexual dysfunction in the couple. In J. Money and H. Musaph (Eds.), *Handbook of sexology.* New York: Elsevier-North Holland Press, 1978. [17]

Lorenz, K. Vergleichende Verhaltensforschung,. *Zoologischer Anzeiger,* 1939, *12,* 69-192. [7]

_____. Die Angeborenen former moglicher Arfahrung. *Zeitschrift fur Tierpsychologie,* 1943, *5,* 233-409. [14]

_____. *Evolution and modification of behavior.* Chicago: University of Chicago Press, 1965. [7]

_____. *On aggression.* New York: Bantam Books, 1969. [28]

Luborsky, L. B., Docherty, J. P., and **Penick, S.** Onset conditions for psychosomatic symptoms: A comparative review of immediate observation with retrospective research. *Psychosomatic Medicine,* May/June 1973, *35,* 187-204. [21]

_____, and **Spence, D. P.** Quantitative research of psychoanalytic therapy. In S. L. Garfield and A. E. Bergin (Eds.), *Handbook of psychotherapy and behavior change: An empirical analysis* (2nd ed.). New York: Wiley, 1978. [24]

Luce, G. G. *Body time.* New York: Random House, 1971. [6]

Luchins, A. S. Classroom experiments on mental set. *American Journal of Psychology,* 1946, *59,* 295-298. [10]

_____. Primacy-recency in impression formation. In C. I. Hovland et al. (Eds.), *The order of presentation in persuasion.* New Haven, Conn.: Yale University Press, 1957. Pp. 33-61. [26]

Luchins, E. H., and **Luchins, A. S.** Letters: Mathematical ability: Is sex a factor? *Science,* 1981, *212,* 114-121. [12]

Luria, A. R. *The mind of a mnemonist.* New York: Basic Books, 1968. [9]

Lykken, D. T. *A tremor in the blood: Uses and abuses of the lie detector.* New York: McGraw-Hill, 1981. [15]

Lynch, G., Rose, G., Gall, C., and **Cottman, C. W.** The response of the dentate gyrus to partial deafferentation. In M. Santini (Ed.), *Golgi Centennial Symposium Proceedings.*

New York: Raven Press, 1975. [3]

Lynch, J. J. *The broken heart: The medical consequences of loneliness.* New York: Basic Books, 1977. [21]

_____, and **McCarthy, J. F.** The effect of petting on a classically conditioned emotional response. *Behaviour Research and Therapy,* 1967, *5,* 55-62. [21]

_____, **Paskewitz, D. A.** and **Orne, M. T.** Some factors in the feedback control of human alpha rhythm. *Psychosomatic Medicine,* September/October 1974, *36,* 5, 399-410. [6]

Macaulay, J. R. A shill for charity. In J. R. Macaulay and L. Berkowitz (Eds.), *Altruism and helping behavior: Social psychological studies of some antecedents and consequences.* New York: Academic Press, 1970. Pp. 43-59. [27]

Maccoby, E. E. Women's intellect. In S. M. Farber and R. H. L. Wilson (Eds.), *The potential of women.* New York: McGraw-Hill, 1963. Pp. 24-39. [16]

_____, and **Jacklin, C. N.** *Psychology of sex differences.* Stanford, Calif.: Stanford University Press, 1974. [14]

_____, and _____. Sex differences in aggression: A rejoinder and reprise. *Child Development,* 1980, *51,* 964-980. [14]

Mackintosh, E., West, S., and **Saegert, S.** Two studies of crowding in urban public spaces. *Environment and Behavior,* 1975, *7,* 159-184. [28]

MacLean, P. D. Contrasting function of limbic and neocortical systems of the brain and their relevance to psychophysiological aspects of medicine. *American Journal of Medicine,* 1958, *25,* 611-626. [3]

MacNichol, E. F., Jr. Three-pigment color vision. *Scientific American,* December 1964, *211,* 48-56. [4]

Magnusson, D., and **Endler, N. S.** Interactional psychology: Present status and future prospects. In D. Magnusson and N. S. Endler (Eds.), *Personality at the crossroads: Current issues in interactional psychology.* Hillsdale, N.J.: Erlbaum, 1977. [19]

Magoun, H. W. *The waking brain.* Springfield, Ill.: Charles C. Thomas, 1963. [3]

Mans, L, Cicchette, D., and **Sroufe, L. A.** Mirror reaction of Down's syndrome infants and toddlers: Cognitive underpinnings of self-recognition. *Child Development,* 1978, *49,* 1247-1250. [11]

Maranon, G. Contribution a etude de l'action emotive de l'adrenaline. *Revue Francaise d' Endocinologie,* 1924, *2,* 301-325. [15]

Marcel, A. Conscious and unconscious reading: The effects of visual masking on work perception. *Cognitive psychology* (in press). [5]

Marcia, J. E. Identity in adolescence. In J. Adelson (Ed.), *Handbook of adolescent psychology.* New York: Wiley-Interscience,

1980. Pp. 159-187. [14]

Mark, V. H. Stimulus/response: A psychosurgeon's case for psychosurgery. *Psychology Today,* July 1974, *8,* 28-33ff. [3]

_____, and **Ervin, F. R.** *Violence and the brain.* New York: Harper & Row, 1970. [15, 27]

Markman, E. M. Realizing that you don't understand: A preliminary investigation. *Child Development,* 1977, *48,* 986-992. [12]

_____, and **Seibert, J.** Classes and collections: Internal organization and resulting holistic properties. *Cognitive Psychology,* 1976, *8,* 561-577. [12]

Marks, G., Miller, N. and **Maruyama, G.** Effect of targets' physical attractiveness on assumptions of similarity. *Journal of Personality and Social Psychology,* 1981, *41,* 198-206. [26]

Markus, H. Self-schemata and processing information about the self. *Journal of Personality and Social Psychology,* 1977, *35,* 63-78. [26]

_____. The effect of mere presence on social facilitation: An unobtrusive test. *Journal of Experimental Social Psychology,* 1978, *14,* 389-397. [27]

_____. Sibling personalities: The luck of the draw. *Psychology Today,* June 1981, *15,* 35-37. [26]

Marler, P. Animal communication signals. *Science,* 1967, *157,* 64-67. [13]

_____. Bird song and speech development: Could there be parallels? *American Scientist,* 1970, *58,* 669-673. [7]

_____. On animal aggression: The roles of strangeness and familiarity. *American Psychologist,* March 1976, *31,* 3, 239-246. [7]

Marlowe, D., and **Gergen, K. J.** Personality and social interaction. In Gardner Lindzey and E. Aronson (Eds.) *Handbook of Social Psychology* (Vol. 3). (2nd ed.). Reading, Mass.: Addison-Wesley, 1969. Pp. 590-665. [25]

Marsh, C. A framework for describing subjective states of consciousness. In N. E. Zinbert (Ed.), *Alternate states of consciousness.* New York: Free Press, 1977. Pp. 145-157. [6]

Marshall, D. S. Sexual behavior on Mangaia. In D. S. Marshall and R. D. Suggs (eds.), *Human Sexual Behavior.* New York: Basic Books, 1971. [17]

Marshall, G., and **Zimbardo, P.** The affective consequences of "inadequately explained" physiological arousal. *Journal of Personality and Social Psychology,* 1979, *37,* 970-988. [15]

Marshall, N. J. Environmental components of orientations toward privacy. In J. Archea and C. Eastman (Eds.), *Proceedings of the 2nd Annual Environmental Design Research Association Conference.* Pittsburgh: Carnegie-Mellon University, 1970. Pp. 246-251. [28]

Martens, R. Palmar sweating and the presence

of an audience. *Journal of Experimental Social Psychology*, 1969, *5*, 371–374. [27]

Martin, B. *Abnormal psychology* (2nd ed.). New York: Holt, Rinehart and Winston, 1981. [21]

Martin, G. B., and **Clark, R. D.** Distress crying in neonates: Species and peer specificity. *Developmental Psychology*, 1982, *18*. [11]

Martin, R. C., and **Melvin, K. B.** Fear response of bobwhite quail (*Colinus viginianus*) to a model and a live red-tailed hawk (*Buteo janicensis*). *Psychologische Forschung*, 1964, *27*, 322–336. [7]

Martindale, C. *Cognition and consciousness*. Homewood, Ill.: Dorsey, 1981. [6, 10]

Martorano, S. C. A developmental analysis of performance on Piaget's formal operations tasks. *Developmental Psychology*, 1977, *13*, 666–672. [12]

Marx, J. L. Neurobiology: Researchers high on endogenous opiates. *Science*, 1976, *193*, 1227–1229. [4]

_____. New information about the development of the autonomic nervous system. *Science*, 1979, *206*, 434–437. [3]

_____. Ape-language controversy flares up. *Science*, 1980, *207*, 1330–1333. [13]

Maslach, C. Negative emotional biasing of unexplained arousal. *Journal of Personality and Social Psychology*, 1979, *37*, 953–969. [15]

Masling, J., Johnson, C., and **Saturansky, C.** Oral imagery, accuracy of perceiving others, and performance in Peace Corps training. *Journal of Personality and Social Psychology*, 1974, *30*, 414–419. [18]

_____, **Price, J. Goldband, S.** and **Katkin, E. S.** Oral imagery and autonomic arousal in social isolation. *Journal of Personality and Social Psychology*, 1981, *40*, 395–400. [18]

Maslow, A. H. *Motivation and personality*. New York: Harper & Row, 1954. [16, 19]

_____. Deficiency motivation and growth motivation. In M. R. Jones (Ed.), *Nebraska symposium on motivation. 1955.* Lincoln: University of Nebraska Press, 1955. [19]

_____. *The psychology of science: A reconnaissance.* New York: Harper & Row, 1966. [19]

_____. *Toward a psychology of being* (2nd ed.). New York: Van Nostrand Reinhold, 1968. [19]

_____. Some basic propositions of a growth and self-actualization psychology. In S. Maddi (Ed.), *Perspectives on personality*. Boston: Little, Brown, 1971b. [19]

_____. *The farther reaches of the human mind*. New York: Viking, 1971. [16,19]

Mason, W. A. The effects of social restriction on the behavior of Rhesus monkeys: III. Tests of gregariousness. *Journal of Comparative and Physiological Psychology*, 1961, *54*, 287–290. [15]

_____, and **Lott, D. F.** Ethology and comparative psychology. *Annual review of psychology* (Vol. 27). Palo Alto, Calif.: Annual

Reviews, 1976. Pp. 129–154. [7]

Massey, M. E. A market analysis of sex-oriented materials in Denver, Colorado, August, 1969—A pilot study. In *Technical reports of the Commission on Obscenity and Pornography* (Vol. 4) . Washington, D.C.: U.S. Government Printing Office, 1970. [17]

Masters, J. C., and **Furman, W.** Popularity, individual friendship selection, and specific peer interaction among children. *Developmental Psychology*, 1981, *17*, 344–350. [14, 26]

Masters, W. H., and **Johnson, V. E.** *Homosexuality in perspective*. Boston: Little, Brown, 1979. [17]

_____, and _____. The sexual response cycle of the human female: III, The clitoris: Anatomic and clinical considerations. *Western Journal of Surgery, Obstetrics, and Gynecology*, 1962, *70*, 248–257. [17]

_____, and _____. *Human sexual response*. Boston: Little Brown, 1966. [17]

_____, and _____. *Human sexual inadequacy*. Boston, Little Brown, 1970. [17]

Matas, L., Arend, R. A., and **Sroufe, L. A.** Continuity of adaptation in the second year: The relationship between quality of attachment and later competence. *Child Development*, 1978, *49*, 547–556. [14]

Maugh, T. H. Marijuana "justifies serious concern." *Science*, 1982, *215*, 1488–1489. [6]

Mauerer, D. Infant visual perception: Methods of study. In L. B. Cohen and P. Salapatek (Eds.), *Infant perception: From sensation to cognition.* (Vol. 1). *Basic visual processes*. New York: Academic Press, 1975. Pp. 1–76. [11]

McArthur, L. A., Solomon, M. R., and **Jaffe, R. H.** Weight and sex differences in emotional responsiveness to proprioceptive and pictorial stimuli. *Journal of Personality and Social Psychology*, 1980, *39*, 308–319. [15]

McCall, R. B., Appelbaum, M. I., and **Hogarty, P. S.** Developmental changes in mental performance. *Monographs of the Society for Research in Child Development*, 1973, *38*, serial no. 150. [20]

_____, **Parke, R. D.**, and **Kavanaugh, R. D.** Imitation of live and televised models by children one to three years of age. *Monographs of the Society for Research in Child Development*, 1978, Whole No. 173. [12]

McCartney, K., Scarr, S., Phillips, D., Grajek, S., and **Schwarz, J. C.** Environmental differences among day care centers and their effects on children's development. In E. F. Zigler and E. W. Gordon (Eds.), *Day care: Scientific and social policy issues*. Boston: Auburn House Publishing Company, 1982. Pp. 126–151. [14]

McCary, J. L. *McCary's human sexuality* (3rd ed.). New York: Van Nostrand, 1978. [17]

McClelland, D. C. Managing motivation to

expand human freedom. *American Psychologist*, 1978, *33*, 201–210. [16]

_____, et al. The achievement motive. New York: Appleton-Century-Crofts, 1953. [16]

_____, and **Atkinson, J. W.** The projective expression of needs. I. The effect of different intensities of the hunger drive on perception. *Journal of Psychology*, 1948, *25*, 205–232. [5]

_____, and **Winter, D. G.** *Motivating economic achievement*. New York: Free Press, 1969. [16]

McDonald, G. E. Imprinting: Drug-produced isolation and the sensitive period. *Nature*, 1968, *217*, 1158–1159. [7]

McDougall, W. *Introduction to social psychology*. London: Methuen, 1908. [7]

McGeoch, J. A. *The psychology of human learning*. New York: Longmans, Green, 1942. [9]

McGlone, J. Sex differences in functional brain asymmetry. *Cortex*, 1978, *14*, 122–128. [3]

McGraw, M. B. *Growth, a study of Johnny and Jimmy*. New York: Appleton-Century-Crofts, 1935. [11]

_____. Later development of children specially trained during infancy: Johnny and Jimmy at school age. *Child Development*, 1939a, *10*, 1–19. [11]

_____. Swimming behavior of the human infant. *Journal of Pediatrics*, 1939b, *15*, 485–490. [11]

McGuinness, D., and **Pribram, K. H.** The origins of sensory bias in the development of gender differences in perception and cognition. In M. Bortner (Ed.), *Cognitive growth and development.* New York: Bruner/Mazel, 1979. [14]

McGuire, R. J., Carlisle, J. M., and **Young, B. G.** Sexual deviations as conditioned behavior: A hypothesis. *Behaviour Research and Therapy*, 1965, *2*, 185–190. [17]

McGuire, W., and **Papageorgis, D.** The relative efficacy of various types of prior belief—defense in producing immunity against persuasion. *Journal of Abnormal and Social Psychology*, 1961, *62*, 327–337. [25]

McNeil, E. B. *The quiet furies*. Englewood Cliffs, N.J.: Prentice-Hall, 1967. [22]

Mead, G. H. *Mind, self and society: From the standpoint of a social behaviorist*. Chicago: University of Chicago Press, 1934. [11]

Mednick, M. T. S. The new psychology of women: A feminist analysis. In J. E. Gullahorn (Ed.), *Psychology and women: In transition*. New York: Wiley, 1979. Pp. 189–211. [16]

Mednick, S. A. Breakdown in individuals at high risk for schizophrenia: Possible predispositional perinatal factors. *Mental Hygiene*, 1970, *54*, 50–63. [23]

_____. Birth defects and schizophrenia. *Psychology Today*, April 1971, *4*, 48–50 passim. [23]

———. The associative basis of the creative process. *Psychological Review*, 1962, *69*, 220-232. [10]

Mehrabian, A. Relationship of attitude to seated posture, orientation, and distance. *Journal of Personality and Social Psychology*, 1968, *10*, 26-30. [28]

Meichenbaum, D. H. *Cognitive behavior modification: An integrative approach*. New York: Plenum Press, 1977. [24]

Meiselman, K. C. *Incest*. San Francisco: Jossey-Bass, 1978. [17]

Meltzoff, A. N., and **Moore, M. K.** Imitation of facial and manual gestures by human neonates. *Science*, 1977, *198*, 75-78. [11, 15]

Melzack, R. *The puzzle of pain*. New York: Basic Books, 1973. [4]

———, **Penick, E.,** and **Beckett, A.** The problem of "innate fear" of the hawk shape: An experimental study with mallard ducks. *Journal of Comparative and Physiological Psychology*, 1959, *52*, 6, 694-698. [7]

———, and **Wall, P. D.** Pain mechanisms: A new theory. *Science*, 1965, *150*, 971. [4]

Mendels, J. Lithium in the treatment of depression. *American Journal of Psychiatry*, 1976, *133*, 373-378. [24]

Menyuk, P. and **Bernholtz, N.** Prosodic features and children's language production. *MIT Research Laboratory of Electronics Quarterly Progress Reports*, 1969, No. 93, 216-219. [13]

Mercer, J. R. I.Q.: The lethal label. *Psychology Today*, September 1972, *6*, 44-47 passim. *[20]*

Merskey, H. The perception and measurement of pain. *Journal of Psychosomatic Research*, 1973, *17*, 251-255. [4]

Messenger, J. C. Sex and repression in an Irish folk community. In D. S. Marshall and R. D. Suggs (Eds.), *Human sexual behavior*. New York: Basic Books, 1971. Pp. 3-37. [17]

Messick, S. Test validity and the ethics of assessment. *American Psychologist*, 1980, *35*, 1012-1027. [20]

Meyer, R. J., and **Haggerty, R. J.** Streptococcal infections in families: Factors altering individual susceptibility. *Pediatrics*, 1962, *29*, 539-549. [21]

Meyer-Bahlburg, H. F. L. Sex hormones and male homosexuality in comparative perspective. *Archives of Sexual Behavior*, 1977, *6*, 297-325. [17]

———. Sex hormones and female homosexuality: A critical examination. *Archives of Sexual Behavior*, 1979, *8*, 101-119. [17]

Meyerowitz, B. E. Psychosocial correlates of breast cancer and its treatments. *Psychological Bulletin*, 1980, *87*, 108-131. [21]

Michael, R. P., Bonsall, R. W. and **Warner, P.** Human vaginal secretions: Volatile fatty acid content. *Science*, 1974, *186*, 1217-1219. [4]

Michaels, R. H., and **Mellin, G. W.** Prospective experience with maternal rubella and the associationed congenital malformations. *Pediatrics*, 1960, *26*, 200-209. [11]

Milgram, S. Behavioral study of obedience. *Journal of Abnormal and Social Psychology*, 1963, *67*, 371-378. [27]

———. Some conditions of obedience and disobedience to authority. In I. D. Steiner and M. Fishbein (Eds.), *Current studies in social psychology*. New York: Holt, Rinehart & Winston, 1965. Pp. 243-262. [27]

———. The experience of living in cities. *Science*, 1970, *167*, 1461-1468. [28]

———. *Obedience to authority*. New York: Harper & Row, 1974. [27]

———, and **Tavris, C.** The frozen world of the familiar stranger: A conversation with Stanley Milgram, by Carol Tavris. *Psychology Today*, June 1974, *8*, 70-80. [27]

Miller, G. A. The magical number seven, plus or minus two: Some limits on our capacity for processing information. *Psychological Review*, 1956, *63*, 81-97. [9]

———. Decision units in the perception of speech. *IRE Transactions on Information Theory*, 1962, *8*, 81-83. [5]

———. Reconsiderations: Language, Thought, and Reality. *Human Nature*, June 1978, *1*, 92-96. [13]

Miller, N. E. Experimental studies of conflict. In J. McV. Hunt (Ed.), *Personality and the behavior disorders* (Vol. 1). New York: Ronald Press, 1944. Pp. 431-465. [19]

———. Theory and experiment relating psychoanalytic displacement to stimulus-response generalization. *Journal of Abnormal and Social Psychology*, 1948, *43*, 155-178. [19]

———. Experiment on motivation. *Science*, 1957, *126*, 1271-1278. [3]

———. Liberalization of basic S-R concepts: Extensions to conflict behavior, social motivation and learning. In S. Koch (Ed.), *Psychology: A study of a science* (Vol. 2). New York: McGraw-Hill, 1959. [19]

———. Biofeedback: Evaluation of a new technique. *New England Journal of Medicine*, 1974, *290*, 684-685. [6]

Miller, N., and **Maruyama, G.** Ordinal position and peer popularity. *Journal of Personality and Social Psychology*, 1976, *33*, 123-131. [26]

Miller, R. E., Caul, W. F., and **Mirsky, I. A.** Communication of affects between feral and socially isolated monkeys. *Journal of Personality and Social Psychology*, 1967, *7*, 231-239. [15]

Mills, M., and **Melhuish, E.** Recognition of mother's voice in early infancy. *Nature*, November 8, 1974, *252*, 5479, 123-124. [11]

Milner, B. Some effects of frontal lobectomy in man. In J. M. Warren and K. Arent (Eds.), *The frontal granular cortex and behavior*. New York: McGraw-Hill, 1964. [3]

———. Amnesia following operation on the temporal lobes. In C. W. M. Whitty and O. L. Zangwill (Eds.), *Amnesia*. London: Butterworths, 1966. Pp. 112-115. [9]

Minkowski, A. *Regional development of the brain in early life*. Oxford: Blackwell, 1967. [11]

Minuchin, S. *Families and family therapy*. Cambridge, Mass.: Harvard University Press, 1974. [24]

———, interviewed by **Marcus, M.** The artificial boundary between self and family. *Psychology Today*, January 1977, *10*, 66-72. [24]

Mischel, W. A social-learning view of sex differences in behavior. In E. E. Maccoby (Ed.), *The development of sex differences*. Stanford, Calif.: Stanford University Press, 1966. pp. 56-81. [14]

———. *Personality and assessment*. New York: Wiley, 1968. [19]

———. Toward a cognitive social-learning reconceptualization of personality. *Psychological Review*, 1973, *80*, 252-283. [14, 19]

———. On the interface of cognition and personality: Beyond the person-situation debate. *American Psychologist*, 1979, *34*, 740-754. [19]

———, and **Peake, P. K.** Beyond deja vu in the search for cross-situational consistency. *Psychological Review* (in press). [19]

Mitler, M. M., Guilleminault, C., Orme, J., Zarcone, V. P., and **Dement, W. C.** Sleeplessness, sleep attacks, and things that go wrong in the night. *Psychology Today*, December 1975, *9*, 45-50. [6]

Moede, W. Die Richtlinien der Leistungs-Psychologie. *Industrielle Psychotechnik*, 1927, *4*, 193-207. [27]

Moir, D. J. Egocentrism and the emergence of conventional morality in preadolescent girls. *Child Development*, 1974, *45*, 299-304. [14]

Molfese, D. L., Freeman, R. B., and **Palermo, D. D.** The ontogeny of brain lateralization for speech and nonspeech stimuli. *Brain and Language*, 1975, *2*, 356-368. [13]

Moncrieff, R. W. *Odour preferences*. New York: Wiley, 1966. [4]

Money, J. Factors in the genesis of homosexuality. In G. Winokur (Ed.), *Determinants of human sexual behavior*. Springfield, Ill.: Charles C. Thomas, 1963. Pp. 19-43. [17]

———, and **Ehrhardt, A. A.** *Man and woman, boy and girl*. Baltimore: Johns Hopkins University Press, 1972. [17]

Monnier, M., Boehmer, A., and **Scholer, A.** Early habituation, dishabituation, and generalization induced in visual center by color stimuli. *Vision Research*, 1976, *16*, 1497-1504. [12]

Montogomery, K. C. The role of the exploratory drive in learning. *Journal of Comparative and Physiological Psychology*, 1954, *47*, 60-64. [16]

Moore, H. T. Further data concerning sex differences. *Journal of Abnormal and Social Psychology*, 1922, *17*, 210-214. [2]

Moore, T. Exclusive early mothering and its alternatives: The outcome to adolescence.

Scandinavian Journal of Psychology, 1975, *16*, 255-272. [14]

Moray, N. Attention in dichotic listening: Affective cues and the influence of instructions. *Quarterly Journal of Experimental Psychology*, 1959, *11*, 56-60. [9]

Moreland, R. L., and **Zajonc, R. B.** Is stimulus recognition a necessary condition for the occurrence of exposure effects? *Journal of Personality and Social Psychology*, 1977, *35*, 191-199. [25]

Morgan, C. L. *Introduction to comparative psychology*. New York: Scribner, 1894. [7]

Morse, P. A. The discrimination of speech and nonspeech stimuli in early infancy. *Journal of Experimental Child Psychology*, 1972, *14*, 477-492. [11]

Moss, H. A. Early sex differences and mother-infant interaction. In R. C. Freedman, R. N. Richards, and R. L. Van de Wiele (Eds.), *Sex differences in behavior*. New York: Wiley, 1974. [14]

Mosteller, F. Innovation and evaluation. *Science*, 1981, *211*, 881-886. [10]

Moyer, K. E. *The physiology of hostility*. Chicago: Markham, 1971. [3]

Muckensturm, B. La signification de la livree nuptiale de l'epinoche. *Revue du comportement animal*, 1969, *3*, 39-64. [7]

Mull, H. K. The effect of repetition upon the enjoyment of modern music. *Journal of Psychology*, 1957, *43*, 155-162. [15]

Murdock, B. B., Jr. The serial position effect of free recall. *Journal of Experimental Psychology*, 1962, *64*, 482-488. [9]

Murphy, H. B. M., Wittkower, E. D., Fried, J., and **Ellenberger, H.** A cross-cultural survey of schizophrenic symptomatology. In *Proceedings of the Third World Congress of Psychiatry* (Vol. 2). Toronto: University of Toronto Press, 1961. Pp. 1309-1315. [22]

Murphy, J. M. Psychiatric labeling in cross-cultural perspective. *Science*, 1976, *191*, 1019-1028. [22]

Murray, H. A. et al. *Explorations in personality*. New York: Oxford University Press, 1938. [16, 20]

Murstein, B. I. Physical attractiveness and marital choice. *Journal of Personality and Social Psychology*, 1972, *22*, 8-12. [25, 26]

Mussen, P., and **Eisenberg-Berg, N.** *Roots of caring, sharing, and helping: The development of prosocial behavior in children*. San Francisco: Freeman, 1977. [14]

Muuss, R. E. *Theories of adolescence* (3rd ed.). New York: Random House, 1975. [14]

Myers, J. K., and **Bean, L. L.** *A decade later: A follow-up of social class and mental illness*. New York: Wiley, 1968. [23]

Naftulin, D. H., Ware, J. E., and **Donnelly, F. A.** The Doctor Fox lecture: A paradigm of educational seduction. *Medical Education*, 1973, *48*, 630-635. [1]

Nathan, P. W. The gate control theory of pain: A critical review. *Brain*, 1976, *99*, 123-158. [4]

National Center for Educational Statistics. Gainful employment among high school youth. *Bulletin*, September 1981, Whole issue. [14]

National Education Association v. *State of South Carolina* 434 U.S. 1026 (1978). [20]

Nawy, H. The San Francisco erotic marketplace. In *Technical reports of the Commission on Obscenity and Pornography* (Vol. 4). Washington, D.C.: U.S. Government Printing Office, 1970. [17]

Needleman, H. L. Lead poisoning in children: Neurologic implications of widespread subclinical intoxications. *Seminars in Psychiatry*, February 1973, *5*, 47-53. [20]

———. Subclinical lead exposure in Philadelphia schoolchildren. *New England Journal of Medicine*, 1974, *290*, 245-248. [20]

Nelson, K. Cognitive development in the first years of life. Report prepared for the National Research Council, 1981. [12]

———, **Rescorla, L., Gruendel, J.,** and **Benedict, H.** Early lexicons: What do they mean? *Child Development*, 1978, *49*, 960-968. [13]

Nelson, K. E. Facilitating children's syntax acquisition. *Developmental Psychology*, 1977, *13*, 101-107. [13]

———, and **Nelson, K.** Cognitive pendulums and their linguistic realization. In K. E. Nelson (Ed.), *Children's language* (Vol. 1). New York: Gardner Press, 1978. Pp. 223-286. [13]

Neugarten, B. L. Dynamics of transition of middle age to old age: Adaptation and the life cycle. *Journal of Geriatric Psychiatry*, 1970, *4*, 71-87. [21]

———. The roles we play. In American Medical Association (ed.), *The quality of life: The middle years*. Acton, Mass.: Publishing Sciences Group, 1974. [21]

———. Adaptation and the life cycle. *The Counseling Psychologist*, 1976, *6*, 16-20. [14]

———. Personality and aging. In J. E. Birren and K. W. Schaie (Eds.), *Handbook of the psychology of aging*. New York: Van Nostrand Rheinhold, 1977. Pp. 626-649. [12]

———. Time, age, and the life cycle. *American Journal of Psychiatry*, 1979, *136*, 887-894. [14]

———, interviewed by **Hall, E.** Acting one's age: New rules for old. *Psychology Today*, April 1980, *13*, 66-80. [14]

Neugebauer, R. Treatment of the mentally ill in medieval and early modern England: A reappraisal. *Journal of the History of the Behavioral Sciences*, 1978, *14*, 158-169. [23]

New York Times News Service. America aging: 25.5 million are over 65. *The New York Times*, May 24, 1981, A-1, 9. [12]

Newcomb, A. F., Brady, J. E., and **Hartup, W. W.** Friendship and incentive condition as determinants of children's task-oriented behavior. *Child Development*, 1979, *50*, 878-881. [14]

Newell, A., and **Simon, H. A.** *Human problem solving*. Englewood Cliffs, N.J.: Prentice-Hall, 1972. [10]

Newman, G., and **Nichols, C. R.** Sexual activities and attitudes in older persons. *Journal of the American Medical Association*, 1960, *173*, 33-35. [17]

Newman, O. *Defensible space*. New York: Collier Books, 1972. [28]

Nicassio, P., and **Bootzin, R.** A comparison of progressive relaxation and autogenic training as treatments for insomnia. *Journal of Abnormal Psychology*, 1974, *83*, 253-260. [21]

Nisbett, R. E. Determinants of food intake in human obesity. *Science*, 1968, *159*, 1245-1255. [16]

———, **Caputo, C., Legant, P.,** and **Moracek, J.** Behavior as seen by the actor and as seen by the observer. *Journal of Personality and Social Psychology*, 1973, *27*, 154-165. [19, 26]

———, and **Ross, L.** *Human inference: Strategies and shortcomings of social judgment*. Englewood Cliffs, N.J.: Prentice-Hall, 1980. [10, 26]

———, and **Wilson, T. C.** Telling more than we can know: Verbal reports on mental processes. *Psychological Review*, 1977, *84*, 231-259. [7]

Norman, D. A. *Memory and attention*. New York: Wiley, 1976. [9]

———. Post-Freudian slips. *Psychology Today*, April 1980, *13*, 42-50. [13]

———, **Rumelhart, D. E.,** and the **LNR Research Group.** *Explorations in cognition*. San Francisco: Freeman, 1975. [9]

Oden, M. H. The fulfillment of promise: 40-year follow-up of the Terman gifted group. *Genetic Psychology Monographs*, 1968, *77*, 3-93. [20]

Offer, D., Ostrov, E., and **Howard, K. I.** *The adolescent: A psychological self-portrait*. New York: Basic Books, 1981. [14, 21]

Ogilvie, B. C. Stimulus addiction: The sweet psychic jolt of danger. *Psychology Today*, October 1974, *8*, 88-94. [16]

Olds, J., and **Milner, P.** Positive reinforcement produced by electrical stimulation of septal area and other regions of rat brain. *Journal of Comparative and Physiological Psychology*, 1954, *47*, 411-427. [3]

Olson, G. M. An information-processing analysis of visual memory and habituation in infants. In T. J. Tighe and R. N. Leaton (Eds.), *Habituation: Perspectives from child development, animal behavior, and neurophysiology*. Hillsdale, N.J.: Erlbaum, 1976. Pp. 239-277. [12]

Olton, D. S. and **Noonberg, A. R.** *Biofeedback: Clinical applications in behavioral medicine*. Englewood Cliffs, N.J.: Prentice-Hall, 1980. [21]

Orlick, T. D. Positive socialization via cooperative games. *Developmental Psychology,* 1981, *17,* 426–429. [14]

Orlinsky, D. E., and **Howard, K. I.** The relation of process to outcome in psychotherapy. In S. L. Garfield and A. E. Bergin (Eds.), *Handbook of psychotherapy and behavior change: An empirical analysis* (2nd ed.). New York: Wiley, 1978. [24]

Orne, M. T. *Demand character and the concept of quasi control.* New York: Academic Press, 1969. [2]

_____. The use and misuse of hypnosis in court. *The International Journal of Clinical and Experimental Hypnosis,* 1979, *27,* 4, 311–341. [6]

_____, and **Evans, F. J.** Inadvertent termination of hypnosis with hypnotized and simulating subjects. *International Journal of Clinical and Experimental Hypnosis,* 1966, *14,* 61–78. [2]

_____, and **Scheibe, K. E.** The contribution of non-deprivation factors in the production of sensory deprivation effects: The psychology of the panic button. *Journal of Abnormal and Social Psychology,* 1964, *68,* 3–12. [6]

Ornstein, R. E. *The psychology of consciousness* (2nd ed.). New York: Harcourt Brace Jovanovich, 1977. [6]

Orwell, G. *Nineteen eighty-four.* New York: Harcourt, Brace, 1949. [13]

Osborne, J. G., Powers, R. B., and **Anderson, E. G.** A lottery to stop littering. *Psychology Today,* August 1974, *8,* 65–66. [8]

Osgood, C. E., Suci, G. J., and **Tannenbaum, P. H.** *The measurement of meaning.* Urbana, Ill.: University of Illinois Press, 1957. [15]

Oskamp, S., and **Kleinke, C.** Amount of reward as a variable in prisoner's dilemma game. *Journal of Personality and Social Psychology,* 1970, *16,* 133–140. [27]

Overmier, J. B., and **Seligman, M. E. P.** Effects of inescapable shock on subsequent escape and avoidance responding. *Journal of Comparative and Physiological Psychology,* 1967, *63,* 28–33. [21]

Padden, C. The eyes have it: Linguistic functions of the eyes in American Sign Language. In *Proceedings of the Second Gallaudet Symposium in Language and Communication Research: Problems in research.* Washington, D.C.: Gallaudet Press, 1976. Pp. 31–35. [13]

Paivio, A. *Imagery and verbal processes.* New York: Holt, Rinehart and Winston, 1971. [9]

Paluck, R. J., and **Esser, A. H.,** Controlled experimental modification of aggressive behavior in territories of severely retarded boys. *American Journal of Mental Deficiency,* 1971, *76,* 23–39. [28]

Papajohn, J. Marital behavior therapy. In D. Upper (Ed.), *Perspectives in behavior therapy.* Kalamazoo, Mich.: Behaviordelia,

1977. Pp. 45–52. [24]

Papousek, H. Individual variability in learned responses in human infants. In R. J. Robinson (Ed.), *Brain and early behaviour: Development in the fetus and infant.* London: Academic Press, 1969. Pp. 251–266. [12]

Parke, R. D., Berkowitz, L., Leyens, J. P., West, S. G., and **Sebastian, R. J.** Some effects of violent and nonviolent movies on the behavior of juvenile delinquents. In L. Berkowitz (Ed.), *Advances in experimental social psychology* (Vol. 10). New York: Academic Press, 1977. Pp. 135–172. [1, 27]

_____, and **Sawin, D. B.** Children's privacy in the home: Developmental, ecological, and child-rearing determinants. *Environment and Behavior,* 1979, *11,* 87–104. [28]

Parker, A. *States of mind: ESP and altered states of consciousness.* New York: Taplinger, 1975. [6]

Parker, E. S., and **Noble, E. P.** Alcohol consumption and cognitive functioning in social drinkers. *Journal of Studies on Alcohol,* 1977, *38,* 1224–1232. [6]

Parkes, M. C., Benjamin, B. and **Fitzgerald, R. G.** Broken heart: A statistical study of increased mortality among widowers. *British Medical Journal,* 1969, *1,* 740–743. [21]

Pase* v. *Hannon 506 F. Supp. 831 (N. D. Ill. 1980). [20]

Patterson, G. R. Mothers: The unacknowledged victims. *Monographs of the Society for Research in Child Development,* 1980, Serial No. 186. [14]

_____, and **Cobb, J. A.** Stimulus control for classes of noxious behaviors. In J. F. Knutson (Ed.), *The control of aggression.* Chicago: Aldine, 1973. Pp. 145–200. [14]

_____, and **Hops, H.** Coercion: A game for two: Intervention techniques for marital conflict. In R. Ulrich and P. Mountjoy (Eds.), *The experimental analysis of social behavior.* New York: Appleton-Century-Crofts, 1972. [24]

_____, **Littman, R. A.,** and **Bricker, W.** Assertive behavior in children: A step toward a theory of aggression. *Monographs of the Society for Research in Child Development,* 1967, *32,* 5, Whole No. 113. [14, 27]

Pattie, F. A. A report of attempts to produce uniocular blindness by hypnotic suggestion. *British Journal of Medical Psychology,* 1935, *15,* 230–241. [6]

Paul, G. L., and **Lentz, R. J.** *Psychosocial treatment of chronic mental patients: Milieu versus social-learning programs.* Cambridge, Mass.: Harvard University Press, 1977. [1, 24]

Paul, S. M. Movement and madness: Toward a biological model of schizophrenia. In J. D. Maser and M. E. P. Seligman (Eds.), *Psychopathology: Experimental models.* San Francisco: Freeman, 1977. Pp. 358–386. [23]

Pavlov, I. P. *Conditioned reflexes.* London: Oxford University Press, 1927. [1, 8]

Paykel, E. S. Life stress and psychiatric dis-

order: Applications of the clinical approach. In B. S. Dohrenwend and B. P. Dohrenwend (Eds.), *Stressful life events: Their nature and effects.* New York: Wiley, 1974. Pp. 135–149. [21]

Pearlman, A. L., Birch, J., and **Meadows, J. C.** Cerebral color blindness: An acquired defect in hue discrimination. *Annals of Neurology,* 1979, *5,* 3, 253–261. [4]

Penfield, W. The interpretive cortex. *Science,* 1959, *70,* 1719–1725. [9]

_____. Consciousness, memory, and man's conditioned reflexes. In K. H. Pribram (Ed.), *On the biology of learning.* New York: Harcourt Brace Jovanovich, 1969. Pp. 127–168. [6]

_____. The mind-brain question. In D. Goleman and R. J. Davidson (Eds.), *Consciousness: Brain, states of awareness, and mysticism.* New York: Harper & Row, 1979. Pp. 29–30. [6]

_____, and **Perot, P.** The brain's record of auditory and visual experience. *Brain,* 1963, *86,* 595–696. [3]

_____, and **Rasmussen, T.** *The cerebral cortex of man.* New York: Macmillan, 1950. [3]

Pennington, N., and **Hastie, R.** Juror decision making models: The generalization gap. *Psychological Bulletin,* 1981, *89,* 246–278. [1]

Perenin, M. T., and **Jeannerod, M.** Subcortical vision in man. *Trends in Neurosciences,* August 1979, *2,* 204–207. [5]

Perls, F. S. Four lectures. In J. Fagan and I. L. Shepherd (Eds.), *Gestalt therapy now: Therapy, techniques, applications.* Palo Alto, Calif.: Science [Behavior Books, 1970. [24]

_____, **Hefferline, R. F.,** and **Goodman, P.** *Gestalt therapy: Excitement and growth in the human personality.* New York: Julian Press, 1951. [24]

Perry, D. G., and **Bussey, K.** The social learning theory of sex differences: Imitation is alive and well. *Journal of Personality and Social Psychology,* 1979, *37,* 1699–1712. [14]

Perry, J. D., and **Whipple, B.** Pelvic muscle strength of female ejaculators: Evidence in support of a new theory of orgasm. *The Journal of Sex Research,* February 1981, *17,* 22–39. [17]

Pessin, J., and **Husband, R. W.,** Effects of social stimulation on human maze learning. *Journal of Abnormal and Social Psychology,* 1933, *28,* 148–154. [27]

Petersen, A. C., and **Taylor, B.** The biological approach to adolescence. In J. Adelson (Ed.), *Handbook of adolescent psychology.* New York: Wiley-Interscience, 1980. Pp. 159–187. [14]

Peterson, L. R., and **Peterson, M.** Short-term retention of individual verbal items. *Journal of Experimental Psychology,* 1959, *58,* 193–198. [9]

Petrig, B., Julesz, B., Kropfl, W., Baumgartner, G., and **Anliker, M.** Development of stereopsis and cortical binocularity in human infants: Electrophysiological evidence. *Science*, 1981, *213*, 1402-1405. [11]

Pfaffman, C. Gustatory nerve impulses in rat, cat and rabbit. *Journal of Neurophysiology*, 1955, *81*, 429-440. [4]

Pfeifer, L. A subjective report of tactile hallucination in schizophrenia. *Journal of Clinical Psychology*, 1970, *26*, 57-60. [22]

Phillips, S., King, S. and **Dubois, L.** Spontaneous activities of female versus male newborns. *Child Development*, 1978, *49*, 590-597. [14]

Piaget, J. *The moral judgment of the child.* Boston: Routledge & Kegan Paul, 1932. [14]

_____. *The child's conception of number.* Boston: Routledge & Kegan Paul,1952a. [12]

_____. *The origins of intelligence in children* (1952b). New York: International Universities Press, 1966. [12]

_____. *The construction of reality in the child.* New York: Basic Books, 1954. [12]

_____. Need and significance of cross-cultural research in genetic psychology. In B. Inhelder and H. H. Chipman (Eds.), *Piaget and his school.* New York: Springer, 1976. Pp. 259-268. [12]

_____. *Success and understanding.* Cambridge, Mass.: Harvard University Press, 1978. [12]

_____, and **Inhelder, B.** *Le development des quantities chez l'enfant; conservation et atomisme.* Neuchatel: Delachaux et Niestle, 1941. [12]

_____, and _____. *The child's conception of space.* London: Routledge & Kegan Paul, 1956. [12]

_____, and _____. *The Psychology of the child.* New York: Basic Books, 1969. [12, 13]

Pilbeam, D. An idea we could live without— The naked ape. *Discovery*, Spring 1972, 63-70. [7]

Piliavin, I. M., Piliavin, J. A., and **Rodin, J.** Costs, diffusion, and the stigmatized victim. *Journal of Personality and Social Psychology*, 1975, *32*, 429-438. [27]

_____, **Rodin, J.,** and **Piliavin, J. A.** Good samaritanism: An underground phenomenon? *Journal of Personality and Social Psychology*, 1969, *13*, 289-299. [27]

Pines, M. Can the brain renew itself? *Psychology*, Trial Issue, Washington, D.C.: American Psychological Association, 1976, 17-19. [3]

Platt, J. R. *Perception and change: Projections for survival.* Ann Arbor: University of Michigan Press, 1970. [27]

_____. Social traps. *American Psychologist*, 1973, *28*, 641-651. [27]

Plotkin, W. B., and **Cohen, R.** Occipital alpha and the attributes of the "Alpha Experience." *Psychological Physiology*, 1976, *13*, 16-21.[6]

Plutchik, R. *Emotion: A psychoevolutionary synthesis.* New York: Harper [Row, 1980a. [15]

_____. A language for the emotions. *Psychology Today*, February 1980b, *13*, 68-78. [15]

_____. A general psychoevolutionary theory of emotion. In R. Plutchik and H. Kellerman (Eds.), *Emotion: Theory, research and experience* (Vol. 1). New York: Academic Press, 1980c. [15]

Poeppel, E., Held, R., and **Frost, D.** Residual visual function after brain wounds involving central pathways in man. *Nature*, 1973, *243*, 295-296. [5]

Poincare, H. *Foundations of science.* Lancaster, Pa.: Science Press, 1913. [10]

Pollack, I., and **Pickett, J. M.** The intelligibility of excerpts from conversations. *Language and Speech*, 1963, *6*, 165-171. [13]

Pomeroy, W. B. The Masters-Johnson report and the Kinsey tradition. In R. Brecher and E. Brecher (Eds.), *An analysis of "Human sexual response."* New York: New American Library, 1966. [17]

Poon, L. W., Fozard, J. L., and **Walsh-Sweeney, L.** Memory training for the elderly: Salient issues on the use of imagery mnemonics. In L. W. Poon, J. L. Fozard, L. S. Cermak, D. Arenberg, and L. W. Thompson (Eds.), *New directions in memory and aging: Proceedings of the George A. Talland Memorial Conference.* Hillsdale, N.J.: Erlbaum, 1980. [12]

Portnoy, F., and **Simmons, C.** Day care and attachment. *Child Development*, 1978, *49*, 239-242. [14]

Posner, M. I., and **Keele, S. W.** On the genesis of abstract ideas. *Journal of Experimental Psychology*, 1968, *77*, 353-363. [10]

_____, and _____. Retention of abstract ideas. *Journal of Experimental Psychology*, 1970, *83*, 304-308. [10]

Postman, L., and **Phillips, L. W.** Short-term temporal changes in free recall. *Quarterly Journal of Experimental Psychology*, 1965, *17*, 132-138. [9]

_____, and **Stark, K.** Role of response availability in transfer and interference. *Journal of Experimental Psychology*, 1969, *79* (pt. 1), 168-177. [9]

Powers, E. A., Goudy, W. J., and **Keith, P. M.** Congruence between panel and recall data in longitudinal research. *Public Opinion Quarterly*, Fall 1978, 380-389. [4]

Prechtl, H. F. R. Problems of behavioral studies in the newborn infant. In D. S. Lehrman, R. A. Hinde, and E. Shaw (Eds.), *Advances in the study of behavior* (Vol. 1). New York: Academic Press, 1965. Pp. 75-98. [11]

Premack, D. Language in the chimpanzee? *Science*, 1971a, *172*, 808-822. [2, 13]

_____. On the assessment of language competence in the chimpanzee. In A. M. Schrier and F. Stollnitz (Eds.), *Behavior of non-human primates.* New York: Academic Press, 1971b. Pp. 185-228. [13]

_____, and **Premack, A. J.** Teaching language to an ape. *Scientific American*, 1972,

227, 92-99. [2]

Price, R. H. *Abnormal behavior: Perspectives in conflict.* (2nd ed.). New York: Holt, Rinehart & Winston, 1978. [23]

Prien, R. F., Klett, C. J., and **Craffey, E. M.** Lithium prophylaxis in recurrent affective illness. *American Journal of Psychiatry*, 1974, *131*, 198-203. [24]

Pruitt, D. G., and **Kimmel, M.** Twenty years of experimental gaming: Critique, synthesis, and suggestions for the future. In M. R. Rosenzweig and L. W. Porter (Eds.), *Annual review of psychology* (Vol. 28). Palo Alto, Calif.: Annual Reviews, 1977. Pp. 363-392. [27]

Rabbie, J. M., and **Horowitz, M.** Arousal of ingroup-outgroup bias by a chance win or loss. *Journal of Personality and Social Psychology*, 1969, *13*, 269-277. [13]

Rabkin, J. G. Stressful life events and schizophrenia: A review of the literature. *Psychological Bulletin*, 1980, *87*, 408-425. [21]

Rachman, S. J. *Fear and courage.* San Francisco: Freeman, 1978. [21]

_____, **Marks, I.,** and **Hodgson, R.** The treatment of obsessive-compulsive neurotics by modeling and flooding *in vivo. Behaviour Research and Therapy*, 1973, *11*, 463-471. [22,24]

_____, and **Wilson, G. T.** *The effects of psychological therapy* (2nd. ed.) Oxford: Pergamon Press, 1980. [24]

Rada, R. T. Psychological factors in rapist behavior. In R. T. Rada (Ed.), *Clinical aspects of the rapist.* New York: Grune & Stratton, 1978. Pp. 21-58. [17]

Rahe, R. H., and **Arthur, R. J.** Life change and illness studies. *Journal of Human Stress*, 1978, *4*, 3-15. [21]

_____, and **Lind, E.** Psychosocial factors and sudden cardiac death: A pilot study. *Journal of Psychosomatic Research*, 1971, *15*, 19-24. [21]

Ray, O. *Drugs, society, and human behavior* (2nd ed.). St. Louis: Mosby, 1978. [24]

Ray, W., and **Ravizza, R.** *Methods.* Belmont, Calif.: Wadsworth, 1981. [2]

Reese, H. W. Imagery and associative memory. In R. V. Kail, Jr., and J. W. Hagen (Eds.), *Perspectives on the development of memory and cognition.* Hillsdale, N.J.: Erlbaum, 1977. Pp. 113-176. [12]

Reid, J. B. (Ed.). *A social learning approach to family intervention* (Vol. II). *Observation in home settings.* Eugene, Ore.: Castalia Publishing, 1978. [20]

Reinisch, J. M. Prenatal exposure to synthetic progestin increases potential for aggression in humans. *Science*, 1981, *211*, 1171-1173. [14]

Reiss, I. L. *Heterosexual relationships inside and outside of marriage.* Morristown, N.J.: General Learning Press, 1973. [17]

Resnick, R. B., Kestenbaum, R. S., and **Schwartz, L. K.** Acute systemic effects of cocaine in man: A controlled study by intranasal and intravenous routes by administration. *Science*, 1977, *195*, 696-698 [6]

Revelle, W., Amaral, P., and **Turriff, S.** Introversion-extraversion, time stress, and caffeine: The effect on verbal performance. *Science*, 1976, *192*, 149-150. [19]

————, **Humphreys, M. S., Simon, L.,** and **Gilliland, K.** The interactive effect of personality, time of day, and caffeine: A test of the arousal model. *Journal of Experimental Psychology: General*, 1980, *109*, 1-31. [19]

Rheingold, H. L., Gewirtz, J. L., and **Ross, H. W.** Social conditioning of vocalizations in infants. *Journal of Comparative and Physiological Psychology*, 1959, *52*, 68-73. [12]

————, and **Eckerman, C. O.** The infant separates himself from his mother. *Science*, 1970, *168*, 78-83. [14]

Rhine, J. B. Telepathy and other untestable hypotheses. *Journal of Parapsychology*, June 1974, *38*, 1, 137-153. [6]

Rhodewalt, F., and **Comer, R.** Induced-compliance attitude change: Once more with feeling. *Journal of Experimental Social Psychology*, 1979, *15*, 35-47. [15]

Rice, B. Between the lines of threatening messages. *Psychology Today*, September 1981, *15*, 52-64. [13]

————. The Hawthorne effect: Persistence of a flawed theory. *Psychology Today*, 1982, *16*, 71-74. [2]

Rice, R. D. Premature infants respond to sensory stimulation. *APA Monitor*, November 1975. [11]

Richards, J. E., and **Rader, N.** Crawling-onset age predicts visual cliff avoidance in infants. *Journal of Experimental Psychology: Human Perception and Performance*, 1981, *7*, 382-387. [11]

Rimm, D. C., and **Masters, J. C.,** *Behavior therapy: Techniques and empirical findings.* New York: Academic Press, 1979. [24]

Risley, T. R. The effects and side-effects of punishing the autistic behavior of a defiant child. *Journal of Applied Behavior Analysis*, 1968, *1*, 21-34. [8]

Robbins, M. B., and **Jensen, G. D.** Multiple orgasm in males. *Journal of Sex Research*, 1978, *14*, 21-26. [17]

Roberts, J. M., and **Gregor, T.** Privacy: A cultural view. In J. R. Pennock and J. W. Chapman (Eds.), *Privacy.* New York: Atherton, 1971. Pp. 189-225. [28]

Robinson, N. M., and **Robinson, H. B.** *The mentally retarded child, A psychological approach* (2nd ed.). New York: McGraw-Hill, 1976. [24]

Rock, I. *The nature of perceptual adaptation.* New York: Basic Books, 1966. [5]

Rodin, J. Current status of the internal-external hypothesis for obesity: What went wrong? *American Psychologist*, 1981, *34*, 361-372. [16]

————, and **Langer, E.** Long-term effects of a control-relevant intervention with the in-stitutionalized aged. *Journal of Personality and Social Psychology*, 1977, *35*, 897-902. [21]

Roff, M., Sells, S. B., and **Golden, M. M.** *Social adjustment and personality development in children.* Minneapolis: University of Minnesota Press, 1972. [14]

Roffwarg, H. P., Muzio, J. N., and **Dement, W. C.** Ontogenetic development of the human sleep-dream cycle. *Science*, 1966, *152*, 604-619. [6]

Rogel, M. J. A critical evaluation of the possibility of higher primate reproductive and sexual pheromones. *Psychological Bulletin*, 1978, *85*, 810-830. [17]

Rogers, C. R. *Client-centered therapy: Its current practice, implications, and theory.* Boston: Houghton Mifflin, 1951. [24]

————. A theory of personality. In S. Maddi (Ed.), *Perspectives on personality.* Boston: Little, Brown, 1971. [19]

Roopnarine, J., and **Lamb, M.** The effects of day care on attachment and exploratory behavior in a strange situation. *Merrill-Palmer Quarterly*, 1978, *24*, 85-95. [14]

Rorschach, H. *Psychodiagnostics: A diagnostic test based on perception.* New York: Grune & Stratton, 1942. [20]

Rose, S. The conscious brain. New York: Knopf, 1973. [3, 6]

Rose, S. A., and **Blank, M.** The potency of context in children's cognition: An illustration through conservation. *Child Development*, 1974, *45*, 499-502. [12]

————, **Schmidt, K., Riese, M. L.,** and **Bridger, W. H.** Effects of prematurity and early intervention on responsivity to actual stimuli: A comparison of preterm and full-term infants. *Child Development*, 1980, *51*, 416-425. [11]

Rosenhan, D. L. On being sane in insane places. *Science*, 1973, *179*, 250-258. [22]

————, **Underwood, B.,** and **Moore, B.** Affect moderates self-gratification and altruism. *Journal of Personality and Social Psychology*, 1974, *30*, 546-552. [27]

Rosenman, R. H., Brand, R. J., Jenkins, C. D., Friedman, M., Straus, R., and **Wurm, M.** Coronary heart disease in the Western Collaborative Group study: Final follow-up experience of 8½ years. *Journal of the American Medical Association*, 1975, *8*, 872-877. [21]

Rosenthal, D., Wender, P. H., Kety, S., Welner, J., and **Schulsinger, F.** The adopted-away offspring of schizophrenics. *American Journal of Psychiatry*, 1971, *128*, 307-311. [23]

Rosenthal, R. *Experimenter effects in behavioral research.* New York: Appleton-Century-Crofts, 1966. [2]

————, and **Fode, K. L.** The effect of experimental bias on the performance of the albino rat. *Behavioral Science*, 1963, *8*, 183-187. [2]

Rosenthal, T., and **Bandura, A.** Psychological modeling: Theory and practice. In S. L. Garfield and A. E. Bergin (Eds.), *Handbook of psychotherapy and behavior change: An empirical analysis.* (2nd. ed.). New York: Wiley, 1978. [19, 23, 24]

Rosenzweig, M. R., Bennett, E. L. and **Diamond, M. C.** Brain changes in response to experience. *Scientific American*, February 1972, *226*, 22-29. [11]

Roskies, E. Teaching healthy managers to control their coronary-prone (Type A) behavior. In K. Blankstein, J. Polivy and P. Pliner (Eds.), *Self-control and self-modification of emotional behavior.* New York: Plenum, 1982. [21]

Ross, E. D., and **Mesulam, M.** Dominant language functioning of the right hemisphere: Prosody and emotional gesturing. *Archives of Neurology*, 1979, *36*, 144-148. [15]

Rotter, J. B. Generalized expectancies for internal versus external control of reinforcement. *Psychological Monographs*, 1966, *80*, 1, Whole No. 609. [20]

Rovee-Collier, C. K., Sullivan, M. W., Enright, M., Lucas, D., and **Fagen, J. W.** Reactivation of infant memory. *Science*, 1980, *208*, 1159-1161. [12]

Rowan, W. *The riddle of migration.* Baltimore: William & Wilkins, 1931. [7]

Rowland, N. E. and **Antelman, S. M.** Stress-induced hyperphagia and obesity in rats: A possible model for understanding human obesity. *Science*, 1976, *191*, 310-312. [3]

Rozin, E., and **Rozin, P.** Culinary themes and variations. *Natural History*, February 1981, *90*, 7-14. [25]

Rozin, P. Specific aversions and neophobia resulting from vitamin deficiency or poisoning in half-wild and domestic rats. *Journal of Comparative and Physiological Psychology*, 1968, *66*, 82-88. [16]

————. The significance of learning mechanisms in food selection: Some biology, psychology, and sociology of science. In L. M. Barker, M. R. Best, and M. Domjan (Eds.), *Learning mechanisms in food selection.* Waco, Tex.: Baylor University Press, 1977. [16]

————, and **Schiller, D.** The nature and acquisition of a preference for chili pepper by humans. *Motivation and Emotion.* 1980, *4*, 77-101. [25]

Rubenstein, C., Shaver, P., and **Peplau, L. A.** Loneliness. *Human Nature*, February 1979, *2*, 58-65. [14]

Rubenstein, R. L. Books: *Beyond freedom and dignity. Psychology Today*, September 1971, *5*, 28-31 *passim*. [19]

Rubin, H. B., and **Henson, D. E.** Voluntary enhancement of penile erection. *Bulletin of the Psychonomic Society*, 1975, *6*, 158-160. [17]

Rubin, L. B. *Women of a certain age: The midlife search for self.* New York: Harper & Row, 1979. [21]

Rubin, Z. Measurement of romantic love.

Journal of Personality and Social Psychology, 1970, *16*, 265-273. [26]

_____. *Liking and loving: An invitation to social psychology*. New York: Holt, Rinehart & Winston, 1973. [26]

_____. *Children's friendships*. Cambridge, Mass.: Harvard University Press, 1980. [14]

Rule, B. G., and Nesdale, A. R. Emotional arousal and aggressive behavior. *Psychological Bulletin*, 1976, *83*, 851-863. [27]

Rumbaugh, D. M., Gill, T. V., and van Glasersfeld, E.C. Reading and sentence completion by a chimpanzee. *Science*, 1963, *182*, 731-733. [13]

Rush, A. J., Beck, A. T., Kovac, M., and Hollon, S. Comparative efficacy of cognitive therapy and imipramine in the treatment of depressed outpatients. *Cognitive Therapy and Research*, 1977, *1*, 17-37. [24]

Rush, F. *The best kept secret: Sexual abuse of children*. Englewood Cliffs, N.J.: Prentice-Hall, 1980. [18]

Rutter, M. Parent-child separation: Psychological effects on the children. *Journal of Child Psychology and Psychiatry*, 1971, *12*, 233-260. [14]

Rycroft, C. Introduction. In M. Prince, *Dissociation of personality*. New York: Oxford University Press, 1978. [22]

Rynders, J. *Annual report of the University of Minnesota Institute of Child Development*, 1975. [11]

Sackett, G. P., Ruppenthal, G. C., Fahrenbruch, C. E., Holm, R. A., and Greenough, W. T. Social isolation rearing effects in monkeys vary with genotype. *Developmental Psychology*, 1981, *17*, 313-318. [14]

Sackheim, H. A., and Gur, R. C. Lateral asymmetry in intensity of emotional expression. *Neuropsychologia*, 1978, *16*, 473-481. [15]

Sadalla, E. K., Burroughs, J., and Quaid, M. House form and social identity: A validity study. In R. R. Stough and A. Wandersman (Eds.), *Optimizing environments: Proceedings of the eleventh annual conference of the Environmental Design Research Association*. Washington, D.C.: Environmental Design Research Association, 1980. Pp. 210-206. [28]

_____, and Loftness, S. Emotional images as mediators in one-trial paired-associate learning. *Journal of Experimental Psychology*, 1972, *95*, 295-298. [9]

Saghir, M. T., and Robins, E. *Male and female homosexuality: A comprehensive investigation*. Baltimore: Williams & Wilkins, 1973. [17]

Sagi, A., and Hoffman, M. L. Empathic distress in the newborn. *Developmental Psychology*, 1967, *12*, 175-176. [11]

Salapatek, P. Pattern perception in early infancy. In L. B. Cohen and P. Salapatek (Eds.), *Infant perception: From sensation to cognition* (Vol. 1). *Basic visual processes*. New York: Academic Press, 1975. Pp. 133-248. [11]

Sales, E. Women's adult development. In I. H. Frieze, J. E. Parsons, P. B. Johnson, D. N. Ruble, and G. L. Zellman (Eds.), *Women and sex roles: A social psychological perspective*. New York: Norton, 1978. Pp. 157-190. [21]

Salk, L. Mothers' heartbeat as an imprinting stimulus. *Transactions of the New York Academy of Sciences*, 1962, *24*, 753-763. [2]

Salzen, E. D., and Meyer, C. C. Reversibility of imprinting. *Journal of Comparative and Physiological Psychology*, 1968, *66*, 269-275. [7]

Sameroff, A. J., and Cavanaugh, P. J. Learning in infancy: A developmental perspective. In J. D. Osofsky (Ed.), *Handbook of infant development*. New York: Wiley-Interscience, 1979. Pp. 344-392. [12]

Sanford, R. R. The effects of abstinence from food upon imaginal processes. *Journal of Psychology*, 1937, *2*, 129-136. [16]

Sarason, I. G. A modeling and informational approach to delinquency. In E. Ribes-Inesta and A. Bandura (Eds.), *Analysis of delinquency and aggression*. Hillsdale, N.J.: Erlbaum, 1976. [24]

Sarason, S. B., Mandler, G., and Craighill, P. G. The effects of differential instructions on anxiety and learning. *Journal of Abnormal and Social Psychology*, 1952, *47*, 561-565. [8]

Sarbin, T. R., and Coe, W. C. *Hypnosis: A social psychological analysis of influence communication*. New York: Holt, Rinehart & Winston, 1972. [6]

Satir, V. *Conjoint family therapy* (Rev. ed.). Palo Alto, Calif.: Science & Behavior Books, 1967. [24]

Savage-Rumbaugh, E. S., Rumbaugh, D. M., and Boysen, S. Do apes use language? *American Scientist*, 1980, *68*, 49-61. [13]

_____, Smith, S. T. and Lawson, J. Reference: The linguistic essential. *Science*, 1980, *210*, 922-924. [13]

Swatzky, H. L., and Lehn, W. H. The Arctic mirage and the early North Atlantic. *Science*, 1976, *192*, 1300-1305. [5]

Scanlon, J., and Chisolm, J. J. Jr. Fetal effects of lead exposure. *Pediatrics*, 1972, *49*, 145-146. [20]

Scared to Death. *Science Digest*, November/December, 1980, 105. [3]

Scarr, S. Outline of developmental contributions to clinical psychology. Paper presented at annual meeting of American Psychological Association, Los Angeles, Calif., August 1981. [11]

_____. *Race, social class, and individual differences in I. Q.* Hillsdale, N.J.: Erlbaum, 1981. [20]

_____, and Grajek, S. Similarities and differences among siblings. In M. E. Lamb and B. Sutton-Smith (Eds.), *Sibling relationships*. Hillsdale, N.J.: Erlbaum, 1982. [11]

_____, and Salapatek, P. Patterns of fear development during infancy. *Merrill-Palmer Quarterly of Behavior and Development*, 1970, *16*, 53-90. [11]

_____, Webber, P. L., Weinberg, R. A., and Wittig, M. A. Personality resemblance among adolescents and their parents in biologically related and adoptive families. *Journal of Personality and Social Psychology*, 1981, *40*. [11]

_____, and Weinberg, R. A. IQ test performance of black children adopted by white families. *American Psychologist*, 1976, *3*, 726-739. [20]

_____, and _____. Attitudes, interests and I.Q.. *Human Nature*, April 1978, *1*, 29-36. [14]

_____, and _____. The influence of "family background" on intellectual attainment. *American Sociological Review*, 1978, *43*, 674-692. [11]

Scarr-Salapatek, S. Unknowns in the IQ equation. *Science*, 1971, *174*, 1223-1228. [20]

_____. An evolutionary perspective on infant intelligence: Species patterns and individual variations. In M. Lewis (Ed.), *Origins of intelligence*. New York: Plenum, 1976. Pp. 165-197. [11]

Schachtel, E. G. *Experimental foundations of Rorschach's test*. New York: Basic Books, 1966. [20]

Schachter, S. *The psychology of affiliation*. Stanford, Calif.: Stanford University Press, 1959. [21]

_____. Some extraordinary facts about obese humans and rats. *American Psychologist*, 1970, *26*, 129-144. [16]

_____. *Emotion, obesity, and crime*. New York: Academic Press, 1971. [16]

_____, Goldman, R., and Gordon, A. Effects of fear, food deprivation, and obesity on eating. *Journal of Personality and Social Psychology*, 1968, *10*, 91-97. [16]

_____, and Singer, J. E. Cognitive, social, and physiological determinants of emotional state. *Psychological Review*, 1962, *69*, 379-399. [15]

_____, and Wheeler, L. Epinephrine, chlorpromazine, and amusement. *Journal of Abnormal and Social Psychology*, 1962, *65*, 121-128. [15]

Schaeffer, J., Andrysiak, T., and Ungerleider, J. T. Cognition and long-term use of ganja (cannabis). *Science*, 1981, *213*, 465-466. [6]

Schaffer, R. *Mothering*. Cambridge, Mass.: Harvard University Press, 1977. [14]

Scheerer, M. Problem-solving. *Scientific American*, April 1963, *208*, 118-128. [10]

Scheff, T. J. *Labeling madness*. Englewood Cliffs, N.J.: Prentice-Hall, 1975. [23]

Scherer, K. R., Abeles, R. P., and Fischer, C. S. *Human aggression and conflict*. Englewood Cliffs, N.J.: Prentice-Hall, 1975. [27]

Schiff, M., Duyme, M., Dumaret, A., Stewart, J., Tomkiewicz, S., and **Feingold, J.** Intellectual status of working-class children adopted early into upper-middle class families. *Science,* 1978, *200,* 1503–1504. [20]

Schildkraut, J. J. The catecholamine hypothesis of affective disorders: A review of supporting evidence. *American Journal of Psychiatry,* 1965, *122,* 509–522. [23]

_____. Neuropharmacological studies of mood disorders. In J. Zubin and F. A. Freyhan (Eds.), *Disorders of mood.* Baltimore: Johns Hopkins Press, 1972. [23]

Schmale, A. Giving up as a final common pathway to changes in health. *Advances in psychosomatic medicine* (Vol. 8), 1972. [21]

Schmidt, D. E., and **Keating, J. P.** Human crowding and personal control: An integration of the research. *Psychological Bulletin,* 1979, *86,* 680–700. [28]

Schmidt, E. E., Goldman, R. D., and **Feimer, N. R.** Perceptions of crowding: Predicting at the residence, neighborhood and city levels. *Environment and Behavior,* 1979, *11,* 105–130. [28]

Schneider, W., and **Shiffrin, R. M.** Controlled and automatic human information processing. I. Detection, search, attention. *Psychological Review,* 1977, *84,* 1–66. [9]

Schultes, R. E. *Hallucinogenic plants.* New York: Golden Press, 1976. [6]

Schultz, J. H., and **Luthe, W. O.** *Autogenic therapy. Vol. I.: Autogenic methods.* New York: Grune & Stratton, 1969. [21]

Schwartz, D. J., Weinstein, L. N., and **Arkin, A. M.** Qualitative aspects of sleep mentation. In A. M. Arkin, J. S. Antrobus, and S. J. Ellman (Eds.), *The mind in sleep: Psychology and psychophysiology.* Hillsdale, N.J.: Erlbaum, 1978. [6]

Schwartz, G. E. Psychosomatic disorders and biofeedback: A psychobiological model of disregulation. In J. D. Maser and M. E. P. Seligman (Eds.), *Psychopathology: Experimental models.* San Francisco: Freeman, 1977. [21]

_____, **Davidson, R. J.,** and **Maer, F.** Right hemisphere lateralization for emotion in the human brain: Interactions with cognition. *Science,* 1975, *190,* 286–288. [2]

_____, **Fair, P. L., Mandel, M. R., Salt, P., Meiske, M.,** and **Klerman, G. L.** Facial electromyography in the assessment of improvement in depression. *Psychosomatic Medicine,* 1978, *40,* 355–360. [15]

Schwartz, J., and **Tallal, P.** Rate of acoustic change may underlie hemispheric specialization for speech perception. *Science,* 1980, *207,* 1380–1381. [3]

Scollan, R. A real early stage: An unzippered condensation of a dissertation on child language. In E. Ochs and B. B. Schieffelin (Eds.), *Developmental pragmatics.* New York: Academic Press, 1979. Pp. 215–227. [13]

Scott, J. P. Critical periods in behavioral development. *Science,* November 30, 1962, *138,* 949–958. [7]

_____, **Stewart, J. M.** and **DeGhett, V. J.** Critical periods in the organization of systems. *Development Psychobiology,* 1974, *7,* 489–513. [11]

Scott, W. E., Jr. The effects of extrinsic rewards on "intrinsic motivation": A critique. *Organizational Behavior and Human Performance,* 1975, *15,* 117–129. [16]

Searle, L. V. The organization of heredity: Maze-brightness and maze-dullness. *Genetic Psychology Monographs,* 1949, *39,* 279–325. [7]

Searle, J. R. *Speech acts: An essay in the philosophy of language.* New York: Cambridge University Press, 1969. [13]

Sears, R. R. Sources of life satisfaction of the Terman gifted men. *American Psychologist,* 1977, *32,* 119–128. [20]

Segal, M. W. Alphabet and attraction: An unobtrusive measure of the effect of propinquity in a field setting. *Journal of Personality and Social Psychology,* 1974, *30,* 654–657. [25, 26]

Segall, M. H., Campbell, D. T., and **Herskovits, M. J.** *The influence of culture on visual perception.* Indianapolis: Bobbs-Merrill, 1966. [5]

Sekuler, R., Hutman, L. P. and **Owsley, C. J.** Human aging and spatial vision. *Science,* 1980, *209,* 1255–1256. [12]

Selfridge, O. G. Pandemonium: A paradigm for learning. In *Symposium on the mechanization of thought processes.* London: HM Stationary Office, 1959. [5]

Seligman, M. E. P., and **Hager, J. L.** The sauce-bernaise syndrome. *Psychology Today,* August 1972, 6, 59–61 *passim.* [8]

Selman, R. L. Toward a structural analysis of developing interpersonal relations concepts. In A. Pick (Ed.), *Minnesota symposia on child psychology* (Vol. 10). Minneapolis: University of Minnesota Press, 1976. [14]

_____. *The growth of interpersonal understanding.* New York: Academic Press, 1980. [14]

_____, and **Jacquette, D.** Stability and oscillation in interpersonal awareness: A clinical-developmental analysis. In C. B. Keasey (Ed.), *Nebraska symposium on motivation* (Vol. 25). Lincoln: University of Nebraska Press, 1977. [14]

Selye, H. *The stress of life.* New York: McGraw-Hill, 1956. [21]

_____. *Stress without distress.* Philadelphia: Lippincott, 1974. [21]

_____, and **Cherry, L.** On the real benefits of eustress. *Psychology Today,* March 1978, *11,* 60–63 *passim.* [21]

Serbin, L. A., Connor, J. M., and **Citron, C. C.** Sex-differentiated free play behavior: Effects of teacher modeling, location, and gender. *Developmental Psychology,* 1981, *17,* 640–646. [14]

_____, **O'Leary, K. D., Kent, R. N.** and **Tonick, I. J.** A comparison of teacher response to the pre-academic and problem behavior of boys and girls. *Child Development,* 1973, *33,* 796–804. [14]

Shank, R., and **Abelson, R.** *Scripts, plans, goals and understanding.* Hillsdale, N.J.: Erlbaum, 1977. [10]

Shapin, B., and **Coly, L.** (Eds.). *PSI and states of awareness.* New York: Parapsychology Foundation, 1978. [6]

Shapiro, C. M., Bortz, R., Mitchell, D., Bartel, P., and **Jooste, P.** Slow-wave sleep: A recovery period after exercise. *Science,* 1981, *214,* 1253–1254. [6]

Shapiro, D. Y. Serial female sex change after simultaneous removal of males from social groups of a coral reef fish. *Science,* 1980, *209,* 1136–1137. [7]

Sheehan, S. *Is there no place on earth for me?* Boston: Houghton Mifflin, 1982. [22]

Sherif, C. W. *Orientation in social psychology.* New York: Harper & Row, 1976. [16]

Sherif, M. *The Psychology of Social Norms.* New York: Harper, 1936. [27]

_____, **Harvey, O. J., White, B. J., Hood, W. R.,** and **Sherif, C. W.** *Intergroup conflict and cooperation: The robber's cave experiment.* Norman: University of Oklahoma Press, 1961. [25, 26]

_____, and **Sherif, C. W.** *Reference Groups.* New York: Harper & Row, 1964. [14]

Sidtis, J. J., Volpe, B. T., Holtzman, J. D., Wilson, D. H., and **Gazzaniga, M. S.** Cognitive interaction after staged collosal section: Evidence for transfer of semantic activation. *Science,* 1981, *212,* 344–346. [3]

Siegel, R. K. Hallucinations. *Scientific American,* October 1977, *237,* 132–140. [6]

Silver, R. L., and **Wortman, C. B.** Coping with undesirable life events. In J. Garber and M. E. P. Seligman (Eds.), *Human helplessness: Theory and applications.* New York: Academic Press, 1980. [21]

Simon, H. A., and **Gilmartin, K. A.** A simulation of memory for chess positions. *Cognitive Psychology,* 1973, *5,* 29–46. [10]

_____, and **Newell, A.** Computer simulation of human thinking and problem solving. In *Cognitive development in children.* Chicago: University of Chicago Press, 1970. Pp. 113–125. [10]

Singer, J. L., and **Singer, D. G.** *Television, imagination, and aggression.* Hillsdale, N.J.: Erlbaum, 1981. [14]

Siqueland, E., and **Delucia, C. A.** Visual reinforcement of non-nutritive sucking in human infants. *Science,* 1969, *165,* 1144–1146. [12]

Sistrunk, F., and **McDavid, J. W.** Sex variables in conforming behavior. *Journal of Personality and Social Psychology,* 1971, *17,* 200–207. [25]

Skinner, B. F. *Behavior of organisms: An experimental analysis.* New York: Appleton-Century-Crofts, 1938. [8]

_____. Superstitious behavior in the pigeon. *Journal of Experimental Psychology,* 1948a, *38,* 168–172. [8]

———. *Walden two*. New York: Macmillan, 1948b. [1, 8]

———, *Walden two* (1948). New York: Macmillan, 1968. [19]

———. *Verbal behavior*. New York: Appleton-Century-Crofts, 1957. [13]

———. *Beyond freedom and dignity*. New York: Knopf, 1971. [1, 8, 19]

———. *Science and human behavior*. New York: Free Press, 1965. [19]

———. The steep and thorny road to a science of behavior. *American Psychologist*, 1975, *30*, 42-49. [19]

———. *Walden two (1949)*. New York: Macmillan, 1968. [19]

Sklar, L. S., and Anisman, H. Stress and cancer. *Psychological Bulletin*, 1981, *89*, 369-406. [21]

Skodak, M., and Skeels, H. M. A final follow-up of one hundred adopted children. *Journal of Genetic Psychology*, 1949, *75*, 85-125. [20]

Slater, E. A review of earlier evidence on genetic factors in schizophrenia. In D. Rosenthal and S. S. Kety (Eds.), *The transmission of schizophrenia*. Elmsford, N.Y.: Pergamon, 1968. [23]

Slobin, D. I. Cognitive prerequisites for the development of grammar. In C. A. Ferguson and D. I. Slobin (Eds.), *Studies of child language development*. New York: Holt, Rinehart [Winston, 1973. [13]

Slovic, P., and Fischoff, B. On the psychology of experimental surprises. *Journal of Experimental Psychology: Human Perception and Performance*, 1977, *3*, 544-551. [10]

———, Fischoff, B., and Lichtenstein, S. Unpublished study. [10]

———, Kunreuther, H., and White, G. F. Decision process, rationality and adjustment to natural hazards. In G. F. White (Ed.), *Natural hazards, local, national and global*. New York: Oxford University Press, 1974. Pp. 187-205. [10]

Smith, A., and Sugar, O. Development of above-normal language and intelligence twenty-one years after left hemispherectomy. *Neurology*, 1975, *25*, 813-818. [13]

Smith, M. L., Glass, G. V., and Miller, T. I. *The benefits of psychotherapy*. Baltimore: Johns Hopkins Press, 1980. [24]

Snodgrass, J. G. *The numbers game—Statistics for psychology*. Baltimore, Md.: Williams and Wilkins, 1977. [2]

Snow, C. E., and Hoefnagel-Hohle, M. The critical period for language acquisition: Evidence from second language learning. *Child Development*, 1978, *49*, 1114-1118. [13]

Snow, C. P. Either-or. *Progressive*, 1961, *25*, 2, 24-25. [27]

Snyder, F. Sleep and dreaming: Progress in the new biology of dreaming. *American Journal of Psychiatry*, 1965, *122*, 377-391. [6]

———. The phenomenology of dreaming. In L. Madow and L. H. Snow (Eds.), *The psychodynamic implications of the physiological studies on dreams*. Springfield, Ill.: Charles C. Thomas, 1970. [6]

Snyder, M. L., Stephan, W. G., and Rosenfield, D. Egotism and attribution. *Journal of Personality and Social Psychology*, 1976, *32*, 637-644. [26]

———, Tanke, E. D., and Berscheid, E. Social perception and interpersonal behavior: On the self-fulfilling nature of social stereotypes. *Journal of Personality and Social Psychology*, 1977, *35*, 656-666. [26]

Snyder, S. H. Catecholamines in the brain as mediators of amphetamine psychosis. *Archives of General Psychiatry*, 1972, *27*, 169-179. [23]

———. The dopamine hypothesis of schizophrenia: Focus on the dopamine receptor. *American Journal of Psychiatry*, 1976, *133*, 197-202. [23]

———. The true speed trip: schizophrenia. In D. Goleman and R. J. Davidson (Eds.), *Consciousness: Brain, states of awareness, and mysticism*. New York: Harper & Row, 1979, Pp. 105-109. [6]

———, interviewed by Goleman, D. Matter over mind: The big issues raised by newly discovered brain chemicals. *Psychology Today*, June 1980, *14*, 66-76. [3]

———. Dopamine receptors, neuroleptics, and schizophrenia. *American Journal of Psychiatry*, 1981, *138*, 460-464. [23]

Sociobiology Study Group of Science for the People. Sociobiology—Another biological determinism. In A. L. Caplan (Ed.), *The sociobiology debate: Readings on ethical and scientific issues*. New York: Harper & Row, 1978. Pp. 280-290. [7]

Soldatos, C. R., Kales, J. D., Scharf, M. B., Bixler, E. O., and Kales, A. Cigarette smoking associated with sleep difficulty. *Science*, 1980, *207*, 551-552. [6]

Solomon, R. L. The opponent-process theory of acquired motivation: The costs of pleasure and the benefits of pain. *American Psychologist*. 1980, *35*, 691-712. [16]

Sommer, R. *Personal space: The behavioral basis of design*. Englewood Cliffs, N.J.: Prentice-Hall, 1969. [28]

Sowell, T. New light on black I.Q.. *The New York Times Magazine*, March 27, 1977, 56-62. [20]

Spence, K. W. *Behavior theory and conditioning*. New Haven: Yale University Press, 1956. [27]

Sperling, G. The information available in brief visual presentation. *Psychological Monographs*, 1960, *74*, Whole No. 498. [9]

Sperry, R. W. The great cerebral commisure. *Scientific American*, January 1964, *110*. [3]

———. A modified concept of consciousness. *Psychological Review*, 1969, *76*, 532-536. [3]

———. Left-brain, right-brain. *Saturday Review*, 1975, *2*, 30-33. [3]

———. Changing concepts of consciousness and free will. *Perspectives in Biology and Medicine*, Autumn 1976, *20*, 1, 9-19. [6]

———. Bridging science and values: A unifying view of mind and brain. *American Psychologist*, April 1977, *32*, 4, 237-245. [6]

Spirduso, W. W. Reaction and movement time as a function of age and physical activity level. *Journal of Gerontology*, 1975, *30*, 435-440. [12]

Spitzer, R. L. More on pseudoscience in science and the case for psychiatric diagnosis: A critique of D. L. Rosenhan's "On being sane in insane places" and "The contextual nature of psychiatric diagnosis." *Archives of General Psychiatry*, 1976, *33*, 459-470. [22]

Springer, S. P., and Deutsch, G. *Left brain, right brain*. San Francisco: Freeman, 1981. [2, 3, 6, 12]

Srole, L., Langner, T. S., Michael, S. T., Opler, M. K., and Rennie, T. A. C. *The Midtown Manhattan study: Mental health in the metropolis* (Vol. 1). New York: McGraw-Hill, 1962. [22]

St. James-Roberts, I. Neurological plasticity, recovery from brain insult, and child development. In H. W. Reese and L. P. Lipsitt (Eds.), *Advances in child development and behavior* (Vol. 14). New York: Academic Press, 1979. Pp. 253-319. [3]

Stallone, F., Shelley, E., Mendlewicz, J., and Fieve, R. R. The use of lithium in affective disorders. III: A double-blind study of prophylaxis in bipolar illness. *American Journal of Psychiatry*, 1973, *130*, 1006-1010. [24]

Stanley, J. C. Test better finder of great math talent than teachers are. *American Psychologist*, April 1976, *31*, 313-314. [20]

———, and George, W. C. SMPY's ever-increasing D_4. *Gifted Child Quarterly*, 1980, *24*, 41-48. [20]

Staub, E. Instigation to goodness: The role of social norms and interpersonal influence. *Journal of Social Issues*, 1972, *28*, 3, 131-150. [27]

Stefanson, V. *Unsolved mysteries of the Arctic*. New York: Macmillan, 1938. [16]

Stein, A. H., and Bailey, M. M. The socialization of achievement orientation in females. *Psychological Bulletin*, 1973, *80*, 345-366. [16]

Steiner, J. E. Facial expressions in response to taste and smell stimulation. In H. W. Reese and L. P. Lipsitt (Eds.), *Advances in child development and behavior* (Vol. 13). New York: Academic Press, 1979. Pp. 257-296. [11]

Sterman, M. B. Biofeedback and epilepsy. *Human Nature*, May 1978, *1*, 50-57. [21]

Stern, W. *The psychological methods of testing inteligence*. Baltimore: Warwick & York, 1914. [20]

Sternberg, S. High-speed scanning in human memory. *Science*, 1966, *153*, 652-654. [9]

Stevens, C. F. *Neurophysiology: A primer*. New York: Wiley, 1966. [3]

———. The Neuron. *Scientific American*, September 1979, *241*, 55-65. [3]

Stevens, S. S. On the psychophysical law. *Psychological Review*, 1957, *64*, 153-181. [4]

_____. The surprising simplicity of sensory metrics. *American Psychologist*, 1962, *17*, 29-39. [4]

Stewart, K. Dream theory in Malaya. In C. T. Tart (Ed.), *Altered states of consciousness.* New York: Doubleday, 1972. [6]

Stokols, D. On the distinction between density and crowding: Some implications for future research. *Psychological Review*, 1972, *79*, 275-277. [28]

Storms, M. D. Videotape and the attribution process: Reversing actors' and observers' points of view. *Journal of Personality and Social Psychology*, 1973, *27*, 167-175. [26]

Stoyva, J. Self-regulation and the stress-related disorders: A perspective on biofeedback. In D. I. Mostofsky (Ed.), *Behavior control and modification of physiological activity.* Englewood Cliffs, N.J.: Prentice-Hall, 1976. Pp. 366-398. [3]

Stratton, G. M. Some preliminary experiments on vision without inversion of the retinal image. *Psychological Review*, 1896, *3*, 611-617. [5]

Strayer, F. D., and **Strayer, J.** An ethological analysis of social agonism and dominance relations among preschool children. *Child Development*, 1976, *47*, 980-989. [14,28]

Strayer, J. Social conflict and peer group status. Paper presented at Biennial Meeting of the Society for Research in Child development, New Orleans, March, 1977. [14]

Strauss, M. E., Foureman, W. C., and **Parwatikar, S. D.** Schizophrenics' size estimations of thematic stimuli. *Journal of Abnormal Psychology*, 1974, *83*, 117-123. [22]

Streissguth, A. P., Landesman-Dwyer, S., and **Smith, D. W.** Teratogenic effects of alcohol in humans and laboratory animals. *Science*, 1980, *209*, 353-361. [11]

Stuart, R. B. Behavioral contracting within the families of delinquents. *Journal of Behavior Therapy and Experimental Psychiatry*, 1971, *2*, 1-11. [24]

Suedfeld, P. Changes in intellectual performance and in susceptibility to influence. In J. P. Zubek (Ed.), *Sensory deprivation: Fifteen years of research.* New York: Appleton-Century-Crofts, 1969. Pp. 126-166. [6]

_____. The Benefits of boredom: Sensory deprivation reconsidered. In I. L. Janis (Ed.), *Current trends in psychology.* Los Altos, Calif.: William Kaufmann, 1977. Pp. 281-290. [6]

_____. Social isolation: A case for interdisciplinary research. In D. Goleman and R. J. Davidson (Eds.), *Consciousness: Brain, states of awareness, and mysticism.* New York: Harper & Row, 1979. Pp. 161-165. [6]

Sugarman, S. Developmental change in early representational intelligence: Evidence from spatial classification strategies and related verbal expressions. *Cognitive Psychology*, 1982, *14*. [12]

Sundstrom, E. An experimental study of crowding: Effects of room size, intrusion, and goal blocking on nonverbal behavior, self-disclosure, and self-reported stress. *Journal of Personality and Social Psychology*, 1975, *32*, 645-654. [28]

_____, and **Altman, I.** Field study of territorial behavior and dominance. *Journal of Personality and Social Psychology*, 1974, *30*, 115-124. [28]

_____, **Burt, R. E.,** and **Kamp, D.** Privacy at work: Architectural correlates of job satisfaction and job performance. *Academy of Management Journal*, 1980, *23*, 101-117. [28]

Suomi, S. J., and **Harlow, H. F.** Depressive behavior in young monkeys subjected to vertical chamber confinement. *Journal of Comparative and Physiological Psychology*, 1972, *80*, 11-18. [14]

Super, C. M. Cognitive development: Looking across at growing up. In C. M. Super and S. Harkness (Eds.), *New directions for child development* (No. 8). *Anthropological perspectives on child development.* San Francisco: Jossey-Bass, 1980. Pp. 59-69. [12]

Suppes, P., and **Morningstar, M.** Computer-assisted instruction. *Science*, 1969, *166*, 343-350. [8]

Surveying Crime. Report of the Panel for the Evaluation of Crime Surveys. Washington, D.C.: National Academy of Sciences, 1976. [2]

Synder, M. Self-monitoring processes. In L. Berkowitz (Ed.), *Advances in experimental social psychology* (Vol. 12). New York: Academic Press, 1979. [25]

_____, and **Kendzierski, D.** Acting on one's attitudes: Procedures for linking attitude and behavior. *Journal of Experimental Social Psychology*, 1982, *18*, 165-183. [25]

Szasz, T. S. *The Myth of Mental Illness: Foundations of a theory of personal conduct.* New York: Harper & Row, 1961. [22, 23]

Tajfel, H. *Human groups and social categories.* Cambridge, Engl.: Cambridge University Press, 1981. [26]

Tanzer, D. Natural childbirth: Pain or peak experience? *Psychology Today*, October 1968, *69*, 16-21. [19]

Tart, C. T. Marijuana intoxication: Common experiences. *Nature*, 1970, *226*, 701-704. [6]

_____. *States of Consciousness.* New York: Dutton, 1975. [6, 19]

_____. PSI functioning and altered states of consciousness: A perspective. In B. Shapin and L. Coly (Eds.), *PSI and states of awareness.* New York: Parapsychology Foundation, 1978. Pp. 180-210. [6]

Tavris, C. A., and **Offir, C.** *The longest war: Sex differences in perspective.* New York: Harcourt Brace Jovanovich, 1977. [14, 17]

Taylor, R. B., and **Stough, R. R.** Territorial cognition: Assessing Altman's typology. *Journal of Personality and Social Psychology*, 1978, *36*, 418-423. [28]

Taylor, S. E., and **Fiske, S. T.** Salience, attention and attribution: Top of the head phenomena. In L. Berkowitz (Ed.), *Advances in experimental social psychology* (Vol. 11). New York: Academic Press, 1978. [10]

Tedeschi, J. T., Schlenker, B. R., and **Bonoma, T. V.** Cognitive dissonance: Private ratiocination or public spectacle? *American Psychologist*, 1971, *26*, 685-695. [16]

Teitelbaum, P. The encephalization of hunger. In E. Stellar and J. M. Sprague (Eds.), *Progress in physiological psychology* (Vol. 4). New York: Academic Press, 1971. [3]

Terman, L. M. *The measurement of intelligence.* Boston: Houghton Mifflin, 1916. [20]

_____, and **Merrill, M. A.** *Stanford-Binet Intelligence Scale: Manual for the third revision, form L-M.* Boston: Houghton Mifflin, 1973. [20]

_____, and _____. *Measuring intelligence.* Boston: Houghton Mifflin, 1937. [20]

_____, and **Oden, M. H.** *Genetic studies of genius. IV. The gifted child grows up.* Stanford, Calif.: Stanford University Press, 1947. [20]

_____, and _____. *Genetic studies of genius. V. The gifted group at mid-life.* Stanford, Calif.: Stanford University Press, 1959. [20]

Terrace, H. S., Petitto, L. A., Sanders, R. J., and **Bever, T. G.** Can an ape create a sentence? *Science*, 1979, *206*, 891-902. [13]

Thackery, W. M. *The Works of W. M. Thackery* (Vol. 12). London: John Murray, 1899. [10]

Thomas, A., and **Chess, S.** *Temperament and development.* New York: Brunner-Mazel, 1977. [14]

Thompson, C. R., and **Church, R. M.** An explanation of the language of a chimpanzee. *Science*, 1980, *208*, 313-314. [13]

Thompson, R. *Introduction to physiological psychology.* New York: Harper & Row, 1975. [3]

Thompson, R. F., Mayers, K. S., Robertson, R. T., and **Patterson, C. J.** Number coding in association cortex of cat. *Science*, 1970, *168*, 271-273. [3]

Thompson, W. C., Reyes, R. M., and **Bower, G. H.** Delayed effects of availability on judgment. Unpublished manuscript, Stanford University, 1979. [10]

Thorndike, E. L. Animal intelligence. *Psychological Review Monograph*, 1898, *2*. [8]

_____. Autobiography. In C. Murchison (Ed.)., *A history of psychology in autobiography* (Vol. 3). Worcester, Mass.: Clark University Press, 1936. [8]

Thorpe, W. H. *Bird song.* London: Cambridge University Press, 1961. [7]

Thurstone, L. L. *A factorial study of perception.* Chicago: University of Chicago Press, 1944. [5]

Tinbergen, N. *The study of instinct.* New

York: Oxford University Press, 1951. [7]

———. The curious behavior of the stickle-back. *Scientific American*, December 1952, *187*, 22-26. [7]

———. *The herring gull's world*. New York: Basic Books, 1961. [7]

———. The releasing and directing stimulus situations of the gaping response in young blackbirds and thrushes. In N. Tinbergen, *The animal in its world* (Vol. 2). Cambridge, Mass.: Harvard University Press, 1973. Pp. 17-51. [11]

Titchener, E. B. *A textbook of psychology*. New York: Macmillan, 1910. [25]

Tollefson, D. J. The relationship between the occurence of fractures and life crisis events. Master of Nursing Thesis, University of Washington, Seattle, 1972. [21]

Toman, W. *Family constellation: Its effect on personality and social behavior* (3rd ed.). New York: Springer, 1976. [26]

Tomizuka, C., and **Tobias, S.** Letters: Math-ematical ability: Is sex a factor? *Science*, 1981, *212*, 114-121. [12]

Tonkova-Yampol'skaya, R. V. Development of speech intonation in infants during the first two years of life. In C. A. Ferguson and D. I. Slobin (Eds.), *Studies of child language development*. New York: Holt, Rinehart & Winston, 1973. Pp. 128-138. [13]

Tosteson, D. C. Lithium and mania. *Scien-tific American*, April 1981, *224*, 164-174. [3]

Tourangeau, R., and **Ellsworth, P. C.** The role of facial response in the experience of emotion. *Journal of Personality and Social Psychology*, 1979, *37*, 1519-1531. [15]

Trabasso, T., McLanahan, A. G., Isen, A. M., Riley, C. A., Dolecki, P., and **Tucker, T.** How do children solve class in-clusion problems? In R. S. Siegler (Ed.), *Children's thinking: What develops?* Hillsdale, N.J.: Erlbaum, 1978. Pp. 151-180. [12]

Tracy, R. L., Lamb, M. E., and **Ainsworth, M. D.** Infant approach behavior as related to attachment. *Child Development*, 1976, *47*, 571-578. [2]

Trask, C. H., and **Cree, E. M.** Oximeter studies on patients with chronic obstructive emphysema, awake and during sleep. *New England Journal of Medicine*, 1962, *266*, 639-642. [6]

Trause, M. A. Stranger responses: Effects of familiarity, strangers' approach, and sex of infant. *Child Development*, 1977, *48*, 1657-1661. [14]

Travis, L. E. The effect of a small audience upon eye-hand coordination. *Journal of Ab-normal and Social Psychology*, 1925, *20*, 142-146. [27]

Trehub, S. E. Infants' sensitivity to vowel and tonal contrast. *Developmental Psychology*, 1973, *9*, 91-96. [11]

———, and **Rabinovitch, M. S.** Auditory-linguistic sensitivity in early infancy. *Devel-opmental Psychology*, 1972, *6*, 74-77. [11]

Treisman, A. M. Contextual cues in selective listening. *Quarterly Journal of Experimental Psychology*, 1960, *12*, 242-248. [9]

Treisman, M. Motion Sickness: An evolu-tionary hypothesis. *Science*, 1977, *197*, 493-495. [7]

Tresemer, D. Fear of success: Popular, but unproven. *Psychology Today*, March 1974, *7*, 82-85. [16]

Triplett, N. The dynamogenic factors in peacemaking and competition. *American Journal of Psychology*, 1897, *9*, 507-533. [27]

Truex, R. C., and **Carpenter, M. B.** *Human neuroanatomy*. Baltimore: Williams & Wilkins, 1969. [3]

Tryon, R. C. Studies in individual differences in maze ability, VII: The specific compo-nents of maze ability, and a general theory of psychological components. *Journal of Com-parative Psychology*, 1940a, *30*, 283-335. [7]

———. Studies in individual differences in maze ability, VIII: Prediction validity of the psychological components of maze ability. *Journal of Comparative Psychology*, 1940b, *30*, 535-582. [7]

———. Genetic differences in maze learning in rats. *Thirty-ninth yearbook, National Society for the Study of Education* (Part I). Bloomington, Ill.: Public School Publishing Co., 1940c. Pp. 111-119. [7]

Tulving, E. Episodic and semantic memory. In E. Tulving and W. Donaldson (Eds.), *Or-ganization of memory*. New York: Academic Press, 1972. [9]

———, and **Kahneman, D.** Judgment under uncertainty: Heuristics and biases. *Science*, 1973a, *185*, 1124-1131. [10]

Tversky, A., and **Kahneman, D.** The fram-ing of decisions and the psychology of choice. *Science*, 1981, *211*, 453-458. [10]

Ullman, C. A. Teachers, peers, and tests as predictors of adjustment. *Journal of Educa-tional Psychology*, 1957, *48*, 257-267. [14]

Ullman, M. Dreaming. Life-style, and physi-ology: A comment on Adler's view of the dream. *Journal of Individual Psychology*, 1962, *18*, 18-25. [6]

Ullmann, L. P., and **Krasner, L.** *A psycho-logical approach to abnormal behavior.* (2nd ed.). Englewood Cliffs, N.J.: Prentice-Hall, 1975. [23]

United States Department of Health and Human Services, Public Health Service, Alcohol, Drug Abuse, and Mental Health Administration. *The fourth special report to the United States Congress on alcohol and health,* January 1981, p. 169. [22]

Valenstein, E. S. *Brain Control.* New York: Wiley-Interscience, 1973. [3, 24]

Valentine, C. W. *Experimental psychology of beauty.* New York: Dodge, 1913. [11]

Valins, S., and **Baum, A.** Residential group size, social interaction, and crowding. *Envi-ronment and Behavior*, 1973, *4*, 421-439. [28]

Vance, E. B., and **Wagner, N. W.** Written descriptions of orgasm: A study of sex differ-ences. *Archives of Sexual Behavior*, 1976, *5*, 87-98. [17]

Van Kammen, D. P. Y-aminobutyric acid (GABA) and the dopamine hypothesis of schizophrenia. *American Journal of Psychiatry*, 1977, *134*, 138-143. [23]

Vassos, J. *Phobia.* New York: Covici and Friede, 1931. [22]

Vernon, P. Psychological effects of air raids. *Journal of Abnormal and Social Psychology*, 1941, *36*, 457-476. [21]

Vinokur, A., and **Selzer, M. L.** Desirable versus undesirable life events: Their relation-ship to stress and mental distress. *Journal of Personality and Social Psychology*, 1975, *32*, 329-337. [21]

Visinteiner, M. A., Volpicelli, J. R., and **Seligman, M. E. P.** Tumor rejection in rats after inescapable or escapable shock. *Science*, 1982, *216*, 437-439. [21]

Vitz, P. C. Affect as a function of stimulus variation. *Journal of Experimental Psychology*, 1966, *71*, 74-79. [16]

von Frisch, K. *Bees: Their vision, chemical senses, and language.* Ithaca, N.Y.: Cornell University Press, 1950. [7]

———. *The dance language and orientation of bees.* Cambridge, Mass.: Belknap Press of Harvard University Press, 1967. [7, 13]

von Holst, E., and **von St. Paul, U.** Electri-cally controlled behavior. *Scientific American*, March 1962, *206*, 50-59.[7]

von Senden, M. *Space and sight: The percep-tion of space and shape in the congenitally blind before and after operations.* New York: Free Press, 1960. [5]

von Uexkull, J. J. *Umwelt und Innenwelt der Tiere* (2nd ed.). Berlin: Springer-Verlag, 1921. [7]

Vygotsky, L. S. *Thought and language.* Cam-bridge, Mass.: MIT Press, 1962. [12]

———. *Mind in society.* Cambridge, Mass.: Harvard University Press, 1978. [14]

Waddington, C. H. *The strategy of the genes.* New York: Macmillan, 1957. [11]

Wade, N. Does man alone have language? Apes reply in riddles, and a horse says neigh. *Science*, 1980, *208*, 1349-1351. [13]

Wagner, R. V. Complementary needs, role ex-pectations, interpersonal attraction, and the stability of working relationships. *Journal of Personality and Social Psychology*, 1975, *32*, 116-124. [26]

Wallace, R. K., and **Benson, H.** The physio-logy of meditation. *Scientific American*, February 1972, *226*, 84-90. [6]

Wallace, W. L. Review of the Scholastic Apti-tude Test. In Oscar K. Buros (Ed.), *The seventh mental measurements yearbook*, 1972, 648-650. [20]

Wallas, G. *The art of thought.* New York: Harcourt Brace and World, 1926. [10]

Walster, E., and **Festinger, L.** The effective-ness of "overheard" persuasive communica-tions. *Journal of Abnormal and Social*

Psychology, 1962, *65*, 395-402. [25]

Ward, L. B. Reminiscence and rote learning. *Psychological Monographs*, 1937, *49*, No. 220. [10]

Warrington, E. K., and Sanders, H. I. The fate of old memories. *Quarterly Journal of Experimental Psychology*, 1971, *23*, 432-442. [12]

Washburn, S. L. Human behavior and the behavior of other animals. *American Psychologist*, May 1978, *33*, 405-418. [7]

Washington v. Davis 426 U.S. 229 (1976). [20]

Wason, P. C., and Johnson-Laird, P. N. *Psychology of reasoning: Structure and content.* Cambridge, Mass.: Harvard University Press, 1972. [12]

Waterman, A. S., Geary, P. S., and Waterman, C. K. Longitudinal study of changes in ego-identity states from the freshman to the senior year of college. *Developmental Psychology*, 1974, *10*, 387-392. [14]

Waters, E., Wippman, J., and Sroufe, L. A. Attachment, positive effect, and competence in the peer group: Two studies in construct. *Child Development*, 1979, *50*, 821-829. [14]

Watson, J. B. *Behaviorism.* New York: Norton, 1930. [10]

_____. *Behaviorism* (1924). New York: Norton, 1970. [7, 8]

_____. Psychology as the behaviorist views it. *Psychological Review*, 1913, *20*, 158-177.[1]

_____, and Rayner, R. Conditioned emotional reactions. *Journal of Experimental Psychology*, 1920, *3*, 1-14. [8]

Watson, J. S. Smiling, cooing, and "the game." *Merrill-Palmer Quarterly of Behavior and Development*, 1972, *18*, 323-339. [12]

_____, Hayes, L. A., Dorman, L., and Vietze, P. Infant sex differences in operant fixation with visual and auditory reinforcement. *Infant Behavior and Development.* 1980, *3*, 107-114. [12]

Watson, R. I. *The great psychologists: From Aristotle to Freud.* Philadelphia: Lippincott, 1963. [1]

Watzlawick, P., Beavin, J. and Jackson, D. *Pragmatics of human communication: A study of interaction patterns, pathologies, and paradoxes.* New York: Norton, 1967. [24]

Webb, E. J., Campbell, D. T., Schwartz, R. D., and Sechrest, L. *Unobtrusive measures: Nonreactive research in the social sciences.* Chicago: Rand McNally, 1966. [2]

Webb, W. B. Sleep and dreams. In B. B. Wolman (Ed.), *Handbook of general psychology.* Englewood Cliffs, N.J.: Prentice-Hall, 1973. Pp. 734-748. [6]

_____. The nature of dreams. In D. Goleman and R. J. Davidson (Eds.), *Consciousness: Brain, states of awareness, and mysticism.* New York: Harper & Row, 1979. Pp. 76-78. [6]

_____, and Kersey, J. Recall of dreams and the probability of stage 1—REM sleep. *Perceptual and Motor Skills*, 1967, *24*, 627-630. [6]

Weber, E. H. *De pulsu, resorptione, auditu et tactu.* Leipzig: Kohler, 1834. [4]

Wechsler, D. *Wechsler adult intelligence scale manual.* New York: Psychological Corporation, 1955. [20]

_____. *The measurement and appraisal of adult intelligence* (14th ed.). Baltimore: William & Wilkins, 1958. [20]

Weil, A. T., Zinberg, N., and Nelsen, J. M. Clinical and psychological effects of marijuana in man. *Science*, 1968, *162*, 1234-1242. [6]

Weinberg, S. K. *Incest behavior.* New York: Citadel, 1955. [17]

Weiner, B. *Theories of motivation: From mechanism to cognition.* Chicago: Markham, 1972. [16]

Weingartner, H., Adefris, W., Eich, J. E., and Murphy, D. Encoding-imagery specificity in alcohol state-dependent learning. *Journal of Experimental Psychology: Human Learning and Memory*, 1976, *2*, 83-87. [9]

Weisberg, R. W. *Memory, thought, and behavior.* New York: Oxford University Press, 1980. [10]

Weiss, J. M. Psychological factors in stress and disease. *Scientific American*, 1972, *226*, 104-113. [21]

_____. Psychosomatic Disorders. In J. D. Maser and M. E. P. Seligman (Eds.), *Psychopathology: Experimental models.* San Francisco: W. H. Freeman, 1977. [21]

Weiss, R. S. *Going it alone: The family life and social situation of the single parent.* New York: Basic Books, 1979. [21]

Weizenbaum, J. *Computer power and human reason.* San Francisco: W. H. Freeman, 1976. [10]

Wells, G. L., and Petty, R. E. The effects of overt head movement on persuasion: Compatibility and incompatibility of responses. *Basic and Applied Social Psychology*, 1980, *1*, 219-230. [15, 25]

Werner, A. Sexual dysfunction in college men and women. *American Journal of Psychiatry*, 1975, *132*, 164-168. [17]

Werner, J. S., and Perlmutter, M. Development of visual memory in infants. In H. W. Reese and L. P. Lipsitt (Eds.), *Advances in child development and behavior* (Vol. 13). New York: Academic Press, 1979. Pp. 1-56. [12]

Wertheimer, M. Untersuchungen zur Lehre von der Gestalt. *Psychologisches Forschung*, 1923, *4*, 301-350. [5]

_____. Psychomotor coordination of auditory and visual space at birth. *Science*, 1961, *134*, 1962. [11]

Werthman, C. The social meaning of the physical environment. Ph.D. dissertation, University of California, Berkeley, 1968. [28]

West, S. G., Gunn, S. P., and Chernicky, P. Ubiquitous Watergate: An Attributional analysis. *Journal of Personality and Social Psychology*, 1975, *32*, 55-65. [2]

Westin, A. *Privacy and freedom.* New York: Atheneum, 1967. [28]

White, B. L. An experimental approach to the effects of experience on early human behavior. In J. P. Hill (Ed.), *Minnesota symposia on child psychology* (Vol. 1). Minneapolis: University of Minnesota Press, 1967. Pp. 201-226. [11]

_____. *Human infants: Experience and psychological development.* Englewood Cliffs, N.J.: Prentice-Hall, 1971. [11]

White, R. W. *The enterprise of living: Growth and organization in personality.* New York: Holt, Rinehart & Winton, 1972. [26]

Whitlock, F. A. The aetiology of hysteria. *Acta Psychiatrica Scandinavica*, 1967, *43*, 144-162. [22]

Whitty, C. W. M., and Zangwill, O. L. *Amnesia: Clinical, psychological and medical aspects* (2nd ed.). Boston: Butterworths, 1977. [3]

Whorf, B. L. Science and linguistics. In J. B. Carroll (Ed.), *Language, thought, and reality: Selected writings of Benjamin Lee Whorf.* Cambridge, Mass.: MIT Press, 1956. Pp. 207-219. [13]

Whybrow, P. C., and Prange, A. J., Jr. A hypothesis of thyroid-catecholamine-receptor interaction. *Archives of General Psychiatry*, 1981, *38*, 106-113. [23]

Wichman, H. Effects of isolation and communication in a two-person game. *Journal of Personality and Social Psychology*, 1970, *16*, 114-120. [27]

Wicker, A. W. An examination of the "other variables" explanation of attitude-behavior inconsistency. *Journal of Personality and Social Psychology*, 1971, *19*, 18-30. [25]

Wicklegren, W. A single trace fragility theory of memory dynamics. *Memory and Cognition*, 1974, *2*, 775-780. [10]

Wicklund, R. A., and Brehm, J. W. *Perspectives on cognitive dissonance.* Hillsdale, N.J.: Erlbaum, 1976. [16]

Williams, B. M. Hypnosis is like a scalpel: You wouldn't want it wielded by your janitor. *Psychology Today*, November 1974, *8*, 126-127. [6]

Williams, D. A., King, P., Foote, D., Abramson, P., and Lord, M. The classroom computers. *Newsweek*, March 9, 1981, 90-91. [8]

Williams, R. H. Hypoglycemosis. In R. H. Williams (Ed.), *Diabetes.* New York: Hoeber, 1960. [16]

Williams, R. L., Karacan, I., and Hursch, C. J. *EEG of human sleep: Clinical applications.* New York: Wiley, 1974. [6]

Wilson, E. O. *Sociobiology: The new synthesis.* Cambridge, Mass.: Harvard University Press, 1975. [4,7,27]

_____. *On human nature.* Cambridge, Mass.: Harvard University Press, 1978. [7,28]

Winch, R. F. *Mate selection: A study of complementary needs.* New York: Harper & Row, 1958. [26]

Winer, G. A. Class-inclusion reasoning in children: A review of the empirical literature. *Child Development*, 1980, *51*, 309-328. [12]

Winget, C., Kramer, M., and **Whitman, R.** Dreams and demography. *Canadian Psychiatric Association Journal,* 1972, *17,* 203-208. [27]

Wingfield, A. *Human learning and memory: An introduction.* New York: Harper and Row, 1979. [9]

———, and **Byrnes, D.** *The psychology of human memory.* New York: Academic Press, 1981. [9]

Winick, C. A. Some observations of patrons of adult theaters and bookstores. In *Technical reports of the Commission on Obscenity and Pornography* (Vol. 4). Washington, D.C.: U.S. Government Printing Office, 1970. [17]

Winick, M., and **Noble, A.** Cellular responses in rats during malnutrition at various ages. *Journal of Nutrition,* 1966, *89,* 300-306. [11]

Winokur, G. Genetic aspects of depression. In J. P. Scott and E. C. Senay (Eds.), *Separation and depression: Clinical and research aspects.* Washington, D.C.: American Association for the Advancement of Science, 1973. [22]

Witkin, H. A., Mednick, S. A., Schulsinger, F., Bakkestom, E., Christiansen, K. O., Goodenough, D. R., Hirchhorn, K., Lunsteen, C., Owen, D. R., Philip, J., Ruben, D. B., and **Stocking, M.** Criminality in XYY and XXY men. *Science,* 1976, *193,* 547-555. [27]

Wolfe, J. B. Effectiveness of token-rewards for chimpanzees. *Comparative Psychological Monographs,* 1936, *12,* Whole No. 5. [8]

Wolfe, M. Childhood and privacy. In I. Altman and J. F. Wohlwill (Eds.), *Human behavior and environment* (Vol. 3). *Children and the environment.* New York: Plenum, 1978. Pp. 175-222. [28]

Wolff, P. H. The natural history of crying and other vocalizations in early infancy. In B. M. Foss (Ed.), *Determinants of infant behavior* (Vol. 4). London: Methuen, 1969. Pp. 81-109. [13]

Wolff, S., and **Wolff, H. G.** *Human gastric function.* New York: Oxford University Press, 1947. [15]

Wolpe, J. *Psychotherapy by reciprocal inhibition.* Stanford.: Stanford University Press, 1958. [24]

———. *The practice of behavior therapy* (2nd ed.). New York: Pergamon Press, 1973. [22]

———. Cognition and causation in human behavior and its therapy. *American Psychologist,* 1978, *33,* 437-446. [24]

———, and **Wolpe, D.** *Our useless fears.* Boston: Houghton Mifflin, 1981. [24]

Woodruff, R. A., Clayton, P. J., and **Guze, S. B.** Is everyone depressed? *American Journal of Psychiatry,* 1975, *132,* 627-628. [22]

Woolfolk, R. L. Psychophysiological correlates of meditation. *Archives of General Psychiatry,* October 1975, *32,* 1326-1333. [6]

Woolsey, C. N. Organization of the cortical auditory system. In W. A. Rosenblith (Ed.), *Sensory communication.* New York: Wiley, 1961. [3]

Wortman, C. B., and **Brehm, J. W.** Responses to uncontrollable outcomes: An investigation of resistance theory and the learned helplessness model. In L. Berkowitz (Ed.), *Advances in experimental social psychology* (Vol. 8). New York: Academic Press, 1975. [21]

———, and **Dintzer, L.** Is an attributional analysis of the learned helplessness phenomenon viable?: A critique of the Abramson-Seligman-Teasdale reformulation. *Journal of Abnormal Psychology,* 1978, *87,* 75-90. [21]

———, and **Loftus, E. F.** *Psychology.* New York: Knopf, 1981. P. 178. [9]

Wynne, L. C., Singer, M. T., Bartko, J. J., and **Toohey, M. L.** Schizophrenics and their families: Recent research on parental communication. In J. M. Tanner (Ed.), *Psychiatric research: The widening perspective.* New York: International Universities Press, 1975. [23]

Yates, A. J. *Biofeedback and the modification of behavior.* New York: Plenum, 1980. [6]

Yerkes, R. M., and **Dodson, J. D.** The relation of strength of stimulus to rapidity of habit formation. *Journal of Comparative Neurology and Psychology,* 1908, *18,* 459-482. [10, 19]

Yonas, A., Oberg, C., and **Norcia, A.** Development of sensitivity to binocular information for the approach of an object. *Developmental Psychology,* 1978, *14,* 147-152. [11]

Youniss, J. *Parents and peers in social development: A Sullivan-Piaget perspective.* Chicago: The University of Chicago Press, 1980. [14]

Zaidel, E. Language comprehension in the right hemisphere following cerebral commissurotomy. In A. Caramazza and E. Zurif (Eds.), *Language acquisition and language breakdown: Parallels and divergences.* Baltimore, Md.: The Johns Hopkins University Press, 1978. [3]

Zajonc, R. B. Attraction, affiliation, and Attachment. In J. F. Eisenberg and W. S. Dillon (Eds.), *Man and beast: Comparative social behavior.* Washington, D.C.: Smithsonian Institution Press, 1971. Pp. 143-179. [25]

———. Altruism, envy, competitiveness, and the common good. In V. Derlaga and J. Grzelak (Eds.), *Cooperation and helping behavior.* New York: Academic Press, 1982. Pp. 417-435. [27]

———. Social facilitation. *Science,* 1965, *149,* 269-274. [27]

———. The attitudinal effects of mere exposure. *Journal of Personality and Social Psychology Monographs,* 1968, *9,* Part 2, 1-27. [5, 15, 25]

———. Compresence. In P.P. Paulus (Ed.), *Psychology of group influence.* Hillsdale,

N.J.: Lawrence Erlbaum Associates, 1980. [27]

———. Family configuration and intelligence. *Science,* 1976, *192,* 227-236. [20]

———. Feeling and thinking: Preferences need no inferences. *American Psychologist,* February 1980, *35,* 151-175. [25]

———, **Heingartner, A.** and **Herman, E. M.** Social enhancement and impairment of performance in the cockroach. *Journal of Personality and Social Psychology,* 1969, *13,* 83-92. [27]

———, and **Markus, G. B.** Birth order and intellectual development. *Psychological Review,* 1975, *82,* 74-88. [20]

———, and **Markus, H.** Affective and cognitive factors in preferences. *Journal of Consumer Research,* 1982, *9,* 123–131. [25]

———, **Wilson, W. R.,** and **Rajecki, D. W.** Affiliation and social discrimination produced by brief exposure in day-old domestic chicks. *Animal Behavior,* 1975, *23,* 131-138. [25, 26]

Zanna, M. P., Kiesler, C. A., and **Pilkonis, P. A.** Positive and negative attitudinal affect established by classical conditioning. *Journal of Personality and Social Psychology,* 1970, *14,* 321-328. [25]

Zelazo, P. R., Zelazo, N. A., and **Kolb, S.** "Walking" in the newborn. *Science,* 1972, *176,* 314-315. [11]

Zeki, S. The representation of colours in the cerebral cortex. *Nature,* April 3, 1980, *284,* 412-418. [4]

Zilboorg, G., and **Henry, G. W.** *A history of medical psychology.* New York: Norton, 1941. [23]

Zillman, D. Excitation transfer in communication-mediated aggressive behavior. *Journal of Experimental Social Psychology,* 1971 *7,* 419-434. [15]

Zimbardo, P. G., Cohen, A., Weisenberg, M., Dworkin, L., and **Firestone, I.** The control of experimental pain. In P. G. Zimbardo, A. Cohen, M. Weisenberg, L. Dworkin, and I. Firestone (Eds.), *The cognitive control of motivation.* Glenview, Ill.: Scott, Foresman, 1969. Pp. 100-125. [16]

Zubin, J., and **Spring, B.** Vulnerability: A new view of schizophrenia. *Journal of Abnormal Psychology,* 1977, *86,* 103-126. [23]

Zuckerman, M. The search for high sensation. *Psychology Today,* February 1978, *11,* 30-46. *passim.* [16]

———, **Klorman, R., Larrance, D. T.,** and **N. H. Spiegel,** Facial, autonomic, and subjective components of emotion: The facial feedback hypothesis versus externalizer-internalizer distinction. *Journal of Personality and Social Psychology,* 1981, *41,* 929-944. [15]

———, and **Wheeler, L.** To dispel fantasies about the fantasy-based measure of fear of success. *Psychological Bulletin,* 1975, *82,* 932-946. [16]

Glossary

The numbers following the entries refer to the chapters of the text in which each term or concept is discussed in detail.

absolute threshold — the weakest stimulus that produces a sensation. [4]

accommodation — the modification of existing schemes to incorporate new knowledge that does not fit them. [12]

achievement motive — the capacity to derive satisfaction by attaining some standard of excellence. [15]

achievement tests — tests constructed to assess the extent of an individual's knowledge about subjects taught in school. [20]

acquisition — the transformation of raw information into the form in which it will be stored.[9]

active phase — that stage in the course of schizophrenia in which psychotic symptoms predominate. [22]

adaptation — adjustment in sensory capacity. [4]

adaptive significance — the importance of behavior in helping the animal to survive and reproduce. [7]

adjustment — a continuous process of interacting with the people, events, and forces that affect our lives. [21]

adrenal glands — a pair of glands that secrete hormones to control emotions and the body's reaction to stress. [3]

affect — emotional response. [22]

affective disorders — disturbances of mood. [22]

afterimage — a sensory impression that persists after removal of the stimulus. [4]

aggression — any act that is intended to cause pain, damage, or suffering to another. [27]

agnosia — an inability to recognize sounds.[3]

aim — in Freud's terms, one of the four characteristic features of an instinct: satisfaction of need and stopping of excitation. [18]

algorithm — a simple set of rules arranged in a logical order that will solve all instances of a particular set of problems. [10]

altricial — helpless (referring to the young of a species) [11]

altruism — prosocial behavior showing unselfish concern springing from a combination of emotional distress at another's plight and an understanding of her or his needs. [14]

amacrine cells — a type of neural cell found in the retina of the eye. [4]

amnesia — partial or total loss of memory. [3, 22]

amniocentesis — a diagnostic technique in which a physician inserts a hollow needle into the maternal abdomen and withdraws some of the amniotic fluid, containing fetal cells, which can then be tested for the presence of abnormal chromosomes. [11]

amygdala — a structure in the limbic system. [3]

anal stage — the stage in psychosexual development during which the child's attention shifts to the anus and the pleasures of holding in and pushing out feces. [10, 18]

analytic psychology — a school of psychoanalysis founded in 1913 by Carl Jung. [18]

anchoring — a bias in judgment, resulting from the effect of the starting point from which the decision was made. [10]

androgen insensitivity syndrome — the condition of a genetically male fetus whose body cells fail to respond to androgen; the baby will be born genetically male but with the external anatomy of a female. [17]

androgens — male sex hormones. [17]

anterograde amnesia — a condition in which people are unable to lay down new memories. [9]

anticipation — a verbal slip in which a produced sound was scheduled to appear later in the utterance. [13]

antisocial personality. [22] See **sociopath.**

anvil — one of the ossicles. [4]

anxiety — in Freudian theory, a state of psychic pain that alerts the ego to danger; it is akin to fear. [18, 22]

anxiety disorder — a condition in which severe and persistent anxiety interferes with daily functioning. [22]

aphasia — an inability to speak or to understand spoken language. [3]

apparent motion — the perception of motion when a rapid succession of motionless stimuli mimic the changes that occur in true movement. [5]

applied science — the use of basic science to accomplish practical goals. [1]

approach-avoidance conflict — a conflict of two motives, so that satisfying one motive frustrates the other. [19]

aptitude tests — tests designed to find out about an individual's talent or capacity for particular lines of work. [20]

archetypes — in Jung's terms, ancient ideas or images common to all human beings in all eras and all regions of the world and that form the collective unconscious. [18]

assimilation — the incorporation of new knowledge through the use of existing schemes. [12]

association cortex — the areas of the somatosensory cortex assumed to be involved in abstract thought. [3]

ataxia — a condition characterized by severe tremors, drunken movements, and loss of balance; due to damage to the cerebellum. [3]

attachment — an emotional bond such as one which is formed between the infant and her or his primary care giver. [14]

attitude — an attraction or aversion toward an object,

together with what we know about that object. [25]

attribution theories—theories that propose to explain how people attribute personality traits or intentions to others to explain their behavior. [26]

audience inhibition—suppression due to concern about others' evaluation of our behavior. [27]

auditory cortex—the area in the temporal lobe of the brain that processes auditory information. [4]

auditory nerve—the nerve that relays auditory information to the brain. [4]

authenticity—living by personal values. [23]

autistic fantasy—a state on the continuum that stretches from normal waking consciousness to dreaming; it lacks any orientation toward reality. [6]

autogenic training—a relaxation procedure that depends on self-suggestion and imagery. [21]

automaticity—automatic actions, such as routine driving. [9]

autonomic nervous system—the division of the PNS that regulates the internal environment and is generally involuntary. [3]

availability—a heuristic in which predictions are based on a comparison of the current situation with past examples that readily come to mind. [10]

aversive conditioning—conditioning that relies on negative reinforcement and punishment. [8, 24]

axon—a long fiber of a neuron that leads away from the cell body. [3]

basic anxiety—in Horney's terms, anxiety arising out of a child's sense of helplessness and isolation. [18]

basic hostility—in Horney's terms, hostility arising from resentment over parental indifference, inconsistency, and interference. [18]

basic needs—fundamental physiological needs and intermediate psychological needs (such as safety and self-esteem). [15]

basic science—fundamental principles that explain a broad range of facts. [1]

basilar membrane—a membrane supporting the organ of Corti. Movements of this membrane stimulate hair cells, which in turn trigger electrical activity in the auditory nerve. [4]

behavior—anything a person does or experiences, including thoughts, feelings, and dreams. [1]

behavior rehearsal—a procedure similar to participant modeling, but applied to social behavior. [24]

behaviorism—the approach to psychology that limits its study to observable, measurable, responses to specific stimuli. [1]

behavioristic theories—situational theories that are primarily based on the principles of learning and reinforcement. [19]

behavior modification—the application of operant techniques to human behavior. [8]

binocular disparity—the difference between the retinal images received by each eye. [5]

biofeedback—the provision of a continuous flow of information regarding some physiological function by electronic devices; a person can then learn to attain voluntary control over the monitored function. [6]

biogenic theory—the view that mental disorder has a physical, or organic, cause. [23]

bipolar cells—a type of neural cell found in the retina of the eye. [4]

bipolar disorder—a disorder characterized by extreme moods, beginning with a manic episode of euphoria, excitement, and activity, followed by a depressive episode. [22]

birth order—the child's rank in the sequence of births. [26]

blind mill—an encounter-group technique in which participants close their eyes and wander around the room, communicating only by touch. [24]

blindsight—the ability of the blind to sense the existence and location of stimuli. [5]

brain stem—a part of the central core of the brain. [3]

cardinal trait—a single trait that directs a major portion of a person's behavior. [19]

case study—a method of collecting data in which researchers conduct an intensive investigation of one or a few individuals, usually with reference to a single psychological phenomenon. [2]

catecholamine hypothesis—the hypothesis that depression results from low levels of norepinephrine (a catecholamine) and mania results from high levels of norepinephrine in the brain. [23]

celibacy—complete abstinence from sexual activity. [17]

cell body—the part of a neuron containing the nucleus. [3]

central core—the area of the brain that carries out functions necessary for survival. [3]

central fissure—in the cortical surface, the separation between the frontal and parietal lobes. [3]

central nervous system (CNS)—the major control center of behavior. It consists of the brain and the spinal cord. [3]

central tendency—a characteristic of frequency distributions indicated by statistics such as the mean, mode, and median. [2]

central traits—characteristic ways of dealing with the world that can be captured by a trait name (honest, loving, gregarious) and that have marked effects on the way other, related traits are perceived. [19, 26]

cerebellum—the area of the brain that coordinates voluntary movement and maintains physical balance. [3]

cerebral cortex—the gray matter that covers the cerebral hemispheres. [3]

cerebral hemisphere—the most prominent layer of the brain; involved in information processing. [3]

chromosome—a coiled, threadlike cellular structure that contains the genes. [11]

clairvoyance—the knowledge of events not detectable by normal senses. [6]

clang association—in schizophrenia, the throwing together of concepts, ideas, and symbols merely because they rhyme. [22]

classical conditioning—a process whereby a neutral stimulus, when repeatedly presented with another stimulus that normally evokes a reflexive response, comes to elicit that response when presented by itself. [8]

client-centered therapy—a humanistic therapy in which the client learns to reintegrate self and organism, to accept all experiences as genuine, and to establish an unconditional positive regard. [19, 24]

clinical psychologist—a mental-health professional who has earned a doctorate (PhD or PsyD) in clinical psychology and has completed a one-year clinical internship. [24]

clinical psychology—the approach to psychology concerned with the study, diagnosis, and treatment of abnormal behavior. [1]

cochlea—the portion of the inner ear containing receptors for converting acoustic energy into sound. [4]

cognition—the process of knowing; the higher mental processes that human beings engage in, including problem solving, knowing, thinking, decision making, reasoning, judging, imagining. [10]

cognitive balance theory—the theory proposing that information about people's inconsistent relationships with each other leads to a conflict that the individual seeks to resolve. [15]

cognitive control—the guidance and maintenance of behavior through self-reinforcement. [19]

cognitive dissonance theory—the theory proposing that contradictory thoughts cause a state of psychological distress known as dissonance; the individual then attempts to reestablish internal harmony. [15]

cognitive restructuring—a process that focuses on the client's ways of perceiving the world and regards self-defeating behavior as a result of the client's false assumptions. [24]

cognitive therapy—a method of cognitive restructuring that aims to show clients that what they think determines how they feel. [24]

collective unconscious—in Jung's terms, a level of the unconscious; a storehouse of memories and behavior patterns inherited from humanity's remote ancestral past. [18]

colliculus—a structure in the midbrain, concerned with visual reflexes. [4]

color cancellation—the phenomenon occurring when complementary colors are combined and perceived as colorless. [4]

common trait—a basic mode of adjustment that is approximately the same for all individuals. [19]

community psychology—a branch of clinical psychology with the primary aim of preventing mental disorders. [1]

competence—speakers' abstract knowledge of their language's rules and principles. [13]

complexive thinking—in cognitive development, a child's tendency to jump from one idea to another without coordinating them. [12]

compulsion—an action that a person uncontrollably performs again and again, although she or he has no conscious desire to do so. [22]

computer-assisted instruction (CAI)—a teaching technique in which a student alone at a computer terminal gets immediate feedback for answers and moves ahead at her or his own pace. [8]

computer simulation—the construction of computer programs that act as much like people as possible.[10]

concrete-operational period—the period of cognitive development characterized by logical thought—but only in regard to concrete objects. [12]

concurrent validity—the correlation of a test's scores with other existing measures and standards. [20]

conditional positive regard—the withholding of love and praise when a child does not conform to parental or social standards. [19]

conditioned reinforcer—a stimulus that signals that a primary reinforcer will soon appear. [8]

conditioned response (CR)—a response to a CS. [8]

conditioned stimulus (CS)—a new stimulus that elicits behavior after repeated association with the UCS. [8]

conditions of worth—extraneous standards whose attainment ensures positive regard. [19]

cones—receptor cells in the eye operating in bright light. Cones are responsible for detailed vision and color perception. [4]

confabulation—a memory error in which a person who is unable to retrieve an item from memory constructs an appropriate recollection. [9]

conformity—the tendency to shift one's views or behavior closer to the norms expressed by other people. [27]

congruence—genuineness; the therapist's ability to share her or his own feelings with the client in an open and spontaneous manner. [24]

consciousness—an awareness of the thoughts, images, sensations, and emotions that flow through the mind at any given moment. [6]

conservation—the principle that irrelevant changes in the external appearance of objects have no effect on the object's quantity. [12]

constituent—a major subdivision of a sentence, such as a noun phrase or a prepositional phrase. [13]

constraints—biological limitations. [12]

construct validity—a test's measurement of the trait or theoretical construct it claims to measure. [20]

consumer psychology—a branch of industrial psychology concerned with preferences, buying habits, and responses to advertising of consumers. [1]

content validity—a test's coverage of a representative sample of the measured attribute. [20]

context—the setting in which stimuli appear; a retrieval cue for memory. [5, 9]

continuity—a principle of grouping. [5]

continuous reinforcement schedule—a schedule

of reinforcement in which the subject is rewarded for every response. [8]

control group—in an experiment, the group *not* exposed to the independent variable. [2]

conventional level—Kohlberg's stage of moral development in which the child or adult decides moral issues in terms of maintaining the social order and meeting the expectations of others. [14]

conversion disorders—disorders in which an individual develops some physical dysfunction—such as blindness, deafness, paralysis, or loss of sensation in some part of the body—that has no organic basis and apparently expresses some psychological conflict. [22]

cornea—the transparent covering in front of the eye. [4]

corpus callosum—a thick band of neural fibers that carries messages between the left and right sides of the brain. [3]

correlation—an indication of the degree of linear relatedness between two variables. [2]

correlational coefficient—the descriptive statistic indicating the degree of linear relatedness. A perfect positive correlation is indicated by the coefficient +1; a perfect negative correlation is indicated by −1. [2]

correlational study—a method of collecting data in which researchers select a group and assess the relationship between already existing variables. [2]

covert sensitization—a technique in which clients are asked to visualize the behavior they are trying to eliminate and then to conjure up the image of an extremely painful or revolting stimulus. [24]

cranium—the portion of the skull that houses the brain. [3]

creative thinking—the generation of new rules based on stores of information other than previously learned rules. [10]

creativity—the combination of previously unconnected elements in a new and useful way. [10]

crowding—the perception of restricted space and the limits it places on action. [28]

cultural relativism—the development of biases from culturally normal experience. [5]

decibel (dB)—a unit of measurement used to express perceived sound intensity. [4]

defense mechanism—an intrapsychic scheme to conceal the source of anxiety from the self and from the world. [18]

deferred imitation—the ability to mimic in play on one occasion actions observed at an earlier time. [12]

deficiency needs. [19] See **basic needs.**

delusions—irrational beliefs that are maintained despite overwhelming evidence that they have no basis in reality. [22]

demand characteristics—a methodological problem in which a subject's response is strongly determined by the research setting. [2]

dendrites—short fibers that branch out from the cell body. [3]

density—the physical conditions of a setting expressed in terms of the number of people in a given space. [28]

dependent variable—the event that is being studied and that is expected to change when the independent variable is altered. [2]

depressant—a drug that retards the action of the central nervous system so that neurons fire more slowly. [6]

depth perception—the ability to tell how far away an object is. [5]

descriptive statistics—data used to describe the central tendency and variability of a sample. [2]

developmental psychology—the approach to psychology that is concerned with all aspects of behavioral development over the entire life span. [1]

diathesis-stress model—the view that genes establish a diathesis, or predisposition, to schizophrenia, but that the disorder will not develop unless the predisposition is combined with certain stressful environmental factors. [23]

dichotic listening—a process in which a person wearing a set of earphones hears two different messages played simultaneously, one in each ear. [9]

dichromats—people who have difficulty discriminating color in certain regions of the wavelength spectrum. [4]

difference threshold—the smallest change in a stimulus that produces a change in sensation. [4]

diffusion of responsibility—spreading the responsibility for intervening over all the bystanders. [27]

discreteness—a major characteristic of human language; the distinctness of its units. [13]

discrimination—(1) differentiation among similar stimuli, with response to one and no response to others. (2) the behavioral expression of prejudice. [8,26]

discrimination training—a procedure in which the organism is reinforced for responding to one stimulus but not reinforced for responding to a slightly different stimulus. [8]

discriminative stimuli—stimuli that an organism learns to respond to or to ignore in discrimination training. [8]

displacement—(1) a major characteristic of language; transmission of information about distant objects or events. (2) in Freud's terms, transference of psychic energy from the original object to a variety of substitute objects. [13, 18]

disregulation model—a model suggesting that physical disorders arise when the body's internal regulatory systems fail to operate properly. [21]

dissociative disorders—the dissociation, or splitting off, of certain aspects of memory and identity. [22]

dominance—the ability to influence others. [28]

dominant responses—the responses most likely to be made by an organism in a given situation. [27]

dopamine — a neurotransmitter thought to regulate emotional response and complex movements. [3]

dopamine hypothesis — the view that schizophrenia is associated with excessive activity in those parts of the brain that use dopamine to transmit neural impulses. [23]

double-blind hypothesis — the theory that faulty family communication, so that a child never learns to distinguish among the meanings expressed in normal language and behavior, is at the root of schizophrenia. [23]

double-blind technique — a method of avoiding experimenter bias in which neither researcher nor subjects know which group is the experimental group and which the control group. [2]

Down's syndrome — the most common chromosomal cause of retardation; caused by cell division of the parental ovum or sperm resulting in an extra chromosome 21. [11, 20]

drive — an internal motivational factor. [15]

drug — any inorganic substance that can interact with a biological system. [6]

dual-code theory — the theory proposing that information is represented by visual images and by words. [9]

duplication hypothesis — a theory proposing that people are happiest when they re-create their birth-order position in their marital relationship. [26]

dynamics — (of personality) motivating or driving forces. [18]

echoic memory — the auditory form of sensory memory. [9]

educational psychology — the approach to psychology that investigates all the psychological aspects of the learning process. [1]

efficacy expectations — people's beliefs that they can successfully execute whatever behavior is required to produce a desired outcome. [24]

ego — according to Freud, a psychic component serving as mediator between the id and reality. [18]

egocentrism — in cognitive development, a child's belief that others literally see things as the child does. [12]

ego ideal — in Freud's terms, our values and abstract moral ideals. [18]

ego identity — in Erikson's terms, an integrated, autonomous, unique "self." [18]

ego-psychologist — a psychoanalytic investigator who considers herself or himself a Freudian but who elaborates on Freud's theory, emphasizing ego functions. [18]

eidetic imagery — the unique ability to visualize a remembered scene with almost photographic clarity. [9]

ejaculation — the discharge of fluid during orgasm. [17]

elaborative rehearsal — a form of rehearsal that transfers information into long-term memory so that it may later be retrieved. [9]

electroconvulsive therapy — "shock treatment"; administering a series of brief electrical shocks of approximately 70 to 130 volts, spaced over a period of several weeks. The shock induces a convulsion similar to an epileptic seizure. [24]

electroencephalogram (EEG) — a recording of the brain's electrical activity. [6]

electromyographic recording (EMG) — measurements of electrical activity from muscles. [16]

embryo — the developing organism in the womb from the fourth to the eighth week. [11]

empathic understanding — the therapist's ability to see the world through the eyes of the client. [24]

encoding. [9] See **acquisition.**

endocrine glands — glands that produce hormones. [3]

endocrine system — a set of glands which secretes hormones carried in the bloodstream. They influence neural and muscular tissue in other parts of the body. [3]

endorphins — a variety of neurotransmitter similar in structure to opiates; implicated in pain and pleasure. [3]

end state — a goal or the satisfaction of some need. [15]

environmental psychology — the approach to psychology that studies the relationship between people and their physical settings. [1, 28]

epidemiology — the study of the range of occurrence, distribution, and control of illness in a population. [22]

episodic memory — a form of memory recording the things we see and hear and do. [9]

equilibration — in cognitive development, a continual search for a balance between assimilation and accommodation. [12]

equilibrium — a state of balance (of hormones in the bloodstream). [3]

erectile failure — a man's inability to achieve or maintain an erection. [17]

erogenous zone — an area of the body that is particularly sensitive to touch; a focus of pleasure. [14, 17]

Eros — according to Freud, one of two broad types of instincts in the id; the constructive life instinct responsible for survival, self-propagation, and creativity. [18]

ethology — a scientific study developed by European scientists who sought to explain animal behavior in evolutionary and physiological terms. [7]

evoked potential — changes in the brain's electrical activity in response to stimulation presented by a researcher. [3]

excitatory — a message that causes a receiving neuron to fire. [3]

excitement phase — the first phase of sexual response. [17]

exhibitionism — sexual gratification obtained through exhibiting the genitals to an involuntary bystander. [22]

existential frustration — a major source of abnormal behavior arising from an inability to find meaning in life. [23]

experiment — a method of collecting data in which researchers actively control the presence, absence, or intensity of factors that may affect the behavior under study. [2]

experimental group—in an experiment, the group exposed to the independent variable. [2]

experimental psychology—the approach to psychology that investigates basic behavioral processes that are shared by several species. [1]

experimenter bias—a methodological problem in which researchers inadvertently influence the subjects' responses or perceive the subjects' actions in terms of their own hypothesis. [2]

exposure effect—repeated neutral encounters with an object that produce a positive attitude. [25]

extinction—the slow decline and eventual disappearance of a conditioned response. [8]

extrasensory perception (ESP)—the reception of knowledge about the environment that does not arrive through a known sensory channel. [6]

extraversion—in Jung's terms, a major personality orientation in which the person is overly interested in the external world and thus is outgoing, sociable, and excitement-seeking. [18]

extrinsic motivation—the process by which external rewards lead an individual to undertake a behavior. [15]

eyeball-to-eyeball—an encounter-group therapy in which pairs of participants stare into each other's eyes. [24]

face validity—a test's appearance of validity to the people taking it. [20]

facial-feedback hypothesis—the hypothesis that our subjective experience of emotion comes from an awareness of our facial expressions. [16]

factor analysis—a statistical method that analyzes responses to a host of possible scale items and reduces them to a few underlying factors. [20]

fan effect—a feature of memory: the more we know about a subject, the longer it takes us to retrieve specific items of information about it. [9]

fear of success—the motive to avoid success. [15]

feature analysis—the process by which sensory information is identified according to its distinctive characteristics or features. [5]

Fechner's law—the law stating that the magnitude of a sensation increases in proportion to the logarithm of the physical intensity of a stimulus (expressed in the equation $S = k \log I$). [4]

feedback—reinforcement in the form of information about past performance that is used to alter future behavior. [8]

fetishism—sexual gratification that is dependent on an inanimate object or some part of the body other than the genitals. [22]

fetus—the developing organism in the womb from the eighth week to birth. [11]

field studies—experiments in which researchers can introduce the independent variable but cannot control other variables and often cannot assign subjects to the experimental group. [2]

figure—in a scene, the region that represents an object. [5]

fixation—(1) an automatic application of an inappropriate strategy and a rigid clinging to the obviously ineffective approach. (2) a halt in psychosexual development caused by failure to resolve the conflict between impulse and control. [10, 14, 18]

fixed action patterns—relatively stereotyped and often-repeated patterns of movement. [7]

fixed interval schedule—a partial reinforcement schedule in which reinforcement comes for the first response after a specified period. [8]

fixed ratio schedule—a partial reinforcement schedule in which the subject is rewarded each time it makes a specific number of responses. [8]

flashbulb memory—a brief, clear memory of a moment of the past. [9]

flooding—an intensive extinction therapy. [24]

forensic psychology—the approach to psychology that applies psychological principles to the problems of law enforcement and the courts. [1]

formal-operational period—the culmination of cognitive development, characterized by abstract reasoning and the ability to assume artificial premises that are known to be false. [12]

fovea—the retinal area that lies almost directly opposite the pupil of the eye. It contains only cone receptors and is the area of the highest visual acuity. [4]

frame—the way a problem is phrased. [10]

free association—an indirect therapeutic technique employed to study unconscious processes. The patient will say anything that comes to mind, making no attempt to produce logical statements, and the psychoanalyst will attempt to interpret the associations. [1, 18]

free-floating anxiety—an inability to specify the source of the fear. [22]

free recall—an experimental technique in which a person hears a list of words read one at a time. After the last word is read, the person recalls as many words as possible. [9]

frequency—the number of waves passing a given point in a given period. [4]

frequency distribution—an arrangement of data that shows the number of instances of each value of a variable. [2]

frontal lobes—the area of the brain generally involved in behavior. [3]

frustration—interference with any form of goal-directed behavior. [27]

frustration-aggression hypothesis—the idea that "aggression is always a consequence of frustration" and, conversely, "frustration always leads to some form of aggression" (Dollard, 1939). [27]

fugue—a dissociative disorder in which individuals flee from the home as well as from the self. [22]

fully functioning—psychologically adjusted, open to experience, undefensive, accurately aware, unconditionally positive in self-regard, harmonious in relations with other people. [19]

functional fixedness—the inability to use a familiar object in an unfamiliar way. [10]

galvanic skin response (GSR)—a decrease in the resistance of the skin to electrical conduction. [16]

ganglia—collections of neuron cell bodies found principally along the spinal column. [3]

ganglion cells—a type of neural cell found in the retina of the eye. [4]

gate-control theory—the theory asserting that the sensation of pain depends on the balance of activity between large- and small-diameter nerve fibers within the spinal cord. [4]

gender identity—the child's understanding that she or he is female or male and will always remain so. [14]

gender roles—attitudes and patterns of behavior that society considers acceptable for each gender. [14]

gene—the unit of hereditary information. [11]

generalization—the tendency for a response learned in one situation to be elicited by other, similar situations. [8]

generalization gradient—the increased tendency to respond as the resemblance between a new stimulus and a conditioned stimulus becomes closer. [8]

generalized anxiety disorder—anxiety disorder characterized by diffuse and generalized anxiety that is impossible to manage by avoiding specific situations. [22]

genital stage—the final stage of psychosexual development, in which the focus is on the pleasures of sexual intercourse. [14, 18]

gestalt—a meaningful pattern or figure into which human beings group perceptual information. [5]

Gestalt therapy—a blend of Freudian concepts with humanistic philosophy and radically different therapeutic techniques. [24]

given-new strategy—a decoding technique, essential to comprehending speech, in which the listener takes the new information in the utterance and integrates it with old information. [13]

glia—structural units of the nervous system; they provide nutrients and structural support to neurons and bar certain substances from the bloodstream. [3]

global motion parallax—a constant flux in what is seen that produces the perception that the observer is moving through space. [5]

gonads—the sex glands. [3]

grammar—the structure of language. [13]

gray matter—nonmyelinated axons, dendrites, and cell bodies. [3]

ground—in a scene, the region that represents spaces between objects. [5]

grouping—the organizing of sensory data. [5]

growth needs. [19] See **metaneeds.**

habituation—a procedure in which a stimulus is presented until the subject stops responding to it, used to demonstrate the presence of recognition. [11, 12]

hair cells—the receptors in the organ of Corti. [4]

hallucinations—spontaneous sensory perceptions—usually of sounds—that are unrelated to external stimuli. [22]

hallucinogen—a drug with the ability to produce hallucinations. [6]

hammer—one of the ossicles in the middle ear. [4]

Hawthorne effect—a demand characteristic; the influence of the attention paid to subjects during an experiment. [2]

health psychology—a branch of clinical psychology with the aim of preventing and treating disease that involves psychological factors. [1]

heritability—the extent to which observed variation of a trait can be attributed to genetic differences. [20]

heuristic—a rule of thumb that provides a general direction for solving problems. [10]

hindsight—a bias in judgment resulting from looking back on events after they have already occurred. [10]

hippocampus—a structure in the limbic system. [3]

homeostasis—a process of self-regulation to maintain a balanced internal environment; a state of equilibrium. [3, 18]

homing—an internal sense of navigation; not considered a human sense. [4]

homosexual—a person whose primary source of sexual gratification is members of the same sex. [17]

horizontal cells—a type of neural cell found in the retina of the eye. [4]

hormones—chemical substances used by the endocrine system to transmit messages. [3]

hostile aggression—aggression that aims at hurting another person. [14]

human-factors psychology—a branch of industrial psychology that considers the purpose of a particular machine or environment, the capabilities of the probable user, and the most efficient design that matches the two. [1]

humanistic-existential perspective—a psychogenic approach to psychological disorder that includes both humanistic and existential theories. [23]

humanistic theories—person-centered theories that emphasize the potential of human beings for growth, creativity, and spontaneity. [19]

hypnagogic state—the state lying between waking and sleep. [6]

hypochondriasis—the preoccupation with bodily symptoms as possible signs of serious illness. [22]

hypothalamus—a small structure in the brain that monitors changes in internal environment and sends signals to maintain equilibrium. [3]

hypotheses—propositions or beliefs to be tested. [2]

hypothesis testing—a strategy commonly used by scientists in which the various ways a goal can be reached are formulated and then tested. [10]

iconic memory—the visual form of sensory memory. [9]

id—according to Freud, the biological drives with which the infant is born. [18]

identification—the child's wish to be like the parent and her or his adoption of whatever behavior the parent consistently displays. [14]

identity—an individual's sense of personal sameness and continuity. [14]

identity crisis—an internal conflict that requires the adolescent to develop a new self-concept. [14, 18]

illusion—a perception that does not correspond to a real object or event; it is produced by physical or psychological distortion. [5]

impetus—in Freud's terms, one of the four characteristic features of an instinct: a force whose strength is determined by the intensity of the need. [18]

impression management theory—the theory that maintains that a person's attitudes remain impervious to the effects of dissonance and that the insufficient reward affects only the expression of attitudes to others. [15]

imprinting—the process by which some species of birds and mammals form early social attachments. [7]

incentive—an external motivational stimulus. [15]

incest—sexual activity between closely related persons. [17, 22]

inclusive fitness—the idea that an individual may sacrifice its own life to protect others who share the individual's genes. [7]

independent variable—any factor whose change is expected to affect the event being studied. [2]

individual psychology—the school of psychology founded by Alfred Adler in 1911. [18]

individual trait—a unique way of organizing the world that cannot be applied to all people. [19]

individuation—in Jung's terms, a process of developing all parts of the personality. [18]

industrial psychology—the approach to psychology that considers the relationship between people and their jobs. [1]

inferential statistics—methods that allow researchers to judge how likely it is that their findings did not occur simply by chance. [2]

inferiority complex—in Adler's terms, the feelings and actions that characterize a person with an inability to overcome a childhood sense of incompleteness. [18]

inflection—a formal unit added to a word to indicate a syntactical usage. [13]

information overload—a constant flood of information that confronts the individual with inputs (bits of information) at a rate that exceeds the human ability to process them. [28]

inhibited ejaculation—a condition in which men are unable to ejaculate during sexual activity. [17]

inhibitory—a message that prevents a receiving neuron from firing. [3]

innate releasers—specific stimuli in the environment of a given species that release a chain of behavior. [7]

insight—the sudden perception of a new relationship that leads to an innovative solution. [10]

instinct—in Freud's terms, the psychological expression of a biologically based physical need. [18]

instrumental aggression—aggression that aims at acquiring or retrieving objects, territory, or privileges. [14]

instrumental conditioning. [8] See **operant conditioning.**

intelligence quotient (IQ)—the ratio of mental age to chronological age. [20]

intensity—the strength of a stimulus such as the amplitude of the air-pressure wave. [4]

interference—the theoretical blocking out of old memories by new material. [9]

interjudge reliability—the extent to which the scoring or interpretation of a test by different judges will produce the same results. [20]

internal consistency reliability—the extent to which different parts of a test produce the same results. [20]

internalization—the child's incorporation of society's values to such an extent that violation of these standards produces a sense of guilt. [14]

internalize—to incorporate (standards) into one's own personality. [18]

interneurons—neurons that connect only sensory and motor neurons. [3]

interposition—a monocular depth cue in which one object partially blocks the view of another object. [5]

intersubject replication—replication with different subjects. [2]

intimate distance—the distance, of up to about eighteen inches from the individual, that is reserved for the expression of deep emotion. [28]

intonation—the use of pitch to indicate meaning. [13]

intrasubject replication—replication with the same subjects. [2]

intrinsic motivation—the process by which long-term goals or preferences lead an individual to undertake a behavior. [15]

introspection—a method of psychological study in which trained observers report their own mental activities under controlled conditions. [10]

introversion—in Jung's terms, a major personality orientation in which the person withdraws interest from the external world and consequently is quiet, reserved, and cautious. [18]

iris—the pigmented portion of the eye that surrounds the pupil of the eye. [4]

iteration—a major characteristic of human language; the capacity to add constituents to old sentences in order to form new statements. [13]

James-Lange theory of emotion—the view that emotion results from the perception of bodily changes. [16]

just noticeable difference (JND). [4] See **difference threshold.**

kinesthesis—the sense of body movement and position. [4]

latency period or **stage**—the period in psychosexual

development in which libidinal dynamics are more or less stabilized; children busy themselves exploring the world and learning new things. [14, 18]

latent content of dreams—according to Freud, the unconscious wishes, primarily derived from unresolved early emotional conflicts, veiled by symbolic images in dreams. [6, 18]

lateral fissure—in the cortical surface, the separation marking the top boundary of the temporal lobe. [3]

lateral geniculate nucleus—a grouping of cell bodies in the thalamus. [4]

lateralization—the establishment of functions in one hemisphere or the other. [3]

law of effect—the law stating that responses that are followed by a satisfying consequence tend to be repeated, while responses that are followed by annoying consequences tend to disappear. [8]

learned helplessness—the acquired belief that one cannot exert any control over the environment. [21]

learning—a relatively enduring change in behavior caused by experience or practice. [8]

lens—a transparent structure behind the pupil of the eye. [4]

lesion—an injury created by selective destruction or removal of brain tissue. [3]

levels of processing—the theory that memory depends on human beings processing information at increasingly deeper levels; retention depends on the depth of processing and extent of elaboration. [9]

libido—a driving force permeating the entire personality and propelling it through life. [18]

life structure—an account of the major periods of a subject's life, as determined by activities, associations, and parental, marital, and familial relationships. [21]

limbic system—the layer of the brain involved in motivational and emotional processes. [3]

linear perspective—the apparent convergence of parallel lines in the distance. [5]

linguistic relativity hypothesis—Whorf's hypothesis that language determines our ideas, thoughts, and perceptions. [13]

localization of function—the idea that different parts of the brain appear to be involved in different types of behavior. [3]

long-term memory—the type of memory storage capable of storing a limitless amount of information indefinitely. [9]

maintenance rehearsal—a form of rehearsal to maintain information in short-term memory. [9]

major depression—one or more major depressive episodes with no intervening episodes of euphoria. [22]

manifest content of dreams—according to Freud, that level of content in dreams that is a weaving of daily events, sensations during sleep, and memories; the surface meaning. [6, 18]

mantra—a sound that the meditator chants over and over. [6]

marital schism—a basic family pattern, thought to produce schizophrenia, in which the parents of the schizophrenic are bitterly divided. [23]

marital skew—a basic family pattern, thought to produce schizophrenia, in which one parent of the schizophrenic totally dominates the other. [23]

masochism—sexual gratification obtained through having pain inflicted on oneself. [22]

mean—a measure of central tendency; the arithmetic average. [2]

measures of variability—measures that show how closely clustered or how widely spread any distribution of scores is. [2]

median—a measure of central tendency; the score that falls in the exact middle of a distribution, when all scores are arranged from highest to lowest. [2]

medical model—a model of abnormal behavior that views psychological problems in the same way as it views physical problems—as diseases. [22]

meditation—a retraining of attention that induces an altered state of consciousness. [6]

medulla—the part of the brain stem involved in breathing, circulation, chewing, salivation, and facial movements. [3]

meiosis—the process in which the twenty-three chromosome pairs of a single cell are split apart, rearranged, and distributed to two germ cells, each having twenty-three single chromosomes. [11]

memory—the function or capacity to register, retain, and retrieve information. [9]

memory trace—a physiological change theoretically formed in the brain to record information; as time passes, the trace decays. [9]

mental retardation—"significantly subaverage general intellectual functioning existing concurrently with deficits in adaptive behavior, and manifested during the developmental period" (American Association on Mental Deficiency, 1977). [20]

mental set—a tendency to keep repeating solutions that worked in other situations. [21]

metacognition—an understanding of the cognitive processes. [12]

metaneeds—the highest motives, having to do with creativity and self-actualization. [15]

metapathologies—crises (such as alienation and apathy) that result when metaneeds are not fulfilled. [19]

method of loci—a mnemonic system involving the use of a series of loci, or places, that are firmly implanted in memory. [9]

methodology—methods used in an investigation. [2]

microinterpersonal behavior—face-to-face interaction that is affected by the physical environment itself and by people's active use of that environment. [28]

midbrain—the part of the brain stem that contains centers for visual and auditory reflexes. [3]

mild retardation—mental retardation in which the (Stanford-Binet) IQ is between 52 and 67; mild retardates can hold undemanding jobs, marry, and have children. [20]

Minnesota Multiphasic Personality Inventory (MMPI)— an empirically constructed personality inventory, valuable for diagnostic purposes. [20]

mnemonic—memory-assisting. [9]

mode—a measure of central tendency; the score that most frequently appears in a distribution. [2]

modeling—the process by which a person learns some new behavior by watching another person perform it. [24]

moderate retardation—mental retardation in which the (Stanford-Binet) IQ is between 36 and 51; although moderate retardates can take care of themselves, they must live in sheltered workshops. [20]

monochromats—people who are totally color-blind. Monochromats see the world in shades of gray. [4]

monocular cues—information that does not require the cooperation of both eyes. [5]

moral anxiety—(1) In Freud's terms, anxiety over danger that comes from the superego. (2) generally, anxiety caused by the superego's demands for moral behavior. [18, 23]

motion parallax—differences that occur in the relative movement of retinal images when the observer or objects move. [5]

motivation—the process corresponding to the property of behavior called "motive." [15]

motive—the dynamic property of behavior that gives it organization over time and that defines its end states. [15]

motor cells—the specialized cells that control muscle movements and glandular secretions. [3]

motor cortex—the area of the frontal lobes involved in regulation of voluntary movement. [3]

motor neurons—neurons that carry messages from the spinal cord to muscles or glands. [3]

multiple orgasms—a series of orgasms that women may experience without going through the resolution phase between each orgasm. [17]

multiple personality—a division into two or more complete behavior organizations, each well-defined and highly distinct from the others; a rare dissociative disorder. [22]

myelin sheath—a fatty, whitish substance that wraps around some axons and that serves as insulation. [3]

naturalistic observation—a method of collecting data in which researchers carefully observe and record behavior in natural settings. [2]

nature versus nurture—the controversy among psychologists over whether human behavior is essentially instinctive or almost entirely learned. [7]

negative correlation—a relationship between two variables in which a high rank on one measure is accompanied by a low rank on the other. [2]

negative discriminative stimulus—a stimulus that an organism learns to ignore in discrimination training. [8]

negative reinforcement—the strengthening of a re-

sponse by the removal or termination of a stimulus. [8]

neodissociation theory—a theory of hypnosis based on the notion that consciousness depends on multiple systems that are coordinated through hierarchies of control, and that during hypnosis the controls shift. [6]

neo-Freudians—students of Freud who disagree with Freud's theory but retain some of his insights. [18]

nerves—bundles of neuron fibers. [3]

nervous system—a network of communication channels that spreads into every part of the body. [3]

neurons—the specialized cells that connect motor and receptor cells and transmit information throughout the body. [3]

neuropsychologists—specialists who study the relationships between the brain and behavior, examining the structure of the nervous system and how it relates to other organs and parts of the body. [3]

neuropsychology. [1] See **physiological psychology.**

neurosis—any condition in which a person develops some maladaptive behavior as a protection against unconscious anxiety. [22]

neurotic anxiety—in Freud's terms, anxiety over danger that comes from the id. [18, 23]

neurotransmitters—chemicals, stored in sacs at the tip of the axon, that transmit messages across the synapse. [3]

nondirective counseling or **therapy.** [19, 24] See **client-centered therapy.**

non-REM (NREM) sleep—the stages of sleep other than REM sleep. [6]

norm—a normative distribution that shows the frequency with which particular scores on a test are made. [20]

normal distribution—a ball-shaped, symmetrical distribution, in which mean, median, and mode are the same. [2]

norms—(1) averages derived from observing many individuals. (2) a society's rules that prescribe "right" and "wrong" behavior. [11, 20]

null hypothesis—the statement that all differences between the experimental and the control group were due to chance. [2]

obedience—any behavior that complies with the explicit commands of a person in authority. [27]

object—in Freud's terms, one of the four characteristic features of an instinct: the means used to satisfy the need. [18]

object concept—an understanding that objects have an existence of their own. [12]

object permanence—the awareness that objects continue to exist when out of sight. [12]

observational learning—a learning process in which the individual pays attention to what other people do and say and notices the consequences for them of their behavior. [8]

obsession—an involuntary, irrational thought that occurs repeatedly. [22]

obsessive-compulsive disorders—disorders characterized by rituals of orderliness or cleanliness, such as continual hand washing. [23]

occipital lobe—the area in the brain for reception and analysis of visual information. [3]

Oedipal conflict—the most important conflict in the child's psychological development, in which children perceive themselves as rivals of their same-sex parents for the affection of the parent of the opposite sex. [14]

olfaction—the sense of smell. [4]

olfactory epithelium—the sense organ for olfaction. [4]

operant behavior—voluntary response to a stimulus. [8]

operant conditioning—conditioning in which learning is explained by the way the consequences of behavior affect the organism's behavior in the future. [8]

opponent-process theory—(1) the theory of color vision proposing the existence of three antagonistically organized systems, with two of the systems composed of pairs of opposite colors. (2) the theory explaining acquired motivations as the result of two opposing processes. [4, 15]

optic chiasm—the junction where the nerves meet and are rerouted. [4]

optic disc—the "blind spot" in the eye; the area on the retina through which the optic nerve passes. [4]

optic nerve—the nerve that relays visual information to the brain. [4]

optimal arousal level—the level of motivation at which performance is at its best. [10]

optimal-level theories—theories proposing that activities seemingly unrelated to specific primary needs are based on a built-in tendency to maintain a certain level of stimulation.[15]

oral stage—that stage in psychosexual development that occupies the first year of life and during which the baby's mouth is the primary source of sensual pleasure. [14, 18]

organic brain syndromes—disorders directly traceable to the destruction of brain tissue or to biochemical imbalance in the brain. [22]

organism—the total range of a person's possible experiences. [19]

organizational psychology. [1] see **industrial psychology.**

organ of Corti—the actual organ of hearing. [4]

orgasm—the climactic phase of sexual response. [17]

ossicles—a series of bones in the middle ear. [4]

oval window—the flexible membrane that divides the middle ear from the inner ear. [4]

overextension—a child's tendency to extend the meanings of words to cover objects or actions for which they have no words. [13]

overinclusion—a loosening of associations, so that each sentence is generated from some mental stimulus in the preceding sentence. [22]

overregulation—extension of a grammatical rule to cases where it does not apply. [13]

pain thresholds—points at which pains are first perceived. [4]

panic attacks—episodes in which an already heightened state of tension mounts to an acute and overwhelming level. [22]

panic disorder—panic attacks preceded by no specific stimulus. [22]

papillae—groupings of taste buds. [4]

paradoxical cold—the phenomenon of feeling a cold sensation when a cold spot on the skin is stimulated with a hot stimulus. [4]

paranormal phenomena—phenomena outside the range of normal events. [6]

parapsychology—the study of ESP; the psychology of events that go beyond what is probable. [6]

parasympathetic nervous system—the division of the autonomic nervous system that dominates in relaxed situations. [3]

parietal lobe—the area of the brain behind the central fissure. [3]

partial reinforcement schedule—a schedule of reinforcement in which the subject is rewarded after only some of its responses. [8]

participant modeling—a therapeutic technique in which the therapist models the feared activity and then helps the client to confront and master a graduated series of threatening activities. [24]

participant observation—a form of naturalistic observation in which researchers actually join an existing group to record events that are accessible only to group members. [2]

peak experiences—profound moments when a person feels in complete harmony with the world. [19]

pedophilia—sexual gratification obtained through sexual contacts with children. [22]

peptides—neurotransmitters thought to regulate pain, mental disorders, sexual drive, thirst, hunger, drowsiness, and perhaps the ability to learn and remember. [3]

percentile system—a system of scoring tests in which the group of scores is divided into one hundred equal parts. [20]

perception—an organism's awareness of objects and events in the environment, brought about by stimulation of the organism's sense organs. [5]

perceptual constancy—the tendency to perceive objects as having certain constant or stable properties. [5]

perceptual set—the readiness to perceive stimuli in a specific way, ignoring some types of stimulation and becoming sensitive to others. [5]

performance—an aspect of language; the way we use our knowledge of language in listening or in speaking. [13]

peripheral nervous system (PNS)—the relay system connecting the CNS and all parts of the body. [3]

perseveration—(1) a verbal slip in which a produced

sound is erroneously repeated later in the utterance. (2) a tendency to dwell on the primary association to a given stimulus. [13, 22]

personal disposition. [19] See **individual trait.**

personal distance — the distance from about one and a half to four feet that is considered appropriate spacing for close friends and for conversations that concern personal matters. [28]

personality — the differences among people plus the stability of any individual's behavior over long periods. [14, 18]

personality disorders — disorders involving inflexible and maladaptive personality traits that impair functioning. [22]

personality psychology — the approach to psychology in which individual differences in behavior are studied. [1]

personal space — the zone around each individual into which other people may not trespass uninvited. [28]

personal unconscious — in Jung's terms, a level of the unconscious similar to the unconscious as depicted by Freud. [18]

personnel psychology — a branch of industrial psychology. Personnel psychologists screen job applicants, evaluate job performance, and recommend employees for promotion. [1]

persuasive communication — a direct, overt attempt to change attitudes. [25]

phallic stage — the third stage of psychosexual development, during which the child's attention is focused on the genitals and the pleasures of fondling them. [14, 18]

phenomenological approach — an approach in the humanistic-existential perspective that stresses the individual's own perception of events as opposed to a therapist's interpretation of hidden causes. [23]

phenylketonuria (PKU) — a rare abnormality caused by a defect in a single gene and resulting in progressive mental retardation. [11]

pheromones — chemicals that trigger a behavioral reaction in other animals of the same species. [4]

phi phenomenon — an example of apparent motion in which the illusion is created by rapidly flashing still pictures. [5]

phobia — an anxiety irrationally centered on a particular object or situation. [22]

phonemes — the smallest sound units in the language. [13]

phonology — the ordering of meaningful sounds to form words. [13]

photopigment — a light-sensitive molecule. [4]

phototaxis — movement toward light. [7]

physiological psychology — the approach to psychology that attempts to untangle the connections between the endocrine and nervous systems and behavior. [1]

physiological zero — the temperature at which there is no sensation. [4]

pitch — the attribute of tones in terms of which they may be described as high or low. This attribute is closely related to frequency of the sound waves. [4]

pituitary gland — the "master gland" of the endocrine system. [3]

placebo — a substance that has no direct physiological effect. [2]

place theory — the theory stating that the site of maximum displacement on the basilar membrane indicates to the brain the specific frequency of sound. [4]

plateau phase — the second phase of sexual response. [17]

pleasure principle — according to Freud, the tendency of the id to devote itself exclusively to the immediate reduction of tension. [18]

polarized — a description of a cell when its interior is negatively charged and its exterior is positively charged. [3]

pons — the part of the brain stem that connects the two halves of the cerebellum and that acts as a relay station. [3]

positive correlation — a relationship between two variables in which a high rank on one measure is accompanied by a high rank on the other. [2]

positive discriminative stimulus — a stimulus that an organism learns to respond to in discrimination training. [8]

positive reinforcement — the strengthening of a response by the presentation of a stimulus. [8]

pragmatics — the study of linguistic function. [13]

precocial — competent (referring to the young of a species). [11]

precognition — the ability to see the future. [6]

preconventional level — Kohlberg's stage of moral development in which children judge moral issues in terms of pain or pleasure or of the physical power of authority. [14]

predictive validity — a test's ability to produce scores that show a relationship to future performance on a job. [20]

prefrontal lobotomy — a surgical procedure in which a surgical instrument is inserted into the brain and rotated to sever nerve fibers connecting the frontal lobe (thought center) and the thalamus (emotional center). [24]

pregenital stage — a collective term for Freud's first three psychosexual stages. [18]

prejudice — negatively toned attitudes and opinions about an entire group, such as a racial minority or women, developed in the absence of sufficient knowledge. [26]

premature ejaculation — a condition in which men ejaculate rapidly, before they or their partners would like. [17]

preoperational period — the period of cognitive development characterized by the development of language, elaborate symbolic play, and the absence of logic; the preschool years. [12]

primacy effect — a process in which the personality traits that are detected first influence subsequent information about the person. [26]

primary drives — internal motivational factors that seek fulfillment of basic needs. [15]

primary erectile failure—the condition of a man who has never been able to achieve or maintain an erection sufficient for intercourse. [17]

primary orgasmic dysfunction—the situation of women who have never experienced orgasm through any means. [17]

primary reinforcer—a stimulus that fulfills some basic need. [8]

primary territory—a region whose ownership is clearly recognized, that is controlled by its users for long periods of time, and that is central to its occupants' daily lives. [28]

principled level—Kohlberg's stage of moral development in which the person judges moral issues in terms of self-chosen principles and standards based on universal ethical principles and on the ideals of reciprocity and human equality. [14]

principle of parsimony—the general scientific principle that, given two equally reasonable explanations of any situation, one should always choose the simpler. [7]

privacy—the selective control of access to the self or to the social group. [28]

proactive interference—interference in which earlier learning blocks out subsequent learning. [9]

probability—a tool of inferential statistics. It allows researchers to estimate reasonably accurately the chances that a particular event will occur. [2]

prodromal phase—a phase of deterioration, in which a person becomes increasingly withdrawn, eccentric in behavior, and unable to carry out daily functions, before schizophrenia becomes active. [22]

productivity—a major characteristic of human language; the capacity to allow individual units to be combined into an unlimited number of messages. [13]

profound retardation—mental retardation in which the (Stanford-Binet) IQ is below 20; profoundly retarded persons usually remain in institutions but can sometimes carry out a few tasks under close supervision; some cannot speak, although they may understand simple communication. [20]

program evaluation—evaluation by psychologists of the cost and effectiveness of applied programs. [1]

progressive relaxation—a relaxation technique in which the individual tenses and then releases different muscle groups in sequence. [21]

projection—the unknowing attribution of one's own impulses or fears onto others. [18]

projective tests—tests whose overall assessment depends upon clinical interpretation. [20]

propositional-code theory—the theory proposing that information is represented in an abstract manner that uses neither sounds nor sights nor motor acts, and that the abstractions take the form of rule-governed propositions. [9]

prosocial behavior—action intended to benefit another person, taken without expectation of external reward, and generally involving some cost to the individual. [14]

prostitution—the emotionally indifferent sale of sex on a promiscuous basis. [17]

prototype—a hypothetical best—or most typical—example of a category. [10]

proximity—a principle of grouping; how close together people live and work. [5, 26]

psychiatric nurse—a registered nurse who has specialized in psychiatric nursing. [24]

psychiatric social worker—a professional who has earned a master's degree in social work and has specialized in psychiatric social work. [24]

psychiatrist—a physician (MD) who specializes in the diagnosis and treatment of mental illness. [24]

psychoactive drug—a drug that interacts with the central nervous system to alter mood, perception, and behavior. [6]

psychoanalysis—the process by which Freud attempted to bring unconscious material into the patient's awareness, where it could be examined rationally. [18]

psychoanalyst—a person with special training in the technique of psychoanalysis and who has been psychoanalyzed as part of the training. [24]

psychogenic theory—the view that mental disturbances result primarily from psychological factors. [23]

psychohistory—the application of psychoanalytic principles to the study of historical figures. [18]

psychokinesis (PK)—the ability to move objects without touching them. [6]

psychological test—an objective and standardized measure of a sample of behavior that provides a systematic basis for making inferences about people. [20]

psychology—the study of behavior. [1]

psychometric function—a plot depicting the change in an individual's performance that takes place as some aspect of a situation varies. [4]

psychopharmacology—the study of the relationship between drugs and behavior. [1]

psychophysics—the branch of the study of sensory processes devoted to establishing the relationship between physical stimulation and the resulting sensory experience. [4]

psychosis—a condition in which the person's perceptions of reality are highly distorted. [22]

psychosurgery—the destruction or removal of brain tissue to change behavior. [3]

psychotherapy—a systematic series of interactions between a therapist trained to aid in solving psychological problems and a person who is troubled or who is troubling others. [24]

psychotic disorder—a disorder characterized by a generalized failure of functioning in all areas of a person's life. [22]

puberty—the period of sexual maturation that transforms a child into a physical adult. [14]

public distance—the zone from twelve to twenty-five feet from the individual; individuals interacting at this range are not personally involved. [28]

public territory—a region to which there is free access. [28]

punishment—a consequence that leads to the suppression of or to a decrease in the frequency of a behavior. [8]

pupil—the opening in the center of the iris of the eye. [4]

qualitative change—change in cognitive development, considered as involving a radical restructuring of the mind. [12]

quantitative change—change in cognitive development, considered as resulting from the accumulation of knowledge. [12]

quantitative psychology—the approach to psychology that specializes in measurement and statistics. [1]

racism—a doctrine that inherent differences among the various human races determine cultural or individual achievement. [26]

random sample—a method of selection in which every member of the population has an equal chance of being included in the sample. [2]

range—the difference between the smallest and the largest scores in a statistical distribution. [2]

rape—nonconsenting sexual intercourse with another person as the result of force, threat, or intimidation. [17, 22]

rational-emotive therapy—a therapy in which clients are first led to recognize the irrational nature of previously unexamined beliefs and then are aided in establishing a more realistic cognitive framework; a method of cognitive restructuring. [24]

reaction formation—the replacement of an anxiety-producing impulse by its opposite. [18]

reaction range—the unique range of responses to the environment possible for the genetic make-up of each person. [20]

realistic fantasy—a state on the continuum that stretches from normal waking consciousness to dreaming; it is most like normal consciousness. [6]

reality anxiety—in Freud's terms, anxiety over danger that comes from the outside world. [18, 23]

reality principle—according to Freud, the principle based on the need for safety, on which the ego operates. [18]

recall—a measure of memory that asks people to remember particular information, either spontaneously or after prompting with a clue. [9]

receptive field—the restricted region of the retina within which a neural response may be generated by light. [4]

receptor cells—the specialized cells that receive sensory information from the environment. [3]

recognition—a measure of memory that asks people to choose a familiar item from a set of presented items. [9]

recursion—a major characteristic of human language; the capacity to embed one structure of meaning within another. [13]

reflex arc—the basic functional unit of the nervous system; a connection between sensory and motor signals. [3]

refractory period—(1) a short period after a cell has fired, during which it cannot transmit an impulse. (2) a period of time tht must pass after a man's orgasm before he can become sexually aroused again. [3, 17]

regression—a return to an earlier stage of development in response to some perceived threat. [18]

reinforcement—a consequence that leads to an increase in the frequency of a behavior. [8]

reinforcement control—a way of regulating and maintaining behavior by rewarding an individual after he or she has behaved in a particular way. [19]

relative size—the relationship between the size of the retinal image produced by an object and the apparent distance of that object from an observer. [5]

relearning score—a measurement of relearning speed. [9]

reliable—a test, measuring something consistently. [20]

REM sleep—a stage of sleep associated with dreams in which the eyes move rapidly back and forth under closed eyelids. [6]

replication—duplication of a study with the same results. [2]

representational thought—thinking in which one mentally represents objects not directly in front of one. [12]

representativeness—a heuristic in which predictions are based on resemblances between the predicted event and a typical example. [10]

representative sample—a method of selection in which people known to possess certain characteristics are included in proportion to their numbers in the population being studied. [2]

repression—the fundamental defense mechanism, one that keeps threatening thoughts and memories from consciousness and pushes them back into the unconscious. [18]

reproductive thinking—the direct application of previous knowledge to a new problem. [10]

residual phase—a period following the active phase of schizophrenia in which behavior resembles that of the prodromal phase. [22]

resistance—a client's attempts to block the therapist's treatment. [24]

resolution phase—the final phase of sexual response. [17]

respondent behavior—involuntary response to a stimulus. [8]

retention—the maintenance of information in storage. [9]

reticular formation—the part of the brain stem that arouses higher brain areas to incoming information and maintains the sleep-waking cycle. [3]

retina—the layer of cells at the back of the eye composed of receptors and neurons. [4]

retrieval—the ability to get encoded information out of storage and back into awareness. [9]

retrieval cue—a piece of information that helps us to retrieve information from long-term memory. [9]

retroactive interference—interference in which subsequent learning blocks out earlier learning. [9]

retrograde amnesia—a condition in which people are unable to remember events preceding some kind of brain insult. [9]

reverie—a state on the continuum that stretches from normal waking consciousness to dreaming; it consists of unrelated images, scenes, or memories. [6]

reversal—a verbal slip in which sounds are exchanged. [13]

reward. [8] See **reinforcement.**

rhodopsin—a highly sensitive photopigment found in rods. [4]

rods—receptor cells in the eye responsible for vision in dim light. Rods signal information about brightness. [4]

role enactment theory—the theory that hypnosis is simply a special case of role playing. [6]

role taking—being able to imagine oneself in another's place. [14]

Rorschach Inkblot Test—a test in which a person is handed a series of symmetrical inkblots, one at a time, and is asked to report what she or he sees, using free association. [20]

rough-and-tumble play—a sort of social play concentrated among boys. [14]

round window—a membranous spot on the cochlea. [4]

sadism—sexual gratification obtained through inflicting pain on another person. [22]

sample—a selected segment of the data pertaining to a hypothesis. [2]

savings score. [9] See **relearning score.**

schedule of reinforcement—the basis on which a subject is rewarded for a behavior. [8]

schemes—action patterns that consist of whatever in an action can be repeated and generalized to other situations. [12]

schizophrenia—a group of disorders characterized by thought disturbance that may be accompanied by delusions, hallucinations, attention deficits, and bizarre motor activity. [22]

Scholastic Aptitude Test (SAT)—a test designed to measure "aptitude for college studies" rather than school achievement or general intelligence. [20]

school psychology—the approach to psychology concerned with assessment of children with learning or emotional problems. The school psychologist will then work out ways for parents and teachers to help these children. [1]

secondary erectile failure—a condition in which men who have experienced no erectile failure with a partner in the past are unable to achieve or maintain an erection in some or all sexual situations. [17]

secondary (situational) orgasmic dysfunction—the situation of women who experience orgasms sometimes, but not with their primary sexual partner or not during sexual intercourse. [17]

secondary reinforcer. [8] See **conditioned reinforcer.**

secondary territory—a semipublic place whose ownership is neither permanent nor exclusive. [28]

secondary trait—a characteristic mode of behavior that is less prominent than a central trait and is seen in fewer situations. [19]

selective attention—the process of controlling the selection of material from sensory memory. [9]

self—the parts of the total range of a person's possible experiences that the individual recognizes and accepts. [19]

self-actualization—fulfillment of an individual's capabilities. [19]

self-disclosure—what we tell another person about ourselves. [28]

self-instructional training—a method of cognitive restructuring that gives clients new ways of thinking and talking about their problems. [24]

self-schemata—clusters of generalizations about the self based on past experiences that organize, summarize, and explain our behavior in specific domains. [26]

semantic differential—a rating scale presenting pairs of polar adjectives (good/bad, nice/nasty). [16]

semanticity—a major characteristic of human language; the meaningfulness of words and sentences. [13]

semantic memory—organized knowledge about words and symbols and their meanings, relationships, and referents, and the rules for manipulating them. [9]

semantic network model—the model of memory that sees it as a network of interconnected nodes, each node being an idea, a concept, or an event. [9]

semantics—rules that prescribe the meaning of words and sentences. [13]

semen—the fluids discharged by males in ejaculation. [17]

semicircular canals—the three fluid-filled canals in the inner ear that make up the vestibular organ. [4]

senility—the loss of physical and mental ability that sometimes accompanies old age. [12]

sensitive period—a relatively restricted interval during which an animal is especially susceptible to particular influences that may have lasting effects on behavior. [7]

sensorimotor period—the period of cognitive development in which the infant relies on action schemes; the first two years of life. [12]

sensory deprivation—alteration of consciousness by sharp reduction of all sensory stimulation. [6]

sensory memory—the momentary persistence of sensory information after stimulation has ceased. [9]

sensory neurons—neurons that carry messages from the sense organs to the spinal cord. [3]

sensory physiology—the branch of the study of sensory processes that investigates the means by which environmental information is captured and transformed by receptors and then processed in the nervous system. [4]

separation distress—an infant's protesting when parted from the mother and expressing joy when the mother returns. [14]

septal area—a structure in the limbic system. [3]

sequential stimuli—a chain of environmental stimuli that is required to trigger behavior. [7]

serial-position curve—a curve showing the probability of recalling a word in relation to its position on the list in free recall. [9]

serotonin—a neurotransmitter that may play an important role in the regulation of sleep and emotion. [6]

severe retardation—mental retardation in which the (Stanford-Binet) IQ is between 20 and 35; severe retardates can learn to care for some of their physical needs. [20]

sexism—discrimination on the basis of gender. [26]

sex-typed behavior—behavior that is regarded as appropriate for only one sex. [14]

sexual dysfunction—any recurring problem that prevents an individual from engaging in sexual relations or from reaching orgasm during sex. [17]

shaping—a form of operant conditioning based on the reinforcement of ever-closer approximations of a desired behavior. [8]

short-term memory—the type of memory storage capable of retaining information for about fifteen seconds. [9]

signal detection theory—the theory proposing that there is no single absolute threshold for a stimulus. [4]

sign stimulus—a stimulus (odor, color, or shape) that releases a fixed action pattern in an animal. [7]

similarity—a principle of grouping. [5]

simplicity—the concept integrating all the principles of grouping. [5]

simultaneous color contrast—the tendency of a color in one part of a visual scene to cause a shift in the perceived color of a neighboring area. [4]

single-unit recording—placement of an electrode to allow researchers to record the electrical activity of a single neuron. [3]

size constancy—the tendency to perceive the size of an object as constant regardless of its distance and, hence, the size of its retinal image. [5]

social distance—the space that extends from four to twelve feet around an individual, in which most business contacts take place. [28]

social facilitation—enhanced performance in the presence of others. [27]

social-impact theory—the theory that when social forces affect a situation, the larger the group, the less pressure on any one member because the impact of the forces is spread over the entire group. [27]

social influence—waiting for others to define the situation as an emergency. [27]

social interest—in Adler's terms, the inborn desire to strive for the public good. [18]

socialization—the process of absorbing society's attitudes, values, and customs. [14]

social learning theory—the theory proposing that learning is not simply a matter of reacting to stimuli; rather, people apply cognitive processes to the stimuli they encounter, selecting, organizing, and transforming them. [8]

social psychology—the approach to psychology concerned with the study of the behavior of people in groups. In social psychology, special attention is paid to the influence of other people on individuals. [1]

social trap—a situation in which as a result of personal decisions, people, organizations, or societies start moving in some direction or initiate some relationship whose consequences become collectively harmful or lethal but that seems virtually impossible to stop. [27]

sociobiology—according to Wilson, "the systematic study of the biological basis of all social behavior" (1975, p. 4). [7]

sociopath—one who is indifferent to the rights of others. [22]

somatic nervous system—the division of the PNS related to the external world and generally under voluntary control. [3]

somatoform disorders—disorders whose distinguishing feature is the persistence of symptoms that have a somatic or physical form, but in which there is no physiological malfunction. [22]

somatosensory cortex—the area of the parietal lobe involved in reception and interpretation of touch and positional information. [3]

source—in Freud's terms, one of the four characteristic features of an instinct: a bodily condition or need. [18]

source trait—an underlying root or cause of a surface trait. [19]

species-specific behavior—behavior typical of a particular species whose members share a common genetic background and a common environment that provides similar influences and experiences. [7]

speech act—an utterance. [13]

stages—cumulative periods of development. [12]

standard deviation—the preferred measure of variability. It shows how much figures in a given set of data vary from the mean. [2]

standardization group—a large and well-defined group of people to which a test is given to establish the test's norms. [20]

standard score system—a system of scoring tests in which standard scores represent points on a bell-shaped curve that reflects the normal pattern of distribution of scores on almost any test. [20]

Stanford-Binet Test—a revision of Binet's test of intelligence; devised at Stanford University. [20]

state-dependent memory—memory more easily recalled when a person is in the same physiological state as when she or he acquired the information. [9]

statistical significance—a tool of inferential statistics that allows researchers to determine exactly how small the probability is that their results have come about by chance. [2]

stereoblindness — blindness to binocular disparity. [5]

stereopsis — perception of depth based on binocular disparity. [5]

stereotypes — standardized beliefs about a certain group. [26]

Stevens' power law — the law stating that different sensory domains have different exponents. [4]

stimulant — a drug that increases heart rate, blood pressure, and muscle tension by stimulating the central nervous system. [6]

stimulus — any form of energy that can evoke a response. [4]

stimulus control — a particular behavior taking place only when a particular stimulus in the environment evokes it at the appropriate time. [19]

stimulus substitution — a tendency to react to a previously neutral stimulus as though it were an unconditioned stimulus with which it had been repeatedly associated. [8]

stirrup — one of the ossicles. [4]

stress — a term without precise meaning; sometimes defined as any stimulus that places a strain on a person's physical or psychological capacity to adjust; sometimes defined as an internal response to some disruptive or disquieting situation. [21]

stress syndrome — the body's response to continuing stress: enlarged adrenal glands, shrunken thymus gland and lymph nodes, and ulcerated stomach. [21]

stroke — a common cause of brain damage. In a stroke, blood vessels on the surface of the brain rupture. [3]

subgoal analysis — the division of a difficult problem into a series of smaller problems, or subgoals, that are relatively easy to solve. [10]

subjective contours — lines or shapes that appear to be part of a figure but are actually not physically present. [5]

sublimation — in Freud's terms, the diversion of instinctual energy from original object choices to social organization and cultural development. [18]

subliminal perception — the registration of sensory information that influences behavior without producing any conscious experience of the stimulus. [5]

superego — according to Freud, that part of the personality that represents the moral standards of the society as conveyed to the child by the parents. [18]

superstitious behavior — the increase of a response owing to a coincidental relationship between the behavior and a reinforcer. [8]

surface traits — clusters of behavior that tend to go together. [19]

surveys — methods of collecting data in which researchers obtain information about people's characteristics, attitudes, opinions, or behavior by asking them questions. [2]

swinging — a pattern of extramarital sex in which a couple incorporates outside sexual experiences into the marriage. [17]

sympathetic nervous system — the division of the autonomic nervous system that dominates in emergencies or stressful situations. [3]

synapse — a small gap between neurons. [3]

synergistic — a combined action of drugs. For example, the effect of two depressants taken together is greater than the sum of the two drugs' effects. [6]

syntax — the rules for combining words to form sentences. [13]

systematic desensitization — a procedure aiming at the gradual extinction of anxiety, in which the relaxed client is gradually exposed to anxiety-producing stimuli. [24]

tardive dyskinesia — a muscle disorder in which patients grimace and smack their lips uncontrollably. [24]

taste buds — the structures in the mouth and tongue that contain receptor cells for taste stimuli. [4]

tectorial membrane — a membrane in the organ of Corti. [4]

telegraphic speech — a child's utterances in the language-acquisition stage, characterized by two-word sentences. [13]

teleology — purposiveness. [7]

telepathy — the transference of thought from one person to another; mind reading. [6]

temperament — the individual's pattern of activity, susceptibility to emotional stimulation, response to stimuli, and general mood. [14]

temporal lobe — the area in the brain involved in auditory reception and processing of visual information. [3]

territoriality — behavior that is displayed in connection with the ownership of a place or a geographic area by an individual or a group. [28]

test-retest reliability — the extent to which repeated administration of a test to the same group of people produces the same results. [20]

texture gradient — the graduated differences in texture that occur as distance increases. [5]

thalamus — a pair of structures in the brain that provides a link between the cerebral hemispheres and the sense organs. [3]

Thanatos — according to Freud, one of two broad types of instincts in the id; the death instinct. [18]

Thematic Apperception Test (TAT) — a test consisting of a series of cards depicting ambiguous scenes involving one, two, or three people. The subject is asked to tell a story about each picture. [20]

theories — in psychology, sets of logically related statements that help explain human behavior. [2]

theory of psychosexual development — Freud's theory that from earliest infancy people are motivated by powerful biological instincts to seek pleasure and that at different ages, different parts of the body are the focus of this pleasure. [14]

thyroid gland — the gland that regulates body metabolism. [3]

thyroxin — the hormone produced by the thyroid gland. [3]

"tip-of-the-tongue" phenomenon—the condition of knowing that the information is known, while retrieval cues fail to produce the information. [9]

token economy—a therapeutic technique, used primarily in institutions, in which a wide range of appropriate behavior is rewarded with tangible conditioned reinforcers, or "tokens." [24]

trait—"any relatively enduring way in which one individual differs from another" (Guilford, 1959). [19]

trait theories—theories stating that human behavior can be organized according to enduring characteristics that are called traits—for example, aggression, friendliness, and honesty. [19]

transactional analysis—a psychotherapeutic approach based on psychodynamic theory; often used with groups of married couples. [24]

transduction—conversion of environmental stimuli into neural impulses. [4]

transference—a client's transfer to the analyst of childhood feelings toward important people in his or her life, particularly the parents. [24]

transference neurosis—the stage of therapy in which the client reenacts with the analyst childhood conflicts with the parents. [24]

transsexualism—gender identification with the opposite sex. [17, 22]

transvestism—sexual gratification obtained through dressing in clothing of the opposite sex. [22]

traumatic—psychologically damaging. [18]

trichromatic theory—the theory proposing that color vision is based on three types of cones thought to be mingled in a mosaic pattern throughout the central retina. [4]

trimester—one-third of the period of pregnancy. [11]

Turner's syndrome—the condition of a fetus that has received only a single X chromosome and no Y chromosome. [17]

two-factor theory of emotion—the theory that the experience of an emotion is based on a physiological change plus a cognitive interpretation of that change. [16]

tympanic canal—a division of the cochlea. [4]

tympanic membrane—the membrane separating the outer ear and the inner ear; the eardrum. [4]

Type A behavior—a personality pattern; people who fit this pattern are highly competitive, hostile when thwarted, and their behavior shows the urgency of working against the pressures of time. [21]

unconditional positive regard—continued support of a person (by the self or others) regardless of what the person says or does. [19]

unconditioned response (UCR)—an unlearned response to a stimulus. [8]

unconditioned stimulus (UCS)—a stimulus that evokes a response without having been learned. [8]

unconscious—an aspect of personality unknown to the mind of the subject. [18]

vaginismus—a condition in which involuntary muscle spasms cause the vagina to shut tightly so that penetration by the penis is extremely painful or impossible. [17]

valid—of a test, measuring what it purports to measure. [20]

variable interval schedule—a partial reinforcement schedule in which reinforcement comes at unpredictable times. [8]

variable ratio schedule—a partial reinforcement schedule in which reinforcement comes after an unpredictable number of responses. [8]

variables—any factors or events in an experiment that are capable of change. [2]

vestibular apparatus—the organ in the inner ear that provides a sense of balance and equilibrium. [4]

vestibular canal—a division of the cochlea. [4]

vestibular sense—the sense of balance. [4]

visual cortex—the area in the brain where the processing associated with the emergence of conscious visual perception occurs. [4]

volley theory—the theory stating that the entire basilar membrane vibrates at the resonant frequency, causing the auditory nerve to fire in synchrony, thus signaling pitch. [4]

voyeurism—sexual gratification obtained through secret observations of another person's sexual activities or genitals. [22]

wariness of strangers—a baby's responding to strangers with, for example, fear or withdrawal. [14]

wavelength—a unit of scale of the electromagnetic spectrum. [4]

Weber's law—the law stating that the amount of stimulus needed to produce a just noticeable difference is a constant fraction of the intensity of the stimulus. [4]

Wechsler Adult Intelligence Scale (WAIS)—a test for adults that measures both performance and verbal ability. [20]

Wechsler Intelligence Scale for Children (WISC)—a test of children that measures both verbal and performance ability. [20]

Wechsler Preschool and Primary Scale of Intelligence (WPPSI)—a test that measures both verbal and performance ability of children from four to six and a half years old. [20]

white matter—myelinated axons. [3]

word order—a basic syntactical rule prescribing the order of words in most sentences. [13]

Yerkes-Dodson law—an inverted relationship between motivation and performance. [10]

zazen—a set of meditation techniques used by Zen Buddhists. [6]

Index of Names

Index of Subjects

Credits and Acknowledgments

CHAPTER 1
2— © Rick Smolan 1980
6—*Fingerprint Landscape* (1950). © Saul Steinberg. Collection of the Artist.
8— © Sepp Seitz 1979/Woodfin Camp & Associates
10—George N. Peet/The Picture Cube
11—Rene Burri/Magnum
13—Fred R. Conrad/NYT Pictures
15— © Catherine Ursillo/Photo Researchers, Inc.

CHAPTER 2
20—Jim Holland/Stock, Boston
23— © Shelly Katz 1982/Black Star
26— © Danny Lyon/Magnum
31—After M. Kramer, Statistics of mental disorders in the U.S.: current status, some urgent needs, and suggested solutions, *Journal of the Royal Statistical Society, Series A,* 132 (1969), Part 3, 353-407.
40— © John Troha 1980/Black Star
41—RH Picture Collection

CHAPTER 3
46—Arthur Tress
50—Julius Weber (top left); Lester V. Bergman & Associates (top center); UPI/COMPIX (top right)
58— © Leonard Speier 1982
64— © Martin M. Rotker 1981/Taurus Photos
65—Courtesy, Neal Miller

CHAPTER 4
74—*Ice*, 1966 by Richard Lindner. Collection of The Whitney Museum of American Art, New York.
77— © Leonard Speier 1982
82—Jay Braun
89— © Gilles Peress/Magnum
91— © Leonard Speier 1977
93— © Elinor S. Beckwith/Taurus Photos
96— © Leonard Speier 1982

CHAPTER 5
102— © Janet S. Mendes 1981/The Picture Cube
106— © Karsh, Ottawa/Woodfin Camp & Associates
114—(top) Frank Siteman/Stock, Boston
114—(bottom) *Entry Into Jerusalem* (Detail from the *Maesta Altar*). Duccio. Scala/EPA
115—*Delivery of the Keys*. Perugino. Vatican Museum. Scala/EPA
117—B—Philip Clark; D—Bob Ward
118—Photo by Robert Berger, reprinted with permission of *Science Digest* © Hearst Corporation

CHAPTER 6
126— © Michael de Camp/The Image Bank
128—James H. Karales/Peter Arnold, Inc.
132— © Arthur Tress
134—Detail, *Queen Katherine's Dream*. William Blake. National Gallery of Art, Washington, D.C. Rosenwald Collection.
142—After "The Pathology of Boredom," by Woodburn Heron © 1957 by *Scientific American, Inc.* All rights reserved.
147—Frank Siteman/The Picture Cube

CHAPTER 7
154© Edith G. Haun/Stock, Boston
156—Peter Southwick/Stock, Boston
159—Russ Kinne/Photo Researchers, Inc.
163—(top) Yva Momatiuk/Photo Researchers, Inc.
163—(bottom) Thomas McAvoy/LIFE MAGAZINE © Time, Inc.
167—Thomas McAvoy/LIFE MAGAZINE © Time, Inc.
169—Helen Csuickshank/National Audubon Society/Photo Researchers, Inc.
171— © R. Lynn Goldberg 1980

CHAPTER 8
176—James R. Smith
180—After I. Pavlov, *Conditioned Reflexes* (G. V. Antep, translator), Oxford University Press, 1927.
182— © Leonard Speier 1982
184—Alex Webb/Magnum
186—After B. F. Skinner, Superstitious behavior in the pigeon, *Journal of Experimental Psychology*, 38 (1948), 168-172, © 1948 by the American Psychological Association. Reprinted by permission.
188—Bruce Davidson/Magnum
189—Alan Clifton/Black Star
192— © Leonard Speier 1982
195— © Watriss-Baldwin 1980/Woodfin Camp & Associates

CHAPTER 9
198— © Arthur Tress
200— © Ed Hof/The Picture Cube
201— © Bruce D. Rosenblum/The Picture Cube
206—After L. R. Peterson and M. G. Peterson, Short-term retention of experimental verbal items, *Journal of Experimental Psychology*, 58 (1959), 193-198, © 1959 by the American Psychological Association. Reprinted by permission.
209—After B. Murdok, Jr., The serial position effect of free recall, *Journal of Experimental Psychology*, 64: 5, fig. 1, © 1962 by the American Psychological Association, and L. Postman and L. W. Philips, Short-term temporal changes in free recall, *Quarterly Journal of Experimental Psychology*, 17 (1965), 132-138.
217—Courtesy, Professor Elizabeth F. Loftus
221— © Rick Smolan

CHAPTER 10
226— © Nicholas Foster 1976/The Image Bank
235—(bottom) Adapted from A. S. Luchins and E. H. Luchins, *Rigidity of Behavior: A Variational Approach to the Effect Einstellary*, University of Oregon Books, 1959, 109.
236— © Leonard Speier 1982
238— © Richard Kalvar/Magnum
245— © Leonard Speier 1982

CHAPTER 11
250— © Joan Liftin/Archive Pictures
254—Marcia Keegan
258— © Rick Winsor 1981/Woodfin Camp & Associates
262—Courtesy, Dr. Richard Walk
267—Suzanne Szasz

CHAPTER 12
270— © Abigail Heyman/Archive Pictures
272—Courtesy, Downstate Medical Center. Photo by Camilla Smith
274—George Zimbel/Monkmeyer Press Photo Service
276—Dr. Carolyn Rovel-Collier, Rutgers University, Department of Psychology
281—Steve Wells
284—William MacDonald
285— © Leonard Speier 1982

CHAPTER 13
294— © Arthur Tress
297— © Richard Kalvar/Magnum
302—Tom Bledsoe
303— © David Cupp 1982/Woodfin Camp & Associates
304— © Paul Fusco/Magnum
312—William MacDonald
314— © Barbara Alper 1982
317—Courtesy, Munsell Color, Baltimore, Md.

CHAPTER 14
320— © Leonard Speier 1982
325— © Ira Berger 1981/Woodfin Camp & Associates
331— © Frank Siteman/The Picture Cube
333—Jeffrey Foxx/Woodfin Camp & Associates
336— © Lawrence Frank 1978
339— © Betty Barry/The Picture Cube

CHAPTER 15
344—*No Thank You*, 1964, Roy Lichtenstein. Collection Max Palevsky. Courtesy, Leo Castelli Gallery.
347— © Harry Wilks/Stock, Boston
349—With permission, Copyright © Paul Ekman 1972
352— © Susan Shapiro
353—(left) © Ron Alexander/Stock, Boston; (right) After R. Lazarus and E. Alfert, The short-circuiting of threat by experimentally altering cognitive appraisal, *Journal of Abnormal and Social Psychology*, 69 (1964), 195-205, © 1964 by the American Psychological Association. Reprinted by permission.

357 — With permission, Copyright © Paul Ekman 1972
359 — © Daniel S. Brody/Stock, Boston

CHAPTER 16
366 — © Frank Siteman/The Picture Cube
373 — Courtesy, R. A. Butler
374 — A. Devaney, Inc.
377 — Harry Crosby

CHAPTER 17
388 — *Persimmon*, 1964. Robert Rauschenberg. Collection of Mrs. Leo Castelli. Courtesy, Leo Castelli Gallery.
391 — Jaye R. Phillips/The Picture Cube
396 — © Leonard Speier 1981
400 — © Sepp Seitz 1980/Woodfin Camp & Associates
401 — © Arthur Tress

CHAPTER 18
410 — © Joan Menschenfreund
415 — © Hazil Hankin 1981
420 — © Frank Siteman 1979/The Picture Cube
423 — © Lawrence Frank 1978

CHAPTER 19
432 — A. Gesar/The Image Bank
434 — © Mitchell Funk/The Image Bank
436 — © Owen Franken/Stock, Boston
442 — © Arthur Tress
443 — Burk Uzzle/Magnum
446 — © Judith Golden

CHAPTER 20
454 — © David F. Hughes 1981/The Picture Cube
460 — Photos by John Oldenkamp with permission of the Houghton Mifflin Company, from Terman and Merrill, Stanford-Binet Intelligence Scale
464 — © J. Berndt 1982/The Picture Cube
465 — From A. Dove in Taking the Chitling Test, *Newsweek*, 7/15, © 1968 by Newsweek, Inc. All rights reserved. Reprinted by permission.

468 — Michael Weisbrot & Family/Stock, Boston

CHAPTER 21
480 — © Leonard Speier 1982
483 — © Frank Siteman 1982/The Picture Cube
486 — © Lawrence Frank 1980
488 — © Arthur Tress
489 — © Arthur Tress
491 — (top) Adapted from J. E. Singer, D. C. Glass, and B. Reim, Behavioral consequences of adaptation to controllable and uncontrollable noise, *Journal of Experimental Social Psychology*, 7 (1971), 244–257. Reprinted by permission of Academic Press and J. E. Singer, D. C. Glass, and B. Reim; (bottom) © Ted Spiegel/Black Star
493 — © Barbara Alper 1982
494 — © Alan Carey/The Image Works
495 — Jim Anderson/Woodfin Camp & Associates

CHAPTER 22
504 — *Standing Man*, W. De Kooning. Wadsworth Atheneum, Hartford, Connecticut; Ellen Gallup and Mary Catlin Summer Collection
507 — © Barbara Alper 1982
511 — © Barbara Alper 1982
514 — *Birthday*, Marc Chagall. Oil on canvas. The Solomon R. Guggenheim Museum, New York.
515 — © Arthur Tress
519 — Courtesy of Al Vercoutere, Camarillo State Hospital

CHAPTER 23
526 — © Arthur Tress
528 — *The Trial of George Jacobs for Witchcraft*. Painting by T. H. Matteson. Courtesy of the Essex Institute, Salem, Massachusetts
531 — © Chris Alan Wilton/The Image Bank
534 — Bruce Davidson/Magnum
536 — © Leonard Speier 1980

540 — © Arthur Tress/Woodfin Camp & Associates

CHAPTER 24
544 — © Dan McCoy/Rainbow
546 — © Arthur Tress
548 — © Gil Spitzer
558 — Bruce Hoertel
560 — © Leonard Speier 1979
563 — (top) © Ann Chwatsky
563 — (bottom) © Leonard Speier 1980

CHAPTER 25
568 — © Erich Lessing/Magnum
570 — Phillip Jones Griffiths/Magnum
572 — © Leonard Speier 1982
576 — © Ann Chwatsky
582 — © Alan Carey/The Image Works

CHAPTER 26
586 — © Jim Leach
589 — © Eric Kroll 1979/Taurus Photos
592 — © Rick Smolan
594 — Bill Call
596 — © Alan Carey/The Image Works
600 — © Neal Slavin
604 — © Sharon Fox/The Picture Cube

CHAPTER 27
608 — © Douglas Kirkland 1981/Contact Press Images
610 — © Alan Macweeney/Archive Pictures
615 — Focus On Sports
621 — UPI
627 — Mark Jury Communications

CHAPTER 28
634 — © Leonard Speier 1982
636 — © Arthur Tress
637 — © Rick Smolan/Stock, Boston
638 — © Ira Kirschenbaum/Stock, Boston
641 — © Barbara Alper 1982
644 — © Alan Carey/The Image Works
646 — © Rick Smolan 1980
647 — © Donald C. Dietz/Stock, Boston
650 — © Leonard Speier 1982